Look for this iPod icon throughout the text.

Icons connect textbook content to your iPod or other MP3 device.

Images courtesy of Apple.

What if I Don't Have an iPod?

Content can be downloaded and viewed on any computer, with or without an iPod.

Visit this text's Web site for directions or use the DVD available for purchase with this text.

iPod content includes:

- Lecture presentations
  - *Audio-based*
  - *Video-based*
  - *Slideshow only*
- Demonstration problems+
- Interactive self quizzes
- Videos on various course topics

+Available with some textbooks

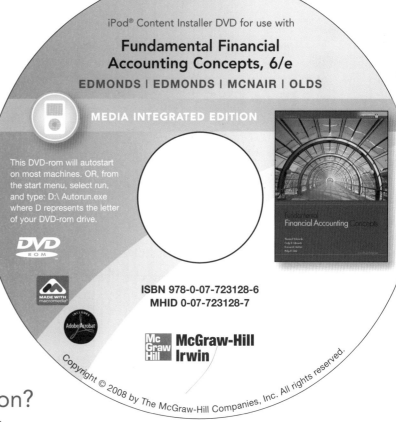

iPod® Content Installer DVD for use with

Fundamental Financial Accounting Concepts, 6/e

EDMONDS | EDMONDS | MCNAIR | OLDS

MEDIA INTEGRATED EDITION

This DVD-rom will autostart on most machines. OR, from the start menu, select run, and type: D:\ Autorun.exe where D represents the letter of your DVD-rom drive.

DVD ROM

MADE WITH macromedia

INCLUDES Adobe Acrobat

ISBN 978-0-07-723128-6
MHID 0-07-723128-7

Mc Graw Hill **McGraw-Hill Irwin**

Copyright © 2008 by The McGraw-Hill Companies, Inc. All rights reserved.

Want to see iPod in action?

Visit **www.mhhe.com/ipod** to view a demonstration of our iPod® content.

McGraw-Hill's
HOMEWORK PLUS ™
MANAGER

online

THE COMPLETE SOLUTION

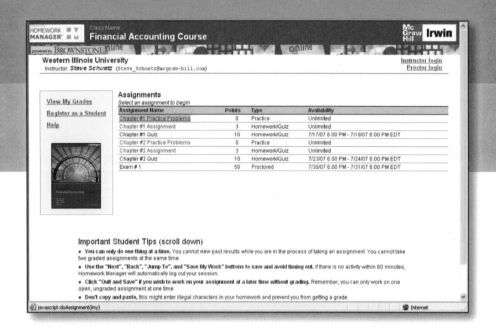

McGraw-Hill's
Homework Manager®

This online homework management solution contains the textbook's end-of-chapter material. Now you have the option to build assignments from static and algorithmic versions of the text problems and exercises or to build self-graded quizzes from the additional questions provided in the online test bank.

Features:
- Assigns book-specific problems/exercises to students
- Provides integrated test bank questions for quizzes and tests
- Automatically grades assignments and quizzes, storing results in one grade book
- Dispenses immediate feedback to students regarding their work

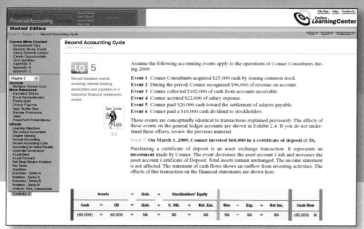

Interactive Online Version
of the Textbook

In addition to the textbook, students can rely on this online version of the text for a convenient way to study. The interactive content is fully integrated with McGraw-Hill's Homework Manager® to give students quick access to relevant content as they work through problems, exercises, and practice quizzes.

Features:

- Online version of the text integrated with McGraw-Hill's Homework Manager

- Students referred to appropriate sections of the online book as they complete an assignment or take a practice quiz

- Direct link to related material that corresponds with the learning objective within the text

McGraw-Hill's Homework Manager Plus™ combines the power of McGraw-Hill's Homework Manager® with the latest interactive learning technology to create a comprehensive, fully integrated online study package. Students working on assignments in McGraw-Hill's Homework Manager can click a simple hotlink and instantly review the appropriate material in the Interactive Online Textbook.

By including McGraw-Hill's Homework Manager Plus with your textbook adoption, you're giving your students a vital edge as they progress through the course and ensuring that the help they need is never more than a mouse click away. Contact your McGraw-Hill representative or visit the book's Web site to learn how to add McGraw-Hill's Homework Manager Plus to your adoption.

Sixth Edition

Fundamental Financial Accounting Concepts

Thomas P. Edmonds
University of Alabama—Birmingham

Cindy D. Edmonds
University of Alabama—Birmingham

Frances M. McNair
Mississippi State University

Edward E. Milam
Mississippi State University

Philip R. Olds
Virginia Commonwealth University

McGrawHill **McGraw-Hill**
Irwin

Boston   Burr Ridge, IL   Dubuque, IA   New York   San Francisco   St. Louis
Bangkok   Bogotá   Caracas   Kuala Lumpur   Lisbon   London   Madrid   Mexico City
Milan   Montreal   New Delhi   Santiago   Seoul   Singapore   Sydney   Taipei   Toronto

McGraw-Hill
Irwin

FUNDAMENTAL FINANCIAL ACCOUNTING CONCEPTS
Published by McGraw-Hill/Irwin, a business unit of The McGraw-Hill Companies, Inc., 1221
Avenue of the Americas, New York, NY, 10020. Copyright © 2008 by The McGraw-Hill
Companies, Inc. All rights reserved. No part of this publication may be reproduced or distributed
in any form or by any means, or stored in a database or retrieval system, without the prior written
consent of The McGraw-Hill Companies, Inc., including, but not limited to, in any network or
other electronic storage or transmission, or broadcast for distance learning.

Some ancillaries, including electronic and print components, may not be available to customers
outside the United States.

This book is printed on acid-free paper.

2 3 4 5 6 7 8 9 0 DOW/DOW 0 9 8

ISBN   978-0-07-352678-2
MHID   0-07-352678-9

Editorial director: *Stewart Mattson*
Senior sponsoring editor: *Steve Schuetz*
Managing developmental editor: *Gail Korosa*
Editorial assistant: *Colleen Honan*
Marketing manager: *Melissa Larmon*
Lead project manager: *Pat Frederickson*
Senior production supervisor: *Debra R. Sylvester*
Lead designer: *Matthew Baldwin*
Senior designer: *Artemio Ortiz Jr.*
Senior photo research coordinator: *Jeremy Cheshareck*
Photo researcher: *Editorial Image, LLC*
Senior media technology producer: *Victor Chiu*
Media producer: *Lynn M. Bluhm*
Media project manager: *Matthew Perry*
Cover: *Dave Seidler*
Typeface: *10/12 Times New Roman*
Compositor: *Aptara, Inc.*
Printer: *R. R. Donnelley*

Library of Congress Cataloging-in-Publication Data

Fundamental financial accounting concepts / Thomas P. Edmonds ... [et al.].—6th ed.
        p. cm.
    Includes index.
    ISBN-13: 978-0-07-352678-2 (alk. paper)
    ISBN-10: 0-07-352678-9 (alk. paper)
    1. Accounting. I. Edmonds, Thomas P.
HF5636.F86 2008
    657—dc22   2007024947

www.mhhe.com

This book is dedicated to our students, whose questions have so frequently caused us to reevaluate our method of presentation that they have, in fact, become major contributors to the development of this text.

NOTE FROM THE AUTHORS

Over the past 15 years, major changes in accounting education have impacted the way most college and university professors teach introductory accounting. We are gratified that our concepts approach has been so effective it has become a market leader in the change movement. The concepts approach takes traditional accounting to the next level. We not only cover debits and credits, but more importantly explain how those debits and credits impact financial statements.

How have we become market leaders in the introductory accounting course?

We look at ourselves as innovative traditionalists. We don't aim to radically transform accounting education, but instead to make it more effective. Students who use this text follow a different path toward the accomplishment of a conventional set of learning objectives. However, the path is easier to walk; and students complete the journey with a far greater understanding of accounting.

In contrast to traditional textbooks, this is a concepts-based text that focuses on the big picture. Recording procedures and other details are presented after a conceptual foundation has been established. This approach enables students to understand rather than memorize. What do we mean by a concepts-based textbook? We mean the text stresses the relationships between business events and financial statements. The primary objective is to develop students who can explain how any given business event affects the income statement, balance sheet, and statement of cash flows. Do assets increase, decrease, or remain unchanged? What effect does the event have on liabilities, equity, revenue, expense, gains, losses, net income, and dividends? Furthermore, how does the event affect cash flows? In summary, the focus is on learning how business events affect financial statements.

Balance Between Theory and Practice

The big picture approach enables professors to focus on developing skills as well as covering content. Students who understand concepts are better able to communicate ideas and more effective at solving unstructured problems. Students who understand concepts are also better prepared to learn technical content. Students using this text will learn the basics of double-entry bookkeeping, including debits and credits, journal entries, T-accounts, and trial balances. This text maintains an appropriate balance between skill development and technical competence.

This is not a user or preparer approach. Indeed, the concepts approach serves both users and preparers. In order to function effectively in today's business world, both preparers and users must understand event/statement relationships.

Implementing the concepts approach is surprisingly simple.

Instead of teaching students to record transactions in journals or T-accounts, teach them to record transactions directly into financial statements. Making a direct connection between business events and financial statements encourages students to analyze conceptual relationships rather than memorize procedures. Early in the course, students develop a conceptual framework that supports critical thinking and communication.

But don't take our word for it.

With over 200 colleges and universities successfully making the change to the concepts approach, we feel confident you will experience the same success as many of your colleagues have across the country. We would like to thank all of those who have been supportive of our teaching philosophy, and we highly encourage you to contact the author team or your local McGraw-Hill/Irwin representative to learn more about our texts.

Tom Edmonds • Cindy Edmonds • Frances McNair • Phil Olds • Edd Milan

---

Thomas P. Edmonds

Thomas P. Edmonds, Ph.D., is the Friends and Alumni Professor of Accounting at the University of Alabama at Birmingham (UAB). Dr. Edmonds has taught in the introductory area throughout his career. He has coordinated the accounting principles courses at the University of Houston and UAB. He currently teaches introductory accounting in mass sections and in UAB's distance learning program. He is actively involved in the accounting education change movement. He has conducted more that 50 workshops related to teaching introductory accounting during the last decade. Dr. Edmonds has received numerous prestigious teaching awards including the 2005 Alabama Society of CPAs Outstanding Educator Award and the UAB President's Excellence in Teaching Award. Dr. Edmonds' current research is education based. He has written articles that appeared in many publications including among others the *Accounting Review, Issues in Accounting, Journal of Accounting Education,* and *Advances in Accounting Education.* Dr. Edmonds has been a successful entrepreneur. He has worked as a management accountant for a transportation company and as a commercial lending office for the Federal Home Loan Bank. Dr. Edmonds began his academic training at Young Harris Community College. His Ph.D. degree was awarded by Georgia State University. Dr. Edmonds' work experience and academic training has enabled him to bring a unique perspective to the classroom.

Cindy D. Edmonds

Cindy D. Edmonds, Ph.D., is an Associate Professor of Accounting at the University of Alabama at Birmingham. She serves as the coordinator of the introductory accounting courses at UAB. Dr. Edmonds has received five prestigious teaching awards. Dr. Edmonds' articles appear in numerous publications including *Advances in Accounting Education, Journal of Education for Business, Journal of Accounting Regulation, Advances in Accounting, Management Accounting, CMA Journal, Disclosures,* and *Business & Professional Ethics Journal.* Dr. Edmonds is heavily involved in service activities. She is a past president of the Birmingham Chapter of the American Society of Women Accountants. Dr. Edmonds has worked in the insurance industry, in a manufacturing company, and in a governmental agency. This work experience has enabled her to bring a real-world flavor to her writing. Dr. Edmonds holds a B.S. degree from Auburn University, an M.B.A degree from the University of Houston, and a Ph.D. degree from the University of Alabama.

Frances M. McNair

Frances M. McNair holds the KPMG Peat Marwick Professorship in Accounting at Mississippi State University (MSU). She has been involved in teaching principles of accounting for the past 12 years and currently serves as the coordinator for the principles of accounting courses at MSU. She joined the MSU faculty in 1987 after receiving her Ph.D. from the University of Mississippi. The author of various articles that have appeared in the *Journal of Accountancy, Management Accounting, Business and Professional Ethics Journal, The Practical Accountant, Taxes,* and other publications, she also coauthored the book *The Tax Practitioner* with Dr. Denzil Causey. Dr. McNair is currently serving on committees of the American Taxation Association, the American Accounting Association, and the Institute of Management Accountants as well as numerous School of Accountancy and MSU committees.

AUTHORS

Edward E. Milam

Edward E. Milam, Ph.D., CPA, is a Professor of Accounting at Mississippi State University (MSU). Dr. Milam has been the recipient of several prestigious teaching awards including the Federation of Schools of Accountancy Outstanding Educator Award, and the Mississippi Society of CPA's Educator of the Year Award. Dr. Milam is a past President of the Federation of Schools of Accountancy, and has served on various committees of the ATA, FSA, AICPA, American Accounting Association, and the Mississippi Society of Certified Public Accountants. He has authored numerous articles that appeared in publications including *Journal of Accountancy, Taxes, Management Accounting, Financial Executive, Estate Planning, Trusts and Estates,* the *CPA Journal,* and others. He has also coauthored seven books.

Philip R. Olds

Philip R. Olds is Associate Professor of Accounting at Virginia Commonwealth University (VCU). He serves as the coordinator of the introduction to accounting courses at VCU. Professor Olds received his A.S. degree from Brunswick Junior College in Brunswick, Georgia (now Costal Georgia Community College). He received a B.B.A. in Accounting from Georgia Southern College (now Georgia Southern University) and his M.P.A. and Ph.D. degrees from Georgia State University. After graduating from Georgia Southern, he worked as an auditor with the U.S. Department of Labor in Atlanta, Georgia. A CPA in Virginia, Professor Olds has published articles in various professional journals and presented papers at national and regional conferences. He also served as the faculty adviser to the VCU chapter of Beta Alpha Psi for five years. In 1989, he was recognized with an Outstanding Faculty Vice-President Award by the national Beta Alpha Psi organization.

HOW DOES THE BOOK HELP
STUDENTS SEE THE BIG PICTURE?

PRINCIPAL FEATURES

Horizontal Financial Statements Model

A horizontal financial statements model replaces the accounting equation as the predominant teaching platform in this text. The model arranges the balance sheet, income statement and statement of cash flows horizontally across a single line of text as shown below.

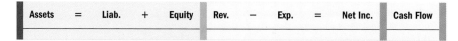

Assets	=	Liab.	+	Equity	Rev.	−	Exp.	=	Net Inc.	Cash Flow

The statements model approach enables students to more clearly see how accounting relates to real-world decision making. Under the traditional approach students learn to journalize a series of events and to present summarized information in financial statements. They never see how individual transactions affect financial statements. In contrast, when students record transactions into a statements model, they see a direct connection between business events and financial statements. Most business people think "if I take this particular action, how will it affect my financials," not "if I do these fifteen things how will they be journalized." Accordingly, the statements model approach provides a learning experience that is more intuitive and relevant than the one provided by traditional teaching methodology.

Establishing the Conceptual Framework

Chapter 1 introduces the key components of the conceptual framework for financial accounting. Accruals are introduced in Chapter 2, deferrals in Chapter 3. The first three chapters use only nontechnical terms (increase/decrease rather than debit/credit) to discuss the effects of events on the financial statements. Chapter 4 introduces recording procedures, including debits and credits. By the end of the first four chapters, students using this text will have been exposed to the same accounting content as those who use traditional books.

After Chapter 4, the text demonstrates both the conceptual structure and the recording procedures in tandem. For example, the purchase of treasury stock would be shown as follows:

Assets	=	Liab.	+	Equity	Rev.	−	Exp.	=	Net Inc.	Cash Flow
(8,400)	=	NA	+	(8,400)	NA	−	NA	=	NA	8,400 FA

Account Title	Debit	Credit
Treasury Stock	8,400	
Cash		8,400

Effects of Cash Flows Through the Entire Text

The statement of cash flows is introduced in the first chapter and included throughout the text. Students learn to prepare a statement of cash flows in the first chapter by learning to analyze each increase and decrease in the cash account. They can prepare a statement of cash flows by classifying each entry in the cash account as an operating, investing, or financing activity.

Effects on Financial Statements over Multiple Accounting Cycles

The text uses a vertical statements model that shows financial statements from top to bottom on a single page. This model displays financial results for consecutive accounting cycles in adjacent columns, thereby enabling the instructor to show how related events are reported *over multiple accounting cycles.*

EXHIBIT 9.6	Financial Statements under Units-of-Production Depreciation				
DRYDEN ENTERPRISES Financial Statements					
	2008	2009	2010	2011	2012
Income Statements					
Rent revenue	$11,000	$ 7,000	$ 9,000	$ 5,000	$ 0
Depreciation expense	(8,000)	(4,000)	(6,000)	(2,000)	0
Operating income	3,000	3,000	3,000	3,000	0
Gain on sale of van	0	0	0	0	500
Net income	$ 3,000	$ 3,000	$ 3,000	$ 3,000	$ 500
Balance Sheets					
Assets					
Cash	$12,000	$19,000	$28,000	$33,000	$37,500
Van	24,000	24,000	24,000	24,000	0
Accumulated depreciation	(8,000)	(12,000)	(18,000)	(20,000)	0
Total assets	$28,000	$31,000	$34,000	$37,000	$37,500
Stockholders' equity					
Common stock	$25,000	$25,000	$25,000	$25,000	$25,000
Retained earnings	3,000	6,000	9,000	12,000	12,500
Total stockholders' equity	$28,000	$31,000	$34,000	$37,000	$37,500
Statements of Cash Flows					
Operating Activities					
Inflow from customers	$11,000	$ 7,000	$ 9,000	$ 5,000	$ 0
Investing Activities					
Outflow to purchase van	(24,000)				
Inflow from sale of van					4,500
Financing Activities					
Inflow from stock issue	25,000				
Net Change in Cash	12,000	7,000	9,000	5,000	4,500
Beginning cash balance	0	12,000	19,000	28,000	33,000
Ending cash balance	$12,000	$19,000	$28,000	$33,000	$37,500

WHAT WE DID TO MAKE IT BETTER!

You spoke, we listened. The primary changes in this edition were motivated by comments and suggestions provided by our existing and potential new adopters. The most significant changes are as follows:

- **Restructured text materials to clearly distinguish revenue, expense, and dividend accounts from the retained earnings account.** We introduced the term "accounts" in Chapter 1 and clearly defined revenue, expense, dividend, and retained earnings as separate accounts. Also, we introduced the closing process in Chapter 1 and expanded coverage of this topic in Chapters 2, 3 and 4. We added several new exercises and added new requirements to existing problems that deal specifically with the issue of account classification and the closing process.
- **Expanded and updated coverage of ethics to include other features of corporate governance.** Indeed, the heading in Chapter 2 formerly titled "Importance of Ethics" is now titled "Corporate Governance." More specifically, we expanded the coverage of Sarbanes-Oxley. We replaced the content related to Cressey's common features of ethical misconduct with content that covers the primary features of the fraud triangle. The reference to the fraud triangle is more current and germane because it is found directly in contemporary accounting literature.
- **Moved coverage of gains and losses from Chapter 3 to Chapter 5.** This enabled us to use single-step income statements in Chapters 1 through 4. The single-step income statement is simpler and avoids the conflict in how interest is reported on the income statement versus the statement of cash flows. The multi-step income statement is introduced in Chapter 5.
- **Replaced coverage of the *net method* of accounting for cash discounts with coverage of the *gross method*.** While we remain convinced that the net method is theoretically preferable, we recognize that the gross method is easier to teach and used more frequently in the real world.
- **Added coverage of the effective interest rate method for amortizing bond discounts and premiums to an end-of-chapter appendix.** We continue to use the straight-line method in the main body of the text because of its simplicity. However, several instructors expressed the desire to include the effective interest rate method because of its theoretical superiority and widespread use in practice.
- **Rewrote Chapter 12 to shift the focus from the *direct method* of accounting for cash flows from operating activities to the *indirect method*.** We continue to use the direct method in Chapters 1 through 11 while students are forming their knowledge of the statement of cash flows. However, we believe that indirect method is more appropriate at an advanced level because of its wide spread use in practice.
- **Added a full featured separate chapter covering financial statement analysis which is available online.** We continue to cover financial statement analysis in each chapter of the text. However, some instructors prefer to cover financial statement analysis in more detail and as a separate subject. Making a financial statement analysis chapter available online enables us to provide the detailed coverage that some instructors prefer while keeping the hard copy of the text at a reasonable length. Please review the table of contents to familiarize yourself with the financial statement analysis coverage that is included in the text.
- **Streamlined the text by more effective use of appendices.** We moved content related to the audit function to an appendix. Content related to investment securities and time-value-of-money was moved to appendices located at the end of the book. The appendix covering not-for-profit accounting was deleted. A new appendix covering the effective interest rate method of accounting for bond discounts and premiums was added.

Chapter Specific Changes

Chapter 1 An Introduction to Accounting

- Changed chapter title to **An Introduction to Accounting.**
- Redesigned chapter to enhance clarity and readability.
- Defined the term "accounts" and clearly distinguished revenue, expense, and dividend accounts from the retained earnings account.
- Added an introduction to the closing process.
- Added a new Check Yourself problem to highlight account classification and the closing process.
- Added new exercises and changed requirements to several of the exercises and problems to provide coverage of the closing process.
- Added a section covering careers in accounting.
- Added a new Reality Bytes.
- Redesigned formulas and graphics to promote clarity.
- Moved discussion of the Price/Earnings ratio to an end of chapter Appendix.

Chapter 2 Accounting for Accruals

- Expanded coverage of ethics to include other features of corporate governance. Broadened coverage of Sarbanes-Oxley and replaced coverage of common features of ethical misconduct (Cressey) with coverage of the fraud triangle.
- Expanded coverage of closing process. Rewrote the section on closing and added a new Check Yourself exercise. Added exercises and problems that emphasize closing.
- Moved coverage of auditing to appendix.

Chapter 3 Accounting for Deferrals

- Moved coverage of gains and losses to Chapter 5. This enables the use of the single step income statement and avoids the conflict between how interest is reported on the income statement versus the statement of cash flows.

- Replaced the Focus on International Issues textbox discussion with new scenario.
- Added exercises and problems related to financial statement analysis.

Chapter 4 The Double-Entry Accounting System

- Replaced Reality Bytes sidebar with new scenario.

Chapter 5 Accounting for Merchandising Businesses

- Extensive chapter rewrite to enhance organizational structure and readability.
- Replaced coverage of the *net method* of accounting for cash discounts with coverage of the *gross method.*
- Added coverage of gains and losses.
- Expanded coverage of multistep versus single step income statements.
- Expanded the end-of-chapter materials by adding twelve new exercises.

Chapter 6 Accounting for Inventories

- Changed title from *Accounting for Merchandising Businesses—Advanced Topics* to *Accounting for Inventories.*
- Moved appendix on investments in marketable securities to appendix at end of book.
- Streamlined exhibits to highlight the key elements affecting the financial statements.
- Expanded the end-of-chapter materials by adding twelve new exercises.

Chapter 7 Internal Control and Accounting for Cash

- Added exercises and problems related to financial statement analysis.

Chapter 8 Accounting for Receivables and Payables

- Changed title from *Accounting for Accruals—Advanced Topics* to *Accounting for Receivables and Payables.*
- Added exercises and problems related to financial statement analysis.

Chapter 9 Accounting for Long-Term Operational Assets

- Replaced Reality Bytes sidebar with new scenario.
- Added exercises and problems related to financial statement analysis.

Chapter 10 Accounting for Long-Term Debt

- Added coverage of the effective interest rate method for amortizing bond premiums and discounts to an end-of-chapter appendix.
- Moved coverage of time value of money to an appendix.
- Expanded the end-of-chapter materials by adding twelve new exercises.

Chapter 11 Accounting for Equity Transactions

- Deleted appendix related to not-for-profit accounting.
- Updated exercises, problems, and cases.
- Added exercises and problems related to financial statement analysis.

Chapter 12 Statement of Cash Flows

- Extensive chapter rewrite to shift focus from the *direct method* of accounting for cash flows from operating activities to the *indirect method.*
- Created new end-of-chapter materials to reflect emphasis on indirect method.

Chapter 13 Financial Statement Analysis (on the text Web site, www.mhhe.com/edmonds6e)

- Added a full-featured separate chapter covering financial statement analysis which is available online.
- Updated Financial Analyst section of each chapter with current data and new companies where appropriate. Added end-of-chapter materials to assure that all chapters contained exercises and problems related to financial analysis.
- Updated the annual reports for The Topps Company, Inc., and Harley-Davidson, Inc., that accompany the text.
- Updated ATC Problems 1 and 2 in each chapter that relate to the annual reports that accompany the text.
- Updated the summary of financial ratios section in Appendix C.
- Updated the Annual Report Projects with new solutions for (1) The Topps Company, Inc., (2) Harley-Davidson, Inc., and (3) professor-selected companies.

Real-World Examples

The text provides a variety of real-world examples of financial accounting as an essential part of the management process. There are descriptions of accounting practices from real organizations such as Coca-Cola, Enron, General Motors, and Amazon.com. These companies are highlighted in blue in the text.

The Curious Accountant

Each chapter opens with a short vignette. These pose a question about a real-world accounting issue related to the topic of the chapter. The answer to the question appears in a separate sidebar a few pages further into the chapter.

The Curious Accountant

Suppose Sarah Greenwood wishes to purchase a subscription to *American Baby* for her sister who is scheduled to give birth to her first child in early September 2010. She pays $12 for a one-year subscription to the Meredith Corporation, the company that publishes *American Baby, Better Homes and Gardens, The Ladies Home Journal,* and several other magazines. It also owns 13 television stations. Her sister will receive her first issue of the magazine in September.

How should Meredith Corporation account for the receipt of this cash? How would this event be reported on its December 31, 2010, financial statements? (Answer on page 127.)

CHAPTER OPENING

LO 1

Distinguish among accruals, deferrals, and allocations.

In Chapter 2, we defined accruals as the recognition of revenue and expense before the receipt or payment of cash. In this chapter, you will learn that accrual accounting involves deferrals and allocations as well as accruals. A **deferral** involves recognizing a revenue or expense at some time after cash has been collected or paid. For example, if a business collects cash in 2008 for services it will perform in 2009, the revenue is recognized in 2009 even though the cash was collected in 2008. When recognition comes after cash is exchanged, the event is a deferral. When recognition comes before cash is exchanged, the event is an accrual.

Deferred amounts may be recognized over several accounting periods. The process of assigning the total deferral to different accounting periods is called **allocation**. To illustrate, assume an attorney received a retainer fee of $30,000 from a client at the beginning of 2008. In exchange for the cash, the attorney agreed to act as a trustee for the client's children for the years 2008, 2009, and 2010. The recognition of the $30,000 of revenue would be deferred until it was earned. A portion of the revenue would then be allocated to each of the three accounting periods based on the amount earned each year. If the work were spread evenly over the three years, $10,000 would be recognized in each period. ∎

Focus on International Issues

These boxed inserts expose students to international issues in accounting.

FOCUS ON   INTERNATIONAL ISSUES

IS THERE GLOBAL GAAP?

As explained in this chapter, financial reporting is a measurement and communication discipline based on rules referred to as *generally accepted accounting principles.* The accounting rules described in this text are based on GAAP used in the United States. Not all economies throughout the world use the same accounting rules. Although there are many similarities among the accounting principles used in different countries, there also are major differences. In recent years, however, there has been a concerted effort to bring the accounting standards of the major industrialized nations into uniformity, or at least, to have less diversity. This process is usually referred to as *harmonization,* but simply put, there is no "global GAAP." Examples of how financial reporting in other countries differs from that in the United States are presented throughout this book.

Accounting rules differ among countries for a variety of reasons, including the economic and legal environments in each country and how the GAAP in that country is established. Generally accepted accounting principles in the United States are primarily established by the Financial Accounting Standards Board (FASB). The FASB is a nongovernment rule-making body established by the accounting profession. In some countries, such as Japan for example, the GAAP is established by government bodies. In these countries GAAP is established more like the way federal laws and regulations are established in the United States.

Furthermore, in the United States any connection between GAAP established by the FASB and tax accounting rules established by Congress and the Internal Revenue Service (IRS) is coincidental, not deliberate. In some countries there is a close connection be-

The Financial Analyst

Financial statement analysis is highlighted in each chapter under this heading.

THE FINANCIAL   ANALYST

This section of each chapter introduces topics related to analyzing real world financial reports. We focus first on the types of businesses that operate in the real world. We also discuss the annual report that is used to communicate information to stakeholders.

Real-World Financial Reports

As previously indicated, organizations exist in many different forms, including *business entities* and *not-for-profit* entities. Business entities are typically service, merchandising, or manufacturing companies. **Service businesses,** which include doctors, attorneys, accountants, dry cleaners, and maids, provide services to their customers. **Merchandising businesses,** sometimes called *retail* or *wholesale companies,* sell goods to customers that other entities make. **Manufacturing businesses** make the goods that they sell to their customers.

Some business operations include combinations of these three categories. For example, an automotive repair shop might change oil (service function), sell parts such as oil filters

"This is a well-written book. The real-life examples, pictures and illustrations especially provide an interesting perspective of accounting. This is a book that combines user approach and preparer approach in an effective manner."
Bea Chiang,
College of New Jersey

MOTIVATE STUDENTS?

Reality Bytes

This feature expands on the topics by showing how companies use the concepts discussed in the chapter to make business decisions.

Topic Tackler Plus

A logo indicates a topic explained on Topic Tackler Plus software. It includes two hard-to-learn topics for each chapter explained with video, PowerPoint, practice quizzes, self tests, and an audio-narrated demonstration problem walk-through.

Annual Reports

Two annual reports accompany the text.

- The 2005 annual report for Harley-Davidson, Inc., is packaged with the text.
- The 2006 annual report for The Topps Company, Inc. is printed in Appendix B.

Business Application Problems related to the annual reports are included at the end of each chapter.

Projects for each of these companies are included in the Annual Report and Financial Statement Analysis Projects, located in Appendix D. Also, a general purpose annual report project is included for instructors to assign for any company.

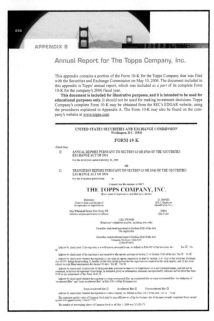

"This is a great textbook. I do like the approach of the first four chapters showing the financial statement effect of each transaction and the incorporation of cash flows in the discussions. The graphics are bright and relevant and some of the other pedagogical elements are great (real world, check yourself, etc.)."
Mark Fronke, Cerritos College

Focus Companies

Each chapter introduces important topics within the context of a realistic, though hypothetical company. Students see the impact of financial accounting decisions on the company as they work through the chapter. When the focus company is presented in the chapter, a logo representing the Focus Company is shown so the students see its application to the text topics.

Name and Type of Company Used as Main Chapter Example

Chapter Title	Company Used as Main Chapter Example	Company Logo	Type of Company
1. An Introduction to Accounting	Rustic Camp Sites	Rustic camp sites	Rents land
2. Accounting for Accruals	Conner Consultants	C·C Conner Consultants	Provides training services
3. Accounting for Deferrals	Marketing Magic, Inc. (MMI)	MMI Marketing Magic, Inc.	Advertising agency
4. The Double-Entry Accounting System	Collins Consultants	Collins Consultants	Provides accounting advisory services
5. Accounting for Merchandising Businesses	June's Plant Shop	June's PLANT SHOP	Sells gardening supplies
6. Accounting for Inventories	The Mountain Bike Company	The Mountain Bike	Sells bicycles

Event 1 **Rustic Camp Sites (RCS) was formed on January 1, 2008, when it acquired $120,000 cash from issuing common stock.**

When RCS issued stock, it received cash and gave each investor (owner) a stock certificate as a receipt. Since this transaction provided $120,000 of assets (cash) to the business, it is an **asset source transaction.** It increases the business's assets (cash) and its stockholders' equity (common stock).

Check Yourself

These short question/answers occur at the end of each main topic and ask students to stop and think about the material just covered. The answer follows to provide immediate feedback before students go on to a new topic.

CHECK YOURSELF 1.4

To gain a clear understanding of the balance sheet, try to create one that describes your personal financial condition. First list your assets, then your liabilities. Determine the amount of your equity by subtracting your liabilities from your assets.

Answer

Answers for this exercise will vary depending on the particular assets and liabilities each student identifies. Common student assets include automobiles, computers, stereos, TVs, phones, CD players, clothes, and textbooks. Common student liabilities include car loans, mortgages, student loans, and credit card debt. The difference between the assets and the liabilities is the equity.

"This is an excellent textbook. It strikes a great balance between understandability and readability, while still covering the topics in a thorough enough manner. It has many excellent features such as The Curious Accountant. It has included discussions of many pertinent, up-to-date topics such as ethics."
Sharon Jackson,
Samford University

ATC 5-10 Spreadsheet Analysis *Mastering Excel*

At the end of 2008, the following information is available for Short and Wise Companies:

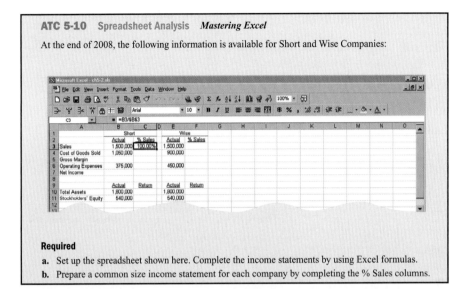

Required

a. Set up the spreadsheet shown here. Complete the income statements by using Excel formulas.

b. Prepare a common size income statement for each company by completing the % Sales columns.

<< A Look Back

This chapter introduced the principle of deferring revenue and expense recognition. *Deferrals* involve recognizing revenue or expense at some time *after* cash has been collected or paid. Deferrals cause significant differences in the amount of revenue and expenses reported on the income statement and the amount of cash flow from operating activities. These differences are readily apparent when deferral events are viewed in a horizontal financial statements model. To illustrate, review the following transactions and the statements model that follows them. To reinforce your understanding, draw a statements model on a piece of paper and try to record the effects of each event before reading the

A Look Forward >>

To this point, we have used plus and minus signs to illustrate the effects of business events on financial statements. In real businesses, so many transactions occur that recording them with simple mathematical notations is impractical. In practice, accountants usually maintain records using a system of rules known as *double-entry bookkeeping*. Chapter 4 introduces the basic components of this bookkeeping system. You will learn how to record business events using a debit/credit format. You will be introduced to ledgers, journals, and trial balances. When you finish Chapter 4, you will have a clear understanding of how accountants maintain records of business activity.

"The authors have done an excellent job teaching the subject matter in a very simple, understandable, yet accurate and knowledgeable way. Pedagogically excellent."
**Catherine Eason,
Queens University of Charlotte**

Regardless of the instructional approach, there is no shortcut to learning accounting. Students must practice to master basic accounting concepts. The text includes a prodigious supply of practice materials and exercises and problems.

Self-Study Review Problem

These example problems include a detailed, worked-out solution and provide support for students before they work problems on their own. These review problems are included in an animated audio presentation, on the text Web site.

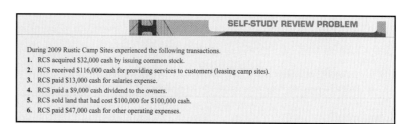

SELF-STUDY REVIEW PROBLEM

During 2009 Rustic Camp Sites experienced the following transactions.
1. RCS acquired $32,000 cash by issuing common stock.
2. RCS received $116,000 cash for providing services to customers (leasing camp sites).
3. RCS paid $13,000 cash for salaries expense.
4. RCS paid a $9,000 cash dividend to the owners.
5. RCS sold land that had cost $100,000 for $100,000 cash.
6. RCS paid $47,000 cash for other operating expenses.

Exercise Series A & B and Problem Series A & B

There are two sets of problems and exercises, Series A and B. Instructors can assign one set for homework and another set for classwork.

• Check figures

The figures provide key answers for selected problems.

• Excel

Many problems can be solved using the Excel™ templates contained on the text's Online Learning Center. A logo appears in the margins next to these problems.

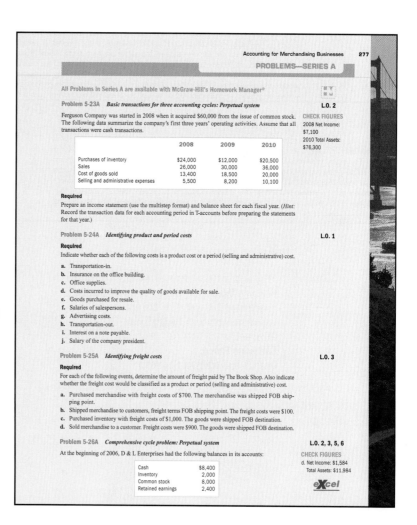

Accounting for Merchandising Businesses **277**

PROBLEMS—SERIES A

All Problems in Series A are available with McGraw-Hill's Homework Manager®

Problem 5-23A *Basic transactions for three accounting cycles: Perpetual system*   L.O. 2

Ferguson Company was started in 2008 when it acquired $60,000 from the issue of common stock. The following data summarize the company's first three years' operating activities. Assume that all transactions were cash transactions.

CHECK FIGURES
2008 Net Income:
$7,100
2010 Total Assets:
$76,300

	2008	2009	2010
Purchases of inventory	$24,000	$12,000	$20,500
Sales	26,000	30,000	36,000
Cost of goods sold	13,400	18,500	20,000
Selling and administrative expenses	5,500	8,200	10,100

Required
Prepare an income statement (use the multistep format) and balance sheet for each fiscal year. (*Hint:* Record the transaction data for each accounting period in T-accounts before preparing the statements for that year.)

Problem 5-24A *Identifying product and period costs*   L.O. 1

Required
Indicate whether each of the following costs is a product cost or a period (selling and administrative) cost.

a. Transportation-in.
b. Insurance on the office building.
c. Office supplies.
d. Costs incurred to improve the quality of goods available for sale.
e. Goods purchased for resale.
f. Salaries of salespersons.
g. Advertising costs.
h. Transportation-out.
i. Interest on a note payable.
j. Salary of the company president.

Problem 5-25A *Identifying freight costs*   L.O. 3

Required
For each of the following events, determine the amount of freight paid by The Book Shop. Also indicate whether the freight cost would be classified as a product or period (selling and administrative) cost.

a. Purchased merchandise with freight costs of $700. The merchandise was shipped FOB shipping point.
b. Shipped merchandise to customers, freight terms FOB shipping point. The freight costs were $100.
c. Purchased inventory with freight costs of $1,000. The goods were shipped FOB destination.
d. Sold merchandise to a customer. Freight costs were $900. The goods were shipped FOB destination.

Problem 5-26A *Comprehensive cycle problem: Perpetual system*   L.O. 2, 3, 5, 6

At the beginning of 2006, D & L Enterprises had the following balances in its accounts:

CHECK FIGURES
d. Net Income: $1,584
Total Assets: $11,984

Cash	$8,400
Inventory	2,000
Common stock	8,000
Retained earnings	2,400

eXcel

CONCEPTS REINFORCED?

Analyze, Think, Communicate (ATC)

Each chapter includes an innovative section entitled Analyze, Think, Communicate (ATC). This section offers Business Applications Cases, Group Assignments, Real World Cases, Writing Assignments, Ethical Dilemma Problems, Research Assignments and Spreadsheet Assignments.

We use logos to help students identify the type of question being asked.

- **Topps**
  Harley-Davidson

- **Group Work**

- **Real World Company**

- **Ethics**

- **Research**

- **Writing**

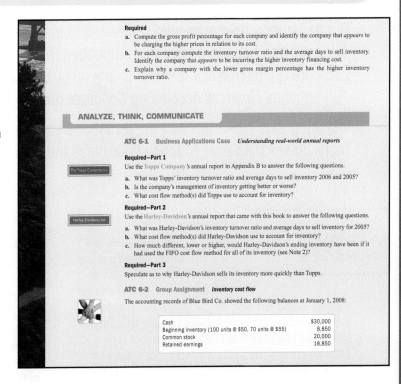

> "Thanks for such a great text. I see a significant difference in enthusiasm and success in my students with your text."
> **Denise English,**
> **Boise State University**

Comprehensive Problem

Beginning in Chapter 5, a comprehensive problem builds in each successive chapter, with the ending account balances in one chapter becoming the beginning account balances in the next chapter.

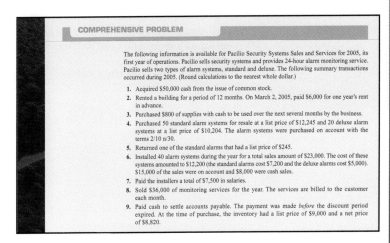

HOW CAN TECHNOLOGY

Our technology resources help students and instructors focus on learning success. By using the Internet and multimedia students get book-specific help at their convenience. Compare our technology to those of any other book and we're confident you'll agree that *Fundamental Financial Accounting Concepts* has the best in the market.

Teaching aids make in-class presentations easy and stimulating. These aids give you more power than ever to teach your class the way you want.

McGraw-Hill's Homework Manager®

is a Web-based supplement that duplicates problem structures directly from the end-of-chapter material in your textbook, using algorithms to provide a limitless supply of online self-graded assignments that can be used for student practice, homework, or testing. Each assignment has a unique solution. Say goodbye to cheating in your classroom; say hello to the power and flexibility you've been waiting for in creating assignments. All Exercises and Problems in Series A are available with Homework Manager.

McGraw-Hill's Homework Manager is also a useful grading tool. All assignments can be delivered over the Web and are graded automatically, with the results stored in your private grade book. Detailed results let you see at a glance how each student does on an assignment or an individual problem—you can even see how many tries it took them to solve it.

McGraw-Hill's Homework Manager Plus™

combines the power of McGraw-Hill's Homework Manager with the latest interactive learning technology to create a comprehensive, fully integrated online study package.

Students using McGraw-Hill's Homework Manager Plus can access not only McGraw-Hill's Homework Manager™ itself, but the interactive Online Textbook as well. Far more than a textbook on a screen, this resource is completely integrated into McGraw-Hill's Homework Manager, allowing students working on assignments to click a hotlink and instantly review the appropriate material in the textbook.

By including McGraw-Hill's Homework Manager Plus with your textbook adoption, you're giving your students a vital edge as they progress through the course and ensuring that the help they need is never more than a mouse click away.

Students receive full access to McGraw-Hill's Homework Manager when they purchase Homework Manager Plus.

"A well-written text with supplements that cover any aspect one would need. It will appeal to the students with the use of video and practice tests. The homework manager is a great plus and instructors will wonder what they did before it."
Terry Elliott,
Morehead State University

HELP STUDENT SUCCESS?

iPod® Content

Harness the power of one of the most popular technology tools today—the Apple iPod. Our innovative approach allows students to download audio and video presentations right into their iPod and take learning materials with them wherever they go.

Students can visit the Online Learning Center at www.mhhe.com/edmonds6e to download our iPod content. For each chapter of the book they will be able to download narrated lecture presentations, financial accounting videos, and even self-quizzes. It makes review and study time as easy as putting on earphones.

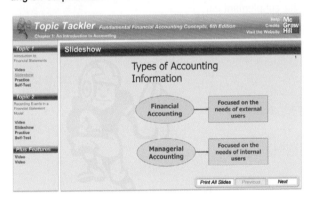

Topic Tackler Plus

This software is a complete tutorial focusing on areas in the course that give students the most trouble. It provides help on two key topics for each chapter by use of:

- Video clips
- PowerPoint slide shows
- Interactive exercises
- Self-grading quizzes

Topic Tackler Plus also includes the Self-Study Review Problems in the book presented in an audio-narrated PowerPoint slide presentation.

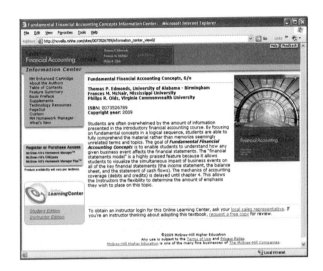

Online Learning Center (OLC)

www.mhhe.com/edmonds6e

More and more students are studying online. That's why we offer an Online Learning Center (OLC) that follows Fundamental Financial Accounting Concepts chapter by chapter. The OLC includes:

- Topic Tackler Plus
- iPod® Content
- Excel Spreadsheets
- Spreadsheet Tips
- Glossary
- Key Term Flashcards
- Interactive Quizzes
- Narrated PowerPoints
- Narrated Self Study Review Problem
- Financial Statement Analysis Chapter
- Accounting Resources
- Videos
- Sample Study Guide Chapter
- Text Updates/Errata

How Can Technology Enhance Your Course?

For instructors, the book's secured Online Learning Center (OLC) contains essential course materials. You can pull all of this material into your PageOut course syllabus or use it as part of another online course management system. It includes all of the student assets, as well as:

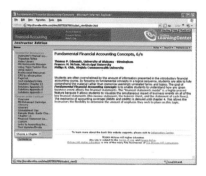

- Instructor's Manual
- Solutions Manual
- Solutions to Excel Assignments
- Sample Syllabi
- Transition Notes
- Text Updates/Errata

Enhanced Course Cartridge

The Enhanced Course Cartridge is developed to help you get your course up and running with much less time and effort. The content, enhanced with more assignments and more study materials than a standard cartridge, is pre-populated into appropriate chapters and content categories. Now there's not a need to cut and paste our content into your course—it's already there! In addition to the standard instructor supplement content, this cartridge also includes:

- Pre-populated course syllabus
- iPod®/MP3 content
- Chapter pretests and posttests
- Mid-term and Final tests
- Discussion boards
- Additional assignments
- Personalized graphics/banners/icons for your school
- Gradebook functionality

The Enhanced Cartridge allows students to access their course anytime, anywhere, including:

- Key term flashcards
- Excel templates
- Narrated review problems
- Topic Tackler Plus
- PowerPoint slides

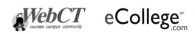

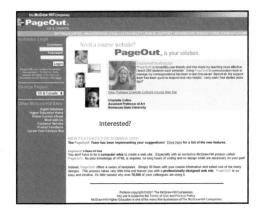

Online Course Management
WebCT, eCollege, and Blackboard

We've heard you tell us about the importance of course management systems. In response, McGraw-Hill/Irwin is pleased to offer a new, ENHANCED COURSE CARTRIDGE that populates your CMS with instructor and student supplements, directly from *Fundamental Financial Accounting Concepts*. There is no need to upload content unless you want to! But you still have the capability to add any of your own material or hide the material that we provide. Our content includes all the material on the OLC plus a wealth of study material for students. See our description on the previous page.

PageOut

McGraw-Hill's Course Management System Pageout is the easiest way to create a Web site for your accounting course. Just fill in a series of boxes with plain English and click on one of our professional designs. In no time your course is online with a Web site that contains your syllabus. If you need help, our team of specialists is ready to take your course materials and build a custom Web site to your specifications. To learn more visit *www.pageout.net*.

CPS Classroom Performance System by eInstruction

This is a revolutionary system that brings ultimate interactivity to the classroom. CPS is a wireless response system that gives you immediate feedback from every student in the class. CPS units include easy-to-use software for creating and delivering questions and assessments to your class. With CPS you can ask subjective and objective questions. Then every student simply responds with their individual, wireless response pad, providing instant results. CPS is the perfect tool for engaging students while gathering important assessment data.

Instructors Resource CD

This CD includes:

- Solutions Manual
- Instructors Manual
- Test Bank
- EZ Test Computerized Test Bank
- PowerPoint slides
- Video clips
- Exhibits from the text

SUPPLEMENTS for Instructors

Instructor's Resource CD

ISBN-10: 0073218383 ISBN-13: 9780073218380

This CD includes electronic versions of the Instructor's Manual, Solutions Manual, Test Bank, and computerized Test Bank, as well as PowerPoint slides, video clips, all exhibits in the text in PowerPoint, and spreadsheet templates with solutions. This CD-ROM makes it easy for instructors to create multimedia presentations.

Instructor's Manual

(Available on the password-protected Instructor Online Learning Center (OLC) and Instructor's Resource CD)

This comprehensive manual includes step-by-step, explicit instructions on how the text can be used to implement alternative teaching methods. It also provides guidance for instructors who use the traditional lecture method. The guide includes lesson plans and demonstration problems with student work papers, as well as solutions.

Solutions Manual

(Available on the password-protected Instructor OLC and Instructor Resource CD)

Prepared by the authors, the manual contains complete solutions to all the text's end-of-chapter exercises, problems, and cases.

PowerPoint Presentation

(Available on the OLC and Instructor's Resource CD-ROM)

These audio-narrated slides can serve as interactive class discussions and were prepared by Jon A. Booker and Charles W. Caldwell of Tennessee Technological University and Susan Galbreath of David Lipscomb University.

Test Bank

(Available on the Instructor's Resource CD)

This test bank in Word™ format contains multiple-choice questions, essay questions, and short problems. Each test item is coded for level of difficulty and learning objective. In addition to an expansive array of traditional test questions, the test bank includes questions that focus exclusively on how business events affect financial statements.

Computerized Test Bank

(Available on the Instructor's Resource CD)

This test bank utilizes McGraw-Hill's EZ Test software to quickly create customized exams. This user-friendly program allows instructors to sort questions by format; edit existing questions or add new ones. It also can scramble questions for multiple versions of the same test.

Algorithmic-Diploma Test Bank

ISBN-10: 0073334340 ISBN-13: 9780073334349

Assurance-of-Learning Ready

Many educational institutions today are focused on the notion of assurance of learning, an important element of some accreditation standards. *Fundamental Financial Accounting Concepts* is designed specifically to support your assurance of learning initiatives with a simple, yet powerful, solution.

Each test bank question for *Fundamental Financial Accounting Concepts* maps to a specific chapter learning outcome/objective listed in the text. You can use our test bank software, *EZ Test* to easily query for learning outcomes/objectives that directly relate to the learning objectives for your course. You can then use the reporting features of *EZ Test* to aggregate student results in similar fashion, making the collection and presentation of assurance of learning data simple and easy. You can also use our Algorithmic-Diploma Test Bank to do this.

AACSB Statement

McGraw-Hill Companies is a proud corporate member of AACSB International. Recognizing the importance and value of AACSB accreditation, the authors of *Fundamental Financial Accounting Concepts*, Sixth Edition, have sought to recognize the curricula guidelines detailed in AACSB standards for business accreditation by connecting selected questions in *Fundamental Financial Accounting Concepts* the general knowledge and skill guidelines found in the AACSB standards. It is important to note that the statements contained in *Fundamental Financial Accounting Concepts,* Sixth Edition are provided only as a guide for the users of this text.

The statements contained in *Fundamental Financial Accounting Concepts*, Sixth Edition are provided only as a guide for the users of this text. The AACSB leaves content coverage and assessment clearly within the realm and control of individual schools, the mission of the school, and the faculty. The AACSB does also charge schools with the obligation of doing assessment against their own content and learning goals. While *Fundamental Financial Accounting Concepts*, Sixth Edition and its teaching package make no claim of any specific AACSB qualification or evaluation, we have labeled selected questions according to the six general knowledge and skills areas. The labels or tags within *Fundamental Financial Accounting Concepts*, Sixth Edition are as indicated. There are of course, many more within the test bank, the text, and the teaching package which might be used as a "standard" for your course. However, the labeled questions are suggested for your consideration.

> "Edmonds is contemporary, engaging, different, and well-written. It has excellent support materials for students and faculty."
>
> **Joseph Onyeocha,**
> **South Carolina State University**

SUPPLEMENTS for Students

McGraw-Hill's Homework Manager Plus™
One Pass integrates all of the text's multimedia resources. With just one access code, students can-obtain state of the art study aids, including Homework Manager, NetTutor and an online version of the text.

McGraw-Hill's Homework Manager®
This web-based software duplicates problem structures directly from the end-of-chapter material in the textbook. It uses algorithms to provide a limitless supply of self-graded practice for students. It shows students where they made errors. All Exercises and Problems in Series A are available with Homework Manager.

Study Guide
ISBN-10: 0073218332
ISBN-13: 9780073218335
Each chapter contains a review and explanation of the chapter's learning objectives, as well as multiple-choice problems and short exer- cises. Unique to this Study Guide is a series of problems that require students to indicate how accounting events affect the elements of financial statements. The guide includes appropriate working papers and a complete set of solutions.

Excel Templates
(Available on the Online Learning Center (OLC))
These templates allow students to develop spreadsheet skills to solve selected assignments identified by an icon in the end-of-chapter material.

Working Papers
ISBN-10: 0073218324
ISBN-13: 9780073218328
Working papers are available to direct students in solving text assignments.

Computerized Practice Sets
Wheels Exquisite, Level 1
Student ISBN-10: 0072428457
ISBN-13: 9780072428452
Instructor ISBN-10: 0072427531
ISBN-13: 9780072427530

Gold Run Snowmobile
Student ISBN-10: 0072957883
ISBN-13: 9780072957884
Instructor ISBN-10: 0072947683
ISBN-13: 9780072947687

Topic Tackler Plus
(Available on the Online Learning Center (OLC))
This tutorial offers a virtual helping hand in understanding the most challenging topics in the financial accounting course. Through a step-by-step sequence of video clips, PowerPoint slides, interactive practice exercises, and self tests, Topic Tackler Plus offers help on two key topics for each chapter. These topics are indicated by a logo in the text. Another component takes the Self-Study Review Problem in the book and demonstrates how to solve it in an animated audio presentation.

Narrated PowerPoint
(Available on the Online Learning Center (OLC))
These PowerPoint slides cover key chapter topics in an audio-narrated presentation sure to help students learn.

ALEKS for Financial Accounting
ISBN-10: 0072859598
ISBN-13: 9780072841961

Online Learning Center (OLC)
www.mhhe.com/edmonds6e
See page xix for details

iPod® Content
See page xix for details

Tom Edmonds / Cindy Edmonds / Frances McNair / Phil Olds / Edd Milan

ACKNOWLEDGMENTS

Our grateful appreciation is extended to those who reviewed previous editions:

Special thanks to the talented people who prepared the supplements. These take a great deal of time and effort to write and we appreciate their efforts. Sue Cullers of Tarleton State University prepared the Test Bank. Nancy Schneider of Lynchburg College wrote the Instructors Manual. Steven Muller of Valencia Community College prepared the narrated Self-Review Problem PowerPoint slides. Jack Terry of ComSource Associates developed the Excel Templates. Amelia Baldwin of the University of Alabama-Huntsville did the PowerPoint slide presentation. Linda Schain of Hofstra University prepared the Topic Tackler Plus material. Nina Collum of Mississippi State University prepared the online quizzes. We also thank our accuracy checkers Beth Woods and Nina Collum. Other accuracy checkers include Ann DeCapite of Coastal Carolina Community College, and Teressa Farough. A special thanks to Linda Bell of William Jewell College for her contribution to the Financial Statement Analysis material that appears in Appendix D.

We are most grateful to Melissa Larmon and the sales staff for providing the informative advertising that has so accurately communicated the unique features of the concepts approach to accounting educators. Many others at McGraw-Hill/Irwin at a moment's notice redirected their attention to focus their efforts on the development of this text. We extend our sincere appreciation to Pat Frederickson, Debra Sylvester, Artemio Ortiz, Jeremy Cheshareck, Victor Chiu, Lynn Bluhm and Matthew Perry. We deeply appreciate the long hours that you committed to the formation of a high-quality text.

Thomas P. Edmonds • Cindy P. Edmonds • Frances M. McNair • Philip R. Olds • Edward M. Milan

---

We would like to express our appreciation to the people who have provided assistance in the development of this textbook.

We express our sincere thanks to the following individuals who provided extensive reviews for the sixth edition:

Reviewers

Marie Archambault, *Marshall University*

Kashi Balachandran, *Stern School, New York University*

Cheryl Bartlett, *Albuquerque TVI Community College*

Ira Bates, *Florida A&M University*

Deborah Beard, *Southeast Missouri State University*

Judy Beebe, *Western Oregon University*

Judy Benish, *Fox Valley Tech*

Connie Buchanan, *Southwest Texas Junior College*

Jacqueline Burke, *Hofstra University*

Valrie Chambers, *Texas A&M University, Corpus Christi*

Bea Chiang, *College of New Jersey*

Cheryl Corke, *Genesse Community College*

Samantha Cox, *Wake Technical Community College*

Kathy Crusto-Way, *Tarrant County College Southeast*

Sue Cullers, *Tarleton State University*

Jill D'Aquila, *Iona College*

Catherine Eason, *Queens University of Charlotte*

Alan Eastman, *Indiana University of Pennsylvania*

Susan Eldridge, *University of Nebraska, Omaha*

Terry Elliott, *Morehead State University*

Tom English, *Boise State University*

Denise English, *Boise State University*

John Farlin, *Ohio Dominican University*

Philip Fink, *University of Toledo*

Peter Frischmann, *Idaho State University*

Mark Fronke, *Cerritos College*

Ross Fuerman, *Suffolk University*

Daniel Gibbons, *Waubonsee Community College*

Frank Giove, *Niagara University*

Diana Glowacki, *Tarrant County College*

Joseph Guardino, *Kingsborough Community College*

Jeffry Haber, *Iona College*

Coby Harmon, *University of California, Santa Barbara*

Judith Harris, *Nova Southeastern University*

Paul Haugen, *Wisconsin Indianhead Technical College*

Thomas Hayes, *University of Louisiana, Monroe*

Bambi Hora, *University of Central Oklahoma*

M. A. Houston, *Wright State University*

Susan Hughes, *Butler University*

Kurt Hull, *California State University, Los Angeles*

Sharon Jackson, *Samford University*

Gary Todd Jackson, *Northeastern State University*

Agatha Jeffers, *Montclair State University*

Scott Jerris, *San Francisco State University*

Cindi Khanlarian, *University of North Carolina, Greensboro*

Bonita Kramer, *Montana State University*

Ellen Landgraf, *Loyola University, Chicago*

Doug Laufer, *Metropolitan State College of Denver*

Daniel Law, *Gonzaga University*

Marilynn Leathart, *John Carroll University*

Patsy Lee, *University of Texas, Arlington*

June Li, *University of Minnesota, Duluth*

James Lukawitz, *University of Memphis*

Mary MacAusland, *Reading Area Community College*

Mostafa Maksy, *Northeastern Illinois University*

Elizabeth Matz, *University of Pittsburgh, Bradford*

Ruth Ann McEwen, *Suffolk University*

Shaen McMurtrie, *Northern Oklahoma College*

Trini Melcher, *California State University, San Marcos*

Pam Meyer, *University of Louisiana, Lafayette*

R. L. C. Miller, *California State University, Fullerton*

Susan Minke, *Indiana University-Purdue University, Ft. Wayne*

Bruce Neumann, *University of Colorado, Denver*

Bruce Oliver, *Rochester Institute of Technology*

Joseph Onyeocha, *South Carolina State University*

Ashton Oravetz, *Tyler Junior College*

Stephen Owusu-Ansah, *University of Texas, Pan American*

Cynthia Phipps, *Lake Land College*

Ronald Pierno, *Florida State University*

Thomas Rearick, *Indiana University*

Ann Rich, *Quinnipiac University*

Laura Rickett, *Kent State University*

Luther Ross, *Central Piedmont Community College*

Nadine Russell

P. N. Saksena, *Indiana University, South Bend*

Henry Schulman, *Grossmont College*

Carol Shaver, *Louisiana Tech University*

Lewis Shaw, *Suffolk University*

Talitha Smith, *Auburn University*

Jill Smith, *Idaho State University*

Mary Soroko, *St. Cloud State University*

Linda Specht, *Trinity University*

Shelley Stall Kane, *Wake Technical Community College*

Vic Stanton, *University of California, Berkeley*

Scott Steinkamp, *College of Lake County*

Rasoul Taghizadeh, *Lexington Community College*

Bill Talbot, *Montgomery College*

James Thompson, *Oklahoma City University*

Karen Turner, *University of Northern Colorado*

Thomas Whalen, *Suffolk University*

Jennifer Wilbanks, *State Fair Community College*

Marvin Williams, *University of Houston*

Gail Wright, *Bryant University*

Judith Zander, *Grossmont College*

Haiwen Zhang, *University of Minnesota*

Ping Zhon, *Baruch College*

Focus Group

R. E. (Gene) Bryson, *University of Alabama*

Kang Cheng, *Towson University*

Keith Harrison, *Truman State University*

Kenneth Heaslip, *Seton Hall University*

Byron Henry, *Howard University*

Margaret Hicks, *Howard University*

Richard Newmark, *University of Northern Colorado*

Emeka Ofobike, *University of Akron*

Past Edition Reviewers

Our grateful appreciation is extended to those who reviewed previous editions:

Charles Richard Aldridge, *Western Kentucky University*

Mary Allen, *Boise State University*

Sheila Ammons, *Austin Community College*

Debra Barbeau, *Southern Illinois University-Carbondale*

Charles Baril, *James Madison University*

Beryl Barkman, *University of Massachusetts-Dartmouth*

Jim Bates, *Mountain Empire Community College*

Linda Bell, *William Jewell College*

Wilbur Berry, *Jacksonville State University*

Nancy Bledsoe, *Millsaps College*

Cendy Boyd, *Northeast Louisiana State*

Arthur Boyett, *Francis Marion University*

Cassie Bradley, *Troy State University*

Rodger Brannan, *University of Minnesota, Duluth*

Radie Bunn, *Southwest Missouri State University*

Jacqueline Burke, *Hofstra University*

Gregory Bushong, *Wright State University*

Judith Cadle, *Tarleton State University*

James Cahsell, *Miami University*

Scott Cairns, *Shippensburg College*

Eric Carlsen, *Kean University*

Frederic J. Carlson, *LeTourneau University*

Joan Carroll, *SUNY-College at Oswego*

Bruce Chase, *Radford University*

Alan Cherry, *Loyola Marymount University*

Ginger Clark, *University of Cincinnati*

Paul Clikeman, *University of Richmond*

Ronald Colley, *State University of West Georgia*

William Cress, *University of Wisconsin-La Cross*

Wagih Dafashy, *College of William & Mary*

Laura DeLaune, *Louisiana State University*

Robert Derstine, *Villanova University*

Walter Doehring, *Genesee Community College*

George Dow, *Valencia Community College*

Lola Dudley, *Eastern Illinois University*

Melanie Earls, *Mississippi State University*

M. J. Edwards, *Adirondack Community College*

Ruth Epps, *Virginia Commonwealth University*

Ralph Fritzsch, *Midwestern State University*

David Fordham, *James Madison University*

Ken Fowler, *San Jose State University*

Lou Fowler, *Missouri Western State College*

Mary Anne Gaffney, *Temple University*

David Ganz, *University of Missouri-Saint Louis*

Michael Garner, *Salisbury State University*

William T. Geary, *College of William and Mary*

Lucille Genduso, *Nova Southeastern University*

Frank Gersich, *Gustavus Adolphus College*

Claudia Gilbertson, *North Hennepin Community College*

Lorraine Glasscock, *University of North Alabama*

Diane Glowacki, *Tarrant County College*

John Gould, *Western Carolina University*

Larry Hagler, *East Carolina University*

Penny Hanes, *Virginia Tech University*

Leon Hanouille, *Syracuse University*

Phillip Harsha, *Southwest Missouri State University*

Charles Hart, *Copiah-Lincoln Community College*

Inez Heal, *Youngstown State University*

Kenneth Hiltebeitel, *Villanova*

Nitham Hindi, *Shippensburg College*

Jan Holmes, *Louisiana State University*

Karen Hull, *Kansas Wesleyan University*

Richard Hulme, *California State Polytechnic University-Pomona*

Scott Jerris, *San Francisco State University.*

Pamela Jones, *Mississippi State University*

Khondkar Karim, *Monmouth University*

Nathan Kranowski, *Radford University*

Helen LaFrancois, *University of Massachusetts-Dartmouth*

Robert Landry, *Massasoit Community College*

William Lathen, *Boise State University*

David Law, *Youngstown State University*

William Link, *University of Missouri-Saint Louis*

Larry Logan, *University of Massachusetts-Dartmouth*

Patricia Lopez, *Valencia Community College*

James Lukawitz, *University of Memphis*

Catherine Lumbattis, *Southern Illinois University-Carbondale*

Joseph Marcheggiani, *Butler University*

Herb Martin, *Hope College*

Alan Mayer-Sommer, *Georgetown University*

Dwight McIntyre, *Clemson University*

Dawn McKinley, *William Rainey Harper College*

Nancy Meade, *Radford University*

Elizabeth Minbiole, *Northwood University*

George Minmier, *University of Memphis*

Cheryl Mitchem, *Virginia State University*

Lu Montondon, *Southwest Texas State University*

Elizabeth Mulig, *Columbus State University*

Steven Muller, *Valencia Community College*

Carol Murphy, *Quinsigamond Community College*

Irvin Nelson, *Utah State University*

Tim Nygaard, *Madisonville Community College*

Brian O'Doherty, *East Carolina University*

Joseph Onyeocha, *South Carolina State University*

Ashton Oravetz, *Tyler Junior College*

Lawrence Ozzello, *University of Wisconsin-Eau Claire*

Eileen Peacock, *Oakland University*

Kathy Perdue, *DeVry Institute of Technology at Decatur*

Thomas Phillips, Jr., *Louisiana Tech University*

Cathy Pitts, *Highline Community College*

Mary Raven, *Mount Mary College*

Craig Reeder, *Florida A&M University*

Jane Reimers, *Florida State University*

Michael Riordan, *James Madison University*

Patricia Robinson, *Johnson and Wales University*

Ken Ruby, *Idaho State University*

Nancy Schneider, *Lynchburg College*

Jeffrey Schwartz, *Montgomery College*

Cindy Seipel, *New Mexico State University*

Suzanne Sevalstad, *University of Nevada-Las Vegas*

Kim Shaughnessy, *James Madison University*

John Shaver, *Louisiana Tech University*

Lewis Shaw, *Suffolk University*

Jill Smith, *Idaho State University*

Talitha Smith, *Auburn University*

Paul E. Solomon

John Sperry, *Virginia Commonwealth University*

Barbara Squires, *Corning Community College*

Paul Steinbart, *Saint Louis University-Saint Louis*

Tim Stephens, *DeVry Institute of Technology at Addison*

Mary Stevens, *University of Texas-El Paso*

Sue Stickland, *University of Texas, Arlington*

Leonard Stokes, *Siena College*

Janice Swanson, *Southern Oregon University*

James Swayze, *University of Nevada, Las Vegas*

Ellen Sweatt, *Georgia Perimeter College*

Maurice Tassin, *Louisiana Tech University*

Kim Temme, *Maryville University*

Peter Theuri, *Northern Kentucky University*

Bor-Yi Tsay, *University of Alabama-Birmingham*

Suneel Udpa, *St. Mary's College of California*

Donna Ulmer, *St. Louis Community College, Meramec*

Denise Dickins Veitch, *Florida Atlantic University*

George Violette, *University of Southern Maine*

Beth Vogel, *Mount Mary College*

Sharon Walters, *Morehead State University*

Andrea Weickgenannt, *Northern Kentucky University*

J. D. Weinhold, *Concordia College*

Judith Welch, *University of Central Florida*

T. Sterling Wetzel, *Oklahoma State University, Stillwater*

Thomas Whitacre, *University of South Carolina*

Macil C. Wilkie, Jr., *Grambling State University*

Stephen Willits, *Bucknell University*

Marie Winks, *Lynchburg College*

Kenneth Winter, *University of Wisconsin-La Cross.*

Alan Winters, *Clemson University*

Gail Wright, *Bryant College*

Haiwen Zhang, *University of Minnesota*

Brief Contents

Chapter 1   An Introduction to Accounting   2

Chapter 2   Accounting for Accruals   60

Chapter 3   Accounting for Deferrals   120

Chapter 4   The Double-Entry Accounting System   170

Chapter 5   Accounting for Merchandising Businesses   238

Chapter 6   Accounting for Inventories   298

Chapter 7   Internal Control and Accounting for Cash   342

Chapter 8   Accounting for Receivables and Payables   390

Chapter 9   Accounting for Long-Term Operational Assets   442

Chapter 10   Accounting for Long-Term Debt   500

Chapter 11   Accounting for Equity Transactions   558

Chapter 12   Statement of Cash Flows   604

Chapter 13   (Online) Financial Statement Analysis

Appendix A   Accessing the EDGAR Database Through the Internet   655

Appendix B   Annual Report for The Topps Company, Inc.   656

Appendix C   Summary of Financial Ratios   711

Appendix D   Annual Report and Financial Statement Analysis Projects   714

Appendix E   Accounting for Investment Securities   725

Appendix F   Time Value of Money   734

Contents

Chapter 1 An Introduction to Accounting 2

Chapter Opening 3

Role of Accounting in Society 4

Using Free Markets to Set Resource
Priorities 4

Accounting Provides Information 5

Types of Accounting Information 6

Nonbusiness Resource Allocations 6

Careers in Accounting 7

Measurement Rules 8

Reporting Entities 9

Elements of Financial Statements 10

Accounting Equation 11

**Recording Business Events Under the
Accounting Equation 12**

Asset Source Transactions 12

Asset Exchange Transactions 13

Another Asset Source Transaction 14

Asset Use Transactions 14

**Historical Cost and Reliability
Concepts 15**

Recap: Types of Transactions 16

Summary of Transactions 16

Preparing Financial Statements 17

Income Statement and the Matching
Concept 17

Statement of Changes in Stockholders'
Equity 19

Balance Sheet 19

Statement of Cash Flows 20

The Closing Process 21

**The Horizontal Financial
Statements Model 21**

The Financial Analyst 22

A Look Back 24

A Look Forward 25

Appendix 25

Self-Study Review Problem 27

Key Terms 28

Questions 28

Multiple-Choice Questions 29

Exercises—Series A 29

Problems—Series A 37

Exercises—Series B 41

Problems—Series B 48

Analyze, Think, Communicate 53

Chapter 2 Accounting for Accruals 60

Chapter Opening 61

Accrual Accounting 62

Transaction Data in Ledger
Accounts 64

2008 Financial Statements 65

The Closing Process 67

Matching Concept 67

Second Accounting Cycle 70

Adjusting the Accounts 71

Summary of 2009 Transactions 72

2009 Financial Statements 72

Closing the Temporary (Nominal)
Accounts 74

Steps in an Accounting Cycle 74

Accounting for Notes Payable 74

Vertical Statements Model 76

The Financial Analyst   78

A Look Back   82

A Look Forward   83

Appendix   83

Self-Study Review Problem   86

Key Terms   88

Questions   88

Multiple-Choice Questions   89

Exercises—Series A   89

Problems—Series A   97

Exercises—Series B   103

Problems—Series B   110

Analyze, Think, Communicate   116

Chapter 3   Accounting for Deferrals   120

Chapter Opening   121

Accounting for Deferrals Illustrated   122

   Summary of Events and Ledger
   Accounts   124

   The 2007 Financial
   Statements   125

   The Matching Concept   125

Second Accounting Cycle   127

   Effect of 2008 Transactions on the
   Accounting Equation and the Financial
   Statements   130

Third Accounting Cycle   132

   Effect of 2009 Transactions on the
   Accounting Equation and the Financial
   Statements   134

The Financial Analyst   136

A Look Back   140

A Look Forward   141

Self-Study Review Problem   141

Key Terms   143

Questions   143

Multiple-Choice Questions   143

Exercises—Series A   144

Problems—Series A   149

Exercises—Series B   154

Problems—Series B   159

Analyze, Think, Communicate   164

Chapter 4   The Double-Entry Accounting System   170

Chapter Opening   171

Debit/Credit Terminology   172

Collins Consultants Case   172

   Asset Source Transactions   172

   Asset Exchange Transactions   176

   Asset Use Transactions   177

   Claims Exchange Transactions   179

   Adjusting the Accounts   180

Overview of Debit/Credit
Relationships   183

Summary of T-Accounts   184

The Ledger   184

The General Journal 186

Financial Statements 188

Closing Entries 188

Trial Balance 190

The Financial Analyst 191

A Look Back 194

A Look Forward 194

Self-Study Review Problem 195

Key Terms 197

Questions 198

Multiple-Choice Questions 198

Exercises—Series A 198

Problems—Series A 207

Exercises—Series B 215

Problems—Series B 223

Analyze, Think, Communicate 231

Chapter 5 Accounting for Merchandising Businesses 238

Chapter Opening 239

Product Costs Versus Selling and Administrative Costs 241

Allocating Inventory Cost Between Asset and Expense Accounts 241

Perpetual Inventory System 241

Effects of 2008 Events on Financial Statements 242

Recording and Reporting Inventory Events in the Double-Entry System 243

Financial Statements for 2008 244

Transportation Cost, Purchase Returns and Allowances, and Cash Discounts Related to Inventory Purchases 245

Effects of 2009 Events on Financial Statements 246

Accounting for Purchase Returns and Allowances 246

Purchase Discounts 247

The Cost of Financing Inventory 248

Accounting for Transportation Costs 248

Recognizing Gains and Losses 251

Recording and Reporting Inventory Events in the Double-Entry System 251

Multistep Income Statement 253

Lost, Damaged, or Stolen Inventory 255

Adjustment for Lost, Damaged, or Stolen Inventory 255

Events Affecting Sales 256

Accounting for Sales Returns and Allowances 257

Accounting for Sales Discounts 258

The Financial Analyst 259

A Look Back 263

A Look Forward 263

Appendix 264

Self-Study Review Problem 265

Key Terms 267

Questions 267

Multiple-Choice Questions 268

Exercises—Series A 269

Problems—Series A 277

Exercises—Series B 280

Problems—Series B 288

Analyze, Think, Communicate 291

Comprehensive Problem 296

Chapter 6 Accounting for Inventories 298

Chapter Opening 299

Inventory Cost Flow Methods 300

 Specific Identification 300

 First-In, First-Out (FIFO) 300

 Last-In, First-Out (LIFO) 300

 Weighted Average 300

 Physical Flow 300

Effect of Cost Flow on Financial Statements 300

 Effect on Income Statement 300

 Effect on Balance Sheet 301

Inventory Cost Flow under a Perpetual System 302

 Multiple Layers with Multiple Quantities 302

 Allocating Cost of Goods Available for Sale 302

 Effect of Cost Flow on Financial Statements 303

Inventory Cost Flow When Sales and Purchases Occur Intermittently 306

 FIFO Cost Flow 306

 Weighted-Average and LIFO Cost Flows 307

Lower-of-Cost-or-Market Rule 308

Avoiding Fraud in Merchandising Businesses 309

Estimating the Ending Inventory Balance 310

The Financial Analyst 312

Effects of Cost Flow on Ratio Analysis 314

A Look Back 314

A Look Forward 314

Self-Study Review Problem 315

Key Terms 316

Questions 316

Multiple-Choice Questions 317

Exercises—Series A 317

Problems—Series A 323

Exercises—Series B 326

Problems—Series B 332

Analyze, Think, Communicate 336

Comprehensive Problem 340

Chapter 7 Internal Control and Accounting for Cash 342

Chapter Opening 343

Key Features of Internal Control Systems 344

 Separation of Duties 344

 Quality of Employees 344

 Bonded Employees 344

 Required Absences 344

 Procedures Manual 345

 Authority and Responsibility 345

 Prenumbered Documents 345

 Physical Control 345

 Performance Evaluations 346

 Limitations 346

Accounting for Cash 346

 Controlling Cash 346

 Cash Payments 347

 Checking Account Documents 348

Reconciling the Bank
Statement   350

Illustrating a Bank Reconciliation   351

Cash Short and Over   354

Using Petty Cash Funds   355

The Financial Analyst   357

A Look Back   360

A Look Forward   361

Self-Study Review Problem   362

Key Terms   362

Questions   363

Multiple-Choice Questions   364

Exercises—Series A   364

Problems—Series A   368

Exercises—Series B   373

Problems—Series B   378

Analyze, Think, Communicate   383

Comprehensive Problem   387

Chapter 8   Accounting for Receivables and Payables   390

Chapter Opening   391

**Allowance Method of Accounting for
Bad Debts   392**

Accounting Events Affecting the 2008
Period   392

Accounting for Bad Debts
Expense   392

General Ledger T-Accounts   394

Financial Statements   395

Estimating Bad Debts
Expense   396

Accounting Events Affecting the 2009
Period   396

Year-End Adjusting Entries   398

General Ledger T-Accounts   398

Analysis of Financial Statements   399

**Recognition of Bad Debts Expense Using
the Direct Write-Off Method   400**

Accounting for Credit Card Sales   401

Warranty Obligations   402

General Ledger T-Accounts and
Financial Statements   403

The Financial Analyst   405

Costs of Credit Sales   405

A Look Back   408

A Look Forward   409

Appendix   409

Self-Study Review Problem   414

Key Terms   414

Questions   415

Multiple-Choice Questions   416

Exercises—Series A   416

Problems—Series A   421

Exercises—Series B   426

Problems—Series B   432

Analyze, Think, Communicate   437

Comprehensive Problem   440

Chapter 9 Accounting for Long-Term Operational Assets 442

Chapter Opening 443

Tangible Versus Intangible Assets 444

   Tangible Long-Term Assets 444

   Intangible Assets 444

Determining the Cost of Long-Term Assets 445

   Basket Purchase Allocation 445

Life Cycle of Operational Assets 446

Methods of Recognizing Depreciation Expense 446

   Straight-Line Depreciation 447

   Double-Declining-Balance Depreciation 450

   Units-of-Production Depreciation 452

   Comparing the Depreciation Methods 453

Income Tax Considerations 455

Revision of Estimates 456

   Revision of Life 456

   Revision of Salvage 456

Continuing Expenditures for Plant Assets 457

   Costs that Are Expensed 457

   Costs that Are Capitalized 457

Natural Resources 459

Intangible Assets 460

   Trademarks 460

   Patents 460

   Copyrights 460

   Franchises 460

   Goodwill 461

Expense Recognition for Intangible Assets 462

   Expensing Intangible Assets with Identifiable Useful Lives 462

   Impairment Losses for Intangible Assets with Indefinite Useful Lives 463

Balance Sheet Presentation 464

The Financial Analyst 464

A Look Back 466

A Look Forward 467

Self-Study Review Problem 467

Key Terms 468

Questions 468

Multiple-Choice Questions 469

Exercises—Series A 469

Problems—Series A 475

Exercises—Series B 481

Problems—Series B 486

Analyze, Think, Communicate 492

Comprehensive Problem 498

Chapter 10 Accounting for Long-Term Debt 500

Chapter Opening 501

Installment Notes Payable 502

Line of Credit 505

Bond Liabilities 505

   Advantages of Issuing Bonds 506

   Security of Bonds 507

   Timing of Maturity 507

   Special Features 508

   Bond Ratings 508

   Bonds Issued at Face Value 509

   Recording Procedures 509

Effect of Events on Financial Statements   510

Financial Statements   511

Bonds Issued at a Discount   512

Effective Interest Rate   512

Bond Prices   513

Mason Company Revisited   513

Effect on Financial Statements   515

Effect of Semiannual Interest Payments   517

Bonds Issued at a Premium   517

The Market Rate of Interest   518

Bond Redemptions   518

Security for Loan Agreements   519

The Financial Analyst   519

A Look Back   522

A Look Forward   522

Appendix   523

Self-Study Review Problem   527

Key Terms   527

Questions   528

Multiple-Choice Questions   529

Exercises—Series A   529

Problems—Series A   536

Exercises—Series B   539

Problems—Series B   546

Analyze, Think, Communicate   550

Comprehensive Problem   556

Chapter 11   Accounting for Equity Transactions   558

Chapter Opening   560

Formation of Business Organizations   560

Ownership Agreements   560

Advantages and Disadvantages of Different Forms of Business Organization   560

Regulation   560

Double Taxation   561

Limited Liability   562

Continuity   562

Transferability of Ownership   563

Management Structure   563

Ability to Raise Capital   563

Appearance of Capital Structure in Financial Statements   563

Presentation of Equity in Proprietorships   563

Presentation of Equity in Partnerships   564

Presentation of Equity in Corporations   565

Characteristics of Capital Stock   565

Par Value   565

Stated Value   565

Other Valuation Terminology   566

Stock: Authorized, Issued, and Outstanding   566

Classes of Stock   566

Common Stock   566

Preferred Stock   567

Accounting for Stock Transactions on the Day of Issue   568

Issuing Par Value Stock   568

Stock Clarification   568

Stock Issued at Stated Value   569

Stock Issued with No-Par Value   569

Financial Statement Presentation   570

Stockholders' Equity Transactions after the Day of Issue   570
   Treasury Stock   570
   Cash Dividend   572
   Stock Dividend   573
   Stock Split   573
   Appropriation of Retained Earnings   574
Financial Statement Presentation   574
The Financial Analyst   575
A Look Back   577
A Look Forward   578

Self-Study Review Problem   578
Key Terms   579
Questions   579
Multiple-Choice Questions   580
Exercises—Series A   581
Problems—Series A   585
Exercises—Series B   588
Problems—Series B   593
Analyze, Think, Communicate   596
Comprehensive Problem   602

Chapter 12   Statement of Cash Flows   604

Chapter Opening   605
   Operating Activities   606
   Investing Activities   606
   Financing Activities   606
   Noncash Investing and Financing Activities   606
Reporting Format for the Statement of Cash Flows   606
Converting from Accrual to Cash-Basis Accounting   607
   Operating Activities   609
   Procedures for Determining Cash Flow from Operating Activities under the Indirect Method   610
Preparing the Operating Activities Section of the Statement of Cash Flows Using the Direct Method   612
   Preparing the Investing Activities Section of the Statement of Cash Flows   615
   Preparing the Financing Activities Section of the Statement of Cash Flows   617

   Preparing the Schedule of Noncash Investing and Financing Activities for the Statement of Cash Flows   621
The Financial Analyst   621
A Look Back   623
A Look Forward   623
Appendix   624
Self-Study Review Problem   625
Key Terms   628
Questions   628
Multiple-Choice Questions   629
Exercises—Series A   629
Problems—Series A   633
Exercises—Series B   639
Problems—Series B   643
Analyze, Think, Communicate   649

Chapter 13   (Online) Financial Statement Analysis

Appendix A   Accessing the EDGAR
Database Through the Internet   655

Appendix B   Annual Report for The Topps
Company, Inc.   656

Appendix C   Summary of Financial
Ratios   711

Appendix D   Annual Report and Financial
Statement Analysis Projects   714

Appendix E   Accounting for Investment
Securities   725

Appendix F   Time Value of Money   734

Glossary   742
Photo Credits   753
Index   754

CHAPTER 1

An Introduction to Accounting

After you have mastered the material in this chapter you will be able to:

1. Explain the role of accounting in society.

2. Distinguish among the different accounting entities involved in business events.

3. Name and define the major elements of financial statements.

4. Describe the relationships expressed in the accounting equation.

5. Record business events in general ledger accounts organized under an accounting equation.

6. Explain how the historical cost and reliability concepts affect amounts reported in financial statements.

7. Classify business events as asset source, use, or exchange transactions.

8. Use general ledger account information to prepare four financial statements.

9. Record business events using a horizontal financial statements model.

10. Explain the price-earnings ratio (Appendix).

LP1

The Curious Accountant

Who owns McDonald's? Who owns the American Red Cross (ARC)? Many people and organizations other than owners are interested in the operations of McDonald's and the ARC. These parties are called *stakeholders.* Among others, they include lenders, employees, suppliers, customers, benefactors, research institutions, local governments, flood victims, lawyers, bankers, financial analysts, and government agencies such as the Internal Revenue Service and the Securities and Exchange Commission. Organizations communicate information to stakeholders through *financial reports.*

How do you think the financial reports of McDonald's differ from those of the ARC? (Answer on page 10.)

CHAPTER OPENING

Why should you study accounting? You should study accounting because it can help you succeed in business. Businesses use accounting to keep score. Imagine trying to play football without knowing how many points a touchdown is worth. Like sports, business is competitive. If you do not know how to keep score, you are not likely to succeed.

* **Accounting** is an information system that reports on the economic activities and financial condition of a business or other organization. Do not underestimate the importance of accounting information. If you had information that enabled you to predict business success, you could become a very wealthy Wall Street investor. Communicating economic information is so important that accounting is frequently called the language of business.* ■

Role of Accounting in Society

Explain the role of accounting in society.

Video 1.1

How should society allocate its resources? Should we spend more to harvest food or cure disease? Should we build computers or cars? Should we invest money in IBM or General Motors? Accounting provides information that helps answer such questions.

Using Free Markets to Set Resource Priorities

Suppose you want to start a business. You may have heard "you have to have money to make money." In fact, you will need more than just money to start and operate a business. You will likely need such resources as equipment, land, materials, and employees. If you do not have these resources, how can you get them? In the United States, you compete for resources in open markets.

A **market** is a group of people or entities organized to exchange items of value. The market for business resources involves three distinct participants: consumers, conversion agents, and resource owners. *Consumers* use resources. Resources are frequently not in a form consumers want. For example, nature provides trees but consumers want furniture. *Conversion agents* (businesses) transform resources such as trees into desirable products such as furniture. *Resource owners* control the distribution of resources to conversion agents. Thus resource owners provide resources (inputs) to conversion agents who provide goods and services (outputs) to consumers.

For example, a home builder (conversion agent) transforms labor and materials (inputs) into houses (output) that consumers use. The transformation adds value to the inputs, creating

outputs worth more than the sum of the inputs. A house that required $220,000 of materials and labor to build could have a market value of $250,000.

Common terms for the added value created in the transformation process include **profit, income,** or **earnings.** Accountants measure the added value as the difference between the cost of a product or service and the selling price of that product or service. The profit on the house described above is $30,000, the difference between its $220,000 cost and $250,000 market value.

Conversion agents who successfully and efficiently (at low cost) satisfy consumer preferences are rewarded with high earnings. These earnings are shared with resource owners, so conversion agents who exhibit high earnings potential are more likely to compete successfully for resources.

Return to the original question. How can you get the resources you need to start a business? You must go to open markets and convince resource owners that you can produce profits. Exhibit 1.1 illustrates the market trilogy involved in resource allocation.

The specific resources businesses commonly use to satisfy consumer demand are financial resources, physical resources, and labor resources.

Financial Resources

Businesses (conversion agents) need **financial resources** (money) to get started and to operate. *Investors* and *creditors* provide financial resources.

- **Investors** provide financial resources in exchange for ownership interests in businesses. Owners expect businesses to return to them a share of the business income earned.

- **Creditors** lend financial resources to businesses. Instead of a share of business income, creditors expect businesses to repay borrowed resources at a future date.

The resources controlled by a business are called **assets.** If a business ceases to operate, its remaining assets are sold and the sale proceeds are returned to the investors and creditors through a process called business **liquidation.** Creditors have a priority claim on assets in business liquidations. After creditor claims are satisfied, any remaining assets are distributed to investors (owners).

EXHIBIT 1.1

Market Trilogy in Resource Allocation

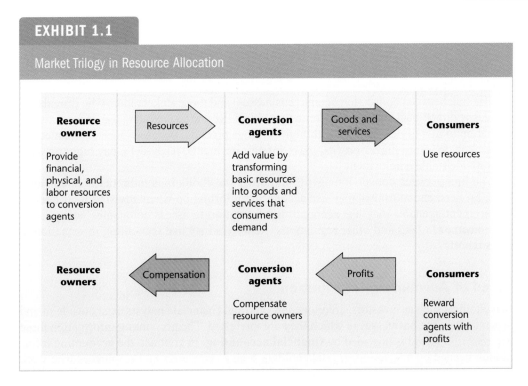

To illustrate, suppose a business acquired $100 cash from investors and $200 cash from creditors. Assume the business lost $75 and returned the remaining $225 ($300 − $75) to the resource providers. The creditors would receive $200; the owners would receive only $25. If the business lost $120, the creditors would receive only $180 ($300 − $120); the investors would receive nothing.

As this illustration suggests, both creditors and investors can lose resources when businesses fail. Creditors, however, are in a more secure position because of their priority claim on resources. In exchange for their more secure position, creditors normally do not share business profits. Instead, they receive a fixed amount of money called **interest**.

Investors and creditors prefer to provide financial resources to businesses with high earnings potential because such companies are better able to share profits and make interest payments. Profitable businesses are also less likely to experience bankruptcy and liquidation.

Physical Resources

In their most primitive form, **physical resources** are natural resources. Physical resources often move through numerous stages of transformation. For example, standing timber may be successively transformed into harvested logs, raw lumber, and finished furniture. Owners of physical resources seek to sell those resources to businesses with high earnings potential because profitable businesses are able to pay higher prices and make repeat purchases.

Labor Resources

Labor resources include both intellectual and physical labor. Like other resource providers, workers prefer businesses that have high income potential because these businesses are able to pay higher wages and offer continued employment.

Accounting Provides Information

How do providers of financial, physical, and labor resources identify conversion agents (businesses) with high profit potential? Investors, creditors, and workers rely heavily on accounting information to evaluate which businesses are worthy of receiving resources. In addition, other people and organizations have an interest in accounting information about businesses. The many **users** of accounting information are commonly called **stakeholders.** Stakeholders include resource providers, financial analysts, brokers, attorneys, government regulators, and news reporters.

The link between conversion agents (businesses) and those stakeholders who provide resources is direct: businesses pay resource providers. Resource providers use accounting information to identify companies with high earnings potential because those companies are more likely to return higher profits, make interest payments, repay debt, pay higher prices, and provide stable employment.

The link between conversion agents and other stakeholders is indirect. Financial analysts, brokers, and attorneys may use accounting information when advising their clients. Government agencies may use accounting information to assess companies' compliance with income tax laws and other regulations. Reporters may use accounting information in news reports.

Types of Accounting Information

Stakeholders such as investors, creditors, lawyers, and financial analysts exist outside of and separate from the businesses in which they are interested. The accounting information these *external users* need is provided by **financial accounting.** In contrast, the accounting information needed by *internal users,* stakeholders such as managers and employees who work within a business, is provided by **managerial accounting.**

The information needs of external and internal users frequently overlap. For example, external and internal users are both interested in the amount of income a business earns. Managerial accounting information, however, is usually more detailed than financial accounting reports. Investors are concerned about the overall profitability of Wendy's versus Burger King; a Wendy's regional manager is interested in the profits of individual Wendy's restaurants. In fact, a regional manager is also interested in nonfinancial measures, such as the number of employees needed to operate a restaurant, the times at which customer demand is high versus low, and measures of cleanliness and customer satisfaction.

Nonbusiness Resource Usage

The U.S. economy is not *purely* market based. Factors other than profitability often influence resource allocation priorities. For example, governments allocate resources to national defense, to redistribute wealth, or to protect the environment. Foundations, religious groups, the Peace Corps, and various benevolent organizations prioritize resource usage based on humanitarian concerns.

Like profit-oriented businesses, civic or humanitarian organizations add value through resource transformation. For example, a soup kitchen adds value to uncooked meats and vegetables by converting them into prepared meals. The individuals who consume the meals, however, are unable to pay for the kitchen's operating costs, much less for the added value. The soup kitchen's motivation is to meet humanitarian needs, not to earn profits. Organizations that are not motivated by profit are called **not-for-profit entities** (also called *nonprofit* or *nonbusiness organizations*).

Stakeholders interested in nonprofit organizations also need accounting information. Accounting systems measure the cost of the goods and services not-for-profit organizations provide, the efficiency and effectiveness of the organizations' operations, and the ability of the organizations to continue to provide goods and services. This information serves a host of stakeholders, including taxpayers, contributors, lenders, suppliers, employees, managers, financial analysts, attorneys, and beneficiaries.

The focus of accounting, therefore, is to provide information useful to making decisions for a variety of business and nonbusiness user groups. The different types of accounting information and the stakeholders that commonly use the information are summarized in Exhibit 1.2.

EXHIBIT 1.2

Accounting as Information Provider

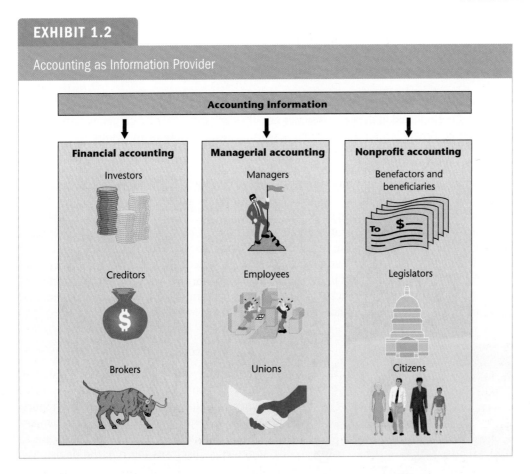

Careers in Accounting

An accounting career can take you to the top of the business world. *BusinessWeek* studied the backgrounds of the chief executive officers (CEOs) of the 1,000 largest public corporations. More CEOs had backgrounds in finance and accounting than any other field. Exhibit 1.3 provides additional detail regarding the career paths followed by these executives.

What do accountants do? Accountants identify, record, analyze, and communicate information about the economic events that affect organizations. They may work in either public accounting or private accounting.

Public Accounting

You are probably familiar with the acronym CPA. CPA stands for certified *public* accountant. Public accountants provide services to various clients. They are usually paid a fee that varies depending on the service provided. Services typically offered by public accountants include (1) audit services, (2) tax services, and (3) consulting services.

- *Audit services* involve examining a company's accounting records in order to issue an opinion about whether the company's financial statements conform to generally accepted accounting principles. The auditor's opinion adds credibility to the statements, which are prepared by the company's management.

- *Tax services* include both determining the amount of tax due and tax planning to help companies minimize tax expense.

- *Consulting services* cover a wide range of activities that includes everything from installing sophisticated computerized accounting systems to providing personal financial advice.

EXHIBIT 1.3

Career Paths of Chief Executive Officers

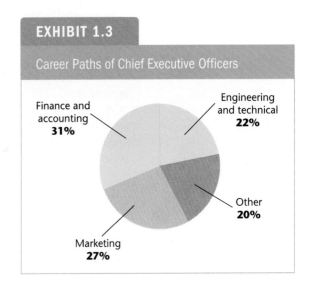

All public accountants are not certified. Each state government establishes certification requirements applicable in that state. Although the requirements vary from state to state, CPA candidates normally must have a college education, pass a demanding technical examination, and obtain work experience relevant to practicing public accounting.

Private Accounting

Accountants employed in the private sector usually work for a specific company or nonprofit organization. Private sector accountants perform a wide variety of functions for their employers. Their duties include classifying and recording transactions, billing customers and collecting amounts due, ordering merchandise, paying suppliers, preparing and analyzing financial statements, developing budgets, measuring costs, assessing performance, and making decisions.

Private accountants may earn any of several professional certifications. For example, the Institute of Certified Management Accountants issues the *Certified Management Accounting (CMA)* designation. The Institute of Internal Auditors issues the *Certified Internal Auditor (CIA)* designation. These designations are widely recognized indicators of technical competence and integrity on the part of individuals who hold them. All professional accounting certifications call for meeting education requirements, passing a technical examination, and obtaining relevant work experience.

Measurement Rules

Suppose a store sells a compact disk player in December to a customer who agrees to pay for it in January. Should the business *recognize* (report) the sale as a December transaction or as a January transaction? It really does not matter as long as the storeowner discloses the rule the decision is based on and applies it consistently to other transactions. Because businesses may use different reporting rules, however, clear communication also requires full and fair disclosure of the accounting rules chosen.

Communicating business results would be simpler if each type of business activity were reported using only one measurement method. World economies and financial reporting practices, however, have not evolved uniformly. Even in highly sophisticated countries such as the United States, companies exhibit significant diversity in reporting methods. Providers of accounting reports assume that users are educated about accounting practices.

The **Financial Accounting Standards Board (FASB)**[1] is a privately funded organization with the primary authority for establishing accounting standards in the United States. The measurement rules established by the FASB are called **generally accepted accounting principles (GAAP).** Financial reports issued to the public must follow GAAP. This textbook introduces these principles so you will be able to understand business activity reported by companies in the USA.

Companies are not required to follow GAAP when preparing *management accounting* reports. Although there is considerable overlap between financial and managerial accounting, managers are free to construct internal reports in whatever fashion best suits the effective operation of their companies.

---

[1]The FASB consists of seven full-time members appointed by the supporting organization, the Financial Accounting Foundation (FAF). The FAF membership is intended to represent the broad spectrum of individuals and institutions that have an interest in accounting and financial reporting. FAF members include representatives of the accounting profession, industry, financial institutions, the government, and the investing public.

FOCUS ON INTERNATIONAL ISSUES

IS THERE GLOBAL GAAP?

As explained in this chapter, financial reporting is a measurement and communication discipline based on rules referred to as *generally accepted accounting principles.* The accounting rules described in this text are based on GAAP used in the United States. Not all economies throughout the world use the same accounting rules. Although there are many similarities among the accounting principles used in different countries, there also are major differences. In recent years, however, there has been a concerted effort to bring the accounting standards of the major industrialized nations into uniformity, or at least, to have less diversity. This process is usually referred to as *harmonization,* but simply put, there is no "global GAAP." Examples of how financial reporting in other countries differs from that in the United States are presented throughout this book.

Accounting rules differ among countries for a variety of reasons, including the economic and legal environments in each country and how the GAAP in that country is established. Generally accepted accounting principles in the United States are primarily established by the Financial Accounting Standards Board (FASB). The FASB is a nongovernment rule-making body established by the accounting profession. In some countries, such as Japan for example, the GAAP is established by government bodies. In these countries GAAP is established more like the way federal laws and regulations are established in the United States.

Furthermore, in the United States any connection between GAAP established by the FASB and tax accounting rules established by Congress and the Internal Revenue Service (IRS) is coincidental, not deliberate. In some countries there is a close connection between tax accounting rules and GAAP.

Reporting Entities

Financial accounting reports disclose the financial activities of particular individuals or organizations described as **reporting entities.** Each entity is a separate reporting unit. For example, a business, the person who owns the business, and a bank that loans money to the business are viewed as three separate reporting entities. Accountants would prepare three separate sets of financial reports to describe the economic activities of each of the three entities.

LO 2

Distinguish among the different accounting entities involved in business events.

This text describes accounting from the perspective of a business entity. This point of view may require that you mentally adjust the way you look at business transactions. You likely think from a customer perspective. For example, as a customer you consider a sales discount a great bargain. The view is different, however, from the perspective of the business granting the discount. A sales discount means an item did not sell at the expected price. To move the item, the business had to accept less money than it originally planned to accept. From this perspective, a sales discount is not a good thing. To understand accounting, train yourself to interpret transactions from the perspective of a business rather than a consumer.

CHECK YOURSELF 1.1

In a recent business transaction, land was exchanged for cash. Did the amount of cash increase or decrease?

Answer

The answer depends on the reporting entity to which the question pertains. One entity sold land. The other entity bought land. For the entity that sold land, cash increased. For the entity that bought land, cash decreased.

Elements of Financial Statements

Name and define the major elements of financial statements.

Video 1.1 · Topic Tackler PLUS

1-1

Business entities communicate economic information about their activities to the public through four **financial statements:**[2] (1) an income statement, (2) a statement of changes in equity, (3) a balance sheet, and (4) a statement of cash flows.

The information reported in financial statements is organized into categories known as **elements.** Eight financial statement elements are discussed in this chapter: assets, liabilities, equity, contributed capital, revenue, expenses, distributions, and net income. The other two elements, gains and losses, are discussed in a later chapter. In practice, the business world uses various titles to identify several of the financial statement elements. For example, business people use net income, net earnings, and net profit interchangeably to describe the same element. Contributed capital may be called *common stock* and equity may be called *stockholders' equity, owner's capital,* and *partners' equity.* Furthermore, the transfer of assets from a business to its owners may be called *distributions, withdrawals,* or *dividends.*

Detailed information about the elements is maintained in records commonly called **accounts.** For example, information regarding the element *assets* may be organized in separate accounts for cash, equipment, buildings, land, and so forth. The types and number of accounts used by a business depends on the information needs of its stakeholders. Some businesses provide very detailed information; others report highly summarized information. The more detail desired, the greater number of accounts needed. Think of accounts like the notebooks students keep for their classes. Some students keep detailed notes about every class they take in a separate notebook. Other students keep only the key points for all of their classes in a single notebook. Similarly, some business use more accounts than other businesses.

Diversity also exists regarding the names used for various accounts. For example, employee pay may be called salaries, wages, commissions, and so forth. Do not become frustrated with the diversity of terms used in accounting. Remember, accounting is a language. The same word can have different meanings. Similarly, different words can be used to describe the same phenomenon. The more you study and use accounting, the more familiar it becomes to you.

---

[2]In practice these statements have alternate names. For example, the income statement may be called *results of operations* or *statement of earnings.* The balance sheet is sometimes called the *statement of financial position.* The statement of changes in equity might be called *statement of capital* or *statement of stockholders' equity.* Since the Financial Accounting Standards Board (FASB) called for the title *statement of cash flows,* companies do not use alternate names for that statement.

Answers to The Curious Accountant

Anyone who owns stock in **McDonald's** owns a part of the company. McDonald's has many owners. In contrast, nobody actually owns the **American Red Cross** (ARC). The ARC has a board of directors that is responsible for overseeing its operations, but the board is not its owner.

Ultimately, the purpose of a business entity is to increase the wealth of its owners. To this end, it "spends money to make money." The expense that McDonald's incurs for advertising is a cost incurred in the hope that it will generate revenues when it sells hamburgers. The financial statements of a business show, among other things, whether and how the company made a profit during the current year.

The ARC is a not-for-profit entity. It operates to provide services to society at large, not to make a profit. It cannot increase the wealth of its owners, because it has no owners. When the ARC spends money to assist flood victims, it does not spend this money in the expectation that it will generate revenues. The revenues of the ARC come from contributors who wish to support efforts related to assisting disaster victims. Because the ARC does not spend money to make money, it has no reason to prepare an *income statement* like that of McDonald's.

Not-for-profit entities do prepare financial statements that are similar in appearance to those of commercial enterprises. The financial statements of not-for-profit entities are called the *statement of financial position,* the *statement of activities,* and the *cash flow statement.*

The resources that a business uses to produce earnings are called *assets*. Examples of assets include land, buildings, equipment, materials, and supplies. Assets result from historical events. For example, if a business owns a truck that it purchased in a past transaction, the truck is an asset of the business. A truck that a business *plans* to purchase in the future, however, is not an asset of that business, no matter how certain the future purchase might be.

The assets of a business belong to the resource providers (creditors and investors). These resource providers have **claims** on the assets. The relationship between the assets and the providers' claims is described by the **accounting equation:**

$$\text{Assets} = \text{Claims}$$

Describe the relationships expressed in the accounting equation.

Video 1.1

Creditor claims are called **liabilities** and investor claims are called **equity.** Substituting these terms into the accounting equation produces the following expanded form:

$$\overbrace{\text{Assets} = \text{Liabilities} + \text{Equity}}^{\text{Claims}}$$

Liabilities can also be viewed as future *obligations of the enterprise.* To settle the obligations, the business will probably either relinquish some of its assets (e.g., pay off its debts with cash), provide services to its creditors (e.g., work off its debts), or accept other obligations (e.g., trade short-term debt for long-term debt).

As indicated by the accounting equation, the amount of total assets is equal to the total of the liabilities plus the equity. To illustrate, assume that Hagan Company has assets of $500, liabilities of $200, and equity of $300. These amounts appear in the accounting equation as follows:

$$\overbrace{\begin{array}{ccccc} \text{Assets} & = & \text{Liabilities} & + & \text{Equity} \\ \$500 & = & \$200 & + & \$300 \end{array}}^{\text{Claims}}$$

The claims side of the accounting equation (liabilities plus equity) may also be viewed as listing the sources of the assets. For example, when a bank loans assets (money) to a business, it establishes a claim to have those assets returned at some future date. Liabilities can therefore be viewed as sources of assets.

Equity can also be viewed as a source of assets. In fact, equity represents two distinct sources of assets. First, businesses typically acquire assets from their owners (investors). Many businesses issue **common stock**[3] certificates as receipts to acknowledge assets received from owners. The owners of such businesses are often called **stockholders,** and the ownership interest in the business is called **stockholders' equity.**

Second, businesses usually obtain assets through their earnings activities (the business acquires assets by working for them). Assets a business has earned can either be distributed to the owners or kept in the business. The portion of assets that has been provided by earnings activities and not returned as dividends is called **retained earnings.** Since stockholders own the business, they are entitled to assets acquired through its earnings activities. Retained earnings is therefore a

---

[3]This presentation assumes the business is organized as a corporation. Other forms of business organization include proprietorships and partnerships. The treatment of equity for these types of businesses is slightly different from that of corporations. A detailed discussion of the differences is included in a later chapter of the text.

component of stockholders' equity. Further expansion of the accounting equation can show the three sources of assets (liabilities, common stock, and retained earnings):

$$\underset{\text{Stockholders' equity}}{\text{Assets} = \text{Liabilities} + \underbrace{\text{Common stock} + \text{Retained earnings}}}$$

CHECK YOURSELF 1.2

Gupta Company has $250,000 of assets, $60,000 of liabilities, and $90,000 of common stock. What percentage of the assets was provided by retained earnings?

Answer

First, using algebra, determine the dollar amount of retained earnings:
Assets = Liabilities + Common stock + Retained earnings
Retained earnings = Assets − Liabilities − Common stock
Retained earnings = $250,000 − $60,000 − $90,000
Retained earnings = $100,000

Second, determine the percentage:
Percentage of assets provided by retained earnings = Retained earnings/Total assets
Percentage of assets provided by retained earnings = $100,000/$250,000 = 40%

Recording Business Events under the Accounting Equation

Record business events in general ledger accounts organized under an accounting equation.

Video 1.2   Topic Tackler PLUS

1-2

An **accounting event** is an economic occurrence that changes an enterprise's assets, liabilities, or stockholders' equity. A **transaction** is a particular kind of event that involves transferring something of value between two entities. Examples of transactions include acquiring assets from owners, borrowing money from creditors, and purchasing or selling goods and services. The following section of the text explains how several different types of accounting events affect a company's accounting equation.

Asset Source Transactions

As previously mentioned, businesses obtain assets (resources) from three sources. They acquire assets from owners (stockholders); they borrow assets from creditors; and they earn assets through profitable operations. Asset source transactions increase total assets and total claims. A more detailed discussion of the effects of asset source transactions is provided below:

Event 1 Rustic Camp Sites (RCS) was formed on January 1, 2008, when it acquired $120,000 cash from issuing common stock.

When RCS issued stock, it received cash and gave each investor (owner) a stock certificate as a receipt. Since this transaction provided $120,000 of assets (cash) to the business, it is an **asset source transaction.** It increases the business's assets (cash) and its stockholders' equity (common stock).

	Assets		=	Liab.	+	Stockholders' Equity		
	Cash	+ Land	=	N. Pay.	+	Com. Stk.	+	Ret. Earn.
Acquired cash through stock issue	120,000	+ NA	=	NA	+	120,000	+	NA

Notice the elements have been divided into accounts. For example, the element *assets* is divided into a Cash account and a Land account. Do not be concerned if some of these account titles are unfamiliar. They will be explained as new transactions are presented. Recall that the number of accounts a company uses depends on the nature of its business and the level of detail management needs to operate the business. For example, Sears would have an account called Cost of Goods Sold although GEICO Insurance would not. Why? Because Sears sells goods (merchandise) but GEICO does not.

Also, notice that a stock issue transaction affects the accounting equation in two places, both under an asset (cash) and also under the source of that asset (common stock). All transactions affect the accounting equation in at least two places. It is from this practice that the **double-entry bookkeeping** system derives its name.

Event 2 RCS acquired an additional $400,000 of cash by borrowing from a creditor.

This transaction is also an asset source transaction. It increases assets (cash) and liability claims (notes payable). The account title Notes Payable is used because the borrower (RCS) is required to issue a promissory note to the creditor (a bank). A promissory note describes, among other things, the amount of interest RCS will pay and for how long it will borrow the money.[4] The effect of the borrowing transaction on the accounting equation is indicated below.

	Assets			=	Liab.	+	Stockholders' Equity		
	Cash	+	Land	=	N. Pay.	+	Com. Stk.	+	Ret. Earn.
Beginning balances	120,000	+	NA	=	NA	+	120,000	+	NA
Acquired cash by issuing note	400,000	+	NA	=	400,000	+	NA	+	NA
Ending balances	520,000	+	NA	=	400,000	+	120,000	+	NA

The beginning balances above came from the ending balances produced by the prior transaction. This practice is followed throughout the illustration.

Asset Exchange Transactions

Businesses frequently trade one asset for another asset. In such cases, the amount of one asset decreases and the amount of the other asset increases. Total assets are unaffected by asset exchange transactions. Event 3 is an asset exchange transaction.

Event 3 RCS paid $500,000 cash to purchase land.

This asset exchange transaction reduces the asset account Cash and increases the asset account Land. The amount of total assets is not affected. An **asset exchange transaction** simply reflects changes in the composition of assets. In this case, the company traded cash for land. The amount of cash decreased by $500,000 and the amount of land increased by the same amount.

	Assets			=	Liab.	+	Stockholders' Equity		
	Cash	+	Land	=	N. Pay.	+	Com. Stk.	+	Ret. Earn.
Beginning balances	520,000	+	NA	=	400,000	+	120,000	+	NA
Paid cash to buy land	(500,000)	+	500,000	=	NA	+	NA	+	NA
Ending balances	20,000	+	500,000	=	400,000	+	120,000	+	NA

---

[4]For simplicity, the effects of interest are ignored in this chapter. We discuss accounting for interest in future chapters.

Another Asset Source Transaction

 Event 4 **RCS obtained $85,000 cash by leasing camp sites to customers.**

Revenue represents an economic benefit a company obtains by providing customers with goods and services. In this example the economic benefit is an increase in the asset cash. Revenue transactions can therefore be viewed as *asset source transactions*. The asset increase is balanced by an increase in the retained earnings section of stockholders' equity because producing revenue increases the amount of earnings that can be retained in the business.

	Assets			=	Liab.	+	Stockholders' Equity			
	Cash	+	Land	=	N. Pay.	+	Com. Stk.	+	Ret. Earn.	Acct. Title
Beginning balances	20,000	+	500,000	=	400,000	+	120,000	+	NA	
Acquired cash by earning revenue	85,000	+	NA	=	NA	+	NA	+	85,000	Revenue
Ending balances	105,000	+	500,000	=	400,000	+	120,000	+	85,000	

Note carefully that the $85,000 ending balance in the retained earnings column is *not* in the Retained Earnings account. It is in the Revenue account. It will be transferred to the Retained Earnings account at the end of the accounting period. Transferring the Revenue account balance to the Retained Earnings account is part of a process called *closing the accounts.*

Asset Use Transactions

Businesses use assets for a variety of purposes. For example, assets may be used to pay off liabilities or they may be transferred to owners. Assets may also be used in the process of generating earnings. All **asset use transactions** decrease the total amount of assets and the total amount of claims on assets (liabilities or stockholders' equity).

Event 5 **RCS paid $50,000 cash for operating expenses such as salaries, rent, and interest. (RCS could establish a separate account for each type of expense. However, the management team does not currently desire this level of detail. Remember, the number of accounts a business uses depends on the level of information managers need to make decisions.)**

In the normal course of generating revenue, a business consumes various assets and services. The assets and services consumed to generate revenue are called **expenses.** Revenue results from providing goods and services to customers. In exchange, the business acquires assets from its customers. Since the owners bear the ultimate risk and reap the rewards of operating the business, revenues increase stockholders' equity (retained earnings), and expenses decrease retained earnings. In this case, the asset account, Cash, decreased. This decrease is balanced by a decrease in the retained earnings section of stockholders' equity because expenses decrease the amount of earnings retained in the business.

	Assets			=	Liab.	+	Stockholders' Equity			
	Cash	+	Land	=	N. Pay.	+	Com. Stk.	+	Ret. Earn.	Acct. Title
Beginning balances	105,000	+	500,000	=	400,000	+	120,000	+	85,000	
Used cash to pay expenses	(50,000)	+	NA	=	NA	+	NA	+	(50,000)	Expense
Ending balances	55,000	+	500,000	=	400,000	+	120,000	+	35,000	

Like revenues, expenses are not recorded directly into the Retained Earnings account. The $50,000 of expense is recorded in the Expense account. It will be transferred to the Retained Earnings account at the end of the accounting period as part of the closing process. The $35,000 ending balance in the retained earnings column shows what would be in the Retained Earnings account after the balances in the Revenue and Expense accounts have been closed. The current balance in the Retained Earnings account is zero.

Event 6 RCS paid $4,000 in cash dividends to its owners.

To this point the enterprise's total assets and equity have increased by $35,000 ($85,000 of revenue − $50,000 of expense) as a result of its earnings activities. RCS can keep the additional assets in the business or transfer them to the owners. If a business transfers some or all of its earned assets to owners, the transfer is frequently called a **dividend.** Since assets distributed to stockholders are not used for the purpose of generating revenue, *dividends are not expenses.* Furthermore, dividends are a transfer of *earnings,* not a return of the assets acquired from the issue of common stock.

	Assets			=	Liab.	+	Stockholders' Equity			
	Cash	+	Land	=	N. Pay.	+	Com. Stk.	+	Ret. Earn.	Acct. Title
Beginning balances	55,000	+	500,000	=	400,000	+	120,000	+	35,000	
Used cash to pay dividends	(4,000)	+	NA	=	NA	+	NA	+	(4,000)	Dividends
Ending balances	51,000	+	500,000	=	400,000	+	120,000	+	31,000	

Like revenues and expenses, dividends are not recorded directly into the Retained Earnings account. The $4,000 dividend is recorded in the Dividends account. It will be transferred to retained earnings at the end of the accounting period as part of the closing process. The $31,000 ending balance in the retained earnings column shows what would be in the Retained Earnings account after the balances in the Revenue, Expense, and Dividend accounts have been closed. The current balance in the Retained Earnings account is zero.

Historical Cost and Reliability Concepts

Event 7 The land that RCS paid $500,000 to purchase had an appraised market value of $525,000 on December 31, 2008.

Although the appraised value of the land is higher than the original cost, RCS will not increase the amount recorded in its accounting records above the land's $500,000 historical cost. In general, accountants do not recognize changes in market value. The **historical cost concept** requires that most assets be reported at the amount paid for them (their historical cost) regardless of increases in market value.

Explain how the historical cost and reliability concepts affect amounts reported in financial statements.

Surely investors would rather know what an asset is worth instead of how much it originally cost. So why do accountants maintain records and report financial information based on historical cost? Accountants rely heavily on the **reliability concept.** Information is reliable if it can be independently verified. For example, two people looking at the legal documents associated with RCS's land purchase will both conclude that RCS paid $500,000 for the land. That historical cost is a verifiable fact. The appraised value, in contrast, is an opinion. Even two persons who are experienced appraisers are not likely to come up with the same amount for the land's market value. Accountants do not report market values in financial statements because such values are not reliable.

Recap: Types of Transactions

Classify business events as asset source, use, or exchange transactions.

The transactions described above have each been classified into one of three categories: (1) asset source transactions; (2) asset exchange transactions; and (3) asset use transactions. A fourth category, claims exchange transactions, is introduced in a later chapter. In summary

- **Asset source transactions** increase the total amount of assets and increase the total amount of claims. In its first year of operation, RCS acquired assets from three sources: first, from owners (Event 1); next, by borrowing (Event 2); and finally, through earnings activities (Event 4).

- **Asset exchange transactions** decrease one asset and increase another asset. The total amount of assets is unchanged by asset exchange transactions. RCS experienced one asset exchange transaction; it used cash to purchase land (Event 3).

- **Asset use transactions** decrease the total amount of assets and the total amount of claims. RCS used assets to pay expenses (Event 5) and to pay dividends (Event 6).

As you proceed through this text, practice classifying transactions into one of the four categories. Businesses engage in thousands of transactions every day. It is far more effective to learn how to classify the transactions into meaningful categories than to attempt to memorize the effects of thousands of transactions.

Summary of Transactions

Record business events in general ledger accounts organized under an accounting equation.

The complete collection of a company's accounts is called the **general ledger.** The general ledger account information for RCS's 2008 accounting period is shown in Exhibit 1.4. The revenue, expense, and dividend account data appear in the retained earnings column. These account titles are shown immediately to the right of the dollar amounts listed in the retained earnings column. To help you review RCS's general ledger, the business events that the company experienced during 2008 are summarized below.

1. RCS issued common stock, acquiring $120,000 cash from its owners.
2. RCS borrowed $400,000 cash.
3. RCS paid $500,000 cash to purchase land.

EXHIBIT 1.4

General Ledger Accounts Organized Under the Accounting Equation

| Event No. | Assets | | | = Liabilities | + | Stockholders' Equity | | | Other Account Titles |
	Cash	+	Land	= Notes Payable	+	Common Stock	+	Retained Earnings	
Beg. bal.	0		0	0		0		0	
1.	120,000					120,000			
2.	400,000			400,000					
3.	(500,000)		500,000						
4.	85,000							85,000	Revenue
5.	(50,000)							(50,000)	Expense
6.	(4,000)							(4,000)	Dividend
7.	NA		NA	NA		NA		NA	
	51,000	+	500,000	= 400,000	+	120,000	+	31,000	

4. RCS received $85,000 cash from earning revenue.

5. RCS paid $50,000 cash for expenses.

6. RCS paid dividends of $4,000 cash to the owners.

7. The land that RCS paid $500,000 to purchase had an appraised market value of $525,000 on December 31, 2008.

As indicated earlier, accounting information is normally presented to external users in four general-purpose financial statements. The information in the ledger accounts is used to prepare these financial statements. The data in the above ledger accounts are color coded to help you understand the source of information in the financial statements. The numbers in *green* are used in the *statement of cash flows*. The numbers in *red* are used to prepare the *balance sheet*. Finally, the numbers in *blue* are used to prepare the *income statement*. The numbers reported in the statement of changes in stockholders' equity have not been color coded because they appear in more than one statement. The next section explains how the information in the accounts is presented in financial statements.

Preparing Financial Statements

The financial statements for RCS are shown in Exhibit 1.5. The information used to prepare these statements was drawn from the ledger accounts. Information in one statement may relate to information in another statement. For example, the amount of net income reported on the income statement also appears on the statement of changes in stockholders' equity. Accountants use the term **articulation** to describe the interrelationships among the various elements of the financial statements. The key articulated relationships in RCS's financial statements are highlighted with arrows (Exhibit 1.5). A description of each statement follows.

LO 8

Use general ledger account information to prepare four financial statements.

Video 1.2

Income Statement and the Matching Concept

Businesses consume assets and services in order to generate revenues, thereby creating greater quantities of other assets. For example, RCS may pay cash (asset use) to an employee who maintains the camp sites. Maintaining the sites is necessary in order to collect cash (obtain assets) from customers. The **income statement** *matches* asset increases from operating a business with asset decreases from operating the business.[5] Asset increases resulting from providing goods and services to customers in the course of normal operations are called *revenues*. Asset decreases resulting from consuming assets and services for the purpose of generating revenues are called *expenses*. If revenues are greater than expenses, the difference is called **net income.** If expenses exceed revenues, the difference is a **net loss.**

The income statement in Exhibit 1.5 indicates that RCS has earned more assets than it has used. The statement shows that RCS has increased its assets by $35,000 (net income) as a result of operating its business. Observe the phrase *For the Year Ended December 31, 2008,* in the heading of the income statement. Income is measured for a span of time called the **accounting period.** While accounting periods of one year are normal for external financial reporting, income can be measured weekly, monthly, quarterly, semiannually, or over any other desired time period. Notice that the cash RCS paid to its stockholders (dividends) is not reported as expense. The decrease in assets for dividend payments is not incurred for the purpose of generating revenue. Instead, dividends are transfers of wealth to the owners of the business. Dividend payments are not reported on the income statement.

---

[5]This description of the income statement is expanded in subsequent chapters as additional relationships among the elements of financial statements are introduced.

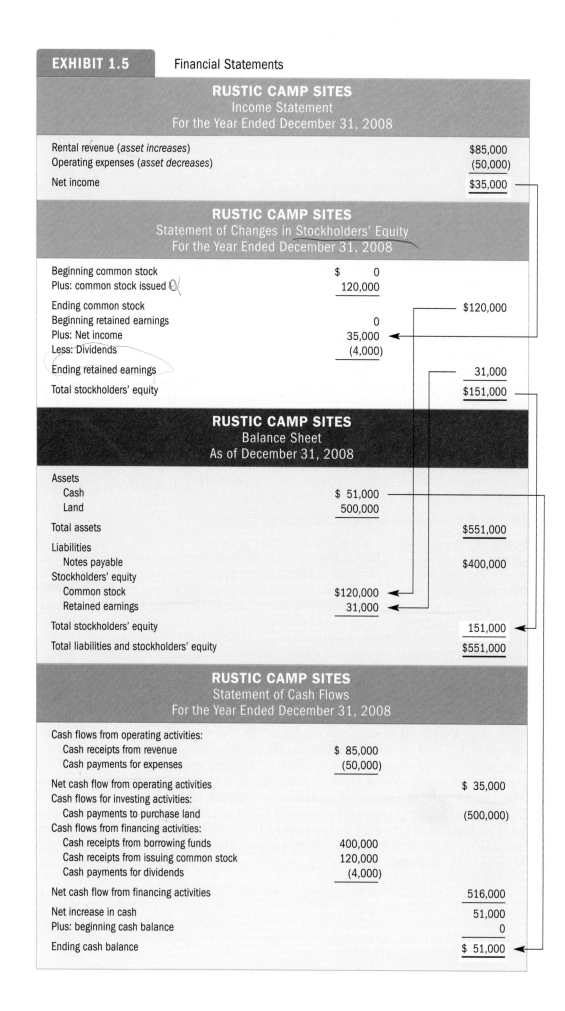

EXHIBIT 1.5   Financial Statements

RUSTIC CAMP SITES
Income Statement
For the Year Ended December 31, 2008

Rental revenue (*asset increases*)	$85,000
Operating expenses (*asset decreases*)	(50,000)
Net income	$35,000

RUSTIC CAMP SITES
Statement of Changes in Stockholders' Equity
For the Year Ended December 31, 2008

Beginning common stock	$ 0	
Plus: common stock issued	120,000	
Ending common stock		$120,000
Beginning retained earnings	0	
Plus: Net income	35,000	
Less: Dividends	(4,000)	
Ending retained earnings		31,000
Total stockholders' equity		$151,000

RUSTIC CAMP SITES
Balance Sheet
As of December 31, 2008

Assets		
Cash	$ 51,000	
Land	500,000	
Total assets		$551,000
Liabilities		
Notes payable		$400,000
Stockholders' equity		
Common stock	$120,000	
Retained earnings	31,000	
Total stockholders' equity		151,000
Total liabilities and stockholders' equity		$551,000

RUSTIC CAMP SITES
Statement of Cash Flows
For the Year Ended December 31, 2008

Cash flows from operating activities:		
Cash receipts from revenue	$ 85,000	
Cash payments for expenses	(50,000)	
Net cash flow from operating activities		$ 35,000
Cash flows for investing activities:		
Cash payments to purchase land		(500,000)
Cash flows from financing activities:		
Cash receipts from borrowing funds	400,000	
Cash receipts from issuing common stock	120,000	
Cash payments for dividends	(4,000)	
Net cash flow from financing activities		516,000
Net increase in cash		51,000
Plus: beginning cash balance		0
Ending cash balance		$ 51,000

Mahoney, Inc., was started when it issued common stock to its owners for $300,000. During its first year of operation Mahoney received $523,000 cash for services provided to customers. Mahoney paid employees $233,000 cash. Advertising costs paid in cash amounted to $102,000. Other cash operating expenses amounted to $124,000. Finally, Mahoney paid a $25,000 cash dividend to its stockholders. What amount of net income would Mahoney's report on its earnings statement?

Answer

The amount of net income is $64,000 ($523,000 Revenue − $233,000 Salary Expense − $102,000 Advertising Expense − $124,000 Other Operating Expenses). The cash received from issuing stock is not revenue because it was not acquired from earnings activities. In other words, Mahoney did not work (perform services) for this money; it was contributed by owners of the business. The dividends are not expenses because the decrease in cash was not incurred for the purpose of generating revenue. Instead, the dividends represent a transfer of wealth to the owners.

Statement of Changes in Stockholders' Equity

The **statement of changes in stockholders' equity** explains the effects of transactions on stockholders' equity during the accounting period. It starts with the beginning balance in the common stock account. In the case of RCS, the beginning balance in the common stock account is zero because the company did not exist before the 2008 accounting period. The $120,000 of stock issued during the accounting period is added to the beginning balance to determine the ending balance in the common stock account.

In addition to reporting the changes in common stock, the statement describes the changes in retained earnings for the accounting period. RCS had no beginning balance in retained earnings. During the period, the company earned $35,000 and paid $4,000 in dividends to the stockholders, producing an ending retained earning balance of $31,000 ($0 + $35,000 − $4,000). Since equity consists of common stock and retained earnings, the ending total equity balance is $151,000 ($120,000 + $31,000). This statement is also dated with the phrase *For the Year Ended December 31, 2008,* because it describes what happened to stockholders' equity during 2008.

Balance Sheet

The **balance sheet** draws its name from the accounting equation. Total assets balances with (equals) claims (liabilities and stockholders' equity) on those assets. The balance sheet for RCS is shown in Exhibit 1.5. Note that total claims (liabilities plus stockholders' equity) are equal to total assets ($551,000 = $551,000).

Note the order of the assets in the balance sheet. Cash appears first, followed by land. Assets are displayed in the balance sheet based on their level of **liquidity.** This means that assets are listed in order of how rapidly they will be converted to cash. Finally, note that the balance sheet is dated with the phrase *As of December 31, 2008,* indicating that it describes the company's financial condition on the last day of the accounting period.

To gain a clear understanding of the balance sheet, try to create one that describes your personal financial condition. First list your assets, then your liabilities. Determine the amount of your equity by subtracting your liabilities from your assets.

Answer

Answers for this exercise will vary depending on the particular assets and liabilities each student identifies. Common student assets include automobiles, computers, stereos, TVs, phones, CD players, clothes, and textbooks. Common student liabilities include car loans, mortgages, student loans, and credit card debt. The difference between the assets and the liabilities is the equity.

Statement of Cash Flows

The **statement of cash flows** explains how a company obtained and used *cash* during the accounting period. Receipts of cash are called *cash inflows,* and payments are *cash outflows.* The statement classifies cash receipts (inflows) and payments (outflows) into three categories: financing activities, investing activities, and operating activities.

Businesses normally start with an idea. Implementing the idea usually requires cash. For example, suppose you decide to start an apartment rental business. First, you would need cash to finance acquiring the apartments. Acquiring cash to start a business is a financing activity. **Financing activities** include obtaining cash (inflow) from owners or paying cash (outflow) to owners (dividends). Financing activities also include borrowing cash (inflow) from creditors and repaying the principal (outflow) to creditors. Because interest on borrowed money is an expense, however, cash paid to creditors for interest is reported in the operating activities section of the statement of cash flows.

After obtaining cash from financing activities, you would invest the money by building or buying apartments. **Investing activities** involve paying cash (outflow) to purchase productive assets or receiving cash (inflow) from selling productive assets. **Productive assets** are sometimes called long-term assets because businesses normally use them for more than one year. Cash outflows to purchase land or cash inflows from selling a building are examples of investing activities.

After investing in the productive assets (apartments), you would engage in operating activities. **Operating activities** involve receiving cash (inflow) from revenue and paying cash (outflow) for expenses. Note that cash spent to purchase short-term assets such as office supplies is reported in the operating activities section because the office supplies would likely be used (expensed) within a single accounting period.

The primary cash inflows and outflows related to the types of business activity introduced in this chapter are summarized in Exhibit 1.6. The exhibit will be expanded as additional types of events are introduced in subsequent chapters.

The statement of cash flows for Rustic Camp Sites in Exhibit 1.5 shows that the amount of cash increased by $51,000 during the year. The beginning balance in the Cash account was zero; adding the $51,000 increase to the beginning balance results in a $51,000 ending balance. Notice that the $51,000 ending cash balance on the statement of cash flows is the same as the amount of cash reported in the asset section on the December 31 year-end balance sheet. Also, note that the statement of cash flows is dated

---

EXHIBIT 1.6

Classification Scheme for Statement of Cash Flows

Cash flows from operating activities:
Cash receipts (inflows) from revenue (including interest)
Cash payments (outflows) for expenses (including interest)

Cash flows from investing activities:
Cash receipts (inflows) from the sale of long-term assets
Cash payments (outflows) for the purchase of long-term assets

Cash flows from financing activities:
Cash receipts (inflows) from borrowing funds
Cash receipts (inflows) from issuing common stock
Cash payments (outflows) to repay borrowed funds
Cash payments (outflows) for dividends

CHECK YOURSELF 1.5

Classify each of the following cash flows as an operating activity, investing activity, or financing activity.

1. Acquired cash from owners.
2. Borrowed cash from creditors.
3. Paid cash to purchase land.
4. Earned cash revenue.
5. Paid cash for salary expenses.
6. Paid cash dividend.
7. Paid cash for interest.

Answer

(1) financing activity; (2) financing activity; (3) investing activity; (4) operating activity; (5) operating activity; (6) financing activity; (7) operating activity.

with the phrase *For the Year Ended December 31, 2008,* because it describes what happened to cash over the span of the year.

The Closing Process

As previously indicated transaction data are recorded in the Revenue, Expense, and Dividend accounts during the accounting period. At the end of the accounting period the data in theses accounts is transferred to the Retained Earnings account. The process of transferring the balances is called **closing.** Since the Revenue, Expense, and Dividend accounts are closed each period, they are called **temporary accounts.** At the beginning of each new accounting period, the temporary accounts have zero balances. The Retained Earnings account carries forward from one accounting period to the next. Since this account is not closed, it is called a **permanent account.**

CHECK YOURSELF 1.6

After closing on December 31, 2008, Walston Company had $4,600 of assets, $2,000 of liabilities, and $700 of common stock. During January of 2009, Walston earned $750 of revenue and incurred $300 of expense. Walston closes it books each year on December 31.

1. Determine the balance in the Retained Earnings account as of December 31, 2008.
2. Determine the balance in the Retained Earnings account as of January 1, 2009.
3. Determine the balance in the Retained Earnings account as of January 31, 2009.

Answer

1. Assets = Liabilities + Common Stock + Retained Earnings

   $4,600 = $2,000 + $700 + Retained Earnings

   Retained Earnings = $1,900

2. The balance in the Retained Earnings account on January 1, 2009, is the same as it was on December 31, 2008. This year's ending balance becomes next year's beginning balance. Therefore, the balance in the Retained Earnings account on January 1, 2009, is $1,900.

3. The balance in the Retained Earnings account on January 31, 2009, is still $1,900. The revenue earned and expenses incurred during January are not recorded in the Retained Earnings account. Revenue is recorded in a Revenue account and expenses are recorded in an Expense account during the accounting period. The balances in the Revenue and Expense accounts are transferred to the Retained Earnings account during the closing process at the end of the accounting period (December 31, 2009).

The Horizontal Financial Statements Model

Financial statements are the scorecard for business activity. If you want to succeed in business, you must know how your business decisions affect your company's financial statements. This text uses a **horizontal statements model** to help you understand how business events affect financial statements. This model shows a set of financial statements horizontally across a single page of paper. The balance sheet is displayed first, adjacent to the income statement, and then the statement of cash flows. Because the effects of equity transactions can be analyzed by referring to certain balance sheet columns, and because of limited space, the statement of changes in stockholders' equity is not shown in the horizontal statements model.

LO 9

Record business events using a horizontal financial statements model.

The model frequently uses abbreviations. For example, activity classifications in the statement of cash flows are identified using OA for operating activities, IA for investing activities, and FA for financing activities. NC designates the net change in cash. The statements model uses "NA" when an account is not affected by an event. The background of the *balance sheet* is red, the *income statement* is blue, and the *statement of cash flows* is green. To demonstrate the usefulness of the horizontal statements model, we use it to display the seven accounting events that RCS experienced during its first year of operation (2008).

1. RCS acquired $120,000 cash from the owners.
2. RCS borrowed $400,000 cash.

3. RCS paid $500,000 cash to purchase land.

4. RCS received $85,000 cash from earning revenue.

5. RCS paid $50,000 cash for expenses.

6. RCS paid $4,000 of cash dividends to the owners.

7. The market value of the land owned by RCS was appraised at $525,000 on December 31, 2008.

Event No.	Balance Sheet										Income Statement					Statement of Cash Flows	
	Assets			=	Liab.	+	Stockholders' Equity										
	Cash	+	Land	=	N. Pay.	+	Com. Stk.	+	Ret. Earn.		Rev.	−	Exp.	=	Net Inc.		
Beg. bal.	0	+	0	=	0	+	0	+	0		0	−	0	=	0	NA	
1.	120,000	+	NA	=	NA	+	120,000	+	NA		NA	−	NA	=	NA	120,000	FA
2.	400,000	+	NA	=	400,000	+	NA	+	NA		NA	−	NA	=	NA	400,000	FA
3.	(500,000)	+	500,000	=	NA	+	NA	+	NA		NA	−	NA	=	NA	(500,000)	IA
4.	85,000	+	NA	=	NA	+	NA	+	85,000		85,000	−	NA	=	85,000	85,000	OA
5.	(50,000)	+	NA	=	NA	+	NA	+	(50,000)		NA	−	50,000	=	(50,000)	(50,000)	OA
6.	(4,000)	+	NA	=	NA	+	NA	+	(4,000)		NA	−	NA	=	NA	(4,000)	FA
7.	NA	+	NA	=	NA	+	NA	+	NA		NA	−	NA	=	NA	NA	
Totals	51,000	+	500,000	=	400,000	+	120,000	+	31,000		85,000	−	50,000	=	35,000	51,000	NC

Recognize that statements models are learning tools. Because they are helpful in understanding how accounting events affect financial statements, they are used extensively in this book. However, the models omit many of the details used in published financial statements. For example, the horizontal model shows only a partial set of statements. Also, since the statements are presented in aggregate, the description of dates (i.e., "as of" versus "for the period ended") does not distinguish periodic from cumulative data.

THE FINANCIAL ANALYST

This section of each chapter introduces topics related to analyzing real world financial reports. We focus first on the types of businesses that operate in the real world. We also discuss the annual report that is used to communicate information to stakeholders.

Real-World Financial Reports

As previously indicated, organizations exist in many different forms, including *business* entities and *not-for-profit* entities. Business entities are typically service, merchandising, or manufacturing companies. **Service businesses,** which include doctors, attorneys, accountants, dry cleaners, and maids, provide services to their customers. **Merchandising businesses,** sometimes called *retail* or *wholesale companies,* sell goods to customers that other entities make. **Manufacturing businesses** make the goods that they sell to their customers.

Some business operations include combinations of these three categories. For example, an automotive repair shop might change oil (service function), sell parts such as oil filters

Service   **Merchandising**   **Manufacturing**

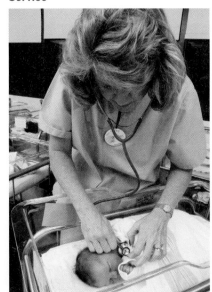

(retail function), and rebuild engines (manufacturing function). The nature of the reporting entity affects the form and content of the information reported in an entity's financial statements. For example, not-for-profit entities provide statements of revenues, expenditures, and changes in fund equity while business entities provide income statements. Similarly, income statements of retail companies show an expense item called *cost of goods sold,* but service companies that do not sell goods have no such item in their income statements. You should expect some diversity when reviewing real-world financial statements.

Annual Report for The Topps Company, Inc.

Organizations normally provide information, including financial statements, to *stakeholders* yearly in a document known as an **annual report.** The annual report for Topps is reproduced in Appendix B of this text. This report includes the company's financial statements (see pages 15–19 of the report). Immediately following the statements are footnotes that provide additional details about the items described in the statements (see pages 20–47). The annual report contains the *auditors' report,* which is discussed in Chapter 2. Annual reports also include written commentary describing management's assessment of significant events that affected the company during the reporting period. This commentary is called *management's discussion and analysis* (MD&A).

The U.S. Securities and Exchange Commission (SEC) requires public companies to file an annual report on a document known as a 10-K. The SEC is discussed in more detail later. Even though the annual report is usually flashier (contains more color and pictures) than the 10-K, the 10-K is normally more comprehensive with respect to content. As a result, the 10-K report can substitute for the annual report, but the annual report cannot substitute for the 10-K. In an effort to reduce costs, some companies use the 10-K report as their annual report.

Special Terms in Real-World Reports

The financial statements of real-world companies include numerous items relating to advanced topics that are not covered in introductory accounting textbooks, especially the first chapter of an introductory accounting textbook. Do not, however, be discouraged from browsing through real-world annual reports. You will significantly enhance your learning if you look at many annual reports and attempt to identify as many items as you can. As your accounting knowledge grows, you will likely experience increased interest in real-world financial reports and the businesses they describe.

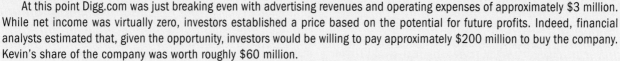

So, how did the kid, Kevin Rose, do it? He built a company investors wanted to buy. So how, in just 18 months, did he build a company so big that only a portion of it was worth $60 million? When investors buy a company they are really buying a right to share in the *future* earnings of that company. The existing company does not have to be so large. It is the potential for future earnings that has to be big.

Kevin risked everything to start his business—"all his time, all his cash, and even his girlfriend, who fought with him after he poured his savings into his company instead of a down payment on a house." Kevin's idea was to use information that others would "dig up" on the Web. Kevin's Web site would allow his users to post links to other Web sites they had found containing interesting stories. The "diggers" would then vote for the best links to be placed onto the front page of Digg.com. As more and more users came to the site to find the most interesting stories, they would also become contributors by listing their favorite links. A snowball effect would make Digg.com a very popular Web site, thereby enabling the company to earn mega revenues from advertising.

Kevin and a small cadre of friends and supporters worked feverishly to establish the hardware and software that would enable the realization of Kevin's dream. The big question was "if we build it, will they come?" Roughly 18 months later they had their answer—a resounding yes. By 4 P.M. on launch day Digg.com had signed up more than 13,000 registered users. Growth continued to soar. Shortly thereafter Digg.com was ranked the 24th most popular Web site in the United States.

At this point Digg.com was just breaking even with advertising revenues and operating expenses of approximately $3 million. While net income was virtually zero, investors established a price based on the potential for future profits. Indeed, financial analysts estimated that, given the opportunity, investors would be willing to pay approximately $200 million to buy the company. Kevin's share of the company was worth roughly $60 million.

As this story illustrates, investors frequently use information that is not reported in a company's annual report. The annual report focuses on historical data. This information is important because the past is frequently a strong predictor of what will happen in the future. However, innovative ideas may generate companies that have little or no history but that nevertheless have very promising futures. Also, investors and creditors may be motivated by nonfinancial considerations such as social consciousness, humanitarian ideals, or personal preferences. While accounting information is critically important, it is only one dimension of the information pool that investors and creditors use to make decisions.

We encourage you to look for annual reports in the library or ask your employer for a copy of your company's report. The Internet is another excellent source for obtaining annual reports. Most companies provide links to their annual reports on their home pages. Look for links labeled "about the company" or "investor relations" or other phrases that logically lead to the company's financial reports. The best way to learn accounting is to use it. Accounting is the language of business. Learning the language will serve you well in almost any area of business that you pursue.

« A Look Back

This chapter introduced the role of accounting in society and business: to provide information helpful to operating and evaluating the performance of organizations. Accounting is a measurement discipline. To communicate effectively, users of accounting must agree on the rules of measurement. *Generally accepted accounting principles (GAAP)* constitute the rules used by the accounting profession in the United States to govern financial reporting. GAAP is a work in progress that continues to evolve.

This chapter has discussed eight elements of financial statements: *assets, liabilities, equity, common stock (contributed capital), revenue, expenses, dividends (distributions),* and *net income.* The elements represent broad classifications reported on financial statements. Four basic financial statements appear in the reports of public companies: the *balance sheet,* the *income statement,* the *statement of changes in stockholders' equity,* and the *statement of cash flows.* The chapter discussed the form and content of each statement as well as the interrelationships among the statements.

This chapter introduced a *horizontal financial statements model* as a tool to help you understand how business events affect a set of financial statements. This model is used throughout the text. You should carefully study this model before proceeding to Chapter 2.

A Look Forward

To keep matters as simple as possible and to focus on the interrelationships among financial statements, this chapter considered only cash events. Obviously, many real-world events do not involve an immediate exchange of cash. For example, customers use telephone service throughout the month without paying for it until the next month. Such phone usage represents an expense in one month with a cash exchange in the following month. Events such as this are called *accruals.* Understanding the effects that accrual events have on the financial statements is included in Chapter 2.

GROWTH AND THE PRICE-EARNINGS RATIO **APPENDIX**

When you buy a share of stock, what do you really get? The stock certificate you receive is evidence of your right to share in the earnings of the company that issued the stock. The more the company earns, the more your wealth increases. This explains why investors are willing to pay higher prices for companies with higher earnings potential.

Explain the price-earnings ratio.

Price-Earnings Ratio

The **price-earnings ratio,** frequently called the *P/E ratio,* is the most commonly reported measure of a company's value. The P/E ratio is a company's market price per share of stock divided by the company's annual earnings per share (EPS).[6]

Assume Western Company recently reported annual earnings per share of $3. Western's stock is currently selling for $54 per share. Western's stock is therefore selling at a P/E ratio of 18 ($54 market price / $3 EPS). What does a P/E ratio of 18 mean? If Western continued earning $3 per share of stock each year and paid all its earnings out to stockholders in the form of cash dividends, it would take 18 years for an investor to recover the price paid for the stock.

In contrast, assume the stock of Eastern Company, which reported EPS of $4, is currently selling for $48 per share. Eastern's P/E ratio is 12 ($48 market price / $4 EPS). Investors who buy Eastern Company stock would get their money back six years faster (18 − 12) than investors who buy Western Company stock.

Why would investors buy a stock with a P/E ratio of 18 when they could buy one with a P/E ratio of 12? If investors expect Western Company's earnings to grow faster than Eastern Company's earnings, the higher P/E ratio makes sense. For example, suppose Western Company's earnings were to double to $6 per share while Eastern's remained at $4 per share. Western's P/E ratio would drop to 9 ($54 market price / $6 EPS) while Eastern's remains at 12. This explains why high-growth companies sell for higher P/E multiples than do low-growth companies.

---

[6]The amount of earnings per share is provided in the company's annual report. In its simplest form, it is computed by dividing the company's net income (net earnings) by the number of shares of common stock outstanding.

Measuring Growth Through Percentage Analysis

The income statements for Cammeron, Inc., show that earnings increased by $4.2 million from 2008 to 2009. Comparable data for Diller Enterprises indicate earnings growth of $2.9 million. Is Cammeron a better-managed company than Diller? Not necessarily; perhaps Cammeron is simply a larger company than Diller. Investors frequently use percentage analysis to level the playing field when comparing companies of differing sizes. Consider the following actual earnings data for the two companies:

	2008*	2009*	Growth[†]
Cammeron	$42.4	$46.6	$4.2
Diller	9.9	12.8	2.9

*Earnings data shown in millions.

[†]Growth calculated by subtracting 2008 earnings from 2009 earnings.

The percentage growth in earnings between 2008 and 2009 for each of the companies can be measured with the following formula:

$$\frac{\text{Alternative year earnings} - \text{Base year earnings}}{\text{Base year earnings}} = \text{Percentage growth rate}$$

Cammeron, Inc.:

$$\frac{\$46.6 - \$42.4}{\$42.4} = 9.9\%$$

Diller Enterprises:

$$\frac{\$12.8 - \$9.9}{\$9.9} = 29.3\%$$

This analysis shows that Cammeron is the larger company, but Diller is growing much more rapidly. If this trend continues, Diller will eventually become the larger company and have higher earnings than Cammeron. This higher earnings potential is why investors value fast-growing companies. The P/E ratios of real-world companies are often correlated with their growth rates, as demonstrated in the data reported in Exhibit 1.7. The data in this exhibit are based on the closing stock prices on June 29, 2006.

EXHIBIT 1.7

Real-World Price-Earnings Ratios and Growth Rates

Company	P/E Ratio	Average Annual Earnings Growth 2003–2005
High growth companies:		
Coldwater Creek	48	121.2 %
Google	71	196.5
Medium growth companies:		
Oracle	23	9.1
Wal-Mart	18	8.0
Low growth companies:		
Radio Shack	8	0.3
Talbots	11	(1.1)

During 2009 Rustic Camp Sites experienced the following transactions.

1. RCS acquired $32,000 cash by issuing common stock.
2. RCS received $116,000 cash for providing services to customers (leasing camp sites).
3. RCS paid $13,000 cash for salaries expense.
4. RCS paid a $9,000 cash dividend to the owners.
5. RCS sold land that had cost $100,000 for $100,000 cash.
6. RCS paid $47,000 cash for other operating expenses.

Required

a. Record the transaction data in a horizontal financial statements model like the following one. In the Cash Flow column, classify the cash flows as operating activities (OA), investing activities (IA), or financing activities (FA). The beginning balances have been recorded as an example. They are the ending balances shown on RCS's December 31, 2008, financial statements illustrated in the chapter. Note that the revenue and expense accounts have a zero beginning balance. Amounts in these accounts apply only to a single accounting period. Revenue and expense account balances are not carried forward from one accounting period to the next.

	Balance Sheet											Income Statement					Statement of Cash Flows
	Assets			=	Liab.	+	Stockholders' Equity										
Event No.	Cash	+	Land	=	N. Pay.	+	Com. Stk.	+	Ret. Earn.			Rev.	−	Exp.	=	Net Inc.	
Beg. bal.	51,000	+	500,000	=	400,000	+	120,000	+	31,000			NA	−	NA	=	NA	NA

b. Explain why there are no beginning balances in the Income Statement columns.
c. What amount of net income will RCS report on the 2009 income statement?
d. What amount of total assets will RCS report on the December 31, 2009, balance sheet?
e. What amount of retained earnings will RCS report on the December 31, 2009, balance sheet?
f. What amount of net cash flow from operating activities will RCS report on the 2009 statement of cash flows?

Solution

a.

	Balance Sheet											Income Statement					Statement of Cash Flows
	Assets			=	Liab.	+	Stockholders' Equity										
Event No.	Cash	+	Land	=	N. Pay.	+	Com. Stk.	+	Ret. Earn.			Rev.	−	Exp.	=	Net Inc.	
Beg. bal.	51,000	+	500,000	=	400,000	+	120,000	+	31,000			NA	−	NA	=	NA	NA
1.	32,000	+	NA	=	NA	+	32,000	+	NA			NA	−	NA	=	NA	32,000 FA
2.	116,000	+	NA	=	NA	+	NA	+	116,000			116,000	−	NA	=	116,000	116,000 OA
3.	(13,000)	+	NA	=	NA	+	NA	+	(13,000)			NA	−	13,000	=	(13,000)	(13,000) OA
4.	(9,000)	+	NA	=	NA	+	NA	+	(9,000)			NA	−	NA	=	NA	(9,000) FA
5.	100,000	+	(100,000)	=	NA	+	NA	+	NA			NA	−	NA	=	NA	100,000 IA
6.	(47,000)	+	NA	=	NA	+	NA	+	(47,000)			NA	−	47,000	=	(47,000)	(47,000) OA
Totals	230,000	+	400,000	=	400,000	+	152,000	+	78,000			116,000	−	60,000	=	56,000	179,000 NC*

*The letters NC on the last line of the column designate the net change in cash.

b. The revenue and expense accounts are temporary accounts used to capture data for a single accounting period. They are closed (amounts removed from the accounts) to retained earnings at the end of the accounting period and therefore always have zero balances at the beginning of the accounting cycle.

c. RCS will report net income of $56,000 on the 2009 income statement. Compute this amount by subtracting the expenses from the revenue ($116,000 Revenue − $13,000 Salaries expense − $47,000 Other operating expense).

d. RCS will report total assets of $630,000 on the December 31, 2009, balance sheet. Compute total assets by adding the cash amount to the land amount ($230,000 Cash + $400,000 Land).

e. RCS will report retained earnings of $78,000 on the December 31, 2009, balance sheet. Compute this amount using the following formula: Beginning retained earnings + Net income − Dividends = Ending retained earnings. In this case, $31,000 + $56,000 − $9,000 = $78,000.

f. Net cash flow from operating activities is the difference between the amount of cash collected from revenue and the amount of cash spent for expenses. In this case, $116,000 cash inflow from revenue − $13,000 cash outflow for salaries expense − $47,000 cash outflow for other operating expenses = $56,000 net cash inflow from operating activities.

KEY TERMS

accounts 11
accounting 3
accounting equation 11
accounting event 12
accounting period 17
annual report 23
articulation 17
assets 4
asset exchange transaction 13
asset source transaction 12
asset use transaction 14
balance sheet 19
claims 11
closing 21
common stock 11
creditors 4
dividend 15
double-entry
   bookkeeping 13

earnings 4
elements 10
equity 11
expenses 14
financial accounting 6
Financial Accounting
   Standards Board
   (FASB) 8
financial resources 4
financial statements 10
financing activities 20
general ledger 16
generally accepted
   accounting principles
   (GAAP) 8
historical cost concept 15
horizontal statements
   model 21
income 4

income statement 17
interest 5
investing activities 20
investors 4
labor resources 5
liabilities 11
liquidation 4
liquidity 19
managerial accounting 6
manufacturing businesses 22
market 4
merchandising businesses 22
net income 17
net loss 17
not-for-profit entities 6
operating activities 20
permanent accounts 21
physical resources 5
price-earnings ratio 25

productive assets 20
profit 4
reliability concept 15
reporting entities 9
retained earnings 11
revenue 14
service businesses 22
stakeholders 6
statement of cash flows 20
statement of changes in
   stockholders' equity 19
stockholders 11
stockholders' equity 11
temporary accounts 21
transaction 12
users 6

QUESTIONS

1. Explain the term *stakeholder*. Distinguish between stakeholders with a direct versus an indirect interest in the companies that issue accounting reports.

2. Why is accounting called the *language of business?*

3. What is the primary mechanism used to allocate resources in the United States?

4. In a business context, what does the term *market* mean?

5. What market trilogy components are involved in the process of transforming resources into finished products?

6. Give an example of a financial resource, a physical resource, and a labor resource.

7. What type of income or profit does an investor expect to receive in exchange for providing financial resources to a business? What type of income does a creditor expect from providing financial resources to an organization or business?

8. How do financial and managerial accounting differ?

9. Describe a not-for-profit or nonprofit enterprise. What is the motivation for this type of entity?

10. What are the U.S. rules of accounting information measurement called?

11. How does establishing GAAP in the United States differ from establishing accounting principles in Japan and Germany?

12. What body has the primary responsibility for establishing GAAP in the United States?

13. Distinguish between elements of financial statements and accounts.

14. What is the most basic form of the accounting equation?

15. What role do assets play in business profitability?

16. To whom do the assets of a business belong?

17. What is the nature of creditors' claims on assets?

18. How do temporary accounts differ from permanent accounts? Name three temporary accounts. Is retained earnings a temporary or a permanent account?

19. What term describes creditors' claims on the assets of a business?

20. What is the accounting equation? Describe each of its three components.

21. Who ultimately bears the risk and collects the rewards associated with operating a business?

22. What does a *double-entry bookkeeping system* mean?

23. Identify the three types of accounting transactions discussed in this chapter. Provide an example of each type of transaction, and explain how it affects the accounting equation.

24. How does acquiring capital from owners affect the accounting equation?

25. What is the difference between assets that are acquired by issuing common stock and those that are acquired using retained earnings?

26. How does earning revenue affect the accounting equation?

27. What are the three primary sources of assets?

28. What is the source of retained earnings?

29. How does distributing assets (paying dividends) to owners affect the accounting equation?

30. What are the similarities and differences between dividends and expenses?

31. Discuss the term *articulation* as it relates to financial statements.

32. What four general-purpose financial statements do business enterprises use?

33. Which of the general-purpose financial statements provides information about the enterprise at a specific designated date?

34. What causes a net loss?

35. What three categories of cash receipts and cash payments do businesses report on the statement of cash flows? Explain the types of cash flows reported in each category.

36. How are asset accounts usually arranged in the balance sheet?

37. How is the price-earnings ratio computed? What does it measure?

38. What information can be learned from analyzing the percentage growth in earnings of a company?

39. What type of information does a business typically include in its annual report?

MULTIPLE-CHOICE QUESTIONS

Multiple-choice questions are provided on the text Web site at www.mhhe.com/edmonds6e.

Quiz 1

EXERCISES—SERIES A

All Exercises in Series A are available with McGraw-Hill's Homework Manager®

Exercise 1-1A   *The role of accounting in society*   **L.O. 1**

Resource owners provide three types of resources to conversion agents that transform the resources into products or services that satisfy consumer demands.

Required

Identify the three types of resources. Write a brief memo explaining how resource owners select the particular conversion agents to which they will provide resources. Your memo should include answers to the following questions: If you work as a private accountant, what role would you play in the allocation of resources? Which professional certification would be most appropriate to your career?

L.O. 1

Exercise 1-2A *Distributions in a business liquidation*

Assume that Brandy Company acquires $1,400 cash from creditors and $1,800 cash from investors (stockholders). The company then has an operating loss of $2,000 cash and goes out of business.

Required

a. Define the term *business liquidation*.

b. What amount of cash will Brandy's creditors receive?

c. What amount of cash will Brandy's investors (stockholders) receive?

L.O. 2

Exercise 1-3A *Identifying the reporting entities*

Carlos Bueso recently started a business. During the first few days of operation, Mr. Bueso transferred $30,000 from his personal account into a business account for a company he named Bueso Enterprises. Bueso Enterprises borrowed $40,000 from the State Bank of Texas. Mr. Bueso's father-in-law, James Bright, invested $64,000 into the business for which he received a 25 percent ownership interest. Bueso Enterprises purchased a building from Leigh Realty Company. The building cost $120,000 cash. Bueso Enterprises earned $28,000 in revenue from the company's customers and paid its employees $25,000 for salaries expense.

Required

Identify the entities that were mentioned in the scenario and explain what happened to the cash accounts of each entity that you identify.

L.O. 3

Exercise 1-4A *Retained earnings and the closing process*

Firwood Company was started on January 1, 2008. During the month of January, Firwood earned $4,600 of revenue and incurred $3,000 of expense. Firwood closes its books on December 31 of each year.

Required

a. Determine the balance in the Retained Earnings account as of January 31, 2008.

b. Comment on whether retained earnings is an element of financial statements or an account.

c. What happens to the Retained Earnings account at the time expenses are recognized?

L.O. 3

Exercise 1-5A *Titles and accounts appearing on financial statements*

Annual reports normally include an income statement, statement of changes in equity, balance sheet, and statement of cash flows.

Required

Identify the financial statements on which each of the following titles or accounts would appear. If a title or an account appears on more than one statement, list all statements that would include it.

a. Retained Earnings

b. Revenue

c. Common Stock

d. Financing Activities

e. Salaries Expense

f. Land

g. Ending Cash Balance

h. Beginning Cash Balance

i. Notes Payable

j. Dividends

Exercise 1-6A   *Components of the accounting equation*   **L.O. 4**

Required

The following three requirements are independent of each other.

a. Michael's Motors has assets of $4,550 and net assets of $3,200. What is the amount of liabilities? What is the amount of claims?

b. Sweet Tooth Bakery has liabilities of $4,800 and equity of $5,400. What is the amount of assets? What is the amount of net assets?

c. Pam's Candy Co. has assets of $49,200 and liabilities of $28,200. What is the amount of equity? What is the amount of net assets?

Exercise 1-7A   *Effect of events on the accounting equation*   **L.O. 4, 5**

Olive Enterprises experienced the following events during 2007.

1. Acquired cash from the issue of common stock.
2. Paid cash to reduce the principal on a bank note.
3. Sold land for cash at an amount equal to its cost.
4. Provided services to clients for cash.
5. Paid utilities expenses with cash.
6. Paid a cash dividend to the stockholders.

Required

Explain how each of the events would affect the accounting equation by writing the letter I for increase, the letter D for decrease, and NA for does not affect under each of the components of the accounting equation. The first event is shown as an example.

Event Number	Assets	=	Liabilities	+	Stockholders' Equity	
					Common Stock	Retained Earnings
1	I		NA		I	NA

Exercise 1-8A   *Effects of issuing stock*   **L.O. 4, 5**

Joseph Company was started in 2009 when it acquired $15,000 cash by issuing common stock. The cash acquisition was the only event that affected the business in 2009.

Required

Write an accounting equation, and record the effects of the stock issue under the appropriate general ledger account headings.

Exercise 1-9A   *Effects of borrowing*   **L.O. 4, 5**

East Asia Company was started in 2008 when it issued a note to borrow $6,200 cash.

Required

Write an accounting equation, and record the effects of the borrowing transaction under the appropriate general ledger account headings.

Exercise 1-10A   *Effects of revenue, expense, dividend, and the closing process*   **L.O. 3, 4, 5, 8**

Ruff Company was started on January 1, 2009. During 2009, the company experienced the following three accounting events: (1) earned cash revenues of $13,500, (2) paid cash expenses of $9,200, and (3) paid a $500 cash dividend to its stockholders. These were the only events that affected the company during 2009.

Required

a. Write an accounting equation, and record the effects of each accounting event under the appropriate general ledger account headings.

b. Prepare an income statement for the 2009 accounting period and a balance sheet at the end of 2009 for Ruff Company.

c. What is the balance in the Retained Earnings account immediately after the cash revenue is recognized?

d. What is the balance in the Retained Earnings account after the closing process is complete?

L.O. 3

Exercise 1-11A   *Classifying items for the statement of cash flows*

Required

Indicate how each of the following would be classified on the statement of cash flows as operating activities (OA), investing activities (IA), financing activities (FA), or not applicable (NA).

a. Borrowed $8,000 cash from State Bank.

b. Paid $5,000 cash for salary expense.

c. Signed a contract to provide services in the future.

d. Performed services for $25,000 cash.

e. Paid $9,000 cash to purchase land.

f. Paid $1,500 cash for utilities expense.

g. Sold land for $5,000 cash.

h. Paid $4,000 cash on the principal of a bank loan.

i. Paid a $2,000 cash dividend to the stockholders.

j. Received $30,000 cash from the issue of common stock.

L.O. 3, 4, 5, 6

Exercise 1-12A   *Effect of transactions on general ledger accounts*

At the beginning of 2011, T & M Corp.'s accounting records had the following general ledger accounts and balances.

T & M CORP.								
Accounting Equation								
Event	Assets		=	Liabilities	+	Stockholders' Equity		Acct. Titles for RE
	Cash	Land		Notes Payable		Common Stock	Retained Earnings	
Balance 1/1/2011	10,000	20,000		12,000		7,000	11,000	

T & M Corp. completed the following transactions during 2011.

1. Purchased land for $5,000 cash.

2. Acquired $25,000 cash from the issue of common stock.

3. Received $75,000 cash for providing services to customers.

4. Paid cash operating expenses of $42,000.

5. Borrowed $10,000 cash from the bank.

6. Paid a $5,000 cash dividend to the stockholders.

7. Determined that the market value of the land is $35,000.

Required

a. Record the transactions in the appropriate general ledger accounts. Record the amounts of revenue, expense, and dividends in the Retained Earnings column. Provide the appropriate titles for these accounts in the last column of the table.

b. Determine the net cash flow from financing activities.

c. What is the balance in the Retained Earnings accounts as of January 1, 2012?

Exercise 1-13A *Preparing financial statements*

Dakota Company experienced the following events during 2008.

1. Acquired $30,000 cash from the issue of common stock.
2. Paid $12,000 cash to purchase land.
3. Borrowed $10,000 cash.
4. Provided services for $20,000 cash.
5. Paid $1,000 cash for rent expense.
6. Paid $15,000 cash for other operating expenses.
7. Paid a $2,000 cash dividend to the stockholders.
8. Determined that the market value of the land purchased in Event 2 is now $12,700.

Required

a. The January 1, 2008, general ledger account balances are shown in the following accounting equation. Record the eight events in the appropriate general ledger accounts. Record the amounts of revenue, expense, and dividends in the Retained Earnings column. Provide the appropriate titles for these accounts in the last column of the table. The first event is shown as an example.

DAKOTA COMPANY
Accounting Equation

Event	Assets		=	Liabilities	+	Stockholders' Equity		Acct. Titles for RE
	Cash	Land		Notes Payable		Common Stock	Retained Earnings	
Balance 1/1/2008	2,000	12,000		0		6,000	8,000	
1.	30,000					30,000		

b. Prepare an income statement, statement of changes in equity, year-end balance sheet, and statement of cash flows for the 2008 accounting period.
c. Determine the percentage of assets that were provided by retained earnings. How much cash is in the retained earnings account?

Exercise 1-14A *Classifying events as asset source, use, or exchange*

Vera Company experienced the following events during its first year of operations.

1. Acquired $16,000 cash from the issue of common stock.
2. Paid $3,500 cash for salary expenses.
3. Borrowed $10,000 cash from New South Bank.
4. Paid $6,000 cash to purchase land.
5. Provided boarding services for $10,500 cash.
6. Acquired an additional $1,000 cash from the issue of common stock.
7. Paid $2,400 cash for utilities expense.
8. Paid a $1,500 cash dividend to the stockholders.
9. Provided additional services for $6,000 cash.
10. Purchased additional land for $2,500 cash.
11. The market value of the land was determined to be $24,000 at the end of the accounting period.

Required

Classify each event as an asset source, use, or exchange transaction.

L.O. 4

Exercise 1-15A   *Relationship between assets and retained earnings*

West Company was organized when it acquired $2,000 cash from the issue of common stock. During its first accounting period the company earned $800 of cash revenue and incurred $500 of cash expenses. Also, during the accounting period the company paid its owners a $200 cash dividend.

Required

a. Determine the balance in the Retained Earnings account before and after the temporary accounts are closed.

b. As of the end of the accounting period, determine what percentage of total assets were provided by earnings.

L.O. 6

Exercise 1-16A   *Historical cost versus market value*

Sarah Company purchased land in April 2004 at a cost of $600,000. The estimated market value of the land is $700,000 as of December 31, 2008. Sarah purchased marketable equity securities (bought the common stock of a company that is independent of Sarah) in May 2004 at a cost of $320,000. These securities have a market value of $360,000 as of December 31, 2008. Generally accepted accounting principles require that the land be shown on the December 31, 2008, balance sheet at $600,000, while the marketable equity securities are required to be reported at $360,000.

Required

Write a brief memo that explains the contradiction regarding why GAAP requires Sarah to report historical cost with respect to the land versus market value with respect to the marketable securities. This answer may require speculation on your part. Use your knowledge about the historical cost and reliability concepts to formulate a logical response.

L.O. 2, 7

Exercise 1-17A   *Relating accounting events to entities*

Sharp Company was started in 2009 when it acquired $25,000 cash by issuing common stock to Katie Sharp.

Required

a. Was this event an asset source, use, or exchange transaction for Sharp Company?

b. Was this event an asset source, use, or exchange transaction for Katie Sharp?

c. Was the cash flow an operating, investing, or financing activity on Sharp Company's 2009 statement of cash flows?

d. Was the cash flow an operating, investing, or financing activity on Katie Sharp's 2009 statement of cash flows?

L.O. 4

Exercise 1-18A   *Missing information in the accounting equation*

Required

Calculate the missing amounts in the following table:

Company	Assets	=	Liabilities	+	Common Stock	+	Retained Earnings
A	$?		$48,000		59,000		$36,000
B	90,000		?		25,000		50,000
C	95,000		15,000		?		37,000
D	102,000		29,000		35,000		?

L.O. 4

Exercise 1-19A   *Missing information in the accounting equation*

As of December 31, 2008, Thomas Company had total assets of $156,000, total liabilities of $85,600, and common stock of $52,400. During 2009 Thomas earned $36,000 of cash revenue, paid $20,000 for cash expenses, and paid a $2,000 cash dividend to the stockholders.

Required

a. Determine the amount of retained earnings as of December 31, 2008, after closing.
b. Determine the amount of net income earned in 2009.
c. Determine the amount of retained earnings as of December 31, 2009, after closing.
d. Determine the amount of cash that is in the retained earnings account as of December 31, 2009.

Exercise 1-20A   *Missing information for determining net income*   **L.O. 3, 4**

The December 31, 2009, balance sheet for Crow Company showed total stockholders' equity of $82,500. Total stockholders' equity increased by $53,400 between December 31, 2009, and December 31, 2010. During 2010 Crow Company acquired $13,000 cash from the issue of common stock. Crow Company paid an $8,000 cash dividend to the stockholders during 2010.

Required

Determine the amount of net income or loss Crow reported on its 2010 income statement. (*Hint:* Remember that stock issues, net income, and dividends all change total stockholders' equity.)

Exercise 1-21A   *Effect of events on a horizontal financial statements model*   **L.O. 6, 9**

Tim's Auto Service experienced the following events during 2011.

1. Purchased land for cash.
2. Issued common stock for cash.
3. Collected cash for providing auto repair services to customers.
4. Paid a cash dividend to the stockholders.
5. Paid cash for operating expenses.
6. Paid cash to reduce the principal balance on a liability.
7. Determined that the market value of the land is higher than its historical cost.

Required

Use a horizontal statements model to show how each event affects the balance sheet, income statement, and statement of cash flows. Indicate whether the event increases (I), decreases (D), or does not affect (NA) each element of the financial statements. Also, in the Cash Flows column, classify the cash flows as operating activities (OA), investing activities (IA), or financing activities (FA). The first transaction is shown as an example.

Event No.	Balance Sheet											Income Statement					Statement of Cash Flows
	Cash	+	Land	=	N. Pay	+	C. Stock.	+	Ret. Ear.			Rev.	−	Exp.	=	Net Inc.	
1.	D	+	I	=	NA	+	NA	+	NA			NA	−	NA	=	NA	D IA

Exercise 1-22A   *Record events in the horizontal statements model*   **L.O. 3, 9**

Arnett Co. was started in 2011. During 2011, the company (1) acquired $11,000 cash from the issue of common stock, (2) earned cash revenue of $18,000, (3) paid cash expenses of $10,500, and (4) paid a $1,000 cash dividend to the stockholders.

Required

a. Record these four events in a horizontal statements model. Also, in the Cash Flows column, classify the cash flows as operating activities (OA), investing activities (IA), or financing activities (FA). The first event is shown as an example.

Event No.	Balance Sheet								Income Statement					Statement of Cash Flows
	Cash	=	N. Pay	+	C. Stock.	+	Ret. Ear.		Rev.	−	Exp.	=	Net Inc.	
1.	11,000	=	NA	+	11,000	+	NA		NA	−	NA	=	NA	11,000 FA

b. What does the income statement tell you about the assets of this business?

L.O. 6, 9

Exercise 1-23A *Effect of events on a horizontal statements model*

Holiday, Inc., was started on January 1, 2009. The company experienced the following events during its first year of operation.

1. Acquired $50,000 cash from the issue of common stock.
2. Paid $12,000 cash to purchase land.
3. Received $50,000 cash for providing tax services to customers.
4. Paid $9,500 cash for salary expenses.
5. Acquired $5,000 cash from the issue of additional common stock.
6. Borrowed $10,000 cash from the bank.
7. Purchased additional land for $10,000 cash.
8. Paid $8,000 cash for other operating expenses.
9. Paid a $2,800 cash dividend to the stockholders.
10. Determined that the market value of the land is $25,000.

Required

a. Record these events in a horizontal statements model. Also, in the Cash Flows column, classify the cash flows as operating activities (OA), investing activities (IA), or financing activities (FA). The first event is shown as an example.

Event No.	Balance Sheet												Income Statement						Statement of Cash Flows
	Cash	+	Land	=	N. Pay	+	C. Stock.	+	Ret. Ear.				Rev.	−	Exp.	=	Net Inc.		
1.	50,000	+	NA	=	NA	+	50,000	+	NA				NA	−	NA	=	NA		50,000 FA

b. What is the net income earned in 2009?
c. What is the amount of total assets at the end of 2009?
d. What is the net cash flow from operating activities for 2009?
e. What is the net cash flow from investing activities for 2009?
f. What is the net cash flow from financing activities for 2009?
g. What is the cash balance at the end of 2009?
h. As of the end of the year 2009, what percentage of total assets were provided by creditors, investors, and earnings?
i. What is the balance in the Retained Earnings account immediately after Event 4 is recorded?

L.O. 6, 7, 9

Exercise 1-24A *Types of transactions and the horizontal statements model*

Jodi's Pet Store experienced the following events during its first year of operations, 2009.

1. Acquired cash by issuing common stock.
2. Purchased land with cash.
3. Borrowed cash from a bank.
4. Signed a contract to provide services in the future.
5. Paid a cash dividend to the stockholders.
6. Paid cash for operating expenses.
7. Determined that the market value of the land is higher than the historical cost.

Required

a. Indicate whether each event is an asset source, use, or exchange transaction.
b. Use a horizontal statements model to show how each event affects the balance sheet, income statement, and statement of cash flows. Indicate whether the event increases (I), decreases (D), or does not affect (NA) each element of the financial statements. Also, in the Cash Flows column, classify the cash flows as operating activities (OA), investing activities (IA), or financing activities (FA). The first transaction is shown as an example.

Event No.	Balance Sheet								Income Statement						Statement of Cash Flows
	Cash	+	Land	=	N. Pay	+	C. Stock.	+	Ret. Ear.	Rev.	−	Exp.	=	Net Inc.	
1.	I	+	NA	=	NA	+	I	+	NA	NA	−	NA	=	NA	I FA

Exercise 1-25A *Price-earnings ratio (Appendix)*

L.O. 10

The following information is available for two companies.

	Wilson Company	Taylor Company
Earnings per share	$ 1.05	$ 3.50
Market price per share	40.50	108.00

Required

a. Compute the price-earnings ratio for each company.
b. Explain why one company would have a higher price-earnings ratio than the other.

PROBLEMS—SERIES A

All Problems in Series A are available with McGraw-Hill's Homework Manager®

Problem 1-26A *Applying GAAP to financial reporting*

L.O. 1

Syble Denson is a business consultant. She analyzed the business processes of one of her clients, Camry Companies, in November 2010. She prepared a report containing her recommendation for changes in some of the company's business practices. She presented Camry with the report in December 2010. Syble guarantees that her clients will save money by following her advice. She does not collect for the services she provides until the client is satisfied with the results of her work. In this case she received cash payment from Camry in February 2011.

Required

a. Define the acronym GAAP.
b. Assume that Syble's accountant tells her that GAAP permits Syble to recognize the revenue from Camry in either 2010 or 2011. What GAAP rule would justify reporting the same event in two different ways? Write a brief memo explaining the logic behind this rule.
c. If Syble were keeping records for managerial reporting purposes, would she be bound by GAAP rules? Write a brief memo to explain how GAAP applies to financial versus managerial reporting.

Problem 1-27A *Accounting entities*

L.O. 2

The following business scenarios are independent from one another.

1. Mary Poort purchased an automobile from Hayney Bros. Auto Sales for $9,000.
2. John Rodman loaned $15,000 to the business in which he is a stockholder.
3. First State Bank paid interest to Caleb Co. on a certificate of deposit that Caleb Co. has invested at First State Bank.
4. Parkside Restaurant paid the current utility bill of $128 to Gulf Utilities.
5. Gatemore, Inc., borrowed $50,000 from City National Bank and used the funds to purchase land from Morgan Realty.
6. Steven Wong purchased $10,000 of common stock of International Sales Corporation from the corporation.
7. Dan Dow loaned $4,000 cash to his daughter.
8. Mega Service Co. earned $5,000 in cash revenue.

CHECK FIGURE
a1. Entities mentioned:
Mary Poort and
Hayney Bros. Auto
Sales

9. McCloud Co. paid $1,500 for salaries to each of its four employees.

10. Shim Inc. paid a cash dividend of $3,000 to its sole shareholder, Marcus Shim.

Required

a. For each scenario, create a list of all of the entities that are mentioned in the description.

b. Describe what happens to the cash account of each entity that you identified in Requirement *a*.

L.O. 3

Problem 1-28A *Relating titles and accounts to financial statements*

A random list of various financial statements components follows: (1) Retained Earnings account ending balance, (2) revenues, (3) Common Stock account beginning balance, (4) Common Stock account ending balance, (5) assets, (6) expenses, (7) operating activities, (8) dividends, (9) Retained Earnings beginning balance, (10) investing activities, (11) common stock issued during the period, (12) liabilities, and (13) financing activities.

Required

Set up a table with the following headings. Identify the financial statements on which each of the preceding components appears by placing a check mark in the appropriate column. If an item appears on more than one statement, place the reference number in every applicable column. The first component is shown as an example.

Income Statement	Statement of Changes in Stockholders' Equity	Balance Sheet	Statement of Cash Flows
	✓	✓	

L.O. 3, 4, 5, 6, 8

eXcel

CHECK FIGURES
a. Net Income 2008: $13,000
b. Retained Earnings 2009: $33,500

Problem 1-29A *Preparing financial statements for two complete accounting cycles*

Johnson Consulting experienced the following transactions for 2008, its first year of operations, and 2009. *Assume that all transactions involve the receipt or payment of cash.*

Transactions for 2008

1. Acquired $20,000 by issuing common stock.
2. Received $35,000 cash for providing services to customers.
3. Borrowed $25,000 cash from creditors.
4. Paid expenses amounting to $22,000.
5. Purchased land for $30,000 cash.

Transactions for 2009

Beginning account balances for 2007 are:

Cash	$28,000
Land	30,000
Notes payable	25,000
Common stock	20,000
Retained earnings	13,000

1. Acquired an additional $24,000 from the issue of common stock.
2. Received $95,000 for providing services.
3. Paid $15,000 to creditors to reduce loan.
4. Paid expenses amounting to $71,500.
5. Paid a $3,000 dividend to the stockholders.
6. Determined that the market value of the land is $47,000.

Required

a. Write an accounting equation, and record the effects of each accounting event under the appropriate headings for each year. Record the amounts of revenue, expense, and dividends in the Retained Earnings column. Provide appropriate titles for these accounts in the last column of the table.

b. Prepare an income statement, statement of changes in stockholders' equity, year-end balance sheet, and statement of cash flows for each year.

c. Determine the amount of cash that is in the retained earnings account at the end of 2008 and 2009.

d. Examine the balance sheets for the two years. How did assets change from 2008 to 2009?

e. Determine the balance in the Retained Earnings account immediately after Event 2 in 2008 and in 2009 are recorded.

Problem 1-30A *Interrelationships among financial statements*

Crawford Enterprises started the 2009 accounting period with $50,000 of assets (all cash), $18,000 of liabilities, and $4,000 of common stock. During the year, Crawford earned cash revenues of $38,000, paid cash expenses of $32,000, and paid a cash dividend to stockholders of $2,000. Crawford also acquired $15,000 of additional cash from the sale of common stock and paid $10,000 cash to reduce the liability owed to a bank.

CHECK FIGURE
a. Net Income: $6,000
   Total Assets: $59,000

Required

a. Prepare an income statement, statement of changes in stockholders' equity, period-end balance sheet, and statement of cash flows for the 2009 accounting period. (*Hint:* Determine the amount of beginning retained earnings before considering the effects of the current period events. It also might help to record all events under an accounting equation before preparing the statements.)

b. Determine the percentage of total assets that were provided by creditors, investors, and earnings.

Problem 1-31A *Classifying events as asset source, use, or exchange*

The following unrelated events are typical of those experienced by business entities:

1. Acquire cash by issuing common stock.
2. Borrow cash from the local bank.
3. Pay office supplies expense.
4. Make plans to purchase office equipment.
5. Trade a used car for a computer with the same value.
6. Pay other operating supplies expense.
7. Agree to represent a client in an IRS audit and to receive payment when the audit is complete.
8. Receive cash from customers for services rendered.
9. Pay employee salaries with cash.
10. Pay back a bank loan with cash.
11. Pay interest to a bank with cash.
12. Transfer cash from a checking account to a money market account.
13. Sell land for cash at its original cost.
14. Pay a cash dividend to stockholders.
15. Learn that a financial analyst determined the company's price-earnings ratio to be 26.

CHECK FIGURE
Event 2: Asset Source

Required

Identify each of the events as an asset source, asset use, or asset exchange transaction. If an event would not be recorded under generally accepted accounting principles, identify it as not applicable (NA). Also indicate for each event whether total assets would increase, decrease, or remain unchanged. Organize your answer according to the following table. The first event is shown in the table as an example.

Event No.	Type of Event	Effect on Total Assets
1	Asset source	Increase

Problem 1-32A *Recording the effect of events in a horizontal statements model*

Doyer Corporation experienced the following transactions during 2010.

1. Paid a cash dividend to the stockholders.
2. Acquired cash by issuing additional common stock.

3. Signed a contract to perform services in the future.
4. Performed services for cash.
5. Paid cash expenses.
6. Sold land for cash at an amount equal to its cost.
7. Borrowed cash from a bank.
8. Determined that the market value of the land is higher than its historical cost.

Required

Use a horizontal statements model to show how each event affects the balance sheet, income statement, and statement of cash flows. Indicate whether the event increases (I), decreases (D), or does not affect (NA) each element of the financial statements. Also, in the Cash Flows column, classify the cash flows as operating activities (OA), investing activities (IA), or financing activities (FA). The first transaction is shown as an example.

Event No.	Balance Sheet											Income Statement					Statement of Cash Flows
	Cash	+	Land	=	N. Pay	+	C. Stock.	+	Ret. Ear.			Rev.	−	Exp.	=	Net Inc.	
1.	D	+	NA	=	NA	+	NA	+	D			NA	−	NA	=	NA	D FA

L.O. 4, 6, 9

Problem 1-33A *Recording events in a horizontal statements model*

Madden Company was started on January 1, 2007, and experienced the following events during its first year of operation.

1. Acquired $30,000 cash from the issue of common stock.
2. Borrowed $40,000 cash from National Bank.
3. Earned cash revenues of $48,000 for performing services.
4. Paid cash expenses of $45,000.
5. Paid a $1,000 cash dividend to the stockholders.
6. Acquired an additional $20,000 cash from the issue of common stock.
7. Paid $10,000 cash to reduce the principal balance of the bank note.
8. Paid $53,000 cash to purchase land.
9. Determined that the market value of the land is $75,000.

Required

a. Record the preceding transactions in the horizontal statements model. Also, in the Cash Flows column, classify the cash flows as operating activities (OA), investing activities (IA), or financing activities (FA). The first event is shown as an example.

Event No.	Balance Sheet											Income Statement					Statement of Cash Flows
	Cash	+	Land	=	N. Pay	+	C. Stock.	+	Ret. Ear.			Rev.	−	Exp.	=	Net Inc.	
1.	30,000	+	NA	=	NA	+	30,000	+	NA			NA	−	NA	=	NA	30,000 FA

b. Determine the amount of total assets that Madden would report on the December 31, 2007, balance sheet.
c. Identify the sources of the assets that Madden would report on the December 31, 2007, balance sheet. Determine the amount of each of these sources.
d. Determine the net income that Madden would report on the 2007 income statement. Explain why dividends do not appear on the income statement.
e. Determine the net cash flows from operating activities, financing activities, and investing activities that Madden would report on the 2007 statement of cash flows.
f. Determine the percentage of assets that were provided by investors, creditors, and earnings.
g. What is the balance in the Retained Earnings account immediately after Event 3 is recorded.

Problem 1-34A   *Price-earnings relationships (Appendix)*   **L.O. 10**

Earnings per share and market price per share data for Parker Corp. and Tabor Corp. follow.

Parker Corp.	2008	2009	2010
Earnings per share	$ 4.22	$ 4.13	$ 4.15
Market price per share	52.14	45.43	45.98
Tabor Corp.	**2008**	**2009**	**2010**
Earnings per share	$ 3.27	$ 4.45	$ 5.81
Market price per share	110.52	129.89	220.78

CHECK FIGURE
b. Parker Corp. 2008
  P/E ratio: 12.36
  Tabor Corp. 2010 P/E
  ratio: 38.00

Required

a. Calculate the annual percentage growth rate in the earnings per share of each company from 2008 to 2009 and from 2009 to 2010.

b. Calculate the price-earnings ratio for each company for all three years.

c. Explain what the price-earnings ratio means.

d. Why would the price-earnings ratios of the two companies be different?

EXERCISES—SERIES B

Exercise 1-1B   *The role of accounting in society*   **L.O. 1**

Free economies use open markets to allocate resources.

Required

Identify the three participants in a free business market. Write a brief memo explaining how these participants interact to ensure that goods and services are distributed in a manner that satisfies consumers. Your memo should include answers to the following questions: If you work as a public accountant, what role would you play in the allocation of resources? Which professional certification would be most appropriate to your career?

Exercise 1-2B   *Distributions in a business liquidation*   **L.O. 1**

Assume that Jones Company acquires $1,600 cash from creditors and $1,800 cash from investors. The company then has operating losses of $1,200 cash and goes out of business.

Required

a. Explain the primary differences between investors and creditors.

b. What amount of cash will Jones's creditors receive?

c. What amount of cash will Jones's investors (stockholders) receive?

Exercise 1-3B   *Identifying the reporting entities*   **L.O. 2**

Karen White helped organize a charity fund to help cover the medical expenses of a friend of hers who was seriously injured in a bicycle accident. The fund was named Vicki Holland Recovery Fund (VHRF). Karen contributed $1,000 of her own money to the fund. The $1,000 was paid to WRCK, a local radio station that designed and played an advertising campaign to educate the public as to the need for help. The campaign resulted in the collection of $15,000 cash. VHRF paid $10,000 to the Shelby Hospital to cover Vicki's outstanding hospital cost. The remaining $5,000 was contributed to the National Cyclist Fund.

Required

Identify the entities that were mentioned in the scenario and explain what happened to the cash accounts of each entity that you identify.

L.O. 3   **Exercise 1-4B**   *Financial statement elements and accounts*

Required

Write a brief memo that distinguishes between the *elements* of financial statements and the *accounts* that appear on financial statements. Also, distinguish between temporary and permanent accounts.

L.O. 3   **Exercise 1-5B**   *Titles and accounts appearing on financial statements*

Annual reports normally include an income statement, a statement of changes in stockholders' equity, a balance sheet, and a statement of cash flows.

Required

Identify the financial statements on which each of the following titles or accounts would appear. If a title or an account appears on more than one statement, list all statements that would include it.

a. Common Stock
b. Land
c. Ending Cash Balance
d. Beginning Cash Balance
e. Notes Payable
f. Retained Earnings
g. Revenue
h. Dividends
i. Financing Activities
j. Salary Expense

L.O. 4   **Exercise 1-6B**   *Components of the accounting equation*

Required

The following three requirements are independent of each other.

a. Best Pizza Co. has assets of $8,500 and net assets of $6,200. What is the amount of liabilities? What is the amount of claims?
b. Mollie's Ice Cream has liabilities of $1,200 and equity of $4,400. What is the amount of assets? What is the amount of net assets?
c. Fireworks, Inc., has assets of $98,300 and liabilities of $44,700. What is the amount of equity? What is the amount of residual interest?

L.O. 4, 5   **Exercise 1-7B**   *Effect of events on the accounting equation*

Star Co. experienced the following events during 2006.

1. Acquired cash from the issue of common stock.
2. Provided services to clients for cash.
3. Borrowed cash.
4. Paid operating expenses with cash.
5. Paid a cash dividend to the stockholders.
6. Purchased land with cash.

Required

Explain how each of these events affect the accounting equation by writing the letter I for increase, the letter D for decrease, and NA for does not affect under each of the components of the accounting equation. The first event is shown as an example.

Event Number	Assets	=	Liabilities	+	Common Stock	+	Retained Earnings
					Stockholders' Equity		
1	I		NA		I		NA

Exercise 1-8B   *Effects of issuing stock*

L.O. 3

Sigma Company was started in 2009 when it acquired $48,000 cash by issuing common stock. The cash acquisition was the only event that affected the business in 2009.

Required

Which financial statements would be affected by this event?

Exercise 1-9B   *Effects of borrowing*

L.O. 3

Northeast Company was started in 2010 when it borrowed $25,000 from National Bank.

Required

Which financial statements would be affected by this event?

Exercise 1-10B   *Effects of revenue, expense, and dividend events*

L.O. 3, 4, 5, 8

Morgan Company was started on January 1, 2008. During 2008, the company completed three accounting events: (1) earned cash revenues of $12,500, (2) paid cash expenses of $6,400, and (3) paid a $1,000 cash dividend to the owner. These were the only events that affected the company during 2008.

Required

a. Write an accounting equation, and record the effects of each accounting event under the appropriate general ledger account headings.
b. Prepare an income statement for the 2008 accounting period and a balance sheet at the end of 2008 for Morgan Company.
c. What is the balance in the Retained Earnings account immediately after the cash revenue is recognized?
d. What is the balance in the Retained Earnings account after the closing process is complete?

Exercise 1-11B   *Classifying items for the statement of cash flows*

L.O. 3

Required

Indicate how each of the following would be classified on the statement of cash flows as operating activities (OA), investing activities (IA), financing activities (FA), or not applicable (NA).

a. Paid $4,000 cash for salary expense.
b. Borrowed $8,000 cash from State Bank.
c. Received $30,000 cash from the issue of common stock.
d. Purchased land for $8,000 cash.
e. Performed services for $14,000 cash.
f. Paid $4,200 cash for utilities expense.
g. Sold land for $7,000 cash.
h. Paid a cash dividend of $1,000 to the stockholders.
i. Hired an accountant to keep the books.
j. Paid $3,000 cash on the loan from State Bank.

Exercise 1-12B   *Effect of transactions on general ledger accounts*

L.O. 3, 4, 5, 6

At the beginning of 2009, Quick Service Company's accounting records had the following general ledger accounts and balances.

QUICK SERVICE COMPANY
Accounting Equation

Event	Assets		=	Liabilities	+	Stockholders' Equity		Acct. Titles for RE
	Cash	Land		Notes Payable		Common Stock	Retained Earnings	
Balance 1/1/2009	20,000	50,000		35,000		25,000	10,000	

Quick completed the following transactions during 2009:

1. Purchased land for $12,000 cash.
2. Acquired $20,000 cash from the issue of common stock.
3. Received $50,000 cash for providing services to customers.
4. Paid cash operating expenses of $42,000.
5. Paid $20,000 cash on notes payable.
6. Paid a $2,000 cash dividend to the stockholders.
7. Determined that the market value of the land is $75,000.

Required

a. Record the transactions in the appropriate general ledger accounts. Record the amounts of revenue, expense, and dividends in the Retained Earnings column. Provide the appropriate titles for these accounts in the last column of the table.

b. Determine the amount of net income for the 2009 period.

c. What is the amount of total assets at the end of 2009? What is the amount of net assets at the end of 2009?

L.O. 3, 4, 5, 6, 8   **Exercise 1-13B**   *Preparing financial statements*

Lee, Inc., experienced the following events during 2008.

1. Acquired $55,000 cash from the issue of common stock.
2. Paid $15,000 cash to purchase land.
3. Borrowed $10,000 cash from First Bank.
4. Provided services for $28,000 cash.
5. Paid $2,500 cash for utilities expense.
6. Paid $11,000 cash for other operating expenses.
7. Paid a $2,000 cash dividend to the stockholders.
8. Determined that the market value of the land purchased in Event 2 is $23,000.

Required

a. The January 1, 2008, general ledger account balances are shown in the following accounting equation. Record the eight events in the appropriate general ledger accounts. Record the amounts of revenue, expense, and dividends in the Retained Earnings column. Provide the appropriate titles for these accounts in the last column of the table. The first event is shown as an example.

			LEE, INC.					
			Accounting Equation					
Event	Assets		=	Liabilities	+	Stockholders' Equity		Acct. Titles for RE
	Cash	Land		Notes Payable		Common Stock	Retained Earnings	
Balance 1/1/2008	12,000	25,000		0		15,000	22,000	
1.	55,000					55,000		

b. Prepare an income statement, statement of changes in stockholders' equity, year-end balance sheet, and statement of cash flows for the 2008 accounting period.

c. Determine the percentage of assets that were provided by retained earnings. How much cash is in the retained earnings account?

Exercise 1-14B   *Classifying events as asset source, use, or exchange*   **L.O. 7**

California Company experienced the following events during its first year of operations.

1. Acquired $10,000 cash from the issue of common stock.
2. Borrowed $8,000 cash from First Bank.
3. Paid $4,000 cash to purchase land.
4. Received $5,000 cash for providing boarding services.
5. Acquired an additional $2,000 cash from the issue of common stock.
6. Purchased additional land for $3,500 cash.
7. Paid $2,500 cash for salary expenses.
8. Signed a contract to provide additional services in the future.
9. Paid $1,000 cash for rent expense.
10. Paid a $1,000 cash dividend to the stockholders.
11. Determined the market value of the land to be $8,000 at the end of the accounting period.

Required

Classify each event as an asset source, use, or exchange transaction or as not applicable (NA).

Exercise 1-15B   *Financial statement elements*   **L.O. 3**

Carolina Company was organized by issuing $750 of common stock and by borrowing $450. During the accounting period, the company earned cash revenue of $900 and paid cash expenses of $500. Also during the accounting period, the company purchased land for $1,150.

Required

a. What asset accounts would appear on the company's balance sheet? What are the balance sheet amounts in these accounts?
b. Determine the percentage of total assets that were provided by investors, creditors, and earnings.
c. How much cash is in the Retained Earnings account?
d. Determine the balance in the Retained Earnings account before and after the temporary accounts are closed.

Exercise 1-16B   *Historical cost versus market value*   **L.O. 6**

JMD, Inc., purchased land in January 2009 at a cost of $270,000. The estimated market value of the land is $350,000 as of December 31, 2011.

Required

a. Name the December 31, 2011, financial statement(s) on which the land will be shown.
b. At what dollar amount will the land be shown in the financial statement(s)?
c. Name the key concept that will be used in determining the dollar amount that will be reported for land that is shown in the financial statement(s).

Exercise 1-17B   *Relating accounting events to entities*   **L.O. 2, 7**

Parker Company sold land for $100,000 cash to Stewart Company in 2010.

Required

a. Was this event an asset source, use, or exchange transaction for Parker Company?
b. Was this event an asset source, use, or exchange transaction for Stewart Company?
c. Was the cash flow an operating, investing, or financing activity on Parker Company's 2010 statement of cash flows?
d. Was the cash flow an operating, investing, or financing activity on Stewart Company's 2010 statement of cash flows?

L.O. 4

Exercise 1-18B   *Missing information in the accounting equation*

Required

Calculate the missing amounts in the following table.

Company	Assets	=	Liabilities	+	Common Stock	+	Retained Earnings
					Stockholders' Equity		
A	$?		$25,000		$48,000		$50,000
B	40,000		?		7,000		30,000
C	75,000		15,000		?		42,000
D	125,000		45,000		60,000		?

L.O. 4

Exercise 1-19B   *Missing information in the accounting equation*

As of December 31, 2008, Coleman Company had total assets of $132,000, retained earnings of $79,600, and common stock of $45,000. During 2009 Coleman earned $42,000 of cash revenue, paid $17,500 for cash expenses, and paid a $1,000 cash dividend to the stockholders. Coleman also paid $5,000 to reduce its debt during 2009.

Required

a. Determine the amount of liabilities at December 31, 2008.
b. Determine the amount of net income earned in 2009.
c. Determine the amount of total assets as of December 31, 2009.
d. Determine the amount of total liabilities as of December 31, 2009.

L.O. 3, 4

Exercise 1-20B   *Missing information for determining revenue*

Total stockholders' equity of Hunter Company increased by $42,250 between December 31, 2009, and December 31, 2010. During 2010 Hunter acquired $15,000 cash from the issue of common stock. The company paid a $2,500 cash dividend to the stockholders during 2010. Total expenses during 2010 amounted to $18,000.

Required

Determine the amount of revenue that Hunter reported on its 2010 income statement. (*Hint:* Remember that stock issues, net income, and dividends all change total stockholders' equity.)

L.O. 6, 9

Exercise 1-21B   *Effect of events on a horizontal financial statements model*

Green Consulting Services experienced the following events during 2008.

1. Acquired cash by issuing common stock.
2. Collected cash for providing tutoring services to clients.
3. Borrowed cash from a local government small business foundation.
4. Purchased land for cash.
5. Paid cash for operating expenses.
6. Paid a cash dividend to the stockholders.
7. Determined that the market value of the land is higher than its historical cost.

Required

Use a horizontal statements model to show how each event affects the balance sheet, income statement, and statement of cash flows. Indicate whether the event increases (I), decreases (D), or does not affect (NA) each element of the financial statements. Also, in the Cash Flows column, classify the cash flows as operating activities (OA), investing activities (IA), or financing activities (FA). The first transaction is shown as an example.

Event No.	Balance Sheet										Income Statement					Statement of Cash Flows
	Cash	+	Land	=	N. Pay	+	C. Stock.	+	Ret. Ear.		Rev.	−	Exp.	=	Net Inc.	
1.	I	+	NA	=	NA	+	I	+	NA		NA	−	NA	=	NA	I IA

Exercise 1-22B *Record events in the horizontal statements model*

L.O. 3, 9

Adam's Boat Shop was started in 2012. During 2012, the company (1) acquired $5,000 cash from the issue of common stock, (2) earned cash revenue of $22,000, (3) paid cash expenses of $9,300, and (4) paid an $800 cash dividend to the stockholders.

Required

a. Record these four events in a horizontal statements model. Also, in the Cash Flows column, classify the cash flows as operating activities (OA), investing activities (IA), or financing activities (FA). The first event is shown as an example.

Event No.	Balance Sheet								Income Statement					Statement of Cash Flows
	Cash	=	N. Pay	+	C. Stock.	+	Ret. Ear.		Rev.	−	Exp.	=	Net Inc.	
1.	5,000	=	NA	+	5,000	+	NA		NA	−	NA	=	NA	5,000 FA

b. Why is the net income different from the net increase in cash for this business?

Exercise 1-23B *Effect of events on a horizontal statements model*

L.O. 6, 9

Elliott James started Computers Inc. on January 1, 2008. The company experienced the following events during its first year of operation.

1. Acquired $15,000 cash by issuing common stock.
2. Paid $5,000 cash to purchase land.
3. Received $42,000 cash for providing computer consulting services to customers.
4. Paid $12,500 cash for salary expenses.
5. Acquired $4,000 cash from the issue of additional common stock.
6. Borrowed $15,000 cash from the bank.
7. Purchased additional land for $15,000 cash.
8. Paid $16,000 cash for other operating expenses.
9. Paid a $2,500 cash dividend to the stockholders.
10. Determined that the market value of the land is $18,000.

Required

a. Record these events in a horizontal statements model. Also, in the Cash Flows column, classify the cash flows as operating activities (OA), investing activities (IA), or financing activities (FA). The first event is shown as an example.

Event No.	Balance Sheet										Income Statement					Statement of Cash Flows
	Cash	+	Land	=	N. Pay	+	C. Stock.	+	Ret. Ear.		Rev.	−	Exp.	=	Net Inc.	
1.	15,000	+	NA	=	NA	+	15,000	+	NA		NA	−	NA	=	NA	15,000 FA

b. What is the net income earned in 2008?
c. What is the amount of total assets at the end of 2008?
d. What is the net cash flow from operating activities for 2008?
e. What is the net cash flow from investing activities for 2008?
f. What is the net cash flow from financing activities for 2008?
g. What is the cash balance at the end of 2008?
h. As of the end of the year 2008, what percentage of total assets were provided by creditors, investors, and earnings?
i. What is the balance in the Retained Earnings account immediately after Event 4 is recorded?

L.O. 6, 7, 9

Exercise 1-24B *Types of transactions and the horizontal statements model*

The Candle Shop experienced the following events during its first year of operations, 2010.

1. Acquired cash by issuing common stock.
2. Provided services and collected cash.
3. Borrowed cash from a bank.
4. Paid cash for operating expenses.
5. Purchased land with cash.
6. Paid a cash dividend to the stockholders.
7. Determined that the market value of the land is higher than the historical cost.

Required

a. Indicate whether each event is an asset source, use, or exchange transaction.
b. Use a horizontal statements model to show how each event affects the balance sheet, income statement, and statement of cash flows. Indicate whether the event increases (I), decreases (D), or does not affect (NA) each element of the financial statements. Also, in the Cash Flows column, classify the cash flows as operating activities (OA), investing activities (IA), or financing activities (FA). The first transaction is shown as an example.

Event No.	Balance Sheet										Income Statement					Statement of Cash Flows
	Cash	+	Land	=	N. Pay	+	C. Stock.	+	Ret. Ear.		Rev.	−	Exp.	=	Net Inc.	
1.	I	+	NA	=	NA	+	I	+	NA		NA	−	NA	=	NA	I FA

L.O. 10

Exercise 1-25B *Price-earnings ratio (Appendix)*

The following information is available for two companies:

	ABC Company	XYZ Company
Earnings per share	$ 0.92	$ 2.25
Market price per share	46.50	68.40

Required

a. Compute the price-earnings ratio for each company.
b. Which company would you expect to have the higher earnings growth potential?

PROBLEMS—SERIES B

L.O. 1

Problem 1-26B *Accounting's role in not-for-profits*

Jill Smith is struggling to pass her introductory accounting course. Jill is intelligent but she likes to party. Studying is a low priority for Jill. When one of her friends tells her that she is going to have trouble in business if she doesn't learn accounting, Jill responds that she doesn't plan to go into business. She says that she is arts oriented and plans someday to be a director of a museum. She is in the school of business to develop her social skills, not her quantitative skills. Jill says she won't have to worry about accounting, since museums are not intended to make a profit.

Required

a. Write a brief memo explaining whether you agree or disagree with Jill's position regarding accounting and not-for-profit organizations.
b. Distinguish between financial accounting and managerial accounting.
c. Identify some of the stakeholders of not-for-profit institutions that would expect to receive financial accounting reports.
d. Identify some of the stakeholders of not-for-profit institutions that would expect to receive managerial accounting reports.

Problem 1-27B   *Accounting entities*

The following business scenarios are independent from one another.

1. Tilly Jensen starts a business by transferring $5,000 from her personal checking account into a checking account for the business.
2. A business that Bart Angle owns earns $2,300 of cash revenue.
3. Phil Culver borrows $20,000 from the National Bank and uses the money to purchase a car from Henderson Ford.
4. Lipka Company pays its five employees $2,000 each to cover their salaries.
5. Kevin Dow loans his son Brian $5,000 cash.
6. Asthana, Inc., paid $150,000 cash to purchase land from Waterbury, Inc.
7. Moshe Liu and Chao Porat form a partnership by contributing $30,000 each from their personal bank accounts to a partnership bank account.
8. Ken Stanga pays cash to purchase $2,000 of common stock that is issued by Krishnan, Inc.
9. Omni Company pays a $42,000 cash dividend to each of its seven shareholders.
10. McCann, Inc., borrowed $5,000,000 from the National Bank.

Required
a. For each scenario create a list of all of the entities that are mentioned in the description.
b. Describe what happens to the cash account of each entity that you identified in Requirement *a*.

Problem 1-28B   *Relating titles and accounts to financial statements*

Required
Identify the financial statements on which each of the following items (titles, date descriptions, and accounts) appears by placing a check mark in the appropriate column. If an item appears on more than one statement, place a check mark in every applicable column.

Item	Income Statement	Statement of Changes in Stockholders' Equity	Balance Sheet	Statement of Cash Flows
Notes payable				
Beginning common stock				
Service revenue				
Utility expense				
Cash from stock issue				
Operating activities				
For the period ended (date)				
Net income				
Investing activities				
Net loss				
Ending cash balance				
Salary expense				
Consulting revenue				
Dividends				
Financing activities				

continued

Item	Income Statement	Statement of Changes in Stockholders' Equity	Balance Sheet	Statement of Cash Flows
Ending common stock				
Interest expense				
As of (date)				
Land				
Beginning cash balance				

L.O. 3, 4, 5, 6, 8

Problem 1-29B *Preparing financial statements for two complete accounting cycles*

Susan's Consulting Services experienced the following transactions for 2010, the first year of operations, and 2011. *Assume that all transactions involve the receipt or payment of cash.*

Transactions for 2010

1. Acquired $50,000 by issuing common stock.
2. Received $100,000 for providing services to customers.
3. Borrowed $15,000 cash from creditors.
4. Paid expenses amounting to $60,000.
5. Purchased land for $40,000 cash.

Transactions for 2011

Beginning account balances for 2011 are:

Cash	$65,000
Land	40,000
Notes payable	15,000
Common stock	50,000
Retained earnings	40,000

1. Acquired an additional $20,000 from the issue of common stock.
2. Received $130,000 for providing services in 2011.
3. Paid $10,000 to reduce notes payable.
4. Paid expenses amounting to $75,000.
5. Paid a $15,000 dividend to the stockholders.
6. Determined that the market value of the land is $50,000.

Required

a. Write an accounting equation, and record the effects of each accounting event under the appropriate headings for each year. Record the amounts of revenue, expense, and dividends in the Retained Earnings column. Provide appropriate titles for these accounts in the last column of the table.

b. Prepare an income statement, statement of changes in stockholders' equity, year-end balance sheet, and statement of cash flows for each year.

c. Determine the amount of cash that is in the retained earnings account at the end of 2010 and 2011.

d. Compare the information provided by the income statement with the information provided by the statement of cash flows. Point out similarities and differences.

e. Determine the balance in the Retained Earnings account immediately after Event 2 in 2010 and in 2011 are recorded.

L.O. 3, 5, 8

Problem 1-30B *Interrelationships among financial statements*

Todd Corp. started the accounting period with $15,000 of assets, $2,200 of liabilities, and $4,550 of retained earnings. During the period, the Retained Earnings account increased by $3,565. The bookkeeper reported that Todd paid cash expenses of $5,010 and paid a $6,000 cash dividend to stockholders, but she could not find a record of the amount of cash that Todd received for performing services. Todd also paid $1,500 cash to reduce the liability owed to a bank, and the business acquired $2,000 of additional cash from the issue of common stock.

Required

a. Prepare an income statement, statement of changes in stockholders' equity, year-end balance sheet, and statement of cash flows for the accounting period. (*Hint:* Determine the beginning balance in the common stock account before considering the effects of the current period events. It also might help to record all events under an accounting equation before preparing the statements.)

b. Determine the percentage of total assets that were provided by creditors, investors, and earnings.

Problem 1-31B   *Classifying events as asset source, use, or exchange*   L.O. 4, 7

The following unrelated events are typical of those experienced by business entities.

1. Acquire cash by issuing common stock.
2. Purchase land with cash.
3. Purchase equipment with cash.
4. Pay monthly rent on an office building.
5. Hire a new office manager.
6. Borrow cash from a bank.
7. Pay a cash dividend to stockholders.
8. Pay cash for operating expenses.
9. Pay an office manager's salary with cash.
10. Receive cash for services that have been performed.
11. Pay cash for utilities expense.
12. Acquire land by accepting a liability (financing the purchase).
13. Pay cash to purchase a new office building.
14. Discuss plans for a new office building with an architect.
15. Repay part of a bank loan.

Required

Identify each of the events as an asset source, use, or exchange transaction. If an event would not be recorded under generally accepted accounting principles, identify it as not applicable (NA). Also indicate for each event whether total assets would increase, decrease, or remain unchanged. Organize your answer according to the following table. The first event is shown in the table as an example.

Event No.	Type of Event	Effect on Total Assets
1	Asset source	Increase

Problem 1-32B   *Recording the effect of events in a horizontal statements model*   L.O. 6, 9

Doyer Consulting experienced the following transactions during 2010.

1. Acquired cash by issuing common stock.
2. Received cash for performing services.
3. Paid cash expenses.
4. Borrowed cash from the local bank.
5. Purchased land for cash.
6. Paid cash to reduce the principal balance of the bank loan.
7. Paid a cash dividend to the stockholders.
8. Determined that the market value of the land is higher than its historical cost.

Required

Use a horizontal statements model to show how each event affects the balance sheet, income statement, and statement of cash flows. Indicate whether the event increases (I), decreases (D), or does not affect (NA) each element of the financial statements. Also, in the Cash Flows column, classify the cash flows as operating activities (OA), investing activities (IA), or financing activities (FA). The first transaction is shown as an example.

Event No.	Balance Sheet									Income Statement						Statement of Cash Flows	
	Cash	+	Land	=	N. Pay	+	C. Stock.	+	Ret. Ear.	Rev.	−	Exp.	=	Net Inc.			
1.	I	+	NA	=	NA	+	I	+	NA	NA	−	NA	=	NA		I	FA

L.O. 4, 6, 9

Problem 1-33B   *Recording events in a horizontal statements model*

Davidson Company was started January 1, 2009, and experienced the following events during its first year of operation.

1. Acquired $52,000 cash from the issue of common stock.
2. Borrowed $20,000 cash from National Bank.
3. Earned cash revenues of $42,000 for performing services.
4. Paid cash expenses of $23,000.
5. Paid a $6,000 cash dividend to the stockholders.
6. Acquired $10,000 cash from the issue of additional common stock.
7. Paid $10,000 cash to reduce the principal balance of the bank note.
8. Paid $45,000 cash to purchase land.
9. Determined that the market value of the land is $55,000.

Required

a. Record the preceding transactions in the horizontal statements model. Also, in the Cash Flows column, classify the cash flows as operating activities (OA), investing activities (IA), or financing activities (FA). The first event is shown as an example.

Event No.	Balance Sheet									Income Statement						Statement of Cash Flows	
	Cash	+	Land	=	N. Pay	+	C. Stock.	+	Ret. Ear.	Rev.	−	Exp.	=	Net Inc.			
1.	52,000	+	NA	=	NA	+	52,000	+	NA	NA	−	NA	=	NA		52,000	FA

b. Determine the amount of total assets that Davidson would report on the December 31, 2009, balance sheet.

c. Identify the asset source transactions and related amounts for 2009.

d. Determine the net income that Davidson would report on the 2009 income statement. Explain why dividends do not appear on the income statement.

e. Determine the net cash flows from operating activities, investing activities, and financing activities that Davidson would report on the 2009 statement of cash flows.

f. Determine the percentage of assets that were provided by investors, creditors, and earnings.

g. What is the balance in the Retained Earnings account immediately after Event 3 is recorded?

L.O. 10

Problem 1-34B   *Price-earnings relationships (Appendix)*

Shim, Inc., is a pharmaceutical company heavily involved in research leading to the development of genealogy-based medicines. While the company has several promising research studies in progress, it has brought only two viable products to market during the last decade. Earnings per share and market price per share data for the latest three years of operation follow.

Shim, Inc.	2008	2009	2010
Earnings per share	$ 1.22	$ 1.17	$ 1.20
Market price per share	86.20	84.49	86.80

Required

a. Calculate the company's annual growth rate in earnings per share from 2008 to 2009 and from 2009 to 2010.

b. Based on the data shown in Exhibit 1–7, identify the company as a high-, medium-, or low-growth company.

c. Calculate the company's price-earnings ratio for all three years.

d. Explain the size of the price-earnings ratio.

ANALYZE, THINK, COMMUNICATE

ATC 1-1   Business Applications Case   *Understanding real-world annual reports*

Required—Part 1

Use the Topps Company's annual report in Appendix B to answer the following questions.

a. What was Topps' net income for 2006?

b. Did Topps' net income increase or decrease from 2005 to 2006, and by how much?

c. What was Topps' accounting equation for 2006?

d. Which of the following had the largest percentage change from 2005 to 2006: net sales, cost of sales, or selling, general, and administrative expenses? Show all computations.

Required—Part 2

Use the Harley-Davidson's annual report that came with this book to answer the following questions.

a. What was Harley-Davidson's net income for 2005?

b. Did Harley-Davidson's net income increase or decrease from 2004 to 2005, and by how much?

c. What was Harley-Davidson's accounting equation for 2005?

d. Which of the following had the largest percentage increase from 2004 to 2005: net revenue, cost of goods sold, or selling, general, and engineering expenses? Show all computations.

ATC 1-2   Group Assignment   *Missing information*

The following selected financial information is available for ROC, Inc. Amounts are in millions of dollars.

Income Statements	2009	2008	2007	2006
Revenue	$ 860	$1,520	$ (a)	$1,200
Cost and expenses	(a)	(a)	(2,400)	(860)
Income from continuing operations	(b)	450	320	(a)
Unusual items	-0-	175	(b)	(b)
Net income	$ 20	$ (b)	$ 175	$ 300
Balance Sheets				
Assets				
Cash and marketable securities	$ 350	$1,720	$ (c)	$ 940
Other assets	1,900	(c)	2,500	(c)
Total assets	2,250	$2,900	$ (d)	$3,500
Liabilities	$ (c)	$ (d)	$1,001	$ (d)
Stockholders' equity				
Common stock	600	720	(e)	800
Retained earnings	(d)	(e)	800	(e)
Total stockholders' equity	1,520	1,345	(f)	2,200
Total liabilities and stockholders' equity	$2,250	$ (f)	$3,250	$3,500

Required

a. Divide the class into groups of four or five students each. Organize the groups into four sections. Assign Task 1 to the first section of groups, Task 2 to the second section, Task 3 to the third section, and Task 4 to the fourth section.

Group Tasks

(1) Fill in the missing information for 2006.

(2) Fill in the missing information for 2007.

(3) Fill in the missing information for 2008.

(4) Fill in the missing information for 2009.

b. Each section should select two representatives. One representative is to put the financial statements assigned to that section on the board, underlining the missing amounts. The second representative is to explain to the class how the missing amounts were determined.

c. Each section should list events that could have caused the unusual item category on the income statement.

ATC 1-3   Real-World Case   *Classifying cash flow activities at five companies*

The following cash transactions occurred in five real-world companies during 2004:

1. FedEx Corp. which is the holding company of Federal Express, purchased Kinko's, Inc., on February 12, 2004, for $2.4 billion.

2. Google, Inc., issued 14.1 million shares of its stock on August 18, 2004, for $85 per share. On that same day, a few major shareholders of Google, including its founders sold 5.5 million shares of its stock at the same price.

3. Payless Shoe Source, Inc., had cash sales of $2.8 billion during its fiscal year ending on January 31, 2004.

4. Red Hat, Inc., the leading provider of the open-source operating system Linux, issued $600 million of "convertible debentures" in January 2004. Convertible debentures are a form of long-term debt that is explained in more detail in Chapter 10.

5. Sears, Roebuck and Company completed the sale of its domestic Credit and Financial Products business to Citicorp on November 3, 2004, for $32 billion, $22 billion of which was received in cash.

Required

Determine if each of the above transactions should be classified as an *operating, investing,* or *financing* activity. Also, identify the amount of each cash flow and whether it was an *inflow* or an *outflow.*

ATC 1-4   Business Applications Case   *Use of real-world numbers for forecasting (Appendix)*

The following information was drawn from the annual report of Machine Import Company (MIC):

	For the Years	
	2006	**2007**
Income Statements		
Revenue	$600,000	$690,000
Operating expenses	480,000	552,000
Income from continuing operations	120,000	138,000
*Extraordinary item—lottery win		62,000
Net income	$120,000	$200,000

continued

Balance Sheets		
Assets	$880,000	$880,000
Liabilities	$200,000	$ 0
Stockholders' equity		
Common stock	380,000	380,000
Retained earnings	300,000	500,000
Total liabilities and stockholders' equity	$880,000	$880,000

*By definition, extraordinary items are not likely to reoccur in the future.

Required

a. Compute the percentage of growth in net income from 2006 to 2007. Can stockholders expect a similar increase between 2007 and 2008?

b. Assuming that MIC collected $200,000 cash from earnings (i.e., net income), explain how this money was spent in 2007.

c. Assuming that MIC experiences the same percentage of growth from 2007 to 2008 as it did from 2006 to 2007, determine the amount of income from continuing operations that the owners can expect to see on the 2008 income statement.

d. During 2008, MIC experienced a $40,000 loss due to storm damage (note that this would be shown as an extraordinary loss on the income statement). Liabilities and common stock were unchanged from 2007 to 2008. Use the information that you computed in Requirement *c* plus the additional information provided in the previous two sentences to prepare an income statement and balance sheet as of December 31, 2008.

ATC 1-5   Writing Assignment   *Elements of financial statements defined*

Bob and his sister Marsha both attend the state university. As a reward for their successful completion of the past year (Bob had a 3.2 GPA in business, and Marsha had a 3.7 GPA in art), their father gave each of them 100 shares of The Walt Disney Company stock. They have just received their first annual report. Marsha does not understand what the information means and has asked Bob to explain it to her. Bob is currently taking an accounting course, and she knows he will understand the financial statements.

Required

Assume that you are Bob. Write Marsha a memo explaining the following financial statement items to her. In your explanation, describe each of the two financial statements and explain the financial information each contains. Also define each of the elements listed for each financial statement and explain what it means.

Balance Sheet
Assets
Liabilities
Stockholders' equity

Income Statement
Revenue
Expense
Net income

ATC 1-6   Ethical Dilemma   *Loyalty versus the bottom line*

Assume that Jones has been working for you for five years. He has had an excellent work history and has received generous pay raises in response. The raises have been so generous that Jones is quite overpaid for the job he is required to perform. Unfortunately, he is not qualified to take on other, more responsible jobs available within the company. A recent job applicant is willing to accept a salary $5,000 per year less than the amount currently being paid to Jones. The applicant is well qualified to take over Jones's duties and has a very positive attitude. The following financial statements were reported by your company at the close of its most recent accounting period.

Required

a. Reconstruct the financial statements, assuming that Jones was replaced at the beginning of the most recent accounting period. Both Jones and his replacement are paid in cash. No other changes are to be considered.

b. Discuss the short- and long-term ramifications of replacing Jones. There are no right answers. However, assume that you are required to make a decision. Use your judgment and common sense to support your choice.

Financial Statements

Income Statement

Revenue	$ 57,000
Expense	(45,000)
Net income	$ 12,000

Statement of Changes in Stockholders' Equity

Beginning common stock	$ 20,000	
Plus: stock issued	5,000	
Ending common stock		$ 25,000
Beginning retained earnings	50,000	
Net income	12,000	
Dividends	(2,000)	
Ending retained earnings		60,000
Total stockholders' equity		$ 85,000

Balance Sheet

Assets	
Cash	$ 85,000
Equity	
Common stock	$ 25,000
Retained earnings	60,000
Total stockholders' equity	$ 85,000

Statement of Cash Flows

Operating activities		
Inflow from customers	$ 57,000	
Outflow for expenses	(45,000)	
Net inflow from operations		$ 12,000
Investing activities		0
Financing activities		
Inflow from stock issue	5,000	
Outflow for dividends	(2,000)	
Net Inflow from financing activities		3,000
Net change in cash		15,000
Plus: beginning cash balance		70,000
Ending cash balance		$85,000

ATC 1-7   Research Assignment   *Finding real-world accounting information*

The Curious Accountant story at the beginning of this chapter referred to McDonald's Corporation and discussed who its stakeholders are. This chapter introduced the basic four financial statements companies use annually to keep their stakeholders informed of their accomplishments and financial situation. Complete the requirements below using the most recent (20xx) financial statements available on the McDonald's website. Obtain the statements on the Internet by following the steps below. (The formatting of the company's Web site may have changed since these instructions were written.)

1. Go to www.mcdonalds.com.
2. Click on the "Corporate" link at the bottom of the page. (Most companies have a link titled "investors relations" that leads to their financial statements; McDonald's uses "corporate" instead.)
3. Click on the "INVESTORS" link at the top of the page.
4. Click on *"Publications"* and then on *"Annual Report Archives."*
5. Click on *"McDonald's 20xx Annual Report"* and then on *"20xx Financial Report."*
6. Go to the company's financial statements on pages 17 through 20 of the annual report.

Required

a. What was the company's net income in each of the last 3 years?
b. What amount of total assets did the company have at the end of the most recent year?
c. How much retained earnings did the company have at the end of the most recent year?
d. For the most recent year, what was the company's cash flow from operating activities, cash flow from investing activities, and cash flow from financing activities?

ATC 1-8   Spreadsheet Assignment   *Using Excel*

The financial statements for Simple Company are reported here using an Excel spreadsheet.

Required

Recreate the financial statements using your own Excel spreadsheet.

a. For each number with an arrow by it, enter a formula in that particular cell address to solve for the number shown. (Do not enter the arrow.)
b. When complete, print the spreadsheet with formulas rather than absolute numbers.

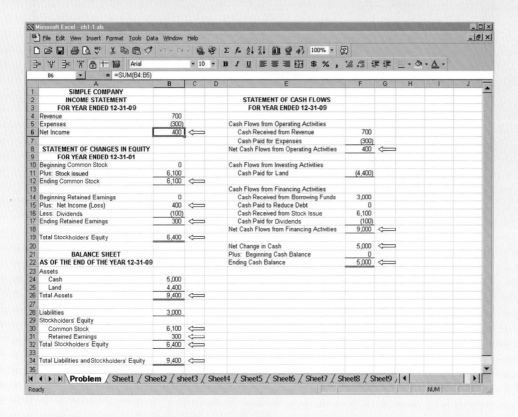

Spreadsheet Tips

(1) Widen a column by positioning the cursor on the vertical line between two column headings until cross-hairs appear. Either double click to automatically widen or click and drag the crosshair to the desired width.

(2) Negative numbers can be parenthesized by choosing Format and then Cells. Under Category, choose Custom and under Type, choose the first option containing parentheses.

(3) The SUM function is one way to add a series of numbers. For example, the formula for net income in cell B6 is =SUM(B4:B5).

(4) Single and double lines can be drawn using the Borders icon.

(5) Print a spreadsheet on one page by choosing File, Page Setup, and Fit to 1.

(6) Print without gridlines by choosing File, Page Setup, and Sheet and uncheck Gridlines. Another option is to choose Tools and Options and uncheck Gridlines.

(7) Print formulas by choosing Tools, Options, and Formulas.

ATC 1-9 Spreadsheet Assignment *Mastering Excel*

Required

a. Enter the following headings for the horizontal statements model onto a blank spreadsheet.

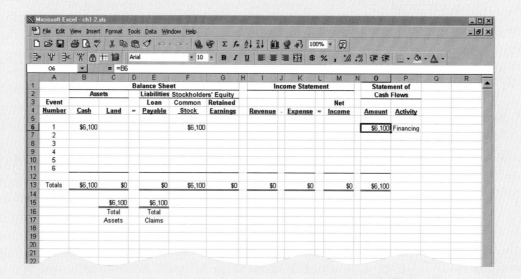

b. Under the appropriate headings, record the effects of each of the following accounting events for the first month of operations. The first event has been recorded as an example.

(1) Acquired $6,100 from the issue of common stock.

(2) Paid $4,400 to purchase land.

(3) Borrowed $3,000 cash.

(4) Provided services to customers and received $700 in cash.

(5) Paid $300 for expenses.

(6) Paid a $100 dividend to the stockholders.

> (*Note:* The amounts on the statement of cash flows can be referenced to the Cash account on the balance sheet. In other words, recording the cash amounts twice is not necessary. Instead enter formulas in the Statement of Cash Flows column equating those cell addresses to the respective cell in the Cash column. Notice that the formula in cell O6 (statement of cash flows) is set equal to cell B6 (cash on the balance sheet). Once the formula is completed for cell O6, it can be easily copied to cells O7 through O11.)

c. Using formulas, sum each of the quantitative columns to arrive at the end-of-month amounts reported on the financial statements.

Spreadsheet Tips

(1) Center the heading *Balance Sheet* across columns by entering the entire heading in cell B1. Position the cursor on B1 until a fat cross appears. Click and drag the cursor across B1 through G1. Click on the Merge and Center icon (it is highlighted in the screen in the computer display).

(2) Enter arithmetic signs as headings by placing an apostrophe in front of the sign. For example, to enter the equals sign in cell D4, enter '=.

(3) Copy cells by positioning the cursor in the bottom right corner of the cell to copy from (such as cell O6) until a thin cross appears. Click and drag the cursor down through the desired locations to copy to (through cell O11).

(4) To enter the dollar sign, choose Format, Cells, and Currency.

CHAPTER 2

Accounting for Accruals

After you have mastered the material in this chapter, you will be able to:

1. Record basic accrual events in a horizontal financial statements model.

2. Organize general ledger accounts under an accounting equation.

3. Prepare financial statements based on accrual accounting.

4. Describe the matching concept, the accounting cycle, and the closing process.

5. Record business events involving interest-bearing receivables and payables in a horizontal financial statements model.

6. Prepare a vertical financial statements model.

7. Explain how business events affect financial statements over multiple accounting cycles.

LP2

8. Discuss the primary components of corporate governance.

9. Classify accounting events into one of four categories:
   a. asset source transactions.
   b. asset use transactions.
   c. asset exchange transactions.
   d. claims exchange transactions.

10. Describe the auditor's role in financial reporting (Appendix).

27. What type of entry is the entry to record accrued interest expense? How does it affect the accounting equation?

28. Is land purchased in 1920 reported on a current balance sheet at its current value? If not, at what value is it shown?

29. The after-closing balance in the Retained Earnings account on December 31, 2008, is $35,780. What is the balance in the Retained Earnings account on January 1, 2009?

30. The before-closing balance in the Revenue account was $22,880 on December 31, 2007. What is the balance in the Revenue account on January 1, 2008?

31. What types of accounts are closed at the end of the accounting period? Why is it necessary to close these accounts?

32. Give several examples of period costs.

33. Give an example of a cost that can be directly matched with the revenue produced by an accounting firm from preparing a tax return.

34. List and describe the four stages of the accounting cycle discussed in Chapter 2.

35. Name and comment on the three elements of the fraud triangle.

36. What is the maximum penalty and prison term that can be charged to a CEO and/or CFO under the Sarbanes-Oxley Act?

37. Appendix: What is a financial audit? Who is qualified to perform it?

38. Appendix: What is an independent auditor? Why must auditors be independent?

39. Appendix: What makes an error in the financial statements material?

40. Appendix: What three basic types of auditors' opinions can be issued on audited financial statements? Describe each.

41. Appendix: What are the implications of an unqualified audit opinion?

42. Appendix: When might an auditor issue a disclaimer on financial statements?

43. Appendix: In what circumstances can an auditor disclose confidential information about a client without the client's permission?

44. What are the six articles of ethical conduct set out under section I of the AICPA's Code of Professional Conduct?

MULTIPLE-CHOICE QUESTIONS

Multiple-choice questions are provided on the text Web site at www.mhhe.com/edmonds6e.

Quiz 2

www.mhhe.com/edmonds6e

EXERCISES—SERIES A

All Exercises in Series A are available with McGraw-Hill's Homework Manager®

Where applicable in all exercises, round computations to the nearest dollar.

Exercise 2-1A *Effect of accruals on the financial statements*   **L.O. 2, 3**

Maddox, Inc., experienced the following events in 2007, in its first year of operation.

1. Received $20,000 cash from the issue of common stock.
2. Performed services on account for $40,000.
3. Paid the utility expense of $3,500.
4. Collected $36,000 of the accounts receivable.
5. Recorded $8,000 of accrued salaries at the end of the year.
6. Paid a $2,000 cash dividend to the shareholders.

Required

a. Record the events in general ledger accounts under an accounting equation. In the last column of the table, provide appropriate account titles for the Retained Earnings amounts. The first transaction has been recorded as an example.

	MADDOX, INC. General Ledger Accounts							
Event	Assets		=	Liabilities	+	Stockholders' Equity		Acct. Titles for RE
	Cash	Accounts Receivable		Notes Payable		Common Stock	Retained Earnings	
1.	20,000					20,000		

b. What is the balance in the Retained Earnings account immediately after Event 2 has been recorded? What is the balance in the Retained Earnings account after the temporary accounts are closed on December 31, 2007? What is the balance in the Revenue account on January 1, 2008?

c. Prepare the income statement, statement of changes in stockholders' equity, balance sheet, and statement of cash flows for the 2007 accounting period.

d. Why is the amount of net income different from the amount of net cash flow from operating activities?

L.O. 2, 3

Exercise 2-2A *Effect of collecting accounts receivable on the accounting equation and financial statements*

Venture Company earned $8,000 of service revenue on account during 2008. The company collected $5,200 cash from accounts receivable during 2008.

Required

Based on this information alone, determine the following. (*Hint:* Record the events in general ledger accounts under an accounting equation before satisfying the requirements.)

a. The balance of the accounts receivable that Venture would report on the December 31, 2008, balance sheet.

b. The amount of net income that Venture would report on the 2008 income statement.

c. The amount of net cash flow from operating activities that Venture would report on the 2008 statement of cash flows.

d. The amount of retained earnings that Venture would report on the 2008 balance sheet.

e. Why are the answers to Requirements *b* and *c* different?

f. What is the before- and after-closing balance in the Revenue and Retained Earnings accounts on December 31, 2008.

L.O. 1

Exercise 2-3A *Effect of earning revenue on account on the financial statements*

M. Jones started a computer training center in 2007. The only accounting event in 2007 was the recognition of $9,600 of service revenue earned on account.

Required

Use the following horizontal statements model to show how this event affects the balance sheet, income statement, and statement of cash flows. Indicate whether the event increases (I), decreases (D), or does not affect (NA) each element of the financial statements. Also, in the Cash Flows column, designate the classification of any cash flows using the letters OA for operating activities, IA for investing activities, and FA for financing activities.

Balance Sheet					Income Statement			Statement of Cash Flows
Cash	+ Accts. Rec.	= C. Stk.	+ Ret. Ear.		Rev.	− Exp.	= Net Inc.	

Exercise 2-4A *Effects of revenue and expense recognition on the income statement and statement of cash flows*

The following transactions pertain to the operations of Howard & Co., CPAs.

1. Acquired $50,000 cash from the issue of common stock.
2. Performed accounting services and billed clients $67,000.
3. Paid a $5,000 cash dividend to the stockholders.
4. Collected $45,000 cash from accounts receivable.
5. Paid $49,000 cash for operating expenses.
6. Performed accounting services for $10,000 cash.

Required

a. Identify which of these transactions result in revenue or expense recognition for Howard & Co., CPAs.

b. Based on your response to Requirement *a,* determine the amount of net income Howard will report on its income statement.

c. Identify which of the preceding transactions affect(s) cash flow from operating activities.

d. Based on your response to Requirement *c,* determine the amount of net cash flow from operating activities Howard will report on the statement of cash flows.

e. What is the before- and after-closing balance in the Accounting Services Revenue account? What other accounts would be closed at the end of the accounting cycle?

Exercise 2-5A *Classifying events on the statement of cash flows*

The following transactions pertain to the operations of Traci Company for 2008:

1. Acquired $30,000 cash from the issue of common stock.
2. Provided $40,000 of services on account.
3. Incurred $25,000 of other operating expenses on account.
4. Collected $37,000 cash from accounts receivable.
5. Paid a $2,000 cash dividend to the stockholders.
6. Paid $18,000 cash on accounts payable.
7. Performed services for $9,000 cash.
8. Paid $2,000 cash for rent expense.

Required

a. Classify the cash flows from these transactions as operating activities (OA), investing activities (IA), or financing activities (FA). Use NA for transactions that do not affect the statement of cash flows.

b. Prepare a statement of cash flows. (There is no beginning cash balance.)

Exercise 2-6A *Effect of accounts receivable and accounts payable transactions on financial statements*

The following events apply to Brown and Birgin, a public accounting firm, for the 2007 accounting period.

1. Performed $96,000 of services for clients on account.
2. Performed $65,000 of services for cash.
3. Incurred $45,000 of other operating expenses on account.
4. Paid $26,000 cash to an employee for salary.
5. Collected $70,000 cash from accounts receivable.
6. Paid $38,000 cash on accounts payable.
7. Paid a $10,000 cash dividend to the stockholders.
8. Accrued salaries were $3,000 at the end of 2007.

Required

a. Show the effects of the events on the financial statements using a horizontal statements model like the following one. In the Cash Flow column, use OA to designate operating activity, IA for investment activity, FA for financing activity, and NC for net change in cash. Use NA to indicate the element is not affected by the event. The first event is recorded as an example.

Event No.	Assets		=	Liabilities		+	Equity		Rev.	−	Exp.	=	Net Inc.	Cash Flow
	Cash	+ Accts. Rec.	=	Accts. Pay.	+ Sal. Pay.	+	Ret. Earn.							
1	NA	+ 96,000	=	NA	+ NA	+	96,000		96,000	− NA		=	96,000	NA

b. What is the amount of total assets at the end of 2007?

c. What is the balance of accounts receivable at the end of 2007?

d. What is the balance of accounts payable at the end of 2007?

e. What is the difference between accounts receivable and accounts payable?

f. What is net income for 2007?

g. What is the amount of net cash flow from operating activities for 2007?

L.O. 2, 3

Exercise 2-7A   *Net income versus changes in cash*

In 2008, Puckett Inc. billed its customers $60,000 for services performed. The company collected $42,000 of the amount billed. Puckett incurred $38,000 of other operating expenses on account. Puckett paid $30,000 of the accounts payable. Puckett acquired $35,000 cash from the issue of common stock. The company invested $15,000 cash in the purchase of land.

Required

Use the preceding information to answer the following questions. (*Hint:* Identify the six events described in the paragraph and record them in general ledger accounts under an accounting equation before attempting to answer the questions.)

a. What amount of revenue will Puckett report on the 2008 income statement?

b. What amount of cash flow from revenue will Puckett report on the statement of cash flows?

c. What is the net income for the period?

d. What is the net cash flow from operating activities for the period?

e. Why is the amount of net income different from the net cash flow from operating activities for the period?

f. What is the amount of net cash flow from investing activities?

g. What is the amount of net cash flow from financing activities?

h. What amounts of total assets, liabilities, and equity will Puckett report on the year-end balance sheet?

L.O. 4

Exercise 2-8A   *Closing the accounts*

The following information was drawn from the accounting records of Spartan Company as of December 31, 2007, before the temporary accounts had been closed. The Cash balance was $3,000, and Notes Payable amounted to $1,300. The company had revenues of $4,500 and expenses of $2,000. The company's Land account had a $5,000 balance. Dividends amounted to $300. There was $1,000 of common stock issued.

Required

a. Identify which accounts would be classified as permanent and which accounts would be classified as temporary.

b. Assuming that Spartan's beginning balance (as of January 1, 2007) in the Retained Earnings account was $3,500, determine its balance after the nominal accounts were closed at the end of 2007.

c. What amount of net income would Spartan Company report on its 2007 income statement?

d. Explain why the amount of net income differs from the amount of the ending Retained Earnings balance.

e. What are the balances in the revenue, expense, and dividend accounts on January 1, 2008?

L.O. 4

Exercise 2-9A   *Closing accounts and the accounting cycle*

Required

a. Identify which of the following accounts are temporary (will be closed to Retained Earnings at the end of the year) and which are permanent.

(1) Common Stock

(2) Notes Payable

(3) Cash

(4) Service Revenue

(5) Dividends

(6) Land

(7) Salaries Expense

(8) Retained Earnings

(9) Utilities Expense

(10) Interest Revenue

b. Bill bragged that he had five years of accounting experience. Jane disagreed, responding, "No. You have had one year of accounting experience five times." Explain what Jane meant. (*Hint:* Refer to the accounting cycle.)

Exercise 2-10A   *Closing entries*

L.O. 4

Comador Company's accounting records show an after-closing balance of $16,800 in its Retained Earnings account on December 31, 2008. During the 2008 accounting cycle, Comador earned $12,600 of revenue, incurred $9,700 of expense, and paid $1,400 of dividends. Revenues and expenses were recognized evenly throughout the accounting period.

Required

a. Determine the balance in the Retained Earnings account as of January 1, 2009.

b. Determine the balance in the temporary accounts as of January 1, 2009.

c. Determine the after-closing balance in the Retained Earnings account as of December 31, 2007.

d. Determine the balance in the Retained Earnings account as of June 30, 2008.

Exercise 2-11A   *Matching concept*

L.O. 4

Companies make sacrifices known as *expenses* to obtain benefits called *revenues*. The accurate measurement of net income requires that expenses be matched with revenues. In some circumstances matching a particular expense directly with revenue is difficult or impossible. In these circumstances, the expense is matched with the period in which it is incurred.

Required

Distinguish the following items that could be matched directly with revenues from the items that would be classified as period expenses.

a. Sales commissions paid to employees.

b. Advertising expense.

c. Interest expense.

d. The cost of land that has been sold.

Exercise 2-12A   *Complete accounting cycle*

L.O. 2, 3

The following information is available for Todd Co. for the year 2009:

1. Acquired $50,000 cash from the issue of common stock.

2. Performed $120,000 of services on account.

3. Incurred other operating expenses on account in the amount of $90,000.

4. Purchased land for $20,000 cash.

5. Collected $100,000 cash from accounts receivable.

6. Paid $50,000 cash on accounts payable.

7. Performed services for $26,000 cash.

8. Paid $12,000 cash for salaries expense.

9. Paid a $5,000 cash dividend to the stockholders.

10. Borrowed $15,000 cash from State Bank.

Information for Adjusting Entry

11. Accrued interest expense at the end of the accounting period was $900.

Required

a. Explain how each of the transactions affects the elements of the accounting equation by placing a +
for *increase,* − for *decrease,* and NA for *not affected* under each of the elements. Also record the dollar amount of the effect of each event on the accounting equation. In the last column of the table, provide appropriate account titles for Retained Earnings accounts. The first event is recorded as an
example.

						Stockholders' Equity		
Event No.	Assets	=	Liabilities	+	Common Stock	+	Retained Earnings	Acct. Title for RE
1	+50,000		NA		+50,000		NA	

b. What is the amount of net income for 2008?

c. What is the amount of total assets at the end of 2008?

d. What is the amount of total liabilities at the end of 2008?

e. What is the before-closing balance in the Retained Earnings account on December 31, 2008.

L.O. 1, 5   **Exercise 2-13A**   *Effects of recognizing accrued interest on financial statements*

Joe Hughes started Hughes Company on January 1, 2007. The company experienced the following
events during its first year of operation.

1. Earned $1,500 of cash revenue for performing services.
2. Borrowed $3,000 cash from the bank.
3. Adjusted the accounting records to recognize accrued interest expense on the bank note. The note,
   issued on August 1, 2007, had a one-year term and a 6 percent annual interest rate.

Required

a. What is the amount of interest expense in 2007?

b. What amount of cash was paid for interest in 2007?

c. Use a horizontal statements model to show how each event affects the balance sheet, income statement, and statement of cash flows. Indicate whether the event increases (I), decreases (D), or does
not affect (NA) each element of the financial statements. Also, in the Cash Flows column, designate the cash flows as operating activities (OA), investing activities (IA), or financing activities
(FA). The first transaction has been recorded as an example.

Event No.	Balance Sheet										Income Statement					Statement of Cash Flows
	Cash	=	Note Pay.	+	Int. Pay.	+	C. Stk.	+	Ret. Earn.		Rev.	−	Exp.	=	Net Inc.	
1	I	=	NA	+	NA	+	NA	+	I		I	−	NA	=	I	I OA

L.O. 5, 7   **Exercise 2-14A**   *Recognizing accrued interest revenue*

Leach Company invested $80,000 in a certificate of deposit on June 1, 2008. The certificate had a
6 percent annual rate of interest and a one-year term to maturity.

Required

a. What amount of interest revenue will Leach recognize for the year ending December 31, 2008?

b. Show how the December 31, 2008, adjusting entry to recognize the accrued interest revenue
affects the accounting equation.

c. What amount of cash will Leach collect for interest revenue in 2008?

d. What is the amount of interest receivable as of December 31, 2008?

e. What amount of cash will Leach collect for interest revenue in 2009, assuming it does not renew
the CD?

f. What amount of interest revenue will Leach recognize in 2009, assuming it does not renew the CD?

g. What is the amount of interest receivable as of December 31, 2009, assuming it does not renew
the CD?

Exercise 2-15A   *Recognizing accrued interest expense*   **L.O. 5, 7**

Flash Corporation borrowed $90,000 from the bank on November 1, 2007. The note had a 7 percent annual rate of interest and matured on April 30, 2008. Interest and principal were paid in cash on the maturity date.

Required

a. What amount of interest expense was paid in cash in 2007?

b. What amount of interest expense was reported on the 2007 income statement?

c. What amount of total liabilities was reported on the December 31, 2007, balance sheet?

d. What total amount of cash was paid to the bank on April 30, 2008, for principal and interest?

e. What amount of interest expense was reported on the 2008 income statement?

Exercise 2-16A   *Effect of transactions on the balance sheet*   **L.O. 2, 3**

Cowboy Corp. was formed on January 1, 2009. The business acquired $80,000 cash from the issue of common stock. The business performed $210,000 of services on account and collected $180,000 of the amount due. Other operating expenses incurred on account amounted to $185,000. By the end of 2009, $170,000 of that amount had been paid with cash. The business paid $20,000 cash to purchase land. Cowboy borrowed $40,000 cash from the bank. On December 31, 2009, there was $2,500 of accrued interest expense.

Required

Using the preceding information, answer the following questions. (*Hint:* Identify the eight events described in the preceding paragraph and record them in general ledger accounts under an accounting equation before answering the questions.)

a. What is the cash balance at the end of 2009?

b. What is the balance of accounts receivable at the end of 2009?

c. What is the amount of total assets at the end of 2009?

d. What is the amount of total liabilities at the end of 2009?

e. What is the amount of common stock at the end of 2009?

f. What is the amount of retained earnings at the end of 2009?

Exercise 2-17A   *Identifying source, use, and exchange transactions*   **L.O. 9**

Required

Indicate whether each of the following transactions is an asset source (AS), asset use (AU), asset exchange (AE), or claims exchange (CE) transaction.

a. Performed services for cash.

b. Performed services for clients on account.

c. Collected cash from accounts receivable.

d. Invested cash in a certificate of deposit.

e. Purchased land with cash.

f. Acquired cash from the issue of stock.

g. Paid a cash dividend to the stockholders.

h. Paid cash on accounts payable.

i. Incurred other operating expenses on account.

j. Paid cash for rent expense.

k. Closed the Revenue account.

Exercise 2-18A   *Identifying asset source, use, and exchange transactions* **L.O. 9**

Required

a. Name an asset use transaction that will affect the income statement.

b. Name an asset use transaction that will *not* affect the income statement.

c. Name an asset exchange transaction that will *not* affect the statement of cash flows.

d. Name an asset exchange transaction that will affect the statement of cash flows.

e. Name an asset source transaction that will *not* affect the income statement.

L.O. 3

Exercise 2-19A *Relation of elements to financial statements*

Required

Identify whether each of the following items would appear on the income statement (IS), statement of changes in stockholders' equity (SE), balance sheet (BS), or statement of cash flows (CF). Some items may appear on more than one statement; if so, identify all applicable statements. If an item would not appear on any financial statement, label it NA.

a. Accounts Receivable

b. Accounts Payable

c. Interest Payable

d. Dividends

e. Beginning Cash Balance

f. Ending Retained Earnings

g. Interest Expense

h. Ending Cash Balance

i. Salaries Expense

j. Net Income

k. Utilities Expense

l. Interest Revenue

m. Cash Flow from Operating Activities

n. Service Revenue

o. Auditor's Opinion

L.O. 7

Exercise 2-20A *Evaluating cash management*

The data in the following table apply to Cardinal, Incorporated.

	2007	2008
Accounts receivable	$ 25,800,000	$ 27,060,000
Sales	332,700,000	382,606,000
Accounts payable	15,800,000	18,644,000
Operating expenses	257,300,000	285,603,000

Required

a. What is the percentage growth in the Accounts Receivable, Sales, Accounts Payable, and Operating Expenses accounts from 2007 to 2008?

b. Companies must incur interest expense to obtain cash. To minimize interest expense, companies attempt to collect cash from receivables as quickly as possible and to delay the payment of cash to settle payables as long as possible. Based on your answers to Requirement *a,* comment on Cardinal's cash management.

L.O. 8

Exercise 2-21A *Ethical conduct*

In February 2006, former senator Warren Rudman of New Hampshire completed a 17-month investigation of an $11 billion accounting scandal at Fannie Mae (a major enterprise involved in home-mortgage financing). The Rudman investigation concluded that Fannie Mae's CFO and controller used an accounting gimmick to manipulate financial statements in order to meet earning-per-share (EPS) targets. Meeting the EPS targets triggered bonus payments for the executives.

Required

Comment on the provisions of SOX that pertain to intentional misrepresentation and describe the maximum penalty that the CFO could face.

L.O. 8, 10

Exercise 2-22A *Materiality and the auditor (Appendix)*

Krystal Jerry is an auditor. Her work at two companies disclosed inappropriate recognition of revenue. Both cases involved dollar amounts in the $100,000 range. In one case, Jerry considered the item material and required her client to restate earnings. In the other case, Jerry dismissed the misstatement as being immaterial.

Required

Write a memo that explains how a $100,000 misstatement of revenue is acceptable for one company but unacceptable for a different company.

PROBLEMS—SERIES A

All Problems in Series A are available with McGraw-Hill's Homework Manager®

Problem 2-23A *Effect of events on the accounting equation*

L.O. 2

Required

Explain how each of the following independent accounting events would affect the accounting equation by writing the letter I for increase, the letter D for decrease, and NA for no affect under the appropriate columns. The effects of the first event are shown for you.

Letter of Event	Assets	=	Liabilities	+	Common Stock	+	Retained Earnings
a	I				I		

a. Received cash from the issue of common stock.

b. Paid cash for interest expense accrued in a previous period.

c. Purchased land with cash.

d. Repaid borrowed funds with cash.

e. Collected cash from accounts receivable.

f. Paid cash for salaries.

g. Recognized service revenue on account.

h. Received utility bill; cash payment will be made in the future.

i. Borrowed cash from creditors.

j. Paid a cash dividend to the stockholders.

k. Accrued interest expense on note payable at the end of the accounting period.

Problem 2-24A *Classifying events as source, use, or exchange and effect of events on financial statements—horizontal statements model*

L.O. 1, 4, 9

The following transactions pertain to D&H Advisory Services for 2009:

1. Business started when it acquired $40,000 cash from the issue of common stock.

2. Paid $25,000 cash to purchase land.

3. Paid $3,000 cash for rent expense.

4. Performed services for clients and billed them $15,800. Expected to collect cash at a later date (the revenue was earned on account).

5. Incurred $11,200 of other operating expenses on account (expected to make cash payment at a later date).

6. Received $700 bill for utilities. The amount due was payable within 30 days.

7. Collected $9,400 cash from accounts receivable.

8. Paid $3,800 cash on the account payable.

9. Acquired an additional $6,000 cash from the issue of common stock.

10. Paid $7,600 cash on the balance of the account payable created in Event 5.

CHECK FIGURES
b. Total cash: $18,900
Net income: $5,300

11. Performed additional services for $6,200 cash.

12. Paid $1,500 cash dividend to the stockholders.

Required

a. Classify each of D&H's transactions as asset source (AS), asset use (AU), asset exchange (AE), or claims exchange (CE).

b. Show the effects of the events on the financial statements using a horizontal statements model like the following one. In the Cash Flow column, use the initials OA for operating activity, IA for investing activity, FA for financing activity, and NC for net change in cash. Use NA to indicate accounts not affected by the transaction. The first event is recorded as an example.

| Event No. | Assets | | | = | Liab. | + | Stk. Equity | | | | | | |
	Cash	+ Accts. Rec.	+ Land	=	Accts. Pay.	+	C. Stock	+ Ret. Earn.	Rev.	− Exp.	= Net Inc.	Cash Flow
1	40,000	+ NA	+ NA	=	NA	+	40,000	+ NA	NA	− NA	= NA	40,000 FA

c. What is the amount of net income for 2009?

d. What is the amount of net cash flow from operating activities for 2009?

e. Explain how the closing entries affect the retained earnings account.

L.O. 1, 4, 5

CHECK FIGURES
b. Ending Balance in Retained Earnings: $17,790
Net Income: $17,790

Problem 2-25A *Effect of events on the financial statements*

Expert Auto experienced the following transactions during 2008.

1. Provided services to customers and billed them $18,000.

2. Borrowed $9,000 from the bank on September 1, 2008. The note had a 7 percent annual interest rate and a one-year term to maturity.

3. Paid $3,000 of salary expense.

4. Provided services to customers and collected $12,000 cash.

5. Incurred $9,000 of other operating expenses on account.

6. Collected $17,000 of the accounts receivable.

7. Paid $8,100 of the accounts payable.

8. Recognized the accrued interest on the note payable at December 31, 2008.

Required

a. Show the effects of the transactions on the financial statements using a horizontal statements model like the following one. In the Cash Flows column, use the letters OA for operating activity, IA for investing activity, FA for financing activity, and NC for net change in cash. Use NA to indicate not affected by the transaction. The first one is recorded as an example.

| Event No. | Balance Sheet | | | | | | Income Statement | | | Statement of Cash Flows |
| | Assets | | = | Liab. | | + Stk. Equity | | | | |
	Cash	+ Accts. Rec.	= Accts. Pay.	Note Pay.	Int. Pay.	+ Ret. Earn.	Rev.	− Exp.	= Net Inc.	
1.	NA	+ 18,000	= NA	NA	NA	18,000	18,000	− NA	= 18,000	NA

b. What is the ending balance of Retained Earnings? What is the amount of net income? Why are these amounts the same in this problem? Is the balance in Retained Earnings likely to be the same as the amount of net income at the end of 2009? Explain your answer.

c. Determine the balances that would appear in the revenue and expense accounts at the beginning of the 2009 accounting period.

Problem 2-26A *Identifying and arranging elements on financial statements*

The following information was drawn from the records of Ruth & Associates at December 31, 2008:

Consulting revenue	$100,000	Notes payable	$32,000
Land	63,000	Salaries payable	7,000
Dividends	10,000	Salary expense	47,000
Cash flow from fin. activities	20,000	Common stock issued	15,000
Interest revenue	4,000	Beginning common stock	25,000
Ending retained earnings	60,000	Accounts receivable	26,000
Cash	52,000	Cash flow from inv. activities	(30,000)
Interest payable	2,000	Cash flow from oper. activities	32,000
Interest expense	5,000		

CHECK FIGURES
2008 Net Income: $52,000
2008 Total Assets: $141,000

Required

Use the preceding information to construct an income statement, statement of changes in stockholders' equity, balance sheet, and statement of cash flows. (Show only totals for each activity on the statement of cash flows).

Problem 2-27A *Two complete accounting cycles*

The following accounting events apply to Schultz Company, which began operations in 2009.

Accounting Events for 2009

1. Acquired $50,000 cash from the issue of common stock.
2. Recognized $86,000 of revenue on account during the period for services performed.
3. Collected $76,000 cash from accounts receivable.
4. Paid $5,000 cash dividend.
5. Paid $42,500 cash for salaries expense.
6. Paid $11,000 cash for other operating expenses.
7. Invested $30,000 in a certificate of deposit with an 18-month term.

CHECK FIGURES
a. 2009 Ending Retained
Earnings: $25,850
2010 Ending Retained
Earnings: $45,370

Information for Adjusting Entries (Books are closed on December 31)

8. Accrued salaries expense of $2,400.
9. Recorded accrued interest on the certificate of deposit. The certificate was purchased on June 30, 2009, and had a 5 percent annual rate of interest.

Accounting Events for 2010

1. Made cash payment of $2,400 for salaries payable.
2. Borrowed $28,000 from a local bank.
3. Received an additional $10,000 cash from the issue of common stock.
4. Recognized $120,000 of revenue on account during 2010 for services performed.
5. Collected $108,000 of cash on accounts receivable during the period.
6. Purchased land for the company that cost $32,000 cash. A few months later, the land was appraised at $45,000.
7. Paid a $10,000 cash dividend to the stockholders of the company.
8. Received the principal amount plus the interest earned on the certificate of deposit. (See Events 7 and 9 in year 2009 for details regarding the original investment.)
9. Paid cash of $40,000 for salaries expense.
10. Paid $46,000 cash for other operating expenses.

Information for Adjusting Entries

11. Accrued salaries expense was $5,000.
12. Recorded accrued interest expense on the bank note (see Event 2 in 2010). The note was issued to the bank on June 1, 2010. It had a 6 percent annual rate of interest and a two-year term to maturity.

Required

a. Record the effect of each of the events in general ledger accounts under an accounting equation for the 2009 and 2010 fiscal years. In the last column of the table, provide appropriate account titles for Retained Earning accounts.

b. Prepare an income statement, statement of changes in stockholders' equity, balance sheet, and statement of cash flows for the 2009 and 2010 calendar years using the vertical statement format.

c. Determine the balances that would appear in the temporary accounts at the beginning of 2011.

L.O. 2, 3, 5, 7

CHECK FIGURES
a. $8,000
b. $900

Problem 2-28A   *Effect of accrued interest on financial statements*

Dana Co. borrowed $15,000 from the local bank on April 1, 2008, when the company was started. The note had an 8 percent annual interest rate and a one-year term to maturity. Dana Co. recognized $50,000 of revenue on account in 2008 and $60,000 of revenue on account in 2009. Cash collections from accounts receivable were $38,000 in 2008 and $62,000 in 2009. Dana Co. paid $30,000 of salaries expense in 2008 and $32,000 of salaries expense in 2009. Repaid loan and interest occurred at maturity date.

Required

Based on the preceding information, answer the following questions. (*Hint:* Record the events in general ledger accounts under an accounting equation before answering the questions.)

a. What amount of net cash flow from operating activities would Dana report on the 2008 cash flow statement?

b. What amount of interest expense would Dana report on the 2008 income statement?

c. What amount of total liabilities would Dana report on the December 31, 2008, balance sheet?

d. What amount of retained earnings would Dana report on the December 31, 2008, balance sheet?

e. What amount of cash flow from financing activities would Dana report on the 2008 statement of cash flows?

f. What amount of interest expense would Dana report on the 2009 income statement?

g. What amount of cash flows from operating activities would Dana report on the 2009 cash flow statement?

h. What amount of total assets would Dana report on the December 31, 2009, balance sheet?

i. What amount of cash flow from investing activities would Dana report on the 2009 cash flow statement?

j. If Dana Co. paid a $700 dividend during 2009, what retained earnings balance would it report on the December 31, 2009, balance sheet?

L.O. 3, 4

Problem 2-29A   *Closing the accounts*

The following accounts and account balances were taken from the records of Black Company. Except as otherwise indicated, all balances are as of December 31, 2009, before the closing entries had been recorded.

CHECK FIGURES
Net Income: $2,900
Ending Retained
Earnings: $17,300

Cash received from common stock issued during 2009	$ 3,500
Cash	7,800
Revenue	8,000
Salary expense	2,900
Cash flow from operating activities	2,500
Notes payable	2,000
Utility expense	800
Dividends	1,200
Cash flow from financing activities	2,300
Rent expense	1,400
Land	20,200
Retained earnings, January 1, 2009	15,600
Common stock, December 31, 2009	10,000

Required

a. Prepare the income statement Black would include in its 2009 annual report.

b. Identify the accounts that should be closed to the Retained Earnings account.

c. Determine the Retained Earnings account balance at December 31, 2009. Identify the reasons for the difference between net income and the ending balance in Retained Earnings.

d. What are the balances in the Revenue, Expense, and Dividend accounts on January 1, 2010? Explain.

Problem 2-30A   *Missing information in financial statements*

L.O. 6, 7

Required

Fill in the blanks (indicated by the alphabetic letters in parentheses) in the following financial statements. Assume the company started operations January 1, 2008 and all transactions involve cash.

CHECK FIGURES
n. $75
t. $9,710

	For the Years		
	2008	**2009**	**2010**
Income Statements			
Revenue	$ 400	$ 500	$ 800
Expense	(250)	(l)	(425)
Net income	$ (a)	$ 100	$ 375
Statement of Changes in Stockholders' Equity			
Beginning common stock	$ 0	$ (m)	$ 9,100
Plus: Common stock issued	(b)	1,100	310
Ending common stock	8,000	9,100	(s)
Beginning retained earnings	0	25	75
Plus: Net income	(c)	100	375
Less: Dividends	(d)	(50)	(150)
Ending retained earnings	25	(n)	300
Total stockholders' equity	$ (e)	$ 9,175	$ (t)
Balance Sheets			
Assets			
Cash	$ (f)	$ (o)	$ (u)
Land	0	(p)	2,500
Total assets	$11,000	$11,650	$10,550
Liabilities	$ (g)	$ (q)	$ 840
Stockholders equity			
Common stock	(h)	(r)	9,410
Retained earnings	(i)	75	300
Total stockholders' equity	8,025	9,175	9,710
Total liabilities and stockholders' equity	$11,000	$11,650	$10,550
Statements of Cash Flows			
Cash flows from operating activities			
Cash receipts from revenue	$ (j)	$ 500	$ (v)
Cash payments for expenses	(k)	(400)	(w)
Net cash flows from operating activities	150	100	375

continued

Cash flows from investing activities			
Cash payments for land	0	(5,000)	0
Cash receipt from sale of land	0	0	2,500
Net cash flows from investing activities	0	(5,000)	2,500
Cash flows from financing activities			
Cash receipts from borrowed funds	2,975	0	0
Cash payments to reduce debt	0	(500)	(x)
Cash receipts from stock issue	8,000	1,100	(y)
Cash payments for dividends	(125)	(50)	(z)
Net cash flows from financing activities	10,850	550	(1,475)
Net change in cash	11,000	(4,350)	1,400
Beginning cash balance	0	11,000	6,650
Ending cash balance	$11,000	$ 6,650	$ 8,050

L.O. 2, 3, 5

Problem 2-31A   *Missing information in financial statements*

Beach Properties had the following assets at the beginning of the accounting period (January 1, 2008): Cash—$21,000, Accounts Receivable—$36,000, Certificate of Deposit—$16,000, and Land—$70,000. The beginning balances in the liability accounts were Accounts Payable—$27,000 and Notes Payable—$20,000. A $61,000 balance was in Common Stock at the beginning of the accounting period. During the accounting period, service revenue earned on account was $44,000. The ending balance in the Accounts Receivable account was $34,000. Operating expenses incurred on account amounted to $35,000. There was $33,000 paid on accounts payable. In addition, there was $1,200 of accrued interest revenue and $1,700 of accrued interest expense as of the end of the accounting period (December 31, 2008). Finally, a $2,500 cash dividend was paid to the stockholders. (*Hint:* Record the events in general ledger accounts under an accounting equation before satisfying the requirements.)

Required

a. Determine the amount of cash collected from accounts receivable.

b. Prepare a balance sheet as of January 1, 2008.

c. Prepare an income statement, statement of changes in stockholders' equity, balance sheet, and statement of cash flows for the 2008 accounting period.

d. Determine the interest rate earned on the certificate of deposit.

e. Determine the interest rate paid on the note payable.

f. Determine the balances of the revenue, expense, and dividends accounts on January 1, 2009.

L.O. 8

Problem 2-32A   *Ethics*

Pete Chalance is an accountant with a shady past. Suffice it to say that he owes some very unsavory characters a lot of money. Despite his past, Pete works hard at keeping up a strong professional image. He is a manager at Smith and Associates, a fast-growing CPA firm. Pete is highly regarded around the office because he is a strong producer of client revenue. Indeed, on several occasions he exceeded his authority in establishing prices with clients. This is typically a partner's job but who could criticize Pete, who is most certainly bringing in the business. Indeed, Pete is so good that he is able to pull off the following scheme. He bills clients at inflated rates and then reports the ordinary rate to his accounting firm. Say for example, the normal charge for a job is $2,500. Pete will smooth talk the client, then charge him $3,000. He reports the normal charge of $2,500 to his firm and keeps the extra $500 for himself. He knows it isn't exactly right because his firm gets its regular charges and the client willingly pays for the services rendered. He thinks to himself, as he pockets his ill-gotten gains, who is getting hurt anyway?

Required

The text discusses three common features (conditions) that motivate ethical misconduct. Identify and explain each of the three features as they appear in the above scenario.

L.O. 10

Problem 2-33A   *Auditor responsibilities (Appendix)*

The historical cost principle requires assets to be reported at their original cost until they are sold or retired. However, under certain circumstances some assets may be reported at their market value with the difference between the historical cost and the market value being recognized as profit or loss.

Reporting assets at market value is frequently called *mark to market accounting.* Executives at Enron abused mark to market accounting to intentionally misrepresent the company's financial condition. More specifically, they inflated market values to achieve the desired net income. In other words, they reported earnings that simply did not exist. The independent auditors signed off on the mark to market accounting practice even though it was obvious that the practice was being abused.

Required

a. Comment on how a mark to market overstatement of earnings may affect the balance sheet, income statement, and statement of cash flows.

b. Speculate as to why the independent auditors were willing to approve the use of mark to market accounting even though it was an inappropriate accounting practice in the circumstances.

c. Identify and describe three key provisions in the Sarbanes-Oxley Act that are designed to strengthen the audit function.

EXERCISES—SERIES B

Where applicable in all exercises, round computations to the nearest dollar.

Exercise 2-1B   *Effect of accruals on the financial statements*

L.O. 2, 3

Chef, Inc., experienced the following events in 2009, its first year of operations.

1. Received $17,000 cash from the issue of common stock.
2. Performed services on account for $42,000.
3. Paid the utility expense of $1,300.
4. Collected $32,000 of the accounts receivable.
5. Recorded $7,000 of accrued salaries at the end of the year.
6. Paid a $1,000 cash dividend to the stockholders.

Required

a. Record these events in general ledger accounts under an accounting equation. In the last column of the table, provide appropriate account titles for the Retained Earnings amounts. The first transaction has been recorded as an example.

CHEF, INC.
General Ledger Accounts

Event	Assets		=	Liabilities	+	Stockholders' Equity		Acct. Titles for RE
	Cash	Accounts Receivable		Salaries Payable		Common Stock	Retained Earnings	
1.	17,000					17,000		

b. What is the balance in the Retained Earnings Account immediately after Event 2 has been recorded? What is the balance in the Retained Earnings account after the temporary accounts are closed on December 31, 2009? What is the balance in the Revenue account on January 1, 2010?

c. Prepare the income statement, statement of changes in stockholders' equity, balance sheet, and statement of cash flows for the 2009 accounting period.

d. Why is the ending cash balance the same as the net change in cash on the statement of cash flows?

Exercise 2-2B   *Effect of collecting accounts receivable on the accounting equation and financial statements*

L.O. 2, 3

Ramsey Company earned $15,000 of revenue on account during 2008. The company collected $7,000 cash from accounts receivable during 2008.

Required

Based on this information alone, determine the following. (*Hint:* It may be helpful to record the events in general ledger accounts under an accounting equation before satisfying the requirements.)

a. The balance of accounts receivable that Ramsey would report on the December 31, 2008, balance sheet.

b. The amount of net income that Ramsey would report on the 2008 income statement.

c. The amount of net cash flow from operating activities that Ramsey would report on the 2008 statement of cash flows.

d. The amount of retained earnings that Ramsey would report on the December 31, 2008, balance sheet.

e. Why are the answers to Requirements *b* and *c* different?

f. What is the before- and after-closing balances in the Service Revenue and Retained Earnings accounts on December 31, 2008?

L.O. 1

Exercise 2-3B   *Effect of accrued salaries on the financial statements*

B. Karim recorded $8,700 of accrued salaries expense at the end of 2009.

Required

Use the following horizontal statements model to show how this event affects the balance sheet, income statement, and statement of cash flows. Indicate whether the event increases (I), decreases (D), or does not affect (NA) each element of the financial statements. Also, in the Cash Flows column, designate the classification of any cash flows using the letters OA for operating activities, IA for investing activities, and FA for financing activities.

Balance Sheet								Income Statement			Statement of Cash Flows
Cash	=	Sal. Pay	+	C. Stk.	+	Ret. Ear.		Rev.	− Exp.	= Net Inc.	

L.O. 3

Exercise 2-4B   *Effects of revenue and expense recognition on the income statement and statement of cash flows*

The following transactions pertain to the operations of Derek & Co., CPAs for 2009, its first year of operation.

1. Acquired $110,000 cash from the issue of common stock.
2. Performed accounting services and billed clients $130,000.
3. Paid $8,000 cash dividend to the stockholders.
4. Collected $80,000 cash from accounts receivable.
5. Paid $72,000 cash for operating expenses.
6. Performed accounting services for $5,000 cash.

Required

a. Which of these transactions resulted in revenue or expense recognition for Derek & Co., CPAs?

b. Based on your response to Requirement *a,* determine the amount of net income that Derek will report on the income statement.

c. Determine the net cash flow from operating activities for each of the preceding transactions.

d. What is the before- and after-closing balances in the Accounting Services Revenue account on December 31, 2009? What other account(s) would be closed at the end of the accounting cycle?

L.O. 3

Exercise 2-5B   *Classifying events on the statement of cash flows*

The following transactions pertain to the operations of Rush Company for 2008:

1. Acquired $35,000 cash from the issue of common stock.
2. Provided $80,000 of services on account.
3. Paid $22,000 cash on accounts payable.
4. Performed services for $5,000 cash.
5. Collected $71,000 cash from accounts receivable.

6. Incurred $42,000 of operating expenses on account.
7. Paid $3,200 cash for expenses.
8. Paid a $5,000 cash dividend to the stockholders.

Required

a. Classify the cash flows from each of these transactions as operating activities (OA), investing activities (IA), or financing activities (FA). Use NA for transactions that do not affect the statement of cash flows.
b. Prepare a statement of cash flows. (This is the first year of operations.)

Exercise 2-6B   *Effect of accounts receivable and accounts payable transactions on financial statements*   **L.O. 1**

The following events apply to Culvin and Piper, a public accounting firm, for the 2008 accounting period.

1. Performed $70,000 of services for clients on account.
2. Performed $40,000 of services for cash.
3. Incurred $36,000 of other operating expenses on account.
4. Paid $10,000 cash to an employee for salary.
5. Collected $47,000 cash from accounts receivable.
6. Paid $16,000 cash on accounts payable.
7. Paid an $8,000 cash dividend to the stockholders.
8. Accrued salaries were $2,000 at the end of 2008.

Required

a. Show the effects of the events on the financial statements using a horizontal statements model like the following one. In the Cash Flow column, use OA to designate operating activity, IA for investment activity, FA for financing activity, and NC for net change in cash. Use NA to indicate the element is not affected by the event. The first event is recorded as an example.

| Event No. | Assets | | = | Liabilities | | | + | Stk. Equity | Rev. | − | Exp. | = | Net Inc. | Cash Flow |
	Cash	+ Accts. Rec.	=	Accts. Pay.	+	Sal. Pay.	+	Ret. Earn.						
1	NA	+ 70,000	=	NA	+	NA	+	70,000	70,000	−	NA	=	70,000	NA

b. What is the amount of total assets at the end of 2008?
c. What is the balance of accounts receivable at the end of 2008?
d. What is the balance of accounts payable at the end of 2008?
e. What is the difference between accounts receivable and accounts payable?
f. What is net income for 2008?
g. What is the amount of net cash flow from operating activities for 2008?

Exercise 2-7B   *Net income versus changes in cash*   **L.O. 2, 3**

In 2009, Sol Company billed its customers $120,000 for services performed. The company subsequently collected $73,000 of the amount billed. Sol incurred $69,000 of operating expenses on account. Sol paid $65,000 of that amount. Sol acquired $30,000 cash from the issue of common stock. The company invested $36,000 cash in the purchase of land.

Required

Use the preceding information to answer the following questions. (*Hint:* It may be helpful to identify the six events described in the paragraph and to record them in general ledger accounts under an accounting equation before answering the questions.)

a. What amount of revenue will Sol report on the 2009 income statement?
b. What is the net income for the period?
c. What amount of cash flow from revenue will Sol report on the statement of cash flows?
d. What is the net cash flow from operating activities for the period?
e. Why is the amount of net income different from the net cash flow from operating activities for the period?

f. What is the amount of net cash flow from investing activities?

g. What is the amount of net cash flow from financing activities?

h. What amount of total equity will Sol report on the year-end balance sheet?

L.O. 4

Exercise 2-8B *Closing the accounts*

The following information was drawn from the accounting records of Croom Company as of December 31, 2008, before the nominal accounts had been closed. The company's cash balance was $2,000, and its land account had a $7,000 balance. Notes payable amounted to $3,000. The balance in the Common Stock account was $1,500. The company had revenues of $5,500 and expenses of $2,000, and dividends amounted to $900.

Required

a. Identify the accounts that would be closed to Retained Earnings at the end of the accounting period.

b. Assuming that Croom's beginning balance (as of January 1, 2008) in the Retained Earnings account was $1,900, determine its balance after the nominal accounts were closed at the end of 2008.

c. What amount of net income would Croom Company report on its 2008 income statement?

d. Explain why the amount of net income differs from the amount of the ending Retained Earnings balance.

e. What are the balances in the revenue, expense, and dividend accounts on January 1, 2009?

L.O. 4

Exercise 2-9B *Closing accounts and the accounting cycle*

Required

a. Identify which of the following accounts are temporary (will be closed to Retained Earnings at the end of the year) and which are permanent.

(1) Cash

(2) Salaries Expense

(3) Notes Payable

(4) Utilities Expense

(5) Service Revenue

(6) Dividends

(7) Common Stock

(8) Land

(9) Interest Revenue

(10) Retained Earnings

b. List and explain the four stages of the accounting cycle. Which stage must be first? Which stage is last?

L.O. 4

Exercise 2-10B *Closing entries*

Lotus Company's accounting records show a $27,400 balance in its Retained Earnings account on January 1, 2008. During the 2008 accounting cycle Lotus earned $15,200 of revenue, incurred $10,700 of expense, and paid $600 of dividends. Revenues and expenses were recognized evenly throughout the accounting period.

Required

a. Determine the after-closing balance in the Retained Earnings account as of December 31, 2007.

b. Determine the before-closing balance in the temporary accounts as of December 31, 2008.

c. Determine the after-closing balance in the Retained Earnings account as of December 31, 2008.

d. Determine the balance in the Retained Earnings account as of June 30, 2008.

L.O. 4

Exercise 2-11B *Matching concept*

Companies make sacrifices known as *expenses* to obtain benefits called *revenues*. The accurate measurement of net income requires that expenses be matched with revenues. In some circumstances matching a particular expense directly with revenue is difficult or impossible. In these circumstances, the expense is matched with the period in which it is incurred.

Required

a. Identify an expense that could be matched directly with revenue.

b. Identify a period expense that would be difficult to match with revenue. Explain why.

Exercise 2-12B   *Complete accounting cycle*   **L.O. 2, 3**

The following information is available for Eagle Co. for the year 2010. The business had the following transactions:

1. Performed $150,000 of services on account.
2. Acquired $70,000 cash from the issue of common stock.
3. Purchased land for $20,000 cash.
4. Incurred other operating expenses on account in the amount of $91,000.
5. Performed services for $18,000 cash.
6. Paid $60,000 cash on accounts payable.
7. Collected $85,000 cash from accounts receivable.
8. Paid $20,000 cash dividend to the stockholders.
9. Paid $9,000 cash for salaries.
10. Borrowed $30,000 cash from National Bank.

Information for Adjusting Entry

11. Accrued interest expense at the end of the accounting period was $1,500.

Required

a. Explain how each of the transactions affects the elements of the accounting equation by placing a + for *increase*, − for *decrease*, and NA for *not affected* under each of the elements. Also record the dollar amount of the effect of each event on the accounting equation. In the last column of the table, provide appropriate account titles for Retained Earnings amounts. The first event is recorded as an example.

					Stockholders' Equity		
Event No.	Assets	=	Liabilities	+	Common Stock	+	Retained Earnings	Acct. Titles for RE
1	+150,000		NA		NA		+150,000	Service Revenue

b. What is the amount of net income for 2010?

c. What is the amount of total assets at the end of 2010?

d. What is the amount of total liabilities at the end of 2010?

e. What is the before- and after-closing balance in the Revenue account on December 31, 2010?

Exercise 2-13B   *Effects of recognizing accrued interest on financial statements*   **L.O. 1, 5**

Arthur Troy started Troy Company on January 1, 2009. The company experienced the following events during its first year of operation.

1. Earned $6,200 of cash revenue.
2. Borrowed $5,000 cash from the bank.
3. Adjusted the accounting records to recognize accrued interest expense on the bank note. The note, issued on September 1, 2009, had a one-year term and a 9 percent annual interest rate.

Required

a. What is the amount of interest payable at December 31, 2009?

b. What is the amount of interest expense in 2009?

c. What is the amount of interest paid in 2009?

d. Use a horizontal statements model to show how each event affects the balance sheet, income statement, and statement of cash flows. Indicate whether the event increases (I) decreases (D), or does not affect (NA) each element of the financial statements. Also, in the Cash Flows column, designate the cash flows as operating activities (OA), investing activities (IA), or financing activities (FA). The first transaction has been recorded as an example.

Event No.	Balance Sheet											Income Statement						Statement of Cash Flows
	Cash	=	Note Pay.	+	Int. Pay.	+	C. Stk.	+	Ret. Earn.			Rev.	−	Exp.	=	Net Inc.		
1	I	=	NA	+	NA	+	NA	+	I			I	−	NA	=	I		I OA

L.O. 5, 7   **Exercise 2-14B**   *Recognizing accrued interest revenue*

Texas Company invested $90,000 in a certificate of deposit on August 1, 2008. The certificate had a 6 percent annual rate of interest and a one-year term to maturity.

Required

a. What amount of interest revenue will Texas recognize for the year ending December 31, 2008?

b. Show how the December 31, 2008, adjusting entry to recognize the accrued interest revenue affects the accounting equation.

c. What amount of cash will Texas collect for interest revenue in 2008?

d. What is the amount of interest receivable as of December 31, 2008?

e. What amount of cash will Texas collect for interest revenue in 2009, assuming it does not renew the CD?

f. What amount of interest revenue will Texas recognize in 2009, assuming it does not renew the CD?

g. What is the amount of interest receivable as of December 31, 2009, assuming it does not renew the CD?

L.O. 5, 7   **Exercise 2-15B**   *Recognizing accrued interest expense*

Polar Corporation borrowed $50,000 from the bank on October 1, 2009. The note had a 9 percent annual rate of interest and matured on March 31, 2010. Interest and principal were paid in cash on the maturity date.

Required

a. What amount of interest expense was paid in cash in 2009?

b. What amount of interest expense was recognized on the 2009 income statement?

c. What amount of total liabilities was reported on the December 31, 2009, balance sheet?

d. What total amount of cash was paid to the bank on March 31, 2010, for principal and interest?

e. What amount of interest expense was reported on the 2010 income statement?

L.O. 2, 3   **Exercise 2-16B**   *Effect of transactions on the balance sheet*

Neely Corp. was formed on January 1, 2008. The business acquired $110,000 cash from the issue of common stock. The business performed $300,000 of services on account and collected $260,000 of the amount due. Operating expenses incurred on account amounted to $185,000. By the end of 2008, $100,000 of that amount had been paid with cash. The business paid $20,000 cash to purchase land. The business borrowed $50,000 cash from the bank. On December 31, 2008, there was $900 of accrued interest expense.

Required

Using the preceding information, answer the following questions. (*Hint:* Identify the eight events described in the preceding paragraph and record them in general ledger accounts under an accounting equation before answering the questions.)

a. What is the cash balance at the end of 2008?

b. What is the balance of accounts receivable at the end of 2008?

c. What is the amount of total assets at the end of 2008?

d. What is the amount of total liabilities at the end of 2008?

e. What is the amount of common stock at the end of 2008?

f. What is the amount of net income for 2008?

Exercise 2-17B   *Identifying source, use, and exchange transactions*   L.O. 9

Required

Indicate whether each of the following transactions is an asset source (AS), asset use (AU), asset exchange (AE), or claims exchange (CE) transaction.

a. Paid cash on accounts payable.

b. Collected cash from accounts receivable.

c. Paid a cash dividend to the stockholders.

d. Borrowed cash from the bank.

e. Purchased land with cash.

f. Closed the temporary accounts.

g. Performed services for clients on account.

h. Paid cash for salary expense.

i. Acquired cash from the issue of common stock.

j. Incurred other operating expenses on account.

k. Performed services for cash.

Exercise 2-18B   *Identifying asset source, use, and exchange transactions*   L.O. 9

Required

a. Name an asset use transaction that will *not* affect the income statement.

b. Name an asset exchange transaction that will affect the statement of cash flows.

c. Name an asset source transaction that will *not* affect the income statement.

d. Name an asset source transaction that will *not* affect the statement of cash flows.

e. Name an asset source transaction that will affect the income statement.

Exercise 2-19B   *Relation of elements to financial statements*   L.O. 3

Required

Identify whether each of the following items would appear on the income statement (IS), statement of changes in stockholders' equity (SE), balance sheet (BS), or statement of cash flows (CF). Some items may appear on more than one statement; if so, identify all applicable statements. If an item would not appear on any financial statement, label it NA.

a. Land

b. Interest Revenue

c. Dividends

d. Salaries Expense

e. Net Income

f. Interest Payable

g. Ending Cash Balance

h. Cash Flow from Investing Activities

i. Note Payable

j. Notes Receivable

k. Accounts Receivable

l. Retained Earnings

m. Interest Receivable

n. Utilities Payable

o. Auditor's Opinion

L.O. 7

Exercise 2-20B   *Evaluating cash management*

The data in the following table apply to Melvin, Incorporated.

	2009	2010
Accounts receivable	$ 13,700,000	$ 14,736,000
Sales	232,100,000	251,800,000
Accounts payable	5,872,000	4,527,000
Operating expenses	146,800,000	150,900,000

Required

a. The accounts receivable balance is what percent of sales in 2009 and 2010?

b. The accounts payable balance is what percent of operating expenses in 2009 and 2010?

c. Companies must incur interest expense to obtain cash. To minimize interest expense, companies attempt to collect cash from receivables as quickly as possible and to delay the payment of cash to settle payables as long as possible. Based on your answers to Requirements *a* and *b*, comment on Melvin's cash management.

L.O. 8

Exercise 2-21B   *Ethical conduct*

Required

Name and provide a brief explanation of the six articles of the AICPA Code of Professional Conduct.

L.O. 8, 10

Exercise 2-22B   *Confidentiality and the auditor (Appendix)*

Ben Harpo discovered a significant fraud in the accounting records of a high-profile client. The story has been broadcast on national airways. Harpo was unable to resolve his remaining concerns with the company's management team and ultimately resigned from the audit engagement. Harpo knows that he will be asked by several interested parties, including his friends and relatives, the successor auditor, and prosecuting attorneys in a court of law, to tell what he knows. He has asked you for advice.

Required

Write a memo that explains his disclosure responsibilities to each of the interested parties.

PROBLEMS—SERIES B

Where applicable in all problems, round computations to the nearest dollar.

L.O. 2

Problem 2-23B   *Effect of events on the accounting equation*

Required

Explain how each of the following independent accounting events would affect the accounting equation by writing the letter I for increase, the letter D for decrease, and NA for does not affect under the appropriate columns. The effects of the first event are shown for you.

Letter of Event	Assets	=	Liabilities	+	Common Stock	+	Retained Earnings
a	I/D		NA		NA		NA

a. Collected cash from accounts receivable.

b. Paid a cash dividend to the stockholders.

c. Performed services for cash.

d. Paid cash to creditors on account.

e. Bought equipment by issuing a note payable.

f. Acquired cash from the issue of common stock.

g. Paid cash for salary expense.

h. Performed services for clients on account.

i. Incurred operating expenses on account.

j. Repaid note payable and interest expense with cash.

k. Paid monthly rent expense.

l. Accrued interest expense on a note payable.

Problem 2-24B   *Classifying events as source, use, or exchange and effect of events on financial statements—horizontal statements model*   L.O. 1, 4, 9

The following transactions pertain to Banjo Financial Services for 2009.

1. Business started when it acquired $20,000 cash from the issue of common stock.

2. Paid $1,200 cash for rent expense.

3. Performed services for clients and billed them $10,000. Expected to collect cash at a later date (the revenue was earned on account).

4. Incurred $2,500 of other operating expenses on account (expected to make cash payment at a later date).

5. Paid $1,400 cash on the account payable created in Event 4.

6. Acquired $1,500 cash from the issue of additional common stock.

7. Paid $350 cash on the balance of the account payable created in Event 4.

8. Performed additional services for $4,000 cash.

9. Paid a $500 cash dividend to the stockholders.

10. Collected $8,500 cash from accounts receivable.

Required

a. Classify each of Banjo's transactions as asset source (AS), asset use (AU), asset exchange (AE), or claims exchange (CE).

b. Show the effects of the events on the financial statements using a horizontal statements model like the following one. In the Cash Flow column, use the initials OA for operating activity, IA for investing activity, FA for financing activity, and NC for net change in cash flow. Use NA to indicate accounts not affected by the transaction. The first one has been recorded as an example.

	Assets			=	Liab.	+	Stockholders' Equity								
Event No.	Cash	+	Accts. Rec.	=	Accts. Pay.	+	Common Stock	+	Ret. Earn.	Rev.	−	Exp.	=	Net Inc.	Cash Flow
1	20,000	+	NA	=	NA	+	20,000	+	NA	NA	−	NA	=	NA	20,000 FA

c. What is the amount of net income for 2009?

d. What is the amount of net cash flow from operating activities for 2009?

e. Explain how the closing entries affect the retained earnings account.

Problem 2-25B   *Effect of events on the financial statements*   L.O. 1, 4, 5

Oaks Services experienced the following transactions during 2010.

1. Provided services to customers and received $7,000 cash.

2. Paid $1,000 cash for other operating expenses.

3. Borrowed $15,000 from the bank on March 1, 2010. The note had an 8 percent annual interest rate and a one-year term to maturity.

4. Provided services to customers and billed them $30,000.

5. Incurred $6,000 of other operating expenses on account.

6. Collected $14,000 of accounts receivable.

7. Paid $4,000 of the amount due on accounts payable.

8. Recognized the accrued interest on the note payable at December 31, 2010.

Required

a. Show the effects of the transactions on the financial statements using a horizontal statements model like the following one. In the Cash Flows column, use the letters OA for operating activity, IA for investing activity, FA for financing activity, and NC for net change in cash. Use NA to indicate accounts not affected by the transaction. The first one is recorded as an example.

	Balance Sheet								Income Statement			
	Assets		=	Liab.			+ Stk. Equity					
Event No.	Cash	+ Accts. Rec.	=	Accts. Pay.	Note Pay.	Int. Pay.	+	Ret. Earn.	Rev.	− Exp.	= Net Inc.	Statement of Cash Flows
1.	7,000 +	NA	=	NA	NA	NA	+	7,000	7,000 −	NA	= 7,000	7,000 OA

b. What is the ending balance of retained earnings? What is the amount of net income? Why are these amounts the same in this problem? Give an example of a transaction that would cause these amounts to be different.

c. Determine the balances that would appear in the revenue and expense accounts at the beginning of the 2011 accounting period.

L.O. 3   **Problem 2-26B** *Identifying and arranging elements on financial statements*

The following information was drawn from the records of Irvin & Associates on December 31, 2008:

Land	$97,500	Common stock issued	$10,000
Salaries payable	17,000	Salary expense	22,500
Interest expense	1,375	Beginning common stock	12,000
Accounts receivable	20,600	Ending retained earnings	60,500
Notes payable	35,000	Cash flow from inv. activities	(7,700)
Cash flow from oper. activities	30,800	Interest payable	300
Cash	16,700	Interest revenue	375
Service revenue	51,000	Dividends	2,000
Cash flow from fin. activities	(8,400)		

Required

Use the preceding information to construct an income statement, statement of changes in stockholders' equity, balance sheet, and statement of cash flows. (Show only totals for each activity on the statement of cash flows.)

L.O. 2, 3, 4, 6, 7   **Problem 2-27B** *Two complete accounting cycles*

The following accounting events apply to Hutch Co., which began operation in 2007.

Accounting Events for 2007

1. Acquired $100,000 cash from the issue of common stock.

2. Recognized $190,000 of service revenue on account.

3. Collected $175,000 cash from accounts receivable.

4. Paid the stockholders a $10,000 cash dividend.

5. Paid $90,000 cash for salaries expense.

6. Invested $48,000 cash in a 12–month certificate of deposit.

Information for December 31, 2007, End-of-Year Adjusting Entries

7. Accrued salary expense of $7,000.

8. Recorded accrued interest on the certificate of deposit. The CD was purchased on July 1, 2007, and had a 10 percent annual rate of interest.

Accounting Events for 2008

1. Paid cash for salaries payable of $7,000.

2. Received an additional $60,000 cash from the issue of common stock.

3. Earned service revenue on account of $230,000 for the year.

4. Received cash collections of accounts receivable of $224,000.

5. Paid a $40,000 cash dividend.

6. Paid $70,000 cash for salaries expense.

7. Purchased for $280,000 cash a plot of land on May 31, 2008. The value of the land rose to $300,000 by December 31.

8. Borrowed on June 1, 2008, $84,000 cash on a two-year, 8 percent note issued to State Bank.

9. Received cash for the principal and interest due on the certificate of deposit of $52,800 when it matured on June 30, 2008.

Information for Dec. 31, 2008 Adjusting Entries

10. Accrued salary expenses of $12,000.

11. Recorded accrued interest expense on the bank note (see Event 8 in 2008).

Required

a. Record the effect of each of the events in general ledger accounts under an accounting equation for the 2007 and 2008 fiscal years. In the last column of the table, provide appropriate account titles for retained earnings amounts.

b. Prepare an income statement, statement of changes in stockholders' equity, balance sheet, and statement of cash flows for the 2007 and 2008 calendar years.

c. Determine the balance that would appear in the temporary accounts at the beginning of 2009.

Problem 2-28B   *Effect of accrued interest on financial statements*   **L.O. 2, 3, 5, 7**

Dill Enterprises borrowed $18,000 from a local bank on July 1, 2008, when the company was started. The note had a 10 percent annual interest rate and a one-year term to maturity. Dill Enterprises recognized $52,000 of revenue on account in 2008 and $65,000 of revenue on account in 2009. Cash collections of accounts receivable were $40,000 in 2008 and $50,000 in 2009. Dill paid $24,000 of other operating expenses in 2008 and $28,000 of other operating expenses in 2009. Dill repaid the loan and interest at the maturity date.

Required

Based on this information, answer the following questions. (*Hint:* Record the events in the general ledger accounts under an accounting equation before answering the questions.)

a. What amount of interest expense would Dill report on the 2008 income statement?

b. What amount of net cash flow from operating activities would Dill report on the 2008 statement of cash flows?

c. What amount of total liabilities would Dill report on the December 31, 2008, balance sheet?

d. What amount of retained earnings would Dill report on the December 31, 2008, balance sheet?

e. What amount of net cash flow from financing activities would Dill report on the 2008 statement of cash flows?

f. What amount of interest expense would Dill report on the 2009 income statement?

g. What amount of net cash flow from operating activities would Dill report on the 2009 statement of cash flows?

h. What amount of total assets would Dill report on the December 31, 2009, balance sheet?

i. What amount of net cash flow from investing activities would Dill report on the 2009 statement of cash flows?

j. If Dill Enterprises paid a $1,500 dividend during 2009, what retained earnings balance would it report on the December 31, 2009, balance sheet?

Problem 2-29B *Closing the accounts*

The following data were taken from the records of Valley Company. Except as otherwise indicated, all balances are as of December 31, 2010, before the closing entries had been recorded.

Consulting revenue	$14,500
Cash	28,500
Cash received from common stock issued during 2010	4,500
Travel expense	1,500
Dividends	8,000
Cash flow from investing activities	3,400
Rent expense	2,100
Payment to reduce debt principal	8,000
Retained earnings, January 1, 2010	19,000
Salary expense	6,900
Cash flow from operating activities	1,500
Common stock, December 31, 2010	10,000
Other operating expenses	1,900

Required

a. Identify the accounts that should be closed to the Retained Earnings account.

b. Prepare the income statement that Valley would include in its 2010 annual report.

c. Determine the Retained Earnings account balance at December 31, 2010. Explain how the company could pay cash dividends in excess of the amount of net income earned in 2010.

d. Name the stages of the accounting cycle in the order in which they normally occur.

Problem 2-30B *Missing information in financial statements*

Required

Fill in the blank (as indicated by the alphabetic letters in parentheses) in the following financial statements. Assume the company started operations January 1, 2008, and that all transactions involve cash.

		For the Years	
	2008	**2009**	**2010**
Income Statements			
Revenue	$ 700	$ 1,300	$ 2,000
Expense	(a)	(700)	(1,300)
Net income	$ 200	$ (m)	$ 700
Statement of Changes in Stockholders' Equity			
Beginning common stock	$ 0	$ (n)	$ 6,000
Plus: Common stock issued	5,000	1,000	2,000
Ending common stock	5,000	6,000	(t)
Beginning retained earnings	0	100	200
Plus: Net income	(b)	(o)	700
Less: Dividends	(c)	(500)	(300)
Ending retained earnings	100	(p)	600
Total stockholders' equity	$ (d)	$ 6,200	$ 8,600

continued

Balance Sheets

Assets			
Cash	$ (e)	$ (q)	$ (u)
Land	0	(r)	8,000
Total assets	$ (f)	$11,200	$10,600
Liabilities	$ (g)	$ 5,000	$ 2,000
Stockholders' equity			
Common stock	(h)	(s)	8,000
Retained earnings	(i)	200	600
Total stockholders' equity	(j)	6,200	8,600
Total liabilities and stockholders' equity	$8,100	$11,200	$10,600

Statements of Cash Flows

Cash flows from operating activities			
Cash receipts from revenue	$ (k)	$ 1,300	$ (v)
Cash payments for expenses	(l)	(700)	(w)
Net cash flows from operating activities	200	600	700
Cash flows from investing activities			
Cash payments for land	0	(8,000)	0
Cash flows from financing activities			
Cash receipts from loan	3,000	3,000	0
Cash payments to reduce debt	0	(1,000)	(x)
Cash receipts from stock issue	5,000	1,000	(y)
Cash payments for dividends	(100)	(500)	(z)
Net cash flows from financing activities	7,900	2,500	(1,300)
Net change in cash	8,100	(4,900)	(600)
Plus: Beginning cash balance	0	8,100	3,200
Ending cash balance	$8,100	$ 3,200	$ 2,600

Problem 2-31B   *Missing information in financial statements*   **L.O. 2, 3, 5**

Contour Properties had the following assets at the beginning of the accounting period (January 1, 2008): Cash—$2,000, Accounts Receivable—$2,400, Certificate of Deposit—$5,000, and Land—$22,000. The beginning balances in the liability accounts were Accounts Payable—$1,400, and Notes Payable—$8,000. A $6,000 balance was in the Common Stock account at the beginning of the accounting period. During the accounting period, $3,600 of service revenue was earned on account. The ending balance in the Accounts Receivable account was $4,000. Operating expenses incurred on account amounted to $2,100. There was $2,300 paid on accounts payable. In addition, there was $400 of accrued interest revenue and $700 of accrued interest expense as of the end of the accounting period (December 31, 2008). Finally, a $1,000 cash dividend was paid to the stockholders. (*Hint:* Record the events in general ledger accounts under an accounting equation before satisfying the requirements.)

Required

a. Determine the amount of cash collected from accounts receivable.

b. Prepare a balance sheet as of January 1, 2008.

c. Prepare an income statement, statement of changes in stockholders' equity, balance sheet, and statement of cash flows for December 31, 2008.

d. Determine the interest rate earned on the certificate of deposit.

e. Determine the interest rate charged on the note payable.

f. Determine the balance of the revenues, expenses, and dividends accounts at January 1, 2009.

L.O. 8

Problem 2-32B *Ethics*

Raula Kato discovered a material reporting error in accounting records of Sampoon, Inc. (SI). The error was so significant that it will certainly have an adverse effect on the price of the client's stock which is actively traded on the western stock exchange. After talking to his close friend, and president of SI, Kato agreed to withhold the information until the president had time to sell his SI stock. Kato leaked the information to his parents so that they could sell their shares of stock as well. The reporting matter was a relatively complex issue that involved recently issued reporting standards. Kato told himself that if he were caught he would simply plead ignorance. He would simply say that he did not have time to keep up with the rapidly changing standards and he would be off the hook.

Required

a. Write a memo that identifies specific articles of the AICPA Code of Professional Conduct that were violated by Kato.

b. Would pleading ignorance relieve Kato from his audit responsibilities?

L.O. 10

Problem 2-33B *Types of audit reports (Appendix)*

Lee Moak is a partner of a regional accounting firm. Ms. Moak was hired by a potential client to audit the company's books. After extensive work, Ms. Moak determined that she was unable to perform the appropriate audit procedures.

Required

a. Name the type of audit report that Ms. Moak should issue with respect to the work that she did accomplish.

b. If Ms. Moak had been able to perform the necessary audit procedures, there are three types of audit reports that could have been issued depending on the outcome of the audit. Name and describe these three types of audit reports.

ANALYZE, THINK, COMMUNICATE

ATC 2-1 **Business Applications Case** *Understanding real-world annual reports*

Required—Part 1

Use the Topps Company's annual report in Appendix B to answer the following questions.

a. Who are the independent auditors for Topps?

b. What type of opinion did the independent auditors issue on Topps' financial statements?

c. On what date does it appear the independent auditors completed their work related to Topps' 2006 financial statements?

d. Does the auditors' report give any information about how the audit was conducted? If so, what does it suggest was done?

e. Does the auditors' report tell the reader that the audit was concerned with materiality rather than absolute accuracy in the financial statements?

Required—Part 2

Use the Harley-Davidson's annual report that came with this book to answer the following questions.

a. Who are the independent auditors for Harley-Davidson?

b. What type of opinion did the independent auditors issue on Harley-Davidson's financial statements?

c. On what date does it appear the independent auditors completed their work related to Harley-Davidson's 2005 financial statements?

d. Does the auditors' report tell the reader that the audit was concerned with materiality rather than absolute accuracy in the financial statements?

ATC 2-2   Group Assignment   *Missing information*

Verizon Communications, Inc., is one of the world's largest providers of communication services. The following information, taken from the company's annual reports, is available for the years 2005, 2004, and 2003.

	2005	2004	2003
Revenue	$75,112	$71,283	$67,468
Operating expenses	60,298	58,166	60,061
Interest expense	2,180	2,384	2,797
All dollar amounts are shown in millions.			

Required

a. Divide the class into groups of four or five students. Organize the groups into three sections. Assign each section of groups the financial data for one of the preceding accounting periods.

Group Tasks

(1) Determine the amount of net income for the year assigned.

(2) How does the result in Requirement *a* affect the retained earnings of the company?

(3) If the average interest rate is 7 percent, what is the average amount of debt for the year?

(4) Have representatives from each section put the income statement for their respective year on the board.

Class Discussion

b. Have the class discuss the trend in revenue and net income.

ATC 2-3   Real-World Case   *Unusual types of liabilities*

In the liabilities section of its 2005 balance sheet, Wachovia Corporation reported "noninterest-bearing deposits" of over $67 billion. Wachovia is a very large banking company. In the liabilities section of its 2005 balance sheet, Newmont Mining Corporation reported "reclamation and remediation liabilities" of $445 million. Newmont Mining is involved in gold mining and refining activities. In the accrued liabilities reported on its 2005 balance sheet, Conoco Phillips included $989 million for "accrued environmental costs."

Required

a. For each of the preceding liabilities, write a brief explanation of what you believe the nature of the liability to be and how the company will pay it off. To develop your answers, think about the nature of the industry in which each of the companies operates.

b. Of the three liabilities described, which do you think poses the most risk for the company? In other words, for which liability are actual costs most likely to exceed the liability reported on the balance sheet? Uncertainty creates risk.

ATC 2-4   Business Applications Case   *Decisions about materiality*

The accounting firm of Tucker & Connley, CPAs, recently completed the audits of three separate companies. During these audits, the following events were discovered, and Tucker & Connley is trying to decide if each event is material. If an item is material, the CPA firm will insist that the company modify the financial statements.

1. In 2008, Grant Company reported service revenues of $4,000,000 and net earnings of $240,000. Because of an accounting error, the company recorded $24,000 as revenue in 2008 for services that will not be performed until early 2009.

2. Harris Company plans to report a cash balance of $210,000. Because of an accounting error, this amount is $15,000 too high. Harris also plans to report total assets of $12,000,000 and net earnings of $1,245,000.

3. Morton Company's 2008 balance sheet shows a cash balance of $250,000 and total assets of $9,500,000. For 2008, the company had a net income of $850,000. These balances are all correct,

but they would have been $7,000 higher if the president of the company had not claimed business travel expenses that were, in fact, the cost of personal vacations for him and his family. He charged the costs of these trips on the company's credit card. The president of Morton Company owns 25 percent of the business.

Required

Write a memorandum to the partners of Tucker & Connley, explaining whether each of these events is material.

ATC 2-5   Business Applications Case   *Limitations of audit opinion (Appendix)*

The statement of financial position (balance sheet) of Interlock Company reports assets of $5,500,000. Pam Patel advises you that a major accounting firm has audited the statements and attested that they were prepared in accordance with generally accepted accounting principles. She tells you that she can buy the total owner's interest in the business for only $3,800,000 and is seriously considering the opportunity. She says that the auditor's unqualified opinion validates the $5,500,000 value of the assets. Ms. Patel believes she would be foolish to pass up the opportunity to purchase the assets at a price of only $3,800,000.

Required

a. What part of the accounting equation is Ms. Patel failing to consider?

b. Comment on Ms. Patel's misconceptions regarding the auditor's role in providing information that is useful in making investment decisions.

ATC 2-6   Writing Assignment   *Definition of elements of financial statements*

Putting "yum" on people's faces around the world is the mission of Yum! Brands, Inc. Yum was spun off from PepsiCo in 1997. A spin-off occurs when a company separates its operations into two or more distinct companies. The company was originally composed of KFC, Pizza Hut, and Taco Bell and was operated as a part of PepsiCo prior to the spin-off. In 2002 YUM acquired A&W All American Foods and Long John Silver's units. The acquisition pushed YUM's debt to $4.8 billion. The debt had decreased to $4.25 billion in 2005. YUM's net income before interest and taxes in 2005 was $1.07 billion.

Required

a. If Yum's debt remains constant at $4.25 billion for 2006, how much interest will Yum incur in 2006, assuming the average interest rate is 7 percent?

b. Does the debt seem excessive compared with the amount of 2005 net income before interest and taxes? Explain.

c. Assume Yum pays tax at the rate of 30 percent, what amount of tax will Yum pay in 2005?

d. Assume that you are the president of the company. Write a memo to the shareholders explaining how Yum is able to meet its obligations and increase stockholders' equity.

ATC 2-7   Ethical Dilemma   *Am I being tested?*

In her senior year, Sarah Culver accepted a job as an intern working for a big four accounting firm. The internship provides an opportunity for both the firm and the student to examine long-term employment possibilities. Both parties are on their best behavior hoping that the end result will be permanent employment. Interns typically work a 40-hour week and are paid according to the number of hours worked. Recently, the firm decided that all interns would spend Friday mornings in a training session. The firm planned for the interns to work 9-hour days Monday through Thursday and 4 hours Friday morning to complete a 40-hour work week. Unfortunately, the audit engagement on which Sarah was working was ahead of schedule and everyone was putting in eight-hour days. She would be left alone with nothing to do if she were to stay an extra hour. To resolve the issue, Sarah's senior manager told her to leave with everyone else but to go ahead and report the extra hour per day on her time card. He said that he approved the time cards and no one would know the difference. At first, Sarah was elated. She thought to herself, "I get Friday afternoons off and still get paid for a 40-hour week. How lucky I am to be on this engagement!" However, as she thought about it further, she realized that she was being told to report hours worked that were not worked. It slowly sank in that she was, in fact, being told to overbill the client. She knew the amount was small. Certainly, the senior manager was not trying to rip off the client in some major fraud scheme, but was he testing her ethical standing? Now she was worried.

Required

a. Identify the elements of the fraud triangle that are present in this case.

b. Identify the breaches in the Articles of AICPA Code of Professional Conduct.

c. Speculate on how this real-world case was ultimately resolved.

ATC 2-8 Spreadsheet Assignment *Using Excel*

Required

a. Refer to Problem 2-26A. Use an Excel spreadsheet to construct the required financial statements. To complete Requirement *b,* use formulas where normal arithmetic calculations are made within the financial statements (in particular the statement of changes in stockholders' equity).

b. It is interesting to speculate about what would happen if certain operating results change for better or worse. After completing Requirement *a,* change certain account balances for each of the following independent operating adjustments. After each adjustment, notice how the financial statements would differ if the change in operations were to occur. After noting the effect of each adjustment, return the data to the original amounts in Problem 2-26A and then go to the next operating adjustment.

In the following table, note the new amounts on the financial statements for the various operating changes listed.

Original	1	2	3	4	5
Net income					
Total assets					
Total liabilities					
Total stockholders' equity					
Total liabilities & stockholders' equity					

Independent Operating Adjustments

1. Revenue and the related Accounts Receivable increased $10,000.

2. Revenue and the related Accounts Receivable decreased $10,000.

3. Salary Expense and the related Salaries Payable decreased $4,000.

4. Salary Expense and the related Salaries Payable increased $4,000.

5. Dividends paid decreased $500 and cash changed accordingly.

ATC 2-9 Spreadsheet Assignment *Mastering Excel*

Refer to Problem 2-24A. Complete Requirements *b, c,* and *d* using an Excel spreadsheet. Refer to Chapter 1 problem ATC 1-8 for ideas on how to structure the spreadsheet.

CHAPTER 3

Accounting for Deferrals

The Curious Accountant

Suppose Sarah Greenwood wishes to purchase a subscription to *American Baby* for her sister who is scheduled to give birth to her first child in early September 2010. She pays $12 for a one-year subscription to the **Meredith Corporation**, the company that publishes *American Baby*, *Better Homes and Gardens*, *The Ladies Home Journal*, and several other magazines. It also owns 13 television stations. Her sister will receive her first issue of the magazine in September.

How should Meredith Corporation account for the receipt of this cash? How would this event be reported on its December 31, 2010, financial statements? (Answer on page 127.)

CHAPTER OPENING

LO 1

Distinguish among accruals, deferrals, and allocations.

*In Chapter 2, we defined accruals as the recognition of revenue and expense before the receipt or payment of cash. In this chapter, you will learn that accrual accounting involves deferrals and allocations as well as accruals. A **deferral** involves recognizing a revenue or expense at some time after cash has been collected or paid. For example, if a business collects cash in 2008 for services it will perform in 2009, the revenue is recognized in 2009 even though the cash was collected in 2008. When recognition comes after cash is exchanged, the event is a deferral. When recognition comes before cash is exchanged, the event is an accrual.*

*Deferred amounts may be recognized over several accounting periods. The process of assigning the total deferral to different accounting periods is called **allocation**. To illustrate, assume an attorney received a retainer fee of $30,000 from a client at the beginning of 2008. In exchange for the cash, the attorney agreed to act as a trustee for the client's children for the years 2008, 2009, and 2010. The recognition of the $30,000 of revenue would be deferred until it was earned. A portion of the revenue would then be allocated to each of the three accounting periods based on the amount earned each year. If the work were spread evenly over the three years, $10,000 would be recognized in each period.* ∎

Accounting for Deferrals Illustrated

Record accruals, deferrals, and allocations in a financial statements model.

Topic Tackler

PLUS

3-1

Marketing Magic, Inc.

Stephen Peck is a brilliant young advertising executive employed by Westberry Corporation. Over a three-year period, he created ad campaigns that doubled Westberry's sales. Peck always wanted to start his own advertising agency. He believed his success with Westberry gave him the credibility necessary to attract a respectable client base. When Peck informed his employer of his plans and resigned, Westberry was stunned. The company's executives urged Peck to reconsider and offered a generous raise. Peck declined the offer. In desperation, Westberry agreed to become Peck's first client, paying Peck's new business $72,000 in advance to develop ad campaigns for Westberry. Peck's company, Marketing Magic, Inc. (MMI), began operations on January 1, 2007. The company experienced the following accounting events during its first year.

Event 1   MMI acquired $1,000 cash from issuing common stock.

As discussed in previous chapters, issuing stock is an asset source transaction. If you need help understanding the effects of this event, see Chapters 1 and 2. The impact of the stock issue on the financial statements follows:

Assets				=	Liab.	+	Stockholders' Equity			Rev.	−	Exp.	=	Net Inc.	Cash Flow
Cash	+	Comp. Equip.	−	Acc. Dep.	=	Unear. Rev.	+	C. Stk.	+	Ret. Ear.					
1,000	+	NA	−	NA	=	NA	+	1,000	+	NA	NA	−	NA	=	NA	1,000 FA

The statements model includes several accounts that have not been discussed previously. These accounts are described as additional accounting events are introduced.

Event 2   On January 1, 2007, MMI received $72,000 cash in advance from Westberry for services to be performed from March 1, 2007, through February 28, 2008.

MMI must defer (delay) the revenue recognition until the services are performed (the work is done). The deferred revenue represents a liability to Marketing Magic because the company is *obligated* to perform services in the future. The liability is called **unearned revenue.** The cash receipt is an *asset source* transaction. The asset, Cash, and the liability account, Unearned Revenue, both increase by $72,000. Collecting the cash has no effect on the income statement. The revenue will be reported on the income statement after the service has been rendered. The statement of cash flows reflects a $72,000 cash inflow from operating activities. The effects of this transaction on the financial statements are shown here:

Assets				=	Liab.	+	Stockholders' Equity			Rev.	−	Exp.	=	Net Inc.	Cash Flow
Cash	+	Comp. Equip.	−	Acc. Dep.	=	Unear. Rev.	+	C. Stk.	+	Ret. Ear.					
72,000	+	NA	−	NA	=	72,000	+	NA	+	NA	NA	−	NA	=	NA	72,000 OA

Event 3   MMI signed contracts to provide $58,000 of marketing services in 2008.

Even though contracts for $58,000 of services to be performed in 2008 were signed, MMI did not receive any of the cash due from these contracts, nor has it provided any services related to them. There is no historical activity to record in the accounting records. The effect of the contracts will be reported when cash is received or when services are performed. There is no realization or recognition to report in the financial statements merely upon signing the contract agreements.

Assets			=	Liab.	+	Stockholders' Equity		Rev.	−	Exp.	=	Net Inc.	Cash Flow
Cash	+ Comp. Equip.	− Acc. Dep.	=	Unear. Rev.	+	C. Stk.	+ Ret. Ear.						
NA	+ NA	− NA	=	NA	+	NA	+ NA	NA	−	NA	=	NA	NA

Event 4 **MMI paid $12,000 cash to purchase computer equipment.**

Purchasing equipment is an *asset exchange* transaction. The asset, cash, decreases and the asset, computer equipment, increases. Total assets are unchanged. The income statement is not affected. An expense will be recognized later to reflect use of the equipment. The statement of cash flows shows a $12,000 outflow for investing activities. The effects of this transaction on the financial statements are shown here:

Assets			=	Liab.	+	Stockholders' Equity		Rev.	−	Exp.	=	Net Inc.	Cash Flow
Cash	+ Comp. Equip.	− Acc. Dep.	=	Unear. Rev.	+	C. Stk.	+ Ret. Ear.						
(12,000)	+ 12,000	− NA	=	NA	+	NA	+ NA	NA	−	NA	=	NA	(12,000) IA

Event 5 **MMI adjusted its accounts to recognize the revenue earned in 2007.**

MMI must recognize the revenue earned on the Westberry contract (see Event 2) during the 2007 accounting period. MMI began earning revenue on March 1, 2007. Assuming the work is performed relatively evenly throughout the one-year contract period, the earnings process can be viewed as continual. Recording revenue as it is earned (continually) is impractical, if not impossible. A more reasonable approach is to make a single adjustment to the accounting records at the end of the accounting period to recognize the amount of revenue earned for the entire accounting period. In this case MMI would recognize revenue for 10 months (March 1 through December 31). The amount of the adjustment is computed as follows:

$72,000 ÷ 12 months = $6,000 revenue to be recognized per month

$6,000 × 10 months = $60,000 revenue to be recognized in 2007

The adjusting entry moves $60,000 from the Unearned Revenue account to the Service Revenue account. This entry is a *claims exchange:* the liability account Unearned Revenue decreases, and equity increases (recognizing that the revenue increases net income and ultimately retained earnings). Total claims remain unchanged. The effect of the revenue recognition on the financial statements follows:

Assets			=	Liab.	+	Stockholders' Equity		Rev.	−	Exp.	=	Net Inc.	Cash Flow
Cash	+ Comp. Equip.	− Acc. Dep.	=	Unear. Rev.	+	C. Stk.	+ Ret. Ear.						
NA	+ NA	− NA	=	(60,000)	+	NA	+ 60,000	60,000	−	NA	=	60,000	NA

This effect is consistent with the definition of revenue. Revenue is an economic benefit (an increase in assets or a decrease in liabilities) that results from providing goods and services to customers.

Event 6 **MMI adjusted its accounts to recognize the expense of using the computer equipment during 2007. The equipment was purchased on January 1, 2007. It had an expected useful life of four years and a $2,000 salvage value.**

To measure the net economic benefit of running the business, MMI must estimate how much of the cost of the computer equipment it used in the process of earning revenue. Since the

LO 3

Explain how unearned revenue affects financial statements.

LO 4

Explain how straight-line depreciation affects financial statements.

$2,000 salvage value is expected to be recovered at the end of the equipment's useful life, only $10,000 ($12,000 − $2,000) worth of the equipment is ultimately expected to be used. Assuming the equipment is used evenly over its four-year life, it is logical to allocate an equal amount of the $10,000 to expense each year the equipment is used. The allocation is computed as follows:

$$(\text{Cost} - \text{Salvage}) \div \text{Useful life} = \text{Depreciation expense}$$
$$(\$12,000 - \$2,000) \div \quad 4 \quad = \quad \$2,500$$

This method of allocation is commonly referred to as **straight-line.** The allocated cost of using a long-term tangible asset is commonly called **depreciation expense.** *Long-term* is usually defined as a period longer than one year. Recognizing depreciation expense is an *asset use* transaction. Recall that incurring an expense *decreases* assets or *increases* liabilities. The effects of the expense recognition on the financial statements follow.

Assets				=	Liab.	+	Stockholders' Equity			Rev.	−	Exp.	=	Net Inc.	Cash Flow
Cash	+	Comp. Equip.	− Acc. Dep.	=	Unear. Rev.	+	C. Stk.	+	Ret. Ear.						
NA	+	NA	− 2,500	=	NA	+	NA	+	(2,500)	NA	−	2,500	=	(2,500)	NA

The asset account, Computer Equipment, is not decreased directly. Instead, the asset reduction is recorded in a **contra asset account** called **Accumulated Depreciation.** This approach is used because it increases the usefulness of the information. The **book value** of the asset is the difference between the balances in the Computer Equipment account and the related Accumulated Depreciation account as follows:

$$\text{Book value} = \text{Original cost} - \text{Accumulated depreciation}$$

Both the historical cost of the asset and the amount of accumulated depreciation are reported in the financial statements. This presentation is shown in the financial statements in Exhibit 3.1.

Event 7 **MMI paid a $50,000 cash dividend to the stockholders.**

As discussed in Chapters 1 and 2, the dividend represents an *asset use* transaction. Its effect on the financial statements is shown here:

Assets				=	Liab.	+	Stockholders' Equity			Rev.	−	Exp.	=	Net Inc.	Cash Flow
Cash	+	Comp. Equip.	− Acc. Dep.	=	Unear. Rev.	+	C. Stk.	+	Ret. Ear.						
(50,000)	+	NA	− NA	=	NA	+	NA	+	(50,000)	NA	−	NA	=	NA	(50,000) FA

Summary of Events and Ledger Accounts

Marketing Magic experienced seven business events during 2007. These events are summarized here.

1. Acquired $1,000 cash from issuing common stock.
2. Obtained $72,000 cash in advance from Westberry for services to be performed from March 1, 2007, through February 28, 2008.
3. Obtained contracts to provide $58,000 of marketing services in 2008.
4. Paid $12,000 cash to purchase computer equipment.
5. Adjusted the accounting records to recognize the revenue earned in 2007.
6. Adjusted the accounting records to recognize the expense for 2007 of using the computer equipment purchased on January 1, 2007. The equipment has an expected useful life of four years and a $2,000 salvage value.
7. Paid a $50,000 cash dividend to the stockholders.

The accounting events have been recorded in the following ledger accounts.

Assets			=	Liabilities	+	Stockholders' Equity	
Cash		**Computer Equipment**		**Unearned Revenue**		**Common Stock**	**Retained Earnings**
(1)	1,000	(4) 12,000		(2) 72,000		(1) 1,000	0
(2)	72,000			(5) (60,000)			**Service Revenue**
(4)	(12,000)	**Accumulated Depreciation**		Bal. 12,000			(5) 60,000
(7)	(50,000)						**Depreciation Expense**
Bal.	11,000	(6) (2,500)					(6) (2,500)
							Dividends
							(7) (50,000)

The information in the accounts has been used to prepare the financial statements in Exhibit 3.1.

The 2007 Financial Statements

Exhibit 3.1 shows the 2007 financial statements for Marketing Magic. You should be familiar with most of the components of the financial statements by now. It is still important to trace the effects of all the described transactions to the financial statements. Especially observe that deferrals as well as accruals cause the amount of reported net income to differ from the amount of cash flow from operating activities.

The income statement displays revenue of $60,000 and depreciation expense of $2,500, while the operating activities section of the statement of cash flows shows the $72,000 of cash received from the Westberry contract. The $12,000 cash paid for computer equipment is reported in the investing activities section rather than the operating activities section. The cash effects of purchasing or selling any long-term asset are always reported as investing activities.

Observe the statement presentation for the computer equipment that is shown in the balance sheet (Exhibit 3.1). The accumulated depreciation is subtracted from the original cost to determine the carrying value (book value) of the asset ($12,000 − $2,500 = $9,500). The carrying value ($9,500) is added to the other assets to determine total assets on the balance sheet.

Prepare financial statements that include accruals, deferrals, and allocations.

Video 3.1

CHECK YOURSELF 3.1

Sanderson & Associates received a $24,000 cash advance as a retainer to provide legal services to a client. The contract called for Sanderson to render services during a one-year period beginning October 1, 2008. Based on this information alone, determine the cash flow from operating activities Sanderson would report on the 2008 and 2009 statements of cash flows. Also determine the amount of revenue Sanderson would report on the 2008 and 2009 income statements.

Answer

Since Sanderson collected all of the cash in 2008, the 2008 statement of cash flows would report a $24,000 cash inflow from operating activities. The 2009 statement of cash flows would report zero cash flow from operating activities. Revenue is recognized in the period in which it is earned. In this case revenue is earned at the rate of $2,000 per month ($24,000 ÷ 12 months = $2,000 per month). Sanderson rendered services for three months in 2008 and nine months in 2009. Sanderson would report $6,000 (3 months × $2,000) of revenue on the 2008 income statement and $18,000 (9 months × $2,000) of revenue on the 2009 income statement.

The Matching Concept

You may have noticed that the recognition of 12 months of computer depreciation expense use does not match with the 10 months of revenue recognition. Certainly, the computer may have been used in ways that do not directly match with the generation of revenue. For example, the computer may be used in the current period to generate advertising ideas that

Explain the matching concept.

EXHIBIT 3.1	Vertical Statements Model

MARKETING MAGIC
Financial Statements

Income Statement for the Year Ended December 31, 2007

Service revenue	$60,000
Depreciation expense	(2,500)
Net income	$57,500

Statement of Changes in Stockholders' Equity for the Year Ended December 31, 2007

Beginning common stock	$ 0	
Plus: Issue of stock	1,000	
Ending common stock		$1,000
Beginning retained earnings	0	
Plus: Net income	57,500	
Less: Dividends	(50,000)	
Ending retained earnings		7,500
Total stockholders' equity		$8,500

Balance Sheet as of December 31, 2007

Assets		
Cash		$11,000
Computer equipment	$12,000	
Less: Accumulated depreciation	(2,500)	9,500
Total assets		$20,500
Liabilities		
Unearned revenue		$12,000
Stockholders' equity		
Common stock	$ 1,000	
Retained earnings	7,500	
Total stockholders' equity		8,500
Total liabilities and stockholders' equity		$20,500

Statement of Cash Flows for the Year Ended December 31, 2007

Cash Flows from Operating Activities		
Cash receipts from customers		$72,000
Cash Flows from Investing Activities		
Cash payment for computer equipment		(12,000)
Cash Flows from Financing Activities		
Cash receipt from issue of stock	$ 1,000	
Cash payment for dividends	(50,000)	
Net cash outflow from financing activities		(49,000)
Net increase in cash		11,000
Plus: Beginning cash balance		0
Ending cash balance		$11,000

are sold to customers several years in the future. In the real world, perfect matching is virtually impossible. Accountants must settle for the "best fit" rather than the attainment of perfection. The **matching concept** is applied in alternative ways in order to attain the best fit. Three common matching practices include:

1. Costs may be matched directly with the revenues they generate. An example would be matching cost of goods sold with sales revenue.

Answers to The Curious Accountant

Because the Meredith Corporation receives cash from customers before actually providing any magazines to them, the company has not earned any revenue when it receives the cash. Thus, Meredith has a liability called *unearned revenue*. If it closed its books on December 31, then $3 of Sarah's subscription would be recognized as revenue in 2010. The remaining $9 would appear on the balance sheet as a liability.

Meredith Corporation actually ends its accounting year on June 30 each year. A copy of the June 30, 2005, balance sheet for the company is presented in Exhibit 3.2. The liability for unearned subscription revenue was $239.8 ($127.4 + $112.4) million—which represented about 28.5 percent of Meredith's total liabilities!

Will Meredith need cash to pay these subscription liabilities? Not exactly. The liabilities will not be paid directly with cash. Instead, they will be satisfied by providing magazines to the subscribers. However, Meredith will need cash to pay for producing and distributing the magazines supplied to the customers. Even so, the amount of cash required to provide magazines will probably differ significantly from the amount of unearned revenues. In most cases, subscription fees do not cover the cost of producing and distributing magazines. By collecting significant amounts of advertising revenue, publishers can provide magazines to customers at prices well below the cost of publication. The amount of unearned revenue is not likely to coincide with the amount of cash needed to cover the cost of satisfying the company's obligation to produce and distribute magazines. Even though the association between unearned revenues and the cost of providing magazines to customers is not direct, a knowledgeable financial analyst can use the information to make estimates of future cash flows and revenue recognition.

2. The costs of items with short or undeterminable useful lives are matched with the period in which they are incurred. Examples of period expenses include advertising, rent, and utilities.

3. The costs of long-term assets with identifiable useful lives are systematically allocated over the assets' useful lives. In other words, expenses are spread over the periods in which the assets are used. Depreciation is an example of an expense that is recognized through the **systematic allocation of cost.**

Accountants may use all three approaches within the same company to attain the best possible matching of revenues with expenses.

Beyond matching inconsistencies, you should be aware that some information in financial reports is based on estimated rather than exact measures. For example, the determination of depreciation expense is based on the asset's salvage value and its expected useful life, both of which are estimated amounts. The book value of the asset and the amounts of depreciation expense, net income, and retained earnings are therefore estimated, not exact, amounts.

Finally, the application of the **concept of materiality** may cause inaccuracies in financial reporting. Recall that generally accepted accounting principles (GAAP) apply only to material items. For example, accountants may expense a pencil sharpener in the period in which it is purchased, even though theoretically it should be capitalized and expensed over its useful life. Recall that an omission or misstatement is considered material if the decision of a reasonable person would be influenced by the omission or misstatement. As a result, the reporting of many insignificant items is determined by practicality rather than theoretical accuracy.

Second Accounting Cycle

Marketing Magic experienced the following transactions during 2008.

1. Acquired an additional $5,000 cash from issuing more common stock.
2. Paid $400 cash for supplies.
3. Paid $1,200 cash for an insurance policy that provided coverage for one year, beginning February 1, 2008.

Distinguish among accruals, deferrals, and allocations.

EXHIBIT 3.2 2005 Balance Sheet for Meredith Corporation

CONSOLIDATED BALANCE SHEETS
Meredith Corporation and Subsidiaries
As of June 30 (amounts in thousands)

	2005	2004-Restated
Assets		
Current assets		
Cash and cash equivalents	$ 29,788	$ 58,723
Accounts receivable (net of allowances of $15,205 in 2005 and $14,844 in 2004)	176,669	164,876
Inventories	41,562	31,262
Current portion of subscription and acquisition costs	27,777	35,716
Current portion of broadcast rights	13,539	11,643
Other current assets	15,160	11,794
Total current assets	304,495	314,014
Property, plant and equipment		
Land	19,261	19,454
Buildings and improvements	106,112	110,010
Machinery and equipment	256,380	245,535
Leasehold improvements	8,863	8,819
Construction in progress	8,266	9,313
Total property, plant and equipment	398,882	393,131
Less accumulated depreciation	(205,926)	(197,332)
Net property, plant and equipment	192,956	195,799
Subscription acquisition costs	24,722	26,280
Broadcast rights	7,096	5,293
Other assets	58,589	59,270
Intangibles, net	707,068	673,968
Goodwill	196,382	191,303
Total assets	$1,491,308	$1,465,927
Liabilities and Shareholders' Equity		
Current liabilities		
Current portion of long-term debt	$ 125,000	$ 75,000
Current portion of long-term broadcast rights payable	18,676	19,929
Accounts payable	48,462	42,684
Accrued expenses		
Compensation and benefits	42,162	48,679
Distribution expenses	17,546	19,406
Other taxes and expenses	59,818	32,863
Total accrued expenses	119,526	100,948
Current portion of unearned subscription revenues	127,416	132,189
Total current liabilities	439,080	370,750
Long-term debt	125,000	225,000
Long-term broadcast rights payable	17,208	13,024
Unearned subscription revenues	112,358	120,998
Deferred income taxes	93,929	76,828
Other noncurrent liabilities	51,906	49,356
Total liabilities	839,481	855,956
Shareholders' equity		
Common stock, par value $1 per share	39,700	40,802
Class B stock, par value $1 per share, convertible to common stock	9,596	9,683
Additional paid-in capital	55,346	66,229
Retained earnings	550,115	495,808
Accumulated other comprehensive loss	(1,025)	(427)
Unearned compensation	(1,905)	(2,124)
Total shareholders' equity	651,827	609,971
Total liabilities and shareholders' equity	$1,491,308	$1,465,927

4. Recognized revenue for $108,000 of services provided on account.

5. Collected $89,000 of the receivables due from customers.

6. Recognized $32,000 of operating expenses purchased on account. These are other operating expenses in addition to supplies and insurance and are classified as other operating expenses.

7. Paid suppliers $28,000 of the amount owed on accounts payable.

8. Paid a $70,000 cash dividend to stockholders.

9. Purchased land for $3,000 cash.

Adjusting Entries

10. Recognized the remainder of the unearned revenue. All services had been provided by February 28, 2008, as specified in the original contract with Westberry.

11. Recognized 2008 depreciation expense.

12. Recognized supplies expense; $150 of supplies was on hand at the close of business on December 31, 2008.

13. Recognized insurance expense for 11 months.

Exhibit 3.3 shows these transactions recorded in accounts that are organized under an accounting equation. The transactions are referenced by the transaction number shown in parentheses to the left of the amount. The beginning balances were carried forward from the 2007 ending balances. The parentheses in the expense and dividend accounts indicate the effect of the account balance on retained earnings. For example, the ($32,000) balance in operating expenses does not imply that expenses were negative. In fact, operating

EXHIBIT 3.3

Effect of 2008 Transactions on the Accounting Equation

Assets		=	Liabilities	+	Stockholders' Equity	

Cash

Bal.	11,000
(1)	5,000
(2)	(400)
(3)	(1,200)
(5)	89,000
(7)	(28,000)
(8)	(70,000)
(9)	(3,000)
Bal.	2,400

Accounts Receivable

Bal.	0
(4)	108,000
(5)	(89,000)
Bal.	19,000

Supplies

Bal.	0
(2)	400
(12)	(250)
Bal.	150

Prepaid Insurance

Bal.	0
(3)	1,200
(13)	(1,100)
Bal.	100

Computer Equipment

| Bal. | 12,000 |

Accumulated Depreciation

Bal.	(2,500)
(11)	(2,500)
Bal.	(5,000)

Land

Bal.	0
(9)	3,000
Bal.	3,000

Accounts Payable

Bal.	0
(6)	32,000
(7)	(28,000)
Bal.	4,000

Unearned Revenue

Bal.	12,000
(10)	(12,000)
Bal.	0

Common Stock

Bal.	1,000
(1)	5,000
Bal.	6,000

Retained Earnings

| Bal. | 7,500 |

Dividends

| (8) | (70,000) |

Service Revenue

(4)	108,000
(10)	12,000
Bal.	120,000

Other Operating Expenses

| (6) | (32,000) |

Depreciation Expense

| (11) | (2,500) |

Supplies Expense

| (12) | (250) |

Insurance Expense

| (13) | (1,100) |

expenses increased during the period, which caused net income and ultimately retained earnings to decrease.

Effect of 2008 Transactions on the Accounting Equation and the Financial Statements

LO 7

Explain how supplies affect financial statements.

The effects of many of the 2008 transactions have been explained in previous sections of this book. Those transactions that are new are discussed in the following section of the text.

Accounting for Supplies

Transaction 2 is a deferral. To understand this event, it is helpful to distinguish between the terms *cost* and *expense*. A cost can be either an asset or an expense. If a purchased item has already been used in the process of earning revenue, its cost represents an *expense*. If the item will be used in the future to generate revenue, its cost represents an *asset*. Storing the cost in an asset account enables the accountant to *defer* the recognition of an expense until the future time when the item is used. This explains why assets are sometimes called deferred expenses. Exhibit 3.4 demonstrates the relationship between a cost and an expense. With respect to Event 2, the cost of supplies is placed in an asset account. The expense recognition is deferred until the supplies are used to produce revenue.

Impact on Accounting Equation   It is impractical to expense supplies as they are being used. For example, it is too tedious to record an expense every time a pencil, a piece of paper, or an envelope is used. Instead, accountants expense the total cost of all supplies used during the entire accounting period in a single year-end adjusting entry. The cost of supplies used is determined by the following formula:

$$\frac{\text{Beginning}}{\text{balance}} + \text{Purchases} = \frac{\text{Supplies}}{\text{available for use}} - \frac{\text{Ending}}{\text{balance}} = \frac{\text{Supplies}}{\text{used}}$$

In practice, the cost of supplies on hand at the end of the period (ending balance) is determined by physically counting them. We can now determine that Marketing Magic used $250 (zero beginning balance + $400 purchase = $400 available for use − $150 ending balance). This explains the year-end adjusting entry (Transaction 12) that transfers $250 from the Supplies account to the Supplies Expense account. This treatment is consistent with our previous definition of an expense. Recall that an expense is defined as a decrease in assets or increase in liabilities that results from using assets and services to generate revenue. In this case, recognizing the expense decreases the asset, supplies. The $150 of supplies on hand at the end of the accounting period is reported as an asset on the balance sheet.

Impact on Financial Statements   Observe how the deferral causes differences between the amount of income reported on the income statement and the amount of cash flow from operating activities shown on the statement of cash flows. Of the $400 cash paid for supplies, only $250 is recognized as expense. The remaining $150 is deferred as an asset. Verify these effects by reviewing the financial statements in Exhibit 3.5.

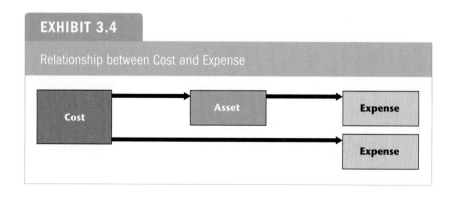

EXHIBIT 3.4

Relationship between Cost and Expense

EXHIBIT 3.5 Vertical Statements Model

MARKETING MAGIC
Financial Statements

Income Statement for the Year Ended December 31, 2008

Service revenue		$120,000
Other operating expenses	$32,000	
Depreciation expense	2,500	
Supplies expense	250	
Insurance expense	1,100	
Total expenses		(35,850)
Net income		$ 84,150

Statement of Changes in Stockholders Equity for the Year Ended December 31, 2008

Beginning common stock	$ 1,000	
Plus: Issue of stock	5,000	
Ending common stock		$ 6,000
Beginning retained earnings	7,500	
Plus: Net income	84,150	
Less: Dividends	(70,000)	
Ending retained earnings		21,650
Total stockholders' equity		$ 27,650

Balance Sheet as of December 31, 2008

Assets		
Cash		$ 2,400
Accounts receivable		19,000
Supplies		150
Prepaid insurance		100
Computer equipment	$12,000	
Less: Accumulated depreciation	(5,000)	7,000
Land		3,000
Total assets		$ 31,650
Liabilities		
Accounts payable		$ 4,000
Stockholders' equity		
Common stock	$ 6,000	
Retained earnings	21,650	
Total stockholders' equity		27,650
Total liabilities and stockholders' equity		$ 31,650

Statement of Cash Flows for the Year Ended December 31, 2008

Cash Flows from Operating Activities		
Cash receipts from customers	$89,000	
Cash payment for supplies	(400)	
Cash payment for insurance	(1,200)	
Cash payment for operating expenses	(28,000)	
Net cash flow from operating activities		$ 59,400
Cash Flows from Investing Activities		
Cash outflow to purchase land		(3,000)
Cash Flows from Financing Activities		
Cash receipt from issue of stock	5,000	
Cash payment for dividends	(70,000)	
Net cash outflow from financing activities		(65,000)
Net decrease in cash		(8,600)
Plus: Beginning cash balance		11,000
Ending cash balance		$ 2,400

LO 8

Explain how prepaid items affect financial statements.

Accounting for Prepaid Insurance

Event 3 is also a deferral. The cost of the insurance is placed in an asset account called Prepaid Insurance (Transaction 3 in Exhibit 3.3). The expense recognition is deferred until the insurance is used.

Impact on Accounting Equation   The amount of the $1,200 cost that represents insurance that was used during the accounting period is transferred from the Prepaid Insurance account to the Insurance Expense account in a single adjusting entry made at the end of the accounting period. In this case the amount of insurance used during the accounting period is computed as follows:

$$\text{Cost of annual policy} \div 12 = \text{Cost per month} \times \text{Months used} = \text{Insurance expense}$$

$$\$1,200 \text{ cost of policy} \div 12 = \$100 \text{ per month} \times 11 \text{ months} = \$1,100 \text{ insurance expense}$$

This explains MMI's $1,100 ($100 × 11) charge to expense for the 2008 accounting period (Event 13 in Exhibit 3.3). The remaining $100 represents an asset, prepaid insurance, that is shown on the balance sheet. Other recording schemes are possible. Some sophisticated computer programs can continually allocate costs between asset and expense accounts. Regardless of the recording method, the ultimate impact on the financial statements is the same.

Impact on Financial Statements   Deferring the insurance cost causes the amount of insurance expense to differ from the amount of cash paid for insurance. The $1,200 cash payment is reported as an operating activities outflow on the statement of cash flows. The used portion of the cost is a $1,100 expense on the income statement, and the remaining $100 is deferred as an asset, prepaid insurance, on the balance sheet. Verify these effects by reviewing the financial statements in Exhibit 3.5.

CHECK YOURSELF 3.2

Rujoub, Inc., paid $18,000 cash for one year of insurance coverage that began on November 1, 2008. Based on this information alone, determine the cash flow from operating activities that Rujoub would report on the 2008 and 2009 statements of cash flows. Also, determine the amount of insurance expense Rujoub would report on the 2008 income statement and the amount of prepaid insurance (an asset) that Rujoub would report on the December 31, 2008, balance sheet.

Answer

Since Rujoub paid all of the cash in 2008, the 2008 statement of cash flows would report an $18,000 cash outflow from operating activities. The 2009 statement of cash flows would report zero cash flow from operating activities. The expense would be recognized in the periods in which the insurance is used. In this case, insurance expense is recognized at the rate of $1,500 per month ($18,000 ÷ 12 months). Rujoub used two months of insurance coverage in 2008 and therefore would report $3,000 (2 months × $1,500) of insurance expense on the 2008 income statement. Rujoub would report a $15,000 (10 months × $1,500) asset, prepaid insurance, on the December 31, 2008, balance sheet. The $15,000 of prepaid insurance would be recognized as insurance expense in 2009 when the insurance coverage is used.

Third Accounting Cycle

LO 1

Distinguish among accruals, deferrals, and allocations.

Marketing Magic experienced the following transactions during 2009.

1. Acquired $1,000 cash from issuing common stock to additional stockholders.
2. Purchased land for $2,000 cash.
3. Paid $400 cash for more supplies.
4. Borrowed $20,000 from a local bank on February 1, 2009. The note issued had a 9 percent interest rate and a one-year term.

5. Paid $1,200 cash to renew the insurance policy for a one-year term beginning February 1, 2009.

6. Recognized revenue for $167,000 of services provided on account.

7. Collected $129,000 of the receivables due from customers.

8. Recognized $62,000 of accrued operating expenses, other than supplies and insurance, charged on account.

9. Paid suppliers $65,000 of the amount owed on accounts payable.

10. Received $18,000 cash in advance from a customer for marketing services to be performed for a one-year period beginning December 1, 2009.

11. Paid an $80,000 cash dividend to stockholders.

Adjusting Entries

12. Recognized one month of the unearned revenue.

13. Recognized 2009 depreciation expense.

14. Recognized supplies expense; $200 of supplies was on hand at the close of business on December 31, 2009.

15. Recognized insurance expense for 12 months.

16. Recognized the accrued interest on the bank note.

The effects of the 2009 accounting events on the accounting equation are shown in Exhibit 3.6.

EXHIBIT 3.6

Effect of 2009 Transactions on the Accounting Equation

Assets			=	Liabilities		+	Stockholders' Equity		

Cash

Bal.	2,400
(1)	1,000
(2)	(2,000)
(3)	(400)
(4)	20,000
(5)	(1,200)
(7)	129,000
(9)	(65,000)
(10)	18,000
(11)	(80,000)
Bal.	21,800

Accounts Receivable

Bal.	19,000
(6)	167,000
(7)	(129,000)
Bal.	57,000

Supplies

Bal.	150
(3)	400
(14)	(350)
Bal.	200

Prepaid Insurance

Bal.	100
(5)	1,200
(15)	(1,200)
Bal.	100

Computer Equipment

Bal.	12,000

Accumulated Depreciation

Bal.	(5,000)
(13)	(2,500)
Bal.	(7,500)

Land

Bal.	3,000
(2)	2,000
Bal.	5,000

Accounts Payable

Bal.	4,000
(8)	62,000
(9)	(65,000)
Bal.	1,000

Unearned Revenue

Bal.	0
(10)	18,000
(12)	(1,500)
Bal.	16,500

Interest Payable

(16)	1,650

Notes Payable

(4)	20,000

Common Stock

Bal.	6,000
(1)	1,000
Bal.	7,000

Retained Earnings

Bal.	21,650

Dividends

(11)	(80,000)

Service Revenue

(6)	167,000
(12)	1,500
Bal.	168,500

Operating Expenses

(8)	(62,000)

Depreciation Expense

(13)	(2,500)

Supplies Expense

(14)	(350)

Insurance Expense

(15)	(1,200)

Interest Expense

(16)	(1,650)

Effect of 2009 Transactions on the Accounting Equation and the Financial Statements

The transactions are recorded in the ledger accounts shown in Exhibit 3.6. The associated financial statements are shown in Exhibit 3.7. Again, you should already be familiar with many of these transactions. Those requiring additional commentary are discussed in the following section of the chapter.

EXHIBIT 3.7	Vertical Statements Model

MARKETING MAGIC
Financial Statements

Income Statement for the Year Ended December 31, 2009

Service revenue		$168,500
Other operating expenses	$62,000	
Depreciation expense	2,500	
Supplies expense	350	
Insurance expense	1,200	
Interest expense	1,650	
Total expenses		(67,700)
Net income		$100,800

Statement of Changes in Stockholders Equity for the Year Ended December 31, 2009

Beginning common stock	$ 6,000	
Plus: Issue of stock	1,000	
Ending common stock		$ 7,000
Beginning retained earnings	21,650	
Plus: Net income	100,800	
Less: Dividends	(80,000)	
Ending retained earnings		42,450
Total stockholders' equity		$ 49,450

Balance Sheet as of December 31, 2009

Assets		
Cash		$21,800
Accounts receivable		57,000
Supplies		200
Prepaid insurance		100
Computer equipment	$12,000	
Less: Accumulated depreciation	(7,500)	4,500
Land		5,000
Total assets		$88,600
Liabilities		
Accounts payable	$ 1,000	
Unearned revenue	16,500	
Interest payable	1,650	
Notes payable	20,000	
Total liabilities		$39,150
Stockholders' equity		
Common stock	7,000	
Retained earnings	42,450	
Total stockholders' equity		49,450
Total liabilities and stockholders' equity		$88,600

continued

Statement of Cash Flows for the Year Ended December 31, 2009		
Cash Flows from Operating Activities		
Cash receipts from customers	$147,000	
Cash payment for supplies	(400)	
Cash payment for insurance	(1,200)	
Cash payment for operating expenses	(65,000)	
Net cash flow from operating activities		$ 80,400
Cash Flows from Investing Activities		
Cash payment to purchase land		(2,000)
Cash Flows from Financing Activities		
Cash receipt from bank loan	20,000	
Cash receipt from issue of stock	1,000	
Cash payment for dividends	(80,000)	
Net cash outflow from financing activities		(59,000)
Net increase in cash		19,400
Plus: Beginning cash balance		2,400
Ending cash balance		$ 21,800

Accounting Treatment for Stock Issue

Transaction 1 demonstrates that ownership interests may be shared by two or more individuals. Millions of individuals and institutions hold ownership interests in major corporations such as General Motors, Sears, Roebuck, and International Business Machines (IBM). The effect of the $1,000 cash acquired from issuing more common stock is no different from the effect of the acquisitions shown previously. The acquisition is an *asset source* transaction recorded with increases in the asset account, Cash, and the stockholders' equity account, Common Stock.

Accounting Treatment for Supplies

The amount of supplies expense is determined as in 2008 except that in 2009 there is a beginning balance of $150 in the Supplies account. Specifically, the amount of supplies used is $350 ($150 beginning balance + $400 purchases = $550 supplies available for use − $200 ending balance). The year-end adjusting entry (Transaction 14) transfers $350 from the asset account, Supplies, to the Supplies Expense account. Again, the amount of supplies expense differs from the amount of cash spent. The operating activities section of the statement of cash flows reports the $400 cash outflow to purchase supplies while the income statement shows a $350 expense.

Accounting Treatment for Prepaid Insurance

The $1,200 policy renewal (Transaction 5) on February 1, 2009, increased the Prepaid Insurance account. Combined with the $100 beginning balance in the Prepaid Insurance account, MMI had $1,300 of insurance coverage for a 13-month period. Since 12 months of insurance were used in 2009, the year-end adjusting entry transfers $1,200 from the Prepaid Insurance account to the Insurance Expense account (Transaction 15).

Accounting Treatment for Bank Loan

The bank loan (Transaction 4) requires recognizing interest expense for the 11 months since MMI received the funds. Interest expense is determined by multiplying the principal by the rate and by the length of time the money has been used ($20,000 × 0.09 × [11 ÷ 12] = $1,650). Because interest accrues as time passes, MMI has a liability at December 31, 2009, for interest expense incurred but not yet paid. Recording the accrual increases liabilities and interest expense as shown in Transaction 16 in Exhibit 3.6.

Accounting Treatment for Unearned Revenue

The cash collection (Transaction 10) is a deferral. Upon receiving the cash, MMI recorded a liability, unearned revenue. Assuming work under the contract is performed evenly over the one-year period, the monthly allocation for revenue recognition is $1,500 ($18,000 ÷ 12). Since one month of service has been provided by December 31, 2009, the year-end adjusting entry (Transaction 12) transfers $1,500 from the liability account to the revenue account. This example shows how revenue recognition may coincide with a decrease in liabilities. Only $1,500 of the $18,000 cash received is recognized as revenue in 2009 ($1,500 is included in the $168,500 of revenue reported on the income statement) but the entire $18,000 is reported in the operating activities section of the statement of cash flows ($18,000 is included in the $147,000 cash receipts from customers). Trace the effects of these transactions to the financial statements.

CHECK YOURSELF 3.3

On January 1, 2008, Lambert Company paid $28,000 cash to purchase office furniture. The furniture has a $3,000 salvage value and a five-year useful life. Explain how Lambert would report this asset purchase on the 2008 statement of cash flows. Also, determine the amount of depreciation expense and accumulated depreciation Lambert would report in the *2010* financial statements.

Answer

Lambert would report a $28,000 cash outflow in the investing activities section of the 2008 statement of cash flows. During 2010 and every other year of the asset's useful life, Lambert would report $5,000 ([$28,000 − $3,000] ÷ 5) of depreciation expense on the income statement. The accumulated depreciation would increase by $5,000 each year of the asset's useful life. As of December 31, 2010, Lambert would report accumulated depreciation on the balance sheet of $15,000 (3 years × $5,000 per year).

THE FINANCIAL ANALYST

Topic Tackler

PLUS

3-2

Suppose a company earned net income of $1,000,000. Is the company's performance good or poor? If the company is Time Warner, the performance is poor. If it is a small shoe store, the performance is outstanding. So, how do financial analysts compare the performance of differing size companies? Financial ratios are very helpful in this regard.

Assessing the Effective Use of Assets

LO 9

Analyze financial statements and make meaningful comparisons between companies by using a debt to assets ratio, a return on assets ratio, and a return on equity ratio.

Evaluating performance requires considering the size of the investment base used to produce the income. In other words, you expect someone who has a ten million dollar investment base to earn more than someone who has a ten thousand dollar base. The relationship between the level of income and the size of the investment can be expressed as the **return on assets ratio,** as follows:

$$\frac{\text{Net income}^1}{\text{Total assets}}$$

---

[1]The use of net income in this ratio ignores the effects of debt financing and income taxation. The effect of these variables on the return on assets ratio is explained in Chapter 10.

This ratio permits meaningful comparisons between different-size companies. Compare Aldila, Inc., a company that manufactures graphite shafts for golf clubs that it sells to other companies such as Callaway Golf and TaylorMade Golf, to Time Warner (TW). In 2005, Aldila's net income was $13.4 million. TW's was $2.9 billion, more than 216 times the earnings of Aldila. However, the return on assets ratios for the two companies reveal that Aldila produced higher earnings relative to the assets it invested. TW's return on assets ratio was 2.9 percent while Aldila's was 27.9 percent. Even though Aldila earned fewer dollars of net income, the company used its assets more efficiently than TW.

Assessing Debt Risk

Borrowing money can be a risky business. To illustrate, assume two companies have the following financial structures:

	Assets	=	Liabilities	+	Stockholders' Equity
Eastern Company	100	=	20	+	80
Western Company	100	=	80	+	20

Which company has the greater financial risk? If each company incurred a $30 loss, the financial structures would change as follows:

	Assets	=	Liabilities	+	Stockholders' Equity
Eastern Company	70	=	20	+	50
Western Company	70	=	80	+	(10)

Clearly, Western Company is at greater risk. Eastern Company could survive a $30 loss that reduced assets and stockholders' equity. It would still have a $50 balance in stockholders' equity and more than enough assets ($70) to satisfy the creditors' $20 claim. In contrast, a $30 loss would throw Western Company into bankruptcy. The company would have a $10 deficit (negative) balance in stockholders' equity and the remaining assets ($70) would be less than the creditors' $80 claim on assets.

The level of debt risk can be measured in part by using a **debt to assets ratio,** as follows:

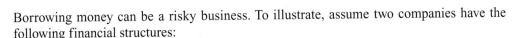

$$\frac{\text{Total debt}}{\text{Total assets}}$$

For example, Eastern Company's debt to assets ratio is 20 percent ($20 ÷ $100) while Western Company's is 80 percent ($80 ÷ $100). Why would the owners of Western Company be willing to accept greater debt risk? Assume that both companies produce $12 of revenue and each must pay 10 percent interest on money owed to creditors. Income statements for the two companies appear as follows:[2]

	Eastern Company	Western Company
Revenue	$12	$12
Interest expense	2	8
Net income	$10	$ 4

---

[2]This illustration ignores the effect of income taxes on debt financing. This subject is discussed in Chapter 10.

At first glance, the owners of Eastern Company appear better off because Eastern produced higher net income. In fact, however, the owners of *Western* Company are better off. The owners of Eastern Company get $10 of income for investing $80 of their own money into the business, a return on their invested funds of 12.5 percent ($10 ÷ $80). In contrast, the owners of Western Company obtain $4 of net income for their $20 investment, a return on invested funds of 20 percent ($4 ÷ $20).

The relationship between net income and the stockholders' equity used above is the **return on equity ratio,** computed as:

$$\frac{\text{Net income}}{\text{Stockholders' equity}}$$

Using borrowed money to increase the return on stockholders' investment is called **financial leverage.** Financial leverage explains why companies are willing to accept the risk of debt. Companies borrow money to make money. If a company can borrow money at 10 percent and invest it at 12 percent, the owners will be better off by 2 percent of the amount borrowed. A business that does not borrow may be missing an opportunity to increase its return on equity.

Real-World Data

Exhibit 3.8 shows the debt to assets, return on assets, and return on equity ratios for six real-world companies in two different industries. The data are drawn from the companies' 2005 financial reports. Notice Hartford's return on assets ratio was 0.5 percent and MetLife's

EXHIBIT 3.8

Three Ratios (in Percentages) for Six Real-World Companies

Industry	Company	Debt to Assets	Return on Assets	Return on Equity
Insurance	Hartford	96	0.5	12.3
	MetLife	94	1.0	15.4
	Nationwide	96	0.5	12.3
Oil	Chevron	50	11.2	22.5
	Conoco Phillips	50	12.6	25.1
	Marathon Oil	57	10.6	25.0

was 1.0 percent. Neither ratio seems good; banks often pay more than 1.0 percent interest on deposits in savings accounts. The *return on equity* ratios, however, show a different picture; Hartford's was 12.3 percent and MetLife's was 15.4 percent—much better than banks pay depositors.

Exhibit 3.8 also shows that while Chevron's return on assets ratio was 23 times higher than Hartford's (11.2 percent versus 0.5 percent), its return on equity ratio was less than double that of Hartford (22.5 percent versus 12.3 percent). How can this happen? Compare the debt to assets ratios. Hartford financed 96 percent of its assets with debt compared to Chevron's 50 percent. This suggests that financial leverage is a contributing factor. While financial leverage can boost the return on equity, it is not the only factor that effects this ratio. For example, notice that compared to all of the companies shown in Exhibit 3.8, Marathon Oil had the highest return on equity ratio, but not the highest return on debt to assets ratio. Certainly, many factors other than debt management affect profitability.

Since financial leverage offers the opportunity to increase return on equity, why doesn't every company leverage itself to the maximum? There is a down side. When the economy turns down, companies may not be able to produce investment returns that exceed interest rates. A company that has borrowed money at a fixed rate of 8 percent, but can only earn 6 percent on its investments will suffer from financial leverage. In other words, financial leverage is a double-edged sword. It can have a negative as well as a positive impact on a company's return on equity ratio.

Finally, compare the ratios in Exhibit 3.8 for companies in the oil industry to the same ratios for companies in the insurance industry. There are significant differences *between* industries, but there are considerable similarities *within* each industry. The debt to assets ratio is much higher for the insurance industry than for the oil industry. However, within each industry, the ratios are clustered fairly together. Distinct differences between industries and similarities within industries are common business features. When you compare accounting information for different companies, you must consider the industries in which those companies operate.

Scope of Coverage

Throughout this text, ratios directly related to chapter topics are introduced. Even so, only a few of the many ratios available to users of financial statements are introduced. Introductory finance courses typically include a more extensive study of ratios and other topics related to financial statement analysis. Many business programs offer an entire course on financial statement analysis. These courses help students learn to judge whether the ratio results signal good or poor performance. Developing such judgment requires understanding how accounting policies and procedures can affect financial ratios. The ratios introduced in this text will enhance your understanding of accounting as a basis for studying more advanced topics in subsequent courses.

<< A Look Back

This chapter introduced the principle of deferring revenue and expense recognition. *Deferrals* involve recognizing revenue or expense at some time *after* cash has been collected or paid. Deferrals cause significant differences in the amount of revenue and expenses reported on the income statement and the amount of cash flow from operating activities. These differences are readily apparent when deferral events are viewed in a horizontal financial statements model. To illustrate, review the following transactions and the statements model that follows them. To reinforce your understanding, draw a statements model on a piece of paper and try to record the effects of each event before reading the explanation in the text.

List of Events

1. Received an advance payment of $1,200 cash for services to be performed in the future.
2. Provided $800 of the services agreed on in Event 1.
3. Paid $900 in advance for a one-year contract to rent office space.
4. Used eight months (that is, $600) of the office space leased in Event 3.

Event No.	Balance Sheet								Income Statement					Statement of Cash Flows	
	Assets			=	Liab.	+	Stockholders' Equity		Rev.	−	Exp.	=	Net Inc.		
	Cash	+	P. Rent	=	U. Rev.	+	Ret. Earn								
1	1,200	+	NA	=	1,200	+	NA		NA	−	NA	=	NA	1,200	OA
2	NA	+	NA	=	(800)	+	800		800	−	NA	=	800	NA	
3	(900)	+	900	=	NA	+	NA		NA	−	NA	=	NA	(900)	OA
4	NA	+	(600)	=	NA	+	(600)		NA	−	600	=	(600)	NA	
Totals	300	+	300	=	400	+	200		800	−	600	=	200	300	NC

The $200 of net income differs from the $300 of cash flow from operating activities. The entries in the statements model make the reasons for the difference clear. Although $1,200 of cash was collected, only $800 of revenue was recognized. The remaining $400 will be recognized in the future when the rest of the work is done. The $400 obligation to provide future services is currently reported on the balance sheet as unearned revenue. Also, although $900 cash was paid for rent, only $600 of rent expense was recognized. The remaining $300 is shown on the balance sheet as the asset *prepaid rent*. In general, costs are **capitalized** (recorded) in asset accounts when cash is paid. Expense recognition is deferred until the time that the assets (capitalized costs) are used to produce revenue. This principle applies to many costs, including those incurred for supplies, insurance, equipment, and buildings. Study these relationships carefully to develop a clear understanding of how deferrals affect financial reporting.

A Look Forward

To this point, we have used plus and minus signs to illustrate the effects of business events on financial statements. In real businesses, so many transactions occur that recording them with simple mathematical notations is impractical. In practice, accountants usually maintain records using a system of rules known as *double-entry bookkeeping*. Chapter 4 introduces the basic components of this bookkeeping system. You will learn how to record business events using a debit/credit format. You will be introduced to ledgers, journals, and trial balances. When you finish Chapter 4, you will have a clear understanding of how accountants maintain records of business activity.

SELF-STUDY REVIEW PROBLEM

Gifford Company experienced the following accounting events during 2008.

1. Started operations on January 1 when it acquired $20,000 cash by issuing common stock.
2. On January 1 paid $15,000 cash to purchase computer equipment.
3. On March 1 collected $36,000 cash as an advance for services to be performed in the future.
4. Paid cash operating expenses of $17,000.
5. Paid a $2,700 cash dividend to the stockholders.
6. On December 31, 2008, adjusted the books to recognize the revenue earned by providing services related to the advance described in Event 3. The contract required Gifford to provide services for a one-year period starting March 1.
7. On December 31, 2008, Gifford adjusted the books to recognize depreciation expense on the computer equipment. The equipment has a three-year useful life and a $3,000 salvage value.

Gifford Company experienced the following accounting events during 2009.

1. Recognized $38,000 of cash revenue.
2. Paid cash operating expenses of $21,000.
3. Paid a $5,000 cash dividend to the stockholders.
4. On December 31, 2009, adjusted the books to recognize the remaining revenue earned by providing services related to the advance described in Event 3 of 2008.
5. On December 31, 2009, Gifford adjusted the books to recognize depreciation expense on the computer equipment purchased in Event 2 of 2008. The equipment has a three-year useful life and a $3,000 salvage value.

Required

a. Record the events in a financial statements model like the following one. The first event is recorded as an example.

Event No.	Assets			=	Liab.	+	Stockholders' Equity			Rev. − Exp. = Net Inc.	Cash Flow
	Cash	+ Comp. Equip.	− Acc. Dep.	=	Unear. Rev.	+	C. Stk.	+ Ret. Ear.			
1	20,000 +	NA	− NA	=	NA	+	20,000 +	NA		NA − NA = NA	20,000 FA

b. What amount of depreciation expense would Gifford report on the 2008 and 2009 income statements?
c. What amount of cash flow for depreciation would Gifford report on the 2009 statement of cash flows?
d. What amount of unearned revenue would Gifford report on the 2008 and 2009 year-end balance sheets?

e. What are the 2009 opening balances for the revenue and expense accounts?

f. What amount of total assets would Gifford report on the December 31, 2008, balance sheet?

g. What claims on the assets would Gifford report on the December 31, 2009, balance sheet?

Solution to Requirement a

The financial statements model follows.

Event No.	Cash	+	Comp. Equip.	−	Acc. Dep.	=	Unear. Rev.	+	C. Stk.	+	Ret. Ear.	Rev.	−	Exp.	=	Net Inc.	Cash Flow	
												Assets = Liab. + Stockholders' Equity						
2008																		
1	20,000	+	NA	−	NA	=	NA	+	20,000	+	NA	NA	−	NA	=	NA	20,000	FA
2	(15,000)	+	15,000	−	NA	=	NA	+	NA	+	NA	NA	−	NA	=	NA	(15,000)	IA
3	36,000	+	NA	−	NA	=	36,000	+	NA	+	NA	NA	−	NA	=	NA	36,000	OA
4	(17,000)	+	NA	−	NA	=	NA	+	NA	+	(17,000)	NA	−	17,000	=	(17,000)	(17,000)	OA
5	(2,700)	+	NA	−	NA	=	NA	+	NA	+	(2,700)	NA	−	NA	=	NA	(2,700)	FA
6*	NA	+	NA	−	NA	=	(30,000)	+	NA	+	30,000	30,000	−	NA	=	30,000	NA	
7†	NA	+	NA	−	4,000	=	NA	+	NA	+	(4,000)	NA	−	4,000	=	(4,000)	NA	
Bal.	21,300	+	15,000	−	4,000	=	6,000	+	20,000	+	6,300	30,000	−	21,000	=	9,000	21,300	NC
	Asset, Liability, and Equity Account Balances Carry Forward											**Rev. & Exp. Accts. Are Closed**						
2009																		
Bal.	21,300	+	15,000	−	4,000	=	6,000	+	20,000	+	6,300	NA	−	NA	=	NA	NA	
1	38,000	+	NA	−	NA	=	NA	+	NA	+	38,000	38,000	−	NA	=	38,000	38,000	OA
2	(21,000)	+	NA	−	NA	=	NA	+	NA	+	(21,000)	NA	−	21,000	=	(21,000)	(21,000)	OA
3	(5,000)	+	NA	−	NA	=	NA	+	NA	+	(5,000)	NA	−	NA	=	NA	(5,000)	FA
4*	NA	+	NA	−	NA	=	(6,000)	+	NA	+	6,000	6,000	−	NA	=	6,000	NA	
5†	NA	+	NA	−	4,000	=	NA	+	NA	+	(4,000)	NA	−	4,000	=	(4,000)	NA	
Bal.	33,300	+	15,000	−	8,000	=	0	+	20,000	+	20,300	44,000	−	25,000	=	19,000	12,000	NC

*Revenue is earned at the rate of $3,000 ($36,000 ÷ 12 months) per month. Revenue recognized in 2008 is $30,000 ($3,000 × 10 months). Revenue recognized in 2009 is $6,000 ($3,000 × 2 months).

†Depreciation expense is $4,000 ([$15,000 − $3,000] ÷ 3 years) per year.

Solutions to Requirements b–g

b. Gifford would report depreciation expense in 2008 of $4,000 ([$15,000 − $3,000] ÷ 3 years). This same amount would be recognized in 2009 and 2010.

c. There is no cash flow for depreciation in 2009 or any other year. The total cash outflow from purchasing the computer equipment ($15,000) would be reported as a cash outflow from investing activities in the year in which the equipment was purchased.

d. The December 31, 2008, balance sheet will report $6,000 of unearned revenue, which is the amount of the cash advance less the amount of revenue recognized in 2008 ($36,000 − $30,000). The December 31, 2009, balance is zero.

e. Since revenue and expense accounts are closed at the end of each accounting period, the beginning balances in these accounts are always zero.

f. Assets on the December 31, 2008, balance sheet consist of Gifford's cash at year end and the book value (cost − accumulated depreciation) of the computer equipment. Specifically, the amount of total assets is $32,300 ($21,300 + [$15,000 − $4,000]).

g. Since all unearned revenue would be recognized before the financial statements were prepared at the end of 2009, there would be no liabilities on the 2009 balance sheet. Common Stock and Retained Earnings would be the only claims as of December 31, 2009, for a claims total of $40,300 ($20,000 + $20,300).

KEY TERMS

Accumulated
  depreciation 124
Allocation 121
Book value 124
Capitalized 140

Concept of materiality 127
Contra asset account 124
Debt to assets ratio 137
Deferral 121
Depreciation expense 124

Financial leverage 138
Matching concept 126
Return on assets ratio 136
Return on equity ratio 138
Straight-line method 124

Systematic allocation
  of cost 127
Unearned revenue 122

QUESTIONS

1. What is the process of assigning the total deferral amounts to different accounting periods called?
2. What role do assets play in business profitability?
3. What does the term *deferral* mean?
4. If cash is collected in advance of performing services, when is the associated revenue recognized?
5. What does the term *salvage value* mean?
6. What is the effect on the claims side of the accounting equation when cash is collected in advance of performing services?
7. What does the term *unearned revenue* mean?
8. How is straight-line depreciation computed?
9. Define the term *depreciation expense.* On what type of asset is depreciation recognized?
10. Define the term *contra asset account.* What is an example?
11. How is the book value of an asset determined?
12. If a piece of equipment originally cost $12,000, has an estimated salvage value of $1,000, and has accumulated depreciation of $10,000, what is the book value of the equipment?
13. What does the term *financial leverage* mean?
14. In which section of the statement of cash flows is cash paid for office equipment reported?
15. What is the difference between a cost and an expense?
16. When does a cost become an expense? Do all costs become expenses?
17. How and when is the cost of the *supplies used* recognized in an accounting period?
18. Give an example of an asset whose cost is systematically allocated over several accounting periods.
19. Explain the *matching concept.*
20. Why is prepaid insurance called a deferral expense?
21. List the three ways in which expenses are matched with the revenues they produce.
22. MSB had $400 of supplies on hand on 1/1/07. It purchased another $1,250 of supplies during the year. If an inventory on 12/31/07 indicates that there were $525 of supplies on hand, how much is its supplies expense for 2007?
23. Explain the *concept of materiality.*
24. What are several factors that prevent the establishment of a global GAAP?
25. How is the return on assets ratio computed? How is this measure useful in comparing two companies?
26. How is the debt to assets ratio computed? What does this ratio measure?
27. How can financial leverage increase the return on equity ratio?

MULTIPLE-CHOICE QUESTIONS

**Multiple-choice questions are provided on the text Web site at
www.mhhe.com/edmonds6e.**

Quiz 3

www.mhhe.com/edmonds6e

EXERCISES—SERIES A

All Exercises in Series A are available with McGraw-Hill's Homework Manager®

L.O. 1

Exercise 3-1A   *Transactions that affect the elements of financial statements*

Required

Give an example of a transaction that will

a. Increase an asset and decrease another asset (asset exchange event).
b. Increase an asset and increase a liability (asset source event).
c. Decrease an asset and decrease a liability (asset use event).
d. Decrease an asset and decrease equity (asset use event).
e. Increase a liability and decrease equity (claims exchange event).
f. Increase an asset and increase equity (asset source event).
g. Decrease a liability and increase equity (claims exchange event).

L.O. 1, 2

Exercise 3-2A   *Identifying deferral and accrual events*

Required

Identify each of the following events as an accrual, deferral, or neither.

a. Incurred other operating expenses on account.
b. Recorded expense for salaries owed to employees at the end of the accounting period.
c. Paid a cash dividend to the stockholders.
d. Paid cash to purchase supplies to be used over the next several months.
e. Purchased a delivery van with a five-year life.
f. Provided services on account.
g. Recognized interest income on a certificate of deposit before receiving the cash.
h. Paid one year's rent in advance.
i. Paid cash for utilities expense.
j. Collected $2,400 in advance for services to be performed over the next 12 months.

L.O. 3, 6

Exercise 3-3A   *Effect of deferrals on the accounting equation*

Required

For each of the following independent cases, show the effect on the accounting equation of both the deferral and the related December 31, 2008, adjustment.

a. Amerigo paid $48,000 for a 12-month lease on warehouse space on September 1, 2008.
b. Earth Services purchased a new computer system for $29,000 on January 1, 2008. The computer system has an estimated useful life of three years and a $2,000 salvage value.
c. Anthony Park, attorney, accepted $22,000 in advance from his client on September 1, 2008, for services to be performed over the next eight months.

L.O. 3

Exercise 3-4A   *Identifying transaction type and effect on the financial statements*

Required

Identify whether each of the following transactions is an asset source (AS), asset use (AU), asset exchange (AE), or claims exchange (CE). Also show the effects of the events on the financial statements using the horizontal statements model. Indicate whether the event increases (I), decreases (D), or does not affect (NA) each element of the financial statements. In the Cash Flows column, designate the cash flows as operating activities (OA), investing activities (IA), or financing activities (FA). The first two transactions have been recorded as examples.

Event No.	Type of Event	Assets	=	Liabilities	+	Common Stock	+	Retained Earnings	Rev.	−	Exp.	=	Net Inc.	Cash Flows	
						Stockholders' Equity									
a	AE	I D		NA		NA		NA	NA		NA		NA	D	IA
b	AS	I		NA		I		NA	NA		NA		NA	I	FA

a. Purchased land for cash.

b. Acquired cash from the issue of common stock.

c. Collected cash from accounts receivable.

d. Paid cash for operating expenses.

e. Recorded accrued salaries.

f. Paid cash to purchase office equipment.

g. Performed services on account.

h. Paid cash advance for rent on office space.

i. Recorded depreciation expense on office equipment.

j. Performed services for cash.

k. Purchased a building with cash *and* issued a note payable.

l. Paid cash for salaries accrued at the end of a prior period.

m. Paid a cash dividend to the stockholders.

n. Adjusted books to reflect the amount of prepaid rent expired during the period.

o. Incurred operating expenses on account.

p. Paid cash on accounts payable.

q. Received cash advance for services to be provided in the future.

Exercise 3-5A *Effect of prepaid rent on the accounting equation and financial statements*

L.O. 3, 4, 6

The following events apply to 2009, the first year of operations of Howard Services:

1. Acquired $30,000 cash from the issue of common stock.

2. Paid $12,000 cash in advance for one-year rental contract for office space.

3. Provided services for $23,000 cash.

4. Adjusted the records to recognize the use of the office space. The one-year contract started on May 1, 2009. The adjustment was made as of December 31, 2009.

Required

a. Write an accounting equation and record the effects of each accounting event under the appropriate general ledger account headings.

b. Prepare an income statement and statement of cash flows for the 2009 accounting period.

c. Explain the difference between the amount of net income and amount of net cash flow from operating activities.

Exercise 3-6A *Effect of supplies on the financial statements*

L.O. 5, 6, 10

Kim's Copy Service, Inc., started the 2009 accounting period with $9,000 cash, $6,000 of common stock, and $3,000 of retained earnings. Kim's Copy Service was affected by the following accounting events during 2009:

1. Purchased $11,500 of paper and other supplies on account.

2. Earned and collected $31,000 of cash revenue.

3. Paid $9,000 cash on accounts payable.

4. Adjusted the records to reflect the use of supplies. A physical count indicated that $3,000 of supplies was still on hand on December 31, 2009.

Required

a. Show the effects of the events on the financial statements using a horizontal statements model like the following one. In the Cash Flows column, use OA to designate operating activity, IA for investing activity, FA for financing activity, and NC for net change in cash. Use NA to indicate accounts not affected by the event. The beginning balances are entered in the following example.

Event No.	Assets		=	Liab.	+	Stockholders' Equity			Rev.	−	Exp.	=	Net Inc.	Cash Flows
	Cash	+ Supplies	=	Accts. Pay	+	C. Stock	+	Ret. Earn.						
Beg. Bal.	9,000	+ 0	=	0	+	6,000	+	3,000	0	−	0	=	0	0

b. Explain the difference between the amount of net income and amount of net cash flow from operating activities.

L.O. 3, 5, 6   **Exercise 3-7A** *Effect of depreciation on the accounting equation and financial statements*

The following events apply to The Taco Factory for the 2008 fiscal year:

1. Started the company when it acquired $21,000 cash from the issue of common stock.
2. Purchased a new cooktop that cost $18,000 cash.
3. Earned $32,000 in cash revenue.
4. Paid $16,000 cash for salaries expense.
5. Paid $7,000 cash for operating expenses.
6. Adjusted the records to reflect the use of the cooktop. The cooktop, purchased on January 1, 2008, has an expected useful life of five years and an estimated salvage value of $3,000. Use straight-line depreciation. The adjusting entry was made as of December 31, 2008.

Required

a. Write an accounting equation and record the effects of each accounting event under the appropriate general ledger account headings.
b. What amount of depreciation expense would The Taco Factory report on the 2009 income statement?
c. What amount of accumulated depreciation would The Taco Factory report on the December 31, 2009, balance sheet?
d. Would the cash flow from operating activities be affected by depreciation in 2009?

L.O. 5, 10   **Exercise 3-8A** *Effect of unearned revenue on financial statements*

Jordan Michael started a personal financial planning business when she accepted $80,000 cash as advance payment for managing the financial assets of a large estate. Michael agreed to manage the estate for a one-year period, beginning April 1, 2009.

Required

a. Show the effects of the advance payment and revenue recognition on the 2009 financial statements using a horizontal statements model like the following one. In the Cash Flows column, use OA to designate operating activity, IA for investing activity, FA for financing activity, and NC for net change in cash. Use NA if the account is not affected.

Event No.	Assets	=	Liab.	+	Stockholders' Equity	Rev.	−	Exp.	=	Net Inc.	Cash Flows
	Cash	=	Unearn. Rev.	+	Ret. Earn.						

b. How much revenue would Jordan recognize on the 2010 income statement?
c. What is the amount of cash flow from operating activities in 2010?

L.O. 3, 4   **Exercise 3-9A** *Effects of deferrals on the accounting equation*

Brawner Consulting Company started the period with cash of $15,000, common stock of $13,000, and retained earnings of $2,000. Brawner engaged in the following transactions in 2008:

1. On January 1, 2008, purchased a copier for $12,000.
2. On February 1, paid $5,400 for insurance for a 12-month period.
3. Purchased $1,800 of supplies for cash.

4. Provided $36,000 of services for cash.

5. Paid $9,000 for salaries expense.

6. On May 1, received $12,000 for services that will be performed over the next 12 months.

Information for Adjusting Entries

7. The copier had an estimated life of four years and a $2,000 salvage value.

8. Recognized the expired insurance.

9. An inventory of supplies showed $250 of supplies still on hand.

10. Recognized the revenue from Event 6.

Required

a. Write an accounting equation and record the effects of accounting events under the appropriate general ledger account heading. (Be sure to enter the beginning balances in the appropriate general ledger accounts.)

b. Prepare an income statement and a statement of cash flows for 2008.

Exercise 3-10A   *Effect of accounting events on the income statement and statement of cash flows*   **L.O. 5, 6, 8**

Required

Explain how each of the following events and the related adjusting entry will affect the amount of *net income* and the amount of *cash flow from operating activities* reported on the year-end financial statements. Identify the direction of change (increase, decrease, or NA) and the amount of the change. Organize your answers according to the following table. The first event is recorded as an example. If an event does not have a related adjusting entry, record only the effects of the event.

	Net Income		Cash Flows from Operating Activities	
Event No.	Direction of Change	Amount of Change	Direction of Change	Amount of Change
a	NA	NA	NA	NA

a. Acquired $70,000 cash from the issue of common stock.

b. Earned $15,000 of revenue on account. Collected $12,000 cash from accounts receivable.

c. Paid $3,600 cash on October 1 to purchase a one-year insurance policy.

d. Collected $9,600 in advance for services to be performed in the future. The contract called for services to start on September 1 and to continue for one year.

e. Accrued salaries amounting to $6,000.

f. Paid $22,000 cash to purchase equipment. The equipment, purchased on January 1, had an estimated salvage value of $2,000 and an expected useful life of four years.

g. Provided services for $9,000 cash.

h. Purchased $1,200 of supplies on account. Paid $1,000 cash on accounts payable. The ending balance in the Supplies account, after adjustment, was $400.

i. Paid cash for other operating expenses of $2,600.

Exercise 3-11A   *Effect of accruals and deferrals on financial statements: the horizontal statements model*   **L.O. 10**

G. Gabe, Attorney at Law, experienced the following transactions in 2009, the first year of operations:

1. Purchased $1,500 of office supplies on account.

2. Accepted $24,000 on February 1, 2009, as a retainer for services to be performed evenly over the next 12 months.

3. Performed legal services for cash of $66,000.

4. Paid cash for salaries expense of $22,500.

5. Paid a cash dividend to the stockholders of $5,000.

6. Paid $1,000 of the amount due on accounts payable.

7. Determined that at the end of the accounting period, $125 of office supplies remained on hand.
8. On December 31, 2008, recognized the revenue that had been earned for services performed in accordance with Transaction 2.

Required

Show the effects of the events on the financial statements using a horizontal statements model like the following one. In the Cash Flow column, use the initials OA to designate operating activity, IA for investing activity, FA for financing activity, and NC for net change in cash. Use NA to indicate accounts not affected by the event. The first event has been recorded as an example.

Event No.	Assets		=	Liabilities			+	Stk. Equity	Rev.	−	Exp.	=	Net Inc.	Cash Flow
	Cash	+ Supp.	=	Accts. Pay.	+	Unearn. Rev.	+	Ret. Earn.						
1	NA	+ 1,500	=	1,500	+	NA	+	NA	NA	−	NA	=	NA	NA

L.O. 7

Exercise 3-12A *Asset versus expense*

A cost can be either an asset or an expense.

Required

a. Distinguish between a cost that is an asset and a cost that is an expense.
b. List three costs that are assets.
c. List three costs that are expenses.

L.O. 6

Exercise 3-13A *Matching concept*

Required

Place a check mark in the appropriate cell of the following table to indicate whether each of the following costs would be expensed through (1) direct matching, (2) period matching, or (3) systematic allocation.

Cost	Matched Directly with Revenue	Matched with the Period Incurred	Systematically Allocated
Delivery van			
Office manager's salary			
Office supplies			
Insurance			
Office building			
Loss on the sale of a warehouse			
Sales commissions			

L.O. 3, 5, 6

Exercise 3-14A *Effect of an error on financial statements*

On May 1, 2009, Tennessee Corporation paid $12,000 cash in advance for a one-year lease on an office building. Assume that Tennessee records the prepaid rent and that the books are closed on December 31.

Required

a. Show the payment for the one-year lease and the related adjusting entry to rent expense in the accounting equation.
b. Assume that Tennessee Corporation failed to record the adjusting entry to reflect using the office building. How would the error affect the company's 2009 income statement and balance sheet?

L.O. 1

Exercise 3-15A *Revenue and expense recognition*

Required

a. Describe a revenue recognition event that results in a decrease in liabilities.
b. Describe a revenue recognition event that results in an increase in assets.
c. Describe an expense recognition event that results in an increase in liabilities.
d. Describe an expense recognition event that results in a decrease in assets.

Exercise 3-16A   *Unearned revenue defined as a liability*

Martin Gantt received $600 in advance for tutoring fees when he agreed to help Josh Smith with his introductory accounting course. Upon receiving the cash, Martin mentioned that he would have to record the transaction as a liability on his books. Smith asked, "Why a liability? You don't owe me any money, do you?"

Required

Respond to Smith's question regarding Gantt's liability.

Exercise 3-17A   *Using ratio analysis to assess financial risk*

The following information was drawn from the balance sheets of two companies.

Company	Assets	=	Liabilities	+	Equity
New	$100,000		$ 24,500		$ 75,500
Old	500,000		220,000		280,000

Required

a. Compute the debt to assets ratio to measure the level of financial risk of both companies.

b. Compare the two ratios computed in Requirement *a* to identify which company has the higher level of financial risk.

PROBLEMS—SERIES A

All Problems in Series A are available with McGraw-Hill's Homework Manager®

Problem 3-18A   *Recording events in a horizontal statements model*

The following events pertain to The Mesa Company:

CHECK FIGURES
Net Income: $10,700
Ending Cash Balance: $21,600

1. Acquired $15,000 cash from the issue of common stock.
2. Provided services for $4,000 cash.
3. Provided $13,000 of services on account.
4. Collected $9,000 cash from the account receivable created in Event 3.
5. Paid $1,100 cash to purchase supplies.
6. Had $100 of supplies on hand at the end of the accounting period.
7. Received $2,400 cash in advance for services to be performed in the future.
8. Performed one-half of the services agreed to in Event 7.
9. Paid $5,000 for salaries expense.
10. Incurred $1,500 of other operating expenses on account.
11. Paid $1,200 cash on the account payable created in Event 10.
12. Paid a $1,500 cash dividend to the stockholders.

Required

Show the effects of the events on the financial statements using a horizontal statements model like the following one. In the Cash Flows column, use the letters OA to designate operating activity, IA for investing activity, FA for financing activity, and NC for net change in cash. Use NA to indicate accounts not affected by the event. The first event is recorded as an example.

Event No.		Assets		=	Liabilities		+	Stockholders' Equity		Rev.	−	Exp.	=	Net Inc.	Cash Flows
	Cash	Accts. Rec.	Supp.	= Pay.	Accts.	Unearn. Rev.	+	Com. Stk.	Ret. Earn.						
1	15,000 +	NA +	NA	= NA +		NA	+ 15,000 +		NA	NA −		NA =		NA	15,000 FA

L.O. 3, 4, 10

CHECK FIGURES

a. Net Income: $52,000

b. Net Income: $15,000

Problem 3-19A   *Effect of deferrals on financial statements: three separate single-cycle examples*

Required

a. On February 1, 2010, Moore, Inc., was formed when it received $70,000 cash from the issue of common stock. On May 1, 2010, the company paid $42,000 cash in advance to rent office space for the coming year. The office space was used as a place to consult with clients. The consulting activity generated $80,000 of cash revenue during 2010. Based on this information alone, record the events and related adjusting entry in the general ledger accounts under the accounting equation. Determine the amount of net income and cash flows from operating activities for 2010.

b. On January 1, 2010, the accounting firm of Wayne & Associates was formed. On August 1, 2010, the company received a retainer fee (was paid in advance) of $36,000 for services to be performed monthly during the next 12 months. Assuming that this was the only transaction completed in 2010, prepare an income statement, statement of changes in stockholders' equity, balance sheet, and statement of cash flows for 2010.

c. Hal's Trees was started when it received $62,000 cash from the issue of common stock on January 1, 2010. The cash received by the company was immediately used to purchase a $30,000 asset that had a $5,000 salvage value and an expected useful life of five years. The company earned $11,000 of cash revenue during 2010. Show the effects of these transactions on the financial statements using the horizontal statements model.

L.O. 3, 6

CHECK FIGURE

b. Adjustment Amount: $4,500

Problem 3-20A   *Effect of adjusting entries on the accounting equation*

Required

Each of the following independent events requires a year-end adjusting entry. Show how each event and its related adjusting entry affect the accounting equation. Assume a December 31 closing date. The first event is recorded as an example.

	Total Assets				Stockholders' Equity	
Event/ Adjustment	Cash	+ Other Assets	= Liabilities	+	Common Stock	+ Retained Earnings
a	−20,000	+20,000	NA		NA	NA
Adj.	NA	+200	NA		NA	+200

a. Invested $20,000 cash in a certificate of deposit that paid 3 percent annual interest. The certificate was acquired on September 1 and had a one-year term to maturity.

b. Paid $6,000 cash in advance on April 1 for a one-year insurance policy.

c. Purchased $1,600 of supplies on account. At year's end, $100 of supplies remained on hand.

d. Paid $9,000 cash in advance on March 1 for a one-year lease on office space.

e. Borrowed $12,000 by issuing a one-year note with 8 percent annual interest to National Bank on May 1.

f. Paid $36,000 cash to purchase a delivery van on January 1. The van was expected to have a four-year life and a $4,000 salvage value. Depreciation is computed on a straight-line basis.

g. Received an $18,000 cash advance for a contract to provide services in the future. The contract required a one-year commitment starting September 1.

L.O. 3, 4

CHECK FIGURES

a. Net Income, 2009: $23,900

b. Net Income, 2010: $22,750

Problem 3-21A   *Events for two complete accounting cycles*

Ohio Mining Company was formed on January 1, 2009.

Events Affecting the 2009 Accounting Period

1. Acquired cash of $60,000 from the issue of common stock.
2. Purchased office equipment that cost $27,000 cash.
3. Purchased land that cost $17,000 cash.
4. Paid $800 cash for supplies.
5. Recognized revenue on account of $46,000.

6. Paid $15,000 cash for other operating expenses.
7. Collected $26,000 cash from accounts receivable.

Information for Adjusting Entries

8. Incurred accrued salaries of $1,800 on December 31, 2009.
9. Had $300 of supplies on hand at the end of the accounting period.
10. Used the straight-line method to depreciate the equipment acquired in Event 2. Purchased on January 1, it had an expected useful life of five years and a $3,000 salvage value.

Events Affecting the 2010 Accounting Period

1. Acquired an additional $15,000 cash from the issue of common stock.
2. Paid $1,800 cash to settle the salaries payable obligation.
3. Paid $3,600 cash in advance for a lease on office facilities.
4. Received $5,400 cash in advance for services to be performed in the future.
5. Purchased $1,000 of supplies on account during the year.
6. Provided services on account of $31,000.
7. Collected $28,000 cash from accounts receivable.
8. Paid a cash dividend of $7,000 to the stockholders.

Information for Adjusting Entries

9. The advance payment for rental of the office facilities (see Event 3) was made on May 1 for a one-year lease term.
10. The cash advance for services to be provided in the future was collected on September 1 (see Event 4). The one-year contract started September 1.
11. Had $250 of supplies on hand at the end of the period.
12. Recorded depreciation on the office equipment for 2010.
13. Incurred accrued salaries of $1,800 at the end of the accounting period.

Required

a. Identify each event affecting the 2009 and 2010 accounting periods as asset source (AS), asset use (AU), asset exchange (AE), or claims exchange (CE). Record the effects of each event under the appropriate general ledger account headings of the accounting equation.
b. Prepare an income statement, statement of changes in stockholders' equity, balance sheet, and statement of cash flows for 2009 and 2010, using the vertical statement model.

Problem 3-22A *Effect of events on financial statements*

L.O. 3, 5, 6

Oaks Company had the following balances in its accounting records as of December 31, 2008:

CHECK FIGURES
b. $1,400
h. $(81,000)

Assets		Claims	
Cash	$ 61,000	Accounts payable	$ 25,000
Accounts receivable	45,000	Common stock	90,000
Land	27,000	Retained earnings	18,000
Totals	$133,000		$133,000

The following accounting events apply to Oak's 2008 fiscal year:

Jan.	1	Acquired an additional $70,000 cash from the issue of common stock.
	1	Purchased a delivery van that cost $26,000 and that had an $7,000 salvage value and a five-year useful life.
Mar.	1	Borrowed $21,000 by issuing a note that had an 8 percent annual interest rate and a one-year term.
April	1	Paid $6,600 cash in advance for a one-year lease for office space.
June	1	Paid a $3,000 cash dividend to the stockholders.
July	1	Purchased land that cost $25,000 cash.
Aug.	1	Made a cash payment on accounts payable of $13,000.

Sept. 1 Received $8,400 cash in advance as a retainer for services to be performed monthly during the next eight months.

Oct. 1 Purchased $900 of supplies on account.

Nov. 1 Purchased a one-year $30,000 certificate of deposit that paid a 4 percent annual rate of interest.

Dec. 31 Earned $80,000 of service revenue on account during the year.

31 Received $56,000 cash collections from accounts receivable.

31 Incurred $16,000 other operating expenses on account during the year.

31 Incurred accrued salaries expense of $5,000.

31 Had $250 of supplies on hand at the end of the period.

Required

Based on the preceding information, answer the following questions. All questions pertain to the 2009 financial statements. (*Hint:* Record the events in general ledger accounts under an accounting equation before answering the questions.)

a. What additional five adjusting entries are required at the end of the year?

b. What amount of interest expense would Oaks report on the income statement?

c. What amount of net cash flow from operating activities would Oaks report on the statement of cash flows?

d. What amount of rent expense would Oaks report in the income statement?

e. What amount of total liabilities would Oaks report on the balance sheet?

f. What amount of supplies expense would Oaks report on the income statement?

g. What amount of unearned revenue would Oaks report on the balance sheet?

h. What amount of net cash flow from investing activities would Oaks report on the statement of cash flows?

i. What amount of interest payable would Oaks report on the balance sheet?

j. What amount of total expenses would Oaks report on the income statement?

k. What amount of retained earnings would Oaks report on the balance sheet?

l. What total amount of service revenues would Oaks report on the income statement?

m. What amount of cash flows from financing activities would Oaks report on the statement of cash flows?

n. What amount of net income would Oaks report on the income statement?

L.O. 4

Problem 3-23A *Preparing financial statements*

e**X**cel

CHECK FIGURES
Net Income: $43,900
Total Assets: $63,900

The following information was drawn from the records of Molina Company at December 31, 2011:

Cash	$13,700	Cash flow from operating act.	$ 7,500
Land	10,800	Beginning retained earnings	8,000
Insurance expense	1,200	Beginning common stock	1,000
Dividends	8,000	Service revenue	90,000
Prepaid insurance	2,500	Cash flow from financing act.	7,000
Notes payable	13,000	Ending common stock	7,000
Supplies	900	Accumulated depreciation	5,000
Supplies expense	400	Cash flow from investing act.	(5,000)
Depreciation expense	2,500	Operating expenses	42,000
Accounts receivable	19,000	Office equipment	22,000

Required

Use the accounts and balances from Molina Company to construct an income statement, statement of changes in stockholders' equity, balance sheet, and statement of cash flows (show only totals for each activity on the statement of cash flows).

L.O. 5

Problem 3-24A *Relationship of accounts to financial statements*

Required

Identify whether each of the following items would appear on the income statement (IS), statement of changes in stockholders' equity (SE), balance sheet (BS), or statement of cash flows (CF). If some items appear on more than one statement, identify all applicable statements. If an item will not appear on any financial statement, label it NA.

a.	Depreciation expense	**t.**	Cash
b.	Interest receivable	**u.**	Supplies
c.	Certificate of deposit	**v.**	Cash flow from financing activities
d.	Unearned revenue	**w.**	Interest revenue
e.	Service revenue	**x.**	Ending retained earnings
f.	Cash flow from investing activities	**y.**	Net income
g.	Consulting revenue	**z.**	Dividends
h.	Interest expense	**aa.**	Office equipment
i.	Ending common stock	**bb.**	Debt to equity ratio
j.	Total liabilities	**cc.**	Land
k.	Debt to assets ratio	**dd.**	Interest payable
l.	Cash flow from operating activities	**ee.**	Rent expense
m.	Operating expenses	**ff.**	Notes receivable
n.	Supplies expense	**gg.**	Accounts payable
o.	Beginning retained earnings	**hh.**	Total assets
p.	Beginning common stock	**ii.**	Salaries payable
q.	Prepaid insurance	**jj.**	Insurance expense
r.	Salary expense	**kk.**	Notes payable
s.	Accumulated depreciation	**ll.**	Accounts receivable

Problem 3-25A   *Missing information in financial statements*

L.O. 4, 5

The following data are relevant to the revenue and expense accounts of Woods Corporation during 2009. The Accounts Receivable balance was $15,000 on January 1, 2009. Consulting services provided to customers on account during the year were $80,000. The receivables balance on December 31, 2009, amounted to $12,000. Woods received $33,000 in advance payment for training services to be performed over a 24-month period beginning March 1, 2009. Furthermore, Woods purchased a $60,000 certificate of deposit on September 1, 2009. The certificate paid 6 percent interest, which was payable in cash on August 31 of each year. During 2009, Woods recorded depreciation expense of $7,000. Salaries paid to employees during 2009 were $32,000. The Salaries Payable account increased by $4,000 during the year. Other operating expenses paid in cash during 2009 amounted to $51,000. No other revenue or expense transactions occurred during 2009. (*Hint:* Compute the amounts that will affect the income statement and statement of cash flows before answering questions.)

CHECK FIGURES
a. Net Income: $950
b. Net Cash Flow from Operating Activities: $33,000

Required

a. Prepare an income statement, assuming that Woods uses the accrual basis of accounting.

b. Determine the net cash flows from operating activities for 2009.

Problem 3-26A   *Using accounting information*

L.O. 5

Jon Richfield told his friend that he was very angry with his father. He had asked his father for a sports car, and his father had replied that he did not have the cash. Richfield said that he knew his father was not telling the truth because he had seen a copy of his father's business records, which included a balance sheet that showed a Retained Earnings account of $650,000. He said that anybody with $650,000 had enough cash to buy his son a car.

Required

Explain why Richfield's assessment of his father's cash position may be invalid. What financial statements and which items on those statements would enable him to make a more accurate assessment of his father's cash position?

Problem 3-27A   *Using ratio analysis to make comparisons between companies*

L.O. 9

At the end of 2010 the following information is available for the Rand Company and the Wolfe Company.

	Rand Co.	Wolfe Co.
Total assets	$245,000	$926,000
Total liabilities	152,000	501,000
Stockholders' equity	93,000	425,000
Net income	20,000	65,000

Required

a. For each company, compute the debt to assets ratio and the return on equity ratio.

b. Determine what percentage of each company's assets were financed by the owners.

c. Which company has the greatest level of financial risk?

d. Based on profitability alone, which company performed better?

e. Do the above ratios support the concept of financial leverage? Explain.

EXERCISES—SERIES B

L.O. 1   **Exercise 3-1B**   *Transactions that affect the elements of financial statements*

Required

Give an example of a transaction that will do the following:

a. Increase an asset and increase equity (asset source event).

b. Decrease an asset and decrease equity (asset use event).

c. Increase an asset and decrease another asset (asset exchange event).

d. Decrease a liability and increase equity (claims exchange event).

e. Increase a liability and decrease equity (claims exchange event).

f. Increase an asset and increase a liability (asset source event).

g. Decrease an asset and decrease a liability (asset use event).

L.O. 1, 2   **Exercise 3-2B**   *Identifying deferral and accrual events*

Required

Identify each of the following events as an accrual, a deferral, or neither.

a. Paid cash in advance for a one-year insurance policy.

b. Recognized interest income from a certificate of deposit before the cash was received.

c. Collected accounts receivable.

d. Paid cash for current salaries expense.

e. Purchased supplies to be used in the future on account.

f. Provided services on account.

g. Provided services and collected cash.

h. Purchased a delivery van that has a four-year useful life.

i. Recognized accrued salaries at the end of the accounting period.

j. Paid a cash dividend to the stockholders.

L.O. 3, 6   **Exercise 3-3B**   *Effect of deferrals on the accounting equation*

Required

For each of the following independent cases, show the effects on the accounting equation of both the deferral and the related December 31, 2009, adjustment.

a. Sandra Dee, owner of Dee's Business Services, purchased a new computer system for $14,600 on January 1, 2009. The computer system has an estimated useful life of five years and a $1,400 salvage value.

b. Queen Supply paid $18,000 for a 12-month lease on warehouse space on October 1, 2009.

c. Bob Sanders, J.D., accepted a $72,000 advance from a client on November 1, 2009. The services are to be performed over the next six months.

Exercise 3-4B   *Identifying transaction type and effect on the financial statements*

Required

Identify whether each of the following transactions is an asset source (AS), asset use (AU), asset exchange (AE), or claims exchange (CE). Also show the effects of the events on the financial statements using the horizontal statements model. Indicate whether the event increases (I), decreases (D), or does not affect (NA) each element of the financial statements. In the Cash Flows column, designate the cash flows as operating activities (OA), investing activities (IA), or financing activities (FA). The first two transactions have been recorded as examples.

Event No.	Type of Event	Assets	=	Liabilities	+	Common Stock	+	Retained Earnings	Rev.	−	Exp.	=	Net Inc.	Cash Flows
a	AS	I		NA		NA		I	I		NA		I	I OA
b	AS	I		I		NA		NA	NA		NA		NA	NA

The columns Assets=Liabilities+Common Stock+Retained Earnings are grouped under **Stockholders' Equity** (Common Stock and Retained Earnings).

a. Provided services and collected cash.

b. Purchased supplies on account to be used in the future.

c. Paid cash in advance for one year's rent.

d. Purchased office equipment for cash.

e. Paid a cash dividend to the stockholders.

f. Received cash from the issue of common stock.

g. Paid cash on accounts payable.

h. Collected cash from accounts receivable.

i. Received cash advance for services to be provided in the future.

j. Incurred other operating expenses on account.

k. Performed services on account.

l. Adjusted books to reflect the amount of prepaid rent expired during the period.

m. Paid cash for operating expenses.

n. Recorded depreciation expense on office equipment.

o. Recorded accrued salaries.

p. Paid cash for salaries accrued at the end of a prior period.

q. Purchased a building with cash *and* issued a note payable.

Exercise 3-5B   *Effect of prepaid rent on the accounting equation and financial statements*

The following events apply to 2009, the first year of operations of Clark Services:

1. Acquired $31,000 cash from the issue of common stock.

2. Paid $21,000 cash in advance for one-year rental contract for office space.

3. Provided services for $28,000 cash.

4. Adjusted the records to recognize the use of the office space. The one-year contract started on April 1, 2009. The adjustment was made as of December 31, 2009.

Required

a. Write an accounting equation and record the effects of each accounting event under the appropriate general ledger account headings.

b. Prepare a balance sheet at the end of the 2009 accounting period.

c. What amount of rent expense will Clark report on the 2009 income statement?

d. What amount of net cash flow from operating activities will Clark report on the 2009 statement of cash flows?

Exercise 3-6B   *Effect of supplies on the financial statements*

Delivery Express started the 2010 accounting period with $1,500 cash, $700 of common stock, and $800 of retained earnings. Delivery was affected by the following accounting events during 2010:

1. Purchased $3,000 of copier toner and other supplies on account.

2. Earned and collected $11,200 of cash revenue.

3. Paid $1,800 cash on accounts payable.
4. Adjusted the records to reflect the use of supplies. A physical count indicated that $600 of supplies was still on hand on December 31, 2010.

Required

a. Show the effects of the events on the financial statements using a horizontal statements model like the following one. In the Cash Flows column, use OA to designate operating activity, IA for investing activity, FA for financing activity, and NC for net change in cash. Use NA to indicate accounts not affected by the event. The beginning balances are entered in the following example.

Event No.	Assets			=	Liab.	+	Stockholders' Equity			Rev.	−	Exp.	=	Net Inc.	Cash Flows
	Cash	+	Supplies	=	Accts. Pay	+	C. Stock	+	Ret. Earn.						
Beg. Bal.	1,500	+	0	=	0	+	700	+	800	0	−	0	=	0	0

b. Explain the difference between the amount of net income and amount of net cash flow from operating activities.

L.O. 3, 4, 5, 6

Exercise 3-7B *Effect of depreciation on the accounting equation and financial statements*

The following events apply to Dill's Diner for the 2008 fiscal year:

1. Started the company when it acquired $40,000 cash by issuing common stock.
2. Purchased a new stove that cost $26,000 cash.
3. Earned $21,000 in cash revenue.
4. Paid $3,500 of cash for salaries expense.
5. Adjusted the records to reflect the use of the stove. Purchased on January 1, 2008, the stove has an expected useful life of four years and an estimated salvage value of $4,000. Use straight-line depreciation. The adjusting entry was made as of December 31, 2008.

Required

a. Write an accounting equation and record the effects of each accounting event under the appropriate general ledger account headings.
b. Prepare a balance sheet and a statement of cash flows for the 2008 accounting period.
c. What is the net income for 2008?
d. What is the amount of depreciation expense Dill's would report on the 2009 income statement?
e. What amount of accumulated depreciation would Dill's report on the December 31, 2009, balance sheet?
f. Would the cash flow from operating activities be affected by depreciation in 2009?

L.O. 5, 10

Exercise 3-8B *Effect of unearned revenue on financial statements*

Albert Suppen started a personal financial planning business when he accepted $40,000 cash as advance payment for managing the financial assets of a large estate. Albert agreed to manage the estate for a 12-month period, beginning April 1, 2008.

Required

a. Show the effects of the advance payment and revenue recognition on the 2008 financial statements using a horizontal statements model like the following one. In the Cash Flows column, use OA to designate operating activity, IA for investing activity, FA for financing activity, and NC for net change in cash. Use NA if the account is not affected.

Event No.	Assets	=	Liab.	+	Stockholders' Equity	Rev.	−	Exp.	=	Net Inc.	Cash Flows
	Cash	=	Unearn. Rev.	+	Ret. Earn.						

b. How much revenue would Suppen recognize on the 2009 income statement?
c. What is the amount of cash flow from operating activities in 2009?

Exercise 3-9B   *Effects of deferrals on the accounting equation*   **L.O. 3, 4**

Lee Company started the period with cash of $22,000, common stock of $12,000 and retained earnings of $10,000. Lee engaged in the following transactions in 2008:

1. On January 1, 2008, purchased a computer for $7,500.
2. On February 1, paid $6,600 for rent for a 12-month period.
3. Purchased $1,100 of supplies for cash.
4. Provided $56,000 of services for cash.
5. Paid $18,000 for salaries expense.
6. On May 1, received $9,000 for services that will be performed over the next 12 months.

Information for Adjusting Entries

7. The computer had an estimated life of three years and a $2,400 salvage.
8. Recognized the expired rent.
9. An inventory of supplies showed $120 of supplies still on hand.
10. Recognized the revenue from Event 6.

Required

a. Write an accounting equation and record the effects of accounting events under the appropriate general ledger account heading. (Be sure to enter the beginning balances in the appropriate general ledger accounts.)
b. Prepare an income statement and a statement of cash flows for 2008.

Exercise 3-10B   *Effect of accounting events on the income statement and statement of*   **L.O. 5, 6**
                     cash flows

Required

Explain how each of the following events and any related adjusting entry will affect the amount of *net income* and the amount of *cash flow from operating activities* reported on the year-end financial statements. Identify the direction of change (increase, decrease, or NA) and the amount of the change. Organize your answers according to the following table. The first event is recorded as an example. If an event does not have a related adjusting entry, record only the effects of the event.

	Net Income		Cash Flows from Operating Activities	
Event No.	Direction of Change	Amount of Change	Direction of Change	Amount of Change
a	NA	NA	Decrease	$3,600
Adj	Decrease	$600	NA	NA

a. Paid $3,600 cash on November 1 to purchase a one-year insurance policy.
b. Purchased $1,000 of supplies on account. Paid $700 cash on accounts payable. The ending balance in the Supplies account, after adjustment, was $100.
c. Paid $42,000 cash to purchase machinery on January 1. It had an estimated salvage value of $6,000 and an expected useful life of four years.
d. Provided services for $9,000 cash.
e. Collected $1,800 in advance for services to be performed in the future. The contract called for services to start on May 1 and to continue for one year.
f. Accrued salaries amounting to $4,000.
g. Acquired $30,000 cash from the issue of common stock.
h. Earned $8,000 of revenue on account. Collected $5,000 cash from accounts receivable.
i. Paid cash operating expenses of $2,500.

L.O. 10

Exercise 3-11B   *Effect of accruals and deferrals on financial statements: horizontal statements model*

Hardin Attorney at Law experienced the following transactions in 2010, the first year of operations:

1. Accepted $32,000 on April 1, 2010, as a retainer for services to be performed evenly over the next 12 months.
2. Performed legal services for cash of $29,000.
3. Purchased $1,600 of office supplies on account.
4. Paid $1,000 of the amount due on accounts payable.
5. Paid a cash dividend to the stockholders of $7,000.
6. Paid cash for operating expenses of $16,200.
7. Determined that at the end of the accounting period $250 of office supplies remained on hand.
8. On December 31, 2010, recognized the revenue that had been earned for services performed in accordance with Transaction 1.

Required

Show the effects of the events on the financial statements using a horizontal statements model like the following one. In the Cash Flows column, use the initials OA to designate operating activity, IA for investing activity, FA for financing activity, and NC for net change in cash. Use NA to indicate accounts not affected by the event. The first event has been recorded as an example.

| Event No. | Assets | | = | Liabilities | | + | Stk. Equity | Rev. | − | Exp. | = | Net Inc. | Cash Flow |
	Cash	+ Supp.	=	Accts. Pay.	+ Unearn. Rev.	+	Ret. Earn.						
1	32,000 +	NA	=	NA	+ 32,000	+		NA	−	NA	=	NA	32,000 OA

L.O. 7

Exercise 3-12B   *Distinguishing between an expense and a cost*

Christy Byrd tells you that the accountants where she works are real hair splitters. For example, they make a big issue over the difference between a cost and an expense. She says the two terms mean the same thing to her.

Required

a. Explain to Christy the difference between a cost and an expense from an accountant's perspective.
b. Explain whether each of the following events produces an asset or an expense.
   (1) Purchased a building for cash.
   (2) Purchased equipment on account.
   (3) Used supplies on hand to produce revenue.
   (4) Paid in advance for insurance on the building.
   (5) Recognized accrued salaries.

L.O. 6

Exercise 3-13B   *Matching concept*

Required

Place a check mark in the appropriate cell of the following table to indicate whether each of the following costs would be expensed through (1) direct matching, (2) period matching, or (3) systematic allocation.

Cost	Matched Directly with Revenue	Matched with the Period Incurred	Systematically Allocated
Expired insurance			
Delivery van			
Land that has been sold			
Office supplies expense			
Sales commissions			
Building			
Supplies used			

Exercise 3-14B   *Effect of an error on financial statements*   L.O. 3, 5, 6

On May 1, 2008, Dobler Corporation paid $10,800 to purchase a 24-month insurance policy. Assume that Dobler records the purchase as an asset and that the books are closed on December 31.

Required

a. Show the purchase of the insurance policy and the related adjusting entry to insurance expense in the accounting equation.

b. Assume that Dobler Corporation failed to record the adjusting entry to reflect the expiration of insurance. How would the error affect the company's 2008 income statement and balance sheet?

Exercise 3-15B   *Revenue and expense recognition*   L.O. 1

Required

a. Describe an expense recognition event that results in an increase in liabilities.

b. Describe an expense recognition event that results in a decrease in assets.

c. Describe a revenue recognition event that results in an increase in assets.

d. Describe a revenue recognition event that results in a decrease in liabilities.

Exercise 3-16B   *Unearned revenue defined as a liability*   L.O. 1, 2

Lei, an accounting major, and Jim, a marketing major, are watching a *Matlock* rerun on late-night TV. Of course, there is a murder and the suspect wants to hire Matlock as the defense attorney. Matlock will take the case but requires an advance payment of $100,000. Jim remarks that Matlock has earned a cool $100,000 without lifting a finger. Lei tells Jim that Matlock has not earned anything but has a $100,000 liability. Jim asks "How can that be?"

Required

Assume you are Lei. Explain to Jim why Matlock has a liability and when Matlock would actually earn the $100,000.

Exercise 3-17B   *Using ratio analysis to assess financial risk*   L.O. 9

The following information was drawn from the balance sheets of two companies.

Company	Assets	=	Liabilities	+	Equity
Termite Terminators	$215,000		$ 58,000		$157,000
Pests Police	675,000		256,500		418,500

Required

a. Compute the debt to assets ratio to measure the level of financial risk of both companies.

b. Compare the two ratios computed in Requirement *a* to identify which company has the higher level of financial risk.

PROBLEMS—SERIES B

Problem 3-18B   *Recording events in a horizontal statements model*   L.O. 10

The following events pertain to Patriot, Inc.:

1. Acquired $9,000 cash from the issue of common stock.

2. Provided $9,000 of services on account.

3. Provided services for $4,000 cash.

4. Received $2,500 cash in advance for services to be performed in the future.

5. Collected $7,000 cash from the account receivable created in Event 2.
6. Paid $1,100 for cash expenses.
7. Performed $1,500 of the services agreed to in Event 4.
8. Incurred $2,800 of expenses on account.
9. Paid $3,600 cash in advance for one-year contract to rent office space.
10. Paid $2,200 cash on the account payable created in Event 8.
11. Paid a $2,000 cash dividend to the stockholders.
12. Recognized rent expense for nine months' use of office space acquired in Event 9.

Required

Show the effects of the events on the financial statements using a horizontal statements model like the following one. In the Cash Flows column, use the letters OA to designate operating activity, IA for investing activity, FA for financing activity, and NC for net change in cash. Use NA to indicate accounts not affected by the event. The first event is recorded as an example.

Event No.	Assets			=	Liabilities		+	Stockholders' Equity		Rev.	−	Exp.	=	Net Inc.	Cash Flows	
	Cash +	Accts. Rec. +	Prep. Rent =		Accts. Pay. +	Unearn. Rev. +		Common Stock +	Ret. Earn.							
1	9,000 +	NA +	NA =		NA +	NA +		9,000 +	NA	NA	−	NA =		NA	9,000	FA

L.O. 3, 4, 10   **Problem 3-19B**   *Effect of deferrals on financial statements: three separate single-cycle examples*

Required

a. On February 1, 2009, Best Company was formed when it acquired $12,000 cash from the issue of common stock. On June 1, 2009, the company paid $3,300 cash in advance to rent office space for 12 months. The office space was used as a place to consult with clients. The consulting activity generated $5,200 of cash revenue during 2009. Based on this information alone, record the events in general ledger accounts under the accounting equation. Determine the amount of net income and cash flows from operating activities for 2009.

b. On August 1, 2010, the consulting firm of Tucker & Associates was formed. On September 1, 2010, the company received a $15,000 retainer (was paid in advance) for monthly services to be performed over a one-year period. Assuming that this was the only transaction completed in 2010, prepare an income statement, statement of changes in stockholders' equity, balance sheet, and statement of cash flows for 2010.

c. Hawk Company was started when it acquired $8,000 cash from the issue of common stock on January 1, 2008. The company immediately used the cash received to purchase an $8,000 machine that had a $500 salvage value and an expected useful life of four years. The machine was used to produce $6,000 of cash revenue during the accounting period. Show the effects of these transactions on the financial statements using the horizontal statements model.

L.O. 3, 6   **Problem 3-20B**   *Effect of adjusting entries on the accounting equation*

Required

Each of the following independent events requires a year-end adjusting entry. Show how each event and its related adjusting entry affects the accounting equation. Assume a December 31 closing date. The first event is recorded as an example.

Event/ Adjustment	Total Assets					Stockholders' Equity		
	Cash	+	Other Assets	=	Liabilities	+	Common Stock	+ Retained Earnings
a	−6,000	+	+6,000	=	NA	+	NA	+ NA
Adj.	NA		−1,500		NA		NA	−1,500

a. Paid $6,000 cash in advance on October 1 for a one-year insurance policy.

b. Borrowed $20,000 by issuing a one-year note with 9 percent annual interest to National Bank on April 1.

c. Paid $21,000 cash to purchase a delivery van on January 1. The van was expected to have a four-year life and a $3,000 salvage value. Depreciation is computed on a straight-line basis.

d. Received an $1,800 cash advance for a contract to provide services in the future. The contract required a one-year commitment, starting April 1.

e. Purchased $900 of supplies on account. At year's end, $210 of supplies remained on hand.

f. Invested $8,000 cash in a certificate of deposit that paid 6 percent annual interest. The certificate was acquired on May 1 and had a one-year term to maturity.

g. Paid $8,400 cash in advance on August 1 for a one-year lease on office space.

Problem 3-21B *Events for two complete accounting cycles*

L.O. 3, 4

Covington Company was formed on January 1, 2008.

Events Affecting the 2005 Accounting Period

1. Acquired $30,000 cash from the issue of common stock.
2. Purchased communication equipment that cost $6,000 cash.
3. Purchased land that cost $18,000 cash.
4. Paid $500 cash for supplies.
5. Recognized revenue on account of $12,000.
6. Paid $2,400 cash for other operating expenses.
7. Collected $9,000 cash from accounts receivable.

Information for Adjusting Entries

8. Incurred accrued salaries of $3,500 on December 31, 2008.
9. Had $50 of supplies on hand at the end of the accounting period.
10. Used the straight-line method to depreciate the equipment acquired in Event 2. Purchased on January 1, the equipment had an expected useful life of four years and a $2,000 salvage value,

Events Affecting the 2009 Accounting Period

1. Acquired $9,000 cash from the issue of common stock.
2. Paid $3,500 cash to settle the salaries payable obligation.
3. Paid $7,200 cash in advance for a lease on computer equipment.
4. Received $8,400 cash in advance for services to be performed in the future.
5. Purchased $1,500 of supplies on account during the year.
6. Provided services on account of $11,000.
7. Collected $10,000 cash from accounts receivable.
8. Paid a cash dividend of $2,000 to the stockholders.

Information for Adjusting Entries

9. The advance payment for rental of the computer equipment (see Event 3) was made on February 1 for a one-year term.
10. The cash advance for services to be provided in the future was collected on October 1 (see Event 4). The one-year contract started on October 1.
11. Had $200 of supplies remaining on hand at the end of the period.
12. Recorded depreciation on the computer equipment for 2009.
13. Incurred accrued salaries of $6,000 at the end of the accounting period.

Required

a. Identify each event affecting the 2008 and 2009 accounting periods as an asset source (AS), asset use (AU), asset exchange (AE), or claims exchange (CE). Record the effects of each event under the appropriate general ledger account headings of the accounting equation.

b. Prepare an income statement, statement of changes in stockholders' equity, balance sheet, and statement of cash flows for 2008 and 2009, using the vertical statements model.

L.O. 3, 5, 6

Problem 3-22B   *Effect of events on financial statements*

Porser Company had the following balances in its accounting records as of December 31, 2008:

Assets		Claims	
Cash	$26,000	Accounts payable	$ 5,000
Accounts receivable	9,000	Common stock	28,000
Land	42,000	Retained earnings	44,000
Total	$77,000	Total	$77,000

The following accounting events apply to Porser Company's 2009 fiscal year:

Jan.	1	Acquired $15,000 cash from the issue of common stock.
	1	Purchased a truck that cost $22,000 and had a $2,000 salvage value and a four-year useful life.
Feb.	1	Borrowed $12,000 by issuing a note that had a 9 percent annual interest rate and a one-year term.
	1	Paid $3,000 cash in advance for a one-year lease for office space.
Mar.	1	Paid a $2,000 cash dividend to the stockholders.
April	1	Purchased land that cost $28,000 cash.
May	1	Made a cash payment on accounts payable of $4,000.
July	1	Received $5,400 cash in advance as a retainer for services to be performed monthly over the next 12 months.
Sept.	1	Sold land for $42,000 that originally cost $42,000.
Oct.	1	Purchased $5,000 of supplies on account.
Nov.	1	Purchased a one-year $50,000 certificate of deposit that paid a 6 percent annual rate of interest.
Dec.	31	Earned $42,000 of service revenue on account during the year.
	31	Received cash collections from accounts receivable amounting to $40,000.
	31	Incurred other operating expenses on account during the year that amounted to $6,000.
	31	Incurred accrued salaries expense of $5,200.
	31	Had $200 of supplies on hand at the end of the period.

Required

Based on the preceding information, answer the following questions. All questions pertain to the 2009 financial statements. (*Hint:* Enter items in general ledger accounts under the accounting equation before answering the questions.)

a. Based on the preceding transactions, identify five additional adjustments and describe them.

b. What amount of interest expense would Porser report on the income statement?

c. What amount of net cash flow from operating activities would Porser report on the statement of cash flows?

d. What amount of rent expense would Porser report in the income statement?

e. What amount of total liabilities would Porser report on the balance sheet?

f. What amount of supplies expense would Porser report on the income statement?

g. What amount of unearned revenue would Porser report on the balance sheet?

h. What amount of net cash flow from investing activities would Porser report on the statement of cash flows?

i. What amount of interest payable would Porser report on the balance sheet?

j. What amount of total expenses would Porser report on the income statement?

k. What amount of retained earnings would Porser report on the balance sheet?

l. What amount of service revenues would Porser report on the income statement?

m. What amount of cash flows from financing activities would Porser report on the statement of cash flows?

n. What amount of net income would Porser report on the income statement?

L.O. 4

Problem 3-23B   *Preparing financial statements*

The following accounts and balances were drawn from the records of State Company:

Required

Use the accounts and balances from State Company to construct an income statement, statement of changes in stockholders' equity, balance sheet, and statement of cash flows. (Show only totals for each activity on the statement of cash flows.)

Supplies	$ 500	Beginning retained earnings	$16,000
Cash flow from investing act.	(8,800)	Cash flow from financing act.	–0–
Prepaid insurance	600	Depreciation expense	1,800
Service revenue	48,600	Dividends	6,000
Operating expenses	35,000	Cash	9,000
Supplies expense	900	Accounts receivable	6,000
Insurance expense	2,100	Office equipment	16,000
Beginning common stock	28,000	Accumulated depreciation	8,000
Cash flow from operating act.	11,200	Land	41,000
Common stock issued	8,000	Accounts payable	10,300

Problem 3-24B *Relationship of accounts to financial statements*

L.O. 5

Required

Identify whether each of the following items would appear on the income statement (IS), statement of changes in stockholders' equity (SE), balance sheet (BS), or statement of cash flows (CF). Some items may appear on more than one statement; if so, identify all applicable statements. If an item would not appear on any financial statement, label it NA.

a. Interest receivable
b. Salary expense
c. Notes receivable
d. Unearned revenue
e. Cash flow from investing activities
f. Insurance expense
g. Ending retained earnings
h. Accumulated depreciation
i. Supplies
j. Beginning retained earnings
k. Certificate of deposit
l. Cash flow from financing activities
m. Accounts receivable
n. Prepaid insurance
o. Cash
p. Interest expense
q. Accounts payable
r. Beginning common stock
s. Dividends

t. Total assets
u. Consulting revenue
v. Depreciation expense
w. Supplies expense
x. Salaries payable
y. Notes payable
z. Ending common stock
aa. Interest payable
bb. Office equipment
cc. Interest revenue
dd. Land
ee. Operating expenses
ff. Total liabilities
gg. Debt to equity ratio
hh. Rent expense
ii. Net income
jj. Service revenue
kk. Cash flow from operating activities
ll. Return on assets ratio

Problem 3-25B *Missing information in financial statements*

L.O. 4, 5

Vision Technology started the 2009 accounting period with $7,000 cash, accounts receivable of $9,000, prepaid rent of $4,500, supplies of $150, computers that cost $35,000, accumulated depreciation on computers of $7,000, accounts payable of $12,000, and common stock of $15,000. During 2009, Vision recognized $95,000 of revenue on account and collected $84,000 of cash from accounts receivable. It paid $5,000 cash for rent in advance and reported $7,000 of rent expense on the income statement. Vision paid $1,200 cash for supplies, and the income statement reported supplies expense of $1,100. Depreciation expense reported on the income statement amounted to $3,500. It incurred $38,600 of operating expenses on account and paid $34,000 cash toward the settlement of accounts payable. The company acquired capital of $10,000 cash from the issue of common stock. A $700 cash dividend was paid. (*Hint:* Record the events under the general ledger accounts of an accounting equation before satisfying the requirements.)

Required

a. Determine the balance in the Retained Earnings account at the beginning of the accounting period.
b. Prepare an income statement, statement of changes in stockholders' equity, balance sheet, and statement of cash flows as of the end of the accounting period.

L.O. 5

Problem 3-26B *Using accounting information*

Rene Hugh is trying to decide whether to start a small business or put her capital into a savings account. To help her make a decision, two of her friends shared their investing experiences with her. Tom Eubanks had started a small business three years ago. As of the end of the most recent year of operations, Eubanks's business had total assets of $225,000 and net income of $27,000. The second friend, Elaine Parker, had deposited $40,000 in a bank savings account that paid $2,000 in interest during the last year.

Required

a. Assume you are an investment counselor. Explain to Hugh how the return on assets ratio shows whether Eubanks's or Parker's investment is producing a higher return.

b. Using your personal judgment, identify any other factors that Hugh should consider before she decides whether to start her own business or deposit her money in a savings account. Recommend to Hugh which alternative you think she should accept.

L.O. 9

Problem 3-27B *Using ratio analysis to make comparisons between companies*

At the end of 2010, the following information is available for Richard's Rocks and Jenny's Gems.

	Richard's Rocks	Jenny's Gems
Total assets	$127,000	$753,000
Total liabilities	93,000	452,000
Stockholders' equity	34,000	301,000
Net income	8,000	45,000

Required

a. For each company, compute the debt to assets ratio and the return on equity ratio.

b. Determine what percentage of each company's assets were financed by the owners.

c. Which company has the greatest level of financial risk?

d. Based on profitability alone, which company performed better?

e. Do the above ratios support the concept of financial leverage? Explain.

ANALYZE, THINK, COMMUNICATE

ATC 3-1 **Business Applications Case** *Understanding real-world annual reports*

Required—Part 1

Use the Topps Company's annual report in Appendix B to answer the following questions.

a. What was Topps' debt to assets ratio for 2006 and 2005?

b. What was Topps' return on assets ratio for 2006 and 2005?

c. What was Topps' return on equity ratio for 2006 and 2005?

d. Why was Topps' return on equity ratio higher than its return on assets ratio for 2006 and 2005?

Required—Part 2

Use the Harley-Davidson's annual report that came with this book to answer the following questions.

a. What was Harley-Davidson's debt to assets ratio for 2005 and 2004? (Note, total liabilities must be computed.)

b. What was Harley-Davidson's return on assets ratio for 2005 and 2004?

c. What was Harley-Davidson's return on equity ratio for 2005 and 2004?

d. The difference between Harley-Davidson's return on equity ratio and its return on assets ratio for 2005 was greater than in 2004. What explains this?

Required—Part 3

a. Looking only at the debt to assets ratios for Topps and Harley-Davidson, which company appears to have the higher financial risk?

b. Looking only at the return on assets ratios and return on equity ratios for Topps and Harley-Davidson, which company appears to be the more profitable?

ATC 3-2   Group Assignment   *Missing information*

Little Theater Group is a local performing arts group that sponsors various theater productions. The company sells season tickets for the regular performances. It also sells tickets to individual perform-ances called *door sales*. The season tickets are sold in June, July, and August for the season that runs from September through April of each year. The season tickets package contains tickets to eight per-formances, one per month. The first year of operations was 2008. All revenue not from season ticket sales is from door sales. The following selected information was taken from the financial records for December 31, 2008, 2009, and 2010, at the company's year end:

	2008	2009	2010
Revenue (per income statement)	$450,000	$575,000	$625,000
Unearned revenue (per balance sheet)	127,000	249,000	275,000
Operating expense	231,000	326,000	428,000

Required

a. Divide the class into groups consisting of four or five students. Organize the groups into three sec-tions. Assign the groups in each section the financial data for one of the preceding accounting periods.

Group Tasks

1. Determine the total amount of season ticket sales for the year assigned.
2. Determine the total amount of door sales for the year assigned.
3. Compute the net income for the year assigned.
4. Have a representative of each section put its income statement on the board.

Class Discussion

b. Compare the income statements for 2008, 2009, and 2010. Discuss the revenue trend; that is, are door sales increasing more than season ticket sales? What is the company's growth pattern?

ATC 3-3   Real-World Case   *Ratio analysis to assess profitability and risk*

The following table provides the net earnings, total assets, and total liabilities for four companies from two different industries. The data are for the fiscal years ending in 2005. *All numbers are millions of dollars.*

	Net Earnings	Total Assets	Total Liabilities
Banking Industry			
Sun Trust Bank	$1,987	$179,713	$162,825
Wells Fargo & Co.	7,671	481,741	441,081
Home Construction Industry			
Pulte Homes	1,492	13,048	7,091
Ryland Group	447	3,387	1,836

Required

a. Compute the debt to assets ratio, return on assets ratio, and the return on equity ratio for each com-pany. Show all computations.

b. Which company appears to be using its assets most efficiently?

c. Which company appears to be earning the best return for its owners?

d. Which company appears to have the greatest financial risk?

e. Use the information developed for Requirement *a* to demonstrate the concept of financial leverage.

ATC 3-4   Business Applications Case   *Performing ratio analysis using real-world data*

The following data were taken from Yahoo, Inc.'s 2005 annual report. *All dollar amounts are in millions.*

	Fiscal Years Ending	
	December 31, 2005	December 31, 2004
Total assets	$10,831.8	$9,178.2
Total liabilities		
Stockholders' equity	8,566.4	7,101.4
Net income	1,896.2	839.6

Required

a. For each year, compute Yahoo's debt to assets ratio, return on assets ratio, and return on equity ratio. You will need to compute total liabilities.

b. Did the company's level of financial risk increase or decrease from 2004 to 2005?

c. In which year did the company appear to manage its assets most efficiently?

d. Do the above ratios support the concept of financial leverage? Explain.

ATC 3-5   Business Applications Case   *Performing ratio analysis using real-world data*

The following data were taken from the 2005 annual reports of Biogen Idec, Inc., and Genentech, Inc. Both companies are leaders in biotechnology. *All dollar amounts are in millions.*

	Biogen Idec	Genentech
	December 31, 2005	December 31, 2005
Total assets	$8,366.9	$12,146.9
Total liabilities	1,461.0	4,677.3
Stockholders' equity	6,905.9	7,469.6
Net income	160.7	1,279.0

Required

a. For each company, compute the debt to assets ratio, return on assets ratio, and return on equity ratio.

b. Which company has the greatest level of financial risk? Explain.

c. Which company appears to have managed its assets most efficiently? Explain.

d. Which company performed better from the perspective of the owners? Explain.

ATC 3-6   Writing Assignment   *Effect of land sale on return on assets*

Custom Builders is holding land that cost $1,200,000 for future use. However, plans have changed and the company may not need the land in the foreseeable future. The president is concerned about the return on assets. Current net income is $570,000 and total assets are $4,700,000.

Required

a. Write a memo to the company president explaining the effect of disposing of the land, assuming that it has a current value of $2,000,000.

b. Write a memo to the company president explaining the effect of disposing of the land, assuming that it has a current value of $800,000.

ATC 3-7   Ethical Dilemma   *What is a little deceit among friends?*

Glenn's Cleaning Services Company is experiencing cash flow problems and needs a loan. Glenn has a friend who is willing to lend him the money he needs provided she can be convinced that he will be able to repay the debt. Glenn has assured his friend that his business is viable, but his friend has asked to see the company's financial statements. Glenn's accountant produced the following financial statements:

Income Statement		Balance Sheet	
Service Revenue	$ 38,000	Assets	$85,000
Operating Expenses	(70,000)	Liabilities	$35,000
Net Loss	$(32,000)	Stockholders' Equity	
		Common Stock	82,000
		Retained Earnings	(32,000)
		Total Liabilities and	
		Stockholders' Equity	$85,000

Glenn made the following adjustments to these statements before showing them to his friend. He recorded $82,000 of revenue on account from Barrymore Manufacturing Company for a contract to clean its headquarters office building that was still being negotiated for the next month. Barrymore had scheduled a meeting to sign a contract the following week, so he was sure that he would get the job. Barrymore was a reputable company, and Glenn was confident that he could ultimately collect the $82,000. Also, he subtracted $30,000 of accrued salaries expense and the corresponding liability. He reasoned that since he had not paid the employees, he had not incurred any expense.

Required

a. Reconstruct the income statement and balance sheet as they would appear after Glenn's adjustments. Comment on the accuracy of the adjusted financial statements.

b. Comment on the ethical implications of Glenn's actions. Before you answer, consider the following scenario. Suppose you are Glenn and the $30,000 you owe your employees is due next week. If you are unable to pay them, they will quit and the business will go bankrupt. You are sure you will be able to repay your friend when your employees perform the $82,000 of services for Barrymore and you collect the cash. However, your friend is risk averse and is not likely to make the loan based on the financial statements your accountant prepared. Would you make the changes that Glenn made to get the loan and thereby save your company? Defend your position with a rational explanation.

ATC 3-8   Research Assignment   *Identifying accruals and deferrals at Reader's Digest.*

Chapter 2 defined and discussed accrual transactions, and Chapter 3 defined and discussed deferral transactions. Complete the requirements below using the most recent financial statements available on the Internet for Reader's Digest Association, Inc. Obtain the statements by following the steps below. (Be aware that the formatting of the company's website may have changed since these instructions were written.)

1. Go to www.rd.com.
2. Click on the "Investors Relations" link under "Corporate:" which are at the bottom of the page in very small print.
3. Click on the "Annual Report" link at the left side of the page.
4. Under the "20XX Annual Report" heading, click on either "Full Annual Report" or Form 10-K.
5. Find the company's balance sheet and complete the requirements below. In recent years this has been shown around page 50 in the Form 10-K section of the company's annual report.

Required

a. Make a list of all the accounts on the balance sheet that you believe are accrual type accounts.

b. Make a list of all the accounts on the balance sheet that you believe are deferral type accounts.

ATC 3-9 Spreadsheet Assignment *Using Excel*

Set up the following spreadsheet for Hubbard Company to calculate financial ratios based on given financial information.

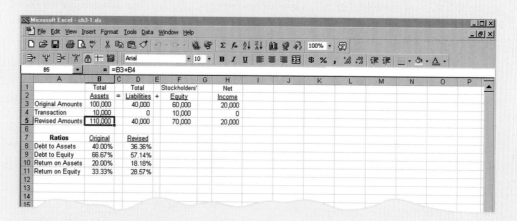

Steps to Prepare Spreadsheet

1. Enter the information in Column A.
2. Enter the headings in rows 1 and 2.
3. In row 3, enter the numbers for the Original Amounts.
4. In Column B, beginning with row 8, formulate the ratios based on the Original Amounts. Format the ratios as percentages.
5. The following independent transactions apply to Hubbard Company.
   a. Acquired $10,000 cash from the issue of common stock.
   b. Borrowed $10,000 cash.
   c. Earned $5,000 revenue and received cash.
   d. Accrued $3,000 of expenses.
   e. Incurred and paid $3,000 of expenses.

Required

a. In row 4, enter the effect of Transaction *a* on both the accounting equation and net income.
b. Formulate the revised amounts in row 5 for each heading after considering the effect of Transaction *a* on the original amounts.
c. Design formulas for the ratios in Column D based on the Revised Amounts.
d. Enter the ratios for the Original and Revised Transaction *a* amounts in the following table.

		Ratios for Various Transactions				
Ratios	Original	a	b	c	d	e
Debt to assets						
Debt to equity						
Return on assets						
Return on equity						

e. Delete the effect of Transaction *a* in row 4. Enter the effect of Transaction *b* in row 4. Notice that Excel automatically recalculates the Revised Amounts and Ratios on your spreadsheet as the result of the changed data.
f. Continue to delete transactions in row 4 as completed and enter the effect of each subsequent Transaction *c* through *e* one at a time. Enter the ratios for each independent transaction in the preceding table.

Spreadsheet Tip

Format percentages by choosing Format, Cells, and Percentage.

ATC 3-10 Spreadsheet Assignment *Mastering Excel*

a. Refer to Problem 3-23A. Using an Excel spreadsheet, prepare the financial statements as indicated. To complete Requirement *b* here, use formulas where normal arithmetic calculations are made in the financial statements.

b. It is interesting to speculate what would happen if certain operating results change for better or worse. After completing Requirement *a*, change certain account balances for each of the following independent operating adjustments. After each adjustment, note how the financial statements would differ if the change in operations were to occur. After the effect of each adjustment is noted, return the data to the original amounts in Problem 3-23A, and then go to the next operating adjustment.

   In the following table, record the new amounts on the financial statements for the various operating changes listed.

	Original	1	2	3	4	5
Net income						
Total assets						
Total liabilities						
Total stockholders' equity						
Total liabilities & stockholders' equity						

Independent Operating Adjustments

1. Service Revenue increased $7,500. Assume that all services are provided on account.
2. Insurance Expense decreased $500. The related Prepaid Insurance account changed accordingly.
3. Supplies Expense decreased $100. The related Supplies account changed accordingly.
4. Depreciation Expense increased $300. The related Accumulated Depreciation account changed accordingly.
5. Dividends paid decreased $1,000 and the Cash account changed accordingly.

CHAPTER 4

The Double-Entry Accounting System

LEARNING OBJECTIVES

After you have mastered the material in this chapter, you will be able to:

1. Explain the fundamental concepts associated with double-entry accounting systems.

2. Describe business events using debit/credit terminology.

3. Record transactions in T-accounts.

4. Identify the events that need adjusting entries and record them.

5. State the need for and record closing entries.

6. Prepare and interpret a trial balance.

7. Record transactions using the general journal format.

8. Describe the components of an annual report, including the management, discussion, and analysis section and the footnotes to financial statements.

9. Describe the role of the Securities and Exchange Commission in financial reporting.

LP4

The Curious Accountant

As previously indicated, most companies prepare financial statements at least once a year. The year for which accounting records are maintained is called the company's **fiscal year.** This book usually assumes that the fiscal year is the same as a calendar year; that is, it ends on December 31. In practice, many companies have fiscal years that do not end on December 31. For example, Polo Ralph Lauren, a company that produces clothing, has a fiscal year that ends the first Saturday in April. Abercrombie & Fitch, a company that sells clothing, has a fiscal year that ends on the last Sunday in January.

Why do you think these companies choose these dates to end their fiscal years? (Answers on pages 191 and 192.)

CHAPTER OPENING

This chapter explains how to record transactions using double-entry accounting. It is insightful to draw a parallel between the requirements of the double-entry system and those of a traffic light. Red could mean "go" rather than "stop." In fact, it makes no difference whether red means go or stop. What is important is that drivers agree on what red means. Similarly, the rules of double-entry accounting could be written differently. In fact, the rules may seem backward to you. You are accustomed to hearing accounting terms like "debit" or "credit" from a customer perspective. You must now reorient yourself to a business perspective. Regardless of how awkward the rules may seem to you, you must accept them as they are. In time, they will become second nature to you. With practice, you can learn to navigate the double-entry accounting system just as effortlessly as you respond to traffic lights. ■

Debit/Credit Terminology

Explain the fundamental concepts associated with double-entry accounting systems.

Describe business events using debit/credit terminology.

Video 4.1

An account form known as a **T-account** is a good starting point for learning double-entry recording procedures. A T-account looks like the letter "T" drawn on a piece of paper. The account title is written across the top of the horizontal bar of the T. The left side of the vertical bar is the **debit** side, and the right side is the **credit** side. An account has been *debited* when an amount is written on the left side and *credited* when an amount is written on the right side. Accountants often abbreviate the term *debit* as "dr." and *credit* as "cr." For any given account, the difference between the total debit and credit amounts is the **account balance.**

The **double-entry accounting** system requires that total debits always equal total credits. This feature is so powerful in promoting accuracy that it has been used for hundreds of years. If debits do not equal credits, accountants know to search for an error. However, an equality of debits and credits does not prove accuracy. For example, an accountant may record the debit and credit of a $500 transaction as $5,000. Total debits and credits will be equal, but the accounting records will be inaccurate. On the other hand, if a debit is recorded as $680 and the corresponding credit as $860, the error will be caught. The system is not flawless, but it is highly effective in reducing errors.

To begin: debits increase asset accounts and credits decrease asset accounts. In T-account form, this rule is expressed as follows:

Asset	
Debit	Credit
+	−

The pluses and minuses are reversed for liability and stockholders' equity accounts. This is algebraically correct because those accounts are on the other side of the equal sign in the accounting equation. In T-account form, these debit and credit rules are as follows:

			Claims			
Assets		=	Liabilities	+	Equity	
Debit	Credit		Debit	Credit	Debit	Credit
+	−		−	+	−	+

Notice that a debit can represent an increase or a decrease. Likewise, a credit can represent an increase or a decrease. Whether a debit or credit is an increase or a decrease depends on the type of account (asset, liability, or stockholders' equity) in question. The rules of debits and credits are summarized as follows:

1. Debits increase asset accounts; credits decrease asset accounts.
2. Debits decrease liability and stockholders' equity accounts; credits increase liability and stockholders' equity accounts.

Collins Consultants Case

Record transactions in T-accounts.

We will record the accounting events for a small business, Collins Consultants, to show how the rules for debits and credits work. Each event falls into one of the four transaction types:

1. Asset source transactions
2. Asset exchange transactions
3. Asset use transactions
4. Claims exchange transactions

Asset Source Transactions

A business may obtain assets from three primary sources: (1) from stockholders, (2) from creditors, or (3) through operating activities (earning revenue). An asset source transaction increases an asset account and a corresponding liability or stockholders' equity account. The increase in the asset account is recorded with a debit entry. The increase in a liability or stockholders' equity account is recorded with a credit entry. The following section demonstrates recording procedures for common asset source transactions.

Event 1 Owners Contribute Assets

Collins Consultants was established on January 1, 2008, when it acquired $15,000 cash from Collins.

This accounting event increases both assets and stockholders' equity. The increase in assets (Cash) is recorded with a debit, and the increase in stockholders' equity (Common Stock) with a credit, shown in T-account form as follows:

Assets		=	Liabilities	+	Equity	
Cash					**Common Stock**	
Debit	Credit				Debit	Credit
+						+
(1) 15,000						15,000 (1)

This entry has the following effects on the financial statements:

Assets	=	Liab.	+	Equity	Rev.	−	Exp.	=	Net Inc.	Cash Flow
15,000	=	NA	+	15,000	NA	−	NA	=	NA	15,000 FA

Event 2 Creditor Provides Assets

On February 1, Collins Consultants issued a $10,000 note payable to the National Bank to borrow cash.

The interest rate and maturity date of the note are discussed later. Borrowing the cash increases both assets and liabilities. The increase in assets (Cash) is recorded with a debit, and the increase in liabilities (Notes Payable) is recorded with a credit, as illustrated in the following T-accounts:

Assets		=	Liabilities		+	Equity
Cash			**Notes Payable**			
Debit	Credit		Debit	Credit		
+				+		
(2) 10,000				10,000 (2)		

This illustration shows only the accounts affected by the borrowing event. Throughout the chapter, the effects of each event are labeled with the event number shown in parentheses, in this case (2). Later in the chapter we illustrate the cumulative effect of all the events on each account.

This entry has the following effects on the financial statements:

Assets	=	Liab.	+	Equity	Rev.	−	Exp.	=	Net Inc.	Cash Flow
10,000	=	10,000	+	NA	NA	−	NA	=	NA	10,000 FA

Event 3 Creditor Provides Assets

On February 17, Collins Consultants purchased $850 of office supplies on account (agreed to pay for the supplies at a later date) from Morris Supply Company.

Purchasing supplies on account increases both assets and liabilities. The increase in assets (Supplies) is recorded with a debit, and the increase in liabilities (Accounts Payable) is recorded with a credit, as shown in the following T-accounts:

Assets		=	Liabilities		+	Equity
Supplies			**Accounts Payable**			
Debit	Credit		Debit	Credit		
+				+		
(3) 850				850 (3)		

This entry has the following effects on the financial statements:

Assets	=	Liab.	+	Equity	Rev.	−	Exp.	=	Net Inc.	Cash Flow
850	=	850	+	NA	NA	−	NA	=	NA	NA

Event 4   Creditor Provides Assets

On February 28, Collins Consultants signed a contract to evaluate the internal control system used by Kendall Food Stores. Kendall paid Collins $5,000 in advance for these future services.

Accepting the $5,000 in advance creates an obligation for Collins Consultants. The obligation is to provide future services to Kendall Food Stores. Collins will recognize a liability called *unearned revenue.* Recording the event increases both assets and liabilities. The increase in assets (Cash) is recorded with a debit, and the increase in liabilities (Unearned Revenue) is recorded with a credit, as shown in the following T-accounts:

Assets		=	Liabilities		+	Equity
Cash			**Unearned Revenue**			
Debit	Credit		Debit	Credit		
+				+		
(4) 5,000				5,000 (4)		

This entry has the following effects on the financial statements:

Assets	=	Liab.	+	Equity	Rev.	−	Exp.	=	Net Inc.	Cash Flow
5,000	=	5,000	+	NA	NA	−	NA	=	NA	5,000 OA

Event 5   Creditor Provides Assets

On March 1, Collins Consultants received $18,000 from signing a contract to provide professional advice to Harwood Corporation over a one-year period.

The event increases both assets and liabilities. The increase in assets (Cash) is recorded with a debit, and the increase in liabilities (Unearned Revenue) is recorded with a credit, as shown in the following T-accounts:

Assets		=	Liabilities		+	Equity
Cash			**Unearned Revenue**			
Debit	Credit		Debit	Credit		
+				+		
(5) 18,000				18,000 (5)		

This entry has the following effects on the financial statements:

Assets	=	Liab.	+	Equity	Rev.	−	Exp.	=	Net Inc.	Cash Flow
18,000	=	18,000	+	NA	NA	−	NA	=	NA	18,000 OA

Event 6 Operating Activity Provides Assets
On April 10, Collins Consultants provided $2,000 of services to Rex Company on account (agreed to let the customer pay at a future date).

Recognizing revenue earned on account increases both assets and stockholders' equity. The increase in assets (Accounts Receivable) is recorded with a debit, and the increase in stockholders' equity (Consulting Revenue) is recorded with a credit, as shown in the following T-accounts:

Assets	=	Liabilities	+	Equity
Accounts Receivable				Consulting Revenue

Debit	Credit			Debit	Credit
+					+
(6) 2,000					2,000 (6)

This entry has the following effects on the financial statements:

Assets	=	Liab.	+	Equity	Rev.	−	Exp.	=	Net Inc.	Cash Flow
2,000	=	NA	+	2,000	2,000	−	NA	=	2,000	NA

Event 7 Operating Activity Provides Assets
On April 29, Collins performed services and received $8,400 cash.

Recognizing the revenue increases both assets and stockholders' equity. The increase in assets (Cash) is recorded with a debit, and the increase in stockholders' equity (Consulting Revenue) is recorded with a credit, as shown in the following T-accounts:

Assets	=	Liabilities	+	Equity
Cash				Consulting Revenue

Debit	Credit			Debit	Credit
+					+
(7) 8,400					8,400 (7)

This entry has the following effects on the financial statements:

Assets	=	Liab.	+	Equity	Rev.	−	Exp.	=	Net Inc.	Cash Flow
8,400	=	NA	+	8,400	8,400	−	NA	=	8,400	8,400 OA

Summary of the Previous Asset Source Transactions

Events 1 through 7 are asset source transactions. In each case, an asset account and a corresponding claims account increased. The increase in the asset account was recorded with a debit and the increase in the liability or stockholders' equity account was recorded with a credit. Any transaction that provides assets to a business is recorded similarly.

CHECK YOURSELF 4.1

What are the three sources of assets? Which accounts are debited and credited when a business acquires an asset?

Answer

The three sources of assets are creditors, investors, and earnings. When a company acquires an asset, the asset account is debited and the source account is credited. For example, if a company earns revenue on account, the receivables account is debited and the revenue account is credited.

Asset Exchange Transactions

Asset exchange transactions involve trading one asset for another asset. One asset account increases; the other decreases. The total amount of assets remains unchanged. Asset exchange transactions are recorded by debiting the asset account that is increasing and crediting the asset account that is decreasing. In T-account form, asset exchange transactions have the following effects on the accounting equation:

Assets				=	Claims
Asset 1		**Asset 2**			
Debit	Credit	Debit	Credit		
+			−		

Event 8 Exchange Cash for Note Receivable
On May 1, Collins Consultants loaned Reston Company $6,000. Reston issued a note to Collins.

The terms of the note are discussed later. The note receivable represents an investment to Collins. Recognizing the investment (loan) increases one asset account and decreases another. The increase in assets (Notes Receivable) is recorded with a debit, and the decrease in assets (Cash) is recorded with a credit, as shown in the following T-accounts:

Assets				=	Claims
Cash		**Notes Receivable**			
Debit	Credit	Debit	Credit		
	−	+			
	6,000 (8)	(8) 6,000			

This entry has the following effects on the financial statements:

Assets			= Liab. + Equity	Rev. − Exp. = Net Inc.	Cash Flow
Cash	**+**	**Note Rec.**			
(6,000)	+	6,000	= NA + NA	NA − NA = NA	(6,000) IA

Event 9 Exchange Cash for Office Equipment
On June 30, Collins purchased office equipment for $42,000 cash.

The increase in assets (Office Equipment) is recorded with a debit, and the decrease in assets (Cash) is recorded with a credit, as shown in the following T-accounts:

Assets				=	Claims
Cash		**Office Equipment**			
Debit	Credit	Debit	Credit		
	−	+			
	42,000 (9)	(9) 42,000			

This entry has the following effects on the financial statements:

Assets			= Liab. + Equity	Rev. − Exp. = Net Inc.	Cash Flow
Cash	**+**	**Office Equip.**			
(42,000)	+	42,000	= NA + NA	NA − NA = NA	(42,000) IA

Event 10 Exchange Cash for Prepaid Rent
On July 31, Collins paid $3,600 cash in advance for a one-year lease to rent office space beginning August 1.

The increase in assets (Prepaid Rent) is recorded with a debit, and the decrease in assets (Cash) is recorded with a credit, as shown in the following T-accounts:

Assets				=	Claims
Cash		**Prepaid Rent**			
Debit	Credit	Debit	Credit		
	−	+			
	3,600 (10)	(10) 3,600			

This entry has the following effects on the financial statements:

Assets			= Liab. + Equity			Rev. − Exp. = Net Inc.			Cash Flow
Cash	+	Prep. Rent							
(3,600)	+	3,600	= NA	+	NA	NA − NA =		NA	(3,600) OA

Event 11 Exchange Receivable for Cash
On August 8, Collins Consultants collected $1,200 from Rex Company as partial payment of the account receivable (see Event 6).

The increase in assets (Cash) is recorded with a debit, and the decrease in assets (Accounts Receivable) is recorded with a credit, as shown in the following T-accounts:

Assets				=	Claims
Cash		**Accounts Receivable**			
Debit	Credit	Debit	Credit		
+			−		
(11) 1,200			1,200 (11)		

This entry has the following effects on the financial statements:

Assets			= Liab. + Equity			Rev. − Exp. = Net Inc.			Cash Flow
Cash	+	Accts. Rec.							
1,200	+	(1,200)	= NA	+	NA	NA − NA =		NA	1,200 OA

Summary of the Previous Asset Exchange Transactions

Events 8 through 11 are all asset exchange transactions. In each case, one asset account increased and another decreased. The asset account that increased was debited, and the asset account that decreased was credited. These asset exchange transactions did not affect the total amounts of either assets or claims.

Asset Use Transactions

There are three primary asset use transactions: (1) expenses may use assets, (2) settling liabilities may use assets, or (3) paying dividends may use assets. An asset use transaction decreases an asset account and also decreases a claims account. The decrease in the asset account is recorded with a credit and the decrease in the claims account is recorded with a debit.

Event 12 Assets Used to Produce Revenue (Expenses)
On September 4, Collins Consultants paid employees who worked for the company $2,400 in salaries.

The decrease in assets (Cash) is recorded with a credit, and the decrease in stockholders' equity (Salaries Expense) is recorded with a debit, as shown in the following T-accounts:

Assets		=	Liabilities	+	Equity	
Cash					**Salaries Expense**	
Debit	Credit				Debit	Credit
	–				+ Expense	
	2,400 (12)				– Equity	
					(12) 2,400	

The debit to Salaries Expense represents an *increase* in the Salaries Expense account, which is actually a *decrease* in stockholders' equity (Retained Earnings). Debit entries increase expense accounts. Expenses, however, decrease stockholders' equity (Retained Earnings). Debiting an expense account, therefore, reduces stockholders' equity.

This entry has the following effects on the financial statements:

Assets	=	Liab.	+	Equity	Rev.	–	Exp.	=	Net Inc.	Cash Flow	
(2,400)	=	NA	+	(2,400)	NA	–	2,400	=	(2,400)	(2,400)	OA

Event 13 Assets Transferred to Owners (Dividends)
On September 20, Collins Consultants paid a $1,500 cash dividend to its owner.

The decrease in assets (Cash) is recorded with a credit, and the decrease in stockholders' equity (Dividends) is recorded with a debit, as shown in the following T-accounts:

Assets		=	Liabilities	+	Equity	
Cash					**Dividends**	
Debit	Credit				Debit	Credit
	–				+ Div.	
	1,500 (13)				– Equity	
					(13) 1,500	

The debit to Dividends represents both an increase in the Dividends account and a decrease in stockholders' equity (Retained Earnings). Since dividends decrease stockholders' equity, an increase in the Dividends account reduces stockholders' equity.

This entry has the following effects on the financial statements:

Assets	=	Liab.	+	Equity	Rev.	–	Exp.	=	Net Inc.	Cash Flow	
(1,500)	=	NA	+	(1,500)	NA	–	NA	=	NA	(1,500)	FA

Event 14 Assets Used to Pay Liabilities
On October 10, Collins Consultants paid Morris Supply Company the $850 owed from purchasing office supplies on account (see Event 3).

The decrease in assets (Cash) is recorded with a credit, and the decrease in liabilities (Accounts Payable) is recorded with a debit, as shown in the following T-accounts:

Assets		=	Liabilities		+	Equity
Cash			**Accounts Payable**			
Debit	Credit		Debit	Credit		
	–		+			
	850 (14)		(14) 850			

This entry has the following effects on the financial statements:

Assets	=	Liab.	+	Equity	Rev.	−	Exp.	=	Net Inc.	Cash Flow
(850)	=	(850)	+	NA	NA	−	NA	=	NA	(850) OA

Summary of Asset Use Transactions

Events 12 through 14 each reduced both an asset account and either a liability or stockholders' equity account. Even though debit entries to expense and dividends accounts represent increases in those accounts, the balances in expense and dividends accounts reduce stockholders' equity. Any asset use transaction is recorded with a debit to a liability or a stockholders' equity account and a credit to an asset account.

Claims Exchange Transactions

Certain transactions involve exchanging one claims account for another claims account. The total amount of claims remains unchanged. Such transactions are recorded by debiting the claims account which is decreasing and crediting the claims account which is increasing.

Event 15 Recognizing Revenue (Unearned to Earned)
On November 15, Collins completed its consulting evaluation of the internal control system used by Kendall Food Stores (see Event 4).

Kendall expressed satisfaction with Collins's report. Recall Kendall had paid $5,000 in advance for the consulting services. Upon completing the project, Collins will recognize the revenue earned. Kendall's advance payment had created a liability; recognizing the revenue decreases liabilities and increases stockholders' equity. The decrease in liabilities (Unearned Revenue) is recorded with a debit, and the increase in stockholders' equity (Consulting Revenue) is recorded with a credit, as shown in the following T-accounts:

Assets	=	Liabilities	+	Equity
		Unearned Revenue		**Consulting Revenue**
		Debit | Credit		Debit | Credit
		− |		| +
		(15) 5,000 |		| 5,000 (15)

This entry has the following effects on the financial statements:

Assets	=	Liab.	+	Equity	Rev.	−	Exp.	=	Net Inc.	Cash Flow
NA	=	(5,000)	+	5,000	5,000	−	NA	=	5,000	NA

Event 16 Recognizing Expense
On December 18, Collins Consultants received a $900 bill from Creative Ads for advertisements which had appeared in regional magazines. Collins plans to pay the bill later.

The event increases liabilities and decreases stockholders' equity. The increase in liabilities (Accounts Payable) is recorded with a credit, and the decrease in stockholders' equity (Advertising Expense) is recorded with a debit, as shown in the following T-accounts:

Assets	=	Liabilities	+	Equity
		Accounts Payable		**Advertising Expense**
		Debit | Credit		Debit | Credit
		| +		+ Expense |
		| 900 (16)		− Equity |
		|		(16) 900 |

This entry has the following effects on the financial statements:

Assets	=	Liab.	+	Equity	Rev.	−	Exp.	=	Net Inc.	Cash Flow
NA	=	900	+	(900)	NA	−	900	=	(900)	NA

Summary of Claims Exchange Transactions

Events 15 and 16 reflect exchanges on the claims side of the accounting equation. In each case, one claims account was debited, and another claims account was credited. Claims exchange transactions do not affect the total amounts of either assets or claims.

Adjusting the Accounts

Identify the events that need adjusting entries and record them.

Assume that Collins Consultants' fiscal year ends on December 31, 2008. In order to prepare the financial statements, Collins must first adjust its accounting records to recognize any unrecorded accruals and or deferrals. The appropriate adjustments are discussed in the next section of this chapter. Notice that adjusting entries do not affect the cash account.

Adjustment 1 **Accrual of Interest Revenue**
Collins Consultants recognized accrued interest on the $6,000 note receivable from Reston (see Event 8).

The note was issued on May 1, 2008. It had a 9 percent annual rate of interest and a one-year term to maturity. Collins therefore earned $360 ([$6,000 × 0.09] × [8 ÷ 12]) of interest revenue during 2008. The required adjusting entry increases both assets and stockholders' equity. The increase in assets (Interest Receivable) is recorded with a debit, and the increase in stockholders' equity (Interest Revenue) is recorded with a credit, as shown in the following T-accounts:

Assets	=	Liabilities	+	Equity
Interest Receivable				**Interest Revenue**
Debit	Credit			Debit	Credit
+					+
(A1) 360					360 (A1)

The label (A1) indicates this is the first adjusting entry. The second adjusting entry is labeled (A2). Subsequent adjusting entries follow this referencing scheme.

This adjustment has the following effects on the financial statements:

Assets	=	Liab.	+	Equity	Rev.	−	Exp.	=	Net Inc.	Cash Flow
360	=	NA	+	360	360	−	NA	=	360	NA

Adjustment 2 **Accrual of Interest Expense**
Collins Consultants recognized accrued interest expense on the $10,000 note payable it issued to the National Bank (see Event 2).

The note was issued on February 1, 2008. It had a 12 percent annual interest rate and a one-year term to maturity. Interest expense on the note for the 2008 accounting period is $1,100 ([$10,000 × 0.12] × [11 ÷ 12]). The required adjusting entry increases liabilities and decreases stockholders' equity. The increase in liabilities (Interest Payable) is recorded with a credit, and the decrease in stockholders' equity (Interest Expense) is recorded with a debit, as shown in the following T-accounts:

Assets	=	Liabilities	+	Equity	
		Interest Payable		**Interest Expense**	
		Debit / Credit		Debit / Credit	
		+		+ Expense	
		1,100 (A2)		− Equity	
				(A2) 1,100	

This adjustment has the following effects on the financial statements:

Assets	=	Liab.	+	Equity	Rev.	−	Exp.	=	Net Inc.	Cash Flow
NA	=	1,100	+	(1,100)	NA	−	1,100	=	(1,100)	NA

Adjustment 3 Accrual of Salary Expense
Collins recognized accrued but unpaid salaries.

Collins Consultants last paid salaries to employees on September 4 (see Event 12). Assume that Collins owes $800 more to employees for work done in 2008 since September 4. Collins will pay these salaries in 2009. The required adjusting entry increases liabilities and decreases stockholders' equity. The increase in liabilities (Salaries Payable) is recorded with a credit, and the decrease in stockholders' equity (Salaries Expense) is recorded with a debit, as shown in the following T-accounts:

Assets	=	Liabilities	+	Equity	
		Salaries Payable		**Salaries Expense**	
		Debit / Credit		Debit / Credit	
		+		+ Expense	
		800 (A3)		− Equity	
				(A3) 800	

This adjustment has the following effects on the financial statements:

Assets	=	Liab.	+	Equity	Rev.	−	Exp.	=	Net Inc.	Cash Flow
NA	=	800	+	(800)	NA	−	800	=	(800)	NA

Adjustment 4 Equipment Used to Produce Revenue (Depreciation Expense)
Collins recognized depreciation on the office equipment it had purchased on June 30 (see Event 9).

Collins expects the equipment to have a five-year life and a $2,000 salvage value. Since the equipment was purchased at midyear, Collins should recognize a half-year of depreciation expense, which is $4,000 ([$42,000 − $2,000] ÷ 5 = $8,000 ÷ 2 = $4,000). The adjusting entry necessary to record depreciation decreases both assets and stockholders' equity. The decrease in assets (Office Equipment) is recorded with a credit to the contra asset account Accumulated Depreciation and the decrease in stockholders' equity (Depreciation Expense) is recorded with a debit, as shown in the following T-accounts:

Assets	=	Liabilities	+	Equity	
Accumulated Depreciation				**Depreciation Expense**	
Debit / Credit				Debit / Credit	
+ Acc. Depr.				+ Expense	
− Assets				− Equity	
4,000 (A4)				(A4) 4,000	

The credit entry to the Accumulated Depreciation account represents an increase in that account. Accumulated Depreciation, however, reduces total assets. The Accumulated Depreciation account is classified as a **contra account** because it normally has a credit balance while most asset accounts have debit balances. Accumulated depreciation increases each time additional amounts of depreciation are recorded.

This adjustment has the following effects on the financial statements:

Assets	=	Liab.	+	Equity	Rev.	−	Exp.	=	Net Inc.	Cash Flow
(4,000)	=	NA	+	(4,000)	NA	−	4,000	=	(4,000)	NA

Adjustment 5 Office Space Used to Produce Revenue (Rent Expense)
Collins recognized rent expense for the portion of prepaid rent used up since entering the lease agreement on July 31 (see Event 10).

Recall that Collins paid $3,600 in advance to lease office space for one year. The monthly rental cost is therefore $300 ($3,600 ÷ 12 months). By December 31, Collins had *used* the office for five months in 2008. Rent expense for those 5 months is therefore $1,500 ($300 × 5). Recognizing the rent expense decreases both assets and stockholders' equity. The decrease in assets (Prepaid Rent) is recorded with a credit, and the decrease in stockholders' equity (Rent Expense) is recorded with a debit, as shown in the following T-accounts:

Assets	=	Liabilities	+	Equity
Prepaid Rent				**Depreciation Expense**

Debit	Credit				Debit	Credit
	—				+ Expense	
	1,500 (A5)				− Equity	
					(A5) 1,500	

This adjustment has the following effects on the financial statements:

Assets	=	Liab.	+	Equity	Rev.	−	Exp.	=	Net Inc.	Cash Flow
(1,500)	=	NA	+	(1,500)	NA	−	1,500	=	(1,500)	NA

Adjustment 6 Supplies Used to Produce Revenue (Supplies Expense)
A physical count at the end of the year indicates that $125 worth of the supplies purchased on February 17 is still on hand (see Event 3).

Collins used $725 ($850 − $125) of supplies during the period. Recognizing the supplies expense decreases both assets and stockholders' equity. The decrease in assets (Supplies) is recorded with a credit and the decrease in stockholders' equity (Supplies Expense) is recorded with a debit, as shown in the following T-accounts:

Assets	=	Liabilities	+	Equity
Supplies				**Supplies Expense**

Debit	Credit				Debit	Credit
	—				+ Expense	
	725 (A6)				− Equity	
					(A6) 725	

This adjustment has the following effects on the financial statements:

Assets	=	Liab.	+	Equity	Rev.	−	Exp.	=	Net Inc.	Cash Flow
(725)	=	NA	+	(725)	NA	−	725	=	(725)	NA

Adjustment 7 Recognition of Revenue (Unearned to Earned)

Collins Consultants adjusted its accounting records to reflect revenue earned to date on the contract to provide services to Harwood Corporation for a one-year period beginning March 1 (see Event 5).

Recall that Collins collected $18,000 in advance for this contract. By December 31, 2008, Collins would have provided Harwood professional services for 10 months, earning $15,000 ($18,000 ÷ 12 = $1,500 × 10 = $15,000) of the contract revenue during 2008. This amount must be transferred from the liability account (Unearned Revenue) to an equity account (Consulting Revenue). Recognizing the revenue decreases liabilities and increases stockholders' equity. The decrease in liabilities (Unearned Revenue) is recorded with a debit, and the increase in stockholders' equity (Consulting Revenue) is recorded with a credit, as shown in the following T-accounts:

Assets	=	Liabilities		+	Equity	
		Unearned Revenue			**Consulting Revenue**	
		Debit	Credit		Debit	Credit
		−				+
		(A7) 15,000				15,000 (A7)

This adjustment has the following effects on the financial statements:

Assets	=	Liab.	+	Equity	Rev.	−	Exp.	=	Net Inc.	Cash Flow
NA	=	(15,000)	+	15,000	15,000	−	NA	=	15,000	NA

CHECK YOURSELF 4.2

Can an asset exchange transaction be an adjusting entry?

Answer

No. Adjusting entries always involve revenue or expense accounts. Since an asset exchange transaction involves only asset accounts, it cannot be an adjusting entry.

Overview of Debit/Credit Relationships

The transactions presented in this chapter illustrate the relationships summarized in Panel A of Exhibit 4.1. Panel B illustrates these relationships in T-account form. Debit/credit terminology is fundamental to understanding and communicating accounting information. Practice using the terminology until it becomes second nature to you.

LO **2**

Describe business events using debit/credit terminology.

EXHIBIT 4.1

Debit/Credit Relationships

Panel A

Account	Debits	Credits
Assets	Increase	Decrease
Contra Assets	Decrease	Increase
Liabilities	Decrease	Increase
Equity	Decrease	Increase
Common Stock	Decrease	Increase
Revenue	Decrease	Increase
Expenses	Increase	Decrease
Dividends	Increase	Decrease

Panel B

Assets		=	Liabilities		+	Equity	
Debit	Credit		Debit	Credit		Debit	Credit
+	−		−	+		−	+

Contra Assets	
Debit	Credit
+ Assets	− Assets
− Contra	+ Contra

Common Stock	
Debit	Credit
−	+

Dividends	
Debit	Credit
− Equity	+ Equity
+ Div.	− Div.

Revenue	
Debit	Credit
−	+

Expense	
Debit	Credit
− Equity	+ Equity
+ Exp.	− Exp.

Summary of T-Accounts

LO 3

Record transactions in T-accounts.

Exhibit 4.2 summarizes in T-account form all the activity in the Collins Consultants example. Verify that the accounting equation is in balance. In this case, the total of all asset balances is $48,635, which is equal to the total of all liability and stockholders' equity account balances. The balance in each account, which is the difference between all the debit entries and all the credit entries, is written on the plus (increase) side of that account. Asset, expense, and dividend accounts normally have *debit balances;* liability, stockholders' equity, and revenue accounts normally have *credit balances.*

The Ledger

LO 1

Explain the fundamental concepts associated with double-entry accounting systems.

The collection of all the accounts used by a particular business is called the **ledger.** The ledger for Collins Consultants is displayed in Exhibit 4.2. In a manual system, the ledger could be a book with pages for each account where entries are recorded by hand. In the more sophisticated systems, the ledger is maintained in electronic form. Data is entered into electronic ledgers using computer keyboards or scanners. Companies typically assign each ledger account a name and a number. A list of all ledger accounts and their account numbers is called the **chart of accounts.**

EXHIBIT 4.2

Ledger Accounts

Video 4.1

Assets			=	Liabilities			+	Equity		

Cash

(1)	15,000	6,000	(8)
(2)	10,000	42,000	(9)
(4)	5,000	3,600	(10)
(5)	18,000	2,400	(12)
(7)	8,400	1,500	(13)
(11)	1,200	850	(14)
Bal.	1,250		

Accounts Receivable

(6)	2,000	1,200	(11)
Bal.	800		

Supplies

(3)	850	725	(A6)
Bal.	125		

Prepaid Rent

(10)	3,600	1,500	(A5)
Bal.	2,100		

Notes Receivable

(8)	6,000		
Bal.	6,000		

Interest Receivable

(A1)	360		
Bal.	360		

Office Equipment

(9)	42,000		
Bal.	42,000		

Accumulated Depreciation

		4,000	(A4)
		4,000	Bal.

Accounts Payable

(14)	850	850	(3)
		900	(16)
		900	Bal.

Unearned Revenue

(15)	5,000	5,000	(4)
(A7)	15,000	18,000	(5)
		3,000	Bal.

Notes Payable

		10,000	(2)
		10,000	Bal.

Interest Payable

		1,100	(A2)
		1,100	Bal.

Salaries Payable

		800	(A3)
		800	Bal.

Common Stock

		15,000	(1)
		15,000	Bal.

Dividends

(13)	1,500		
Bal.	1,500		

Consulting Revenue

		2,000	(6)
		8,400	(7)
		5,000	(15)
		15,000	(A7)
		30,400	Bal.

Interest Revenue

		360	(A1)
		360	Bal.

Salaries Expense

(12)	2,400		
(A3)	800		
Bal.	3,200		

Advertising Expense

(16)	900		
Bal.	900		

Interest Expense

(A2)	1,100		
Bal.	1,100		

Depreciation Expense

(A4)	4,000		
Bal.	4,000		

Rent Expense

(A5)	1,500		
Bal.	1,500		

Supplies Expense

(A6)	725		
Bal.	725		

Total Assets	=	Total Liabilities	+	Total Equity
		15,800		32,835

Total Claims

48,635	48,635

REALITY BYTES

Do all accounting systems require the use of debits and credits? The answer is a definite no. Indeed, many small businesses use a single-entry system. A checkbook constitutes a sufficient accounting system for many business owners. Deposits represent revenues, and payments constitute expenses. Many excellent automated accounting systems do not require data entry through a debit/credit recording scheme. QuickBooks is a good example of this type of system. Data are entered into the QuickBooks software program through a user-friendly computer interface that does not require knowledge of debit/credit terminology. Even so, the QuickBooks program produces traditional financial reports such as an income statement, balance sheet, and statement of cash flows. How is this possible? Before you become too ingrained in the debit/ credit system, recall that throughout the first three chapters of this text, we maintained accounting records without using debits and credits. Financial reports can be produced in many ways without using a double-entry system. Having recognized this point, we also note the fact that the vast majority of medium- to large-size companies use the double-entry system. Indeed, debit/credit terminology is a part of common culture. Most people have an understanding of what is happening when a business tells them that their account is being debited or credited. Accordingly, it is important for you to embrace the double-entry system as well as other financial reporting systems.

The General Journal

LO 7

Record transactions using the general journal format.

It is impractical for most businesses to enter transaction data directly into ledger accounts. Imagine the number of entries involved in a single day's cash transactions for a grocery store. To simplify recordkeeping, a salesclerk may record data on a cash register tape. The tape is a **source document** that the accountant uses to enter the transaction data into the accounting system. Other source documents include invoices, time cards, check stubs, and deposit tickets.

To further simplify the recording process, accountants initially record data from source documents into a **journal.** In other words, *transactions are recorded in journals before they are entered into the ledger accounts.* Journals are therefore called **books of original entry.** A company may use **special journals** to record specific types of repetitive transactions. For example, a company may use a special journal to record cash receipts, another to record cash payments, a third to record purchases on account, and yet another to record sales on account. Transactions that don't fit into any of the special journals are recorded in the **general journal.** Although special journals can be helpful, their use is not required. A business can choose to record all transactions in its general journal. For simplicity, this text uses only the general journal format.

At a minimum, the general journal shows the dates, the account titles, and the amounts of each transaction. The date is recorded in the first column, followed by the title of the account to be debited. The title of the account to be credited is indented and written on the line directly below the account to be debited. The dollar amount of the transaction is recorded in the Debit and Credit columns. For example, providing services for $1,000 cash on August 1 would be recorded in general journal format as follows:

Date	Account Title	Debit	Credit
Aug. 1	Cash	1,000	
	Service Revenue		1,000

Exhibit 4.3 shows the general journal entries for all the Collins Consultants' transactions discussed thus far. After transactions have been recorded in a journal, the dollar amounts of the debits and credits are copied into the ledger accounts. The process of copying information from journals to ledgers is called **posting.**

EXHIBIT 4.3

General Journal			
Date	Account Titles	Debit	Credit
Jan. 1	Cash	15,000	
	Common Stock		15,000
Feb. 1	Cash	10,000	
	Notes Payable		10,000
17	Supplies	850	
	Accounts Payable		850
28	Cash	5,000	
	Unearned Revenue		5,000
Mar. 1	Cash	18,000	
	Unearned Revenue		18,000
April 10	Accounts Receivable	2,000	
	Consulting Revenue		2,000
29	Cash	8,400	
	Consulting Revenue		8,400
May 1	Notes Receivable	6,000	
	Cash		6,000
June 30	Office Equipment	42,000	
	Cash		42,000
July 31	Prepaid Rent	3,600	
	Cash		3,600
Aug. 8	Cash	1,200	
	Accounts Receivable		1,200
Sept. 4	Salaries Expense	2,400	
	Cash		2,400
20	Dividends	1,500	
	Cash		1,500
Oct. 10	Accounts Payable	850	
	Cash		850
Nov. 15	Unearned Revenue	5,000	
	Consulting Revenue		5,000
Dec. 18	Advertising Expense	900	
	Accounts Payable		900
Dec. 31	**Adjusting Entries** Interest Receivable	360	
	Interest Revenue		360
31	Interest Expense	1,100	
	Interest Payable		1,100
31	Salaries Expense	800	
	Salaries Payable		800
31	Depreciation Expense	4,000	
	Accumulated Depreciation		4,000
31	Rent Expense	1,500	
	Prepaid Rent		1,500
31	Supplies Expense	725	
	Supplies		725
31	Unearned Revenue	15,000	
	Consulting Revenue		15,000

Most companies today use computer technology to record transactions and prepare financial statements. Computers can record and post data pertaining to vast numbers of transactions with incredible speed and unparalleled accuracy. Both manual and computerized accounting systems, however, use the same underlying design. Analyzing a manual accounting system is a useful way to gain insight into how computer-based systems work.

Financial Statements

The general ledger provides the information needed to prepare the financial statements for Collins Consultants. The income statement, statement of changes in stockholders' equity, balance sheet, and statement of cash flows are shown in Exhibits 4.4, 4.5, 4.6, and 4.7.

Closing Entries

Video 4.2

State the need for and record closing entries.

Exhibit 4.8 shows the **closing entries** for Collins Consultants. These entries move all 2008 data from the Revenue, Expense, and Dividend (temporary) accounts into the Retained Earnings account. For example, the first entry moves the balance in the Consulting Revenue account to the Retained Earnings account. Recall that the Consulting Revenue account has a $30,400 credit balance before it is closed. Debiting the account by that amount brings its after-closing balance to zero. The corresponding $30,400 credit to Retained Earnings increases the balance in that account. Similarly, the second entry (debiting the Interest Revenue account and crediting the Retained Earnings account for $360) moves the balance from the Interest Revenue account to the Retained Earnings account. The third entry moves the balance in the Salaries Expense account to the Retained Earnings account. Since the Salaries Expense account has a before-closing debit balance, crediting the account for $3,200 leaves it with an after-closing balance of zero. The corresponding $3,200 debit to the Retained Earnings account reduces the balance in that account. The remaining entries close the other expense or dividend accounts by crediting them and debiting the Retained Earnings account.

Notice that the closing entries can be made in a more efficient manner. For example, the two revenue accounts can be closed simultaneously in the following compound journal entry.

Date	Account Title	Debit	Credit
Dec. 31	Consulting Revenue	30,400	
	Interest Revenue	360	
	Retained Earnings		30,760

EXHIBIT 4.4

COLLINS CONSULTANTS
Income Statement
For the Year Ended December 31, 2008

Revenue		
Consulting revenue	$30,400	
Interest revenue	360	
Total revenue		$30,760
Less: Expenses		
Salaries expense	3,200	
Advertising expense	900	
Interest expense	1,100	
Depreciation expense	4,000	
Rent expense	1,500	
Supplies expense	725	
Total expenses		(11,425)
Net income		$19,335

EXHIBIT 4.5

COLLINS CONSULTANTS
Statement of Changes in Stockholders' Equity
For the Year Ended December 31, 2008

Beginning common stock	$ 0	
Plus: Stock issued	15,000	
Ending common stock		$15,000
Beginning retained earnings	0	
Plus: Net income	19,335	
Less: Dividends	(1,500)	
Ending retained earnings		17,835
Total stockholders' equity		$32,835

EXHIBIT 4.6

COLLINS CONSULTANTS
Balance Sheet
As of December 31, 2008

Assets		
Cash		$ 1,250
Accounts receivable		800
Supplies		125
Prepaid rent		2,100
Notes receivable		6,000
Interest receivable		360
Office equipment	$42,000	
Less: Accumulated depreciation	(4,000)	38,000
Total assets		$48,635
Liabilities		
Accounts payable	$ 900	
Unearned revenue	3,000	
Notes payable	10,000	
Interest payable	1,100	
Salaries payable	800	
Total liabilities		$15,800
Stockholders' equity		
Common stock	15,000	
Retained earnings	17,835	
Total stockholders' equity		32,835
Total liabilities and stockholders' equity		$48,635

EXHIBIT 4.7

COLLINS CONSULTANTS
Statement of Cash Flows
For the Year Ended December 31, 2008

Cash Flow from Operating Activities		
Inflow from customers*	$32,600	
Outflow for rent	(3,600)	
Outflow for salaries	(2,400)	
Outflow for supplies	(850)	
Net cash inflow from operating activities		$25,750
Cash Flow from Investing Activities		
Outflow for loan	(6,000)	
Outflow to purchase equipment	(42,000)	
Net cash outflow for investing activities		(48,000)
Cash Flow from Financing Activities		
Inflow from issue of stock	15,000	
Inflow from borrowing	10,000	
Outflow for dividends	(1,500)	
Net cash inflow from financing activities		23,500
Net change in cash		1,250
Plus: Beginning cash balance		0
Ending cash balance		$ 1,250

*The sum of cash inflows from Events 4, 5, 7, and 11.

EXHIBIT 4.8

Closing Entries			
Date	Account Title	Debit	Credit
Dec. 31	Consulting Revenue	30,400	
	Retained Earnings		30,400
31	Interest Revenue	360	
	Retained Earnings		360
31	Retained Earnings	3,200	
	Salaries Expense		3,200
31	Retained Earnings	900	
	Advertising Expense		900
31	Retained Earnings	1,100	
	Interest Expense		1,100
31	Retained Earnings	4,000	
	Depreciation Expense		4,000
31	Retained Earnings	1,500	
	Rent Expense		1,500
31	Retained Earnings	725	
	Supplies Expense		725
31	Retained Earnings	1,500	
	Dividends		1,500

Distribution of Fiscal Closing Dates

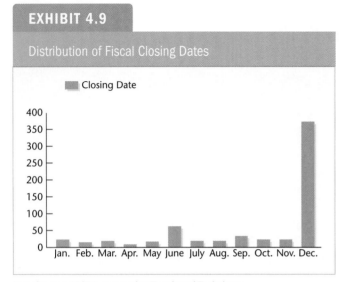

Data Source: AICPA Accounting Trends and Techniques

The expense and dividend accounts could also be closed in a compound journal entry. Other even more efficient recording schemes are possible. For example, revenue, expense, and dividend accounts could all be closed in a single compound journal entry. The exact form of the closing entries is not important. What is important is that the entries move the balances from the revenue, expense, and dividend accounts to the Retained Earnings account. After the closing entries are posted to the ledger accounts, the revenue, expense, and dividend accounts have zero balances. The temporary accounts are then ready to capture revenue, expense, and dividend data for the 2004 fiscal year.

If all companies closed their books on December 31 each year, accountants, printers, lawyers, government agencies, and others would be overburdened by the effort to produce the accounting reports of all companies at the same time. Furthermore, there would be little work to do at other times of the year. In an effort to balance the workload, many companies choose to close their books at the end of the natural business year. A natural business year ends when the operating activities are at their lowest point. For many companies the lowest point in the operating cycle occurs on a date other than December 31. A recent survey found that almost one-half of the companies sampled closed their books in months other than December (see Exhibit 4.9).

Video 4.1

Trial Balance

LO 6

Prepare and interpret a trial balance.

Companies frequently prepare a **trial balance** to verify the equality of debits and credits in the ledger. A trial balance is a list of all ledger accounts and their balances. The debit and credit balances are listed in separate columns. Each column is totaled, and the two totals are compared for equality. Exhibit 4.10 displays the trial balance for Collins Consultants after the closing entries have been posted to the ledger.

If the debit total does not equal the credit total, the accountant knows to search for an error. However, as previously indicated, equal debit and credit totals does not assure accuracy. For example, the trial balance would not disclose errors like the following: failure to record transactions; misclassifications, such as debiting the wrong account; or incorrectly recording the amount of a transaction, such as recording a $200 transaction as $2,000. Equal debits and credits in a trial balance should be viewed as evidence rather than proof of accuracy.

How often should a trial balance be prepared? A company can test the equality of debits and credits as often as desired. Some companies prepare a trial balance daily; others may prepare one monthly, quarterly, or annually, depending on the needs of management.

After Closing Trial Balance

Account Titles	Debit	Credit
Cash	$ 1,250	
Accounts receivable	800	
Supplies	125	
Prepaid rent	2,100	
Notes receivable	6,000	
Interest receivable	360	
Office equipment	42,000	
Accumulated depreciation		$4,000
Accounts payable		900
Unearned revenue		3,000
Notes payable		10,000
Interest payable		1,100
Salaries payable		800
Common stock		15,000
Retained earnings		17,835
Totals	$52,635	$52,635

Answers to The Curious Accountant

Part 1

The process of closing the books and going through a year-end audit is time consuming for a business. Also, it is time spent that does not produce revenue. Thus, companies whose business is highly seasonal often choose "slow" periods to end their fiscal year. Abercrombie & Fitch does heavy business during the Christmas season, so it might find December 31 an inconvenient time to close its books. Toward the end of January, business activity is slow, and

inventory levels are at their low points. This is a good time to count the inventory and to assess the financial condition of the company. For these reasons, the company has chosen to close its books to end its fiscal year around the end of January.

Now that you know why a business like Abercrombie & Fitch might choose to end its fiscal year at the end of January, can you think of a reason why Polo Ralph Lauren closes its books at the end of April? (See page 192.)

CHECK YOURSELF 4.3

Describe an error that would not cause a trial balance to be out of balance.

Answer

Many potential errors would not cause a trial balance to be out of balance, such as debiting or crediting the wrong account. For example, if revenue earned on account were recorded with a debit to Cash instead of Accounts Receivable, total assets would be correct and the totals in the trial balance would equal each other even though the balances in the Cash and Accounts Receivable accounts would be incorrect. Recording the same incorrect amount in both the debit and credit part of an entry also would not cause a trial balance to be out of balance. For example, if $20 of revenue earned on account were recorded as a $200 debit to Accounts Receivable and a $200 credit to Consulting Revenue, the totals in the trial balance would equal each other although Accounts Receivable and Consulting Revenue amounts would be incorrect.

THE FINANCIAL ANALYST

Companies communicate information to analysts and other users through a document called the *annual report*. These reports are usually printed in color on high quality paper and contain lots of photographs. However, in an effort to reduce cost, some companies issue their annual reports in black and white on low grade paper or in electronic form. A company's annual report contains much more than the financial statements. Annual reports often have 40 or more pages. The financial statements require only four to six pages. What is printed on all those other pages? In general, the annual report of a large company has four major sections: (1) financial statements, (2) footnotes to the financial statements, (3) management's discussion and analysis, and (4) auditors' report. The footnotes and management's discussion and analysis make up the bulk of the report.

LO 8

Describe the components of an annual report, including the management, discussion, and analysis section and the footnotes to financial statements.

Footnotes to the Financial Statements

Accountants frequently have to make estimates when preparing financial statements. Also, GAAP may offer alternative ways of reporting certain transactions. **Footnotes to the financial statements** explain some of the estimates that were made as well as which reporting options were used. Reading the footnotes is critical to understanding the financial statements. The financial statements often include a caveat such as "the accompanying footnotes are an integral part of these financial statements."

Answers to The Curious Accountant

Part 2

Early April probably is a relatively slow time of year for **Polo Ralph Lauren**. Polo sells most of its goods through retailers. It must deliver clothing to stores such as **Abercrombie & Fitch** weeks before they will be sold to holiday shoppers. By

April the Christmas season has passed and much of the spring clothing will have already been shipped to retailers, so this is a good time for Polo to close its books. **Tommy Hilfiger**, another clothing manufacturer, closes its books on March 31 of each year.

Management's Discussion and Analysis

Management's discussion and analysis (MD&A) is usually located at the beginning of the annual report. MD&A is the section of the annual report in which management explains the company's past performance and future plans. For example, MD&A typically compares current year earnings with those of past periods and explains the reasons for significant changes. If the company is planning significant acquisitions of assets or other businesses, this information is usually included in MD&A. Likewise, any plans to discontinue part of the existing business are outlined in MD&A.

Role of the Independent Auditor Revisited

The auditors' role was introduced in Chapter 2. The auditors' responsibilities differ for various parts of the annual report. The auditors' primary responsibility is to express an opinion regarding whether the financial statements conform to GAAP. Since the footnotes are a part of the financial statements, the auditors' opinion extends to the footnotes as well as the statements.

Auditors have less responsibility for information reported in MD&A. Auditors *review* the MD&A section to be sure it does not contain comments that conflict with information in the financial statements. For example, if the current year's net income is down from last year's, management cannot say that "earnings continue to grow." However, MD&A can contain expressions of opinion. If current earnings are down relative to last year's, management could say, "We *believe* the decline to be temporary and expect substantial growth in the coming year." Auditors are not responsible for validating such opinions.

The Securities and Exchange Commission

Describe the role of the Securities and Exchange Commission in financial reporting.

The annual reports of public companies often differ from those of private companies because public companies are registered with the **Securities and Exchange Commission (SEC).** Public companies, sometimes called SEC companies, have to follow the reporting rules of the SEC as well as GAAP. SEC rules require some additional disclosures not required by GAAP. For example, an MD&A section is required by the SEC, but not by GAAP. As a result, annual reports of non-SEC companies usually do not include MD&A.

The SEC is a government agency authorized to establish and enforce the accounting rules for public companies. Although the SEC can overrule GAAP, it has very seldom done so. Recall that GAAP is established by the Financial Accounting Standards Board, a private professional accounting organization. While SEC rules seldom conflict with GAAP, they frequently require additional disclosures. All companies whose stock trades on public stock exchanges, and some whose do not, are required to register with the SEC. The SEC has no jurisdiction over non-SEC companies.

SEC companies must file specific information directly with the SEC annually, quarterly, and in-between if required. The most common reports are filed on Form 10-K (annually) and

FOCUS ON INTERNATIONAL ISSUES

IS THERE A GLOBAL ACCOUNTING LEADER?

Chapter 3 discussed some reasons that there is no single set of global GAAP. Nevertheless, one may wonder if there are certain countries that tend to take the lead in the establishment of GAAP. Although no single country has led in the overall development of accounting rule making, a few countries have led in some specific areas of accounting development.

For example, details about the double-entry bookkeeping system explained in this chapter were first published in Italy. This system was first formally publicized in the late 1400s by an Italian monk, Luca Pacioli. Pacioli did not actually develop the double-entry system; he published an explanation of the system as he had observed it in use by Italian merchants of his day. The use of the terms *debit* and *credit* results from the Italian origins of the bookkeeping system. Today, this system is used throughout the world.

As another example, consider that the public accounting profession as we know it in the United States and many other countries originated in the United Kingdom. The idea of an independent auditing professional (the CPA in the United States) came to the United States from the United Kingdom around the turn of the twentieth century. Not all countries have the strong nongovernment accounting profession that exists in the United Kingdom and United States, but those that do can trace their roots back to the United Kingdom.

Form 10-Q (quarterly). The *10-Q*s are less detailed than the 10-Ks. While there is significant overlap between the 10-Ks (SEC report) and the annual reports that companies issue directly to the public, the 10-Ks usually contain more information but fewer pictures. Most of the reports filed with the SEC are available electronically through the SEC's EDGAR database. EDGAR is an acronym for Electronic Data Gathering, Analysis, and Retrieval system, and it

REALITY BYTES

Imagine you were required to e-mail your family every time something unusual happened in your college studies. Even worse, what if you had to immediately inform your family if there even were a reasonable possibility something negative might happen in the future. For example, if you did not study for an upcoming accounting exam, suppose you had to tell your family before you took the test that your future exam grade might be low because you did not study for it. Essentially, public companies are required to provide just that type of disclosure by filing a Form 8-K with the SEC whenever any significant event occurs.

Anyone with even a casual interest in the business world knew that many automobile manufacturers, and General Motors in particular, were having problems making a profit selling cars in 2005 and 2006. Therefore, it came as no surprise to many investors on March 29, 2006, when the two largest corporate-credit ratings services in the United States, Standard & Poor's and Moody's, announced concerns about GM's credit worthiness. Nevertheless, GM felt an obligation to file an 8-K report with the SEC the very next day officially repeating the unpleasant news about itself. In part, this 8-K read:

> On March 29, 2006, Standard & Poor's Ratings Services placed all its ratings on General Motors Corp. (GM), . . . on CreditWatch with negative implications. This action stems from GM's disclosure in its 2005 10-K that the recent restatement of its previous financial statements raises potential issues regarding access to its $5.6 billion standby credit facility, as well as the possibility that certain lease obligations of as much as $3 billion could be subject to possible claims of acceleration, termination, or other remedies. At a minimum, GM could have to seek waivers on financial reporting requirements from lenders, which could put pressure on its liquidity.

For more information on these matters, use EDGAR to download the 8-K report that GM filed with the SEC on March 30, 2006.

is accessible through the World Wide Web on the Internet. Appendix A provides instructions for using EDGAR.

The SEC regulates audit standards as well as financial reporting. Prior to passage of the Sarbanes-Oxley Act in July 2002, the SEC left much of the regulation and oversight of independent auditors to the American Institute of Certified Public Accountants, a private professional organization. However, a key provision of Sarbanes-Oxley establishes the Public Company Accounting Oversight Board (PCAOB). This board assumes the primary responsibility for establishing and enforcing auditing standards for CPAs who audit SEC companies. The board has five financially astute members, three of whom cannot be CPAs.

◄◄ A Look Back

This chapter introduced the *double-entry accounting system*. This system was first documented in the 1400s, and is used by most companies today. Key components of the double-entry system are summarized below.

1. Business events can be classified concisely using debit/credit terminology. *Debits* are used to record increases in asset accounts and decreases in liability and stockholders' equity accounts. *Credits* are used to record decreases in asset accounts and increases in liability and stockholders' equity accounts.

2. *T-accounts* are frequently used to analyze and communicate account activity. The account title is placed at the top of the horizontal bar of the T, and increases and decreases are placed on either side of the vertical bar. In a T-account, debits are recorded on the left side and credits are recorded on the right side.

3. Accountants initially record transaction data in journals. The *general journal* format is used not only for data entry but also as a shorthand communication tool. Each journal entry includes at least one debit and one credit. An entry is recorded using at least two lines, with the debit recorded on the top line and the credit on the bottom line. The credit is indented to distinguish it from the debit. The general journal format is illustrated here:

4. Information is posted (copied) from the journals to *ledger* accounts. The ledger accounts provide the information used to prepare the financial statements.

5. *Trial balances* are used to check the mathematical accuracy of the recording process. Ledger accounts with their associated debit and credit balances are listed in the trial balance. The debit and credit amounts are totaled and compared. An equal amount of debits and credits provides evidence that transactions have been recorded correctly, although errors may still exist. If the debits and credits are *not* equal, it is proof that errors exist.

The double-entry system is just a way to organize accounting data. No matter how we organize the data, the objective is to summarize and report it in a way that is useful for making decisions.

►► A Look Forward

Chapters 1 through 4 focused on businesses that generate revenue by providing services to their customers. Examples of these types of businesses include consulting, real estate sales, medical services, and legal services. The next chapter introduces accounting practices for businesses that generate revenue by selling goods. Examples of these companies include **Wal-Mart**, **Circuit City**, **Office Depot**, and **Lowes**.

The   events apply to the first year of operations for Mestro Financial Services Company:

1.   d $28,000 cash by issuing common stock on January 1, 2008.
2.   sed $1,100 of supplies on account.
          12,000 cash in advance for a one-year lease on office space.
          d $23,000 of consulting revenue on account.
          red $16,000 of general operating expenses on account.
          cted $20,000 cash from receivables.
          $13,000 cash on accounts payable.
8. Paid a $1,000 cash dividend to the stockholders.

Information for Adjusting Entries

9. There was $200 of supplies on hand at the end of the accounting period.
10. The one-year lease on the office space was effective beginning on October 1, 2008.
11. There was $1,200 of accrued salaries at the end of 2008.

Required

a. Record the preceding events in ledger T-accounts.
b. Prepare a trial balance.
c. Prepare an income statement, statement of changes in stockholders' equity, balance sheet, and statement of cash flows.
d. Prepare the appropriate closing entries in general journal format.

Solution to Requirement a

MESTRO FINANCIAL SERVICES COMPANY
T-Accounts, 2008

Assets			=	Liabilities			+	Equity		

Cash

1.	28,000	3.	12,000
6.	20,000	7.	13,000
		8.	1,000
Bal.	22,000		

Accounts Receivable

4.	23,000	6.	20,000
Bal.	3,000		

Supplies

2.	1,100	9.	900
Bal.	200		

Prepaid Rent

3.	12,000	10.	3,000
Bal.	9,000		

Accounts Payable

7.	13,000	2.	1,100
		5.	16,000
		Bal.	4,100

Salaries Payable

		11.	1,200
		Bal.	1,200

Common Stock

		1.	28,000
		Bal.	28,000

Dividends

8.	1,000	

Consulting Revenue

		4.	23,000

General Operating Expenses

5.	16,000	

Salaries Expense

11.	1,200	

Supplies Expense

9.	900	

Rent Expense

10.	3,000	

Solution to Requirement b

MESTRO FINANCIAL SERVICES COMPANY
Trial Balance
December 31, 2008

Account Titles	Debit	Credit
Cash	$22,000	
Accounts receivable	3,000	
Supplies	200	
Prepaid rent	9,000	
Accounts payable		$ 4,100
Salaries payable		1,200
Common stock		28,000
Dividends	1,000	
Consulting revenue		23,000
General operating expenses	16,000	
Salaries expense	1,200	
Supplies expense	900	
Rent expense	3,000	
Totals	$56,300	$56,300

Solution to Requirement c

MESTRO FINANCIAL SERVICES COMPANY
Financial Statements
For 2008

Income Statement

Consulting revenue		$23,000
Expenses		
General operating expenses	$16,000	
Salaries expense	1,200	
Supplies expense	900	
Rent expense	3,000	
Total expenses		(21,100)
Net income		$ 1,900

Statement of Changes in Stockholders' Equity

Beginning common stock	$ 0	
Plus: Common stock issued	28,000	
Ending common stock		$28,000
Beginning retained earnings	0	
Plus: Net income	1,900	
Less: Dividends	(1,000)	
Ending retained earnings		900
Total stockholders' equity		$28,900

continued

Balance Sheet		
Assets		
Cash	$22,000	
Accounts receivable	3,000	
Supplies	200	
Prepaid rent	9,000	
Total assets		$34,200
Liabilities		
Accounts payable	$ 4,100	
Salaries payable	1,200	
Total liabilities		$ 5,300
Stockholders' equity		
Common stock	28,000	
Retained earnings	900	
Total stockholders' equity		28,900
Total liabilities and stockholders' equity		$34,200

Statement of Cash Flows		
Cash flows from operating activities		
Inflow from customers	$20,000	
Outflow for expenses	(25,000)	
Net cash flow from operating activities		$ (5,000)
Cash flows from investing activities		0
Cash flows from financing activities		
Inflow from issue of common stock	28,000	
Outflow for dividends	(1,000)	
Net cash flow from financing activities		27,000
Net change in cash		22,000
Plus: Beginning cash balance		0
Ending cash balance		$22,000

Solution to Requirement d   *closing entries*

Date	Account Titles	Debit	Credit
Dec. 31	Closing Entries		
	Consulting Revenue	*total* 23,000	
	Retained Earnings		23,000
Dec. 31	Retained Earnings	*total* 21,100	
	General Operating Expenses		16,000
	Salaries Expense		1,200
	Supplies Expense		900
	Rent Expense		3,000
Dec. 31	Retained Earnings	*total* 1,000	
	Dividends		1,000

KEY TERMS

Account balance 172
Books of original entry 186
Chart of accounts 184

Closing entries 188
Contra account 182
Credit 172

Debit 172
Double-entry
  accounting 172

Fiscal year 171
Footnotes to the financial
  statements 191

General journal 186	Management's Discussion and	Securities and Exchange	Special journals 186
Journal 186	Analysis (MD&A) 192	Commission (SEC) 192	T-account 172
Ledger 184	Posting 186	Source document 186	Trial balance 190

QUESTIONS

1. What are the two fundamental equality requirements of the double-entry accounting system?
2. Define *debit* and *credit*. How are assets, liabilities, common stock, retained earnings, revenues, expenses, and dividends affected (increased or decreased) by debits and by credits?
3. How is the balance of an account determined?
4. What are the three primary sources of business assets?
5. What are the three primary ways a business may use assets?
6. Why is an adjusting entry necessary to record depreciation expense? What accounts are affected? How are the account balances affected?
7. How does a debit to an expense account ultimately affect retained earnings? Stockholders' equity?
8. What accounts normally have debit balances? What accounts normally have credit balances?
9. What is the primary source of information for preparing the financial statements?
10. What is the purpose of a journal?
11. What is the difference between the *general journal* and special journals?
12. What is a ledger? What is its function in the accounting system?
13. What is the purpose of closing entries?
14. At a minimum, what information is recorded in the general journal?
15. What is the purpose of a trial balance?
16. When should a trial balance be prepared?
17. What does the term *posting* mean?
18. Where did the terms *debit* and *credit* originate?
19. What country is responsible for the accounting profession's having "independent accounting professionals"?
20. What type of information is found in the footnotes to the financial statements?
21. What type of information is found in the MD&A section of the annual report?
22. What is the Securities and Exchange Commission? What are its responsibilities concerning a company's financial statements? What types of companies are under the SEC's jurisdiction?

MULTIPLE-CHOICE QUESTIONS

Quiz 4

Multiple-choice questions are provided on the text Web site at www.mhhe.com/edmonds6e.

EXERCISES—SERIES A

All Exercises in Series A are available with McGraw-Hill's Homework Manager®

L.O. 1

Exercise 4-1A *Matching debit and credit terminology with accounting elements*

Required

Complete the following table by indicating whether a debit or credit is used to increase or decrease the balance of accounts belonging to each category of accounting elements. The appropriate debit/credit terminology has been identified for the first category (assets) as an example.

Category of Elements	Used to Increase This Element	Used to Decrease This Element
Assets	Debit	Credit
Contra asset		
Liabilities		
Common stock		
Retained earnings		
Revenue		
Expense		
Dividends		

Exercise 4-2A   *Debit/credit terminology*

L.O. 1, 2

Two introductory accounting students were arguing about how to record a transaction involving an exchange of cash for land. Trisha stated that the transaction should have a debit to Land and a credit to Cash; Tony argued that the reverse (debit to Cash and credit to Land) represented the appropriate treatment.

Required

Which student was correct? Defend your position.

Exercise 4-3A   *Matching debit and credit terminology with account titles*

L.O. 2

Required

Indicate whether each of the following accounts normally has a debit balance or a credit balance.

a. Cash
b. Interest Expense
c. Depreciation Expense
d. Accumulated Depreciation
e. Accounts Payable

f. Unearned Revenue
g. Service Revenue
h. Dividends
i. Land
j. Accounts Receivable

Exercise 4-4A   *Identifying increases and decreases in T-accounts*

L.O. 1

Required

For each of the following T-accounts, write "increase" or "decrease" under the terms "debit" and "credit" to indicate how debit and credit entries affect the account balance.

Cash		Accounts Payable		Common Stock	
Debit	Credit	Debit	Credit	Debit	Credit

Accounts Receivable		Notes Payable		Dividends	
Debit	Credit	Debit	Credit	Debit	Credit

Accumulated Depreciation				Service Revenue	
Debit	Credit			Debit	Credit

				Other Operating Expense	
				Debit	Credit

Exercise 4-5A   *Applying debit/credit terminology to accounting events*

L.O. 2

Required

In parallel columns, list the accounts that would be debited and credited for each of the following unrelated transactions:

a. Provided services on account.
b. Paid cash for operating expense.

   c. Acquired cash from the issue of common stock.
   d. Purchased supplies on account.
   e. Purchased equipment for cash.
   f. Paid a cash dividend to the stockholders.
   g. Provided services for cash.
   h. Recognized accrued salaries at the end of the period.

L.O. 2, 3

Exercise 4-6A   *T-accounts and the accounting equation*

Required

Record each of the following Holder Co. events in T-accounts and then explain how the event affects the accounting equation.

   a. Received $30,000 cash by issuing common stock.
   b. Purchased supplies for $1,100 cash.
   c. Performed services on account for $6,000.
   d. Purchased land for $10,000, paying $4,000 cash and issuing a note payable for the balance.

L.O. 3

Exercise 4-7A   *Recording transactions in T-accounts*

The following events apply to Clark Delivery Co. for 2010, its first year of operation.

   1. Received cash of $50,000 from the issue of common stock.
   2. Purchased a delivery van for $30,000 cash on January 1, 2010. The delivery van has a salvage value of $6,000 and a three-year useful life.
   3. Performed $90,000 worth of services on account.
   4. Paid $53,000 cash for salaries expense.
   5. Purchased supplies for $12,000 on account.
   6. Collected $62,000 of accounts receivable.
   7. Paid $8,500 of the accounts payable.
   8. Paid a $5,000 dividend to the stockholders.
   9. Recorded depreciation expense for the year on the delivery van.
   10. Had $1,500 of supplies on hand at the end of the period.

Required

   a. Record these events in the appropriate T-accounts and determine the ending balance in each account.
   b. Determine the amount of total assets at the end of 2010.
   c. Determine the amount of net income for 2010.

L.O. 2

Exercise 4-8A   *Debit/credit terminology*

Required

For each of the following independent events, identify the account that would be debited and the account that would be credited. The accounts for the first event are identified as an example.

Event	Account Debited	Account Credited
a	Cash	Notes Payable

   a. Borrowed cash by issuing a note.
   b. Received cash for services to be performed in the future.
   c. Recognized depreciation expense.
   d. Paid salaries payable.
   e. Provided services on account.
   f. Repaid principal balance on note payable.

g. Paid cash for operating expenses.

h. Purchased supplies on account.

i. Recognized accrued interest expense.

j. Recognized revenue for services completed. Cash had been collected in Event *b*.

k. Paid accounts payable.

l. Purchased office equipment with cash.

m. Received cash in payment of accounts receivable.

n. Recognized accrued interest revenue.

o. Paid a cash dividend to the stockholders.

Exercise 4-9A   *Identification of the type of transaction, its effect on the accounting equation, and whether the effect is recorded with a debit or credit*   **L.O. 1, 2**

Required

Identify whether each of the following transactions is an asset source (AS), asset use (AU), asset exchange (AE), or claims exchange (CE). Also explain how each event affects the accounting equation by placing a + for *increase,* − for *decrease,* and NA for *not affected* under each of the components of the accounting equation. Finally, indicate whether the effect requires a debit or credit entry. The first event is recorded as an example.

| | | | | | | Stockholders' Equity | |
| | Type of | | | | | Common | | Retained |
Event	Event	Assets	=	Liabilities	+	Stock	+	Earnings
a	AE	+ Debit − Credit		NA		NA		NA

a. Purchased office equipment with cash.

b. Provided services for cash.

c. Repaid principal balance on note payable.

d. Purchased supplies on account.

e. Paid accounts payable.

f. Acquired cash from the issue of common stock.

g. Received cash in payment of accounts receivable.

h. Paid cash in advance for one year of rent.

i. Paid salaries payable.

j. Received cash for services to be performed in the future.

k. Recognized accrued interest expense.

l. Paid a cash dividend to the stockholders.

m. Recognized revenue for services completed for which cash had been collected previously.

n. Recognized depreciation expense on the equipment.

o. Recognized accrued interest revenue.

Exercise 4-10A   *Recording events in the general journal*   **L.O. 7**

Required

Record each of the following transactions in general journal form.

a. Received $12,000 cash for services to be performed at a later date.

b. Purchased supplies for $1,200 cash.

c. Performed $25,000 worth of services on account.

d. Purchased equipment that cost $54,000 by paying $12,000 cash and issuing a $42,000 note for the balance.

e. Charged $1,200 on account for repairs expense.

f. Collected $19,000 cash on accounts receivable.

g. Paid $900 on accounts payable.

h. Paid $4,800 cash in advance for an insurance policy on the equipment.

i. Recorded accrued interest expense of $1,400.

j. Recorded $5,000 depreciation expense on the equipment.

k. Recorded the adjusting entry to recognize $3,600 of insurance expense.

L.O. 6

Exercise 4-11A *Preparing a trial balance*

Required

On December 31, 2009, Parks Company had the following account balances in its general ledger. Use this information to prepare a trial balance.

Common stock	$32,000
Salaries expense	16,000
Office supplies	2,400
Advertising expense	5,000
Retained earnings, 1/1/2009	46,200
Unearned revenue	18,000
Office equipment	53,000
Accounts receivable	6,500
Accumulated depreciation	16,000
Cash	65,000
Service revenue	93,000
Dividends	7,500
Depreciation expense	6,000
Prepaid insurance	6,400
Land	26,400
Rent expense	15,000
Accounts payable	4,000

L.O. 5, 7

Exercise 4-12A *Preparing closing entries*

The following financial information was taken from the books of Lee Spa.

Account Balances as of December 31, 2008	
Accounts receivable	$29,000
Accounts payable	7,500
Advertising expense	2,500
Accumulated depreciation	13,500
Cash	19,800
Certificate of deposit	22,000
Common stock	24,000
Depreciation expense	7,200
Dividends	5,000
Equipment	35,000
Interest receivable	600
Interest revenue	2,800
Notes payable	10,000
Prepaid rent	3,200
Rent expense	7,800
Retained earnings 1/1/2008	17,600
Salaries expense	32,000
Salaries payable	9,800
Service revenue	82,500
Supplies	400
Supplies expense	3,200

Required

a. Prepare the necessary closing entries at December 31, 2008, for Lee Spa.

b. What is the balance in the Retained Earnings account after the closing entries are posted?

Exercise 4-13A   *Recording events in T-accounts and preparing a trial balance*   **L.O. 3, 6**

The following events apply to Ted's Electronics in its first year of operations.

1. Received $30,000 cash from the issue of common stock.
2. Earned $25,000 of service revenue on account.
3. Incurred $15,000 of operating expenses on account.
4. Borrowed $20,000 from First Bank.
5. Paid $8,000 cash to purchase office equipment.
6. Collected $20,000 of cash from accounts receivable.
7. Received a $6,000 cash advance for services to be provided in the future.
8. Purchased $1,200 of supplies on account.
9. Made an $7,500 payment on accounts payable.
10. Paid a $7,000 cash dividend to the stockholders.
11. Recognized $500 of supplies expense.
12. Recognized $5,000 of revenue for services provided to the customer in Event 7.
13. Recorded accrued interest expense of $600.
14. Recognized $2,000 of depreciation expense.

Required

a. Record the events in T-accounts and determine the ending account balances.

b. Test the equality of the debit and credit balances of the T-accounts by preparing a trial balance.

Exercise 4-14A   *Determining the effect of errors on the trial balance*   **L.O. 6**

Required

Explain how each of the following posting errors affects a trial balance. State whether the trial balance will be out of balance because of the posting error, and indicate which side of the trial balance will have a higher amount after each independent entry is posted. If the posting error does not affect the equality of debits and credits shown in the trial balance, state that the error will not cause an inequality and explain why.

a. A $400 debit to Rent Expense was posted twice.
b. A $1,200 credit to Accounts Payable was not posted.
c. A $400 credit to Notes Payable was credited to Revenue.
d. A $200 debit to Cash was posted as a $2,000 debit.
e. A $520 debit to Office Supplies was debited to Office Equipment.

Exercise 4-15A   *Recording events in the general journal, posting to T-accounts,*   **L.O. 3, 5, 7**
                      and preparing closing entries

At the beginning of 2012, Oliver Cleaning Service had the following balances in its accounts:

Account	Balance
Cash	$25,000
Accounts receivable	19,000
Accounts payable	12,400
Common stock	18,000
Retained earnings	13,600

The following events apply to Oliver for 2012.

1. Provided $75,000 of services on account.
2. Incurred $3,100 of operating expenses on account.
3. Collected $56,000 of accounts receivable.
4. Paid $42,000 cash for salaries expense.
5. Paid $15,000 cash as a partial payment on accounts payable.
6. Paid a $12,000 cash dividend to the stockholders.

Required

a. Record these events in a general journal.
b. Open T-accounts and post the beginning balances and the preceding transactions to the appropriate accounts. Determine the balance of each account.
c. Record the beginning balances and the events in a horizontal statements model such as the following one:

Assets		=	Liab.	+	Equity		Rev.	−	Exp.	=	Net Inc.	Cash Flow
Cash	+ Accts. Rec.	=	Accts. Pay.	+	Common Stock	+ Ret. Earn.						

d. Record the closing entries in the general journal and post them to the T-accounts. What is the amount of net income for the year?
e. What is the amount of *change* in retained earnings for the year? Is the change in retained earnings different from the amount of net income? If so, why?

L.O. 3, 5

Exercise 4-16A *Recording receivables and identifying their effect on financial statements*

Ross Company performed services on account for $30,000 in 2009, its first year of operations. Ross collected $24,000 cash from accounts receivable during 2009 and the remaining $6,000 in cash during 2010.

Required

a. Record the 2009 transactions in T-accounts.
b. Record the 2009 transactions in a horizontal statements model like the following one:

Assets		=	Liab.	+	Equity	Rev.	−	Exp.	=	Net Inc.	Cash Flow
Cash	+ Accts. Rec.	=	NA	+	Ret. Earn.						

c. Determine the amount of revenue Ross would report on the 2009 income statement.
d. Determine the amount of cash flow from operating activities Ross would report on the 2009 statement of cash flows.
e. Open a T-account for Retained Earnings, and close the 2009 Service Revenue account to the Retained Earnings account.
f. Record the 2010 cash collection in the appropriate T-accounts.
g. Record the 2010 transaction in a horizontal statements model like the one shown in Requirement b.
h. Assuming no other transactions occur in 2010, determine the amount of net income and the net cash flow from operating activities for 2010.

L.O. 3–6

Exercise 4-17A *Recording supplies and identifying their effect on financial statements*

Andrea Greg started and operated a small family consulting firm in 2011. The firm was affected by two events: (1) Greg provided $24,000 of services on account, and (2) she purchased $8,000 of supplies on account. There were $900 of supplies on hand as of December 31, 2011.

Required

a. Open T-accounts and record the two transactions in the accounts.

b. Record the required year-end adjusting entry to reflect the use of supplies.

c. Record the above transactions in a horizontal statements model like the following one.

Assets			=	Liab.	+	Equity	Rev.	−	Exp.	=	Net Inc.	Cash Flow
Accts.				Accts.								
Rec.	+	Supp.	=	Pay.	+	Ret. Earn.						

d. Explain why the amount of net income and the net cash flow from operating activities differ.

e. Record and post the required closing entries, and prepare an after-closing trial balance.

Exercise 4-18A   *Recording prepaids and identifying their effect on financial statements*

L.O. 4, 7

Orchard Fresh began operations in 2009 by issuing common stock for $150,000. The company paid $120,000 cash in advance for a one-year contract to lease machinery for the business. The lease agreement was signed on March 1, 2009, and was effective immediately. Orchard Fresh earned $115,000 of cash revenue in 2009.

Required

a. Record the March 1 cash payment in general journal format.

b. Record in general journal format the adjustment required as of December 31, 2009.

c. Record all 2009 events in a horizontal statements model like the following one:

Assets			=	Liab.	+	Equity	Rev.	−	Exp.	=	Net Inc.	Cash Flow
Cash	+	PrPd. Rent				Ret. Earn.						

d. What amount of net income would Orchard Fresh report on the 2009 income statement? What is the amount of net cash flow from operating activities for 2009?

e. Determine the amount of prepaid rent Orchard Fresh would report on the December 31, 2009, balance sheet.

Exercise 4-19A   *Recording accrued salaries and identifying their effect on financial statements*

L.O. 4, 7

On December 31, 2012, Kim's Dance Company had accrued salaries of $12,500.

Required

a. Record in general journal format the adjustment required as of December 31, 2012.

b. Determine the amount of net income Kim's Dance would report on the 2012 income statement, assuming that Kim's Dance earns $25,000 of cash revenue. What is the amount of net cash flow from operating activities for 2012?

c. What amount of Salaries Payable would Kim's Dance report on the December 31, 2012, balance sheet?

Exercise 4-20A   *Recording depreciation and identifying its effect on financial statements*

L.O. 3, 4

On January 1, 2010, Allison bought a computer system for $35,000 cash. The computer had a useful life of five years and a salvage value of $3,000.

Required

a. Record in T-accounts Allison's purchase of the computer system.

b. Record in T-accounts the adjustment required on December 31, 2010.

c. Determine the book value of the computer Allison would report on the December 31, 2010, balance sheet.

d. Determine the amount of net income Allison would report on the 2010 income statement, assuming that Allison earned $15,000 of cash revenue in 2010.

e. What is the amount of net cash flow from operating activities for 2010?

f. What amount of depreciation expense would Allison report on the 2011 income statement?

g. Determine the book value of the computer Allison would report on the December 31, 2011, balance sheet.

L.O. 3, 4

Exercise 4-21A *Recording a note payable and identifying its effect on financial statements*

On May 1, 2009, Tabor Company borrowed $80,000 from First Bank. The note had a 6 percent annual interest rate and a one-year term to maturity.

Required

a. Identify the transaction type (asset source, use, or exchange or claims exchange) and record in T-accounts the entry for the financing event on May 1, 2009.

b. Identify the transaction type and record in T-accounts the adjustment as of December 31, 2009.

c. Determine the amount of net income on the 2009 income statement, assuming Tabor Company earned $35,000 of cash revenue.

d. What is the amount of net cash flow from operating activities for 2009?

e. Determine the total liabilities on the December 31, 2009, balance sheet.

f. Record (1) the 2010 accrual of interest and (2) the cash payment of principal and interest on May 1, 2010.

g. Are the May 1, 2010, transactions asset source, asset use, asset exchange, or claims exchange transactions?

L.O. 3, 4

Exercise 4-22A *Recording unearned revenue and identifying its effect on financial statements*

Jamie received a $90,000 cash advance on March 1, 2010, for legal services to be performed in the future. Services were to be provided for a one-year term beginning March 1, 2010.

Required

a. Record the March 1 cash receipt in T-accounts.

b. Record in T-accounts the adjustment required as of December 31, 2010.

c. Record the preceding transaction and related adjustment in a horizontal statements model like the following one:

Assets	=	Liab.	+	Equity	Rev.	−	Exp.	=	Net Inc.	Cash Flow

d. Determine the amount of net income on the 2010 income statement. What is the amount of net cash flow from operating activities for 2010?

e. What amount of Unearned Revenue would Jamie report on the December 31, 2010, balance sheet?

L.O. 3

Exercise 4-23A *Using a T-account to determine cash flow from operating activities*

Taylor, Inc., began the accounting period with a $75,000 debit balance in its Accounts Receivable account. During the accounting period, Taylor earned revenue on account of $280,000. The ending Accounts Receivable balance was $62,000.

Required

Based on this information alone, determine the amount of cash inflow from operating activities during the accounting period. (*Hint:* Use a T-account for Accounts Receivable. Enter the debits and credits for the given events, and solve for the missing amount.)

L.O. 3

Exercise 4-24A *Using a T-account to determine cash flow from operating activities*

Adams Company began the accounting period with an $18,000 credit balance in its Accounts Payable account. During the accounting period, Adams incurred expenses on account of $54,000. The ending Accounts Payable balance was $12,000.

Required

Based on this information, determine the amount of cash outflow for expenses during the accounting period. (*Hint:* Use a T-account for Accounts Payable. Enter the debits and credits for the given events, and solve for the missing amount.)

All Problems in Series A are available with McGraw-Hill's Homework Manager®

Problem 4-25A *Identifying debit and credit balances*

L.O. 2

Required

Indicate whether each of the following accounts normally has a debit or credit balance.

a. Common Stock
b. Retained Earnings
c. Certificate of Deposit
d. Interest Expense
e. Accounts Receivable
f. Interest Revenue
g. Insurance Expense
h. Interest Payable
i. Cash
j. Dividends
k. Unearned Revenue
l. Operating Expense
m. Accumulated Depreciation
n. Accounts Payable
o. Office Equipment

p. Depreciation Expense
q. Service Revenue
r. Notes Payable
s. Notes Receivable
t. Supplies
u. Utilities Payable
v. Consulting Revenue
w. Interest Receivable
x. Supplies Expense
y. Salaries Expense
z. Equipment
aa. Salaries Payable
bb. Land
cc. Prepaid Insurance

Problem 4-26A *Transaction type and debit/credit terminology*

L.O. 1, 2

The following events apply to Hunter Enterprises.

1. Acquired $50,000 cash from the issue of common stock.
2. Paid salaries to employees, $1,750 cash.
3. Collected $8,100 cash for services to be performed in the future.
4. Paid cash for utilities expense, $804.
5. Recognized $22,500 of service revenue on account.
6. Purchased equipment costing $15,000 by paying cash of $6,000 and borrowing the balance from First National Bank by issuing a four-year note.
7. Paid a $1,250 cash dividend to the stockholders.
8. Purchased $2,500 of supplies on account.
9. Received $6,250 cash for services rendered.
10. Paid cash to rent office space for the next 12 months, $6,000.
11. Made a $3,750 principal payment on the bank note.
12. Paid cash of $8,750 for other operating expenses.
13. Paid on account payable, $620.
14. Paid cash to purchase office furniture, $5,000.
15. Recognized $3,750 of depreciation expense.
16. Recognized $1,500 of rent expense. Cash had been paid in a prior transaction (see Event 10).
17. Recognized $2,500 of revenue for services performed. Cash had been previously collected (see Event 3).
18. Recognized $425 of accrued interest expense.

Required

Identify each event as asset source (AS), asset use (AU), asset exchange (AE), or claims exchange (CE). Also identify the account that is to be debited and the account that is to be credited when the transaction is recorded. The first event is recorded as an example.

Event No.	Type of Event	Account Debited	Account Credited
1	AS	Cash	Common Stock

Problem 4-27A *Recording adjusting entries in general journal format*

Required

Each of the following independent events requires a year-end adjusting entry. Record each event and the related adjusting entry in general journal format. The first event is recorded as an example. Assume a December 31 closing date.

Date	Account Titles	Debit	Credit
Oct. 1	Prepaid Rent	9,600	
	Cash		9,600
Dec. 31	Rent Expense (9,600 × 3/12)	2,400	
	Prepaid Rent		2,400

a. Paid $9,600 cash in advance on October 1 for a one-year lease on office space.

b. Borrowed $70,000 cash by issuing a note to Third National Bank on May 1. The note had a one-year term and a 6 percent annual rate of interest.

c. Paid $46,000 cash to purchase equipment on October 1. The equipment was expected to have a four-year useful life and a $6,000 salvage value. Depreciation is computed on a straight-line basis.

d. Invested $14,000 cash in a certificate of deposit that paid 4 percent annual interest. The certificate was acquired on April 1 and had a one-year term to maturity.

e. Purchased $3,200 of supplies on account on June 15. At year end, $500 of supplies remained on hand.

f. Received a $9,600 cash advance on August 1 for a contract to provide services for one year.

g. Paid $3,600 cash in advance on May 1 for a one-year insurance policy.

Problem 4-28A *One complete accounting cycle*

The following events apply to Rick's Vacations' first year of operations:

1. Acquired $20,000 cash from the issue of common stock on January 1, 2009.
2. Purchased $1,200 of supplies on account.
3. Paid $4,200 cash in advance for a one-year lease on office space.
4. Earned $35,000 of revenue on account.
5. Incurred $12,500 of other operating expenses on account.
6. Collected $28,000 cash from accounts receivable.
7. Paid $9,000 cash on accounts payable.
8. Paid a $5,000 cash dividend to the stockholders.

Information for Adjusting Entries

9. There was $150 of supplies on hand at the end of the accounting period.
10. The lease on the office space covered a one-year period beginning September 1.
11. There was $3,600 of accrued salaries at the end of the period.

Required

a. Record these transactions in general journal form.
b. Post the transaction data from the journal to ledger T-accounts.
c. Prepare a trial balance.
d. Prepare an income statement, statement of changes in stockholders' equity, a balance sheet, and a statement of cash flows.

e. Record the entries to close the temporary accounts (Revenue, Expense, and Dividends) to Retained Earnings in general journal form.

f. Post the closing entries to the T-accounts, and prepare an after-closing trial balance.

Problem 4-29A *Two complete accounting cycles*   T - accounts

Laura's Salon experienced the following events during 2008.

1. Started operations by acquiring $50,000 of cash from the issue of common stock.
2. Paid $6,000 cash in advance for rent during the period from March 1, 2008, to March 1, 2009.
3. Received $5,400 cash in advance for services to be performed evenly over the period from September 1, 2008, to September 1, 2009.
4. Performed services for customers on account for $65,200.
5. Incurred operating expenses on account of $31,500.
6. Collected $58,400 cash from accounts receivable.
7. Paid $26,000 cash for salaries expense.
8. Paid $28,000 cash as a partial payment on accounts payable.

CHECK FIGURES
b. Ending Cash Balance, 2008: $53,800
g. Net Income, 2009: $36,100

Adjusting Entries

9. Made the adjusting entry for the expired rent (see Event 2).
10. Recognized revenue for services performed in accordance with Event 3.
11. Recorded $2,100 of accrued salaries at the end of 2008.

Events for 2009

1. Paid $2,100 cash for the salaries accrued at the end of the previous year.
2. Performed services for cash, $46,500.
3. Borrowed $20,000 cash from the local bank by issuing a note.
4. Paid $25,000 cash to purchase land.
5. Paid $6,000 cash in advance for rent during the period from March 1, 2009, to March 1, 2010.
6. Performed services for customers on account for $82,000.
7. Incurred operating expenses on account of $47,500.
8. Collected $76,300 cash from accounts receivable.
9. Paid $46,000 cash as a partial payment on accounts payable.
10. Paid $41,000 cash for salaries expense.
11. Paid a $5,000 cash dividend to the stockholders.

Adjusting Entries

12. Recognized revenue for services performed in accordance with Event 3 in 2008.
13. Made the adjusting entry for the expired rent. (*Hint:* Part of the rent was paid in 2008.)
14. Recorded accrued interest. The note was issued on March 1, 2009, for a one-year term and had an interest rate of 9 percent (see Event 3).

Required

a. Record the events and adjusting entries for 2008 in general journal form.
b. Post the events for 2008 to T-accounts.
c. Prepare a trial balance for 2008.
d. Prepare an income statement, statement of changes in stockholders' equity, balance sheet, and statement of cash flows for 2008.
e. Record the entries to close the 2008 temporary accounts to Retained Earnings in the general journal and post to the T-accounts.
f. Prepare an after-closing trial balance for December 31, 2008.
g. Repeat requirements *a* through *f* for 2009.

Problem 4-30A *Identifying accounting events from journal entries*

Required

The following information is from the records of attorney Tim Boone. Write a brief description of the accounting event represented in each of the general journal entries.

Date	Account Titles	Debit	Credit
Jan. 1	Cash	40,000	
	Common Stock		40,000
Feb. 10	Cash	4,000	
	Unearned Revenue		4,000
Mar. 5	Supplies	1,000	
	Cash		1,000
Apr. 10	Office Equipment	12,000	
	Cash		3,000
	Note Payable		9,000
Apr. 30	Prepaid Rent	800	
	Cash		800
May 1	Accounts Receivable	20,000	
	Service Revenue		20,000
June 1	Salaries Expense	2,000	
	Cash		2,000
Aug. 5	Accounts Receivable	12,000	
	Service Revenue		12,000
10	Dividends	2,000	
	Cash		2,000
Sept. 10	Cash	4,400	
	Accounts Receivable		4,400
Oct. 1	Property Tax Expense	2,800	
	Cash		2,800
Dec. 31	Depreciation Expense	1,000	
	Accumulated Depreciation		1,000
31	Supplies Expense	800	
	Supplies		800
31	Rent Expense	2,200	
	Prepaid Rent		2,200
31	Unearned Revenue	6,240	
	Service Revenue		6,240

L.O. 3, 4, 6

Problem 4-31A   *Recording events in statements model and T-accounts and preparing a trial balance*

The following accounting events apply to Chang Co. for the year 2008:

Asset Source Transactions

1. Began operations when the business acquired $20,000 cash from the issue of common stock.
2. Purchased $6,500 of equipment on account.
3. Performed services and collected cash of $2,000.
4. Collected $4,500 of cash in advance for services to be provided over the next 12 months.
5. Provided $12,000 of services on account.
6. Purchased supplies of $650 on account.

Asset Exchange Transactions

7. Purchased $4,000 of equipment for cash.
8. Collected $6,000 of cash from accounts receivable.
9. Loaned $1,000 to Ted Marples, who issued a 12-month, 9 percent note.
10. Purchased $500 of supplies with cash.
11. Purchased a $4,200 certificate of deposit that had a six-month term and paid 4 percent annual interest.

Asset Use Transactions

12. Paid $4,500 cash for salaries of employees.
13. Paid a cash dividend of $2,000 to the stockholders.

14. Paid for the equipment that had been purchased on account (see Event 2).
15. Paid $650 for supplies that had been purchased on account.

Claims Exchange Transactions

16. Placed an advertisement in the local newspaper for $100 and agreed to pay for the ad later.
17. Incurred utilities expense of $125 on account.

Adjusting Entries

18. Recognized $3,000 of revenue for performing services. The collection of cash for these services occurred in a prior transaction. (See Event 4.)
19. Recorded $45 of interest revenue that had accrued on the note receivable from Marples (see Event 9).
20. Recorded $84 of interest revenue that had accrued on the certificate of deposit (see Event 11).
21. Recorded $600 of accrued salary expense at the end of 2008.
22. Recognized $1,200 of depreciation on the equipment (see Events 2 and 7).
23. Recorded supplies expense. Had $120 of supplies on hand at the end of the accounting period.

Required

a. Use a horizontal statements model to show how each event affects the balance sheet, income statement, and statement of cash flows. Indicate whether the event increases (+), decreases (−), or does not affect (NA) each element of the financial statements. Also, in the Cash Flow column, use the letters OA to designate operating activity, IA for investing activity, and FA for financing activity. The first event is recorded as an example.

Assets	=	Liab.	+	Equity	Rev.	−	Exp.	=	Net Inc.	Cash Flow
+		NA		+	NA		NA		NA	+ FA

b. Record each of the preceding transactions in T-accounts and determine the balance of each account.
c. Prepare a before-closing trial balance.

Problem 4-32A   *Effect of journal entries on financial statements*   L.O. 1, 7

Entry No.	Account Titles	Debit	Credit
1	Cash	xxx	
	Common Stock		xxx
2	Office Equipment	xxx	
	Cash		xxx
	Note Payable		xxx
3	Prepaid Rent	xxx	
	Cash		xxx
4	Dividends	xxx	
	Cash		xxx
5	Utility Expense	xxx	
	Cash		xxx
6	Accounts Receivable	xxx	
	Service Revenue		xxx
7	Salaries Expense	xxx	
	Cash		xxx
8	Cash	xxx	
	Service Revenue		xxx

continued

Entry No.	Account Titles	Debit	Credit
9	Cash	xxx	
	Unearned Revenue		xxx
10	Supplies	xxx	
	Accounts Payable		xxx
11	Depreciation Expense	xxx	
	Accumulated Depreciation		xxx
12	Cash	xxx	
	Accounts Receivable		xxx
13	Rent Expense	xxx	
	Prepaid Rent		xxx
14	Supplies Expense	xxx	
	Supplies		xxx
15	Unearned Revenue	xxx	
	Service Revenue		xxx

Required

The preceding 15 different accounting events are presented in general journal format. Use a horizontal statements model to show how each event affects the balance sheet, income statement, and statement of cash flows. Indicate whether the event increases (+), decreases (−), or does not affect (NA) each element of the financial statements. Also, in the Cash Flow column, use the letters OA to designate operating activity, IA for investing activity, and FA for financing activity. The first event is recorded as an example.

Assets	=	Liab.	+	Equity	Rev.	−	Exp.	=	Net Inc.	Cash Flow
+		NA		+	NA		NA		NA	+ FA

L.O. 6

CHECK FIGURE
Error (e): Yes,
$3,000 debit

Problem 4-33A *Effect of errors on the trial balance*

Required

Consider each of the following errors independently (assume that each is the only error that has occurred). Complete the following table. The first error is recorded as an example.

Error	Is the Trial Balance Out of Balance?	By What Amount?	Which Is Larger, Total Debits or Credits?
a	yes	90	credit

a. A credit of $820 to Accounts Payable was recorded as $870.
b. A credit of $500 to Accounts Receivable was not recorded.
c. A debit of $900 to Rent Expense was recorded as a debit of $600 to Salaries Expense.
d. An entry requiring a debit of $450 to Cash and a credit of $450 to Accounts Receivable was not posted to the ledger accounts.
e. A credit of $1,500 to Prepaid Insurance was recorded as a debit of $1,500 to Prepaid Insurance.
f. A debit of $600 to Cash was recorded as a credit of $600 to Cash.

Problem 4-34A   *Effect of errors on the trial balance*

The following trial balance was prepared from the ledger accounts of Zhen Company.

ZHEN COMPANY
Trial Balance
April 30, 2010

Account Title	Debit	Credit
Cash	$ 7,150	
Accounts receivable	42,500	
Supplies	1,200	
Prepaid insurance	3,200	
Equipment	56,800	
Accounts payable		$ 8,950
Notes payable		32,000
Common stock		94,800
Retained earnings		56,720
Dividends	6,000	
Service revenue		42,500
Rent expense	7,200	
Salaries expense	26,400	
Operating expense	74,880	
Totals	$225,330	$234,970

When the trial balance failed to balance, the accountant reviewed the records and discovered the following errors:

1. The company received $235 as payment for services rendered. The credit to Service Revenue was recorded correctly, but the debit to Cash was recorded as $370.
2. A $215 receipt of cash that was received as a payment on accounts receivable was not recorded.
3. A $225 purchase of supplies on account was properly recorded as a debit to the Supplies account. However, the credit to Accounts Payable was not recorded.
4. Equipment valued at $5,000 was contributed to the business in exchange for common stock. The entry to record the transaction was recorded as a $5,000 credit to both the Equipment account and the Common Stock account.
5. A $100 rent payment was properly recorded as a credit to Cash. However, the Salaries Expense account was incorrectly debited for $100.

Required

Based on this information, prepare a corrected trial balance for Zhen Company.

Problem 4-35A   *Comprehensive problem: single cycle*

The following transactions pertain to Jones Corporation for 2009.

Jan.	1	Began operations when the business acquired $50,000 cash from the issue of common stock.
Mar.	1	Paid rent for office space for two years, $18,000 cash.
Apr.	1	Borrowed $40,000 cash from First National Bank. The note issued had an 8 percent annual rate of interest and matured in one year.
	14	Purchased $950 of supplies on account.
June	1	Paid $27,000 cash for a computer system. The computer system had a five-year useful life and no salvage value.
	30	Received $26,000 cash in advance for services to be provided over the next year.
July	5	Paid $600 of the accounts payable from April 14.
Aug.	1	Billed a customer $9,600 for services provided during July.
	8	Completed a job and received $4,500 cash for services rendered.

Sept.	1	Paid employee salaries of $36,000 cash.
	9	Received $10,500 cash from accounts receivable.
Oct.	5	Billed customers $34,000 for services rendered on account.
Nov.	2	Paid a $2,000 cash dividend to the stockholders.
Dec.	31	Adjusted records to recognize the services provided on the contract of June 30.
	31	Recorded the accrued interest on the note to First National Bank. (See April 1.)
	31	Recorded depreciation on the computer system used in the business. (See June 1.)
	31	Recorded $4,500 of accrued salaries as of December 31.
	31	Recorded the rent expense for the year. (See March 1.)
	31	Physically counted supplies; $200 was on hand at the end of the period. (See April 14.)

Required

a. Record the preceding transactions in the general journal.

b. Post the transactions to T-accounts and calculate the account balances.

c. Prepare a trial balance.

d. Prepare the income statement, statement of changes in stockholders' equity, balance sheet, and statement of cash flows.

e. Prepare the closing entries at December 31.

f. Prepare a trial balance after the closing entries are posted.

L.O. 3–7

CHECK FIGURES
b. Cash, April 30, 2011: $4,240
f. Net Income: $1,602

Problem 4-36A *Comprehensive problem: two cycles*

This is a two-cycle problem. The second cycle is in Problem 4-36B. The first cycle *can* be completed without referring to the second cycle.

Will and Tyler organized a rental shop that began operations on April 1, 2011. Baker Rentals consummated the following transactions during the first month of operation.

April	1	Acquired $40,000 to establish the company, $20,000 from the issue of common stock and $20,000 from issuing a bank note. The note had a five-year term and a 6 percent annual interest rate. Interest is payable in cash on March 31 of each year.
	1	Paid $4,500 in advance rent for a one-year lease on office space.
	1	Paid $32,000 to purchase rental tools. The tools were expected to have a useful life of five years and a salvage value of $2,000.
	6	Purchased supplies for $260 cash.
	9	Received $500 cash as an advance payment from Don Orr to reserve tools to be used in May.
	10	Recorded rentals to customers. Cash receipts were $950, and invoices for rentals on account were $1,200.
	15	Paid $960 cash for employee salaries.
	16	Collected $560 from accounts receivable.
	23	Received monthly utility bills amounting to $233. The bills will be paid during May.
	25	Paid advertising expense for advertisements during April, $240.
	30	Recorded rentals to customers. Cash sales were $1,150 and invoices for rentals on account were $1,850.
	30	Paid $960 cash for employee salaries.

Information for April 30 Adjusting Entries

1. Counted the supplies inventory. Had $80 of supplies on hand.

2. Make adjustments for interest expense, rent expense, and depreciation expense.

Required

a. Record the transactions for April in general journal format.

b. Open a general ledger, using T-accounts, and post the general journal entries to the ledger.

c. Prepare a trial balance.

d. Record and post the appropriate adjusting entries.

e. Prepare a before-closing trial balance.

f. Prepare an income statement, statement of changes in stockholders' equity, balance sheet, and statement of cash flows.

g. Record and post the closing entries.

h. Prepare an after-closing trial balance.

Exercise 4-1B   *Matching debit and credit terminology with accounts*   **L.O. 2**

Required

Complete the following table by indicating whether a debit or credit is used to increase or decrease the balance of the following accounts. The appropriate debit/credit terminology has been identified for the first account as an example.

Account Title	Used to Increase This Account	Used to Decrease This Account
Accounts receivable	Debit	Credit
Accounts payable		
Common stock		
Land		
Interest expense		
Accumulated depreciation		
Unearned revenue		
Service revenue		
Retained earnings		
Insurance expense		

Exercise 4-2B   *Debit/credit rules*   **L.O. 1, 2**

Matt, Allison, and Sarah, three accounting students, were discussing the rules of debits and credits. Matt says that debits increase account balances and credits decrease account balances. Allison says that Matt is wrong, that credits increase account balances and debits decrease account balances. Sarah interrupts and declares that they are both correct.

Required

Explain what Sarah meant and give examples of transactions where debits increase account balances, credits decrease account balances, credits increase account balances, and debits decrease account balances.

Exercise 4-3B   *Matching debit and credit terminology with account titles*   **L.O. 1, 2**

Required

Indicate whether each of the following accounts normally has a debit balance or a credit balance.

a. Salaries Expense   **f.** Land
b. Accumulated Depreciation **g.** Dividends
c. Cash   **h.** Accounts Payable
d. Prepaid Insurance   **i.** Unearned Revenue
e. Common Stock   **j.** Consulting Revenue

Exercise 4-4B   *Identifying increases and decreases in T-accounts*   **L.O. 1**

Required

For each of the following T-accounts, write "increase" or "decrease" under the terms "debit" and "credit" to indicate how debit and credit entries affect the account balance.

Assets		=	Liabilities		+	Stockholders' Equity	
Debit	Credit		Debit	Credit		Debit	Credit

Contra Assets						Revenue	
Debit	Credit					Debit	Credit

						Expense	
						Debit	Credit

L.O. 2

Exercise 4-5B *Applying debit/credit terminology to accounting events*

Required

In parallel columns, list the accounts that would be debited and credited for each of the following unrelated transactions:

  a. Provided services for cash.
  b. Paid cash for salaries expense.
  c. Borrowed cash from a local bank.
  d. Acquired cash from the issue of common stock.
  e. Provided services on account.
  f. Purchased supplies for cash.
  g. Purchased equipment for cash.
  h. Recorded accrued salaries at the end of the accounting period.

L.O. 2, 3

Exercise 4-6B *T-accounts and the accounting equation*

Required

Record each of the following Cole Co. events in T-accounts, and then explain how the event affects the accounting equation.

  a. Borrowed $10,000 cash by issuing a note to a bank.
  b. Purchased supplies for $250 cash.
  c. Purchased land for $15,000. The company paid $6,000 cash and issued a note for the balance.
  d. Performed services for $800 cash.

L.O. 3

Exercise 4-7B *Recording transactions in T-accounts*

The following events apply to Hunt Company for 2010, its first year of operation.

  1. Received cash of $48,000 from the issue of common stock.
  2. Purchased a delivery van on January 1 for $30,000 cash that has a salvage value of $5,000 and a four-year useful life.
  3. Performed $85,000 of services on account.
  4. Incurred $9,000 of other operating expenses on account.
  5. Paid $34,000 cash for salaries expense.
  6. Collected $70,000 of accounts receivable.
  7. Paid a $5,000 dividend to the stockholders.
  8. Performed $9,200 of services for cash.
  9. Paid $5,200 of the accounts payable.
  10. Recorded depreciation expense for the year on the delivery van.

Required

  a. Record the preceding transactions in the appropriate T-accounts and determine the ending balance in each account.
  b. Determine the amount of total assets at the end of 2010.
  c. Determine the amount of net income for 2010.

L.O. 2

Exercise 4-8B *Debit/credit terminology*

Required

For each of the following independent events, identify the account that would be debited and the account that would be credited. The accounts for the first event are identified as an example.

Event	Account Debited	Account Credited
a	Cash	Common Stock

a. Received cash by issuing common stock.
b. Received cash for services to be performed in the future.
c. Provided services on account.
d. Paid accounts payable.
e. Purchased office equipment with cash.
f. Recognized accrued interest revenue.
g. Paid cash for operating expenses.
h. Recognized depreciation expense.
i. Paid salaries payable.
j. Purchased supplies on account.
k. Paid cash dividends to the stockholders.
l. Recognized revenue for services completed; collected the cash in Event *b*.
m. Received cash in payment of accounts receivable.
n. Recognized accrued interest expense.
o. Repaid principal balance on note payable.

Exercise 4-9B   *Identifying transaction type, its effect on the accounting equation, and whether*   **L.O. 1, 2**
                    the effect is recorded with a debit or credit

Required

Identify whether each of the following transactions is an asset source (AS), asset use (AU), asset exchange (AE), or claims exchange (CE). Also explain how each event affects the accounting equation by placing a + for *increase*, − for *decrease*, and NA for *not affected* under each of the components of the accounting equation. Finally, indicate whether the effect requires a debit or credit entry. The first event is recorded as an example.

						Stockholders' Equity		
Event	Type of Event	Assets	=	Liabilities	+	Common Stock	+	Retained Earnings
a	AS	+ Debit		NA		NA		+ Credit

a. Provided services on account.
b. Received cash in payment of accounts receivable.
c. Borrowed cash by issuing a note.
d. Purchased land by issuing a note.
e. Paid interest payable.
f. Recognized accrued interest revenue.
g. Recognized revenue for services completed; cash collected previously.
h. Paid a cash dividend to the stockholders.
i. Recognized depreciation expense on the equipment.
j. Repaid principal balance on note payable.
k. Paid cash in advance for one-year's rent.
l. Received cash for services to be performed in the future.
m. Recognized accrued interest expense.
n. Incurred other operating expense on account.
o. Paid salaries payable.

Exercise 4-10B   *Recording events in the general journal*   **L.O. 7**

Required

Record each of the following transactions in general journal form.

a. Performed $24,000 of services on account.
b. Purchased equipment that cost $20,000 by paying $5,000 cash and issuing a $15,000 note for the balance.

c. Purchased supplies for $530 cash.

d. Received $3,000 cash for services to be performed at a later date.

e. Collected $9,500 cash on accounts receivable.

f. Had repairs made on equipment; the $1,700 for repairs expense was charged on account.

g. Paid $2,300 cash in advance for an insurance policy on the equipment.

h. Paid $1,200 on accounts payable.

i. Recorded the adjusting entry to recognize $800 of insurance expense.

j. Recorded $6,200 depreciation expense on the equipment.

k. Recorded accrued interest expense of $800.

L.O. 6   **Exercise 4-11B**   *Preparing a trial balance*

Required

On December 31, 2009, Bailey Company had the following account balances in its general ledger. Use this information to prepare a trial balance.

Land	$ 75,000
Unearned revenue	48,000
Dividends	20,000
Depreciation expense	6,000
Prepaid rent	19,200
Cash	28,800
Salaries expense	30,000
Accounts payable	12,000
Common stock	80,000
Operating expense	50,000
Office supplies	12,000
Advertising expense	3,500
Retained earnings, 1/1/2009	18,000
Service revenue	175,000
Office equipment	72,000
Accounts receivable	26,000
Accumulated depreciation	9,500

L.O. 5, 7   **Exercise 4-12B**   *Preparing closing entries*

The following financial information was taken from the books of Angela's Fitness Club, a small spa and health club.

Account Balances as of December 31, 2012	
Accounts receivable	$ 8,150
Accounts payable	6,200
Accrued salaries payable	2,150
Accumulated depreciation	7,800
Cash	20,725
Certificate of deposit	9,650
Depreciation expense	2,600
Dividends	2,450
Equipment	16,450
Interest expense	1,150
Interest payable	500
Operating expense	31,550
Prepaid rent	2,600
Rent expense	6,500
Retained earnings 1/1/2012	46,500
Salaries expense	11,200
Service revenue	48,400
Supplies	800
Supplies expense	4,240
Common stock	6,515

Required

a. Prepare the necessary closing entries at December 31, 2012, for Angela's Fitness Club.

b. What is the balance in the Retained Earnings account after the closing entries are posted?

Exercise 4-13B   *Recording events in T-accounts and preparing a trial balance*   **L.O. 3, 6**

The following events apply to Chang, Inc., in its first year of operation.

1. Acquired $80,000 cash from the issue of common stock.
2. Borrowed $64,000 from State Bank.
3. Earned $78,000 of service revenue on account.
4. Incurred $30,400 of operating expenses on account.
5. Collected $52,800 cash from accounts receivable.
6. Made a $32,000 payment on accounts payable.
7. Paid a $4,000 cash dividend to the stockholders.
8. Paid $14,500 cash to purchase office equipment.
9. Received a $14,200 cash advance for services to be provided in the future.
10. Purchased $5,600 of supplies on account.
11. Recorded accrued interest expense of $3,260.
12. Recognized $3,200 of depreciation expense.
13. Recognized $4,800 of revenue for services provided to the customer in Event 9.
14. Recognized $4,200 of supplies expense.

Required

a. Record the events in T-accounts and determine the ending account balances.

b. Test the equality of the debit and credit balances of the T-accounts by preparing a trial balance.

Exercise 4-14B   *Determining the effect of errors on the trial balance*   **L.O. 6**

Required

Explain how each of the following posting errors affects a trial balance. State whether the trial balance will be out of balance because of the posting error, and indicate which side of the trial balance will have a higher amount after each independent entry is posted. If the posting error does not affect the equality of debits and credits shown in the trial balance, state that the error will not cause an inequality and explain why.

a. A $2,000 credit to Notes Payable was not posted.

b. A $2,400 debit to Cash was posted as a $4,200 debit.

c. A $2,000 debit to Prepaid Rent was debited to Rent Expense.

d. The collection of $1,000 of accounts receivable was posted to Accounts Receivable twice.

e. A $4,000 credit to Accounts Payable was posted as a credit to Cash.

Exercise 4-15B   *Recording events in the general journal, posting to T-accounts, and*   **L.O. 3, 5, 7**
                      preparing closing entries

At the beginning of 2010, Joe's Consulting had the following balances in its accounts:

Account	Balance
Cash	$15,000
Accounts receivable	9,500
Accounts payable	3,600
Common stock	9,900
Retained earnings	11,000

The following events apply to Joe's Consulting for 2010.

1. Provided $124,000 of services on account.
2. Incurred $11,980 of operating expenses on account.
3. Collected $112,000 of accounts receivable.
4. Paid $71,000 cash for salaries expense.
5. Paid $13,600 cash as a partial payment on accounts payable.
6. Paid a $9,000 cash dividend to the stockholders.

Required

a. Record these transactions in a general journal.
b. Open T-accounts, and post the beginning balances and the preceding transactions to the appropriate accounts.
c. Record the beginning balances and the transactions in a horizontal statements model such as the following one:

Assets		=	Liab.	+	Equity		Rev.	−	Exp.	=	Net Inc.	Cash Flow
Cash	+ Accts. Rec.	=	Accts. Pay.	+	Common Stock	+ Ret. Earn.						

d. Record the closing entries in the general journal and post them to the T-accounts. What is the amount of net income for the year?
e. What is the amount of *change* in retained earnings for the year? Is the change in retained earnings different from the amount of net income? If so, why?

L.O. 3, 5

Exercise 4-16B   *Recording receivables and identifying their effect on financial statements*

Box Company performed services on account for $80,000 in 2008. Box collected $50,000 cash from accounts receivable during 2008, and the remaining $30,000 was collected in cash during 2009.

Required

a. Record the 2008 transactions in T-accounts.
b. Record the 2008 transactions in a horizontal statements model like the following one:

Assets		=	Liab.	+	Equity	Rev.	−	Exp.	=	Net Inc.	Cash Flow
Cash	+ Accts. Rec.	=	NA	+	Ret. Earn.						

c. Determine the amount of revenue Box would report on the 2008 income statement.
d. Determine the amount of cash flow from operating activities Box would report on the 2008 statement of cash flows.
e. Open a T-account for Retained Earnings, and close the 2008 Revenue account to the Retained Earnings account.
f. Record the 2009 cash collection in the appropriate T-accounts.
g. Record the 2009 transaction in a horizontal statements model like the one shown in Requirement *b*.
h. Assuming no other transactions occur in 2009, determine the amount of net income and the net cash flow from operating activities for 2009.

L.O. 3-6

Exercise 4-17B   *Recording supplies and identifying their effect on financial statements*

Ben Abbott started and operated a small family architectural firm in 2012. The firm was affected by two events: (1) Abbott provided $50,000 of services on account, and (2) he purchased $12,000 of supplies on account. There were $1,000 of supplies on hand as of December 31, 2012.

Required

a. Open T-accounts and record the two transactions in the accounts.
b. Record the required year-end adjusting entry to reflect the use of supplies.
c. Record the preceding transactions in a horizontal statements model like the following one:

Assets			=	Liab.	+	Equity		Rev.	−	Exp.	=	Net Inc.	Cash Flow
Accts. Rec.	Supp.	=	Accts. Pay.	+	Ret. Earn.								

d. Explain why the amount of net income and the net cash flow from operating activities differ.
e. Record and post the required closing entries, and prepare an after-closing trial balance.

Exercise 4-18B   *Recording prepaids and identifying their effect on financial statements*   **L.O. 4, 7**

The South East Company began operations when it issued common stock for $25,000 cash. It paid $24,000 cash in advance for a one-year contract in 2011 to lease delivery equipment for the business. It signed the lease agreement on March 1, 2011, which was effective immediately. South East earned $30,000 of cash revenue in 2011.

Required

a. Record the March 1 cash payment in general journal format.
b. Record in general journal format the adjustment required as of December 31, 2011.
c. Record all events in a horizontal statements model like the following one:

Assets			=	Liab.	+	Equity		Rev.	−	Exp.	=	Net Inc.	Cash Flow
Cash	+	PrPd. Rent	=		+	Ret. Earn.							

d. What amount of net income will South East report on the 2011 income statement? What is the amount of net cash flow from operating activities for 2011?
e. Determine the amount of prepaid rent South East would report on the December 31, 2011, balance sheet.

Exercise 4-19B   *Recording accrued salaries and identifying their effect on financial statements*   **L.O. 4, 7**

On December 31, 2008, MMR Company had accrued salaries of $4,800.

Required

a. Record in general journal format the adjustment required as of December 31, 2008.
b. Determine the amount of net income MMR would report on the 2008 income statement, assuming that MMR earns $6,000 of cash revenue. What is the amount of net cash flow from operating activities for 2008?
c. What amount of Salaries Payable would MMR report on the December 31, 2008, balance sheet?

Exercise 4-20B   *Recording depreciation and identifying its effect on financial statements*   **L.O. 3, 4**

On January 1, 2010, Carlos bought a computer for $20,000 cash. The computer had a useful life of three years and a salvage value of $3,500.

Required

a. Record in T-accounts Carlos' purchase of the computer.
b. Record in T-accounts the adjustment required on December 31, 2010.
c. Determine the book value of the computer Carlos would report on the December 31, 2010, balance sheet.
d. Determine the amount of net income Carlos would report on the 2010 income statement, assuming that Carlos earned $7,000 of cash revenue in 2010.
e. What is the amount of net cash flow from operating activities for 2010?

f. What amount of depreciation expense would Carlos report on the 2011 income statement?

g. Determine the book value of the computer Carlos would report on the December 31, 2011, balance sheet.

L.O. 3, 4   **Exercise 4-21B**   *Recording a note payable and identifying its effect on financial statements*

On April 1, 2009, Toll Co. borrowed $30,000 from First National Bank. The note had a 10 percent annual interest rate and a one-year term to maturity.

Required

a. Identify the transaction type (asset source, use, or exchange or claims exchange) and record in T-accounts the entry for the financing event on April 1, 2009.

b. Identify the transaction type and record in T-accounts the adjustment as of December 31, 2009.

c. Determine the amount of net income on the 2009 income statement, assuming Toll Co. earned $5,000 of cash revenue.

d. What is the amount of net cash flow from operating activities for 2009?

e. Determine the total liabilities on the December 31, 2009, balance sheet.

f. Record in T-accounts (1) the 2010 accrual of interest and (2) the cash payment of principal and interest on April 1, 2010.

g. Are the April 1, 2010, transactions asset source, asset use, asset exchange, or claims exchange transactions?

L.O. 3, 4   **Exercise 4-22B**   *Recording unearned revenue and identifying its effect on financial statements*

Katie received a $120,000 cash advance payment on June 1, 2010, for consulting services to be performed in the future. Services were to be provided for a one-year term beginning June 1, 2010.

Required

a. Record the June 1 cash receipt in T-accounts.

b. Record in T-accounts the adjustment required as of December 31, 2010.

c. Record the preceding transaction and related adjustment in a horizontal statements model like the following one:

Assets	=	Liab.	+	Equity	Rev.	−	Exp.	=	Net Inc.	Cash Flow

d. Determine the amount of net income on the 2010 income statement. What is the amount of net cash flow from operating activities for 2010?

e. What amount of liabilities would Katie report on the 2010 balance sheet?

L.O. 3   **Exercise 4-23B**   *Using a T-account to determine cash flow from operating activities*

XYZ began the accounting period with a $29,000 debit balance in its Accounts Receivable account. During the accounting period, XYZ earned revenue on account of $63,000. The ending accounts receivable balance was $27,000.

Required

Based on this information alone, determine the amount of cash inflow from operating activities during the accounting period. (*Hint:* Use a T-account for Accounts Receivable. Enter the debits and credits for the given events, and solve for the missing amount.)

L.O. 3   **Exercise 4-24B**   *Using a T-account to determine cash flow from operating activities*

The Dance Company began the accounting period with a $20,000 credit balance in its Accounts Payable account. During the accounting period, Dance incurred expenses on account of $47,500. The ending Accounts Payable balance was $14,000.

Required

Based on this information, determine the amount of cash outflow for expenses during the accounting period. (*Hint:* Use a T-account for Accounts Payable. Enter the debits and credits for the given events, and solve for the missing amount.)

Problem 4-25B *Identifying debit and credit balances*

Required

Indicate whether each of the following accounts normally has a debit or credit balance.

a. Interest Receivable
b. Land
c. Notes Payable
d. Salaries Expense
e. Certificate of Deposit
f. Interest Revenue
g. Rent Expense
h. Common Stock
i. Cash
j. Salaries Payable
k. Accounts Receivable
l. Insurance Expense
m. Prepaid Insurance
n. Retained Earnings
o. Supplies Expense
p. Prepaid Rent
q. Accumulated Depreciation
r. Equipment
s. Interest Payable
t. Service Revenue
u. Supplies
v. Accounts Payable
w. Depreciation Expense
x. Unearned Revenue
y. Loss on Sale of Equipment
z. Gain on Sale of Land
aa. Truck
bb. Operating Expense
cc. Dividends

Problem 4-26B *Transaction type and debit/credit terminology*

The following events apply to Wong Enterprises.

1. Acquired $45,000 cash from the issue of common stock.
2. Paid salaries to employees, $8,000 cash.
3. Collected $9,000 cash for services to be performed in the future.
4. Paid cash for utilities expense $3,200.
5. Recognized $28,000 of service revenue on account.
6. Purchased equipment costing $90,000 by paying cash of $25,000 and borrowing the balance from Third National Bank by issuing a four-year note.
7. Paid a $5,000 cash dividend to the stockholders.
8. Purchased $4,000 of supplies on account.
9. Received $18,000 cash for services rendered.
10. Paid cash to rent office space for the next 12 months, $8,400.
11. Made a $5,000 principal payment on the bank note.
12. Paid cash of $9,200 for operating expenses.
13. Paid on accounts payable, $2,400.
14. Paid cash to purchase office furniture, $3,600.
15. Recognized $18,000 of depreciation expense.
16. Recognized $3,250 of rent expense that had been paid in cash in a prior transaction (see Event 10).
17. Recognized $8,000 of revenue for services performed for which cash had been previously collected (see Event 3).
18. Recognized $4,800 of accrued interest expense.

Required

Identify each event as asset source (AS), asset use (AU), asset exchange (AE), or claims exchange (CE). Also identify the account to be debited and the account to be credited when the transaction is recorded. The first event is recorded as an example.

Event No.	Type of Event	Account Debited	Account Credited
1	AS	Cash	Common Stock

L.O. 4, 7

Problem 4-27B *Recording adjusting entries in general journal format*

Required

Each of the following independent events requires a year-end adjusting entry. Record each event and the related adjusting entry in general journal format. The first event is recorded as an example. Assume a December 31 closing date.

Event No.	Date	Account Titles	Debit	Credit
a	Sept. 1	Prepaid Rent	30,000	
		Cash		30,000
a	Dec. 31	Rent Expense (30,000 × ⁴⁄₁₂)	10,000	
		Prepaid Rent		10,000

a. Paid $30,000 cash in advance on September 1 for a one-year lease on office space.

b. Borrowed $22,500 cash by issuing a note to Bay City National Bank on October 1. The note had a one-year term and an 8 percent annual rate of interest.

c. Paid $19,400 cash to purchase equipment on September 1. The equipment was expected to have a five-year useful life and a $5,000 salvage value. Depreciation is computed on a straight-line basis.

d. Invested $11,000 cash in a certificate of deposit that paid 6 percent annual interest rate. The certificate was acquired on June 1 and had a one-year term to maturity.

e. Purchased $4,000 of supplies on account on April 15. At year-end, $600 of supplies remained on hand.

f. Received a $3,600 cash advance on July 1 for a contract to provide services for one year.

g. Paid $10,200 cash in advance on February 1 for a one-year insurance policy.

L.O. 3–7

Problem 4-28B *One complete accounting cycle*

The following events apply to Dunn Company's first year of operations:

1. Acquired $40,000 cash from issuing common stock on January 1, 2009.
2. Purchased $600 of supplies on account.
3. Paid $12,000 cash in advance for a one-year lease on office space.
4. Earned $5,750 of revenue on account.
5. Incurred $4,485 of operating expenses on account.
6. Collected $2,950 cash from accounts receivable.
7. Paid $3,250 cash on accounts payable.

Information for Adjusting Entries

8. There was $50 of supplies on hand at the end of the accounting period.
9. The lease on the office space covered a one-year period beginning September 1, 2009.
10. There was $1,100 of accrued salaries at the end of the period.

Required

a. Record these transactions in general journal form.
b. Post the transaction data from the journal to ledger T-accounts.
c. Prepare a trial balance.
d. Prepare an income statement, statement of changes in stockholders' equity, a balance sheet, and a statement of cash flows.
e. Close the temporary accounts (Revenue, Expense, and Dividends) to Retained Earnings.
f. Post the closing entries to the T-accounts, and prepare an after-closing trial balance.

Problem 4-29B *Two complete accounting cycles*

L.O. 3–7

Holland Enterprises experienced the following events for 2009, the first year of operation.

1. Acquired $26,000 cash from the issue of common stock.
2. Paid $8,000 cash in advance for rent. The payment was for the period April 1, 2009, to March 31, 2010.
3. Performed services for customers on account for $27,000.
4. Incurred operating expenses on account of $9,500.
5. Collected $23,000 cash from accounts receivable.
6. Paid $8,500 cash for salary expense.
7. Paid $9,000 cash as a partial payment on accounts payable.

Adjusting Entries

8. Made the adjusting entry for the expired rent (see Event 2).
9. Recorded $900 of accrued salaries at the end of 2009.

Events for 2010

1. Paid $900 cash for the salaries accrued at the end of the prior accounting period.
2. Performed services for cash of $12,500.
3. Borrowed $6,000 from the local bank by issuing a note.
4. Paid $8,000 cash in advance for rent. The payment was for one year beginning April 1, 2010.
5. Performed services for customers on account for $42,000.
6. Incurred operating expense on account of $24,500.
7. Collected $40,500 cash from accounts receivable.
8. Paid $15,000 cash as a partial payment on accounts payable.
9. Paid $14,000 cash for salary expense.
10. Paid a $6,000 cash dividend to the owners.

Adjusting Entries

11. Made the adjusting entry for the expired rent. (*Hint:* Part of the rent was paid in 2009.)
12. Recorded accrued interest. The note was issued on September 1, 2010, for a one-year term and had an interest rate of 9 percent. (See Event 3.)

Required

a. Record the events and adjusting entries for 2009 in general journal form.
b. Post the 2009 events to T-accounts.
c. Prepare a trial balance for 2009.
d. Prepare an income statement, statement of changes in stockholders' equity, balance sheet, and statement of cash flows for 2009.
e. Record the entries to close the 2009 temporary accounts to Retained Earnings in the general journal and post to the T-accounts.
f. Prepare an after-closing trial balance for December 31, 2009.
g. Repeat Requirements *a* through *f* for 2010.

Problem 4-30B *Identifying accounting events from journal entries*

L.O. 2, 7

Required

The following information is from the records of Pierce Consulting. Write a brief description of the accounting event represented in each of the general journal entries.

Date	Account Titles	Debit	Credit
Jan. 1	Cash	12,500	
	Common Stock		12,500
Feb. 10	Supplies	1,550	
	Accounts Payable		1,550

continued

Date	Account Titles	Debit	Credit
Mar. 1	Cash	13,000	
	Unearned Revenue		13,000
Apr. 1	Prepaid Rent	10,200	
	Cash		10,200
20	Accounts Receivable	18,400	
	Service Revenue		18,400
May 1	Office Equipment	17,000	
	Cash		4,000
	Note Payable		13,000
June 15	Salaries Expense	6,100	
	Cash		6,100
30	Property Tax Expense	3,000	
	Cash		3,000
July 28	Cash	9,300	
	Service Revenue		9,300
Aug. 30	Dividends	3,000	
	Cash		3,000
Sept. 19	Cash	16,000	
	Accounts Receivable		16,000
Dec. 31	Depreciation Expense	2,700	
	Accumulated Depreciation		2,700
31	Supplies Expense	2,025	
	Supplies		2,025
31	Rent Expense	6,400	
	Prepaid Rent		6,400
31	Unearned Revenue	8,500	
	Service Revenue		8,500

L.O. 3, 4, 6

Problem 4-31B *Recording events in statements model and T-accounts and preparing a trial balance*

The following accounting events apply to Miranda's Designs for the year 2009.

Asset Source Transactions

1. Began operations by acquiring $20,000 of cash from the issue of common stock.
2. Purchased $7,000 of equipment on account.
3. Performed services and collected cash of $1,000.
4. Collected $6,000 of cash in advance for services to be provided over the next 12 months.
5. Provided $12,000 of services on account.
6. Purchased supplies of $1,500 on account.

Asset Exchange Transactions

7. Purchased $4,000 of equipment for cash.
8. Collected $7,000 of cash from accounts receivable.
9. Loaned $2,400 to Matt, who issued a 12-month, 7 percent note.
10. Purchased $630 of supplies with cash.
11. Purchased a $4,800 certificate of deposit. The CD had a six-month term and paid 4 percent annual interest.

Asset Use Transactions

12. Paid $4,000 cash for salaries of employees.
13. Paid a cash dividend of $2,000 to the stockholders.

14. Paid for the equipment that had been purchased on account (see Event 2).
15. Paid off $630 of the accounts payable with cash.

Claims Exchange Transactions

16. Placed an advertisement in the local newspaper for $800 on account.
17. Incurred utility expense of $600 on account.

Adjusting Entries

18. Recognized $4,400 of revenue for performing services. The collection of cash for these services occurred in a prior transaction. (See Event 4.)
19. Recorded $100 of interest revenue that had accrued on the note receivable from Matt (see Event 9).
20. Recorded $168 of interest revenue that had accrued on the certificate of deposit (see Event 11).
21. Recorded $1,500 of accrued salary expense at the end of 2009.
22. Recognized $1,400 of depreciation on the equipment (see Events 2 and 7).
23. Recorded supplies expense. Had $600 of supplies on hand at the end of the accounting period.

Required

a. Use a horizontal statements model to show how each event affects the balance sheet, income statement, and statement of cash flows. Indicate whether the event increases (+), decreases (−), or does not affect (NA) each element of the financial statements. Also, in the Cash Flow column, use the letters OA to designate operating activity, IA for investing activity, and FA for financing activity. The first event is recorded as an example.

Assets	=	Liab.	+	Equity	Rev.	−	Exp.	=	Net Inc.	Cash Flow
+	=	NA	+	+	NA	−	NA	=	NA	+ FA

b. Record each of the preceding events in T-accounts.
c. Prepare a before-closing trial balance.

Problem 4-32B   *Effect of journal entries on financial statements*   **L.O. 1, 7**

Entry No.	Account Titles	Debit	Credit
1	Cash	xxx	
	Common Stock		xxx
2	Cash	xxx	
	Unearned Revenue		xxx
3	Supplies	xxx	
	Accounts Payable		xxx
4	Office Equipment	xxx	
	Cash		xxx
	Note Payable		xxx
5	Accounts Receivable	xxx	
	Service Revenue		xxx
6	Cash	xxx	
	Accounts Receivable		xxx
7	Cash	xxx	
	Service Revenue		xxx
8	Salaries Expense	xxx	
	Cash		xxx
9	Dividends	xxx	
	Cash		xxx

continued

Entry No.	Account Titles	Debit	Credit
10	Prepaid Rent	XXX	
	Cash		XXX
11	Property Tax Expense	XXX	
	Cash		XXX
12	Depreciation Expense	XXX	
	Accumulated Depreciation		XXX
13	Supplies Expense	XXX	
	Supplies		XXX
14	Rent Expense	XXX	
	Prepaid Rent		XXX
15	Unearned Revenue	XXX	
	Service Revenue		XXX

Required

The preceding 15 different accounting events are presented in general journal format. Use a horizontal statements model to show how each event affects the balance sheet, income statement, and statement of cash flows. Indicate whether the event increases (+), decreases (−), or does not affect (NA) each element of the financial statements. Also, in the Cash Flow column, use the letters OA to designate operating activity, IA for investing activity, and FA for financing activity. The first event is recorded as an example.

Assets	=	Liab.	+	Equity	Rev.	−	Exp.	=	Net Inc.	Cash Flow
+		NA		+	NA		NA		NA	+ FA

L.O. 6

Problem 4-33B *Effect of errors on the trial balance*

Required

Consider each of the following errors independently (assume that each is the only error that has occurred). Complete the following table. The first error is recorded as an example.

Error	Is the Trial Balance Out of Balance?	By What Amount?	Which Is Larger, Total Debits or Credits?
a	no	NA	NA

a. A debit of $400 to Supplies Expense was recorded as a debit of $400 to Rent Expense.
b. A credit of $500 to Consulting Revenue was not recorded.
c. A credit of $720 to Accounts Payable was recorded as $270.
d. A debit of $3,000 to Cash was recorded as a credit of $3,000 to Cash.
e. An entry requiring a debit to Cash of $1,200 and a credit to Accounts Receivable of $1,200 was not posted to the ledger accounts.
f. A debit of $1,500 to Prepaid Rent was recorded as a credit of $1,500 to Prepaid Rent.

L.O. 6

Problem 4-34B *Effect of errors on the trial balance*

The following trial balance was prepared from the ledger accounts of Lopez, Inc.:

LOPEZ, INC.
Trial Balance
May 31, 2008

Account Title	Debit	Credit
Cash	$ 1,100	
Accounts receivable	1,770	
Supplies	420	
Prepaid insurance	2,400	
Office equipment	10,000	
Accounts payable		$ 1,500
Notes payable		1,000
Common stock		1,800
Retained earnings		7,390
Dividends	400	
Service revenue		19,600
Rent expense	3,600	
Salaries expense	9,000	
Operating expenses	2,500	
Totals	$31,190	$31,290

The accountant for Lopez, Inc., made the following errors during May 2008.

1. The cash purchase of a $2,100 typewriter was recorded as a $2,000 debit to Office Equipment and a $2,100 credit to Cash.
2. An $800 purchase of supplies on account was properly recorded as a debit to the Supplies account but was incorrectly recorded as a credit to the Cash account.
3. The company provided services valued at $8,600 to a customer. The accountant recorded the transaction in the proper accounts but in the incorrect amount of $6,800.
4. An $800 cash receipt for a payment on an account receivable was not recorded.
5. A $400 cash payment of an account payable was not recorded.
6. The May utility bill, which amounted to $780 on account, was not recorded.

Required

a. Identify the errors that would cause a difference in the total amounts of debits and credits that would appear in a trial balance. Indicate whether the Debit or Credit column would be larger as a result of the error.

b. Indicate whether each of the preceding errors would overstate, understate, or have no effect on the amount of total assets, liabilities, and equity. Your answer should take the following form:

Event No.	Assets	=	Liabilities	+	Stockholders' Equity
1	Understate		No effect		No effect

c. Prepare a corrected trial balance.

Problem 4-35B   *Comprehensive problem: single cycle*   **L.O. 3-7**

The following transactions pertain to Legal Services Company for 2008.

Jan. 30	Established the business when it acquired $75,000 cash from the issue of common stock.
Feb. 1	Paid rent for office space for two years, $12,000 cash.
Mar. 1	Borrowed $20,000 cash from National Bank. The note issued had a 9 percent annual rate of interest and matured in one year.
Apr. 10	Purchased $6,500 of supplies on account.

June	1	Paid $27,000 cash for a computer system which had a three-year useful life and no salvage value.
July	1	Received $75,000 cash in advance for services to be provided over the next year.
	20	Paid $2,400 of the accounts payable from April 10.
Aug.	15	Billed a customer $32,000 for services provided during August.
Sept.	15	Completed a job and received $24,000 cash for services rendered.
Oct.	1	Paid employee salaries of $20,000 cash.
	15	Received $32,000 cash from accounts receivable.
Nov.	16	Billed customers $37,000 for services rendered on account.
Dec.	1	Paid a dividend of $8,000 cash to the stockholders.
	31	Adjusted records to recognize the services provided on contract of July 1.
	31	Recorded the accrued interest on the note to National Bank (see March 1).
	31	Recorded depreciation on the computer system used in the business (see June 1).
	31	Recorded $4,500 of accrued salaries as of December 31.
	31	Recorded the rent expense for the year (see February 1).
	31	Physically counted supplies; $480 was on hand at the end of the period (see April 10).

Required

a. Record the preceding transactions in the general journal.

b. Post the transactions to T-accounts and calculate the account balances.

c. Prepare a trial balance.

d. Prepare the income statement, statement of changes in stockholders' equity, balance sheet, and statement of cash flows.

e. Prepare the closing entries at December 31.

f. Prepare a trial balance after the closing entries are posted.

L.O. 3-7   **Problem 4-36B**   *Comprehensive problem: two cycles*

This problem extends Problem 4-36A involving Baker Rentals and *should not* be attempted until that problem has been completed. The transactions consummated by Baker Rentals during May 2011 (the company's second month of operation) consisted of the following:

May	1	Recorded rentals of tools to customers. Cash receipts were $420, and invoices for rentals on account were $1,200.
	2	Purchased supplies on account that cost $300.
	7	Collected $4,000 cash from customer accounts receivable.
	8	Don Orr rented the tools that had been paid for in advance (see April 9 in Problem 4-36A).
	10	Paid the utility company for the monthly utility bills that had been received in the previous month, $233.
	15	Paid $3,200 cash for employee salaries.
	15	Purchased a one-year insurance policy that cost $1,200 with coverage beginning immediately.
	16	Paid $300 on the account payable that was established when supplies were purchased on May 2.
	20	Paid a $300 cash dividend to the stockholders.
	27	Received monthly utility bills amounting to $310. The bills would be paid during the month of June.
	31	Recorded rentals of tools to customers. Cash sales were $625, and invoices for rentals on account were $4,100.
	31	Paid $3,200 cash for employee salaries.
	31	Counted the supplies inventory. Had $40 of supplies on hand.

Required

a. Open a general ledger with T-accounts, using the ending account balances computed in Problem 4-36A.

b. Record the preceding transactions directly into the T-accounts.

c. Record the adjusting entries directly into the T-accounts. (*Note:* Refer to Problem 4-36A to obtain all the information needed to prepare the adjusting entries.)

d. Prepare an income statement, statement of changes in stockholders' equity, balance sheet, and statement of cash flows.

e. Record the closing entries directly into the T-accounts.

f. Answer the following questions.

   (1) Why is the amount in the May 31, 2011, Retained Earnings account not equal to the amount of net income or loss for the month of May?

   (2) Why is the amount of Accumulated Depreciation on the May 31, 2011, balance sheet not equal to the amount of Depreciation Expense for the month of May?

ANALYZE, THINK, COMMUNICATE

ATC 4-1 **Business Applications Case** *Understanding real-world annual reports*

Required

a. Use the Topps Company's annual report in Appendix B to answer the following questions.

   (1) On February 25, 2006, Topps had a balance of $269,954 in Retained Earnings. On February 26, 2005, the balance in Retained Earnings was $275,205. Why did Retained Earnings change during 2006?

   (2) Why did Topps' Net Sales and Net Income decrease so much in 2006 compared to 2005?

   (3) Could Requirement 2 be answered by examining only Topps' income statement, balance sheet, and cash statement? If not, where did you find the information?

   (4) Does the Treasury Stock account in the Stockholders' Equity section of the 2006 balance sheet have a debit or credit balance?

b. Use the Harley-Davidson's annual report that came with this book to answer the following questions.

   (1) On December 31, 2005, Harley-Davidson had a balance of $4,630,390,000 in Retained Earnings. On December 31, 2004, the balance in Retained Earnings was $3,844,571,000. Why did Retained Earnings change during 2005?

   (2) Harley-Davidson's Net Revenue increased during 2005 compared to 2004. The MD&A section of its annual report explains the reasons this occurred. What are these reasons?

   (3) Does the Accumulated and Other Comprehensive Income (Loss) account in the Shareholders' Equity section of the 2004 balance sheet have a debit or credit balance?

ATC 4-2 **Group Assignment** *Financial statement analysis*

The account balances for Crowley Company were as follows:

| | January 1 | | |
	2008	2009	2010
Cash	$ 12,000	$ 5,800	$ 29,400
Accounts receivable	6,000	10,000	6,000
Equipment	25,000	25,000	25,000
Accumulated depreciation	(12,000)	(13,200)	(14,400)
Prepaid rent	0	1,000	1,400
Accounts payable	4,000	3,000	7,000
Notes payable	12,000*	0	0
Interest payable	300	0	0
Salaries payable	0	0	2,100
Common stock	10,000	10,000	10,000
Retained earnings	4,700	15,600	28,300

*Funds were originally borrowed on October 1, 2007, with an interest rate of 10 percent.

Crowley Company experienced the following events for the accounting periods 2008, 2009, and 2010.

2008

1. Performed services for $36,000 on account.
2. Paid rent of $6,000 for the period March 1, 2008, to March 1, 2009.

3. Incurred operating expense of $18,000 on account.

4. Collected $32,000 of accounts receivable.

5. Paid $19,000 of accounts payable.

6. Paid note and interest due on October 1.

7. Recorded expired rent.

8. Recorded depreciation expense of $1,200.

2009

1. Performed services on account of $48,000.

2. Paid rent of $8,400 for the period March 1, 2008, to March 1, 2009, and recorded the expired rent for the period January 1, 2009, to March 1, 2009.

3. Incurred operating expenses of $24,000 on account.

4. Collected $52,000 of accounts receivable.

5. Paid $20,000 of accounts payable.

6. Recorded expired rent.

7. Recorded accrued salaries of $2,100.

8. Recorded depreciation expense of $1,200.

2010

1. Paid accrued salaries.

2. Performed services on account of $56,000.

3. Paid rent of $9,000 for the period March 1, 2010, to March 1, 2011, and recorded the expired rent for the period January 1, 2010, to March 1, 2010.

4. Incurred operating expenses of $32,000 on account.

5. Collected $55,000 of accounts receivable.

6. Paid $33,000 of accounts payable.

7. Sold equipment for $2,000; the equipment had a cost of $5,000 and accumulated depreciation of $4,000.

8. Recorded expired rent.

9. Recorded depreciation expense of $1,000.

Required

a. Divide the class into groups of four or five students. Organize the groups into three sections. Assign each section of groups the financial data for one of the preceding accounting periods.

Group Task

Prepare an income statement, balance sheet, and statement of cash flows. It may be helpful to open T-accounts and post transactions to these accounts before attempting to prepare the statements.

Class Discussion

b. Review the cash flows associated with the collection of receivables and the payment of payables. Comment on the company's collection and payment strategy.

c. Explain why depreciation decreased in 2010.

d. Did net income increase or decrease between 2008 and 2009? What were the primary causes?

e. Did net income increase or decrease between 2009 and 2010? What were the primary causes?

ATC 4-3   Real-World Case   *Choice of fiscal year*

Consider the following brief descriptions of four companies from different industries. Toll Brothers, Inc., is one of the largest homebuilders in the nation, with operations in 21 states. Sharper Image Corp. sells consumer products, especially electronic items, through 183 The Sharper Image stores and its catalogues. Six Flags, Inc., claims to be the world's largest operator of regional theme parks. It operates 29 parks worldwide, including 13 of the largest 50 parks in the United States. Vail Resorts, Inc., operates several ski resorts in Colorado, including Vail Mountain, the largest in the United States, and Breckenridge Mountain Resort.

The chapter explained that companies often choose to close their books when business is slow. Each of these companies ends its fiscal year on a different date. The closing dates, listed chronologically, are:

January 31
July 31
October 31
December 31

Required

a. Try to determine which fiscal year-end matches which company. Write a brief explanation of the reason for your decisions.

b. Because many companies deliberately choose to prepare their financial statements at a slow time of year, try to identify problems this may present for someone trying to analyze the balance sheet for Sharper Image. Write a brief explanation of the issues you identify.

ATC 4-4   Business Applications Case   *Components of financial statements*

A stockbroker handed Dr. Hibert a set of financial statements for a company the broker described as a "sure bet" for a major increase in stock price. The broker assured Hibert that the company was a legitimate business. As proof, she stated that the company was listed with the Securities and Exchange Commission. After looking over the financial statements, Hibert wanted additional information. He has an Internet connection and can access SEC files. Assume that Hibert obtains a 10-K annual report through the EDGAR database.

Required

Identify three major sections of information that are likely to be contained in the 10-K annual report. Describe the content of each section, and explain the independent auditor's role as it relates to each section.

ATC 4-5   Business Applications Case   *Components of financial statements*

LaToya Chase just finished reading the annual report of Dream Time Company. Chase is enthusiastic about the possibility of investing in the company. In the management's discussion and analysis section of the report, Dream Time's new president, Judy Jones, stated that she was committed to an annual growth rate of 25 percent over the next five years. Chase tells you that the company's financial statements received an unqualified audit opinion from a respected firm of CPAs. Based on the audit report, Chase concluded that the auditors agree with Jones's forecast of a five-year, 25 percent growth rate. She tells you, "These accountants are usually very conservative. If they forecast 25 percent growth, actual growth is likely to be close to 35 percent. I'm not going to miss an opportunity like this. I am buying the stock."

Required

Comment on Chase's understanding of the relationship between the auditor's report and management's discussion and analysis in a company's annual report.

ATC 4-6   Writing Assignment   *Fiscal closing date*

Assume you are the auditor for Gourmet Caterers. The company currently has a December 31 year end as of which you perform the audit. You would like for Gourmet to change the year end to another time (almost any time except December 31).

Required

Write a memo to the owners of Gourmet Caterers and propose a new year end. In the memo explain why it would be reasonable or better to have a different year end and specify what the year end would be. Also give reasons that the change would be beneficial from your perspective.

ATC 4-7   Ethical Dilemma   *Choice of brothers: ethics, risk, and accounting numbers in a medieval setting*

In the late 1400s, a wealthy land owner named Caster was trying to decide which of his twin sons, Rogan or Argon, to designate as the first heir to the family fortune. He decided to set up each son with a small farm consisting of 300 sheep and 20 acres of land. Each twin would be allowed to manage his property as he deemed appropriate. After a designated period, Caster would call his sons before him to account for their actions. The heir to the family fortune would be chosen on the basis of which son had produced a larger increase in wealth during the test period.

On the appointed day of reckoning, Argon boasted that he had 714 sheep under his control while Rogan had only 330. Furthermore, Argon stated that he had increased his land holdings to 27 acres. The seven-acre increase resulted from two transactions: first, on the day the contest started, Argon used 20 sheep to buy 10 additional acres; and second, he sold three of these acres for a total of 9 sheep on the day of reckoning. Also, Argon's flock had produced 75 newborn sheep during the period of accounting. He had been able to give his friends 50 sheep in return for the help that they had given him in building a fence, thereby increasing not only his own wealth but the wealth of his neighbors as well. Argon boasted that the fence was strong and would keep his herd safe from predatory creatures for five years (assume the fence had been used for one year during the contest period). Rogan countered that Argon was holding 400 sheep that belonged to another herder. Argon had borrowed these sheep on the day that the contest had started. Furthermore, Argon had agreed to return 424 sheep to the herder. The 24 additional sheep represented consideration for the use of the herder's flock. Argon had agreed to return the sheep immediately after the day of reckoning.

During the test period, Rogan's flock had produced 37 newborn sheep, but 2 sheep had gotten sick and died during the accounting period. Rogan had also lost 5 sheep to predatory creatures. He had no fence, and some of his sheep strayed from the herd, thereby exposing themselves to danger. Knowing that he was falling behind, Rogan had taken a wife in order to boost his productivity. His wife owned 170 sheep on the day they were married; her sheep had produced 16 newborn sheep since the date of her marriage to Rogan. Argon had not included the wife's sheep in his count of Rogan's herd. If his wife's sheep had been counted, Rogan's herd would contain 516 instead of 330 sheep suggested by Argon's count.

Argon charged that seven of Rogan's sheep were sick with symptoms similar to those exhibited by the two sheep that were now dead. Rogan interjected that he should not be held accountable for acts of nature such as illness. Furthermore, he contended that by isolating the sick sheep from the remainder of the herd, he had demonstrated prudent management practices that supported his case to be designated first heir.

Required

a. Prepare an income statement, balance sheet, statement of sheep flow (cash flow) for each twin, using contemporary (20XX) accounting standards. Note that you have to decide whether to include the sheep owned by Rogan's wife when making his financial statements (what is the accounting entity?). (*Hint:* Use the number of sheep rather than the number of dollars as the common unit of measure.)

b. Refer to the statements you prepared in Requirement *a* to answer the following questions:
   (1) Which twin has more owner's equity at the end of the accounting period?
   (2) Which twin produced the higher net income during the accounting period?
   (3) Which son should be designated heir based on conventional accounting and reporting standards?

c. What is the difference in the value of the land of the twins if the land is valued at market value (that is, three sheep per acre) rather than historical cost (that is, two sheep per acre)?

d. Did Argon's decision to borrow sheep increase his profitability? Support your answer with appropriate financial data.

e. Was Argon's decision to build a fence financially prudent? Support your answer with appropriate financial data.

f. Assuming that the loan resulted in a financial benefit to Argon, identify some reasons that the shepherd who owned the sheep may have been willing to loan them to Argon.

g. Which twin is likely to take risks to improve profitability? What would be the financial condition of each twin if one-half of the sheep in both flocks died as a result of illness? How should such risk factors be reported in financial statements?

h. Should Rogan's decision to "marry for sheep" be considered from an ethical perspective, or should the decision be made solely on the basis of the bottom-line net income figure?

i. Prepare a report that recommends which twin should be designated heir to the family business. Include a set of financial statements that supports your recommendation. Since this is a managerial report that will not be distributed to the public, you are not bound by generally accepted accounting principles.

ATC 4-8 Research Assignment *Investigating Nike's 10-K report*

As explained in this chapter, many companies must file financial reports with the SEC. Many of these reports are available electronically through the EDGAR database. EDGAR is an acronym for Electronic Data Gathering, Analysis, and Retrieval system, and it is accessible through the World Wide Web on the Internet. Instructions for using EDGAR are in Appendix A.

Using the most current 10-K available on EDGAR or on the company's Web site at www.nikebiz.com, answer the following questions about Nike Company.

a. In what year did Nike begin operations?

b. Other than athletic shoes and clothing, what business does Nike operate?

c. How many employees does Nike have?

d. Describe, in dollar amounts, Nike's accounting equation at the end of the most recent year.

e. Has Nike's performance been improving or deteriorating over the past three years? Explain your answer.

ATC 4-9   Spreadsheet Assignment   *Use of Excel*

Adams Company started operations on January 1, 2008. Six months later on June 30, 2008, the company decided to prepare financial statements. The company's accountant decided to problem solve for the adjusting journal entries and the final adjusted account balances by using an electronic spreadsheet. Once the spreadsheet is complete, she will record the adjusting entries in the general journal and post to the ledger. The accountant has started the following spreadsheet but wants you to finish it for her.

Required

a. On a blank spreadsheet, enter the following trial balance in Columns A through C. Also enter the headings for Columns E through I.

	Trial Balance			Adjusting Journal Entries		Adjusted Trial Balance	
Account Titles	Debit	Credit		Debit	Credit	Debit	Credit
Cash	1500						
Certificate of Deposit	10000						
Accounts Receivable	12000						
Supplies	1500						
Prepaid Rent	12000						
Office Equipment	9000						
Accounts Payable		2500					
Unearned Revenue		5000	(1)	3000			2000
Common Stock		20000					
Retained Earnings		0					
Service Revenue		35000			(1)	3000	
Salaries Expense	12000						
Operating Expense	4500						
Totals	62500	62500		3000	3000	0	2000

b. Each of the following events requires an adjusting journal entry. Instead of recording entries in general journal format, record the adjusting entries in the Debit and Credit columns under the heading Adjusting Journal Entries. Entry (1) has already been recorded as an example. Be sure to number your adjusting entries on the spreadsheet. It will be necessary to insert new accounts for the adjustments. Recall that the accounting period is for six months.

(1) Received a $5,000 cash advance on April 1 for a contract to provide five months of service.

(2) Had accrued salaries on June 30 amounting to $1,500.

(3) On January 1 invested in a one-year, $10,000 certificate of deposit that had a 5 percent interest rate.

(4) On January 1 paid $12,000 in advance for a one-year lease on office space.

(5) Received in the mail a utility bill dated June 30 for $150.

(6) Purchased $1,500 of supplies on January 1. As of June 30, $700 of supplies remained on hand.

(7) Paid $9,000 for office equipment on January 1. The equipment was expected to have a four-year useful life and a $1,000 salvage value. Depreciation is computed on a straight-line basis.

c. Develop formulas to sum both the Debit and Credit columns under the Adjusting Journal Entries heading.

d. Develop formulas to derive the adjusted balances for the adjusted trial balance. For example, the formula for the ending balance of Unearned Revenue is =C10−E10+G10. In other words, a credit balance minus debit entries plus credit entries equals the ending balance. Once an ending balance is formulated for one credit account, that formula can be copied to all other credit accounts; the same is true for debit accounts. Once an ending balance is formulated for a debit account, that formula can be copied to all other debit accounts.

e. Develop formulas to sum both the Debit and Credit columns under the Adjusted Trial Balance heading.

Spreadsheet Tips

1. Rows and columns can be inserted by positioning the mouse on the immediate row or column after the desired position. Click on the *right* mouse button. With the *left* mouse button, choose Insert and then either Entire Column or Entire Row. Use the same method to delete columns or rows.

2. Enter the sequential numbering of the adjusting entries as labels rather than values by positioning an apostrophe in front of each entry. The first adjusting entry should be labeled '(1).

ATC 4-10   Spreadsheet Assignment   *Mastery of Excel*

At the end of the accounting period, Adams Company's general ledger contained the following adjusted balances.

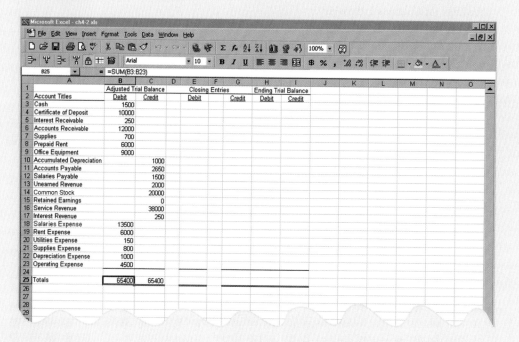

| | Adjusted Trial Balance | | | Closing Entries | | Ending Trial Balance | |
Account Titles	Debit	Credit		Debit	Credit	Debit	Credit
Cash	1500						
Certificate of Deposit	10000						
Interest Receivable	250						
Accounts Receivable	12000						
Supplies	700						
Prepaid Rent	6000						
Office Equipment	9000						
Accumulated Depreciation		1000					
Accounts Payable		2650					
Salaries Payable		1500					
Unearned Revenue		2000					
Common Stock		20000					
Retained Earnings		0					
Service Revenue		38000					
Interest Revenue		250					
Salaries Expense	13500						
Rent Expense	6000						
Utilities Expense	150						
Supplies Expense	800						
Depreciation Expense	1000						
Operating Expense	4500						
Totals	65400	65400					

Required

a. Set up the preceding spreadsheet format. (The spreadsheet tips for ATC 4-9 also apply for this problem.)

b. Record the closing entries in the Closing Entries column of the spreadsheet.

c. Compute the Ending Trial Balance amounts.

CHAPTER 5

Accounting for Merchandising Businesses

LEARNING OBJECTIVES

After you have mastered the material in this chapter you will be able to:

1. Identify and explain the primary features of the perpetual inventory system.

2. Record and report inventory transactions in the double-entry accounting system.

3. Explain the meaning of terms used to describe transportation costs, cash discounts, returns or allowances, and financing costs.

4. Explain how gains and losses differ from revenues and expenses.

5. Compare and contrast single and multistep income statements.

6. Show the effect of lost, damaged, or stolen inventory on financial statements.

7. Use common size financial statements and ratio analysis to evaluate managerial performance.

8. Identify the primary features of the periodic inventory system. (Appendix)

LP5

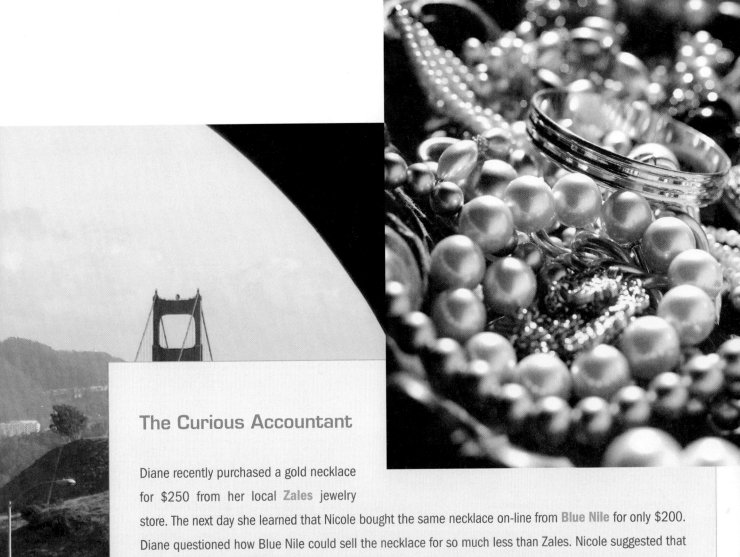

The Curious Accountant

Diane recently purchased a gold necklace for $250 from her local Zales jewelry store. The next day she learned that Nicole bought the same necklace on-line from Blue Nile for only $200. Diane questioned how Blue Nile could sell the necklace for so much less than Zales. Nicole suggested that even though both jewelry sellers purchase their products from the same producers at about the same price, Blue Nile can charge lower prices because it does not have to operate expensive bricks-and-mortar stores, thus lowering its operating costs. Diane disagrees. She thinks the cost of operating large distribution centers and Internet server centers will offset any cost savings Blue Nile enjoys from not owning retail jewelry stores.

Exhibit 5.1 presents the income statements for Zales and Blue Nile. Based on these income statements, do you think Diane or Nicole is correct? (Answer on page 261.)

CHAPTER OPENING

Previous chapters have discussed accounting for service businesses. These businesses obtain revenue by providing some kind of service such as medical or legal advice to their customers. Other examples of service companies include dry cleaning companies, maid service companies, and car washes. This chapter introduces accounting practices for merchandising businesses. **Merchandising businesses** *generate revenue by selling goods. They buy the merchandise they sell from companies called suppliers. The goods purchased for resale are called* **merchandise inventory.** *Merchandising businesses include* **retail companies** *(companies that sell goods to the final consumer) and* **wholesale companies** *(companies that sell to other businesses). Sears, JCPenney, Target, and Sam's Club are real-world merchandising businesses.* ■

EXHIBIT 5.1   Comparative Income Statements

BLUE NILE, INC.
Consolidated Statements of Operations
(dollars in thousands)

| | Fiscal Year Ended | | |
	January 1, 2006	January 2, 2005	December 31, 2003
Net sales	$203,169	$169,242	$128,894
Cost of sales	158,025	131,590	99,476
Gross profit	45,144	37,652	29,418
Operating expenses:			
Selling, general and administrative	27,095	22,795	18,207
Restructuring charges	–	–	(87)
	27,095	22,795	18,120
Operating income	18,049	14,857	11,298
Other income (expense), net:			
Interest income	2,499	709	109
Interest expense	–	–	(209)
Other income	5	63	88
	2,504	772	(12)
Income before income taxes	20,553	15,629	11,286
Income tax expense (benefit)	7,400	5,642	(15,700)
Net income	$ 13,153	$ 9,987	$ 26,986

ZALE CORPORATION AND SUBSIDIARIES
Consolidated Statements of Operations
(dollars in thousands)

| | Fiscal Years Ended July 31, | | |
	2005	2004	2003
Total revenue	$2,383,066	$2,304,440	$2,212,241
Cost and expenses:			
Cost of sales	1,157,226	1,122,946	1,101,030
Selling, general and administrative expenses	982,113	942,796	884,069
Cost of insurance operations	6,084	5,963	8,228
Depreciation and amortization expense	59,840	56,381	55,690
Impairment of goodwill	–	–	136,300
Operating earnings	177,803	176,354	26,924
Interest expense, net	7,725	7,528	6,319
Cost of early retirement of debt	–	–	5,910
Earnings before income taxes	170,078	168,826	14,695
Income taxes	63,303	62,353	55,340
Net earnings (loss)	$ 106,775	$ 106,473	$ (40,645)

Product Costs Versus Selling and Administrative Costs

Companies report inventory costs on the balance sheet in the asset account Merchandise Inventory. All costs incurred to acquire merchandise and ready it for sale are included in the inventory account. Examples of inventory costs include the price of goods purchased, shipping and handling costs, transit insurance, and storage costs. Since inventory items are referred to as products, inventory costs are frequently called **product costs.**

Costs that are not included in inventory are usually called **selling and administrative costs.** Examples of selling and administrative costs include advertising, administrative salaries, sales commissions, insurance, and interest. Since selling and administrative costs are usually recognized as expenses *in the period* in which they are incurred, they are sometimes called **period costs.** In contrast, product costs are expensed when inventory is sold regardless of when it was purchased. In other words, product costs are matched directly with sales revenue, while selling and administrative costs are matched with the period in which they are incurred.

Allocating Inventory Cost Between Asset and Expense Accounts

The cost of inventory that is available for sale during a specific accounting period is determined as follows:

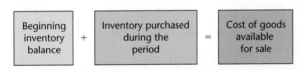

Video 5.1

The **cost of goods available for sale** is allocated between the asset account Merchandise Inventory and an expense account called **Cost of Goods Sold.** The cost of inventory items that have not been sold (Merchandise Inventory) is reported as an asset on the balance sheet, and the cost of the items sold (Cost of Goods Sold) is expensed on the income statement. This allocation is depicted graphically as follows.

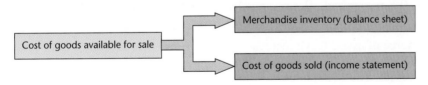

The difference between the sales revenue and the cost of goods sold is called **gross margin** or **gross profit.** The selling and administrative expenses (period costs) are subtracted from gross margin to obtain the net income.

Exhibit 5.1 displays income statements from the annual reports of Blue Nile and Zales. For each company, review the most current income statement and determine the amount of gross margin. You should find a gross profit of $45,144 for Blue Nile and a gross margin of $1,225,840 ($2,383,066 − $1,157,226) for Zales.

Perpetual Inventory System

Most modern companies maintain their inventory records using the **perpetual inventory system,** so-called because the inventory account is adjusted perpetually (continually) throughout the accounting period. Each time merchandise is purchased, the inventory

Video 5.1

Topic Tackler

PLUS

5-1

account is increased; each time it is sold, the inventory account is decreased. The following illustration demonstrates the basic features of the perpetual inventory system.

June Gardener loved plants and grew them with such remarkable success that she decided to open a small retail plant store. She started June's Plant Shop (JPS) on January 1, 2008. The following discussion explains and illustrates the effects of the four events the company experienced during its first year of operation.

June's
PLANT SHOP

Effects of 2008 Events on Financial Statements

Event 1 JPS acquired $15,000 cash by issuing common stock.

This event is an asset source transaction. It increases both assets (cash) and stockholders' equity (common stock). The income statement is not affected. The statement of cash flows reflects an inflow from financing activities. These effects are shown here:

Assets			=	Liab.	+	Stockholders' Equity							
Cash	+	Inventory	+	Land	=	Accts. Pay.	+	Com. Stk.	+	Ret. Earn.	Rev.	−	Exp.	=	Net Inc.	Cash Flow
15,000	+	NA	+	NA	=	NA	+	15,000	+	NA	NA	−	NA	=	NA	15,000 FA

Event 2 JPS purchased merchandise inventory for $14,000 cash.

This event is an asset exchange transaction. One asset, cash, decreases and another asset, merchandise inventory, increases; total assets remain unchanged. Because product costs are expensed when inventory is sold, not when it is purchased, the event does not affect the income statement. The cash outflow, however, is reported in the operating activities section of the statement of cash flows. These effects are illustrated below:

Assets			=	Liab.	+	Stockholders' Equity							
Cash	+	Inventory	+	Land	=	Accts. Pay.	+	Com. Stk.	+	Ret. Earn.	Rev.	−	Exp.	=	Net Inc.	Cash Flow
(14,000)	+	14,000	+	NA	=	NA	+	NA	+	NA	NA	−	NA	=	NA	(14,000) OA

Event 3a JPS recognized sales revenue from selling inventory for $12,000 cash.

The revenue recognition is the first part of a two-part transaction. The *sales part* represents a source of assets (cash increases from earning sales revenue). Both assets (cash) and stockholders' equity (retained earnings) increase. Sales revenue on the income statement increases. The $12,000 cash inflow is reported in the operating activities section of the statement of cash flows. These effects are shown in the following financial statements model:

Assets			=	Liab.	+	Stockholders' Equity							
Cash	+	Inventory	+	Land	=	Accts. Pay.	+	Com. Stk.	+	Ret. Earn.	Rev.	−	Exp.	=	Net Inc.	Cash Flow
12,000	+	NA	+	NA	=	NA	+	NA	+	12,000	12,000	−	NA	=	12,000	12,000 OA

Event 3b JPS recognized $8,000 of cost of goods sold.

The expense recognition is the second part of the two-part transaction. The *expense part* represents a use of assets. Both assets (merchandise inventory) and stockholders' equity (retained earnings) decrease. An expense account, Cost of Goods Sold, is reported on the income statement. This part of the transaction does not affect the statement of cash flows. A cash outflow occurred when the goods were bought, not when they were sold. These effects are shown here:

Assets			=	Liab.	+	Stockholders' Equity			Rev.	−	Exp.	=	Net Inc.	Cash Flow
Cash	+ Inventory	+ Land	=	Accts. Pay.	+	Com. Stk.	+	Ret. Earn.	Rev.	−	Exp.	=	Net Inc.	Cash Flow
NA	+ (8,000)	+ NA	=	NA	+	NA	+	(8,000)	NA	−	18,000	=	(8,000)	NA

Event 4 JPS paid $1,000 cash for selling and administrative expenses.

This event is an asset use transaction. The payment decreases both assets (cash) and stockholders' equity (retained earnings). The increase in selling and administrative expenses decreases net income. The $1,000 cash payment is reported in the operating activities section of the statement of cash flows. These effects are illustrated below:

Assets			=	Liab.	+	Stockholders' Equity			Rev.	−	Exp.	=	Net Inc.	Cash Flow
Cash	+ Inventory	+ Land	=	Accts. Pay.	+	Com. Stk.	+	Ret. Earn.	Rev.	−	Exp.	=	Net Inc.	Cash Flow
(1,000)	+ NA	+ NA	=	NA	+	NA	+	(1,000)	NA	−	1,000	=	(1,000)	(1,000) OA

Event 5 JPS paid $5,500 cash to purchase land for a place to locate a future store.

Buying the land increases the Land account and decreases the Cash account on the balance sheet. The income statement is not affected. The statement of cash flow shows a cash outflow to purchase land in the financing activities section of the statement of cash flows. These effects are shown below:

Assets			=	Liab.	+	Stockholders' Equity			Rev.	−	Exp.	=	Net Inc.	Cash Flow
Cash	+ Inventory	+ Land	=	Accts. Pay.	+	Com. Stk.	+	Ret. Earn.	Rev.	−	Exp.	=	Net Inc.	Cash Flow
(5,500)	+ NA	+ 5,500	=	NA	+	NA	+	NA	NA	−	NA	=	NA	(5,500) IA

Recording and Reporting Inventory Events in the Double-Entry System

The 2008 transactions JPS experienced are summarized below.

Event 1 JPS acquired $15,000 cash by issuing common stock.

Event 2 JPS purchased merchandise inventory (plants) for $14,000 cash.

Event 3a JPS recognized sales revenue from selling inventory for $12,000 cash.

Event 3b JPS recognized $8,000 of cost of goods sold.

Event 4 JPS paid $1,000 cash for selling and administrative expenses.

Event 5 JPS paid $5,500 cash to purchase land.

Record and report inventory transactions in the double-entry accounting system.

Panel A of Exhibit 5.2 shows these transactions recorded in general journal format. Panel B of Exhibit 5.2 shows the general ledger T-accounts after the journal entries have been posted to them. The ledger accounts provide the data for the financial statements in Exhibit 5.3.

EXHIBIT 5.2

Journal Entries and General Ledger Accounts for 2008

Panel A Journal Entries

Event No.	Account Title	Debit	Credit
1	Cash	15,000	
	Common Stock		15,000
2	Merchandise Inventory	14,000	
	Cash		14,000
3a	Cash	12,000	
	Sales Revenue		12,000
3b	Cost of Goods Sold	8,000	
	Merchandise Inventory		8,000
4	Selling and Administrative Expenses	1,000	
	Cash		1,000
5	Land	5,500	
	Cash		5,500

Panel B General Ledger Accounts

Assets	=	Liabilities	+	Equity

Cash

(1)	15,000	14,000	(2)
(3a)	12,000	1,000	(4)
		5,500	(5)
Bal.	6,500		

Accounts Payable

	0	Bal.

Common Stock

	15,000	(1)
	15,000	Bal.

Merchandise Inventory

(2)	14,000	8,000	(3b)
Bal.	6,000		

Retained Earnings

Sales Revenue

	12,000	(3a)

Land

(5)	5,500	

Cost of Goods Sold

(3b)	8,000	

Selling and Admin. Expenses

(4)	1,000	

Although Exhibit 5.2 does not illustrate the 2008 year-end closing entries, recall that the closing entries will transfer the amounts from the revenue and expense accounts to the Retained Earnings account. The balance in the Retained Earnings account after closing will be $3,000. Before reading further, trace the transaction data from each journal entry in Panel A to the ledger accounts in Panel B and then from the ledger accounts to the financial statements in Exhibit 5.3.

Financial Statements for 2008

JPS had no beginning inventory in its first year, so the cost of merchandise inventory available for sale was $14,000 (the amount of inventory purchased during the period). Recall that JPS must allocate the *Cost of Goods (Inventory) Available for Sale* between the *Cost of*

EXHIBIT 5.3

Financial Statements

2008 Income Statement		12/31/08 Balance Sheet			2008 Statement of Cash Flows	
Sales revenue	$12,000	Assets			Operating activities	
Cost of goods sold	(8,000)	Cash	$ 6,500		Inflow from customers	$12,000
		Merchandise inventory	6,000		Outflow for inventory	(14,000)
Gross margin	4,000	Land	5,500		Outflow for selling	
Less: Operating exp.					& admin. exp.	(1,000)
Selling and		Total assets		$18,000		
admin. exp.	(1,000)	Liabilities		$ 0	Net cash outflow for	
Net income	$ 3,000	Stockholders' equity			operating activities	$ (3,000)
		Common stock	$15,000		Investing activities	
		Retained earnings	3,000		Outflow to purchase land	(5,500)
					Financing Activities	
		Total stockholders' equity		18,000	Inflow from stock issue	15,000
		Total liab. and stk. equity		$18,000	Net change in cash	6,500
					Plus: Beginning cash balance	0
					Ending cash balance	$ 6,500

Goods Sold ($8,000) and the ending balance ($6,000) in the **Merchandise Inventory** account. The cost of goods sold is reported as an expense on the income statement and the ending balance of merchandise inventory is reported as an asset on the balance sheet. The difference between the sales revenue ($12,000) and the cost of goods sold ($8,000) is labeled *gross margin* ($4,000) on the income statement.

CHECK YOURSELF 5.1

Phambroom Company began 2009 with $35,600 in its Inventory account. During the year, it purchased inventory costing $356,800 and sold inventory that had cost $360,000 for $520,000. Based on this information alone, determine (1) the inventory balance as of December 31, 2009, and (2) the amount of gross margin Phambroom would report on its 2009 income statement.

Answer

1. Beginning inventory + Purchases = Goods available − Ending inventory = Cost of goods sold

    $35,600 + $356,800 = $392,400 − Ending inventory = $360,000

    Ending inventory = $32,400

2. Sales revenue − Cost of goods sold = Gross margin

    $520,000 − $360,000 = $160,000

Transportation Cost, Purchase Returns and Allowances, and Cash Discounts Related to Inventory Purchases

Purchasing inventory often involves: (1) incurring transportation costs, (2) returning inventory or receiving purchase allowances (cost reductions), and (3) taking cash discounts (also cost reductions). During its second accounting cycle, JPS encountered these kinds of events. The final account balances at the end of the 2008 fiscal year become the beginning balances for 2009: Cash, $6,500; Merchandise Inventory, $6,000; Land, 5,500; Common Stock, $15,000; and Retained Earnings, $3,000.

LO 3

Explain the meaning of terms used to describe transportation costs, cash discounts, returns or allowances, and financing costs.

Effects of 2009 Events on Financial Statements

JPS experienced the following events during its 2009 accounting period. The effects of each of these events are explained and illustrated in the following discussion.

Event 1 JPS borrowed $4,000 cash by issuing a note payable.

JPS borrowed the money to enable it to purchase a plot of land for a future site for a store it planned to build in the near future. Borrowing the money increases the Cash account and the Note Payable account on the balance sheet. The income statement is not affected. The statement of cash flow shows a cash flow from financing activities. These effects are shown below:

Assets				=	Liabilities		+	Stockholders' Equity							
Cash	+	Accts. Rec.	+	Inventory	+	Land	=	Accts. Pay.	+	Notes Pay.	+	Com. Stk.	+	Ret. Earn.		Rev.	−	Exp.	=	Net Inc.		Cash Flow
4,000	+	NA	+	NA	+	NA	=	NA	+	4,000	+	NA	+	NA		NA	−	NA	=	NA		4,000 FA

Event 2 JPS purchased on account merchandise inventory with a list price of $11,000.

The inventory purchase increases both assets (merchandise inventory) and liabilities (accounts payable) on the balance sheet. The income statement is not affected until later, when inventory is sold. Since the inventory was purchased on account, there was no cash outflow. These effects are shown here:

Assets				=	Liab.		+	Stockholders' Equity							
Cash	+	Accts. Rec.	+	Inventory	+	Land	=	Accts. Pay.	+	Notes Pay.	+	Com. Stk.	+	Ret. Earn.		Rev.	−	Exp.	=	Net Inc.		Cash Flow
NA	+	NA	+	11,000	+	NA	=	11,000	+	NA	+	NA	+	NA		NA	−	NA	=	NA		NA

Accounting for Purchase Returns and Allowances

Event 3 JPS returned some of the inventory purchased in Event 2. The list price of the returned merchandise was $1,000.

To promote customer satisfaction, many businesses allow customers to return goods for reasons such as wrong size, wrong color, wrong design, or even simply because the purchaser changed his mind. The effect of a purchase return is the *opposite* of the original purchase. For JPS the **purchase return** decreases both assets (merchandise inventory) and liabilities (accounts payable). There is no effect on either the income statement or the statement of cash flows. These effects are shown below:

	Assets			=	Liab.		+	Stockholders' Equity						
Cash +	Accts. Rec. +	Inventory +	Land =		Accts. Pay. +	Notes Pay. +		Com. Stk. +	Ret. Earn.		Rev. −	Exp. =	Net Inc.	Cash Flow
NA +	NA +	(1,000) +	NA =		(1,000) +	NA +		NA +	NA		NA −	NA =	NA	NA

Sometimes dissatisfied buyers will agree to keep goods instead of returning them if the seller offers to reduce the price. Such reductions are called allowances. **Purchase allowances** affect the financial statements the same way purchase returns do.

Purchase Discounts

Event 4 **JPS received a cash discount on goods purchased in Event 2. The credit terms were 2/10, n/30.**

To encourage buyers to pay promptly, sellers sometimes offer **cash discounts.** To illustrate, assume JPS purchased the inventory in Event 2 under terms **2/10, n/30** (two-ten, net thirty). These terms mean the seller will allow a 2 percent cash discount if the purchaser pays cash within 10 days from the date of purchase. The amount not paid within the first 10 days is due at the end of 30 days from date of purchase. Recall that JPS returned $1,000 of the inventory purchased in Event 1 leaving a $10,000 balance ($11,000 list price − $1,000 purchase return). If JPS pays for the inventory within 10 days, the amount of the discount is $200 ($10,000 × .02).

When cash discounts are applied to purchases they are called **purchases discounts.** When they are applied to sales, they are called sales discounts. Sales discounts will be discussed later in the chapter. A *purchase discount* reduces the cost of the inventory and the associated account payable on the balance sheet. A purchase discount does not directly affect the income statement or the statement of cash flow. These effects are shown here:

	Assets			=	Liab.		+	Stockholders' Equity						
Cash +	Accts. Rec. +	Inventory +	Land =		Accts. Pay. +	Notes Pay. +		Com. Stk. +	Ret. Earn.		Rev. −	Exp. =	Net Inc.	Cash Flow
NA +	NA +	(200) +	NA =		(200) +	NA +		NA +	NA		NA −	NA =	NA	NA

If JPS paid the account payable after 10 days, there would be no purchase discount. In this case the balances in the Inventory and Account Payable accounts would remain at $10,000.

Event 5 **JPS paid the $9,800 balance due on the account payable.**

The remaining balance in the accounts payable is $9,800 ($10,000 list price − $200 purchase discount). Paying cash to settle the liability reduces cash and accounts payable on the balance sheet. The income statement is not affected. The cash outflow is shown in the operating section of the statement of cash flows. These effects are shown below:

	Assets			=	Liab.		+	Stockholders' Equity						
Cash +	Accts. Rec. +	Inventory +	Land =		Accts. Pay. +	Notes Pay. +		Com. Stk. +	Ret. Earn.		Rev. −	Exp. =	Net Inc.	Cash Flow
(9,800) +	NA +	NA +	NA =		(9,800) +	NA +		NA +	NA		NA −	NA =	NA	(9,800) OA

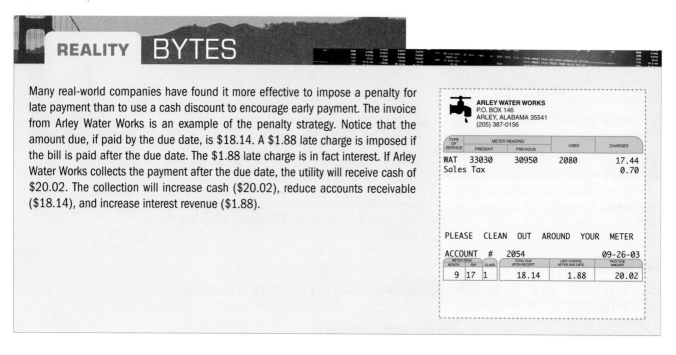

REALITY BYTES

Many real-world companies have found it more effective to impose a penalty for late payment than to use a cash discount to encourage early payment. The invoice from Arley Water Works is an example of the penalty strategy. Notice that the amount due, if paid by the due date, is $18.14. A $1.88 late charge is imposed if the bill is paid after the due date. The $1.88 late charge is in fact interest. If Arley Water Works collects the payment after the due date, the utility will receive cash of $20.02. The collection will increase cash ($20.02), reduce accounts receivable ($18.14), and increase interest revenue ($1.88).

The Cost of Financing Inventory

Suppose you buy inventory this month and sell it next month. Where do you get the money to pay for the inventory at the time you buy it? One way to finance the purchase is to buy it on account and withhold payment until the last day of the term for the account payable. For example, suppose you buy inventory under terms 2/10, net/30. Under these circumstances you could delay payment for 30 days after the day of purchase. This way you may be able to collect enough money from the inventory you sell to pay for the inventory you purchased. Refusing the discount allows you the time needed to generate the cash necessary to pay off the liability (account payable). Unfortunately, this is usually a very expensive way to finance the purchase of inventory.

While the amount of a cash discount may appear small, the discount period is short. Consider the terms 2/10, net/30. Since you can pay on the tenth day and still receive the discount, you obtain financing for only 20 days (30-day full credit term − 10-day discount term). In other words, you must forgo a 2 percent discount to obtain a loan with a 20-day term. What is the size of the discount in annual terms? The answer is determined by the following formula.

$$\text{Annual rate} = \text{Discount rate} \times (365 \text{ days} \div \text{term of the loan})$$

$$\text{Annual rate} = 2\% \times (365 \div 20)$$

$$\text{Annual rate} = 36.5\%$$

This means that a 2 percent discount rate for 20 days is equivalent to a 36.5 percent annual rate of interest. So, if you do not have the money to pay the account payable, but can borrow money from a bank at less than 36.5 percent annual interest, you should borrow the money and pay off the account payable within the discount period.

Accounting for Transportation Costs

Event 6 **The shipping terms for the inventory purchased in Event 2 were FOB shipping point. JPS paid the freight company $300 cash for delivering the merchandise.**

The terms **FOB shipping point** and **FOB destination** identify whether the buyer or the seller is responsible for transportation costs. If goods are delivered FOB shipping point, the buyer is responsible for the freight cost. If goods are delivered FOB destination, the seller is responsible. When the buyer is responsible, the freight cost is called **transportation-in.** When the seller is responsible, the cost is called **transportation-out.** The following table summarizes freight cost terms.

Responsible Party	Buyer	Seller
Freight terms	FOB shipping point	FOB destination
Account title	Merchandise inventory	Transportation-out

Event 6 indicates the inventory was delivered FOB shipping point, so JPS (the buyer) is responsible for the $300 freight cost. Since incurring transportation-in costs is necessary to obtain inventory, these costs are added to the inventory account. The freight cost increases one asset account (Merchandise Inventory) and decreases another asset account (Cash). The income statement is not affected by this transaction because transportation-in costs are not expensed when they are incurred. Instead they are expensed as part of *cost of goods sold* when the inventory is sold. However, the cash paid for transportation-in costs is reported as an outflow in the operating activities section of the statement of cash flows. The effects of *transportation-in costs* are shown here:

		Assets			=	Liab.			+	Stockholders' Equity						
Cash	+	Accts. Rec.	+	Inventory	+	Land	=	Accts. Pay.	+	Notes Pay.	+	Com. Stk.	+	Ret. Earn.		
(300)	+	NA	+	300	+	NA	=	NA	+	NA	+	NA	+	NA		

Rev.	−	Exp.	=	Net Inc.	Cash Flow
NA	−	NA	=	NA	(300) OA

Event 7a JPS recognized $24,750 of revenue on the cash sale of merchandise that cost $11,500.

The sale increases assets (cash) and stockholders' equity (retained earnings). The revenue recognition increases net income. The $24,750 cash inflow from the sale is reported in the operating activities section of the statement of cash flows. These effects are shown below:

Cash	+	Accts. Rec.	+	Inventory	+	Land	=	Accts. Pay.	+	Notes Pay.	+	Com. Stk.	+	Ret. Earn.
24,750	+	NA	+	NA	+	NA	=	NA	+	NA	+	NA	+	24,750

Rev.	−	Exp.	=	Net Inc.	Cash Flow
24,750	−	NA	=	24,750	24,750 OA

Event 7b JPS recognized $11,500 of cost of goods sold.

When goods are sold, the product cost—*including a proportionate share of transportation-in and adjustments for purchase returns and allowances*—is transferred from the Merchandise Inventory account to the expense account, Cost of Goods Sold. Recognizing cost of goods sold decreases both assets (merchandise inventory) and stockholders' equity (retained earnings). The expense recognition for cost of goods sold decreases net income. Cash flow is not affected. These effects are shown here:

Cash	+	Accts. Rec.	+	Inventory	+	Land	=	Accts. Pay.	+	Notes Pay.	+	Com. Stk.	+	Ret. Earn.
NA	+	NA	+	(11,500)	+	NA	=	NA	+	NA	+	NA	+	(11,500)

Rev.	−	Exp.	=	Net Inc.	Cash Flow
NA	−	11,500	=	(11,500)	NA

Event 8 **JPS paid $450 cash for freight costs on inventory delivered to customers.**

Assume the merchandise sold in Event 7a was shipped FOB destination. Also assume JPS paid the freight cost in cash. FOB destination means the seller is responsible for the freight cost, which is called transportation-out. Transportation-out is reported on the income statement as an operating expense in the section below gross margin. The cost of freight on goods shipped to customers is incurred *after* the goods are sold. It is not part of the costs to obtain goods or ready them for sale. Recognizing the expense of transportation-out reduces assets (cash) and stockholders' equity (retained earnings). Operating expenses increase and net income decreases. The cash outflow is reported in the operating activities section of the statement of cash flows. These effects are shown below:

		Assets		=	Liab.		+	Stockholders' Equity						
Cash	+	Accts. Rec.	+ Inventory + Land	=	Accts. Pay.	+ Notes Pay.	+	Com. Stk.	+ Ret. Earn.	Rev.	− Exp.	= Net Inc.		Cash Flow
(450)	+	NA	+ NA + NA	=	NA	+ NA	+	NA	+ (450)	NA	− 450	= (450)		(450) OA

If the terms had been FOB shipping point, the customer would have been responsible for the transportation cost and JPS would not have recorded an expense.

Event 9 **JPS paid $5,000 cash for selling and administrative expenses.**

The effect on the balance sheet is to decrease both assets (cash) and stockholders' equity (retained earnings). Recognizing the selling and administrative expenses decreases net income. The $5,000 cash outflow is reported in the operating activities section of the statement of cash flows. These effects are shown below:

		Assets		=	Liab.		+	Stockholders' Equity						
Cash	+	Accts. Rec.	+ Inventory + Land	=	Accts. Pay.	+ Notes Pay.	+	Com. Stk.	+ Ret. Earn.	Rev.	− Exp.	= Net Inc.		Cash Flow
(5,000)	+	NA	+ NA + NA	=	NA	+ NA	+	NA	+ (5,000)	NA	− 5,000	= (5,000)		(5,000) OA

Event 10 **JPS paid $360 cash for interest expense on the note described in Event 1.**

The effect on the balance sheet is to decrease both assets (cash) and stockholders' equity (retained earnings). Recognizing the interest expense decreases net income. The $360 cash outflow is reported in the operating activities section of the statement of cash flows. These effects are shown below:

		Assets		=	Liab.		+	Stockholders' Equity						
Cash	+	Accts. Rec.	+ Inventory + Land	=	Accts. Pay.	+ Notes Pay.	+	Com. Stk.	+ Ret. Earn.	Rev.	− Exp.	= Net Inc.		Cash Flow
(360)	+	NA	+ NA + NA	=	NA	+ NA	+	NA	+ (360)	NA	− 360	= (360)		(360) OA

Recognizing Gains and Losses

Event 11 JPS sold the land that had cost $5,500 for $6,200 cash.

When JPS sells merchandise inventory for more than it cost, the difference between the sales revenue and the cost of the goods sold is called the *gross margin.* In contrast, when JPS sells land for more than it cost, the difference between the sales price and the cost of the land is called a **gain.** Why is one called *gross margin* and the other a *gain?* The terms are used to alert financial statement users to the fact that the nature of the underlying transactions is different.

LO 4

Explain how gains and losses differ from revenues and expenses.

JPS' primary business is selling inventory, not land. The term *gain* indicates profit resulting from transactions that are not likely to regularly recur. Similarly, had the land sold for less than cost the difference would have been labeled **loss** rather than expense. This term also indicates the underlying transaction is not from normal, recurring operating activities. Gains and losses are shown separately on the income statement to communicate the expectation that they are nonrecurring.

The presentation of gains and losses in the income statement is discussed in more detail in a later section of the chapter. At this point note that the sale increases cash, decreases land, and increases retained earnings on the balance sheet. The income statement shows a gain on the sale of land and net income increases. The $6,200 cash inflow is shown as an investing activity on the statement of cash flows. These effects are shown below:

Assets				=	Liab.			+	Stockholders' Equity						
Cash	+ Accts. Rec.	+ Inventory	+ Land	=	Accts. Pay.	+ Notes Pay.	+	Com. Stk.	+ Ret. Earn.	Gain	− Exp.	= Net Inc.	Cash Flow
6,200	+ NA	+ NA	+ (5,500)	=	NA	+ NA	+	NA	+ 700	700	− NA	= 700	6,200 IA

CHECK YOURSELF 5.2

Tsang Company purchased $32,000 of inventory on account with payment terms of 2/10, n/30 and freight terms FOB shipping point. Freight costs were $1,100. Tsang obtained a $2,000 purchase allowance because the inventory was damaged upon arrival. Tsang paid for the inventory within the discount period. Based on this information alone, determine the balance in the inventory account.

Answer

List price of inventory	$32,000
Plus: Transportation-in costs	1,100
Less: Purchase returns and allowances	(2,000)
Less: Purchase discount [($32,000 − $2,000) × .02]	(600)
Balance in inventory account	$30,500

Recording and Reporting Inventory Events in the Double-Entry System

LO 2

Exhibit 5.4 summarizes the journal entries and ledger T-accounts for the 2009 accounting events just described. A summary of these events follows here for your convenience. Before reading further, trace the effects of each event to the journal and ledger accounts. Then trace the information in the ledger accounts to the 2009 financial statements displayed in Exhibits 5.5, 5.7, and 5.8.

Record and report inventory transactions in the double-entry accounting system.

Event 1 JPS borrowed $4,000 cash by issuing a note payable.

Event 2 JPS purchased on account merchandise inventory with a list price of $11,000.

Event 3 JPS returned some of the inventory purchased in Event 2. The list price of the returned merchandise was $1,000.

Event 4 JPS received a cash discount on goods purchased in Event 2. The credit terms were 2/10, n/30.

Event 5 JPS paid the $9,800 balance due on the account payable.

Event 6 The inventory purchased in Event 2 was delivered FOB shipping point. JPS paid the freight company $300 cash for delivering the merchandise.

Event 7a JPS recognized $24,750 of revenue on the cash sale of merchandise that cost $11,500.

Event 7b JPS recognized $11,500 of cost of goods sold.

Event 8 JPS paid $450 cash for freight costs on inventory delivered to customers.

Event 9 JPS paid $5,000 cash for selling and administrative expenses.

Event 10 JPS paid $360 cash for interest expense on the note described in Event 1.

Event 11 JPS sold the land that had cost $5,500 for $6,200 cash.

EXHIBIT 5.4

Journal Entries and Ledger Accounts for 2009

Panel A Journal Entries

Event No.	Account Title	Debit	Credit
1	Cash	4,000	
	Note Payable		4,000
2	Merchandise Inventory	11,000	
	Accounts Payable		11,000
3	Accounts Payable	1,000	
	Merchandise Inventory		1,000
4	Accounts Payable	200	
	Merchandise Inventory		200
5	Accounts Payable	9,800	
	Cash		9,800
6	Merchandise Inventory	300	
	Cash		300
7a	Cash	24,750	
	Sales		24,750
7b	Cost of Goods Sold	11,500	
	Merchandise Inventory		11,500
8	Transportation-Out	450	
	Cash		450
9	Selling and Administrative Expenses	5,000	
	Cash		5,000
10	Interest Expense	360	
	Cash		360
11	Cash	6,200	
	Land		5,500
	Gain on Sale of Land		700

continued

Panel B Ledger Accounts

Assets	=	Liabilities	+	Equity

Cash

Bal.	6,500	9,800	(5)
(1)	4,000	300	(6)
(7a)	24,750	450	(8)
(11)	6,200	5,000	(9)
		360	(10)
Bal.	25,540		

Merchandise Inventory

Bal.	6,000	1,000	(3)
(2)	11,000	200	(4)
(6)	300	11,500	(7b)
Bal.	4,600		

Land

Bal.	5,500	5,500	(11)
Bal.	0		

Accounts Payable

(3)	1,000	11,000	(2)
(4)	200		
(5)	9,800		
		0	Bal.

Notes Payable

		4,000	(1)
		4,000	Bal.

Common Stock

	15,000	Bal.

Retained Earnings

	3,000	Bal.
	8,140	(Cl)
	11,140	Bal.

Sales Revenue

(Cl)	24,750	24,750	(7a)
		-0-	Bal.

Gain on Sale of Land

(Cl)	700	700	(11)
		-0-	Bal.

Cost of Goods Sold

(7b)	11,500	11,500	(Cl)
Bal.	-0-		

Transportation-out

(8)	450	450	(Cl)
Bal.	-0-		

Selling and Admin. Expenses

(9)	5,000	5,000	(Cl)
Bal.	-0-		

Interest Expense

(10)	360	360	(Cl)
Bal.	-0-		

Total Assets	=	Total Liabilities	+	Total Equity
$30,140		$4,000		$26,140

Multistep Income Statement

JPS' 2009 income statement is shown in Exhibit 5.5. Observe the form of this statement carefully. It is more informative than one which simply subtracts expenses from revenues. First, it compares sales revenue with the cost of the goods that were sold to produce that revenue. The difference between the sales revenue and the cost of goods sold is called *gross margin*. Next, the operating expenses are subtracted from the gross margin to determine the *operating income*. **Operating income** is the amount of income that is generated from the normal recurring operations of a business. Items that are not expected to recur on a regular basis are subtracted from the operating income to determine the amount of *net income*.[1]

Compare and contrast single and multistep income statements.

Video 5.1

---

[1]Revenue and expense items with special characteristics may be classified as discontinued or extraordinary items. These items are shown separately just above net income regardless of whether a company uses a single-step or multistep format. Further discussion of these items is beyond the scope of this text.

EXHIBIT 5.5

JUNE'S PLANT SHOP
Income Statement
For the Period Ended December 31, 2009

Sales revenue	$ 24,750
Cost of goods sold	(11,500)
Gross margin	13,250
Less: Operating expenses	
Selling and administrative expense	(5,000)
Transportation-out	(450)
Operating income	7,800
Nonoperating items	
Interest expense	(360)
Gain on the sale of land	700
Net income	$ 8,140

EXHIBIT 5.6

Income Statement Format
Used by U.S. Companies

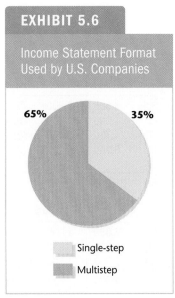

65%   35%

Single-step

Multistep

Data Source: AICPA, *Accounting Trends and Techniques,* 2006.

EXHIBIT 5.7

JUNE'S PLANT SHOP
Balance Sheet
As of December 31, 2009

Assets		
Cash	$25,540	
Merchandise inventory	4,600	
Total assets		$30,140
Liabilities		
Notes payable		$ 4,000
Stockholders' equity		
Common stock	$15,000	
Retained earnings	11,140	
Total stockholders' equity		26,140
Total liabilities and stockholders' equity		$30,140

Income statements that show these additional relationships are called **multistep income statements.** Income statements that display a single comparison of all revenues minus all expenses are called **single-step income statements.** To this point in the text we have shown only single-step income statements to promote simplicity. However, the multistep form is used more frequently in practice. Exhibit 5.6 shows the percentage of companies that use the multistep versus the single-step format. Go to Exhibit 5.1 and identify the company that presents its income statement in the multistep format. You should have identified Blue Nile as the company using the multistep format. Zale's statement is shown in the single-step format.

Note that interest is reported as a *nonoperating* item on the income statement in Exhibit 5.5. In contrast, it is shown in the *operating* activities section of the statement of cash flows in Exhibit 5.8. When the FASB issued Statement of Financial Accounting Standard (SFAS) 95, it required interest to be reported in the operating activities section of the statement of cash flows. There was no corresponding requirement for the treatment of interest on the income statement. Prior to SFAS 95, interest was considered to be a nonoperating item. Most companies continued to report interest as a nonoperating item on their income statements even though they were required to change how it was reported on the statement of cash flows. As a result, there is frequent inconsistency in the way interest is reported on the two financial statements.

EXHIBIT 5.8

JUNE'S PLANT SHOP
Statement of Cash Flows
For the Period Ended December 31, 2009

Operating activities		
Inflow from customers	$ 24,750	
Outflow for inventory*	(10,100)	
Outflow for transportation-out	(450)	
Outflow for selling and administrative expense	(5,000)	
Outflow for interest expense	(360)	
Net cash outflow for operating activities		$ 8,840
Investing activities		
Inflow from sale of land		6,200
Financing activities		
Inflow from issue of note payable		4,000
Net change in cash		19,040
Plus beginning cash balance		6,500
Ending cash balance		$25,540

*Net cost on inventory 9,800 + transportation-in $300 = $10,100

Also note that while the gain on the sale of land is shown on the income statement, it is not included in the operating activities section of the statement of cash flows. Since the gain is a nonoperating item, it is included in the cash inflow from the sale of land shown in the investing activities section. In this case the full cash inflow from the sale of land ($6,200) is shown in the investing activities section of the statement of cash flows in Exhibit 5.8.

Lost, Damaged, or Stolen Inventory

Show the effect of lost, damaged, or stolen inventory on financial statements.

Video 5.1

Most merchandising companies experience some level of inventory **shrinkage,** a term that reflects decreases in inventory for reasons other than sales to customers. Inventory may be stolen by shoplifters, damaged by customers or employees, or even simply lost or misplaced. Since the *perpetual* inventory system is designed to record purchases and sales of inventory as they occur, the balance in the merchandise inventory account represents the amount of inventory that *should* be on hand at any given time. By taking a physical count of the merchandise inventory at the end of the accounting period and comparing that amount with the book balance in the Merchandise Inventory account, managers can determine the amount of any inventory shrinkage. If goods have been lost, damaged, or stolen, the book balance will be higher than the actual amount of inventory on hand and an adjusting entry is required to reduce assets and equity. The Merchandise Inventory account is reduced, and an expense for the amount of the lost, damaged, or stolen inventory is recognized.

Adjustment for Lost, Damaged, or Stolen Inventory

To illustrate, assume that Midwest Merchandising Company maintains perpetual inventory records. Midwest determined, through a physical count, that it had $23,500 of merchandise inventory on hand at the end of the accounting period. The balance in the Inventory account was $24,000. Midwest must make an adjusting entry to write down the Inventory account so the amount reported on the financial statements agrees with the amount actually on hand at the end of the period. The write-down decreases both assets (inventory) and stockholders' equity (retained earnings). The write-down increases

expenses and decreases net income. Cash flow is not affected. The effects on the statements are as follows:

Assets	=	Liab.	+	Equity	Rev.	−	Exp.	=	Net Inc.	Cash Flow
(500)	=	NA	+	(500)	NA	−	500	=	(500)	NA

In general journal form, the entry is as follows:

Account Title	Debit	Credit
Inventory Loss (Cost of Goods Sold)	500	
Inventory		500

Theoretically, inventory losses are operating expenses. However, because such losses are normally immaterial in amount, they are usually added to cost of goods sold for external reporting purposes.

Events Affecting Sales

Record and report inventory transactions in the double-entry accounting system.

To this point we assumed JPS did not offer cash discounts to its customers. However, sales, as well as purchases of inventory can be affected by returns, allowances, and discounts. **Sales discounts** are price reductions offered by sellers to encourage buyers to pay promptly. To illustrate, assume JPS engaged in the following selected events during January 2008.

Event 1a **JPS sold on account merchandise with a list price of $8,500. Payment terms were 1/10, n/30. The merchandise had cost JPS $4,000.**

The sale increases both assets (accounts receivable) and shareholders' equity (retained earnings). Recognizing revenue increases net income. The statement of cash flows is not affected. The journal entry for this event and its effects on the financial statements follow:

Event No.	Account Title	Debit	Credit
1a	Accounts Receivable	8,500	
	Sales Revenue		8,500

Assets				=	Liab.	+	Stockholders' Equity			Rev.	−	Exp.	=	Net Inc.	Cash Flow
Cash	+	Accts. Rec.	+ Inventory =	Note Pay.	+	Com. Stk.	+	Retained Earnings							
NA	+	8,500	+ NA =	NA	+	NA	+	8,500	8,500	−	NA	=	8,500	NA	

Event 1b JPS recognized $4,000 of cost of goods sold.

Recognizing the expense decreases assets (merchandise inventory) and stockholders' equity (retained earnings). Cost of goods sold increases and net income decreases. Cash flow is not affected. The journal entry for this event and its effects on the financial statements follow:

Event No.	Account Title	Debit	Credit
1b	Cost of Goods Sold	4,000	
	Merchandise Inventory		4,000

Assets				=	Liab.	+	Stockholders' Equity			Rev.	−	Exp.	=	Net Inc.	Cash Flow
Cash	+	Accts. Rec.	+ Inventory =	Note Pay.	+	Com. Stk.	+	Retained Earnings							
NA	+	NA	+ (4,000) =	NA	+	NA	+	(4,000)	NA	−	4,000	=	(4,000)	NA	

Accounting for Sales Returns and Allowances

Event 2a A customer from Event 1a returned inventory with a $1,000 list price. The merchandise had cost JPS $450.

The sales return decreases both assets (accounts receivable) and stockholders' equity (retained earnings) on the balance sheet. Sales and net income decrease. Cash flow is not affected. The journal entry for this event and its effects on the financial statements follow:

Event No.	Account Title	Debit	Credit
2a	Sales Revenue	1,000	
	Accounts Receivable		1,000

Assets				=	Liab.	+	Stockholders' Equity			Rev.	−	Exp.	=	Net Inc.	Cash Flow
Cash	+	Accts. Rec.	+ Inventory =	Note Pay.	+	Com. Stk.	+	Retained Earnings							
NA	+	(1,000)	+ NA =	NA	+	NA	+	(1,000)	(1,000)	−	NA	=	(1,000)	NA	

Event 2b The cost of the goods ($450) is returned to the inventory account.

Since JPS got the inventory back, the sales return increases both assets (merchandise inventory) and stockholders' equity (retained earnings). The expense (cost of goods sold) decreases and net income increases. Cash flow is not affected. The journal entry for this event and its effects on the financial statements follow:

Event No.	Account Title	Debit	Credit
2b	Merchandise Inventory	450	
	Cost of Goods Sold		450

	Assets				=	Liab.	+	Stockholders' Equity			Rev.	−	Exp.	=	Net Inc.	Cash Flow
Cash	+	Accts. Rec.	+	Inventory	=	Note Pay.	+	Com. Stk.	+	Retained Earnings						
NA	+	NA	+	450	=	NA	+	NA	+	450	NA	−	(450)	=	450	NA

Accounting for Sales Discounts

Event 3 **JPS collected the balance of the accounts receivable generated in Event 1a. Recall the goods were sold under terms 1/10, net/30.**

Alternative 1 **The collection occurs before the discount period has expired (within 10 days from the date of the sale).**

JPS would give the buyer a 1 percent discount. Given the original sales amount of $8,500 and a sales return of $1,000, the amount of the discount is $75 [($8,500 − $1,000) × .01]. The sales discount reduces the amount of accounts receivable and retained earnings on the balance sheet. It also reduces the amount of revenue and the net income shown on the balance sheet. It does not affect the statement of cash flows. These effects are shown below.

Event No.	Account Title	Debit	Credit
3	Sales Revenue	75	
	Accounts Receivable		75

	Assets				=	Liab.	+	Stockholders' Equity			Rev.	−	Exp.	=	Net Inc.	Cash Flow
Cash	+	Accts. Rec.	+	Inventory	=	Note Pay.	+	Com. Stk.	+	Retained Earnings						
NA	+	(75)	+	NA	=	NA	+	NA	+	(75)	(75)	−	NA	=	(75)	NA

The balance due on the account receivable is $7,425 ($8,500 original sales − $1,000 sales return − $75 discount). The collection increases the Cash account and decreases the Accounts Receivable account. The income statement is not affected. The cash inflow is shown in the operating activities section of the statement of cash flows. The journal entry for this event and its effects on the financial statements follow:

Event No.	Account Title	Debit	Credit
3	Cash	7,425	
	Accounts Receivable		7,425

	Assets			=	Liab.	+	Stockholders' Equity			Rev.	−	Exp.	=	Net Inc.	Cash Flow
Cash	+	Accts. Rec.	+	Inventory	=	Accts. Pay.	+	Com. Stk.	+	Retained Earnings					
7,425	+	(7,425)	+	NA	=	NA	+	NA	+	NA	NA	−	NA	=	NA	7,425 OA

Net Sales

The gross amount of sales minus **sales returns and allowance** and sales discounts is commonly called **net sales.** Companies are not required by GAAP to show sales returns and allowance and sales discount on their income statement. Indeed, most companies show only the amount of *net sales* on the income statement. In this case the net sales amount to $7,425 ($8,500 original sales − $1,000 sales return − $75 discount).

Alternative 2 **The collection occurs after the discount period has expired (after 10 days from the date of the sale).**

Under these circumstances there is no sales discount. The amount collected is $7,500 ($8,500 original sale − $1,000 sales return). Net sales shown on the income statement would also be $7,500.

THE FINANCIAL ANALYST

Merchandising is a highly competitive business. In order to succeed, merchandisers develop different strategies to distinguish themselves in the marketplace. For example, some companies like Wal-Mart, Kmart, and Costco focus on price competition while others such as Neiman Marcus and Saks Fifth Avenue sell high price goods that offer high quality, style, and strong guaranties. Financial analysts have developed specific tools that are useful in scrutinizing the success or failure of a company's sales strategy. The first step in the analytical process is to develop common size statements so that comparisons can be made between companies.

Use common size financial statements and ratio analysis to evaluate managerial performance.

Common Size Financial Statements

How good is a $1,000,000 increase in net income? The answer is not clear because there is no indication as to the size of the company. A million dollar increase may be excellent for a small company but would be virtually meaningless for a company the size of Exxon. To enable meaningful comparisons analysts prepare **common size financial statements.** Common size statements display information in percentages as well as absolute dollar amounts.

To illustrate, we expand the income statements for JPS to include percentages. The results are shown in Exhibit 5.9. The percentage data are computed by defining net sales as the base figure, or 100 percent. The other amounts on the statements are then shown as a percentage of net sales. For example, the *cost of goods sold percentage* is the dollar amount of *cost of goods sold* divided by the dollar amount of *net sales,* which produces a percentage of 67.7 percent ($8,000 ÷ $12,000) for 2008 and 46.6 percent ($11,500 ÷ $24,750) for 2009. Other income statement items are computed using the same approach.

EXHIBIT 5.9	Common Size Financial Statements

JUNE'S PLANT SHOP
Income Statement
For the Period Ended

	2008		2009	
Net sales*	$12,000	100.0%	$24,750	100.0%
Cost of goods sold	(8,000)	67.7	(11,500)	46.5
Gross margin	4,000	33.3	13,250	53.5
Less: Operating expenses				
Selling and administrative expense	(1,000)	8.3	(5,000)	20.2
Transportation-out			(450)	1.8
Operating income	3,000	25.0	7,800	31.5
Nonoperating items				
Interest expense			(360)	(1.5)
Gain on the sale of land			700	2.8
Net income	$ 3,000	25.0	$ 8,140	32.9

*Since JPS did not offer sales discounts or have sales returns and allowances during 2008 or 2009, the amount of sales revenue is equal to the amount of net sales. We use the term *net sales* here because it is more commonly used in business practice. Percentages do not add exactly because they have been rounded.

Ratio Analysis

Two of the percentages shown in Exhibit 5.9 are used frequently in business to make comparisons within a specific company or between two or more different companies. These two commonly used percentages are the **gross margin percentage** and the **net income percentage.** These percentages are calculated as follows:

$$\text{Gross margin percentage} = \frac{\text{Gross margin}}{\text{Net sales}}$$

The gross margin percentage provides insight about a company's pricing strategy. All other things being equal, a high gross margin percentage means that a company is charging high prices in relation to its cost of goods sold.

$$\text{Net income percentage} = \frac{\text{Net income}}{\text{Net sales}}$$

In practice, the *net income percentage* is frequently called the **return on sales** ratio. The return on sales ratio provides insight as to how much of each sales dollar is left as net income after all expenses are paid. All other things being equal, companies with high ratios are doing a better job of controlling expenses.

Comparisons within a Particular Company

To illustrate comparisons within a particular company, assume that JPS relocated its store in an upscale mall in early 2009. Management realized that the company would have to pay more for operating expenses but believed those expenses could be offset by charging significantly higher prices. We use the gross margin percentage and the net income percentage to assess the success of JPS's strategy. Exhibit 5.9 shows an increase in the *gross margin percentage* from 33.3 to 53.5. This confirms that JPS was able to increase prices relative to its cost of goods sold. The increase in the *return on sales* ratio (25 percent to 32.9 percent) confirms that the increase in gross margin was larger than the increase in total expenses. We therefore conclude that JPS's strategy to relocate was successful. As a side note this may also explain why JPS sold its land in late 2009. Considering the success the company experienced at the new location, there was no motive to build a store on the land.

Since net income is affected by nonoperating items, some financial analysts would prefer to use *operating income* instead of *net income* when computing the *return on sales* ratio. In this case the nonoperating items were immaterial. Indeed, to simplify the discussion in this chapter we always assume immateriality when computing this ratio. However, when nonoperating items are significant, it is more insightful to use *operating income* as the numerator of the *return on sales* ratio.

Comparisons between Companies

Does Wal-Mart sell merchandise at a higher or lower price than Target? The *gross margin percentage* is useful in answering questions such as this. Since Wal-Mart's 2005 annual report shows a gross margin percentage of 22.9 while Target's 2005 report shows a gross margin percentage of 33.6, we conclude that there is validity to Wal-Mart's claim of "always the low price." The next section of the chapter provides insight as to how the *gross margin percentage* and the *return on sales* ratio can be used to gain insight about the operations of several real world companies.

CHECK YOURSELF 5.3

The following sales data are from the records of two retail sales companies. All amounts are in thousands.

	Company A	Company B
Sales	$21,234	$43,465
Cost of goods sold	(14,864)	(34,772)
Gross margin	$ 6,370	$ 8,693

One company is an upscale department store, and the other is a discount store. Which company is the upscale department store?

Answer

The gross margin percentage for Company A is approximately 30 percent ($6,370 ÷ $21,234). The gross margin percentage for Company B is 20 percent ($8,693 ÷ $43,465). These percentages suggest that Company A is selling goods with a higher markup than Company B, which implies that Company A is the upscale department store.

Answers to The Curious Accountant

The income statement data show that compared to Zales, Blue Nile does save money by not operating bricks-and-mortar stores. The *gross margin percentage* gives some indication of how much a company is charging in relation to what it pays to purchase the goods it is selling (its cost of goods sold). The *return on sales ratio* reveals how much profit, as a percentage of sales, a company is making after *all* its expenses have been taken into account. For the most recent year shown, Zales' gross margin was 51.4 percent while Blue Nile's was 22.3%, indicating that Blue Nile really does charge less for its jewelry. However, the return on sales for Blue Nile was 6.5% while Zales was only 4.5 percent. This shows that while Blue Nile charges less for its products, it makes up for the lower gross margin with lower operating expenses. In fact, as a percentage of sales, Zales' operating expenses were over three times higher than those of Blue Nile. Excluding costs of goods sold, the operating expenses at Blue Nile were 13.4 percent of sales; Zales were 44.0 percent.

Real-World Data

Exhibit 5.10 shows the gross margin percentages and return on sales ratios for 10 companies. Three of the companies are manufacturers that produce pharmaceutical products, and the remaining seven companies sell various products at the retail level. These data are for the companies' fiscal years that ended in late 2005 or early 2006.

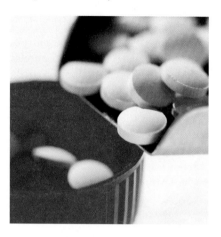

A review of the data confirms our earlier finding that ratios for companies in the same industry are often more similar than are ratios for companies from different industries. For example, note that the manufacturers have much higher margins, both for gross profit and for net earnings, than do the retailers. Manufacturers are often able to charge higher prices than are retailers because they obtain patents which give them a legal monopoly on the products they create. When a company such as Merck develops a new drug, no one else can produce that drug until the patent expires, giving it lots of control over its price at the wholesale level. Conversely, when Walgreens sells Merck's drug at the retail level, it faces price competition from CVS, a company that is trying to sell the same drug to the same consumers. One way CVS can try to get customers to shop at its store is to charge lower prices than its competitors, but this reduces its profit margins, since it must pay the same price to get Merck's drug as did Walgreens. As the data in Exhibit 5.10 show, in 2005 CVS had a lower gross margin percentage than did Walgreens, indicating it is charging slightly lower prices for similar goods.

In the examples presented in Exhibit 5.10, the companies with higher gross margin percentages usually had higher return on sales ratios than their competitors, but this was not always the case. In the office supplies business, Office Depot's gross margin percentage was significantly higher than that of its rival, Staples, but its return on sales ratio was considerably lower. Federated Department Stores, the company that owns Macy's, among others, had a gross margin percentage that was 81 percent greater than Wal-Mart's ([41.6 − 23.0] ÷ 23.0) and its return on sales ratio was 75 percent higher. This is not surprising when you consider how much more luxurious, and costly, the interior of a Macy's store is compared to a Wal-Mart.

EXHIBIT 5.10

Industry/Company	Gross Margin %	Return on Sales
Pharmaceutical manufacturers		
GlaxoSmithKline	78.0%	21.6%
Johnson & Johnson	72.4	20.6
Merck & Co.	76.6	21.0
Retail pharmacies		
CVS	26.8	3.3
Rite Aid	25.0	1.8
Walgreens	27.9	3.7
Department stores		
Federated	41.6	6.3
Wal-Mart	23.0	3.6
Office supplies		
Office Depot	30.8	1.9
Staples	28.5	5.2

A Look Back <<

Merchandising companies earn profits by selling inventory at prices that are higher than the cost paid for the goods. Merchandising companies include *retail companies* (companies that sell goods to the final consumer) and *wholesale companies* (companies that sell to other merchandising companies). The products sold by merchandising companies are called *inventory.* The costs to purchase inventory, to receive it, and to ready it for sale are *product costs,* which are first accumulated in an inventory account (balance sheet asset account) and then recognized as cost of goods sold (income statement expense account) in the period in which goods are sold. Purchases and sales of inventory can be recorded continually as goods are bought and sold (perpetual system) or at the end of the accounting period (periodic system, discussed in the chapter appendix).

Accounting for inventory includes the treatment of cash discounts, transportation costs, and returns and allowances. The cost of inventory is the list price less any purchase returns and allowances and purchase discounts, plus transportation-in costs. The cost of freight paid to acquire inventory (*transportation-in*) is considered a product cost. The cost of freight paid to deliver inventory to customers (*transportation-out*) is a selling expense. *Sales returns and allowances* and *sales discounts* are subtracted from sales revenue to determine the amount of *net sales* reported on the income statement. Purchase returns and allowances reduce product cost. Theoretically, the cost of lost, damaged, or stolen inventory is an operating expense. However, because these costs are usually immaterial in amount they are typically included as part of cost of goods sold on the income statement.

Some companies use a *multistep income statement* which reports product costs separately from selling and administrative costs. Cost of goods sold is subtracted from sales revenue to determine *gross margin.* Selling and administrative expenses are subtracted from gross margin to determine income from operations. Other companies report income using a *single-step format* in which the cost of goods sold is listed along with selling and administrative items in a single expense category that is subtracted in total from revenue to determine income from operations.

Managers of merchandising businesses operate in a highly competitive environment. They must manage company operations carefully to remain profitable. *Common size financial statements* (statements presented on a percentage basis) and ratio analysis are useful monitoring tools. Common size financial statements permit ready comparisons among different-size companies. Although a $1 million increase in sales may be good for a small company and bad for a large company, a 10 percent increase can apply to any size company. The two most common ratios used by merchandising companies are the *gross margin percentage* (gross margin ÷ net sales) and the *net income percentage* (net income ÷ net sales). Interpreting these ratios requires an understanding of industry characteristics. For example, a discount store such as Wal-Mart would be expected to have a much lower gross margin percentage than an upscale store such as Neiman Marcus.

Managers should be aware of the financing cost of carrying inventory. By investing funds in inventory, a firm loses the opportunity to invest them in interest-bearing assets. The cost of financing inventory is an *opportunity cost.* To minimize financing costs, a company should minimize the amount of inventory it carries, the length of time it holds the inventory, and the time it requires to collect accounts receivable after the inventory is sold.

A Look Forward

To this point, the text has explained the basic accounting cycle for service and merchandising businesses. Future chapters more closely address specific accounting issues. For example, in Chapter 6 you will learn how to deal with inventory items that are purchased at differing prices. Other chapters will discuss a variety of specific practices that are widely used by real-world companies.

APPENDIX

PERIODIC INVENTORY SYSTEM

LO 8

Identify the primary features of the periodic inventory system.

Under certain conditions, it is impractical to record inventory sales transactions as they occur. Consider the operations of a fast-food restaurant. To maintain perpetual inventory records, the restaurant would have to transfer from the Inventory account to the Cost of Goods Sold account the *cost* of each hamburger, order of fries, soft drink, or other food items as they were sold. Obviously, recording the cost of each item at the point of sale would be impractical without using highly sophisticated computer equipment. Recording the selling price the customer pays is captured by cash registers; the difficulty lies in capturing inventory cost.

The **periodic inventory system** offers a practical solution for recording inventory transactions in a low-technology, high-volume environment. As shown in Exhibit 5.11, inventory costs are recorded in a Purchases account at the time of purchase. Purchase returns and allowances and transportation-in

EXHIBIT 5.11

General Journal Entries for 2009 (Periodic Method)

Event No.	Account Title	Debit	Credit
1	Cash	4,000	
	Note Payable		4,000
2	Purchases	11,000	
	Accounts Payable		11,000
3	Accounts Payable	1,000	
	Purchase Returns and Allowances		1,000
4	Accounts Payable	200	
	Purchase Discounts		200
5	Accounts Payable	9,800	
	Cash		9,800
6	Transportation-In	300	
	Cash		300
7a	Cash	24,750	
	Sales		24,750
8	Transportation-Out	450	
	Cash		450
9	Selling and Administrative Expenses	5,000	
	Cash		5,000
10	Interest Expense	360	
	Cash		360
11	Cash	6,200	
	Land		5,500
	Gain on Sale of Land		700
Adj	Cost of Goods Sold	11,500	
	Merchandise Inventory (Ending Balance)	4,600	
	Purchase Returns and Allowances	1,000	
	Purchase Discounts	200	
	Purchases		11,000
	Transportation-In		300
	Merchandise Inventory (Beginning Balance)		6,000
CL	Revenue	24,750	
	Gain on Sale of Land	700	
	Cost of Goods Sold		11,500
	Transportation-Out		450
	Selling and Administrative Expenses		5,000
	Interest Expense		360
	Retained Earnings		8,140

are recorded in separate accounts. No entries for the cost of merchandise purchases or sales are recorded in the Inventory account during the period. The cost of goods sold is determined at the end of the period as shown in Exhibit 5.12.

The perpetual and periodic inventory systems represent alternative procedures for recording the same information. The amounts of cost of goods sold and ending inventory reported in the financial statements will be the same regardless of the method used. Exhibit 5.11 presents the general journal entries JPS would make if it used the periodic inventory method for the 2009 transactions. Cost of goods sold is recorded in an adjusting entry at the end of the accounting period.

The **schedule of cost of goods sold** presented in Exhibit 5.12 is used for internal reporting purposes. It is normally not shown in published financial statements. The amount of cost of goods sold is reported as a single line item on the income statement. The income statement in Exhibit 5.5 will be the same whether JPS maintains perpetual or periodic inventory records.

EXHIBIT 5.12

Schedule of Cost of Goods Sold for 2009

Beginning inventory	$ 6,000
Purchases	11,000
Purchase returns and allowances	(1,000)
Purchase discounts	(200)
Transportation-in	300
Cost of goods available for sale	16,100
Ending inventory	(4,600)
Cost of goods sold	$11,500

Advantages and Disadvantages of the Periodic System versus the Perpetual System

The chief advantage of the periodic method is recording efficiency. Recording inventory transactions occasionally (periodically) requires less effort than recording them continually (perpetually). Historically, practical limitations offered businesses like fast-food restaurants or grocery stores no alternative to using the periodic system. The sheer volume of transactions made recording individual decreases to the Inventory account balance as each item was sold impossible. Imagine the number of transactions a grocery store would have to record every business day to maintain perpetual records.

Although the periodic system provides a recordkeeping advantage over the perpetual system, perpetual inventory records provide significant control advantages over periodic records. With perpetual records, the book balance in the Inventory account should agree with the amount of inventory in stock at any given time. By comparing that book balance with the results of a physical inventory count, management can determine the amount of lost, damaged, destroyed, or stolen inventory. Perpetual records also permit more timely and accurate reorder decisions and profitability assessments.

When a company uses the *periodic* inventory system, lost, damaged, or stolen merchandise is automatically included in cost of goods sold. Because such goods are not included in the year-end physical count, they are treated as sold regardless of the reason for their absence. Since the periodic system does not separate the cost of lost, damaged, or stolen merchandise from the cost of goods sold, the amount of any inventory shrinkage is unknown. This feature is a major disadvantage of the periodic system. Without knowing the amount of inventory losses, management cannot weigh the costs of various security systems against the potential benefits.

Advances in such technology as electronic bar code scanning and increased computing power have eliminated most of the practical constraints that once prevented merchandisers with high-volume, low dollar-value inventories from recording inventory transactions on a continual basis. As a result, use of the perpetual inventory system has expanded rapidly in recent years and continued growth can be expected. This text, therefore, concentrates on the perpetual inventory system.

SELF-STUDY REVIEW PROBLEM

Academy Sales Company (ASC) started the 2008 accounting period with the balances given in the financial statements model shown below. During 2008 ASC experienced the following business events.

1. Purchased $16,000 of merchandise inventory on account, terms 2/10, n/30.
2. The goods that were purchased in Event 1 were delivered FOB shipping point. Freight costs of $600 were paid in cash by the responsible party.
3. Returned $500 of goods purchased in Event 1
4a. Recorded the cash discount on the goods purchased in Event 1
4b. Paid the balance due on the account payable within the discount period.

5a. Recognized $21,000 of cash revenue from the sale of merchandise.

5b. Recognized $15,000 of cost of goods sold.

6. The merchandise in Event 5a was sold to customers FOB destination. Freight costs of $950 were paid in cash by the responsible party.

7. Paid cash of $4,000 for selling and administrative expenses.

8. Sold the land for $5,600 cash.

Required

a. Record the above transactions in a financial statements model like the one shown below.

Event No.	Cash	+	Inventory	+	Land	=	Accts. Pay.	+	Com. Stk.	+	Ret. Earn.	Rev./ Gain	−	Exp.	=	Net Inc.	Cash Flow
Bal.	25,000	+	3,000	+	5,000	=	-0-	+	18,000	+	15,000	NA	−	NA	=	NA	NA

b. Prepare a schedule of cost of goods sold. (Appendix)

c. Prepare a multistep income statement. Include common size percentages on the income statement.

d. ASC's gross margin percentage in 2007 was 22%. Based on the common size data in the income statement, did ASC raise or lower its prices in 2008? (Appendix)

e. Assuming a 10 percent rate of growth, what is the amount of net income expected for 2009?

Answer

a.

Event No.	Cash	+	Inventory	+	Land	=	Accts. Pay.	+	Com. Stk.	+	Ret. Earn.	Rev./ Gain	−	Exp.	=	Net Inc.	Cash Flow	
Bal.	25,000	+	3,000	+	5,000	=	-0-	+	18,000	+	15,000	NA	−	NA	=	NA	NA	
1		+	16,000			=	16,000	+		+			−		=			
2	(600)	+	600			=		+		+			−		=		(600)	OA
3		+	(500)			=	(500)	+		+			−		=			
4a		+	(310)			=	(310)	+		+			−		=			
4b	(15,190)	+				=	(15,190)	+		+			−		=		(15,190)	OA
5a	21,000	+				=		+		+	21,000	21,000	−		=	21,000	21,000	OA
5b		+	(15,000)			=		+		+	(15,000)		−	15,000	=	(15,000)		
6	(950)	+				=		+		+	(950)		−	950	=	(950)	(950)	OA
7	(4,000)	+				=		+		+	(4,000)		−	4,000	=	(4,000)	(4,000)	OA
8	5,600	+			(5,000)	=		+		+	600	600	−		=	600	5,600	IA
Bal.	30,860	+	3,790		-0-	=	-0-	+	18,000	+	16,650	21,600	−	19,950	=	1,650	5,860	NC

b.

ACADEMY SALES COMPANY
Schedule of Cost of Goods Sold
For the Period Ended December 31, 2008

Beginning inventory	$ 3,000
Plus purchases	16,000
Less: Purchase returns and allowances	(500)
Less: Purchases discounts	(310)
Plus: Transportation-in	600
Goods available for sale	18,790
Less: Ending inventory	3,790
Cost of goods sold	$(15,000)

c.

ACADEMY SALES COMPANY Income Statement* For the Period Ended December 31, 2008		
Net sales	$21,000	100.0%
Cost of goods sold	(15,000)	71.4
Gross margin	6,000	28.6
Less: Operating expenses		
Selling and administrative expense	(4,000)	19.0
Transportation-out	(950)	4.5
Operating income	1,050	5.0
Nonoperating items		
Gain on the sale of land	600	2.9
Net income	$ 1,650	7.9

*Percentages do not add exactly because they have been rounded.

d. All other things being equal, the higher the gross margin percentage, the higher the sales prices. Since the gross margin percentage increased from 22% to 28.6%, the data suggest that Academy raised its sales prices.

e. $1,155 [$1,050 + (.10 × $1,050)]. Note that the gain is not expected to recur.

KEY TERMS

cash discount 247
common size financial statements 259
cost of goods available for sale 241, 244
cost of goods sold 241, 244
FOB (free on board) destination 248
FOB (free on board) shipping point 248
gain 251
gross margin 241, 244
gross margin percentage 260

gross profit 241
loss 251
merchandise inventory 239, 245
merchandising businesses 239
multistep income statement 254
net income percentage 260
net sales 259
operating income (or loss) 253
period costs 241

periodic inventory system 264
perpetual inventory system 241
product costs 241
purchase discount 247
purchase returns and allowances 246, 247
retail companies 239
return on sales 260
sales discounts 256
sales returns and allowances 259

schedule of cost of goods sold 265
selling and administrative costs 241
shrinkage 255
single-step income statement 254
transportation-in (freight-in) 248
transportation-out (freight-out) 248
2/10, n/30 247
wholesale companies 239

QUESTIONS

1. Define *merchandise inventory*. What types of costs are included in the Merchandise Inventory account?

2. What is the difference between a product cost and a selling and administrative cost?

3. How is the cost of goods available for sale determined?

4. What portion of cost of goods available for sale is shown on the balance sheet? What portion is shown on the income statement?

5. When are period costs expensed? When are product costs expensed?

6. If PetCo had net sales of $600,000, goods available for sale of $450,000, and cost of goods sold of $375,000, what is its gross margin? What amount of inventory will be shown on its balance sheet?

7. Describe how the perpetual inventory system works. What are some advantages of using the perpetual inventory system? Is it necessary to take a physical inventory when using the perpetual inventory system?

8. What are the effects of the following types of transactions on the accounting equation? Also identify the financial statements that are affected. (Assume that the perpetual inventory system is used.)

   a. Acquisition of cash from the issue of common stock.

   b. Contribution of inventory by an owner of a company.

   c. Purchase of inventory with cash by a company.

   d. Sale of inventory for cash.

9. Northern Merchandising Company sold inventory that cost $12,000 for $20,000 cash. How does this event affect the accounting equation? What financial statements and accounts are affected? (Assume that the perpetual inventory system is used.)

10. If goods are shipped FOB shipping point, which party (buyer or seller) is responsible for the shipping costs?

11. Define *transportation-in*. Is it a product or a period cost?

12. Quality Cellular Co. paid $80 for freight on merchandise that it had purchased for resale to customers (transportation-in) and paid $135 for freight on merchandise delivered to customers (transportation-out). What account is debited for the $80 payment? What account is debited for the $135 payment?

13. Why would a seller grant an allowance to a buyer of the seller's merchandise?

14. Dyer Department Store purchased goods with the terms 2/10, n/30. What do these terms mean?

15. Eastern Discount Stores incurred a $5,000 cash cost. How does the accounting for this cost differ if the cash were paid for inventory versus commissions to sales personnel?

16. What is the purpose of giving a cash discount to charge customers?

17. Define *transportation-out*. Is it a product cost or a period cost for the seller?

18. Ball Co. purchased inventory with a list price of $4,000 with the terms 2/10, n/30. What amount will be debited to the Merchandise Inventory account?

19. Explain the difference between gains and revenues.

20. Explain the difference between losses and expenses.

21. Suda Company sold land that cost $40,000 for $37,000 cash. Explain how this transaction would be shown on the statement of cash flows.

22. Explain the difference between purchase returns and sales returns. How do purchase returns affect the financial statements of both buyer and seller? How do sales returns affect the financial statements of both buyer and seller?

23. How is net sales determined?

24. What is the difference between a multistep income statement and a single-step income statement?

25. What is the advantage of using common size income statements to present financial information for several accounting periods?

26. What information is provided by the net income percentage (return on sales ratio)?

27. What is the purpose of preparing a schedule of cost of goods sold? (Appendix)

28. Explain how the periodic inventory system works. What are some advantages of using the periodic inventory system? What are some disadvantages of using the periodic inventory system? Is it necessary to take a physical inventory when using the periodic inventory system? (Appendix)

29. Why does the periodic inventory system impose a major disadvantage for management in accounting for lost, stolen, or damaged goods? (Appendix)

MULTIPLE-CHOICE QUESTIONS

Multiple-choice questions are provided on the text Web site at www.mhhe.com/edmonds6e.

When the instructions for *any* exercise or problem call for the preparation of an income statement, use the *multistep format* unless otherwise indicated.

Exercise 5-1A *Comparing a merchandising company with a service company*   L.O. 1, 2

The following information is available for two different types of businesses for the 2009 accounting period. Madison Consulting is a service business that provides consulting services to small businesses. Books For Less is a merchandising business that sells books to college students.

Data for Madison Consulting

1. Borrowed $40,000 from the bank to start the business.
2. Performed services for customers and collected $30,000 cash.
3. Paid salary expense of $19,200.

Data for Books For Less

1. Borrowed $40,000 from the bank to start the business.
2. Purchased $19,000 of inventory for cash.
3. Inventory costing $16,800 was sold for $30,000 cash.
4. Paid $2,400 cash for operating expenses.

Required

a. Prepare an income statement, balance sheet, and statement of cash flows for each of the companies.
b. What is different about the income statements of the two businesses?
c. What is different about the balance sheets of the two businesses?
d. How are the statements of cash flow different for the two businesses?

Exercise 5-2A *Effect of inventory transactions on journals, ledgers, and financial statements: Perpetual system*   L.O. 2

Chris Daniels started a small merchandising business in 2010. The business experienced the following events during its first year of operation. Assume that Daniels uses the perpetual inventory system.

1. Acquired $60,000 cash from the issue of common stock.
2. Purchased inventory for $50,000 cash.
3. Sold inventory costing $36,000 for $56,000 cash.

Required

a. Record the events in general journal format.
b. Post the entries to T-accounts.
c. Prepare an income statement for 2010 (use the multistep format).
d. What is the amount of total assets at the end of the period?

Exercise 5-3A *Effect of inventory transactions on the income statement and statement of cash flows: Perpetual system*   L.O. 2

During 2011, Lang Merchandising Company purchased $20,000 of inventory on account. The company sold inventory on account that cost $15,000 for $22,500. Cash payments on accounts payable were $12,500. There was $20,000 cash collected from accounts receivable. Lang also paid $4,000 cash for operating expenses. Assume that Lang started the accounting period with $18,000 in both cash and common stock.

Required

a. Identify the events described in the preceding paragraph and record them in a horizontal statements model like the following one:

Assets			=	Liab.	+	Equity			Rev.	−	Exp.	=	Net Inc.	Cash Flow
Cash	+ Accts. Rec.	+ Inv.	=	Accts. Pay.	+	Com. Stk.	+	Ret. Earn.						
18,000 +	NA	+ NA =		NA	+	18,000	+	NA	NA	−	NA	=	NA	NA

b. What is the balance of accounts receivable at the end of 2011?

c. What is the balance of accounts payable at the end of 2011?

d. What are the amounts of gross margin and net income for 2011?

e. Determine the amount of net cash flow from operating activities.

f. Explain any differences between net income and net cash flow from operating activities.

L.O. 2

Exercise 5-4A   Recording inventory transactions in the general journal and posting entries to T-accounts: Perpetual system

David's Paint Supply experienced the following events during 2008, its first year of operation:

1. Acquired $30,000 cash from the issue of common stock.
2. Purchased inventory for $24,000 cash.
3. Sold inventory costing $13,000 for $22,000 cash.
4. Paid $1,600 for advertising expense.

Required

a. Record the general journal entries for the preceding transactions.

b. Post each of the entries to T-accounts.

c. Prepare a trial balance to prove the equality of debits and credits.

L.O. 3

Exercise 5-5A   Understanding the freight terms FOB shipping point and FOB destination

Required

For each of the following events, indicate whether the freight terms are FOB destination or FOB shipping point.

a. Sold merchandise and paid the freight costs.

b. Purchased merchandise and paid the freight costs.

c. Sold merchandise and the buyer paid the freight costs.

d. Purchased merchandise and the seller paid the freight costs.

L.O. 2, 3

Exercise 5-6A   Effect of purchase returns and allowances and freight costs on the journal, ledger, and financial statements: Perpetual system

The trial balance for The Photo Hut as of January 1, 2009 was as follows:

Account Titles	Debit	Credit
Cash	$6,000	
Inventory	3,000	
Common Stock		$7,500
Retained Earnings		1,500
Total	$9,000	$9,000

The following events affected the company during the 2009 accounting period:

1. Purchased merchandise on account that cost $4,100.
2. Purchased goods in Event 1. FOB shipping point with freight cost of $300 cash.

3. Returned $500 of damaged merchandise for credit on account.
4. Agreed to keep other damaged merchandise for which the company received a $250 allowance.
5. Sold merchandise that cost $2,750 for $4,750 cash.
6. Delivered merchandise to customers under terms FOB destination with freight costs amounting to $200 cash.
7. Paid $3,000 on the merchandise purchased in Event 1.

Required

a. Record the transactions in general journal format.
b. Open general ledger T-accounts with the appropriate beginning balances, and post the journal entries to the T-accounts.
c. Prepare an income statement and statement of cash flows for 2009.
d. Explain why a difference does or does not exist between net income and net cash flow from operating activities.

Exercise 5-7A *Accounting for product costs: Perpetual inventory system*　　　　　　**L.O. 2, 3**

Which of the following would be *debited* to the Inventory account for a merchandising business using the perpetual inventory system?

Required

a. Purchase of inventory.
b. Allowance received for damaged inventory.
c. Transportation-in.
d. Cash discount given on goods sold.
e. Transportation-out.
f. Purchase of office supplies.

Exercise 5-8A *Effect of product cost and period cost: Horizontal statements model*　　　　**L.O. 1, 2, 3**

Nigil Co. experienced the following events for the 2010 accounting period:

1. Acquired $10,000 cash from the issue of common stock.
2. Purchased $18,000 of inventory on account.
3. Received goods purchased in Event 2 FOB shipping point. Freight cost of $500 paid in cash.
4. Returned $4,000 of goods purchased in Event 2 because of poor quality.
5. Sold inventory on account that cost $14,300 for $44,000.
6. Freight cost on the goods sold in Event 5 was $100. The goods were shipped FOB destination. Cash was paid for the freight cost.
7. Collected $16,500 cash from accounts receivable.
8. Paid $12,000 cash on accounts payable.
9. Paid $2,200 for advertising expense.
10. Paid $4,400 cash for insurance expense.

Required

a. Which of these transactions result in period (selling and administrative) costs? Which result in product costs? If neither, label the transaction NA.
b. Record each event in a horizontal statements model like the following one. The first event is recorded as an example.

Assets			=	Liab.	+	Equity			Rev.	−	Exp.	=	Net Inc.	Cash Flow
Cash	+ Accts. Rec.	+ Inv.	=	Accts. Pay.	+	C. Stk.	+	Ret. Earn.						
10,000 +	NA	+ NA =		NA	+	10,000	+	NA	NA	−	NA	=	NA	10,000 FA

L.O. 3

Exercise 5-9A   *Cash discounts and purchase returns*

On March 6, 2009, Ed's Imports purchased merchandise from Watches Inc. with a list price of $31,000, terms 2/10, n/45. On March 10, Ed's returned merchandise to Watches Inc. for credit. The list price of the returned merchandise was $6,400. Ed's paid cash to settle the accounts payable on March 15, 2009.

Required

a. What is the amount of the check that Ed's must write to Watches Inc. on March 15?

b. Record the events in a horizontal statements model like the following one.

Assets	=	Liab.	+	Equity			Rev.	−	Exp.	=	Net Inc.	Cash Flow
Cash	+	Inv.	=	Accts. Pay.	+	C. Stk.	+	Ret. Earn.				

c. How much would Ed's pay for the merchandise purchased if the payment is not made until March 20, 2009?

d. Record the payment of the merchandise in Event *c* in a horizontal statements model like the one shown above.

e. Why would Watches Inc. sell merchandise with the terms 2/10, n/45?

L.O. 2, 3

Exercise 5-10A   *Effect of sales returns and allowances and freight costs on the journal, ledger, and financial statements: Perpetual system*

Sans Company began the 2009 accounting period with $18,000 cash, $60,000 inventory, $50,000 common stock, and $28,000 retained earnings. During the 2009 accounting period, Sans experienced the following events:

1. Sold merchandise costing $38,200 for $74,500 on account to Hughes's General Store.
2. Delivered the goods to Hughes under terms FOB destination. Freight costs were $400 cash.
3. Received returned goods from Hughes. The goods cost Sans $2,000 and were sold to Hughes for $3,800.
4. Granted Hughes a $1,000 allowance for damaged goods that Hughes agreed to keep.
5. Collected partial payment of $52,000 cash from accounts receivable.

Required

a. Record the transactions in general journal format.

b. Open general ledger T-accounts with the appropriate beginning balances and post the journal entries to the T-accounts.

c. Prepare an income statement, balance sheet, and statement of cash flows.

d. Why would Sans grant the $1,000 allowance to Hughes? Who benefits more?

L.O. 3

Exercise 5-11A   *Purchase discounts and transportation costs*

Bettino Basket Company had a $6,200 beginning balance in its Merchandise Inventory account. The following information regarding Bettino's purchases and sales of inventory during its 2009 accounting period were drawn from the company's accounting records.

1. Purchased $22,500 of inventory under terms 1/10, net/60. Transportation costs amounted to $400. The goods were delivered FOB shipping point. Bettino paid for the inventory within the discount period.
2. Purchased $24,000 of inventory under terms 2/10, net/30. Transportation costs amounted to $600. The goods were delivered FOB destination. Bettino paid for the inventory after the discount period had expired.
3. Sold inventory that cost $48,000 for $64,000. Transportation costs for goods delivered to customers amounted to $2,400. The goods were delivered FOB destination.

Required

a. Determine the balance in the Inventory account at the end of the accounting period.

b. Is Bettino or its customers responsible for the transportation costs described in Event 3?

c. Determine the gross margin.

Exercise 5-12A   *Purchase returns, discounts, and a multistep income statement*   **L.O. 3, 4, 5**

The following information was drawn from the 2008 accounting records of Bartlett Merchandisers.

1. Inventory with a list price of $30,000 was purchased under terms 2/10, net/30.
2. Bartlett returned $2,500 of the inventory to the supplier.
3. The accounts payable was settled within the discount period.
4. The inventory was sold for $43,000.
5. Selling and administrative expenses amounted to $8,000.
6. Interest expense amounted to $1,000.
7. Land that cost $12,000 was sold for $10,000 cash.

Required
a. Determine the cost of the inventory sold.
b. Prepare a multistep income statement.
c. Where would the interest expense be shown on the statement of cash flows?
d. How would the sale of the land be shown on the statement of cash flows?
e. Explain the difference between a loss and an expense.

Exercise 5-13A   *Comprehensive exercise with purchases discounts*   **L.O. 3, 4, 5, 7**

The Little Black Dress Shop (TLBDS) started the 2008 accounting period with the balances given in the financial statements model shown below. During 2008 TLBDS experienced the following business events.

1. Purchased $32,000 of merchandise inventory on account, terms 2/10, n/30.
2. The goods that were purchased in Event 1 were delivered FOB shipping point. Freight costs of $1,200 were paid in cash by the responsible party.
3. Returned $1,000 of goods purchased in Event 1.
4a. Recorded the cash discount on the goods purchased in Event 1.
4b. Paid the balance due on the account payable within the discount period.
5a. Recognized $42,000 of cash revenue from the sale of merchandise.
5b. Recognized $30,000 of cost of goods sold.
6. The merchandise in Event 5a was sold to customers FOB destination. Freight costs of $1,900 were paid in cash by the responsible party.
7. Paid cash of $8,000 for selling and administrative expenses.
8. Sold the land for $11,200 cash.

Required
a. Record the above transactions in a financial statements model like the one shown below.

Event No.	Cash	+	Inventory	+	Land	=	Accts. Pay.	+	Com. Stk.	+	Ret. Earn.	Rev./ Gain	−	Exp.	=	Net Inc.	Cash Flow
Bal.	50,000	+	6,000	+	10,000	=	-0-	+	36,000	+	30,000	NA	−	NA	=	NA	NA

b. Prepare a multistep income statement. Include common size percentages on the income statement.
c. TLBDS's gross margin percentage in 2007 was 34%. Based on the common size data in the income statement, did TLBDS raise or lower its prices in 2008?
d. Assuming a 5 percent rate of growth, what is the amount of net income expected for 2009?

Exercise 5-14A   *Inventory financing costs*   **L.O. 3**

Jerry Guardino comes to you for advice. He has just purchased a large amount of inventory with the terms 1/10, n/30. The amount of the invoice is $320,000. He is currently short of cash but has good credit. He can borrow the money needed to settle the account payable at an annual interest rate of 7%. Guardino is sure he will have the necessary cash by the due date of the invoice but not by the last day of the discount period.

Required

a. Convert the discount rate into an annual interest rate.

b. Make a recommendation regarding whether Guardino should borrow the money and pay off the account payable within the discount period.

L.O. 2, 6

Exercise 5-15A   *Effect of inventory losses: Perpetual system*

Cox Sales experienced the following events during 2010, its first year of operation:

1. Started the business when it acquired $50,000 cash from the issue of common stock.
2. Paid $21,000 cash to purchase inventory.
3. Sold inventory costing $12,500 for $26,500 cash.
4. Physically counted inventory showing $7,900 inventory was on hand at the end of the accounting period.

Required

a. Open appropriate ledger T-accounts, and record the events in the accounts.

b. Prepare an income statement and balance sheet for 2010.

c. Explain how differences between the book balance and the physical count of inventory could arise. Why is being able to determine whether differences exist useful to management?

L.O. 2

Exercise 5-16A   *Determining the effect of inventory transactions on the accounting equation: Perpetual system*

Ramsey Company experienced the following events:

1. Purchased merchandise inventory on account.
2. Purchased merchandise inventory for cash.
3. Sold merchandise inventory on account. Label the revenue recognition 3a and the expense recognition 3b.
4. Returned merchandise purchased on account.
5. Sold merchandise inventory for cash. Label the revenue recognition 5a and the expense recognition 5b.
6. Paid cash on accounts payable within the discount period.
7. Paid cash for selling and administrative expenses.
8. Collected cash from accounts receivable not within the discount period.
9. Paid cash for transportation-out.
10. Paid cash for transportation-in.

Required

Identify each event as asset source (AS), asset use (AU), asset exchange (AE), or claims exchange (CE). Also explain how each event affects the financial statements by placing a + for increase, − for decrease, or NA for not affected under each of the components in the following statements model. Assume the company uses the perpetual inventory system. The first event is recorded as an example.

Event No.	Event Type	Assets	=	Liab.	+	Equity	Rev.	−	Exp.	=	Net Inc.	Cash Flow
1	AS	+	=	+	+	NA	NA	−	NA	=	NA	NA

L.O. 5

Exercise 5-17A   *Single-step and multistep income statements*

The following information was taken from the accounts of Helen's Groceries, a delicatessen. The accounts are listed in alphabetical order, and each has a normal balance.

Accounts payable	$600
Accounts receivable	400
Accumulated depreciation	100
Advertising expense	200
Cash	410
Common stock	200
Cost of goods sold	600
Interest expense	70
Merchandise inventory	450
Prepaid rent	40
Retained earnings	450
Sales revenue	1,000
Salaries expense	130
Supplies expense	110
Loss on sale of land	25

Required

First, prepare an income statement using the single-step approach. Then prepare another income statement using the multistep approach.

Exercise 5-18A   *Using ratios to make comparisons*   L.O. 7

The following income statements were drawn from the annual reports of the Eckert Company and the Ragland Company.

	Eckert*	Ragland*
Net sales	$32,600	$86,200
Cost of goods sold	(17,930)	(64,650)
Gross margin	14,670	21,550
Less: Operating exp.		
Selling and admin. exp.	(13,040)	(18,960)
Net income	$ 1,630	$ 2,590

*All figures are reported in thousands of dollars.

Required

a. One of the companies is a high-end retailer that operates in exclusive shopping malls. The other operates discount stores that are located in low-cost, stand-alone buildings. Identify the high-end retailer and the discounter. Support your answer with appropriate ratios.

b. If Eckert and Ragland have equity of $16,200 and $20,400, respectively, which company is in the more profitable business?

Exercise 5-19A   *Using common size statements and ratios to make comparisons*   L.O. 7

At the end of 2008 the following information is available for Lewis and Clark companies.

	Lewis	Clark
Sales	$1,000,000	$1,000,000
Cost of goods sold	700,000	600,000
Operating expenses	250,000	300,000
Total assets	1,200,000	1,200,000
Stockholders' equity	360,000	360,000

Required

a. Prepare a common size income statement for each company.

b. Compute the return on assets and return on equity for each company.

c. Which company is more profitable from the stockholders' perspective?

d. One company is a high-end retailer, and the other operates a discount store. Which is the discounter? Support your selection by referring to the appropriate ratios.

L.O. 8   **Exercise 5-20A**   *Effect of inventory transactions on the income statement and balance sheet: Periodic system (Appendix)*

Daniel Jackson is the owner of ABC Cleaning. At the beginning of the year, Jackson had $2,400 in inventory. During the year, Jackson purchased inventory that cost $13,000. At the end of the year, inventory on hand amounted to $3,600.

Required

Calculate the following:

a. Cost of goods available for sale during the year.

b. Cost of goods sold for the year.

c. Inventory amount ABC Cleaning would report on its year-end balance sheet.

L.O. 8   **Exercise 5-21A**   *Determining cost of goods sold: Periodic system (Appendix)*

Laura's Clothing Co. uses the periodic inventory system to account for its inventory transactions. The following account titles and balances were drawn from Laura's records for the year 2009: beginning balance in inventory, $24,900; purchases, $306,400; purchase returns and allowances, $12,400; sales, $720,000; sales returns and allowances, $6,370; transportation-in, $1,820; and operating expenses, $51,400. A physical count indicated that $24,800 of merchandise was on hand at the end of the accounting period.

Required

a. Prepare a schedule of cost of goods sold.

b. Prepare a multistep income statement.

L.O. 8   **Exercise 5-22A**   *Basic transactions: Periodic system, single cycle (Appendix)*

The following events apply to Patrick's Dive Shop for 2010, its first year of operation:

1. Acquired $45,000 cash from the issue of common stock.

2. Issued common stock to Grace Haynes, one of the owners, in exchange for merchandise inventory worth $2,500 Haynes had acquired prior to opening the shop.

3. Purchased $46,500 of inventory on account.

4. Paid $2,750 for advertising expense.

5. Sold inventory for $82,500.

6. Paid $8,000 in salary to a part-time salesperson.

7. Paid $30,000 on accounts payable (see Event 3).

8. Physically counted inventory, which indicated that $7,000 of inventory was on hand at the end of the accounting period.

Required

a. Record each of these events in general journal form. Patrick's Dive Shop uses the periodic system.

b. Post each of the events to ledger T-accounts.

c. Prepare an income statement, statement of changes in stockholders' equity, balance sheet, and statement of cash flows for 2010.

d. Prepare the necessary closing entries at the end of 2010, and post them to the appropriate T-accounts.

e. Prepare an after-closing trial balance.

f. Discuss an advantage of using the periodic system instead of the perpetual system.

g. Why is the common stock issued on the statement of changes in stockholders' equity different from the common stock issued in the cash flow from financing activities section of the cash flow statement?

Problem 5-23A   *Basic transactions for three accounting cycles: Perpetual system*

L.O. 2

Ferguson Company was started in 2008 when it acquired $60,000 from the issue of common stock. The following data summarize the company's first three years' operating activities. Assume that all transactions were cash transactions.

	2008	2009	2010
Purchases of inventory	$24,000	$12,000	$20,500
Sales	26,000	30,000	36,000
Cost of goods sold	13,400	18,500	20,000
Selling and administrative expenses	5,500	8,200	10,100

Required

Prepare an income statement (use the multistep format) and balance sheet for each fiscal year. (*Hint:* Record the transaction data for each accounting period in T-accounts before preparing the statements for that year.)

Problem 5-24A   *Identifying product and period costs*

L.O. 1

Required

Indicate whether each of the following costs is a product cost or a period (selling and administrative) cost.

a. Transportation-in.
b. Insurance on the office building.
c. Office supplies.
d. Costs incurred to improve the quality of goods available for sale.
e. Goods purchased for resale.
f. Salaries of salespersons.
g. Advertising costs.
h. Transportation-out.
i. Interest on a note payable.
j. Salary of the company president.

Problem 5-25A   *Identifying freight costs*

L.O. 3

Required

For each of the following events, determine the amount of freight paid by The Book Shop. Also indicate whether the freight cost would be classified as a product or period (selling and administrative) cost.

a. Purchased merchandise with freight costs of $700. The merchandise was shipped FOB shipping point.
b. Shipped merchandise to customers, freight terms FOB shipping point. The freight costs were $100.
c. Purchased inventory with freight costs of $1,000. The goods were shipped FOB destination.
d. Sold merchandise to a customer. Freight costs were $900. The goods were shipped FOB destination.

Problem 5-26A   *Comprehensive cycle problem: Perpetual system*

L.O. 2, 3, 5, 6

At the beginning of 2006, D & L Enterprises had the following balances in its accounts:

Cash	$8,400
Inventory	2,000
Common stock	8,000
Retained earnings	2,400

During 2006, D & L Enterprises experienced the following events:

1. Purchased inventory costing $5,600 on account from Smoot Company under terms 2/10, n/30. The merchandise was delivered FOB shipping point. Freight costs of $500 were paid in cash.

2. Returned $400 of the inventory that it had purchased because the inventory was damaged in transit. The freight company agreed to pay the return freight cost.

3. Paid the amount due on its account payable to Smoot Company within the cash discount period.

4. Sold inventory that had cost $6,000 for $9,000. The sale was on account under terms 2/10, n/45.

5. Received returned merchandise from a customer. The merchandise had originally cost $520 and had been sold to the customer for $840 cash. The customer was paid $840 cash for the returned merchandise.

6. Delivered goods in Event 4 FOB destination. Freight costs of $600 were paid in cash.

7. Collected the amount due on accounts receivable within the discount period.

8. Took a physical count indicating that $1,800 of inventory was on hand at the end of the accounting period.

Required

a. Identify each of these events as asset source (AS), asset use (AU), asset exchange (AE), or claims exchange (CE). Also explain how each event affects the financial statements by placing a + for increase, − for decrease, or NA for not affected under each of the components in the following statements model. Assume that the perpetual inventory method is used. When an event has more than one part, use letters to distinguish the effects of each part. The first event is recorded as an example.

Event No.	Event Type	Assets	=	Liab.	+	Stk. Equity	Rev.	−	Exp.	=	Net Inc.	Cash Flow
1a	AS	+	=	+	+	NA	NA	−	NA	=	NA	NA
1b	AE	+ −	=	NA	+	NA	NA	−	NA	=	NA	− OA

b. Record the events in general journal format.

c. Open ledger T-accounts and post the beginning balances and the events to the accounts.

d. Prepare a multistep income statement, statement of changes in stockholders' equity, balance sheet, and statement of cash flows.

e. Record and post the closing entries, and prepare an after-closing trial balance.

L.O. 5, 7   **Problem 5-27A**   *Multistep and common size income statements*

The following information was drawn from the records of Pierno Sales Company.

	2008	2009
Net sales	$50,000	$50,000
Cost of goods sold	(20,000)	(22,500)
Operating expenses	(12,500)	(15,000)
Gain on the sale of land	0	8,000

Required

a. Prepare a multistep income statement for each year.

b. Prepare a common size income statement for each year.

c. Assume that the operating trends between 2008 and 2009 continue through 2010. Write a brief memo indicating whether you expect net income to increase or decrease in 2010.

Problem 5-28A *Preparing a schedule of cost of goods sold and multistep and single-step income statements: Periodic system (Appendix)*

The following account titles and balances were taken from the adjusted trial balance of Wright Sales Co. at December 31, 2008. The company uses the periodic inventory method.

Account Title	Balance
Advertising expense	$ 10,400
Depreciation expense	3,000
Income taxes	8,200
Interest expense	5,000
Merchandise inventory, January 1	18,000
Merchandise inventory, December 31	20,100
Miscellaneous expense	800
Purchases	150,000
Purchase returns and allowances	2,700
Rent expense	18,000
Salaries expense	53,000
Sales	320,000
Sales returns and allowances	8,000
Transportation-in	6,200
Transportation-out	10,800
Gain on sale of land	4,000

Required

a. Prepare a schedule to determine the amount of cost of goods sold.
b. Prepare a multistep income statement.
c. Prepare a single-step income statement.

Problem 5-29A *Comprehensive cycle problem: Periodic system (Appendix)*

The following trial balance pertains to Mitchell Home Products as of January 1, 2009:

Account Title	Debit	Credit
Cash	$14,000	
Accounts receivable	9,000	
Merchandise inventory	60,000	
Accounts payable		$ 5,000
Common stock		70,000
Retained earnings		8,000
Total	$83,000	$83,000

The following events occurred in 2009. Assume that Mitchell Home Products uses the periodic inventory system.

1. Purchased land for $8,000 cash and a building for $45,000 by paying $5,000 cash and issuing a 20-year note with an annual interest rate of 8 percent. The building has a 40-year estimated life with no salvage value.
2. Purchased merchandise on account for $23,000, terms 2/10 n/30.
3. The merchandise purchased was shipped FOB shipping point for $230 cash.
4. Returned $2,000 of defective merchandise purchased in Event 2.
5. Sold merchandise for $27,000 cash.
6. Sold merchandise on account for $50,000, terms 1/20 n/30.

7. Paid cash within the discount period on accounts payable due on merchandise purchased in Event 2.
8. Paid $1,200 cash for selling expenses.
9. Collected $35,000 of accounts receivable within the discount period.
10. Collected $12,000 of accounts receivable but not within the discount period.
11. Paid cash to the bank for one full year's interest on the note issued in Event 1.
12. Paid $2,000 on the principal of the note issued in Event 1.
13. Recorded one full year's depreciation on the building purchased in Event 1.
14. Performed a physical count indicating that $30,000 of inventory was on hand at the end of the accounting period.

Required

a. Record these transactions in a general journal.
b. Post the transactions to ledger T-accounts.
c. Prepare a schedule of cost of goods sold, an income statement, a statement of changes in stockholders' equity, a balance sheet, and a statement of cash flows for 2009.

EXERCISES—SERIES B

When the instructions for *any* exercise or problem call for the preparation of an income statement, use the *multistep format* unless otherwise indicated.

L.O. 1, 2

Exercise 5-1B *Comparing a merchandising company with a service company*

The following information is available for two different types of businesses for the 2009 accounting period. Eady CPAs is a service business that provides accounting services to small businesses. Campus Clothing is a merchandising business that sells diving gear to college students.

Data for Eady CPAs

1. Borrowed $40,000 from the bank to start the business.
2. Provided $30,000 of services to customers and collected $30,000 cash.
3. Paid salary expense of $20,000.

Data for Campus Clothing

1. Borrowed $40,000 from the bank to start the business.
2. Purchased $25,000 inventory for cash.
3. Inventory costing $16,400 was sold for $30,000 cash.
4. Paid $3,600 cash for operating expenses.

Required

a. Prepare an income statement, balance sheet, and statement of cash flows for each of the companies.
b. Which of the two businesses would have product costs? Why?
c. Why does Eady CPAs not compute gross margin on its income statement?
d. Compare the assets of both companies. What assets do they have in common? What assets are different? Why?

L.O. 2

Exercise 5-2B *Effect of inventory transactions on journals, ledgers, and financial statements: Perpetual system*

John Selma started a small merchandising business in 2010. The business experienced the following events during its first year of operation. Assume that Selma uses the perpetual inventory system.

1. Acquired $40,000 cash from the issue of common stock.
2. Purchased inventory for $30,000 cash.
3. Sold inventory costing $20,000 for $32,000 cash.

Required

a. Record the events in general journal format.
b. Post the entries to T-accounts.
c. Prepare an income statement for 2010 (use the multistep format).
d. What is the amount of net cash flow from operating activities for 2010?

Exercise 5-3B   *Effect of inventory transactions on the income statement and statement of cash flows: Perpetual system*

L.O. 2

During 2011, Knight Merchandising Company purchased $15,000 of inventory on account. Knight sold inventory on account that cost $12,500 for $17,500. Cash payments on accounts payable were $10,000. There was $11,000 cash collected from accounts receivable. Knight also paid $3,500 cash for operating expenses. Assume that Knight started the accounting period with $14,000 in both cash and common stock.

Required

a. Identify the events described in the preceding paragraph and record them in a horizontal statements model like the following one:

Assets			=	Liab.	+	Equity			Rev.	−	Exp.	=	Net Inc.	Cash Flow
Cash	+ Accts. Rec.	+ Inv.	=	Accts. Pay.	+	Com. Stk.	+	Ret. Earn.						
14,000 +	NA	+ NA =		NA	+	14,000	+	NA	NA	−	NA	=	NA	NA

b. What is the balance of accounts receivable at the end of 2011?
c. What is the balance of accounts payable at the end of 2011?
d. What are the amounts of gross margin and net income for 2011?
e. Determine the amount of net cash flow from operating activities.
f. Explain why net income and retained earnings are the same for Knight. Normally would these amounts be the same? Why or why not?

Exercise 5-4B   *Recording inventory transactions in the general journal and posting entries to T-accounts: Perpetual system*

L.O. 2

Kona Clothing experienced the following events during 2010, its first year of operation:

1. Acquired $14,000 cash from the issue of common stock.
2. Purchased inventory for $8,000 cash.
3. Sold inventory costing $6,000 for $9,000 cash.
4. Paid $800 for advertising expense.

Required

a. Record the general journal entries for the preceding transactions.
b. Post each of the entries to T-accounts.
c. Prepare a trial balance to prove the equality of debits and credits.

Exercise 5-5B   *Determining which party is responsible for freight cost*

L.O. 3

Required

Determine which party, buyer or seller, is responsible for freight charges in each of the following situations:

a. Sold merchandise, freight terms, FOB destination.
b. Sold merchandise, freight terms, FOB shipping point.
c. Purchased merchandise, freight terms, FOB destination.
d. Purchased merchandise, freight terms, FOB shipping point.

L.O. 2, 3

Exercise 5-6B *Effect of purchase returns and allowances and freight costs on the journal, ledger, and financial statements: Perpetual system*

The trial balance for Jerry's Auto Shop as of January 1, 2011 follows:

Account Titles	Debit	Credit
Cash	$28,000	
Inventory	14,000	
Common stock		$36,000
Retained earnings		6,000
Total	$42,000	$42,000

The following events affected the company during the 2011 accounting period:

1. Purchased merchandise on account that cost $18,000.
2. Purchased goods in Event 1 FOB shipping point with freight cost of $1,000 cash.
3. Returned $3,600 of damaged merchandise for credit on account.
4. Agreed to keep other damaged merchandise for which the company received a $1,400 allowance.
5. Sold merchandise that cost $16,000 for $34,000 cash.
6. Delivered merchandise to customers in Event 5 under terms FOB destination with freight costs amounting to $800 cash.
7. Paid $12,000 on the merchandise purchased in Event 1.

Required

a. Record the events in general journal format.
b. Open general ledger T-accounts with the appropriate beginning balances, and post the journal entries to the T-accounts.
c. Prepare an income statement, balance sheet, and statement of cash flows. (Assume that closing entries have been made.)
d. Explain why a difference does or does not exist between net income and net cash flow from operating activities.

L.O. 2, 3

Exercise 5-7B *Accounting for product costs: Perpetual inventory system*

Which of the following would be *debited* to the Inventory account for a merchandising business using the perpetual inventory system?

Required

a. Transportation-out.
b. Purchase discount.
c. Transportation-in.
d. Purchase of a new computer to be used by the business.
e. Purchase of inventory.
f. Allowance received for damaged inventory.

L.O. 1, 2, 3

Exercise 5-8B *Effect of product cost and period cost: Horizontal statements model*

The Toy Store experienced the following events for the 2010 accounting period:

1. Acquired $20,000 cash from the issue of common stock.
2. Purchased $56,000 of inventory on account.
3. Received goods purchased in Event 2 FOB shipping point; freight cost of $600 paid in cash.
4. Sold inventory on account that cost $35,000 for $57,400.
5. Freight cost on the goods sold in Event 4 was $420. The goods were shipped FOB destination. Cash was paid for the freight cost.
6. Customer in Event 4 returned $4,000 worth of goods that had a cost of $1,400.
7. Collected $47,000 cash from accounts receivable.

8. Paid $44,000 cash on accounts payable.
9. Paid $1,100 for advertising expense.
10. Paid $2,000 cash for insurance expense.

Required

a. Which of these events result in period (selling and administrative) costs? Which result in product costs? If neither, label the transaction NA.

b. Record each event in a horizontal statements model like the following one. The first event is recorded as an example.

Assets				=	Liab.	+	Equity			Rev.	−	Exp.	=	Net Inc.	Cash Flow
Cash	+ Accts. Rec.	+ Inv.	=	Accts. Pay.	+	C. Stk.	+	Ret. Earn.							
20,000 +	NA	+ NA =		NA	+	20,000 +		NA		NA	−	NA =		NA	10,000 FA

Exercise 5-9B   *Cash discounts and purchase returns*   L.O. 3

On April 6, 2008, Taylor Furnishings purchased $12,400 of merchandise from Bergin's Imports, terms 2/10 n/45. On April 5, Taylor returned $1,200 of the merchandise to Bergin's Imports for credit. Taylor paid cash for the merchandise on April 15, 2008.

Required

a. What is the amount that Taylor must pay Bergin's Imports on April 15?

b. Record the events in a horizontal statements model like the following one.

Assets			=	Liab.	+	Equity			Rev.	−	Exp.	=	Net Inc.	Cash Flow
Cash	+ Inv.	=	Accts. Pay.	+	C. Stock.	+	Ret. Earn.							

c. How much must Taylor pay for the merchandise purchased if the payment is not made until April 20, 2008?

d. Record the payment in event (c) in a horizontal statements model like the one above.

e. Why would Taylor want to pay for the merchandise by April 15?

Exercise 5-10B   *Effect of sales returns and allowances and freight costs on the journal, ledger,*   L.O. 2, 3
and financial statements: Perpetual system

Stark Company began the 2011 accounting period with $10,000 cash, $38,000 inventory, $25,000 common stock, and $23,000 retained earnings. During 2011, Stark experienced the following events:

1. Sold merchandise costing $28,000 for $46,000 on account to Jack's Furniture Store.
2. Delivered the goods to Jack's under terms FOB destination. Freight costs were $500 cash.
3. Received returned goods from Jack's. The goods cost Stark $2,000 and were sold to Jack's for $3,000.
4. Granted Jack's a $2,000 allowance for damaged goods that Jack's agreed to keep.
5. Collected partial payment of $25,000 cash from accounts receivable.

Required

a. Record the events in general journal format.

b. Open general ledger T-accounts with the appropriate beginning balances and post the journal entries to the T-accounts.

c. Prepare an income statement, balance sheet, and statement of cash flows.

d. Why would Jack's agree to keep the damaged goods? Who benefits more?

L.O. 3

Exercise 5-11B *Determining the cost of inventory*

Required

For each of the following cases determine the ending balance in the inventory account. (*Hint:* First, determine the total cost of inventory available for sale. Next, subtract the cost of the inventory sold to arrive at the ending balance.)

a. Kay's Dress Shop had a beginning balance in its inventory account of $10,000. During the accounting period Kay's purchased $34,000 of inventory, returned $2,000 of inventory, and obtained $320 of purchases discounts. Kay's incurred $800 of transportation-in cost and $1,200 of transportation-out cost. Salaries of sales personnel amounted to $13,400. Administrative expenses amounted to $21,000. Cost of goods sold amounted to $33,200.

b. Sam's Soap Shop had a beginning balance in its inventory account of $4,000. During the accounting period Sam's purchased $18,600 of inventory, obtained $600 of purchases allowances, and received $180 of purchases discounts. Sales discounts amounted to $320. Sam's incurred $450 of transportation-in cost and $130 of transportation-out cost. Selling and administrative cost amounted to $6,900. Cost of goods sold amounted to $17,000.

L.O. 3, 4, 5

Exercise 5-12B *Sales returns, discounts, and a multistep income statement*

The following information was drawn from the 2008 accounting records of Goldstein Merchandisers.

1. Inventory that had cost $22,400 was sold for $34,000 under terms 2/20, net/30.
2. Customers returned merchandise to Goldstein. The merchandise had been sold for a price of $1,400. The merchandise had cost Goldstein $840.
3. All customers paid their accounts within the discount period.
4. Selling and administrative expenses amounted to $5,600.
5. Interest expense amounted to $350.
6. Land that had cost $8,000 was sold for $9,500 cash.

Required

a. Determine the amount of net sales.
b. Prepare a multistep income statement.
c. Where would the interest expense be shown on the statement of cash flows?
d. How would the sale of the land be shown on the statement of cash flows?
e. Explain the difference between a gain and revenue.

L.O. 3, 4, 5, 7

Exercise 5-13B *Comprehensive exercise with sales discounts*

Super Buys started the 2009 accounting period with the balances given in the financial statements model shown below. During 2009 Super Buys experienced the following business events.

1. Paid cash to purchase $40,000 of merchandise inventory.
2. The goods that were purchased in Event 1 were delivered FOB destination. Freight costs of $900 were paid in cash by the responsible party.
3a. Sold merchandise for $53,000 under terms 1/10, n/30.
3b. Recognized $36,000 of cost of good sold.
4a. Super Buys customers returned merchandise that was sold for $2,500.
4b. The merchandise returned in Event 4a had cost Super Buys $1,500.
5. The merchandise in Event 3a was sold to customers FOB destination. Freight costs of $2,200 were paid in cash by the responsible party.
6a. The customers paid for the merchandise sold in Event 4a within the discount period. Recognized the sales discount.
6b. Collected the balance in the accounts receivable account.
7. Paid cash of $7,000 for selling and administrative expenses.
8. Sold the land for $8,400 cash.

Required

a. Record the above transactions in a financial statements model like the one shown below.

Event No.	Cash	+	Accts. Rec.	+	Inventory	+	Land	=	Com. Stk.	+	Ret. Earn.	Rev/ Gain	−	Exp.	=	Net Inc.	Cash Flow
Bal.	50,000	+	0	+	6,000	+	10,000	=	36,000	+	30,000	NA	−	NA	=	NA	NA

b. Determine the amount of net sales.

c. Prepare a multistep income statement. Include common size percentages on the income statement.

d. Super Buys return on sales ratio in 2008 was 12 percent. Based on the common size data in the income statement, did Super Buys' expenses increase or decrease in 2009?

e. Explain why the term *loss* is used to describe the results due to the sale of land?

Exercise 5-14B *Inventory financing costs*   L.O. 3

Joan Sweatt comes to you for advice. She has just purchased a large amount of inventory with the terms 2/10, n/60. The amount of the invoice is $540,000. She is currently short of cash and her company's credit rating is weak. However, she can borrow the money needed to settle the account payable but the required interest rate is 18 percent. Sweatt is confident she will have the necessary cash by the due date of the invoice but not by the last day of the discount period.

Required

a. Convert the discount rate into an annual interest rate.

b. Make a recommendation regarding whether Sweatt should borrow the money and pay off the account payable within the discount period.

Exercise 5-15B *Effect of inventory losses: Perpetual system*   L.O. 2, 6

Reeves Designs experienced the following events during 2010, its first year of operation:

1. Started the business when it acquired $40,000 cash from the issue of common stock.
2. Paid $28,000 cash to purchase inventory.
3. Sold inventory costing $21,500 for $34,200 cash.
4. Physically counted inventory; had inventory of $5,800 on hand at the end of the accounting period.

Required

a. Open appropriate ledger T-accounts, and record the events in the accounts.

b. Prepare an income statement and balance sheet.

c. If all purchases and sales of merchandise are reflected as increases or decreases to the Merchandise Inventory account, why is it necessary for management to even bother to take a physical count of goods on hand (ending inventory) at the end of the year?

Exercise 5-16B *Determining the effect of inventory transactions on the horizontal statements model: Perpetual system*   L.O. 2

Lopez Sales Company experienced the following events:

1. Purchased merchandise inventory for cash.
2. Purchased merchandise inventory on account.
3. Sold merchandise inventory for cash. Label the revenue recognition 3a and the expense recognition 3b.
4. Sold merchandise inventory on account. Label the revenue recognition 4a and the expense recognition 4b.
5. Returned merchandise purchased on account.
6. Paid cash for selling and administrative expenses.
7. Paid cash on accounts payable not within the discount period.
8. Paid cash for transportation-in.

9. Collected cash from accounts receivable.

10. Paid cash for transportation-out.

Required

Identify each event as asset source (AS), asset use (AU), asset exchange (AE), or claims exchange (CE). Also explain how each event affects the financial statements by placing a + for increase, − for decrease, or NA for not affected under each of the components in the following statements model. Assume the use of the perpetual inventory system. The first event is recorded as an example.

Event No.	Event Type	Assets	=	Liab.	+	Equity	Rev.	−	Exp.	=	Net Inc.	Cash Flow
1	AE	+ −	=	NA	+	NA	NA	−	NA	=	NA	− OA

L.O. 5

Exercise 5-17B   Single-step and multistep income statements

The following information was taken from the accounts of Healthy Foods Market, a small grocery store. The accounts are listed in alphabetical order, and all have normal balances.

Accounts payable	$ 300
Accounts receivable	1,040
Accumulated depreciation	200
Advertising expense	200
Cash	820
Common stock	600
Cost of goods sold	900
Interest expense	140
Merchandise inventory	500
Prepaid rent	280
Retained earnings	1,050
Sales revenue	2,400
Salaries expense	260
Supplies expense	210
Gain on sale of land	75

Required

First, prepare an income statement using the single-step approach. Then prepare another income statement using the multistep approach.

L.O. 7

Exercise 5-18B   Using ratios to make comparisons

The following income statements were drawn from the annual reports of the Rivers Company and the Wells Company.

	Rivers*	Wells*
Net sales	$ 32,600	$ 86,200
Cost of goods sold	(24,450)	(47,410)
Gross margin	8,150	38,790
Less: Operating exp.		
Selling and admin. exp.	(6,520)	(30,170)
Net income	$ 1,630	$ 8,620

*All figures are reported in thousands of dollars.

Required

a. One of the companies is a high-end retailer that operates in exclusive shopping malls. The other operates discount stores that are located in low-cost, stand-alone buildings. Identify the high-end retailer and the discounter. Support your answer with appropriate ratios.

b. If Rivers and Wells have equity of $14,100 and $95,800, respectively, which company is in the more profitable business?

Exercise 5-19B *Using common size statements and ratios to make comparisons*

L.O. 7

At the end of 2008 the following information is available for Chicago and St. Louis companies.

	Chicago	St. Louis
Sales	$3,000,000	$3,000
Cost of goods sold	1,800,000	2,100
Operating expenses	960,000	780
Total assets	3,750,000	3,750
Stockholders' equity	1,000,000	1,200

Required

a. Prepare a common size income statement for each company.

b. Compute the return on assets and return on equity for each company.

c. Which company is more profitable from the stockholders' perspective?

d. One company is a high-end retailer, and the other operates a discount store. Which is the discounter? Support your selection by referring to the appropriate ratios.

Exercise 5-20B *Effect of inventory transactions on the income statement and balance sheet: Periodic system (Appendix)*

L.O. 8

Joe Dodd owns Joe's Sporting Goods. At the beginning of the year, Joe's had $8,400 in inventory. During the year, Joe's purchased inventory that cost $42,000. At the end of the year, inventory on hand amounted to $17,600.

Required

Calculate the following:

a. Cost of goods available for sale during the year.

b. Cost of goods sold for the year.

c. Amount of inventory Joe's would report on the year-end balance sheet.

Exercise 5-21B *Determining cost of goods sold: Periodic system (Appendix)*

L.O. 8

Lane Antiques uses the periodic inventory system to account for its inventory transactions. The following account titles and balances were drawn from Lane's records: beginning balance in inventory, $24,000; purchases, $150,000; purchase returns and allowances, $10,000; sales, $400,000; sales returns and allowances, $2,500; freight-in, $750; and operating expenses, $26,000. A physical count indicated that $18,000 of merchandise was on hand at the end of the accounting period.

Required

a. Prepare a schedule of cost of goods sold.

b. Prepare a multistep income statement.

Exercise 5-22B *Basic transactions: Periodic system, single cycle (Appendix)*

L.O. 8

The following transactions apply to Sarah's Specialties Shop for 2010, its first year of operations:

1. Acquired $70,000 cash from the issue of common stock.
2. Acquired $16,000 of merchandise from Sarah Hill, the owner, who had acquired the merchandise prior to opening the shop. Issued common stock to Sarah in exchange for the merchandise inventory.
3. Purchased $90,000 of inventory on account.
4. Paid $3,000 for radio ads.

5. Sold inventory for $220,000 cash.

6. Paid $20,000 in salary to a part-time salesperson.

7. Paid $65,000 on accounts payable (see Event 3).

8. Physically counted inventory, which indicated that $40,000 of inventory was on hand at the end of the accounting period.

Required

a. Record each of these transactions in general journal form using the periodic method.

b. Post each of the transactions to ledger T-accounts.

c. Prepare an income statement, statement of changes in stockholders' equity, balance sheet, and statement of cash flows for 2010.

d. Prepare the necessary closing entries at the end of 2010, and post them to the appropriate T-accounts.

e. Prepare an after-closing trial balance.

f. Give an example of a business that may want to use the periodic system. Give an example of a business that may use the perpetual system.

g. Give some examples of assets other than cash that are commonly contributed to a business in exchange for stock.

PROBLEMS—SERIES B

L.O. 2

Problem 5-23B *Basic transactions for three accounting cycles: Perpetual system*

Ginger's Flower Company was started in 2009 when it acquired $80,000 cash from the issue of common stock. The following data summarize the company's first three years' operating activities. Assume that all transactions were cash transactions.

	2009	2010	2011
Purchases of inventory	$ 60,000	$ 90,000	$130,000
Sales	102,000	146,000	220,000
Cost of goods sold	54,000	78,000	140,000
Selling and administrative expenses	40,000	52,000	72,000

Required

Prepare an income statement (use multistep format) and balance sheet for each fiscal year. (*Hint:* Record the transaction data for each accounting period in T-accounts before preparing the statements for that year.)

L.O. 1

Problem 5-24B *Identifying product and period costs*

Required

Indicate whether each of the following costs is a product cost or a period cost:

a. Depreciation on office equipment.

b. Insurance on vans used to deliver goods to customers.

c. Salaries of sales supervisors.

d. Monthly maintenance expense for a copier.

e. Goods purchased for resale.

f. Cleaning supplies for the office.

g. Freight on goods purchased for resale.

h. Salary of the marketing director.

i. Freight on goods sold to customer with terms FOB destination.

j. Utilities expense incurred for office building.

Problem 5-25B   *Identifying freight cost*

Required

For each of the following events, determine the amount of freight paid by Tom's Parts House. Also indicate whether the freight is classified as a product or period cost.

a. Purchased inventory with freight costs of $1,400, FOB destination.

b. Shipped merchandise to customers with freight costs of $300, FOB destination.

c. Purchased additional merchandise with costs of $500, FOB shipping point.

d. Sold merchandise to a customer. Freight costs were $800, FOB shipping point.

Problem 5-26B   *Comprehensive cycle problem: Perpetual system*

At the beginning of 2009, the Jeater Company had the following balances in its accounts:

Cash	$ 4,300
Inventory	9,000
Common stock	10,000
Retained earnings	3,300

During 2009, the company experienced the following events.

1. Purchased inventory that cost $2,200 on account from Blue Company under terms 1/10, n/30. The merchandise was delivered FOB shipping point. Freight costs of $110 were paid in cash.

2. Returned $200 of the inventory that it had purchased because the inventory was damaged in transit. The freight company agreed to pay the return freight cost.

3. Paid the amount due on its account payable to Blue Company within the cash discount period.

4. Sold inventory that had cost $3,000 for $5,500 on account, under terms 2/10, n/45.

5. Received returned merchandise from a customer. The merchandise originally cost $400 and was sold to the customer for $710 cash. The customer was paid $710 cash for the returned merchandise.

6. Delivered goods FOB destination in Event 4. Freight costs of $60 were paid in cash.

7. Collected the amount due on the account receivable within the discount period.

8. Took a physical count indicating that $7,970 of inventory was on hand at the end of the accounting period.

Required

a. Identify each of these events as asset source (AS), asset use (AU), asset exchange (AE), or claims exchange (CE). Also explain how each event would affect the financial statements by placing a + for increase, − for decrease, or NA for not affected under each of the components in the following statements model. Assume that the perpetual inventory method is used. When an event has more than one part, use letters to distinguish the effects of each part. The first event is recorded as an example.

Event No.	Event Type	Assets	=	Liab.	+	Stk. Equity	Rev.	−	Exp.	=	Net Inc.	Cash Flow
1a	AS	+	=	+	+	NA	NA	−	NA	=	NA	NA
1b	AE	+ −	=	NA	+	NA	NA	−	NA	=	NA	− OA

b. Record the events in general journal format.

c. Open ledger T-accounts, and post the beginning balances and the events to the accounts.

d. Prepare a multistep income statement, a statement of changes in stockholders' equity, a balance sheet, and a statement of cash flows.

e. Record and post the closing entries, and prepare an after-closing trial balance.

L.O. 5, 7   **Problem 5-27B**   *Multistep and common size income statements*

The following information was drawn from the records of Laufer Sales Company.

	2008	2009
Net sales	$100,000	$100,000
Cost of goods sold	(45,000)	(40,000)
Operating expenses	(30,000)	(25,000)
Loss on the sale of land	-0-	(12,000)

Required

a. Prepare a multistep income statement for each year.

b. Prepare a common size income statement for each year.

c. At a recent meeting of the stockholders, Laufer's president stated 2010 would be a very good year with net income rising significantly. Write a brief memo explaining whether you agree or disagree with the president. Assume that the operating trends between 2008 and 2009 continue through 2010.

L.O. 5, 8   **Problem 5-28B**   *Preparing schedule of cost of goods sold and multistep and single-step income statements: Periodic system (Appendix)*

The following account titles and balances were taken from the adjusted trial balance of Brisco Farm Co. for 2012. The company uses the periodic inventory system.

Account Title	Balance
Sales returns and allowances	$ 3,250
Miscellaneous expense	400
Transportation-out	700
Sales	69,750
Advertising expense	2,750
Salaries expense	8,500
Transportation-in	1,725
Purchases	42,000
Interest expense	360
Merchandise inventory, January 1	6,200
Rent expense	5,000
Merchandise inventory, December 31	4,050
Purchase returns and allowances	1,250
Depreciation expense	710
Loss on sale of land	3,400

Required

a. Prepare a schedule to determine the amount of cost of goods sold.

b. Prepare a multistep income statement.

c. Prepare a single-step income statement.

L.O. 8   **Problem 5-29B**   *Comprehensive cycle problem: Periodic system (Appendix)*

The following trial balance pertains to Nate's Grocery as of January 1, 2009:

Account Title	Debit	Credit
Cash	$26,000	
Accounts receivable	4,000	
Merchandise inventory	50,000	
Accounts payable		$ 4,000
Common stock		43,000
Retained earnings		33,000
Totals	$80,000	$80,000

The following events occurred in 2009. Assume that Nate's uses the periodic inventory method.

1. Purchased land for $20,000 cash and a building for $90,000 by paying $10,000 cash and issuing a 20-year note with an annual interest rate of 8 percent. The building has a 40-year estimated life with no residual value.
2. Purchased merchandise on account for $126,000, terms 1/10 n/45.
3. Paid freight of $1,000 cash on merchandise purchased FOB shipping point.
4. Returned $3,600 of defective merchandise purchased in Event 2.
5. Sold merchandise for $86,000 cash.
6. Sold merchandise on account for $120,000, terms 2/10 n/30.
7. Paid cash within the discount period on accounts payable due on merchandise purchased in Event 2.
8. Paid $11,600 cash for selling expenses.
9. Collected $50,000 of the accounts receivable from Event 6 within the discount period.
10. Collected $60,000 of the accounts receivable but not within the discount period.
11. Paid cash to the bank for one full year's interest on the note issued in Event 1.
12. Paid $10,000 on the principal of the note issued in Event 1.
13. Recorded one full year's depreciation on the building purchased in Event 1.
14. A physical count indicated that $27,600 of inventory was on hand at the end of the accounting period.

Required

a. Record these transactions in a general journal.
b. Post the transactions to ledger T-accounts.
c. Prepare a schedule of costs of goods sold, an income statement, statement of changes in stockholders' equity, balance sheet, and statement of cash flows for 2009.

ANALYZE, THINK, COMMUNICATE

ATC 5-1 Business Applications Case *Understanding real-world annual reports*

Required

a. Use the Topps Company's annual report in Appendix B to answer the following questions.
   (1) What was Topps' gross margin percentage for 2006 and 2005?
   (2) What was Topps' return on sales percentage for 2006 and 2005?
   (3) Topps' Gross Profit on Sales was about $9 million lower in 2006 than in 2005 and this caused its Net Income to be lower as well. However, its gross margin percentage also decreased in 2006. Ignoring taxes, how much higher would its 2006 net income have been if the gross margin percentage in 2006 had been the same as for 2005?

b. Use the Harley-Davidson's annual report that came with this book to answer the following questions.
   (1) What was Harley-Davidson's gross margin percentage for 2005 and 2004?
   (2) What was Harley-Davidson's return on sales percentage for 2005 and 2004?
   (3) Harley-Davidson's gross margin percentage increased during 2005 compared to 2004. The MD&A section of its annual report explains the reasons this occurred. What are these reasons?

ATC 5-2 Group Exercise *Multistep income statement*

The following quarterly information is given for Raybon for the year ended 2008 (amounts shown are in millions).

	First Quarter	Second Quarter	Third Quarter	Fourth Quarter
Net sales	$736.0	$717.4	$815.2	$620.1
Gross margin	461.9	440.3	525.3	252.3
Net income	37.1	24.6	38.6	31.4

Required

a. Divide the class into groups and organize the groups into four sections. Assign each section financial information for one of the quarters.

   (1) Each group should compute the cost of goods sold and operating expenses for the specific quarter assigned to its section and prepare a multistep income statement for the quarter.

   (2) Each group should compute the gross margin percentage and cost of goods sold percentage for its specific quarter.

   (3) Have a representative of each group put that quarter's sales, cost of goods sold percentage, and gross margin percentage on the board.

Class Discussion

b. Have the class discuss the change in each of these items from quarter to quarter and explain why the change might have occurred. Which was the best quarter and why?

ATC 5-3   Real-World Case   *Identifying companies based on financial statement information*

Presented here is selected information from the 2005 fiscal-year 10-K reports of four companies. The four companies, in alphabetical order, are Caterpillar, Inc., a manufacturer of heavy machinery; Oracle Corporation, a company that develops software; Starbucks, a company that sells coffee products; and Tiffany & Company, a company that operates high-end jewelry and department stores. The data for the companies, presented in the order of the amount of their sales in millions of dollars, follow:

	A	B	C	D
Sales	$2,395	$6,369	$11,799	$36,339
Cost of goods sold	1,052	2,605	2,651	26,558
Net earnings	255	495	2,886	2,854
Inventory	1,060	546	0	5,224
Accounts receivable	142	191	2,900	13,968
Total assets	$2,777	$3,514	$20,687	$47,069

Required

Based on these financial data and your knowledge and assumptions about the nature of the businesses that the companies operate, determine which data relate to which companies. Write a memorandum explaining your decisions. Include a discussion of which ratios you used in your analysis, and show the computations of these ratios in your memorandum.

ATC 5-4   Business Applications Case   *Performing ratio analysis using real-world data*

The following data were taken from Microsoft Corporation's 2004 annual report. All dollar amounts are in millions.

	Fiscal Years Ending	
	June 30, 2004	June 30, 2003
Revenue	$36,835	$32,187
Cost of goods sold	6,716	6,059
Net income	8,168	7,531

Required

a. Compute Microsoft's gross margin percentage for 2004 and 2003.

b. Compute Microsoft's return on sales percentage for 2004 and 2003.

c. Based on the percentages computed in Requirements *a* and *b*, did Microsoft's performance get better or worse from 2003 to 2004?

d. Compare Microsoft's gross margin percentages and return on sales percentages to those of the other real-world companies discussed in this chapter and discuss whether or not it appears to have better than average financial performance or not.

ATC 5-5 **Business Applications Case** *Performing ratio analysis using real-world data*

Supervalu, Inc., claims to be the largest publicly held food wholesaler in the United States. In addition to being a food wholesaler, it operates "extreme value" retail grocery stores under the name Save-A-Lot. Most of these discount stores are located in inner-city areas not served by others.

Whole Food Markets claims to be the world's largest retailer of natural and organic foods. Unlike Save-A-Lot stores that focus on low-income customers. Whole Foods offers specialty products to customers with sufficient disposal income to spend on such goods.

The following data were taken from these companies' 2005 and 2004 annual reports. All dollar amounts are in thousands.

	Supervalu, Inc. February 26, 2005	Whole Foods September 26, 2004
Sales	$19,543,240	$3,864,950
Cost of goods sold	16,681,472	2,523,816
Net income	385,823	129,512

Required

a. Before performing any calculations, speculate as to which company will have the highest gross margin and return on sales percentage. Explain the rationale for your decision.

b. Calculate the gross margin percentages for Supervalu and Whole Foods Market.

c. Calculate the return on sales percentages for Supervalu and Whole Foods Market.

d. Do the calculations from Requirements *b* and *c* confirm your speculations in Requirement *a*?

ATC 5-6 **Written Assignment, Critical Thinking** *Effect of sales returns on financial statements*

Bell Farm and Garden Equipment reported the following information for 2008:

Net sales of equipment	$2,450,567
Other income	6,786
Cost of goods sold	(1,425,990)
Selling, general, and administrative expense	(325,965)
Depreciation and amortization	(3,987)
Net operating income	$ 701,411

Selected information from the balance sheet as of December 31, 2008 follows:

Cash and marketable securities	$113,545
Inventory	248,600
Accounts receivable	82,462
Property, plant, and equipment—net	335,890
Other assets	5,410
Total assets	$785,907

Assume that a major customer returned a large order to Bell on December 31, 2008. The amount of the sale had been $146,800 with a cost of sales of $94,623. The return was recorded in the books on January 1, 2009. The company president does not want to correct the books. He argues that it makes no difference as to whether the return is recorded in 2008 or 2009. Either way, the return has been duly recognized.

Required

a. Assume that you are the CFO for Bell Farm and Garden Equipment Co. Write a memo to the president explaining how omitting the entry on December 31, 2008, could cause the financial statements to be misleading to investors and creditors. Explain how omitting the return from the customer would affect net income and the balance sheet.

b. Why might the president want to record the return on January 1, 2009, instead of December 31, 2008?

c. Would the failure to record the customer return violate the AICPA Code of Professional Conduct? (See Exhibit 2.7 in Chapter 2.)

d. If the president of the company refuses to correct the financial statements, what action should you take?

ATC 5-7   Ethical Dilemma   *Wait until I get mine*

Ada Fontanez is the president of a large company that owns a chain of athletic shoe stores. The company was in dire financial condition when she was hired three years ago. In an effort to motivate Fontanez, the board of directors included a bonus plan as part of her compensation package. According to her employment contract, on January 15 of each year, Fontanez is paid a cash bonus equal to 5 percent of the amount of net income reported on the preceding December 31 income statement. Fontanez was sufficiently motivated. Through her leadership, the company prospered. Her efforts were recognized throughout the industry, and she received numerous lucrative offers to leave the company. One offer was so enticing that she decided to change jobs. Her decision was made in late December 2008. However, she decided to resign effective February 1, 2009, to ensure the receipt of her January bonus. On December 31, 2008, the chief accountant, Walter Smith, advised Fontanez that the company had a sizable quantity of damaged inventory. A warehouse fire had resulted in smoke and water damage to approximately $600,000 of inventory. The warehouse was not insured, and the accountant recommended that the loss be recognized immediately. After examining the inventory, Fontanez argued that it could be sold as *damaged goods* to customers at reduced prices. Accordingly, she refused to allow the write-off the accountant recommended. She stated that so long as she is president, the inventory stays on the books at cost. She told the accountant that he could take up the matter with the new president in February.

Required

a. How would an immediate write-off of the damaged inventory affect the December 31, 2008, income statement, balance sheet, and statement of cash flows?

b. How would the write-off affect Fontanez's bonus?

c. If the new president is given the same bonus plan, how will Fontanez's refusal to recognize the loss affect his or her bonus?

d. Assuming that the damaged inventory is truly worthless, comment on the ethical implications of Fontanez's refusal to recognize the loss in the 2008 accounting period.

e. Assume that the damaged inventory is truly worthless and that you are Smith. How would you react to Fontanez's refusal to recognize the loss?

ATC 5-8   Research Assignment   *Analyzing Alcoa's profit margins*

Using either Alcoa's most current Form 10-K or the company's annual report, answer the questions below. To obtain the Form 10-K you can use either use the EDGAR system following the instructions in Appendix A, or it can be found on the company's website. The company's annual report is available on its website.

Required

a. What was Alcoa's gross margin percentage for the most current year?

b. What was Alcoa's gross margin percentage for the previous year? Has it changed significantly?

c. What was Alcoa's return on sales percentage for the most current year?

d. What percentage of Alcoa's total sales for the most current year was from operations in the United States?

e. Comment on the appropriateness of comparing Alcoa's gross margin with that of Ford Motor Company. If Ford has a higher/lower margin, does that mean that Ford is a better managed company?

ATC 5-9 Spreadsheet Analysis *Using Excel*

The following accounts, balances, and other financial information are drawn from the records of Vong Company for the year 2008:

Net sales revenue	$18,800	Beginning common stock	$ 9,000
Unearned revenue	2,600	Land	8,000
Accounts receivable	6,000	Certificate of deposit	10,000
Cost of goods sold	6,000	Interest revenue	100
Inventory	5,000	Interest receivable	100
Accounts payable	5,800	Dividends	1,500
Notes payable	6,000	Beginning retained earnings	8,500
Interest expense	550	Cash from stock issued	3,000
Accrued interest payable	550	Cash	7,200
Supplies	50	Gain on sale of land	1,050
Supplies expense	750	Loss on sale of property	50
Office equipment	3,500	Salaries expense	1,400
Depreciation expense	500	Accrued salaries payable	400
Accumulated depreciation	1,000	Rent expense	1,100
Transportation-out expense	500	Prepaid rent	100
Miscellaneous operating expense	4,500		

The Cash account revealed the following cash flows:

Received cash from advances from customers	$ 2,600
Purchased office equipment	(3,500)
Received cash from issuing stock	3,000
Collected cash from accounts receivable	3,800
Purchased land	(8,000)
Received cash from borrowing funds	6,000
Paid cash for rent	(1,200)
Sold land	10,000
Paid cash for dividends	(1,500)
Paid cash for operating expenses	(1,000)
Purchased certificate of deposit	(10,000)

Required

Build an Excel spreadsheet to construct a multistep income statement, statement of changes in stockholders' equity, balance sheet, and statement of cash flows for the year 2008.

ATC 5-10   Spreadsheet Analysis   *Mastering Excel*

At the end of 2008, the following information is available for Short and Wise Companies:

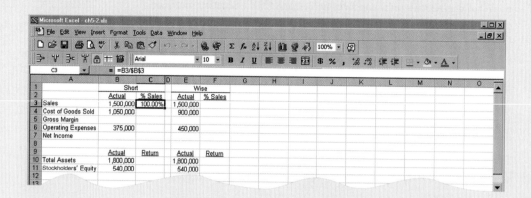

Required

a. Set up the spreadsheet shown here. Complete the income statements by using Excel formulas.

b. Prepare a common size income statement for each company by completing the % Sales columns.

c. One company is a high-end retailer, and the other operates a discount store. Which is the discounter? Support your selection by referring to the common size statements.

d. Compute the return on assets and return on equity for each company.

e. Which company is more profitable from the stockholders' perspective?

f. Assume that a shortage of goods from suppliers is causing cost of goods sold to increase 10 percent for each company. Change the respective cost of goods sold balances in the Actual income statement column for each company. Note the new calculated amounts on the income statement and in the ratios. Which company's profits and returns are more sensitive to inventory price hikes?

COMPREHENSIVE PROBLEM

The following information is available for Pacilio Security Systems Sales and Service, Inc., for 2005, its first year of operations. Pacilio sells security systems and provides 24-hour alarm monitoring service. Pacilio sells two types of alarm systems, standard and deluxe. The following summary transactions occurred during 2005. (Round calculations to the nearest whole dollar.)

1. Acquired $50,000 cash from the issue of common stock.

2. Rented a building for a period of 12 months. On March 2, 2005, paid $6,000 for one year's rent in advance.

3. Purchased $800 of supplies with cash to be used over the next several months by the business.

4. Purchased 50 standard alarm systems for resale at a list price of $12,200 and 20 deluxe alarm systems at a list price of $10,160. The alarm systems were purchased on account with the terms 2/10 n/30.

5. Returned one of the standard alarms that had a list price of $240.

6. Installed 40 alarm systems during the year for a total sales amount of $23,000. The cost of these systems amounted to $12,200 (the standard alarms cost $7,220 and the deluxe alarms cost $5,160). $15,000 of the sales were on account and $8,000 were cash sales.

7. Paid the installers a total of $7,500 in salaries.

8. Sold $36,000 of monitoring services for the year. The services are billed to the customer each month.

9. Paid cash to settle part accounts payable in event 4. The payment was made *before* the discount period expired. At the time of purchase, the inventory had a list price of $9,000 and a net price of $8,820.

10. Paid cash to settle additional accounts payable. The payment was made *after* the discount period expired. At the time of purchase, the inventory had a list price of $9,000 and a net price of $8,820.

11. Collected $43,000 of accounts receivable during the year.

12. Paid advertising cost of $1,400 for the year.

13. Paid $1,100 for utilities expense for the year.

14. Paid a cash dividend of $2,000 to the shareholders.

Adjustments

15. There was $150 of supplies on hand at the end of the year.

16. Recognized the expired rent for the year.

Required

a. Record the above transactions in general journal form.

b. Post the transactions to T-accounts.

c. Prepare a trial balance.

d. Prepare an income statement, statement of changes in stockholders' equity, balance sheet, and statement of cash flows.

e. Close the temporary accounts to retained earnings.

f. Post the closing entries to T-accounts and prepare an after-closing trial balance.

CHAPTER 6

Accounting for Inventories

LEARNING OBJECTIVES

After you have mastered the material in this chapter, you will be able to:

1. Explain how different inventory cost flow methods (specific identification, FIFO, LIFO, and weighted average) affect financial statements.

2. Demonstrate the computational procedures for FIFO, LIFO, and weighted average.

3. Apply the lower-of-cost-or-market rule to inventory valuation.

4. Explain how fraud can be avoided through inventory control.

5. Use the gross margin method to estimate ending inventory.

6. Explain the importance of inventory turnover to a company's profitability.

The Curious Accountant

Albertson's is one of the largest food store chains in the United States, operating about 2,500 stores. As of February 2, 2006, the company had approximately $3 billion of inventory reported on its balance sheet. In the footnotes to its financial statements, Albertson's reported that it uses an inventory method that assumes its newest goods are sold first and its oldest goods are kept in inventory.

Can you think of any reason why a company selling perishable goods such as milk and vegetables uses an inventory method that assumes older goods are kept while newer goods are sold? (Answer on page 312.)

CHAPTER OPENING

In the previous chapter, we used the simplifying assumption that identical inventory items cost the same amount. In practice, businesses often pay different amounts for identical items. Suppose The Mountain Bike Company (TMBC) sells high-end Model 201 helmets. Since all Model 201 helmets are identical, does the helmet supplier charge TMBC the same amount for each helmet? Probably not. You have likely observed that prices change frequently.

Assume TMBC purchases one Model 201 helmet at a cost of $100. Two weeks later, TMBC purchases a second Model 201 helmet. Because the supplier has raised prices, the second helmet costs $110. If TMBC sells one of its two helmets, should it record $100 or $110 as cost of goods sold? The following section of this chapter discusses several acceptable alternative methods for determining the amount of cost of goods sold from which companies may choose under generally accepted accounting principles. ■

Inventory Cost Flow Methods

Recall that when goods are sold, product costs flow (are transferred) from the Inventory account to the Cost of Goods Sold account. Four acceptable methods for determining the amount of cost to transfer are (1) specific identification; (2) first-in, first-out (FIFO); (3) last-in, first-out (LIFO); and weighted average.

Specific Identification

Suppose TMBC tags inventory items so that it can identify which one is sold at the time of sale. TMBC could then charge the actual cost of the specific item sold to cost of goods sold. Recall that the first inventory item TMBC purchased cost $100 and the second item cost $110. Using **specific identification,** cost of goods sold would be $100 if the first item purchased were sold or $110 if the second item purchased were sold.

When a company's inventory consists of many low-priced, high-turnover goods, the record keeping necessary to use specific identification isn't practical. Imagine the difficulty of recording the cost of each specific food item in a grocery store. Another disadvantage of the specific identification method is the opportunity for managers to manipulate the income statement. For example, TMBC can report a lower cost of goods sold by selling the first instead of the second item. Specific identification is, however, frequently used for high-priced, low-turnover inventory items such as automobiles. For big ticket items like cars, customer demands for specific products limit management's ability to select which merchandise is sold and volume is low enough to manage the recordkeeping.

First-In, First-Out (FIFO)

The **first-in, first-out (FIFO) cost flow method** requires that the cost of the items purchased *first* be assigned to cost of goods sold. Using FIFO, TMBC's cost of goods sold is $100.

Last-In, First-Out (LIFO)

The **last-in, first-out (LIFO) cost flow method** requires that the cost of the items purchased *last* be charged to cost of goods sold. Using LIFO, TMBC's cost of goods sold is $110.

Weighted Average

To use the **weighted-average cost flow method,** first calculate the average cost per unit by dividing the *total cost* of the inventory available by the *total number* of units available. In the case of TMBC, the average cost per unit of the inventory is $105 ([$100 + $110] ÷ 2). Cost of goods sold is then calculated by multiplying the average cost per unit by the number of units sold. Using weighted average, TMBC's cost of goods sold is $105 ($105 × 1).

Physical Flow

The preceding discussion pertains to the flow of *costs* through the accounting records, *not* the actual **physical flow of goods.** Goods usually move physically on a FIFO basis, which means that the first items of merchandise acquired by a company (first-in) are the first items sold to its customers (first-out). The inventory items on hand at the end of the accounting period are typically the last items in (the most recently acquired goods). If companies did not sell their oldest inventory items first, inventories would include dated, less marketable merchandise. *Cost flow,* however, can differ from *physical flow.* For example, a company may use LIFO or weighted average for financial reporting even if its goods flow physically on a FIFO basis.

Effect of Cost Flow on Financial Statements

Effect on Income Statement

The cost flow method a company uses can significantly affect the gross margin reported in the income statement. To demonstrate, assume that TMBC sold the inventory item discussed previously for $120. The amounts of gross margin using the FIFO, LIFO, and weighted-average cost flow assumptions are shown in the following table:

	FIFO	LIFO	Weighted Average
Sales	$120	$120	$120
Cost of goods sold	(100)	(110)	(105)
Gross margin	$ 20	$ 10	$ 15

Even though the physical flow is assumed to be identical for each method, the gross margin reported under FIFO is double the amount reported under LIFO. Companies experiencing identical economic events (same units of inventory purchased and sold) can report significantly different results in their financial statements. Meaningful financial analysis requires an understanding of financial reporting practices.

Effect on Balance Sheet

Since total product costs are allocated between costs of goods sold and ending inventory, the cost flow method a company uses affects its balance sheet as well as its income statement. Since FIFO transfers the first cost to the income statement, it leaves the last cost on the balance sheet. Similarly, by transferring the last cost to the income statement, LIFO leaves the first cost in ending inventory. The weighted-average method bases both cost of goods sold and ending inventory on the average cost per unit. To illustrate, the ending inventory TMBC would report on the balance sheet using each of the three cost flow methods is shown in the following table:

	FIFO	LIFO	Weighted Average
Ending inventory	$110	$100	$105

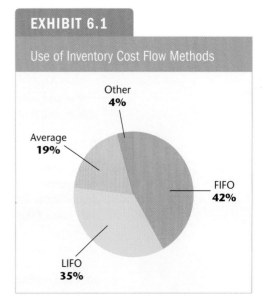

EXHIBIT 6.1

Use of Inventory Cost Flow Methods

Other 4%
Average 19%
FIFO 42%
LIFO 35%

Data Source: AICPA, *Accounting Trends and Techniques*, 2006.

The FIFO, LIFO, and weighted-average methods are all used extensively in business practice. The same company may even use one cost flow method for some of its products and different cost flow methods for other products. Exhibit 6.1 illustrates the relative use of the different cost flow methods among U.S. companies.

CHECK YOURSELF 6.1

Nash Office Supply (NOS) purchased two Model 303 copiers at different times. The first copier purchased cost $400 and the second copier purchased cost $450. NOS sold one of the copiers for $600. Determine the gross margin on the sale and the ending inventory balance assuming NOS accounts for inventory using (1) FIFO, (2) LIFO, and (3) weighted average.

Answer

	FIFO	LIFO	Weighted Average
Sales	$600	$600	$600
Cost of goods sold	(400)	(450)	(425)
Gross margin	$200	$150	$175
Ending inventory	$450	$400	$425

Demonstrate the computational procedures for FIFO, LIFO, and weighted average.

Multiple Layers with Multiple Quantities

The previous example illustrates different **inventory cost flow methods** using only two cost layers ($100 and $110) with only one unit of inventory in each layer. Actual business inventories are considerably more complex. Most real-world inventories are composed of multiple cost layers with different quantities of inventory in each layer. The underlying allocation concepts, however, remain unchanged.

For example, a different inventory item The Mountain Bike Company (TMBC) carries in its stores is a bike called the Eraser. TMBC's beginning inventory and two purchases of Eraser bikes are described below.

Jan. 1	Beginning inventory	10 units @ $200	=	$ 2,000
Mar. 18	First purchase	20 units @ $220	=	4,400
Aug. 21	Second purchase	25 units @ $250	=	6,250
Total cost of the 55 bikes available for sale				$12,650

The accounting records for the period show that TMBC paid cash for all Eraser bike purchases and that it sold 43 bikes at a cash price of $350 each.

Allocating Cost of Goods Available for Sale

The following discussion shows how to determine the cost of goods sold and ending inventory amounts under FIFO, LIFO, and weighted average. We show all three methods to demonstrate how they affect the financial statements differently; TMBC would actually use only one of the methods.

Regardless of the cost flow method chosen, TMBC must allocate the cost of goods available for sale ($12,650) between cost of goods sold and ending inventory. The amounts assigned to each category will differ depending on TMBC's cost flow method. Computations for each method are shown below.

FIFO Inventory Cost Flow

Recall that TMBC sold 43 Eraser bikes during the accounting period. The FIFO method transfers to the Cost of Goods Sold account the *cost of the first 43 bikes* TMBC had available to sell. The first 43 bikes acquired by TMBC were the 10 bikes in the beginning inventory (these were purchased in the prior period) plus the 20 bikes purchased in March and 13 of the bikes purchased in August. The expense recognized for the cost of these bikes ($9,650) is computed as follows:

Jan. 1	Beginning inventory	10 units @ $200	=	$2,000
Mar. 18	First purchase	20 units @ $220	=	4,400
Aug. 21	Second purchase	13 units @ $250	=	3,250
Total cost of the 43 bikes sold				$9,650

Since TMBC had 55 bikes available for sale it would have 12 bikes (55 available − 43 sold) in ending inventory. The cost assigned to these 12 bikes (the ending balance in the Inventory account) equals the cost of goods available for sale minus the cost of goods sold as shown below:

Cost of goods available for sale	$12,650
Cost of goods sold	(9,650)
Ending inventory balance	$ 3,000

We show the allocation of the cost of goods available for sale between cost of goods sold and ending inventory graphically below.

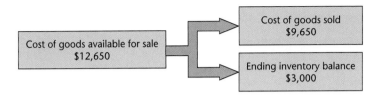

LIFO Inventory Cost Flow

Under LIFO, the cost of goods sold is the cost of the last 43 bikes acquired by TMBC, computed as follows:

Aug. 21	Second purchase	25 units @ $250 =	$ 6,250
Mar. 18	First purchase	18 units @ $220 =	3,960
Total cost of the 43 bikes sold			$10,210

The LIFO cost of the 12 bikes in ending inventory is computed as shown below:

Cost of goods available for sale	$12,650
Cost of goods sold	(10,210)
Ending inventory balance	$ 2,440

We show the allocation of the cost of goods available for sale between cost of goods sold and ending inventory graphically below.

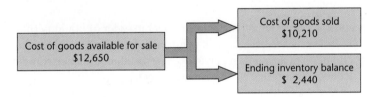

Weighted-Average Cost Flow

The weighted-average cost per unit is determined by dividing the *total cost of goods available for sale* by the *total number of units* available for sale. For TMBC, the weighted-average cost per unit is $230 ($12,650 ÷ 55). The weighted-average cost of goods sold is determined by multiplying the average cost per unit by the number of units sold ($230 × 43 = $9,890). The cost assigned to the 12 bikes in ending inventory is $2,760 (12 × $230).

We show the allocation of the cost of goods available for sale between cost of goods sold and ending inventory graphically below.

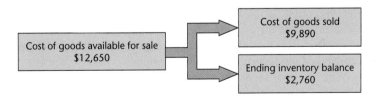

Effect of Cost Flow on Financial Statements

Exhibit 6.2 displays partial financial statements for The Mountain Bike Company (TMBC). This exhibit includes only information pertaining to the Eraser bikes inventory item described above. Other financial statement data are omitted.

Explain how different inventory cost flow methods (specific identification, FIFO, LIFO, and weighted average) affect financial statements.

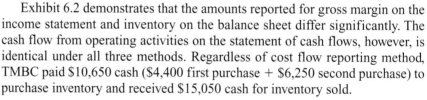

EXHIBIT 6.2

TMBC Company
Comparative Financial Statements

Partial Income Statements

	FIFO	LIFO	Weighted Average
Sales	$15,050	$15,050	$15,050
Cost of goods sold	(9,650)	(10,210)	(9,890)
Gross margin	5,400	4,840	5,160

Partial Balance Sheets

	FIFO	LIFO	Weighted Average
Assets			
Cash	$ XX	$ XX	$ XX
Accounts receivable	XX	XX	XX
Inventory	3,000	2,440	2,760

Partial Statements of Cash Flows

	FIFO	LIFO	Weighted Average
Operating Activities			
Cash inflow from customers	$15,050	$15,050	$15,050
Cash outflow for inventory	(10,650)	(10,650)	(10,650)

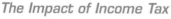

Recall that assets are reported on the balance sheet in order of liquidity (how quickly they are expected to be converted to cash). Since companies frequently sell inventory on account, inventory is less liquid than accounts receivable. As a result, companies commonly report inventory below accounts receivable on the balance sheet.

Exhibit 6.2 demonstrates that the amounts reported for gross margin on the income statement and inventory on the balance sheet differ significantly. The cash flow from operating activities on the statement of cash flows, however, is identical under all three methods. Regardless of cost flow reporting method, TMBC paid $10,650 cash ($4,400 first purchase + $6,250 second purchase) to purchase inventory and received $15,050 cash for inventory sold.

The Impact of Income Tax

Based on the financial statement information in Exhibit 6.2, which cost flow method should TMBC use? Most people initially suggest FIFO because FIFO reports the highest gross margin and the largest balance in ending inventory. However, other factors are relevant. FIFO produces the highest gross margin; it also produces the highest net income and the highest income tax expense. In contrast, LIFO results in recognizing the lowest gross margin, lowest net income, and the lowest income tax expense.

Will investors favor a company with more assets and higher net income or one with lower tax expense? Recognize that specific identification, FIFO, LIFO, and weighted average are *different methods of reporting the same information.* TMBC experienced only one set of events pertaining to Eraser bikes. Exhibit 6.2 reports those same events three different ways. However, if the FIFO reporting method causes TMBC to pay more taxes than the LIFO method, using FIFO will cause a real reduction in the value of the company. Paying more money in taxes leaves less money in the company.

Knowledgeable investors would be more attracted to TMBC if it uses LIFO because the lower tax payments allow the company to keep more value in the business.

Research suggests that, as a group, investors are knowledgeable. They make investment decisions based on economic substance regardless of how information is reported in financial statements.

The Income Statement versus the Tax Return

In some instances companies may use one accounting method for financial reporting and a different method to compute income taxes (the tax return must explain any differences). With respect to LIFO, however, the Internal Revenue Service requires that companies using LIFO for income tax purposes must also use LIFO for financial reporting. A company could not, therefore, get both the lower tax benefit provided by LIFO and the financial reporting advantage offered under FIFO.

Inflation versus Deflation

Our illustration assumes an inflationary environment (rising inventory prices). In a deflationary environment, the impact of using LIFO versus FIFO is reversed. LIFO produces tax advantages in an inflationary environment, while FIFO produces tax advantages in a deflationary environment. Companies operating in the computer industry where prices are falling would obtain a tax advantage by using FIFO. In contrast, companies that sell medical supplies in an inflationary environment would obtain a tax advantage by using LIFO.

Full Disclosure and Consistency

Generally accepted accounting principles allow each company to choose the inventory cost flow method best suited to its reporting needs. Because results can vary considerably among methods, however, the GAAP principle of **full disclosure** requires that financial statements disclose the method chosen. In addition, so that a company's financial statements are comparable from year to year, the GAAP principle of **consistency** generally requires that companies use the same cost flow method each period. The limited exceptions to the consistency principle are described in more advanced accounting courses.

Video 6.1

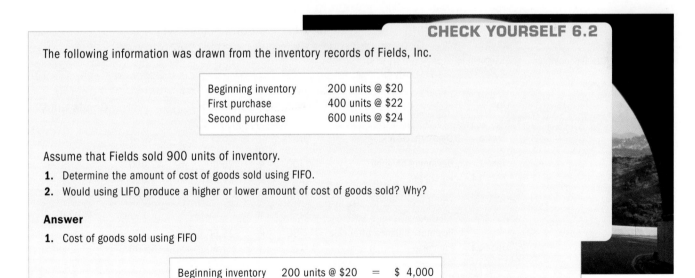

CHECK YOURSELF 6.2

The following information was drawn from the inventory records of Fields, Inc.

Beginning inventory	200 units @ $20
First purchase	400 units @ $22
Second purchase	600 units @ $24

Assume that Fields sold 900 units of inventory.

1. Determine the amount of cost of goods sold using FIFO.

2. Would using LIFO produce a higher or lower amount of cost of goods sold? Why?

Answer

1. Cost of goods sold using FIFO

Beginning inventory	200 units @ $20	=	$ 4,000
First purchase	400 units @ $22	=	8,800
Second purchase	300 units @ $24	=	7,200
Total cost of goods sold			$20,000

2. The inventory records reflect an inflationary environment of steadily rising prices. Since LIFO charges the latest costs (in this case the highest costs) to the income statement, using LIFO would produce a higher amount of cost of goods sold than would using FIFO.

Inventory Cost Flow When Sales and Purchases Occur Intermittently

Demonstrate the computational procedures for FIFO, LIFO, and weighted average.

In the previous illustrations, all purchases were made before any goods were sold. This section addresses more realistic conditions, when sales transactions occur intermittently with purchases. Consider a third product The Mountain Bike Company (TMBC) carries in its inventory, an energy bar called NeverStop. NeverStop is sold at concession booths sponsored by TMBC at bike races. TMBC purchases and sells NeverStop in bulk boxes. It refers to each box as a unit of product. TMBC's beginning inventory, purchases, and sales of NeverStop for the period are described below.

Date	Transaction	Description
Jan. 1	Beginning inventory	100 units @ $20.00
Feb. 14	Purchased	200 units @ $21.50
Apr. 5	Sold	220 units @ $30.00
June 21	Purchased	160 units @ $22.50
Aug. 18	Sold	100 units @ $30.00
Sept. 2	Purchased	280 units @ $23.50
Nov. 10	Sold	330 units @ $30.00

FIFO Cost Flow

Exhibit 6.3 displays the computations for cost of goods sold and inventory if TMBC uses the FIFO cost flow method. The inventory records are maintained in layers. Each time a sales transaction occurs, the unit cost in the first layer of inventory is assigned to the items sold. If the number of items sold exceeds the number of items in the first layer, the unit cost of the

EXHIBIT 6.3

Inventory Balance and Cost of Goods Sold using FIFO Cost Flow

Date	Description	Inventory Units		Cost		Total	Cost of Goods Sold
Jan. 1	Beginning balance	100	@	$20.00	=	$2,000	
Feb. 14	Purchase	200	@	21.50	=	4,300	
Apr. 5	Sale of 220 units	(100)	@	20.00	=	(2,000)	
		(120)	@	21.50	=	(2,580)	$ 4,580
	Inventory balance after sale	80	@	21.50	=	1,720	
June 21	Purchase	160	@	22.50	=	3,600	
Aug. 18	Sale of 100 units	(80)	@	21.50	=	(1,720)	
		(20)	@	22.50	=	(450)	2,170
	Inventory balance after sale	140	@	22.50	=	3,150	
Sept. 2	Purchase	280	@	23.50	=	6,580	
Nov. 10	Sale of 330 units	(140)	@	22.50	=	(3,150)	
		(190)	@	23.50	=	(4,465)	7,615
	Ending inventory balance	90	@	23.50	=	$2,115	
	Total cost of goods sold						$14,365

next layer is assigned to the remaining number of units sold, and so on. For example, the cost assigned to the 220 units of inventory sold on April 5 is determined as follows:

100 units of inventory in the first layer $\times$ $20.00 per unit	=	$2,000
+ 120 units of inventory in the second layer $\times$ $21.50 per unit	=	2,580
220 units for total cost of goods sold for the April 5 sale	=	$4,580

The cost of goods sold for subsequent sales transactions is similarly computed.

Using FIFO, and assuming a selling price of $30 per unit, gross margin for the period is computed as follows:

Sales (650 units @ $30 each)	$19,500
Cost of goods sold	(14,365)
Gross margin	$ 5,135

Weighted-Average and LIFO Cost Flows

When maintaining perpetual inventory records, using the weighted-average or LIFO cost flow methods leads to timing difficulties. For example, under LIFO, the cost of the *last* items purchased *during an accounting period* is the first amount transferred to cost of goods sold. When sales and purchases occur intermittently, the cost of the last items purchased isn't known at the time earlier sales occur. For example, when TMBC sold merchandise in April, it did not know what the replacement inventory purchased in September would cost.

Accountants can solve cost flow timing problems by keeping perpetual records of the quantities (number of units) of items purchased and sold separately from the related costs. Keeping records of quantities moving in and out of inventory, even though cost information is unavailable, provides many of the benefits of a perpetual inventory system. For example, management can determine the quantity of lost, damaged, or stolen goods and the point at which to reorder merchandise. At the end of the accounting period, when the cost of all inventory purchases is available, costs are assigned to the quantity data that have been maintained perpetually. Although further discussion of the weighted-average and LIFO cost flow methods is beyond the scope of this text, recognize that timing problems associated with intermittent sales are manageable.

FOCUS ON   INTERNATIONAL ISSUES

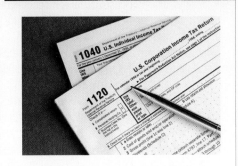

THE INFLUENCE OF TAX ACCOUNTING ON GAAP

As noted in this chapter, a U.S. company can use LIFO for income tax reporting *only* if it also uses LIFO for GAAP. This is unusual because tax accounting in the United States is separate and distinct from financial reporting under GAAP; the Internal Revenue Service has no formal power to establish GAAP. In the case of LIFO, however, the IRS has an indirect influence on the inventory method that a company chooses for financial reporting. The tax accounting rules of most other countries do not allow the use of the LIFO cost flow method, even if the country's GAAP does allow its use. If U.S. tax rules did not allow the use of LIFO under any circumstances, how many companies would use it for financial reporting? Very few!

The separation between tax accounting and GAAP accounting that exists in the United States does not exist in many other countries. In some countries, a company cannot deduct a cost for tax purposes unless the same cost is shown as an expense on the company's GAAP-based income statement. In other words, the unusual situation that exists in the United States only for the use of LIFO is the general rule in many countries. Countries whose tax laws greatly influence GAAP reporting include France, Germany, and Japan.

Lower-of-Cost-or-Market Rule

LO 3

Apply the lower-of-cost-or-market rule to inventory valuation.

Regardless of whether a company uses FIFO, LIFO, weighted average, or specific identification, once the cost of ending inventory has been determined, generally accepted accounting principles require that the cost be compared with the end of period market value and that the inventory be reported at *lower of cost or market. Market* is defined as the amount the company would have to pay to *replace* the merchandise. If the replacement cost is less than the actual cost, regardless of whether the decline in market value is due to physical damage, deterioration, obsolescence, or a general price-level decline, the loss must be recognized in the current period.

The **lower-of-cost-or-market rule** can be applied to (1) each individual inventory item, (2) major classes or categories of inventory, or (3) the entire stock of inventory in the aggregate. The most common practice is the individualized application. To illustrate applying the rule to individual inventory items, assume that The Mountain Bike Company (TMBC) has in ending inventory 100 T-shirts it purchased at a cost of $14 each. If the year-end replacement cost of the shirts is above $14, TMBC will report the ending inventory at cost (100 × $14 = $1,400). However, if outsourcing permits the manufacturer to reduce the unit price of the shirts to $11, then TMBC's replacement cost falls below the historical cost, and the inventory must be written down to $1,100 (100 × $11).

Exhibit 6.4 illustrates computing the ending inventory value on an item-by-item basis for a company that has four different inventory items. The company must write down the $30,020 historical cost of its ending inventory to $28,410. This $1,610 write-down reduces the company's gross margin for the period. If the company keeps perpetual inventory records, the effect of the write-down and the journal entry to record it are as follows:

Assets	=	Liab.	+	Equity	Rev.	−	Exp.	=	Net Inc.	Cash Flow
(1,610)	=	NA	+	(1,610)	NA	−	1,610	=	(1,610)	NA

Account Title	Debit	Credit
Cost of Goods Sold (Inventory Loss)	1,610	
Inventory		1,610

REALITY BYTES

To avoid spoilage or obsolescence, most companies use a first-in, first-out (FIFO) approach for the flow of physical goods. The older goods (first units purchased) are sold before the newer goods are sold. For example, Albertson's and other food stores stack older merchandise at the front of the shelf where customers are more likely to pick it up first. As a result, merchandise is sold before it becomes dated. However, when timing is not an issue, convenience may dictate the use of the last-in, first-out (LIFO) method. Examples of products that frequently move on a LIFO basis include rock, gravel, dirt, or other nonwasting assets. Indeed, rock, gravel, and dirt are normally stored in piles that are unprotected from weather. New inventory is simply piled on top of the old. Inventory that is sold is taken from the top of the pile because it is convenient to do so. Accordingly, the last inventory purchased is the first inventory sold. For example, Vulcan Materials Co., which claims to be the nation's largest producer of construction aggregates (stone and gravel), uses LIFO. Regardless of whether the flow of physical goods occurs on a LIFO or FIFO basis, costs can flow differently. The flow of inventory through the physical facility is a separate issue from the flow of costs through the accounting system.

EXHIBIT 6.4

Determination of Ending Inventory at Lower of Cost or Market

Item	Quantity (a)	Unit Cost (b)	Unit Market (c)	Total Cost (a × b)	Total Market (a × c)	Lower of Cost or Market
A	320	$21.50	$22.00	$ 6,880	$ 7,040	$ 6,880
B	460	18.00	16.00	8,280	7,360	7,360
C	690	15.00	14.00	10,350	9,660	9,660
D	220	20.50	23.00	4,510	5,060	4,510
				$30,020	$29,120	$28,410

Conceptually, the loss should be reported as an operating expense on the income statement. However, if the amount is immaterial, it can be included in cost of goods sold.

Avoiding Fraud in Merchandising Businesses

For merchandising businesses, inventory is often the largest single asset reported on the balance sheet and cost of goods sold is normally the largest single expense reported on the income statement. For example, the 2002 income statement for Publix (a large grocery store chain) reported $16.0 billion of sales and approximately $11.6 billion of cost of goods sold, which means cost of goods sold for Publix was about 72 percent of revenue. In contrast, the next largest expense (operating and administrative expense) was approximately $3.4 billion, or 21 percent of revenue. While cost of goods sold represents only one expense account, the operating and administrative expense category actually combines many, perhaps hundreds, of individual expense accounts, such as depreciation, salaries, utilities, and so on. Because the inventory and cost of goods sold accounts are so significant, they are attractive targets for concealing fraud. For example, suppose a manager attempts to perpetrate a fraud by deliberately understating expenses. The understatement is less likely to be detected if it is hidden in the $11.6 billion Cost of Goods Sold account than if it is recorded in one of the smaller operating expense accounts.

Because the inventory and cost of goods sold accounts are susceptible to abuse, auditors and financial analysts carefully examine them for signs of fraud. Using tools to detect possible inventory misstatements requires understanding how overstatement or understatement of inventory affects the financial statements. To illustrate, assume that a company overstates its year-end inventory balance by $1,000. This inventory overstatement results in a $1,000 understatement of cost of goods sold, as shown in the following schedule:

LO 4

Explain how fraud can be avoided through inventory control.

Topic Tackler

PLUS

6-2

	Ending Inventory Is Accurate	Ending Inventory Is Overstated	Effect
Beginning inventory	$ 4,000	$ 4,000	
Purchases	6,000	6,000	
Cost of goods available for sale	10,000	10,000	
Ending inventory	(3,000)	(4,000)	$1,000 Overstated
Cost of goods sold	$ 7,000	$ 6,000	$1,000 Understated

The understatement of cost of goods sold results in the overstatement of gross margin, which leads to an overstatement of net earnings, as indicated in the following income statement:

	Ending Inventory Is Accurate	Ending Inventory Is Overstated	Effect
Sales	$11,000	$11,000	
Cost of goods sold	(7,000)	(6,000)	$1,000 Understated
Gross margin	$ 4,000	$ 5,000	$1,000 Overstated

On the balance sheet, assets (inventory) and stockholders' equity (retained earnings) are overstated as follows:

	Ending Inventory Is Accurate	Ending Inventory Is Overstated	Effect
Assets			
Cash	$1,000	$ 1,000	
Inventory	3,000	4,000	$1,000 Overstated
Other assets	5,000	5,000	
Total assets	$9,000	$10,000	
Stockholders' equity			
Common stock	$5,000	$ 5,000	
Retained earnings	4,000	5,000	$1,000 Overstated
Total stockholders' equity	$9,000	$10,000	

Managers may be tempted to overstate the physical count of the ending inventory in order to report higher amounts of gross margin on the income statement and larger amounts of assets on the balance sheet. How can companies discourage managers from deliberately overstating the physical count of the ending inventory? The first line of defense is to assign the task of recording inventory transactions to different employees from those responsible for counting inventory.

Recall that under the perpetual system, increases and decreases in inventory are recorded at the time inventory is purchased and sold. If the records are maintained accurately, the balance in the inventory account should agree with the amount of physical inventory on hand. If a manager were to attempt to manipulate the financial statements by overstating the physical count of inventory, there would be a discrepancy between the accounting records and the physical count. In other words, a successful fraud requires controlling both the physical count and the recording process. If the counting and recording duties are performed by different individuals, fraud requires collusion, which reduces the likelihood of its occurrence. The separation of duties is an internal control procedure discussed further in the next chapter.

Because motives for fraud persist, even the most carefully managed companies cannot guarantee that no fraud will ever occur. As a result, auditors and financial analysts have developed tools to test for financial statement manipulation. The gross margin method of estimating the ending inventory balance is such a tool.

Estimating the Ending Inventory Balance

LO 5

Use the gross margin method to estimate ending inventory.

The **gross margin method** assumes that the percentage of gross margin to sales remains relatively stable over time. To the extent that this assumption is accurate, the gross margin ratio from prior periods can be used to accurately estimate the current period's ending inventory. To illustrate, first review the information in Exhibit 6.5 which pertains to the T-Shirt Company.

EXHIBIT 6.5

THE T-SHIRT COMPANY
Schedule for Estimating the Ending Inventory Balance
For the Six Months Ending June 30, 2008

Beginning inventory	$ 5,100	
Purchases	18,500	
Cost of goods available for sale		$23,600
Sales through June 30, 2008	22,000	
Less: Estimated gross margin*	?	
Estimated cost of goods sold		?
Estimated ending inventory		$?

*Historically, gross margin has amounted to approximately 25 percent of sales.

The estimated cost of ending inventory can be computed as follows:

1. Calculate the expected gross margin ratio using financial statement data from prior periods. Accuracy may be improved by averaging gross margin and sales data over several accounting periods. For the T-Shirt Company, assume the average gross margin for the prior five years ÷ the average sales for the same five-year period = 25% expected gross margin ratio.

2. Multiply the expected gross margin ratio by the current period's sales ($22,000 × 0.25 = $5,500) to estimate the amount of gross margin.

3. Subtract the estimated gross margin from sales ($22,000 − $5,500 = $16,500) to estimate the amount of cost of goods sold.

4. Subtract the estimated cost of goods sold from the amount of goods available for sale ($23,600 − $16,500 = $7,100) to estimate the amount of ending inventory.

The estimated amount of ending inventory ($7,100) can be compared to the book balance and the physical count of inventory. If the book balance or the physical count is significantly higher than the estimated inventory balance, the analysis suggests the possibility of financial statement manipulation.

Other analytical comparisons are also useful. For example, the current year's gross margin ratio can be compared to last year's ratio. If cost of goods sold has been understated (ending inventory overstated), the gross margin ratio will be inflated. If this year's ratio is significantly higher than last year's, further analysis is required.

Although it may seem common because of the intense publicity generated when it occurs, fraud is the exception rather than the norm. In fact, growth in the inventory account balance usually results from natural business conditions. For example, a company that is adding new stores is expected to report growth in its inventory balance. Nevertheless, significant growth in inventory that is not explained by accompanying sales growth signals the need to analyze further for evidence of manipulation.

Since one year's ending inventory balance becomes the next year's beginning inventory balance, inaccuracies carry forward from one accounting period to the next. Persistent inventory overstatements result in an inventory account balance that spirals higher and higher. A fraudulently increasing inventory balance is likely to be discovered eventually.

To avoid detection, a manager who has previously overstated inventory will need to write the inventory back down in a subsequent accounting period. Therefore significant decreases, as well as increases, in the inventory balance or the gross margin ratio should be investigated. A manager may try to justify inventory write-downs by claiming that the inventory was lost, damaged, stolen, or had declined in value below historical cost. While there are valid reasons for writing down inventory, the possibility of fraud should be investigated.

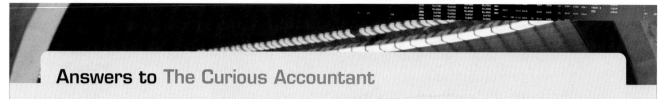

Answers to The Curious Accountant

Even though **Albertson's** uses the last-in, first-out *cost flow assumption* for financial reporting purposes, it, like most other companies, actually sells its oldest inventory first. As explained in the text material, GAAP allows a company to report its costs of goods sold in an order that is different from the actual physical flow of its goods. The primary reason some companies use the LIFO assumption is to reduce income taxes. Over the years, Albertson's has saved approximately $100 million in taxes by using the LIFO versus the FIFO cost flow assumption when computing its taxable income.

CHECK YOURSELF 6.3

A physical count of Cantrell Inc.'s inventory revealed an ending balance of $6,020. The company's auditor decided to use the gross margin method to test the accuracy of the physical count. The accounting records indicate that the beginning inventory balance had been $20,000. During the period Cantrell had purchased $70,000 of inventory and had recognized $140,000 of sales revenue. Cantrell's gross margin percentage is normally 40 percent of sales. Develop an estimate of the amount of ending inventory and comment on the accuracy of the physical count.

Answer

Goods available for sale is $90,000 ($20,000 beginning inventory + $70,000 purchases). Estimated cost of goods sold is $84,000 ($140,000 sales − [$140,000 × 0.40] gross margin). Estimated ending inventory is $6,000 ($90,000 goods available for sale − $84,000 cost of goods sold). The difference between the physical count and the estimated balance ($6,020 − $6,000 = $20) is immaterial. Therefore the gross margin estimate is consistent with the physical count.

THE FINANCIAL ANALYST

Explain the importance of inventory turnover to a company's profitability.

Assume a grocery store sells two brands of kitchen cleansers, Zjax and Cosmos. Zjax costs $1 and sells for $1.25, resulting in a gross margin of $0.25 ($1.25 − $1.00). Cosmos costs $1.20 and sells for $1.60, resulting in a gross margin of $0.40 ($1.60 − $1.20). Is it more profitable to stock Cosmos than Zjax? Not if the store can sell significantly more cans of Zjax.

Suppose the lower price results in higher customer demand for Zjax. If the store can sell 7,000 units of Zjax but only 3,000 units of Cosmos, Zjax will provide a total gross profit of $1,750 (7,000 units × $0.25 per unit), while Cosmos will provide only $1,200 (3,000 units × $0.40 per unit). How fast inventory sells is as important as the spread between cost and selling price. To determine how fast inventory is selling, financial analysts calculate a ratio that measures the *average number of days it takes to sell inventory.*

Average Number of Days to Sell Inventory

The first step in calculating the average number of days it takes to sell inventory is to compute the **inventory turnover,** as follows:

$$\frac{\text{Cost of goods sold}}{\text{Inventory}}$$

The result of this computation is the number of times the balance in the Inventory account is turned over (sold) each year. To more easily interpret the inventory turnover ratio, analysts often take a further step and determine the **average number of days to sell inventory** (also called the **average days in inventory**), computed as

$$\frac{365}{\text{Inventory turnover}}$$

Is It a Marketing or an Accounting Decision?

As suggested, overall profitability depends upon two elements: gross margin and inventory turnover. The most profitable combination would be to carry high-margin inventory that turns over rapidly. To be competitive, however, companies must often concentrate on one or the other of the elements. For example, *discount merchandisers* such as Costco offer lower prices to stimulate greater sales. In contrast, fashionable stores such as Neiman Marcus charge higher prices to compensate for their slower inventory turnover. These upscale stores justify their higher prices by offering superior style, quality, convenience, service, etc. While decisions about pricing, advertising, service, and so on are often viewed as marketing decisions, effective choices require understanding the interaction between the gross margin percentage and inventory turnover.

Real-World Data

Exhibit 6.6 shows the *average number of days to sell inventory* for eight real-world companies in three different industries. The numbers pertain to fiscal years that ended in late 2005 or early 2006. The data raise several questions.

Explain the importance of inventory turnover to a company's profitability.

First, why do Concha y Toro and Willamette Valley Vineyards take so long to sell their inventories compared to the other companies? Both of these companies produce and sell wine. Quality wine is aged before it is sold; time spent in inventory is actually a part of the production process. In the wine world, wines produced by Willamette Valley are, on average, considered to be of higher quality than those produced by Concha y Toro. This higher quality results, in part, from the longer time Willamette Valley wines spend aging prior to sale.

Why does Starbucks hold its inventory so much longer than the other two fast-food businesses? Starbucks' inventory is mostly coffee. It is more difficult for Starbucks to obtain coffee than it is for McDonald's to obtain beef or Yum! Brands to obtain flour, cheese, and fresh vegetables. Very little coffee is grown in the United States (Hawaii is the only state that produces coffee). Since purchasing coffee requires substantial delivery time, Starbucks cannot order its inventory at the last minute. This problem is further complicated by the fact that coffee harvests are seasonal. Cattle, on the other hand, can be processed into hamburgers year-round. As a result, Starbucks must hold inventory longer than McDonald's or Yum! Brands.

EXHIBIT 6.6

Industry	Company	Average Number of Days to Sell Inventory
Fast Food	McDonald's	10
	Starbucks	77
	Yum! Brands	12
Office Supplies	Office Depot	50
	OfficeMax	50
	Staples	54
Wine	Concha y Toro	203
	Willamette Valley Vineyards	348

Finally, why do companies in the office supply business take longer to sell inventory than those in the fast-food business? Part of the answer is that food is perishable and stationery is not. But there is also the fact that office supply stores carry many more inventory items than do fast-food restaurants. It is much easier to anticipate customer demand if a company sells only 20 different items than if the company sells 20,000 different items. The problem of anticipating customer demand is solved by holding larger quantities of inventory.

Effects of Cost Flow on Ratio Analysis

Since the amounts of ending inventory and cost of goods sold are affected by the cost flow method (FIFO, LIFO, etc.) a company uses, the gross margin and inventory turnover ratios are also affected by the cost flow method used. Further, since cost of goods sold affects the amount of net income and retained earnings, many other ratios are also affected by the inventory cost flow method that a company uses. Financial analysts must consider that the ratios they use can be significantly influenced by which accounting methods a company chooses.

‹‹ A Look Back

This chapter discussed the inventory cost flow methods of first-in, first-out (FIFO), last-in, first-out (LIFO), weighted average, and specific identification. Under *FIFO,* the cost of the items purchased first is reported on the income statement, and the cost of the items purchased last is reported on the balance sheet. Under *LIFO,* the cost of the items purchased last is reported on the income statement, and the cost of the items purchased first is reported on the balance sheet. Under the *weighted-average method,* the average cost of inventory is reported on both the income statement and the balance sheet. Finally, under specific identification, the actual cost of the goods is reported on the income statement and the balance sheet.

Generally accepted accounting principles often allow companies to account for the same types of events in different ways. The different cost flow methods presented in this chapter—FIFO, LIFO, weighted average, and specific identification—are examples of alternative accounting procedures allowed by GAAP. Financial analysts must be aware that financial statement amounts are affected by the accounting methods that a company uses as well as the economic activity it experiences.

This chapter also explained how to calculate the time it takes a company to sell its inventory. The measure of how fast inventory sells is called *inventory turnover;* it is computed by dividing cost of goods sold by inventory. The result of this computation is the number of times the balance in the inventory account is turned over each year. The *average number of days to sell inventory* can be determined by dividing the number of days in a year (365) by the inventory turnover ratio.

›› A Look Forward

Chapter 7 examines accounting for cash and the system of internal controls. Internal controls are the accounting practices and procedures that companies use to protect assets and to ensure that transactions are recorded accurately. You will learn that companies account for small disbursements of cash, called *petty cash disbursements,* differently than they do for large disbursements. You will also learn how to prepare a formal bank reconciliation.

Erie Jewelers sells gold earrings. Its beginning inventory of Model 407 gold earrings consisted of 100 pairs of earrings at $50 per pair. Erie purchased two batches of Model 407 earrings during the year. The first batch purchased consisted of 150 pairs at $53 per pair; the second batch consisted of 200 pairs at $56 per pair. During the year, Erie sold 375 pairs of Model 407 earrings.

Required

Determine the amount of product cost Erie would allocate to cost of goods sold and ending inventory assuming that Erie uses (a) FIFO, (b) LIFO, and (c) weighted average.

Solution to Requirements a–c

Goods Available for Sale

Beginning inventory	100	@	$50	=	$ 5,000
First purchase	150	@	53	=	7,950
Second purchase	200	@	56	=	11,200
Goods available for sale	450				$24,150

a. FIFO

Cost of Goods Sold	Pairs		Cost per Pair		Cost of Goods Sold
From beginning inventory	100	@	$50	=	$ 5,000
From first purchase	150	@	53	=	7,950
From second purchase	125	@	56	=	7,000
Total pairs sold	375				$19,950

Ending inventory = Goods available for sale − Cost of goods sold

Ending inventory = $24,150 − $19,950 = $4,200

b. LIFO

Cost of Goods Sold	Pairs		Cost per Pair		Cost of Goods Sold
From second purchase	200	@	$56	=	$11,200
From first purchase	150	@	53	=	7,950
From beginning inventory	25	@	50	=	1,250
Total pairs sold	375				$20,400

Ending inventory = Goods available for sale − Cost of goods sold

Ending inventory = $24,150 − $20,400 = $3,750

c. Weighted average

Goods available for sale ÷ Total pairs = Cost per pair

$24,150   ÷   450   = $53.6667

Cost of goods sold   375 units @ $53.6667 = $20,125

Ending inventory   75 units @ $53.6667 = $4,025

KEY TERMS

average days in inventory
  ratio (sometimes called
  average number of days
  to sell inventory
  ratio) 313
consistency 305

first-in, first-out (FIFO) cost
  flow method 300
full disclosure 305
gross margin method 310
inventory cost flow
  methods 302

inventory turnover 312
last-in, first-out (LIFO) cost
  flow method 300
lower-of-cost-or-market
  rule 308
physical flow of goods 300

specific identification 300
weighted-average cost flow
  method 300

QUESTIONS

1. Name and discuss the four cost flow methods discussed in this chapter.

2. What are some advantages and disadvantages of the specific identification method of accounting for inventory?

3. What are some advantages and disadvantages of using the FIFO method of inventory valuation?

4. What are some advantages and disadvantages of using the LIFO method of inventory valuation?

5. In an inflationary period, which inventory cost flow method will produce the highest net income? Explain.

6. In an inflationary period, which inventory cost flow method will produce the largest amount of total assets on the balance sheet? Explain.

7. What is the difference between the flow of costs and the physical flow of goods?

8. Does the choice of cost flow method (FIFO, LIFO, or weighted average) affect the statement of cash flows? Explain.

9. Assume that Key Co. purchased 1,000 units of merchandise in its first year of operations for $25 per unit. The company sold 850 units for $40. What is the amount of cost of goods sold using FIFO? LIFO? Weighted average?

10. Assume that Key Co. purchased 1,500 units of merchandise in its second year of operation for $27 per unit. Its beginning inventory was determined in Question 9. Assuming that 1,500 units are sold, what is the amount of cost of goods sold using FIFO? LIFO? Weighted average?

11. Refer to Questions 9 and 10. Which method might be preferable for financial statements? For income tax reporting? Explain.

12. In an inflationary period, which cost flow method, FIFO or LIFO, produces the larger cash flow? Explain.

13. Which inventory cost flow method produces the highest net income in a deflationary period?

14. How does the phrase *lower-of-cost-or-market* apply to inventory valuation?

15. If some merchandise declined in value because of damage or obsolescence, what effect will the lower-of-cost-or-market rule have on the income statement? Explain.

16. What is a situation in which estimates of the amount of inventory may be useful or even necessary?

17. How can management manipulate net income using inventory fraud?

18. If the amount of goods available for sale is $123,000, the amount of sales is $130,000, and the gross margin is 25 percent of sales, what is the amount of estimated ending inventory?

19. Assume that inventory is overstated by $1,500 at the end of 2008 but is corrected in 2009. What effect will this have on the 2008 income statement? The 2008 balance sheet? The 2009 income statement? The 2009 balance sheet?

20. What information does inventory turnover provide?

21. What is an example of a business that would have a high inventory turnover? A low inventory turnover?

Multiple-choice questions are provided on the text Web site at www.mhhe.com/edmonds6e.

Quiz 6

All Exercises in Series A are available with McGraw-Hill's Homework Manager®

Exercise 6-1A   *Understanding the need for cost flow*

L.O. 1

Carol Hudson says cost flow doesn't make any difference in her business. Her company operates in a market of rapidly declining prices. If she holds inventory for any extended period of time, it will be worth less than she paid for it. She is able to earn a good profit by selling inventory rapidly. Indeed, she frequently has firm sales orders before she confirms her purchases. In 2008, she bought and sold 8,000 units of product. There was no beginning or ending inventory.

Required

a. Will cost of goods sold be higher, lower, or the same if Carol uses FIFO versus LIFO?

b. Write a brief memo that explains your response to Requirement *a*.

Exercise 6-2A   *Determine the cost of goods sold*

L.O. 1, 2

The following information applies to Westward Company.

Beginning inventory	200 units @ $23 each
Purchases	600 units @ $25 each

Westward sold 700 units of inventory during the year.

Required

a. Determine the cost of goods sold assuming a FIFO cost flow.

b. Determine the cost of goods sold assuming a LIFO cost flow.

c. Determine the cost of goods sold assuming a weighted-average cost flow.

Exercise 6-3A   *Determine the ending inventory balance*

L.O. 1, 2

The following information applies to Kassouf Company.

Beginning inventory	100 units @ $10 each
Purchases	400 units @ $12 each

Kassouf sold 420 units of inventory during the year.

Required

a. Determine the balance in ending inventory assuming a FIFO cost flow.

b. Determine the balance in ending inventory assuming a LIFO cost flow.

c. Determine the balance in ending inventory assuming a weighted-average cost flow.

Exercise 6-4A   *Cost flow versus cash flow*

L.O. 1, 2

Hagel Company had beginning inventory of 100 units that cost $5 each. These items were purchased with cash in the previous accounting period. During the current accounting period, Hagel paid cash to purchase 500 units of inventory at a price of $6 each. Hagel sold 520 units of inventory at a cash price of $10 per unit.

Required

a. Determine the gross margin under FIFO and LIFO.

b. Determine the cash flow from operating activities under FIFO and LIFO.

L.O. 1, 2   **Exercise 6-5A**   *Cost flow versus physical flow*

Kelly Sales Company purchased two identical inventory items. The first item purchased cost $58; the second item purchased several months later when prices had fallen cost $52. Kelly sold the item purchased second for $70.

Required

a. Determine the cost of goods sold and the amount of ending inventory under FIFO, LIFO, weighted average (WA), and specific identification (SI).

b. How would your answer to Requirement *a* differ if Kelly had sold the item purchased first instead of the one purchased second?

L.O. 1, 2   **Exercise 6-6A**   *Allocating product cost between cost of goods sold and ending inventory*

Ming Co. started the year with no inventory. During the year, it purchased two identical inventory items. The inventory was purchased at different times. The first purchase cost $2,400 and the other, $3,000. One of the items was sold during the year.

Required

Based on this information, identify the cost flow method that will produce:

a. The highest amount of net income.

b. The lowest balance in the Inventory account shown on the balance sheet.

c. The highest amount of cash flow from operating activities.

L.O. 1, 2   **Exercise 6-7A**   *Allocating product cost between cost of goods sold and ending inventory: Multiple purchases*

Rainey Company sells coffee makers used in business offices. Its beginning inventory of coffee makers was 200 units at $25 per unit. During the year, Rainey made two batch purchases of coffee makers. The first was a 300-unit purchase at $30 per unit; the second was a 250-unit purchase at $35 per unit. During the period, Rainey sold 700 coffee makers.

Required

Determine the amount of product costs that would be allocated to cost of goods sold and ending inventory, assuming that Rainey uses

a. FIFO.

b. LIFO.

c. Weighted average.

L.O. 1, 2   **Exercise 6-8A**   *Effect of inventory cost flow (FIFO, LIFO, and weighted average) on gross margin*

The following information pertains to Boone Company for 2009.

Beginning inventory	70 units @ $26
Units purchased	280 units @ $30

Ending inventory consisted of 30 units. Boone sold 320 units at $40 each. All purchases and sales were made with cash.

Required

a. Compute the gross margin for Boone Company using the following cost flow assumptions: (1) FIFO, (2) LIFO, and (3) weighted average.

b. What is the dollar amount of difference in net income between using FIFO versus LIFO? (Ignore income tax considerations.)

c. Determine the cash flow from operating activities, using each of the three cost flow assumptions listed in Requirement *a*. Ignore the effect of income taxes. Explain why these cash flows have no differences.

Exercise 6-9A   *Effect of inventory cost flow on ending inventory balance and gross margin*   **L.O. 1, 2**

Ross Sales had the following transactions for DVDs in 2010, its first year of operations.

Jan. 20	Purchased 75 units @ $15	=	$1,125
Apr. 21	Purchased 450 units @ $20	=	9,000
July 25	Purchased 300 units @ $23	=	6,900
Sept. 19	Purchased 100 units @ $26	=	2,600

During the year, Ross Sales sold 850 DVDs for $60 each.

Required

a. Compute the amount of ending inventory Ross would report on the balance sheet, assuming the following cost flow assumptions: (1) FIFO, (2) LIFO, and (3) weighted average.

b. Compute the difference in gross margin between the FIFO and LIFO cost flow assumptions.

Exercise 6-10A   *Income tax effect of shifting from FIFO to LIFO*   **L.O. 1, 2**

The following information pertains to the inventory of the Eaton Company:

Jan. 1	Beginning Inventory	600 units @ $22
Apr. 1	Purchased	2,500 units @ $25
Oct. 1	Purchased	700 units @ $28

During the year, Eaton sold 3,300 units of inventory at $40 per unit and incurred $15,000 of operating expenses. Eaton currently uses the FIFO method but is considering a change to LIFO. All transactions are cash transactions. Assume a 30 percent income tax rate.

Required

a. Prepare income statements using FIFO and LIFO.

b. Determine the amount of income taxes Eaton would save if it changed cost flow methods.

c. Determine the cash flow from operating activities under FIFO and LIFO.

d. Explain why cash flow from operating activities is lower under FIFO when that cost flow method produced the higher gross margin.

Exercise 6-11A   *Effect of inventory cost flow assumption on financial statements*   **L.O. 1**

Required

For each of the following situations, fill in the blank with *FIFO, LIFO,* or *weighted average.*

a. _____ would produce the highest amount of net income in an inflationary environment.

b. _____ would produce the highest amount of assets in an inflationary environment.

c. _____ would produce the lowest amount of net income in a deflationary environment.

d. _____ would produce the same unit cost for assets and cost of goods sold in an inflationary environment.

e. _____ would produce the lowest amount of net income in an inflationary environment.

f. _____ would produce an asset value that was the same regardless of whether the environment was inflationary or deflationary.

g. _____ would produce the lowest amount of assets in an inflationary environment.

h. _____ would produce the highest amount of assets in a deflationary environment.

Exercise 6-12A   *Effect of FIFO versus LIFO on income tax expense*   **L.O. 1, 2**

Beth Porter, Inc., had sales of $225,000 for 2009, its first year of operation. On April 2, the company purchased 200 units of inventory at $210 per unit. On September 1, an additional 150 units were purchased for $230 per unit. The company had 50 units on hand at the end of the year. The company's income tax rate is 35 percent. All transactions are cash transactions.

Required

a. The preceding paragraph describes five accounting events: (1) a sales transaction, (2) the first purchase of inventory, (3) a second purchase of inventory, (4) the recognition of cost of goods sold expense, and (5) the payment of income tax expense. Record the amounts of each event in horizontal statements models like the following ones, assuming first a FIFO and then a LIFO cost flow.

Effect of Events on Financial Statements
Panel 1: FIFO Cost Flow

Event No.	Balance Sheet									Income Statement						Statement of Cash Flows
	Cash	+	Inventory	=	C. Stk.	+	Ret. Earn.			Rev.	−	Exp.	=	Net Inc.		

Panel 2: LIFO Cost Flow

Event No.	Balance Sheet									Income Statement						Statement of Cash Flows
	Cash	+	Inventory	=	C. Stk.	+	Ret. Earn.			Rev.	−	Exp.	=	Net Inc.		

b. Compute net income using FIFO.

c. Compute net income using LIFO.

d. Explain the difference, if any, in the amount of income tax expense incurred using the two cost flow assumptions.

e. How does the use of the FIFO versus the LIFO cost flow assumptions affect the statement of cash flows?

L.O. 2

Exercise 6-13A *Recording inventory transactions using the perpetual system:
Intermittent sales and purchases*

The following inventory transactions apply to IBC Company for 2010.

Jan. 1	Purchased	300 units @ $10
Apr. 1	Sold	125 units @ $15
Aug. 1	Purchased	450 units @ $11
Dec. 1	Sold	500 units @ $18

The beginning inventory consisted of 175 units at $12 per unit. All transactions are cash transactions.

Required

a. Record these transactions, in general journal format, assuming that IBC uses the FIFO cost flow assumption and keeps perpetual records.

b. Compute the ending balance in the Inventory account.

L.O. 2

Exercise 6-14A *Effect of cost flow on ending inventory: Intermittent sales and purchases*

Nick's Boating Company had the following series of transactions for 2011:

Date	Transaction	Description
Jan. 1	Beginning inventory	100 units @ $20
Mar. 15	Purchased	200 units @ $22
May 30	Sold	150 units @ $40
Aug. 10	Purchased	225 units @ $25
Nov. 20	Sold	360 units @ $40

Required

a. Determine the quantity and dollar amount of inventory at the end of the year, assuming Nick's Boating Company uses the FIFO cost flow assumption and keeps perpetual records.

b. Write a memo explaining why Nick's Boating Company would have difficulty applying the LIFO method on a perpetual basis. Include a discussion of how to overcome these difficulties.

Exercise 6-15A   *Lower-of-cost-or-market rule: Perpetual system*   L.O. 3

The following information pertains to Bill's Auto Parts ending inventory for the current year.

Item	Quantity	Unit Cost	Unit Market Value
P	75	$5	$7
D	50	8	5
S	20	7	8
J	10	8	7

Required

a. Determine the value of the ending inventory using the lower-of-cost-or-market rule applied to each individual inventory item.

b. Prepare any necessary journal entries, assuming the decline in value is immaterial, using the individual method. Bill's Auto Parts uses the perpetual inventory system.

Exercise 6-16A   *Lower-of-cost-or-market rule*   L.O. 3

Craft Company carries three inventory items. The following information pertains to the ending inventory:

Item	Quantity	Unit Cost	Unit Market Value
O	150	$10	$ 8
J	250	18	14
R	175	5	10

Required

a. Determine the ending inventory that will be reported on the balance sheet, assuming that Craft applies the lower-of-cost-or-market rule to individual inventory items.

b. Explain how the write-down would be recorded under the perpetual inventory system.

Exercise 6-17A   *Estimating ending inventory using the gross margin method*   L.O. 4, 5

Tom Clark, the owner of Tom's Fishing Supplies, is surprised at the amount of actual inventory at the end of the year. He thought there should be more inventory on hand based on the amount of sales for the year. The following information is taken from the books of Tom's Fishing Supplies:

Beginning Inventory	$200,000
Purchases for the year	300,000
Sales for the year	500,000
Inventory at the end of the year (based on actual count and the balance in the inventory account)	125,000

Historically, Tom has made a 30 percent gross margin on his sales. Tom thinks there may be some problem with the inventory. Evaluate the situation based on the historical gross profit percentage.

Required

Estimate the following:

a. Gross margin in dollars.

b. Cost of goods sold in dollars.

c. Estimated ending inventory.

d. Inventory shortage.

e. Give an explanation for the shortage.

L.O. 4, 5

Exercise 6-18A   *Estimating ending inventory: Perpetual system*

Kayla Smith owned a small company that sold boating equipment. The equipment was expensive, and a perpetual system was maintained for control purposes. Even so, lost, damaged, and stolen merchandise normally amounted to 5 percent of the inventory balance. On June 14, Kayla's warehouse was destroyed by fire. Just prior to the fire, the accounting records contained a $300,000 balance in the Inventory account. However, inventory costing $30,000 had been sold and delivered to customers the day of the fire but had not been recorded in the books at the time of the fire. The fire did not affect the showroom, which contained inventory that cost $80,000.

Required

Estimate the amount of inventory destroyed by fire.

L.O. 4, 5

Exercise 6-19A   *Effect of inventory error on financial statements: Perpetual system*

Ellis Company failed to count $24,000 of inventory in its 2009 year-end physical count.

Required

Explain how this error will affect Ellis' 2009 financial statements, assuming that Ellis uses the perpetual inventory system.

L.O. 4, 5

Exercise 6-20A   *Effect of inventory error on elements of financial statements*

The ending inventory for Ivy Co. was incorrectly adjusted, which caused it to be understated by $12,500 for 2011.

Required

Was each of the following amounts overstated, understated, or not affected by the error?

Item No.	Year	Amount
1	2011	Beginning inventory
2	2011	Purchases
3	2011	Goods available for sale
4	2011	Cost of goods sold
5	2011	Gross margin
6	2011	Net income
7	2012	Beginning inventory
8	2012	Purchases
9	2012	Goods available for sale
10	2012	Cost of goods sold
11	2012	Gross margin
12	2012	Net income

L.O. 6

Exercise 6-21A   *Using the average number of days to sell inventory ratio to make a lending decision*

Carter's Produce has applied for a loan and has agreed to use its inventory as collateral. The company currently has an inventory balance of $289,000. The cost of goods sold for the past year was $7,518,000. The average shelf life for the produce that Carter's sells is 10 days, after which time the fruit begins to spoil and must be sold at drastically reduced prices in order to dispose of it rapidly. The company had maintained steady sales over the past three years and expects to continue at current levels for the foreseeable future.

Required

Based on your knowledge of inventory turnover, evaluate the quality of the inventory as collateral for the loan.

All Problems in Series A are available with McGraw-Hill's Homework Manager®

Problem 6-22A *Effect of different inventory cost flow methods on financial statements*

L.O. 1, 2

The accounting records of Brooks Photography, Inc., reflected the following balances as of January 1, 2012:

Cash	$19,000
Beginning inventory	6,750 (75 units @ $90)
Common stock	7,500
Retained earnings	18,250

The following five transactions occurred in 2012:

1. First purchase (cash)   100 units @ $92
2. Second purchase (cash)   175 units @ $100
3. Sales (all cash)   300 units @ $170
4. Paid $15,000 cash for operating expenses.
5. Paid cash for income tax at the rate of 30 percent of income before taxes.

Required

a. Compute the cost of goods sold and ending inventory, assuming (1) FIFO cost flow, (2) LIFO cost flow, and (3) weighted-average cost flow.
b. Use a vertical model to prepare the 2012 income statement, balance sheet, and statement of cash flows under FIFO, LIFO, and weighted average. (*Hint:* Record the events under an accounting equation before preparing the statements.)

Problem 6-23A *Allocating product costs between cost of goods sold and ending inventory: Intermittent purchases and sales of merchandise*

L.O. 1, 2

Porter, Inc., had the following sales and purchase transactions during 2009. Beginning inventory consisted of 80 items at $120 each. Porter uses the FIFO cost flow assumption and keeps perpetual inventory records. Assume all transactions are cash.

Date	Transaction	Description
Mar. 5	Purchased	100 items @ $125
Apr. 10	Sold	60 items @ $240
June 19	Sold	75 items @ $245
Sept. 16	Purchased	40 items @ $130
Nov. 28	Sold	50 items @ $255

Required

a. Record the inventory transactions in general journal format.
b. Calculate the gross margin Porter would report on the 2009 income statement.
c. Determine the ending inventory balance Porter would report on the December 31, 2009, balance sheet.

Problem 6-24A *Inventory valuation based on the lower-of-cost-or-market rule*

L.O. 3

At the end of the year, Regan Computer Repair had the following items in inventory:

Item	Quantity	Unit Cost	Unit Market Value
D1	70	$20	$26
D2	30	52	48
D3	50	35	42
D4	40	60	43

Required

a. Determine the amount of ending inventory using the lower-of-cost-or-market rule applied to each individual inventory item.

b. Provide the general journal entry necessary to write down the inventory based on Requirement *a*. Assume that Regan Computer Repair uses the perpetual inventory system.

c. Determine the amount of ending inventory, assuming that the lower-of-cost-or-market rule is applied to the inventory in aggregate.

d. Provide the general journal entry necessary to write down the inventory based on Requirement *c*. Assume that Regan Computer Repair uses the perpetual inventory system.

L.0. 4, 5

CHECK FIGURES
a. Gross Margin:
$157,500
b. Total Inventory Loss:
$92,500

Problem 6-25A   *Estimating ending inventory: Gross margin method*

Tokro Supplies had its inventory destroyed by a fire on September 21 of the current year. Although some of the accounting information was destroyed, the following information was discovered for the period of January 1 through September 21:

Beginning inventory, January 1	$ 70,000
Purchases through September 21	400,000
Sales through September 21	525,000

The gross margin for Tokro Supplies has traditionally been 30 percent of sales.

Required

a. For the period ending September 21, compute the following:

  (1) Estimated gross margin.

  (2) Estimated cost of goods sold.

  (3) Estimated inventory at September 21.

b. Assume that $10,000 of the inventory was not damaged. What is the amount of the loss from the fire?

c. Tokro Supplies uses the perpetual inventory system. If some of the accounting records had not been destroyed, how would Tokro determine the amount of the inventory loss?

L.0. 4, 5

CHECK FIGURE
b. Estimated Ending
Inventory: $115,600

Problem 6-26A   *Estimating ending inventory: Gross margin method*

Mark Knight, owner of Knight Company, is reviewing the quarterly financial statements and thinks the cost of goods sold is out of line with past years. The following historical data is available for 2009 and 2010:

	2009	2010
Net sales	$140,000	$200,000
Cost of goods sold	60,000	90,000

At the end of the first quarter of 2011, Knight Company's ledger had the following account balances:

Sales	$260,000
Purchases	160,000
Beginning Inventory, January 1, 2011	70,000

Required

Using the information provided, estimate the following for the first quarter of 2011:

a. Cost of goods sold. (Use average cost of goods sold percentage for 2009 and 2010.)

b. Ending inventory at March 31 based on historical cost of goods sold percentage.

c. Inventory shortage if the inventory balance as of March 31 is $100,000.

L.0. 4

Problem 6-27A   *Effect of inventory errors on financial statements*

The following income statement was prepared for Hunter Company for the year 2010:

BELL COMPANY
Income Statement
For the Year Ended December 31, 2010

Sales	$104,000
Cost of goods sold	(53,700)
Gross margin	50,300
Operating expenses	(10,600)
Net income	$ 39,700

During the year-end audit, the following errors were discovered.

1. A $2,800 payment for repairs was erroneously charged to the Cost of Goods Sold account. (Assume that the perpetual inventory system is used.)

2. Sales to customers for $1,200 at December 31, 2010, were not recorded in the books for 2010. Also, the $1,944 cost of goods sold was not recorded. The error was not discovered in the physical count because the goods had not been delivered to the customer.

3. A mathematical error was made in determining ending inventory. Ending inventory was understated by $600. (The Inventory account was written down in error to the Cost of Goods Sold account.)

Required

Determine the effect, if any, of each of the errors on the following items. Give the dollar amount of the effect and whether it would overstate (+), understate (−), or not affect (NA) the account. The effect on sales is recorded as an example.

Error No. 1	Amount of Error	Effect
Sales, 2010	NA	NA
Ending inventory, December 31, 2010		
Gross margin, 2010		
Beginning inventory, January 1, 2011		
Cost of goods sold, 2010		
Net income, 2010		
Retained earnings, December 31, 2010		
Total assets, December 31, 2010		

Error No. 2	Amount of Error	Effect
Sales, 2010	$1,200	
Ending inventory, December 31, 2010		
Gross margin, 2010		
Beginning inventory, January 1, 2011		
Cost of goods sold, 2010		
Net income, 2010		
Retained earnings, December 31, 2010		
Total assets, December 31, 2010		

Error No. 3	Amount of Error	Effect
Sales, 2010	NA	NA
Ending inventory, December 31, 2010		
Gross margin, 2010		
Beginning inventory, January 1, 2011		
Cost of goods sold, 2010		
Net income, 2010		
Retained earnings, December 31, 2010		
Total assets, December 31, 2010		

L.O. 6

Problem 6-28A   *Using ratios to make comparisons*

The following accounting information pertains to Sweet Treats and Cindy's Candy companies at the end of 2010. The only difference between the two companies is that Sweet Treats uses FIFO while Cindy's Candy uses LIFO.

	Sweet Treats	Cindy's Candy
Cash	$ 80,000	$ 80,000
Accounts receivable	320,000	320,000
Merchandise inventory	240,000	180,000
Accounts payable	220,000	220,000
Cost of goods sold	1,200,000	1,260,000
Building	400,000	400,000
Sales	2,000,000	2,000,000

Required

a. Compute the gross profit percentage for each company and identify the company that *appears* to be charging the higher prices in relation to its cost.

b. For each company, compute the inventory turnover ratio and the average days to sell inventory. Identify the company that *appears* to be incurring the higher inventory financing cost.

c. Explain why a company with the lower gross margin percentage has the higher inventory turnover ratio.

EXERCISES—SERIES B

L.O. 1

Exercise 6-1B   *Understanding the need for cost flow*

Ganyon Company had 250 units of inventory that had cost $22 per unit at the beginning of 2008. During 2008, Ganyon purchased 650 units of inventory at $22 per unit. Ganyon sold 800 units during 2008.

Required

a. Determine the amount of cost of goods sold assuming FIFO, LIFO, and weighted average.

b. Explain why the amount of cost of foods sold is the same regardless of the cost flow method used.

L.O. 1, 2

Exercise 6-2B   *Determine the cost of goods sold*

The following information applies to Roseman Sales Company.

Beginning inventory	300 units @ $7 each
Purchases	1,700 units @ $8 each

Roseman sold 1,800 units of inventory during the year.

Required

a. Determine the cost of goods sold assuming a FIFO cost flow.

b. Determine the cost of goods sold assuming a LIFO cost flow.

c. Determine the cost of goods sold assuming a weighted-average cost flow.

Exercise 6-3B   *Determine the ending inventory balance*   L.O. 1, 2

The following information applies to Color Guard Companies.

Beginning inventory	200 units @ $32 each
Purchases	800 units @ $36 each

Color Guard sold 840 units of inventory during the year.

Required

a. Determine the balance in ending inventory assuming a FIFO cost flow.

b. Determine the balance in ending inventory assuming a LIFO cost flow.

c. Determine the balance in ending inventory assuming a weighted-average cost flow.

Exercise 6-4B   *Cost flow versus cash flow*   L.O. 1, 2

Hagel Company had beginning inventory of 250 units that cost $22 each. These items were purchased with cash in the previous accounting period. During the current accounting period, Hagel paid cash to purchase 750 units of inventory at a price of $26 each. Hagel sold 800 units of inventory at a cash price of $30 per unit.

Required

a. Determine the gross margin under FIFO and LIFO.

b. Determine the cash flow from operating activities under FIFO and LIFO.

Exercise 6-5B   *Cost flow versus physical flow*   L.O. 1, 2

Ryan Sales Company purchased two identical inventory items. The first item purchased cost $46; the second item purchased several months later when prices had risen cost $50. Ryan sold the item purchased first for $60.

Required

a. Determine the cost of goods sold and the amount of ending inventory under FIFO, LIFO, weighted average (WA), and specific identification (SI).

b. How would your answer to Requirement *a* differ if Ryan had sold the item purchased second instead of the one purchased first?

Exercise 6-6B   *Allocating product cost between cost of goods sold and ending inventory*   L.O. 1, 2

Marshall Co. started the year with no inventory. During the year, it purchased two identical inventory items at different times. The first purchase cost $1,500 and the other, $2,000. Marshall sold one of the items during the year.

Required

Based on this information, identify the cost flow method that will produce:

a. The lowest amount of net income.

b. The highest balance in the Inventory account on the balance sheet.

c. The lowest amount of cash flow from operating activities.

Exercise 6-7B   *Allocating product cost between cost of goods sold and ending inventory:*   L.O. 1, 2
                     Multiple purchases

Barnett Company sells chairs that are used at computer stations. Its beginning inventory of chairs was 200 units at $40 per unit. During the year, Barnett made two batch purchases of this chair. The first was a 150-unit purchase at $55 per unit; the second was a 100-unit purchase at $60 per unit. During the period, it sold 360 chairs.

Required

Determine the amount of product costs that would be allocated to cost of goods sold and ending inventory, assuming that Barnett uses:

a. FIFO.

b. LIFO.

c. Weighted average.

L.O. 1, 2   **Exercise 6-8B**   *Effect of inventory cost flow (FIFO, LIFO, and weighted average) on gross margin*

The following information pertains to Bell Company for 2010.

Beginning inventory	60 units @ $20
Units purchased	200 units @ $23

Ending inventory consisted of 30 units. Bell sold 230 units at $50 each. All purchases and sales were made with cash.

Required

a. Compute the gross margin for Bell Company using the following cost flow assumptions: (1) FIFO, (2) LIFO, and (3) weighted average.

b. What is the amount of net income using FIFO, LIFO, and weighted average? (Ignore income tax considerations.)

c. Compute the amount of ending inventory using (1) FIFO, (2) LIFO, and (3) weighted average.

L.O. 1, 2   **Exercise 6-9B**   *Effect of inventory cost flow on ending inventory balance and gross margin*

Hayes Sales had the following transactions for T-shirts for 2008, its first year of operations.

Jan. 20	Purchased 450 units @ $6	=	$2,700
Apr. 21	Purchased 200 units @ $8	=	1,600
July 25	Purchased 150 units @ $10	=	1,500
Sept. 19	Purchased 75 units @ $9	=	675

During the year, Hayes Sales sold 775 T-shirts for $20 each.

Required

a. Compute the amount of ending inventory Hayes would report on the balance sheet, assuming the following cost flow assumptions: (1) FIFO, (2) LIFO, and (3) weighted average.

b. Compute the difference in gross margin between the FIFO and LIFO cost flow assumptions.

L.O. 1, 2   **Exercise 6-10B**   *Income tax effect of shifting from FIFO to LIFO*

The following information pertains to the inventory of the Ping Company:

Jan. 1	Beginning Inventory	500 units @ $18
Apr. 1	Purchased	2,000 units @ $22
Oct. 1	Purchased	1,200 units @ $28

During the year, Ping sold 3,400 units of inventory at $50 per unit and incurred $17,000 of operating expenses. Ping currently uses the FIFO method but is considering a change to LIFO. All transactions are cash transactions. Assume a 35 percent income tax rate.

Required

a. Prepare income statements using FIFO and LIFO.

b. Determine the amount of income taxes that Ping would pay using each cost flow method.

c. Determine the cash flow from operating activities under FIFO and LIFO.

d. Why is the cash flow from operating activities different under FIFO and LIFO?

Exercise 6-11B   *Effect of inventory cost flow assumption on financial statements*   L.O. 1

Required

For each of the following situations, indicate whether FIFO, LIFO, or weighted average applies.

a. In a period of rising prices, net income would be highest.
b. In a period of rising prices, cost of goods sold would be highest.
c. In a period of rising prices, ending inventory would be highest.
d. In a period of falling prices, net income would be highest.
e. In a period of falling prices, the unit cost of goods would be the same for ending inventory and cost of goods sold.

Exercise 6-12B   *Effect of FIFO versus LIFO on income tax expense*   L.O. 1, 2

The Oliver Company had sales of $300,000 for 2011, its first year of operation. On April 2, the company purchased 200 units of inventory at $300 per unit. On September 1, an additional 250 units were purchased for $350 per unit. The company had 100 units on hand at the end of the year. The company's income tax rate is 30 percent. All transactions are cash transactions.

Required

a. The preceding paragraph describes five accounting events: (1) a sales transaction, (2) the first purchase of inventory, (3) a second purchase of inventory, (4) the recognition of cost of goods sold expense, and (5) the payment of income tax expense. Record the amounts of each event in horizontal statements models like the following ones, assuming first a FIFO and then a LIFO cost flow.

										Statement of
			Effect of Events on Financial Statements							
			Panel 1: FIFO Cost Flow							
Event No.			**Balance Sheet**					**Income Statement**		**Statement of Cash Flows**
	Cash	+	Inventory	=	Ret. Earn.	Rev.	−	Exp.	= Net Inc.	
			Panel 2: LIFO Cost Flow							
Event No.			**Balance Sheet**					**Income Statement**		**Statement of Cash Flows**
	Cash	+	Inventory	=	Ret. Earn.	Rev.	−	Exp.	= Net Inc.	

b. Compute net income using FIFO.
c. Compute net income using LIFO.
d. Explain the difference, if any, in the amount of income tax expense incurred using the two cost flow assumptions.
e. Which method, FIFO or LIFO, produced the larger amount of assets on the balance sheet?

Exercise 6-13B   *Recording inventory transactions using the perpetual method: Intermittent sales and purchases*   L.O. 2

The following inventory transactions apply to Parker Company for 2009.

Jan. 1	Purchased	250 units @ $42
Apr. 1	Sold	125 units @ $73
Aug. 1	Purchased	450 units @ $44
Dec. 1	Sold	550 units @ $76

The beginning inventory consisted of 175 units at $40 per unit. All transactions are cash transactions.

Required

a. Record these transactions, in general journal format, assuming that Parker uses the FIFO cost flow assumption and keeps perpetual records.

b. Compute cost of goods sold for 2009.

L.O. 2

Exercise 6-14B *Effect of cost flow on ending inventory: Intermittent sales and purchases*

Alfonza Co. had the following series of transactions for 2008:

Date	Transaction	Description
Jan. 1	Beginning inventory	50 units @ $30
Mar. 15	Purchased	250 units @ $35
May 30	Sold	200 units @ $70
Aug. 10	Purchased	275 units @ $42
Nov. 20	Sold	325 units @ $75

Required

a. Determine the quantity and dollar amount of inventory at the end of the year, assuming Alfonza Co. uses the FIFO cost flow assumption and keeps perpetual records.

b. Write a memo explaining why Alfonza Co. would have difficulty applying the weighted-average method on a perpetual basis.

L.O. 3

Exercise 6-15B *Lower-of-cost-or-market rule: Perpetual system*

The following information pertains to North Street Market's ending inventory for the current year.

Item	Quantity	Unit Cost	Unit Market Value
P	75	$16	$12
D	50	19	16
S	20	24	27
J	30	20	22

Required

a. Determine the value of the ending inventory using the lower-of-cost-or-market rule applied to each individual inventory item.

b. Prepare any necessary journal entries, assuming the decline in value is immaterial. North Street Market uses the perpetual inventory system.

L.O. 3

Exercise 6-16B *Lower-of-cost-or-market rule*

Jacobs Company carries three inventory items. The following information pertains to the ending inventory:

Item	Quantity	Unit Cost	Unit Market Value
B	100	$40	$34
C	150	62	56
D	80	20	30

Required

a. Determine the ending inventory that Jacobs will report on the balance sheet, assuming that it applies the lower-of-cost-or-market rule to individual inventory items.

b. Explain how adjustments to ending inventory would be recorded.

Exercise 6-17B   *Estimating ending inventory*

L.O. 4, 5

A substantial portion of inventory owned by Steve's Garden Shop was recently destroyed when the roof collapsed during a rainstorm. It also lost some of its accounting records. Steve's must estimate the loss from the storm for insurance reporting and financial statement purposes. Steve's uses the periodic inventory system. The following accounting information was recovered from the damaged records.

Beginning inventory	$ 30,000
Purchases to date of storm	150,000
Sales to date of storm	137,500

The value of undamaged inventory counted was $1,500. Historically Steve's gross margin percentage has been approximately 30 percent of sales.

Required

Estimate the following:

a. Gross margin in dollars.

b. Cost of goods sold.

c. Ending inventory.

d. Amount of lost inventory.

Exercise 6-18B   *Estimating ending inventory: Perpetual system*

L.O. 4, 5

Ross Eady owned a small company that sold building equipment. The equipment was expensive, and a perpetual system was maintained for control purposes. Even so, lost, damaged, and stolen merchandise normally amounted to 4 percent of the inventory balance. On June 14, Eady's warehouse was destroyed by fire. Just prior to the fire, the accounting records contained a $338,000 balance in the Inventory account. However, inventory costing $51,000 had been sold and delivered to customers but had not been recorded in the books at the time of the fire. The fire did not affect the showroom, which contained inventory that cost $68,000.

Required

Estimate the amount of inventory destroyed by fire.

Exercise 6-19B   *Effect of inventory error on financial statements: Perpetual system*

L.O. 4, 5

Naro Company failed to count $100,000 of inventory in its 2010 year-end physical count.

Required

Write a memo explaining how Naro Company's balance sheet will be affected in 2010. Assume Naro uses the perpetual inventory system.

Exercise 6-20B   *Effect of inventory misstatement on elements of financial statements*

L.O. 4, 5

The ending inventory for Fulton Co. was erroneously written down causing an understatement of $10,400 at the end of 2010.

Required

Was each of the following amounts overstated, understated, or not affected by the error?

Item No.	Year	Amount
1	2010	Beginning inventory
2	2010	Purchases
3	2010	Goods available for sale
4	2010	Cost of goods sold
5	2010	Gross margin
6	2010	Net income
7	2011	Beginning inventory
8	2011	Purchases
9	2011	Goods available for sale
10	2011	Cost of goods sold
11	2011	Gross margin
12	2011	Net income

L.O. 6

Exercise 6-21B   *Using the average number of days to sell inventory ratio to make a lending decision*

Fashion Trends is a clothing store catering to high-school-aged girls who are very style conscious. Since this group consists mainly of what marketers call early adopters, the clothes they buy tend to go out of style very quickly, and Fashion Trends' ability to remain profitable depends on correctly predicting the next trend, and then selling its clothing very quickly. To finance its inventory purchases for the upcoming back-to-school season, Fashion Trends has applied for a loan and wishes to use its inventory as part of the collateral for the loan.

The company's inventory balance averages around $262,500, and its cost of goods sold for the past year was $1,752,000. Its sales in the past year totaled $2,803,200. The life cycle for the clothes that Fashion trend sells is about 60 days, after which time the clothes must be sold at significantly reduced prices.

Required

Based on your knowledge of inventory turnover, evaluate the quality of the inventory as collateral for the loan.

PROBLEMS—SERIES B

L.O. 1, 2

Problem 6-22B   *Effect of different inventory cost flow methods on financial statements*

The accounting records of Lauren's Dive Shop reflected the following balances as of January 1, 2009.

Cash	$50,800
Beginning inventory	58,000 (200 units @ $290)
Common stock	45,000
Retained earnings	63,800

The following five transactions occurred in 2009:

1. First purchase (cash)   100 units @ $300
2. Second purchase (cash)   140 units @ $320
3. Sales (all cash)   400 units @ $475

4. Paid $30,000 cash for salaries expense.
5. Paid cash for income tax at the rate of 30 percent of income before taxes.

Required

a. Compute the cost of goods sold and ending inventory, assuming (1) FIFO cost flow, (2) LIFO cost flow, and (3) weighted-average cost flow.
b. Use a vertical model to prepare the 2009 income statement, balance sheet, and statement of cash flows under FIFO, LIFO, and weighted average. (*Hint:* Record the events under an accounting equation before preparing the statements.)

Problem 6-23B   *Allocating product costs between cost of goods sold and ending inventory:*   **L.O. 1, 2**
                    Intermittent purchases and sales of merchandise

Elm Company had the following sales and purchase transactions during 2012. Beginning inventory consisted of 50 items at $350 each. The company uses the FIFO cost flow assumption and keeps perpetual inventory records. Assume all transactions are cash.

Date	Transaction	Description
Mar. 5	Purchased	50 items @ $360
Apr. 10	Sold	40 items @ $450
June 19	Sold	50 items @ $450
Sept. 16	Purchased	50 items @ $380
Nov. 28	Sold	25 items @ $470

Required

a. Record the inventory transactions in general journal format.
b. Calculate the gross margin Elm Company would report on the 2012 income statement.
c. Determine the ending inventory balance Elm Company would report on the December 31, 2012, balance sheet.

Problem 6-24B   *Inventory valuation based on the lower-of-cost-or-market rule*   **L.O. 3**

At the end of the year, Chase Repair Service had the following items in inventory:

Item	Quantity	Unit Cost	Unit Market Value
P1	80	$ 80	$ 95
P2	70	60	66
P3	100	145	130
P4	40	130	140

Required

a. Determine the amount of ending inventory using the lower-of-cost-or-market rule applied to each individual inventory item.
b. Provide the general journal entry necessary to write down the inventory based on Requirement *a.* Assume that Chase Repair Service uses the perpetual inventory system.
c. Explain how the inventory loss would be reported when the periodic inventory system is used.

Problem 6-25B   *Estimating ending inventory: Gross margin method*

Far East Company had its inventory destroyed by a tornado on October 6 of the current year. Fortunately, some of the accounting records were at the home of one of the owners and were not damaged. The following information was available for the period of January 1 through October 6:

Beginning inventory, January 1	$ 146,000
Purchases through October 6	720,000
Sales through October 6	1,140,000

Gross margin for Far East has traditionally been 35 percent of sales.

Required

a. For the period ending October 6, compute the following:
   (1) Estimated gross margin.
   (2) Estimated cost of goods sold.
   (3) Estimated inventory at October 6.
b. Assume that $20,000 of the inventory was not damaged. What is the amount of the loss from the tornado?
c. If Far East Company had used the perpetual inventory system, how would it have determined the amount of the inventory loss?

Problem 6-26B   *Estimating ending inventory: Gross margin method*

Sue's Market Place wishes to produce quarterly financial statements, but it takes a physical count of inventory only at year end. The following historical data were taken from the 2008 and 2009 accounting records:

	2008	2009
Net sales	$30,000	$35,000
Cost of goods sold	15,500	18,250

At the end of the first quarter of 2010, Sue's ledger had the following account balances:

Sales	$28,250
Purchases	20,500
Beginning inventory 1/1/2010	6,250
Ending inventory 3/31/2010	7,500

Sue thinks her inventory is low based on purchases and sales.

Required

Using the information provided, estimate the following for the first quarter of 2010:

a. Cost of goods sold. (Use average cost of goods sold percentage for 2008 and 2009.)
b. Ending inventory at March 31.
c. What could explain the difference in actual and estimated inventory?

Problem 6-27B   *Effect of inventory errors on financial statements*

The following income statement was prepared for John's Building Supply for the year 2011:

JOHN'S BUILDING SUPPLY
Income Statement
For the Year Ended December 31, 2011

Sales	$120,000
Cost of goods sold	(77,200)
Gross margin	42,800
Operating expenses	(21,300)
Net income	$ 21,500

During the year-end audit, the following errors were discovered:

1. A $4,000 payment for repairs was erroneously charged to the Cost of Goods Sold account. (Assume that the perpetual inventory system is used.)

2. Sales to customers for $1,000 at December 31, 2011, were not recorded in the books for 2011. Also, the $600 cost of goods sold was not recorded. The error was not discovered in the physical count because the goods had not been delivered to the customers.

3. A mathematical error was made in determining ending inventory. Ending inventory was understated by $3,600. (The Inventory account was written down in error to the Cost of Goods Sold account.)

Required

Determine the effect, if any, of each of the errors on the following items. Give the dollar amount of the effect and whether it would overstate (+), understate (−), or not affect (NA) the account. The first item for each error is recorded as an example.

Error No. 1	Amount of Error	Effect
Sales, 2011	NA	NA
Ending inventory, December 31, 2011		
Gross margin, 2011		
Beginning inventory, January 1, 2012		
Cost of goods sold, 2011		
Net income, 2011		
Retained earnings, December 31, 2011		
Total assets, December 31, 2011		

Error No. 2	Amount of Error	Effect
Sales, 2011	$1,000	−
Ending inventory, December 31, 2011		
Gross margin, 2011		
Beginning inventory, January 1, 2012		
Cost of goods sold, 2011		
Net income, 2011		
Retained earnings, December 31, 2011		
Total assets, December 31, 2011		

Error No. 3	Amount of Error	Effect
Sales, 2011	NA	NA
Ending inventory, December 31, 2011		
Gross margin, 2011		
Beginning inventory, January 1, 2012		
Cost of goods sold, 2011		
Net income, 2011		
Retained earnings, December 31, 2011		
Total assets, December 31, 2011		

L.O. 6

Problem 6-28B   *Using ratios to make comparisons*

The following accounting information pertains to Clemens and Twain companies at the end of 2010. The only difference between the two companies is that Clemens uses FIFO while Twain uses LIFO.

	Clemens	Twain
Cash	$ 75,000	$ 75,000
Accounts receivable	200,000	200,000
Merchandise inventory	150,000	100,000
Accounts payable	160,000	160,000
Cost of goods sold	600,000	650,000
Building	250,000	250,000
Sales	1,000,000	1,000,000

Required

a. Compute the gross profit percentage for each company and identify the company that *appears* to be charging the higher prices in relation to its cost.
b. For each company, compute the inventory turnover ratio and the average days to sell inventory. Identify the company that *appears* to be incurring the higher inventory financing cost.
c. Explain why a company with the lower gross margin percentage has the higher inventory turnover ratio.

ANALYZE, THINK, COMMUNICATE

ATC 6-1   **Business Applications Case**   *Understanding real-world annual reports*

Required—Part 1

Use the Topps Company's annual report in Appendix B to answer the following questions.

a. What was Topps' inventory turnover ratio and average days to sell inventory 2006 and 2005?
b. Is the company's management of inventory getting better or worse?
c. What cost flow method(s) did Topps use to account for inventory?

Required—Part 2

Use the Harley-Davidson's annual report that came with this book to answer the following questions.

a. What was Harley-Davidson's inventory turnover ratio and average days to sell inventory for 2005?
b. What cost flow method(s) did Harley-Davidson use to account for inventory?
c. How much different, lower or higher, would Harley-Davidson's ending inventory have been if it had used the FIFO cost flow method for all of its inventory (see Note 2)?

Required—Part 3

Speculate as to why Harley-Davidson sells its inventory more quickly than Topps.

ATC 6-2   **Group Assignment**   *Inventory cost flow*

The accounting records of Blue Bird Co. showed the following balances at January 1, 2008:

Cash	$30,000
Beginning inventory (100 units @ $50, 70 units @ $55)	8,850
Common stock	20,000
Retained earnings	18,850

Transactions for 2008 were as follows:

> Purchased 100 units @ $54 per unit.
> Purchased 250 units @ $58 per unit.
> Sold 220 units @ $80 per unit.
> Sold 200 units @ $90 per unit.
> Paid operating expenses of $3,200.
> Paid income tax expense. The income tax rate is 30%.

Required

a. Organize the class into three sections, and divide each section into groups of three to five students. Assign each section one of the cost flow methods, FIFO, LIFO, or weighted average.

Group Tasks

Determine the amount of ending inventory, cost of goods sold, gross margin, and net income after income tax for the cost flow method assigned to your section. Also prepare an income statement using that cost flow assumption.

Class Discussion

b. Have a representative of each section put its income statement on the board. Discuss the effect that each cost flow method has on assets (ending inventory), net income, and cash flows. Which method is preferred for tax reporting? For financial reporting? What restrictions are placed on the use of LIFO for tax reporting?

ATC 6-3   Real-World Case   *Analyzing inventory management issues at Campbell's Soup*

After more than a decade of generally good economic news, the economy of the United States began to slow in 2000. At that time, the Campbell Soup Company (Campbell's), like many other companies, saw its earnings decline. Campbell's net earnings fell from $714 million in its 2000 fiscal year to $525 million in 2002, but then it began to improve. By 2004, its earnings were back up to $647 million.

The data below, for Campbell's fiscal years ending on August 3, 2003, and August 1, 2004, pertain to analyzing the company's management of inventory. All dollar amounts are in millions.

	2004	2003
Sales	$7,109	$6,678
Cost of goods sold	4,187	3,805
Ending inventory	795	709
Income before taxes	947	924
Net earnings	647	595*
Income tax rate	32%	32%

*Includes a special charge for a change in accounting principle of ($31). This expense does not affect the requirements below.

Required

a. Compute Campbell's gross margin percentage for 2004 and 2003.

b. Compute Campbell's average days to sell inventory for 2004 and 2003.

c. Did Campbell's earnings improve from 2003 to 2004 due to either better gross margins or better inventory management (turnover)? Explain.

d. How much higher or lower would Campbell's *earnings before taxes* have been in 2004 if its gross margin percentage had been the same as it was in 2003? Show all supporting computations.

e. How much higher or lower would Campbell's *net earnings* have been in 2004 if its gross margin percentage had been the same as it was in 2003? Show all supporting computations.

ATC 6-4   Business Applications Case   *Performing ratio analysis using real-world data*

Safeway, Inc., operated 1,802 stores as of January 1, 2005. The following data were taken from the company's annual report. All dollar amounts are in thousands.

	Fiscal Years Ending	
	January 1, 2005	**January 3, 2004**
Revenue	$35,822,900	$35,727,200
Cost of goods sold	25,227,600	25,003,000
Net income	560,200	(169,800)
Merchandise inventory	2,740,700	2,642,200

Required

a. Compute Safeway's inventory turnover ratio for 2005 and 2004.

b. Compute Safeway's average days to sell inventory for 2005 and 2004.

c. Based on your computations in Requirements *a* and *b*, did Safeway's inventory management get better or worse from 2004 to 2005?

ATC 6-5   Business Applications Case   *Performing ratio analysis using real-world data*

Ruby Tuesday's, Inc., operated 484 casual dining restaurants across the United States as of June 1, 2004. Zale Corporation claims to be "North America's largest specialty retailer of fine jewelry." The following data were taken from these companies' 2004 annual reports. All dollar amounts are in thousands.

	Ruby Tuesday's **June 1, 2004**	**Zale Corporation** **July 31, 2004**
Sales	$1,023,342*	$2,304,440
Cost of goods sold	263,033	1,122,946
Net income	110,009	106,473
Merchandise inventory	8,068	826,824

*Excludes franchise revenue.

Required

a. Before performing any calculations, speculate as to which company will take the longest to sell its inventory. Explain the rationale for your decision.

b. Calculate the inventory turnover ratios for Ruby Tuesday's and Zale Corporation.

c. Calculate the average days to sell inventory for Ruby Tuesday's and Zale Corporation.

d. Do the calculations from Requirements *b* and *c* confirm your speculations in Requirement *a*?

ATC 6-6   Writing Assignment   *Inventory cost flow versus cash flow*

Required

Write a brief paragraph in response to each of the following items:

a. If the costs of inventory purchased remain constant, the amounts in cost of goods sold and ending inventory would be the same regardless of which inventory cost flow method is applied. Do you agree or disagree? Why or why not?

b. The amount of cash flow is not affected by the inventory cost flow method used by a company. Do you agree or disagree? Why or why not?

c. Explain how a manager could use specific identification to manipulate financial statements.

ATC 6-7   Ethical Dilemma   *Show them only what you want them to see*

Clair Coolage is the chief accountant for a sales company called Far Eastern Imports. The company has been highly successful and is trying to increase its capital base by attracting new investors. The company operates in an inflationary environment and has been using the LIFO inventory cost flow method to minimize its net earnings and thereby reduce its income taxes. Katie Bailey, the vice president of finance, asked Coolage to estimate the change in net earnings that would occur if the company switched to FIFO. After reviewing the company's books, Coolage estimated that pretax income would increase by $1,200,000 if the company adopted the FIFO cost flow method. However, the switch would result in approximately $400,000 of additional taxes. The overall effect would result in an increase of $800,000 in net earnings. Bailey told Coolage to avoid the additional taxes by preparing the tax return on a LIFO basis but to prepare a set of statements on a FIFO basis to be distributed to potential investors.

Required

a. Comment on the legal and ethical implications of Bailey's decision.

b. How will the switch to FIFO affect Far Eastern's balance sheet?

c. If Bailey reconsiders and makes a decision to switch to FIFO for tax purposes as well as financial reporting purposes, net income will increase by $800,000. Comment on the wisdom of paying $400,000 in income taxes to obtain an additional $800,000 of net income.

ATC 6-8   Research Assignment   *Analyzing inventory at Gap, Inc.*

Required

Using the most current 10-K available on EDGAR or the company's annual report, answer the following questions about Gap, Inc., Instructions for using EDGAR are in Appendix A.

a. What was the average amount of inventory per store? Use *all* stores operated by Gap, not just those called *The Gap*. (*Hint:* The answer to this question must be computed. The number of stores in operation at the end of the most recent year can be found in the MD&A section.)

b. How many *new* stores did Gap open during the year?

c. Using the quarterly financial information contained in the 10-K, complete the following chart.

Quarter	Sales During Each Quarter
1	
2	
3	
4	

d. Referring to the chart in Requirement *c*, explain why Gap's sales vary so widely throughout its fiscal year. Do you believe that Gap's inventory level varies throughout the year in relation to sales?

ATC 6-9   Spreadsheet Analysis   *Using Excel*

At January 1, 2008, the accounting records of Bronco Boutique had the following balances:

Cash	$1,000
Inventory	2,250 (150 units @ $15)
Common stock	2,000
Retained earnings	1,250

During January, Bronco Boutique entered into five cash transactions:

1. Purchased 120 units of inventory @ $16 each.
2. Purchased 160 units of inventory @ $17 each.
3. Sold 330 units of inventory @ $30 each.
4. Incurred $1,700 of operating expenses.
5. Paid income tax at the rate of 30 percent of income before taxes.

Required

a. Set up rows 1 through 10 of the following spreadsheet to compute cost of goods sold and ending inventory, assuming (1) FIFO, (2) LIFO, and (3) weighted-average cost flows. Notice that the FIFO cost flow has already been completed for you. Use columns O through W to complete the LIFO and weighted-average cost flow computations. Be sure to use formulas for all calculations.

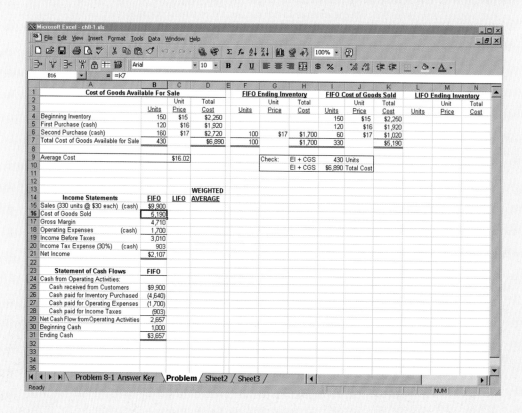

b. In rows 13 through 31, compute the amount of net income and net cash flow from operations under FIFO, LIFO, and weighted average. The FIFO column has been provided as an example.

ATC 6-10   Spreadsheet Assignment   *Mastering Excel*

Required

Complete ATC 6-5 using an Excel spreadsheet. Use Excel problem ATC 6-9 as a resource for structuring the spreadsheet.

COMPREHENSIVE PROBLEM

The trial balance of Pacilio Security System Sales and Service as on January 1, 2006, was as follows:

Cash	$64,380
Accounts receivable	8,000
Supplies	150
Prepaid rent	1,000
Merchandise inventory–std. alarms 19 @ $240	4,560
Merchandise inventory–deluxe alarms 10 @ $500	5,000
Accounts payable	4,120
Common stock	50,000
Retained earnings	28,970

During 2006, Pacilio Security Services, Inc., experienced the following transactions:

1. On January 1, 2006, purchased a company van for $9,200 cash. The van had an estimated life of three years and estimated salvage value of $2,000.
2. On January 15, purchased 20 standard alarm systems for cash at a cost of $250 each.
3. On February 1, paid $4,120 on accounts payable, but not within the discount period. Total cash paid was $4,120.
4. Paid $7,200 on March 2, 2006, for one year's rent in advance.
5. Purchased $500 of office supplies for cash.
6. Purchased 10 deluxe alarm systems for cash on April 1 at a cost of $550 each.
7. Purchased another 25 standard alarm systems on August 1 for resale at a cost of $260 each.
8. On September 5, purchased on account 30 standard alarm systems at a cost of $265 each and 20 deluxe alarm systems at a cost of $575 each.
9. Installed 60 standard alarm systems for $33,000 and 30 deluxe alarm systems for $27,000. $45,000 of the sales were on account and $15,000 were cash sales. (*Note:* Be sure to record cost of goods sold using FIFO method.)
10. Made a full refund to a dissatisfied customer who returned her deluxe system. The sale had been a cash sale for $900 with a cost of $575.
11. Paid installers a total of $16,200 cash for salaries.
12. Sold $68,000 of monitoring services during the year on account. The services are billed to the customers each month.
13. Collected $98,000 of accounts receivable during the year.
14. Paid $10,880 on accounts payable during the year.
15. Paid $3,500 of advertising expense during the year.
16. Paid $2,384 of utilities expense for the year.

Adjustments

17. $200 of supplies were on hand at the end of the year.
18. Recognized the expired rent for the year.
19. Recognized depreciation expense for 2006.

Required

a. Record the above transactions in general journal form. Pacilio uses FIFO cost flow assumption.
b. Post the transactions to the T-accounts.
c. Prepare a trial balance.
d. Prepare an income statement, statement of changes in stockholders' equity, balance sheet, and statement of cash flows.
e. Close the temporary accounts to retained earnings.
f. Post the closing entries to the T-accounts and prepare a after-closing trial balance.

CHAPTER 7

Internal Control and Accounting for Cash

LEARNING OBJECTIVES

After you have mastered the material in this chapter, you will be able to:

1. Identify the key elements of a strong system of internal control.

2. Identify special internal controls for cash.

3. Prepare a bank reconciliation.

4. Explain the use of a petty cash fund.

5. Prepare a classified balance sheet.

6. Use the current ratio to assess the level of liquidity.

LP7

The Curious Accountant

On June 25, 2002, WorldCom, the second largest long-distance telecommunications company in the United States, announced that its expenses had been incorrectly understated by approximately $3.6 billion. This understatement occurred because certain costs that should have been recorded as expenses were, instead, recorded as assets. On June 26, the company, which was experiencing difficulties before the revelation of its accounting problems, announced it would lay off 17,000 of its 80,000 employees, and the NASDAQ stopped trading of its stock. The company predicted its accounting misstatements would total over $11 billion by August 2003.

The restatement of WorldCom's earnings resulting from this discovery was the largest in corporate history, replacing the previous record set by Waste Management in 1998. Obviously, this is not a record a company wants to hold. As a result of these accounting irregularities, some members of management were fired or asked to resign.

How do you think such a large understatement of expenses goes undetected? Try to *speculate as to how it was ultimately discovered.* (Answer on page 347.)

CHAPTER OPENING

*To operate successfully, businesses must employ systems of control. How can Wal-Mart's upper-level managers ensure that every store will open on time? How can the president of General Motors be confident that the company's financial reports fairly reflect the company's operations? How can the owner of a restaurant prevent a waiter from serving food to his friends and relatives without charging them for it? The answer: by exercising effective control over the enterprise. The policies and procedures used to provide reasonable assurance that the objectives of an enterprise will be accomplished are called **internal controls.**[1]*

---

[1]*AICPA Professional Standards,* vol. 1, sec. 320, par. 6 (June 1, 1989).

*Internal controls can be divided into two categories: (1) **accounting controls** are designed to safeguard company assets and ensure reliable accounting records; and (2) **administrative controls** are concerned with evaluating performance and assessing the degree of compliance with company policies and public laws.* ■

Key Features of Internal Control Systems

Topic Tackler

PLUS

7-1

LO 1

Identify the key elements of a strong system of internal control.

Video 7.1

Internal control systems vary from company to company. However, most systems include certain basic policies and procedures that have proven effective over time. A discussion of the more common features of a strong system of internal control follows.

Separation of Duties

The likelihood of fraud or theft is reduced if collusion is required to accomplish the act. As a result, a clear **separation of duties** is frequently used as a deterrent to corruption. When duties are separated, the work of one employee can act as a check on the work of another employee. For example, a person selling seats to a movie may be tempted to steal money received from customers who enter the theater. This temptation is reduced if the person staffing the box office is required to issue tickets that a second employee collects as people enter the theater. If ticket stubs collected by the second employee are compared with the cash receipts from ticket sales, any cash shortages would become apparent. Furthermore, friends and relatives of the ticket agent could not easily enter the theater without paying. Theft or unauthorized entry would require collusion between the ticket agent and the usher who collects the tickets. Both individuals would have to be dishonest enough to steal, yet trustworthy enough to convince each other they would keep the embezzlement secret. Whenever possible, the functions of *authorization, recording,* and *custody* should be performed by separate individuals.

Quality of Employees

A business is only as good as the people who run it. Cheap labor is not a bargain if the employees are incompetent. Employees should be properly trained. In fact, they should be trained to perform a variety of tasks. The ability of employees to substitute for one another prevents disruptions when co-workers are absent because of illnesses, vacations, or other commitments. The capacity to rotate jobs also relieves boredom and increases respect for the contributions of other employees. Every business should strive to maximize the productivity of each and every employee. Ongoing training programs are essential to a strong system of internal control.

Bonded Employees

The best way to ensure employee honesty is to hire individuals with *high levels of personal integrity.* Employers should screen job applicants using interviews, background checks, and recommendations from prior employers or educators. Even so, screening programs may fail to identify character weaknesses. Further, unusual circumstances may cause honest employees to go astray. Therefore, employees in positions of trust should be bonded. A **fidelity bond** provides insurance that protects a company from loss caused by employee dishonesty.

Required Absences

Employees should be required to take regular vacations and their duties should be rotated periodically. Employees may be able to cover up fraudulent activities if they are always present at work. Consider the case of a parking meter collection agent who covered the same route for several years with no vacation. When the agent became sick, a substitute collected more money each day than the regular reader usually reported. Management checked past records and found that the ill meter reader had been understating the cash receipts and pocketing the difference. If management had required vacations or rotated the routes, the embezzlement would have been discovered much earlier.

Nordstrom, known for its service, empowers its employees to make on-the-spot decisions to satisfy customers.

Procedures Manual

Appropriate accounting procedures should be documented in a **procedures manual.** The manual should be routinely updated. Periodic reviews should be conducted to ensure that employees are following the procedures outlined in the manual.

Authority and Responsibility

Employees are motivated by clear lines of authority and responsibility. They work harder when they have the authority to use their own judgment and they exercise reasonable caution when they are held responsible for their actions. Businesses should prepare an **authority manual** that establishes a definitive *chain of command.* The authority manual should guide both specific and general authorizations. **Specific authorizations** apply to specific positions within the organization. For example, investment decisions are authorized at the division level while hiring decisions are authorized at the departmental level. In contrast, **general authority** applies across different levels of management. For example, employees at all levels may be required to fly coach or to make purchases from specific vendors.

Prenumbered Documents

How would you know if a check were stolen from your checkbook? If you keep a record of your check numbers, the missing number would tip you off immediately. Businesses also use prenumbered checks to avoid the unauthorized use of their bank accounts. In fact, prenumbered forms are used for all important documents such as purchase orders, receiving reports, invoices, and checks. To reduce errors, prenumbered forms should be as simple and as easy to use as possible. Also, the documents should allow for authorized signatures. For example, credit sales slips should be signed by the customer to clearly establish who made the purchase. Thus, the likelihood of unauthorized transactions is reduced.

Physical Control

Employees walk away with billions of dollars of business assets each year. To limit losses, companies should establish adequate physical control over valuable assets. For example, inventory should be kept in a storeroom and not released without proper authorization. Serial numbers on equipment should be recorded along with the name of the individual who is responsible for the equipment. Unannounced physical counts should be conducted randomly to verify the presence of company-owned equipment. Certificates of deposit and marketable securities should be kept in fireproof vaults. Access to these vaults should be limited to authorized personnel. These procedures protect the documents from fire and limit access to only those individuals who have the appropriate security clearance to handle the documents.

In addition to safeguarding assets, there should be physical control over the accounting records. The accounting journals, ledgers, and supporting documents should be kept in a fireproof safe. Only personnel responsible for recording transactions in the journals should have access to them. With limited access, there is less chance that someone will change the records to conceal fraud or embezzlement.

Performance Evaluations

Because few people can evaluate their own performance objectively, internal controls should include independent verification of employee performance. For example, someone other than the person who has control over inventory should take a physical count of inventory. Internal and external audits serve as independent verification of performance. Auditors should evaluate the effectiveness of the internal control system as well as verify the accuracy of the accounting records. In addition, the external auditors attest to the company's use of generally accepted accounting principles in the financial statements.

Limitations

A system of internal controls is designed to prevent or detect errors and fraud. However, no control system is foolproof. Internal controls can be circumvented by collusion among employees. Two or more employees working together can hide embezzlement by covering for each other. For example, if an embezzler goes on vacation, fraud will not be reported by a replacement who is in collusion with the embezzler. No system can prevent all fraud. However, a good system of internal controls minimizes illegal or unethical activities by reducing temptation and increasing the likelihood of early detection.

CHECK YOURSELF 7.1

What are nine features of an internal control system?

Answer

The nine features follow.

1. Separating duties so that fraud or theft requires collusion.
2. Hiring and training competent employees.
3. Bonding employees to recover losses through insurance.
4. Requiring employees to be absent from their jobs so that their replacements can discover errors or fraudulent activity that might have occurred.
5. Establishing proper procedures for processing transactions.
6. Establishing clear lines of authority and responsibility.
7. Using prenumbered documents.
8. Implementing physical controls such as locking cash in a safe.
9. Conducting performance evaluations through independent internal and external audits.

Accounting for Cash

Identify special internal controls for cash.

Video 7.1

For financial reporting purposes, **cash** generally includes currency and other items that are payable *on demand,* such as checks, money orders, bank drafts, and certain savings accounts. Savings accounts that impose substantial penalties for early withdrawal should be classified as *investments* rather than cash. Postdated checks or IOUs represent *receivables* and should not be included in cash. As illustrated in Exhibit 7.1, most companies combine currency and other payable on demand items in a single balance sheet account with varying titles.

Companies must maintain a sufficient amount of cash to pay employees, suppliers, and other creditors. When a company fails to pay its legal obligations, the creditors can force the company into bankruptcy. Even so, management should avoid accumulating more cash than is needed. The failure to invest excess cash in earning assets reduces profitability. Cash inflows and outflows must be managed to prevent a shortage or surplus of cash.

Controlling Cash

Controlling cash, more than any other asset, requires strict adherence to internal control procedures. Cash has universal appeal. A relatively small suitcase filled with high-denomination

Answers to The Curious Accountant

Bernie Ebbers, founder of WorldCom, is quoted as once having ordered Cynthia Cooper, WorldCom's vice president of internal audit, never to use the phrase *internal control*. Ebbers said he didn't understand it. Apparently, he was right. It was Mrs. Cooper and her team of internal auditors who ultimately uncovered the vast fraud. Perhaps a different attitude at the top about internal control could have avoided this fiasco.

As noted earlier, WorldCom had been experiencing difficulties prior to June 2002. In April 2002 its longtime CEO was ousted, and its board of directors launched an internal investigation of the company's operations. Mrs. Cooper found and reported the questionable accounting procedures to the company's audit committee. The chief financial officer at WorldCom, Scott Sullivan, was fired upon discovery of the accounting fraud. He and a few other key executives were ultimately indicted on criminal charges. After others had pled guilty to the fraud charges, the chief financial officer

reportedly continued to claim the company was within the rules to record the costs in question as assets and depreciate them in future periods, rather than recognize them immediately as expenses. The company's external auditor and board of directors did not agree with him.

Another question to consider is why no one asked to see the $3.6 billion of assets the company was supposed to be purchasing. The answer to this is not as obvious as one might expect. In the telecommunications business, many legitimate assets do not have any physical existence; they are said to be intangible assets, so it is not surprising that no one noticed they did not exist. Intangible assets are discussed in Chapter 9. In 2005, Mr. Ebbers was sentenced to 25 years in prison for his part in the accounting fraud at WorldCom. Mr. Sullivan, who eventually pled guilty and agreed to cooperate with prosecutors, was sentenced to five years in prison. WorldCom has since changed its name to MCI.

currency can represent significant value. Furthermore, the rightful owner of currency is difficult to prove. In most cases, possession constitutes ownership. As a result, cash is highly susceptible to theft and must be carefully protected. Cash is most susceptible to embezzlement when it is received or disbursed. The following controls should be employed to reduce the likelihood of theft.

Cash Receipts

A record of all cash collections should be prepared immediately upon receipt. The amount of cash on hand should be counted regularly. Missing amounts of money can be detected by comparing the actual cash on hand with the book balance. Employees who receive cash should give customers a copy of a written receipt. Customers usually review their receipts to ensure they have gotten credit for the amount paid and call any errors to the receipts clerk's attention. This not only reduces errors but also provides a control on the clerk's honesty. Cash receipts should be deposited in a bank on a timely basis. Cash collected late in the day should be deposited in a night depository. Every effort should be made to minimize the amount of cash on hand. Keeping large amounts of cash on hand not only increases the risk of loss from theft but also places employees in danger of being harmed by criminals who may be tempted to rob the company.

Cash Payments

To effectively control cash, a company should make all disbursements using checks, thereby providing a record of cash payments. All checks should be prenumbered, and unused checks should be locked up. Using prenumbered checks allows companies to easily identify lost or stolen checks by comparing the numbers on unused and canceled checks with the numbers used for legitimate disbursements.

The duties of approving disbursements, signing checks, and recording transactions should be separated. If one person is authorized to approve, sign, and record checks, he or she could falsify supporting documents, write an unauthorized check, and record a cover-up transaction in the accounting records. By separating these duties, the check signer reviews the documentation provided by the approving individual before signing the check. Likewise, the recording clerk reviews the

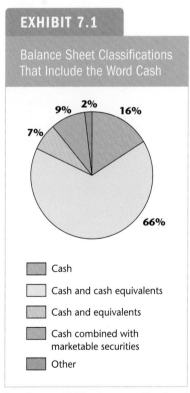

EXHIBIT 7.1

Balance Sheet Classifications That Include the Word Cash

- Cash
- Cash and cash equivalents
- Cash and equivalents
- Cash combined with marketable securities
- Other

Data Source: AICPA, *Accounting Trends and Techniques,* 2006.

REALITY BYTES

The Cost of Protecting Cash

Could you afford to buy a safe like the one shown here? The vault is only one of many expensive security devices used by banks to safeguard cash. By using checking accounts, companies are able to avoid many of the costs associated with keeping cash safe. In addition to providing physical control, checking accounts enable companies to maintain a written audit trail regarding cash receipts and payments. Indeed, checking accounts represent the most widely used internal control device in modern society. It is difficult to imagine a business operating without the use of checking accounts.

work of both the approving person and the check signer when the disbursement is recorded in the accounting records. Thus, writing unauthorized checks requires trilevel collusion.

Supporting documents with authorized approval signatures should be required when checks are presented to the check signer. For example, a warehouse receiving order should be matched with a purchase order before a check is approved to pay a bill from a supplier. Before payments are approved, invoice amounts should be checked and payees verified as valid vendors. Matching supporting documents with proper authorization discourages employees from creating phony documents for a disbursement to a friend or fictitious business. Also, the approval process serves as a check on the accuracy of the work of all employees involved.

Supporting documents should be marked *Paid* when the check is signed. If the documents are not indelibly marked, they could be retrieved from the files and resubmitted for a duplicate, unauthorized payment. A payables clerk could collude with the payee to split extra cash paid out by submitting the same supporting documents for a second payment.

All spoiled and voided checks should be defaced and retained. If defaced checks are not retained, an employee could steal a check and then claim that it was written incorrectly and thrown away. The clerk could then use the stolen check to make an unauthorized payment.

Checking Account Documents

The previous section explained the need for businesses to use checking accounts. A description of four main types of forms associated with a bank checking account follows:

Signature Card

A bank **signature card** shows the bank account number and the signatures of the people authorized to sign checks. The card is retained in the bank's files. If a bank employee is unfamiliar with the signature on a check, he or she can refer to the signature card to verify the signature before cashing the check.

Deposit Ticket

Each deposit of cash or checks is accompanied by a **deposit ticket,** which normally identifies the account number and the name of the account. The depositor lists the individual amounts of currency, coins, and checks, as well as the total deposited, on the deposit ticket.

Bank Check

A written check affects three parties: (1) the person or business writing the check (the *payer*); (2) the bank on which the check is drawn; and (3) the person or business to whom the check is payable (the *payee*). Companies often write **checks** using multicopy, prenumbered forms, with the name of the issuing business preprinted on the face of each check. A remittance notice is usually attached to the check forms. This portion of the form provides the issuer space to record what the check is for (e.g., what invoices are being paid), the amount being disbursed, and the date of payment. When signed by the person whose signature is on the signature card, the check authorizes the bank to transfer the face amount of the check from the payer's account to the payee.

Bank Statement

Periodically, the bank sends the depositor a **bank statement.** The bank statement is presented from the bank's point of view. Checking accounts are liabilities to a bank because the bank is obligated to pay back the money that customers have deposited in their accounts. Therefore, in the bank's accounting records a customer's checking account has a *credit* balance. As a result, **bank statement debit memos** describe transactions that reduce the customer's account balance (the bank's liability). **Bank statement credit memos** describe activities that increase the customer's account balance (the bank's liability). Since a checking account is an asset (cash) to the depositor, a *bank statement debit memo* requires a *credit entry* to the cash account on the depositor's books. Likewise, when a bank tells you that it has credited your account, you will debit your cash account in response.

Bank statements normally report (a) the balance of the account at the beginning of the period; (b) additions for customer deposits made during the period; (c) other additions described in credit memos (e.g., for interest earned); (d) subtractions for the payment of checks drawn on the account during the period; (e) other subtractions described in debit memos (e.g., for service charges); (f) a running balance of the account; and (g) the balance of the account at the end of the period. The sample bank statement in Exhibit 7.2 illustrates these

EXHIBIT 7.2

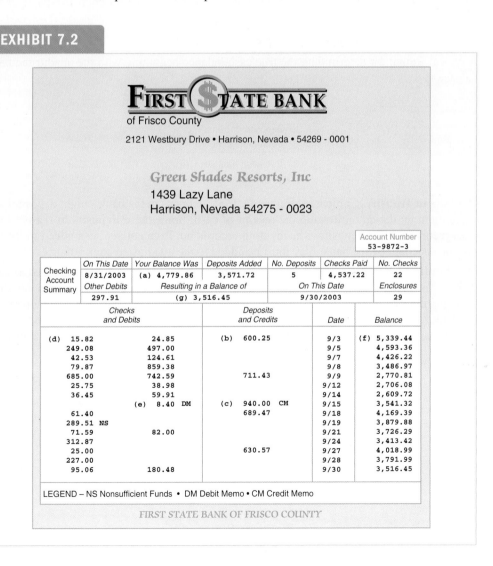

Checking Account Summary	On This Date	Your Balance Was	Deposits Added	No. Deposits	Checks Paid	No. Checks
	8/31/2003	(a) 4,779.86	3,571.72	5	4,537.22	22
	Other Debits	Resulting in a Balance of		On This Date		Enclosures
	297.91	(g) 3,516.45		9/30/2003		29

Checks and Debits		Deposits and Credits		Date	Balance
(d) 15.82	24.85	(b) 600.25		9/3	(f) 5,339.44
249.08	497.00			9/5	4,593.36
42.53	124.61			9/7	4,426.22
79.87	859.38			9/8	3,486.97
685.00	742.59	711.43		9/9	2,770.81
25.75	38.98			9/12	2,706.08
36.45	59.91			9/14	2,609.72
	(e) 8.40 DM	(c) 940.00 CM		9/15	3,541.32
61.40		689.47		9/18	4,169.39
289.51 NS				9/19	3,879.88
71.59	82.00			9/21	3,726.29
312.87				9/24	3,413.42
25.00		630.57		9/27	4,018.99
227.00				9/28	3,791.99
95.06	180.48			9/30	3,516.45

LEGEND – NS Nonsufficient Funds • DM Debit Memo • CM Credit Memo

FIRST STATE BANK OF FRISCO COUNTY

items with references to the preceding letters in parentheses. Normally, the canceled checks or copies of them are enclosed with the bank statement.

Reconciling the Bank Statement

Prepare a bank reconciliation.

Topic Tackler
PLUS

7-2

Usually the ending balance reported on the bank statement differs from the balance in the depositor's cash account as of the same date. The discrepancy is normally attributable to timing differences. For example, a depositor deducts the amount of a check from its cash account at the same time the check is written. However, the bank does not deduct the amount of the check from the depositor's account until the payee presents it for payment, which may be days, weeks, or even months after the check is written. As a result, the balance on the depositor's books is lower than the balance on the bank's books. Companies prepare a **bank reconciliation** to explain the differences between the cash balance reported on the bank statement and the cash balance recorded in the depositor's accounting records.

Determining True Cash Balance

A bank reconciliation normally begins with the cash balance reported by the bank which is called the **unadjusted bank balance.** The adjustments necessary to determine the amount of cash that the depositor actually owns as of the date of the bank statement are then added to and subtracted from the unadjusted bank balance. The final total is the **true cash balance.** The true cash balance is independently reached a second time by making adjustments to the **unadjusted book balance.** The bank account is reconciled when the true cash balance determined from the perspective of the unadjusted *bank* balance agrees with the true cash balance determined from the perspective of the unadjusted *book* balance. The procedures a company uses to determine the *true cash balance* from the two different perspectives are outlined here.

Adjustments to the Bank Balance

A typical format for determining the true cash balance beginning with the unadjusted bank balance is

> Unadjusted bank balance
> + Deposits in transit
> − Outstanding checks
> _____
> = True cash balance

Deposits in Transit   Companies frequently leave deposits in the bank's night depository or make them on the day following the receipt of cash. Since these **deposits in transit** have been recorded in the depositor's accounting records but have not yet been added to the depositor's account by the bank, they must be added to the unadjusted bank balance.

Outstanding Checks   These are disbursements that have been properly recorded as cash deductions on the depositor's books. However, the bank has not deducted the amounts from the depositor's bank account because the checks have not yet been presented by the payee to the bank for payment; that is, the checks have not "cleared" the bank. **Outstanding checks** must be subtracted from the unadjusted bank balance to determine the true cash balance.

Adjustments to the Book Balance

A typical format for determining the true cash balance beginning with the unadjusted book balance is as follows:

> Unadjusted book balance
> + Accounts receivable collections
> + Interest earned
> − Bank service charges
> − Non-sufficient-funds (NSF) checks
> _____
> = True cash balance

Accounts Receivable Collections To collect cash as quickly as possible, many companies have their customers send payments directly to the bank. The bank adds the collection directly to the depositor's account and notifies the depositor about the collection through a credit memo that is included on the bank statement. The depositor adds the amount of the cash collections to the unadjusted book balance in the process of determining the true cash balance.

Interest Earned Banks pay interest on certain checking accounts. The amount of the interest is added directly to the depositor's bank account. The bank notifies the depositor about the interest through a credit memo that is included on the bank statement. The depositor adds the amount of the interest revenue to the unadjusted book balance in the process of determining the true cash balance.

Service Charges Banks frequently charge depositors fees for services performed. They may also charge a penalty if the depositor fails to maintain a specified minimum cash balance throughout the period. Banks deduct such fees and penalties directly from the depositor's account and advise the depositor of the deduction through a debit memo that is included on the bank statement. The depositor deducts such **service charges** from the unadjusted book balance to determine the true cash balance.

Non-Sufficient-Funds (NSF) Checks **NSF checks** are checks that a company obtains from its customers. The checks are then deposited in the company's checking account. However, when the checks are submitted to the customers' banks for payment, the banks refuse payment because there is insufficient money in the customers' accounts. When such checks are returned, the amounts of the checks are deducted from the company's bank account balance. The company is advised of NSF checks through debit memos that appear on the bank statement. The depositor deducts the amounts of the NSF checks from the unadjusted book balance in the process of determining the true cash balance.

Correction of Errors

In the course of reconciling the bank statement with the cash account, the depositor may discover errors in the bank's records, the depositor's records, or both. If an error is found on the bank statement, an adjustment for it is made to the unadjusted bank balance to determine the true cash balance, and the bank should be notified immediately to correct its records. Errors made by the depositor require adjustments to the book balance to arrive at the true cash balance.

Certified Checks

A **certified check** is guaranteed for payment by a bank. Whereas a regular check is deducted from the customer's account when it is presented for payment, a certified check is deducted from the customer's account when the bank certifies that the check is good. Certified checks, therefore, *have* been deducted by the bank in determining the unadjusted bank balance, whether they have cleared the bank or remain outstanding as of the date of the bank statement. Since certified checks are deducted both from bank and depositor records immediately, they do not cause differences between the depositor and bank balances. As a result, certified checks are not included in a bank reconciliation.

Illustrating a Bank Reconciliation

The following example illustrates preparing the bank reconciliation for Green Shades Resorts, Inc. (GSRI). The bank statement for GSRI is displayed in Exhibit 7.2. Exhibit 7.3 illustrates the completed bank reconciliation. The items on the reconciliation are described below.

GREEN SHADES
RESORTS, INC.

Adjustments to the Bank Balance

As of September 30, 2008, the bank statement showed an unadjusted balance of $3,516.45. A review of the bank statement disclosed three adjustments that had to be made to the unadjusted bank balance to determine GSRI's true cash balance.

1. Comparing the deposits on the bank statement with deposits recorded in GSRI's accounting records indicated there was $724.11 of deposits in transit.

EXHIBIT 7.3

GREEN SHADES RESORTS, INC.
Bank Reconciliation
September 30, 2008

Unadjusted bank balance, September 30, 2008	$3,516.45
Add: Deposits in transit	724.11
Bank error: Check drawn on Green Valley Resorts charged to GSRI	25.00
Less: Outstanding checks	

Check No.	Date	Amount
639	Sept. 18	$ 13.75
646	Sept. 20	29.00
672	Sept. 27	192.50

Total	(235.25)
True cash balance, September 30, 2008	$4,030.31
Unadjusted book balance, September 30, 2008	$3,361.22
Add: Receivable collected by bank	940.00
Error made by accountant (Check no. 633 recorded as $63.45 instead of $36.45)	27.00
Less: Bank service charges	(8.40)
NSF check	(289.51)
True cash balance, September 30, 2008	$4,030.31

2. An examination of the returned checks disclosed that the bank had erroneously deducted a $25 check written by Green Valley Resorts from GSRI's bank account. This amount must be added back to the unadjusted bank balance to determine the true cash balance.

3. The checks returned with the bank statement were sorted and compared to the cash records. Three checks with amounts totaling $235.25 were outstanding.

After these adjustment are made GSRI's true cash balance is determined to be $4,030.31.

Adjustments to the Book Balance

As indicated in Exhibit 7.3, GSRI's unadjusted book balance as of September 30, 2008, was $3,361.22. This balance differs from GSRI's true cash balance because of four unrecorded accounting events:

1. The bank collected a $940 account receivable for GSRI.

2. GSRI's accountant made a $27 recording error.

3. The bank charged GSRI an $8.40 service fee.

4. GSRI had deposited a $289.51 check from a customer who did not have sufficient funds to cover the check.

Two of these four adjustments increase the unadjusted cash balance. The other two decrease the unadjusted cash balance. After the adjustments have been recorded, the cash account reflects the true cash balance of $4,030.31 ($3,361.22 unadjusted cash balance + $940.00 receivable collection + $27.00 recording error − $8.40 service charge − $289.51 NSF check). Since the true balance determined from the perspective of the bank statement agrees with the true balance determined from the perspective of GSRI's books, the bank statement has been successfully reconciled with the accounting records.

Updating GSRI's Accounting Records

Each of the adjustments to the book balance must be recorded in GSRI's financial records. The effects of each adjustment on the financial statements are as follows.

Adjustment 1 **Recording the $940 receivable collection increases cash and reduces accounts receivable.**

The event is an asset exchange transaction. The effect of the collection on GSRI's financial statements is:

Assets			=	Liab.	+	Equity	Rev.	−	Exp.	=	Net Inc.	Cash Flow
Cash	+	Accts. Rec.										
940	+	(940)	=	NA	+	NA	NA	−	NA	=	NA	940 OA

Adjustment 2 **Assume the $27 recording error occurred because GSRI's accountant accidentally transposed two numbers when recording check no. 633 for utilities expense.**

The check was written to pay utilities expense of $36.45 but was recorded as a $63.45 disbursement. Since cash payments are overstated by $27.00 ($63.45 − $36.45), this amount must be added back to GSRI's cash balance and deducted from the utilities expense account, which increases net income. The effects on the financial statements are:

Assets	=	Liab.	+	Equity	Rev.	−	Exp.	=	Net Inc.	Cash Flow
Cash	=			Ret. Earn.						
27	=	NA	+	27	NA	−	(27)	=	27	27 OA

Adjustment 3 **The $8.40 service charge is an expense that reduces assets, stockholders' equity, net income, and cash.**

The effects are:

Assets	=	Liab.	+	Equity	Rev.	−	Exp.	=	Net Inc.	Cash Flow
Cash	=			Ret. Earn.						
(8.40)	=	NA	+	(8.40)	NA	−	8.40	=	(8.40)	(8.40) OA

Adjustment 4 **The $289.51 NSF check reduces GSRI's cash balance.**

When it originally accepted the customer's check, GSRI increased its cash account. Since there is not enough money in the customer's bank account to pay the check, GSRI didn't actually receive cash so GSRI must reduce its cash account. GSRI will still try to collect the money from the customer. In the meantime, it will show the amount of the NSF check as an account receivable. The adjusting entry to record the NSF check is an asset exchange transaction. Cash decreases and accounts receivable increases. The effect on GSRI's financial statements is:

Assets			=	Liab.	+	Equity	Rev.	−	Exp.	=	Net Inc.	Cash Flow
Cash	+	Accts. Rec.										
(289.51)	+	289.51	=	NA	+	NA	NA	−	NA	=	NA	(289.51) OA

Journal Entries

The journal entries for the four adjustments described above are as follows:

Account Title	Debit	Credit
Cash	940.00	
Accounts receivable		940.00
To record the account receivable collected by the bank		
Cash	27.00	
Utilities expense		27.00
To correct error on recording check no. 633		
Bank service charge expense	8.40	
Cash		8.40
To record service charge expense		
Accounts receivable	289.51	
Cash		289.51
To establish receivable due from customer who wrote the bad check		

Cash Short and Over

Sometimes employees make mistakes when collecting cash from or making change for customers. When such errors occur, the amount of money in the cash register will not agree with the amount of cash receipts recorded on the cash register tape. For example, suppose that when a customer paid for $17.95 of merchandise with a $20 bill, the sales clerk returned $3.05 in change instead of $2.05. If, at the end of the day, the cash register tape shows total receipts of $487.50, the cash drawer would contain only $486.50. The actual cash balance is less than the expected cash balance by $1. Any shortage of cash or excess of cash is recorded in a special account called **Cash Short and Over.** In this example, the shortage is recorded with the following journal entry:

Account Title	Debit	Credit
Cash	486.50	
Cash short and over	1.00	
Sales		487.50

A cash shortage is an expense. It is recorded by debiting the Cash Short and Over account. An overage of cash represents revenue and is recorded by crediting the Cash Short and Over account. As with other expense and revenue items, the balance of the Cash Short and Over account is closed to the Retained Earnings account at the end of the accounting period.

CHECK YOURSELF 7.2

The following information was drawn from Reliance Company's October bank statement. The unadjusted bank balance on October 31 was $2,300. The statement showed that the bank had collected a $200 account receivable for Reliance. The statement also included $20 of bank service charges for October and a $100 check payable to Reliance that was returned NSF. A comparison of the bank statement with company accounting records indicates that there was a $500 deposit in transit and $1,800 of checks outstanding at the end of the month. Based on this information, determine the true cash balance on October 31.

Answer

Since the unadjusted book balance is not given, start with the unadjusted bank balance to determine the true cash balance. The collection of the receivable, the bank service charges, and the NSF check are already recognized in the unadjusted bank balance, so these items are not used to determine the true cash balance. Determine the true cash balance by adding the deposit in transit to and subtracting the outstanding checks from the unadjusted bank balance. The true cash balance is $1,000 ($2,300 unadjusted bank balance + $500 deposit in transit − $1,800 outstanding checks).

Using Petty Cash Funds

LO 4

Explain the use of a petty cash fund.

While checks are used for most disbursements, payments for small items such as postage, delivery charges, taxi fares, employees' supper money, and so on are frequently made with currency. Companies frequently establish a **petty cash fund** to maintain effective control over these small cash disbursements. The fund is established for a specified dollar amount, such as $300, and is controlled by one employee, called the *petty cash custodian.*

Petty cash funds are usually maintained on an **imprest basis,** which means that the money disbursed is replenished on a periodic basis. The fund is created by drawing a check on the regular checking account, cashing it, and giving the currency to the petty cash custodian. The custodian normally keeps the currency under lock and key. The amount of the petty cash fund depends on what it is used for, how often it is used, and how often it is replenished. It should be large enough to handle disbursements for a reasonable time period, such as several weeks or a month.

Establishing a petty cash fund merely transfers cash from a bank account to a safety box inside the company offices. The establishment is an asset exchange event. The cash account decreases, and an account called Petty Cash increases. The effects on the financial statements of establishing a $300 petty cash fund and the related journal entry are shown here:

Assets			=	Liab.	+	Equity	Rev.	−	Exp.	=	Net Inc.	Cash Flow
Cash	+	Petty Cash										
(300)	+	300	=	NA	+	NA	NA	−	NA	=	NA	NA

Account Title	Debit	Credit
Petty cash	300.00	
Cash		300.00

When money is disbursed from the petty cash fund, the custodian should complete a **petty cash voucher,** such as the one in Exhibit 7.4. Any supporting documents, such as an invoice, restaurant bill, or parking fee receipt, should be attached to the petty cash voucher. The person who receives the cash should sign the voucher as evidence of receiving the money. The total of the amounts recorded on the petty cash vouchers plus the remaining coins and currency should equal the balance of the petty cash ledger account. *No journal entry is made in the accounting records when petty cash funds are disbursed.* The effects on the financial statements are recorded at the time when the petty cash fund is replenished (when additional currency is put into the petty cash safety box).

When the amount of currency in the petty cash fund is relatively low, the fund is replenished. The petty cash vouchers are totaled, the amount of any cash short or over is determined, and a check is issued to the bank to obtain the currency needed to return the fund to its imprest balance. For example, suppose the $300 petty cash fund is replenished when the

EXHIBIT 7.4

Petty cash voucher no. _____

To: _____ Date _____, 20 _____

Explanation: Account No. _____ Amount _____

Approved by _____ Received by _____

total of the petty cash vouchers is $216. The vouchers can be classified according to different types of expenses or listed in total as miscellaneous expense. Assuming the company classifies petty cash expenditures as miscellaneous expense, the journal entries to record replenishing the fund are as follows:

Account Title	Debit	Credit
Miscellaneous expense	216.00	
Petty cash		216.00
To record expenses paid from the petty cash fund		
Petty cash	216.00	
Cash		216.00
To replenish the petty cash fund		

If desired, the effect of the entries could be recorded more efficiently. Since the credit to the Petty Cash account is offset by a debit to the same account, a single entry debiting miscellaneous expense and crediting cash would have the same effect on the accounts. The entry more frequently used in practice to record replenishing petty cash is:

Account Title	Debit	Credit
Miscellaneous expense	216.00	
Cash		216.00

The replenishment affects the financial statements in the same manner as any other cash expense. It reduces assets, stockholders' equity, net income, and cash flow, as follows:

Assets	=	Liab.	+	Equity	Rev.	−	Exp.	=	Net Inc.	Cash Flow
Cash	=			Ret. Earn.						
(216)	=	NA	+	(216)	NA	−	216	=	(216)	(216) OA

If management desires more detailed information about petty cash expenditures, the vouchers can be sorted into postage, $66; delivery charges, $78.40; taxi fares, $28; and supper money, $43.60, in which case the journal entry to replenish the fund could be recorded as follows:

Account Title	Debit	Credit
Postage expense	66.00	
Delivery expense	78.40	
Taxi fares expense	28.00	
Employee meal expense	43.60	
Cash		216.00

Once the vouchers are checked, the fund replenished, and the journal entry recorded, the vouchers should be indelibly marked *Paid* so they cannot be reused.

Sometimes, cash shortages and overages are discovered when the money in the petty cash fund is physically counted. Suppose that a physical count discloses $212.30 in petty cash vouchers and only $87 in currency and coins. Assuming an imprest petty cash balance of $300, the journal entries necessary to replenish the fund are as follows:

Account Title	Debit	Credit
Miscellaneous expense	212.30	
Cash short and over	.70	
Cash		213.00
To replenish the petty cash fund		

If cash shortages or overages do not occur frequently and are of insignificant amounts, companies are likely to include them in miscellaneous expense or miscellaneous revenue.

CHECK YOURSELF 7.3

Cornerstone Corporation established a $400 petty cash fund that was replenished when it contained $30 of currency and coins and $378 of receipts for miscellaneous expenses. Based on this information, determine the amount of cash short or over to be recognized. Explain how the shortage or overage would be reported in the financial statements. Also determine the amount of petty cash expenses that were recognized when the fund was replenished.

Answer

The fund contained $408 of currency and receipts ($30 currency + $378 of receipts), resulting in a cash overage of $8 ($408 − $400). The overage would be reported as miscellaneous revenue on the income statement. The amount of petty cash expenses recognized would equal the amount of the expense receipts, which is $378.

THE FINANCIAL ANALYST

Current versus Noncurrent

Having enough money to pay bills is critical to business survival. To assess the ability of a business to pay its bills, financial analysts frequently classify assets and liabilities according to their liquidity. The more quickly an asset is converted to cash, the more *liquid* it is. To assist analysts in assessing a company's liquidity, assets are usually divided into two major classifications: *current* and *noncurrent.* Current items are also referred to as *short term* and noncurrent items as *long term.*

LO 5

Prepare a classified balance sheet.

A **current (short-term) asset** is expected to be converted to cash or consumed within one year or an operating cycle, whichever is longer. An **operating cycle** is defined as the average time it takes a business to convert cash to inventory, inventory to accounts receivable, and accounts receivable back to cash. The financial tools used to measure the length of an operating cycle for particular businesses are discussed in Chapter 8. For most businesses, the operating cycle is less than one year. As a result, the one-year rule normally prevails with respect to classifying assets as current. The current assets section of a balance sheet typically includes the following items:

> Current assets
>   Cash
>   Marketable securities
>   Accounts receivable
>   Short-term notes receivable
>   Interest receivable
>   Inventory
>   Supplies
>   Prepaids

Given the definition of current assets, it seems reasonable to assume that **current (short-term) liabilities** would be those due within one year or an operating cycle, whichever is longer. This assumption is usually correct. However, an exception is made for long-term renewable debt. For example, consider a liability that was issued with a 20-year term to maturity. After 19 years, the liability becomes due within one year and is, therefore, a current liability. Even so, the liability will be classified as long term if the company plans to issue new long-term debt and to use the proceeds from that debt to repay the maturing liability.

This situation is described as *refinancing short-term debt on a long-term basis.* In general, if a business does not plan to use any of its current assets to repay a debt, that debt is listed as long term even if it is due within one year. The current liabilities section of a balance sheet typically includes the following items:

Current liabilities
    Accounts payable
    Short-term notes payable
    Wages payable
    Taxes payable
    Interest payable

Balance sheets that distinguish between current and noncurrent items are called **classified balance sheets.** To enhance the usefulness of accounting information, most real-world balance sheets are classified. Exhibit 7.5 displays an example of a classified balance sheet.

EXHIBIT 7.5

LIMBAUGH COMPANY
Classified Balance Sheet
As of December 31, 2008
Assets

Current Assets		
Cash	$ 20,000	
Accounts receivable	35,000	
Inventory	230,000	
Prepaid rent	3,600	
Total current assets		$288,600
Property, Plant, and Equipment		
Office equipment	$ 80,000	
Less: Accumulated depreciation	(25,000)	55,000
Building	340,000	
Less: Accumulated depreciation	(40,000)	300,000
Land	120,000	
Total property, plant, and equipment		475,000
Total assets		$763,600

Liabilities and Stockholders' Equity

Current Liabilities		
Accounts payable	$ 32,000	
Notes payable (short-term)	120,000	
Salaries payable	32,000	
Unearned revenue	9,800	
Total current liabilities		$193,800
Long-Term Liabilities		
Note payable		100,000
Total liabilities		293,800
Stockholders' Equity		
Common stock	200,000	
Retained earnings	269,800	469,800
Total liabilities and stockholders' equity		$763,600

Liquidity describes the ability to generate sufficient short-term cash flows to pay obligations as they come due. **Solvency** is the ability to repay liabilities in the long run. Liquidity and solvency are both important to the survival of a business. Financial analysts rely on several ratios to help them evaluate a company's liquidity and solvency. The *debt to assets* ratio introduced in Chapter 3 is one tool used to measure solvency. The primary ratio used to evaluate liquidity is the current ratio.

Use the current ratio to assess the level of liquidity.

Current Ratio

The **current ratio** is defined as:

$$\frac{\text{Current assets}}{\text{Current liabilities}}$$

Since current assets normally exceed current liabilities, this ratio is usually greater than 100 percent. For example, if a company has $250 in current assets and $100 in current liabilities, current assets are 250 percent of current liabilities. The current ratio is traditionally expressed as a decimal rather than as a percentage, however; most analysts would describe this example as a current ratio of 2.5 to 1 ($250 ÷ $100 = $2.50 in current assets for every $1 in current liabilities). This book uses the traditional format when referring to the current ratio.

The current ratio is among the most widely used ratios in analyzing financial statements. Current ratios can be too high as well as too low. A low ratio suggests that the company may have difficulty paying its short-term obligations. A high ratio suggests that a company is not maximizing its earnings potential because investments in liquid assets usually do not earn as much money as investments in other assets. Companies must try to maintain an effective balance between liquid assets (so they can pay bills on time) and nonliquid assets (so they can earn a good return).

Real-World Data

Exhibit 7.6 presents the current ratios and debt to assets ratios for six companies in three different industries. These data are for fiscal years ending in late 2005 or early 2006.

Which of these companies has the highest level of financial risk? Perhaps Dominion Resources because it has the highest debt to assets ratio. Notice that the electric utilities have higher debt to assets ratios and lower current ratios than those of the companies in the building supplies business. Does this mean that electric utilities are riskier investments? Not necessarily; since the companies are in different industries, the ratios may not be comparable. Utility companies have a more stable revenue base than building companies. If the economy turns downward, people are likely to continue to use utilities. However, they are less likely to buy a new home or to add on to their existing home. Because utility companies have a stable source of revenue, creditors are likely to feel comfortable with higher levels of debt for them than they would for building companies. As previously stated, the industry must be considered when interpreting ratios, but of the companies shown in Exhibit 7.6, Whole Foods Market appears to have the lowest financial risk.

EXHIBIT 7.6			
Industry	**Company**	**Current Ratio**	**Debt to Assets Ratio**
Electric utilities	American Electric Power	0.72	0.75
	Dominion Resources	0.70	0.80
Grocery stores	Kroger	0.96	0.79
	Whole Foods Market	1.61	0.28
Building supplies	Home Depot	1.19	0.40
	Lowe's	1.34	0.42

FOCUS ON INTERNATIONAL ISSUES

WHY ARE THESE BALANCE SHEETS BACKWARD?

Many of the differences in accounting rules used around the world would be difficult to detect by merely comparing financial statements from companies in different countries. For example, if a balance sheet for a U.S. company and one for a U.K. company both report an asset called *land,* it might not be clear whether the reported amounts were computed by using the same measurement rules or different measurement rules. Did both companies use historical cost as a basis for measurement? Perhaps not, but this would be difficult to determine by merely comparing balance sheets from two countries.

However, one difference between financial reporting in the United Kingdom and the United States that is very obvious is the arrangement of assets on the balance sheet. In this chapter, we explain that U.S. GAAP requires current assets to be shown first and noncurrent assets second; the same is true of liabilities. In the United Kingdom, noncurrent assets appear first, followed by current assets; however, liabilities are shown in the same order as in the United States. In other countries (e.g., France), both assets and liabilities are shown with noncurrent items first. The accounting rules of some countries require that equity be shown before liabilities; this is the opposite of U.S. GAAP. Therefore, to someone who learned accounting in the United States, the balance sheets of companies from some countries may appear "backward" or "upside down."

No matter in what order the assets, liabilities, and equity accounts are arranged on a company's balance sheet, one accounting concept is true throughout the free world:

Assets = Liabilities + Equity

For a real-world example of the items discussed here, look up the financial statements of ITV, the largest commercial television network in the United Kingdom. Go to www.itvplc.com. Click on "Company reports" under "Financial information." Next, click on "Annual reports 2005," or whatever is the most current fiscal year.

Finally, note that the debt to assets ratios, with the exception of the grocery stores, tend to be grouped by industry. Current ratios do vary somewhat among different industries, but they probably do not vary as much as the debt to assets ratios. Why? Because all companies, regardless of how they finance their total assets, must keep sufficient current assets on hand to repay current liabilities.

◀◀ A Look Back

The policies and procedures used to provide reasonable assurance that the objectives of an enterprise will be accomplished are called *internal controls,* which can be subdivided into two categories: accounting controls and administrative controls. *Accounting controls* are composed of procedures designed to safeguard the assets and ensure that the accounting records contain reliable information. *Administrative controls* are designed to evaluate performance and the degree of compliance with company policies and public laws. While the mechanics of internal control systems vary from company to company, the more prevalent features include the following:

1. *Separation of duties.* Whenever possible, the functions of authorization, recording, and custody should be exercised by different individuals.

2. *Quality of employees.* Employees should be qualified to competently perform the duties that are assigned to them. Companies must establish hiring practices to screen out unqualified candidates. Furthermore, procedures should be established to ensure that employees receive appropriate training to maintain their competence.

3. *Bonded employees.* Employees in sensitive positions should be covered by a fidelity bond that provides insurance to reimburse losses due to illegal actions committed by employees.

4. *Required absences.* Employees should be required to take extended absences from their jobs so that they are not always present to hide unscrupulous or illegal activities.

5. *Procedures manual.* To promote compliance, the procedures for processing transactions should be clearly described in a manual.

6. *Authority and responsibility.* To motivate employees and promote effective control, clear lines of authority and responsibility should be established.

7. *Prenumbered documents.* Prenumbered documents minimize the likelihood of missing or duplicate documents. Prenumbered forms should be used for all important documents such as purchase orders, receiving reports, invoices, and checks.

8. *Physical control.* Locks, fences, security personnel, and other physical devices should be employed to safeguard assets.

9. *Performance evaluations.* Because few people can evaluate their own performance objectively, independent performance evaluations should be performed. Substandard performance will likely persist unless employees are encouraged to take corrective action.

Because cash is such an important business asset and because it is tempting to steal, much of the discussion of internal controls in this chapter focused on cash controls. Special procedures should be employed to control the receipts and payments of cash. One of the most common control policies is to use *checking accounts* for all except petty cash disbursements.

A *bank reconciliation* should be prepared each month to explain differences between the bank statement and a company's internal accounting records. A common reconciliation format determines the true cash balance based on both bank and book records. Items that typically appear on a bank reconciliation include the following:

Unadjusted bank balance	XXX	Unadjusted book balance	XXX
Add		Add	
Deposits in transit	XXX	Interest revenue	XXX
		Collection of receivables	XXX
Subtract		Subtract	
Outstanding checks	XXX	Bank service charges	XXX
		NSF checks	XXX
True cash balance	XXX	True cash balance	XXX

Agreement of the two true cash balances provides evidence that accounting for cash transactions has been accurate.

Another common internal control policy for protecting cash is using a *petty cash fund.* Normally, an employee who is designated as the petty cash custodian is entrusted with a small amount of cash. The custodian reimburses employees for small expenditures made on behalf of the company in exchange for authorized receipts from the employees at the time they are reimbursed. The total of these receipts plus the remaining currency in the fund should always equal the amount of funds entrusted to the custodian. Journal entries to recognize the expenses incurred are made at the time the fund is replenished.

Finally, the chapter discussed assessing organizational *liquidity.* The *current ratio* is determined by dividing current assets by current liabilities. The higher the ratio, the more liquid the company's assets.

A Look Forward >>

Accounting for receivables and payables was introduced in Chapter 2 using relatively simple illustrations. For example, we assumed that customers who purchased services on account always paid their bills. In real business practice, some customers do not pay their bills. Among other topics, Chapter 8 examines how companies account for bad debts.

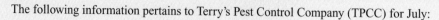

SELF-STUDY REVIEW PROBLEM

The following information pertains to Terry's Pest Control Company (TPCC) for July:

1. The unadjusted bank balance at July 31 was $870.
2. The bank statement included the following items:
   (a) $60 credit memo for interest earned by TPCC.
   (b) A $200 NSF check made payable to TPCC.
   (c) A $110 debit memo for bank service charges.
3. The unadjusted book balance at July 31 was $1,400.
4. A comparison of the bank statement with company accounting records disclosed the following:
   (a) A $400 deposit in transit at July 31.
   (b) Outstanding checks totaling $120 at the end of the month.

Required

a. Prepare a bank reconciliation.
b. Prepare in general journal format the entries necessary to adjust TPCC's cash account to its true balance.

Solution to Requirement a

TERRY'S PEST CONTROL COMPANY Bank Reconciliation July 31	
Unadjusted bank balance	$ 870
Add: Deposits in transit	400
Less: Outstanding checks	(120)
True cash balance	$1,150
Unadjusted book balance	$1,400
Add: Interest revenue	60
Less: NSF check	(200)
Less: Bank service charges	(110)
True cash balance	$1,150

Solution to Requirement b

Ref.	Account Title	Debit	Credit
1.	Cash	60	
	Interest revenue		60
2.	Accounts receivable	200	
	Cash		200
3.	Bank service charge expense	110	
	Cash		110

KEY TERMS

accounting controls 344
administrative controls 344
authority manual 345
bank reconciliation 350
bank statement 349

bank statement credit
   memo 349
bank statement debit
   memo 349
cash 346

cash short and over 354
certified check 351
checks 348
classified balance
   sheet 358

current (short-term)
   asset 357
current (short-term)
   liability 357
current ratio 359

deposit ticket 348
deposits in transit 350
fidelity bond 344
general authority 345
imprest basis 355
internal controls 343

liquidity 359
non-sufficient-funds (NSF)
    check 351
operating cycle 357
outstanding checks 350
petty cash fund 355

petty cash voucher 355
procedures manual 345
separation of duties 344
service charges 351
signature card 348
solvency 359

specific authorizations 345
true cash balance 350
unadjusted bank balance 350
unadjusted book balance 350

QUESTIONS

1. What are the policies and procedures called that are used to provide reasonable assurance that the objectives of an enterprise will be accomplished?
2. What is the difference between accounting controls and administrative controls?
3. What are several features of a strong internal control system?
4. What is meant by *separation of duties*? Give an illustration.
5. What are the attributes of a high-quality employee?
6. What is a fidelity bond? Explain its purpose.
7. Why is it important that every employee periodically take a leave of absence or vacation?
8. What are the purpose and importance of a procedures manual?
9. What is the difference between specific and general authorizations?
10. Why should documents (checks, invoices, receipts) be prenumbered?
11. What procedures are important in the physical control of assets and accounting records?
12. What is the purpose of independent verification of performance?
13. What items are considered cash?
14. Why is cash more susceptible to theft or embezzlement than other assets?
15. Giving written copies of receipts to customers can help prevent what type of illegal acts?
16. What procedures can help to protect cash receipts?
17. What procedures can help protect cash disbursements?
18. What effect does a debit memo in a bank statement have on the Cash account? What effect does a credit memo in a bank statement have on the Cash account?
19. What information is normally included in a bank statement?
20. Why might a bank statement reflect a balance that is larger than the balance recorded in the depositor's books? What could cause the bank balance to be smaller than the book balance?
21. What is the purpose of a bank reconciliation?
22. What is an outstanding check?
23. What is a deposit in transit?
24. What is a certified check?
25. How is an NSF check accounted for in the accounting records?
26. What is the purpose of the Cash Short and Over account?
27. What is the purpose of a petty cash fund?
28. What types of expenditures are usually made from a petty cash fund?
29. What is the difference between a current asset and a noncurrent asset?
30. What are some common current assets?
31. What does the term *operating cycle* mean?
32. What are some common current liabilities?
33. What is a classified balance sheet?
34. What is the difference between the liquidity and the solvency of a business?
35. How does the arrangement of assets and liabilities on financial statements differ for the United States, the United Kingdom, and France?
36. The higher the current ratio, the better the company's financial condition. Do you agree or disagree with this statement? Explain.
37. Does a high (80 to 95 percent) debt to assets ratio mean that a business is in financial difficulty? What types of businesses traditionally operate with high debt to assets ratios?

MULTIPLE-CHOICE QUESTIONS

Quiz 7

Multiple-choice questions are provided on the text Web site at www.mhhe.com/edmonds6e.

EXERCISES—SERIES A

All Exercises in Series A are available with McGraw-Hill's Homework Manager®

L.O. 1

Exercise 7-1A   *Internal control procedures*

Required

a. Name and describe the two categories of internal controls.

b. What is the purpose of internal controls?

L.O. 1

Exercise 7-2A   *Internal controls for equipment*

Required

List the internal control procedures that pertain to the protection of business equipment.

L.O. 2

Exercise 7-3A   *Features of internal control procedures for cash*

Required

List and discuss effective internal control procedures that apply to cash.

L.O. 1

Exercise 7-4A   *Internal control procedures*

Dick Haney is opening a new business that will sell sporting goods. It will initially be a small operation, and he is concerned about the security of his assets. He will not be able to be at the business all of the time and will have to rely on his employees and internal control procedures to ensure that transactions are properly accounted for and assets are safeguarded. He will have a store manager and two other employees who will be sales personnel and stock personnel and who will also perform any other duties necessary. Dick will be in the business on a regular basis. He has come to you for advice.

Required

Write a memo to Dick outlining the procedures that he should implement to ensure that his store assets are protected and that the financial transactions are properly recorded.

L.O. 1

Exercise 7-5A   *Internal controls to prevent theft*

Sarah Black worked as the parts manager for Country Automobiles, a local automobile dealership. Sarah was very dedicated and never missed a day of work. Since Country was a small operation, she was the only employee in the parts department. Her duties consisted of ordering parts for stock and as needed for repairs, receiving the parts and checking them in, distributing them as needed to the shop or to customers for purchase, and keeping track of and taking the year-end inventory of parts. Country decided to expand and needed to secure additional financing. The local bank agreed to a loan contingent on an audit of the dealership. One requirement of the audit was to oversee the inventory count of both automobiles and parts on hand. Sarah was clearly nervous, explaining that she had just inventoried all parts in the parts department and supplied the auditors with a detailed list. The inventory showed parts on hand worth $225,000. This seemed a little excessive, and the accountants decided they needed to verify at least a substantial part of the inventory. When the auditors began their counts, a pattern began to develop. Each type of part seemed to be one or two items short when the actual count was taken. This raised more concern. Although Sarah assured the auditors the parts were just misplaced, the auditors continued the count. After completing the count of parts on hand, the auditors could document only $155,000 of actual parts. Suddenly, Sarah quit her job and moved to another state.

Required

a. What do you suppose caused the discrepancy between the actual count and the count that Sarah had supplied?

b. What procedures could be put into place to prevent this type of problem?

Exercise 7-6A   *Treatment of NSF check*

The bank statement of Gear Supplies included a $300 NSF check that one of Gear's customers had written to pay for services that were provided by Gear.

Required

a. Show the effects of recognizing the NSF check on the financial statements by recording the appropriate amounts in a horizontal statements model like the following one.

Assets		=	Liab.	+	Equity	Rev.	−	Exp.	=	Net Inc.	Cash Flow
Cash	+ Accts. Rec.										

b. Is the recognition of the NSF check on Gear's books an asset source, use, or exchange transaction?

c. Suppose the customer redeems the check by giving Gear $325 cash in exchange for the bad check. The additional $25 paid a service fee charged by Gear. Show the effects on the financial statements in the horizontal statements model in Requirement *a*.

d. Is the receipt of cash referred to in Requirement *c* an asset source, use, or exchange transaction?

Exercise 7-7A   *Adjustments to the balance per books*

Required

Identify which of the following items are added to or subtracted from the unadjusted *book balance* to arrive at the true cash balance. Distinguish the additions from the subtractions by placing a + beside the items that are added to the unadjusted book balance and a − beside those that are subtracted from it. The first item is recorded as an example.

Reconciling Items	Book Balance Adjusted?	Added or Subtracted?
Interest revenue	Yes	+
Deposits in transit		
Debit memo		
Bank service charge		
Charge for checks		
NSF check from customer		
Note receivable collected by the bank		
Outstanding checks		
Credit memo		

Exercise 7-8A   *Adjustments to the balance per bank*

Required

Identify which of the following items are added to or subtracted from the unadjusted *bank balance* to arrive at the true cash balance. Distinguish the additions from the subtractions by placing a + beside the items that are added to the unadjusted bank balance and a − beside those that are subtracted from it. The first item is recorded as an example.

Reconciling Items	Bank Balance Adjusted?	Added or Subtracted?
Deposits in transit	Yes	+
Debit memo		
Credit memo		
Certified checks		
Petty cash voucher		
NSF check from customer		
Interest revenue		
Bank service charge		
Outstanding checks		

L.O. 3

Exercise 7-9A   *Adjusting the cash account*

As of May 31, 2009, the bank statement showed an ending balance of $18,500. The unadjusted Cash account balance was $16,950. The following information is available:

1. Deposit in transit, $2,630.
2. Credit memo in bank statement for interest earned in May, $25.
3. Outstanding check, $4,208.
4. Debit memo for bank service charge, $53.

Required

a. Determine the true cash balance by preparing a bank reconciliation as of May 31, 2009, using the preceding information.
b. Record in general journal format the adjusting entries necessary to correct the unadjusted book balance.

L.O. 3

Exercise 7-10A   *Determining the true cash balance, starting with the unadjusted bank balance*

The following information is available for Marble Company for the month of August:

1. The unadjusted balance per the bank statement on August 31 was $57,800.
2. Deposits in transit on August 31 were $2,900.
3. A debit memo was included with the bank statement for a service charge of $20.
4. A $5,620 check written in August had not been paid by the bank.
5. The bank statement included a $1,000 credit memo for the collection of a note. The principal of the note was $950, and the interest collected was $50.

Required

Determine the true cash balance as of August 31. (*Hint:* It is not necessary to use all of the preceding items to determine the true balance.)

L.O. 3

Exercise 7-11A   *Determining the true cash balance, starting with the unadjusted book balance*

Smith Company had an unadjusted cash balance of $8,550 as of April 30. The company's bank statement, also dated April 30, included a $100 NSF check written by one of Smith's customers. There were $920 in outstanding checks and $250 in deposits in transit as of April 30. According to the bank statement, service charges were $75, and the bank collected a $700 note receivable for Smith. The bank statement also showed $12 of interest revenue earned by Smith.

Required

Determine the true cash balance as of April 30. (*Hint:* It is not necessary to use all of the preceding items to determine the true balance.)

Exercise 7-12A   *Effect of establishing a petty cash account*

Southern Pine Company established a $225 petty cash fund on January 1, 2008.

Required

a. Is the establishment of the petty cash fund an asset source, use, or exchange transaction?

b. Record the establishment of the petty cash fund in a horizontal statements model like the following one:

Assets		= Liab.	+ Equity	Rev.	− Exp.	= Net Inc.	Cash Flow
Cash	+ Petty Cash						

c. Record the establishment of the fund in general journal format.

Exercise 7-13A   *Effect of petty cash events on the financial statements*

Nova, Inc., established a petty cash fund of $250 on January 2. On January 31, the fund contained cash of $56.20 and vouchers for the following cash payments:

Postage	$25.00
Office supplies	52.50
Printing expense	30.00
Entertainment expense	84.30

The three distinct accounting events affecting the petty cash fund for the period were (1) establishment of the fund, (2) reimbursements made to employees, and (3) recognition of expenses and replenishment of the fund.

Required

a. Record each of the three events in a horizontal statements model like the following one. In the Cash Flow column, indicate whether the item is an operating activity (OA), investing activity (IA), or a financing activity (FA). Use NA to indicate that an account was not affected by the event.

Assets		= Liab.	+ Equity	Rev.	− Exp.	= Net Inc.	Cash Flow
Cash	+ Petty Cash						

b. Record the events in general journal format.

Exercise 7-14A   *Determining the amount of petty cash expense*

Consider the following events:

1. A petty cash fund of $100 was established on April 1, 2010.
2. Employees were reimbursed when they presented petty cash vouchers to the petty cash custodian.
3. On April 30, 2010, the petty cash fund contained vouchers totaling $85.30 plus $15.50 of currency.

Required

Answer the following questions:

a. How did the establishment of the petty cash fund affect (increase, decrease, or have no effect on) total assets?

b. What is the amount of total petty cash expenses to be recognized during April?

c. When are petty cash expenses recognized (at the time of establishment, reimbursement, or replenishment)?

L.O. 5

Exercise 7-15A   *Preparing a classified balance sheet*

Required

Use the following information to prepare a classified balance sheet for Little Co. at the end of 2008.

Accounts receivable	$42,500
Accounts payable	12,500
Cash	16,230
Common stock	40,000
Long-term notes payable	27,000
Merchandise inventory	31,000
Office equipment (net)	27,000
Retained earnings	40,430
Prepaid insurance	3,200

L.O. 6

Exercise 7-16A   *Operating cycle*

Western Co. sells gifts and novelty items mostly on account. It takes an average of 120 days to sell its inventory and an average of 50 days to collect the accounts receivable.

Required

a. Draw a diagram of the operating cycle for Western Co.
b. Compute the length of the operating cycle based on the information given.

L.O. 6

Exercise 7-17A   *Using the current ratio to make comparisons*

The following information was drawn from the 2009 balance sheets of the Alberta and Ottawa Companies.

	Alberta Company	Ottawa Company
Current assets	$45,000	$72,000
Current liabilities	28,000	54,000

Required

a. Compute the current ratio for each company.
b. Which company has the greater likelihood of being able to pay its bills?
c. Assume that both companies have the same amount of total assets. Speculate as to which company would produce the higher return on assets ratio.

PROBLEMS—SERIES A

All Problems in Series A are available with McGraw-Hill's Homework Manager®

L.O. 1, 2

Problem 7-18A   *Using internal control to restrict illegal or unethical behavior*

Required

For each of the following fraudulent acts, describe one or more internal control procedures that could have prevented (or helped prevent) the problems.

a. Paula Wissel, the administrative assistant in charge of payroll, created a fictional employee, wrote weekly checks to the fictional employee, and then personally cashed the checks for her own benefit.
b. Larry Kent, the receiving manager of Southern Lumber, created a fictitious supplier named F&M Building Supply. F&M regularly billed Southern Lumber for supplies purchased. Kent had printed shipping slips and billing invoices with the name of the fictitious company and opened a post office box as the mailing address. Kent simply prepared a receiving report and submitted it for payment to the accounts payable department. The accounts payable clerk then paid the invoice when it was received because Kent acknowledged receipt of the supplies.

c. Holly Baker works at a local hobby shop and usually operates the cash register. She has developed a way to give discounts to her friends. When they come by, she rings a lower price or does not charge the friend for some of the material purchased. At first, Baker thought she would get caught, but no one seemed to notice. Indeed, she has become so sure that there is no way for the owner to find out that she has started taking home some supplies for her own personal use.

Problem 7-19A *Preparing a bank reconciliation*

L.O. 3

CHECK FIGURE
a. True Cash Balance,
   October 31, 2008:
   $10,950

Tom Landry owns a construction business, Landry Supply Co. The following cash information is available for the month of October 2008.

As of October 31, the bank statement shows a balance of $13,800. The October 31 unadjusted balance in the Cash account of Landry Supply Co. is $12,700. A review of the bank statement revealed the following information:

1. A deposit of $1,600 on October 31, 2008, does not appear on the October 31 bank statement.
2. A debit memo for $250 was included in the bank statement for the purchase of a new supply of checks.
3. When checks written during the month were compared with those paid by the bank, three checks amounting to $4,450 were found to be outstanding.
4. It was discovered that a check to pay for repairs was correctly written and paid by the bank for $3,100 but was recorded on the books as $1,600.

Required

a. Prepare a bank reconciliation at the end of October showing the true cash balance.
b. Prepare any necessary journal entries to adjust the books to the true cash balance.

Problem 7-20A *Missing information in a bank reconciliation*

L.O. 3

CHECK FIGURE
True Cash Balance,
April 30, 2009: $13,370

The following data apply to Owens Sports, Inc., for April 2009:

1. Balance per the bank on April 30, $12,250.
2. Deposits in transit not recorded by the bank, $2,700.
3. Bank error; check written by Owens on his personal checking account was drawn on the Owens Sports, Inc., account, $900.
4. The following checks written and recorded by Owens Sports, Inc., were not included in the bank statement:

1901	$ 250
1920	580
1921	1,650

5. Credit memo for note collected by the bank, $1,100.
6. Service charge for collection of note, $10.
7. The bookkeeper recorded a check written for $560 to pay for April's office supplies as $650 in the cash disbursements journal.
8. Bank service charge in addition to the note collection fee, $40.
9. NSF checks returned by the bank, $150.

Required
Determine the amount of the unadjusted cash balance per Owens Sports, Inc.'s books.

Problem 7-21A *Adjustments to the cash account based on the bank reconciliation*

L.O. 3

CHECK FIGURE
h. Theft Loss: $600

Required
Determine whether the following items in Powers Imports' bank reconciliation require adjusting or correcting entries on Powers Imports' books. When an entry is required, record it in general journal format.

a. The bank collected $7,000 of Powers Imports' accounts receivable. Powers Imports had instructed its customers to send their payments directly to the bank.
b. The bank mistakenly gave Imports, Inc., credit for a $500 deposit made by Powers Imports.

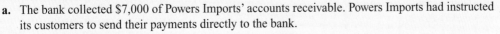

c. Deposits in transit were $5,600.

d. Powers Imports' bank statement contained a $750 NSF check. Powers Imports had received the check from a customer and had included it in one of its bank deposits.

e. The bank statement indicated that Powers Imports earned $80 of interest revenue.

f. Powers Imports' accountant mistakenly recorded a $230 check that was written to purchase supplies as $370.

g. Bank service charges for the month were $50.

h. The bank reconciliation disclosed the fact that $600 had been stolen from Powers Imports' business.

i. Outstanding checks amounted to $1,700.

L.O. 3

CHECK FIGURE
a. True Cash Balance,
July 31, 2009:
$14,929

Problem 7-22A *Bank reconciliation and adjustments to the Cash account*

The following information is available for River Bed Hotel for July 2009:

Bank Statement

STATE BANK

Bolta Vista, NV 10001

River Bed Hotel
10 Main Street
Bolta Vista, NV 10001

Account number
12-4567
July 31, 2009

Beginning balance 6/30/2009	$ 9,031
Total deposits and other credits	28,900
Total checks and other debits	23,902
Ending balance 7/31/2009	14,029

Checks and Debits		Deposits and Credits		
Check No.	Amount	Date		Amount
2350	$3,761	July	1	$1,102
2351	1,643	July	10	6,498
2352	8,000	July	15	4,929
2354	2,894	July	21	6,174
2355	1,401	July	26	5,963
2357	6,187	July	30	2,084
DM	16	CM		2,150

The following is a list of checks and deposits recorded on the books of the River Bed Hotel for July 2009:

Date		Check No.	Amount of Check	Date		Amount of Deposit
July	2	2351	$1,643	July	8	$6,498
July	4	2352	8,000	July	14	4,929
July	10	2353	1,700	July	21	6,174
July	10	2354	2,894	July	26	5,963
July	15	2355	1,401	July	29	2,084
July	20	2356	950	July	30	3,550
July	22	2357	6,187			

Other Information

1. Check no. 2350 was outstanding from June.
2. Credit memo was for collection of notes receivable.
3. All checks were paid at the correct amount.
4. Debit memo was for printed checks.
5. The June 30 bank reconciliation showed a deposit in transit of $1,102.
6. The unadjusted Cash account balance at July 31 was $12,795.

Required

a. Prepare the bank reconciliation for River Bed Hotel at the end of July.

b. Record in general journal form any necessary entries to the Cash account to adjust it to the true cash balance.

Problem 7-23A *Effect of adjustments to cash on the accounting equation*

After reconciling its bank account, Arthur Company made the following adjusting entries:

Entry No.	Account Titles	Debit	Credit
1	Cash	845	
	Accounts receivable		845
	To record bank collection		
2	Cash	44	
	Interest revenue		44
	To record interest revenue		
3	Bank service charge expense	35	
	Cash		35
	To record bank service charge		
4	Accounts receivable	174	
	Cash		174
	To record NSF check from Beat		
5	Cash	20	
	Supplies expense		20
	To correct overstatement of expense		

Required

Identify the event depicted in each journal entry as asset source (AS), asset use (AU), asset exchange (AE), or claims exchange (CE). Also explain how each entry affects the accounting equation by placing a + for increase, − for decrease, or NA for not affected under the following components of the accounting equation. The first event is recorded as an example.

						Stockholders' Equity		
Event No.	Type of Event	Assets	=	Liabilities	+	Common Stock	+	Retained Earnings
1	AE	+ −		NA		NA		NA

Problem 7-24A *Bank reconciliation and internal control*

Following is a bank reconciliation for Fez's Sandwich Shop for May 31, 2009:

	Cash Account	Bank Statement
Balance as of 5/31/09	$25,500	$23,000
Deposit in transit		4,250
Outstanding checks		(1,730)
Note collected by bank	1,050	
Bank service charge	(30)	
Automatic payment on loan	(1,000)	
Adjusted cash balance as of 5/31/09	$25,520	$25,520

Because of limited funds, Fez's employed only one accountant who was responsible for receiving cash, recording receipts and disbursements, preparing deposits, and preparing the bank reconciliation. The accountant left the company on June 8, 2009, after preparing the preceding statement. His replacement compared the checks returned with the bank statement to the cash disbursements journal and found the total of outstanding checks to be $4,200.

Required

a. Prepare a corrected bank reconciliation.

b. What is the total amount of cash missing, and how was the difference between the "true cash" per the bank and the "true cash" per the books hidden on the reconciliation prepared by the former employee?

c. What could Fez's do to avoid cash theft in the future?

L.O. 4

CHECK FIGURE
a. Cash Over: $3

Problem 7-25A   *Petty cash fund*

The following data pertain to the petty cash fund of Easy Company:

1. The petty cash fund was created on an imprest basis at $250 on March 1.
2. On March 31, a physical count of the fund disclosed $18 in currency and coins, vouchers authorizing meal allowances totaling $148, vouchers authorizing purchase of postage stamps of $31, and vouchers for payment of delivery charges of $50.

Required

a. Prepare all general journal entries necessary to (1) establish the fund, (2) reimburse employees, and (3) recognize the expenses and replenish the fund as of March 31. (*Hint:* Journal entries may not be required for all three events.)

b. Explain how the Cash Short and Over account required in this case affects the income statement.

c. Identify the event depicted in each journal entry recorded in Requirement *a* as asset source (AS), asset use (AU), asset exchange (AE), or claims exchange (CE).

d. Record the effects on the financial statements of the events in Requirement *a* using a horizontal statements model like the following one. In the Cash Flow column, indicate whether the item is an operating activity (OA), investing activity (IA), or financing activity (FA). Use NA to indicate that an account was not affected by the event.

Assets		= Liab.	+ Equity	Rev.	− Exp.	= Net Inc.	Cash Flow
Cash	+ Petty Cash						

L.O. 5

CHECK FIGURE
Total Current Assets: $51,300
Net Income: $42,800

Problem 7-26A   *Multistep income statement and classified balance sheet*

Required

Use the following information to prepare a multistep income statement for the year ending December 31, 2010, and a classified balance sheet as of December 31, 2010.

Accounts receivable	$ 6,000
Common stock	68,000
Salaries expense	154,000
Interest expense	5,000
Cash	20,000
Accounts payable	1,800
Retained earnings 12/31/10	76,000
Accumulated depreciation	10,000
Unearned revenue	16,000
Land	90,000
Salaries payable	3,400
Cost of goods sold	175,000

continued

Supplies	900
Note receivable (long term)	10,000
Inventory	16,000
Office equipment	52,000
Gain on sale of equipment	10,000
Interest receivable (short term)	400
Operating expenses	34,000
Sales revenue	400,000
Prepaid rent	8,000
Interest payable (short term)	1,200
Notes payable (long term)	26,900
Interest revenue	800

Problem 7-27A *Using ratios to make comparisons*

L.O. 6

The following accounting information exists for Lockwood and Doggett companies at the end of 2009.

CHECK FIGURE
a. Doggett Current Ratio:
   1.57 to 1

	Lockwood	Doggett
Cash	$ 15,000	$ 25,000
Wages payable	20,000	25,000
Merchandise inventory	30,000	55,000
Building	80,000	80,000
Accounts receivable	35,000	30,000
Long-term notes payable	90,000	120,000
Land	45,000	50,000
Accounts payable	40,000	45,000
Sales revenue	220,000	270,000
Expenses	190,000	245,000

Required

a. Identify the current assets and current liabilities and compute the current ratio for each company.
b. Assuming that all assets and liabilities are listed here, compute the debt to assets ratios for each company.
c. Determine which company has the greater financial risk in both the short term and the long term.

EXERCISES—SERIES B

Exercise 7-1B *Features of a strong internal control system*

L.O. 1

Required

List and describe nine features of a strong internal control system described in this chapter.

Exercise 7-2B *Internal controls for small businesses*

L.O. 1, 2

Required

Assume that you are the owner of a small business that has only two employees.

a. Which of the internal control procedures are most important to you?
b. How can you help overcome the limited separation-of-duties control procedure?

Exercise 7-3B *Internal control for cash*

L.O. 2

Required

a. Why are special controls needed for cash?
b. What is included in the definition of *cash*?

L.O. 1

Exercise 7-4B   *Internal control procedures to prevent embezzlement*

Bell Gates was in charge of the returns department at The Software Company. She was responsible for evaluating returned merchandise. She sent merchandise that was reusable back to the warehouse, where it was restocked in the supply of inventory. Gates was also responsible for taking the merchandise that she determined to be defective to the city dump for disposal. She had agreed to buy a friend a tax planning program at a discount through her contacts at work. That is when the idea came to her. She could simply classify one of the reusable returns as defective and bring it home instead of taking it to the dump. She did so and made a quick $150. She was happy, and her friend was ecstatic; he was able to buy a $400 software package for only $150. He told his friends about the deal, and soon Gates had a regular set of customers. She was caught when a retail store owner complained to the marketing manager that his pricing strategy was being undercut by The Software Company's direct sales to the public. The marketing manager was suspicious because The Software Company had no direct marketing program. When the outside sales were ultimately traced back to Gates, the company discovered that it had lost over $10,000 in sales revenue because of her criminal activity.

Required

Identify an internal control procedure that could have prevented the company's losses. Explain how the procedure would have stopped the embezzlement.

L.O. 1

Exercise 7-5B   *Internal control procedures to prevent deception*

Emergency Care Medical Centers (ECMC) hired a new physician, Ken Major, who was an immediate success. Everyone loved his bedside manner; he could charm the most cantankerous patient. Indeed, he was a master salesman as well as an expert physician. Unfortunately, Major misdiagnosed a case that resulted in serious consequences to the patient. The patient filed suit against ECMC. In preparation for the defense, ECMC's attorneys discovered that Major was indeed an exceptional salesman. He had worked for several years as district marketing manager for a pharmaceutical company. In fact, he was not a physician at all! He had changed professions without going to medical school. He had lied on his application form. His knowledge of medical terminology had enabled him to fool everyone. ECMC was found negligent and lost a $3 million lawsuit.

Required

Identify the relevant internal control procedures that could have prevented the company's losses. Explain how these procedures would have prevented Major's deception.

L.O. 3

Exercise 7-6B   *Treatment of NSF check*

Tipton Stationery's bank statement contained a $300 NSF check that one of its customers had written to pay for supplies purchased.

Required

a. Show the effects of recognizing the NSF check on the financial statements by recording the appropriate amounts in a horizontal statements model like the following one:

Assets			=	Liab.	+	Equity	Rev.	−	Exp.	=	Net Inc.	Cash Flow
Cash	+	Accts. Rec.										

b. Is the recognition of the NSF check on Tipton's books an asset source, use, or exchange transaction?

c. Suppose the customer redeems the check by giving Tipton $320 cash in exchange for the bad check. The additional $20 paid a service fee charged by Tipton. Show the effects on the financial statements in the horizontal statements model in Requirement *a*.

d. Is the receipt of cash referenced in Requirement *c* an asset source, use, or exchange transaction?

L.O. 3

Exercise 7-7B   *Adjustments to the balance per books*

Required

Identify which of the following items are added to or subtracted from the unadjusted *book balance* to arrive at the true cash balance. Distinguish the additions from the subtractions by placing a + beside the items that are added to the unadjusted book balance and a − beside those that are subtracted from it. The first item is recorded as an example.

Reconciling Items	Book Balance Adjusted?	Added or Subtracted?
Outstanding checks	No	N/A
Interest revenue earned on the account		
Deposits in transit		
Bank service charge		
Automatic debit for utility bill		
Charge for checks		
NSF check from customer		
ATM fee		

Exercise 7-8B *Adjustments to the balance per bank*   L.O. 3

Required

Identify which of the following items are added to or subtracted from the unadjusted *bank balance* to arrive at the true cash balance. Distinguish the additions from the subtractions by placing a + beside the items that are added to the unadjusted bank balance and a − beside those that are subtracted from it. The first item is recorded as an example.

Reconciling Items	Book Balance Adjusted?	Added or Subtracted?
Bank service charge	No	N/A
Outstanding checks		
Deposits in transit		
Debit memo		
Credit memo		
ATM fee		
Petty cash voucher		
NSF check from customer		
Interest revenue		

Exercise 7-9B *Adjusting the Cash account*   L.O. 3

As of June 30, 2009, the bank statement showed an ending balance of $12,762.95. The unadjusted Cash account balance was $12,205.73. The following information is available:

1. Deposit in transit, $1,476.30.
2. Credit memo in bank statement for interest earned in June, $47.62.
3. Outstanding check, $1,992.21.
4. Debit memo for bank service charge, $6.31.

Required

a. Determine the true cash balance by preparing a bank reconciliation as of June 30, 2009, using the preceding information.
b. Record in general journal format the adjusting entries necessary to correct the unadjusted book balance.

Exercise 7-10B *Determining the true cash balance, starting with the unadjusted bank balance*   L.O. 3

The following information is available for Fresh Company for the month of June:

1. The unadjusted balance per the bank statement on June 30 was $65,711.41.
2. Deposits in transit on June 30 were $1,464.95.
3. A debit memo was included with the bank statement for a service charge of $25.38.

4. A $5,031.81 check written in June had not been paid by the bank.

5. The bank statement included a $944 credit memo for the collection of a note. The principal of the note was $859, and the interest collected amounted to $85.

Required

Determine the true cash balance as of June 30. (*Hint:* It is not necessary to use all of the preceding items to determine the true balance.)

L.O. 3

Exercise 7-11B *Determining the true cash balance, starting with the unadjusted book balance*

Nifty Company had an unadjusted cash balance of $7,600 as of May 31. The company's bank statement, also dated May 31, included a $38 NSF check written by one of Nifty's customers. There were $548.60 in outstanding checks and $143.74 in deposits in transit as of May 31. According to the bank statement, service charges were $33, and the bank collected a $400 note receivable for Nifty. The bank statement also showed $22 of interest revenue earned by Nifty.

Required

Determine the true cash balance as of May 31. (*Hint:* It is not necessary to use all of the preceding items to determine the true balance.)

L.O. 4

Exercise 7-12B *Effect of establishing a petty cash account*

Ocho Company established a $400 petty cash fund on January 1, 2010.

Required

a. Is the establishment of the petty cash fund an asset source, use, or exchange transaction?

b. Record the establishment of the petty cash fund in a horizontal statements model like the following one:

Assets		=	Liab.	+	Equity	Rev.	−	Exp.	=	Net Inc.	Cash Flow
Cash	+ Petty Cash										

c. Record the establishment of the fund in general journal format.

L.O. 4

Exercise 7-13B *Effect of petty cash events on the financial statements*

General Medical Center established a petty cash fund of $150 on January 2. On January 31, the fund contained cash of $32.60 and vouchers for the following cash payments:

Postage	$64.76
Office supplies	19.16
Printing expense	7.40
Transportation expense	27.18

The three distinct accounting events affecting the petty cash fund for the period were (1) establishment of the fund, (2) reimbursements made to employees, and (3) recognition of expenses and replenishment of the fund.

Required

a. Record each of the three events in a horizontal statements model like the following one. In the Cash Flow column, indicate whether the item is an operating activity (OA), investing activity (IA), or a financing activity (FA). Use NA to indicate that an account was not affected by the event.

Assets		=	Liab.	+	Equity	Rev.	−	Exp.	=	Net Inc.	Cash Flow
Cash	+ Petty Cash										

b. Record the events in general journal format.

Exercise 7-14B *Determining the amount of petty cash expense*   L.O. 4

Consider the following events:

1. A petty cash fund of $250 was established on April 1, 2011.
2. Employees were reimbursed when they presented petty cash vouchers to the petty cash custodian.
3. On April 30, 2011, the petty cash fund contained vouchers totaling $211.71 plus $29.21 of currency.

Required

Answer the following questions:

a. How did the establishment of the petty cash fund affect (increase, decrease, or have no effect on) total assets?
b. What is the amount of total petty cash expenses to be recognized during April?
c. When are petty cash expenses recognized (at the time of establishment, reimbursement, or replenishment)?

Exercise 7-15B *Preparing a classified balance sheet*   L.O. 5

Required

Use the following information to prepare a classified balance sheet for Avalon Co. at the end of 2009.

Accounts receivable	$12,150
Accounts payable	5,500
Cash	11,201
Common stock	12,000
Land	10,000
Long-term notes payable	11,500
Merchandise inventory	18,000
Retained earnings	22,351

Exercise 7-16B *Operating cycle*   L.O. 6

Ozzie Co. sells fine silk articles mostly on account. Ozzie Co. takes an average of 90 days to sell its inventory and an average of 31 days to collect the accounts receivable.

Required

a. Draw a diagram of the operating cycle for Ozzie Co.
b. Compute the length of the operating cycle based on the information given.

Exercise 7-17B *Using the current ratio to make comparisons*   L.O. 6

The following information was drawn from the 2009 balance sheets of the Cyber Security and Virus Blockers companies.

	Cyber Security	Virus Blockers
Current assets	$40,000	$70,000
Current liabilities	25,000	55,000

Required

a. Compute the current ratio for each company.
b. Which company has the greater likelihood of being able to pay its bills?
c. Assume that both companies have the same amount of total assets. Speculate as to which company would produce the higher return on assets ratio.

PROBLEMS—SERIES B

L.O. 1, 2

Problem 7-18B *Using internal control to restrict illegal or unethical behavior*

Required

For each of the following fraudulent acts, describe one or more internal control procedures that could have prevented (or helped prevent) the problems.

a. Everyone in the office has noticed what a dedicated employee Jennifer Reidel is. She never misses work, not even for a vacation. Reidel is in charge of the petty cash fund. She transfers funds from the company's bank account to the petty cash account on an as-needed basis. During a surprise audit, the petty cash fund was found to contain fictitious receipts. Over a three-year period, Reidel had used more than $4,000 of petty cash to pay for personal expenses.

b. Bill Bruton was hired as the vice president of the manufacturing division of a corporation. His impressive resume listed a master's degree in business administration from a large state university and numerous collegiate awards and activities, when in fact Bruton had only a high school diploma. In a short time, the company was in poor financial condition because of his inadequate knowledge and bad decisions.

c. Havolene Manufacturing has good internal control over its manufacturing materials inventory. However, office supplies are kept on open shelves in the employee break room. The office supervisor has noticed that he is having to order paper, tape, staplers, and pens on an increasingly frequent basis.

L.O. 3

Problem 7-19B *Preparing a bank reconciliation*

Bob Carson owns a bait shop, Fish Supplies. The following cash information is available for the month of August, 2006.

As of August 31, the bank statement shows a balance of $18,100. The August 31 unadjusted balance in the Cash account of Fish Supplies is $15,900. A review of the bank statement revealed the following information:

1. A deposit of $2,260 on August 31, 2009, does not appear on the August bank statement.

2. It was discovered that a check to pay for merchandise inventory was correctly written and paid by the bank for $4,040 but was recorded on the books as $4,700.

3. When checks written during the month were compared with those paid by the bank, three checks amounting to $4,000 were found to be outstanding.

4. A debit memo for $200 was included in the bank statement for the purchase of a new supply of checks.

Required

a. Prepare a bank reconciliation at the end of August showing the true cash balance.

b. Prepare any necessary journal entries to adjust the books to the true cash balance.

L.O. 3

Problem 7-20B *Missing information in a bank reconciliation*

The following data apply to Awesome Parts Supply, Inc., for May 2008.

1. Balance per the bank on May 31, $7,700.

2. Deposits in transit not recorded by the bank, $975.

3. Bank error; check written by Allen Auto Supply was drawn on Awesome Parts' account, $500.

4. The following checks written and recorded by Awesome Parts were not included in the bank statement:

3013	$ 300
3054	735
3056	1,800

5. Note collected by the bank, $500.
6. Service charge for collection of note, $10.
7. The bookkeeper recorded a check written for $188 to pay for the May utilities expense as $888 in the cash disbursements journal.
8. Bank service charge in addition to the note collection fee, $25.
9. Customer checks returned by the bank as NSF, $125.

Required

Determine the amount of the unadjusted cash balance per Awesome Parts' books.

Problem 7-21B *Adjustments to the Cash account based on the bank reconciliation*   **L.O. 3**

Required

Determine whether the following items included in Ming Company's bank reconciliation for January 31, 2009, will require adjusting or correcting entries on Ming's books. When an entry is required, record it in general journal format.

a. An $877 deposit was recorded by the bank as $778.
b. Four checks totaling $450 written during the month of January were not included with the January bank statement.
c. A $54 check written to Office Max for office supplies was recorded in the general journal as $45.
d. The bank statement indicated that the bank had collected a $330 note for Ming.
e. Ming recorded $500 of receipts on January 31, 2009, which was deposited in the night depository of the bank. These deposits were not included in the bank statement.
f. Service charges of $30 for the month of January were listed on the bank statement.
g. The bank charged a $297 check drawn on Cave Restaurant to Ming's account. The check was included in Ming's bank statement.
h. A check of $28 was returned to the bank because of insufficient funds and was noted on the bank statement. Ming received the check from a customer and thought that it was good when it was deposited into the account.

Problem 7-22B *Bank reconciliation and adjustments to the Cash account*   **L.O. 3**

The following information is available for Moose Garage for March 2009:

BANK STATEMENT
HAZARD STATE BANK
215 MAIN STREET
HAZARD, GA 30321

Moose Garage
629 Main Street
Hazard, GA 30321

Account number
62-00062
March 31, 2009

Beginning balance 3/1/2009	$15,000.00
Total deposits and other credits	7,000.00
Total checks and other debits	6,000.00
Ending balance 3/31/2009	16,000.00

Checks and Debits		Deposits and Credits	
Check No.	Amount	Date	Amount
1462	$1,163.00	March 1	$1,000.00
1463	62.00	March 2	1,340.00
1464	1,235.00	March 6	210.00
1465	750.00	March 12	1,940.00·
1466	1,111.00	March 17	855.00
1467	964.00	March 22	1,480.00
DM	15.00	CM	175.00
1468	700.00		

The following is a list of checks and deposits recorded on the books of Moose Garage for March 2009:

Date	Check No.	Amount of Check	Date	Amount of Deposit
March 1	1463	$ 62.00	March 1	$1,340.00
March 5	1464	1,235.00	March 5	210.00
March 6	1465	750.00		
March 9	1466	1,111.00	March 10	1,940.00
March 10	1467	964.00		
March 14	1468	70.00	March 16	855.00
March 19	1469	1,500.00	March 19	1,480.00
March 28	1470	102.00	March 29	2,000.00

Other Information

1. Check no. 1462 was outstanding from February.
2. A credit memo for collection of accounts receivable was included in the bank statement.
3. All checks were paid at the correct amount.
4. The bank statement included a debit memo for service charges.
5. The February 28 bank reconciliation showed a deposit in transit of $1,000.
6. Check no. 1468 was for the purchase of equipment.
7. The unadjusted Cash account balance at March 31 was $16,868.

Required

a. Prepare the bank reconciliation for Moose Garage at the end of March.
b. Record in general journal form any necessary entries to the Cash account to adjust it to the true cash balance.

L.O. 3

Problem 7-23B   *Effect of adjustments to cash on the accounting equation*

After reconciling its bank account, Hull Equipment Company made the following adjusting entries:

Entry No.	Account Titles	Debit	Credit
1	Cash	40	
	Interest revenue		40
	To record interest revenue		
2	Accounts receivable	250	
	Cash		250
	To record NSF check from Wilson		
3	Rent expense	35	
	Cash		35
	To correct understatement of expense		
4	Bank service charge expense	15	
	Cash		15
	To record bank service charge		
5	Cash	175	
	Accounts receivable		175
	To record bank collection		

Required

Identify the event depicted in each journal entry as asset source (AS), asset use (AU), asset exchange (AE), or claims exchange (CE). Also explain how each entry affects the accounting equation by placing a + for increase, − for decrease, or NA for not affected under the following components of the accounting equation. The first event is recorded as an example.

Event No.	Type of Event	Assets	=	Liabilities	+	Common Stock	+	Retained Earnings
						Stockholders' Equity		
1	AS	+		NA		NA		+

Problem 7-24B   *Bank reconciliation and internal control*

L.O. 1, 2, 3

Following is a bank reconciliation for Skate Shop for June 30, 2010:

	Cash Account	Bank Statement
Balance as of 6/30/10	$1,618	$3,000
Deposit in transit		600
Outstanding checks		(1,507)
Note collected by bank	2,000	
Bank service charge	(25)	
NSF check	(1,500)	
Adjusted cash balance as of 6/30/10	$2,093	$2,093

When reviewing the bank reconciliation, Skate's auditor was unable to locate any reference to the NSF check on the bank statement. Furthermore, the clerk who reconciles the bank account and records the adjusting entries could not find the actual NSF check that should have been included in the bank statement. Finally, there was no specific reference in the accounts receivables supporting records identifying a party who had written a bad check.

Required

a. Prepare the adjusting entry that the clerk would have made to record the NSF check.

b. Assume that the clerk who prepares the bank reconciliation and records the adjusting entries also makes bank deposits. Explain how the clerk could use a fictitious NSF check to hide the theft of cash.

c. How could Skate avoid the theft of cash that is concealed by the use of fictitious NSF checks?

Problem 7-25B   *Petty cash fund*

L.O. 4

Romo Co. established a petty cash fund by issuing a check for $270 and appointing Bob Potts as petty cash custodian. Potts had vouchers for the following petty cash payments during the month:

Stamps	$17.00
Miscellaneous items	30.00
Employee supper money	82.00
Taxi fare	85.00
Window-washing service	22.00

There was $32 of currency in the petty cash box at the time it was replenished.

Required

a. Prepare all general journal entries necessary to (1) establish the fund, (2) reimburse employees, (3) recognize expenses, and replenish the fund. (*Hint:* Journal entries may not be required for all the events.)

b. Explain how the Cash Short and Over account required in this case will affect the income statement.

c. Identify the event depicted in each journal entry recorded in Requirement *a* as asset source (AS), asset use (AU), asset exchange (AE), or claims exchange (CE).

d. Record the effects of the events in Requirement *a* on the financial statements using a horizontal statements model like the following one. In the Cash Flow column, indicate whether the item is an operating activity (OA), investing activity (IA), or financing activity (FA). Use NA to indicate that an account was not affected by the event.

Assets		= Liab. + Equity	Rev. − Exp. = Net Inc.	Cash Flow
Cash + Petty Cash				

L.O. 5

Problem 7-26B *Multistep income statement and classified balance sheet*

Required

Use the following information to prepare a multistep income statement and a classified balance sheet for Nixon Enterprises for the year end of December 31, 2008.

Accounts receivable	$ 6,000
Common stock	47,000
Salaries expense	118,000
Interest expense	12,200
Cash	3,600
Accounts payable	5,000
Retained earnings, Jan. 1, 2008	20,380
Accumulated depreciation	6,800
Unearned revenue	9,600
Land	50,000
Salaries payable	1,800
Cost of goods sold	185,000
Supplies	500
Note receivable (long term)	6,000
Inventory	9,000
Office equipment	58,000
Gain on sale of equipment	6,400
Interest receivable (short term)	1,240
Operating expenses	19,000
Sales revenue	340,000
Prepaid rent	9,600
Interest payable (short term)	740
Interest revenue	420
Notes payable (long term)	40,000

L.O. 6

Problem 7-27B *Using ratios to make comparisons*

The following accounting information exists for Adams and Hood companies at the end of 2009.

	Adams	Hood
Cash	$ 12,000	$ 15,000
Wages payable	10,000	12,000
Merchandise inventory	20,000	55,000
Building	90,000	80,000
Accounts receivable	22,000	25,000
Long-term notes payable	80,000	100,000
Land	35,000	40,000
Accounts payable	25,000	35,000
Sales revenue	220,000	250,000
Expenses	190,000	230,000

Required

a. Identify the current assets and current liabilities and compute the current ratio for each company.

b. Assuming that all assets and liabilities are listed here, compute the debt to assets ratios for each company.

c. Determine which company has the greater financial risk in both the short term and the long term.

ANALYZE, THINK, COMMUNICATE

ATC 7-1   Business Applications Case   *Understanding real-world annual reports*

Required—Part 1

Use the Topps Company's annual report in Appendix B to answer the following questions.

a. What was Topps' current ratio as of February 25, 2006?

b. Which of Topps' current assets had the largest balance at February 25, 2006?

c. What percentage of Topps' total assets consisted of current assets?

d. Instead of "Cash," Topps' balance sheet shows an account named "Cash and cash equivalents." What do cash equivalents include? (See the footnotes.)

e. Does Topps' have any restrictions placed on it by its creditors? (*Hint:* See Note 11.)

Required—Part 2

Use the Harley-Davidson's annual report that came with this book to answer the following questions.

a. What was Harley-Davidson's current ratio as of December 31, 2005 and December 31, 2004?

b. Did its current ratio get stronger or weaker from 2004 to 2005?

c. Which of Harley-Davidson's current assets had the largest balance at December 31, 2005?

d. What percentage of Harley-Davidson's total assets consisted of current assets at December 31, 2005?

Required—Part 3

Why are Harley-Davidson's receivables, as a percentage of total assets, so much higher than Topps?

ATC 7-2   Group Assignment   *Analyzing financial statements*

The following selected information was taken from the annual reports of three companies: Southwest Airlines, Pier 1 Imports, and Wendy's. Amounts are given in thousands of dollars.

	Company 1	Company 2	Company 3
Accounts receivable	$ 76,530	$ 4,128	$ 66,755
Accounts payable	160,891	105,541	107,157
Other current liabilities	707,622	4,845	105,457
Allowance for depreciation	1,375,631	138,179	537,910
Cash	623,343	32,280	234,262
Property, plant, and equipment	4,811,324	355,015	1,803,410
Inventories	0	220,013	35,633
Retained earnings	1,632,115	118,721	839,215
Common stock	376,903	204,327	345,019
Other current assets	108,543	29,057	44,904
Other long-term assets	4,051	67,954	294,626
Long-term liabilities	1,370,629	136,834	544,832

Required

a. Organize the class into three sections and divide each section into three groups of three to five students. Assign Company 1 to groups in section 1, Company 2 to groups in section 2, and Company 3 to groups in section 3.

Group Tasks

1. Identify the company that is represented by the financial data assigned to your group.

2. Prepare a classified balance sheet for the company assigned to your group.

3. Select a representative from a group in each section and put the balance sheet on the board.

Class Discussion

b. Discuss the balance sheets of each company and the rationale for matching the financial information with the company.

ATC 7-3 Real-World Case *Whose numbers are they anyway?*

The following excerpt, sometimes referred to as *management's statement of responsibility,* was taken from JC Penney's 10-K report for its 2003 fiscal year. The authors have italicized and numbered selected portions of the excerpt.

Company Statement on Financial Information (partial)

[1] *The Company is responsible for the information presented in this Annual Report.* The consolidated financial statements have been prepared in accordance with accounting principles generally accepted in the United States of America and present fairly, in all material respects, the Company's results of operations, financial position and cash flows. The Company's CEO and CFO have signed certification statements as required by Sections 302 and 906 of the Sarbanes-Oxley Act of 2002. These signed certifications have been filed with the Securities and Exchange Commission as part of the Company's 2002 Form 10-K. Certain amounts included in the consolidated financial statements are estimated based on currently available information and judgment as to the outcome of future conditions and circumstances. . . .

The Company's system of internal controls is supported by written policies and procedures and supplemented by a staff of internal auditors. **[2]** *This system is designed to provide reasonable assurance, at suitable costs,* that assets are safeguarded and that transactions are executed in accordance with appropriate authorization and are recorded and reported properly. The system is continually reviewed, evaluated and where appropriate, modified to accommodate current conditions. Emphasis is placed on the careful **[3]** *selection,* **[4]** *training and development of professional finance and internal audit managers.*

An organizational alignment that is premised upon appropriate **[5]** *delegation of authority* and **[6]** *division of responsibility* is fundamental to this system. **[7]** *Communication programs are aimed at assuring that established policies and procedures are disseminated and understood throughout the Company.*

The consolidated financial statements have been audited by independent auditors whose report appears below. Their audit was conducted in accordance with auditing standards generally accepted in the United States of America, which include the consideration of the Company's internal controls to the extent necessary to form an independent opinion on the consolidated financial statements prepared by management.

The Audit Committee of the Board of Directors is composed solely of directors who are not officers or employees of the Company . . .

Required

Assume that a colleague, who has never taken an accounting course, asks you to explain JC Penney's "company statement on financial information." Write a memorandum that explains each of the numbered portions of the material. When appropriate, include examples to explain these concepts of internal control to your colleague.

ATC 7-4 Business Applications Case *Performing ratio analysis using real-world data*

Tupperware Company claims to be "one of the world's leading direct sellers, supplying premium food storage, preparation and serving items to consumers in more than 100 countries through its Tupperware brand." The following data were taken from the company's 2004 annual report. Dollar amounts are in millions.

	Fiscal Years Ending	
	December 31, 2004	**December 31, 2003**
Current assets	$466.0	$411.4
Current liabilities	292.1	290.4
Total assets	983.2	915.9
Total liabilities	692.3	687.7

Required

a. Compute Tupperware's current ratios for 2004 and 2003.

b. Compute Tupperware's debt to assets ratios for 2004 and 2003.

c. Based on the ratios computed in Requirements *a* and *b*, did Tupperware's liquidity get better or worse from 2003 to 2004?

d. Based on the ratios computed in Requirements *a* and *b*, did Tupperware's solvency get better or worse from 2003 to 2004?

ATC 7-5   Business Applications Case   *Performing ratio analysis using real-world data*

Texas Instruments, Inc., claims to be "the world leader in digital signal processing and analog technologies, the semiconductor engines of the Internet age." Eastman Kodak Company manufactures Kodak film, cameras and related products. The following data were taken from the companies' December 31, 2004, annual reports. Dollar amounts are in millions.

	Eastman Kodak	Texas Instruments
Current assets	$ 5,648	$10,190
Current liabilities	4,990	1,925
Total assets	14,737	16,299
Total liabilities	10,926	3,236

Required

a. Compute the current ratio for each company.

b. Compute the debt to assets ratio for each company.

c. Based on the ratios computed in Requirements *a* and *b*, which company had the better liquidity in 2004?

d. Based on the ratios computed in Requirements *a* and *b*, which company had the better solvency in 2004?

ATC 7-6   Writing Assignment   *Internal control procedures*

Alison Marsh was a trusted employee of Small City State Bank. She was involved in everything. She worked as a teller, she accounted for the cash at the other teller windows, and she recorded many of the transactions in the accounting records. She was so loyal that she never would take a day off, even when she was really too sick to work. She routinely worked late to see that all the day's work was posted into the accounting records. She would never take even a day's vacation because they might need her at the bank. Tick and Tack, CPAs, were hired to perform an audit, the first complete audit that had been done in several years. Marsh seemed somewhat upset by the upcoming audit. She said that everything had been properly accounted for and that the audit was a needless expense. When Tick and Tack examined some of the bank's internal control procedures, it discovered problems. In fact, as the audit progressed, it became apparent that a large amount of cash was missing. Numerous adjustments had been made to customer accounts with credit memorandums, and many of the transactions had been posted several days late. In addition, there were numerous cash payments for "office expenses." When the audit was complete, it was determined that more than $200,000 of funds was missing or improperly accounted for. All fingers pointed to Marsh. The bank's president, who was a close friend of Marsh, was bewildered. How could this type of thing happen at this bank?

Required

Prepare a written memo to the bank president, outlining the procedures that should be followed to prevent this type of problem in the future.

ATC 7-7   Ethical Dilemma   *See no evil, hear no evil, report no evil*

Cindy Putman recently started her first job as an accounting clerk with the Wheeler Company. When reconciling Wheeler's bank statement, Putman discovered that the bank had given the company a $42,245 credit for a deposit made in the amount of $24,245. As a result, the bank account was overstated by $18,000. Putman brought the error to the attention of Ed Wheeler, who told her to reconcile the two accounts by subtracting the amount of the error from the unadjusted bank balance. Wheeler told Putman, "Don't bother informing the bank. They'll find the mistake soon enough." Three months later, Putman was still having to include the bank error in the bank reconciliation. She was convinced that the bank would not find the mistake and asked Wheeler what to do. He told Putman that it was not her job to correct bank mistakes. He told her to adjust the company books by making a debit to Cash and a credit to Retained Earnings. He said "We can always reverse the entry if the bank discovers the mistake." Putman was uneasy about this solution. Wheeler told her that his years of business experience had taught him to *go with the flow.* He said, "Sometimes you win, sometimes you lose. I'm sure that we have made mistakes that were to our disadvantage, and no one ever told us about them. We just got a good break. Keep quiet and share in the good fortune." At the end of the month, Putman discovered a $500 cash bonus included in her paycheck. She had been working hard, and she rationalized that she deserved the bonus. She told herself that it had nothing to do with the treatment of the bank error. Anyway, she thought that Wheeler was probably right. The bank would eventually find the mistake, she could reverse the adjusting entry, and everything would be set straight.

Two years later, a tax auditor for the Internal Revenue Service (IRS) discovered the adjusting entry that debited Cash and credited Retained Earnings for $18,000. The IRS agent charged Wheeler Company with income tax evasion. Being unable to identify the source of the increase in cash, the agent concluded that the company was attempting to hide revenue by making direct credits to Retained Earnings. Wheeler denied any knowledge of the entry. He told the agent that Putman rarely brought anything to his attention. He said that Putman was the independent sort who had probably made an honest mistake. He pointed out that at the time the entry was made, Putman had little experience.

Later in a private conversation, Wheeler told Putman to plead ignorance and that they both would get off the hook. He said that if she did not keep quiet, they would go down together. He reminded her of the $500 bonus. Wheeler told Putman that accepting payment to defraud the IRS constituted a crime that would land her in jail. Putman was shocked that Wheeler would not tell the truth. She had expected some loyalty from him, and it was clear that she was not going to get it.

Required

Answer the following questions:

a. Explain how the direct credit to retained earnings understated net income.
b. What course of action would you advise Putman to take?
c. Why was Putman foolish to expect loyalty from Wheeler?
d. Suppose Putman had credited Miscellaneous Revenue instead of Retained Earnings and the company had paid income taxes on the $18,000. Under these circumstances, the bank error would never have been discovered. Is it OK to hide the error from the bank if it is reported on the tax return?

ATC 7-8   Research Assignment   *Analyzing Pep Boys' liquidity*

Required

Using the most current 10-K available on EDGAR, or the company's Web site, answer the following questions about Pep Boys Manny, Moe & Jack, for the most recent year reported. Type in *Pep Boys* as the company name when you search EDGAR. Instructions for using EDGAR are in Appendix A.

a. What is Pep Boys' current ratio?
b. Which of Pep Boys' current assets had the largest balance?
c. What percentage of Pep Boys' total assets consisted of current assets?
d. Did Pep Boys have any "currently maturing" long-term debt included in current liabilities on its balance sheet?
e. If Pep Boys were a company that manufactured auto parts rather than a retailer of auto parts, how do you think its balance sheet would be different?

ATC 7-9   Spreadsheet Assignment   *Using Excel*

At the end of 2008, the following accounting information is available for Bainbridge and Crist Companies.

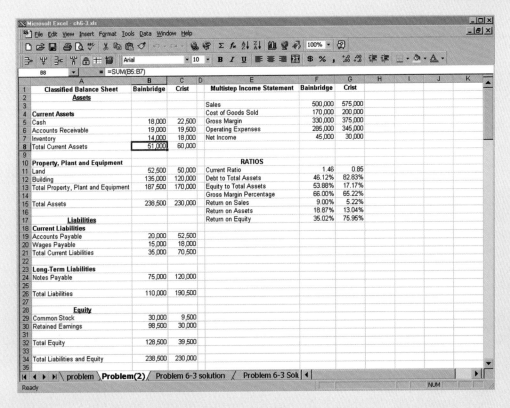

	A	B	C	D	E	F	G	H	I	J	K
1	Classified Balance Sheet	Bainbridge	Crist		Multistep Income Statement	Bainbridge	Crist				
2	Assets										
3					Sales	500,000	575,000				
4	Current Assets				Cost of Goods Sold	170,000	200,000				
5	Cash	18,000	22,500		Gross Margin	330,000	375,000				
6	Accounts Receivable	19,000	19,500		Operating Expenses	285,000	345,000				
7	Inventory	14,000	18,000		Net Income	45,000	30,000				
8	Total Current Assets	51,000	60,000								
9											
10	Property, Plant and Equipment				RATIOS						
11	Land	52,500	50,000		Current Ratio	1.46	0.85				
12	Building	135,000	120,000		Debt to Total Assets	46.12%	82.83%				
13	Total Property, Plant and Equipment	187,500	170,000		Equity to Total Assets	53.88%	17.17%				
14					Gross Margin Percentage	66.00%	65.22%				
15	Total Assets	238,500	230,000		Return on Sales	9.00%	5.22%				
16					Return on Assets	18.87%	13.04%				
17	Liabilities				Return on Equity	35.02%	75.95%				
18	Current Liabilities										
19	Accounts Payable	20,000	52,500								
20	Wages Payable	15,000	18,000								
21	Total Current Liabilities	35,000	70,500								
22											
23	Long-Term Liabilities										
24	Notes Payable	75,000	120,000								
25											
26	Total Liabilities	110,000	190,500								
27											
28	Equity										
29	Common Stock	30,000	9,500								
30	Retained Earnings	98,500	30,000								
31											
32	Total Equity	128,500	39,500								
33											
34	Total Liabilities and Equity	238,500	230,000								
35											

Required

a. Set up the preceding spreadsheet. Complete the balance sheet and income statement. Use Excel formulas for rows that "total" on the balance sheet and for gross margin and net income on the income statement.

b. Calculate the designated ratios using Excel formulas.

c. Which company is more likely to be able to pay its current liabilities?

d. Which company carries a greater financial risk?

e. Which company is more profitable from the stockholders' perspective?

f. Based on profitability alone, which company performed better?

g. Assume that sales increased 10 percent and that the additional sales were made on account. Adjust the balance sheet and income statement for the effects. Notice that Retained Earnings will also need to be adjusted to keep the balance sheet in balance. What is the resultant effect on the ratios?

COMPREHENSIVE PROBLEM

The trial balance of Pacilio Security System Sales and Service as of January 1, 2007, was as follows:

Cash	$105,496
Supplies	200
Accounts receivable	23,000
Merchandise inventory–std. alarms 4 @ $260; 30 @ $265	8,990
Merchandise inventory–deluxe alarms 11 @ $575	6,325
Prepaid rent	1,200
Van	9,200
Accumulated depreciation	2,400
Accounts payable	8,570
Common stock	50,000
Retained earnings	93,441

During 2010, Pacilio Security Services Inc. experienced the following transactions:

1. On March 1, 2010, Pacilio created a petty cash fund for $100 to handle small expenditures.
2. Paid $7,200 on March 2, 2010, for one year's rent in advance.
3. Purchased $400 of supplies on account.
4. Purchased 80 standard alarm systems for $22,400 and 50 deluxe alarm systems for $28,500 during the year for cash.
5. Sold 82 standard alarm systems for $45,920 and 28 deluxe systems for $25,480. All sales were on account. (Be sure to compute cost of goods sold using the FIFO cost flow method.)
6. Paid $6,000 on accounts payable for the year.
7. Replenished the petty cash fund on August 1. At this time, the petty cash fund had only $7 of cash left. It contained the following receipts: office supplies $23, cutting grass $55, and miscellaneous expense $14.
8. Billed $75,000 of monitoring services for the year.
9. Paid installer salaries of $25,000 for the year.
10. Collected $122,300 of accounts receivable for the year.
11. Paid $3,600 of advertising expense for the year.
12. Paid $2,500 of utilities expense for the year.

Adjustments

13. There were $160 of supplies on hand at the end of the year.
14. Recognized expired rent for the year.
15. Recognized depreciation expense for the year.

Required

a. Record the above transactions in general journal form.
b. Post the transactions to the T-accounts.
c. Prepare a bank reconciliation at the end of the year. The following information is available for the bank reconciliation:
   (1) Checks written but not paid by the bank, $8,350.
   (2) A deposit of $6,500 made on December 31, 2010, had been recorded but was not shown on the bank statement.
   (3) A debit memo for $55 for new supply of checks.
   (4) A credit memo for $20 for interest earned on the checking account.
   (5) An NSF check for $120.
   (6) The balance shown on the bank statement was $134,098.
d. Record and post any adjustments necessary from the bank reconciliation.
e. Prepare a trial balance
f. Prepare an income statement, statement of changes in stockholders' equity, balance sheet, and statement of cash flows.
g. Close the temporary accounts to retained earnings.
h. Post the closing entries to the T-accounts and prepare an after-closing trial balance.

CHAPTER 8

Accounting for Receivables and Payables

LEARNING OBJECTIVES

After you have mastered the material in this chapter, you will be able to:

1. Explain how the allowance method of accounting for bad debts affects financial statements.

2. Show how the direct write-off method of accounting for bad debts affects financial statements.

3. Explain how accounting for credit card sales affects financial statements.

4. Explain how accounting for warranty obligations affects financial statements.

5. Explain the effects of the cost of financing credit sales.

6. Show how discount notes and related interest charges affect financial statements. (Appendix)

LP8

The Curious Accountant

Suppose the U.S. government purchases $10 million of fuel from Chevron. Assume the government offers to pay for the fuel on the day it receives it from Chevron (a cash purchase) or 30 days later (a purchase on account).

Assume that Chevron is absolutely sure the government will pay its account when due. Do you think Chevron should care whether the government pays for the goods upon delivery or 30 days later? Why? (Answers on page 393.)

Video 8.1

CHAPTER OPENING

Many people buy on impulse. If they must wait, the desire to buy wanes. To take advantage of impulse buyers, most merchandising companies offer customers credit because it increases their sales. A disadvantage of this strategy occurs when some customers are unable or unwilling to pay their bills. Nevertheless, the widespread availability of credit suggests that the advantages of increased sales outweigh the disadvantages of some uncollectible accounts.

When a company allows a customer to "buy now and pay later," the company's right to collect cash in the future is called an **account receivable.** *Typically, amounts due from individual accounts receivable are relatively small and the terms to maturity are short. Most accounts receivable are collected within 30 days. When a longer credit term is needed or when a receivable is large, the seller usually requires the buyer to issue a note reflecting a credit agreement between the parties. The note specifies the maturity date, interest rate, and other credit terms. Receivables evidenced by such notes are called* **notes receivable.** *Accounts and notes receivable are reported as assets on the balance sheet. For every receivable on one company's books, there is a corresponding* **payable** *on another company's books. If one company expects to collect, another company must be obligated to pay. Accounts payable and notes payable[1] are reported as liabilities on the balance sheet.* ■

---

[1] Notes payable and other liabilities may be classified as short term or long term, depending on the time to maturity. Short-term liabilities mature within one year or the operating cycle, whichever is longer. Liabilities with longer maturities are classified as long term. This chapter focuses on accounting for short-term liabilities; accounting for long-term liabilities is discussed in Chapter 10.

Allowance Method of Accounting for Bad Debts

Explain how the allowance method of accounting for bad debts affects financial statements.

Most companies will not collect cash for the full face value of their receivables because some of their customers will be unable or unwilling to pay. To avoid overstating assets, companies report receivables at **net realizable value,** which is face value less an allowance for doubtful accounts (accounts estimated to be uncollectible). Only the amount actually expected to be collected is included in total assets. Payables, in contrast, are normally reported on the balance sheet at face value because of the **going concern assumption.** Specifically, companies operate under the assumption that they will continue to exist (they are going concerns). Under this assumption, companies expect to pay their obligations in full.

Reporting the net realizable value of receivables in the financial statements is commonly called the **allowance method of accounting for bad debts.** The following section illustrates using the allowance method for Allen's Tutoring Services.

Accounting Events Affecting the 2008 Period

Allen's Tutoring Services is a small company that provides tutoring services to college students. Allen's started operations on January 1, 2008. During 2008, Allen's experienced three types of accounting events. These events are discussed below.

Event 1   Revenue Recognition
Allen's Tutoring Services recognized $14,000 of service revenue earned on account during 2008.

This is an asset source transaction. Allen's Tutoring Services obtained assets (accounts receivable) by providing services to customers. Both assets and stockholders' equity (retained earnings) increase. The event increases revenue and net income. Cash flow is not affected. These effects follow:

| Event No. | Assets | = | Liab. | + | Equity | Rev. | − | Exp. | = | Net Inc. | Cash Flow |
	Accts. Rec.	=			Ret. Earn.						
1	14,000	=	NA	+	14,000	14,000	−	NA	=	14,000	NA

Event 2   Collection of Receivables
Allen's Tutoring Services collected $12,500 cash from accounts receivable in 2008.

This event is an asset exchange transaction. The asset cash increases; the asset accounts receivable decreases. Total assets remains unchanged. Net income is not affected because the revenue was recognized in the previous transaction. The cash inflow is reported in the operating activities section of the statement of cash flows.

| Event No. | Assets | | | = | Liab. | + | Equity | Rev. | − | Exp. | = | Net Inc. | Cash Flow |
	Cash	+	Accts. Rec.										
2	12,500	+	(12,500)	=	NA	+	NA	NA	−	NA	=	NA	12,500 OA

Accounting for Bad Debts Expense[2]

Event 3   Recognizing Bad Debts Expense
Allen's Tutoring Services recognized bad debts expense for accounts expected to be uncollectible in the future.

The year-end balance in the Accounts Receivable account is $1,500 ($14,000 of revenue on account −$12,500 of collections). Although Allen's Tutoring Services has the legal right

---

[2]The term *bad debts* may be misleading. It is some *receivables* that are "bad" rather than some company debt. Businesses, however, commonly refer to bad receivables as bad debts. We believe it is important to use real-world terminology, but be aware of the misleading nature of the term *bad debts expense.*

Answers to The Curious Accountant

Chevron would definitely prefer to make the sale to the government in cash rather than on account. Even though it may be certain to collect its accounts receivable, the sooner Chevron gets its cash, the sooner the cash can be reinvested.

The interest cost related to a small account receivable of $50 that takes 30 days to collect may seem immaterial; at 4 percent, the lost interest amounts to less than $.20. However, when one considers that Chevron had approximately

$17.2 billion of accounts receivable on December 31, 2005, the cost of financing receivables for a real-world company becomes apparent. At 4 percent, the cost of waiting 30 days to collect $17.2 billion of cash is $56.5 million ($17.2 billion × .04 × [30 ÷ 365]). For one full year, the cost to Chevron would be more than $688 million ($17.2 billion × 0.04). In 2005, it took Chevron approximately 32 days to collect its accounts receivable, and the weighted-average interest rate on its debt was approximately 4.2 percent.

to receive this $1,500 in 2009, the company is not likely to collect the entire amount because some of its customers may not pay the amounts due. Allen's will not know the actual amount of uncollectible accounts until some future time when the customers default (fail to pay). However, the company can *estimate* the amount of receivables that will be uncollectible.

Suppose Allen's Tutoring Services estimates that $75 of the receivables is uncollectible. To improve financial reporting, the company can recognize the estimated expense in 2008. In this way, bad debts expense and the matching revenue will be recognized in the same accounting period (2008). Recognizing an estimated expense is better than recognizing no expense. The *matching* of revenues and expenses is improved and the statements are, therefore, more accurate.

The estimated amount of **bad debts expense** is recognized in a year-end adjusting entry. The adjusting entry reduces the book value of total assets, reduces stockholders' equity (retained earnings), and reduces the amount of reported net income. The statement of cash flows is not affected. The effects of recognizing bad debts expense are shown here:

Event No.	Assets	=	Liab.	+	Equity	Rev.	−	Exp.	=	Net Inc.	Cash Flow
	Accts. Rec.	=	Allow.	+	Ret. Earn.						
3	(75)	=	NA	+	(75)	NA	−	75	=	(75)	NA

The amount of receivables expected to be uncollectible ($75) is recorded in a contra asset account called **Allowance for Doubtful Accounts.** The difference between the amount in accounts receivable and the contra account is the *net realizable value* of accounts receivable. In this case, the net realizable value of receivables is:

Accounts receivable	$1,500
Less: Allowance for doubtful accounts	(75)
Net realizable value of receivables	$1,425

The net realizable value of receivables represents the amount of cash the company estimates it will actually collect. Generally accepted accounting principles require disclosure of both the net realizable value of receivables and the amount of the allowance account. Most companies disclose these amounts in their balance sheets. However, a significant number of companies report only the net amount on the balance sheet and report the allowance amount in the footnotes. Typical alternative balance sheet captions that Allen's Tutoring Services could use to report accounts receivable follow:

Alternative 1	
Accounts receivable	$1,500
Less allowance for doubtful accounts	(75)
Net realizable value	$1,425
Alternative 2	
Trade accounts receivable, less allowance of $75	$1,425
Alternative 3	
Receivables, less allowance for losses of $75	$1,425
Alternative 4	
Accounts and notes receivable, net	$1,425
Alternative 5	
Accounts receivable	$1,425

As the different captions indicate, companies report the amount of receivables on their balance sheets in a variety of ways. Exhibit 8.1 identifies the most frequently used captions.

General Ledger T-Accounts

Exhibit 8.2 displays in T-account form the general ledger for the three business events experienced by Allen's Tutoring Services. The transactions data are referenced by the event number shown in parentheses. The entries to close the revenue and expense accounts at the end of the 2008 accounting period are also included. The closing entries are referenced with the letters *cl*. The ledger accounts provide the information to prepare the financial statements in Exhibit 8.3. The accounting events are summarized here:

1. Earned $14,000 of revenue on account.
2. Collected $12,500 cash from accounts receivable.
3. Adjusted the accounts to reflect management's estimate that bad debts expense would be $75.
4. Closed the revenue and expense accounts. (Referenced with letters *cl*.)

EXHIBIT 8.1

Real-World Reporting Practices: Most Frequently Used Titles Related to the Reporting of Accounts Receivable

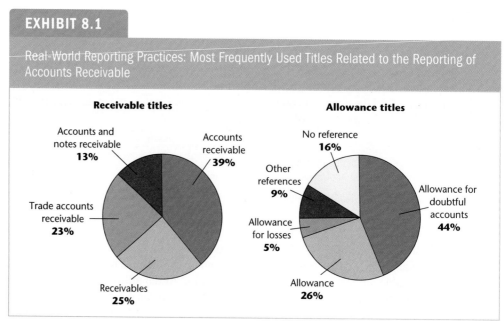

Data Source: AICPA, *Accounting Trends and Techniques, 2006.*

EXHIBIT 8.2

General Ledger

Assets	=	Liabilities	+	Equity

Cash

(2)	12,500	
Bal.	12,500	

Accounts Receivable

(1)	14,000	12,500	(2)
Bal.	1,500		

Allowance for Doubtful Accounts

		75	(3)
		75	Bal.

Liabilities

	0	Bal.

Retained Earnings

		13,925	(cl)
		13,925	Bal.

Service Revenue

(cl.)	14,000	14,000	(1)
		0	Bal.

Bad Debts Expense

(3)	75	75	(cl.)
Bal.	0		

EXHIBIT 8.3

Financial Statements for 2008

Income Statement		Balance Sheet		Statement of Cash Flows	
Service revenue	$14,000	Assets		**Operating Activities**	
Bad debts exp.	(75)	Cash	$12,500	Inflow from customers	$12,500
Net income	$13,925	Accounts receivable	$1,500	**Investing Activities**	0
		Less: Allowance	(75)	**Financing Activities**	0
		Net realizable value	1,425	Net change in cash	12,500
		Total assets	$13,925	Plus: Beginning cash balance	0
		Stockholders' equity		Ending cash balance	$12,500
		Retained earnings	$13,925		

Financial Statements

As previously indicated, estimating bad debts improves the usefulness of the 2008 financial statements in two ways. First, the balance sheet reports the amount of cash ($1,500 − $75 = $1,425) the company actually expects to collect (net realizable value of accounts receivable). Second, the income statement provides a clearer picture of managerial performance because it better *matches* the bad debts expense with the revenue it helped produce. The statements in Exhibit 8.3 show that the cash flow from operating activities ($12,500) differs from net income ($13,925). The statement of cash flows reports only cash collections, whereas the income statement reports revenues earned on account less the estimated amount of bad debts expense.

CHECK YOURSELF 8.1

Pamlico, Inc., began operations on January 1, 2007. During 2007, it earned $400,000 of revenue on account. The company collected $370,000 of accounts receivable. At the end of the year, Pamlico estimates bad debts expense will be 1 percent of sales. Based on this information alone, what is the net realizable value of accounts receivable as of December 31, 2007?

Answer

Accounts receivable at year end are $30,000 ($400,000 sales on account − $370,000 collection of receivables). The amount in the allowance for doubtful accounts would be $4,000 ($400,000 credit sales × 0.01). The net realizable value of accounts receivable is therefore $26,000 ($30,000 − $4,000).

PLUS

8-1

Video 8.1

Estimating Bad Debts Expense

In the Allen's Tutoring Services example, the estimated amount of bad debts expense was simply given. How do practicing accountants make such estimates? They normally base the estimate on the company's actual collection history. For example, assume that in the previous accounting period, Tannon Company was unable to collect $10,000 of $1,000,000 of sales on account. Expressed as a percentage, Tannon's bad debts expense is 1 percent of its credit sales ($10,000 ÷ $1,000,000). Estimates of future bad debts can be made by multiplying the historical percentage by current sales. If sales for the current period are $1,200,000, the estimated bad debts expense would be $12,000 ($1,200,000 × .01).

It may be necessary to adjust the historical percentage for anticipated future circumstances. For example, the percentage would be reduced if a company adopts more rigorous approval standards for new credit applicants. Alternatively, the percentage may be increased if economic forecasts signal an economic downturn that would make future defaults more likely.

Determining the estimated bad debts percentage of credit sales may be difficult when a company is in its first year of operation because it has no credit history. In such cases, accountants can consult with trade associations or business associates (other people in the same industry who do have experience) to develop a reasonable estimate of expected losses.

Accounting Events Affecting the 2009 Period

To further illustrate accounting for bad debts, we discuss eight accounting events affecting Allen's Tutoring Services during 2009.

Event 1 Write-Off of an Uncollectible Account Receivable
Allen's Tutoring Services wrote off an uncollectible account receivable with a $70 balance.

This is an asset exchange transaction. The amount of the uncollectible account is removed from the Accounts Receivable account and from the Allowance for Doubtful Accounts account. Since the balances in both the Accounts Receivable and the Allowance accounts decrease, the net realizable value of receivables—and therefore total assets—remains unchanged. The write-off does not affect the income statement. Since the bad debts expense was recognized in the previous year, the expense would be double counted if it were recognized again at the time the uncollectible account is written off. Finally, the statement of cash flows is not affected by the write-off. These effects are shown in the following statements model:

| Event No. | Assets | | | = | Liab. | + | Equity | Rev. | − | Exp. | = | Net Inc. | Cash Flow |
	Accts. Rec.	−	Allow.										
1	(70)	−	(70)	=	NA	+	NA	NA	−	NA	=	NA	NA

The computation of the *net realizable value,* before and after the write-off, is shown below.

	Before Write-Off	After Write-Off
Accounts receivable	$1,500	$1,430
Less: Allowance for doubtful accounts	(75)	(5)
Net realizable value	$1,425	$1,425

Event 2 Investment in Note Receivable
Allen's Tutoring Services invested in a note receivable.

Mr. Allen realized that he could improve his company's profitability by investing some of the idle cash in his company's growing cash account. On May 1, 2009, Allen's Tutoring Service loaned $12,000 cash to another business. The borrower issued a 9 percent interest-bearing note to Allen's. The note had a one-year term. For Allen's Tutoring Services, the loan represents an investment. The asset account, Cash, decreases; the asset account, Notes Receivable, increases. Total assets are unchanged. The income statement is unaffected. The cash outflow is reported in the investing activities section of the statement of cash flows. These effects are shown here:

Event No.	Assets			=	Liab.	+	Equity	Rev.	−	Exp.	=	Net Inc.	Cash Flow
	Cash	+	Note Rec.										
2	(12,000)	+	12,000	=	NA	+	NA	NA	−	NA	=	NA	(12,000) IA

Event 3　Revenue Recognition
Allen's Tutoring Services provided $10,000 of tutoring services on account during 2009.

Assets (accounts receivable) and stockholders' equity (retained earnings) increase. Recognizing revenue increases net income. Cash flow is not affected. These effects are illustrated below:

Event No.	Assets	=	Liab.	+	Equity	Rev.	−	Exp.	=	Net Inc.	Cash Flow
	Accts. Rec.	=			Ret. Earn.						
3	10,000	=	NA	+	10,000	10,000	−	NA	=	10,000	NA

Event 4　Collection of Accounts Receivable
Allen's Tutoring Services collected $8,430 cash from accounts receivable.

The balance in the Cash account increases, and the balance in the Accounts Receivable account decreases. Total assets are unaffected. Net income is not affected because revenue was recognized previously. The cash inflow is reported in the operating activities section of the statement of cash flows.

Event No.	Assets			=	Liab.	+	Equity	Rev.	−	Exp.	=	Net Inc.	Cash Flow
	Cash	+	Accts. Rec.										
4	8,430	+	(8,430)	=	NA	+	NA	NA	−	NA	=	NA	8,430 OA

Event 5　Recovery of Bad Debt: Reinstate Receivable
Allen's Tutoring Services recovered a bad debt that was previously written off.

Occasionally, a company receives payment from a customer whose account was previously written off. In such cases, the customer's account should be reinstated and the cash received should be recorded the same way as any other collection on account. The account receivable is reinstated because a complete record of the customer's payment history may be useful if the customer requests credit again at some future date. To illustrate, assume that Allen's Tutoring Services received a $10 cash payment from a customer whose account had previously been written off. The first step is to reinstate the account receivable by reversing the previous write-off. The balances in the Accounts Receivable and the Allowance accounts increase. Since the Allowance is a contra asset account, the increase in it offsets the increase in the Accounts Receivable account, and total assets are unchanged. Net income and cash flow are unaffected. These effects are shown here:

Event No.	Assets			=	Liab.	+	Equity	Rev.	−	Exp.	=	Net Inc.	Cash Flow
	Accts. Rec.	−	Allow.										
5	10	−	10	=	NA	+	NA	NA	−	NA	=	NA	NA

Event 6   Recovery of Bad Debt: Collection of Receivable
Allen's Tutoring Services recorded collection of the reinstated receivable.

The collection of $10 is recorded like any other collection of a receivable account. Cash increases and accounts receivable decreases.

Event	Assets			=	Liab.	+	Equity	Rev.	–	Exp.	=	Net Inc.	Cash Flow
No.	Cash	+	Accts. Rec.										
6	10	+	(10)	=	NA	+	NA	NA	–	NA	=	NA	10 OA

Year-End Adjusting Entries

The next two transactions are required to adjust Allen's accounts to make them ready for the preparation of the 2009 financial statements. The adjusting entries are made as of December 31, 2009.

Event 7   Adjustment for Recognition of Bad Debts Expense
Allen's Tutoring Services recognized bad debts expense for 2009.

Assume Allen's estimated 2009 bad debts expense to be 1.35 percent of 2009 credit sales. The amount of bad debts expense would be $135 ($10,000 × 0.0135). Recognizing the $135 bad debts expense decreases both assets (net realizable value of receivables) and stockholders' equity (retained earnings). The expense recognition decreases net income. The statement of cash flows is not affected. The financial statements are affected as shown here:

Event	Assets			=	Liab.	+	Equity	Rev.	–	Exp.	=	Net Inc.	Cash Flow
No.	Accts. Rec.	–	Allow.				Ret. Earn.						
7	NA	–	135	=	NA	+	(135)	NA	–	135	=	(135)	NA

Event 8   Recognition of Interest Revenue
Allen's Tutoring Services recognized interest revenue on the note receivable.

Recall that on May 1, 2009, Allen's Tutoring Services invested $12,000 in a note receivable with a one-year term and a 9 percent annual interest rate. By December 31, 2009, the note had earned $720 ($12,000 × 0.09 × [8 ÷ 12]). Recognizing the earned interest increases assets (interest receivable) and stockholders' equity (retained earnings). The revenue recognition increases net income. Cash flow is not affected. These effects are illustrated below:

Event No.	Assets	=	Liab.	+	Equity	Rev.	–	Exp.	=	Net Inc.	Cash Flow
8	720	=	NA	+	720	720	–	NA	=	720	NA

General Ledger T-Accounts

Exhibit 8.4 displays in T-account form the ledger accounts for the 2009 business events experienced by Allen's Tutoring Services. The entry to close the revenue and expense accounts at the end of the 2009 accounting period is included. The ledger accounts provide the information to prepare the financial statements in Exhibit 8.5. The accounting events are summarized here:

1. Wrote off a $70 uncollectible account receivable.
2. Invested $12,000 in a note receivable.
3. Earned $10,000 of tutoring service revenue on account.
4. Collected $8,430 cash from accounts receivable.
5. Reinstated a $10 account receivable that had previously been written off.
6. Recorded collection of $10 from the reinstated receivable.
7. Adjusted accounts to recognize $135 of estimated bad debts expense.

EXHIBIT 8.4

General Ledger

Assets				=	Liabilities		+	Equity		

Cash

Bal.	12,500	12,000	(2)	
(4)	8,430			
(6)	10			
Bal.	8,940			

Liabilities

	0	Bal.

Retained Earnings

	13,925	Bal.
	10,585	(cl.)
	24,510	Bal.

Accounts Receivable

Bal.	1,500	70	(1)
(3)	10,000	8,430	(4)
(5)	10	10	(6)
Bal.	3,000		

Service Revenue

(cl.)	10,000	10,000	(3)
		0	Bal.

Allowance for Doubtful Accounts

(1)	70	75	Bal.
		10	(5)
		135	(7)
		150	Bal.

Interest Revenue

(cl.)	720	720	(8)
		0	Bal.

Notes Receivable

(2)	12,000
Bal.	12,000

Bad Debts Expense

(7)	135	135	(cl.)
Bal.	0		

Interest Receivable

(8)	720
Bal.	720

8. Adjusted accounts to recognize $720 of accrued interest revenue.

9. Closed the revenue and expense accounts.

The transaction data in the T-accounts for Events 1 through 8 are referenced by event number shown in parentheses. Event 9 is referenced with the letters *cl* indicating that journal entry is for closing the accounts.

Analysis of Financial Statements

Exhibit 8.5 displays the 2009 financial statements. Observe that the amount of bad debts expense ($135) differs from the ending balance of the Allowance account ($150). The balance in the Allowance account was $15 before the 2009 adjusting entry for bad debts expense was recorded. At the end of 2008, Allen's Tutoring Services estimated there would be $75 of uncollectible accounts as a result of 2008 credit sales. Actual write-offs, however, amounted to $70 and $10 of that amount was recovered, indicating the actual bad debts expense for 2008 was only $60. Hindsight shows the expense for 2008 was overstated by $15. However, if no estimate had been made, the amount of bad debts expense would have been understated by $60. In some accounting periods estimated bad debts expense will likely be overstated; in others it may be understated. The allowance method cannot produce perfect results, but it does improve the accuracy of the financial statements.

Since no dividends were paid, retained earnings at the end of 2009 equals 2008's retained earnings plus 2009's net income (that is, $13,925 + $10,585 = $24,510). Again, the cash flow from operating activities ($8,440) differs from net income ($10,585) because the statement of cash flows does not include the effects of revenues earned on account or the recognition of bad debts expense.

EXHIBIT 8.5

Financial Statements for 2009

Income Statement		Balance Sheet		Statement of Cash Flows	
Service revenue	$10,000	Assets		**Operating Activities**	
Bad debts exp.	(135)	Cash	$ 8,940	Inflow from customers	$ 8,440
Operating income	9,865	Accounts receivable	$3,000	**Investing Activities**	
Interest revenue	720	Less: Allowance	(150)	Outflow for the note rec.	(12,000)
Net income	$10,585	Net realizable value	2,850	**Financing Activities**	0
		Note receivable	12,000		
		Interest receivable	720	Net change in cash	(3,560)
		Total assets	$24,510	Plus: Beginning cash balance	12,500
		Stockholders' equity		Ending cash balance	$ 8,940
		Retained earnings	$24,510		

CHECK YOURSELF 8.2

Maher Company had beginning balances in Accounts Receivable and Allowance for Doubtful Accounts of $24,200 and $2,000, respectively. During the accounting period Maher earned $230,000 of revenue on account and collected $232,500 of cash from receivables. The company also wrote off $1,950 of uncollectible accounts during the period. Maher estimates bad debts expense will be 1 percent of credit sales. Based on this information, what is the net realizable value of receivables at the end of the period?

Answer

The balance in the Accounts Receivable account is $19,750 ($24,200 + $230,000 − $232,500 − $1,950). The amount of bad debts expense for the period is $2,300 ($230,000 × 0.01). The balance in the Allowance for Doubtful Accounts is $2,350 ($2,000 − $1,950 + $2,300). The net realizable value of receivables is therefore $17,400 ($19,750 − $2,350).

Recognition of Bad Debts Expense Using the Direct Write-Off Method

Video 8.1

Show how the direct write-off method of accounting for bad debts affects financial statements.

If the amount of uncollectible accounts is immaterial, generally accepted accounting principles allow companies to use the **direct write-off method** of accounting for bad debts, under which bad debts expense is not recognized until accounts are determined to be uncollectible. The direct write-off method fails to match revenues with expenses and it overstates the net realizable value of receivables. However, if the amount of uncollectible accounts is immaterial, the reporting inaccuracies are accepted as a reasonable trade-off for the recording convenience offered by the direct write-off method.

The direct write-off method does not use estimates, an allowance account, or adjusting entries. Instead, bad debts expense is recorded when uncollectible accounts are identified. Sales or services on account are, as always, recognized in the period in which goods are sold or services are provided. Bad debts expense, however, is recognized in a later period when an account is determined to be uncollectible. To illustrate, assume that the following events apply to Dr. Price's optical services business.

Event 1 Recognition of Revenue Earned on Account
During 2008, the company provided $50,000 of services on account.

The effects of this event are:

Event No.	Assets	=	Liab.	+	Equity	Rev.	−	Exp.	=	Net Inc.	Cash Flow
1	50,000	=	NA	+	50,000	50,000	−	NA	=	50,000	NA

The general journal entry to record the transaction is:

Account Title	Debit	Credit
Accounts Receivable	50,000	
Service Revenue		50,000

There is no year-end adjusting entry made for estimated bad debts expense. Instead, bad debts expense will be recognized when an account is determined to be uncollectible.

Event 2 Recognition of Bad Debts Expense
Assume that Price determines in 2009 that a customer who owes $200 for services delivered in 2008 is unable to pay the amount due.

Writing off the account using the direct write-off method results in recognizing bad debts expense in 2009, even though the associated revenue was recognized in 2008. Financial reporting accuracy is compromised because expenses *are not matched* with related revenues. Such inaccuracies are acceptable only to the extent they are deemed immaterial. The effects of the write-off of the uncollectible account on the financial statements are:

Event No.	Assets	=	Liab.	+	Equity	Rev.	−	Exp.	=	Net Inc.	Cash Flow
2	(200)	=	NA	+	(200)	NA	−	200	=	(200)	NA

In general journal form, the entry to recognize bad debts expense in 2009 is recorded as follows:

Account Title	Debit	Credit
Bad Debts Expense	200	
Accounts Receivable		200

Accounting for Credit Card Sales

Maintaining accounts receivable is expensive. In addition to bad debts expense, companies extending credit to their customers incur considerable costs for such clerical tasks as running background checks and maintaining customer records. Many businesses find it more efficient to accept third-party credit cards instead of offering credit directly to their customers. Credit card companies service the merchant's credit sales for a fee that typically ranges between 2 and 8 percent of gross sales.

LO 3

Explain how accounting for credit card sales affects financial statements.

Video 8.1

The credit card company provides customers with plastic cards that permit cardholders to charge purchases at various retail outlets. When a sale takes place, the seller records the transaction on a receipt the customer signs. The receipt is forwarded to the credit card company, which immediately pays the merchant.

The credit card company deducts its service fee from the gross amount of the sale, and pays the merchant the net balance (gross amount of sale less credit card fee) in cash. The credit card company collects the gross sale amount directly from the customer. The merchant avoids the risk of bad debts as well as the cost of maintaining customer credit records. To illustrate, assume that the following events apply to Joan Wilson's consulting practice.

Event 1 Recognition of Revenue and Expense on Credit Card Sales
Wilson accepts a credit card payment for $1,000 of services rendered to one of her customers.

Assume the credit card company charges a 5 percent fee for handling the transaction ($1,000 × 0.05 = $50). Wilson's income increases by the amount of revenue ($1,000) and decreases by the amount of the credit card expense ($50). Net income increases by $950. The event increases an asset, accounts receivable, due from the credit card company, and stockholders' equity (retained earnings) by $950 ($1,000 revenue − $50 credit card expense). Cash flow is not affected. These effects are shown here:

Event No.	Assets	=	Liab.	+	Equity	Rev.	−	Exp.	=	Net Inc.	Cash Flow
1	950	=	NA	+	950	1,000	−	50	=	950	NA

In general journal form, the entry to record the transaction is as follows:

Account Title	Debit	Credit
Accounts Receivable–Credit Card Company	950	
Credit Card Expense	50	
Service Revenue		1,000

Event 2 Collection of Credit Card Receivable
The collection of the receivable due from the credit card company is recorded like any other receivable collection.

When Wilson collects the net amount of $950 ($1,000 − $50) from the credit card company, one asset account (Cash) increases and another asset account (Accounts Receivable) decreases. Total assets are not affected. The income statement is not affected. A $950 cash inflow is reported in the operating activities section of the statement of cash flows. These effects are illustrated below:

Event No.	Assets			=	Liab.	+	Equity	Rev.	−	Exp.	=	Net Inc.	Cash Flow
	Cash	+	Accts. Rec.										
2	950	+	(950)	=	NA	+	NA	NA	−	NA	=	NA	950 OA

The following entry records the transaction in the general journal.

Account Title	Debit	Credit
Cash	950	
Accounts Receivable–Credit Card Company		950

Warranty Obligations

LO 4

Explain how accounting for warranty obligations affects financial statements.

To attract customers, many companies guarantee their products or services. Such guarantees are called **warranties.** Warranties take many forms. Usually, they extend for a specified period of time. Within this period, the seller promises to replace or repair defective products without charge. While the amount and timing of warranty obligations are uncertain, warranties usually represent legal liabilities that must be reported in the financial statements.

To illustrate accounting for warranty obligations, assume Perfect Picture Frame (PPF) Company had cash of $2,000, inventory of $6,000, common stock of $5,000, and retained earnings of $3,000 on January 1, 2009. The 2009 accounting period is affected by three accounting events: (1) sale of merchandise under warranty; (2) recognition of warranty obligations to customers who purchased the merchandise; and (3) settlement of a customer's warranty claim.

Event 1 Sale of Merchandise
PPF sold for $7,000 cash merchandise that had cost $4,000.

In the statements model displayed here, revenue from the sale is referenced as 1a and the cost of the sale as 1b. The effects of the sales transaction on the financial statements are shown below:

Event No.	Assets			=	Liab.	+	Equity	Rev.	−	Exp.	=	Net Inc.	Cash Flow	
	Cash	+	Inventory											
1a	7,000	+	NA	=	NA	+	7,000	7,000	−	NA	=	7,000	7,000	OA
1b	NA	+	(4,000)	=	NA	+	(4,000)	NA	−	4,000	=	(4,000)	NA	

Event 2 Recognition of Warranty Expense
PPF guaranteed the merchandise sold in event 1 to be free from defects for one year following the date of sale.

Although the exact amount of future warranty claims is unknown, PPF must inform financial statement users of the company's obligation. PPF must estimate the amount of the warranty liability and report the estimate in the 2009 financial statements. Assume the warranty obligation is estimated to be $100. Recognizing this obligation increases liabilities (warranties payable) and reduces stockholders' equity (retained earnings). Recognizing the warranty expense reduces net income. The statement of cash flows is not affected when the obligation and the corresponding expense are recognized. These effects follow:

Event No.	Assets	=	Liab.	+	Equity	Rev.	−	Exp.	=	Net Inc.	Cash Flow
2	NA	=	100	+	(100)	NA	−	100	=	(100)	NA

Event 3 Settlement of Warranty Obligation
PPF paid $40 cash to repair defective merchandise returned by a customer.

The cash payment for the repair is not an expense. Warranty expense was recognized in the period in which the sale was made (when the Warranties Payable account was created). The payment reduces an asset (cash) and a liability (warranties payable). The income statement is not affected by the repairs payment. However, there is a $40 cash outflow reported in the operating activities section of the statement of cash flows.

Event No.	Assets	=	Liab.	+	Equity	Rev.	−	Exp.	=	Net Inc.	Cash Flow	
3	(40)	=	(40)	+	NA	NA	−	NA	=	NA	(40)	OA

General Ledger T-Accounts and Financial Statements

Exhibit 8.6 presents in T-account form the ledger accounts for the business events experienced by PPF. The entry to close the revenue and expense accounts at the end of the 2009 accounting period is included. The ledger accounts provide the information to prepare the financial statements in Exhibit 8.7. The accounting events are summarized here:

EXHIBIT 8.6

General Ledger

Assets				=	Liabilities			+	Equity		

Cash

							Warranties Payable			**Common Stock**	
Bal.	2,000	40	(3)	(3)	40	100	(2)		5,000	Bal.
(1a)	7,000					60	Bal.			
Bal.	8,960									

Retained Earnings

	3,000	Bal.
	2,900	(cl.)
	5,900	Bal.

Inventory

Bal.	6,000	4,000	(1b)
Bal.	2,000		

Sales Revenue

(cl.)	7,000	7,000	(1a)
		0	Bal.

Cost of Goods Sold

(1b)	4,000	4,000	(cl.)
Bal.	0		

Warranty Expense

(2)	100	100	(cl.)
Bal.	0		

EXHIBIT 8.7

Financial Statements for 2009

Income Statement

Sales revenue	$7,000
Cost of goods sold	(4,000)
Gross margin	3,000
Warranty exp.	(100)
Net income	$2,900

Balance Sheet

Assets	
Cash	$ 8,960
Inventory	2,000
Total assets	$10,960
Liabilities	
Warranties payable	$ 60
Stockholders' equity	
Common stock	5,000
Retained earnings	5,900
Total liab. and stockholders' equity	$10,960

Statement of Cash Flows

Operating Activities	
Inflow from customers	$7,000
Outflow for warranty	(40)
Net Inflow from operating activities	6,960
Investing Activities	0
Financing Activities	0
Net change in cash	6,960
Plus: Beginning cash balance	2,000
Ending cash balance	$8,960

Transactions for 2009

1. Sold merchandise that cost $4,000 for $7,000 cash.
2. Recognized a $100 warranty obligation and the corresponding expense.
3. Paid $40 to satisfy a warranty claim.
4. Closed the revenue and expense accounts.

The transaction data in the T-accounts for Events 1 through 3 are referenced by event number shown in parentheses. Event 4 is referenced with the letters *cl* indicating that journal entry is for closing the accounts.

THE FINANCIAL ANALYST

Costs of Credit Sales

As mentioned earlier, two costs of extending credit to customers are bad debts expense and record-keeping costs. These costs can be significant. Large companies spend literally millions of dollars to buy the equipment and pay the staff necessary to operate entire departments devoted to managing accounts receivable. Further, there is an implicit interest charge associated with extending credit. When a customer is permitted to delay payment, the creditor foregoes the opportunity to invest the amount the customer owes.

Exhibit 8.8 presents part of a footnote from the 2005 annual report of Rent-A-Center. This excerpt provides insight into the credit costs real companies incur. First, observe that Rent-A-Center was owed $23.7 million of accounts receivable. These receivables represent money that could be in the bank earning interest if all sales had been made in cash. If Rent-A-Center could have earned interest at 5 percent on that money, the opportunity cost of this lost interest is approximately $1.2 million ($23.7 million × .05) a year. Next, observe that Rent-A-Center expects to have uncollectible accounts amounting to $3.3 million (balance in the allowance account). These are indeed significant costs to a company whose net earnings were $135.8 million in 2005.

Topic Tackler

PLUS

8-2

LO 5

Explain the effects of the cost of financing credit sales.

EXHIBIT 8.8

Rent-A-Center, Inc. December 31, 2005
PARTIAL FOOTNOTE B Regarding Accounts Receivable and Allowance for Doubtful Accounts (amounts shown in thousands)

Receivables consist of the following:

	2005	2004
Installment sales receivable	$18,356	$16,919
Financial service loans receivable	2,757	–
Trade receivables	2,607	1,956
Total	23,720	18,875
Less allowance for doubtful accounts	(3,317)	(2,606)
Net receivables	$20,403	$16,269

Changes in the Company's allowance for doubtful accounts are as follows:

	2005	2004
Beginning balance	$2,606	$1,918
Bad debt expense	1,581	1,101
Addition from acquisition	114	–
Accounts written off	(1,271)	(744)
Recoveries	287	331
Ending balance	$3,317	$2,606

Average Number of Days to Collect Accounts Receivable

The longer it takes to collect accounts receivable, the greater the opportunity cost of lost income. Also, business experience indicates that the older an account receivable becomes, the less likely it is to be collected. Finally, taking longer to collect an account typically costs more for salaries, equipment, and supplies used in the process of trying to collect it. Businesses are therefore concerned about how long it takes to collect their receivables.

Two ratios help management, or other users, measure a company's collection period. One is the **accounts receivable turnover ratio,** computed as:[3]

$$\frac{\text{Sales}}{\text{Accounts receivable}}$$

Dividing a company's sales by its accounts receivable tells how many times the accounts receivable balance is "turned over" (converted into cash) each year. The higher the turnover, the shorter the collection period. To simplify its interpretation, the accounts receivable turnover ratio is often taken one step further to determine the **average number of days to collect accounts receivable,** sometimes called the *average collection period.* This is computed as:

$$\frac{365}{\text{Accounts receivable turnover ratio}}$$

[3]To be more precise, the ratio could be computed using only credit sales and average accounts receivable. Usually, however, companies do not report credit sales separately from cash sales in published financial statements. Average accounts receivable, if desired, is computed as ([beginning receivables + ending receivables] ÷ 2). For this course, use the simpler computation shown here (sales ÷ accounts receivable).

REALITY BYTES

Most electrical appliances come with a manufacturer's warranty that obligates the manufacturer to pay for defects that occur during some designated period of time after the point of sale. Why would Circuit City issue warranties that obligate it to pay for defects that occur after the manufacturer's warranty has expired? Warranties are in fact insurance policies that generate profits. Indeed, the Circuit City Group reported that the gross dollar sales from extended warranty programs were 3.8 percent of its domestic sales in fiscal year 2006. Even more important, Circuit City notes that gross profit margins on products sold with extended warranties are higher than the gross profit margins on products sold without extended warranties. It should be noted that warranties produce revenues for manufacturers as well as retailers. The only difference is that the revenues generated from manufacturer's warranties are embedded in the sales price. Indeed, products with longer, more comprehensive warranties usually sell at higher prices than products with shorter, less extensive warranties.

This ratio measures how many days, on average, it takes a company to collect its accounts receivable. Since longer collection periods increase costs, shorter periods are obviously more desirable. To illustrate computing the *average number of days to collect accounts receivable* ratio for Allen's Tutoring Services, refer to the 2009 financial statements in Exhibit 8.5. On average, the company takes 104 days to collect its receivables, computed in two steps:

1. The accounts receivable turnover is 3.509 ($10,000 ÷ $2,850) times.
2. The average number of days to collect receivables is 104 (365 ÷ 3.509) days.

In the preceding computations, the net realizable value of accounts receivable was used because that is the amount typically reported in published financial statements. The results would not have been materially different had total accounts receivable been used.

Real-World Data

What is the collection period for real companies? The time required to collect receivables varies among industries and among companies within industries. Column 4 in Exhibit 8.9 displays the average number of days to collect receivables for eight companies in three different industries. These numbers are for the 2005 calendar year.

Since fast-food restaurants require customers to pay cash when they purchase hamburgers or coffee, why do these companies have accounts receivable? The accounts receivable for Yum! Brands and McDonald's arise because these companies sell goods to restaurants that are independent franchisees. So, for example, Yum's accounts receivable represents future collections from restaurant owners, not customers who purchase pepperoni pizzas at Pizza Hut restaurants.

Are the collection periods for Concha y Toro and Willamette Valley too long? The answer depends on their credit policies. If they are selling goods to customers on net 30-day terms, there may be reason for concern, but if they allow customers 90 days to pay and the cost of this policy has been built into their pricing structure, the collection periods may not be unreasonable.

Some companies allow their customers extended time to pay their bills because the customers would otherwise have difficulty coming up with the money. For example, Concha y Toro may sell to a wine retailer that does not have the cash available to pay immediately. If Concha y Toro allows the retailer sufficient time, the retailer can sell the wine to customers

EXHIBIT 8.9

Industry	Company	Average Days to Sell Inventory	Average Days to Collect Receivables	Length of Operating Cycle
Fast Food	McDonald's	10	14	24
	Starbucks	77	11	88
	Yum! Brands	12	9	21
Office Supplies	Office Depot	50	31	81
	OfficeMax	59	24	83
	Staples	54	13	67
Wine	Concha y Toro	203	92	295
	Willamette Valley Vineyards	348	42	390

and obtain the cash it needs to pay Concha y Toro. Many small companies do not have cash available to pay up front. Buying on credit is the only way they can obtain the inventory they need. If a manufacturer or wholesaler wants to sell to such companies, credit sales represent the only option available.

The **operating cycle** is defined as the average time it takes a business to convert inventory to accounts receivable plus the time it takes to convert accounts receivable into cash. The average number of days to collect receivables ratio is one component of the operating cycle for a particular company. The other component is the average number of days to sell inventory ratio that was explained in Chapter 6. The length of the operating cycles for the real-world companies discussed herein is shown in the last column of Exhibit 8.9.

What is the significance of the different operating cycle lengths in Exhibit 8.9? As previously explained, the longer the operating cycle takes, the more it costs the company. Exhibit 8.9 shows it takes OfficeMax an average of 16 days longer than Staples to complete an operating cycle. All other things being equal, approximately how much did this longer time reduce OfficeMax's earnings? Assume OfficeMax could invest excess cash at 8 percent (or alternatively, assume it pays 8 percent to finance its inventory and accounts receivable). Using the accounting information reported in OfficeMax's December 31, 2005, financial statements, we can answer the question as follows:

$$\text{OfficeMax's investment in inventory} \times \text{Interest rate} \times \text{Time} = \text{Cost}$$

$$\$1,114,570,000 \times 8\% \times 16/365 \quad \$3,908,629$$

With 4.4 operating cycles per year (365 ÷ 83), the extended operating cycle costs OfficeMax $17.2 million annually. Based on the assumptions used here, OfficeMax would increase its after-tax net earnings by approximately 5 percent if it could reduce its operating cycle by 16 days. Although this illustration is a rough estimate, it demonstrates that it is important for businesses to minimize the length of their operating cycles.

CHECK YOURSELF 8.3

Randolph Corporation had sales for the year of $535,333 and an Accounts Receivable balance at year end of $22,000. Determine Randolph's average number of days to collect accounts receivable.

Answer

The accounts receivable turnover is 24.33 ($535,333 ÷ $22,000) times per year. The average number of days to collect accounts receivable is 15 (365 ÷ 24.33).

FOCUS ON   INTERNATIONAL ISSUES

A ROSE BY ANY OTHER NAME . . .

If a person who studied U.S. GAAP wanted to look at the financial statements of a non-U.S. company, choosing statements of a company from another English-speaking country might seem logical. Presumably, this would eliminate language differences, and only the differences in GAAP would remain. Unfortunately, this is not true.

When an accountant in the United States uses the term *turnover,* she or he is usually thinking of a financial ratio, such as the accounts receivable turnover ratio. However, in the United Kingdom, the term *turnover* refers to what U.S. accountants call *sales.* U.K. balance sheets do not usually show an account named *Inventory;* rather, they use the term *Stocks.* In the United States, accountants typically use the term *stocks* to refer to certificates representing ownership in a corporation. Finally, if an accountant or banker from the United Kingdom should ever ask you about your *gearing ratio,* he or she probably is not interested in your bicycle but in your debt to assets ratio.

◀◀ A Look Back

Accounting for receivables and payables was first introduced in Chapter 2. This chapter presented additional complexities related to short-term receivables and payables, such as the *allowance method of accounting for bad debts.* The allowance method improves matching of expenses with revenues. This chapter illustrated the percent of sales method of estimating bad debts expense. Under this method bad debts expense is estimated to be a certain percentage of credit sales. For example, if credit sales were $500,000 and bad debts were estimated to be 1 percent of credit sales, then bad debts expense would be $5,000 ($500,000 × .01). This is an estimate of the uncollectible accounts that will occur in the future. The estimated amount of bad debts expense is recognized in the same period in which the associated revenue is recognized, thereby matching bad debts expense with the revenue. Bad debts expense decreases stockholders' equity, net income, and the net realizable value of receivables (accounts receivable − allowance for doubtful accounts).

The allowance method of accounting for bad debts is contrasted with the *direct write-off method,* which recognizes bad debts expense when an account is determined to be uncollectible. The method is conceptually inferior because it overstates the value of accounts receivable reported on the balance sheet and it fails to match expenses with related revenues. However, the direct write-off method is easier to apply and may be used when the amount of bad debts is insignificant. When bad debts are immaterial, the benefits of recording convenience outweigh a need for conceptual accuracy.

This chapter also discussed accounting for *warranty obligations.* The amount of warranty expense is recognized in the period in which warranted sales are made or services provided. Warranty obligations are reported as liabilities on the balance sheet until the future period when they are settled.

Finally, the chapter discussed the costs of making credit sales. In addition to bad debts, interest is a major cost of financing receivables. Determining the length of the collection period provides a measure of the quality of receivables. Short collection periods usually indicate low amounts of uncollectible accounts and interest cost. Long collection periods imply higher costs. The collection period can be measured in two steps. First, determine the *accounts receivable turnover ratio* by dividing sales by the accounts receivable balance. Next, determine the *average number of days to collect accounts receivable* by dividing the number of days in the year (365) by the accounts receivable turnover ratio.

A Look Forward

Chapter 9 discusses accounting for long-term assets such as buildings and equipment. As with inventory cost flow, discussed in Chapter 6, GAAP allows companies to use different accounting methods to report on similar types of business events. Life would be easier for accounting students if all companies used the same accounting methods. However, the business world is a complicated place. For the foreseeable future, people are likely to continue to have diverse views as to the best way to account for a variety of business transactions. To function effectively in today's business environment, it is important for you to be able to recognize differences in reporting practices.

 DISCOUNT NOTES   **APPENDIX**

Accounting for Discount Notes

All notes payable discussed previously have been "add-on" **interest-bearing notes.** At maturity, the amount due is the *face value* of the note *plus accrued interest.* In contrast, interest on a **discount note** is included in the face value of the note. A $5,000 face value discount note is repaid with $5,000 cash at maturity. This payment includes both principal and accrued interest. To illustrate, assume the following four events apply to Beacon Management Services.

Show how discount notes and related interest charges affect financial statements.

Event 1 **Borrowing by Issuing a Discount Note**
Beacon Management Services was started when it issued a $10,000 face value discount note to State Bank on March 1, 2008.

The note had a 9 percent *discount rate* and a one-year term to maturity. As with interest-bearing notes, the **issuer of the note** exchanges the promissory note for cash. The first step in accounting for the discount note is to divide the face amount between the discount and the principal (amount borrowed). The discount is computed by multiplying the face value of the note by the interest rate by the time period. In this case, the discount is $900 ($10,000 $\times$ 0.09 $\times$ 1). The amount borrowed is determined by subtracting the discount from the face value of the note ($10,000 $-$ $900 = $9,100). In this case the **principal** (the amount of cash borrowed) is $9,100, and the **discount** (the amount of interest to be incurred over the term of the loan) is $900.

On the issue date, assets and liabilities increase by the amount borrowed (the $9,100 principal). The income statement is not affected by the borrowing transaction on the issue date. The $9,100 cash inflow is reported in the financing activities section of the statement of cash flows. These effects follow:

Video 8.3

Event No.	Assets	=	Liab.	+	Equity	Rev.	−	Exp.	=	Net Inc.	Cash Flow
1	9,100	=	9,100	+	NA	NA	−	NA	=	NA	9,100 FA

For internal record-keeping purposes, the amount of the discount is normally recorded in a **contra liability account** titled **Discount on Notes Payable.** The *carrying value* of the liability is the difference between the notes payable account and the discount account. Carrying value, also known as *book value,* is so called because it is the amount at which the liability is shown (carried) on the books. In this case, the Notes Payable account in Beacon's ledger has a $10,000 credit balance and the Discount on Notes Payable account has a $900 debit balance. The carrying value on the issue date is computed as follows:

Notes payable	$10,000
Discount on notes payable	(900)
Carrying value of liability	$ 9,100

Event 2 Recognition of Operating Expenses
Beacon incurred $8,000 of cash operating expenses.

Paying these expenses reduces assets and stockholders' equity. The effect on the income statement is to increase expenses and decrease net income. The cash outflow is reported in the operating activities section of the statement of cash flows. These effects are shown below:

Event No.	Assets	=	Liab.	+	Equity	Rev.	−	Exp.	=	Net Inc.	Cash Flow
2	(8,000)	=	NA	+	(8,000)	NA	−	8,000	=	(8,000)	(8,000) OA

Event 3 Recognition of Revenue
Beacon recognized $12,000 of cash revenue.

Recognizing the revenue increases assets and stockholders' equity. Net income increases. The cash inflow is reported in the operating activities section of the statement of cash flows. These effects follow.

Event No.	Assets	=	Liab.	+	Equity	Rev.	−	Exp.	=	Net Inc.	Cash Flow
3	12,000	=	NA	+	12,000	12,000	−	NA	=	12,000	12,000 OA

Event 4 Adjustment for Accrued Interest
Beacon recognized accrued interest expense.

On December 31, 2008, Beacon must adjust its accounting records to recognize 10 months of interest expense incurred in the 2008 accounting period. For this note, interest expense accrues at $75 per month ($900 discount ÷ 12). As of December 31, $750 ($75 × 10) of interest expense has accrued. Since no cash payment is due until the note matures in 2009, the reduction in equity from recognizing the interest expense is accompanied by an increase in liabilities.

The increase in liabilities is recorded by *reducing the contra liability account,* Discount on Notes Payable. Recall that the carrying value of the liability was $9,100 on the day the note was issued. The adjusting entry to record the accrued interest expense removes $750 from the discount account, leaving a discount balance of $150 ($900 − $750) after the adjusting entry is posted.

The bookkeeping technique of converting the discount to interest expense over the term of the loan is described as **amortizing** the discount. After amortizing 10 months' interest expense, the carrying value of the liability reported on the December 31, 2008, balance sheet in Exhibit 8.11 is $9,850 ($10,000 face value − $150 discount). The effect of the interest recognition on the income statement is to increase expenses and decrease net income by $750. The statement of cash flows is not affected by the accrual. Cash is paid for the interest at the maturity date. The effects of the adjusting entry for accrued interest expense follow.

Event No.	Assets	=	Liab.	+	Equity	Rev.	−	Exp.	=	Net Inc.	Cash Flow
4	NA	=	750	+	(750)	NA	−	750	=	(750)	NA

General Ledger T-Accounts and Financial Statements
Exhibit 8.10 displays in T-account form the ledger accounts for the business events experienced by Beacon Management Services. The entry to close the revenue and expense accounts at the end of the

EXHIBIT 8.10

General Ledger

Assets	=	Liabilities	+	Equity

Cash

(1)	9,100	8,000	(2)
(3)	12,000		
Bal.	13,100		

Notes Payable

		10,000	(1)
		10,000	Bal.

Discount on Notes Payable

(1)	900	750	(4)
Bal.	150		

Retained Earnings

		3,250	(cl.)
		3,250	Bal.

Service Revenue

(cl.)	12,000	12,000	(3)
		0	Bal.

Operating Expenses

(2)	8,000	8,000	(cl.)
Bal.	0		

Interest Expense

(4)	750	750	(cl.)
Bal.	0		

2008 accounting period is included. The ledger accounts provide the information to prepare the financial statements in Exhibit 8.11. The accounting events are summarized here:

1. Issued a $10,000 face value, 1-year, discount note with a 9 percent discount rate.
2. Paid $8,000 cash for operating expenses.
3. Earned $12,000 cash revenue.
4. Recognized $750 of accrued interest expense.
5. Closed the revenue and expense accounts. The letters *cl* are the posting reference for the closing entries.

EXHIBIT 8.11

Financial Statements for 2008

Income Statement

Service revenue	$12,000
Operating exp.	(8,000)
Operating income	4,000
Interest exp.	(750)
Net income	$ 3,250

Balance Sheet

Assets		
Cash		$13,100
Liabilities		
Notes payable	$10,000	
Less: Disc. on notes pay.	(150)	
Total liabilities		$ 9,850
Stockholders' equity		
Retained earnings		3,250
Total liab. and stockholders' equity		$13,100

Statement of Cash Flows

Operating Activities	
Inflow from customers	$12,000
Outflow for expenses	(8,000)
Net inflow from operating activities	4,000
Investing Activities	0
Financing Activities	
Inflow from creditors	9,100
Net change in cash	13,100
Plus: Beginning cash balance	0
Ending cash balance	$13,100

Accounting Events Affecting the 2009 Period

This section illustrates four accounting events that apply to Beacon's 2009 accounting cycle.

Event 1 Accrual of Interest for 2009
Beacon recognized 2 months of accrued interest.

Since the note had a one-year term, interest for two months remains to be accrued at the maturity date on March 1, 2009. Since interest expense accrues at $75 per month ($900 discount ÷ 12), there is $150 ($75 × 2) of interest expense to recognize in 2009. Recognizing the interest increases liabilities (the discount account is reduced to zero) and decreases stockholders' equity. The effect of the interest recognition on the income statement is to increase expenses and decrease net income by $150. The statement of cash flows is not affected by the interest recognition. These effects follow:

Event No.	Assets	=	Liab.	+	Equity	Rev.	−	Exp.	=	Net Inc.	Cash Flow
1	NA	=	150	+	(150)	NA	−	150	=	(150)	NA

Event 2 Payment of Face Value
Beacon repaid the face value of the discount note.

The face value ($10,000) of the note is due on the maturity date. The repayment of the note is an asset use transaction that decreases both assets and liabilities. The income statement is not affected by the repayment. The $10,000 cash payment includes $900 for interest and $9,100 for principal. In the statement of cash flows, a $900 outflow for interest is reported in the operating activities section and a $9,100 outflow for repaying the loan is reported in the financing activities section. These effects follow:

Event No.	Assets	=	Liab.	+	Equity	Rev.	−	Exp.	=	Net Inc.	Cash Flow
2	(10,000)	=	(10,000)	+	NA	NA	−	NA	=	NA	(900) OA (9,100) FA

Event 3 Revenue Recognition
Beacon recognized $13,000 of cash revenue.

Recognizing the revenue increases assets and stockholders' equity. Net income also increases. The cash inflow is reported in the operating activities section of the statement of cash flows. These effects follow:

Event No.	Assets	=	Liab.	+	Equity	Rev.	−	Exp.	=	Net Inc.	Cash Flow
3	13,000	=	NA	+	13,000	13,000	−	NA	=	13,000	13,000 OA

Event 4 Recognition of Operating Expenses
Beacon incurred $8,500 of cash operating expenses.

This event decreases assets and stockholders' equity. Net income also decreases. The cash outflow is reported in the operating activities section of the statement of cash flows. These effects follow:

Event No.	Assets	=	Liab.	+	Equity	Rev.	−	Exp.	=	Net Inc.	Cash Flow
4	(8,500)	=	NA	+	(8,500)	NA	−	8,500	=	(8,500)	(8,500) OA

General Ledger T-Accounts and Financial Statements

Exhibits 8.12 and 8.13 present the relevant ledger T-accounts and financial statements, respectively. Notice in Exhibit 8.13 that no liabilities are reported because both interest and principal have been paid, leaving Beacon with no obligations as of the 2009 fiscal closing date. Since no dividends were paid to owners during 2008 or 2009, retained earnings includes the total of net income for 2008 and 2009.

EXHIBIT 8.12

General Ledger

Assets				=	Liabilities				+	Equity		

Cash

Bal.	13,100	10,000	(2)
(3)	13,000	8,500	(4)
Bal.	7,600		

Notes Payable

(2)	10,000	10,000	Bal.
		0	Bal.

Discount on Notes Payable

Bal.	150	150	(1)
Bal.	0		

Retained Earnings

		3,250	Bal.
		4,350	(cl.)
		7,600	Bal.

Service Revenue

(cl.)	13,000	13,000	(3)
		0	Bal.

Operating Expense

(4)	8,500	8,500	(cl.)
Bal.	0		

Interest Expense

(1)	150	150	(cl.)
Bal.	0		

EXHIBIT 8.13

Financial Statements for 2009

Income Statement			Balance Sheet			Statement of Cash Flows		
Service revenue	$13,000		Assets			**Operating Activities**		
Operating expenses	(8,500)		Cash	$7,600		Inflow from customers	$13,000	
						Outflow for expenses	(8,500)	
Operating income	4,500		Liabilities	$ 0		Outflow for interest	(900)	
Interest exp.	(150)		Stockholders' equity					
			Retained earnings	7,600		Net inflow from		
Net income	$ 4,350					operating activities	3,600	
			Total liab. and stockholders' equity	$7,600		**Investing Activities**	0	
						Financing Activities		
						Outflow to creditors	(9,100)	
						Net change in cash	(5,500)	
						Plus: Beginning cash balance	13,100	
						Ending cash balance	$ 7,600	

During 2008 Calico Company experienced the following accounting events:

1. Provided $120,000 of services on account.
2. Collected $85,000 cash from accounts receivable.
3. Wrote off $1,800 of accounts receivable that were uncollectible.
4. Paid $90,500 cash for operating expenses.
5. Estimated that bad debts expense would be 2 percent of credit sales. Recorded the adjusting entry.
6. Estimated warranty expense would be $900. Recorded the adjusting entry.

The following ledger accounts present the balances in Calico Company's records on January 1, 2008.

Event No.	Cash	+	Accts. Rec.	−	Allow.	=	War. Pay.	+	C. Stk.	+	Ret. Ear.
			Assets			=	Liabilities	+		Equity	
Bal.	12,000	+	18,000	−	2,200	=	NA	+	20,000	+	7,800

Required

a. Record the 2008 accounting events in the accounting equation.
b. Determine net income for 2008.
c. Determine net cash flow from operating activities for 2008.
d. Determine the net realizable value of accounts receivable at December 31, 2008.

Solution to Requirement a.

Event No.	Cash	+	Accts. Rec.	−	Allow.	=	War. Pay.	+	C. Stk.	+	Ret. Ear.
			Assets			=	Liabilities	+		Equity	
Bal.	12,000	+	18,000	−	2,200	=	NA	+	20,000	+	7,800
1	NA	+	120,000	−	NA	=	NA	+	NA	+	120,000
2	85,000	+	(85,000)	−	NA	=	NA	+	NA	+	NA
3	NA	+	(1,800)	−	(1,800)	=	NA	+	NA	+	NA
4	(90,500)	+	NA	−	NA	=	NA	+	NA	+	(90,500)
5	NA	+	NA	−	2,400	=	NA	+	NA	+	(2,400)
6	NA	+	NA	−	NA	=	900	+	NA	+	(900)
Totals	6,500	+	51,200	−	2,800	=	900	+	20,000	+	34,000

Solution to Requirements b–d.

b. Net income is $26,200 ($120,000 − $90,500 − $2,400 − $900).
c. Net cash flow from operating activities is an outflow of $5,500 ($85,000 − $90,500).
d. The net realizable value of accounts receivable is $48,400 ($51,200 − $2,800).

KEY TERMS

accounts receivable 391
accounts receivable turnover ratio 405
Allowance for Doubtful Accounts 393

allowance method of accounting for bad debts 392
amortization 410

average number of days to collect accounts receivable 405
bad debts expense 393
contra liability account 409

direct write-off method 400
discount 409
discount notes 409
Discount on Notes Payable 409

going concern
   assumption 392
interest-bearing notes 409

issuer of the note 409
net realizable value 392
notes receivable 391

operating cycle 407
payables 391
principal 409

warranty 402

1. What is the difference between accounts receivable and notes receivable?
2. What is the *net realizable value* of receivables?
3. Explain the *going concern* assumption. How does it affect the way accounts receivable versus accounts payable are reported in financial statements?
4. What is the difference between the allowance method and the direct write-off method of accounting for bad debts?
5. What is the most common format for reporting accounts receivable on the balance sheet? What information does this method provide beyond showing only the net amount?
6. What are two ways in which estimating bad debts improves the accuracy of the financial statements?
7. Why is it necessary to make an entry to reinstate a previously written off account receivable before the collection is recorded?
8. What are some factors considered in estimating the amount of uncollectible accounts receivable?
9. What is the effect on the accounting equation of recognizing bad debts expense?
10. What is the effect on the accounting equation of writing off an uncollectible account receivable when the allowance method is used? When the direct write-off method is used?
11. How does the recovery of a bad debt affect the income statement when the allowance method is used? How does the recovery of a bad debt affect the statement of cash flows when the allowance method is used?
12. What is the advantage of using the allowance method of accounting for bad debts? What is the advantage of using the direct write-off method?
13. When is it acceptable to use the direct write-off method of accounting for bad debts?
14. Why is it generally beneficial for a business to accept major credit cards as payment for goods and services even when the fee charged by the credit card company is substantial?
15. What types of costs do businesses avoid when they accept major credit cards as compared with handling credit sales themselves?
16. What does the term *warranty* mean?
17. What effect does recognizing warranty expense have on the balance sheet? On the income statement?
18. When is warranty cost reported on the statement of cash flows?
19. How is the accounts receivable turnover ratio computed? What information does the ratio provide?
20. How is the average number of days to collect accounts receivable computed? What information does the ratio provide?
21. Is accounting terminology standard in all countries? What term is used in the United Kingdom to refer to *sales?* What term is used to refer to *inventory?* What is a *gearing ratio?* Is it important to know about these differences?
22. What is the difference between an interest-bearing note and a discount note? (Appendix)
23. How is the carrying value of a discount note computed? (Appendix)
24. Will the effective rate of interest be the same on a $10,000 face value, 12 percent interest-bearing note and a $10,000 face value, 12 percent discount note? Is the amount of cash received upon making these two loans the same? Why or why not? (Appendix)
25. How does the *amortization* of a discount affect the income statement, balance sheet, and statement of cash flows? (Appendix)
26. What is the effect on the accounting equation of borrowing $8,000 by issuing a discount note that has a 10 percent discount rate and a one-year term to maturity? What is the effect on the accounting equation of the periodic amortization of the discount? What is the effect on the accounting equation of the payment of the face value of the note at maturity? (Appendix)
27. What type of account is Discount on Notes Payable? (Appendix)

Quiz 8

Multiple-choice questions are provided on the text Web site at www.mhhe.com/edmonds6e.

EXERCISES—SERIES A

All Exercises in Series A are available with McGraw-Hill's Homework Manager®

L.O. 1

Exercise 8-1A *Effect of recognizing bad debts expense on financial statements: Allowance method*

Pete's Auto Service was started on January 1, 2008. The company experienced the following events during its first year of operation.

Events affecting 2008

1. Provided $50,000 of repair services on account.
2. Collected $35,000 cash from accounts receivable.
3. Adjusted the accounting records to reflect the estimate that bad debts expense would be 1 percent of the service revenue on account.

Events affecting 2009

1. Wrote off a $350 account receivable that was determined to be uncollectible.
2. Provided $65,000 of repair services on account.
3. Collected $66,000 cash from accounts receivable.
4. Adjusted the accounting records to reflect the estimate that bad debts expense would be 1 percent of the service revenue on account.

Required

a. Record the events for 2008 in T-accounts.
b. Determine the following amounts:
   (1) Net income for 2008.
   (2) Net cash flow from operating activities for 2008.
   (3) Balance of accounts receivable at the end of 2008.
   (4) Net realizable value of accounts receivable at the end of 2008.
c. Repeat Requirements *a* and *b* for the 2009 accounting period.

L.O. 1

Exercise 8-2A *Analyzing financial statement effects of accounting for bad debts using the allowance method*

Duffy Bros. uses the allowance method to account for bad debts expense. Duffy experienced the following four events in 2008:

1. Recognition of $64,000 of service revenue on account.
2. Collection of $56,000 cash from accounts receivable.
3. Determination that $900 of its accounts were not collectible and wrote off these receivables.
4. Recognition of bad debts expense for the year. Duffy estimates that bad debts expense will be 2 percent of its sales.

Required

a. Show the effect of each of these events on the elements of the financial statements, using a horizontal statements model like the following one. Use + for increase, − for decrease, and NA for not affected. In the cash flow column, indicate whether the item is an operating activity (OA), investing activity (IA), or financing activity (FA).

Event No.	Assets				=	Liab.	+	Equity		Rev.	−	Exp.	=	Net Inc.	Cash Flow
	Cash	+	A. Rec.	− Allow. =				Ret. Earn.							

b. Prepare the journal entry to record the above transaction.

Exercise 8-3A *Analyzing account balances for a company using the allowance method of accounting for bad debts*   **L.O. 1**

The following account balances come from the records of Springfield Company.

	Beginning Balance	Ending Balance
Accounts receivable	$4,000	$4,500
Allowance for doubtful accounts	550	600

During the accounting period, Springfield recorded $32,000 of service revenue on account. The company also wrote off a $300 account receivable.

Required

a. Determine the amount of cash collected from receivables.

b. Determine the amount of bad debts expense recognized during the period.

Exercise 8-4A *Effect of recovering a receivable previously written off*   **L.O. 1**

The accounts receivable balance for T&M Lumber at December 31, 2009, was $96,000. Also on that date, the balance in Allowance for Doubtful Accounts was $3,600. During 2010, $2,400 of accounts receivable were written off as uncollectible. In addition, T&M Lumber unexpectedly collected $250 of receivables that had been written off in a previous accounting period. Sales on account during 2010 were $265,000, and cash collections from receivables were $275,000. Bad debts expense was estimated to be 1 percent of the sales on account for the period.

Required

(*Hint:* Post the transactions to T-accounts under the accounting equation before completing the requirements.)

a. Based on the preceding information, compute (after year-end adjustment):

   (**1**) Balance of Allowance for Doubtful Accounts at December 31, 2010.

   (**2**) Balance of Accounts Receivable at December 31, 2010.

   (**3**) Net realizable value of Accounts Receivable at December 31, 2010.

b. What amount of bad debts expense will T&M Lumber report for 2010?

c. Explain how the $250 recovery of receivables affected the accounting equation.

Exercise 8-5A *Accounting for bad debts: Allowance versus direct write-off method*   **L.O. 1, 2**

Dixie Auto Parts sells new and used auto parts. Although a majority of its sales are cash sales, it makes a significant amount of credit sales. During 2008, its first year of operations, Dixie Auto Parts experienced the following:

Sales on account	$175,000
Cash sales	550,000
Collections of accounts receivable	168,000
Uncollectible accounts charged off during the year	1,200

Required

a. Assume that Dixie Auto Parts uses the allowance method of accounting for bad debts and estimates that 1 percent of its sales on account will not be collected. Answer the following questions:

   (**1**) What is the Accounts Receivable balance at December 31, 2008?

   (**2**) What is the ending balance of Allowance for Doubtful Accounts at December 31, 2008, after all entries and adjusting entries are posted?

(3) What is the amount of bad debts expense for 2008?

(4) What is the net realizable value of accounts receivable at December 31, 2008?

b. Assume that Dixie Auto Parts uses the direct write-off method of accounting for bad debts. Answer the following questions:

(1) What is the Accounts Receivable balance at December 31, 2008?

(2) What is the amount of bad debts expense for 2008?

(3) What is the net realizable value of accounts receivable at December 31, 2008?

L.O. 2

Exercise 8-6A   *Accounting for bad debts: Direct write-off method*

Buttross Business Systems has mostly a cash business but does have a small number of sales on account. Consequently, it uses the direct write-off method to account for bad debts. During 2009 Buttross Business Systems earned $87,000 of cash revenue and $12,000 of revenue on account. Cash operating expenses were $56,000. After numerous attempts to collect a $520 account receivable from Sam Smart, the account was determined to be uncollectible in 2010.

Required

a. Record the effects of (1) cash revenue, (2) revenue on account, (3) cash expenses, and (4) write-off of the uncollectible account on the financial statements using a horizontal statements model like the one shown here. In the Cash Flow column, indicate whether the item is an operating activity (OA), investing activity (IA), or financing activity (FA). Use NA to indicate that an element is not affected by the event.

Assets		= Liab.	+ Equity	Rev.	− Exp.	= Net Inc.	Cash Flow
Cash	+ Accts. Rec.						

b. What amount of net income did Buttross Business Systems report on the 2009 income statement?

c. Prepare the general journal entries for the four accounting events listed in Requirement *a*.

L.O. 3

Exercise 8-7A   *Effect of credit card sales on financial statements*

Gold Carpet Cleaning provided $86,000 of services during 2009. All customers paid for the services with major credit cards. Gold turned the credit card receipts over to the credit card company immediately. The credit card company paid Gold cash in the amount of face value less a 2 percent service charge.

Required

a. Record the credit card sales and the subsequent collection of accounts receivable in a horizontal statements model like the one shown here. In the Cash Flow column, indicate whether the item is an operating activity (OA), investing activity (IA), or financing activity (FA). Use NA to indicate that an element is not affected by the event.

Assets		= Liab.	+ Equity	Rev.	− Exp.	= Net Inc.	Cash Flow
Cash	+ Accts. Rec.						

b. Answer the following questions:

(1) What is the amount of total assets at the end of the accounting period?

(2) What is the amount of revenue reported on the income statement?

(3) What is the amount of cash flow from operating activities reported on the statement of cash flows?

(4) Why would Gold Carpet Cleaning accept credit cards instead of providing credit directly to its customers? In other words, why would Gold be willing to pay 2 percent of sales to have the credit card company handle its sales on account?

L.O. 3

Exercise 8-8A   *Recording credit card sales*

Posey Company accepted credit cards in payment for $7,250 of merchandise sold during March 2008. The credit card company charged Posey a 3 percent service fee. The credit card company paid Posey as soon as it received the invoices. Cost of goods sold amounted to $4,100.

Required

a. Prepare the general journal entry to record the merchandise sale.

b. Prepare the general journal entry for the collection of the receivable from the credit card company.

c. Based on this information alone, what is the amount of net income earned during the month of March?

Exercise 8-9A *Effect of warranties on income and cash flow*   L.O. 4

To support herself while attending school, Ann Hunt sold computers to other students. During her first year of operation, she sold computers that had cost her $92,000 cash for $180,000 cash. She provided her customers with a one-year warranty against defects in parts and labor. Based on industry standards, she estimated that warranty claims would amount to 5 percent of sales. During the year she paid $870 cash to replace a defective hard drive.

Required

a. Prepare the journal entries to record the:

   (1) Purchase of inventory.

   (2) Sale of computers.

   (3) Warranty expense.

   (4) Payment for repairs.

b. Post the above transactions to the T-accounts.

c. Prepare an income statement and statement of cash flows for Hunt's first year of operation.

d. Explain the difference between net income and the amount of cash flow from operating activities.

Exercise 8-10A *Effect of warranty obligations and payments on financial statements*   L.O. 4

The Pearl River Co. provides a 120-day parts-and-labor warranty on all merchandise it sells. Pearl River estimates the warranty expense for the current period to be $2,650. During the period a customer returned a product that cost $1,980 to repair.

Required

a. Show the effects of these transactions on the financial statements using a horizontal statements model like the example shown here. Use a + to indicate increase, a − for decrease, and NA for not affected. Also, in the Cash Flow column, indicate whether the item is an operating activity (OA), investing activity (IA), or financing activity (FA).

Assets	=	Liab.	+	Equity	Rev.	−	Exp.	=	Net Inc.	Cash Flow

b. Prepare the journal entry to record the warranty expense for the period.

c. Prepare the journal entry to record payment for the actual repair costs.

d. Discuss the advantage of estimating the amount of warranty expense.

Exercise 8-11A *Comprehensive single-cycle problem*   L.O. 1, 4

The following after-closing trial balance was drawn from the accounts of Oak Timber Co. as of December 31, 2009.

	Debit	Credit
Cash	$26,000	
Accounts receivable	28,000	
Allowance for doubtful accounts		$ 3,000
Inventory	25,000	
Accounts payable		19,200
Common stock		20,000
Retained earnings		36,800
Totals	$79,000	$79,000

Transactions for 2010

1. Acquired an additional $20,000 cash from the issue of common stock.
2. Purchased $80,000 of inventory on account.
3. Sold inventory that cost $65,000 for $110,000. Sales were made on account.
4. The products sold in Event 3 were warranted, and Oak estimated future warranty costs would amount to 4 percent of sales.
5. The company wrote off $1,400 of uncollectible accounts.
6. On September 1, Oak issued a $12,000 short-term interest-bearing note with an 8 percent stated rate of interest. The note had a one-year term.
7. Paid $1,150 cash to satisfy warranty claims.
8. Paid $19,600 cash for salaries expense.
9. The company collected $96,000 cash from accounts receivable.
10. A cash payment of $91,000 was paid on accounts payable.
11. The company paid a $5,000 cash dividend to the stockholders.
12. Bad debts are estimated to be 1 percent of sales on account.
13. Recorded the accrued interest at December 31, 2010.

Required

a. Open T-accounts and record the beginning balances and the effects of the 2010 accounting events.
b. Prepare an income statement, statement of changes in stockholders' equity, balance sheet, and statement of cash flows for 2010.

L.O. 5

Exercise 8-12A *Using the average number of days to collect accounts receivable ratio to make comparisons*

The following information was drawn from the accounting records of Joyce Company and Pound Company.

	Joyce Company	Pound Company
Accounts receivable balance	$ 50,000	$ 80,000
Sales	610,000	784,000

Required

a. Determine the average days to collect accounts receivable for each company.
b. Which company is likely to incur more costs associated with extending credit?
c. Identify and discuss some of the costs that are associated with extending credit.
d. Explain why a company would be willing to accept the costs of extending credit to its customers.

L.O. 6

Exercise 8-13A *Effect of a discount note on financial statements (Appendix)*

Kat Tatum started a moving company on January 1, 2009. On March 1, 2009, Tatum borrowed cash from a local bank by issuing a one-year $60,000 face value note with annual interest based on an 8 percent discount. During 2009, Tatum provided services for $43,200 cash.

Required

Answer the following questions. Record the events in T-accounts prior to answering the questions.

a. What is the amount of total liabilities on the December 31, 2009 balance sheet?
b. What is the amount of net income on the 2009 income statement?
c. What is the amount of cash flow from operating activities on the 2009 statement of cash flows?
d. Provide the general journal entries necessary to record issuing the note on March 1, 2009; recognizing accrued interest on December 31, 2009; and repaying the loan on February 28, 2010.

Exercise 8-14A   *Comparing effective interest rates on discount versus interest-bearing notes (Appendix)*   **L.O. 6**

Bill Phillips borrowed money by issuing two notes on January 1, 2009. The financing transactions are described here.

1. Borrowed funds by issuing a $50,000 face value discount note to State Bank. The note had a 6 percent discount rate, a one-year term to maturity, and was paid off on December 31, 2009.
2. Borrowed funds by issuing a $50,000 face value, interest-bearing note to Community Bank. The note had a 6 percent stated rate of interest, a one-year term to maturity, and was paid off on December 31, 2009.

Required

a. Show the effects of issuing the two notes on the financial statements using separate horizontal financial statement models like the ones here. Record the transaction amounts under the appropriate categories. Also, in the Cash Flow column, indicate whether the item is an operating activity (OA), investing activity (IA), or financing activity (FA). Record only the events occurring on the date of issue. Do not record accrued interest or the repayment at maturity.

Discount Note

Assets	=	Liabilities			+	Equity	Rev.	−	Exp.	=	Net Inc.	Cash Flow
Cash	=	Notes Pay.	−	Disc. on Notes Pay.	+	Ret. Ear.						

Interest-Bearing Note

Assets	=	Liabilities	+	Equity	Rev.	−	Exp.	=	Net Inc.	Cash Flow
Cash	=	Notes Pay.	+	Ret. Ear.						

b. What is the total amount of interest to be paid on each note?
c. What amount of cash was received from each note?
d. Which note has the higher effective interest rate? Support your answer with appropriate computations.

Exercise 8-15A   *Recording accounting events for a discount note (Appendix)*   **L.O. 6**

Collins Co. issued a $30,000 face value discount note to First Bank on June 1, 2009. The note had a 7 percent discount rate and a one-year term to maturity.

Required

Prepare general journal entries for the following transactions:

a. The issuance of the note on June 1, 2009.
b. The adjustment for accrued interest at the end of the year, December 31, 2009.
c. Recording interest expense for 2010 and repaying the principal on May 31, 2010.

PROBLEMS—SERIES A

Problem 8-16A   *Accounting for bad debts—Two cycles using the allowance method*   **L.O. 1**

The following transactions apply to Puretz Consulting for 2008, the first year of operation:

1. Recognized $75,000 of service revenue earned on account.
2. Collected $62,000 from accounts receivable.
3. Adjusted accounts to recognize bad debts expense. Puretz uses the allowance method of accounting for bad debts and estimates that bad debts expense will be 2 percent of sales on account.

CHECK FIGURES
d. Ending Accounts
   Receivable, 2008:
   $13,000
d. Net Income, 2009:
   $33,035

The following transactions apply to Puretz Consulting for 2009:

1. Recognized $86,500 of service revenue on account.
2. Collected $85,000 from accounts receivable.
3. Determined that $1,120 of the accounts receivable were uncollectible and wrote them off.
4. Collected $500 of an account that had been written off previously.
5. Paid $52,600 cash for operating expenses.
6. Adjusted accounts to recognize bad debts expense for 2009. Puretz estimates that bad debts expense will be 1 percent of sales on account.

Required

Complete all the following requirements for 2008 and 2009. Complete all requirements for 2008 prior to beginning the requirements for 2009.

a. Identify the type of each transaction (asset source, asset use, asset exchange, or claims exchange).
b. Show the effect of each transaction on the elements of the financial statements, using a horizontal statements model like the one shown here. Use + for increase, − for decrease, and NA for not affected. Also, in the Cash Flow column, indicate whether the item is an operating activity (OA), investing activity (IA), or financing activity (FA). The first transaction is entered as an example. (*Hint:* Closing entries do not affect the statements model.)

Event No.	Assets	=	Liab.	+	Equity	Rev.	−	Exp.	=	Net Inc.	Cash Flow
1	+		NA		+	+		NA		+	NA

c. Record the transactions in general journal form, and post them to T-accounts (begin 2009 with the ending T-account balances from 2008).
d. Prepare the income statement, statement of changes in stockholders' equity, balance sheet, and statement of cash flows.
e. Prepare closing entries and post these closing entries to the T-accounts. Prepare an after-closing trial balance.

L.O. 1

Problem 8-17A *Determining account balances and preparing journal entries: Allowance method of accounting for bad debts*

The following information pertains to Royal Carpet Company's sales on account and accounts receivable:

Accounts receivable balance, January 1, 2008	$ 64,500
Allowance for doubtful accounts, January 1, 2008	2,800
Sales on account, 2008	756,000
Cost of goods sold, 2008	505,000
Collections of accounts receivable, 2008	782,000

CHECK FIGURE
b. Net Realizable Value:
$31,920

After several collection attempts, Royal Carpet Company wrote off $2,600 of accounts that could not be collected. Royal estimates that bad debts expense will be 0.5 percent of sales on account.

Required

a. Prepare the general journal entries to:
   (1) Record sales on account for 2008.
   (2) Record cash collections from accounts receivable for 2008.
   (3) Write off the accounts that are not collectible.
   (4) Record the estimated bad debts expense for 2008.
b. Compute the following amounts:
   (1) Using the allowance method, the amount of bad debts expense for 2008.
   (2) Net realizable value of receivables at the end of 2008.
c. Explain why the bad debts expense amount is different from the amount that was written off as uncollectible.

Problem 8-18A *Accounting for credit card sales, warranties, and bad debts:*   **L.O. 2, 4**
              Direct write-off method

Huggins Supply Company had the following transactions in 2008, its first year of operations:

1. Acquired $50,000 cash from the issue of common stock.
2. Purchased $210,000 of merchandise for cash in 2008.
3. Sold merchandise that cost $140,000 for $265,000 during the year under the following terms:

$ 60,000	Cash sales ~~goes up 60~~
175,000	Credit card sales (The credit card company charges a 3 percent service fee.)
30,000	Sales on account

4. Collected all the amount receivable from the credit card company.
5. Collected $23,000 of accounts receivable.
6. Used the direct write-off method to account for bad debts expense and wrote off $560 of accounts receivable that were uncollectible.
7. Huggins gives a one-year warranty on equipment it sells. It estimated that warranty expense for 2008 would be $795.
8. Paid selling and administrative expenses of $76,000.

Required

a. Show the effects of each of the transactions on the elements of the financial statements, using a horizontal statements model like the one shown here. Use + for increase, − for decrease, and NA for not affected. The first transaction is entered as an example. (*Hint:* Closing entries do not affect the statements model.)

Event No.	Assets	=	Liab.	+	Equity	Rev.	−	Exp.	=	Net Inc.	Cash Flow
1	+		NA		+	NA		NA		NA	+ FA

b. Prepare general journal entries for each of the transactions, and post them to T-accounts.
c. Prepare an income statement, statement of changes in stockholders' equity, balance sheet, and statement of cash flows for 2008.

Problem 8-19A *Effect of transactions on the elements of financial statements*   **L.O. 2, 3, 4**

Required

Identify each of the following independent transactions as asset source (AS), asset use (AU), asset exchange (AE), or claims exchange (CE). Also explain how each event affects assets, liabilities, stockholders' equity, net income, and cash flow by placing a + for increase, − for decrease, or NA for not affected under each of the categories. The first event is recorded as an example.

Event	Type of Event	Assets	Liabilities	Common Stock	Retained Earnings	Net Income	Cash Flow
a	AE	+ −	NA	NA	NA	NA	−

a. Paid cash for equipment.
b. Sold merchandise at a price above cost. Accepted payment by credit card. The credit card company charges a service fee. The receipts have not yet been forwarded to the credit card company for collection.
c. Submitted receipts to the credit card company and collected cash.
d. Realized a gain when equipment was sold for cash.
e. Provided services for cash.
f. Paid cash to satisfy warranty obligations.

g. Paid cash for salaries expense.

h. Recovered a bad debt that had been previously written off (assume the direct write-off method is used to account for bad debts).

i. Paid cash to creditors on accounts payable.

j. Issued a short-term note to State Bank.

k. Provided services on account.

l. Wrote off an uncollectible account (use the direct write-off method).

m. Recorded three months of accrued interest on the note payable.

n. Collected cash from customers paying their accounts.

o. Recognized warranty expense.

L.O. 1, 4

eXcel

CHECK FIGURE
Net Income: $59,400
Total Assets: $316,300

Problem 8-20A   *Multistep income statement and classified balance sheet*

Required

Use the following information to prepare a multistep income statement and a classified balance sheet for Reza Equipment Co. for 2008. (*Hint:* Some of the items will *not* appear on either statement, and ending retained earnings must be calculated.)

Salaries expense	$ 96,000	Interest receivable (short term)	$ 500
Common stock	40,000	Beginning retained earnings	10,400
Notes receivable (short term)	12,000	Warranties payable (short term)	1,300
Allowance for doubtful accounts	4,000	Gain on sale of equipment	6,400
Accumulated depreciation	30,000	Operating expenses	70,000
Notes payable (long term)	103,600	Cash flow from investing activities	80,000
Salvage value of building	4,000	Prepaid rent	9,600
Interest payable (short term)	1,800	Land	36,000
Bad debts expense	10,800	Cash	17,800
Supplies	1,600	Inventory	122,800
Equipment	60,000	Accounts payable	46,000
Interest revenue	4,200	Interest expense	24,000
Sales revenue	396,000	Salaries payable	9,200
Dividends	8,000	Unearned revenue	52,600
Warranty expense	3,400	Cost of goods sold	143,000
		Accounts receivable	90,000

L.O. 1, 4, 5

CHECK FIGURE
a. Bad Debt Expense:
    $1,300

Problem 8-21A   *Missing information*

The following information comes from the accounts of Jersey Company:

	Beginning Balance	Ending Balance
Accounts receivable	$30,000	$34,000
Allowance for doubtful accounts	1,800	1,700
Warranties payable	4,000	3,000
Notes payable	40,000	40,000
Interest payable	1,200	3,600

Required

a. There were $170,000 of sales on account during the accounting period. Write-offs of uncollectible accounts were $1,400. What was the amount of cash collected from accounts receivable? What amount of bad debts expense was reported on the income statement? What was the net realizable value of receivables at the end of the accounting period?

b. Warranty expense for the period was $3,600. How much cash was paid to settle warranty claims?

c. What amount of interest expense was recognized during the period? How much cash was paid for interest? The note payable has a two-year term with a 6 percent interest rate.

Problem 8-22A *Comprehensive accounting cycle problem (Uses direct write-off method)*

L.O. 2, 3, 4

The following trial balance was prepared for Mountain View Sales and Service on December 31, 2008, after the closing entries were posted.

	Debit	Credit
Cash	$ 56,300	
Accounts receivable	22,100	
Inventory	86,400	
Accounts payable		$ 21,900
Common stock		100,000
Retained earnings		42,900
Totals	$164,800	$164,800

Mountain View had the following transactions in 2009:

1. Purchased merchandise on account for $260,000.
2. Sold merchandise that cost $215,000 on account for $320,000.
3. Performed $76,000 of services for cash.
4. Sold merchandise for $80,000 to credit card customers. The merchandise cost $43,000. The credit card company charges a 4 percent fee.
5. Collected $330,000 cash from accounts receivable.
6. Paid $280,000 cash on accounts payable.
7. Paid $126,000 cash for selling and administrative expenses.
8. Collected cash for the full amount due from the credit card company.
9. Issued a $60,000 face value short-term note with a 6 percent interest rate and a one-year term to maturity.
10. Wrote off $650 of accounts as uncollectible (use the direct write-off method).
11. Made the following adjusting entries:
    (a) Recorded three months' interest on the short-term note at December 31, 2009.
    (b) Estimated warranty expense to be $2,600.

Required

Prepare general journal entries for these transactions; post the entries to T-accounts; and prepare an income statement, a statement of changes in stockholders' equity, a balance sheet, and a statement of cash flows for 2009.

Problem 8-23A *Using ratios to make comparisons*

L.O. 5

The following information pertains to Anjou and Bartlett companies at the end of 2010.

	Anjou	Bartlett
Cash	$ 25,000	$ 70,000
Accounts receivable	105,000	260,000
Allowance for doubtful accounts	5,000	10,000
Merchandise inventory	75,000	150,000
Accounts payable	80,000	200,000
Cost of goods sold	475,000	630,000
Building	125,000	200,000
Sales	650,000	1,000,000

Required

a. For each company, compute the gross margin percentage and the average days to collect accounts receivable (use the net realizable value of receivables to compute the average days to collect receivables).
b. In relation to cost, which company is charging more for its merchandise?

c. Which company is likely to incur higher costs associated with the granting of credit to customers? Explain.

d. Which company appears to have more restrictive credit standards when authorizing credit to its customers? (*Hint:* There is no specific answer to this question. You are expected to use your judgment and general knowledge of ratios to answer).

L.O. 6

CHECK FIGURES
c. Net Income, 2008:
$53,650
Total Assets, 2009:
$110,200

Problem 8-24A *Accounting for a discount note—Two accounting cycles (Appendix)*

Aba Corp. was started in 2008. The following summarizes transactions that occurred during 2008:

1. Issued a $30,000 face value discount note to Golden Savings Bank on April 1, 2008. The note had a 6 percent discount rate and a one-year term to maturity.
2. Recognized revenue from services performed for cash, $150,000.
3. Incurred and paid $95,000 cash for selling and administrative expenses.
4. Amortized the discount on the note at the end of the year, December 31, 2008.
5. Prepared the necessary closing entries at December 31, 2008.

The following summarizes transactions that occurred in 2009:

1. Recognized $195,000 of service revenue in cash.
2. Incurred and paid $138,000 for selling and administrative expenses.
3. Amortized the remainder of the discount for 2009 and paid the face value of the note.
4. Prepared the necessary closing entries at December 31, 2009.

Required

a. Show the effects of each of the transactions on the elements of the financial statements, using a horizontal statements model like the one shown here. Use + for increase, − for decrease, and NA for not affected. The first transaction is entered as an example. (*Hint:* Closing entries do not affect the statements model.)

Event No.	Assets	=	Liab.	+	Equity	Rev.	−	Exp.	=	Net Inc.	Cash Flow
1	+		+		NA	NA		NA		NA	+ FA

b. Prepare the entries in general journal form for the transactions for 2008 and 2009, and post them to T-accounts.

c. Prepare an income statement, statement of changes in stockholders' equity, balance sheet, and statement of cash flows for 2008 and 2009.

EXERCISES—SERIES B

L.O. 1

Exercise 8-1B *Effect of recognizing bad debts expense on financial statements: Allowance method*

Magnolia Dry Cleaning was started on January 1, 2008. It experienced the following events during its first year of operation.

Events affecting 2008

1. Provided $20,000 of cleaning services on account.
2. Collected $16,000 cash from accounts receivable.
3. Adjusted the accounting records to reflect the estimate that bad debts expense would be 1 percent of the service revenue on account.

Events affecting 2009

1. Wrote off an $80 account receivable that was determined to be uncollectible.
2. Provided $32,000 of cleaning services on account.

3. Collected $28,000 cash from accounts receivable.
4. Adjusted the accounting records to reflect the estimate that bad debts expense would be 1 percent of the service revenue on account.

Required

a. Record the events for 2008 in T-accounts.

b. Determine the following amounts:

   (1) Net income for 2008.

   (2) Net cash flow from operating activities for 2008.

   (3) Balance of accounts receivable at the end of 2008.

   (4) Net realizable value of accounts receivable at the end of 2008.

c. Repeat Requirements *a* and *b* for the 2009 accounting period.

Exercise 8-2B *Analyzing financial statement effects of accounting for bad debts using the allowance method*

L.O. 1

Businesses using the allowance method to account for bad debts expense routinely experience four accounting events:

1. Recognition of revenue on account.
2. Collection of cash from accounts receivable.
3. Recognition of bad debts expense through a year-end adjusting entry.
4. Write-off of uncollectible accounts.

Required

Show the effect of each event on the elements of the financial statements, using a horizontal statements model like the one shown here. Use + for increase, − for decrease, and NA for not affected. In the Cash Flow column, indicate whether the item is an operating activity (OA), investing activity (IA), or financing activity (FA). The first transaction is entered as an example.

Event No.	Assets	=	Liab.	+	Equity	Rev.	−	Exp.	=	Net Inc.	Cash Flow
1	+		NA		+	+		NA		+	NA

Exercise 8-3B *Analyzing account balances for a company using the allowance method of accounting for bad debts*

L.O. 1

The following account balances come from the records of Aspen Company.

	Beginning Balance	Ending Balance
Accounts receivable	$3,000	$3,500
Allowance for doubtful accounts	300	320

During the accounting period, Aspen recorded $15,000 of sales revenue on account. The company also wrote off a $120 account receivable.

Required

a. Determine the amount of cash collected from receivables.

b. Determine the amount of bad debts expense recognized during the period.

Exercise 8-4B *Effect of recovering a receivable previously written off*

L.O. 1

The accounts receivable balance for Trendsetters Spa at December 31, 2008, was $76,000. Also on that date, the balance in Allowance for Doubtful Accounts was $3,000. During 2009, $4,200 of accounts receivable were written off as uncollectible. In addition, Trendsetters unexpectedly collected $900 of receivables that had been written off in a previous accounting period. Sales on account during 2009 were $220,000, and cash collections from receivables were $205,000. Bad debts expense was estimated to be 2 percent of the sales on account for the period.

Required

(*Hint:* Post the transactions to T-accounts before you complete the requirements.)

a. Based on the preceding information, compute (after year-end adjustment):
   (1) Balance of Allowance for Doubtful Accounts at December 31, 2009.
   (2) Balance of Accounts Receivable at December 31, 2009.
   (3) Net realizable value of Accounts Receivable at December 31, 2009.
b. What amount of bad debts expense will Trendsetters report for 2009?
c. Explain how the $900 recovery of receivables affects the income statement.

L.O. 1, 2

Exercise 8-5B *Accounting for bad debts: Allowance versus direct write-off method*

Cal's Bike Shop sells new and used bicycle parts. Although a majority of its sales are cash sales, it makes a significant amount of credit sales. During 2008, its first year of operations, Cal's Bike Shop experienced the following:

Sales on account	$320,000
Cash sales	575,000
Collections of accounts receivable	285,000
Uncollectible accounts charged off during the year	300

Required

a. Assume that Cal's Bike Shop uses the allowance method of accounting for bad debts and estimates that 1 percent of its sales on account will not be collected. Answer the following questions:
   (1) What is the Accounts Receivable balance at December 31, 2008?
   (2) What is the ending balance of the Allowance for Doubtful Accounts at December 31, 2008, after all entries and adjusting entries are posted?
   (3) What is the amount of bad debts expense for 2008?
   (4) What is the net realizable value of accounts receivable at December 31, 2008?
b. Assume that Cal's Bike Shop uses the direct write-off method of accounting for bad debts. Answer the following questions:
   (1) What is the Accounts Receivable balance at December 31, 2008?
   (2) What is the amount of bad debts expense for 2008?
   (3) What is the net realizable value of accounts receivable at December 31, 2008?

L.O. 2

Exercise 8-6B *Accounting for bad debts: Direct write-off method*

Hindi Service Co. does mostly a cash business but does make a few sales on account. Consequently, it uses the direct write-off method to account for bad debts. During 2008, Hindi Service Co. earned $25,000 of cash revenue and $4,000 of revenue on account. Cash operating expenses were $18,000. After numerous attempts to collect a $120 account receivable from Bill Smith, the account was determined to be uncollectible in 2008.

Required

a. Record the effects of (1) cash revenue, (2) revenue on account, (3) cash expenses, and (4) write-off of the uncollectible account on the financial statements using a horizontal statements model like the one shown here. In the Cash Flow column, indicate whether the item is an operating activity (OA), investing activity (IA), or financing activity (FA). Use NA to indicate that an element is not affected by the event.

Assets			=	Liab.	+	Equity	Rev.	−	Exp.	=	Net Inc.	Cash Flow
Cash	+	Accts. Rec.										

b. What amount of net income did Hindi Service Co. report on the 2008 income statement?
c. Prepare the general journal entries for the four accounting events listed in Requirement *a*.

Exercise 8-7B *Effect of credit card sales on financial statements*

Tiki Day Spa provided $120,000 of services during 2008. All customers paid for the services with credit cards. Tiki turned the credit card receipts over to the credit card company immediately. The credit card company paid Tiki cash in the amount of face value less a 5 percent service charge.

Required

a. Record the credit card sales and the subsequent collection of accounts receivable in a horizontal statements model like the one shown here. In the Cash Flow column, indicate whether the item is an operating activity (OA), investing activity (IA), or financing activity (FA). Use NA to indicate that an element is not affected by the event.

Assets			=	Liab.	+	Equity		Rev.	−	Exp.	=	Net Inc.		Cash Flow
Cash	+	Accts. Rec.												

b. Answer the following questions:

(1) What is the amount of total assets at the end of the accounting period?

(2) What is the amount of revenue reported on the income statement?

(3) What is the amount of cash flow from operating activities reported on the statement of cash flows?

(4) What costs would a business incur if it maintained its own accounts receivable? What cost does a business incur by accepting credit cards?

Exercise 8-8B *Recording credit card sales*

Bison Company accepted credit cards in payment for $6,000 of services performed during July 2008. The credit card company charged Bison a 4 percent service fee; it paid Bison as soon as it received the invoices.

Required

a. Prepare the general journal entry to record the service revenue.

b. Prepare the general journal entry for the collection of the receivable from the credit card company.

c. Based on this information alone, what is the amount of net income earned during the month of July?

Exercise 8-9B *Effect of warranties on income and cash flow*

To support herself while attending school, Patty Rich sold stereo systems to other students. During her first year of operation, she sold systems that had cost her $95,000 cash for $140,000 cash. She provided her customers with a one-year warranty against defects in parts and labor. Based on industry standards, she estimated that warranty claims would amount to 3 percent of sales. During the year she paid $1,100 cash to replace a defective tuner.

Required

Prepare an income statement and statement of cash flows for Rich's first year of operation. Based on the information given, what is Rich's total warranties liability at the end of the accounting period?

Exercise 8-10B *Effect of warranty obligations and payments on financial statements*

The Bicycle Company provides a 120-day parts-and-labor warranty on all merchandise it sells. The Bicycle Company estimates the warranty expense for the current period to be $1,800. During the period a customer returned a product that cost $975 to repair.

Required

a. Show the effects of these transactions on the financial statements using a horizontal statements model like the example shown here. Use a + to indicate increase, a − for decrease, and NA for not affected. Also, in the Cash Flow column, indicate whether the item is an operating activity (OA), investing activity (IA), or financing activity (FA).

Assets	=	Liab.	+	Equity		Rev.	−	Exp.	=	Net Inc.		Cash Flow

b. Prepare the journal entry to record the warranty expense for the period.

c. Prepare the journal entry to record payment for the actual repair costs.

d. Why do companies estimate warranty expense and record the expense before the repairs are actually made?

L.O. 1, 4

Exercise 8-11B *Comprehensive single-cycle problem*

The following after-closing trial balance was drawn from the accounts of Baker's Brick Co. (BBC) as of December 31, 2008.

	Debit	Credit
Cash	$ 8,000	
Accounts receivable	24,000	
Allowance for doubtful accounts		$ 1,800
Inventory	42,000	
Accounts payable		12,000
Common stock		30,000
Retained earnings		30,200
Totals	$74,000	$74,000

Transactions for 2009

1. Acquired an additional $4,000 cash from the issue of common stock.
2. Purchased $80,000 of inventory on account.
3. Sold inventory that cost $76,000 for $128,000. Sales were made on account.
4. The products sold in Event 3 were warranted, and BBC estimated future warranty costs would amount to 5 percent of sales.
5. The company wrote off $800 of uncollectible accounts.
6. On September 1, BBC issued a $12,000 face value, 8 percent interest-bearing note. The note had a one-year term.
7. Paid $2,000 cash to satisfy warranty claims.
8. Paid $16,000 cash for operating expenses.
9. The company collected $133,200 cash from accounts receivable.
10. A cash payment of $68,000 was paid on accounts payable.
11. The company paid a $2,000 cash dividend to the stockholders.
12. Bad debts are estimated to be 1 percent of sales on account.
13. Recorded the accrued interest at December 31, 2009.

Required

a. Open T-accounts and record the beginning balances and the effects of the 2009 accounting events.

b. Prepare an income statement, statement of changes in stockholders' equity, balance sheet, and statement of cash flows for 2009.

L.O. 5

Exercise 8-12B *Using the average number of days to collect accounts receivable ratio to make comparisons*

The following information was drawn from the accounting records of Hedges Company and Latour Company.

	Hedges	Latour
Accounts receivable balance	$ 80,000	$ 50,000
Sales	920,000	450,000

Required

a. Determine the average days to collect accounts receivable for each company.

b. Which company is likely to incur more costs associated with extending credit?

c. Identify and discuss some of the costs that are associated with extending credit.

d. Explain why a company would be willing to accept the costs of extending credit to its customers.

Exercise 8-13B   *Effect of a discount note on financial statements (Appendix)*

L.O. 6

Grace Cox started a design company on January 1, 2008. On April 1, 2008, Cox borrowed cash from a local bank by issuing a one-year $200,000 face value note with annual interest based on an 8 percent discount. During 2008, Cox provided services for $75,000 cash.

Required

Answer the following questions. (*Hint:* Record the events in T-accounts prior to answering the questions.)

a. What is the amount of total liabilities on the December 31, 2008 balance sheet?

b. What is the amount of net income on the 2008 income statement?

c. What is the amount of cash flow from operating activities on the 2008 statement of cash flows?

d. Provide the general journal entries necessary to record issuing the note on April 1, 2008; recognizing accrued interest on December 31, 2008; and repaying the loan on March 31, 2009.

Exercise 8-14B   *Comparing effective interest rates on discount versus interest-bearing notes (Appendix)*

L.O. 6

Jimmy Jones borrowed money by issuing two notes on March 1, 2008. The financing transactions are described here.

1. Borrowed funds by issuing a $30,000 face value discount note to Farmers Bank. The note had an 8 percent discount rate, a one-year term to maturity, and was paid off on March 1, 2009.

2. Borrowed funds by issuing a $30,000 face value, interest-bearing note to Valley Bank. The note had an 8 percent stated rate of interest, a one-year term to maturity, and was paid off on March 1, 2009.

Required

a. Show the effects of issuing the two notes on the financial statements using separate horizontal financial statement models like the ones here. Record the transaction amounts under the appropriate categories. Also, in the Cash Flow column, indicate whether the item is an operating activity (OA), investing activity (IA), or financing activity (FA). Record only the events occurring on the date of issue. Do not record accrued interest or the repayment at maturity.

Discount Note

Assets	=	Liabilities			+	Equity	Rev.	−	Exp.	=	Net Inc.	Cash Flow
Cash	=	Notes Pay.	−	Disc. on Notes Pay.	+	Ret. Ear.						

Interest-Bearing Note

Assets	=	Liabilities	+	Equity	Rev.	−	Exp.	=	Net Inc.	Cash Flow
Cash	=	Notes Pay.	+	Ret. Ear.						

b. What is the total amount of interest to be paid on each note?

c. What amount of cash was received from each note?

d. Which note has the higher effective interest rate? Support your answer with appropriate computations.

Exercise 8-15B   *Recording accounting events for a discount note (Appendix)*

L.O. 6

Swanson Co. issued a $40,000 face value discount note to National Bank on July 1, 2008. The note had an 8 percent discount rate and a one-year term to maturity.

Required

Prepare general journal entries for the following:

a. The issuance of the note on July 1, 2008.

b. The adjustment for accrued interest at the end of the year, December 31, 2008.

c. Recording interest expense for 2009 and repaying the principal on June 30, 2009.

PROBLEMS—SERIES B

L.O. 1

Problem 8-16B   *Accounting for bad debts: Two cycles using the allowance method*

The following transactions apply to BR Company for 2008, the first year of operation:

1. Recognized $225,000 of service revenue earned on account.
2. Collected $210,000 from accounts receivable.
3. Paid $175,000 cash for operating expenses.
4. Adjusted the accounts to recognize bad debts expense. BR uses the allowance method of accounting for bad debts and estimates that bad debts expense will be 1 percent of sales on account.

The following transactions apply to BR for 2009:

1. Recognized $420,000 of service revenue on account.
2. Collected $422,000 from accounts receivable.
3. Determined that $1,800 of the accounts receivable were uncollectible and wrote them off.
4. Collected $800 of an account that had previously been written off.
5. Paid $126,000 cash for operating expenses.
6. Adjusted the accounts to recognize bad debts expense for 2009. BR estimates bad debts expense will be 0.5 percent of sales on account.

Required

Complete the following requirements for 2008 and 2009. Complete all requirements for 2008 prior to beginning the requirements for 2009.

a. Identify the type of each transaction (asset source, asset use, asset exchange, or claims exchange).

b. Show the effect of each transaction on the elements of the financial statements, using a horizontal statements model like the one shown here. Use + for increase, − for decrease, and NA for not affected. Also, in the Cash Flow column, indicate whether the item is an operating activity (OA), investing activity (IA), or financing activity (FA). The first transaction is entered as an example. (*Hint:* Closing entries do not affect the statements model.)

Event No.	Assets	=	Liab.	+	Equity	Rev.	−	Exp.	=	Net Inc.	Cash Flow
1	+		NA		+	+		NA		+	NA

c. Record the transactions in general journal form, and post them to T-accounts (begin 2009 with the ending T-account balances from 2008).

d. Prepare the income statement, statement of changes in stockholders' equity, balance sheet, and statement of cash flows.

e. Prepare closing entries and post these closing entries to the T-accounts. Prepare the after-closing trial balance.

L.O. 1

Problem 8-17B   *Determining account balances and preparing journal entries: Allowance method of accounting for bad debts*

During the first year of operation, 2009, Holt Appliance Co. recognized $300,000 of service revenue on account. At the end of 2009, the accounts receivable balance was $58,000. For this first year in business, the owner believes bad debts expense will be about 1 percent of sales on account.

Required

a. What amount of cash did Holt collect from accounts receivable during 2009?

b. Assuming Holt uses the allowance method to account for bad debts, what amount should Holt record as bad debts expense for 2009?

c. Prepare the journal entries to:

   (1) Record service revenue on account.

   (2) Record collections from accounts receivable.

   (3) Record the entry to recognize bad debts expense.

d. What is the net realizable value of receivables at the end of 2009?

e. Show the effects of the transactions in Requirement *c* on the financial statements by recording the appropriate amounts in a horizontal statements model like the one shown here. In the Cash Flow column, indicate whether the item is an operating activity (OA), investing activity (IA), or financing activity (FA). Use NA for not affected.

Assets			=	Liab.	+	Equity	Rev.	−	Exp.	=	Net Inc.	Cash Flow
Cash	+	Accts. Rec. − Allow.										

Problem 8-18B   *Accounting for credit card sales, warranties, and bad debts:*   **L.O. 2, 3, 4**
                     Direct write-off method

Southwest Sales had the following transactions in 2008:

1. The business was started when it acquired $500,000 cash from the issue of common stock.

2. Southwest purchased $950,000 of merchandise for cash in 2008.

3. During the year, the company sold merchandise for $1,250,000. The merchandise cost $750,000. Sales were made under the following terms:

a.	$600,000	Cash sales
b.	500,000	Credit card sales (The credit card company charges a 4 percent service fee.)
c.	150,000	Sales on account

4. The company collected all the amount receivable from the credit card company.

5. The company collected $135,000 of accounts receivable.

6. Southwest used the direct write-off method to account for bad debts expense and wrote off $2,000 of accounts receivable that were uncollectible.

7. Southwest gives a one-year warranty on equipment it sells. It estimated that warranty expense for 2008 would be $4,500.

8. The company paid $100,000 cash for selling and administrative expenses.

Required

a. Show the effects of each of the transactions on the elements of the financial statements, using a horizontal statements model like the one shown here. Use + for increase, − for decrease, and NA for not affected. The first transaction is entered as an example. (*Hint:* Closing entries do not affect the statements model.)

Event No.	Assets	=	Liab.	+	Equity	Rev.	−	Exp.	=	Net Inc.	Cash Flow
1	+		NA		+	NA		NA		NA	+ FA

b. Prepare general journal entries for each of the transactions, and post them to T-accounts.

c. Prepare an income statement, statement of changes in stockholders' equity, balance sheet, and statement of cash flows for 2008.

L.O. 2, 3, 4   **Problem 8-19B**   *Effect of transactions on the elements of financial statements*

Required

Identify each of the following independent transactions as asset source (AS), asset use (AU), asset exchange (AE), or claims exchange (CE). Also explain how each event affects assets, liabilities, stockholders' equity, net income, and cash flow by placing a + for increase, − for decrease, or NA for not affected under each of the categories. The first event is recorded as an example.

Event	Type of Event	Assets	Liabilities	Common Stock	Retained Earnings	Net Income	Cash Flow
a	AE	+/−	NA	NA	NA	NA	+

a. Collected cash from customers paying their accounts.

b. Recovered a bad debt that was previously written off (assume direct write-off method was used).

c. Paid cash for equipment.

d. Recognized warranty expense.

e. Sold merchandise at a price above cost. Accepted payment by credit card. The credit card company charges a service fee. The receipts have not yet been forwarded to the credit card company for collection.

f. Realized a gain when equipment was sold for cash.

g. Paid cash to satisfy warranty obligations.

h. Submitted receipts to the credit card company in Requirement *e* above and collected cash.

i. Issued a short-term note to First National Bank.

j. Paid cash to creditors on accounts payable.

k. Accrued three months' interest on the short-term note payable.

l. Provided services for cash.

m. Paid cash for salaries expense.

n. Provided services on account.

o. Wrote off an uncollectible account (use direct write-off method).

L.O. 1, 4   **Problem 8-20B**   *Multistep income statement and classified balance sheet*

Required

Use the following information to prepare a multistep income statement and a classified balance sheet for Matson Company for 2009. (*Hint:* Some of the items will *not* appear on either statement, and ending retained earnings must be calculated.)

Operating expenses	$ 90,000	Cash	$ 23,000
Land	50,000	Interest receivable (short term)	800
Accumulated depreciation	38,000	Cash flow from investing activities	102,000
Accounts payable	60,000	Allowance for doubtful accounts	7,000
Unearned revenue	58,000	Interest payable (short term)	3,000
Warranties payable (short term)	2,000	Sales revenue	500,000
Equipment	77,000	Bad debts expense	14,000
Notes payable (long term)	129,000	Interest expense	32,000
Salvage value of equipment	7,000	Accounts receivable	113,000
Dividends	12,000	Salaries payable	12,000
Warranty expense	5,000	Supplies	3,000
Beginning retained earnings	28,800	Prepaid rent	14,000
Interest revenue	6,000	Common stock	52,000
Gain on sale of equipment	10,000	Cost of goods sold	179,000
Inventory	154,000	Salaries expense	122,000
Notes receivable (short term)	17,000		

Problem 8-21B   *Missing information*

The following information comes from the accounts of Frye Company:

	Beginning Balance	Ending Balance
Accounts receivable	$30,000	$36,000
Allowance for doubtful accounts	1,800	2,400
Warranties payable	3,000	3,600
Notes payable	50,000	50,000
Interest payable	1,000	5,000

Required

a. There were $180,000 in sales on account during the accounting period. Write-offs of uncollectible accounts were $2,100. What was the amount of cash collected from accounts receivable? What amount of bad debts expense was reported on the income statement? What was the net realizable value of receivables at the end of the accounting period?

b. Warranty expense for the period was $2,100. How much cash was paid to settle warranty claims?

c. What amount of interest expense was recognized during the period? How much cash was paid for interest? The note has an 8 percent interest rate and 24 months to maturity.

Problem 8-22B   *Comprehensive accounting cycle problem (Uses allowance method)*

The following trial balance was prepared for Gifts, Etc., Inc., on December 31, 2008, after the closing entries were posted.

	Debit	Credit
Cash	$110,000	
Accounts receivable	136,000	
Allowance for doubtful accounts		$ 10,000
Inventory	690,000	
Accounts payable		98,000
Common stock		720,000
Retained earnings		108,000
Totals	$936,000	$936,000

Gifts, Etc. had the following transactions in 2009:

1. Purchased merchandise on account for $360,000.
2. Sold merchandise that cost $250,000 for $465,000 on account.
3. Sold for $240,000 cash merchandise that had cost $144,000.
4. Sold merchandise for $180,000 to credit card customers. The merchandise had cost $108,000. The credit card company charges a 3 percent fee.
5. Collected $526,000 cash from accounts receivable.
6. Paid $430,000 cash on accounts payable.
7. Paid $134,000 cash for selling and administrative expenses.
8. Collected cash for the full amount due from the credit card company.
9. Issued a $48,000 face value, interest-bearing note with an 8 percent interest rate and a one-year term to maturity.
10. Wrote off $7,200 of accounts as uncollectible.
11. Made the following adjusting entries:
    (a) Recorded bad debts expense estimated at 1 percent of sales on account.
    (b) Recorded seven months of accrued interest on the note at December 31, 2009.
    (c) Estimated warranty expense to be $1,800.

Required

a. Prepare general journal entries for these transactions; post the entries to T-accounts; and prepare an income statement, a statement of changes in stockholders' equity, a balance sheet, and a statement of cash flows for 2009.

b. Compute the net realizable value of accounts receivable at December 31, 2009.

c. If Gifts, Etc. used the direct write-off method, what amount of bad debts expense would it report on the income statement?

L.O. 5

Problem 8-23B *Using ratios to make comparisons*

The following accounting information exists for West and East companies at the end of 2010.

	West	East
Cash	$ 100,000	$ 40,000
Accounts receivable	300,000	184,000
Allowance for doubtful accounts	15,000	4,000
Merchandise inventory	200,000	150,000
Accounts payable	280,000	140,000
Cost of goods sold	900,000	850,000
Building	185,000	175,000
Sales	1,500,000	1,200,000

Required

a. For each company, compute the gross margin percentage and the average days to collect accounts receivable (use the net realizable value of receivables to compute the average days to collect receivables).

b. In relation to cost, which company is charging more for its merchandise?

c. Which company is likely to incur higher costs associated with the granting of credit to customers? Explain.

d. Which company appears to have more restrictive credit standards when authorizing credit to its customers? (*Hint:* There is no specific answer to this question. You are expected to use your judgment and general knowledge of ratios to answer).

L.O. 6

Problem 8-24B *Accounting for a discount note across two accounting cycles (Appendix)*

Mike Estes opened Estes & Company, an accounting practice, in 2008. The following summarizes transactions that occurred during 2008:

1. Issued a $200,000 face value discount note to First National Bank on July 1, 2008. The note had a 9 percent discount rate and a one-year term to maturity.
2. Recognized cash revenue of $452,000.
3. Incurred and paid $230,000 of operating expenses.
4. Adjusted the books to recognize interest expense at December 31, 2008.
5. Prepared the necessary closing entries at December 31, 2008.

The following summarizes transactions that occurred in 2009:

1. Recognized $875,000 of cash revenue.
2. Incurred and paid $620,000 of operating expenses.
3. Recognized the interest expense for 2009 and paid the face value of the note.
4. Prepared the necessary closing entries at December 31, 2009.

Required

a. Show the effects of each of the transactions on the elements of the financial statements, using a horizontal statements model like the one shown here. Use + for increase, − for decrease, and NA for not affected. The first transaction is entered as an example. (*Hint:* Closing entries do not affect the statements model.)

Event No.	Assets	=	Liab.	+	Equity	Rev.	−	Exp.	=	Net Inc.	Cash Flow
1	+		+		NA	NA		NA		NA	+ FA

b. Prepare entries in general journal form for the transactions for 2008 and 2009, and post them to T-accounts.

c. Prepare an income statement, statement of changes in stockholders' equity, balance sheet, and statement of cash flows for 2008 and 2009.

ANALYZE, THINK, COMMUNICATE

ATC 8-1   Business Applications Case   *Understanding real-world annual reports*

Required—Part 1

Use the Topps Company's annual report in Appendix B to answer the following questions.

a. How long did it take Topps to collect accounts receivable during the year ended February 25, 2006?

b. Approximately what percentage of accounts receivable, as of February 25, 2006, does the company think will not be collected (see Note 4)? Caution, "Reserve for returns," also shown in Note 4, is not related to uncollectible accounts receivable.

c. What do you think the balance in the Reserve for Returns account represents?

Required—Part 2

Use the Harley-Davidson's annual report that came with this book to answer the following questions.

a. How long did it take Harley-Davidson to collect receivables during the year ended December 31, 2005? Note: For the purposes of this computation, use all three receivables accounts shown on Harley-Davidson's balance sheet.

b. Why does Harley-Davidson take so long to collect its receivables? Does this indicate the company has a problem with its receivables?

c. Approximately what percentage of accounts receivable, as of December 31, 2005, does the company think will not be collected (see Note 2)?

d. How much warranty liability did Harley-Davidson have as of December 31, 2005 (see Note 1)?

ATC 8-2   Group Assignment   *Missing information*

The following selected financial information is available for three companies:

	Bell	Card	Zore
Total sales	$125,000	$210,000	?
Cash sales	?	26,000	$120,000
Sales on account	40,000	?	75,000
Accounts receivable, January 1, 2008	6,200	42,000	?
Accounts receivable, December 31, 2008	5,600	48,000	7,500
Allowance for doubtful accounts, January 1, 2008	?	?	405
Allowance for doubtful accounts, December 31, 2008	224	1,680	?
Bad debt expense, 2008	242	1,200	395
Uncollectible accounts written off	204	1,360	365
Collections of accounts receivable, 2008	?	?	75,235

Required

a. Divide the class into three sections and divide each section into groups of three to five students. Assign one of the companies to each of the sections.

Group Tasks

   (1) Determine the missing amounts for your company.

   (2) Determine the percentage of accounts receivable estimated to be uncollectible at the end of 2007 and 2008 for your company.

   (3) Determine the percentage of total sales that are sales on account for your company.

   (4) Determine the accounts receivable turnover for your company.

Class Discussion

b. Have a representative of each section put the missing information on the board and explain how it was determined.

c. Which company has the highest percentage of sales that are on account?

d. Which company is doing the best job of collecting its accounts receivable? What procedures and policies can a company use to better collect its accounts receivable?

ATC 8-3 Real-World Case *Time needed to collect accounts receivable*

Presented here are the average days to collect accounts receivable ratios for four companies in different industries. The data are for 2002.

Company	Average Days to Collect Accounts Receivable
Boeing (aircraft manufacturer)	34
Ford (automobile manufacturer)	6
Haverty's (furniture retailer)	81
Colgate Palmolive (consumer products manufacturer)	45

Required

Write a brief memorandum that provides possible answers to each of the following questions:

a. Why would a company that manufactures cars (Ford) collect its accounts receivable faster than a company that sells furniture (Haverty's)? (*Hint:* Ford sells cars to dealerships, not to individual customers.)

b. Why would a company that manufactures and sells large airplanes (Boeing) collect its accounts receivable faster than a company that sells toothpaste and soap (Colgate Palmolive)?

ATC 8-4 Business Applications Case *Performing ratio analysis using real-world data*

The following data were taken from Hershey Foods Corporation's 2004 annual report. All dollar amounts are in thousands.

	Fiscal Years Ending	
	December 31, 2004	December 31, 2003
Sales	$4,429,248	$4,172,551
Accounts receivable	408,930	407,612

Required

a. Compute Hershey's accounts receivable turnover ratios for 2004 and 2003.

b. Compute Hershey's average days to collect accounts receivables for 2004 and 2003.

c. Based on the ratios computed in Requirements *a* and *b*, did Hershey's performance get better or worse from 2003 to 2004?

d. In 2004 the average interest rate on Hershey's long-term debt was approximately 7.2 percent. Assume it took Hershey 30 days to collect its receivables. Using an interest rate of 7.2 percent, calculate how much it cost Hershey's to finance its receivables for 30 days in 2004.

ATC 8-5 Business Applications Case *Performing ratio analysis using real-world data*

AutoZone, Inc., claims to be "the nation's leading auto parts retailer." It sells replacement auto parts directly to the consumer. BorgWarner, Inc., has over 17,000 employees and produces automobile parts, such as transmissions and cooling systems, for the world's vehicle manufacturers. The following data were taken from these companies' 2004 annual reports. All dollar amounts are in thousands.

	AutoZone August 28, 2004	BorgWarner December 31, 2004
Sales	$5,637,025	$3,525,300
Accounts receivable	68,372	499,100

Required

a. Before performing any calculations, speculate as to which company will take the longest to collect its accounts receivables. Explain the rational for your decision.

b. Calculate the accounts receivable turnover ratios for AutoZone and BorgWarner.

c. Calculate the average days to collect accounts receivables for AutoZone and BorgWarner.

d. Do the calculations from Requirements *b* and *c* confirm your speculations in Requirement *a*?

ATC 8-6   Writing Assignment   *Elements of financial statements*

Paul South is opening a men's clothing store in University City. He has some of the necessary funds to lease the building and purchase the inventory but will need to borrow between $45,000 and $50,000. He has talked with two financial institutions that have offered the money according to the following terms:

1. South can borrow the money from Bank 1 by issuing a $50,000, one-year note with an interest rate of 10 percent.

2. South can borrow the money from Bank 2 by issuing a $50,000 face value discount note. The note will have a 9.5 percent discount rate and a one-year term to maturity.

Required

Write a memo to South explaining the difference in the two types of notes. Also advise him regarding the best alternative and why. Include in your explanation the true cost of each of the loans.

ATC 8-7   Ethical Dilemma   *What they don't know won't hurt them, right?*

Alonzo Saunders owns a small training services company that is experiencing growing pains. The company has grown rapidly by offering liberal credit terms to its customers. While his competitors require payment for services provided within 30 days, Saunders permits his customers to delay payment for up to 90 days. This extended delay allows his customers time to fully evaluate the training that employees receive before being required to pay for that training. Saunders guarantees satisfaction. If the customer is unhappy, the customer does not have to pay. Saunders works with reputable companies, provides top quality training, and rarely encounters dissatisfied customers. However, the long collection period has left Saunders with a cash flow problem. He has a large accounts receivable balance, but needs cash to pay the current bills. He has recently negotiated a loan agreement with National Bank of Brighton County that should solve his cash flow problems. A condition of the loan is that the accounts receivable be pledged as collateral for the loan. The bank agreed to loan Saunders 70 percent of the value of his receivables balance. The current balance in the receivables account is approximately $100,000, thereby giving him access to $70,000 cash. Saunders feels very comfortable with this arrangement because he estimates that he needs approximately $60,000, which is well within the range permitted by the bank. Unfortunately, on the day Saunders was scheduled to execute the loan agreement, he heard a rumor that his largest customer was experiencing financial problems and was considering the declaration of bankruptcy. The customer owed Saunders $45,000. Saunders immediately called the company's chief accountant and was told "off the record" that the rumor was true. The accountant advised Saunders that the company had a substantial negative net worth and that most of the valuable assets were collateralized against bank loans. He said that, in his opinion, Saunders was unlikely to be able to collect the balance due. Saunders' immediate concern was the impact that the situation would have on his loan agreement with the bank. Removing the receivable from the collateral pool would leave only $55,000 in the pool and thereby reduce his available credit to $38,500 ($55,000 × 0.70). Even worse, the recognition of the bad debts expense would so adversely affect his income statement that the bank might decide to reduce the available credit by lowering the percentage of receivables allowed under the current loan agreement. As Saunders heads for the bank, he wonders how he will make ends meet. If he cannot obtain the cash he needs, he will soon be declaring bankruptcy himself. He wonders whether he should even tell the bank about the bad debt or just let the bank discover the situation after the fact. He knows that he will have to sign an agreement attesting to the quality of the receivables at the date of the loan. However, he reasons that the information he received is off the record and that therefore he *may not* be legally bound to advise the bank of the condition of the receivables balance. He wishes that he had gone to the bank before he called to confirm the rumor.

Required

a. Assuming that Saunders uses the direct write-off method of accounting for bad debts, explain how the $45,000 write-off of the uncollectible account affects his financial statements.

b. Should Saunders advise the bank of the condition of the receivables? What are the ethical implications associated with telling or not telling the bank about the uncollectible account?

ATC 8-8 Research Assignment *Analyzing Toro's accounts receivable*

Required

Using the most current 10-K available on EDGAR or the company's Web site, answer the following questions about Toro Company for the most recent year reported. Instructions for using EDGAR are in Appendix A.

a. What was Toro's average days to collect accounts receivable?

b. What percentage of accounts receivable did Toro estimate would not be collected?

c. Did Toro provide any information about warranties that it provides to customers? If so, what information was provided? (*Hint:* Look in the accrued warranty footnote.)

d. Toro Company manufactures products under brand names other than *Toro*. What are these brand names?

e. Does it appear that Toro's warranty costs have been decreasing or increasing? Explain why this may have occurred.

ATC 8-9 Spreadsheet Analysis *Using Excel*

Set up the following spreadsheet comparing Vong and Crist Companies.

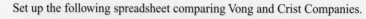

	Vong	Crist
Sales	$800,000	$1,100,000
Cost of Goods Sold	600,000	660,000
Gross Profit		
Gross Profit Percentage		
Accounts Receivable	130,000	270,000
Allowance for Doubtful Accounts	10,000	27,000
Net Realizable Value		
Accounts Receivable Turnover		
Average Days to Collect		

Required

a. For each company, compute gross profit, gross profit percentage, net realizable value, accounts receivable turnover, and average days to collect.

b. In relation to cost, which company is charging more for its merchandise?

c. Which company is likely to incur higher financial costs associated with granting credit to customers? Explain the reasons for your answer.

d. Which company appears to have more restrictive credit standards when authorizing credit to customers? How do you know?

COMPREHENSIVE PROBLEM

The trial balance of Pacilio Security Sales and Services, Inc., as of January 1, 2008, was:

Cash	$132,248
Petty cash	100
Accounts receivable	47,220
Supplies	160
Inventory—standard alarm (32 @ $280)	8,960
Inventory—deluxe alarm (33 @ $570)	18,810
Prepaid rent	1,200
Van	9,200
Accumulated depreciation	4,800
Accounts payable	2,970
Common stock	50,000
Retained earnings	160,128

During 2008, Pacilio Security Sales and Services, Inc., experienced the following transactions:

1. Paid $8,400 on March 2, 2008, for one year's rent in advance.
2. Purchased $550 of supplies for cash.
3. Purchased 45 standard alarm systems on March 30 at a cost of $265 each, and 30 deluxe alarm systems at a cost of $580 each. Cash was paid for the purchase. Purchased 30 more standard alarm systems on November 3, at a cost of $275 each. Paid cash for the purchase.
4. Paid the balance of the accounts payable.
5. Pacilio has noticed that its accounts receivable are rising more than desired and some collection problems exist. It feels that its bad accounts are approximately 2 percent of total credit sales. Pacilio has decided that this year it will use the allowance method of accounting for bad debts. The estimate will be made at the end of the year.
6. Pacilio has tried to collect several of its delinquent accounts and has learned that these customers have either taken bankruptcy or have moved and left no forwarding address. These accounts amount to $1,900.
7. Installed 100 standard alarm systems for a total of $58,000 and 34 deluxe alarm systems for a total of $32,300. All sales were on account. Cost of goods sold was $27,210 for the standard alarms and $19,390 for the deluxe alarms.
8. Pacilio decided to accept credit cards for some of its monitoring service sales. Total monitoring services for the year were $82,000, of which Pacilio accepted credit cards for $24,000 of this amount. The credit card company charges a fee of 4 percent. The balance of $58,000 was sales on accounts.
9. July 1, 2008, Pacilio replenished the petty cash fund. The fund had $21 cash and receipts of $50 for yard mowing, $22 for office supplies, and $9 for miscellaneous expense.
10. Collected the amount due from the credit card company.
11. Collected $146,000 of accounts receivable for the year.
12. Paid installers $32,000 for salaries.
13. Paid $4,500 for advertising expense.
14. Paid $3,100 for utilities expense for the year.

Adjustments

15. Supplies of $250 were on hand at the end of the year.
16. Recognized expired rent for the year.
17. Recognized depreciation expense for the year.
18. Recognized bad debt expense for the year using the allowance method.
19. Pacilio has decided to provide a one-year warranty on its deluxe alarm systems. It estimates that its warranty expense will be 5 percent of its deluxe alarm sales.

Required

a. Record the above transactions in general journal form. Pacilio uses FIFO cost flow assumption.
b. Post the transactions to the T-accounts.
c. Prepare a trial balance.
d. Prepare an income statement, statement of changes in stockholders' equity, balance sheet, and statement of cash flows.
e. Close the temporary accounts to retained earnings.
f. Post the closing entries to the T-accounts and prepare an after-closing trial balance.

CHAPTER 9

Accounting for Long-Term Operational Assets

LP9

LEARNING OBJECTIVES

After you have mastered the material in this chapter, you will be able to:

1. Identify different types of long-term operational assets.

2. Determine the cost of long-term operational assets.

3. Explain how different depreciation methods affect financial statements.

4. Determine how gains and losses on disposals of long-term operational assets affect financial statements.

5. Identify some of the tax issues which affect long-term operational assets.

6. Show how revising estimates affects financial statements.

7. Explain how continuing expenditures for operational assets affect financial statements.

8. Explain how expense recognition for natural resources (depletion) affects financial statements.

9. Explain how expense recognition for intangible assets (amortization) affects financial statements.

10. Understand how expense recognition choices and industry characteristics affect financial performance measures.

The Curious Accountant

In the normal course of operations, most companies acquire long-term assets each year. The way in which a company hopes to make money with these assets varies according to the type of business and the asset acquired. During 2005, Weyerhaeuser Company made cash acquisitions of property and equipment of $861 million and paid $96 million of cash to acquire and reforest timberlands.

In Chapter 3 you learned the basics of accounting for equipment, such as trucks. Can you think of how Weyerhaeuser's use of trees to produce revenue differs from its use of trucks? Do you think the procedures used to account for timber should be similar to or different from those used to account for trucks, and if so, how? (Answers on page 447.)

CHAPTER OPENING

Companies use assets to produce revenue. Some assets, like inventory or office supplies, are called **current assets** *because they are used relatively quickly (within a single accounting period). Other assets, like equipment or buildings, are used for extended periods of time (two or more accounting periods). These assets are called* **long-term operational assets.** *Accounting for long-term assets raises several interesting questions. For example, what is the cost of the asset? Is it the list price only or should the cost of transportation, transit insurance, set up, and so on be added to the list price? Should the cost of a long-term asset be recognized as expense in the period the asset is purchased or should the cost be expensed over the useful life of the asset? What happens to the accounting records when a long-term asset is retired from use? This chapter answers these questions. It explains the accounting treatment for long-term operational assets from the date of purchase through the date of disposal.* ■

Tangible Versus Intangible Assets

Identify different types of
long-term operational assets.

Topic Tackler

§PLUS

9-1

Video 9.1

Long-term assets may be tangible or intangible. **Tangible assets** have a physical presence; they can be seen and touched. Tangible assets include equipment, machinery, natural resources, and land. In contrast, intangible assets have no physical form. While they may be represented by physical documents, **intangible assets** are, in fact, rights or privileges. They cannot be seen or touched. For example, a **patent** represents an exclusive legal *privilege* to produce and sell a particular product. It protects inventors by making it illegal for others to profit by copying their inventions. While a patent may be represented by legal documents, the privilege is the actual asset. Since the privilege cannot be seen or touched, the patent is an intangible asset.

Tangible Long-Term Assets

Tangible long-term assets are classified as (1) property, plant, and equipment; (2) natural resources; or (3) land.

Property, Plant, and Equipment

Property, plant, and equipment is sometimes called *plant assets* or *fixed assets.* Examples of property, plant, and equipment include furniture, cash registers, machinery, delivery trucks, computers, mechanical robots, and buildings. The level of detail used to account for these assets varies. One company may include all office equipment in one account, whereas another company might divide office equipment into computers, desks, chairs, and so on. The term used to recognize expense for property, plant, and equipment is **depreciation.**

Natural Resources

Mineral deposits, oil and gas reserves, timber stands, coal mines, and stone quarries are examples of **natural resources.** Conceptually, natural resources are inventories. When sold, the cost of these assets is frequently expensed as *cost of goods sold.* While inventories are usually classified as short-term assets, natural resources are normally classified as long term because the resource deposits generally have long lives. For example, it may take decades to extract all of the diamonds from a diamond mine. The term used to recognize expense for natural resources is **depletion.**

Land

Land is classified separately from other property because land is not subject to depreciation or depletion. Land has an infinite life. In other words, land is not worn out or consumed as it is used. When buildings or natural resources are purchased simultaneously with land, the amount paid must be divided between the land and the other assets because of the nondepreciable nature of the land.

Intangible Assets

Intangible assets fall into two categories, those with *identifiable useful lives* and those with *indefinite useful lives.*

Intangible Assets with Identifiable Useful Lives

Intangible assets with identifiable useful lives include patents and copyrights. These assets may become obsolete (a patent may become worthless if new technology provides a superior product) or may reach the end of their legal lives. The term used when recognizing expense for intangible assets with identifiable useful lives is called **amortization.**

Intangible Assets with Indefinite Useful Lives

The benefits of some intangible assets may extend so far into the future that their useful lives cannot be estimated. For how many years will the Coca-Cola trademark attract customers? When will the value of a McDonald's franchise end? There are no answers to these questions. Intangible assets such as renewable franchises, trademarks, and goodwill have indefinite useful lives. The costs of such assets are not expensed unless the value of the assets becomes impaired.

Determining the Cost of Long-Term Assets

The **historical cost concept** requires that an asset be recorded at the amount paid for it. This amount includes the purchase price plus any costs necessary to get the asset in the location and condition for its intended use. Common examples are:

Determine the cost of long-term operational assets.

Buildings: (1) purchase price, (2) sales taxes, (3) title search and transfer document costs, (4) realtor's and attorney's fees, and (5) remodeling costs.

Land: (1) purchase price, (2) sales taxes, (3) title search and transfer document costs, (4) realtor's and attorney's fees, (5) costs for removal of old buildings, and (6) grading costs.

Equipment: (1) purchase price (less discounts), (2) sales taxes, (3) delivery costs, (4) installation costs, and (5) costs to adapt for intended use.

The cost of an asset does not include payments for fines, damages, and so on that could have been avoided.

CHECK YOURSELF 9.1

Sheridan Construction Company purchased a new bulldozer that had a $260,000 list price. The seller agreed to allow a 4 percent cash discount in exchange for immediate payment. The bulldozer was delivered FOB shipping point at a cost of $1,200. Sheridan hired a new employee to operate the dozer for an annual salary of $36,000. The employee was trained to operate the dozer for a one-time training fee of $800. The cost of the company's theft insurance policy increased by $300 per year as a result of adding the dozer to the policy. The dozer had a five-year useful life and an expected salvage value of $26,000. Determine the asset's cost.

Answer

List price	$260,000
Less: Cash discount ($260,000 × 0.04)	(10,400)
Shipping cost	1,200
Training cost	800
Total asset cost (amount capitalized)	$251,600

Basket Purchase Allocation

Acquiring a group of assets in a single transaction is known as a **basket purchase.** The total price of a basket purchase must be allocated among the assets acquired. Accountants commonly allocate the purchase price using the **relative fair market value method.** To illustrate, assume that Beatty Company purchased land and a building for $240,000 cash. A real estate appraiser determined the fair market value of each asset to be:

Building	$270,000
Land	90,000
Total	$360,000

The appraisal indicates that the land is worth 25 percent ($90,000 ÷ $360,000) of the total value and the building is worth 75 percent ($270,000 ÷ $360,000). Using these percentages, the actual purchase price is allocated as follows:

Building	0.75 × $240,000 =	$180,000
Land	0.25 × $240,000 =	60,000
Total		$240,000

Life Cycle of Operational Assets

LO 3

Explain how different depreciation methods affect financial statements.

The life cycle of an operational asset involves (1) acquiring the funds to buy the asset, (2) purchasing the asset, (3) using the asset, and finally, (4) retiring (disposing of) the asset. The revenue generated from using the asset plus the funds acquired from its disposal should be sufficient to replace the asset and to provide a reasonable profit. Exhibit 9.1 depicts the life cycle of an operational asset.

Methods of Recognizing Depreciation Expense

Topic Tackler

PLUS

9-2

The method used to recognize depreciation expense should match the asset's usage pattern. More expense should be recognized in periods when the asset is used more and less in periods when the asset is used less. Since assets are used to produce revenue, matching expense recognition with asset usage also matches expense recognition with revenue recognition. Three alternative methods for recognizing depreciation expense are (1) straight-line, (2) double-declining-balance, and (3) units-of-production.

The **straight-line** method produces the same amount of depreciation each accounting period. **Double-declining-balance,** an accelerated method, produces more depreciation expense in the early years of an asset's life, with a declining amount of expense in later years. **Units-of-production** produces varying amounts of depreciation in different accounting periods (more in some accounting periods and less in others). Exhibit 9.2 contrasts the different depreciation methods that U.S. companies use.

To illustrate the different depreciation methods, consider the accounting treatment for a van purchased by Dryden Enterprises. Dryden plans to use the van as rental property. The

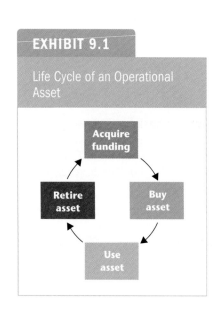

EXHIBIT 9.1

Life Cycle of an Operational Asset

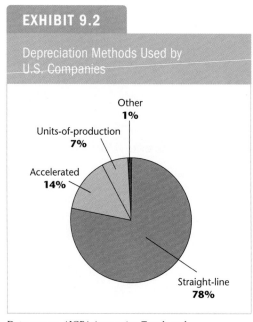

EXHIBIT 9.2

Depreciation Methods Used by U.S. Companies

Data source: *AICPA Accounting Trends and Techniques*, 2006.

Answers to The Curious Accountant

Equipment is a long-term asset used for the purpose of producing revenue. The portion of the equipment used each accounting period is recognized as depreciation expense. Accordingly, the expense recognition for the cost of equipment is spread over the useful life of the asset. Timber, however, is not used until the trees are grown. Conceptually, the cost of the trees should be treated as inventories and expensed as cost of goods sold at the time the products made from trees are sold. Even so, some timber companies recognize a periodic charge called *depletion* in a manner similar to that used for depreciation.

Accounting for unusual long-term assets such as timber requires an understanding of specialized "industry practice" accounting rules that are beyond the scope of this course. Be aware that many industries have unique accounting problems, and business managers in such industries must make the effort to understand specialized accounting rules that relate to their companies.

van had a list price of $23,500. Dryden obtained a 10 percent cash discount from the dealer. The van was delivered FOB shipping point, and Dryden paid an additional $250 for transportation costs. Dryden also paid $2,600 for a custom accessory package to increase the van's appeal as a rental vehicle. The cost of the van is computed as follows:

List price	$23,500	
Less: Cash discount	(2,350)	$23,500 × 0.10
Plus: Transportation costs	250	
Plus: Cost of customization	2,600	
Total	$24,000	

The van has an estimated **salvage value** of $4,000 and an **estimated useful life** of four years. The following section examines three different patterns of expense recognition for this van.

Straight-Line Depreciation

The first scenario assumes the van was used evenly over its four-year life. Specifically, the revenue from renting the van is assumed to be $8,000 per year. The matching concept calls for the expense recognition pattern to match the revenue stream. Since the same amount of revenue is recognized in each accounting period, Dryden should use straight-line depreciation because it recognizes equal amounts of depreciation expense each year.

Life Cycle Phase 1

The first phase of the asset life cycle is to acquire funds to purchase the asset. Assume Dryden acquired $25,000 cash on January 1, 2008, by issuing common stock. The effect of this stock issue on the financial statements follows:

Assets				=	Equity			Rev.	−	Exp.	=	Net Inc.	Cash Flow
Cash	+	Van	− Acc. Dep.	=	Com. Stk.	+	Ret. Earn.						
25,000	+	NA	− NA	=	25,000	+	NA	NA	−	NA	=	NA	25,000 FA

Exhibit 9.3 displays financial statements for the life of the asset. The $25,000 cash inflow from the stock issue appears in the financing activities section of the 2008 statement of cash flows. Also, the balance sheet shows a $25,000 balance in Common Stock. The Cash account does not have a $25,000 balance because it is affected by other events in addition to the stock issue. For example, Dryden used cash to buy the asset and Dryden collected cash from rent revenue.

EXHIBIT 9.3	Financial Statements under Straight-Line Depreciation

DRYDEN ENTERPRISES
Financial Statements

	2008	2009	2010	2011	2012
Income Statements					
Rent revenue	$ 8,000	$ 8,000	$ 8,000	$ 8,000	$ 0
Depreciation expense	(5,000)	(5,000)	(5,000)	(5,000)	0
Operating income	3,000	3,000	3,000	3,000	0
Gain on sale of van	0	0	0	0	500
Net income	$ 3,000	$ 3,000	$ 3,000	$ 3,000	$ 500
Balance Sheets					
Assets					
Cash	$ 9,000	$17,000	$25,000	$33,000	$37,500
Van	24,000	24,000	24,000	24,000	0
Accumulated depreciation	(5,000)	(10,000)	(15,000)	(20,000)	0
Total assets	$28,000	$31,000	$34,000	$37,000	$37,500
Stockholders' equity					
Common stock	$25,000	$25,000	$25,000	$25,000	$25,000
Retained earnings	3,000	6,000	9,000	12,000	12,500
Total stockholders' equity	$28,000	$31,000	$34,000	$37,000	$37,500
Statements of Cash Flows					
Operating Activities					
Inflow from customers	$ 8,000	$ 8,000	$ 8,000	$ 8,000	$ 0
Investing Activities					
Outflow to purchase van	(24,000)				
Inflow from sale of van					4,500
Financing Activities					
Inflow from stock issue	25,000				
Net Change in Cash	9,000	8,000	8,000	8,000	4,500
Beginning cash balance	0	9,000	17,000	25,000	33,000
Ending cash balance	$ 9,000	$17,000	$25,000	$33,000	$37,500

Life Cycle Phase 2

The second phase of the life cycle is to purchase the van. The cost of the van, previously computed, was $24,000 cash. The effect of the investment on the financial statements follows:

Assets				=	Equity			Rev.	−	Exp.	=	Net Inc.	Cash Flow
Cash	+	Van	− Acc. Dep.	=	Com. Stk.	+	Ret. Earn.						
(24,000)	+	24,000	− NA	=	NA	+	NA	NA	−	NA	=	NA	(24,000) IA

Trace the effects of this event to the financial statements in Exhibit 9.3. The cash outflow occurs only in 2008 (see the investing activities section of the statement of cash flows). However, the $24,000 cost of the asset is reported on the balance sheet throughout the van's entire life cycle (2008–2011). The historical cost is removed from the asset account when the van is retired in 2012.

Life Cycle Phase 3

Using the asset generates $8,000 revenue per year. Depreciation expense calculated on a straight-line basis is determined as follows:

$$(\text{Asset cost} - \text{Salvage value}) \div \text{Useful life} = \text{Depreciation expense}$$

$$(\$24{,}000 - \$4{,}000) \div 4 \text{ years} = \$5{,}000 \text{ per year.}$$

Recognizing the depreciation expense is an asset use transaction that reduces assets and equity. The reduction in assets is reported using a **contra asset account** called **Accumulated Depreciation.** These effects are shown in the following statements model. Although illustrated only once, these effects actually would occur four times—once for each year the asset is in use.

Assets				=	Equity			Rev.	−	Exp.	=	Net Inc.	Cash Flow
Cash	+	Van	− Acc. Dep.	=	Com. Stk.	+	Ret. Earn.						
8,000	+	NA	− NA	=	NA	+	8,000	8,000	−	NA	=	8,000	8,000 OA
NA	+	NA	− 5,000	=	NA	+	(5,000)	NA	−	5,000	=	(5,000)	NA

As shown in Exhibit 9.3, the same amount of depreciation expense ($5,000) is recognized on the income statement each year throughout the life cycle (2008–2011). The accumulated depreciation is reported on the balance sheet, increasing from $5,000 to $10,000 to $15,000 and finally to $20,000 between 2008 and 2011. Trace these effects to the financial statements.

Recognizing depreciation expense does not affect cash flow. The entire cash outflow for this asset occurred in 2008 when it was purchased. Depreciation reflects using plant assets rather than spending cash to purchase them.

Life Cycle Phase 4

The final stage in the life cycle of an operational asset is its retirement and removal from the company's records. Dryden retired the van from service on January 1, 2012, selling it for $4,500 cash. The van's book value when it was sold was $4,000 ($24,000 cost − $20,000 accumulated depreciation), so Dryden recognized a $500 gain ($4,500 − $4,000) on the sale. The effects of the retirement on the financial statements are shown here:

Determine how gains and losses on disposals of long-term operational assets affect financial statements.

Assets				=	Equity			Rev. or Gain	−	Exp. or Loss	=	Net Inc.	Cash Flow
Cash	+	Van	− Acc. Dep.	=	Com. Stk.	+	Ret. Earn.						
4,500	+	(24,000)	− (20,000)	=	NA	+	500	500	−	NA	=	500	4,500 IA

Although the gain reported on the 2012 income statement is $500, the cash inflow from selling the van is $4,500. Gains and losses are not reported separately on the statement of cash flows. Instead they are included in the total amount of cash collected from the sale of the asset. In this case, the entire $4,500 is shown in the cash flow from investing activities section of the 2012 statement of cash flows.

Tracing the effects of these events to the financial statements in Exhibit 9.3 illustrates how businesses recover their invested funds. The total cash inflow from using and retiring the van is $36,500 ([$8,000 revenue × 4 years] + $4,500 actual salvage value). Dryden not only recovered the cost of the asset ($24,000) but also generated a $12,500 ($36,500 − $24,000) return on its investment. This is consistent with the total amount of net income that was earned over the life cycle ([$3,000 × 4 years] + $500 gain). The difference between net income and cash flow is a matter of timing.

Finally, note that the amount of retained earnings shown on the 2012 balance sheet is also $12,500. Since the amount of retained earnings equals the sum of the amounts of net income reported on the 2008 through 2012 income statements, we conclude that Dryden paid no dividends to its stockholders.

EXHIBIT 9.4

General Journal Entries

Account Title	Debit	Credit
Cash	25,000	
Common Stock		25,000
Entry on January 1, 2008, to record capital acquisition		
Van	24,000	
Cash		24,000
Entry on January 1, 2008, to record investment in van		
Cash	8,000	
Rent Revenue		8,000
Revenue recognition entries on December 31, 2008–2011		
Depreciation Expense	5,000	
Accumulated Depreciation		5,000
Expense recognition entries on December 31, 2008–2011		
Cash	4,500	
Accumulated Depreciation	20,000	
Van		24,000
Gain on Sale of Van		500
Entry on January 1, 2012, to record asset disposal		

Recording Procedures

Exhibit 9.4 displays the general journal entries to record the transactions over the life cycle of the van.

Double-Declining-Balance Depreciation

LO 3

Explain how different depreciation methods affect financial statements.

For the second scenario, assume demand for the van is strong when it is new, but fewer people rent the van as it ages. As a result, the van produces smaller amounts of revenue as time goes by. To match expenses with revenues, it is reasonable to recognize more depreciation expense in the van's early years and less as it ages.

Double-declining-balance depreciation produces a large amount of depreciation in the first year of an asset's life and progressively smaller levels of expense in each succeeding year. Since the double-declining-balance method recognizes depreciation expense more rapidly than the straight-line method does, it is called an **accelerated depreciation method.** Depreciation expense recognized using double-declining-balance is computed in three steps.

1. *Determine the straight-line rate.* Divide one by the asset's useful life. Since the estimated useful life of Dryden's van is four years, the straight-line rate is 25 percent (1 ÷ 4) per year.

2. *Determine the double-declining-balance rate.* Multiply the straight-line rate by 2 (*double* the rate). The double-declining-balance rate for the van is 50 percent (25 percent × 2).

3. *Determine the depreciation expense.* Multiply the double-declining-balance rate by the book value of the asset *at the beginning of the period* (recall that **book value** is historical cost minus *accumulated depreciation*). The following table shows the amount of depreciation expense Dryden will recognize over the van's useful life (2008–2011).

Year	Book Value at Beginning of Period	×	Double the Straight-Line Rate	=	Annual Depreciation Expense	
2008	($24,000 − $ 0)	×	0.50	=	$12,000	
2009	(24,000 − 12,000)	×	0.50	=	6,000	
2010	(24,000 − 18,000)	×	0.50	=	~~3,000~~	2,000
2011	(24,000 − 20,000)	×	0.50	=	~~2,000~~	0

Regardless of the depreciation method used, *an asset cannot be depreciated below its salvage value.* This restriction affects depreciation computations for the third and fourth years. Because the van had a cost of $24,000 and a salvage value of $4,000, the total amount of **depreciable cost** (historical cost − salvage value) is $20,000 ($24,000 − $4,000). Since $18,000 ($12,000 + $6,000) of the depreciable cost is recognized in the first two years, only $2,000 ($20,000 − $18,000) remains to be recognized after the second year. Depreciation expense recognized in the third year is therefore $2,000 even though double-declining-balance computations suggest that $3,000 should be recognized. Similarly, zero depreciation expense is recognized in the fourth year even though the computations indicate a $2,000 charge.

Effects on the Financial Statements

Exhibit 9.5 displays financial statements for the life of the asset assuming Dryden uses double-declining-balance depreciation. The illustration assumes a cash revenue stream of

EXHIBIT 9.5	Financial Statements under Double-Declining-Balance Depreciation				

DRYDEN ENTERPRISES
Financial Statements

	2008	2009	2010	2011	2012
Income Statements					
Rent revenue	$15,000	$ 9,000	$ 5,000	$ 3,000	$ 0
Depreciation expense	(12,000)	(6,000)	(2,000)	0	0
Operating income	3,000	3,000	3,000	3,000	0
Gain on sale of van	0	0	0	0	500
Net income	$ 3,000	$ 3,000	$ 3,000	$ 3,000	$ 500
Balance Sheets					
Assets					
Cash	$16,000	$25,000	$30,000	$33,000	$37,500
Van	24,000	24,000	24,000	24,000	0
Accumulated depreciation	(12,000)	(18,000)	(20,000)	(20,000)	0
Total assets	$28,000	$31,000	$34,000	$37,000	$37,500
Stockholders' equity					
Common stock	$25,000	$25,000	$25,000	$25,000	$25,000
Retained earnings	3,000	6,000	9,000	12,000	12,500
Total stockholders' equity	$28,000	$31,000	$34,000	$37,000	$37,500
Statements of Cash Flows					
Operating Activities					
Inflow from customers	$15,000	$ 9,000	$ 5,000	$ 3,000	$ 0
Investing Activities					
Outflow to purchase van	(24,000)				
Inflow from sale of van					4,500
Financing Activities					
Inflow from stock issue	25,000				
Net Change in Cash	16,000	9,000	5,000	3,000	4,500
Beginning cash balance	0	16,000	25,000	30,000	33,000
Ending cash balance	$16,000	$25,000	$30,000	$33,000	$37,500

$15,000, $9,000, $5,000, and $3,000 for the years 2008, 2009, 2010, and 2011, respectively. Trace the depreciation expense from the table above to the income statements. Reported depreciation expense is greater in the earlier years and smaller in the later years of the asset's life.

The double-declining-balance method smoothes the amount of net income reported over the asset's useful life. In the early years, when heavy asset use produces higher revenue, depreciation expense is also higher. Similarly, in the later years, lower levels of revenue are matched with lower levels of depreciation expense. Net income is constant at $3,000 per year.

CHECK YOURSELF 9.2

Olds Company purchased an asset that cost $36,000 on January 1, 2008. The asset had an expected useful life of five years and an estimated salvage value of $5,000. Assuming Olds uses the double-declining-balance method, determine the amount of depreciation expense and the amount of accumulated depreciation Olds would report on the 2010 financial statements.

Answer

Year	Book Value at the Beginning of the Period	×	Double the Straight-Line Rate*	=	Annual Depreciation Expense
2008	($36,000 − $ 0)	×	0.40	=	$14,400
2009	(36,000 − 14,400)	×	0.40	=	8,640
2010	(36,000 − 23,040)	×	0.40	=	5,184
Total accumulated depreciation at December 31, 2010					$28,224

*Double-declining-balance rate = 2 × Straight-line rate = 2 × (1 ÷ 5 years) = 0.40

The depreciation method a company uses *does not* affect how it acquires the financing, invests the funds, and retires the asset. For Dryden's van, the accounting effects of these life cycle phases are the same as under the straight-line approach. Similarly, the *recording procedures* are not affected by the depreciation method. Different depreciation methods affect only the amounts of depreciation expense recorded each year, not which accounts are used. The general journal entries are therefore not illustrated for the double-declining-balance or the units-of-production depreciation methods.

Units-of-Production Depreciation

Explain how different depreciation methods affect financial statements.

Suppose rental demand for Dryden's van depends on general economic conditions. In a robust economy, travel increases, and demand for renting vans is high. In a stagnant economy, demand for van rentals declines. In such circumstances, revenues fluctuate from year to year. To accomplish the matching objective, depreciation should also fluctuate from year to year. A method of depreciation known as units-of-production accomplishes this goal by basing depreciation expense on actual asset usage.

Computing depreciation expense using units-of-production begins with identifying a measure of the asset's productive capacity. For example, the number of miles Dryden expects its van to be driven may be a reasonable measure of its productive capacity. If the depreciable asset were a saw, an appropriate measure of productive capacity could be the number of board feet the saw was expected to cut during its useful life. In other words, the basis for measuring production depends on the nature of the depreciable asset.

To illustrate computing depreciation using the units-of-production depreciation method, assume that Dryden measures productive capacity based on the total number of miles the van will be driven over its useful life. Assume Dryden estimates this productive capacity to be 100,000 miles. The first step in determining depreciation expense is to compute the cost per unit of production. For Dryden's van, this amount is total depreciable cost (historical cost − salvage value) divided by total units of expected productive capacity (100,000 miles). The depreciation cost per mile is therefore $0.20 ([$24,000 cost − $4,000 salvage] ÷ 100,000 miles). Annual depreciation expense is computed by multiplying the depreciable cost per mile by the number of miles driven. Odometer readings indicate the van was driven 40,000 miles, 20,000 miles, 30,000 miles, and 15,000 miles in 2008, 2009, 2010, and 2011, respectively. Dryden developed the following schedule of depreciation charges.

Year	Cost per Mile (a)	Miles Driven (b)	Depreciation Expense (a × b)
2008	$0.20	40,000	$8,000
2009	0.20	20,000	4,000
2010	0.20	30,000	6,000
2011	0.20	15,000	~~3,000~~ 2,000

As pointed out in the discussion of the double-declining-balance method, an asset cannot be depreciated below its salvage value. Since $18,000 of the $20,000 ($24,000 cost − $4,000 salvage) depreciable cost is recognized in the first three years of using the van, only $2,000 ($20,000 − $18,000) remains to be charged to depreciation in the fourth year, even though the depreciation computations suggest the charge should be $3,000. As the preceding table indicates, the general formula for computing units-of-production depreciation is:

$$\frac{\text{Cost} - \text{Salvage value}}{\text{Total estimated units of production}} \times \frac{\text{Units of production in current accounting period}}{} = \frac{\text{Annual depreciation expense}}{}$$

Exhibit 9.6 displays financial statements that assume Dryden uses units-of-production depreciation. The exhibit assumes a cash revenue stream of $11,000, $7,000, $9,000, and $5,000 for 2008, 2009, 2010, and 2011, respectively. Trace the depreciation expense from the schedule above to the income statements. Depreciation expense is greater in years the van is driven more and smaller in years the van is driven less, providing a reasonable matching of depreciation expense with revenue produced. Net income is again constant at $3,000 per year.

Comparing the Depreciation Methods

The total amount of depreciation expense Dryden recognized using each of the three methods was $20,000 ($24,000 cost − $4,000 salvage value). The different methods affect the *timing,* but not the *total amount,* of expense recognized. The different methods simply assign the $20,000 to different accounting periods. Exhibit 9.7 presents graphically the differences among the three depreciation methods discussed above. A company should use the method that most closely matches expenses with revenues.

Explain how different depreciation methods affect financial statements.

| EXHIBIT 9.6 | Financial Statements under Units-of-Production Depreciation |

DRYDEN ENTERPRISES
Financial Statements

	2008	2009	2010	2011	2012
Income Statements					
Rent revenue	$11,000	$ 7,000	$ 9,000	$ 5,000	$ 0
Depreciation expense	(8,000)	(4,000)	(6,000)	(2,000)	0
Operating income	3,000	3,000	3,000	3,000	0
Gain on sale of van	0	0	0	0	500
Net income	$ 3,000	$ 3,000	$ 3,000	$ 3,000	$ 500
Balance Sheets					
Assets					
Cash	$12,000	$19,000	$28,000	$33,000	$37,500
Van	24,000	24,000	24,000	24,000	0
Accumulated depreciation	(8,000)	(12,000)	(18,000)	(20,000)	0
Total assets	$28,000	$31,000	$34,000	$37,000	$37,500
Stockholders' equity					
Common stock	$25,000	$25,000	$25,000	$25,000	$25,000
Retained earnings	3,000	6,000	9,000	12,000	12,500
Total stockholders' equity	$28,000	$31,000	$34,000	$37,000	$37,500
Statements of Cash Flows					
Operating Activities					
Inflow from customers	$11,000	$ 7,000	$ 9,000	$ 5,000	$ 0
Investing Activities					
Outflow to purchase van	(24,000)				
Inflow from sale of van					4,500
Financing Activities					
Inflow from stock issue	25,000				
Net Change in Cash	12,000	7,000	9,000	5,000	4,500
Beginning cash balance	0	12,000	19,000	28,000	33,000
Ending cash balance	$12,000	$19,000	$28,000	$33,000	$37,500

| EXHIBIT 9.7 | Depreciation Expense under Different Depreciation Methods |

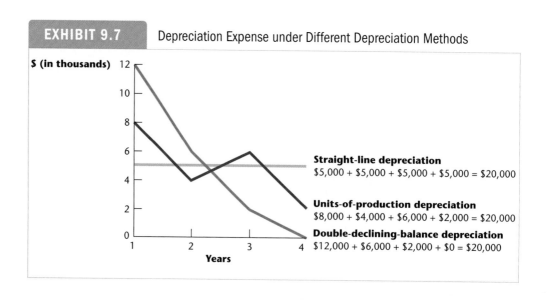

Straight-line depreciation
$5,000 + $5,000 + $5,000 + $5,000 = $20,000

Units-of-production depreciation
$8,000 + $4,000 + $6,000 + $2,000 = $20,000

Double-declining-balance depreciation
$12,000 + $6,000 + $2,000 + $0 = $20,000

Income Tax Considerations

The matching principle is not relevant to income tax reporting. The objective of tax reporting is to minimize tax expense. For tax purposes the most desirable depreciation method is the one that produces the highest amount of depreciation expense. Higher expenses mean lower taxes.

LO 5

Identify some of the tax issues which affect long-term operational assets.

The maximum depreciation currently allowed by tax law is computed using an accelerated depreciation method known as the **modified accelerated cost recovery system (MACRS).** MACRS specifies the useful life for designated categories of assets. For example, under the tax law, companies must base depreciation computations for automobiles, light trucks, technological equipment, and other similar asset types on a 5-year useful life. In contrast, a 7-year life must be used for office furniture, fixtures, and many types of conventional machinery. The law classifies depreciable property, excluding real estate, into one of six categories: 3-year property, 5-year property, 7-year property, 10-year property, 15-year property, and 20-year property. Tables have been established for each category that specify the percentage of cost that can be expensed (deducted) in determining the amount of taxable income. A MACRS tax table for 5- and 7-year property is shown here as an example.

Year	5-Year Property, %	7-Year Property, %
1	20.00	14.29
2	32.00	24.49
3	19.20	17.49
4	11.52	12.49
5	11.52	8.93
6	5.76	8.92
7		8.93
8		4.46

The amount of depreciation a company can deduct each year for tax purposes is determined by multiplying the cost of a depreciable asset by the percentage shown in the table. For example, the depreciation expense for year 1 of a 7-year property asset is the cost of the property multiplied by 14.29 percent. Depreciation for year 2 is the cost multiplied by 24.49 percent.

The tables present some apparent inconsistencies. For example, if MACRS is an accelerated depreciation method, why is less depreciation permitted in year 1 than in years 2 and 3? Also, why is depreciation computed in year 6 for property with a 5-year life and in year 8 for property with a 7-year life? In fact, these conditions are the consequence of using the **half-year convention.**

The half-year convention is designed to simplify computing taxable income. Instead of requiring taxpayers to calculate depreciation from the exact date of purchase to the exact date of disposal, the tax code requires one-half year's depreciation to be charged in the year in which an asset is acquired and one-half year's depreciation in the year of disposal. As a result, the percentages shown in the table for the first and last years represent depreciation for one-half year instead of the actual time of usage.

To illustrate computing depreciation using MACRS, assume that Wilson Company purchased furniture (7-year property) for $10,000 cash on July 21. Tax depreciation charges over the useful life of the asset are computed as shown:

Year	Table Factor, % ×	Cost =	Depreciation Amount
1	14.29	$10,000	$ 1,429
2	24.49	10,000	2,449
3	17.49	10,000	1,749
4	12.49	10,000	1,249
5	8.93	10,000	893
6	8.92	10,000	892
7	8.93	10,000	893
8	4.46	10,000	446
Total over recovery period			$10,000

As an alternative to MACRS, the tax code permits using straight-line depreciation. For certain types of assets such as real property (buildings), the tax code requires using straight-line depreciation.

There is no requirement that depreciation methods used for financial reporting be consistent with those used in preparing the income tax return. For example, a company may use straight-line depreciation in its financial statements and MACRS for the tax return. A company making this choice would reduce taxes in the early years of an asset's life because it would report higher depreciation charges on the tax return than in the financial statements. In later years, however, taxes will be higher because under MACRS, the amount of depreciation declines as the asset becomes older. Taxes are delayed but not avoided. The amount of taxes delayed for future payment represent a **deferred tax liability.** Delaying tax payments is advantageous. During the delay period, the money that would have been used to pay taxes can be used instead to make revenue-generating investments.

Revision of Estimates

Show how revising estimates affects financial statements.

In order to report useful financial information on a timely basis, accountants must make many estimates of future results, such as the salvage value and useful life of depreciable assets, bad debts expense, and warranty obligations. Estimates are frequently revised when new information surfaces. Because revisions of estimates are common, generally accepted accounting principles call for incorporating the revised information into present and future calculations. Prior reports are not corrected.

To illustrate, assume that McGraw Company purchased a machine on January 1, 2008, for $50,000. McGraw estimated the machine would have a useful life of eight years and a salvage value of $3,000. Using the straight-line method, McGraw determined the annual depreciation charge as follows:

$$(\$50,000 - \$3,000) \div 8 \text{ years} = \$5,875 \text{ per year}$$

At the beginning of the fifth year, accumulated depreciation on the machine is $23,500 ($5,875 × 4). The machine's book value is $26,500 ($50,000 − $23,500). At this point, what happens if McGraw changes its estimates of useful life or the salvage value? Consider the following revision examples independently of each other.

Revision of Life

Assume McGraw revises the expected life to 14, rather than 8, years. The machine's *remaining* life would then be 10 more years instead of 4 more years. Assume salvage value remains $3,000. Depreciation for each remaining year is:

$$(\$26,500 \text{ book value} - \$3,000 \text{ salvage}) \div 10\text{-year remaining life} = \$2,350$$

Revision of Salvage

Alternatively, assume the original expected life remained eight years, but McGraw revised its estimate of salvage value to $6,000. Depreciation for each of the remaining four years would be

$$(\$26,500 \text{ book value} - \$6,000 \text{ salvage}) \div 4\text{-year remaining life} = \$5,125$$

Note that the revised amounts are determined for the full year, regardless of when McGraw revised its estimates. For example, if McGraw decides to change the estimated useful life on October 1, 2013, the change would be effective as of January 1, 2013. The year-end adjusting entry for depreciation would include a full year's depreciation calculated on the basis of the new estimated useful life.

Continuing Expenditures for Plant Assets

Most plant assets require additional expenditures for maintenance or improvement during their useful lives. Accountants must determine if these expenditures should be expensed or capitalized.

LO 7

Explain how continuing expenditures for operational assets affect financial statements.

Video 9.1

Costs that Are Expensed

The cost of routine maintenance and minor repairs that are incurred to *keep* an asset in good working order are expensed in the period in which they are incurred. With respect to the previous example, assume McGraw spent $500 for routine lubrication and to replace minor parts. The effect of the expenditure on the financial statements and the journal entry necessary to record it follow:

Assets	=	Equity			Rev.	−	Exp.	=	Net Inc.	Cash Flow
Cash	=	Com. Stk.	+	Ret. Earn.						
(500)	=	NA	+	(500)	NA	−	500	=	(500)	(500) OA

Account Title	Debit	Credit
Repairs Expense	500	
Cash		500

Costs that Are Capitalized

Substantial amounts spent to improve the quality or extend the life of an asset are described as **capital expenditures.** Capital expenditures are accounted for in one of two ways, depending on whether the cost incurred *improves the quality* or *extends the life* of the asset.

Improving Quality

If the expenditure improves the quality of the asset, the amount is added to the historical cost of the asset. The additional cost is then expensed through higher depreciation charges over the asset's remaining useful life.

To demonstrate, return to the McGraw Company example. Recall that the machine originally cost $50,000, had an estimated salvage of $3,000, and had a predicted life of eight years. Recall further that accumulated depreciation at the beginning of the fifth year is $23,500 ($5,875 × 4) so the book value is $26,500 ($50,000 − $23,500). Assume McGraw makes a major expenditure of $4,000 in the machine's fifth year to improve its productive capacity. The effect of the $4,000 expenditure on the financial statements and the journal entry necessary to record it follow:

Assets					=	Equity			Rev.	−	Exp.	=	Net Inc.	Cash Flow
Cash	+	Mach.	−	Acc. Dep.	=	Com. Stk.	+	Ret. Earn.						
(4,000)	+	4,000	−	NA	=	NA	+	NA	NA	−	NA	=	NA	(4,000) IA

Account Title	Debit	Credit
Machine	4,000	
Cash		4,000

After recording the expenditure, the machine account balance is $54,000 and the asset's book value is $30,500 ($54,000 − $23,500). The depreciation charges for the remaining four years are:

($30,500 book value − $3,000 salvage) ÷ 4-year remaining life = $6,875

Extending Life

When a company makes a capital expenditure that extends the life of an asset but not its quality, accountants view the expenditure as canceling some of the depreciation previously charged to expense. The event is still an asset exchange; cash decreases, and the book value of the machine increases. However, the increase in the book value of the machine results from reducing the balance in the contra asset account, Accumulated Depreciation.

To illustrate, assume that instead of increasing productive capacity, McGraw's $4,000 expenditure had extended the useful life of the machine by two years. The effect of the expenditure on the financial statements and the journal entry necessary to record it follow:

Assets				=	Equity			Rev.	−	Exp.	=	Net Inc.	Cash Flow
Cash	+	Mach.	−	Acc. Dep.	=	Com. Stk.	+	Ret. Earn.					
(4,000)	+	NA	−	(4,000)	=	NA	+	NA	NA	−	NA	=	NA	(4,000) IA

Account Title	Debit	Credit
Accumulated Depreciation—Machine	4,000	
Cash		4,000

After the expenditure is recorded, the book value is the same as if the $4,000 had been added to the Machine account ($50,000 cost − $19,500 adjusted balance in Accumulated Depreciation = $30,500). Depreciation expense for each of the remaining six years follows:

($30,500 book value − $3,000 salvage) ÷ 6-year remaining life = $4,583

CHECK YOURSELF 9.3

On January 1, 2008, Dager, Inc., purchased an asset that cost $18,000. It had a five-year useful life and a $3,000 salvage value. Dager uses straight-line depreciation. On January 1, 2010, it incurred a $1,200 cost related to the asset. With respect to this asset, determine the amount of expense and accumulated depreciation Dager would report in the 2010 financial statements under each of the following assumptions.

1. The $1,200 cost was incurred to repair damage resulting from an accident.
2. The $1,200 cost improved the operating capacity of the equipment. The total useful life and salvage value remained unchanged.
3. The $1,200 cost extended the useful life of the asset by one year. The salvage value remained unchanged.

Answer

1. Dager would report the $1,200 repair cost as an expense. Dager would also report depreciation expense of $3,000 ([$18,000 − $3,000] ÷ 5). Total expenses related to this asset in 2010 would be $4,200 ($1,200 repair expense + $3,000 depreciation expense). Accumulated depreciation at the end of 2010 would be $9,000 ($3,000 depreciation expense × 3 years).
2. The $1,200 cost would be capitalized in the asset account, increasing both the book value of the asset and the annual depreciation expense.

continued

	After Effects of Capital Improvement
Amount in asset account ($18,000 + $1,200)	$19,200
Less: Salvage value	(3,000)
Accumulated depreciation on January 1, 2010	(6,000)
Remaining depreciable cost before recording 2010 depreciation	$10,200
Depreciation for 2010 ($10,200 ÷ 3 years)	$ 3,400
Accumulated depreciation at December 31, 2010 ($6,000 + $3,400)	$ 9,400

3. The $1,200 cost would be subtracted from the Accumulated Depreciation account, increasing the book value of the asset. The remaining useful life would increase to four years, which would decrease the depreciation expense.

	After Effects of Capital Improvement
Amount in asset account	$18,000
Less: Salvage value	(3,000)
Accumulated depreciation on January 1, 2010 ($6,000 − $1,200)	(4,800)
Remaining depreciable cost before recording 2010 depreciation	$10,200
Depreciation for 2010 ($10,200 ÷ 4 years)	$ 2,550
Accumulated depreciation at December 31, 2010 ($4,800 + $2,550)	$ 7,350

Natural Resources

The cost of natural resources includes not only the purchase price but also related items such as the cost of exploration, geographic surveys, and estimates. The process of expensing natural resources is commonly called *depletion*.[1] The most common method used to calculate depletion is units-of-production.

Explain how expense recognition for natural resources (depletion) affects financial statements.

To illustrate, assume Apex Coal Mining paid $4,000,000 cash to purchase a mine with an estimated 16,000,000 tons of coal. The unit depletion charge is:

$$\$4,000,000 \div 16,000,000 \text{ tons} = \$0.25 \text{ per ton}$$

If Apex mines 360,000 tons of coal in the first year, the depletion charge is:

$$360,000 \text{ tons} \times \$0.25 \text{ per ton} = \$90,000$$

The depletion of a natural resource has the same effect on the accounting equation as other expense recognition events. Assets (in this case, a *coal mine*) and stockholders' equity decrease. The depletion expense reduces net income. The effect on the financial statements and the journal entries necessary to record the acquisition and depletion of the coal mine follow:

Assets			=	Equity			Rev.	−	Exp.	=	Net Inc.	Cash Flow
Cash	+	Coal Mine	=	Com. Stk.	+	Ret. Earn.						
(4,000,000)	+	4,000,000	=	NA	+	NA	NA	−	NA	=	NA	(4,000,000) IA
NA	+	(90,000)	=	NA	+	(90,000)	NA	−	90,000	=	(90,000)	NA

---

[1]In practice, the depletion charge is considered a product cost and allocated between inventory and cost of goods sold. This text uses the simplifying assumption that all resources are sold in the same accounting period in which they are extracted. The full depletion charge is therefore expensed in the period in which the resources are extracted.

Account Title	Debit	Credit
Coal Mine	4,000,000	
Cash		4,000,000
Depletion Expense	90,000	
Coal Mine		90,000

Intangible Assets

LO 9

Explain how expense recognition for intangible assets (amortization) affects financial statements.

Intangible assets provide rights, privileges, and special opportunities to businesses. Common intangible assets include trademarks, patents, copyrights, franchises, and goodwill. Some of the unique characteristics of these intangible assets are described in the following sections.

Trademarks

A **trademark** is a name or symbol that identifies a company or a product. Familiar trademarks include the Polo emblem, the name Coca-Cola, and the Nike slogan, "Just do it." Trademarks are registered with the federal government and have an indefinite legal lifetime.

The costs incurred to design, purchase or defend a trademark are capitalized in an asset account called Trademarks. Companies want their trademarks to become familiar but also face the risk of a trademark being used as the generic name for a product. To protect a trademark, companies in this predicament spend large sums on legal fees and extensive advertising programs to educate consumers. Well-known trademarks that have been subject to this problem include Coke, Xerox, Kleenex, and Vaseline.

Patents

Video 9.1

A **patent** grants its owner an exclusive legal right to produce and sell a product that has one or more unique features. Patents issued by the U.S. Patent Office have a legal life of 20 years. Companies may obtain patents through purchase, lease, or internal development. The costs capitalized in the Patent account are usually limited to the purchase price and legal fees to obtain and defend the patent. The research and development costs that are incurred to develop patentable products are usually expensed in the period in which they are incurred.

Copyrights

A **copyright** protects writings, musical compositions, works of art, and other intellectual property for the exclusive benefit of the creator or persons assigned the right by the creator. The cost of a copyright includes the purchase price and any legal costs associated with obtaining and defending the copyright. Copyrights granted by the federal government extend for the life of the creator plus 75 years. A radio commercial could legally use a Bach composition as background music; it could not, however, use the theme song from the movie, *The Matrix*, without obtaining permission from the copyright owner. The cost of a copyright is often expensed early because future royalties may be uncertain.

Franchises

Franchises grant exclusive rights to sell products or perform services in certain geographic areas. Franchises may be granted by governments or private businesses. Franchises granted by governments include federal broadcasting licenses. Private business franchises include fast-food restaurant chains and brand labels such as Healthy Choice. The legal and useful lives of a franchise are frequently difficult to determine. Judgment is often crucial to establishing the estimated useful life for franchises.

Goodwill

Goodwill is the value attributable to favorable factors such as reputation, location, and superior products. Consider the most popular restaurant in your town. If the owner sold the restaurant, do you think the purchase price would be simply the total value of the chairs, tables, kitchen equipment, and building? Certainly not, because much of the restaurant's value lies in its popularity; in other words, its ability to generate a high return is based on the goodwill (reputation) of the business.

Calculating goodwill can be very complex; here we present a simple example to illustrate how it is determined. Suppose the accounting records of a restaurant named Bendigo's show:

$$\text{Assets} = \text{Liabilities} + \text{Stockholders' Equity}$$

$$\$200,000 = \$50,000 + \$150,000$$

Assume a buyer agrees to purchase the restaurant by paying the owner $300,000 cash and assuming the existing liabilities. In other words, the restaurant is purchased at a price of $350,000 ($300,000 cash + $50,000 assumed liabilities). Now assume that the assets of the business (tables, chairs, kitchen equipment, etc.) have a fair market value of only $280,000. Why would the buyer pay $350,000 to purchase assets with a market value of $280,000? Obviously, the buyer is purchasing more than just the assets. Indeed, the buyer is purchasing the business's goodwill. The amount of the goodwill is the difference between the purchase price and the fair market value of the assets. In this case, the goodwill is

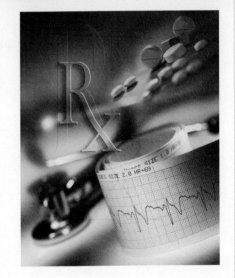

FOCUS ON INTERNATIONAL ISSUES

U.S. GAAP: A COMPETITIVE DISADVANTAGE?

As discussed earlier in this textbook, the diversity of accounting rules is decreasing among industrialized nations. This is due in large part to the fact that so many countries require their publicly listed companies to follow the accounting rules of the International Accounting Standards Board (IASB) and the efforts between the FASB and the IASB to bring their rules into closer agreement. However, there continue to be areas where significant differences exist between the accounting rules for companies in the United States and companies in other countries. Furthermore, in the opinion of the managers of some companies involved in global competition, these differences put U.S. companies at a competitive disadvantage. Accounting for research and development costs (R&D) is a good example of this situation.

Suppose that Microbiotech, Inc., is a pharmaceutical company that spent $10 million in 2009 on R&D of a new drug. If Microbiotech is a U.S. company, it is required to expense the $10 million immediately under U.S. GAAP. However, if Microbiotech is a Japanese company, using Japanese GAAP, it is allowed to capitalize the costs in an asset account and then expense it gradually, through amortization, over the useful life of the asset. As a result, in the year the R&D costs are incurred a U.S. company reports more expense, and less earnings, than its Japanese counterpart.

Some businesspeople believe that U.S. GAAP can put U.S. companies at a competitive disadvantage in the search for capital. Certainly the rules pertaining to R&D demonstrate how Microbiotech, as a U.S. company, may be required to report lower earnings in 2009 than if it had been a Japanese company, even though each company is in the same economic position. South Korea, whose companies present significant competition to U.S. companies, also permits R&D costs to be capitalized.

Keep in mind that well-informed business professionals know how different accounting rules affect a company's financial statements. If they believe that U.S. GAAP cause a company's earnings to be understated, they can take this into consideration when making business decisions.

$70,000 ($350,000 – $280,000). The effects of the purchase on the financial statements of the buyer follow:

Assets					=	Liab.	+	Equity	Rev.	–	Exp.	=	Net Inc.	Cash Flow
Cash	+	Rest. Assets	+	Goodwill										
(300,000)	+	280,000	+	70,000	=	50,000	+	NA	NA	–	NA	=	NA	(300,000) IA

The journal entry to record the purchase of the restaurant is:

Account Title	Debit	Credit
Restaurant Assets	280,000	
Goodwill	70,000	
Cash		300,000
Liabilities		50,000

The fair market value of the restaurant assets represents the historical cost to the new owner. It becomes the basis for future depreciation charges.

Expense Recognition for Intangible Assets

As mentioned earlier, intangible assets fall into two categories, those with *identifiable useful lives* and those with *indefinite useful lives*. Expense recognition for intangible assets depends on which classification applies.

Expensing Intangible Assets with Identifiable Useful Lives

The costs of intangible assets with identifiable useful lives are normally expensed on a straight-line basis using a process called *amortization*. An intangible asset should be amortized over the shorter of two possible time periods: (1) its legal life or (2) its useful life.

To illustrate, assume that Flowers Industries purchased a newly granted patent for $44,000 cash. Although the patent has a legal life of 17 years, Flowers estimates that it will be useful for only 11 years. The annual amortization charge is therefore $4,000 ($44,000 ÷ 11 years). The effect on the financial statements of the patent purchase and first year amortization and the journal entries to record these events follow:

Assets			=	Equity			Rev.	−	Exp.	=	Net Inc.	Cash Flow	
Cash	+	Patent	=	Com. Stk.	+	Ret. Earn.							
(44,000)	+	44,000	=	NA	+	NA	NA	−	NA	=	NA	(44,000)	IA
NA	+	(4,000)	=	NA	+	(4,000)	NA	−	4,000	=	(4,000)	NA	

Account Title	Debit	Credit
Patent	44,000	
Cash		44,000
Amortization Expense, Patent	4,000	
Patent		4,000

Impairment Losses for Intangible Assets with Indefinite Useful Lives

Intangible assets with indefinite useful lives must be tested for impairment annually. The impairment test consists of comparing the fair value of the intangible asset to its carrying value (book value). If the fair value is less than the book value, an impairment loss must be recognized.

To illustrate, return to the example of the Bendigo's restaurant purchase. Recall that the buyer of Bendigo's paid $70,000 for goodwill. Assume the restaurant experiences a significant decline in revenue because many of its former regular customers are dissatisfied with the food prepared by the new chef. Suppose the decline in revenue is so substantial that the new owner believes the Bendigo's name is permanently impaired. The owner decides to hire a different chef and change the name of the restaurant. In this case, the business has suffered a permanent decline in value of goodwill. The company must recognize an impairment loss.

The restaurant's name has lost its value, but the owner believes the location continues to provide the opportunity to produce above-average earnings. Some, but not all, of the goodwill has been lost. Assume the fair value of the remaining goodwill is determined to be $40,000. The impairment loss to recognize is $30,000 ($70,000 − $40,000). The loss reduces the intangible asset (goodwill), stockholder's equity (retained earnings), and net income. The statement of cash flows would not be affected. These effects on the financial statements follow:

Assets	=	Liab.	+	Equity	Rev.	−	Exp./Loss	=	Net Inc.	Cash Flow
Goodwill	=			Ret. Earn.						
(30,000)	=	NA	+	(30,000)	NA	−	30,000	=	(30,000)	NA

The journal entry to recognize the impairment loss is:

Account Title	Debit	Credit
Impairment Loss	30,000	
Goodwill		30,000

Balance Sheet Presentation

This chapter explained accounting for the acquisition, expense recognition, and disposal of a wide range of long-term assets. Exhibit 9.8 illustrates typical balance sheet presentation of many of the assets discussed.

EXHIBIT 9.8

Balance Sheet Presentation of Operational Assets

Balance Sheet			
Long-Term Assets			
Plant and equipment			
Buildings	$4,000,000		
Less: Accumulated depreciation	(2,500,000)	$1,500,000	
Equipment	1,750,000		
Less: Accumulated depreciation	(1,200,000)	550,000	
Total plant and equipment			$2,050,000
Land			850,000
Natural resources			
Mineral deposits (Less: Depletion)		2,100,000	
Oil reserves (Less: Depletion)		890,000	
Total natural resources			2,990,000
Intangibles			
Patents (Less: Amortization)		38,000	
Goodwill		175,000	
Total intangible assets			213,000
Total long-term assets			$6,103,000

THE FINANCIAL ANALYST

LO 10

Understand how expense recognition choices and industry characteristics affect financial performance measures.

Managers may have differing opinions about which allocation method (straight-line, accelerated, or units-of-production) best matches expenses with revenues. As a result, one company may use straight-line depreciation while another company in similar circumstances uses double-declining-balance. Since the allocation method a company uses affects the amount of expense it recognizes, analysts reviewing financial statements must consider the accounting procedures companies use in preparing the statements.

Effect of Judgment and Estimation

Assume that two companies, Alpha and Zeta, experience identical economic events in 2008 and 2009. Both generate revenue of $50,000 and incur cost of goods sold of $30,000 during each year. In 2008, each company pays $20,000 for an asset with an expected useful life of five years and no salvage value. How will the companies' financial statements differ if one uses straight-line depreciation and the other uses the double-declining-balance method? To answer this question, first compute the depreciation expense for both companies for 2008 and 2009.

If Alpha Company uses the straight-line method, depreciation for 2008 and 2009 is:

(Cost − Salvage) ÷ Useful life = Depreciation expense per year

($20,000 − $0) ÷ 5 years = $4,000

In contrast, if Zeta Company uses the double-declining-balance method, Zeta recognizes the following amounts of depreciation expense for 2008 and 2009:

	(Cost − Accumulated Depreciation) × 2 ×		(Straight-Line Rate) =	Depreciation Expense
2008	($20,000 − $0)	×	(2 × [1 ÷ 5]) =	$8,000
2009	($20,000 − $8,000)	×	(2 × [1 ÷ 5]) =	$4,800

Based on these computations, the income statements for the two companies are:

Income Statements				
	2008		2009	
	Alpha Co.	Zeta Co.	Alpha Co.	Zeta Co.
Sales	$50,000	$50,000	$50,000	$50,000
Cost of goods sold	(30,000)	(30,000)	(30,000)	(30,000)
Gross margin	20,000	20,000	20,000	20,000
Depreciation expense	(4,000)	(8,000)	(4,000)	(4,800)
Net income	$16,000	$12,000	$16,000	$15,200

The relevant sections of the balance sheets are:

Plant Assets				
	2008		2009	
	Alpha Co.	Zeta Co.	Alpha Co.	Zeta Co.
Asset	$20,000	$20,000	$20,000	$20,000
Accumulated depreciation	(4,000)	(8,000)	(8,000)	(12,800)
Book value	$16,000	$12,000	$12,000	$ 7,200

The depreciation method is not the only aspect of expense recognition that can vary between companies. Companies may also make different assumptions about the useful lives and salvage values of long-term operational assets. Thus, even if the same depreciation method is used, depreciation expense may still differ.

Since the depreciation method and the underlying assumptions regarding useful life and salvage value affect the determination of depreciation expense, they also affect the amounts of net income, retained earnings, and total assets. Financial statement analysis is affected if it is based on ratios that include these items. Previously defined ratios that are affected include the (1) debt to assets ratio, (2) return on assets ratio, (3) return on equity ratio, and (4) return on sales ratio.

To promote meaningful analysis, public companies are required to disclose all significant accounting policies used to prepare their financial statements. This disclosure is usually provided in the footnotes that accompany the financial statements.

Effect of Industry Characteristics

As indicated in previous chapters, industry characteristics affect financial performance measures. For example, companies in manufacturing industries invest heavily in machinery while insurance companies rely more on human capital. Manufacturing companies therefore have relatively higher depreciation charges than insurance companies. To illustrate how the type of industry affects financial reporting, examine Exhibit 9.9. This exhibit compares the ratio of sales to property, plant, and equipment for two companies in each of three different industries. These data are for 2005.

The table indicates that for every $1.00 invested in property, plant, and equipment, Kelly Services produced $31.91 of sales. In contrast, Cox Communications and United Airlines produced only $0.73 and $1.31, respectively, for each $1.00 they invested in operational assets. Does this mean the management of Kelly is doing a better job than the management of Cox Communications or United Airlines? Not necessarily. It means that these companies operate in different economic environments. In other words, it takes significantly more equipment to operate a cable company or an airline than it takes to operate an employment agency.

Effective financial analysis requires careful consideration of industry characteristics, accounting policies, and the reasonableness of assumptions such as useful life and salvage value.

EXHIBIT 9.9

Industry Data Reflecting the Use of Operational Assets

Industry	Company	Sales ÷ Property, Plant, and Equipment
Cable Companies	Charter Communications	0.90
	Cox Communications	0.73
Airlines	American	1.35
	United	1.31
Employment Agencies	Kelly Services	31.91
	Robert Half	30.20

« A Look Back

Chapter 3 explained that the primary objective of recognizing depreciation is to match the cost of a long-term operational asset with the revenues the asset is expected to generate. This chapter extended applications of the matching concept to natural resources (depletion) and intangible assets (amortization). This chapter also explained how alternative methods can be used to account for the same event. Companies experiencing exactly the same business events could produce different financial statements. The alternative accounting methods for depreciating, depleting, or amortizing assets include the (1) straight-line, (2) double-declining-balance, and (3) units-of-production methods.

The *straight-line method* recognizes equal amounts of expense in each accounting period. The amount of the expense recognized is determined using the formula [(cost − salvage) ÷ number of years of useful life]. The *double-declining-balance method* recognizes proportionately larger amounts of expense in the early years of an asset's useful life and increasingly smaller amounts of expense in the later years of the asset's useful life. The formula for calculating double-declining-balance depreciation is [book value at beginning of period × (2 × the straight-line rate)]. The *units-of-production method* recognizes expense in direct proportion to the number of units produced during an accounting period. The formula for the amount of expense recognized each period is [(cost − salvage) ÷ total estimated units of production = allocation rate x units of production in current accounting period].

The chapter also discussed *MACRS depreciation,* an accelerated tax reporting method. MACRS is not acceptable under GAAP for public reporting. A company may use MACRS depreciation for tax purposes and straight-line or one of the other methods for public reporting. As a result, differences may exist between the amount of tax expense and the amount of tax liability. Such differences are reported as *deferred income taxes.*

This chapter showed how to account for *changes in estimates* such as the useful life or the salvage value of a depreciable asset. Changes in estimates do not affect the amount of depreciation recognized previously. Instead, the remaining book value of the asset is expensed over its remaining useful life.

After an asset has been placed into service, companies typically incur further costs for maintenance, quality improvement, and extensions of useful life. *Maintenance costs* are expensed in the period in which they are incurred. *Costs that improve the quality* of an asset are added to the cost of the asset, increasing the book value and the amount of future depreciation charges. *Costs that extend the useful life* of an asset are subtracted from the asset's Accumulated Depreciation account, increasing the book value and the amount of future depreciation charges.

A Look Forward

In Chapter 10, we move from the assets section of the balance sheet to issues in accounting for long-term liabilities. You will also learn how income tax regulations influence the consequences of borrowing money.

SELF-STUDY REVIEW PROBLEM

The following information pertains to a machine purchased by Bakersfield Company on January 1, 2008.

Purchase price	$ 63,000
Delivery cost	$ 2,000
Installation charge	$ 3,000
Estimated useful life	8 years
Estimated units the machine will produce	130,000
Estimated salvage value	$ 3,000

The machine produced 14,400 units during 2008 and 17,000 units during 2009.

Required

Determine the depreciation expense Bakersfield would report for 2008 and 2009 using each of the following methods.

a. Straight-line.
b. Double-declining-balance.
c. Units-of-production.
d. MACRS assuming that the machine is classified as seven-year property.

Solution to Requirements a–d.

a. Straight-line

Purchase price	$63,000
Delivery cost	2,000
Installation charge	3,000
Total cost of machine	68,000
Less: Salvage value	(3,000)
	 $65,000 ÷ 8 = $8,125 Depreciation per year
2008	$ 8,125
2009	$ 8,125

b. Double-declining-balance

Year	Cost	−	Accumulated Depreciation at Beginning of Year	×	2 × S-L Rate	=	Annual Depreciation
2008	$68,000	−	$ 0	×	(2 × 0.125)	=	$17,000
2009	68,000	−	17,000	×	(2 × 0.125)	=	12,750

c. Units-of-production

(1) (Cost − Salvage value) ÷ Estimated units of production = Depreciation cost per unit produced

$$\frac{\$68,000 - \$3,000}{130,000} = \$0.50 \text{ per unit}$$

(2) Cost per unit × Annual units produced = Annual depreciation expense

2008 $0.50 × 14,400 = $7,200

2009   0.50 × 17,000 = 8,500

d. MACRS

Cost × MACRS percentage = Annual depreciation

2008 $68,000 × 0.1429 = $ 9,717

2009   68,000 × 0.2449 =   16,653

KEY TERMS

accelerated depreciation method 450
accumulated depreciation 449
amortization 444
basket purchase 445
book value 450
capital expenditures 457
contra asset account 449
copyright 460

current assets 443
deferred tax liability 456
depletion 444
depreciable cost 451
depreciation 444
double-declining-balance depreciation 446
estimated useful life 447
franchise 460
goodwill 461

half-year convention 455
historical cost concept 445
intangible assets 444
long-term operational assets 443
modified accelerated cost recovery system (MACRS) 455
natural resources 444
patent 444, 460

property, plant, and equipment 444
relative fair market value method 445
salvage value 447
straight-line depreciation 446
tangible assets 444
trademark 460
units-of-production depreciation 446

QUESTIONS

1. What is the difference in the functions of long-term operational assets and investments?
2. What is the difference between tangible and intangible assets? Give an example of each.
3. What is the difference between goodwill and specifically identifiable intangible assets?
4. Define *depreciation*. What kind of asset is depreciated?
5. Why are natural resources called *wasting assets?*
6. Is land a depreciable asset? Why or why not?
7. Define *amortization*. What kind of assets are amortized?
8. Explain the historical cost concept as it applies to long-term operational assets. Why is the book value of an asset likely to be different from the current market value of the asset?
9. What different kinds of expenditures might be included in the recorded cost of a building?
10. What is a basket purchase of assets? When a basket purchase is made, how is cost assigned to individual assets?
11. What is the life cycle of a long-term operational asset?

12. Explain straight-line, units-of-production, and double-declining-balance depreciation. When is it appropriate to use each of these depreciation methods?

13. What effect does the recognition of depreciation expense have on total assets? On total equity?

14. Does the recognition of depreciation expense affect cash flows? Why or why not?

15. MalMax purchased a depreciable asset. What would be the difference in total assets at the end of the first year if MalMax chooses straight-line depreciation versus double-declining-balance?

16. John Smith mistakenly expensed the cost of a long-term tangible fixed asset. Specifically, he charged the cost of a truck to a delivery expense account. How will this error affect the income statement and the balance sheet in the year in which the mistake is made?

17. What is *salvage value?*

18. What type of account (classification) is accumulated depreciation?

19. Why is depreciation that has been recognized over the life of an asset shown in a contra account? Why not just reduce the asset account?

20. Assume that a piece of equipment cost $5,000 and had accumulated depreciation recorded of $3,000. What is the book value of the equipment? Is the book value equal to the fair market value of the equipment? Explain.

21. Why would a company choose to depreciate one piece of equipment using the double-declining-balance method and another piece of equipment using straight-line depreciation?

22. Explain MACRS depreciation. When is its use appropriate?

23. Does the method of depreciation required to be used for tax purposes reflect the use of a piece of equipment? Can you use double-declining-balance depreciation for tax purposes?

24. Define *deferred taxes*. Where does the account *Deferred Taxes* appear in the financial statements?

25. Why may it be necessary to revise the estimated life of a plant asset? When the estimated life is revised, does it affect the amount of depreciation per year? Why or why not?

26. How are capital expenditures made to improve the quality of a capital asset accounted for? Would the answer change if the expenditure extended the life of the asset but did not improve quality? Explain.

27. When a long-term operational asset is sold at a gain, how is the balance sheet affected? Is the statement of cash flows affected? If so, how?

28. Define *depletion*. What is the most commonly used method of computing depletion?

29. List several of the most common intangible assets. How is the life determined that is to be used to compute amortization?

30. List some differences between U.S. GAAP and GAAP of other countries.

31. How do differences in expense recognition and industry characteristics affect financial performance measures?

MULTIPLE-CHOICE QUESTIONS

Multiple-choice questions are provided on the text Web site at www.mhhe.com/edmonds6e.

Quiz 9

EXERCISES—SERIES A

All Exercises in Series A are available with McGraw-Hill's Homework Manager®

Unless specifically included, income tax considerations should be ignored in all exercises and problems.

Exercise 9-1A   *Long-term operational assets used in a business*   **L.O. 1**

Required

Give some examples of long-term operational assets that each of the following companies is likely to own: *(a)* Chico's, *(b)* John Deere, *(c)* Amtrak, and *(d)* Malco Theatre.

L.O. 1

Exercise 9-2A *Identifying long-term operational assets*

Required

Which of the following items should be classified as long-term operational assets?

a. Prepaid insurance
b. Coal mine
c. Office equipment
d. Notes receivable (short-term)
e. Supplies
f. Copyright

g. Delivery van
h. Land held for investment
i. 10-year treasury note
j. Cash
k. Filing cabinet
l. Tax library of accounting firm

L.O. 1

Exercise 9-3A *Classifying tangible and intangible assets*

Required

Identify each of the following long-term operational assets as either tangible (T) or intangible (I).

a. Pizza oven
b. Land
c. Franchise
d. Filing cabinet
e. Copyright
f. Silver mine

g. Office building
h. Drill press
i. Patent
j. Oil well
k. Desk
l. Goodwill

L.O. 2

Exercise 9-4A *Determining the cost of an asset*

Pine Logging Co. purchased an electronic saw to cut various types and sizes of logs. The saw had a list price of $160,000. The seller agreed to allow a 5 percent discount because Pine paid cash. Delivery terms were FOB shipping point. Freight cost amounted to $4,200. Pine had to hire an individual to operate the saw. Pine had to build a special platform to mount the saw. The cost of the platform was $2,500. The saw operator was paid an annual salary of $65,000. The cost of the company's theft insurance policy increased by $2,000 per year as a result of the acquisition of the saw. The saw had a four-year useful life and an expected salvage value of $10,000.

Required

Determine the amount to be capitalized in an asset account for the purchase of the saw.

L.O. 2

Exercise 9-5A *Allocating costs on the basis of relative market values*

Illinois Company purchased a building and the land on which the building is situated for a total cost of $1,200,000 cash. The land was appraised at $600,000 and the building at $1,000,000.

Required

a. What is the accounting term for this type of acquisition?
b. Determine the amount of the purchase cost to allocate to the land and the amount to allocate to the building.
c. Would Illinois Company recognize a gain on the purchase? Why or why not?
d. Record the purchase in a statements model like the following one.

Assets			=	Liab.	+	Equity	Rev.	−	Exp.	=	Net Inc.	Cash Flow
Cash	+ Land	+ Building										

Exercise 9-6A *Allocating costs for a basket purchase*   **L.O. 2**

Keenum Company purchased a restaurant building, land, and equipment for $900,000. Keenum paid $100,000 in cash and issued a 20-year, 8 percent note to First Bank for the balance. The appraised value of the assets was as follows:

Land	$ 240,000
Building	600,000
Equipment	360,000
Total	$1,200,000

Required

a. Compute the amount to be recorded on the books for each of the assets.

b. Record the purchase in a horizontal statements model like the following one.

Assets				=	Liab.	+	Equity	Rev.	−	Exp.	=	Net Inc.	Cash Flow
Cash + Land + Building + Equip.					N. Payable								

c. Prepare the general journal entry to record the purchase.

Exercise 9-7A *Effect of double-declining-balance depreciation on financial statements*   **L.O. 3**

Miller Company started operations by acquiring $200,000 cash from the issue of common stock. The company purchased equipment that cost $200,000 cash on January 1, 2008. The equipment had an expected useful life of five years and an estimated salvage value of $20,000. Miller Company earned $92,000 and $76,000 of cash revenue during 2008 and 2009, respectively. Miller Company uses double-declining-balance depreciation.

Required

Prepare income statements, balance sheets, and statements of cash flows for 2008 and 2009. Use a vertical statements format. (*Hint:* Record the events in T-accounts prior to preparing the statements.)

Exercise 9-8A *Events related to the acquisition, use, and disposal of a tangible plant asset:*   **L.O. 3, 4**
                  Straight-line depreciation

Mike's Pizza purchased a delivery van on January 1, 2008, for $24,000. In addition, Mike's paid sales tax and title fees of $1,200 for the van. The van is expected to have a four-year life and a salvage value of $2,200.

Required

a. Using the straight-line method, compute the depreciation expense for 2008 and 2009.

b. Prepare the general journal entry to record the 2008 depreciation.

c. Assume the van was sold on January 1, 2011, for $12,000. Prepare the journal entry for the sale of the van in 2011.

Exercise 9-9A *Computing and recording straight-line versus double-declining-balance*   **L.O. 3**
                  depreciation

At the beginning of 2009, Expert Manufacturing purchased a new computerized drill press for $65,000. It is expected to have a five-year life and a $5,000 salvage value.

Required

a. Compute the depreciation for each of the five years, assuming that the company uses

   (1) Straight-line depreciation.

   (2) Double-declining-balance depreciation.

b. Record the purchase of the drill press and the depreciation expense for the first year under the straight-line and double-declining-balance methods in a financial statements model like the following one:

Assets			=	Equity		Rev.	−	Exp.	=	Net Inc.	Cash Flow
Cash	+	Drill Press	−	Acc. Dep.	=	Ret. Earn.					

c. Prepare the journal entries to recognize depreciation for each of the five years, assuming that the company uses
   (1) Straight-line depreciation.
   (2) Double-declining-balance depreciation.

L.O. 4

Exercise 9-10A *Effect of the disposal of plant assets on the financial statements*

A plant asset with a cost of $50,000 and accumulated depreciation of $42,000 is sold for $6,000.

Required

a. What is the book value of the asset at the time of sale?
b. What is the amount of gain or loss on the disposal?
c. How would the sale affect net income (increase, decrease, no effect) and by how much?
d. How would the sale affect the amount of total assets shown on the balance sheet (increase, decrease, no effect) and by how much?
e. How would the event affect the statement of cash flows (inflow, outflow, no effect) and in what section?

L.O. 3, 4

Exercise 9-11A *Double-declining-balance and units-of-production depreciation:*
                    Gain or loss on disposal

Copy Service Co. purchased a new color copier at the beginning of 2008 for $42,000. The copier is expected to have a five-year useful life and a $6,000 salvage value. The expected copy production was estimated at 2,000,000 copies. Actual copy production for the five years was as follows:

2008	550,000
2009	480,000
2010	380,000
2011	390,000
2012	240,000
Total	2,040,000

The copier was sold at the end of 2012 for $5,200.

Required

a. Compute the depreciation expense for each of the five years, using double-declining-balance depreciation.
b. Compute the depreciation expense for each of the five years, using units-of-production depreciation. (Round cost per unit to three decimal places.)
c. Calculate the amount of gain or loss from the sale of the asset under each of the depreciation methods.

L.O. 5

Exercise 9-12A *Computing depreciation for tax purposes*

Quality Lumber Company purchased $140,000 of equipment on September 1, 2008.

Required

a. Compute the amount of depreciation expense that is deductible under MACRS for 2008 and 2009, assuming that the equipment is classified as seven-year property.
b. Compute the amount of depreciation expense that is deductible under MACRS for 2008 and 2009, assuming that the equipment is classified as five-year property.

Exercise 9-13A   *Revision of estimated useful life*

On January 1, 2008, Miller Machining Co. purchased a compressor and related installation equipment for $56,000. The equipment had a three-year estimated life with a $5,000 salvage value. Straight-line depreciation was used. At the beginning of 2010, Miller revised the expected life of the asset to four years rather than three years. The salvage value was revised to $4,000.

Required

Compute the depreciation expense for each of the four years.

Exercise 9-14A   *Distinguishing between maintenance costs and capital expenditures*

Uber's Shredding Service has just completed a minor repair on a shredding machine. The repair cost was $1,200, and the book value prior to the repair was $5,000. In addition, the company spent $9,000 to replace the roof on a building. The new roof extended the life of the building by five years. Prior to the roof replacement, the general ledger reflected the Building account at $90,000 and related Accumulated Depreciation account at $36,000.

Required

After the work was completed, what book value should Uber's report on the balance sheet for the shredding machine and the building?

Exercise 9-15A   *Effect of maintenance costs versus capital expenditures on financial statements*

Commercial Construction Company purchased a forklift for $115,000 cash. It had an estimated useful life of four years and a $5,000 salvage value. At the beginning of the third year of use, the company spent an additional $10,000 that was related to the forklift. The company's financial condition just prior to this expenditure is shown in the following statements model.

Assets				=	Equity			Rev.	−	Exp.	=	Net Inc.	Cash Flow
Cash	+	Forklift	−	Acc. Dep.	=	Com. Stk.	+	Ret. Earn.					
12,000	+	115,000	−	55,000	=	24,000	+	48,000	NA	−	NA	=	NA	NA

Required

Record the $10,000 expenditure in the statements model under each of the following *independent* assumptions:

a. The expenditure was for routine maintenance.
b. The expenditure extended the forklift's life.
c. The expenditure improved the forklift's operating capacity.

Exercise 9-16A   *Effect of maintenance costs versus capital expenditures on financial statements*

On January 1, 2009, Grayson Construction Company overhauled four cranes resulting in a slight increase in the life of the cranes. Such overhauls occur regularly at two-year intervals and have been treated as maintenance expense in the past. Management is considering whether to capitalize this year's $26,000 cash cost in the Cranes asset account or to expense it as a maintenance expense. Assume that the cranes have a remaining useful life of two years and no expected salvage value. Assume straight-line depreciation.

Required

a. Determine the amount of additional depreciation expense Grayson would recognize in 2009 and 2010 if the cost were capitalized in the Cranes account.
b. Determine the amount of expense Grayson would recognize in 2009 and 2010 if the cost were recognized as maintenance expense.
c. Determine the effect of the overhaul on cash flow from operating activities for 2009 and 2010 if the cost were capitalized and expensed through depreciation charges.
d. Determine the effect of the overhaul on cash flow from operating activities for 2009 and 2010 if the cost were recognized as maintenance expense.

L.O. 8   **Exercise 9-17A**   *Computing and recording depletion expense*

Southwest Sand and Gravel paid $800,000 to acquire 1,000,000 cubic yards of sand reserves. The following statements model reflects Southwest's financial condition just prior to purchasing the sand reserves. The company extracted 420,000 cubic yards of sand in year 1 and 360,000 cubic yards in year 2.

Assets			=	Equity			Rev.	−	Exp.	=	Net Inc.	Cash Flow
Cash	+	Sand Res.	=	Com. Stk.	+	Ret. Earn.						
900,000	+	NA	=	900,000	+	NA	NA	−	NA	=	NA	NA

Required

a. Compute the depletion charge per unit.
b. Record the acquisition of the sand reserves and the depletion expense for years 1 and 2 in a financial statements model like the preceding one.
c. Prepare the general journal entries to record the depletion expense for years 1 and 2.

L.O. 9   **Exercise 9-18A**   *Computing and recording the amortization of intangibles*

Nevada's Manufacturing paid cash to purchase the assets of an existing company. Among the assets purchased were the following items:

Patent with 5 remaining years of legal life	$32,000
Goodwill	36,000

Nevada's financial condition just prior to the purchase of these assets is shown in the following statements model:

Assets					=	Liab.	+	Equity	Rev.	−	Exp.	=	Net Inc.	Cash Flow
Cash	+	Patent	+	Goodwill										
94,000	+	NA	+	NA	=	NA	+	94,000	NA	−	NA	=	NA	NA

Required

a. Compute the annual amortization expense for these items if applicable.
b. Record the purchase of the intangible assets and the related amortization expense for year 1 in a horizontal statements model like the preceding one.
c. Prepare the journal entries to record the purchase of the intangible assets and the related amortization for year 1.

L.O. 9   **Exercise 9-19A**   *Computing and recording goodwill*

Ben Sands purchased the business Regional Supply Co. for $285,000 cash and assumed all liabilities at the date of purchase. Regional's books showed assets of $280,000, liabilities of $40,000, and equity of $240,000. An appraiser assessed the fair market value of the tangible assets at $270,000 at the date of purchase. Sands's financial condition just prior to the purchase is shown in the following statements model:

Assets					=	Liab.	+	Equity	Rev.	−	Exp.	=	Net Inc.	Cash Flow
Cash	+	Assets	+	Goodwill										
325,000	+	NA	+	NA	=	NA	+	325,000	NA	−	NA	=	NA	NA

Required

a. Compute the amount of goodwill purchased.

b. Record the purchase in a financial statements model like the preceding one.

Exercise 9-20A   *The effect of depreciation on the return on assets ratio*   **L.O. 10**

Campus Video Games, Inc., (CVG) was started on January 1, 2008, when it acquired $62,500 from the issue of common stock. The company immediately purchased video games that cost $62,500 cash. The games had total estimated salvage values of $7,500 and expected useful lives of five years. CVG used the video games during 2008 to produce $25,000 of cash revenue. Assume that these were the only events affecting CVG during 2008.

Required

(*Hint:* It may be helpful to prepare an income statement and a balance sheet prior to completing the following requirements.)

a. Compute the return on assets ratio as of December 31, 2008 under the assumption that CVG uses the straight-line-depreciation method.

b. Recompute the ratio assuming that CVG uses the double-declining-balance method.

c. Which depreciation method makes it *appear* that CVG is utilizing its assets more effectively?

PROBLEMS—SERIES A

All Problems in Series A are available with McGraw-Hill's Homework Manager®

Problem 9-21A   *Accounting for acquisition of assets including a basket purchase*   **L.O. 2**

Moon Co., Inc., made several purchases of long-term assets in 2009. The details of each purchase are presented here.

New Office Equipment

1. List price: $60,000; terms: 2/10 n/30; paid within discount period.
2. Transportation-in: $1,600.
3. Installation: $2,200.
4. Cost to repair damage during unloading: $1,000.
5. Routine maintenance cost after six months: $300.

Basket Purchase of Copier, Computer, and Scanner for $15,000 with Fair Market Values

1. Copier, $10,000.
2. Computer, $6,000.
3. Scanner, $4,000.

Land for New Warehouse With an Old Building Torn Down

1. Purchase price, $200,000.
2. Demolition of building, $10,000.
3. Lumber sold from old building, $7,000.
4. Grading in preparation for new building, $14,000.
5. Construction of new building, $500,000.

Required

In each of these cases, determine the amount of cost to be capitalized in the asset account.

Problem 9-22A   *Accounting for depreciation over multiple accounting cycles*   **L.O. 3, 4**

NEC Company began operations when it acquired $60,000 cash from the issue of common stock on January 1, 2008. The cash acquired was immediately used to purchase equipment for $60,000 that had a $5,000 salvage value and an expected useful life of four years. The equipment was used to produce the following revenue stream (assume all revenue transactions are for cash). At the beginning of the fifth year, the equipment was sold for $4,500 cash. NEC uses straight-line depreciation.

	2008	2009	2010	2011	2012
Revenue	$15,000	$16,000	$16,400	$14,000	$0

Required

Prepare income statements, statements of changes in stockholders' equity, balance sheets, and statements of cash flows for each of the five years.

Problem 9-23A   *Purchase and use of tangible asset: Three accounting cycles, double-declining-balance depreciation*

The following transactions pertain to ALFA Solutions, Inc. Assume the transactions for the purchase of the computer and any capital improvements occur on January 1 each year.

2008

1. Acquired $50,000 cash from the issue of common stock.
2. Purchased a computer system for $30,000. It has an estimated useful life of five years and a $5,000 salvage value.
3. Paid $2,000 sales tax on the computer system.
4. Collected $40,000 in data entry fees from clients.
5. Paid $1,800 in fees to service the computers.
6. Recorded double-declining-balance depreciation on the computer system for 2008.
7. Closed the revenue and expense accounts to Retained Earnings at the end of 2008.

2009

1. Paid 1,000 for repairs to the computer system.
2. Bought a case of toner cartridges for the printers that are part of the computer system, $1,500.
3. Collected $38,000 in data entry fees from clients.
4. Paid $1,100 in fees to service the computers.
5. Recorded double-declining-balance depreciation for 2009.
6. Closed the revenue and expense accounts to Retained Earnings at the end of 2009.

2010

1. Paid $4,800 to upgrade the computer system, which extended the total life of the system to six years.
2. Paid $1,100 in fees to service the computers.
3. Collected $35,000 in data entry fees from clients.
4. Recorded double-declining-balance depreciation for 2010.
5. Closed the revenue and expense accounts at the end of 2010.

Required

a. Use a horizontal statements model like the following one to show the effect of these transactions on the elements of financial statements. Use + for increase, − for decrease, and NA for not affected. The first event is recorded as an example.

2008 Event No.	Assets	=	Liabilities	+	Equity	Net Inc.	Cash Flow
1	+		NA		+	NA	+ FA

b. Use a vertical model to present financial statements for 2008, 2009, and 2010. (Record the transactions in T-accounts before attempting to prepare the financial statements.)

Problem 9-24A *Calculating depreciation expense using four different methods*

Swanson Service Company purchased a copier on January 1, 2009, for $18,000 and paid an additional $500 for delivery charges. The copier was estimated to have a life of four years or 800,000 copies. Salvage was estimated at $2,500. The copier produced 230,000 copies in 2009 and 250,000 copies in 2010.

CHECK FIGURES
b. Depreciation Expense, 2009: $4,600
c. Depreciation Expense, 2010: $4,625

Required

Compute the amount of depreciation expense for the copier for calendar years 2009 and 2010, using these methods:

a. Straight-line.
b. Units-of-production.
c. Double-declining-balance.
d. MACRS, assuming that the copier is classified as five-year property.

Problem 9-25A *Effect of straight-line versus double-declining-balance depreciation on the recognition of expense and gains or losses*

One Hour Laundry Services purchased a new steam press machine on January 1, for $45,000. It is expected to have a five-year useful life and a $5,000 salvage value. One Hour expects to use the equipment more extensively in the early years.

CHECK FIGURES
a. Depreciation Expense, Year 2: $8,000
b. Depreciation Expense, Year 2: $10,800

Required

a. Calculate the depreciation expense for each of the five years, assuming the use of straight-line depreciation.
b. Calculate the depreciation expense for each of the five years, assuming the use of double-declining-balance depreciation.
c. Would the choice of one depreciation method over another produce a different amount of annual cash flow for any year? Why or why not?
d. Assume that One Hour Laundry Services sold the steam press machine at the end of the third year for $26,000. Compute the amount of gain or loss using each depreciation method.

Problem 9-26A *Computing and recording units-of-production depreciation*

Brees Corporation purchased a delivery van for $35,500 in 2008. The firm's financial condition immediately prior to the purchase is shown in the following horizontal statements model:

Assets				=	Equity			Rev.	−	Exp.	=	Net Inc.	Cash Flow
Cash	+	Van	−	Acc. Dep.	=	Com. Stk.	+	Ret. Earn.					
50,000	+	NA	−	NA	=	50,000	+	NA	NA	−	NA	=	NA	NA

The van was expected to have a useful life of 150,000 miles and a salvage value of $5,500. Actual mileage was as follows:

CHECK FIGURES
a. Depreciation Expense, 2008: $10,000
c. Loss on Sale: $(1,500)

2008	50,000
2009	70,000
2010	58,000

Required

a. Compute the depreciation for each of the three years, assuming the use of units-of-production depreciation.
b. Assume that Brees earns $21,000 of cash revenue during 2008. Record the purchase of the van and the recognition of the revenue and the depreciation expense for the first year in a financial statements model like the preceding one.
c. Assume that Brees sold the van at the end of the third year for $4,000. Record the general journal entry for the sale.

L.O. 3

CHECK FIGURES
a. Company A, Net
   Income: $22,000
c. Company C, Highest
   Book Value: $13,000

Problem 9-27A *Determining the effect of depreciation expense on financial statements*

Three different companies each purchased a machine on January 1, 2008, for $42,000. Each machine was expected to last five years or 200,000 hours. Salvage value was estimated to be $2,000. All three machines were operated for 50,000 hours in 2008, 55,000 hours in 2009, 40,000 hours in 2010, 44,000 hours in 2011, and 31,000 hours in 2012. Each of the three companies earned $30,000 of cash revenue during each of the five years. Company A uses straight-line depreciation, company B uses double-declining-balance depreciation, and company C uses units-of-production depreciation.

Required

Answer each of the following questions. Ignore the effects of income taxes.

a. Which company will report the highest amount of net income for 2008?
b. Which company will report the lowest amount of net income for 2010?
c. Which company will report the highest book value on the December 31, 2010, balance sheet?
d. Which company will report the highest amount of retained earnings on the December 31, 2011, balance sheet?
e. Which company will report the lowest amount of cash flow from operating activities on the 2010 statement of cash flows?

L.O. 6, 8

CHECK FIGURES
a. Coal Mine Depletion,
   2008: $315,000
b. Total Natural
   Resources:
   $1,991,000

Problem 9-28A *Accounting for depletion*

Favre Exploration Corporation engages in the exploration and development of many types of natural resources. In the last two years, the company has engaged in the following activities:

Jan. 1, 2008   Purchased a coal mine estimated to contain 200,000 tons of coal for $900,000.
July 1, 2008   Purchased for $2,500,000 a tract of timber estimated to yield 3,000,000 board feet of lumber and to have a residual land value of $250,000.
Feb. 1, 2009   Purchased a silver mine estimated to contain 30,000 tons of silver for $750,000.
Aug. 1, 2009   Purchased for $720,000 oil reserves estimated to contain 380,000 barrels of oil, of which 20,000 would be unprofitable to pump.

Required

a. Prepare the journal entries to account for the following:
   (1) The 2008 purchases.
   (2) Depletion on the 2008 purchases, assuming that 70,000 tons of coal were mined and 1,000,000 board feet of lumber were cut.
   (3) The 2009 purchases.
   (4) Depletion on the four reserves, assuming that 62,000 tons of coal, 1,200,000 board feet of lumber, 9,000 tons of silver, and 80,000 barrels of oil were extracted.
b. Prepare the portion of the December 31, 2009, balance sheet that reports natural resources.
c. Assume that in 2010 the estimates changed to reflect only 50,000 tons of coal remaining. Prepare the depletion journal entry for 2010 to account for the extraction of 35,000 tons of coal.

L.O. 3, 4, 6, 7

CHECK FIGURES
b. 2010 Depreciation
   Expense: $8,000
d. Loss on Sale: $4,000

Problem 9-29A *Recording continuing expenditures for plant assets*

Sam's Outdoor, Inc., recorded the following transactions over the life of a piece of equipment purchased in 2008:

Jan. 1, 2008   Purchased the equipment for $39,000 cash. The equipment is estimated to have a five-year life and $4,000 salvage value and was to be depreciated using the straight-line method.
Dec. 31, 2008   Recorded depreciation expense for 2008.
May 5, 2009   Undertook routine repairs costing $800.
Dec. 31, 2009   Recorded depreciation expense for 2009.
Jan. 1, 2010   Made an adjustment costing $3,000 to the equipment. It improved the quality of the output but did not affect the life estimate.
Dec. 31, 2010   Recorded depreciation expense for 2010.

Mar. 1, 2011   Incurred $520 cost to oil and clean the equipment.
Dec. 31, 2011   Recorded depreciation expense for 2011.
Jan. 1, 2012   Had the equipment completely overhauled at a cost of $9,000. The overhaul was esti-
                mated to extend the total life to seven years and revised the salvage value to $3,000.
Dec. 31, 2012   Recorded depreciation expense for 2012.
July 1, 2013   Sold the equipment for $8,000 cash.

Required

a. Use a horizontal statements model like the following one to show the effects of these transactions
   on the elements of the financial statements. Use + for increase, − for decrease, and NA for not affected. The first event is recorded as an example.

Date	Assets	=	Liabilities	+	Equity	Net Inc.	Cash Flow
Jan. 1, 2008	+ −		NA		NA	NA	− IA

b. Determine the amount of depreciation expense Sam's will report on the income statements for the
   years 2008 through 2012.
c. Determine the book value (cost − accumulated depreciation) Sam's will report on the balance
   sheets at the end of the years 2008 through 2012.
d. Determine the amount of the gain or loss Sam's will report on the disposal of the equipment on
   July 1, 2013.

Problem 9-30A   *Accounting for continuing expenditures*

L.O. 6, 7

Shaw Manufacturing paid $62,000 to purchase a computerized assembly machine on January 1, 2005.
The machine had an estimated life of eight years and a $2,000 salvage value. Shaw's financial condi-
tion as of January 1, 2008, is shown in the following financial statements model. Shaw uses the
straight-line method for depreciation.

	Assets			=	Equity			Rev.	−	Exp.	=	Net Inc.	Cash Flow
Cash	+	Mach.	−	Acc. Dep.	=	Com. Stk.	+	Ret. Earn.					
15,000	+	62,000	−	22,500	=	8,000	+	46,500	NA	−	NA	=	NA	NA

Shaw Manufacturing made the following expenditures on the computerized assembly machine
in 2008.

Jan. 2   Added an overdrive mechanism for $6,000 that would improve the overall quality of the
          performance of the machine but would not extend its life. The salvage value was revised
          to $3,000.
Aug. 1   Performed routine maintenance, $1,150.
Oct. 2   Replaced some computer chips (considered routine), $950.
Dec. 31   Recognized 2008 depreciation expense.

CHECK FIGURE
b. Depreciation Expense:
$8,500

Required

a. Record the 2008 transactions in a statements model like the preceding one.
b. Prepare journal entries for the 2008 transactions.

Problem 9-31A   *Accounting for intangible assets*

L.O. 9
CHECK FIGURE
a. Goodwill Purchased:
$210,000

Le Gormet Company purchased a fast-food restaurant for $1,700,000. The fair market values of the as-
sets purchased were as follows. No liabilities were assumed.

Equipment	$420,000
Land	300,000
Building	650,000
Franchise (5-year life)	120,000

Required

a. Calculate the amount of goodwill purchased.

b. Prepare the journal entry to record the amortization of the franchise fee at the end of year 1.

L.O. 9

CHECK FIGURE
b. Impairment Loss:
$100,000

Problem 9-32A *Accounting for goodwill*

Green Leaf purchased the assets of Flower Co. for $1,200,000 in 2008. The estimated fair market value of the assets at the purchase date was $1,000,000. Goodwill of $200,000 was recorded at purchase. In 2010, because of negative publicity, one-half of the goodwill purchased from Flower Co. was judged to be permanently impaired.

Required

a. How will Green Leaf account for the impairment of the goodwill?

b. Prepare the journal entry to record the permanent impairment of goodwill.

L.O. 10

CHECK FIGURE
b. (1) Peng: 34.42%

Problem 9-33A *The effect of depreciation on financial statement analysis: Straight-line versus double-declining-balance*

Peng Company and Bradley Company experienced the exact same set of economic events during 2010. Both companies purchased a machine on January 1, 2010. Except for the effects of this purchase, the accounting records of both companies had the following accounts and balances.

As of January 1, 2010	
Total assets	$400,000
Total liabilities	160,000
Total equity	240,000
During 2010	
Total sales revenue	200,000
Total expenses (not including depreciation)	120,000

Liabilities were not affected by transactions in 2010

The machines purchased by the companies each cost $80,000 cash. The machines had expected useful lives of five years and estimated salvage values of $8,000. Peng uses straight-line depreciation. Bradley uses double-declining-balance.

Required

a. For both companies, calculate the balances in the preceding accounts on December 31, 2010, after the effects of the purchase and depreciation of the machine have been applied. (*Hint:* The purchases of the machines are asset exchange transactions that do not affect total assets. However, the effect of depreciating the machine will change the amounts in total assets, expense, and equity [i.e., retained earnings]).

b. Based on the revised account balances determined in Requirement *a,* calculate the following ratios for both companies:

   (1) Debts to assets ratio.

   (2) Return on assets ratio.

   (3) Return on equity ratio.

c. Disregarding the effects of income taxes, which company produced the higher increase in real economic wealth during 2010?

Unless specifically included, income tax considerations should be ignored in all exercises and problems.

Exercise 9-1B   *Using long-term operational assets used in a business*   **L.O. 1**

Required

Give some examples of long-term operational assets that each of the following companies is likely to own: *(a)* Texas Farms, *(b)* Delta Airlines, *(c)* IBM, and *(d)* State Farm Insurance Co.

Exercise 9-2B   *Identifying long-term operational assets*   **L.O. 1**

Required

Which of the following items should be classified as long-term operational assets?

a. Cash	**g.** Inventory
b. Buildings	**h.** Patent
c. Production machinery	**i.** Tract of timber
d. Accounts receivable	**j.** Land
e. Certificate of deposit (6 months)	**k.** Computer
f. Franchise	**l.** Goodwill

Exercise 9-3B   *Classifying tangible and intangible assets*   **L.O. 1**

Required

Identify each of the following long-term operational assets as either tangible (T) or intangible (I).

a. Retail store building	**g.** 18-wheel truck
b. Shelving for inventory	**h.** Timber
c. Trademark	**i.** Log loader
d. Gas well	**j.** Dental chair
e. Drilling rig	**k.** Goodwill
f. FCC license for TV station	**l.** Business Web page

Exercise 9-4B   *Determining the cost of an asset*   **L.O. 2**

Crest Milling Co. purchased a front-end loader to move stacks of lumber. The loader had a list price of $100,000. The seller agreed to allow a 4 percent discount because Crest Milling paid cash. Delivery terms were FOB shipping point. Freight cost amounted to $500. Crest Milling had to hire a consultant to train an employee to operate the loader. The training fee was $1,000. The loader operator is paid an annual salary of $30,000. The cost of the company's theft insurance policy increased by $800 per year as a result of the acquisition of the loader. The loader had a four-year useful life and an expected salvage value of $6,500.

Required

Determine the amount to be capitalized in an asset account for the purchase of the loader.

Exercise 9-5B   *Allocating costs on the basis of relative market values*   **L.O. 2**

Pizzazz, Inc., purchased a building and the land on which the building is situated for a total cost of $800,000 cash. The land was appraised at $270,000 and the building at $630,000.

Required

a. Determine the amount of the purchase cost to allocate to the land and the amount to allocate to the building.

b. Would the company recognize a gain on the purchase? Why or why not?

c. Record the purchase in a statements model like the following one.

Assets			=	Liab.	+	Equity	Rev.	−	Exp.	=	Net Inc.	Cash Flow
Cash	+ Land	+ Building										

L.O. 2 Exercise 9-6B *Allocating costs for a basket purchase*

Royal Co. purchased an office building, land, and furniture for $400,000. It paid $50,000 in cash and issued a 20-year, 6 percent note to First Bank for the balance. The appraised value of the assets was as follows:

Land	$135,000
Building	270,000
Furniture	45,000
Total	$450,000

Required

a. Compute the amount to be recorded on the books for each asset.
b. Record the purchase in a horizontal statements model like the following one.

Assets				=	Liab.	+	Equity	Rev.	−	Exp.	=	Net Inc.	Cash Flow
Cash	+ Land	+ Building	+ Furn.		N. Pay.								

c. Prepare the general journal entry to record the purchase.

L.O. 3 Exercise 9-7B *Effect of double-declining-balance depreciation on financial statements*

Carousel Manufacturing Company started operations by acquiring $120,000 cash from the issue of common stock. The company purchased equipment that cost $120,000 cash on January 1, 2008, that had an expected useful life of six years and an estimated salvage value of $6,000. Carousel Manufacturing earned $76,000 and $85,200 of cash revenue during 2008 and 2009, respectively. Carousel Manufacturing uses double-declining-balance depreciation.

Required

Prepare income statements, balance sheets, and statements of cash flows for 2008 and 2009. Use a vertical statements format. (*Hint:* Record the events in T-accounts prior to preparing the statements.)

L.O. 3, 4 Exercise 9-8B *Events related to the acquisition, use, and disposal of a tangible plant asset: Straight-line depreciation*

24-Hour Taxi Service purchased a new van to use as a taxi on January 1, 2008, for $27,000. In addition, 24-Hour paid sales tax and title fees of $500 for the van. The taxi is expected to have a five-year life and a salvage value of $2,500.

Required

a. Using the straight-line method, compute the depreciation expense for 2008 and 2009.
b. Prepare the general journal entry to record the 2008 depreciation.
c. Assume that the taxi was sold on January 1, 2010, for $16,000. Prepare the journal entry for the sale of the taxi in 2010.

L.O. 3 Exercise 9-9B *Computing and recording straight-line versus double-declining-balance depreciation*

At the beginning of 2008, Angles Drugstore purchased a new computer system for $36,000. It is expected to have a five-year life and a $1,000 salvage value.

Required

a. Compute the depreciation for each of the five years, assuming that the company uses
   (1) Straight-line depreciation.
   (2) Double-declining-balance depreciation.

b. Record the purchase of the computer system and the depreciation expense for the first year under straight-line and double-declining-balance methods in a financial statements model like the following one:

		Assets				=	Equity		Rev.	−	Exp.	=	Net Inc.		Cash Flow
Cash	+	Comp. Sys.	−	Acc. Dep.		=	Ret. Earn.								

c. Prepare the journal entries to recognize depreciation for each of the five years, assuming that the company uses

   (1) Straight-line depreciation.

   (2) Double-declining-balance depreciation.

Exercise 9-10B *Effect of the disposal of plant assets on the financial statements*   **L.O. 4**

Plow Company sold office equipment with a cost of $35,000 and accumulated depreciation of $20,000 for $14,000.

Required

a. What is the book value of the asset at the time of sale?

b. What is the amount of gain or loss on the disposal?

c. How would the sale affect net income (increase, decrease, no effect) and by how much?

d. How would the sale affect the amount of total assets shown on the balance sheet (increase, decrease, no effect) and by how much?

e. How would the event affect the statement of cash flows (inflow, outflow, no effect) and in what section?

Exercise 9-11B *Double-declining-balance and units-of-production depreciation: Gain or*   **L.O. 3, 4**
               loss on disposal

Shay's Photo Service purchased a new color printer at the beginning of 2008 for $28,000. It is expected to have a four-year useful life and a $2,000 salvage value. The expected print production is estimated at 1,300,000 pages. Actual print production for the four years was as follows:

2008	350,000
2009	370,000
2010	280,000
2011	320,000
Total	1,320,000

The printer was sold at the end of 2011 for $1,500.

Required

a. Compute the depreciation expense for each of the four years, using double-declining-balance depreciation.

b. Compute the depreciation expense for each of the four years, using units-of-production depreciation. (Round cost per unit to two decimal places.)

c. Calculate the amount of gain or loss from the sale of the asset under each of the depreciation methods.

Exercise 9-12B *Computing depreciation for tax purposes*   **L.O. 5**

Expert Eye Care Company purchased $52,000 of equipment on March 1, 2009.

Required

a. Compute the amount of depreciation expense that is deductible under MACRS for 2009 and 2010, assuming that the equipment is classified as seven-year property.

b. Compute the amount of depreciation expense that is deductible under MACRS for 2009 and 2010, assuming that the equipment is classified as five-year property.

L.O. 6

Exercise 9-13B *Revision of estimated useful life*

On January 1, 2008, Mini Storage Company purchased a freezer and related installation equipment for $36,000. The equipment had a three-year estimated life with a $6,000 salvage value. Straight-line depreciation was used. At the beginning of 2010, Mini revised the expected life of the asset to four years rather than three years. The salvage value was revised to $4,000.

Required

Compute the depreciation expense for each of the four years.

L.O. 7

Exercise 9-14B *Distinguishing between maintenance costs and capital expenditures*

Cook Wrecker Service has just completed a minor repair on a tow truck. The repair cost was $620, and the book value prior to the repair was $5,600. In addition, the company spent $4,000 to replace the roof on a building. The new roof extended the life of the building by five years. Prior to the roof replacement, the general ledger reflected the Building account at $90,000 and related Accumulated Depreciation account at $26,500.

Required

After the work was completed, what book value should appear on the balance sheet for the tow truck and the building?

L.O. 7

Exercise 9-15B *Effect of maintenance costs versus capital expenditures on financial statements*

Chow Construction Company purchased a compressor for $42,000 cash. It had an estimated useful life of four years and a $4,000 salvage value. At the beginning of the third year of use, the company spent an additional $3,000 related to the equipment. The company's financial condition just prior to this expenditure is shown in the following statements model.

Assets					=	Equity			Rev.	−	Exp.	=	Net Inc.	Cash Flow
Cash	+	Compressor	−	Acc. Dep.	=	Com. Stk.	+	Ret. Earn.						
37,000	+	42,000	−	19,000	=	40,000	+	20,000	NA	−	NA	=	NA	NA

Required

Record the $3,000 expenditure in the statements model under each of the following *independent* assumptions:

a. The expenditure was for routine maintenance.
b. The expenditure extended the compressor's life.
c. The expenditure improved the compressor's operating capacity.

L.O. 7

Exercise 9-16B *Effect of maintenance costs versus capital expenditures on financial statements*

On January 1, 2008, Mountain Power Company overhauled four turbine engines that generate power for customers. The overhaul resulted in a slight increase in the capacity of the engines to produce power. Such overhauls occur regularly at two-year intervals and have been treated as maintenance expense in the past. Management is considering whether to capitalize this year's $25,000 cash cost in the engine asset account or to expense it as a maintenance expense. Assume that the engines have a remaining useful life of two years and no expected salvage value. Assume straight-line depreciation.

Required

a. Determine the amount of additional depreciation expense Mountain would recognize in 2008 and 2009 if the cost were capitalized in the engine account.
b. Determine the amount of expense Mountain would recognize in 2008 and 2009 if the cost were recognized as maintenance expense.

c. Determine the effect of the overhaul on cash flow from operating activities for 2008 and 2009 if the cost were capitalized and expensed through depreciation charges.

d. Determine the effect of the overhaul on cash flow from operating activities for 2008 and 2009 if the cost were recognized as maintenance expense.

Exercise 9-17B   *Computing and recording depletion expense*   L.O. 8

Valley Coal paid $450,000 to acquire a mine with 22,500 tons of coal reserves. The following statements model reflects Valley's financial condition just prior to purchasing the coal reserves. The company extracted 10,000 tons of coal in year 1 and 8,000 tons in year 2.

Assets			=	Equity			Rev.	—	Exp.	=	Net Inc.	Cash Flow
Cash	+	Coal Res.	=	Com. Stk.	+	Ret. Earn.						
600,000	+	NA	=	600,000	+	NA	NA	—	NA	=	NA	NA

Required

a. Compute the depletion charge per unit.

b. Record the acquisition of the coal reserves and the depletion expense for years 1 and 2 in a financial statements model like the preceding one.

c. Prepare the general journal entries to record the depletion expense for years 1 and 2.

Exercise 9-18B   *Computing and recording the amortization of intangibles*   L.O. 9

Horne Manufacturing paid cash to purchase the assets of an existing company. Among the assets purchased were the following items:

Patent with 2 remaining years of legal life	$48,000
Goodwill	20,000

Horne's financial condition just prior to the purchase of these assets is shown in the following statements model:

Assets					=	Liab.	+	Equity	Rev.	—	Exp.	=	Net Inc.	Cash Flow
Cash	+	Patent	+	Goodwill										
90,000	+	NA	+	NA	=	NA	+	90,000	NA	—	NA	=	NA	NA

Required

a. Compute the annual amortization expense for these items.

b. Record the purchase of the intangible assets and the related amortization expense for year 1 in a horizontal statements model like the preceding one.

c. Prepare the journal entries to record the purchase of the intangible assets and the related amortization for year 1.

Exercise 9-19B   *Computing and recording goodwill*   L.O. 9

Rose Corp purchased the business Design Resources for $250,000 cash and assumed all liabilities at the date of purchase. Design Resource's books showed assets of $200,000, liabilities of $60,000, and stockholders' equity of $140,000. An appraiser assessed the fair market value of the tangible assets at

$220,000 at the date of purchase. Rose Corp's financial condition just prior to the purchase is shown in the following statements model:

Assets					=	Liab.	+	Equity	Rev.	−	Exp.	=	Net Inc.	Cash Flow
Cash	+	Assets	+	Goodwill										
300,000	+	NA	+	NA	=	NA	+	300,000	NA	−	NA	=	NA	NA

Required

a. Compute the amount of goodwill purchased.

b. Record the purchase in a financial statements model like the preceding one.

c. When will the goodwill be written off under the impairment rules?

L.O. 10

Exercise 9-20B *The effect of depreciation on the return on assets ratio*

The Freedom Publishing Company (FPC) was started on January 1, 2008, when it acquired $160,000 from the issue of common stock. The company immediately purchased a printing press that cost $160,000 cash. The press had an estimated salvage value of $20,000 and an expected useful life of eight years. FPC used the asset during 2008 to produce $60,000 of cash revenue. Assume that these were the only events affecting FPC during 2008.

Required

(*Hint:* It may be helpful to prepare an income statement and a balance sheet prior to completing the following requirements.)

a. Compute the return on assets ratio as of December 31, 2008, under the assumption that FPC uses the straight-line-depreciation method.

b. Recompute the ratio assuming that FPC uses the double-declining-balance method.

c. Which depreciation method makes it *appear* that FPC is utilizing its assets more effectively?

PROBLEMS—SERIES B

L.O. 2

Problem 9-21B *Accounting for acquisition of assets including a basket purchase*

Khan Company made several purchases of long-term assets in 2009. The details of each purchase are presented here.

New Office Equipment

1. List price: $40,000; terms: 1/10 n/30; paid within the discount period.
2. Transportation-in: $800.
3. Installation: $500.
4. Cost to repair damage during unloading: $500.
5. Routine maintenance cost after eight months: $120.

Basket Purchase of Office Furniture, Copier, Computers, and Laser Printers for $50,000 With Fair Market Values

1. Office furniture, $24,000.
2. Copier, $9,000.
3. Computers and printers, $27,000.

Land for New Headquarters With Old Barn Torn Down

1. Purchase price, $80,000.
2. Demolition of barn, $5,000.
3. Lumber sold from old barn, $2,000.

4. Grading in preparation for new building, $8,000.

5. Construction of new building, $250,000.

Required

In each of these cases, determine the amount of cost to be capitalized in the asset account.

Problem 9-22B   *Accounting for depreciation over multiple accounting cycles:*   **L.O. 3, 4**
                    Straight-line depreciation

LHR Group started business by acquiring $60,000 cash from the issue of common stock on January 1, 2008. The cash acquired was immediately used to purchase equipment for $60,000 that had a $12,000 salvage value and an expected useful life of four years. The equipment was used to produce the following revenue stream (assume that all revenue transactions are for cash). At the beginning of the fifth year, the equipment was sold for $6,800 cash. LHR Group uses straight-line depreciation.

	2008	2009	2010	2011	2012
Revenue	$15,200	$14,400	$13,000	$12,000	$0

Required

Prepare income statements, statements of changes in stockholders' equity, balance sheets, and statements of cash flows for each of the five years. Present the statements in the form of a vertical statements model.

Problem 9-23B   *Purchase and use of tangible asset: Three accounting cycles,*   **L.O. 3, 6, 7**
                    straight-line depreciation

The following transactions relate to Al's Towing Service. Assume the transactions for the purchase of the wrecker and any capital improvements occur on January 1 of each year.

2007

1. Acquired $40,000 cash from the issue of common stock.

2. Purchased a used wrecker for $26,000. It has an estimated useful life of three years and a $2,000 salvage value.

3. Paid sales tax on the wrecker of $1,800.

4. Collected $17,600 in towing fees.

5. Paid $3,000 for gasoline and oil.

6. Recorded straight-line depreciation on the wrecker for 2007.

7. Closed the revenue and expense accounts to Retained Earnings at the end of 2007.

2008

1. Paid for a tune-up for the wrecker's engine, $400.

2. Bought four new tires, $600.

3. Collected $18,000 in towing fees.

4. Paid $4,200 for gasoline and oil.

5. Recorded straight-line depreciation for 2008.

6. Closed the revenue and expense accounts to Retained Earnings at the end of 2008.

2009

1. Paid to overhaul the wrecker's engine, $1,400, which extended the life of the wrecker to a total of four years.

2. Paid for gasoline and oil, $3,600.

3. Collected $30,000 in towing fees.

4. Recorded straight-line depreciation for 2009.

5. Closed the revenue and expense accounts at the end of 2009.

Required

a. Use a horizontal statements model like the following one to show the effect of these transactions on the elements of financial statements. Use + for increase, − for decrease, and NA for not affected. The first event is recorded as an example.

2007 Event No.	Assets	=	Liabilities	+	Equity	Net Inc.	Cash Flow
1	+		NA		+	NA	+ FA

b. Use a vertical model to present financial statements for 2007, 2008, and 2009. (*Hint:* Record the transactions in T-accounts before attempting to prepare the financial statements.)

L.O. 3

Problem 9-24B *Calculating depreciation expense using four different methods*

Reese Inc., manufactures sporting goods. The following information applies to a machine purchased on January 1, 2008:

Purchase price	$ 60,000
Delivery cost	$ 1,500
Installation charge	$ 2,000
Estimated life	5 years
Estimated units	140,000
Salvage estimate	$ 2,500

During 2008, the machine produced 26,000 units and during 2009, it produced 21,000 units.

Required

Determine the amount of depreciation expense for 2008 and 2009 using each of the following methods:

a. Straight-line.
b. Double-declining-balance.
c. Units-of-production. (Round cost per unit to two decimal points.)
d. MACRS, assuming that the machine is classified as seven-year property.

L.O. 3, 4

Problem 9-25B *Effect of straight-line versus double-declining-balance depreciation on the recognition of expense and gains or losses*

Briner Office Service purchased a new computer system in 2008 for $70,000. It is expected to have a five-year useful life and a $5,000 salvage value. The company expects to use the equipment more extensively in the early years.

Required

a. Calculate the depreciation expense for each of the five years, assuming the use of straight-line depreciation.
b. Calculate the depreciation expense for each of the five years, assuming the use of double-declining-balance depreciation.
c. Would the choice of one depreciation method over another produce a different amount of cash flow for any year? Why or why not?
d. Assume that Briner Office Service sold the computer system at the end of the fourth year for $20,000. Compute the amount of gain or loss using each depreciation method.
e. Explain any differences in gain or loss due to using the different methods.

Problem 9-26B *Computing and recording units-of-production depreciation* L.O. 3, 4

Kabodles purchased assembly equipment for $700,000 on January 1, 2008. Kabodles' financial condition immediately prior to the purchase is shown in the following horizontal statements model:

Assets			=	Equity			Rev.	−	Exp.	=	Net Inc.	Cash Flow
Cash	+ Equip.	− Acc. Dep.	=	C. Stk.	+	Ret. Earn.						
800,000	+ NA	− NA	=	800,000	+	NA	NA	− NA	=		NA	NA

The equipment is expected to have a useful life of 100,000 machine hours and a salvage value of $20,000. Actual machine-hour use was as follows:

2008	32,000
2009	33,000
2010	35,000
2011	28,000
2012	12,000

Required

a. Compute the depreciation for each of the five years, assuming the use of units-of-production depreciation.

b. Assume that Kabodles earns $320,000 of cash revenue during 2008. Record the purchase of the equipment and the recognition of the revenue and the depreciation expense for the first year in a financial statements model like the preceding one.

c. Assume that Kabodles sold the equipment at the end of the fifth year for $18,000. Record the general journal entry for the sale.

Problem 9-27B *Determining the effect of depreciation expense on financial statements* L.O. 3

Three different companies each purchased trucks on January 1, 2008, for $40,000. Each truck was expected to last four years or 200,000 miles. Salvage value was estimated to be $5,000. All three trucks were driven 66,000 miles in 2008, 42,000 miles in 2009, 40,000 miles in 2010, and 60,000 miles in 2011. Each of the three companies earned $30,000 of cash revenue during each of the four years. Company A uses straight-line depreciation, company B uses double-declining-balance depreciation, and company C uses units-of-production depreciation.

Required

Answer each of the following questions. Ignore the effects of income taxes.

a. Which company will report the highest amount of net income for 2008?

b. Which company will report the lowest amount of net income for 2011?

c. Which company will report the highest book value on the December 31, 2010, balance sheet?

d. Which company will report the highest amount of retained earnings on the December 31, 2011, balance sheet?

e. Which company will report the lowest amount of cash flow from operating activities on the 2010 statement of cash flows?

Problem 9-28B *Accounting for depletion* L.O. 6, 8

Pujols Company engages in the exploration and development of many types of natural resources. In the last two years, the company has engaged in the following activities:

Jan. 1, 2008 Purchased for $1,600,000 a silver mine estimated to contain 100,000 tons of silver ore.
July 1, 2008 Purchased for $1,500,000 a tract of timber estimated to yield 1,000,000 board feet of lumber and the residual value of the land was estimated at $100,000.

Feb. 1, 2009   Purchased for $1,800,000 a gold mine estimated to yield 30,000 tons of gold-veined ore.
Sept. 1, 2009   Purchased oil reserves for $1,360,000. The reserves were estimated to contain 282,000
                 barrels of oil, of which 10,000 would be unprofitable to pump.

Required

a. Prepare the journal entries to account for the following:

  (1) The 2008 purchases.

  (2) Depletion on the 2008 purchases, assuming that 12,000 tons of silver were mined and 500,000
       board feet of lumber were cut.

  (3) The 2009 purchases.

  (4) Depletion on the four natural resource assets, assuming that 20,000 tons of silver ore, 300,000
       board feet of lumber, 4,000 tons of gold ore, and 50,000 barrels of oil were extracted.

b. Prepare the portion of the December 31, 2009, balance sheet that reports natural resources.

c. Assume that in 2010 the estimates changed to reflect only 20,000 tons of gold ore remaining.
    Prepare the depletion journal entry in 2010 to account for the extraction of 6,000 tons of gold ore.

L.O. 3, 4, 6, 7   **Problem 9-29B** *Recording continuing expenditures for plant assets*

Cooper, Inc., recorded the following transactions over the life of a piece of equipment purchased
in 2009:

Jan. 1, 2009   Purchased equipment for $80,000 cash. The equipment was estimated to have a five-
                 year life and $5,000 salvage value and was to be depreciated using the straight-line
                 method.
Dec. 31, 2009   Recorded depreciation expense for 2009.
Sept. 30, 2010   Undertook routine repairs costing $750.
Dec. 31, 2010   Recorded depreciation expense for 2010.
Jan. 1, 2011   Made an adjustment costing $3,000 to the equipment. It improved the quality of the
                 output but did not affect the life estimate.
Dec. 31, 2011   Recorded depreciation expense for 2011.
June 1, 2012   Incurred $620 cost to oil and clean the equipment.
Dec. 31, 2012   Recorded depreciation expense for 2012.
Jan. 1, 2013   Had the equipment completely overhauled at a cost of $8,000. The overhaul was
                 estimated to extend the total life to seven years.
Dec. 31, 2013   Recorded depreciation expense for 2013.
Oct. 1, 2014   Received and accepted an offer of $18,000 for the equipment.

Required

a. Use a horizontal statements model like the following one to show the effects of these transactions
    on the elements of the financial statements. Use + for increase, − for decrease, and NA for not
    affected. The first event is recorded as an example.

Date	Assets	=	Liabilities	+	Equity	Net Inc.	Cash Flow
Jan. 1, 2009	+ −		NA		NA	NA	− IA

b. Determine the amount of depreciation expense to be reported on the income statements for the
    years 2009 through 2013.

c. Determine the book value (cost − accumulated depreciation) Cooper will report on the balance
    sheets at the end of the years 2009 through 2013.

d. Determine the amount of the gain or loss Cooper will report on the disposal of the equipment on
    October 1, 2014.

L.O. 6, 7   **Problem 9-30B** *Continuing expenditures with statements model*

Pluto Company owned a service truck that was purchased at the beginning of 2007 for $20,000. It
had an estimated life of three years and an estimated salvage value of $2,000. Pluto uses straight-line

depreciation. Its financial condition as of January 1, 2009, is shown in the following financial statements model:

Assets				=	Equity			Rev.	−	Exp.	=	Net Inc.	Cash Flow
Cash	+	Truck	− Acc. Dep.	=	Com. Stk.	+	Ret. Earn.						
14,000	+	20,000	− 12,000	=	4,000	+	18,000	NA	−	NA	=	NA	NA

In 2009, Pluto spent the following amounts on the truck:

Jan. 4   Overhauled the engine for $4,000. The estimated life was extended one additional year, and the salvage value was revised to $3,000.
July 6   Obtained oil change and transmission service, $160.
Aug. 7   Replaced the fan belt and battery, $360.
Dec. 31   Purchased gasoline for the year, $5,000.
      31   Recognized 2009 depreciation expense.

Required

a. Record the 2009 transactions in a statements model like the preceding one.
b. Prepare journal entries for the 2009 transactions.

Problem 9-31B   *Accounting for intangible assets*

L.O. 9

Wie Company purchased Atlantic Transportations Co. for $1,200,000. The fair market values of the assets purchased were as follows. No liabilities were assumed.

Equipment	$400,000
Land	100,000
Building	400,000
Franchise (10-year life)	20,000

Required

a. Calculate the amount of goodwill purchased.
b. Prepare the journal entry to record the amortization of the franchise fee at the end of year 1.

Problem 9-32B   *Accounting for goodwill*

L.O. 9

Mason Equipment Manufacturing Co. purchased the assets of Falcon Inc., a competitor, in 2009. It recorded goodwill of $50,000 at purchase. Because of defective machinery Falcon had produced prior to the purchase, it has been determined that all of the purchased goodwill has been permanently impaired.

Required

Prepare the journal entry to record the permanent impairment of the goodwill.

Problem 9-33B   *The effect of depreciation on financial statement analysis: Straight-line versus double-declining-balance*

L.O. 10

Baggins Company and Gandalf Company experienced the exact same set of economic events during 2009. Both companies purchased a machine on January 1, 2009. Except for the effects of this purchase, the accounting records of both companies had the following accounts and balances.

As of January 1, 2009	
Total assets	$50,000
Total liabilities	20,000
Total equity	30,000
During 2009	
Total sales revenue	30,000
Total expenses (not including depreciation)	20,000

Liabilities were not affected by transactions in 2009

The machines purchased by the companies each cost $14,000 cash. The machines had expected useful lives of five years and estimated salvage values of $2,000. Baggins uses straight-line depreciation. Gandalf uses double-declining-balance.

Required

a. For both companies, calculate the balances in the preceding accounts on December 31, 2009, after the effects of the purchase and depreciation of the machine have been applied. (*Hint:* The purchases of the machines are asset exchange transactions that do not affect total assets. However, the effect of depreciating the machine will change the amounts in total assets, expense, and equity [i.e., retained earnings]).

b. Based on the revised account balances determined in Requirement *a,* calculate the following ratios for both companies:

   (1) Debts to assets ratio.

   (2) Return on assets ratio.

   (3) Return on equity ratio.

c. Disregarding the effects of income taxes, which company produced the higher increase in real economic wealth during 2009?

ANALYZE, THINK, COMMUNICATE

ATC 9-1   Business Applications Case   *Understanding real-world annual reports*

Required—Part 1

The Topps Company, Inc.

Use the Topps Company's annual report in Appendix B to answer the following questions.

a. What method of depreciation does Topps use?

b. What types of intangible assets does Topps have?

c. What are the estimated lives that Topps uses for the various types of long-term assets?

d. As of February 25, 2006, what is the original cost of Topps': Land; Buildings and improvements; and Machinery, equipment and software (see the footnotes)?

e. What was Topps' depreciation expense and amortization expense for 2006 (see the footnotes)?

Required—Part 2

Harley-Davidson, Inc.

Use the Harley-Davidson's annual report that came with this book to answer the following questions.

a. What method of depreciation does Harley-Davidson use?

b. What types of intangible assets, if any, does Harley-Davidson have?

c. What are the estimated lives that Harley-Davidson uses for of the various types of long-term assets?

d. What dollar amount of Harley-Davidson's "identifiable assets" is associated with its Motorcycles Segment and what amount is associated with its Financial Services segment (see Note 12)?

e. What dollar amount of Harley-Davidson's "long-lived assets" is located in the United States and what amount is located in other countries (see Note 12)?

ATC 9-2   Group Assignment   *Different depreciation methods*

Sweet's Bakery makes cakes, pies, and other pastries that it sells to local grocery stores. The company experienced the following transactions during 2008.

1. Started business by acquiring $60,000 cash from the issue of common stock.
2. Purchased bakery equipment for $46,000.
3. Had cash sales in 2008 amounting to $42,000.
4. Paid $8,200 of cash for supplies expense used to make baked goods.
5. Paid other operating expenses of $12,000 for 2008.
6. Recorded depreciation assuming the equipment had a four-year life and a $6,000 salvage value. The MACRS recovery period is five years.
7. Paid income tax. The rate is 30 percent.

Required

a. Organize the class into three sections and divide each section into groups of three to five students. Assign each section a depreciation method: straight-line, double-declining-balance, or MACRS.

Group Task

Prepare an income statement and balance sheet using the preceding information and the depreciation method assigned to your group.

Class Discussion

b. Have a representative of each section put its income statement on the board. Are there differences in net income? In the amount of income tax paid? How will these differences in the amount of depreciation expense change over the life of the equipment?

ATC 9-3   Real-World Case   *Identifying companies based on financial statement information*

The following ratios are for four companies in different industries. Some of these ratios have been discussed in the textbook, others have not, but their names explain how the ratio was computed. The four sets of ratios, presented randomly are:

Ratio	Company 1	Company 2	Company 3	Company 4
Current assets ÷ total assets	10%	11%	15%	74%
Operating cycle	21 days	41 days	31 days	192 days
Return-on-assets	12%	11%	21%	4%
Gross margin	23%	36%	55%	31%
Sales ÷ property, plant and equipment	2.06 times	1.66 times	55.42 times	5.92 times
Sales ÷ number of full-time employees	$37,714	$477,551	$25,027	$461,867

The four companies to which these ratios relate, listed in alphabetical order, are:

Anheuser Bush Companies, Inc., is a company that produces beer and related products. Its fiscal year-end was December 31, 2005.

Applebee's International operates over 1,800 restaurants worldwide. Its fiscal year-end was December 25, 2005.

Deere & Company is a company that manufactures heavy construction equipment. Its fiscal year-end was December 31, 2005.

Weight Watchers International, Inc., is a company that provides weight loss services and products. Its fiscal year-end was December 31, 2005, during which 59 percent of its revenues came from meeting fees, 31 percent came from product sales, and 10 percent came from online services.

Required

Determine which company should be matched with each set of ratios. Write a memorandum explaining the rational for your decisions.

ATC 9-4   **Business Applications Case**   *Performing ratio analysis using real-world data*

American Greetings Corporation manufactures and sells greeting cards and related items such as gift wrapping paper. CSX Corporation is one of the largest railway networks in the nation. The following data were taken from one of the companies' December 31, 2004, annual report and from the other's February 28, 2005, annual report. Revealing which data relate to which company was intentionally omitted. For one company, the dollar amounts are in thousands, while for the other they are in millions.

	Company 1	Company 2
Sales	$ 8,020	$1,902,727
Depreciation costs	730	57,045
Net earnings	339	95,279
Current assets	2,987	1,281,639
Property, plant, and equipment	19,945	339,792
Total assets	24,581	2,535,628

Required

a. Calculate depreciation costs as a percentage of sales for each company.

b. Calculate property, plant, and equipment as a percentage of total assets for each company.

c. Based on the information now available to you, decide which data relate to which company. Explain the rationale for your decision.

d. Which company appears to be using its assets most efficiently? Explain your answer.

ATC 9-5   **Business Applications Case**   *Performing ratio analysis using real-world data*

Cooper Tire Rubber Company claims to be the fourth-largest tire manufacturer in North America. Goodyear Tire & Rubber Company is the largest tire manufacturer in North America. The following information was taken from these companies' December 31, 2004, annual reports. All dollar amounts are in thousands.

	Cooper Tire	Goodyear Tire
Sales	$2,081,609	$18,370,400
Depreciation costs	109,805	628,700
Buildings, machinery, and equipment (net of accumulated depreciation)	694,386	4,629,800
Total assets	2,668,084	16,533,300
Depreciation method	Straight-line or accelerated	Straight-line
Estimated life of assets:		
Buildings	10 to 40 years	40 years
Machinery and equipment	4 to 14 years	15 years

Required

a. Calculate depreciation costs as a percentage of sales for each company.

b. Calculate buildings, machinery, and equipment as a percentage of total assets for each company.

c. Which company appears to be using its assets most efficiently? Explain your answer.

d. Identify some of the problems a financial analyst encounters when trying to compare the use of long-term assets of Cooper versus Goodyear.

ATC 9-6   **Writing Assignment**   *Impact of historical cost on asset presentation on the balance sheet*

Assume that you are examining the balance sheets of two companies and note the following information:

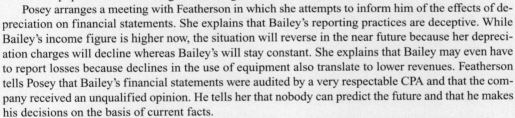

	Company A	Company B
Equipment	$1,130,000	$900,000
Accumulated depreciation	(730,000)	(500,000)
Book value	$ 400,000	$400,000

Maxie Smith, a student who has had no accounting courses, remarks that Company A and Company B have the same amount of equipment.

Required

In a short paragraph, explain to Maxie that the two companies do not have equal amounts of equipment. You may want to include in your discussion comments regarding the possible age of each company's equipment, the impact of the historical cost concept on balance sheet information, and the impact of different depreciation methods on book value.

ATC 9-7   Ethical Dilemma   *Good standards/bad people or just plain bad standards?*

Eleanor Posey has been reading the financial statements of her fiercest competitor, Barron Bailey, who like herself owns a regionally based heating and cooling services company. The statements were given to her by a potential investor, Jim Featherson, who told her that the statements convinced him to put his investment money in Bailey's business instead of Posey's. Bailey's statements show a net income figure 10 percent higher than that reported by Posey's company. When analyzing the footnotes to the financial statements, Posey noticed that Bailey depreciates all property, plant, and equipment on a straight-line basis. In contrast, she depreciates only her building on a straight-line basis. All her equipment is depreciated by the double-declining-balance method, which she believes matches the pattern of use of equipment in the heating and cooling services business.

Posey arranges a meeting with Featherson in which she attempts to inform him of the effects of depreciation on financial statements. She explains that Bailey's reporting practices are deceptive. While Bailey's income figure is higher now, the situation will reverse in the near future because her depreciation charges will decline whereas Bailey's will stay constant. She explains that Bailey may even have to report losses because declines in the use of equipment also translate to lower revenues. Featherson tells Posey that Bailey's financial statements were audited by a very respectable CPA and that the company received an unqualified opinion. He tells her that nobody can predict the future and that he makes his decisions on the basis of current facts.

After Featherson leaves, Posey becomes somewhat resentful of the rules of accounting. Reporting depreciation in the way that she and her accountant believe to be consistent with actual use has caused her to lose an investor with a significant base of capital. She writes a letter to the chairperson of the Financial Accounting Standards Board in which she suggests that the Board establish a single depreciation method that is required to be used by all companies. She argues that this approach would be better for investors who know little about accounting alternatives. If all companies were required to use the same accounting rules, comparability would be significantly improved.

Required

Answer the following questions under the assumption that actual use is, in fact, greater in the earlier part of the life of equipment in the heating and cooling services business.

a. Are Posey's predictions regarding Bailey's future profitability accurate? Explain.

b. Comment on the ethical implications associated with Bailey's decision to depreciate his equipment using the straight-line method.

c. Comment on Posey's recommendation that the FASB eliminate alternative depreciation methods to improve comparability.

d. Comment on Featherson's use of accounting information.

ATC 9-8   Research Assignment   *Comparing Intel and Microsoft*

Required

a. Fill in the missing data in the following table using the most current Form 10-Ks available for Intel Corporation and Microsoft Corporation, or the companies' annual reports. To obtain the Form 10-Ks you can use either the EDGAR system, following the instructions in Appendix A, or they can be found on the companies' Web sites. The companies' annual reports are available on their Web sites. The percentages must be computed; they are not included in the companies' reports. (*Note:* The percentages for current assets and property, plant, and equipment will not sum to 100.)

	Current Assets		Property, Plant, and Equipment		Total Assets	
Microsoft						
Dollar Amount	$		$		$	
% of Total Assets		%		%		100%
Intel						
Dollar Amount	$		$		$	
% of Total Assets		%		%		100%

b. Briefly explain why these two companies have different percentages of their assets in current assets versus property, plant, and equipment.

ATC 9-9 Spreadsheet Assignment *Reporting to the IRS versus financial statement reporting*

Crist Company operates a lawn mowing service. Crist has chosen to depreciate its equipment for financial statement purposes using the straight-line method. However, to save cash in the short run, Crist has elected to use the MACRS method for income tax reporting purposes.

Required

a. Set up the following spreadsheet to reflect the two different methods of reporting. Notice that the first two years of revenues and operating expenses are provided.

b. Enter in the effects of the following items for 2008.

   (1) At the beginning of 2008, Crist purchased for $10,000 cash a lawn mower it expects to use for five years. Salvage value is estimated to be $2,000. As stated, Crist uses the straight-line method of depreciation for financial statement purposes and the MACRS method for income tax purposes. Use formulas to calculate depreciation expense for each method.

   (2) No equipment was sold during 2008; therefore, no gain or loss would be reported this year.

   (3) The income tax rate is 30 percent. For simplicity, assume that the income tax payable was paid in 2008.

   (4) Complete the schedules for income reporting, reporting of equipment, and reporting of cash flows for 2008. Use formulas for all calculations.

c. Enter in the effects of the following items for 2009.

   (1) Crist used the mower for the entire 2009 year. Enter 2009 depreciation expense amounts for the income reporting section of your spreadsheet.

   (2) At December 31, Crist sold the lawn mower for $7,000. Calculate the gain or loss on the sale for the income reporting section. Use formulas to make the calculations.

   (3) The income tax rate is 30 percent. For simplicity, assume that the income tax payable was paid in 2009.

   (4) Complete the schedules for income reporting and reporting of cash flows for 2009.

d. Calculate the Total columns for the income reporting and reporting of cash flows sections.

e. Respond to the following.

   (1) In 2008, by adopting the MACRS method of depreciation for tax purposes instead of the straight-line method, what is the difference in the amount of cash paid for income taxes?

   (2) In the long term, after equipment has been disposed of, is there any difference in total income under the two methods?

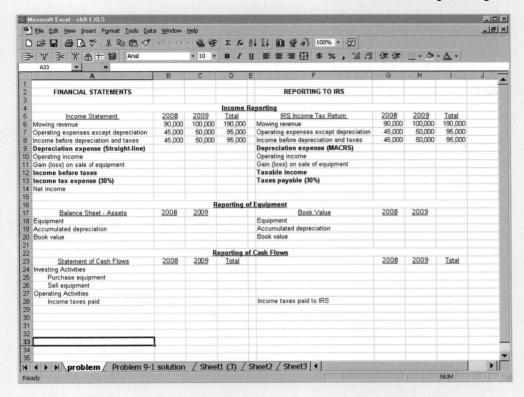

(3) In the long term, after equipment has been disposed of, is there any difference between total income tax expense and total income tax paid?

(4) Explain why Crist Company would use two different depreciation methods, particularly the straight-line method for the financial statements and an accelerated method (MACRS) for reporting to the IRS.

ATC 9-10 Spreadsheet Assignment *Alternative methods of depreciation*

Short Company purchased a computer on January 1, 2001, for $5,000. An additional $100 was paid for delivery charges. The computer was estimated to have a life of five years or 10,000 hours. Salvage value was estimated at $300. During the five years, the computer was used as follows:

2001	2,500 hours
2002	2,400 hours
2003	2,000 hours
2004	1,700 hours
2005	1,400 hours

Required

a. Prepare a five-year depreciation schedule for the computer using the straight-line depreciation method. Be sure to use formulas for all computations including depreciation expense. Set up the following headings for your schedule:

		Beginning				Ending	
Year	Cost	Accumulated Depreciation	Book Value	Depreciation Expense	Cost	Accumulated Depreciation	Book Value

b. Prepare another five-year depreciation schedule for the computer using the units-of-production method. Use (copy) the headings used in Requirement *a*.

c. Prepare another five-year depreciation schedule for the computer using the double-declining-balance method. Use (copy) the headings used in Requirement *a*.

d. Prepare another five-year depreciation schedule for the computer using the MACRS method. Use (copy) the headings used in Requirement *a*.

Spreadsheet Tip

After the year 2001, enter subsequent dates automatically. Position the mouse in the lower right-hand corner of the highlighted cell "2001" until a thin cross appears. Click and drag down four additional rows.

COMPREHENSIVE PROBLEM

The trial balance of Pacilio Security Systems Sales and Service as of January 1, 2009, was:

Cash	$212,114
Petty cash	100
Accounts receivable	47,620
Allowance for doubtful accounts	1,066
Supplies	250
Prepaid rent	1,400
Inventory—standard alarms (7 @ $275)	1,925
Inventory—deluxe alarms (29 @ $580)	16,820
Van	9,200
Accumulated depreciation	7,200
Warranties payable	1,615
Common stock	50,000
Retained earnings	229,548

During 2009, Pacilio Security Systems Sales and Service experienced the following transactions:

1. Purchased a building, land, and office equipment on January 2, 2009, for a total cost of $120,000. The equipment was appraised at $14,000, the building was appraised at $84,000 and the land was appraised at $42,000. Pacilio paid a cash down payment of $80,000 and issued a mortgage for the balance. The mortgage is a 20-year loan with a 6 percent interest rate. Interest is payable annually on December 31 along with a $2,000 payment on principal.

2. Purchased $300 of supplies for cash.

3. Purchased for cash 100 standard alarm systems at a cost of $280 each and 40 deluxe alarms systems at a cost of $590 each.

4. Replenished the petty cash fund on June 30. At this time petty cash had $12 cash and receipts for $28 office supplies, $45 for cutting grass, and $11 for miscellaneous expense.

5. Sold 95 standard alarm systems for $580 each on account and 55 deluxe alarm systems for $960 each on account. (Be sure to record cost of goods sold.)

6. Billed $96,000 in monitoring services for the year. Credit card sales amounted to $36,000, and the credit-card company charged a 4 percent fee. The remaining $60,000 were sales on account.

7. Collected amount due from the credit card company.

8. Paid $900 to repair deluxe alarm systems that were still under warranty.

9. After numerous attempts to collect from customers, wrote off $2,350 of accounts receivable.

10. Collected $162,000 of accounts receivable for the year.

11. Paid installers $35,000 for salaries for the year.

12. Paid $4,200 in advertising expense for the year.

13. Paid $4,800 of utilities expense for the year.

14. On December 31, 2009, paid the interest and principal due on the note payable.

Adjustments

15. Office supplies of $180 were on hand at the end of the year.

16. Recognized expired rent for the year.

17. Recognized warranty expense for the year at 4 percent of the deluxe alarm sales.

18. Recognized bad debt expense for the year. Pacilio uses the allowance method and estimates that 2 percent of sales on account will not be collected.

19. Recognized depreciation expense on the building and equipment. The equipment has a 5-year life and a $2,000 salvage value. The building has a 30-year life with a $12,000 salvage value. The company uses double-declining-balance depreciation for the equipment and straight-line depreciation for the building.

Required

a. Record the above transactions in general journal form. Pacilio uses FIFO cost flow assumption.

b. Post the transactions to the T-accounts.

c. Prepare a trial balance.

d. Prepare an income statement, statement of changes in stockholders' equity, balance sheet, and statement of cash flows.

e. Close the nominal accounts to retained earnings.

f. Post the closing entries to the T-accounts and prepare an after-closing trial balance.

CHAPTER 10

Accounting for Long-Term Debt

LEARNING OBJECTIVES

After you have mastered the material in this chapter, you will be able to:

1. Show how the amortization of long-term notes affects financial statements.

2. Show how a line of credit affects financial statements.

3. Explain how bond liabilities and their related interest costs affect financial statements.

4. Use the straight-line method to amortize bond discounts and premiums.

LP10

5. Explain the advantages and disadvantages of debt financing.

6. Use the effective interest rate method to amortize bond discounts and premiums. (Appendix)

The Curious Accountant

For its 2005 fiscal year, **CBS Corporation** reported a net loss of $7.1 billion. The previous year it had reported an even greater loss, $17.5 billion. The company had $721 million of interest expense in 2005 and $694 million in 2004.

With such huge losses on its income statements, do you think CBS was able to make the interest payments on its debt? If so, how? (Answers on page 503.)

CHAPTER OPENING

Most businesses finance their investing activities with long-term debt. Recall that current liabilities mature within one year or a company's operating cycle, whichever is longer. Other liabilities are **long-term liabilities.** *Long-term debt agreements vary with respect to requirements for paying interest charges and repaying principal (the amount borrowed). Interest payments may be due monthly, annually, at some other interval, or at the maturity date. Interest charges may be based on a* **fixed interest rate** *that remains constant during the term of the loan or may be based on a* **variable interest rate** *that fluctuates up or down during the loan period.*

Principal repayment is generally required either in one lump sum at the maturity date or in installments that are spread over the life of the loan. For example, each monthly payment on your car loan probably includes both paying interest and repaying some of the principal. Repaying a portion of the principal with regular payments that also include interest is often called loan **amortization.**[1] *This chapter explains accounting for interest and principal with respect to the major forms of long-term debt financing.* ■

---

[1]In Chapter 8 the term *amortization* described the expense recognized when the *cost of an intangible asset* is systematically allocated to expense over the useful life of the asset. This chapter shows that the term amortization refers more broadly to a variety of allocation processes. Here it means the systematic process of allocating the *principal repayment* over the life of a loan.

Installment Notes Payable

Show how the amortization of long-term notes affects financial statements.

Topic Tackler

PLUS

10-1

Loans that require payments of principal and interest at regular intervals (amortizing loans) are typically represented by **installment notes.** The terms of installment notes usually range from two to five years. To illustrate accounting for installment notes, assume Blair Company was started on January 1, 2008, when it borrowed $100,000 cash from the National Bank. In exchange for the money, Blair issued the bank a five-year installment note with a 9 percent fixed interest rate. The journal entry to record issuing the note and its effects on the financial statements are as follows:

Date	Account Title	Debit	Credit
2008 Jan. 1	Cash	100,000	
	Installment Note Payable		100,000

	Assets	=	Liab.	+		Equity			Rev.	−	Exp.	=	Net Inc.		Cash Flow
Date	Cash	=	Note Pay.	+	Com. Stk.	+	Ret. Earn.							
2008 Jan. 1	100,000	=	100,000	+	NA	+	NA	NA	−	NA	=	NA		100,000 FA

The loan agreement required Blair to pay five equal installments of $25,709[2] on December 31 of each year from 2008 through 2012. Exhibit 10.1 shows the allocation of each payment between principal and interest. When Blair pays the final installment, both the principal and interest will be paid in full. The amounts shown in Exhibit 10.1 are computed as follows:

1. The Interest Expense (Column D) is computed by multiplying the Principal Balance on Jan. 1 (Column B) by the interest rate. For example, interest expense for 2008 is $100,000 × .09 = $9,000; for 2009 it is $83,291 × .09 = $7,496; and so on.

2. The Principal Repayment (Column E) is computed by subtracting the Interest Expense (Column D) from the Cash Payment on Dec. 31 (Column C). For example, the Principal

EXHIBIT 10.1

Amortization Schedule for Installment Note Payable

Accounting Period Column A	Principal Balance on Jan. 1 Column B	Cash Payment on Dec. 31 Column C	Interest Expense Column D	Principal Repayment Column E	Principal Balance on Dec. 31 Column F
2008	$100,000	$25,709	$9,000	$16,709	$83,291
2009	83,291	25,709	7,496	18,213	65,078
2010	65,078	25,709	5,857	19,852	45,226
2011	45,226	25,709	4,070	21,639	23,587
2012	23,587	25,710*	2,123	23,587	0

*All computations are rounded to the nearest dollar. To fully liquidate the liability, the final payment is one dollar more than the others because of rounding differences.

[2]The amount of the annual payment is determined using the present value concepts presented in Appendix F (page 734) in the back of this text. Usually the lender (bank or other financial institution) calculates the amount of the payment for the customer.

Answers to The Curious Accountant

CBS Corporation was able to make its interest payments in 2004 and 2005 for two reasons. (1) Remember that interest is paid with cash, not accrual earnings. Many of the expenses on the company's income statement did not require the use of cash. Indeed, the company's statement of cash flows shows that net cash flows from operating activities, *after making interest payments*, was a positive $3.5 billion in 2005 and $3.6 billion in 2004. (2) The net loss the company incurred was *after* interest expense had been deducted. The capacity of operations to support interest payments is measured by the amount of earnings before interest deductions. For example, look at the 2008 income statement for Blair Company in Exhibit 10.2. This statement shows only $3,000 of net income, but $12,000 of cash revenue was available for the payment of interest. Similarly, CBS's net losses are not an indication of the company's ability to pay interest in the short run.

Repayment for 2008 is $25,709 − $9,000 = $16,709; for 2009 it is $25,709 − $7,496 = $18,213; and so on.

3. The Principal Balance on Dec. 31 (Column F) is computed by subtracting the Principal Repayment (Column E) from the Principal Balance on Jan. 1 (Column B). For example, the Principal Balance on Dec. 31 for 2008 is $100,000 − $16,709 = $83,291; on December 31, 2009, the principal balance is $83,291 − $18,213 = $65,078; and so on. The Principal Balance on Dec. 31 (ending balance) for 2008 ($83,291) is also the Principal Balance on Jan. 1 (beginning balance) for 2009; the principal balance on December 31, 2009, is the principal balance on January 1, 2010; and so on.

Although the amounts for interest expense and principal repayment differ each year, the effects of the annual payment on the financial statements are the same. On the balance sheet, assets (cash) decrease by the total amount of the payment; liabilities (note payable) decrease by the amount of the principal repayment; and stockholders' equity (retained earnings) decreases by the amount of interest expense. Net income decreases from recognizing interest expense. On the statement of cash flows, the portion of the cash payment applied to interest is reported in the operating activities section and the portion applied to principal is reported in the financing activities section. The journal entry to record the December 31, 2008, cash payment and its effects on the financial statements is as follows:

Date	Account Title	Debit	Credit
2008 Dec. 31	Interest Expense	9,000	
	Installment Note Payable	16,709	
	Cash		25,709

	Assets	=	Liab.	+		Equity		Rev.	−	Exp.	=	Net Inc.	Cash Flow	
Date	Cash	=	Note Pay.	+	Com. Stk.	+	Ret. Earn.							
2008 Dec. 31	(25,709)	=	(16,709)	+	NA	+	(9,000)	NA	−	9,000	=	(9,000)	(9,000) OA (16,709) FA	

Exhibit 10.2 displays income statements, balance sheets, and statements of cash flows for Blair Company for the accounting periods 2008 through 2012. The illustration assumes that Blair earned $12,000 of rent revenue each year. Since some of the principal is repaid each

EXHIBIT 10.2

BLAIR COMPANY
Financial Statements

	2008	2009	2010	2011	2012
Income Statements					
Rent revenue	$12,000	$12,000	$12,000	$12,000	$12,000
Interest expense	(9,000)	(7,496)	(5,857)	(4,070)	(2,123)
Net income	$ 3,000	$ 4,504	$ 6,143	$ 7,930	$ 9,877
Balance Sheets					
Assets					
Cash	$86,291	$72,582	$58,873	$45,164	$31,454
Liabilities					
Note payable	$83,291	$65,078	$45,226	$23,587	$ 0
Stockholders' equity					
Retained earnings	3,000	7,504	13,647	21,577	31,454
Total liabilities and stk. equity	$86,291	$72,582	$58,873	$45,164	$31,454
Statements of Cash Flows					
Operating Activities					
Inflow from customers	$ 12,000	$12,000	$12,000	$12,000	$12,000
Outflow for interest	(9,000)	(7,496)	(5,857)	(4,070)	(2,123)
Investing Activities	0	0	0	0	0
Financing Activities					
Inflow from note issue	100,000	0	0	0	0
Outflow to repay note	(16,709)	(18,213)	(19,852)	(21,639)	(23,587)
Net change in cash	86,291	(13,709)	(13,709)	(13,709)	(13,710)
Plus: Beginning cash balance	0	86,291	72,582	58,873	45,164
Ending cash balance	$ 86,291	$72,582	$58,873	$45,164	$31,454

year, the note payable amount reported on the balance sheet and the amount of the interest expense on the income statement both decline each year.

CHECK YOURSELF 10.1

On January 1, 2008, Krueger Company issued a $50,000 installment note to State Bank. The note had a 10-year term and an 8 percent interest rate. Krueger agreed to repay the principal and interest in 10 annual payments of $7,451.47 at the end of each year. Determine the amount of principal and interest Krueger paid during the first and second year that the note was outstanding.

Answer

Accounting Period	Principal Balance January 1 A	Cash Payment December 31 B	Applied to Interest C = A × 0.08	Applied to Principal B − C
2008	$50,000.00	$7,451.47	$4,000.00	$3,451.47
2009	46,548.53	7,451.47	3,723.88	3,727.59

Line of Credit

Show how a line of credit affects financial statements.

A **line of credit** enables a company to borrow or repay funds as needed. For example, a business may borrow $50,000 one month and make a partial repayment of $10,000 the next month. Credit agreements usually specify a limit on the amount that can be borrowed. Exhibit 10.3 shows that credit agreements are widely used.

Interest rates on lines of credit normally vary with fluctuations in some designated interest rate benchmark such as the rate paid on U.S. Treasury bills. For example, a company may pay 4 percent interest one month and 4.5 percent the next month, even if the principal balance remains constant.

Lines of credit typically have one-year terms. Although they are classified on the balance sheet as short-term liabilities, lines of credit are frequently extended indefinitely by simply renewing the credit agreement.

To illustrate accounting for a line of credit, assume Lagoon Company owns a wholesale jet-ski distributorship. In the spring, Lagoon borrows money using a line of credit to finance building up its inventory. Lagoon repays the loan over the summer months using cash generated from jet-ski sales. Borrowing or repaying events occur on the first of the month. Interest payments occur at the end of each month. Exhibit 10.4 presents all 2008 line of credit events.

Each borrowing event (March 1, April 1, and May 1) is an asset source transaction. Both cash and the line of credit liability increase. Each repayment (June 1, July 1, and August 1) is an asset use transaction. Both cash and the line of credit liability decrease. Each month's interest expense recognition and payment is an asset use transaction. Assets (cash) and stockholders' equity (retained earnings) decrease, as does net income. The journal entries to record the events are shown in Panel A of Exhibit 10.5. The effects of the events on the financial statements are shown in Panel B.

EXHIBIT 10.3

Percentage of U.S. Companies Disclosing Credit Agreements

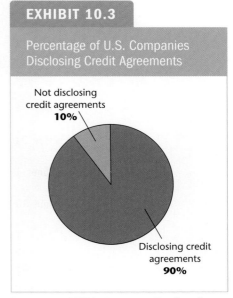

Not disclosing credit agreements **10%**

Disclosing credit agreements **90%**

Data source: AICPA, *Accounting Trends and Techniques,* 2006.

EXHIBIT 10.4

Summary of Line of Credit Events

Date	Amount Borrowed (Repaid)	Loan Balance at End of Month	Effective Interest Rate per Month (%)	Interest Expense (rounded to nearest $1)
Mar. 1	$20,000	$ 20,000	0.09 ÷ 12	$150
Apr. 1	30,000	50,000	0.09 ÷ 12	375
May 1	50,000	100,000	0.105 ÷ 12	875
June 1	(10,000)	90,000	0.10 ÷ 12	750
July 1	(40,000)	50,000	0.09 ÷ 12	375
Aug. 1	(50,000)	0	0.09 ÷ 12	0

Bond Liabilities

Explain how bond liabilities and their related interest costs affect financial statements.

Many companies borrow money directly from the public by selling **bond certificates,** otherwise called *issuing* bonds. Bond certificates describe a company's obligation to pay interest and to repay the principal. The seller, or **issuer,** of a bond is the borrower; the buyer of a bond, or **bondholder,** is the lender.

From the issuer's point of view, a bond represents an obligation to pay a sum of money to the bondholder on the bond's maturity date. The amount due at maturity is the **face value** of the bond. Most bonds also require the issuer to make cash interest payments based on a

EXHIBIT 10.5

Panel A Journal Entries

Date	Account Title	Debit	Credit
Mar. 1	Cash	20,000	
	Note Payable		20,000
Mar. 31	Interest Expense	150	
	Cash		150
Apr. 1	Cash	30,000	
	Note Payable		30,000
Apr. 30	Interest Expense	375	
	Cash		375
May 1	Cash	50,000	
	Note Payable		50,000
May 31	Interest Expense	875	
	Cash		875
June 1	Note Payable	10,000	
	Cash		10,000
June 30	Interest Expense	750	
	Cash		750
July 1	Note Payable	40,000	
	Cash		40,000
July 31	Interest Expense	375	
	Cash		375
Aug. 1	Note Payable	50,000	
	Cash		50,000

Panel B Effects on Financial Statements

Date	Assets	=	Liabilities	+	Equity	Rev.	−	Exp.	=	Net Inc.	Cash Flow	
Mar. 1	20,000	=	20,000	+	NA	NA	−	NA	=	NA	20,000	FA
31	(150)	=	NA	+	(150)	NA	−	150	=	(150)	(150)	OA
Apr. 1	30,000	=	30,000	+	NA	NA	−	NA	=	NA	30,000	FA
30	(375)	=	NA	+	(375)	NA	−	375	=	(375)	(375)	OA
May 1	50,000	=	50,000	+	NA	NA	−	NA	=	NA	50,000	FA
31	(875)	=	NA	+	(875)	NA	−	875	=	(875)	(875)	OA
June 1	(10,000)	=	(10,000)	+	NA	NA	−	NA	=	NA	(10,000)	FA
30	(750)	=	NA	+	(750)	NA	−	750	=	(750)	(750)	OA
July 1	(40,000)	=	(40,000)	+	NA	NA	−	NA	=	NA	(40,000)	FA
31	(375)	=	NA	+	(375)	NA	−	375	=	(375)	(375)	OA
Aug. 1	(50,000)	=	(50,000)	+	NA	NA	−	NA	=	NA	(50,000)	FA
31	NA	=	NA	+	NA	NA	−	NA	=	NA	NA	

stated interest rate at regular intervals over the life of the bond. Exhibit 10.6 shows a typical bond certificate.

Topic Tackler

PLUS

10-2

Advantages of Issuing Bonds

Bond financing offers companies the following advantages.

EXHIBIT 10.6

Bond Certificate

1. Bonds usually have longer terms than notes issued to banks. While typical bank loan terms range from 2 to 5 years, bonds normally have 20-year terms to maturity. Longer terms to maturity allow companies to implement long-term strategic plans without having to worry about frequent refinancing arrangements.

2. Bond interest rates may be lower than bank interest rates. Banks earn profits by borrowing money from the public (depositors) at low interest rates, then loaning that money to companies at higher rates. By issuing bonds directly to the public, companies can pay lower interest costs by eliminating the middleman (banks).

Security of Bonds

Bonds may be either secured or unsecured.

1. **Secured bonds** grant their holders a priority legal claim on specified identifiable assets should the issuer default. A common type of secured bond is a **mortgage bond,** which conditionally transfers the title of designated property to the bondholder until the bond is paid.

2. **Unsecured bonds,** also called **debentures,** are issued based on the general strength of the borrower's credit. Bond certificates often specify the priority of debenture holders' claims relative to other creditors. Holders of **subordinated debentures** have lower priority claims than other creditors, whereas holders of **unsubordinated debentures** have equal claims.

Timing of Maturity

The maturity dates of bonds can be specified in various ways. Even bonds sold as separate components of a single issue may have different maturity dates.

1. **Term bonds** mature on a specified date in the future.

2. **Serial bonds** mature at specified intervals throughout the life of the total issue. For example, bonds with a total face value of $1,000,000 may mature in increments of $100,000 every year for 10 years.

REALITY BYTES

On November 8, 2001, Enron Corporation announced that it would have to reduce its stockholders' equity by approximately $1.2 billion. On December 2, 2001, the company filed for Chapter 11 bankruptcy protection.

When covering this story, most of the media's attention focused on the overstatement of earnings that resulted from Enron's improper use of a form of partnerships called "special purpose entities." However, these entities were also used to improperly keep as much as $1 billion of debt off of Enron's balance sheet. Why did this matter to Enron? Enron was a very rapidly growing company and it used lots of debt to finance this growth. From 1999 to 2000 its assets grew from $33.4 billion to $65.5 billion, but its debt grew from $23.8 billion to $54.0 billion. This caused its debt to assets ratio to rise from 71.3 percent to 82.4 percent. The higher debt burden put Enron at risk of having to pay higher interest rates, an unattractive option for a company with this much debt.

To ensure there is enough cash available at maturity to pay off the debt, a bond agreement may require the issuer to make regular payments into a **sinking fund.** Money deposited in the sinking fund is usually managed by an independent trustee who invests the funds until the bonds mature. At maturity, the funds and the proceeds from the investments are used to repay the bond debt.

Special Features

Some bonds feature one or both of the following characteristics.

1. **Convertible bonds** are liabilities that can be exchanged at the option of the bondholder for common stock or some other specified ownership interest. The issuing company benefits because bondholders (investors) are willing to accept a lower interest rate in exchange for the conversion feature. Bondholders benefit because they obtain the option to share in potential rewards of ownership. If the market value of the company's stock increases, bondholders can convert their bonds to stock. If the stock price does not increase, bondholders are still guaranteed interest payments and priority claims in bankruptcy settlements.

2. **Callable bonds** allow the issuing company to redeem (pay off) the bond debt before the maturity date. If interest rates decline, this feature benefits the issuing company because it could borrow additional money at a lower rate and use the proceeds to pay off its higher rate bonds. Since an early redemption would eliminate their higher interest bond investments, bondholders consider call features undesirable. To encourage investors to buy callable bonds, the **call price** normally exceeds the *face value* of the bonds. For example, the issuing company may agree to pay the holder of a $1,000 face value bond a call price of $1,050 if the bond is redeemed before its maturity date. The difference between the call price and the face value ($50 [$1,050 − $1,000] in this case) is commonly called a **call premium.**

Bond Ratings

Video 10.2

Various financial services, such as Moody's, analyze the risk of default for corporate bond issues and publish ratings of the risk as guides to bond investors. The highest rating (lowest risk) a company can achieve is AAA, the next highest AA, and so forth. Bond issuers try to maintain high credit ratings because lower ratings require them to pay higher interest rates.

Bonds Issued at Face Value

Assume Marsha Mason needs cash in order to seize a business opportunity. Mason knows of a company seeking a plot of land on which to store its inventory of crushed stone. Mason also knows of a suitable tract of land she could purchase for $100,000. The company has agreed to lease the land it needs from Mason for $12,000 per year. Mason lacks the funds to buy the land.

Some of Mason's friends recently complained about the low interest rates banks were paying on certificates of deposit. Mason suggested that her friends invest in bonds instead of CDs. She offered to sell them bonds with a 9 percent stated interest rate. The terms specified in the bond agreement Mason drafted included making interest payments in cash on December 31 of each year, a five-year term to maturity, and pledging the land as collateral for the bonds.[3] Her friends were favorably impressed, and Mason issued the bonds to them in exchange for cash on January 1, 2008.

Mason used the bond proceeds to purchase the land and immediately contracted to lease it for five years. On December 31, 2012, the maturity date of the bonds, Mason sold the land for its $100,000 book value and used the proceeds from the sale to repay the bond liability.

Mason's business venture involved six distinct accounting events:

1. Received $100,000 cash from issuing five-year bonds at face value.
2. Invested proceeds from the bond issue to purchase land for $100,000 cash.
3. Earned $12,000 cash revenue annually from leasing the land.
4. Paid $9,000 annual interest on December 31 of each year.
5. Sold the land for $100,000 cash.
6. Repaid the bond principal to bondholders.

Recording Procedures

Exhibit 10.7 presents the general journal entries to record the six events that Mason Company experienced.

EXHIBIT 10.7

Event No.	Account Title	Debit	Credit
1	Cash	100,000	
	Bonds Payable		100,000
	Entry on January 1, 2008, to record bond issue		
2	Land	100,000	
	Cash		100,000
	Entry on January 1, 2008, to record investment in land		
3	Cash	12,000	
	Rent Revenue		12,000
	Revenue recognition entries on December 31, 2008–2012		
4	Interest Expense	9,000	
	Cash		9,000
	Expense recognition entries on December 31, 2008–2012		
5	Cash	100,000	
	Land		100,000
	Entry on December 31, 2012, to record sale of land		
6	Bonds Payable	100,000	
	Cash		100,000
	Entry on December 31, 2012, to record bond payment		

[3]In practice, bonds are usually issued for much larger sums of money, often hundreds of millions of dollars. Also, terms to maturity are normally long, with 20 years being common. Using such large amounts for such long terms is unnecessarily cumbersome for instructional purposes. The effects of bond issues can be illustrated efficiently by using smaller amounts of debt with shorter maturities, as assumed in the case of Marsha Mason.

Effect of Events on Financial Statements

Event 1 Issue Bonds for Cash
Issuing bonds is an asset source transaction.

Assets (cash) and liabilities (bonds payable) increase. Net income is not affected. The $100,000 cash inflow is reported in the financing activities section of the statement of cash flows. These effects are shown here:

Assets	=	Liab.	+	Equity	Rev.	−	Exp.	=	Net Inc.	Cash Flow	
Cash	=	Bonds Pay.									
100,000	=	100,000	+	NA	NA	−	NA	=	NA	100,000	FA

Event 2 Investment in Land
Paying $100,000 cash to purchase land is an asset exchange transaction.

The asset cash decreases and the asset land increases. The income statement is not affected. The cash outflow is reported in the investing activities section of the statement of cash flows. These effects are illustrated below:

	Assets			=	Liab.	+	Equity	Rev.	−	Exp.	=	Net Inc.	Cash Flow	
Cash	+	Land												
(100,000)	+	100,000		=	NA	+	NA	NA	−	NA	=	NA	(100,000)	IA

Event 3 Revenue Recognition
Recognizing $12,000 cash revenue from renting the property is an asset source transaction.

This event is repeated each year from 2008 through 2012. The event increases assets and stockholders' equity. Recognizing revenue increases net income. The cash inflow is reported in the operating activities section of the statement of cash flows. These effects follow:

Assets	=	Liab.	+	Equity	Rev.	−	Exp.	=	Net Inc.	Cash Flow	
Cash	=			Ret. Earn.							
12,000	=	NA	+	12,000	12,000	−	NA	=	12,000	12,000	OA

Event 4 Expense Recognition
Mason's $9,000 ($100,000 × 0.09) cash payment represents interest expense.

This event is also repeated each year from 2008 through 2012. The interest payment is an asset use transaction. Cash and stockholders' equity (retained earnings) decrease. The expense recognition decreases net income. The cash outflow is reported in the operating activities section of the statement of cash flows. These effects follow:

Assets	=	Liab.	+	Equity	Rev.	−	Exp.	=	Net Inc.	Cash Flow
Cash	=			Ret. Earn.						
(9,000)	=	NA	+	(9,000)	NA	−	9,000	=	(9,000)	(9,000) OA

Event 5 Sale of Investment in Land

Selling the land for cash equal to its $100,000 book value is an asset exchange transaction.

Cash increases and land decreases. Since there was no gain or loss on the sale, the income statement is not affected. The cash inflow is reported in the investing activities section of the statement of cash flows. These effects follow:

Assets			=	Liab.	+	Equity	Rev.	−	Exp.	=	Net Inc.	Cash Flow
Cash	+	Land										
100,000	+	(100,000)	=	NA	+	NA	NA	−	NA	=	NA	100,000 IA

Event 6 Payoff of Bond Liability

Repaying the face value of the bond liability is an asset use transaction.

Cash and bonds payable decrease. The income statement is not affected. The cash outflow is reported in the financing activities section of the statement of cash flows:

Assets	=	Liab.	+	Equity	Rev.	−	Exp.	=	Net Inc.	Cash Flow
Cash	=	Bonds Pay.								
(100,000)	=	(100,000)	+	NA	NA	−	NA	=	NA	(100,000) FA

Financial Statements

Exhibit 10.8 displays Mason Company's financial statements. For simplicity, the income statement does not distinguish between operating and nonoperating items. Rent revenue and interest expense are constant across all accounting periods, so Mason recognizes $3,000 of net income in each accounting period. On the balance sheet, cash increases by $3,000 each year because cash revenue exceeds cash paid for interest. Land remains constant each year at its $100,000 historical cost until it is sold in 2012. Similarly, the bonds payable liability is reported at $100,000 from the date the bonds were issued in 2008 until they are paid off on December 31, 2012.

Compare Blair Company's income statements in Exhibit 10.2 with Mason Company's income statements in Exhibit 10.8. Both Blair and Mason borrowed $100,000 cash at a 9 percent stated interest rate for five-year terms. Blair, however, repaid its liability under the terms of an installment note while Mason did not repay any principal until the end of the five-year bond term. Because Blair repaid part of the principal balance on the installment loan each year, Blair's interest expense declined each year. The interest expense on Mason's bond liability, however, remained constant because the full principal amount was outstanding for the entire five-year bond term.

EXHIBIT 10.8

Mason Company Financial Statements

	Bonds Issued at Face Value				
	2008	2009	2010	2011	2012
Income Statements					
Rent revenue	$ 12,000	$ 12,000	$ 12,000	$ 12,000	$ 12,000
Interest expense	(9,000)	(9,000)	(9,000)	(9,000)	(9,000)
Net income	$ 3,000	$ 3,000	$ 3,000	$ 3,000	$ 3,000
Balance Sheets					
Assets					
Cash	$ 3,000	$ 6,000	$ 9,000	$ 12,000	$ 15,000
Land	100,000	100,000	100,000	100,000	0
Total assets	$103,000	$106,000	$109,000	$112,000	$ 15,000
Liabilities					
Bonds payable	$100,000	$100,000	$100,000	$100,000	$ 0
Stockholders' equity					
Retained earnings	3,000	6,000	9,000	12,000	15,000
Total liabilities and stockholders' equity	$103,000	$106,000	$109,000	$112,000	$ 15,000
Statements of Cash Flows					
Operating Activities					
Inflow from customers	$ 12,000	$ 12,000	$ 12,000	$ 12,000	$ 12,000
Outflow for interest	(9,000)	(9,000)	(9,000)	(9,000)	(9,000)
Investing Activities					
Outflow to purchase land	(100,000)				
Inflow from sale of land					100,000
Financing Activities					
Inflow from bond issue	100,000				
Outflow to repay bond liab.					(100,000)
Net change in cash	3,000	3,000	3,000	3,000	3,000
Plus: Beginning cash balance	0	3,000	6,000	9,000	12,000
Ending cash balance	$ 3,000	$ 6,000	$ 9,000	$ 12,000	$ 15,000

Bonds Issued at a Discount

LO 4

Use the straight-line method to amortize bond discounts and premiums.

Return to the Mason Company illustration with one change. Assume Mason's bond certificates have a 9 percent stated rate of interest printed on them. Suppose Mason's friends find they can buy bonds from another entrepreneur willing to pay a higher rate of interest. They explain to Mason that business decisions cannot be made on the basis of friendship. Mason provides a counteroffer. There is no time to change the bond certificates, so Mason offers to accept $95,000 for the bonds today and still repay the full face value of $100,000 at the maturity date. The $5,000 difference is called a **bond discount.** Mason's friends agree to buy the bonds for $95,000.

Video 10.2

Effective Interest Rate

The bond discount increases the interest Mason must pay. First, Mason must still make the annual cash payments described in the bond agreement. In other words, Mason must pay cash of $9,000 (.09 × $100,000) annually even though she actually borrowed only $95,000. Second, Mason will have to pay back $5,000 more than she received ($100,000 − $95,000). The extra $5,000 (bond discount) is additional interest. Although the $5,000 of additional interest is not paid until maturity, when spread over the life of the bond it amounts to $1,000 of additional interest expense per year.

The actual rate of interest that Mason must pay is called the **effective interest rate.** A rough estimate of the effective interest rate for the discounted Mason bonds is 10.5 percent [($9,000 annual stated interest + $1,000 annual amortization of the discount) ÷ $95,000 amount borrowed]. Selling the bonds at a $5,000 discount permits Mason to raise the 9 percent stated rate of interest to an effective rate of roughly 10.5 percent. Deeper discounts would raise the effective rate even higher. More shallow discounts would reduce the effective rate of interest. Mason can set the effective rate of interest to any level desired by adjusting the amount of the discount.

Bond Prices

It is common business practice to use discounts to raise the effective rate of interest above the stated rate. Bonds frequently sell for less than face value. Bond prices are normally expressed *as a percentage of the face value.* For example, Mason's discounted bonds sold for 95, meaning the bonds sold at 95 percent of face value ($100,000 × .95 = $95,000). Amounts of less than 1 percentage point are usually expressed as a fraction. Therefore, a bond priced at 98 3/4 sells for 98.75 percent of face value.

Mason Company Revisited

To illustrate accounting for bonds issued at a discount, return to the Mason Company example using the assumption the bonds are issued for 95 instead of face value. We examine the same six events using this revised assumption. This revision changes some amounts reported on the financial statements. For example, Event 1 in year 2008 reflects receiving only $95,000 cash from the bond issue. Since Mason had only $95,000 available to invest in land, the illustration assumes that Mason acquired a less desirable piece of property which generated only $11,400 of rent revenue per year.

Event 1 **Issue Bonds for Cash**
Bonds with a face value of $100,000 are issued at 95.

Because Mason must pay the face value at maturity, the $100,000 face value of the bonds is recorded in the Bonds Payable account. The $5,000 discount is recorded in a separate contra liability account called **Discount on Bonds Payable.** As shown below, the contra account is subtracted from the face value to determine the **carrying value** (book value) of the bond liability on January 1, 2008.

Bonds payable	$100,000
Less: Discount on bonds payable	(5,000)
Carrying value	$ 95,000

The bond issue is an asset source transaction. Both assets and total liabilities increase by $95,000. Net income is not affected. The cash inflow is reported in the financing activities section of the statement of cash flows. The effect of the bond issue on the financial statements and the journal entry to record it follow:

Assets	=	Liabilities			+	Equity	Rev.	−	Exp.	=	Net Inc.	Cash Flow
Cash	=	Bonds Pay.	−	Discount	+	Equity						
95,000	=	100,000	−	5,000	+	NA	NA	−	NA	=	NA	95,000 FA

Account Title	Debit	Credit
Cash	95,000	
Discount on Bonds Payable	5,000	
Bonds Payable		100,000

Event 2 Investment in Land
Paying $95,000 cash to purchase land is an asset exchange transaction.

The asset cash decreases and the asset land increases. The income statement is not affected. The cash outflow is reported in the investing activities section of the statement of cash flows. These effects follow:

Assets			=	Liab.	+	Equity	Rev.	−	Exp.	=	Net Inc.	Cash Flow	
Cash	+	Land											
(95,000)	+	95,000	=	NA	+	NA	NA	−	NA	=	NA	(95,000)	IA

Event 3 Revenue Recognition
Recognizing $11,400 cash revenue from renting the property is an asset source transaction.

This event is repeated each year from 2008 through 2012. The event is an asset source transaction that increases assets and stockholders' equity. Recognizing revenue increases net income. The cash inflow is reported in the operating activities section of the statement of cash flows. These effects follow:

Assets	=	Liab.	+	Equity	Rev.	−	Exp.	=	Net Inc.	Cash Flow	
Cash	=			Ret. Earn.							
11,400	=	NA	+	11,400	11,400	−	NA	=	11,400	11,400	OA

Event 4 Expense Recognition
The interest cost of borrowing has two components: the $9,000 paid in cash each year and the $5,000 discount paid at maturity.

Using **straight-line amortization,** the amount of the discount recognized as expense in each accounting period is $1,000 ($5,000 discount ÷ 5 years). Mason will therefore recognize $10,000 of interest expense each year ($9,000 at the stated interest rate plus $1,000 amortization of the bond discount). On the balance sheet, the asset cash decreases by $9,000, the carrying value of the bond liability increases by $1,000 (through a decrease in the bond discount), and retained earnings (interest expense) decreases by $10,000. The effect on the financial statements of recognizing the interest expense and the journal entry to record it for each accounting period are shown here:

Assets	=	Liabilities			+	Equity	Rev.	−	Exp.	=	Net Inc.	Cash Flow	
Cash	=	Bonds Pay.	−	Discount	+	Ret. Earn.							
(9,000)	=	NA	−	(1,000)	+	(10,000)	NA	−	10,000	=	(10,000)	(9,000)	OA

Account Title	Debit	Credit
Interest Expense	10,000	
Cash		9,000
Discount on Bonds Payable		1,000

Event 5 Sale of Investment in Land
Selling the land for cash equal to its $95,000 book value is an asset exchange transaction.

Cash increases and land decreases. Since there was no gain or loss on the sale, the income statement is not affected. The cash inflow is reported in the investing activities section of the statement of cash flows. These effects follow:

Assets			=	Liab.	+	Equity	Rev.	−	Exp.	=	Net Inc.	Cash Flow	
Cash	+	Land											
95,000	+	(95,000)	=	NA	+	NA	NA	−	NA	=	NA	95,000	IA

Event 6 Payoff of Bond Liability
Repaying the face value of the bond liability is an asset use transaction.

Cash and bonds payable decrease. The income statement is not affected. For reporting purposes, the cash outflow is separated into two parts on the statement of cash flows: $95,000 of the cash outflow is reported in the financing activities section because it represents repaying the principal amount borrowed; the remaining $5,000 cash outflow is reported in the operating activities section because it represents the interest arising from issuing the bonds at a discount. In practice, the amount of the discount is frequently immaterial and is combined in the financing activities section with the principal repayment.

Assets	=	Liab.	+	Equity	Rev.	−	Exp.	=	Net Inc.	Cash Flow	
Cash	=	Bonds Pay.									
										(95,000)	FA
(100,000)	=	(100,000)	+	NA	NA	−	NA	=	NA	(5,000)	OA

Effect on Financial Statements

Exhibit 10.9 displays Mason Company's financial statements assuming the bonds were issued at a discount. Contrast the net income reported in Exhibit 10.9 (bonds issued at a discount) with the net income reported in Exhibit 10.8 (bonds sold at face value). Two factors cause the net income in Exhibit 10.9 to be lower. First, since the bonds were sold at a discount, Mason Company had less money to spend on its land investment. It bought less desirable land which generated less revenue. Second, the effective interest rate was higher than the stated rate, resulting in higher interest expense. Lower revenues coupled with higher expenses result in less profitability.

On the balance sheet, the carrying value of the bond liability increases each year until the maturity date, December 31, 2012, when it is equal to the $100,000 face value of the bonds (the amount Mason is obligated to pay). Because Mason did not pay any dividends, retained earnings ($7,000) on December 31, 2012, is equal to the total amount of net income reported over the five-year period ($1,400 × 5). All earnings were retained in the business.

EXHIBIT 10.9

Mason Company Financial Statements

Bonds Issued at a Discount

	2008	2009	2010	2011	2012
Income Statements					
Rent revenue	$ 11,400	$ 11,400	$ 11,400	$ 11,400	$11,400
Interest expense	(10,000)	(10,000)	(10,000)	(10,000)	(10,000)
Net income	$ 1,400	$ 1,400	$ 1,400	$ 1,400	$ 1,400
Balance Sheets					
Assets					
Cash	$ 2,400	$ 4,800	$ 7,200	$ 9,600	$ 7,000
Land	95,000	95,000	95,000	95,000	0
Total assets	$ 97,400	$ 99,800	$102,200	$104,600	$ 7,000
Liabilities					
Bonds payable	$100,000	$100,000	$100,000	$100,000	$ 0
Discount on bonds payable	(4,000)	(3,000)	(2,000)	(1,000)	0
Carrying value of bond liab.	96,000	97,000	98,000	99,000	0
Stockholders' equity					
Retained earnings	1,400	2,800	4,200	5,600	7,000
Total liabilities and stockholders' equity	$ 97,400	$ 99,800	$102,200	$104,600	$ 7,000
Statements of Cash Flows					
Operating Activities					
Inflow from customers	$ 11,400	$ 11,400	$ 11,400	$ 11,400	$11,400
Outflow for interest	(9,000)	(9,000)	(9,000)	(9,000)	(14,000)
Investing Activities					
Outflow to purchase land	(95,000)				
Inflow from sale of land					95,000
Financing Activities					
Inflow from bond issue	95,000				
Outflow to repay bond liab.					(95,000)
Net change in cash	2,400	2,400	2,400	2,400	(2,600)
Plus: Beginning cash balance	0	2,400	4,800	7,200	9,600
Ending cash balance	$ 2,400	$ 4,800	$ 7,200	$ 9,600	$ 7,000

Several factors account for the differences between net income and cash flow. First, although $10,000 of interest expense is reported on each income statement, only $9,000 of cash was paid for interest each year until 2012, when $14,000 was paid for interest ($9,000 based on the stated rate + $5,000 for discount). The $1,000 difference between interest expense and cash paid for interest in 2008, 2009, 2010, and 2011 results from amortizing the bond discount. The cash outflow for the interest related to the discount is included in the $100,000 payment made at maturity on December 31, 2012. Even though $14,000 of cash is paid for interest in 2012, only $10,000 is recognized as interest expense on the income statement that year. Although the total increase in cash over the five-year life of the business ($7,000) is equal to the total net income reported for the same period, there are significant timing differences between when the interest expense is recognized and when the cash outflows occur to pay for it.

CHECK YOURSELF 10.2

On January 1, 2008, Moffett Company issued bonds with a $600,000 face value at 98. The bonds had a 9 percent annual interest rate and a 10-year term. Interest is payable in cash on December 31 of each year. What amount of interest expense will Moffett report on the 2010 income statement? What carrying value for bonds payable will Moffett report on the December 31, 2010, balance sheet?

Answer

The bonds were issued at a $12,000 ($600,000 × 0.02) discount. The discount will be amortized over the 10-year life at the rate of $1,200 ($12,000 ÷ 10 years) per year. The amount of interest expense for 2010 is $55,200 ($600,000 × .09 = $54,000 annual cash interest + $1,200 discount amortization).

The carrying value of the bond liability is equal to the face value less the unamortized discount. By the end of 2010, $3,600 of the discount will have been amortized ($1,200 × 3 years = $3,600). The unamortized discount as of December 31, 2010, will be $8,400 ($12,000 − $3,600). The carrying value of the bond liability as of December 31, 2010, will be $591,600 ($600,000 − $8,400).

Effect of Semiannual Interest Payments

The previous examples assumed that interest payments were made annually. In practice, most bond agreements call for interest to be paid semiannually, which means that interest is paid in cash twice each year. If Marsha Mason's bond certificate had stipulated semiannual interest payments, her company would have paid $4,500 ($100,000 × 0.09 = $9,000 ÷ 2 = $4,500) cash to bondholders for interest on June 30 and December 31 of each year. The journal entries to record semiannual interest payments each year (for the bonds issued at a discount) are as follows:

Date	Account Title	Debit	Credit
June 30	Interest Expense	5,000	
	Discount on Bonds Payable		500
	Cash		4,500
Dec. 31	Interest Expense	5,000	
	Discount on Bonds Payable		500
	Cash		4,500

Bonds Issued at a Premium

When bonds are sold for more than their face value, the difference between the amount received and the face value is called a **bond premium.** Bond premiums reduce the effective interest rate. For example, assume Mason Company issued its 9 percent bonds at 105, receiving $105,000 cash on the issue date. The company is still only required to repay the $100,000 face value of the bonds at the maturity date. The $5,000 difference between the amount received and the amount repaid at maturity reduces the total amount of interest expense. The premium is recorded in a separate liability account called **Premium on Bonds Payable.** This account is reported on the balance sheet as an addition to Bonds Payable, increasing the carrying value of the bond liability. On the issue date, the bond liability would be reported on the balance sheet as follows:

LO 4

Use the straight-line method to amortize bond discounts and premiums.

Bonds payable	$100,000
Plus: Premium on bonds payable	5,000
Carrying value	$105,000

The effect on the financial statements of issuing the bonds at a premium follows:

Assets	=	Liabilities			+	Equity	Rev.	−	Exp.	=	Net Inc.	Cash Flow
Cash	=	Bonds Pay.	+	Premium								
105,000	=	100,000	+	5,000	+	NA	NA	−	NA	=	NA	105,000 FA

The entire $105,000 cash inflow is reported in the financing activities section of the statement of cash flows even though the $5,000 premium is conceptually an operating activities cash flow because it pertains to interest. In practice, premiums are usually so small they are immaterial and the entire cash inflow is normally classified as a financing activity.

The journal entries to record issuing the bonds at a premium and the first interest payment are as follows (assume annual interest payments):

Date	Account Title	Debit	Credit
Jan. 1	Cash	105,000	
	Bonds Payable		100,000
	Premium on Bonds Payable		5,000
Dec. 31	Interest Expense	8,000	
	Premium on Bonds Payable	1,000	
	Cash		9,000

The Market Rate of Interest

When a bond is issued, the effective interest rate is determined by current market conditions. Market conditions are influenced by many factors such as the state of the economy, government policy, and the law of supply and demand. These conditions are collectively reflected in the **market interest rate.** The *effective rate of interest* investors are willing to accept *for a particular bond* equals the *market rate of interest* for other investments with similar levels of risk at the time the bond is issued. When the market rate of interest is higher than the stated rate of interest, bonds will sell at a discount so as to increase the effective rate of interest to the market rate. When the market rate is lower than the stated rate, bonds will sell at a premium so as to reduce the effective rate to the market rate.

Bond Redemptions

Explain how bond liabilities and their related interest costs affect financial statements.

In the previous illustration, Mason Company's five-year, 9 percent bonds were redeemed (paid off) on the maturity date. After Mason Company paid the bondholders the face value of the bonds, the balance in the bonds payable account was zero. The balance in the fully amortized discount account was also zero.

Companies may redeem bonds with a *call provision* prior to the maturity date. If a company calls bonds prior to maturity, it must pay the bondholders the call price. As explained previously, the call price is normally above face value. For example, suppose Mason Company's bond certificate allows it to call the bonds at 103. Assume Marsha Mason's client breaks the land rental contract two years early, at the end of 2010. Mason is forced to sell the land and pay off the bonds. Assuming the bonds were originally issued at a $5,000 discount, Exhibit 10.9 shows there is a $2,000 balance in the Discount on Bonds Payable account at the end of 2010.

To redeem the bonds on January 1, 2011, Mason must pay the bondholders $103,000 ($100,000 face value × 1.03 call price). Since the book value of the bond liability is $98,000 ($100,000 face value − $2,000 remaining discount), Mason recognizes a $5,000 loss ($103,000 redemption price − $98,000 book value) when the bonds are called. The early redemption decreases cash, the carrying value of the bond liability, and stockholders' equity. The effect of the redemption on the financial statements follows:

Assets	=	Liabilities	+	Equity	Rev.	−	Exp.	=	Net Inc.	Cash Flow	
Cash	=	Bond Pay. − Discount	+	Ret. Earn.							
(103,000)	=	(100,000) − (2,000)	+	(5,000)	NA	−	5,000	=	(5,000)	(103,000)	FA

The entire $103,000 cash outflow is reported in the financing activities section of the statement of cash flows. Conceptually, some of this outflow is attributable to activities other than financing. In practice, the amounts paid in an early redemption which are not attributable to financing activities are usually immaterial and the entire cash outflow is therefore classified as a financing activity.

The general journal entry to record the bond redemption follows:

Account Title	Debit	Credit
Loss on Bond Redemption	5,000	
Bonds Payable	100,000	
Discount on Bonds Payable		2,000
Cash		103,000

Security for Loan Agreements

In general, large loans with long terms to maturity pose more risk to lenders (creditors) than small loans with short terms. To reduce the risk that they won't get paid, lenders frequently require borrowers (debtors) to pledge designated assets as **collateral** for loans. For example, when a bank makes a car loan, it usually retains legal title to the car until the loan is fully repaid. If the borrower fails to make the monthly payments, the bank repossesses the car, sells it to someone else, and uses the proceeds to pay the original owner's debt. Similarly, assets like accounts receivable, inventory, equipment, buildings, and land may be pledged as collateral for business loans.

In addition to requiring collateral, creditors often obtain additional protection by including **restrictive covenants** in loan agreements. Such covenants may restrict additional borrowing, limit dividend payments, or restrict salary increases. If the loan restrictions are violated, the borrower is in default and the loan balance is due immediately.

Finally, creditors often ask key personnel to provide copies of their personal tax returns and financial statements. The financial condition of key executives is important because they may be asked to pledge personal property as collateral for business loans, particularly for small businesses.

THE FINANCIAL ANALYST

Bond financing has advantages and disadvantages for the stockholders of a business. Assessing a company's investment potential requires understanding both the potential rewards and the potential risks of debt financing.

LO 5

Explain the advantages and disadvantages of debt financing.

Financial Leverage and Tax Advantage of Debt Financing

As with other forms of credit, bonds may provide companies increased earnings through **financial leverage.** If a company can borrow money at 7 percent through a bond issue and invest the proceeds at 12 percent, the company's earnings benefit from the 5 percent (12 percent − 7 percent) **spread.**

Also, bond interest expense, like other forms of interest expense, is tax deductible, making the effective cost of borrowing less than the interest expense because the interest expense reduces the tax expense. Because dividend payments are not tax deductible, equity financing (e.g., issuing common stock) does not offer this advantage.

To illustrate, assume its organizers obtain $100,000 to start Maduro Company. During its first year of operation, Maduro earns $60,000 of revenue and incurs $40,000 of expenses other than interest expense. Consider two different forms of financing. First, assume the initial $100,000 is obtained by issuing common stock (equity financing) and Maduro pays an 8 percent dividend ($100,000 × .08 = $8,000 dividend). Second, assume Maduro issues $100,000 of bonds that pay 8 percent annual interest ($100,000 × .08 = $8,000). Assuming a 30 percent tax rate, which form of financing produces the larger increase in retained earnings? Refer to the following computations:

Computation of Addition to Retained Earnings		
	Equity Financing	**Debt Financing**
Revenue	$60,000	$60,000
Expense (excluding interest)	(40,000)	(40,000)
Earnings before interest and taxes	20,000	20,000
Interest ($100,000 × 8%)	0	(8,000)
Pretax income	20,000	12,000
Income tax (30%)	(6,000)	(3,600)
Net income	14,000	8,400
Dividend	(8,000)	0
Addition to retained earnings	$ 6,000	$ 8,400

Debt financing produces $2,400 more retained earnings than equity financing. If equity financing is obtained, the company pays $6,000 in income taxes; debt financing requires only $3,600 of income taxes. Maduro's cost of financing, whether paid in dividends to investors or interest to creditors, is $8,000. With debt financing, however, the Internal Revenue Service receives $2,400 less.

The after-tax interest cost of debt can be computed as:

$$\text{Total interest expense} \times (1.0 - \text{Tax rate})$$

$$\$8,000 \times (1.0 - 0.30) = \$5,600$$

The after-tax interest rate that Maduro is paying can be computed using the same logic:

$$\text{Debt interest rate} \times (1.0 - \text{Tax rate})$$

$$8\% \times (1.0 - 0.30) = 5.6\%$$

Unlike interest expense, there is no difference in the before-tax and after-tax effects of a dividend. For Maduro, $1 of dividends costs the company a full $1 of retained earnings, while $1 of interest has an after-tax cost of only $0.70 (assuming a 30 percent tax rate). This tax benefit only applies to profitable businesses. There are no tax savings if a company has no income because businesses that produce losses pay no taxes.

EBIT and Ratio Analysis

The tax consequences of debt financing can influence ratio analysis. For example, consider the *return on assets* (ROA) ratio discussed in Chapter 3. In that chapter ROA was defined as:

Net income ÷ Total assets

Recall that the ROA ratio is used to measure the effectiveness of asset management. In general, higher ROAs suggest better performance. However, the Maduro example demonstrates that a higher ROA can be obtained by using equity financing rather than debt financing without regard to how assets are managed. Recall that Maduro obtained $100,000 of assets whether through equity or debt financing. The assets were used exactly the same way regardless of the financing method used. With equity financing, Maduro's ROA is 14 percent ($14,000 ÷ $100,000) and with debt financing it is 8.4 percent ($8,400 ÷ $100,000). The difference in the ROA results from the financing approach rather than asset management.

The effects of the financing strategy can be avoided in ROA calculations by using *earnings before interest and taxes* (EBIT) rather than net income when computing the ratio. For example, if Maduro uses EBIT to compute ROA, the result is 20 percent ($20,000 ÷ $100,000) regardless of whether debt or equity financing is used. Using EBIT to compute ROA provides a less biased measure of asset utilization. For simplicity, however, this text uses net income to determine ROA unless otherwise indicated.

Times Interest Earned Ratio

Financing with bonds also has disadvantages. The issuer is legally obligated to make interest payments on time and to repay the principal at maturity. If a company fails to make scheduled payments, the creditors (bondholders) can force the company into bankruptcy. The claims on a company's assets held by bondholders and other creditors have priority over the claims of the owners. If a company in bankruptcy is forced to liquidate its assets, creditor claims must be fully paid before any owner claims can be paid. Bond issues therefore increase the owners' risk.

Financial analysts use several ratios to help assess the risk of bankruptcy. One is the *debt to assets ratio,* explained in Chapter 3. Another is the **times interest earned** ratio, defined as:

EBIT ÷ Interest expense

This ratio measures *how many times* a company would be able to pay its interest using its earnings. The *times interest earned ratio* is based on EBIT rather than net income because it is the amount of earnings before interest and taxes that is available to pay interest. The higher the ratio, the less likely a company will be unable to make its interest payments. Higher times interest earned ratios suggest lower levels of risk. Examples of times interest earned ratios and debt to assets ratios for six real-world companies follow. These numbers are based on financial data for the year 2005.

Industry	Company	Times Interest Earned	Debt to Assets
Breakfast Cereal	Kellogg's	5.55 times	0.78
	General Mills	5.07	0.62
Tools	Black & Decker	11.00	0.74
	Stanley Works	9.87	0.59
Hotel	Hilton Hotels	3.46	0.68
	Marriott	7.76	0.62

Since bills are paid with cash, not income, a company may be able to make interest payments even if it has a negative times interest earned ratio. A company with no EBIT may yet have cash. Meaningful financial statement analysis cannot rely on any single ratio or any set of ratios. Making sound business decisions requires considering other information in addition to the insights provided from analyzing ratios. A company with inferior ratios and a patent on a newly discovered drug that cures cancer may be a far better investment than a company with great ratios and a patent on a chemotherapy product that will soon be out of date. Ratio computations are based on historical data. They are useful only to the extent that history is likely to repeat itself.

CHECK YOURSELF 10.3

Selected financial data pertaining to Shaver and Goode Companies follow (amounts are in thousands):

	Shaver Company	Goode Company
Earnings before interest and taxes	$750,720	$2,970,680
Interest expense	234,600	645,800

Based on this information, which company is more likely to be able to make its interest payments?

Answer

The times interest earned ratio for Shaver Company is 3.2 ($750,720 ÷ $234,600) times. The times interest earned ratio for Goode Company is 4.6 ($2,970,680 ÷ $645,800) times. Based on this data, Goode Company is more likely to be able to make its interest payments.

<< A Look Back

This chapter explained basic accounting for long-term debt. *Long-term notes payable* mature in two to five years and usually require payments that include a return of principal plus interest. *Lines of credit* enable companies to borrow limited amounts on an as-needed basis. Although lines of credit normally have one-year terms, companies frequently renew them, extending the effective maturity date to the intermediate range of five or more years. Interest on a line of credit is normally paid monthly.

Long-term debt financing for more than 10 years usually requires issuing *bonds*. Bond agreements normally commit a company to pay *semiannual interest* at a fixed percentage of the bond face value. The amount of interest required by the bond agreement is based on the *stated interest rate*. If bonds are issued when the *market interest rate* is different from the stated interest rate, companies will receive more or less than the face value in order for the effective rate of interest to be consistent with market conditions. Selling bonds at a *discount* (below face value) increases the effective interest rate above the stated rate. Selling bonds at a *premium* decreases the effective rate of interest.

This chapter explained the tax advantages of using debt versus equity financing. Interest is a *tax-deductible expense* subtracted prior to determining taxable income. In contrast, dividends paid to owners are not deductible in determining taxable income.

>> A Look Forward

A company seeking long-term financing might choose to use debt, such as the types of bonds or term loans that were discussed in this chapter. Owners' equity is another source of long-term financing. Several equity alternatives are available, depending on the type of business organization the owners choose to establish. For example, a company could be organized as a sole proprietorship, partnership, or corporation. Chapter 11 presents accounting issues related to equity transactions for each of these types of business structures.

The Effective Interest Rate Method

In the main body of the text we demonstrated the straight-line method for amortizing bond discounts and premiums. While this method is easy to understand, it is inaccurate because it does not show the correct amount of interest expense incurred during each accounting period. To illustrate, return to the case of Mason Company demonstrated in Exhibit 10.9 (page 516). Recall that the exhibit shows the effects of accounting for a $100,000 face value bond with a 9 percent stated rate of interest that was issued at a price of 95. The carrying value of the bond liability on the January 1, 2008, issue date was $95,000. The bond discount was amortized using the straight-line method.

Use the effective interest rate method to amortize bond discounts and premiums.

Recall that the straight-line method amortizes the discount equally over the life of the bond. Specifically, there is a $5,000 discount which is amortized over a 5-year life resulting in a $1,000 amortization per year. As the discount is amortized the bond liability (carrying value of the bond) increases. Specifically, the carrying value of the bond liability shown in Exhibit 10.9 increases as follows:

Accounting Period	2008	2009	2010	2011
Carrying value as of December 31	$96,000	$97,000	$98,000	$99,000

While the carrying value of the bond liability increases steadily, the straight-line method recognizes the same amount of interest expense ($9,000 stated rate of interest + $1,000 discount amortization = $10,000 interest expense) per year. This straight-line recognition pattern is irrational because the amount of interest expense recognized should increase as the carrying value of the bond liability increases. A more accurate recognition pattern can be accomplished by using an approach called the **effective interest rate method.**

Amortizing Bond Discounts under the Effective Interest Rate Method

The effective interest rate is determined by the price that the buyer of a bond is willing to pay on the issue date. In the case of Mason Company the issue price of $95,000 for bonds with a $100,000 face value, a 9 percent stated rate of interest, and a 5 year term produces an effective interest rate of approximately 10.33 percent.[4] Since the effective interest rate is based on the market price of the bonds on the day of issue, it is sometimes called *the market rate of interest.*

Interest recognition under the effective interest method is accomplished as follows:

1. Determine the cash payment for interest by multiplying the stated rate of interest times the face value of the bonds.

2. Determine the amount of interest expense by multiplying the effective rate of interest times the carrying value of the bond liability.

3. Determine the amount of the amortization of the bond discount by subtracting the cash payment from the interest expense.

4. Update the carrying value of the liability by adding the amount of the discount amortization to the amount of the carrying value at the beginning of the accounting period.

Applying these procedures to the Mason Company illustration produces the amortization schedule shown in Exhibit 10.10.

The recognition of interest expense at the end of each accounting period has the following effects on the financial statements. On the balance sheet, assets decrease, liabilities increase, and retained earnings decrease. On the income statement, expenses increase and net income decreases. There is a

---

[4]In practice the effective rate of interest is calculated using software programs, interest formulas, or interest tables. Further discussion of computational methods is beyond the scope of this text.

EXHIBIT 10.10

Amortization Schedule for Bond Discount

	(A) Cash Payment	(B) Interest Expense	(C) Discount Amortization	(D) Carrying Value
January 1, 2008				$ 95,000
December 31, 2008	$ 9,000	$ 9,814	$ 814	95,814
December 31, 2009	9,000	9,898	898	96,712
December 31, 2010	9,000	9,990	990	97,702
December 31, 2011	9,000	10,093	1,093	98,795
December 31, 2012	9,000	10,205	1,205	100,000
Totals	$45,000	$50,000	$5,000	

(A) Stated rate of interest times the face value of the bonds ($100,000 × .09).
(B) Effective interest times the carrying value at the beginning of the period. For the 2008 accounting period the amount is $9,814 ($95,000 × .1033).
(C) Interest Expense − Cash Payment. For 2008 the discount amortization is $814 ($9,814 − $9,000 = $814).
(D) Carrying value at beginning of period plus portion of discount amortized. For the accounting period ending December 31, 2008, the amount is $95,814 ($95,000 + $814).

cash outflow in the operating activities of the statement of cash flows. These effects and the journal entry necessary to record interest expense for the 2008 accounting period are shown below:

Assets	=	Liabilities	+	Equity	Rev.	−	Exp.	=	Net Inc.	Cash Flow
Cash	=	Bond Liab.	+	Ret. Earn.						
(9,000)	=	814*	+	(9,814)	NA	−	9,814	=	(9,814)	(9,000) OA

*The decrease in the amount of the discount increases the bond liability.

Account Title	Debit	Credit
Interest Expense	9,814	
Cash		9,000
Discount on Bonds Payable		814

Exhibit 10.11 shows the financial statements for Mason Company for 2008 through 2012. The statements assume the same events as described as those used to construct Exhibit 10.9 (page 516). These events are summarized below:

1. Mason issues a $100,000 face value bond with a 9 percent stated rate of interest. The bond has a 5-year term and is issued at a price of 95. Annual interest is paid with cash on December 31 of each year.

2. Mason uses the proceeds from the bond issue to purchase land.

3. Leasing the land produces rent revenue of $11,400 cash per year.

4. On the maturity date of the bond, the land is sold and the proceeds from the sale are used to repay the bond liability.

The only difference between the two exhibits is that Exhibit 10.9 was constructed assuming that the bond discount was amortized using the straight-line method while Exhibit 10.11 assumes that the discount was amortized using the effective interest rate method.

EXHIBIT 10.11

Financial Statements

Under the Assumption that Bonds Are Issued at a Discount

	2008	2009	2010	2011	2012
Income Statements					
Rent revenue	$ 11,400	$ 11,400	$ 11,400	$ 11,400	$ 11,400
Interest expense	(9,814)	(9,898)	(9,990)	(10,093)	(10,205)
Net income	$ 1,586	$ 1,502	$ 1,410	$ 1,307	$ 1,195
Balance Sheets					
Assets:					
Cash	$ 2,400	$ 4,800	$ 7,200	$ 9,600	$ 7,000
Land	95,000	95,000	95,000	95,000	0
Total assets	$ 97,400	$ 99,800	$102,200	$104,600	$ 7,000
Liabilities					
Bond payable	$100,000	$100,000	$100,000	$100,000	$ 0
Discount on bonds payable	(4,186)	(3,288)	(2,298)	(1,205)	0
Carrying value of bond liab.	95,814	96,712	97,702	98,795	0
Equity					
Retained earnings	1,586	3,088	4,498	5,805	7,000
Total liabilities and equity	$ 97,400	$ 99,800	$102,200	$104,600	$ 7,000
Statements of Cash Flows					
Operating Activities					
Inflow from customers	$ 11,400	$ 11,400	$ 11,400	$ 11,400	$ 11,400
Outflow for interest	(9,000)	(9,000)	(9,000)	(9,000)	(14,000)
Investing Activities					
Outflow to purchase land	(95,000)				
Inflow for sale of land					95,000
Financing Activities					
Inflow from bond issue	95,000				
Outflow to repay bond liab.					(95,000)
Net change in cash	2,400	2,400	4,800	7,200	(2,600)
Beginning cash balance	0	2,400	2,400	2,400	9,600
Ending cash balance	$ 2,400	$ 4,800	$ 7,200	$ 9,600	$ 7,000

Notice that interest expense under the effective interest rate method (Exhibit 10.11) increases each year while interest expense under the straight-line method (Exhibit 10.9, page 516) remains constant for all years. This result occurs because the effective interest rate method amortizes increasingly larger amounts of the discount (see Column C of Exhibit 10.10) as the carrying value of the bond liability increases. In contrast, the straight-line method amortized the bond discount at a constant rate of $1,000 per year over the life of the bond. Even so, total amount of interest expense recognized over the life of the bond is the same ($50,000) under both methods. Since the effective interest rate method matches the interest expense with the carrying value of the bond liability, it is the theoretically preferred approach. Indeed, accounting standards require the use of the effective interest rate method when the differences between it and the straight-line method are material.

The amortization of the discount affects the carrying value of the bond as well as the amount of interest expense. Under the effective interest method the rate of growth of the carrying value of the bond increases as the maturity date approaches. In contrast, under the straight-line method the rate of growth of the carrying value of the bond remains constant at $1,000 per year throughout the life of the bond.

Finally, notice that cash flow is not affected by the method of amortization. The exact same cash flow consequences occur under both the straight-line (Exhibit 10.9) and the effective interest rate method (Exhibit 10.11).

Amortizing Bond Premiums under the Effective Interest Rate Method

Bond premiums can also be amortized using the effective interest rate method. To illustrate, assume United Company issued a $100,000 face value bond with a 10 percent stated rate of interest. The bond had a 5-year term. The bond was issued at a price of $107,985. The effective rate of interest is 8 percent. United's accountant prepared the amortization schedule shown in Exhibit 10.12.

The recognition of interest expense at the end of each accounting period has the following effects on the financial statements. On the balance sheet assets decrease, liabilities decrease, and retained earnings decrease. On the income statement expenses increase and net income decreases. There is a cash outflow in the operating activities of the statement of cash flows. These effects and the journal entry necessary to record interest expense for the 2008 accounting period are shown below:

Assets	=	Liabilities	+	Equity	Rev.	−	Exp.	=	Net Inc.	Cash Flow
Cash	=	Bond Liab.	+	Ret. Earn.						
(10,000)	=	(1,361)*	+	(8,639)	NA	−	8,639	=	(8,639)	(10,000) OA

*The decrease in the amount of the premium decreases the bond liability.

Account Title	Debit	Credit
Interest Expense	8,639	
Premium on Bonds Payable	1,361	
Cash		10,000

EXHIBIT 10.12

Amortization Schedule for Bond Premium

	(A) Cash Payment	(B) Interest Expense	(C) Premium Amortization	(D) Carrying Value
January 1, 2008				$107,985
December 31, 2008	$10,000	$ 8,639	$1,361	106,624
December 31, 2009	10,000	8,530	1,470	105,154
December 31, 2010	10,000	8,413	1,587	103,567
December 31, 2011	10,000	8,285	1,715	101,852
December 31, 2012	10,000	8,148	1,852	100,000
Totals	$50,000	$42,015	$7,985	

(A) Stated rate of interest times the face value of the bonds ($100,000 × .10).

(B) Effective interest times the carrying value at the beginning of the period. For the 2008 accounting period the amount is $8,639 ($107,985 × .08).

(C) Cash Payment − Interest Expense. For 2008 the premium amortization is $1,361 ($10,000 − $8,639 = $1,361).

(D) Carrying value at beginning of period minus the portion of premium amortized. For the accounting period ending December 31, 2008, the amount is $106,624 ($107,985 − 1,361).

During 2007 and 2008, Herring Corp. completed the following selected transactions relating to its bond issue. The corporation's fiscal year ends on December 31.

2007

Jan.   1   Sold $400,000 of 10-year, 9 percent bonds at 97. Interest is payable in cash on December 31 each year.

Dec. 31   Paid the bond interest and recorded the amortization of the discount using the straight-line method.

2008

Dec. 31   Paid the bond interest and recorded the amortization of the discount using the straight-line method.

Required

a. Show how these events would affect Herring's financial statements by recording them in a financial statements model like the following one.

	Assets	=		Liab.			+	Equity		Rev.	−	Exp.	=	Net Inc.		Cash Flow
Date	Cash	=	Bond Pay.	−	Discount	+		Ret. Earn.								
1/1/07																
12/31/07																
12/31/08																

b. Determine the carrying value of the bond liability as of December 31, 2008.

c. Assuming Herring had earnings before interest and taxes of $198,360 in 2008, calculate the times interest earned ratio.

Solution

a.

	Assets	=		Liab.			+	Equity		Rev.	−	Exp.	=	Net Inc.		Cash Flow	
Date	Cash	=	Bond Pay.	−	Discount	+		Ret. Earn.									
1/1/07	388,000	=	400,000	−	12,000	+		NA		NA	−	NA	=	NA		388,000	FA
12/31/07	(36,000)	=	NA	−	(1,200)	+		(37,200)		NA	−	37,200	=	(37,200)		(36,000)	OA
12/31/08	(36,000)	=	NA	−	(1,200)	+		(37,200)		NA	−	37,200	=	(37,200)		(36,000)	OA

b. The unamortized discount as of December 31, 2008, is $9,600 ($12,000 − $1,200 − $1,200). The carrying value of the bond liability is $390,400 ($400,000 − $9,600).

c. The times interest earned ratio is 5.3 times ($198,360 ÷ $37,200).

amortization 501
bond certificates 505
bond discount 512
bondholder 505
bond premium 517

call premium 508
call price 508
callable bonds 508
carrying value 513
collateral 519

convertible bonds 508
debentures 507
discount on bonds
 payable 513
effective interest rate 513

effective interest rate
 method 523
face value 505
financial leverage 520
fixed interest rate 501

installment notes 502
issuer 505
line of credit 505
long-term liabilities 501
market interest rate 518
mortgage bond 507

premium on bonds
   payable 517
restrictive covenants 519
secured bonds 507
serial bonds 507
sinking fund 508

spread 520
stated interest rate 506
straight-line
   amortization 514
subordinated
   debentures 507

term bonds 507
times interest earned 521
unsecured bonds 507
unsubordinated
   debentures 507
variable interest rate 501

QUESTIONS

1. What is the difference between classification of a note as short term or long term?

2. At the beginning of year 1, B Co. has a note payable of $72,000 that calls for an annual payment of $16,246, which includes both principal and interest. If the interest rate is 8 percent, what is the amount of interest expense in year 1 and in year 2? What is the balance of the note at the end of year 2?

3. What is the purpose of a line of credit for a business? Why would a company choose to obtain a line of credit instead of issuing bonds?

4. What are the primary sources of debt financing for most large companies?

5. What are some advantages of issuing bonds versus borrowing from a bank?

6. What are some disadvantages of issuing bonds?

7. Why can a company usually issue bonds at a lower interest rate than the company would pay if the funds were borrowed from a bank?

8. What effect does income tax have on the cost of borrowing funds for a business?

9. What is the concept of financial leverage?

10. Which type of bond, secured or unsecured, is likely to have a lower interest rate? Explain.

11. What is the function of restrictive covenants attached to bond issues?

12. What is the difference between term bonds and serial bonds?

13. What is the purpose of establishing a sinking fund?

14. What is the call price of a bond? Is it usually higher or lower than the face amount of the bond? Explain.

15. If Roc Co. issued $100,000 of 5 percent, 10-year bonds at the face amount, what is the effect of the issuance of the bonds on the financial statements? What amount of interest expense will Roc Co. recognize each year?

16. What mechanism is used to adjust the stated interest rate to the market rate of interest?

17. When the effective interest rate is higher than the stated interest rate on a bond issue, will the bond sell at a discount or premium? Why?

18. What type of transaction is the issuance of bonds by a company?

19. What factors may cause the effective interest rate and the stated interest rate to be different?

20. If a bond is selling at 97 ½, how much cash will the company receive from the sale of a $1,000 bond?

21. How is the carrying value of a bond computed?

22. Gay Co. has a balance in the Bonds Payable account of $25,000 and a balance in the Discount on Bonds Payable account of $5,200. What is the carrying value of the bonds? What is the total amount of the liability?

23. When the effective interest rate is higher than the stated interest rate, will interest expense be higher or lower than the amount of interest paid?

24. Assuming that the selling price of the bond and the face value are the same, would the issuer of a bond rather make annual or semiannual interest payments? Why?

25. Rato Co. called some bonds and had a loss on the redemption of the bonds of $2,850. How is this amount reported on the income statement?

26. Which method of financing, debt or equity, is generally more advantageous from a tax standpoint? Why?

27. If a company has a tax rate of 30 percent and interest expense was $10,000, what is the after-tax cost of the debt?

28. Which type of financing, debt or equity, increases the risk factor of a business? Why?

29. What information does the times interest earned ratio provide?

MULTIPLE-CHOICE QUESTIONS

Multiple-choice questions are provided on the text Web site at www.mhhe.com/edmonds6e.

Quiz 10

EXERCISES—SERIES A

Exercise 10-1A   *How credit terms affect financial statements*

L.O. 1

Jensen Co. is planning to finance an expansion of its operations by borrowing $100,000. City Bank has agreed to loan Jensen the funds. Jensen has two repayment options: (1) to issue a note with the principal due in 10 years and with interest payable annually or (2) to issue a note to repay $10,000 of the principal each year along with the annual interest based on the unpaid principal balance. Assume the interest rate is 8 percent for each option.

Required

a. What amount of interest will Jensen pay in year 1
   (1) Under option 1?
   (2) Under option 2?
b. What amount of interest will Jensen pay in year 2
   (1) Under option 1?
   (2) Under option 2?
c. Explain the advantage of each option.

Exercise 10-2A   *Accounting for a long-term note payable with annual payments that include interest and principal*

L.O. 1

On January 1, 2009, Grant Co. borrowed $80,000 cash from First Bank by issuing a four-year, 6 percent note. The principal and interest are to be paid by making annual payments in the amount of $23,087. Payments are to be made December 31 of each year, beginning December 31, 2009.

Required

Prepare an amortization schedule for the interest and principal payments for the four-year period.

Exercise 10-3A   *Long-term installment note payable*

L.O. 1

Jerry Posey started a business by issuing a $50,000 face value note to State National Bank on January 1, 2009. The note had a 5 percent annual rate of interest and a 10-year term. Payments of $6,475 are to be made each December 31 for 10 years.

Required

a. What portion of the December 31, 2009, payment is applied to
   (1) Interest expense?
   (2) Principal?
b. What is the principal balance on January 1, 2010?
c. What portion of the December 31, 2010, payment is applied to
   (1) Interest expense?
   (2) Principal?

L.O. 1

Exercise 10-4A *Amortization of a long-term loan*

A partial amortization schedule for a five-year note payable that Puro Co. issued on January 1, 2008, is shown here:

Accounting Period	Principal Balance January 1	Cash Payment	Applied to Interest	Applied to Principal
2008	$100,000	$25,046	$8,000	$17,046
2009	82,954	25,046	6,636	18,410

Required

a. What rate of interest is Puro Co. paying on the note?

b. Using a financial statements model like the one shown below, record the appropriate amounts for the following two events:

  (1) January 1, 2008, issue of the note payable.

  (2) December 31, 2009, payment on the note payable.

Event No.	Assets	=	Liab.	+	Equity	Rev.	−	Exp.	=	Net Inc.	Cash Flow
1											

c. If the company earned $75,000 cash revenue and paid $35,000 in cash expenses in addition to the interest in 2008, what is the amount of each of the following?

  (1) Net income for 2008.

  (2) Cash flow from operating activities for 2008.

  (3) Cash flow from financing activities for 2008.

d. What is the amount of interest expense on this loan for 2010?

L.O. 2

Exercise 10-5A *Accounting for a line of credit*

Davillo Company has a line of credit with Federal Bank. Davillo can borrow up to $500,000 at any time over the course of the 2008 calendar year. The following table shows the prime rate expressed as an annual percentage along with the amounts borrowed and repaid during the first four months of 2008. Davillo agreed to pay interest at an annual rate equal to 2 percent above the bank's prime rate. Funds are borrowed or repaid on the first day of each month. Interest is payable in cash on the last day of the month. The interest rate is applied to the outstanding monthly balance. For example, Davillo pays 6 percent (4 percent + 2 percent) annual interest on $80,000 for the month of January.

Month	Amount Borrowed or (Repaid)	Prime Rate for the Month, %
January	$80,000	3.0
February	60,000	3.5
March	(20,000)	4.0
April	30,000	4.5

Required

Provide all journal entries pertaining to Davillo's line of credit for the first four months of 2008.

L.O. 3

Exercise 10-6A *Annual versus semiannual interest payments*

Lacky Co. issued bonds with a face value of $120,000 on January 1, 2008. The bonds had a 6 percent stated rate of interest and a five-year term. The bonds were issued at face value.

Required

a. What total amount of interest will Lacky pay in 2008 if bond interest is paid annually each December 31?

b. What total amount of interest will Lacky pay in 2008 if bond interest is paid semiannually each June 30 and December 31?

c. Write a memo explaining which option Lacky would prefer.

Exercise 10-7A *Determining cash receipts from bond issues*   L.O. 3, 4

Required

Compute the cash proceeds from bond issues under the following terms. For each case, indicate whether the bonds sold at a premium or discount.

a. Asa, Inc., issued $300,000 of 8-year, 7 percent bonds at 101.

b. Li Co. issued $150,000 of 4-year, 6 percent bonds at 98.

c. Karl Co. issued $200,000 of 10-year, 7 percent bonds at 102 ¼.

d. Rao, Inc., issued $100,000 of 5-year, 6 percent bonds at 97 ½.

Exercise 10-8A *Identifying the relationship between the stated rate of interest and the market*   L.O. 3, 4
rate of interest

Required

Indicate whether a bond will sell at a premium (P), discount (D), or face value (F) for each of the following conditions:

a. _____ The market rate of interest is equal to the stated rate.

b. _____ The market rate of interest is less than the stated rate.

c. _____ The market rate of interest is higher than the stated rate.

d. _____ The stated rate of interest is higher than the market rate.

e. _____ The stated rate of interest is less than the market rate.

Exercise 10-9A *Identifying bond premiums and discounts*   L.O. 3, 4

Required

In each of the following situations, state whether the bonds will sell at a premium or discount.

a. Stokes issued $200,000 of bonds with a stated interest rate of 8 percent. At the time of issue, the market rate of interest for similar investments was 7 percent.

b. Shaw issued $100,000 of bonds with a stated interest rate of 8 percent. At the time of issue, the market rate of interest for similar investments was 9 percent.

c. Link Inc., issued callable bonds with a stated interest rate of 8 percent. The bonds were callable at 104. At the date of issue, the market rate of interest was 9 percent for similar investments.

Exercise 10-10A *Determining the amount of bond premiums and discounts*   L.O. 3, 4

Required

For each of the following situations, calculate the amount of bond discount or premium, if any.

a. West Co. issued $110,000 of 6 percent bonds at 102.

b. Sarah, Inc., issued $60,000 of 10-year, 8 percent bonds at 98.

c. Pulse, Inc., issued $100,000 of 15-year, 9 percent bonds at 102 ¼.

d. Dunn Co. issued $500,000 of 20-year, 8 percent bonds at 98 ¾.

Exercise 10-11A *Effect of a bond discount on financial statements: Annual interest*   L.O. 3, 4

Miller Company issued $200,000 face value of bonds on January 1, 2008. The bonds had a 6 percent stated rate of interest and a 10-year term. Interest is paid in cash annually, beginning December 31, 2008. The bonds were issued at 98.

Required

a. Use a financial statements model like the one shown below to demonstrate how (1) the January 1, 2008, bond issue and (2) the December 31, 2008, recognition of interest expense, including the amortization of the discount and the cash payment, affects the company's financial statements. Use + for increase, − for decrease, and NA for not affected.

Event No.	Assets	=	Liab.	+	Equity	Rev.	−	Exp.	=	Net Inc.	Cash Flow
1											

b. Determine the amount of interest expense reported on the 2008 income statement.
c. Determine the carrying value (face value less discount or plus premium) of the bond liability as of December 31, 2008.
d. Determine the amount of interest expense reported on the 2009 income statement.
e. Determine the carrying value (face value less discount or plus premium) of the bond liability as of December 31, 2009.

L.O. 3, 4

Exercise 10-12A *Effect of a bond premium on financial statements: Annual interest*

Bush Company issued $100,000 face value of bonds on January 1, 2008. The bonds had a 5 percent stated rate of interest and a 10-year term. Interest is paid in cash annually, beginning December 31, 2008. The bonds were issued at 102.

Required

a. Use a financial statements model like the one shown below to demonstrate how (1) the January 1, 2008 bond issue and (2) the December 31, 2008 recognition of interest expense, including the amortization of the premium and the cash payment, affects the company's financial statements. Use + for increase, − for decrease, and NA for not affected.

Event No.	Assets	=	Liab.	+	Equity	Rev.	−	Exp.	=	Net Inc.	Cash Flow
1											

b. Determine the carrying value (face value less discount or plus premium) of the bond liability as of December 31, 2008.
c. Determine the amount of interest expense reported on the 2008 income statement.
d. Determine the carrying value of the bond liability as of December 31, 2009.
e. Determine the amount of interest expense reported on the 2009 income statement.

L.O. 3, 4

Exercise 10-13A *Effect of bonds issued at a discount on financial statements: Semiannual interest*

Yard Supplies, Inc., issued $250,000 of 10-year, 6 percent bonds on July 1, 2009, at 95. Interest is payable in cash semiannually on June 30 and December 31.

Required

a. Prepare the journal entries to record issuing the bonds and any necessary journal entries for 2009 and 2010. Post the journal entries to T-accounts.
b. Prepare the liabilities section of the balance sheet at the end of 2009 and 2010.
c. What amount of interest expense will Yard Supplies report on the financial statements for 2009 and 2010?
d. What amount of cash will Yard Supplies pay for interest in 2009 and 2010?

L.O. 3

Exercise 10-14A *Recording bonds issued at face value and associated interest for two accounting cycles: Annual interest*

On January 1, 2008, Kaplan Corp. issued $220,000 of 10-year, 6 percent bonds at their face amount. Interest is payable on December 31 of each year with the first payment due December 31, 2008.

Required

Prepare all the general journal entries related to these bonds for 2008 and 2009.

Exercise 10-15A   *Recording bonds issued at a discount: Annual interest*   **L.O. 3, 4**

On January 1, 2009, Tyre Co. issued $200,000 of five-year, 6 percent bonds at 96. Interest is payable annually on December 31. The discount is amortized using the straight-line method.

Required

Prepare the journal entries to record the bond transactions for 2009 and 2010.

Exercise 10-16A   *Recording bonds issued at a premium: Annual interest*   **L.O. 3, 4**

On January 1, 2008, Hill Company issued $210,000 of five-year, 6 percent bonds at 101. Interest is payable annually on December 31. The premium is amortized using the straight-line method.

Required

Prepare the journal entries to record the bond transactions for 2008 and 2009.

Exercise 10-17A   *Two complete accounting cycles: Bonds issued at face value with*   **L.O. 3**
                         annual interest

Dancer Company issued $350,000 of 20-year, 6 percent bonds on January 1, 2008. The bonds were issued at face value. Interest is payable in cash on December 31 of each year. Dancer immediately invested the proceeds from the bond issue in land. The land was leased for an annual $56,000 of cash revenue, which was collected on December 31 of each year, beginning December 31, 2008.

Required

a. Prepare the journal entries for these events, and post them to T-accounts for 2008 and 2009.
b. Prepare the income statement, balance sheet, and statement of cash flows for 2008 and 2009.

Exercise 10-18A   *Recording callable bonds*   **L.O. 3**

Smith Co. issued $180,000 of 6 percent, 10-year, callable bonds on January 1, 2008, for their face value. The call premium was 2 percent (bonds are callable at 102). Interest was payable annually on December 31. The bonds were called on December 31, 2011.

Required

Prepare the journal entries to record the bond issue on January 1, 2008, and the bond redemption on December 31, 2011. Assume that all entries to accrue and pay interest were recorded correctly.

Exercise 10-19A   *Determining the after-tax cost of debt*   **L.O. 5**

The following 2009 information is available for three companies:

	Scott Co.	Doug Co.	Black Co.
Face value of bonds payable	$400,000	$700,000	$600,000
Interest rate	8%	7%	6%
Income tax rate	35%	20%	25%

Required

a. Determine the annual before-tax interest cost for each company *in dollars.*
b. Determine the annual after-tax interest cost for each company *in dollars.*
c. Determine the annual after-tax interest cost for each company as *a percentage* of the face value of the bonds.

L.O. 5

Exercise 10-20A *Determining the effects of financing alternatives on ratios*

Cascades Industries has the following account balances:

Current assets	$20,000	Current liabilities	$10,000
Noncurrent assets	80,000	Noncurrent liabilities	50,000
		Stockholders' equity	40,000

The company wishes to raise $40,000 in cash, and is considering two financing options. Either it can sell $40,000 of bonds payable, or it can issue additional common stock for $40,000. To help in the decision process, Cascades' management wants to determine the effects of each alternative on its current ratio and debt to assets ratio.

Required

a. Help Cascades' management by completing the following chart.

Ratio	Currently	If Bonds Are Issued	If Stock Is Issued
Current ratio			
Debt to asset ratio			

b. Assume that after the funds are invested, EBIT amounts to $12,000. Also assume the company pays $4,000 in dividends or $4,000 in interest depending on which source of financing is used. Based on a 30 percent tax rate, determine the amount of the increase in retained earnings that would result under each financing option.

L.O. 3, 6

Exercise 10-21A *Effective interest amortization of a bond discount (Appendix)*

On January 1, 2008, Sea View Condo Association issued bonds with a face value of $200,000, a stated rate of interest of 8 percent, and a 10-year term to maturity. Interest is payable in cash on December 31 of each year. The effective rate of interest was 10 percent at the time the bonds were issued. The bonds sold for $175,442. Sea View used the effective interest rate method to amortize bond discount.

Required

a. Determine the amount of the discount on the day of issue.
b. Determine the amount of interest expense recognized on December 31, 2008.
c. Determine the carrying value of the bond liability on December 31, 2008.
d. Provide the general journal entry necessary to record the December 31, 2008, interest expense.

L.O. 3, 6

Exercise 10-22A *Effective interest amortization of a bond premium (Appendix)*

On January 1, 2008, Propel Company issued bonds with a face value of $100,000, a stated rate of interest of 9 percent, and a 10-year term to maturity. Interest is payable in cash on December 31 of each year. The effective rate of interest was 8 percent at the time the bonds were issued. The bonds sold for $106,710. Propel used the effective interest rate method to amortize bond discount.

Required

a. Determine the amount of the premium on the day of issue.
b. Determine the amount of interest expense recognized on December 31, 2008.
c. Determine the carrying value of the bond liability on December 31, 2008.
d. Provide the general journal entry necessary to record the December 31, 2008, interest expense.

L.O. 3, 6

Exercise 10-23A *Amortization table and financial statement effects for bond discount (Appendix)*

On January 1, 2008, Woodland Enterprises issued bonds with a face value of $50,000, a stated rate of interest of 8 percent, and a five-year term to maturity. Interest is payable in cash on December 31 of each year. The effective rate of interest was 10 percent at the time the bonds were issued. The bonds sold for $45,209. Woodland used the effective interest rate method to amortize bond discount.

Required

a. Prepare an amortization table as shown below:

	Cash Payment	Interest Expense	Discount Amortization	Carrying Value
January 1, 2008				46,209
December 31, 2008	4,000	4,621	621	46,830
December 31, 2009	?	?	?	?
December 31, 2010	?	?	?	?
December 31, 2011	?	?	?	?
December 31, 2012	?	?	?	?
Totals	20,000	23,791	3,791	

b. What item(s) in the table would appear on the 2009 balance sheet?
c. What item(s) in the table would appear on the 2009 income statement?
d. What item(s) in the table would appear on the 2009 statement of cash flows?

Exercise 10-24A *Amortization table and financial statement effects for bond premium (Appendix)*   L.O. 3, 6

On January 1, 2008, Forsyth Incorporated issued bonds with a face value of $100,000, a stated rate of interest of 9 percent, and a five-year term to maturity. Interest is payable in cash on December 31 of each year. The effective rate of interest was 8 percent at the time the bonds were issued. The bonds sold for $103,993. Forsyth used the effective interest rate method to amortize bond discount.

Required

a. Prepare an amortization table as shown below:

	Cash Payment	Interest Expense	Premium Amortization	Carrying Value
January 1, 2008				103,993
December 31, 2008	9,000	8,319	681	103,312
December 31, 2009	?	?	?	?
December 31, 2010	?	?	?	?
December 31, 2011	?	?	?	?
December 31, 2012	?	?	?	?
Totals	45,000	41,007	3,993	

b. What item(s) in the table would appear on the 2010 balance sheet?
c. What item(s) in the table would appear on the 2010 income statement?
d. What item(s) in the table would appear on the 2010 statement of cash flows?

Exercise 10-25A *Effective interest versus straight-line amortization (Appendix)*   L.O. 3, 6

On January 1, 2007, Scott and Associates issued bonds with a face value of $1,000,000, a stated rate of interest of 9 percent, and a 20-year term to maturity. Interest is payable in cash on December 31 of each year. The effective rate of interest was 11 percent at the time the bonds were issued.

Required

Write a brief memo explaining whether the effective interest rate method or the straight-line method will produce the highest amount of interest expense recognized on the 2007 income statement.

PROBLEMS—SERIES A

All Problems in Series A are available with McGraw-Hill's Homework Manager®

L.O. 1

CHECK FIGURES
a. 2008 Ending Principal
   Balance: $55,116
b. 2010 Net Income:
   $38,006

Problem 10-26A *Effect of a term loan on financial statements*

On January 1, 2008, Holmes Co. borrowed cash from First City Bank by issuing an $80,000 face value, three-year term note that had a 7 percent annual interest rate. The note is to be repaid by making annual payments of $30,484 that include both interest and principal on December 31. Holmes invested the proceeds from the loan in land that generated lease revenues of $40,000 cash per year.

Required

a. Prepare an amortization schedule for the three-year period.

b. Prepare an income statement, balance sheet, and statement of cash flows for each of the three years. (*Hint:* Record the transactions for each year in T-accounts before preparing the financial statements.)

c. Does cash outflow from operating activities remain constant or change each year? Explain.

L.O. 2

CHECK FIGURES
a. Interest Expense:
   $5,650
   Total Assets: $56,350

Problem 10-27A *Effect of a line of credit on financial statements*

Hulse Company has a line of credit with Bay Bank. Hulse can borrow up to $250,000 at any time over the course of the 2008 calendar year. The following table shows the prime rate expressed as an annual percentage along with the amounts borrowed and repaid during 2008. Hulse agreed to pay interest at an annual rate equal to 1 percent above the bank's prime rate. Funds are borrowed or repaid on the first day of each month. Interest is payable in cash on the last day of the month. The interest rate is applied to the outstanding monthly balance. For example, Hulse pays 6 percent (5 percent + 1 percent) annual interest on $70,000 for the month of January.

Month	Amount Borrowed or (Repaid)	Prime Rate for the Month, %
January	$70,000	5
February	40,000	5
March	(20,000)	6
April through October	No change	No change
November	(30,000)	6
December	(20,000)	5

Hulse earned $22,000 of cash revenue during 2008.

Required

a. Prepare an income statement, balance sheet, and statement of cash flows for 2008.

b. Write a memo discussing the advantages to a business of arranging a line of credit.

L.O. 3, 4

eXcel

CHECK FIGURES
2008 Operating Income:
$8,533
2011 Total Assets:
$25,000

Problem 10-28A *Accounting for a bond premium over multiple accounting cycles*

Parrish Company was started when it issued bonds with $200,000 face value on January 1, 2008. The bonds were issued for cash at 104. They had a 15-year term to maturity and an 8 percent annual interest rate. Interest was payable annually. Parrish immediately purchased land with the proceeds (cash received) from the bond issue. Parrish leased the land for $24,000 cash per year. On January 1, 2011, the company sold the land for $211,000 cash. Immediately after the sale, Parrish repurchased its bonds (repaid the bond liability) at 105. Assume that no other accounting events occurred in 2011.

Required

Prepare an income statement, statement of changes in equity, balance sheet and statement of cash flows for each of the 2008, 2009, 2010, and 2011 accounting periods. Assume that the company closes its books on December 31 of each year. Prepare the statements using a vertical statements format. (*Hint:* Record each year's transactions in T-accounts prior to preparing the financial statements.)

Problem 10-29A *Recording and reporting a bond discount over two cycles: Semiannual interest*   **L.O 3, 4**

During 2008 and 2009, Gupta Co. completed the following transactions relating to its bond issue. The company's fiscal year ends on December 31.

2008

Mar. 1 Issued $100,000 of eight-year, 7 percent bonds for $96,000. The semiannual cash payment for interest is due on March 1 and September 1, beginning September 2008.

Sept. 1 Recognized interest expense including the amortization of the discount and made the semi-annual cash payment for interest.

Dec. 31 Recognized accrued interest expense including the amortization of the discount.

Dec. 31 Closed the interest expense account.

2009

Mar. 1 Recognized interest expense including the amortization of the discount and made the semi-annual cash payment for interest.

Sept. 1 Recognized interest expense including the amortization of the discount and made the semi-annual cash payment for interest.

Dec. 31 Recognized accrued interest expense including the amortization of the discount.

Dec. 31 Closed the interest expense account.

Required

a. When the bonds were issued, was the market rate of interest more or less than the stated rate of interest? If the bonds had sold at face value, what amount of cash would Gupta Co. have received?

b. Prepare the general journal entries for these transactions.

c. Prepare the liabilities section of the balance sheet at December 31, 2008 and 2009.

d. Determine the amount of interest expense Gupta would report on the income statements for 2008 and 2009.

e. Determine the amount of interest Gupta would pay to the bondholders in 2008 and 2009.

CHECK FIGURES
d. 2008 Interest
   Expense: $6,250
e. 2008 Interest Paid:
   $3,500

Problem 10-30A *Effect of a bond discount on the elements of financial statements*   **L.O. 3, 4**

Sayles Co. was formed when it acquired cash from the issue of common stock. The company then issued bonds at a discount on January 1, 2008. Interest is payable on December 31 with the first payment made December 31, 2003. On January 2, 2008, Sayles Co. purchased a piece of land that produced rent revenue annually. The rent is collected on December 31 of each year, beginning December 31, 2008. At the end of the six-year period (January 1, 2014), the land was sold at a gain, and the bonds were paid off at face value. A summary of the transactions for each year follows:

2008

1. Acquired cash from the issue of common stock.

2. Issued six-year bonds.

3. Purchased land.

4. Received land-lease income.

5. Recognized interest expense, including the amortization of the discount, and made the cash payment for interest on December 31.

6. Prepared December 31 entry to close Rent Revenue.

7. Prepared December 31 entry to close Interest Expense.

2009–2013

8. Received land-lease income.

9. Recognized interest expense, including the amortization of the discount, and made the cash payment for interest December 31.

10. Prepared December 31 entry to close Rent Revenue.

11. Prepared December 31 entry to close Interest Expense.

2014

12. Sold the land at a gain.

13. Retired the bonds at face value.

Required

Identify each of these 13 transactions as asset source (AS), asset use (AU), asset exchange (AE), or claims exchange (CE). Explain how each event affects assets, liabilities, equity, net income, and cash flow by placing a + for increase, − for decrease, or NA for not affected under each of the categories. In the Cash Flow column, indicate whether the item is an operating activity (OA), investing activity (IA), or financing activity (FA). The first event is recorded as an example.

Event No.	Type of Event	Assets	=	Liabilities	+	Common Stock	+	Retained Earnings	Net Income	Cash Flow
1	AS	+		NA		+		NA	NA	+ FA

L.O. 3

CHECK FIGURE
b. Interest Expense: $12,000
Loss on Bond Redemption: $2,250

Problem 10-31A *Recording transactions for callable bonds*

Porter Co. issued $150,000 of 10-year, 8 percent, callable bonds on January 1, 2010, with interest payable annually on December 31. The bonds were issued at their face amount. The bonds are callable at 101 ½. The fiscal year of the corporation is the calendar year.

Required

a. Show the effect of the following events on the financial statements by recording the appropriate amounts in a horizontal statements model like the following one. In the Cash Flow column, indicate whether the item is an operating activity (OA), investing activity (IA), or financing activity (FA). Use NA if an element was not affected by the event.

   (1) Issued the bonds on January 1, 2010.
   (2) Paid interest due to bondholders on December 31, 2010.
   (3) On January 1, 2014, Porter Co. called the bonds. Assume that all interim entries were correctly recorded.

Event No.	Assets	=	Liab.	+	Equity	Rev.	−	Exp.	=	Net Inc.	Cash Flow
1											

b. Prepare journal entries for the three events listed in Requirement *a*.

L.O. 1, 2, 3, 5

Problem 10-32A *Effect of debt transactions on financial statements*

The three typical accounting events associated with borrowing money through a bond issue are:

1. Exchanging the bonds for cash on the day of issue.
2. Making cash payments for interest expense and recording amortization when applicable.
3. Repaying the principal at maturity.

Required

a. Assuming the bonds are issued at face value, show the effect of each of the three events on the financial statements, using a horizontal statements model like the following one. Use + for increase, − for decrease, and NA for not affected.

Event No.	Assets	=	Liab.	+	Equity	Rev.	−	Exp.	=	Net Inc.	Cash Flow
1											

b. Repeat the requirements in Requirement *a*, but assume instead that the bonds are issued at a discount.
c. Repeat the requirements in Requirement *a*, but assume instead that the bonds are issued at a premium.

Problem 10-33A *Using ratios to make comparisons*

L.O. 5

The following information pertains to Seattle and Portland companies at the end of 2008.

Account Title	Seattle	Portland
Current assets	$ 30,000	$ 30,000
Total assets	200,000	200,000
Current liabilities	20,000	15,000
Total liabilities	150,000	110,000
Stockholders' equity	50,000	90,000
Interest expense	13,000	10,000
Income tax expense	20,000	21,500
Net income	28,500	29,100

CHECK FIGURE
a. Times Interest
Earned–Seattle:
4.7 times

Required

a. Compute each company's debt to assets ratio, current ratio, and times interest earned (EBIT must be computed). Identify the company with the greater financial risk.

b. Compute each company's return on equity ratio and return on assets ratio. Use EBIT instead of net income when computing the return on assets ratio. Identify the company that is managing its assets more effectively. Identify the company that is producing the higher return from the stockholders' perspective. Explain how one company was able to produce a higher return on equity than the other.

Problem 10-34A *Effective interest versus straight-line amortization (Appendix)*

L.O. 3, 4, 6

On January 1, 2009, Roma Corp. sold $200,000 of its own 8 percent, 10-year bonds. Interest is payable annually on December 31. The bonds were sold to yield an effective interest rate of 7 percent. Roma Corp. uses the effective interest rate method. The bonds sold for $214,047.

CHECK FIGURE
c. 2011 Interest
Expense: $14,595

Required

a. Prepare the journal entry for the issuance of the bonds.

b. Prepare the journal entry for the amortization of the bond premium and the payment of the interest on December 31, 2011. (Assume effective interest amortization.)

c. Prepare the journal entry for the amortization of the bond premium and the payment of interest on December 31, 2011. (Assume straight-line amortization.)

d. Calculate the amount of interest expense for 2012. (Assume effective interest amortization.)

e. Calculate the amount of interest expense for 2012. (Assume straight-line amortization.)

EXERCISES—SERIES B

Exercise 10-1B *How credit terms affect financial statements*

L.O. 1

Voss Co. borrowed $60,000 from the National Bank by issuing a note with a five-year term. Voss has two options with respect to the payment of interest and principal. Option 1 requires the payment of interest only on an annual basis with the full amount of the principal due at maturity. Option 2 calls for an annual payment that includes interest due plus a partial repayment of the principal balance. The effective annual interest rate on both notes is identical.

Required

Write a memo explaining how the two alternatives will affect *(a)* the carrying value of liabilities, *(b)* the amount of annual interest expense, *(c)* the total amount of interest that will be paid over the life of the note, and *(d)* the cash flow consequences.

L.O. 1

Exercise 10-2B *Accounting for a long-term note payable with annual payments that include interest and principal*

On January 1, 2008, Rupp Co. borrowed $150,000 cash from Central Bank by issuing a five-year, 8 percent note. The principal and interest are to be paid by making annual payments in the amount of $37,568. Payments are to be made December 31 of each year, beginning December 31, 2008.

Required

Prepare an amortization schedule for the interest and principal payments for the five-year period.

L.O. 1

Exercise 10-3B *Long-term installment note payable*

Fred Blan started a business by issuing a $70,000 face value note to First State Bank on January 1, 2008. The note had a 10 percent annual rate of interest and a five-year term. Payments of $17,072 are to be made each December 31 for five years.

Required

a. What portion of the December 31, 2008, payment is applied to
   (1) Interest expense?
   (2) Principal?
b. What is the principal balance on January 1, 2009?
c. What portion of the December 31, 2009, payment is applied to
   (1) Interest expense?
   (2) Principal?

L.O. 1

Exercise 10-4B *Amortization of a long-term loan*

A partial amortization schedule for a 10-year note payable issued on January 1, 2008, is shown below:

Accounting Period	Principal Balance January 1	Cash Payment	Applied to Interest	Applied to Principal
2008	$200,000	$32,549	$20,000	$12,549
2009	187,451	32,549	18,745	13,804
2010	173,647	32,549	17,365	15,184

Required

a. Using a financial statements model like the one shown here, record the appropriate amounts for the following two events:
   (1) January 1, 2008, issue of the note payable.
   (2) December 31, 2008, payment on the note payable.

Event No.	Assets	=	Liab.	+	Equity	Rev.	−	Exp.	=	Net Inc.	Cash Flow
1											

b. If the company earned $100,000 cash revenue and paid $50,000 in cash expenses in addition to the interest in 2008, what is the amount of each of the following?
   (1) Net income for 2008.
   (2) Cash flow from operating activities for 2008.
   (3) Cash flow from financing activities for 2008.
c. What is the amount of interest expense on this loan for 2011?

L.O. 2

Exercise 10-5B *Accounting for a line of credit*

Shastri Company has a line of credit with United Bank. Shastri can borrow up to $150,000 at any time over the course of the 2009 calendar year. The following table shows the prime rate expressed as an annual percentage along with the amounts borrowed and repaid during the first three months of 2009. Shastri agreed to pay interest at an annual rate equal to 2 percent above the bank's prime rate. Funds are borrowed or repaid on the first day of each month. Interest is payable in cash on the last day of the month. The interest rate is applied to the outstanding monthly balance. For example, Shastri pays 6.5 percent (4.5 percent + 2 percent) annual interest on $80,000 for the month of February.

Month	Amount Borrowed or (Repaid)	Prime Rate for the Month, %
January	$50,000	4.0
February	30,000	4.5
March	(40,000)	4.0

Required

Provide all journal entries pertaining to Shastri's line of credit for the first three months of 2009.

Exercise 10-6B *Annual versus semiannual interest payments*

L.O. 3

Carlin Company issued bonds with a face value of $60,000 on January 1, 2008. The bonds had an 8 percent stated rate of interest and a six-year term. The bonds were issued at face value. Interest is payable on an annual basis.

Required

Write a memo explaining whether the total cash outflow for interest would be more, less, or the same if the bonds pay semiannual versus annual interest.

Exercise 10-7B *Determining cash receipts from bond issues*

L.O. 3, 4

Required

Compute the cash proceeds from bond issues under the following terms. For each case, indicate whether the bonds sold at a premium or discount.

a. Red, Inc., issued $200,000 of 10-year, 8 percent bonds at 104.
b. Blue, Inc., issued $80,000 of five-year, 12 percent bonds at 96 ½.
c. Green Co. issued $100,000 of five-year, 6 percent bonds at 102 ¼.
d. Yellow, Inc., issued $50,000 of four-year, 8 percent bonds at 97.

Exercise 10-8B *Identifying the relationship between the stated rate of interest and the market rate of interest*

L.O. 3, 4

Required

Indicate whether a bond will sell at a premium (P), discount (D), or face value (F) for each of the following conditions:

a. _____ The market rate of interest is less than the stated rate.
b. _____ The market rate of interest is equal to the stated rate.
c. _____ The stated rate of interest is higher than the market rate.
d. _____ The market rate of interest is higher than the stated rate.
e. _____ The stated rate of interest is less than the market rate.

Exercise 10-9B *Identifying bond premiums and discounts*

L.O. 3, 4

Required

In each of the following situations, state whether the bonds will sell at a premium or discount.

a. Han issued $200,000 of bonds with a stated interest rate of 6.5 percent. At the time of issue, the market rate of interest for similar investments was 6 percent.
b. Hall issued $300,000 of bonds with a stated interest rate of 5.5 percent. At the time of issue, the market rate of interest for similar investments was 6 percent.
c. Horne Inc. issued callable bonds with a stated interest rate of 6 percent. The bonds were callable at 101. At the date of issue, the market rate of interest was 6.5 percent for similar investments.

L.O. 3, 4

Exercise 10-10B   *Determining the amount of bond premiums and discounts*

Required

For each of the following situations, calculate the amount of bond discount or premium, if any.

a. Lind Co. issued $60,000 of 7 percent bonds at 101 ¼.
b. Schwarz, Inc., issued $90,000 of 10-year, 6 percent bonds at 95 ½.
c. Zoe, Inc., issued $200,000 of 20-year, 6 percent bonds at 102.
d. Uddin Co. issued $150,000 of 15-year, 7 percent bonds at 98.

L.O. 3, 4

Exercise 10-11B   *Effect of a bond discount on financial statements: Annual interest*

Price Company issued $100,000 face value of bonds on January 1, 2009. The bonds had an 8 percent stated rate of interest and a five-year term. Interest is paid in cash annually, beginning December 31, 2009. The bonds were issued at 98.

Required

a. Use a financial statements model like the one shown below to demonstrate how (1) the January 1, 2009, bond issue and (2) the December 31, 2009, recognition of interest expense, including the amortization of the discount and the cash payment, affects the company's financial statements. Use + for increase, − for decrease, and NA for not affected.

Event No.	Assets	=	Liab.	+	Equity	Rev.	−	Exp.	=	Net Inc.	Cash Flow
1											

b. Determine the carrying value (face value less discount or plus premium) of the bond liability as of December 31, 2009.
c. Determine the amount of interest expense reported on the 2009 income statement.
d. Determine the carrying value (face value less discount or plus premium) of the bond liability as of December 31, 2010.
e. Determine the amount of interest expense reported on the 2010 income statement.

L.O. 3, 4

Exercise 10-12B   *Effect of a bond premium on financial statements: Annual interest*

Polish Company issued $100,000 face value of bonds on January 1, 2009. The bonds had an 8 percent stated rate of interest and a five-year term. Interest is paid in cash annually, beginning December 31, 2009. The bonds were issued at 102.

Required

a. Use a financial statements model like the one shown below to demonstrate how (1) the January 1, 2009, bond issue and (2) the December 31, 2009, recognition of interest expense, including the amortization of the premium and the cash payment, affects the company's financial statements. Use + for increase, − for decrease, and NA for not affected

Event No.	Assets	=	Liab.	+	Equity	Rev.	−	Exp.	=	Net Inc.	Cash Flow
1											

b. Determine the carrying value (face value less discount or plus premium) of the bond liability as of December 31, 2009.
c. Determine the amount of interest expense reported on the 2009 income statement.
d. Determine the carrying value of the bond liability as of December 31, 2010.
e. Determine the amount of interest expense reported on the 2010 income statement.

Exercise 10-13B   *Effect of bonds issued at a premium on financial statements:*   **L.O. 3, 4**
Semiannual interest

Pet Supplies, Inc., issued $200,000 of 10-year, 6 percent bonds on July 1, 2009, at 103. Interest is payable in cash semiannually on June 30 and December 31.

Required

a. Prepare the journal entries to record issuing the bonds and any necessary journal entries for 2009 and 2010. Post the journal entries to T-accounts.
b. Prepare the liabilities section of the balance sheet at the end of 2009 and 2010.
c. What amount of interest expense will Pet report on the financial statements for 2009 and 2010?
d. What amount of cash will Pet pay for interest in 2009 and 2010?

Exercise 10-14B   *Recording bonds issued at face value and associated interest for two*   **L.O. 3**
accounting cycles: Annual interest

On January 1, 2009, Peck Corp. issued $200,000 of 10-year, 9 percent bonds at their face amount. Interest is payable on December 31 of each year with the first payment due December 31, 2009.

Required

Prepare all the general journal entries related to these bonds for 2009 and 2010.

Exercise 10-15B   *Recording bonds issued at a discount: Annual interest*   **L.O. 3, 4**

On January 1, 2008, Hays Co. issued $150,000 of five-year, 8 percent bonds at 98 ½. Interest is payable annually on December 31. The discount is amortized using the straight-line method.

Required

Prepare the journal entries to record the bond transactions for 2008 and 2009.

Exercise 10-16B   *Recording bonds issued at a premium: Semiannual interest*   **L.O. 3, 4**

On January 1, 2009, Caldwell Company issued $200,000 of five-year, 8 percent bonds at 103. Interest is payable semiannually on June 30 and December 31. The premium is amortized using the straight-line method.

Required

Prepare the journal entries to record the bond transactions for 2009 and 2010.

Exercise 10-17B   *Two complete accounting cycles: Bonds issued at face value with*   **L.O. 3**
annual interest

Poole Company issued $1,000,000 of 10-year, 8 percent bonds on January 1, 2009. The bonds were issued at face value. Interest is payable in cash on December 31 of each year. Poole immediately invested the proceeds from the bond issue in land. The land was leased for an annual $140,000 of cash revenue, which was collected on December 31 of each year, beginning December 31, 2009.

Required

a. Prepare the journal entries for these events, and post them to T-accounts for 2009 and 2010.
b. Prepare the income statement, balance sheet, and statement of cash flows for 2009 and 2010.

Exercise 10-18B   *Recording callable bonds*   **L.O. 3**

Huta Co. issued $500,000 of 8 percent, 10-year, callable bonds on January 1, 2008, for their face value. The call premium was 4 percent (bonds are callable at 104). Interest was payable annually on December 31. The bonds were called on December 31, 2012.

Required

Prepare the journal entries to record the bond issue on January 1, 2008, and the bond redemption on December 31, 2012. Assume that all entries for accrual and payment of interest were recorded correctly.

L.O. 5

Exercise 10-19B   *Determining the after-tax cost of debt*

The following 2009 information is available for three companies:

	Hunt Co.	Hand Co.	Hart Co.
Face value of bonds payable	$300,000	$600,000	$500,000
Interest rate	10%	9%	8%
Income tax rate	40%	30%	35%

Required

a. Determine the annual before-tax interest cost for each company *in dollars.*

b. Determine the annual after-tax interest cost for each company *in dollars.*

c. Determine the annual after-tax interest cost for each company as *a percentage* of the face value of the bonds.

L.O. 5

Exercise 10-20B   *Determining the effects of financing alternatives on ratios*

Composite Solutions Company (CSC) has the following account balances:

Current assets	$100,000	Current liabilities	$ 65,000
Noncurrent assets	225,000	Noncurrent liabilities	160,000
		Stockholders' equity	100,000

The company wishes to raise $50,000 in cash, and is considering two financing options. Either it can sell $50,000 of bonds payable, or it can issue additional common stock for $50,000. To help in the decision process, CSC's management wants to determine the effects of each alternative on its current ratio and debt to assets ratio.

Required

a. Help CSC's management by completing the following chart:

Ratio	Currently	If Bonds Are Issued	If Stock Is Issued
Current ratio			
Debt to asset ratio			

b. Assume that after the funds are invested, EBIT amounts to $40,000. Also assume the company pays $4,000 in dividends or $4,000 in interest depending on which source of financing is used. Based on a 40 percent tax rate, determine the amount of the increase in retained earnings that would result under each financing option.

L.O. 3, 6

Exercise 10-21B   *Effective interest amortization of a bond discount (Appendix)*

On January 1, 2008, the Lake Shore Landing Association issued bonds with a face value of $100,000, a stated rate of interest of 9 percent, and a 10-year term to maturity. Interest is payable in cash on December 31 of each year. The effective rate of interest was 11 percent at the time the bonds were issued. The bonds sold for $88,222. Lake Shore used the effective interest rate method to amortize bond discount.

Required

a. Determine the amount of the discount on the day of issue.

b. Determine the amount of interest expense recognized on December 31, 2008.

c. Determine the carrying value of the bond liability on December 31, 2008.

d. Provide the general journal entry necessary to record the December 31, 2008, interest expense.

Exercise 10-22B   *Effective interest amortization of a bond premium (Appendix)*   **L.O. 3, 6**

On January 1, 2008, Glover Company issued bonds with a face value of $500,000, a stated rate of interest of 8 percent, and a 10-year term to maturity. Interest is payable in cash on December 31 of each year. The effective rate of interest was 6 percent at the time the bonds were issued. The bonds sold for $573,601. Glover used the effective interest rate method to amortize bond premium.

Required

a. Determine the amount of the premium on the day of issue.
b. Determine the amount of interest expense recognized on December 31, 2008.
c. Determine the carrying value of the bond liability on December 31, 2008.
d. Provide the general journal entry necessary to record the December 31, 2008, interest expense.

Exercise 10-23B   *Amortization table and financial statement effects for bond discount (Appendix)*   **L.O. 3, 6**

On January 1, 2008, Phillips Company issued bonds with a face value of $300,000, a stated rate of interest of 12 percent, and a five-year term to maturity. Interest is payable in cash on December 31 of each year. The effective rate of interest was 14 percent at the time the bonds were issued. The bonds sold for $279,402. Phillips used the effective interest rate method to amortize bond discount.

Required

a. Prepare an amortization table as shown below:

	Cash Payment	Interest Expense	Discount Amortization	Carrying Value
January 1, 2008				279,402
December 31, 2008	36,000	39,116	3,116	282,518
December 31, 2009	?	?	?	?
December 31, 2010	?	?	?	?
December 31, 2011	?	?	?	?
December 31, 2012	?	?	?	?
Totals	180,000	200,598	20,598	

b. What item(s) in the table would appear on the 2011 balance sheet?
c. What item(s) in the table would appear on the 2011 income statement?
d. What item(s) in the table would appear on the 2011 statement of cash flows?

Exercise 10-24B   *Amortization table and financial statement effects for bond premium (Appendix)*   **L.O. 3, 6**

On January 1, 2008, Kohlbeck Company issued bonds with a face value of $600,000, a stated rate of interest of 13 percent, and a five-year term to maturity. Interest is payable in cash on December 31 of each year. The effective rate of interest was 11 percent at the time the bonds were issued. The bonds sold for $644,351. Kohlbeck used the effective interest rate method to amortize bond premium.

Required

a. Prepare an amortization table as shown below:

	Cash Payment	Interest Expense	Premium Amortization	Carrying Value
January 1, 2008				644,351
December 31, 2008	78,000	70,879	7,121	637,229
December 31, 2009	?	?	?	?
December 31, 2010	?	?	?	?
December 31, 2011	?	?	?	?
December 31, 2012	?	?	?	?
Totals	390,000	345,649	44,351	

b. What item(s) in the table would appear on the 2011 balance sheet?

c. What item(s) in the table would appear on the 2011 income statement?

d. What item(s) in the table would appear on the 2011 statement of cash flows?

L.O. 3, 6

Exercise 10-25B   *Effective interest versus straight-line amortization (Appendix)*

On January 1, 2009, the Martin Companies issued bonds with a face value of $2,000,000, a stated rate of interest of 12 percent, and a 20-year term to maturity. Interest is payable in cash on December 31 of each year. The effective rate of interest was 10 percent at the time the bonds were issued.

Required

Write a brief memo explaining whether the effective interest rate method or the straight-line method will produce the highest amount of interest expense recognized on the 2009 income statement.

PROBLEMS—SERIES B

L.O. 1

Problem 10-26B   *Effect of a long-term note payable on financial statements*

On January 1, 2009, Sneed Co. borrowed cash from Best Bank by issuing a $100,000 face value, four-year term note that had a 10 percent annual interest rate. The note is to be repaid by making annual cash payments of $31,547 that include both interest and principal on December 31 of each year. Sneed used the proceeds from the loan to purchase land that generated rental revenues of $40,000 cash per year.

Required

a. Prepare an amortization schedule for the four-year period.

b. Prepare an income statement, balance sheet, and statement of cash flows for each of the four years. (*Hint:* Record the transactions for each year in T-accounts before preparing the financial statements.)

c. Given that revenue is the same for each period, explain why net income increases each year.

L.O. 2

Problem 10-27B   *Effect of a line of credit on financial statements*

Song Company has a line of credit with State Bank. Song can borrow up to $200,000 at any time over the course of the 2009 calendar year. The following table shows the prime rate expressed as an annual percentage along with the amounts borrowed and repaid during 2009. Song agreed to pay interest at an annual rate equal to 2 percent above the bank's prime rate. Funds are borrowed or repaid on the first day of each month. Interest is payable in cash on the last day of the month. The interest rate is applied to the outstanding monthly balance. For example, Song pays 7 percent (5 percent + 2 percent) annual interest on $100,000 for the month of January.

Month	Amount Borrowed or (Repaid)	Prime Rate for the Month, %
January	$100,000	5
February	50,000	6
March	(40,000)	7
April through October	No change	No change
November	(80,000)	6
December	(20,000)	5

Song earned $30,000 of cash revenue during 2009.

Required

a. Prepare an income statement, balance sheet, and statement of cash flows for 2009. (*Note:* Round computations to the nearest dollar.)

b. Write a memo to explain how the business was able to generate retained earnings when the owner contributed no assets to the business.

Problem 10-28B   *Accounting for a bond discount over multiple accounting cycles*

Vole Company was started when it issued bonds with a $400,000 face value on January 1, 2008. The bonds were issued for cash at 96. They had a 20-year term to maturity and an 8 percent annual interest rate. Interest was payable on December 31 of each year. Vole Company immediately purchased land with the proceeds (cash received) from the bond issue. Vole leased the land for $50,000 cash per year. On January 1, 2011, the company sold the land for $400,000 cash. Immediately after the sale of the land, Vole redeemed the bonds at 98. Assume that no other accounting events occurred during 2011.

Required

Prepare an income statement, statement of changes in equity, balance sheet, and statement of cash flows for the 2008, 2009, 2010, and 2011 accounting periods. Assume that the company closes its books on December 31 of each year. Prepare the statements using a vertical statements format. (*Hint:* Record each year's transactions in T-accounts prior to preparing the financial statements.)

Problem 10-29B   *Recording and reporting bond discount over two cycles*

During 2008 and 2009, Yue Corp. completed the following transactions relating to its bond issue. The corporation's fiscal year is the calendar year.

2008

Jan. 1   Issued $100,000 of ten-year, 10 percent bonds for $96,000. The annual cash payment for interest is due on December 31.

Dec. 31   Recognized interest expense, including the amortization of the discount, and made the cash payment for interest.

Dec. 31   Closed the interest expense account.

2009

Dec. 31   Recognized interest expense, including the amortization of the discount, and made the cash payment for interest.

Dec. 31   Closed the interest expense account.

Required

a. When the bonds were issued, was the market rate of interest more or less than the stated rate of interest? If Yue had sold the bonds at their face amount, what amount of cash would Yue have received?

b. Prepare the general journal entries for these transactions.

c. Prepare the liabilities section of the balance sheet at December 31, 2008 and 2009.

d. Determine the amount of interest expense that will be reported on the income statements for 2008 and 2009.

e. Determine the amount of interest that will be paid in cash to the bondholders in 2008 and 2009.

Problem 10-30B   *Effect of a bond premium on the elements of financial statements*

Paris Land Co. was formed when it acquired cash from the issue of common stock. The company then issued bonds at a premium on January 1, 2008. Interest is payable annually on December 31 of each year, beginning December 31, 2008. On January 2, 2008, Paris Land Co. purchased a piece of land and leased it for an annual rental fee. The rent is received annually on December 31, beginning December 31, 2008. At the end of the eight-year period (December 31, 2015), the land was sold at a gain, and the bonds were paid off. A summary of the transactions for each year follows:

2008

1. Acquired cash from the issue of common stock.

2. Issued eight-year bonds.

3. Purchased land.

4. Received land-lease income.

5. Recognized interest expense including the amortization of the premium and made the cash payment for interest on December 31.

6. Prepared the December 31 entry to close Rent Revenue.

7. Prepared the December 31 entry to close Interest Expense.

2009–2014

8. Received land-lease income.
9. Recognized interest expense including the amortization of the premium and made the cash payment for interest on December 31.
10. Prepared the December 31 entry to close Rent Revenue.
11. Prepared the December 31 entry to close Interest Expense.

2013

12. Sold land at a gain.
13. Retired bonds at face value.

Required

Identify each of these 13 transactions as asset source (AS), asset use (AU), asset exchange (AE), or claims exchange (CE). Explain how each event affects assets, liabilities, equity, net income, and cash flow by placing a + for increase, − for decrease, or NA for not affected under each category. In the Cash Flow column, indicate whether the item is an operating activity (OA), investing activity (IA), or financing activity (FA). The first event is recorded as an example.

Event No.	Type of Event	Assets	=	Liabilities	+	Common Stock	+	Retained Earnings	Net Income	Cash Flow
1	AS	+		NA		+		NA	NA	+ FA

L.O. 3

Problem 10-31B   *Recording transactions for callable bonds*

IHL Corp. issued $300,000 of 20-year, 10 percent, callable bonds on January 1, 2009, with interest payable annually on December 31. The bonds were issued at their face amount. The bonds are callable at 105. The fiscal year of the corporation ends December 31.

Required

a. Show the effect of the following events on the financial statements by recording the appropriate amounts in a horizontal statements model like the following one. In the Cash Flow column, indicate whether the item is an operating activity (OA), investing activity (IA), or financing activity (FA). Use NA if an element was not affected by the event.

   (1) Issued the bonds on January 1, 2009.
   (2) Paid interest due to bondholders on December 31, 2009.
   (3) On January 1, 2014, IHL Corp. called the bonds. Assume that all interim entries were correctly recorded.

Event No.	Assets	=	Liab.	+	Equity	Rev.	−	Exp.	=	Net Inc.	Cash Flow
1											

b. Prepare journal entries for the three events listed in Requirement *a*.

L.O. 1, 2, 3, 5

Problem 10-32B   *Effect of debt transactions on financial statements*

Required

Show the effect of each of the following independent accounting events on the financial statements using a horizontal statements model like the following one. Use + for increase, − for decrease, and NA for not affected. The first event is recorded as an example.

Event No.	Assets	=	Liab.	+	Equity	Rev.	−	Exp.	=	Net Inc.	Cash Flow
1	+		+		NA	NA		NA		NA	FA +

a. Issued a bond at a premium.

b. Made an interest payment on a bond that had been issued at a premium and amortized the premium.

c. Borrowed funds using a line of credit.

d. Made an interest payment for funds that had been borrowed against a line of credit.

e. Made a cash payment on a note payable for both interest and principal.

f. Issued a bond at face value.

g. Made an interest payment on a bond that had been issued at face value.

h. Issued a bond at a discount.

i. Made an interest payment on a bond that had been issued at a discount and amortized the discount.

Problem 10-33B *Using ratios to make comparisons*

L.O. 5

The following information pertains to Allen's Auto Repair and Carl's Car Maintenance at the end of 2008.

Account Title	Allen's Auto Repair	Carl's Car Maintenance
Current assets	$ 45,000	$ 45,000
Total assets	800,000	800,000
Current liabilities	78,000	57,000
Total liabilities	675,000	500,000
Stockholders' equity	125,000	300,000
Interest expense	62,000	45,000
Income tax expense	69,000	75,500
Net income	105,000	115,000

Required

a. Compute each company's debt to assets ratio, current ratio, and times interest earned (EBIT must be computed). Identify the company with the greater financial risk.

b. Compute each company's return on equity ratio and return on assets ratio. Use EBIT instead of net income when computing the return on assets ratio. Identify the company that is managing its assets more effectively. Identify the company that is producing the higher return from the stockholders' perspective. Explain how one company was able to produce a higher return on equity than the other.

Problem 10-34B *Effective interest versus straight-line amortization (Appendix)*

L.O. 3, 4, 6

On January 1, 2009, Mode Corp. sold $500,000 of its own 8 percent, 10-year bonds. Interest is payable annually on December 31. The bonds were sold to yield an effective interest rate of 9 percent. Mode uses the effective interest rate method. The bonds sold for $467,912.

Required

a. Prepare the journal entry for the issuance of the bonds.

b. Prepare the journal entry for the amortization of the bond discount and the payment of the interest at December 31, 2009. (Assume effective interest amortization.)

c. Prepare the journal entry for the amortization of the bond discount and the payment of interest on December 31, 2009. (Assume straight-line amortization.)

d. Calculate the amount of interest expense for 2010. (Assume effective interest amortization.)

e. Calculate the amount of interest expense for 2010. (Assume straight-line amortization.)

ANALYZE, THINK, COMMUNICATE

ATC 10-1 Business Applications Case *Understanding real-world annual reports*

Required—Part 1

Use the Topps Company's annual report in Appendix B to answer the following questions.

a. On its balance sheet Topps shows "Accrued expenses and other liabilities" of $25,345. Does the company explain what these are? If so, what are they?

b. In the footnotes, Topps reveals that it entered into a credit agreement with a bank in 2004. What amount of credit is available to Topps under this agreement, and when does it expire?

c. What restrictions does the credit agreement place on Topps? Be specific.

Required—Part 2

Use the Harley-Davidson's annual report that came with this book to answer the following questions.

a. As of December 31, 2005, Harley-Davidson has $1,204,973 of "finance debt." How much of this is current debt and how much is long-term debt?

b. Specifically, what types of borrowings are included in this $1,204,973 of finance debt (see footnotes)?

c. What is the range of interest rates that Harley-Davidson has to pay on its finance debt (see footnotes)?

ATC 10-2 Group Assignment *Missing information*

The following three companies issued the following bonds:

1. Lot, Inc., issued $100,000 of 8 percent, five-year bonds at 102 ¼ on January 1, 2006. Interest is payable annually on December 31.
2. Max, Inc., issued $100,000 of 8 percent, five-year bonds at 98 on January 1, 2006. Interest is payable annually on December 31.
3. Par, Inc., issued $100,000 of 8 percent, five-year bonds at 104 on January 1, 2006. Interest is payable annually on December 31.

Required

a. Organize the class into three sections and divide each section into groups of three to five students. Assign each of the sections one of the companies.

Group Tasks

(1) Compute the following amounts for your company:
   (a) Cash proceeds from the bond issue.
   (b) Interest paid in 2006.
   (c) Interest expense for 2006.
(2) Prepare the liabilities section of the balance sheet as of December 31, 2006.

Class Discussion

b. Have a representative of each section put the liabilities section for its company on the board.

c. Is the amount of interest expense different for the three companies? Why or why not?

d. Is the amount of interest paid different for each of the companies? Why or why not?

e. Is the amount of total liabilities different for each of the companies? Why or why not?

ATC 10-3 Real-World Case *Using accounting numbers to assess creditworthiness*

Standard & Poor's (S&P) and Moody's are two credit-rating services that evaluate the creditworthiness of various companies. Their "grading" systems are similar, but not exactly the same. S&P's grading scheme works as follows: AAA is the highest rating, followed by AA, then A, then BBB, and so on. For each grade, a "+" or "−" may also be used.

The following are selected financial data for four companies whose overall creditworthiness was rated by S&P. The companies, listed alphabetically, are:

Advance Auto Parts, Inc., operated 2,810 auto-parts stores in the United States in 2005.
Brookstone, Inc., operated 9,042 specialty-stores worldwide in 2005.

Dana Corporation manufactures and markets components used for light duty, commercial, and off-road vehicles. Its customers include DaimlerChrysler, Ford, and GM.

United Parcel Services, Inc. (UPS), operates a bunch of "big brown trucks." What else needs to be said?

Dollar amounts are in thousands.

	Net Income	Cash Flow from Operations	Current Ratio	Debt to Assets Ratio	Times Interest Earned	Return on Assets Ratio
Advance Auto Parts						
2005	$ 234,725	$325,211	1.36	.64	12.70	.09
2004	187,988	263,794	1.43	.67	16.23	.09
Brookstone						
2005	21,362	40,373	2.84	.36	23.73	.08
2004	17,552	38,377	2.71	.34	20.50	.08
Dana Corp.						
2005	(1,605,000)	(216,000)	0.70	.91	(.70)	(.22)
2004	62,000	73,000	1.27	.72	.20	.01
UPS						
2005	3,870,000	5,793,000	1.62	.52	36.32	.11
2004	3,333,000	5,331,000	1.93	.51	34.03	.10

Each company received a different credit rating by S&P. The ratings shown, as of August 7, 2006, in descending order, were AAA, BB+, B, and CCC.

Required

Determine which grade was assigned to each company. Write a memorandum explaining the rationale for your decisions.

ATC 10-4   Business Applications Case   *Performing ratio analysis using real-world data*

Sonic Corporation began business in 1953. In 2005 it was operating 3,039 drive-in hamburger restaurants throughout the United States and Mexico. The following data were taken from the company's 2005 annual report. All dollar amounts are in thousands.

	Fiscal Years Ending	
Account Title	August 31, 2005	August 31, 2004
Current assets	$ 35,249	$ 34,583
Total assets	563,316	518,633
Current liabilities	65,342	49,120
Total liabilities	178,777	183,871
Stockholders' equity	384,539	334,762
Interest expense	6,418	7,684
Income tax expense	43,040	36,721
Net income	75,381	63,015

Required

a. Calculate the EBIT for each year.
b. Calculate the times interest earned ratio for each year.
c. Calculate the current ratio and debt to assets ratio for each year.
d. Did the company's level of financial risk increase or decrease from 2004 to 2005? Explain.

ATC 10-5 Business Applications Case *Performing ratio analysis using real-world data*

Jos. A. Bank Clothiers, Inc., operated 324 retail clothing stores in 40 states and the District of Columbia as of January 28, 2006. The Men's Wearhouse, Inc., operated 603 men's clothing stores in the United States, and 116 in Canada, as of January 28, 2006. These stores do business under the names Men's Wearhouse, K&G Fashion Superstores, and Moores Clothing for Men. The following information was taken from these companies' January 28, 2006 annual reports. All dollar amounts are in thousands.

Account Title	Jos. A. Banks	Men's Wearhouse
Current assets	$203,293	$ 729,612
Total assets	304,832	1,123,274
Current liabilities	107,083	238,085
Total liabilities	151,032	495,741
Stockholders' equity	153,800	627,533
Interest expense	1,794	5,888
Income tax expense	24,751	58,785
Net income	35,250	103,903

Required

a. Calculate the EBIT for each company.

b. Calculate each company's debt to assets ratio and current ratio.

c. Calculate each company's return on assets ratio using EBIT instead of net earnings. Calculate each company's return on equity ratio using net earnings.

d. Men's Wearhouse reported interest expense of $5,888, before taxes. What was its after-tax interest expense in dollars. (*Hint:* You will need to compute its tax rate by dividing income tax expense by *earnings before taxes,* which must be computed.)

ATC 10-6 Writing Assignment *Debt versus equity financing*

Mack Company plans to invest $50,000 in land that will produce annual rent revenue equal to 15 percent of the investment starting on January 1, 2008. The revenue will be collected in cash at the end of each year, starting December 31, 2008. Mack can obtain the cash necessary to purchase the land from two sources. Funds can be obtained by issuing $50,000 of 10 percent, five-year bonds at their face amount. Interest due on the bonds is payable on December 31 of each year with the first payment due on December 31, 2008. Alternatively, the $50,000 needed to invest in land can be obtained from equity financing. In this case, the stockholders (holders of the equity) will be paid a $5,000 annual cash dividend. Mack Company is in a 30 percent income tax bracket.

Required

a. Prepare an income statement and statement of cash flows for 2008 under the two alternative financing proposals.

b. Write a short memorandum explaining why one financing alternative provides more net income but less cash flow than the other.

ATC 10-7 Ethical Dilemma *I don't want to pay taxes*

Dana Harbert recently started a very successful small business. Indeed, the business had grown so rapidly that she was no longer able to finance its operations by investing her own resources in the business. She needed additional capital but had no more of her own money to put into the business. A friend, Gene Watson, was willing to invest $100,000 in the business. Harbert estimated that with Watson's investment, the company would be able to increase revenue by $40,000. Furthermore, she believed that operating expenses would increase by only 10 percent. Harbert and Watson agree that Watson's investment should entitle him to receive a cash dividend equal to 20 percent of net income. A set of forecasted statements with and without Watson's investment is presented here. (Assume that all transactions involving revenue, expense, and dividends are cash transactions.)

Financial Statements

	Forecast 1 Without Watson's Investment	Forecast 2 With Watson's Investment
Income Statement		
Revenue	$120,000	$160,000
Operating expenses	(70,000)	(77,000)
Income before interest and taxes	50,000	83,000
Income tax expense (effective tax rate is 30%)	(15,000)	(24,900)
Net income	$ 35,000	$ 58,100
Statement of Changes in Stockholders' Equity		
Beginning retained earnings	$ 15,000	$ 15,000
Plus: Net income	35,000	58,100
Less: Dividend to Watson (20% of $58,100)	0	(11,620)
Ending retained earnings	$ 50,000	$ 61,480
Balance Sheets		
Assets (computations explained in following paragraph)	$400,000	$511,480
Liabilities	$ 0	$ 0
Equity		
Common stock	350,000	450,000
Retained earnings	50,000	61,480
Total liabilities and equity	$400,000	$511,480

The balance for assets in Forecast 1 is computed as the beginning balance of $365,000 plus net income of $35,000. The balance for assets in Forecast 2 is computed as the beginning balance of $365,000, plus the $100,000 cash investment, plus net income of $58,100, less the $11,620 dividend. Alternatively, total assets can be computed by determining the amount of total claims (total assets = total claims).

Harbert tells Watson that there would be a $3,486 tax advantage associated with debt financing. She says that if Watson is willing to become a creditor instead of an owner, she could pay him an additional $697.20 (that is, 20 percent of the tax advantage). Watson tells Harbert that he has no interest in participating in the management of the business, but Watson wants an ownership interest to guarantee that he will always receive 20 percent of the profits of the business. Harbert suggests that they execute a formal agreement in which Watson is paid 11.62 percent interest on his $100,000 loan to the business. This agreement will be used for income tax reporting. In addition, Harbert says that she is willing to establish a private agreement to write Watson a personal check for any additional amount necessary to make Watson's total return equal to 20 percent of all profits plus a $697.20 bonus for his part of the tax advantage. She tells Watson, "It's just like ownership. The only difference is that we call it debt for the Internal Revenue Service. If they want to have some silly rule that says if you call it debt, you get a tax break, then we are foolish if we don't call it debt. I will call it anything they want, just as long as I don't have to pay taxes on it."

Required

a. Construct a third set of forecasted financial statements (Forecast 3) at 11.62 percent annual interest, assuming that Watson is treated as creditor (he loans the business $100,000).

b. Verify the tax advantage of debt financing by comparing the balances of the Retained Earnings account in Forecast 2 and Forecast 3.

c. If you were Watson, would you permit Harbert to classify the equity transaction as debt to provide a higher return to the business and to you?

d. Comment on the ethical implications of misnaming a financing activity for the sole purpose of reducing income taxes.

ATC 10-8 Research Assignment *Analyzing long-term debt at Union Pacific Railroad*

Many companies have a form of debt called *capital leases*. A capital lease is created when a company agrees to rent an asset, such as equipment or a building, for such a long time that GAAP treats this lease as if the asset was purchased using borrowed funds. A capital lease creates a liability for the company that acquired the leased asset because it has promised to make payments to another company for several years in the future. If a company has any capital leases, it must disclose them in the footnotes to the financial statements, and will sometimes disclose them in a separate account in the liabilities section of the balance sheet.

Using the most current (Forms 10-K) for Union Pacific Corporation, complete the requirements below. To obtain the 10-Ks you can either use the EDGAR system following the instructions in Appendix A, or it can be found on the company's Web site.

Required

a. What was Union Pacific's debt to asset ratio? Total liabilities will need to be computed by subtracting "Common shareholders' equity" from total assets.

b. How much interest expense did Union Pacific's incur?

c. What amount of liabilities did Union Pacific's have as a result of capital leases? Footnote 5 presents information about Union Pacific's leases.

d. What percentage of Union Pacific's long-term liabilities was the result of capital leases?

e. Many companies try to structure (design) leasing agreements so that their leases will *not* be classified as capital leases. Explain why a company such as Union Pacific might want to avoid having capital leases.

ATC 10-9 Spreadsheet Assignment *Using Excel*

On January 1, 2009, Bainbridge Company borrowed $100,000 cash from a bank by issuing a 10-year, 9 percent note. The principal and interest are to be paid by making annual payments in the amount of $15,582. Payments are to be made December 31 of each year beginning December 31, 2009.

Required

a. Set up the spreadsheet as shown on the following page. Notice that Excel can be set up to calculate the loan payment. If you're unfamiliar with this, see the following Spreadsheet Tips section. The Beginning Principal Balance (B12) and Cash Payment (C12) can be referenced from the Loan Information section. The interest rate used to calculate Interest Expense (D12) can also be referenced from the Loan Information section.

b. Complete the spreadsheet for the 10 periods.

c. In Row 23, calculate totals for cash payments, interest expense, and applied to principal.

d. Consider how the amounts would differ if Bainbridge were to borrow the $100,000 at different interest rates and time periods. The results of the original data (option 1) have been entered in the following schedule. In the spreadsheet, delete 9 percent and 10 from cells B4 and B5, respectively. Enter the data for the second option (8 percent and 10 years) in cells B4 and B5. Enter the recomputed payment and total interest in the schedule for the second option. Continue the same process for options 3 through 9 by deleting the prior rate and number of periods in the spreadsheet and entering in the next option's data. The number of years scheduled (rows 12 through 21) will have to be shortened for the 7-year options and lengthened for the 13-year options.

	Option								
	1	**2**	**3**	**4**	**5**	**6**	**7**	**8**	**9**
Rate	9%	8%	10%	9%	8%	10%	9%	8%	10%
Years	10	10	10	7	7	7	13	13	13
Payment	15,582								
Total interest	55,820								

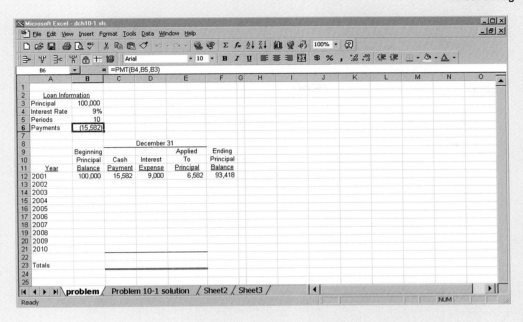

Spreadsheet Tips

1. Excel will calculate an installment loan payment. The interest rate (%), number of periods (nper), and amount borrowed or otherwise known as present value (PV) must be entered in the payment formula. The formula for the payment is =PMT(rate,nper,pv). The rate, number of periods, and amount borrowed (present value) may be entered as actual amounts or referenced to other cells. In the preceding spreadsheet, the payment formula can be either =PMT(9%,10,100000) or =PMT(B4,B5,B3). In our case, the latter is preferred so that variables can be altered in the spreadsheet without also having to rewrite the payment formula. Notice that the payment is a negative number.

2. Using positive numbers is preferred in the amortization schedule. The loan payment (cell B6) in the loan information section shows up as a negative number. Any reference to it in the amortization schedule should be preceded by a minus sign to convert it to a positive number. For example, the formula in cell C12 for the cash payment is =−B6.

3. Recall that to copy a fixed number, a $ sign must be positioned before the column letter and row number. The complete formula then for cell C12 is =−B6.

ATC 10-10 Spreadsheet Analysis *Mastering Excel*

Wise Company was started on January 1, 2008, when it issued 20-year, 10 percent, $200,000 face value bonds at a price of 90. Interest is payable annually at December 31 of each year. Wise immediately purchased land with the proceeds (cash received) from the bond issue. Wise leased the land for $27,000 cash per year. The lease revenue payments are due every December 31.

Required

Set up the following horizontal statements model on a blank spreadsheet. The SCF Activity column is for the classifications operating, financing, or investing.

a. Enter the effects of the 2008 transactions. Assume that both the interest and lease payments occurred on December 31. Notice that the entry for the lease has already been entered as an example. Calculate the ending balances.

b. Enter the effects of the 2009 transactions. Assume that both the interest and lease payments occurred on December 31. Calculate the ending balances.

c. Enter the effects of the 2010 transactions. Assume that both the interest and lease payments occurred on December 31. Calculate the ending balances.

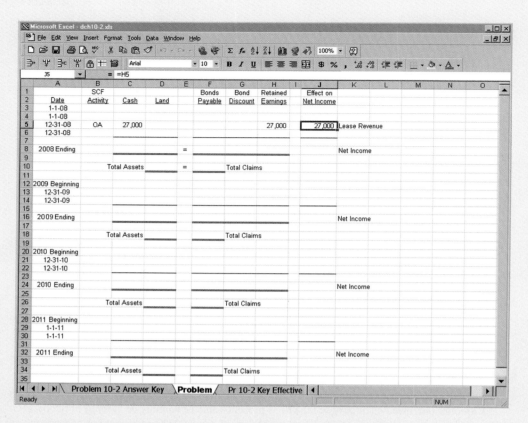

d. On January 1, 2011, Wise Company sold the land for $190,000 cash. Immediately after the sale of the land, Wise repurchased its bond at a price of 93. Assume that no other accounting events occurred during 2011. Enter the effects of the 2011 transactions. Calculate the ending balances.

COMPREHENSIVE PROBLEM

The account balances of Pacilio Security Systems Sales and Service as of January 1, 2010, was:

Cash	$227,386
Petty cash	100
Accounts receivable	51,170
Allowance for doubtful accounts	2,074
Supplies	180
Inventory—standard alarms (12 @ $280)	3,360
Inventory—deluxe alarms (14 @ $590)	8,260
Van	9,200
Equipment	12,000
Building	72,000
Land	36,000
Accumulated depreciation	14,000
Warranties payable	2,827
Notes payable	38,000
Common stock	50,000
Retained earnings	312,755

During 2010, Pacilio Security Systems Sales and Service experienced the following transactions:

1. On January 2, Pacilio refinanced its loan on the building by issuing a new 10-year amortized loan at 5 percent. The amount refinanced was the $38,000 balance of the old notes payable. Pacilio will make annual payments of $4,921 each year.

2. Also on January 2, 2010, Pacilio issued bonds for $80,000 of 4 percent 10-year bonds. The bonds were issued at 98. Interest is payable annually on December 31.

3. On February 1, Pacilio purchased the assets of Safety Alarm System for $110,000 cash. The assets obtained were:

Accounts receivable	$33,500
Inventory (130 standard alarm systems)	35,750
Goodwill	40,750

Pacilio received 320 Safety Alarm monitoring accounts.

4. Purchased $425 of supplies for cash.

5. On May 1, 2010, Pacilio replenished its petty cash fund. The fund had $18 cash and receipts for $26 office supplies and $56 for cutting the grass.

6. Paid cash to purchase 80 standard alarm systems for $285 each and 40 deluxe alarm systems at $600 each.

7. Sold on account 200 standard alarm systems for $120,000 and 45 deluxe alarm systems for $45,000 during the year. (Be sure to record cost of goods sold using the FIFO cost flow method.)

8. Billed $154,000 for monitoring services for the year. Of this amount, $40,000 was credit card sales. The credit card company charges a 4 percent service fee.

9. Collected the amount due from the credit card company.

10. Paid $1,050 to repair deluxe alarm systems that were still under warranty.

11. After numerous attempts to collect from customers, wrote off $1,875 of bad accounts.

12. Collected $305,000 of accounts receivable for the year.

13. Paid $9,000 advertising expense for the year.

14. Paid $6,000 utilities expense during the year.

15. Paid installers $95,000 for salaries for the year.

16. Paid officers $90,000 for salaries for the year.

17. Paid bond interest expense and amortized discount.

18. Paid annual installment on amortized note.

Adjustments

19. There were $210 of office supplies on hand at the end of the year.

20. Recognized warranty expense for the year. Pacilio estimates warranty expense at about 2 percent of its deluxe model alarm sales.

21. Recognized bad debt expense for the year. Bad debt expense is estimated to be 1 percent of sales on account.

22. Recognized depreciation expense for the year. (See chapter 9 problem)

Required

a. Record the above transactions in general journal form. Pacilio uses FIFO cost flow assumption.

b. Post the transactions to the T-accounts.

c. Prepare a trial balance.

d. Prepare an income statement, statement of changes in stockholders' equity, balance sheet, and statement of cash flows.

e. Close the temporary accounts to retained earnings.

f. Post the closing entries to the T-accounts and prepare an after-closing trial balance.

CHAPTER 11

Accounting for Equity Transactions

LEARNING OBJECTIVES

After you have mastered the material in this chapter, you will be able to:

1. Identify the primary characteristics of sole proprietorships, partnerships, and corporations.

2. Analyze financial statements to identify the different types of business organizations.

3. Explain the characteristics of major types of stock issued by corporations.

4. Explain how to account for different types of stock issued by corporations.

5. Show how treasury stock transactions affect a company's financial statements.

6. Explain the effects of declaring and paying cash dividends on a company's financial statements.

7. Explain the effects of stock dividends and stock splits on a company's financial statements.

8. Show how the appropriation of retained earnings affects financial statements.

9. Explain some uses of accounting information in making stock investment decisions.

LP11

The Curious Accountant

Imagine that a rich uncle wanted to reward you for doing so well in your first accounting course, so he gave you $10,000 to invest in the stock of one company. You narrowed your choice to two companies. After reviewing their recent annual reports, you developed the following information:

Mystery Company A: This company's stock has been trading publicly since October 1999, but it only began selling its services in 2001. Although it is an early leader in a business that both you and your grandparents could enjoy, it has not made a profit in a single year of its existence. In fact, each year it has lost more money than the year before. By the end of 2005, it had accumulated losses of $2.2 billion. This stock is currently selling for about $11.40 per share, the same price at which it was offered to the public when it first began trading. At this price, you can buy around 880 shares. A friend told you that at its current price it is a sure winner, especially, since it has recently sold for as much as $38 a share. Your friend, who uses the company's services, says "the sky is the limit for this company; just give it time."

Mystery Company B: This company has been in existence since 1892 and has made a profit most years. From 1998 through 2006, its net earnings totaled $786 million. This company produces products that both you and your grandparents could enjoy. Its stock is selling for about $10.80 per share, so you can buy around 930 shares of it. Your friend says "you would have to be bananas to invest in this company."

The descriptions apply to real-world companies, the names of which will be revealed later. Based on the information provided, which company's stock would you buy? (Answer on page 562.)

CHAPTER OPENING

You want to start a business. How should you structure it? Should it be a sole proprietorship, partnership, or corporation? Each form of business structure presents advantages and disadvantages. For example, a sole proprietorship allows maximum independence and control while partnerships and corporations allow individuals to pool resources and talents with other people. This chapter discusses these and other features of the three primary forms of business structure. ■

Formation of Business Organizations

Identify the primary characteristics of sole proprietorships, partnerships, and corporations.

Topic Tackler
PLUS

11-1

Ownership Agreements

Sole proprietorships are owned by a single individual who is responsible for making business and profit distribution decisions. If you want to be the absolute master of your destiny, you should organize your business as a proprietorship. Establishing a sole proprietorship is usually as simple as obtaining a business license from local government authorities. Usually no legal ownership agreement is required.

Partnerships allow persons to share their talents, capital, and the risks and rewards of business ownership. Since two or more individuals share ownership, partnerships require clear agreements about how authority, risks, and profits will be shared. Prudent partners minimize misunderstandings by hiring attorneys to prepare a **partnership agreement** which defines the responsibilities of each partner and describes how income or losses will be divided. Since the measurement of income affects the distribution of profits, partnerships frequently hire accountants to ensure that records are maintained in accordance with generally accepted accounting principles (GAAP). Partnerships (and sole proprietorships) also may need professional advice to deal with tax issues.

A **corporation** is a separate legal entity created by the authority of a state government. The paperwork to start a corporation is complex. For most laypersons, engaging professional attorneys and accountants to assist with the paperwork is usually well worth the fees charged.

Each state has separate laws governing establishing corporations. Many states follow the standard provisions of the Model Business Corporation Act. All states require the initial application to include **articles of incorporation** which normally include the following information: (1) the corporation's name and proposed date of incorporation; (2) the purpose of the corporation; (3) the location of the business and its expected life (which can be *perpetuity,* meaning *endless*); (4) provisions for capital stock; and (5) the names and addresses of the members of the first board of directors, the individuals with the ultimate authority for operating the business. If the articles are in order, the state establishes the legal existence of the corporation by issuing a charter of incorporation. The charter and the articles are public documents.

Advantages and Disadvantages of Different Forms of Business Organization

Video 11.1

Each form of business organization presents a different combination of advantages and disadvantages. Persons wanting to start a business or invest in one should consider the characteristics of each type of business structure.

Regulation

Few laws specifically affect the operations of proprietorships and partnerships. Corporations, however, are usually heavily regulated. The extent of government regulation depends on the size and distribution of a company's ownership interests. Ownership interests in corporations are normally evidenced by **stock certificates**.

Ownership of corporations can be transferred from one individual to another through exchanging stock certificates. As long as the exchanges (buying and selling of shares of stock, often called *trading*) are limited to transactions between individuals, a company is defined as a **closely held corporation.** However, once a corporation reaches a certain size, it may list

REALITY BYTES

Edward Nusbaum, CEO of Grant Thornton, a Chicago accounting firm, believes that "Sarbanes-Oxley is most likely creating the desired effect in making businesses realize that very strong responsibilities come with being a public company." However, a recent study conducted by Grant Thornton indicates that the cost of regulatory compliance is so significant that many smaller companies are taking their firms' stock off the exchanges. More specifically, the study found that the number of public companies making the switch to private ownership is up 30 percent since the Sarbanes-Oxley Act went into effect July 30, 2002. A different study by Thomson Financial found similar results. The Thomson study found 60 public companies went private in the first nine months of 2003, up from 49 during the same period in 2002 and nearly double the 32 firms that went private in 2001. Clearly, the expense of regulatory compliance is a distinct disadvantage of the corporate form of business. In contrast, ease of formation and light regulation are clear advantages of proprietorships and, to a lesser extent, partnerships.

its stock on a stock exchange such as the New York Stock Exchange or the American Stock Exchange. Trading on a stock exchange is limited to the stockbrokers who are members of the exchange. These brokers represent buyers and sellers who are willing to pay the brokers commissions for exchanging stock certificates on their behalf. Although closely held corporations are relatively free from government regulation, companies whose stock is publicly traded on the exchanges by brokers are subject to extensive regulation.

The extensive regulation of trading on stock exchanges began in the 1930s. The stock market crash of 1929 and the subsequent Great Depression led Congress to the pass the **Securities Act of 1933** and the **Securities Exchange Act of 1934** to regulate issuing stock and to govern the exchanges. The 1934 act also created the Securities and Exchange Commission (SEC) to enforce the securities laws. Congress gave the SEC legal authority to establish accounting principles for corporations that are registered on the exchanges. However, the SEC has generally deferred its rule-making authority to private sector accounting bodies such as the Financial Accounting Standards Board (FASB), effectively allowing the accounting profession to regulate itself.

A number of high-profile business failures around the turn of the century raised questions about the effectiveness of self-regulation and the usefulness of audits to protect the public. The **Sarbanes-Oxley Act of 2002** was adopted to address these concerns. The act creates a five-member Public Company Accounting Oversight Board (PCAOB) with the authority to set and enforce auditing, attestation, quality control, and ethics standards for auditors of public companies. The PCAOB is empowered to impose disciplinary and remedial sanctions for violations of its rules, securities laws, and professional auditing and accounting standards. Public corporations operate in a complex regulatory environment that requires the services of attorneys and professional accountants.

Double Taxation

Corporations pay income taxes on their earnings and then owners pay income taxes on distributions (dividends) received from corporations. As a result, distributed corporate profits are taxed twice—first when income is reported on the corporation's income tax return and a second time when distributions are reported on individual owners' tax returns. This phenomenon is commonly called **double taxation** and is a significant disadvantage of the corporate form of business organization.

Answers to The Curious Accountant

Mystery Company A is XM Satellite Holdings, Inc. (as of November 3, 2006). It is a company that provides XM satellite radio services on a monthly subscription basis. The origins of the company can be traced back to 1992, but it took several years to get its satellite system up and running. On October 5, 1999 XM's stock was sold to the public in an *initial public offering* (IPO) at $12 per share. Its stock, which is traded on NASDAQ,

rose as high as $44.75 in 1999, but in 2002 it traded below $5.00 at times. Obviously, the people trading XM's stock were not paying much attention to its past profits. Instead, they were focusing on what the company might become.

Mystery Company B is Del Monte Foods Company, Inc. (as of November 3, 2006). Of course, only the future will tell which company will be the better investment.

To illustrate, assume Glide Corporation earns pretax income of $100,000. Glide is in a 30 percent tax bracket. The corporation itself will pay income tax of $30,000 ($100,000 × 0.30). If the corporation distributes the after-tax income of $70,000 ($100,000 − $30,000) to individual stockholders in 15 percent tax brackets,[1] the $70,000 dividend will be reported on the individual tax returns, requiring tax payments of $10,500 ($70,000 × .15). Total income tax of $40,500 ($30,000 + $10,500) is due on $100,000 of earned income. In contrast, consider a proprietorship that is owned by an individual in a 30 percent tax bracket. If the proprietorship earns and distributes $100,000 profit, the total tax would be only $30,000 ($100,000 × .30).

Double taxation can be a burden for small companies. To reduce that burden, tax laws permit small closely held corporations to elect "S Corporation" status. S Corporations are taxed as proprietorships or partnerships. Also, many states have enacted laws permitting the formation of **limited liability companies (LLCs)** which offer many of the benefits of corporate ownership yet are in general taxed as partnerships. Since proprietorships and partnerships are not separate legal entities, company earnings are taxable to the owners rather than the company itself.

Limited Liability

Given the disadvantages of increased regulation and double taxation, why would anyone choose the corporate form of business structure over a partnership or proprietorship? A major reason is that the corporate form limits an investor's potential liability as an owner of a business venture. Because a corporation is legally separate from its owners, creditors cannot claim owners' personal assets as payment for the company's debts. Also, plaintiffs must sue the corporation, not its owners. The most that owners of a corporation can lose is the amount they have invested in the company (the value of the company's stock).

Unlike corporate stockholders, the owners of proprietorships and partnerships are *personally liable* for actions they take in the name of their companies. In fact, partners are responsible not only for their own actions but also for those taken by any other partner on behalf of the partnership. The benefit of **limited liability** is one of the most significant reasons the corporate form of business organization is so popular.

Continuity

Unlike partnerships or proprietorships, which terminate with the departure of their owners, a corporation's life continues when a shareholder dies or sells his or her stock. Because of **continuity** of existence, many corporations formed in the 1800s still thrive today.

---

[1]As a result of the Jobs and Growth Tax Relief Reconciliation Act (JGTRRA) of 2003, dividends received in tax years after 2002 are taxed at a maximum rate of 15 percent for most taxpayers. Lower income individuals pay a 5 percent tax on dividends received on December 31, 2007, or earlier. This rate falls to zero in 2008. The provisions of JGTRRA were originally set to expire on December 31, 2008; however, they were extended by the Tax Increase Prevention and Reconciliation Act of 2005 through December 31, 2010.

Transferability of Ownership

The **transferability** of corporate ownership is easy. An investor simply buys or sells stock to acquire or give up an ownership interest in a corporation. Hundreds of millions of shares of stock are bought and sold on the major stock exchanges each day.

Transferring the ownership of proprietorships is much more difficult. To sell an ownership interest in a proprietorship, the proprietor must find someone willing to purchase the entire business. Since most proprietors also run their businesses, transferring ownership also requires transferring management responsibilities. Consider the difference in selling $1 million of ExxonMobil stock versus selling a locally owned gas station. The stock could be sold on the New York Stock Exchange within minutes. In contrast, it could take years to find a buyer who is financially capable of and interested in owning and operating a gas station.

Transferring ownership in partnerships can also be difficult. As with proprietorships, ownership transfers may require a new partner to make a significant investment and accept management responsibilities in the business. Further, a new partner must accept and be accepted by the other partners. Personality conflicts and differences in management style can cause problems in transferring ownership interests in partnerships.

Management Structure

Partnerships and proprietorships are usually managed by their owners. Corporations, in contrast, have three tiers of management authority. The *owners* **(stockholders)** represent the highest level of organizational authority. The stockholders *elect* a **board of directors** to oversee company operations. The directors then *hire* professional executives to manage the company on a daily basis. Since large corporations can offer high salaries and challenging career opportunities, they can often attract superior managerial talent.

Video 11.1

While the management structure used by corporations is generally effective, it sometimes complicates dismissing incompetent managers. The chief executive officer (CEO) is usually a member of the board of directors and is frequently influential in choosing other board members. The CEO is also in a position to reward loyal board members. As a result, board members may be reluctant to fire the CEO or other top executives even if the individuals are performing poorly. Corporations operating under such conditions are said to be experiencing **entrenched management.**

Ability to Raise Capital

Because corporations can have millions of owners (shareholders), they have the opportunity to raise huge amounts of capital. Few individuals have the financial means to build and operate a telecommunications network such as AT&T or a marketing distribution system such as Wal-Mart. However, by pooling the resources of millions of owners through public stock and bond offerings, corporations generate the billions of dollars of capital needed for such massive investments. In contrast, the capital resources of proprietorships and partnerships are limited to a relatively small number of private owners. Although proprietorships and partnerships can also obtain resources by borrowing, the amount creditors are willing to lend them is usually limited by the size of the owners' net worth.

Appearance of Capital Structure in Financial Statements

The ownership interest (equity) in a business is composed of two elements: (1) owner/investor contributions and (2) retained earnings. The way these two elements are reported in the financial statements differs for each type of business structure (proprietorship, partnership, or corporation).

LO 2

Analyze financial statements to identify the different types of business organizations.

Presentation of Equity in Proprietorships

Owner contributions and retained earnings are combined in a single Capital account on the balance sheets of proprietorships. To illustrate, assume that Worthington Sole Proprietorship

EXHIBIT 11.1

		WORTHINGTON SOLE PROPRIETORSHIP Financial Statements As of December 31, 2008				
Income Statement		**Capital Statement**		**Balance Sheet**		
Revenue	$4,000	Beginning capital balance	$ 0	Assets		
Expenses	2,500	Plus: Investment by owner	5,000	Cash		$5,500
Net income	$1,500	Plus: Net income	1,500	Equity		
		Less: Withdrawal by owner	(1,000)	Worthington, Capital		$5,500
		Ending capital balance	$5,500			

was started on January 1, 2008, when it acquired a $5,000 capital contribution from its owner, Phil Worthington. During the first year of operation, the company generated $4,000 of cash revenues, incurred $2,500 of cash expenses, and distributed $1,000 cash to the owner. Exhibit 11.1 displays 2008 financial statements for Worthington's company. Note on the *capital statement* that distributions are called **withdrawals.** Verify that the $5,500 balance in the Capital account on the balance sheet includes the $5,000 owner contribution and the retained earnings of $500 ($1,500 net income − $1,000 withdrawal).

CHECK YOURSELF 11.1

Weiss Company was started on January 1, 2008, when it acquired $50,000 cash from its owners. During 2008 the company earned $72,000 of net income. Explain how the equity section of Weiss's December 31, 2008, balance sheet would differ if the company were a proprietorship versus a corporation.

Answer

Proprietorship records combine capital acquisitions from the owner and earnings from operating the business in a single capital account. In contrast, *corporation* records separate capital acquisitions from the owners and earnings from operating the business. If Weiss were a proprietorship, the equity section of the year-end balance sheet would report a single capital component of $122,000. If Weiss were a corporation, the equity section would report two separate equity components, most likely common stock of $50,000 and retained earnings of $72,000.

Presentation of Equity in Partnerships

The financial statement format for reporting partnership equity is similar to that used for proprietorships. Contributed capital and retained earnings are combined. However, a separate capital account is maintained for each partner in the business to reflect each partner's ownership interest.

To illustrate, assume that Sara Slater and Jill Johnson formed a partnership on January 1, 2009. The partnership acquired $2,000 of capital from Slater and $4,000 from Johnson. The partnership agreement called for each partner to receive an annual distribution equal to 10 percent of her capital contribution. Any further earnings were to be retained in the business and divided equally between the partners. During 2009, the company earned $5,000 of cash revenue and incurred $3,000 of cash expenses, for net income of $2,000 ($5,000 − $3,000). As specified by the partnership agreement, Slater received a $200 ($2,000 × 0.10) cash withdrawal and Johnson received $400 ($4,000 × 0.10). The remaining $1,400 ($2,000 − $200 − $400) of income was retained in the business and divided equally, adding $700 to each partner's capital account.

Exhibit 11.2 displays financial statements for the Slater and Johnson partnership. Again, note that distributions are called *withdrawals*. Also find on the balance sheet a *separate*

EXHIBIT 11.2

SLATER AND JOHNSON PARTNERSHIP
Financial Statements
As of December 31, 2009

Income Statement		Capital Statement		Balance Sheet	
Revenue	$5,000	Beginning capital balance	$ 0	Assets	
Expenses	3,000	Plus: Investment by owners	6,000	Cash	$7,400
Net income	$2,000	Plus: Net income	2,000	Equity	
		Less: Withdrawal by owners	(600)	Slater, Capital	$2,700
		Ending capital balance	$7,400	Johnson, Capital	4,700
				Total capital	$7,400

capital account for each partner. Each capital account includes the amount of the partner's contributed capital plus her proportionate share of the retained earnings.

Presentation of Equity in Corporations

Topic Tackler
PLUS

11-2

Corporations have more complex capital structures than proprietorships and partnerships. Explanations of some of the more common features of corporate capital structures and transactions follow.

Characteristics of Capital Stock

Stock issued by corporations may have a variety of different characteristics. For example, a company may issue different classes of stock that grant owners different rights and privileges. Also, the number of shares a corporation can legally issue may differ from the number it actually has issued. Further, a corporation can even buy back its stock. Finally, a corporation may assign different values to the stock it issues. The accounting treatment for corporate equity transactions is discussed in the next section of the text.

LO 3

Explain the characteristics of major types of stock issued by corporations.

Par Value

Many states require assigning a **par value** to stock. Historically, par value represented the maximum liability of the investors. Par value multiplied by the number of shares of stock issued represents the minimum amount of assets that must be retained in the company as protection for creditors. This amount is known as **legal capital.** To ensure that the amount of legal capital is maintained in a corporation, many states require that purchasers pay at least the par value for a share of stock initially purchased from a corporation. To minimize the amount of assets that owners must maintain in the business, many corporations issue stock with very low par values, often $1 or less. Therefore, *legal capital* as defined by par value has come to have very little relevance to investors or creditors. As a result, many states allow corporations to issue no-par stock.

Video 11.1

Stated Value

No-par stock may have a stated value. Like par value, **stated value** is an arbitrary amount assigned by the board of directors to the stock. It also has little relevance to investors and creditors. Stock with a par value and stock with a stated value are accounted for exactly the same way. When stock has no par or stated value, accounting for it is slightly different. These accounting differences are illustrated later in this chapter.

Other Valuation Terminology

The price an investor must pay to purchase a share of stock is the **market value.** The sales price of a share of stock may be more or less than the par value. Another term analysts frequently associate with stock is *book value.* **Book value per share** is calculated by dividing total stockholders' equity (assets − liabilities) by the number of shares of stock owned by investors. Book value per share differs from market value per share because equity is measured in historical dollars and market value reflects investors' estimates of a company's current value.

Stock: Authorized, Issued, and Outstanding

As part of the regulatory function, states approve the maximum number of shares of stock corporations are legally permitted to issue. This maximum number is called **authorized stock.** Authorized stock that has been sold to the public is called **issued stock.** When a corporation buys back some of its issued stock from the public, the repurchased stock is called **treasury stock.** Treasury stock is still considered to be issued stock, but it is no longer outstanding. **Outstanding stock** (total issued stock minus treasury stock) is stock owned by investors outside the corporation. For example, assume a company that is authorized to issue 150 shares of stock issues 100 shares to investors, and then buys back 20 shares of treasury stock. There are 150 shares authorized, 100 shares issued, and 80 shares outstanding.

Classes of Stock

Video 11.1

The corporate charter defines the number of shares of stock authorized, the par value or stated value (if any), and the classes of stock that a corporation can issue. Most stock issued is either *common* or *preferred.*

Common Stock

All corporations issue **common stock.** Common stockholders bear the highest risk of losing their investment if a company is forced to liquidate. On the other hand, they reap the greatest

FOCUS ON INTERNATIONAL ISSUES

WHO PROVIDES THE FINANCING?

The accounting rules in a country are affected by who provides financing to businesses in that country. Equity (versus debt) financing is a large source of financing for most businesses in the United States. The stock (equity ownership) of most large U.S. companies is said to be *widely held.* This means that many different institutional investors (e.g., pension funds) and individuals own stock. At the other extreme is a country in which the government owns most industries. In between might be a country in which large banks provide a major portion of business financing, such as Japan or Germany.

It is well beyond the scope of this course to explain specifically how a country's GAAP are affected by who provides the financing of the country's major industries. Nevertheless, a businessperson should be aware that the source of a company's financing affects the financial reporting that it must do. Do not assume that business practices or accounting rules in other countries are like those in the United States.

rewards when a corporation prospers. Common stockholders generally enjoy several rights, including: (1) the right to buy and sell stock, (2) the right to share in the distribution of profits, (3) the right to share in the distribution of corporate assets in the case of liquidation, (4) the right to vote on significant matters that affect the corporate charter, and (5) the right to participate in the election of directors.

Preferred Stock

Many corporations issue **preferred stock** in addition to common stock. Holders of preferred stock receive certain privileges relative to holders of common stock. In exchange for special privileges in some areas, preferred stockholders give up rights in other areas. Preferred stockholders usually have no voting rights and the amount of their dividends is usually limited. Preferences granted to preferred stockholders include the following:

1. *Preference as to assets.* Preferred stock often has a liquidation value. In case of bankruptcy, preferred stockholders must be paid the liquidation value before any assets are distributed to common stockholders. However, preferred stockholder claims still fall behind creditor claims.

2. *Preference as to dividends.* Preferred shareholders are frequently guaranteed the right to receive dividends before common stockholders. The amount of the preferred dividend is normally stated on the stock certificate. It may be stated as a dollar value (say, $5) per share or as a percentage of the par value. Most preferred stock has **cumulative dividends,** meaning that if a corporation is unable to pay the preferred dividend in any year, the dividend is not lost but begins to accumulate. Cumulative dividends that have not been paid are called **dividends in arrears.** When a company pays dividends, any preferred stock arrearages must be paid before any other dividends are paid. Noncumulative preferred stock is not often issued because preferred stock is much less attractive if missed dividends do not accumulate.

To illustrate the effects of preferred dividends, consider Dillion, Incorporated, which has the following shares of stock outstanding:

> Preferred stock, 4%, $10 par, 10,000 shares
> Common stock, $10 par, 20,000 shares

Assume the preferred stock dividend has not been paid for two years. If Dillion pays $22,000 in dividends, how much will each class of stock receive? It depends on whether the preferred stock is cumulative.

Allocation of Distribution for Cumulative Preferred Stock		
	To Preferred	**To Common**
Dividends in arrears	$ 8,000	$ 0
Current year's dividends	4,000	10,000
Total distribution	$12,000	$10,000
Allocation of Distribution for Noncumulative Preferred Stock		
	To Preferred	**To Common**
Dividends in arrears	$ 0	$ 0
Current year's dividends	4,000	18,000
Total distribution	$ 4,000	$18,000

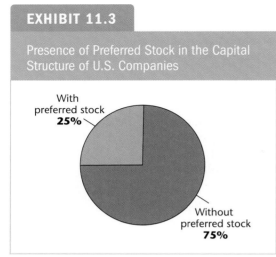

With preferred stock **25%**

Without preferred stock **75%**

Data source: AICPA, *Accounting Trends and Techniques, 2006.*

The total annual dividend on the preferred stock is $4,000 (0.04 × $10 par × 10,000 shares). If the preferred stock is cumulative, the $8,000 in arrears must be paid first. Then $4,000 for the current year's dividend is paid next. The remaining $10,000 goes to common stockholders. If the preferred stock is noncumulative, the $8,000 of dividends from past periods is ignored. This year's $4,000 preferred dividend is paid first, with the remaining $18,000 going to common stockholders.

Other features of preferred stock may include the right to participate in distributions beyond the established amount of the preferred dividend, the right to convert preferred stock to common stock or to bonds, and the potential for having the preferred stock called (repurchased) by the corporation. Detailed discussion of these topics is left to more advanced courses. Exhibit 11.3 indicates that roughly 25 percent of U.S. companies have preferred shares outstanding.

Accounting for Stock Transactions on the Day of Issue

Explain how to account for different types of stock issued by corporations.

NELSON INCORPORATED
Software development company

The issue of stock with a par or stated value is treated differently than no-par stock. For stock with either a par or stated value, the total amount acquired from the owners is divided between two separate equity accounts. The amount of the par or stated value is recorded in the stock account. Any amount received above the par or stated value is recorded in an account called **Paid-in Capital in Excess of Par** (or **Stated**) **Value.**

Issuing Par Value Stock

To illustrate the issue of common stock with a par value, assume that Nelson, Incorporated, is authorized to issue 250 shares of common stock. During 2008, Nelson issued 100 shares of $10 par common stock for $22 per share. The event increases assets and stockholders' equity by $2,200 ($22 × 100 shares). The increase in stockholders' equity is divided into two parts, $1,000 of par value ($10 per share × 100 shares) and $1,200 ($2,200 − $1,000) received in excess of par value. The income statement is not affected. The $2,200 cash inflow is reported in the financing activities section of the statement of cash flows. The effects on the financial statements and the journal entry to record the event follow:

Assets	=	Liab.	+			Equity			Rev.	−	Exp.	=	Net Inc.	Cash Flow
Cash	=	Liab.	+	Com. Stk.	+	Paid-in-Excess								
2,200	=	NA	+	1,000	+	1,200			NA	−	NA	=	NA	2,200 FA

Account Title	Debit	Credit
Cash	2,200	
Common Stock, $10 Par Value		1,000
Paid-in Capital in Excess of Par Value—Common		1,200

The *legal capital* of the corporation is $1,000, the total par value of the issued common stock. The number of shares issued can be easily verified by dividing the total amount in the common stock account by the par value ($1,000 ÷ $10 = 100 shares).

Stock Classification

Assume Nelson, Incorporated, obtains authorization to issue 400 shares of Class B, $20 par value common stock. The company issues 150 shares of this stock at $25 per share. The event increases assets and stockholders' equity by $3,750 ($25 × 150 shares). The increase in stockholders' equity is divided into two parts, $3,000 of par value ($20 per share × 150 shares) and $750 ($3,750 − $3,000) received in excess of par value. The income statement is not affected. The $3,750 cash inflow is reported in the financing activities section of the statement of cash flows. The effects on the financial statements and the journal entry to record the event follow:

Assets	=	Liab.	+		Equity		Rev.	−	Exp.	=	Net Inc.	Cash Flow
Cash	=	Liab.	+	Com. Stk.	+	Paid-in-Excess						
3,750	=	NA	+	3,000	+	750	NA	−	NA	=	NA	3,750 FA

Account Title	Debit	Credit
Cash	3,750	
Common Stock, Class B, $20 Par Value		3,000
Paid-in Capital in Excess of Par Value—Class B Common		750

As the preceding event suggests, companies can issue numerous classes of common stock. The specific rights and privileges for each class are described in the individual stock certificates.

Stock Issued at Stated Value

Assume Nelson is authorized to issue 300 shares of a third class of stock, 7 percent cumulative preferred stock with a stated value of $10 per share. Nelson issued 100 shares of the preferred stock at a price of $22 per share. The effect on the financial statements is identical to that described for the issue of the $10 par value common stock. The journal entry differs only to reflect the name of the different class of stock.

Assets	=	Liab.	+		Equity		Rev.	−	Exp.	=	Net Inc.	Cash Flow
Cash	=	Liab.	+	Pfd. Stk.	+	Paid-in-Excess						
2,200	=	NA	+	1,000	+	1,200	NA	−	NA	=	NA	2,200 FA

Account Title	Debit	Credit
Cash	2,200	
Preferred Stock, $10 Stated Value, 7% Cumulative		1,000
Paid-in Capital in Excess of Stated Value—Preferred		1,200

Stock Issued with No Par Value

Assume that Nelson, Incorporated, is authorized to issue 150 shares of a fourth class of stock. This stock is no-par common stock. Nelson issues 100 shares of this no-par stock at $22 per share. The entire amount received ($22 × 100 = $2,200) is recorded in the stock account. The effects on the financial statements and the journal entry to record the event follow:

Assets	=	Liab.	+		Equity		Rev.	−	Exp.	=	Net Inc.	Cash Flow
Cash	=	Liab.	+	Com. Stk.	+	Paid-in-Excess						
2,200	=	NA	+	2,200	+	NA	NA	−	NA	=	NA	2,200 FA

Account Title	Debit	Credit
Cash	2,200	
Common Stock, No Par		2,200

Financial Statement Presentation

Exhibit 11.4 displays Nelson, Incorporated's balance sheet after the four stock issuances described above. The exhibit assumes that Nelson earned and retained $5,000 of cash income during 2008. The stock accounts are presented first, followed by the paid-in capital in excess accounts. A wide variety of reporting formats is used in practice. For example, another popular format is to group accounts by stock class, with the paid-in capital in excess accounts listed with their associated stock accounts. Alternatively, many companies combine the different classes of stock into a single amount and provide the detailed information in footnotes to the financial statements.

EXHIBIT 11.4

NELSON, INCORPORATED
Balance Sheet
As of December 31, 2008

Assets	
Cash	$15,350
Stockholders' equity	
Preferred stock, $10 stated value, 7% cumulative,	
300 shares authorized, 100 issued and outstanding	$ 1,000
Common stock, $10 par value, 250 shares authorized,	
100 issued and outstanding	1,000
Common stock, class B, $20 par value, 400 shares	
authorized, 150 issued and outstanding	3,000
Common stock, no par, 150 shares authorized,	
100 issued and outstanding	2,200
Paid-in capital in excess of stated value—preferred	1,200
Paid-in capital in excess of par—common	1,200
Paid-in capital in excess of par—class B common	750
Total paid-in capital	10,350
Retained earnings	5,000
Total stockholders' equity	$15,350

Stockholders' Equity Transactions after the Day of Issue

Treasury Stock

LO 5

Show how treasury stock transactions affect a company's financial statements.

When a company buys its own stock, the stock purchased is called *treasury stock.* Why would a company buy its own stock? Common reasons include (1) to have stock available to give employees pursuant to stock option plans, (2) to accumulate stock in preparation for a merger or business combination, (3) to reduce the number of shares outstanding in order to increase earnings per share, (4) to keep the price of the stock high when it appears to be falling, and (5) to avoid a hostile takeover (removing shares from the open market reduces the opportunity for outsiders to obtain enough voting shares to gain control of the company).

Conceptually, purchasing treasury stock is the reverse of issuing stock. When a business issues stock, the assets and equity of the business increase. When a business buys treasury stock, the assets and equity of the business decrease. To illustrate, return to the Nelson, Incorporated, example. Assume that in 2009 Nelson paid $20 per share to buy back 50 shares of the $10 par value common stock that it originally issued at $22 per share. The purchase of treasury stock is an asset use transaction. Assets and stockholders' equity decrease by the cost of the purchase ($20 × 50 shares = $1,000). The income statement is not affected. The cash outflow is reported in the financing activities section of the statement of cash flows. The effects on the financial statements and the journal entry to record the event follow:

Assets	=	Liab.	+	Equity			Rev.	−	Exp.	=	Net Inc.	Cash Flow
Cash	=	Liab.	+	Other Equity Accts.	−	Treasury Stk.						
(1,000)	=	NA	+	NA	−	1,000	NA	−	NA	=	NA	(1,000) FA

Account Title	Debit	Credit
Treasury Stock	1,000	
Cash		1,000

The Treasury Stock account is a contra equity account. It is deducted from the other equity accounts in determining total stockholders' equity. In this example, the Treasury Stock account is debited for the full amount paid ($1,000). The original issue price and the par value of the stock have no effect on the entry. Recording the full amount paid in the Treasury Stock account is called the **cost method of accounting for treasury stock** transactions. Although other methods could be used, the cost method is the most common.

Assume Nelson reissues 30 shares of treasury stock at a price of $25 per share. As with any other stock issue, the sale of treasury stock is an asset source transaction. In this case, assets and stockholders' equity increase by $750 ($25 × 30 shares). The income statement is not affected. The cash inflow is reported in the financing activities section of the statement of cash flows. The effect of this event on the financial statements and the journal entry to record it follow:

Assets	=	Liab.	+	Equity					Rev.	−	Exp.	=	Net Inc.	Cash Flow
Cash	=	Liab.	+	Other Equity Accounts	−	Treasury Stock	+	Paid in from Treasury Stk.						
750	=	NA	+	NA	−	(600)	+	150	NA	−	NA	=	NA	750 FA

Account Title	Debit	Credit
Cash	750	
Treasury Stock		600
Paid-in Capital in Excess of Cost of Treasury Stock		150

The decrease in the Treasury Stock account increases stockholders' equity. The $150 difference between the cost of the treasury stock ($20 per share × 30 shares = $600) and the sales price ($750) is *not* reported as a gain. The sale of treasury stock is a capital acquisition, not a revenue transaction. The $150 is additional paid-in capital. *Corporations do not recognize gains or losses on the sale of treasury stock.*

After selling 30 shares of treasury stock, 20 shares remain in Nelson's possession. These shares cost $20 each, so the balance in the Treasury Stock account is now $400 ($20 × 20 shares). Treasury stock is reported on the balance sheet directly below retained earnings.

Although this placement suggests that treasury stock reduces retained earnings, the reduction actually applies to the entire stockholders' equity section. Exhibit 11.5 (page 575) shows the presentation of treasury stock in the balance sheet.

CHECK YOURSELF 11.2

On January 1, 2008, Janell Company's Common Stock account balance was $20,000. On April 1, 2008, Janell paid $12,000 cash to purchase some of its own stock. Janell resold this stock on October 1, 2008, for $14,500. What is the effect on the company's cash and stockholders' equity from both the April 1 purchase and the October 1 resale of the stock?

Answer

The April 1 purchase would reduce both cash and stockholders' equity by $12,000. The treasury stock transaction represents a return of invested capital to those owners who sold stock back to the company.

The sale of the treasury stock on October 1 would increase both cash and stockholders' equity by $14,500. The difference between the sales price of the treasury stock and its cost ($14,500 − $12,000) represents additional paid-in capital from treasury stock transactions. The stockholders' equity section of the balance sheet would include Common Stock, $20,000, and Additional Paid-in Capital from Treasury Stock, $2,500.

Video 11.2

Explain the effects of declaring and paying cash dividends on a company's financial statements.

Cash Dividend

Cash dividends are affected by three significant dates: *the declaration date, the date of record,* and *the payment date.* Assume that on October 15, 2009, the board of Nelson, Incorporated, declared the cash dividend on the 100 outstanding shares of its $10 stated value preferred stock. The dividend will be paid to stockholders of record as of November 15, 2009. The cash payment will be made on December 15, 2009.

Declaration Date

Although corporations are not required to declare dividends, they are legally obligated to pay dividends once they have been declared. They must recognize a liability on the **declaration date** (in this case, October 15, 2009). The increase in liabilities is accompanied by a decrease in retained earnings. The income statement and statement of cash flows are not affected. The effect on the financial statements of *declaring* the $70 (0.07 × $10 × 100 shares) dividend and the journal entry to record the declaration follow:

Assets	=	Liab.	+		Equity			Rev.	−	Exp.	=	Net Inc.	Cash Flow
Cash	=	Div. Pay.	+	Com. Stk.	+	Ret. Earn.							
NA	=	70	+	NA	+	(70)		NA	−	NA	=	NA	NA

Account Title	Debit	Credit
Dividends	70	
Dividends Payable		70

Date of Record

Cash dividends are paid to investors who owned the preferred stock on the **date of record** (in this case November 15, 2009). Any stock sold after the date of record but before the payment date (in this case December 15, 2009) is traded **ex-dividend,** meaning the buyer will not receive the upcoming dividend. The date of record is merely a cutoff date. It does not affect the financial statements.

Payment Date

Nelson actually paid the cash dividend on the **payment date.** This event has the same effect as paying any other liability. Assets (cash) and liabilities (dividends payable) both decrease. The income statement is not affected. The cash outflow is reported in the financing activities section of the statement of cash flows. The effect of the cash payment on the financial statements and the journal entry to record it follow:

Assets	=	Liab.	+	Equity			Rev.	−	Exp.	=	Net Inc.	Cash Flow
Cash	=	Div. Pay.	+	Com. Stk.	+	Ret. Earn.						
(70)	=	(70)	+	NA	+	NA	NA	−	NA	=	NA	(70) FA

Account Title	Debit	Credit
Dividends Payable	70	
Cash		70

Stock Dividend

Dividends are not always paid in cash. Companies sometimes choose to issue **stock dividends,** wherein they distribute additional shares of stock to the stockholders. To illustrate, assume that Nelson, Incorporated, decided to issue a 10 percent stock dividend on its class B, $20 par value common stock. Since dividends apply to outstanding shares only, Nelson will issue 15 (150 outstanding shares × 0.10) additional shares of class B stock.

Assume the new shares are distributed when the market value of the stock is $30 per share. As a result of the stock dividend, Nelson will transfer $450 ($30 × 15 new shares) from retained earnings to paid-in capital.[2] The stock dividend is an equity exchange transaction. The income statement and statement of cash flows are not affected. The effect of the stock dividend on the financial statements and the journal entry to record it follow:

LO 7

Explain the effects of stock dividends and stock splits on a company's financial statements.

Assets	=	Liab.	+	Equity					Rev.	−	Exp.	=	Net Inc.	Cash Flow
	=		+	Com. Stk.	+	Paid-in Excess	+	Ret. Earn.						
NA	=	NA	+	300	+	150	+	(450)	NA	−	NA	=	NA	NA

Account Title	Debit	Credit
Retained Earnings	450	
Common Stock, Class B, $20 Par Value		300
Paid-in Capital in Excess of Par Value—Class B Common		150

Stock dividends have no effect on assets. They merely increase the number of shares of stock outstanding. Since a greater number of shares represents the same ownership interest in the same amount of assets, the market value per share of a company's stock normally declines when a stock dividend is distributed. A lower market price makes the stock more affordable and may increase demand for the stock, which benefits both the company and its stockholders.

Stock Split

A corporation may also reduce the market price of its stock through a **stock split.** A stock split replaces existing shares with a greater number of new shares. Any par or stated value of the stock is proportionately reduced to reflect the new number of shares outstanding. For example, assume Nelson, Incorporated, declared a 2-for-1 stock split on the 165 outstanding shares (150 originally issued + 15 shares distributed in a stock dividend) of its $20 par value, class B common stock. Nelson notes in the accounting records that the 165 old

---

[2]The accounting here applies to small stock dividends. Accounting for large stock dividends is explained in a more advanced course.

$20 par shares are replaced with 330 new $10 par shares. Investors who owned the 165 shares of old common stock would now own 330 shares of the new common stock.

Stock splits have no effect on the dollar amounts of assets, liabilities, and stockholders' equity. They only affect the number of shares of stock outstanding. In Nelson's case, the ownership interest that was previously represented by 165 shares of stock is now represented by 330 shares. Since twice as many shares now represent the same ownership interest, the market value per share should be one-half as much as it was prior to the split. However, as with a stock dividend, the lower market price will probably stimulate demand for the stock. As a result, doubling the number of shares will likely reduce the market price to slightly more than one-half of the pre-split value. For example, if the stock were selling for $30 per share before the 2-for-1 split, it might sell for $15.50 after the split.

Appropriation of Retained Earnings

Show how the appropriation of retained earnings affects financial statements.

The board of directors may restrict the amount of retained earnings available to distribute as dividends. The restriction may be required by credit agreements, or it may be completely discretionary. A retained earnings restriction, often called an *appropriation,* is an equity exchange event. It transfers a portion of existing retained earnings to **Appropriated Retained Earnings.** Total retained earnings remains unchanged. To illustrate, assume that Nelson appropriates $1,000 of retained earnings for future expansion. The income statement and the statement of cash flows are not affected. The effect on the financial statements of appropriating $1,000 of retained earnings and the journal entry to record it follow:

Assets	=	Liab.	+	Equity					Rev.	−	Exp.	=	Net Inc.	Cash Flow
	=		+	Com. Stk.	+	Ret. Earn.	+	App. Ret. Earn.						
NA	=	NA	+	NA	+	(1,000)	+	1,000	NA	−	NA	=	NA	NA

Account Title	Debit	Credit
Retained Earnings	1,000	
Appropriated Retained Earnings		1,000

Financial Statement Presentation

The 2008 and 2009 events for Nelson, Incorporated, are summarized below. Events 1 through 8 are cash transactions. The results of the 2008 transactions (Nos. 1–5) are reflected in Exhibit 11.4. The results of the 2009 transactions (Nos. 6–9) are shown in Exhibit 11.5.

1. Issued 100 shares of $10 par value common stock at a market price of $22 per share.
2. Issued 150 shares of class B, $20 par value common stock at a market price of $25 per share.
3. Issued 100 shares of $10 stated value, 7 percent cumulative preferred stock at a market price of $22 per share.
4. Issued 100 shares of no-par common stock at a market price of $22 per share.
5. Earned and retained $5,000 cash from operations.
6. Purchased 50 shares of $10 par value common stock as treasury stock at a market price of $20 per share.
7. Sold 30 shares of treasury stock at a market price of $25 per share.
8. Declared and paid a $70 cash dividend on the preferred stock.
9. Issued a 10 percent stock dividend on the 150 shares of outstanding class B, $20 par value common stock (15 additional shares). The additional shares were issued when the market price of the stock was $30 per share. There are 165 (150 + 15) class B common shares outstanding after the stock dividend.

EXHIBIT 11.5

NELSON, INCORPORATED
Balance Sheet
As of December 31, 2009

Assets		
Cash		**$21,030**
Stockholders' equity		
Preferred stock, $10 stated value, 7% cumulative,		
300 shares authorized, 100 issued and outstanding	$1,000	
Common stock, $10 par value, 250 shares authorized,		
100 issued, and 80 outstanding	1,000	
Common stock, class B, $10 par, 800 shares authorized,		
330 issued and outstanding	3,300	
Common stock, no par, 150 shares authorized,		
100 issued and outstanding	2,200	
Paid-in capital in excess of par—preferred	1,200	
Paid-in capital in excess of par—common	1,200	
Paid-in capital in excess of par—class B common	900	
Paid-in capital in excess of cost of treasury stock	150	
Total paid-in capital		$10,950
Retained earnings		
Appropriated	1,000	
Unappropriated	9,480	
Total retained earnings		10,480
Less: Treasury stock, 20 shares @ $20 per share		(400)
Total stockholders' equity		$21,030

10. Issued a 2-for-1 stock split on the 165 shares of class B, $20 par value common stock. After this transaction, there are 330 shares outstanding of the class B common stock with a $10 par value.

11. Appropriated $1,000 of retained earnings.

The illustration assumes that Nelson earned net income of $6,000 in 2009. The ending retained earnings balance is determined as follows: Beginning Balance $5,000 − $70 Cash Dividend − $450 Stock Dividend + $6,000 Net Income = $10,480.

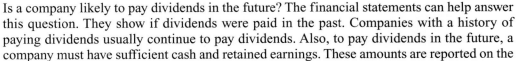

THE FINANCIAL ANALYST

Stockholders may benefit in two ways when a company generates earnings. The company may distribute the earnings directly to the stockholders in the form of dividends. Alternatively, the company may retain some or all of the earnings to finance growth and increase its potential for future earnings. If the company retains earnings, the market value of its stock should increase to reflect its greater earnings prospects. How can analysts use financial reporting to help assess the potential for dividend payments or growth in market value?

LO 9

Explain some uses of accounting information in making stock investment decisions.

Receiving Dividends

Is a company likely to pay dividends in the future? The financial statements can help answer this question. They show if dividends were paid in the past. Companies with a history of paying dividends usually continue to pay dividends. Also, to pay dividends in the future, a company must have sufficient cash and retained earnings. These amounts are reported on the balance sheet and the statement of cash flows.

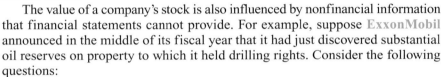

Increasing the Price of Stock

Is the market value (price) of a company's stock likely to increase? Increases in a company's stock price occur when investors believe the company's earnings will grow. Financial statements provide information that is useful in predicting the prospects for earnings growth. Here also, a company's earnings history is an indicator of its growth potential. However, because published financial statements report historical information, investors must recognize their limitations. Investors want to know about the future. Stock prices are therefore influenced more by forecasts than by history.

For example:

- On July 11, 2006, Alcoa, Inc., announced that its profits for the second quarter of the 2006 fiscal year were 62 percent higher than profits in the same quarter of 2005. Its sales were up 19 percent during the second quarter. In reaction to this news, the price of Alcoa's stock *fell* by 4.5 percent. Why did the stock market respond in this way? Because many analysts who follow the company were expecting revenues to grow more than 19 percent.

- On July 26, 2006, General Motors Corporation announced a second quarter *loss* of $3.2 billion. This loss was over three times greater than its loss had been for the second quarter of the 2005 fiscal year. The stock market's reaction to the news was to *increase* the price of GM's stock by over 4 percent to its highest price in ten months. The market reacted this way because in that same announcement the company reported strong revenue growth, which made investors more optimistic about the future, and the investors had expected an even greater second quarter loss.

In each case, the investors reacted not only to the actual accounting information, but also to how they had expected the company to perform, as well as to what the current information suggested about the future.

The value of a company's stock is also influenced by nonfinancial information that financial statements cannot provide. For example, suppose ExxonMobil announced in the middle of its fiscal year that it had just discovered substantial oil reserves on property to which it held drilling rights. Consider the following questions:

- What would happen to the price of ExxonMobil's stock on the day of the announcement?
- What would happen to ExxonMobil's financial statements on that day?

The price of ExxonMobil's stock would almost certainly increase as soon as the discovery was made public. However, nothing would happen to its financial statements on that day. There would probably be very little effect on its financial statements for that year. Only after the company began to develop the oil field and sell the oil would its financial statements reflect the discovery. Changes in financial statements tend to lag behind the announcements companies make regarding their earnings potential.

Stock prices are also affected by general economic conditions and consumer confidence as well as the performance measures reported in financial statements. For example, the stock prices of virtually all companies declined sharply immediately after the September 11, 2001, terrorist attacks on the World Trade Center and the Pentagon. Historical-based financial statements are of little benefit in predicting general economic conditions or changes in consumer confidence.

Price-Earnings Ratio

The most commonly reported measure of a company's value is the price-earnings ratio, frequently called the P/E ratio. The P/E ratio is a company's market price per share of stock divided by the company's annual earnings per share (EPS). In general, high P/E ratios indicate that investors are optimistic about a company's earnings growth potential. For a more detailed discussion of this important ratio refer back to the coverage in Chapter 1.

Exercising Control through Stock Ownership

The more influence an investor has over the operations of a company, the more the investor can benefit from owning stock in the company. For example, consider a power company that needs coal to produce electricity. The power company may purchase some common stock in a coal mining company to ensure a stable supply of coal. What percentage of the mining company's stock must the power company acquire to exercise significant influence over the mining company? The answer depends on how many investors own stock in the mining company and how the number of shares is distributed among the stockholders.

The greater its number of stockholders, the more *widely held* a company is. If stock ownership is concentrated in the hands of a few persons, a company is *closely held.* Widely held companies can generally be controlled with smaller percentages of ownership than closely held companies. Consider a company in which no existing investor owns more one than 1 percent of the voting stock. A new investor who acquires a 5 percent interest would immediately become, by far, the largest shareholder and would likely be able to significantly influence board decisions. In contrast, consider a closely held company in which one current shareholder owns 51 percent of the company's stock. Even if another investor acquired the remaining 49 percent of the company, that investor could not control the company.

Financial statements contain some, but not all, of the information needed to help an investor determine ownership levels necessary to permit control. For example, the financial statements disclose the total number of shares of stock outstanding, but they normally contain little information about the number of shareholders and even less information about any relationships between shareholders. Relationships between shareholders are critically important because related shareholders, whether bound by family or business interests, might exercise control by voting as a block. For publicly traded companies, information about the number of shareholders and the identity of some large shareholders is disclosed in reports filed with the Securities and Exchange Commission.

A Look Back

Starting a business requires obtaining financing; it takes money to make money. Although some money may be borrowed, lenders are unlikely to make loans to businesses that lack some degree of owner financing. Equity financing is therefore critical to virtually all profit-oriented businesses. This chapter has examined some of the issues related to accounting for equity transactions.

The idea that a business must obtain financing from its owners was one of the very first events presented in this textbook. This chapter discussed the advantages and disadvantages of organizing a business as a sole proprietorship versus a partnership versus a corporation. These advantages and disadvantages include the following:

1. *Double taxation*—Income of corporations is subject to double taxation, but that of proprietorships and partnerships is not.

2. *Regulation*—Corporations are subject to more regulation than are proprietorships and partnerships.

3. *Limited liability*—An investor's personal assets are not at risk as a result of owning corporate securities. The investor's liability is limited to the amount of the investment. In general, proprietorships and partnerships do not offer limited liability. However, laws in some states permit the formation of limited liability companies which operate like proprietorships and partnerships yet place some limits on the personal liability of their owners.

4. *Continuity*—Proprietorships and partnerships dissolve when one of the owners leaves the business. Corporations are separate legal entities that continue to exist regardless of changes in ownership.

5. *Transferability*—Ownership interests in corporations are easier to transfer than those of proprietorships or partnerships.

6. *Management structure*—Corporations are more likely to have independent professional managers than are proprietorships or partnerships.

7. *Ability to raise capital*—Because they can be owned by millions of investors, corporations have the opportunity to raise more capital than proprietorships or partnerships.

Corporations issue different classes of common stock and preferred stock as evidence of ownership interests. In general, *common stock* provides the widest range of privileges including the right to vote and participate in earnings. *Preferred stockholders* usually give up the right to vote in exchange for preferences such as the right to receive dividends or assets upon liquidation before common stockholders. Stock may have a *par value* or *stated value,* which relates to legal requirements governing the amount of capital that must be maintained in the corporation. Corporations may also issue *no-par stock*, avoiding some of the legal requirements that pertain to par or stated value stock.

Stock that a company issues and then repurchases is called *treasury stock.* Purchasing treasury stock reduces total assets and stockholders' equity. Reselling treasury stock represents a capital acquisition. The difference between the reissue price and the cost of the treasury stock is recorded directly in the equity accounts. Treasury stock transactions do not result in gains or losses on the income statement.

Companies may issue *stock splits* or *stock dividends*. These transactions increase the number of shares of stock without changing the net assets of a company. The per share market value usually drops when a company issues stock splits or dividends.

>> A Look Forward

Chapter 12 examines the statement of cash flows in more detail than past chapters have provided. It introduces a more practical way to prepare the statement than analyzing every single entry in the cash account, and presents the more formal format for the statement of cash flows used by most real-world companies.

SELF-STUDY REVIEW PROBLEM

Edwards, Inc., experienced the following events:

1. Issued common stock for cash.
2. Declared a cash dividend.
3. Issued noncumulative preferred stock for cash.
4. Appropriated retained earnings.
5. Distributed a stock dividend.
6. Paid cash to purchase treasury stock.
7. Distributed a 2-for-1 stock split.
8. Issued cumulative preferred stock for cash.
9. Paid a cash dividend that had previously been declared.
10. Sold treasury stock for cash at a higher amount than the cost of the treasury stock.

Required

Show the effect of each event on the elements of the financial statements using a horizontal statements model like the one shown here. Use + for increase, − for decrease, and NA for not affected. In the Cash Flow column, indicate whether the item is an operating activity (OA), investing activity (IA), or a financing activity (FA). The first transaction is entered as an example.

Event	Assets	=	Liab.	+	Equity	Rev.	−	Exp.	=	Net Inc.	Cash Flow
1	+		NA		+	NA		NA		NA	+ FA

Solution to Self-Study Review Problem

Event	Assets	=	Liab.	+	Equity	Rev.	−	Exp.	=	Net Inc.	Cash Flow
1	+		NA		+	NA		NA		NA	+ FA
2	NA		+		−	NA		NA		NA	NA
3	+		NA		+	NA		NA		NA	+ FA
4	NA		NA		− +	NA		NA		NA	NA
5	NA		NA		− +	NA		NA		NA	NA
6	−		NA		−	NA		NA		NA	− FA
7	NA		NA		NA	NA		NA		NA	NA
8	+		NA		+	NA		NA		NA	+ FA
9	−		−		NA	NA		NA		NA	− FA
10	+		NA		+	NA		NA		NA	+ FA

KEY TERMS

Appropriated Retained Earnings account 574
articles of incorporation 560
authorized stock 566
board of directors 563
book value per share 566
closely held corporation 560
common stock 566
continuity 562
corporation 560
cost method of accounting for treasury stock 571

cumulative dividends 567
date of record 572
declaration date 572
dividends in arrears 567
double taxation 561
entrenched management 563
ex-dividend 572
issued stock 566
legal capital 565
limited liability 562
limited liability company (LLC) 562

market value 566
outstanding stock 566
paid-in capital in excess of par value 568
par value 565
partnership 560
partnership agreement 560
payment date 572
preferred stock 567
Sarbanes-Oxley Act of 2002 561

Securities Act of 1933 and Securities Exchange Act of 1934 561
sole proprietorship 560
stated value 565
stock certificate 560
stock dividend 573
stockholders 563
stock split 573
transferability 563
treasury stock 566
withdrawals 564

QUESTIONS

1. What are the three major forms of business organizations? Describe each.
2. How are sole proprietorships formed?
3. Discuss the purpose of a partnership agreement. Is such an agreement necessary for partnership formation?
4. What is meant by the phrase *separate legal entity?* To which type of business organization does it apply?
5. What is the purpose of the articles of incorporation? What information do they provide?
6. What is the function of the stock certificate?
7. What prompted Congress to pass the Securities Act of 1933 and the Securities Exchange Act of 1934? What is the purpose of these laws?
8. What are the advantages and disadvantages of the corporate form of business organization?
9. What is a limited liability company? Discuss its advantages and disadvantages.
10. How does the term *double taxation* apply to corporations? Give an example of double taxation.

11. What is the difference between contributed capital and retained earnings for a corporation?

12. What are the similarities and differences in the equity structure of a sole proprietorship, a partnership, and a corporation?

13. Why is it easier for a corporation to raise large amounts of capital than it is for a partnership?

14. What is the meaning of each of the following terms with respect to the corporate form of organization?

    (a) Legal capital

    (b) Par value of stock

    (c) Stated value of stock

    (d) Market value of stock

    (e) Book value of stock

    (f) Authorized shares of stock

    (g) Issued stock

    (h) Outstanding stock

    (i) Treasury stock

    (j) Common stock

    (k) Preferred stock

    (l) Dividends

15. What is the difference between cumulative preferred stock and noncumulative preferred stock?

16. What is no-par stock? How is it recorded in the accounting records?

17. Assume that Best Co. has issued and outstanding 1,000 shares of $100 par value, 10 percent, cumulative preferred stock. What is the dividend per share? If the preferred dividend is two years in arrears, what total amount of dividends must be paid before the common shareholders can receive any dividends?

18. If Best Co. issued 10,000 shares of $20 par value common stock for $30 per share, what amount is credited to the Common Stock account? What amount of cash is received?

19. What is the difference between par value stock and stated value stock?

20. Why might a company repurchase its own stock?

21. What effect does the purchase of treasury stock have on the equity of a company?

22. Assume that Day Company repurchased 1,000 of its own shares for $30 per share and sold the shares two weeks later for $35 per share. What is the amount of gain on the sale? How is it reported on the balance sheet? What type of account is treasury stock?

23. What is the importance of the declaration date, record date, and payment date in conjunction with corporate dividends?

24. What is the difference between a stock dividend and a stock split?

25. Why would a company choose to distribute a stock dividend instead of a cash dividend?

26. What is the primary reason that a company would declare a stock split?

27. If Best Co. had 10,000 shares of $20 par value common stock outstanding and declared a 5-for-1 stock split, how many shares would then be outstanding and what would be their par value after the split?

28. When a company appropriates retained earnings, does the company set aside cash for a specific use? Explain.

29. What is the largest source of financing for most U.S. businesses?

30. What is meant by *equity financing*? What is meant by *debt financing*?

31. What is a widely held corporation? What is a closely held corporation?

32. What are some reasons that a corporation might not pay dividends?

MULTIPLE-CHOICE QUESTIONS

**Multiple-choice questions are provided on the text Web site at
www.mhhe.com/edmonds6e.**

Quiz 11

All Exercises in Series A are available with McGraw-Hill's Homework Manager®

Exercise 11-1A   *Effect of accounting events on the financial statements of a sole proprietorship*   **L.O. 1, 2**

A sole proprietorship was started on January 1, 2009, when it received $80,000 cash from Derek Hughes, the owner. During 2009, the company earned $50,000 in cash revenues and paid $22,400 in cash expenses. Hughes withdrew $5,000 cash from the business during 2009.

Required

Prepare an income statement, capital statement (statement of changes in equity), balance sheet, and statement of cash flows for Hughes's 2009 fiscal year.

Exercise 11-2A   *Effect of accounting events on the financial statements of a partnership*   **L.O. 1, 2**

Wes Poole and Ross King started the PK partnership on January 1, 2009. The business acquired $60,000 cash from Poole and $90,000 from King. During 2009, the partnership earned $56,000 in cash revenues and paid $32,000 for cash expenses. Poole withdrew $2,000 cash from the business, and King withdrew $3,000 cash. The net income was allocated to the capital accounts of the two partners in proportion to the amounts of their original investments in the business.

Required

Prepare an income statement, capital statement, balance sheet, and statement of cash flows for the PK partnership for the 2009 fiscal year.

Exercise 11-3A   *Effect of accounting events on the financial statements of a corporation*   **L.O. 1, 2**

Premo Corporation was started with the issue of 8,000 shares of $10 par common stock for cash on January 1, 2009. The stock was issued at a market price of $18 per share. During 2009, the company earned $58,000 in cash revenues and paid $39,000 for cash expenses. Also, a $4,000 cash dividend was paid to the stockholders.

Required

Prepare an income statement, statement of changes in stockholders' equity, balance sheet, and statement of cash flows for Premo Corporation's 2009 fiscal year.

Exercise 11-4A   *Effect of issuing common stock on the balance sheet*   **L.O. 4**

Newly formed Health First Corporation has 100,000 shares of $5 par common stock authorized. On March 1, 2009, Health First issued 20,000 shares of the stock for $12 per share. On May 2 the company issued an additional 30,000 shares for $15 per share. Health First was not affected by other events during 2009.

Required

a. Record the transactions in a horizontal statements model like the following one. In the Cash Flow column, indicate whether the item is an operating activity (OA), investing activity (IA), or financing activity (FA). Use NA to indicate that an element was not affected by the event.

Assets	=	Liab.	+		Equity		Rev.	−	Exp.	=	Net Inc.	Cash Flow
Cash	=		+	Com. Stk.	+	Paid-in Excess						

b. Determine the amount Health First would report for common stock on the December 31, 2009, balance sheet.

c. Determine the amount Health First would report for paid-in capital in excess of par.

d. What is the total amount of capital contributed by the owners?

e. What amount of total assets would Health First report on the December 31, 2009, balance sheet?

f. Prepare journal entries to record the March 1 and May 2 transactions.

Exercise 11-5A *Recording and reporting common and preferred stock transactions*

Farmer, Inc., was organized on June 5, 2009. It was authorized to issue 400,000 shares of $10 par common stock and 50,000 shares of 5 percent cumulative class A preferred stock. The class A stock had a stated value of $30 per share. The following stock transactions pertain to Farmer, Inc.:

1. Issued 20,000 shares of common stock for $14 per share.
2. Issued 10,000 shares of the class A preferred stock for $32 per share.
3. Issued 30,000 shares of common stock for $18 per share.

Required
a. Prepare general journal entries for these transactions.
b. Prepare the stockholders' equity section of the balance sheet immediately after these transactions.

Exercise 11-6A *Effect of no-par common and par preferred stock on the horizontal statements model*

Collins Corporation issued 10,000 shares of no-par common stock for $20 per share. Collins also issued 2,000 shares of $50 par, 5 percent noncumulative preferred stock at $55 per share.

Required
a. Record these events in a horizontal statements model like the following one. In the Cash Flow column, indicate whether the item is an operating activity (OA), investing activity (IA), or financing activity (FA). Use NA to indicate that an element was not affected by the event.

Assets =	Equity			Rev. − Exp. = Net Inc.	Cash Flow
Cash =	Pfd. Stk. +	Com. Stk. +	Paid-in Excess		

b. Prepare journal entries to record these transactions.

Exercise 11-7A *Issuing stock for assets other than cash*

Gaines Corporation was formed when it issued shares of common stock to two of its shareholders. Gaines issued 5,000 shares of $10 par common stock to S. Gaines in exchange for $75,000 cash (the issue price was $15 per share). Gaines also issued 2,000 shares of stock to J. Caldwell in exchange for a one-year-old delivery van on the same day. Caldwell had originally paid $42,000 for the van.

Required
a. What was the market value of the delivery van on the date of the stock issue?
b. Show the effect of the two stock issues on Gaines's books in a horizontal statements model like the following one. In the Cash Flow column, indicate whether the item is an operating activity (OA), investing activity (IA), or financing activity (FA). Use NA to indicate that an element was not affected by the event.

Assets	=	Equity		Rev. − Exp. = Net Inc.	Cash Flow
Cash + Van	=	Com. Stk. +	Paid-in Excess		

Exercise 11-8A *Treasury stock transactions*

Woodard Corporation repurchased 3,000 shares of its own stock for $40 per share. The stock has a par of $10 per share. A month later Woodard resold 1,500 shares of the treasury stock for $45 per share.

Required
a. Record the two events in general journal format.
b. What is the balance of the treasury stock account after these transactions?

Exercise 11-9A *Recording and reporting treasury stock transactions*

The following information pertains to Kwon Corp. at January 1, 2009.

Common stock, $10 par, 50,000 shares authorized, 2,000 shares issued and outstanding	$20,000
Paid-in capital in excess of par, common stock	15,000
Retained earnings	65,000

Kwon Corp. completed the following transactions during 2009:

1. Issued 2,000 shares of $10 par common stock for $25 per share.
2. Repurchased 200 shares of its own common stock for $22 per share.
3. Resold 50 shares of treasury stock for $26 per share.

Required

a. How many shares of common stock were outstanding at the end of the period?
b. How many shares of common stock had been issued at the end of the period?
c. Prepare journal entries for these transactions.
d. Prepare the stockholders' equity section of the balance sheet reflecting these transactions. Include the number of shares authorized, issued, and outstanding in the description of the common stock.

Exercise 11-10A *Effect of cash dividends on financial statements*

On October 1, 2009, Evans Corporation declared a $50,000 cash dividend to be paid on December 30 to shareholders of record on November 20.

Required

a. Record the events occurring on October 1, November 20, and December 30 in a horizontal statements model like the following one. In the Cash Flow column, indicate whether the item is an operating activity (OA), investing activity (IA), or financing activity (FA).

Date	Assets	=	Liab.	+	C. Stock	+	Ret. Earn	Rev.	−	Exp.	=	Net Inc.	Cash Flow

b. Prepare journal entries for all events associated with the dividend.

Exercise 11-11A *Accounting for cumulative preferred dividends*

When Collum Corporation was organized in January 2009, it immediately issued 10,000 shares of $60 par, 5 percent, cumulative preferred stock and 20,000 shares of $10 par common stock. The company's earnings history is as follows: 2009, net loss of $15,000; 2010, net income of $120,000; 2011, net income of $95,000. The corporation did not pay a dividend in 2009.

Required

a. How much is the dividend arrearage as of January 1, 2010?
b. Assume that the board of directors declares an $80,000 cash dividend at the end of 2010 (remember that the 2009 and 2010 preferred dividends are due). How will the dividend be divided between the preferred and common stockholders?

Exercise 11-12A *Cash dividends for preferred and common shareholders*

J&J Corporation had the following stock issued and outstanding at January 1, 2009:

1. 50,000 shares of $5 par common stock.
2. 5,000 shares of $100 par, 5 percent, noncumulative preferred stock.

On May 10, J&J Corporation declared the annual cash dividend on its 5,000 shares of preferred stock and a $1 per share dividend for the common shareholders. The dividends will be paid on June 15 to the shareholders of record on May 30.

Required

a. Determine the total amount of dividends to be paid to the preferred shareholders and common shareholders.

b. Prepare general journal entries to record the declaration and payment of the cash dividends (be sure to date your entries).

L.O. 6

Exercise 11-13A   *Cash dividends: Common and preferred stock*

Hu Corp. had the following stock issued and outstanding at January 1, 2009:

1. 50,000 shares of no-par common stock.
2. 10,000 shares of $100 par, 3 percent, cumulative preferred stock. (Dividends are in arrears for one year, 2008.)

   On February 1, 2009, Hu declared a $100,000 cash dividend to be paid March 31 to shareholders of record on March 10.

Required

a. What amount of dividends will be paid to the preferred shareholders versus the common shareholders?

b. Prepare the journal entries required for these transactions. (Be sure to include the dates of the entries.)

L.O. 7

Exercise 11-14A   *Accounting for stock dividends*

Magee Corporation issued a 4 percent stock dividend on 30,000 shares of its $10 par common stock. At the time of the dividend, the market value of the stock was $30 per share.

Required

a. Compute the amount of the stock dividend.

b. Show the effects of the stock dividend on the financial statements using a horizontal statements model like the following one.

Assets	=	Liab.	+	Com. Stk.	+	Paid-in Excess	+	Ret. Earn	Rev.	−	Exp.	=	Net Inc.	Cash Flow

c. Prepare the journal entry to record the stock dividend.

L.O. 7

Exercise 11-15A   *Determining the effects of stock splits on the accounting records*

The market value of Lan Corporation's common stock had become excessively high. The stock was currently selling for $160 per share. To reduce the market price of the common stock, Lan declared a 2-for-1 stock split for the 300,000 outstanding shares of its $10 par common stock.

Required

a. How will Lan Corporation's books be affected by the stock split?

b. Determine the number of common shares outstanding and the par value after the split.

c. Explain how the market value of the stock will be affected by the stock split.

L.O. 9

Exercise 11-16A   *Accounting information*

The Cutting Edge (TCE) is one of the world's largest lawn mower distributors. TCE is concerned about maintaining an adequate supply of the economy-line mowers that it sells in its stores. TCE currently obtains its economy-line mowers from two suppliers. To ensure a steady supply of mowers, the management of TCE is considering the purchase of an ownership interest in one of the companies that supply its mowers. More specifically, TCE wants to own enough stock of one of the suppliers to enable it to exercise significant influence over the management of the company. The following is a description of the two suppliers.

   The first supplier, Dobbs, Incorporated, is a closely held company. Large blocks of the Dobbs stock are held by individual members of the Dobbs family. TCE's investment advisor has discovered that one of the members of the Dobbs family is interested in selling her 5 percent share of the company's stock.

The second supplier, National Mowers, Inc., has a widely disbursed ownership with no one single stockholder owning more than 1 percent of the stock. TCE's investment advisor believes that 5 percent of this company's stock could be acquired gradually over an extended period of time without having a significant effect on the company's stock price.

Required

Provide a recommendation to TCE's management as to whether they should pursue the purchase of 5 percent of Dobbs, Incorporated, or 5 percent of National Mowers, Inc. Your answer should be supported by an appropriate logical explanation of your recommendation.

Exercise 11-17A *Using the P/E ratio*

During 2009 Westbrook, Inc., and Greenbank, Inc., reported net incomes of $81,000 and $93,000, respectively. Both companies had 10,000 shares of common stock issued and outstanding. The market price per share of Westbrook's stock was $30, while Greenbank's sold for $120 per share.

Required

a. Determine the P/E ratio for each company.
b. Based on the P/E ratios computed in Requirement *a*, which company do investors believe has the greater potential for growth in income?

Exercise 11-18A *The P/E ratio*

Required

Write a memo explaining why one company's P/E ratio may be higher than another company's P/E ratio.

PROBLEMS—SERIES A

All Problems in Series A are available with McGraw-Hill's Homework Manager®

Problem 11-19A *Effect of business structure on financial statements*

L.O. 1, 2

Upton Company was started on January 1, 2009, when the owners invested $160,000 cash in the business. During 2009, the company earned cash revenues of $120,000 and incurred cash expenses of $82,000. The company also paid cash distributions of $15,000.

CHECK FIGURES
a. Net Income: $38,000
b. Dan Upton Capital: $106,200

Required

Prepare a 2009 income statement, capital statement (statement of changes in equity), balance sheet, and statement of cash flows using each of the following assumptions. (Consider each assumption separately.)

a. Upton is a sole proprietorship owned by J. Upton.
b. Upton is a partnership with two partners, Dan and Nancy Upton. Dan invested $100,000 and Nancy invested $60,000 of the $160,000 cash that was used to start the business. Nancy was expected to assume the vast majority of the responsibility for operating the business. The partnership agreement called for Nancy to receive 60 percent of the profits and Dan the remaining 40 percent. With regard to the $15,000 distribution, Nancy withdrew $6,000 from the business and Dan withdrew $9,000.
c. Upton is a corporation. The owners were issued 10,000 shares of $10 par common stock when they invested the $160,000 cash in the business.

Problem 11-20A *Recording and reporting stock transactions and cash dividends across two accounting cycles*

L.O. 4–6

Flesher Corporation was authorized to issue 100,000 shares of $5 par common stock and 50,000 shares of $50 par, 5 percent, cumulative preferred stock. Flesher Corporation completed the following transactions during its first two years of operation:

CHECK FIGURES
b. Preferred Stock, 2009: $100,000
c. Common Shares Outstanding, 2010: 34,500

2009

Jan. 2   Issued 15,000 shares of $5 par common stock for $8 per share.
     15   Issued 2,000 shares of $50 par preferred stock for $55 per share.
Feb. 14   Issued 20,000 shares of $5 par common stock for $9 per share.

Dec. 31   During the year, earned $310,000 of cash service revenue and paid $240,000 of cash operating expenses.

   31   Declared the cash dividend on outstanding shares of preferred stock for 2009. The dividend will be paid on January 31 to stockholders of record on January 15, 2010.

   31   Closed revenue, expense, and dividend accounts to the retained earnings account.

2010

Jan. 31   Paid the cash dividend declared on December 31, 2008.
Mar. 1   Issued 3,000 shares of $50 par preferred stock for $60 per share.
June 1   Purchased 500 shares of common stock as treasury stock at $9 per share.
Dec. 31   During the year, earned $250,000 of cash service revenue and paid $175,000 of cash operating expenses.

   31   Declared the dividend on the preferred stock and a $0.50 per share dividend on the common stock.

   31   Closed revenue, expense, and dividend accounts to the retained earnings account.

Required

a. Prepare journal entries for these transactions for 2009 and 2010.
b. Prepare the stockholders' equity section of the balance sheet at December 31, 2009.
c. Prepare the balance sheet at December 31, 2010.

L.O. 5, 6, 8

CHECK FIGURE
b. Total Paid-In Capital: $366,900

Problem 11-21A   *Recording and reporting treasury stock transactions*

Millsaps Corp. completed the following transactions in 2009, the first year of operation:

1. Issued 30,000 shares of $10 par common stock at par.
2. Issued 2,000 shares of $30 stated value preferred stock at $33 per share.
3. Purchased 1,000 shares of common stock as treasury stock for $12 per share.
4. Declared a 5 percent dividend on preferred stock.
5. Sold 300 shares of treasury stock for $15 per share.
6. Paid the cash dividend on preferred stock that was declared in Event 4.
7. Earned cash service revenue of $75,000 and incurred cash operating expenses of $42,000.
8. Closed revenue, expense, and dividend accounts to the retained earnings account.
9. Appropriated $6,000 of retained earnings.

Required

a. Prepare journal entries to record these transactions.
b. Prepare the stockholders' equity section of the balance sheet as of December 31, 2009.

L.O. 5

CHECK FIGURE
b. Total Paid-In Capital: $451,200
Total Stockholders' Equity: $569,200

Problem 11-22A   *Recording and reporting treasury stock transactions*

Carter Corporation reports the following information in its January 1, 2009, balance sheet:

Stockholders' equity	
Common stock, $10 par value,	
50,000 shares authorized, 30,000 shares issued and outstanding	$300,000
Paid-in capital in excess of par value	150,000
Retained earnings	100,000
Total stockholders' equity	$550,000

During 2009, Carter was affected by the following accounting events:

1. Purchased 1,000 shares of treasury stock at $20 per share.
2. Reissued 600 shares of treasury stock at $22 per share.
3. Earned $64,000 of cash service revenues.
4. Paid $38,000 of cash operating expenses.

Required

a. Provide journal entries to record these events in the accounting records.
b. Prepare the stockholders' equity section of the year-end balance sheet.

Problem 11-23A   *Recording and reporting stock dividends*

L.O. 4, 6, 7

Davis Corp. completed the following transactions in 2009, the first year of operation:

1. Issued 30,000 shares of $20 par common stock for $30 per share.
2. Issued 5,000 shares of $50 par, 4 percent, preferred stock at $51 per share.
3. Paid the annual cash dividend to preferred shareholders.
4. Issued a 5 percent stock dividend on the common stock. The market value at the dividend declaration date was $40 per share.
5. Later that year, issued a 2-for-1 split on the 21,500 shares of outstanding common stock.
6. Earned $185,000 of cash service revenues and paid $120,000 of cash operating expenses.

CHECK FIGURE
c. Total Paid-In Capital:
$1,215,000
Retained Earnings:
$5,000

Required

a. Record each of these events in a horizontal statements model like the following one. In the Cash Flow column, indicate whether the item is an operating activity (OA), investing activity (IA), or financing activity (FA). Use NA to indicate that an element is not affected by the event.

Assets	=	Liab.	+	Equity						Rev.	−	Exp.	=	Net Inc.	Cash Flow
				Pfd. Stk.	+ Paid-in Excess PS	+ Com. Stk.	+ Paid-in Excess CS	+ Ret. Earn.							

b. Record the 2009 transactions in general journal form.
c. Prepare the stockholders' equity section of the balance sheet at the end of 2009.

Problem 11-24A   *Analyzing the stockholders' equity section of the balance sheet*

L.O. 4, 7

The stockholders' equity section of the balance sheet for Atkins Company at December 31, 2007, is as follows:

Stockholders' Equity		
Paid-in capital		
Preferred stock, ? par value, 6% cumulative,		
50,000 shares authorized,		
40,000 shares issued and outstanding	$400,000	
Common stock, $10 stated value,		
150,000 shares authorized,		
60,000 shares issued and ? outstanding	600,000	
Paid-in capital in excess of par–preferred	30,000	
Paid-in capital in excess of par–common	200,000	
Total paid-in capital		$1,230,000
Retained earnings		250,000
Treasury stock, 2,000 shares		(50,000)
Total stockholders' equity		$1,430,000

CHECK FIGURES
a. Par value per
   share: $10
b. Dividend per
   share: $.60

Note: The market value per share of the common stock is $25, and the market value per share of the preferred stock is $12.

Required

a. What is the par value per share of the preferred stock?
b. What is the dividend per share on the preferred stock?
c. What is the number of common stock shares outstanding?
d. What was the average issue price per share (price for which the stock was issued) of the common stock?
e. Explain the difference between the average issue price and the market price of the common stock.
f. If Atkins declared a 2-for-1 stock split on the common stock, how many shares would be outstanding after the split? What amount would be transferred from the Retained Earnings account because of the stock split? Theoretically, what would be the market price of the common stock immediately after the stock split?

L.O. 1

Problem 11-25A   *Different forms of business organization*

Paul Salvy established a partnership with Lisa Witlow. The new company, S&W Fuels, purchased coal directly from mining companies and contracted to ship the coal via waterways to a seaport where it was delivered to ships that were owned and operated by international utilities companies. Salvy was primarily responsible for running the day-to-day operations of the business. Witlow negotiated the buy-and-sell agreements. She recently signed a deal to purchase and deliver $2,000,000 of coal to Solar Utilities. S&W Fuels purchased the coal on account from Miller Mining Company. After accepting title to the coal, S&W Fuels agreed to deliver the coal under terms FOB destination, Port of Long Beach. Unfortunately, Witlow failed to inform Salvy of the deal in time for Salvy to insure the shipment. While in transit, the vessel carrying the coal suffered storm damage that rendered the coal virtually worthless by the time it reached its destination. S&W Fuels immediately declared bankruptcy. The company not only was responsible for the $2,000,000 due to Miller Mining Company but also was sued by Solar for breach of contract. Witlow had a personal net worth of virtually zero, but Salvy was a wealthy individual with a net worth approaching $2,500,000. Accordingly, Miller Mining and Solar filed suit against Salvy's personal assets. Salvy claimed that he was not responsible for the problem because Witlow had failed to inform him of the contracts in time to obtain insurance coverage. Witlow admitted that she was personally responsible for the disaster.

Required

Write a memo describing Salvy's risk associated with his participation in the partnership. Comment on how other forms of ownership would have affected his level of risk.

L.O. 4–8

Problem 11-26A   *Effects of equity transactions on financial statements*

The following events were experienced by Baskin, Inc.

1. Issued common stock for cash.
2. Paid cash to purchase treasury stock.
3. Declared a cash dividend.
4. Issued cumulative preferred stock.
5. Issued noncumulative preferred stock.
6. Appropriated retained earnings.
7. Sold treasury stock for an amount of cash that was more than the cost of the treasury stock.
8. Distributed a stock dividend.
9. Declared a 2-for-1 stock split on the common stock.
10. Paid a cash dividend that was previously declared.

Required

Show the effect of each event on the elements of the financial statements using a horizontal statements model like the following one. Use + for increase, − for decrease, and NA for not affected. In the Cash Flow column indicate whether the item is an operating activity (OA), investing activity (IA), or financing activity (FA). The first transaction is entered as an example.

Event No.	Assets	=	Liab.	+	Equity	Rev.	−	Exp.	=	Net Inc.	Cash Flow
1	+		NA		+	NA		NA		NA	+ FA

EXERCISES—SERIES B

L.O. 1, 2

Exercise 11-1B   *Effect of accounting events on the financial statements of a sole proprietorship*

A sole proprietorship was started on January 1, 2009, when it received $40,000 cash from Ken Duke, the owner. During 2009, the company earned $24,000 in cash revenues and paid $13,500 in cash expenses. Duke withdrew $500 cash from the business during 2009.

Required

Prepare an income statement, capital statement (statement of changes in equity), balance sheet, and statement of cash flows for Duke's 2009 fiscal year.

Exercise 11-2B   *Effect of accounting events on the financial statements of a partnership*   L.O. 1, 2

Lanna Miller and Traci Price started the M&P partnership on January 1, 2009. The business acquired $30,000 cash from Miller and $50,000 from Price. During 2009, the partnership earned $28,000 in cash revenues and paid $15,200 for cash expenses. Miller withdrew $2,000 cash from the business, and Price withdrew $3,000 cash. The net income was allocated to the capital accounts of the two partners in proportion to the amounts of their original investments in the business.

Required

Prepare an income statement, capital statement, balance sheet, and statement of cash flows for M&P's 2009 fiscal year.

Exercise 11-3B   *Effect of accounting events on the financial statements of a corporation*   L.O. 1, 2

Shay Corporation was started with the issue of 2,000 shares of $5 par stock for cash on January 1, 2009. The stock was issued at a market price of $18 per share. During 2009, the company earned $42,000 in cash revenues and paid $26,000 for cash expenses. Also, a $2,000 cash dividend was paid to the stockholders.

Required

Prepare an income statement, statement of changes in stockholders' equity, balance sheet, and statement of cash flows for Shay Corporation's 2009 fiscal year.

Exercise 11-4B   *Effect of issuing common stock on the balance sheet*   L.O. 4

Newly formed Braddock Corporation has 50,000 shares of $10 par common stock authorized. On March 1, 2009, Braddock issued 10,000 shares of the stock for $20 per share. On May 2 the company issued an additional 6,000 shares for $22 per share. Braddock was not affected by other events during 2009.

Required

a. Record the transactions in a horizontal statements model like the following one. In the Cash Flow column, indicate whether the item is an operating activity (OA), investing activity (IA), or financing activity (FA). Use NA to indicate that an element was not affected by the event.

Assets	=	Liab.	+		Equity			Rev.	−	Exp.	=	Net Inc.		Cash Flow
Cash	=		+	Com. Stk.	+	Paid-in Excess								

b. Determine the amount Braddock would report for common stock on the December 31, 2009, balance sheet.
c. Determine the amount Braddock would report for paid-in capital in excess of par.
d. What is the total amount of capital contributed by the owners?
e. What amount of total assets would Braddock report on the December 31, 2009, balance sheet?
f. Prepare journal entries to record the March 1 and May 2 transactions.

Exercise 11-5B   *Recording and reporting common and preferred stock transactions*   L.O. 4

TNT, Inc., was organized on June 5, 2009. It was authorized to issue 200,000 shares of $5 par common stock and 20,000 shares of 5 percent cumulative class A preferred stock. The class A stock had a stated value of $50 per share. The following stock transactions pertain to TNT, Inc.:

1. Issued 10,000 shares of common stock for $9 per share.
2. Issued 3,000 shares of the class A preferred stock for $55 per share.
3. Issued 50,000 shares of common stock for $10 per share.

Required

a. Prepare general journal entries for these transactions.
b. Prepare the stockholders' equity section of the balance sheet immediately after these transactions.

Exercise 11-6B   *Effect of no-par common and par preferred stock on the horizontal statements model*   L.O. 4

Bates Corporation issued 5,000 shares of no-par common stock for $30 per share. Bates also issued 1,000 shares of $50 par, 6 percent noncumulative preferred stock at $60 per share.

Required

a. Record these events in a horizontal statements model like the following one. In the Cash Flow column, indicate whether the item is an operating activity (OA), investing activity (IA), or financing activity (FA). Use NA to indicate that an element was not affected by the event.

Assets =	Equity			Rev. −	Exp. =	Net Inc.	Cash Flow
Cash =	Pfd. Stk. +	Com. Stk. +	Paid-in Excess				

b. Prepare journal entries to record these transactions.

L.O. 4

Exercise 11-7B *Issuing stock for assets other than cash*

Mark James, a wealthy investor, exchanged a plot of land that originally cost him $30,000 for 1,000 shares of $10 par common stock issued to him by Bay Corp. On the same date, Bay Corp. issued an additional 500 shares of stock to James for $31 per share.

Required

a. What was the value of the land at the date of the stock issue?

b. Show the effect of the two stock issues on Bay's books in a horizontal statements model like the following one. In the Cash Flow column, indicate whether the item is an operating activity (OA), investing activity (IA), or financing activity (FA). Use NA to indicate that an element was not affected by the event.

Assets		=	Equity			Rev. −	Exp. =	Net Inc.	Cash Flow
Cash +	Land	=	Com. Stk. +	Paid-in Excess					

L.O. 5

Exercise 11-8B *Treasury stock transactions*

Stark Corporation repurchased 2,000 shares of its own stock for $38 per share. The stock has a par of $10 per share. A month later Stark resold 500 shares of the treasury stock for $40 per share.

Required

a. Record the two events in general journal format.

b. What is the balance of the treasury stock account after these transactions?

L.O. 5

Exercise 11-9B *Recording and reporting treasury stock transactions*

The following information pertains to Eady Corp. at January 1, 2009.

Common stock, $10 par, 10,000 shares authorized, 800 shares issued and outstanding	$ 8,000
Paid-in capital in excess of par, common stock	12,000
Retained earnings	75,000

Eady Corp. completed the following transactions during 2009:

1. Issued 2,000 shares of $10 par common stock for $35 per share.
2. Repurchased 300 shares of its own common stock for $30 per share.
3. Resold 100 shares of treasury stock for $34 per share.

Required

a. How many shares of common stock were outstanding at the end of the period?

b. How many shares of common stock had been issued at the end of the period?

c. Prepare journal entries for these transactions.

d. Prepare the stockholders' equity section of the balance sheet reflecting these transactions. Include the number of shares authorized, issued, and outstanding in the description of the common stock.

Exercise 11-10B   *Effect of cash dividends on financial statements*   L.O. 6

On May 1, 2009, Potts Corporation declared a $100,000 cash dividend to be paid on May 31 to share-holders of record on May 15.

Required

a. Record the events occurring on May 1, May 15, and May 31 in a horizontal statements model like the following one. In the Cash Flow column, indicate whether the item is an operating activity (OA), investing activity (IA), or financing activity (FA).

Date	Assets	=	Liab.	+	Com. Stock	+	Ret. Earn	Rev.	−	Exp.	=	Net Inc.	Cash Flow

b. Prepare journal entries for all events associated with the dividend.

Exercise 11-11B   *Accounting for cumulative preferred dividends*   L.O. 6

When Shelter Corporation was organized in January 2009, it immediately issued 5,000 shares of $50 par, 5 percent, cumulative preferred stock and 30,000 shares of $20 par common stock. Its earnings history is as follows: 2009, net loss of $25,000; 2010, net income of $120,000; 2011, net income of $250,000. The corporation did not pay a dividend in 2009.

Required

a. How much is the dividend arrearage as of January 1, 2010?

b. Assume that the board of directors declares a $30,000 cash dividend at the end of 2010 (remember that the 2009 and 2010 preferred dividends are due). How will the dividend be divided between the preferred and common stockholders?

Exercise 11-12B   *Cash dividends for preferred and common shareholders*   L.O. 6

Rienzi Corporation had the following stock issued and outstanding at January 1, 2009:

1. 100,000 shares of $1 par common stock.
2. 10,000 shares of $100 par, 8 percent, noncumulative preferred stock.

On June 10, Rienzi Corporation declared the annual cash dividend on its 10,000 shares of pre-ferred stock and a $1 per share dividend for the common shareholders. The dividends will be paid on July 1 to the shareholders of record on June 20.

Required

a. Determine the total amount of dividends to be paid to the preferred shareholders and common shareholders.

b. Prepare general journal entries to record the declaration and payment of the cash dividends (be sure to date your entries).

Exercise 11-13B   *Cash dividends: Common and preferred stock*   L.O. 6

Boxes, Inc., had the following stock issued and outstanding at January 1, 2009:

1. 200,000 shares of no-par common stock.
2. 10,000 shares of $100 par, 8 percent, cumulative preferred stock. (Dividends are in arrears for one year, 2008.)

On March 8, 2009, Boxes declared a $200,000 cash dividend to be paid March 31 to shareholders of record on March 20.

Required

a. What amount of dividends will be paid to the preferred shareholders versus the common shareholders?

b. Prepare the journal entries required for these transactions. (Be sure to include the dates of the entries.)

Exercise 11-14B   *Accounting for stock dividends*   L.O. 7

Farrell Corporation issued a 5 percent stock dividend on 10,000 shares of its $10 par common stock. At the time of the dividend, the market value of the stock was $14 per share.

Required

a. Compute the amount of the stock dividend.

b. Show the effects of the stock dividend on the financial statements using a horizontal statements model like the following one.

Assets	=	Liab.	+	Com. Stock	+	Paid-in Excess	+	Ret. Earn		Rev.	−	Exp.	=	Net Inc.		Cash Flow

c. Prepare the journal entry to record the stock dividend.

L.O. 7

Exercise 11-15B   *Determining the effects of stock splits on the accounting records*

The market value of Horn Corporation's common stock had become excessively high. The stock was currently selling for $240 per share. To reduce the market price of the common stock, Horn declared a 4-for-1 stock split for the 100,000 outstanding shares of its $20 par value common stock.

Required

a. What entry will be made on the books of Horn Corporation for the stock split?

b. Determine the number of common shares outstanding and the par value after the split.

c. Explain how the market value of the stock will be affected by the stock split.

L.O. 9

Exercise 11-16B   *Corporate announcements*

Mighty Drugs (one of the three largest drug makers) just reported that its 2009 third quarter profits are essentially the same as the 2008 third quarter profits. In addition to this announcement, the same day, Mighty Drugs also announced that the Food and Drug Administration has just approved a new drug used to treat high blood pressure that Mighty Drugs developed. This new drug has been shown to be extremely effective and has few or no side effects. It will also be less expensive than the other drugs currently on the market.

Required

Using the above information, answer the following questions:

a. What do you think will happen to the stock price of Mighty Drugs on the day these two announcements are made? Explain your answer.

b. How will the balance sheet be affected on that day by the above announcements?

c. How will the income statement be affected on that day by the above announcements?

d. How will the statement of cash flows be affected on that day by the above announcements?

L.O. 9

Exercise 11-17B   *Using the P/E ratio*

During 2010 the Jason Corporation and the Fitzgerald Corporation reported net incomes of $7,000 and $9,600, respectively. Both companies had 2,000 shares of common stock issued and outstanding. The market price per share of Jason's stock was $50, while Fitzgerald's sold for $85 per share.

Required

a. Determine the P/E ratio for each company.

b. Based on the P/E ratios computed in Requirement *a,* which company do investors believe has the greater potential for growth in income?

L.O. 9

Exercise 11-18B   *The P/E ratio*

Pepper Company's earnings were approximately the same in 2007 and 2008. Even so, the company's P/E ratio dropped significantly.

Required

Speculate about why Pepper's P/E ratio dropped significantly while its earnings remained constant.

Problem 11-19B   *Effect of business structure on financial statements*

Pryor Company was started on January 1, 2009, when it acquired $80,000 cash from the owners. During 2009, the company earned cash revenues of $20,000 and incurred cash expenses of $12,500. The company also paid cash distributions of $5,000.

Required

Prepare a 2009 income statement, capital statement (statement of changes in equity), balance sheet, and statement of cash flows under each of the following assumptions. (Consider each assumption separately.)

a. Pryor is a sole proprietorship owned by Charles Pryor.

b. Pryor is a partnership with two partners, Charles Pryor and Joe Faello. Charles Pryor invested $50,000 and Joe Faello invested $30,000 of the $80,000 cash that was used to start the business. Joe Faello was expected to assume the vast majority of the responsibility for operating the business. The partnership agreement called for J. Faello to receive 60 percent of the profits and C. Pryor to get the remaining 40 percent. With regard to the $5,000 distribution, J. Faello withdrew $2,200 from the business and C. Pryor withdrew $2,800.

c. Pryor is a corporation. It issued 10,000 shares of $5 par common stock for $80,000 cash to start the business.

Problem 11-20B   *Recording and reporting stock transactions and cash dividends across two accounting cycles*

Tye Corporation received a charter that authorized the issuance of 100,000 shares of $10 par common stock and 50,000 shares of $50 par, 6 percent cumulative preferred stock. Tye Corporation completed the following transactions during its first two years of operation.

2008

Jan.	5	Sold 10,000 shares of the $10 par common stock for $28 per share.
	12	Sold 1,000 shares of the 6 percent preferred stock for $70 per share.
Apr.	5	Sold 40,000 shares of the $10 par common stock for $40 per share.
Dec.	31	During the year, earned $170,000 in cash service revenue and paid $110,000 for cash operating expenses.
	31	Declared the cash dividend on the outstanding shares of preferred stock for 2008. The dividend will be paid on February 15 to stockholders of record on January 10, 2009.
	31	Closed the revenue, expense, and dividend accounts to the retained earnings account.

2009

Feb.	15	Paid the cash dividend declared on December 31, 2008.
Mar.	3	Sold 10,000 shares of the $50 par preferred stock for $78 per share.
May	5	Purchased 500 shares of the common stock as treasury stock at $43 per share.
Dec.	31	During the year, earned $210,000 in cash service revenue and paid $140,000 for cash operating expenses.
	31	Declared the annual dividend on the preferred stock and a $0.60 per share dividend on the common stock.
	31	Closed revenue, expense, and dividend accounts to the retained earnings account.

Required

a. Prepare journal entries for these transactions for 2008 and 2009.

b. Prepare the balance sheets at December 31, 2008 and 2009.

c. What is the number of common shares *outstanding* at the end of 2008? At the end of 2009? How many common shares had been *issued* at the end of 2008? At the end of 2009? Explain any differences between issued and outstanding common shares for 2008 and for 2009.

L.O. 4, 5, 8

Problem 11-21B *Recording and reporting treasury stock transactions*

Big Co. completed the following transactions in 2009, the first year of operation:

1. Issued 20,000 shares of $5 par common stock for $5 per share.
2. Issued 1,000 shares of $20 stated value preferred stock for $20 per share.
3. Purchased 1,000 shares of common stock as treasury stock for $7 per share.
4. Declared a $1,500 dividend on preferred stock.
5. Sold 500 shares of treasury stock for $10 per share.
6. Paid $1,500 cash for the preferred dividend declared in Event 4.
7. Earned cash service revenues of $54,000 and incurred cash expenses of $32,000.
8. Closed revenue, expense, and dividend accounts to the retained earnings account.
9. Appropriated $5,000 of retained earnings.

Required

a. Prepare journal entries to record these transactions.
b. Prepare a balance sheet as of December 31, 2009.

L.O. 4, 5

Problem 11-22B *Analyzing journal entries for treasury stock transactions*

The following correctly prepared entries without explanations pertain to Torres Corporation.

	Account Title	Debit	Credit
1.	Cash	2,100,000	
	Common Stock		1,000,000
	Paid-in Capital in Excess of Par Value		1,100,000
2.	Treasury Stock	22,500	
	Cash		22,500
3.	Cash	13,600	
	Treasury Stock		12,000
	Paid-in Capital in Excess of Cost of Treasury Stock		1,600

The original sale (Entry 1) was for 200,000 shares, and the treasury stock was acquired for $15 per share (Entry 2).

Required

a. What was the sales price per share of the original stock issue?
b. How many shares of stock did the corporation acquire in Event 2?
c. How many shares were reissued in Event 3?
d. How many shares are outstanding immediately following Events 2 and 3, respectively?

L.O. 4, 6, 7

Problem 11-23B *Recording and reporting stock dividends*

Arnold Co. completed the following transactions in 2009, the first year of operation:

1. Issued 20,000 shares of no-par common stock for $10 per share.
2. Issued 5,000 shares of $20 par, 6 percent, preferred stock for $20 per share.
3. Paid a cash dividend of $6,000 to preferred shareholders.
4. Issued a 10 percent stock dividend on no-par common stock. The market value at the dividend declaration date was $15 per share.
5. Later that year, issued a 2-for-1 split on the shares of outstanding common stock. The market price of the stock at that time was $35 per share.
6. Produced $145,000 of cash service revenue and incurred $97,000 of cash operating expenses.

Required

a. Record each of the six events in a horizontal statements model like the following one. In the Cash Flow column, indicate whether the item is an operating activity (OA), investing activity (IA), or financing activity (FA). Use NA to indicate that an element is not affected by the event.

Assets =	Equity			Rev. −	Exp. =	Net Inc.	Cash Flow
	Pfd. Stk. +	Com. Stk. +	Ret. Earn.				

b. Record the 2009 transactions in general journal form.

c. Prepare the stockholders' equity section of the balance sheet at the end of 2009. (Include all necessary information.)

d. Theoretically, what is the market value of the common stock after the stock split?

Problem 11-24B *Analyzing the stockholders' equity section of the balance sheet*

L.O. 4, 7

The stockholders' equity section of the balance sheet for City Electric Co. at December 31, 2007, is as follows:

Stockholders' Equity		
Paid-in capital		
Preferred stock, ? par value, 8% cumulative,		
100,000 shares authorized,		
5,000 shares issued and outstanding	$ 300,000	
Common stock, $20 stated value,		
200,000 shares authorized,		
100,000 shares issued and outstanding	3,000,000	
Paid-in capital in excess of par—preferred	100,000	
Paid-in capital in excess of stated value—common	500,000	
Total paid-in capital		$3,900,000
Retained earnings		500,000
Total stockholders' equity		$4,400,000

Note: The market value per share of the common stock is $36, and the market value per share of the preferred stock is $70.

Required

a. What is the par value per share of the preferred stock?

b. What is the dividend per share on the preferred stock?

c. What was the average issue price per share (price for which the stock was issued) of the common stock?

d. Explain the difference between the par value and the market price of the preferred stock.

e. If City declares a 3-for-1 stock split on the common stock, how many shares will be outstanding after the split? What amount will be transferred from the retained earnings account because of the stock split? Theoretically, what will be the market price of the common stock immediately after the stock split?

Problem 11-25B *Different forms of business organization*

L.O. 1

Brian Walters was working to establish a business enterprise with four of his wealthy friends. Each of the five individuals would receive a 20 percent ownership interest in the company. A primary goal of establishing the enterprise was to minimize the amount of income taxes paid. Assume that the five investors are in a 35 percent personal tax bracket and that the corporate tax rate is

25 percent. Also assume that the new company is expected to earn $200,000 of cash income before taxes during its first year of operation. All earnings are expected to be immediately distributed to the owners.

Required

Calculate the amount of after-tax cash flow available to each investor if the business is established as a partnership versus a corporation. Write a memo explaining the advantages and disadvantages of these two forms of business organization. Explain why a limited liability company may be a better choice than either a partnership or a corporation.

L.O. 4–8

Problem 11-26B   *Effects of equity transactions on financial statements*

The following events were experienced by Abbot, Inc.:

1. Issued cumulative preferred stock for cash.
2. Issued common stock for cash.
3. Distributed a 2-for-1 stock split on the common stock.
4. Issued noncumulative preferred stock for cash.
5. Appropriated retained earnings.
6. Sold treasury stock for an amount of cash that was more than the cost of the treasury stock.
7. Distributed a stock dividend.
8. Paid cash to purchase treasury stock.
9. Declared a cash dividend.
10. Paid the cash dividend declared in Event 9.

Required

Show the effect of each event on the elements of the financial statements using a horizontal statements model like the following one. Use + for increase, − for decrease, and NA for not affected. In the Cash Flow column, indicate whether the item is an operating activity (OA), investing activity (IA), or financing activity (FA). The first transaction is entered as an example.

Event No.	Assets	=	Liab.	+	Equity	Rev.	−	Exp.	=	Net Inc.	Cash Flow
1	+		NA		+	NA		NA		NA	+ FA

ANALYZE, THINK, COMMUNICATE

ATC 11-1   **Business Applications Case**   *Understanding real-world annual reports*

Required—Part 1

The Topps Company, Inc.

Use the Topps Company's annual report in Appendix B to answer the following questions.

a. Does Topps' common stock have a par value, and if so how much is it?
b. How many shares of Topps' common stock were *outstanding* as of February 25, 2006? Do not forget to consider treasury stock.
c. The dollar-value balance in Topps' Treasury Stock account is larger than the balance in its Common Stock and Additional Paid-In-Capital accounts. How can this be?
d. How many members of Topps' Board of Directors are also officers (employees) of the company as of February 25, 2006?
e. What was the highest and lowest price per share that Topps' common stock sold for during the fiscal year ending on February 25, 2006?

Required—Part 2

Use the Harley-Davidson's annual report that came with this book to answer the following questions.

a. Does Harley-Davidson's common stock have a par value, and if so how much is it?

b. How many shares of Harley-Davidson's common stock were outstanding as of December 31, 2005?

c. Did Harley-Davidson pay cash dividends in 2005, and if so, how much?

ATC 11-2   Group Assignment   *Missing information*

Listed here are the stockholders' equity sections of three public companies for years ending 2005 and 2004:

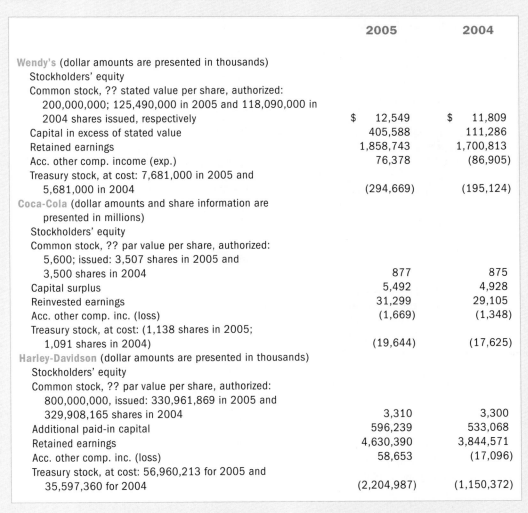

	2005	2004
Wendy's (dollar amounts are presented in thousands)		
Stockholders' equity		
Common stock, ?? stated value per share, authorized: 200,000,000; 125,490,000 in 2005 and 118,090,000 in 2004 shares issued, respectively	$ 12,549	$ 11,809
Capital in excess of stated value	405,588	111,286
Retained earnings	1,858,743	1,700,813
Acc. other comp. income (exp.)	76,378	(86,905)
Treasury stock, at cost: 7,681,000 in 2005 and 5,681,000 in 2004	(294,669)	(195,124)
Coca-Cola (dollar amounts and share information are presented in millions)		
Stockholders' equity		
Common stock, ?? par value per share, authorized: 5,600; issued: 3,507 shares in 2005 and 3,500 shares in 2004	877	875
Capital surplus	5,492	4,928
Reinvested earnings	31,299	29,105
Acc. other comp. inc. (loss)	(1,669)	(1,348)
Treasury stock, at cost: (1,138 shares in 2005; 1,091 shares in 2004)	(19,644)	(17,625)
Harley-Davidson (dollar amounts are presented in thousands)		
Stockholders' equity		
Common stock, ?? par value per share, authorized: 800,000,000, issued: 330,961,869 in 2005 and 329,908,165 shares in 2004	3,310	3,300
Additional paid-in capital	596,239	533,068
Retained earnings	4,630,390	3,844,571
Acc. other comp. inc. (loss)	58,653	(17,096)
Treasury stock, at cost: 56,960,213 for 2005 and 35,597,360 for 2004	(2,204,987)	(1,150,372)

Required

a. Divide the class in three sections and divide each section into groups of three to five students. Assign each section one of the companies.

Group Tasks

Based on the company assigned to your group, answer the following questions.

b. What is the per share par or stated value of the common stock in 2005?

c. What was the average issue price of the common stock for each year?

d. How many shares of stock are outstanding at the end of each year?

e. What is the average cost per share of the treasury stock for 2005?

f. Do the data suggest that your company was profitable in 2005?

g. Can you determine the amount of net income from the information given? What is missing?

h. What is the total stockholders' equity of your company for each year?

Class Discussion

i. Have each group select a representative to present the information about its company. Compare the share issue price and the par or stated value of the companies.

j. Compare the average issue price to the current market price for each of the companies. Speculate about what might cause the difference.

ATC 11-3   Real-World Case   *Which stock is most valuable?*

Listed here are data for five companies. These data are from the companies' annual reports for the fiscal year indicated in the parentheses. The market price per share is the closing price of the companies' stock as of November 3, 2006. Except for the market price per share, all amounts are in thousands. The shares outstanding number is the weighted-average number of shares the company used to compute its basic earnings per share.

Company (Fiscal Year)	Net Earnings	Shares Outstanding	Stockholders' Equity	Market-Price per Share
Brink's (12/31/2005)	$ 142,400	58,700	$ 837,500	$52.50
Carmax (2/28/2006)	148,055	104,954	959,738	43.33
ExxonMobil (12/31/2005)	36,130,000	6,133,000	111,186,000	72.15
Garmin (12/31/2005)	311,219	216,134	1,157,264	46.57
Schering-Plough (12/31/2005)	269,000	1,480,000	7,387,000	22.28

Required

a. Compute the earnings per share (EPS) for each company.

b. Compute the P/E ratio for each company.

c. Using the P/E ratios, rank the companies' stock in the order that the stock market appears to value the companies, from most valuable to least valuable. Identify reasons the ranking based on P/E ratios may not really represent the market's optimism about one or more companies.

d. Compute the book value per share for each company.

e. Compare each company's book value per share to its market-price per share and based on this data, rank them from most valuable to least valuable. (The higher the ratio of market value to book value, the greater the value the stock market appears to be assigning to a company's stock.)

ATC 11-4   Business Applications Case   *Performing ratio analysis using real-world data*

Merck & Company is one of the world's largest pharmaceutical companies. The following data were taken from the company's 2004 annual report.

	Fiscal Years Ending	
	December 31, 2004	December 31, 2003
Net earnings (in millions)	$5,813.4	$6,830.9
Earnings per share	$2.62	$2.95
The following data were taken from public stock-price quotes:		
Stock price per share on March 1, 2005 (Two months after the end of Merck's 2004 fiscal year.)		$32.13
Stock price per share on March 1, 2004 (Two months after the end of Merck's 2003 fiscal year.)		$48.45

Required

a. Compute Merck's price-earnings ratio for March 1, 2005, and March 1, 2004.

b. Did the financial markets appear to be more optimistic about Merck's future performance on March 1, 2004, or March 1, 2005?

c. Based on the information provided, estimate approximately how many shares of stock Merck had outstanding as of December 31, 2004.

ATC 11-5 Business Applications Case *Performing ratio analysis using real-world data*

Google, Inc., operates the world's largest internet search engine. International Business Machines Corporation (IBM) is one of the world's largest computer hardware and software companies. The following data were taken from the companies' December 31, 2004, annual reports.

	Google, Inc.	IBM
Net earnings (in thousands)	$399,119	$8,430,000
Earnings per share	$2.07	$5.03
The following data were taken from public stock-price quotes:		
Stock price per share on March 1, 2005 (Two months after the end of their 2004 fiscal years.)	$186.06	$93.30

Required

a. Compute the price-earnings ratios for each company as of March 1, 2005.

b. Which company's future performance did the financial markets appear to be more optimistic about as of March 1, 2005?

c. Provide some reasons why the market may view one company's future more optimistically than the other.

ATC 11-6 Writing Assignment *Comparison of organizational forms*

Jim Baku and Scott Hanson are thinking about opening a new restaurant. Baku has extensive marketing experience but does not know that much about food preparation. However, Hanson is an excellent chef. Both will work in the business, but Baku will provide most of the funds necessary to start the business. At this time, they cannot decide whether to operate the business as a partnership or a corporation.

Required

Prepare a written memo to Baku and Hanson describing the advantages and disadvantages of each organizational form. Also, from the limited information provided, recommend the organizational form you think they should use.

ATC 11-7 Ethical Dilemma *Bad news versus very bad news*

Louise Stinson, the chief financial officer of Bostonian Corporation, was on her way to the president's office. She was carrying the latest round of bad news. There would be no executive bonuses this year. Corporate profits were down. Indeed, if the latest projections held true, the company would report a small loss on the year-end income statement. Executive bonuses were tied to corporate profits. The executive compensation plan provided for 10 percent of net earnings to be set aside for bonuses. No profits meant no bonuses. While things looked bleak, Stinson had a plan that might help soften the blow.

After informing the company president of the earnings forecast, Stinson made the following suggestion: Since the company was going to report a loss anyway, why not report a big loss? She reasoned that the directors and stockholders would not be much more angry if the company

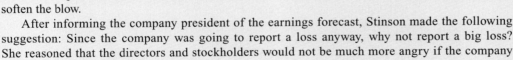

reported a large loss than if it reported a small one. There were several questionable assets that could be written down in the current year. This would increase the current year's loss but would reduce expenses in subsequent accounting periods. For example, the company was carrying damaged inventory that was estimated to have a value of $2,500,000. If this estimate were revised to $500,000, the company would have to recognize a $2,000,000 loss in the current year. However, next year when the goods were sold, the expense for cost of goods sold would be $2,000,000 less and profits would be higher by that amount. Although the directors would be angry this year, they would certainly be happy next year. The strategy would also have the benefit of adding $200,000 to next year's executive bonus pool ($2,000,000 × 0.10). Furthermore, it could not hurt this year's bonus pool because there would be no pool this year since the company is going to report a loss.

Some of the other items that Stinson is considering include (1) converting from straight-line to accelerated depreciation, (2) increasing the percentage of receivables estimated to be uncollectible in the current year and lowering the percentage in the following year, and (3) raising the percentage of estimated warranty claims in the current period and lowering it in the following period. Finally, Stinson notes that two of the company's department stores have been experiencing losses. The company could sell these stores this year and thereby improve earnings next year. Stinson admits that the sale would result in significant losses this year, but she smiles as she thinks of next year's bonus check.

Required

a. Explain how each of the three numbered strategies for increasing the amount of the current year's loss would affect the stockholders' equity section of the balance sheet in the current year. How would the other elements of the balance sheet be affected?

b. If Stinson's strategy were effectively implemented, how would it affect the stockholders' equity in subsequent accounting periods?

c. Comment on the ethical implications of running the company for the sake of management (maximization of bonuses) versus the maximization of return to stockholders.

d. Formulate a bonus plan that will motivate managers to maximize the value of the firm instead of motivating them to manipulate the reporting process.

e. How would Stinson's strategy of overstating the amount of the reported loss in the current year affect the company's current P/E ratio?

ATC 11-8   Research Assignment   *Analyzing PepsiCo's equity structure*

Required

Using the most current 10-K available on EDGAR, or the company's annual report from its Web site, answer the following questions about PepsiCo for the most recent year reported. (PepsiCo is the company that produces Pepsi soft drinks, among other things.) Instructions for using EDGAR are in Appendix A.

a. What is the *book value* of PepsiCo's stockholders' equity that is shown on the company's balance sheet?

b. What is the par value of PepsiCo's common stock?

c. Does PepsiCo have any treasury stock? If so, how many shares of treasury stock does the company hold?

d. Why does the stock of a company such as PepsiCo have a market value that is higher than its book value?

ATC 11-9   Spreadsheet Analysis   *Using Excel*

Annette's Accessories had the following stock issued and outstanding at January 1, 2005.

> 150,000 shares of $1 par common stock
> 10,000 shares of $50 par, 8%, cumulative preferred stock

On March 5, 2005, Annette's declared a $100,000 cash dividend to be paid March 31 to shareholders of record on March 21.

Required

Set up a spreadsheet to calculate the total amount of dividends to be paid to preferred and common shareholders under the following alternative situations:

a. No dividends are in arrears for preferred shareholders.
b. One year's worth of dividends is in arrears for preferred shareholders.
c. Two years' worth of dividends is in arrears for preferred shareholders.
d. Instead of a $100,000 dividend, Annette's paid a $70,000 dividend and one year of dividends was in arrears.

Spreadsheet Tips

The following spreadsheet provides one method of setting up formulas for all possible alternatives. The spreadsheet also reflects the results of Requirement *a*.

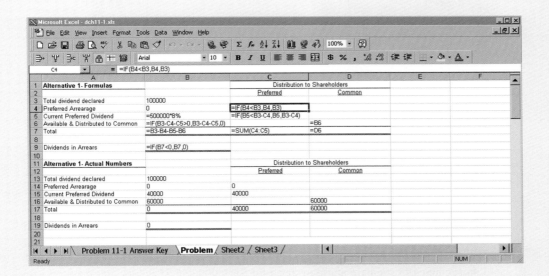

Notice the use of the IF function. The IF function looks like =IF(condition, true, false). To use the IF function, first describe a certain condition to Excel. Next indicate the desired result if that condition is found to be true. Finally, indicate the desired result if that condition is found to be false. Notice in cell C4 of the spreadsheet (dividends in arrears distributed to preferred shareholders) that the condition provided is B4<B3, which is asking whether the dividends in arrears are less than the total dividend. If this condition is true, the formula indicates to display B4, which is the amount of the dividends in arrears. If the condition is false, the formula indicates that B3 should be displayed, which is the total amount of the dividend.

The IF function can also be used to determine the amount of the current dividend distributed to preferred shareholders, the amount available for common shareholders, and the dividends in arrears after the dividend.

ATC 11-10   Spreadsheet Assignment   *Mastering Excel*

Required

Complete Requirement *a* of Problem 11-23B using an Excel spreadsheet.

The account balances of Pacilio Security Systems Sales and Service as of January 1, 2011, was:

Cash	$282,708
Petty cash	100
Accounts receivable	56,795
Allowance for doubtful accounts	2,989
Supplies	210
Inventory—standard alarms (22 @ $285)	6,270
Inventory—deluxe alarms (9 @ $600)	5,400
Van	9,200
Equipment	12,000
Building	72,000
Land	36,000
Accumulated depreciation	18,880
Goodwill	40,750
Warranties payable	2,677
Notes payable	34,979
Bonds payable	80,000
Discount of bonds payable	1,440
Common stock (10,000 shares of $5 par value, common stock)	50,000
Retained earnings	333,348

During 2011, Pacilio Security Systems Sales and Service experienced the following transactions:

1. Pacilio issued 5,000 additional shares of common stock for $8 per share and 1,000 shares of $50 stated value, 5 percent cumulative preferred stock for $52 per share.
2. Purchased $500 of supplies for cash.
3. April 2, 2011, replenished the petty cash fund. The fund had $13 of cash and receipts for $32 office supplies, $40 for cutting the grass, and $12 miscellaneous expense.
4. Purchased 190 standard alarm systems for $290 each and 50 deluxe alarm systems for $605 each.
5. Sold on account 195 standard alarm systems for $130,000 and 52 deluxe alarm systems for $49,000 during the year. (Be sure to record cost of goods sold using the FIFO cost flow method)
6. Billed $160,000 for monitoring services for the year. Of this amount, $46,000 was credit card sales. The credit card company charges a 4 percent service fee.
7. Collected the amount due from the credit card company.
8. Paid $875 to repair deluxe alarm systems that were still under warranty.
9. After numerous attempts to collect from customers, wrote off $2,465 of bad accounts.
10. On September 30, declared a dividend on the preferred stock and a $3 per share dividend on the common stock to be paid to shareholders of record on October 15, payable on October 31, 2011.
11. Collected $302,000 of accounts receivable for the year.
12. On October 31, paid the dividend that had previously been declared.
13. Paid $12,000 of advertising expense for the year.
14. Paid installers $94,000 for salaries for the year.
15. Paid officers $95,000 for salaries for the year.
16. Paid $6,500 utilities expenses for the year.
17. Paid bond interest and amortized the discount. (See Chapter 10.)
18. Paid annual installment on the amortized note.

Adjustments

19. There were $195 of office supplies on hand at the end of the year.

20. Recognized warranty expense for the year. Pacilio estimates warranty expense at 2 percent of deluxe model sales.

21. Recognized bad debt expense for the year. Pacilio uses the allowance method and estimates bad debts at 1 percent of sales on account.

22. Recognized depreciation expense for the year. (See Chapter 9.)

Required

a. Record the above transactions in general journal form. Pacilio uses FIFO cost flow assumption.

b. Post the transactions to the T-accounts.

c. Prepare a trial balance.

d. Prepare an income statement, balance sheet, and statement of cash flows.

e. Close the temporary accounts to retained earnings.

f. Post the closing entries to the T-accounts and prepare an after-closing trial balance.

CHAPTER 12

Statement of Cash Flows

LEARNING OBJECTIVES

After you have mastered the material in this chapter, you will be able to:

1. Name and define the four primary sections of a statement of cash flows.

2. Distinguish between the direct and indirect methods of presenting the operating activities section of a statement of cash flows.

3. Prepare the operating activities section of a statement of cash flows under the indirect method.

4. Prepare the investing activities section of a statement of cash flows.

5. Prepare the financing activities section of a statement of cash flows.

6. Explain how the statement of cash flows could mislead decision makers.

7. Prepare the operating activities section of a statement of cash flows under the direct method. (Appendix)

LP12

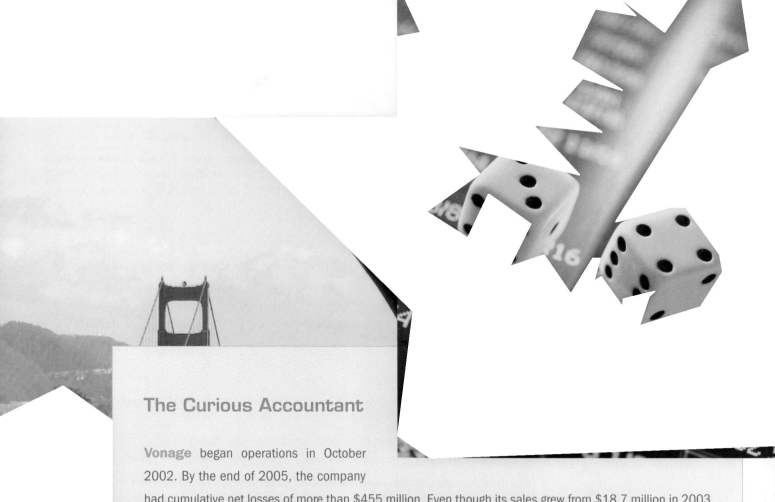

The Curious Accountant

Vonage began operations in October 2002. By the end of 2005, the company had cumulative net losses of more than $455 million. Even though its sales grew from $18.7 million in 2003 to more than $269 million in 2005, it did not make a profit in any of those years.

How could Vonage lose so much money and still be able to pay its bills? (Answer on page 608.)

CHAPTER OPENING

To make informed investment and credit decisions, financial statement users need information to help them assess the amounts, timing, and uncertainty of a company's prospective cash flows. This chapter explains more about the items reported on the statement of cash flows and describes a more practical way to prepare the statement than analyzing every entry in the cash account. As previously shown, the statement of cash flows reports how a company obtained and spent cash during an accounting period. Sources of cash are **cash inflows,** *and uses are* **cash outflows.** *Cash receipts (inflows) and payments (outflows) are reported as either operating activities, investing activities, or financing activities.* ■

Operating Activities

Cash inflows and outflows resulting from running (operating) a business are classified as **operating activities.** Items reported as operating activities include:

1. Cash receipts from sales, commissions, fees, and receipts from interest and dividends.
2. Cash payments for inventories, salaries, operating expenses, interest, and taxes.

Gains and *losses* from disposals of long-term operational assets are not shown on the statement of cash flows. The total amount of cash collected from selling long-term assets (including cash associated with gains and losses) is reported in the investing activities section of the statement of cash flows.

Investing Activities

Investing activities always involve assets. Items reported as investing activities include:

1. Cash receipts (inflows) from selling property, plant, equipment, or marketable securities as well as collecting loans.
2. Cash payments (outflows) for purchasing property, plant, equipment, or marketable securities as well as lending to others.

Financing Activities

Financing activities always involve liabilities or equity. Items reported as financing activities include:

1. Cash receipts (inflows) from issuing stock and borrowing money.
2. Cash payments (outflows) to purchase treasury stock, repay debt, and pay dividends.

It is helpful to note that the classification of cash flows is based on the type of activity rather than the type of account. For example, cash flows involving common stock represent investing activities if the company is purchasing or selling its investment in another company's common stock. In contrast, common stock transactions represent financing activities if the company is issuing or buying back its own stock (treasury stock). Similarly, receiving dividends is an operating activity, but paying dividends is a financing activity. Furthermore, lending cash is an investing activity while borrowing cash is a financing activity.

Noncash Investing and Financing Activities

Occasionally, companies engage in significant **noncash investing and financing activities.** For example, a company could issue common stock in exchange for land or acquire a building by accepting a mortgage obligation. Since these types of transactions do not involve exchanging cash, they cannot be reported in the main body of the statement of cash flows. However, the Financial Accounting Standards Board (FASB) has concluded that full and fair reporting requires disclosing all material investing and financing activities whether or not they involve exchanging cash. Companies must therefore include with the statement of cash flows a separate schedule that reports noncash investing and financing activities.

Reporting Format for the Statement of Cash Flows

Video 12.1

Cash flows are shown on the statement of cash flows in the following order: (1) operating activities, (2) investing activities, and (3) financing activities. At the end of each category, the difference between the inflows and outflows is presented as a net cash inflow or outflow for the category. These net amounts are combined to determine the net change

EXHIBIT 12.1

WESTERN COMPANY
Statement of Cash Flows
For the Year Ended December 31, 2008

Cash Flows from Operating Activities		
Plus: List of individual inflows	$XXX	
Less: List of individual outflows	(XXX)	
Net increase (decrease) from operating activities		$XXX
Cash Flows from Investing Activities		
Plus: List of individual inflows	XXX	
Less: List of individual outflows	(XXX)	
Net increase (decrease) from investing activities		XXX
Cash Flows from Financing Activities		
Plus: List of individual inflows	XXX	
Less: List of individual outflows	(XXX)	
Net increase (decrease) from financing activities		XXX
Net increase (decrease) in cash		XXX
Plus: Beginning cash balance		XXX
Ending cash balance		$XXX
Schedule of Noncash Investing and Financing Activities		
List of noncash transactions		$XXX

(increase or decrease) in the company's cash for the period. The net change in cash is combined with the beginning cash balance to determine the ending cash balance. The ending cash balance on the statement of cash flows is the same as the cash balance shown on the balance sheet. The schedule of noncash investing and financing activities is typically presented at the bottom of the statement of cash flows. Exhibit 12.1 outlines this format.

As indicated in Exhibit 12.2, most companies present the statement of cash flows as the last of the four primary financial statements. However, a sizable number of companies present it after the income statement and balance sheet but before the statement of changes in stockholders' equity. Some companies place the statement of cash flows first, before the other three statements.

EXHIBIT 12.2

Placement of Statement of Cash Flows Relative to Other Financial Statements

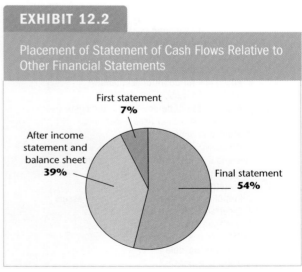

Data source: AICPA, *Accounting Trends and Techniques*, 2006.

Converting from Accrual to Cash-Basis Accounting

The operating activities section of the statement of cash flows is essentially a cash-basis income statement. Since accounting records are normally maintained on an accrual basis, determining the cash flow from operating activities requires converting the accrual based records to cash equivalents.

Answers to The Curious Accountant

First, it should be remembered that GAAP requires that earnings and losses be computed on an accrual basis. A company can have negative earnings and still have positive cash flows from operating activities. This was not the case at Vonage, however. From 2002 through 2005, the company's cash flows from operating activities totaled a negative $256 million. Although this is much less than the $374 million cumulative losses the company incurred during the same period, it still does not pay the bills.

Vonage, like many new companies, was able to stay in business because of the cash it raised through financing activities. These cash flows were a positive $624 million for 2002 through 2005. The company also had some significant noncash transactions. Exhibit 12.3 presents Vonage's statement of cash flows from the first four years (2002–2005) of its life.

EXHIBIT 12.3

VONAGE HOLDINGS CORP.
Consolidated Statements of Cash Flows
(dollars in thousands)

	For the Years Ended December 31			
	2002	2003	2004	2005
Cash Flows from Operating Activities				
Net loss	$(12,742)	$(29,974)	$(69,921)	$(261,334)
Adjustments to reconcile net loss to				
Net cash used in operating activities:				
Depreciation and amortization	1,114	2,367	3,907	11,122
Debt conversion expense	360	1,557	–	–
Change in estimated fair value of embedded derivatives within convertible notes	–	–	–	(66)
Accretion on convertible notes	–	–	–	152
Accrued interest	–	671	(186)	113
Allowance for doubtful accounts	–	–	60	150
Allowance for obsolete inventory	–	24	1,215	625
Amortization of deferred financing costs	–	–	–	75
Loss on disposal of fixed assets	–	–	–	438
Stock option compensation	–	–	–	15
Other	58	(6)	66	(108)
Changes in operating assets and liabilities:				
Accounts receivable	(82)	(326)	(2,100)	(4,888)
Inventory	(1,177)	144	(1,289)	(15,130)
Prepaid expenses and other current assets	(433)	57	(1,518)	(5,765)
Deferred customer acquisition costs	(213)	(2,404)	(5,765)	(17,618)
Due from related parties	(15)	–	15	18
Other assets	(78)	52	(27)	(2,333)
Accounts payable	1,391	6,721	3,016	5,119
Accrued expenses	190	1,404	24,103	71,085
Deferred revenue	487	3,130	9,824	28,565
Net cash used in operating activities	(11,140)	(16,583)	(38,600)	(189,765)
Cash Flows from Investing Activities				
Capital expenditures	(3,348)	(6,430)	(10,867)	(76,261)
Purchase of marketable securities	–	–	(68,798)	(295,341)
Maturities and sales of marketable securities	–	–	6,050	224,249
(Increase) decrease in restricted cash	(1,587)	1,497	(92)	(7,285)
Net cash used in investing activities	(4,935)	(4,933)	(73,707)	(154,638)

continued

	For the Years Ended December 31			
	2002	**2003**	**2004**	**2005**
Cash Flows from Financing Activities				
Principal payments on capital lease obligations	(191)	(158)	(26)	(177)
Proceeds from notes	2,000	20,000	–	247,872
Debt issuance costs	–	–	–	(9,652)
Proceeds from preferred stock issuance, net	12,995	14,110	140,820	195,736
Proceeds from subscription receivable	–	675	300	170
Purchase of treasury stock	–	(403)	–	–
Proceeds from options	–	2	–	57
Net cash provided by financing activities	14,804	34,226	141,094	434,006
Effect of exchange rate changes on cash		–	(3)	(83)
Net change in cash and cash equivalents	(1,271)	12,710	28,784	89,520
Cash and cash equivalents, beginning of period	2,806	1,535	14,245	43,029
Cash and cash equivalents, end of period	$ 1,535	$ 14,245	$ 43,029	$ 132,549
Supplemental disclosures of flow information				
Cash paid during the periods for interest	$ 43	$ 678	$ 5	$ 203
Noncash transactions during the periods for:				
Note payable converted to preferred stock	$ 2,000	$ 20,000	$ –	$ –
Capital lease obligations incurred	$ 136	$ –	$ –	$ 22,603

Operating Activities

The operating activities section of the statement of cash flows can be presented under a *direct* or an *indirect* approach. The **direct method** shows the *sources* and *uses* of cash *directly* from their origins. To illustrate, assume that during 2007 New South Company earns revenue on account of $500 and collects $400 from customers. Further assume the company incurs $390 of expenses on account and pays $350 to settle accounts payable. Exhibit 12.4 shows the operating section of the statement of cash flows under the *direct method*.

Distinguish between the direct and indirect methods of presenting the operating activities section of a statement of cash flows.

New South Corporation
retail gift shop

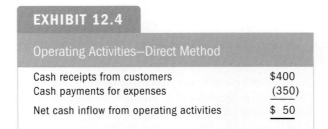

EXHIBIT 12.4

Operating Activities—Direct Method

Cash receipts from customers	$400
Cash payments for expenses	(350)
Net cash inflow from operating activities	$ 50

In contrast, the **indirect method** starts with the amount of net income and makes adjustments to arrive at the amount of cash flow from operations. To illustrate, we begin with New South Company's income statement, which is based on the information described above.

Revenues	$500
Expenses	(390)
Net income	$110

To convert the amount of net income of $110 to the amount of cash flow from operating activities of $50, the following adjustments are necessary:

1. Of the $500 of revenue, only $400 was collected in cash. The portion of the revenue that was not cash (*the $100 increase in accounts receivable*) must be subtracted from net income to arrive at cash flow.

2. Of the $390 of expense, only $350 was paid in cash. The portion of the expense that was not paid in cash (*the $40 increase in accounts payable*) must be added back to net income to arrive at cash flow.

Exhibit 12.5 shows the operating section of the statement of cash flows under the indirect method.

EXHIBIT 12.5

Operating Activities—Indirect Method

Net income	$ 110
Add: Increase in accounts payable	40
Subtract: Increase in accounts receivable	(100)
Net cash flow from operating activities	$ 50

Compare the direct method presented in Exhibit 12.4 with the indirect method presented in Exhibit 12.5. Both methods show $50 of cash flow from operating activities. However, they represent very different approaches to arrive at this conclusion.

Most people find the direct method easier to understand. Indeed, this is why the Financial Accounting Standards Board (FASB) recommends it. Even so, most companies use the indirect method. Why? At the time the FASB required companies to report a statement of cash flows, most companies had accounting systems that were compatible with the indirect method. In other words, it was less expensive to prepare the statement under the indirect method using the existing systems than to create new record-keeping systems that were compatible with the direct method.

The FASB continues to advocate the direct method and a growing number of companies use this reporting format. However, the majority of companies continue to use the indirect method. Given the widespread use of the indirect method, this chapter will focus on that approach. The direct method is covered in the appendix to this chapter.

Procedures for Determining Cash Flow from Operating Activities under the Indirect Method

Topic Tackler

PLUS

12-2

We can use the New South illustration to develop some rules for converting accrual based *net income* to *cash flow from operating activities*. First, recall that the increase in the accounts receivable balance was subtracted from net income when converting to cash flow. The opposite treatment would be required had the balance in the Accounts Receivable account decreased. Generalizing these relationships to other current asset accounts, we develop the following rule:

Rule 1 **Add decreases and subtract increases in noncash current asset account balances to net income.**

Similarly, we note that the increase in accounts payable was added to net income when converting to cash flow. Logically the opposite would be true had the balance in the Accounts Payable account decreased. Generalizing these relationships to other current liability accounts, we develop the following rule:

Rule 2 **Add increases and subtract decreases in current liability account balances to net income.**

In more advanced cases, we note that companies frequently recognize noncash expenses such as depreciation expense when calculating accrual based net income. To convert net income to cash flow from operating activities, these noncash expenses must be added back to the amount of net income. Accordingly, we develop the following rule:

Rule 3 **Add noncash expenses (e.g., depreciation) to net income.**

Finally, we note that gains and losses frequently affect the computation of net income. Since gains and losses are by definition *nonoperating* items, they must be subtracted from or added back to net income to determine cash flow from operating activities. Accordingly, we develop the following rule:

Rule 4 **Add losses to net income and subtract gains from net income.**

For quick reference, the procedures for preparing the operating activities section of the statement of cash flows are summarized in Exhibit 12.6.

EXHIBIT 12.6

Cash Flow from Operating Activities—Indirect Method

	Net income	$XXX
Rule 1	Add decreases and subtract increases in noncash current asset account balances to net income.	XXX
Rule 2	Add increases and subtract decreases in current liability account balances to net income.	XXX
Rule 3	Add noncash expenses (e.g., depreciation) to net income.	XXX
Rule 4	Add losses to net income and subtract gains from net income.	XXX
	Net cash flow from operating activities	$XXX

CHECK YOURSELF 12.1

Hammer, Inc., had a beginning balance of $22,400 in its Accounts Receivable account. During the accounting period, Hammer earned $234,700 of net income. The ending balance in the Accounts Receivable account was $18,200. Based on this information alone, determine the amount of cash flow from operating activities.

Answer

Account Title	Ending	Beginning	Change
Accounts receivable	$18,200	$22,400	$ (4,200)

Applicable Rule	Cash Flow from Operating Activities	Amount
	Net income	$234,700
Rule 1	Add: Decrease in accounts receivable	4,200
	Cash flow from operating activities	$238,900

Preparing the Operating Activities Section of the Statement of Cash Flows Using the Indirect Method

Prepare the operating activities section of a statement of cash flows under the indirect method.

You can prepare the operating activities section of the statement of cash flows by applying the four rules to balance sheet and income statement data. To illustrate, we begin with the financial statements for the New South Company that are shown in Exhibit 12.7. These statements were drawn from New South's 2009 annual report.

Use the balance sheet data to identify the changes in the balances of the current asset and liability accounts. *Do not include the Cash account in this analysis.* The amount of the change in the balance in the Cash account will be discussed later. The *noncash* current asset

EXHIBIT 12.7

Financial Statements for New South Company

NEW SOUTH COMPANY
Balance Sheets

As of December 31	2009	2008
Current assets:		
Cash	$ 300	$ 400
Accounts receivable	1,000	1,200
Interest receivable	400	300
Inventory	8,900	8,200
Prepaid insurance	1,100	1,400
Total current assets	11,700	11,500
Long-term assets		
Marketable securities	5,100	3,500
Store fixtures	5,400	4,800
Accumulated depreciation	(900)	(1,200)
Land	8,200	6,000
Total long-term assets	17,800	13,100
Total assets	$29,500	$24,600
Current liabilities:		
Accounts payable—inventory purchases	$ 800	$ 1,100
Salaries payable	1,000	900
Other operating expenses payable	1,500	1,300
Interest payable	300	500
Unearned rent revenue	600	1,600
Total current liabilities	4,200	5,400
Long-term liabilities		
Mortgage payable	2,200	0
Bonds payable	1,000	4,000
Total long-term liabilities	3,200	4,000
Stockholders' equity		
Common stock	10,000	8,000
Retained earnings	12,700	7,200
Treasury stock	(600)	0
Total stockholders' equity	22,100	15,200
Total liabilities and stockholders' equity	$29,500	$24,600

continued

NEW SOUTH COMPANY
Income Statement
For the Year Ended December 31, 2009

Sales revenue		$20,600
Cost of goods sold		(10,500)
Gross margin		10,100
Operating expenses		
Depreciation expense	$(1,000)	
Salaries expense	(2,700)	
Insurance expense	(1,300)	
Other operating expenses	(1,400)	
Total operating expenses		(6,400)
Income from sales business		3,700
Other income—rent revenue		2,400
Operating income		6,100
Nonoperating revenue and expense		
Interest revenue	700	
Interest expense	(400)	
Gain on sale of store fixtures	600	
Total nonoperating items		900
Net income		$ 7,000

Additional Information Disclosed in the Notes to the Financial Statements

Note 1: There were no sales of marketable securities during 2009.

Note 2: Store fixtures that had originally cost $1,700 were sold. The fixtures had $1,300 of accumulated depreciation at the time they were sold.

Note 3: The land was acquired by issuing a mortgage note payable. There were no sales of land during 2009.

and liability accounts for the New South Company are shown in Exhibit 12.8. The amount of change in each account balance is shown in the column titled *Change*.

EXHIBIT 12.8

Noncash Current Asset and Liability Account Balances

Account Title	2009	2008	Change
Accounts receivable	$ 1,000	$ 1,200	$ (200)
Interest receivable	400	300	100
Inventory	8,900	8,200	700
Prepaid insurance	1,100	1,400	(300)
Accounts payable—inventory purchases	800	1,100	(300)
Salaries payable	1,000	900	100
Other operating expenses payable	1,500	1,300	200
Interest payable	300	500	(200)
Unearned rent revenue	600	1,600	(1,000)

Next, analyze the income statement to identify the amount of net income, noncash expenses, gains, and losses. The income statement for the New South Company contains three items. Specifically, the statement shows net income of $7,000, depreciation expense of $1,000, and a $600 gain on the sale of store fixtures. Applying the procedures shown in Exhibit 12.6 to the information above produces the operating activities section of the statement of cash flows shown in Exhibit 12.9.

EXHIBIT 12.9

Cash Flows from Operating Activities

Applicable Rule	Net income	$ 7,000
	Add:	
Rule 1	Decrease in accounts receivable	200
Rule 1	Decrease in prepaid insurance	300
Rule 1	Increase in salaries payable	100
Rule 1	Increase in other operating expenses payable	200
Rule 3	Depreciation expense	1,000
	Subtract:	
Rule 2	Increase in interest receivable	(100)
Rule 2	Increase in inventory	(700)
Rule 2	Decrease in accounts payable for inventory purchases	(300)
Rule 2	Decrease in interest payable	(200)
Rule 2	Decrease in unearned rent	(1,000)
Rule 4	Gain on sale of equipment	(600)
	Net cash flow from operating activities	$5,900

CHECK YOURSELF 12.2

Q Magazine, Inc., reported $369,000 of net income for the month. At the beginning of the month, its Unearned Revenue account had a balance of $78,000. At the end of the month, the account had a balance of $67,000. Based on this information alone, determine the amount of cash flow from operating activities.

Answer

Account Title	Ending	Beginning	Change
Unearned revenue	$67,000	$78,000	$ (11,000)

Applicable Rule	Cash Flow from Operating Activities	Amount
	Net income	$369,000
Rule 2	Deduct: Decrease in unearned revenue	(11,000)
	Cash flow from operating activities	$358,000

CHECK YOURSELF 12.3

The following account balances were drawn from the accounting records of Loeb, Inc.

Account Title	Ending Balance	Beginning Balance
Prepaid rent	$3,000	$4,200
Interest payable	2,650	2,900

Loeb reported $7,400 of net income during the accounting period. Based on this information alone, determine the amount of cash flow from operating activities.

Answer

Based on Rule 1, the $1,200 decrease ($3,000 − $4,200) in Prepaid Rent (current asset) must be added to net income to determine the amount of cash flow from operating activities. Rule 2 requires that the $250 decrease ($2,650 − $2,900) in Interest Payable (current liability) must be deducted from net income. Accordingly, the cash flow from operating activities is $8,350 ($7,400 + $1,200 − $250). Note that paying interest is defined as an operating activity and should not be confused with dividend payments, which are classified as financing activities.

CHECK YOURSELF 12.4

Arley Company's income statement reported net income (in millions) of $326 for the year. The income statement included depreciation expense of $45 and a net loss on the sale of disposable assets of $22. Based on this information alone, determine the net cash flow from operating activities.

Answer

Based on Rule 3 and Rule 4, both the depreciation expense and the loss would have to be added to net income to determine cash flow from operating activities. Net cash flow from operating activities would be $393 ($326 + $45 + $22).

Preparing the Investing Activities Section of the Statement of Cash Flows

The *investing activities* section of the statement of cash flows does not differ when presented under the direct or indirect approaches. The information necessary to identify cash inflows and outflows from investing activities is obtained by examining the long-term asset section of the balance sheets. More specifically:

Prepare the investing activities section of a statement of cash flows.

- Increases in long-term asset account balances suggest that cash outflows occurred to purchase the assets.

- Decreases in long-term asset account balances suggest that cash inflows occurred from the sale of assets.

To illustrate, return to the financial statements of the New South Company shown in Exhibit 12.7. The following three long-term asset account balances are shown on the New South balance sheets. *Since the accumulated depreciation account does not affect cash flow, it is not necessary to examine this account.*

Account Title	2009	2008
Marketable securities	$5,100	$3,500
Store fixtures	5,400	4,800
Land	8,200	6,000

For each account, organize the information in a table format that shows how purchases and sales affected the account balances. Review the notes to the financial statements in Exhibit 12.7 for additional information. The table for New South's marketable securities is as follows:

Marketable Securities Account Information	
Beginning balance in marketable securities	$3,500
Add: Purchases of marketable securities (cash outflows)	?
Deduct: Sales of marketable securities (cash inflows)	0
Ending balance in marketable securities	$5,100

Note 1 to the financial statements states that there were no sales of marketable securities during 2009. Therefore, a purchase of $1,600 is required to balance the account. The cash outflow associated with this purchase is included in the investing activities section of the statement of cash flows shown in Exhibit 12.10.

Next, examine the information regarding store fixtures.

Store Fixtures Account Information	
Beginning balance in store fixtures	$ 4,800
Add: Purchases of store fixtures (cash outflows)	?
Deduct: Sales of store fixtures (cash inflows)	(1,700)
Ending balance in store fixtures	$ 5,400

Note 2 to the financial statements states that store fixtures that cost $1,700 were sold. The book value of these fixtures was $400 ($1,700 cost − $1,300 accumulated depreciation). Since the income statement shows a $600 gain on the sale of store fixtures, the cash collected from the sale was more than the book value of the store fixtures that were sold. Specifically, the amount of cash collected from the sale of store fixtures is computed as follows:

$$\text{Cash inflow} = \text{book value} + \text{gain} = \$400 + \$600 = \$1,000$$

This explains the $1,000 cash inflow form the sale of store fixtures shown Exhibit 12.10.

Returning to the store fixtures account information table, we note that a $2,300 purchase of store fixtures is required to balance the account. This explains the cash outflow for store fixtures shown in Exhibit 12.10.

Finally, examine the information regarding land.

Land Account Information	
Beginning balance in land	$6,000
Add: Purchases of land (issue of a mortgage note)	?
Deduct: Sales of land	0
Ending balance in land	$8,200

Note 3 to the financial statements states that there were no sales of land during 2009. Therefore, land costing $2,200 must have been purchased. Since the land was purchased by issuing a mortgage note, there were no cash flow effects. Instead this purchase is shown in a separate section on the statement of cash flows titled Noncash Investing and Financing Activities. This section will be discussed in more detail later in the chapter. The cash inflows and outflows from investing activities are summarized in Exhibit 12.10.

EXHIBIT 12.10

Cash Flow from Investing Activities

Cash inflow from the sale of store fixtures	$ 1,000
Cash outflow for the purchase of marketable securities	(1,600)
Cash outflow for the purchase of store fixtures	(2,300)
Net cash outflow from investing activities	$(2,900)

CHECK YOURSELF 12.5

On January 1, 2008, Wyatt Company had a balance of $124,0C0 in its Buildings account. During 2008, Wyatt purchased a building that cost $50,000. The balance in the Buildings account on December 31, 2008, was $90,000. The 2008 income statement contained a loss from the sale of building for $7,000. On the date of sale, accumulated depreciation on the building sold amounted to $49,000.

Required

1. Determine the cost of the building that was sold during 2008.
2. Determine the amount of cash flow from the sale of buildings that should be shown in the investing activities section of the 2008 statement of cash flows.

continued

Answer

1.

Buildings Account Information	
Beginning balance	$124,000
Add: Cost of buildings purchased	50,000
Deduct: Cost of buildings sold	?
Ending balance	$ 90,000

In order to balance the account, buildings with an original cost of $84,000 must have been sold.

2. The book value of the building sold was $35,000 ($84,000 − $49,000 accumulated depreciation). Since a loss was recognized, the building must have been sold for an amount of cash that was less than the book value of the building. Specifically, the cash collected from the sale of the building was $28,000 ($35,000 book value − loss on sale of $7,000).

Preparing the Financing Activities Section of the Statement of Cash Flows

The *financing activities* section of the statement of cash flows does not differ when presented under the direct or indirect approaches. The information necessary to identify cash inflows and outflows from financing activities is obtained by examining the long-term liabilities and stockholders' equity sections of the balance sheets. More specifically:

Prepare the financing activities section of a statement of cash flows.

- Increases in long-term debt account balances suggest that cash inflows occurred from the issuance of debt instruments (notes or bonds).

- Decreases in long-term debt account balances suggest that cash outflows occurred for the payment of debt (notes or bonds).

REALITY BYTES

How did Dillard's, Inc., the department store chain, acquire $22 million of property, plant, and equipment in its 2006 fiscal year *without* spending any cash? Oddly enough, the answer can be found on its statement of cash flows.

The supplemental, "noncash transactions" information included at the bottom of Dillard's statement of cash flows revealed that it acquired the assets by exchanging debt directly for assets. Capital lease transactions, a form of borrowing, were responsible for $19.5 million of these purchases. The remaining $2.5 million was purchased through "accrued capital transactions."

Had Dillard's borrowed $22 million from a bank and then used this cash to purchase $22 million of assets, it would have reported two separate cash events in the body of its statement of cash flows. A cash inflow would have been reported in the financing activities for the borrowing transaction, and a cash outflow would have been reported in the investing activities section for the purchase transaction. Acquiring large amounts of assets is considered important, even if there is no immediate exchange of cash, so generally accepted accounting principles require such events to be reported as a part of the statement of cash flows.

- Increases in contributed capital accounts (common stock, preferred stock, or paid-in capital) suggest that cash inflows occurred from the issue of equity instruments.

- Increases in treasury stock accounts suggest that cash outflows occurred to purchase a company's own stock.

- Decreases in retained earnings resulting from cash dividends suggest that cash outflows occurred to pay dividends.

To illustrate, return to the financial statements of the New South Company shown in Exhibit 12.7. The following long-term liability and stockholders' equity account balances are shown on the New South balance sheets:

Account Title	2009	2008
Mortgage payable	$ 2,200	$ 0
Bonds payable	1,000	4,000
Common stock	10,000	8,000
Retained earnings	12,700	7,200
Treasury stock	(600)	0

Examine each account to determine the causes of the change in the account balance. Organize the information in a table format that explains the changes in the account balances. Review the footnotes to the financial statements for additional information. The table for New South's mortgage payable is as follows:

Mortgage Payable Account Information	
Beginning balance in mortgage payable	$ 0
Add: Mortgage liabilities issues (purchase of land)	2,200
Deduct: Mortgage liabilities repaid	0
Ending balance in mortgage payable	$2,200

As previously indicated, Note 3 to the financial statements states that a $2,200 mortgage was issued to purchase land. Since the mortgage did not involve a cash flow, it is not included in the financing activities section of the statement of cash flows. Instead, it is included in the separate section titled Noncash Investing and Financing Activities.

Information related to the bond liabilities is shown in the following table:

Bond Payable Account Information	
Beginning balance in bond payable	$4,000
Add: Bond liabilities issued (cash inflow)	0
Deduct: Bond liabilities paid off (cash outflow)	?
Ending balance in bond payable	$1,000

Since there is no information to suggest that bonds were issued during 2009, we assume that the amount of bonds issued is zero. A $3,000 payoff of bond liabilities had to occur to balance the account. The associated cash outflow is shown in the financing activities section in Exhibit 12.11.

Information related to the common stock is shown in the following table:

Common Stock Account Information	
Beginning balance in common stock	$ 8,000
Add: Common stock issued	?
Ending balance in common stock	$10,000

A $2,000 issue of common stock is required to balance the account. The associated cash inflow is shown in the financing activities section shown in Exhibit 12.11.

Information related to the Retained Earnings account is shown in the following table:

Retained Earnings Account Information	
Beginning balance in retained earnings	$ 7,200
Add: Net income	7,000
Deduct: Dividends (cash outflow)	?
Ending balance in retained earnings	$12,700

A $1,500 decrease is required to balance the account. In the absence of information to the contrary, we assume that the decrease is due to the payment of dividends. The associated cash outflow for the payment of dividends is shown in the financing activities section in Exhibit 12.11.

Information related to the Treasury Stock account is shown in the following table:

Treasury Stock Account Information	
Beginning balance in treasury stock	$ 0
Add: Purchases of treasury stock (cash outflows)	?
Deduct: Reissue of treasury stock (cash inflows)	0
Ending balance in treasury stock	($600)

Since there is no information to suggest that treasury stock was reissued during 2009, $600 of treasury stock had to be purchased in order to balance the account. The associated cash outflow is shown in the financing activities section in Exhibit 12.11.

EXHIBIT 12.11

Cash Flow from Financing Activities	
Cash inflow from issuing common stock	$ 2,000
Cash outflow to pay off bonds payable	(3,000)
Cash outflow to pay dividends	(1,500)
Cash outflow to purchase treasury stock	(600)
Net cash outflow from financing activities	$ (3,100)

The complete statement of cash flow for the New South Company is shown in Exhibit 12.12. Notice that the combined effects of operating, investing, and financing activities produce a net decrease in cash of $100 for 2009. This is consistent with the difference between the December 31, 2009, and the December 31, 2008, balances in the Cash account shown in balance sheets in Exhibit 12.7. This comparison provides evidence that the statement of cash flows is accurate. A lack of consistency between these amounts would signal an error that requires correction.

EXHIBIT 12.12   Statement of Cash Flows—Indirect Method

NEW SOUTH COMPANY
Statement of Cash Flows
For the Year Ended December 31, 2009

Cash Flows from Operating Activities		
Net income	$ 7,000	
Add:		
Decrease in accounts receivable	200	
Decrease in prepaid insurance	300	
Increase in salaries payable	100	
Increase in other operating expenses payable	200	
Depreciation expense	1,000	
Subtract:		
Increase in interest receivable	(100)	
Increase in inventory	(700)	
Decrease in accounts payable—inventory purchases	(300)	
Decrease in interest payable	(200)	
Gain on sale of store fixtures	(600)	
Decrease in unearned rent	(1,000)	
Net cash flow from operating activities		$5,900
Cash Flows from Investing Activities		
Cash inflow from the sale of store fixtures	1,000	
Cash outflow for the purchase of marketable securities	(1,600)	
Cash outflow for the purchase of store fixtures	(2,300)	
Net cash outflow from investing activities		(2,900)
Cash Flows from Financing Activities		
Cash inflow from issuing common stock	2,000	
Cash outflow to pay off bond liabilities	(3,000)	
Cash outflow to pay dividends	(1,500)	
Cash outflow to purchase treasury stock	(600)	
Net cash outflow from financing activities		(3,100)
Net increase in cash financing		(100)
Plus: Beginning cash balance		400
Ending cash balance		$ 300
Schedule of Noncash Investing and Financing Activities		
Issue of mortgage for land		$2,200

CHECK YOURSELF 12.6

On January 1, 2008, Sterling Company had a balance of $250,000 in its Bonds Payable account. During 2008, Sterling issued bonds with a $75,000 face value. There was no premium or discount associated with the bond issue. The balance in the Bonds Payable account on December 31, 2008, was $150,000.

Required

1. Determine the cash outflow for the repayment of bond liabilities assuming that the bonds were retired at face value.
2. Prepare the financing activities section of the 2008 statement of cash flows.

continued

Answer

1.

Bonds Payable Account Information	
Beginning balance	$250,000
Add: Bond liabilities issued	75,000
Deduct: Bond liabilities repaid	?
Ending balance	$150,000

In order to balance the account, bond liabilities with face value of $175,000 must have been repaid. In the absence of information to the contrary, we assume cash was used to payoff the bond liabilities.

2.

Cash Flow from Financing Activities	
Inflow from the issue of bond liabilities	$ 75,000
Outflow for the payoff of bond liabilities	(175,000)
Net cash outflow from financing activities	$(100,000)

Preparing the Schedule of Noncash Investing and Financing Activities for the Statement of Cash Flows

Occasionally, companies engage in significant noncash investing and financing activities. For example, the New South Company purchased land by issuing a $2,200 mortgage note. Since these types of transactions do not involve exchanging cash, they cannot be reported in the main body of the statement of cash flows. However, the Financial Accounting Standards Board (FASB) requires the disclosure of all material investing and financing activities whether or not they involve exchanging cash. Companies must therefore include with the statement of cash flows a separate schedule that reports noncash investing and financing activities. See the schedule titled *schedule of noncash investing and financing activities* in Exhibit 12.12 as an example.

Video 12.1

THE FINANCIAL ANALYST

Why are financial analysts interested in the statement of cash flows? Understanding the cash flows of a business is essential because cash is used to pay the bills. A company, especially one experiencing rapid growth, can be short of cash in spite of earning substantial net income. To illustrate, assume you start a computer sales business. You borrow $2,000 and spend the money to purchase two computers for $1,000 each. You sell one of the computers on account for $1,500. If your loan required a payment at this time, you could not make it. Even though you have net income of $500 ($1,500 sales − $1,000 cost of goods sold), you have no cash until you collect the $1,500 account receivable. A business cannot survive without managing cash flow carefully. It is little wonder that financial analysts are keenly interested in cash flow.

LO 6

Explain how the statement of cash flows could mislead decision makers.

Real-World Data

The statement of cash flows frequently provides a picture of business activity that would otherwise be lost in the complexities of accrual accounting. For example, IBM Corporation's combined operating losses (before taxes) for 1991, 1992, and 1993 were more than $17.9 *billion.* During this same period, IBM reported "restructuring charges" of more than $24 billion. Restructuring costs relate to reorganizing a company. They may include the costs of closing facilities and losses on asset disposals. Without the restructuring charges, IBM would have reported operating *profits* of about $6 billion (before taxes). Do restructuring charges signal positive or negative changes? Different financial analysts have different opinions about this issue. However, one aspect of IBM's performance during these years is easily understood. The company produced over $21 billion in positive cash flow from operating activities. It had no trouble paying its bills.

Investors consider cash flow information so important that they are willing to pay for it, even when the FASB discourages its use. The FASB *prohibits* companies from disclosing *cash flow per share* in audited financial statements. However, one prominent stock analysis service, *Value Line Investment Survey,* sells this information to a significant customer base. Clearly, Value Line's customers value information about cash flows.

Exhibit 12.13 compares income from operations and cash flow from operating activities for six real-world companies from five different industries for the 2003, 2004, and 2005 fiscal years.

Several things are apparent from Exhibit 12.13. The cash flow from operating activities exceeds income from operations for all of the companies except Pulte Homes. Many real-world companies report such a result because depreciation, a noncash expense, is usually significant. The most dramatic example is for Sprint Nextel in 2004. Even though Sprint

reported a *net loss* from operations of approximately $1.0 billion, it generated *positive* cash flow from operating activities of more than $6.6 *billion.* This difference between cash flow from operating activities and operating income helps explain how some companies can have significant losses over a few years and continue to stay in business and pay their bills.

The exhibit shows that cash flow from operating activities can be more stable than operating income. Results for Sprint also demonstrate this clearly. Although the company's earnings were negative in 2003, more negative in 2004, and positive in 2005, its cash flows from operating activities were always positive. Stability is one of the reasons many financial analysts prefer cash flow over earnings as a predictor of future performance.

EXHIBIT 12.13

Operating Income versus Cash Flow from Operations (Amounts in $000)

Company		2005	2004	2003
Alaska Airlines	Oper. income	$ 77,000	$ (19,100)	$ 3,000
	Cash flow operations	272,800	341,700	318,600
Southwest Airlines	Oper. income	548,000	313,000	442,000
	Cash flow operations	2,229,000	1,157,000	1,336,000
Boeing	Oper. income	2,562,000	1,820,000	685,000
	Cash flow operations	7,000,000	3,504,000	2,776,000
McAfee	Oper. income	138,828	225,065	59,905
	Cash flow operations	419,457	358,913	156,304
Pulte Homes	Oper. income	1,436,888	993,573	617,548
	Cash flow operations	18,704	(692,162)	(336,405)
Sprint Nextel	Oper. income	1,801,000	(1,021,000)	(292,000)
	Cash flow operations	10,678,000	6,625,000	8,748,000

Finally, what could explain why Pulte Homes has *less* cash flow from operating activities than operating income? Does the company have a problem? Not necessarily. Pulte is experiencing the kind of growth described earlier for your computer sales business. Its cash is supporting growth in inventory levels. Pulte is one of the nation's largest new-home construction companies. Its growth rates, based on revenue from sales of new homes, for the 2003, 2004, and 2005 fiscal years were 25 percent, 31 percent, and 28 percent, respectively. When Pulte begins to build new homes, it needs more inventory. Increases in inventory *do* affect cash flow from operating activities. Remember, increases in current assets decrease cash flow from operating activities. This condition alone might explain why the company has less cash flow from operating activities than operating income. Is this situation unfavorable? Chapter 6 made the point that, *other things being equal,* it is better to have less inventory. At Pulte, however, other things are not equal. The company has been growing rapidly.

The Pulte Homes situation highlights a potential weakness in the format of the statement of cash flows. Some accountants consider it misleading to classify all increases in long-term assets as *investing activities* and all changes in inventory as affecting cash flow from operating activities. They argue that the increase in inventory at Pulte that results from building more houses should be classified as an investing activity, just as the cost of a new building is. Although inventory is classified as a current asset and buildings are classified as long-term assets, in reality there is a certain level of inventory a company must permanently maintain to stay in business. The GAAP format of the statement of cash flows penalizes cash flow from operating activities for increases in inventory that are really a permanent investment in assets.

Conversely, the same critics might argue that some purchases of long-term assets are not actually *investments* but merely replacements of old, existing property, plant, and equipment. In other words, the *investing activities* section of the statement of cash flows makes no distinction between expenditures that expand the business and those that simply replace old equipment (sometimes called *capital maintenance* expenditures).

Users of the statement of cash flows must exercise the same care interpreting it as when they use the balance sheet or the income statement. Numbers alone are insufficient. Users must evaluate numbers based on knowledge of the particular business and industry they are analyzing.

Accounting information alone cannot guide a businessperson to a sound decision. Making good business decisions requires an understanding of the business in question, the environmental and economic factors affecting the operation of that business, and the accounting concepts on which the financial statements of that business are based.

A Look Back <<

Thus far in this text, you have considered many different accounting events that businesses experience. You have been asked to consider the effects these events have on a company's balance sheet, income statement, and statement of cash flows. By now, you should recognize that each financial statement shows a different, but equally important, view of a company's financial situation.

This chapter examined in detail only one financial statement, the statement of cash flows. The chapter provided a more comprehensive discussion of how accrual accounting relates to cash-based accounting. Effective use of financial statements requires understanding not only accrual and cash-based accounting systems but also how they relate to each other. That relationship is why a statement of cash flows can begin with a reconciliation of net income, an accrual measurement, to net cash flow from operating activities, a cash measurement. Finally, this chapter explained how the conventions for classifying cash flows as operating, investing, or financing activities require analysis and understanding to make informed decisions with the financial information.

A Look Forward >>

This chapter probably completes your first course in accounting. We sincerely hope that this text has provided you a meaningful learning experience that will serve you well as you progress through your academic training and ultimately, your career. Good luck and best wishes!

APPENDIX

LO 7

Prepare the operating activities section of a statement of cash flows under the direct method.

As previously discussed, the operating activities section of the statement of cash flows can be shown under the indirect or direct approach. The investing and financing sections are the same regardless of whether the direct or indirect approach is used for the operating activities section. The primary focus of the main body of Chapter 12 is on the indirect method. This appendix focuses on the direct method.

The direct method shows the specific sources and uses of cash that are associated with operating activities. It does not make adjustments to net income. Instead, the adjustments necessary to convert accrual-based income to cash flow are made directly to the appropriate revenue and expense accounts.

Just as rules were developed to facilitate the conversions from accrual to cash under the indirect method, rules can be developed for the direct method. Indeed, Exhibit 12.14 provides a quick reference of the procedures for preparing the operating activities section of the statement of cash flows under the direct method.

EXHIBIT 12.14

Cash Flow from Operating Activities

Rule 1	Revenue plus decreases, minus increases in related current asset accounts.	$XXX
Rule 2	Revenue plus increases, minus decreases in related current liability accounts.	XXX
Rule 3	Expense items plus increases, minus decreases in related current asset accounts.	XXX
Rule 4	Expense items minus increases, plus decreases in related current liability accounts.	XXX
Rule 5	Ignore gains, losses, and noncash revenue and expense items shown on the income statement.	XXX
	Net cash flow from operating activities	$XXX

Applying the procedures described in Exhibit 12.14 to the New South Company statements shown in Exhibit 12.7 produces the operating activities section of the statement of cash flows, which is shown in Exhibit 12.15. Note that each item in the operating activities section in Exhibit 12.15 is marked with a reference number. An explanation of how the amount of cash inflow or cash outflow was determined is shown directly below the exhibit. You may find it useful to refer to the list of changes in the account balances shown in Exhibit 12.8 when studying the explanations.

EXHIBIT 12.15   Operating Activities Section of the Statement of Cash Flows—Direct Method

NEW SOUTH COMPANY
Statement of Cash Flows
For the Year Ended December 31, 2009

Cash Flows from Operating Activities	
Inflow from customers (1)	$ 20,800
Inflow from rent (2)	1,400
Inflow from interest (3)	600
Outflow for inventory (4)	(11,500)
Outflow for salary expense (5)	(2,600)
Outflow for insurance expense (6)	(1,000)
Outflow for other operating expenses (7)	(1,200)
Outflow for interest expense (8)	(600)
Net cash flow from operating activities	$5,900

continued

Cash Flows from Investing Activities

Cash inflow from the sale of store fixtures	1,000	
Cash outflow for the purchase of marketable securities	(1,600)	
Cash outflow for the purchase of store fixtures	(2,300)	
Net cash outflow from investing activities		(2,900)

Cash Flows from Financing Activities

Cash inflow from issuing common stock	2,000	
Cash outflow to pay off bond liabilities	(3,000)	
Cash outflow to pay dividends	(1,500)	
Cash outflow to purchase treasury stock	(600)	
Net cash outflow from financing activities		(3,100)
Net increase in cash		(100)
Plus: Beginning cash balance		400
Ending cash balance		$ 300

Schedule of Noncash Investing and Financing Activities

Issue of mortgage for land	$2,200

(1) $20,600 sales revenue + $200 decrease in the Accounts Receivable account balance.

(2) $2,400 rent revenue − $1,000 decrease in the Unearned Rent Revenue account balance.

(3) $700 interest revenue − $100 increase in the Interest Receivable account balance.

(4) Since inventory is purchased on account before being expensed as cost of goods sold, the analysis to determine cash outflow for purchases of inventory must include changes in the account balances of inventory and accounts payable. The result is as follows: $10,500 cost of goods sold + 700 increase in the Inventory account balance + 300 decrease in the Accounts Payable account balance.

(5) $2,700 salary expense − $100 increase in the Salaries Payable account balance.

(6) $1,300 insurance expense − $300 decrease in the Prepaid Insurance account balance.

(7) $1,400 other operating expenses − $200 increase in the Other Operating Expenses Payable account balance.

(8) $400 interest expense + $200 decrease in the Interest Payable account balance.

SELF-STUDY REVIEW PROBLEM

The following financial statements pertain to Schlemmer Company.

Balance Sheets As of December 31		
	2009	**2008**
Cash	$48,400	$ 2,800
Accounts receivable	2,200	1,200
Inventory	5,600	6,000
Equipment	18,000	22,000
Accumulated depreciation—equip.	(13,650)	(17,400)
Land	17,200	10,400
Total assets	$77,750	$25,000
Accounts payable (inventory)	$ 5,200	$ 4,200
Long-term debt	5,600	6,400
Common stock	19,400	10,000
Retained earnings	47,550	4,400
Total liabilities and equity	$77,750	$25,000

Income Statement	
For the Year Ended December 31, 2009	
Sales revenue	$67,300
Cost of goods sold	(24,100)
Gross margin	43,200
Depreciation expense	(1,250)
Operating income	41,950
Gain on sale of equipment	2,900
Loss on disposal of land	(100)
Net income	$44,750

Additional Data

1. During 2009 equipment that had originally cost $11,000 was sold. Accumulated depreciation on this equipment was $5,000 at the time of sale.
2. Common stock was issued in exchange for land valued at $9,400 at the time of the exchange.

Required

Using the indirect method, prepare in good form a statement of cash flows for the year ended December 31, 2009.

Solution

THE SCHLEMMER COMPANY		
Statement of Cash Flows		
For the Year Ended December 31, 2009		
Cash Flows from Operating Activities		
Net income	$44,750	
Add:		
Decrease in inventory (1)	400	
Increase in accounts payable (2)	1,000	
Depreciation expense (3)	1,250	
Loss on disposal of land (4)	100	
Subtract:		
Increase in accounts receivable (1)	(1,000)	
Gain on sale of equipment (4)	(2,900)	
Net cash inflow from operating activities		$43,600
Cash Flows from Investing Activities		
Cash inflow from the sale of equipment (5)	8,900	
Cash outflow for the purchase of equipment (5)	(7,000)	
Cash inflow from sale of land (6)	2,500	
Net cash outflow from investing activities		4,400
Cash Flows from Financing Activities		
Cash outflow to repay long-term debt (7)	(800)	
Cash outflow to pay dividends (8)	(1600)	
Net cash outflow from financing activities		(2,400)
Net Increase in Cash		45,600
Plus: Beginning cash balance		2,800
Ending cash balance		$48,400
Schedule of Noncash Investing and Financing Activities		
Issue of common stock for land (9)		$ 9,400

(1) Add decreases and subtract increases in current asset account balances to net income.

(2) Add increases and subtract decreases in current liability account balances to net income.

(3) Add noncash expenses (e.g., depreciation) to net income.

(4) Add losses on the sale of non current assets to net income and subtract gains on the sale of long-term assets from net income.

(5) Information regarding the Equipment account is summarized in the following table.

Equipment Account Information	
Beginning balance in equipment	$22,000
Purchases of equipment (cash outflows)	?
Sales of equipment (cash inflows)	(11,000)
Ending balance in equipment	$18,000

To balance the account, equipment costing $7,000 must have been purchased. In the absence of information to the contrary, we assume cash was used to make the purchase.

Note 1 to the financial statements states that equipment sold had a book value of $6,000 ($11,000 cost − $5,000 accumulated depreciation). The amount of the cash inflow from this sale is computed as follows:

$$\text{Cash inflow} = \text{book value} + \text{gain} = \$6,000 + \$2,900 = \$8,900$$

(6) The information regarding the Land account is as follows:

Land Account Information	
Beginning balance in land	$10,400
Purchases of land (issue of a mortgage note)	9,400
Sales of land (cash inflows)	?
Ending balance in land	$17,200

Note 2 indicates that land valued at $9,400 was acquired by issuing common stock. Since there was no cash flow associated with this purchase, the event is shown in the *noncash investing and financing activities* section of the statement of cash flows.

To balance the account, the cost (book value) of land sold had to be $2,600. Since the income statement shows a $100 loss on the sale of land, the cash collected from the sale is computed as follows:

$$\text{Cash inflow} = \text{book value} - \text{loss} = \$2,600 - 100 = \$2,500$$

(7) The information regarding the Long-term Debt account is as follows:

Long-term Debt Information	
Beginning balance in long-term debt	$6,400
Issue of long-term debt instruments (cash inflow)	0
Payment of long-term debt (cash outflow)	?
Ending balance in long-term debt	$5,600

There is no information in the financial statements that suggest that long-term debt was issued. Therefore, to balance the account, $800 of long-term debt had to be paid off, thereby resulting in a cash outflow.

(8) The information regarding the Retained Earnings account is as follows:

Retained Earnings Information	
Beginning balance in retained earnings	$ 4,400
Net income	44,750
Dividends (cash outflow)	?
Ending balance in retained earnings	$47,550

To balance the account, $1,600 of dividends had to be paid, thereby resulting in a cash outflow.

(9) Note 2 states that common stock was issue to acquire land valued at $9,400. This is a non-cash investing and financing activity.

KEY TERMS

cash inflows 605	financing activities 606	noncash investing and	operating activities 606
cash outflows 605	indirect method 609	financing activities 606	
direct method 609	investing activities 606		

QUESTIONS

1. What is the purpose of the statement of cash flows?
2. What are the three categories of cash flows reported on the cash flow statement? Discuss each and give an example of an inflow and an outflow for each category.
3. What are noncash investing and financing activities? Provide an example. How are such transactions shown on the statement of cash flows?
4. Albring Company had a beginning balance in accounts receivable of $12,000 and an ending balance of $14,000. Net income amounted to $110,000. Based on this information alone, determine the amount of cash flow from operating activities.
5. Forsyth Company had a beginning balance in utilities payable of $3,300 and an ending balance of $5,200. Net income amounted to $87,000. Based on this information alone, determine the amount of cash flow from operating activities.
6. Clover Company had a beginning balance in unearned revenue of $4,300 and an ending balance of $3,200. Net income amounted to $54,000. Based on this information alone, determine the amount of cash flow from operating activities.
7. Which of the following activities are financing activities?
   (a) Payment of accounts payable.
   (b) Payment of interest on bonds payable.
   (c) Sale of common stock.
   (d) Sale of preferred stock at a premium.
   (e) Payment of a cash dividend.
8. Does depreciation expense affect net cash flow? Explain.
9. If Best Company sold land that cost $4,200 at a $500 gain, how much cash did it collect from the sale of land?
10. If Best Company sold office equipment that originally cost $7,500 and had $7,200 of accumulated depreciation at a $100 loss, what was the selling price for the office equipment?
11. In which section of the statement of cash flows would the following transactions be reported?
    (a) The amount of the change in the balance of accounts receivable.
    (b) Cash purchase of marketable securities.
    (c) Cash purchase of equipment.

  (d) Cash sale of merchandise.

  (e) Cash sale of common stock.

  (f) The amount of net income.

  (g) Cash proceeds from loan.

  (h) Cash payment on bonds payable.

  (i) Cash receipt from sale of old equipment.

  (j) The amount of the change in the balance of accounts payable.

12. What is the difference between preparing the statement of cash flows using the direct method and using the indirect method?

13. Which method (direct or indirect) of presenting the statement of cash flows is more intuitively logical? Why?

14. What is the major advantage of using the indirect method to present the statement of cash flows?

15. What is the advantage of using the direct method to present the statement of cash flows?

16. How would Best Company report the following transactions on the statement of cash flows?

  (a) Purchased new equipment for $46,000 cash.

  (b) Sold old equipment for $8,700 cash. The equipment had a book value of $4,900.

17. Can a company report negative net cash flows from operating activities for the year on the statement of cash flows but still have positive net income on the income statement? Explain.

18. Why does the FASB prohibit disclosing cash flow per share in audited financial statements?

MULTIPLE-CHOICE QUESTIONS

**Multiple-choice questions are provided on the text Web site at
www.mhhe.com/edmonds6e.**

Quiz 12

EXERCISES—SERIES A

All Exercises in Series A are available with McGraw-Hill's Homework Manager®

Exercise 12-1A   *Direct versus indirect method of determining cash flow from operating activities*   **L.O. 2**

Master Mechanics, Inc. (MMI), recognized $1,200 of sales revenue on account and collected $1,100 of cash from accounts receivable. Further, MMI recognized $700 of operating expenses on account and paid $500 cash as partial settlement of accounts payable.

Required

Based on this information alone:

a. Prepare the operating activities section of the statement of cash flows under the direct method.

b. Prepare the operating activities section of the statement of cash flows under the indirect method.

Exercise 12-2A   *Use the indirect method to determine cash flow from operating activities*   **L.O. 3**

An accountant for Golden Enterprise Companies (GEC) computed the following information by making comparisons between GEC's 2009 and 2008 balances sheets. Further information was determined by examining the company's 2009 income statement.

  1. The amount of an increase in the balance of the Accounts Receivable account.

  2. The amount of a loss arising from the sale of land.

  3. The amount of an increase in the balance of the Operating Expenses Payable account.

  4. The amount of a decrease in the balance of the Bonds Payable account.

  5. The amount of depreciation expense shown on the income statement.

6. The amount of cash dividends paid to the stockholders.
7. The amount of a decrease in the balance of an Unearned Revenue account.
8. The amount of an increase in the balance of an Inventory account.
9. The amount of an increase in the balance of a Land account.
10. The amount of a decrease in the balance of a Prepaid Rent account.
11. The amount of an increase in the balance of a Treasury Stock account.

Required

For each item described above indicate whether the amount should be added to or subtracted from the amount of net income when determining the amount of cash flow from operating activities. If an item does not affect cash flow from operating activities, identify it as being not affected.

L.O. 3

Exercise 12-3A   *Use the indirect method to determine cash flow from operating activities*

Mendez Incorporated presents its statement of cash flows using the indirect method. The following accounts and corresponding balances were drawn from the company's 2009 and 2008 year-end balance sheets.

Account Title	2009	2008
Accounts receivable	$15,200	$16,500
Accounts payable	8,800	9,200

The 2009 income statement showed net income of $27,200.

Required

a. Prepare the operating activities section of the statement of cash flows.
b. Explain why the change in the balance in accounts receivable was added to or subtracted from the amount of net income when you completed Requirement *a.*
c. Explain why the change in the balance in accounts payable was added to or subtracted from the amount of net income when you completed Requirement *a.*

L.O. 3

Exercise 12-4A   *Use the indirect method to determine cash flow from operating activities*

Chang Company presents its statement of cash flows using the indirect method. The following accounts and corresponding balances were drawn from Chang's 2009 and 2008 year-end balance sheets.

Account Title	2009	2008
Accounts receivable	$28,000	$32,000
Prepaid rent	1,800	1,500
Interest receivable	700	500
Accounts payable	8,500	9,800
Salaries payable	3,600	3,200
Unearned revenue	4,000	6,000

The income statement contained a $1,200 gain on the sale of equipment, a $900 loss on the sale of land, and $2,500 of depreciation expense. Net income for the period was $52,000.

Required

Prepare the operating activities section of the statement of cash flows.

L.O. 4

Exercise 12-5A   *Determining cash flow from investing activities*

On January 1, 2008, Webber Company had a balance of $278,000 in its Land account. During 2008, Webber sold land that had cost $94,000 for $120,000 cash. The balance in the Land account on December 31, 2008, was $300,000.

Required

a. Determine the cash outflow for the purchase of land during 2008.
b. Prepare the investing activities section of the 2008 statement of cash flows.

Exercise 12-6A   *Determining cash flow from investing activities*   L.O. 4

On January 1, 2008, Duncan Company had a balance of $59,600 in its Delivery Equipment account. During 2008, Duncan purchased delivery equipment that cost $18,500. The balance in the Delivery Equipment account on December 31, 2008, was $60,000. The 2008 income statement contained a gain from the sale of equipment for $3,000. On the date of sale, accumulated depreciation on the equipment sold amounted to $10,000.

Required

a. Determine the cost of the equipment that was sold during 2008.
b. Determine the amount of cash flow from the sale of delivery equipment that should be shown in the investing activities section of the 2008 statement of cash flows.

Exercise 12-7A   *Determining cash flow from investing activities*   L.O. 4

The following accounts and corresponding balances were drawn from Winston Company's 2009 and 2008 year-end balance sheets.

Account Title	2009	2008
Marketable securities	$102,000	$112,000
Machinery	520,000	425,000
Land	140,000	90,000

Other information drawn from the accounting records:

1. Winston incurred a $2,000 loss on the sale of marketable securities during 2009.
2. Old machinery with a book value of $5,000 (cost of $25,000 minus accumulated depreciation of $20,000) was sold. The income statement showed a gain on the sale of machinery of $4,000.
3. Winston did not sell land during the year.

Required

a. Compute the amount of cash flow associated with the sale of marketable securities.
b. Compute the amount of cash flow associated with the purchase of machinery.
c. Compute the amount of cash flow associated with the sale of machinery.
d. Compute the amount of cash flow associated with the purchase of land.
e. Prepare the investing activities section of the statement of cash flows.

Exercise 12-8A   *Determining cash flow from financing activities*   L.O. 5

On January 1, 2008, BGA Company had a balance of $500,000 in its Bonds Payable account. During 2008, BGA issued bonds with a $150,000 face value. There was no premium or discount associated with the bond issue. The balance in the Bonds Payable account on December 31, 2008, was $300,000.

Required

a. Determine the cash outflow for the repayment of bond liabilities assuming that the bonds were retired at face value.
b. Prepare the financing activities section of the 2008 statement of cash flows.

Exercise 12-9A   *Determining cash flow from financing activities*   L.O. 5

On January 1, 2008, Parker Company had a balance of $120,000 in its Common Stock account. During 2008, Parker paid $18,000 to purchase treasury stock. Treasury stock is accounted for using the cost method. The balance in the Common Stock account on December 31, 2008, was $130,000. Assume that the common stock is no par stock.

Required

a. Determine the cash inflow from the issue of common stock.
b. Prepare the financing activities section of the 2008 statement of cash flows.

L.O. 5

Exercise 12-10A   *Determining cash flow from financing activities*

The following accounts and corresponding balances were drawn from Berry Company's 2009 and 2008 year-end balance sheets.

Account Title	2009	2008
Bonds payable	$210,000	$300,000
Common stock	370,000	275,000

Other information drawn from the accounting records:

1. Dividends paid during the period amounted to $30,000.
2. There were no bond liabilities issued during the period.

Required

a. Compute the amount of cash flow associated with the repayment of bond liabilities.
b. Compute the amount of cash flow associated with the issue of common stock.
c. Prepare the financing activities section of the statement of cash flows.

L.O. 7

Exercise 12-11A   *Use the direct method to determine cash flow from operating activities (Appendix)*

The following accounts and corresponding balances were drawn from Widjaja Company's 2009 and 2008 year-end balance sheets.

Account Title	2009	2008
Unearned revenue	$6,500	$5,000
Prepaid rent	1,800	2,400

During the year, $68,000 of unearned revenue was recognized as having been earned. Rent expense for 2009 was $15,000.

Required

Based on this information alone, prepare the operating activities section of the statement of cash flows assuming the indirect approach is used.

L.O. 7

Exercise 12-12A   *Use the direct method to determine cash flow from operating activities (Appendix)*

The following accounts and corresponding balances were drawn from Berry Company's 2009 and 2008 year-end balance sheets.

Account Title	2009	2008
Accounts receivable	$46,000	$42,000
Interest receivable	5,000	6,000
Operating expenses payable	27,000	22,000
Salaries payable	12,000	15,000

The 2009 income statement is shown below:

Income Statement	
Sales	$680,000
Salary expense	(172,000)
Other operating expenses	(270,000)
Operating income	238,000
Nonoperating items: Interest revenue	24,000
Net income	$ 262,000

Required

a. Use the direct method to compute the amount of cash inflow from operating activities.
b. Use the direct method to compute the amount of cash outflow from operating activities.

Exercise 12-13A   *The direct versus the indirect method of determining cash flow from*   **L.O. 2, 7**
operating activities (Appendix)

The following accounts and corresponding balances were drawn from Larry Company's 2009 and 2008 year-end balance sheets.

Account Title	2009	2008
Accounts receivable	$78,000	$75,000
Prepaid rent	800	900
Utilities payable	1,500	1,200
Other operating expenses payable	34,000	33,000

The 2009 income statement is shown below:

Income Statement	
Sales	$272,000
Rent expense	(24,000)
Utilities expense	(36,400)
Other operating expenses	(168,000)
Net Income	$ 43,600

Required

a. Prepare the operating activities section of the statement of cash flows using the direct method.
b. Prepare the operating activities section of the statement of cash flows using the indirect method.

PROBLEMS—SERIES A

All Problems in Series A are available with McGraw-Hill's Homework Manager®

Problem 12-14A   *Preparing a statement of cash flows*   **L.O. 1**

The following information can be obtained by examining a company's balance sheet and income statement information.

a. Decreases in noncash current asset account balances.
b. Cash outflows to repay long-term debt.
c. Increases in noncash current asset account balances.
d. Cash outflows made to purchase long-term assets.
e. Decreases in current liability account balances.
f. Noncash expenses (e.g., depreciation).
g. Cash outflows to purchase treasury stock.
h. Gains recognized on the sale of long-term assets.
i. Cash outflows to pay dividends.
j. Cash inflows from the issue of contributed capital (common stock).
k. Cash inflows from the sale of long-term assets.
l. Increases in current liability account balances.
m. Cash inflows from the issue of long-term debt.
n. Losses incurred from the sale of long-term assets.

Required

Construct a table like the one shown below. For each item, indicate whether it would be used in the computation of net cash flows from operating, investing, or financing activities. Also, indicate whether the item would be added or subtracted when determining the net cash flow from operating, investing, or financing activities. Assume the indirect method is used to prepare the operating activities section of the statement of cash flows. The first item has been completed as an example.

Item	Type of Activity	Add or Subtract
a.	Operating	Add
b.		
c.		
d.		
e.		
f.		
g.		
h.		
i.		
j.		
k.		
l.		
m.		
n.		

L.O. 3

Problem 12-15A *Use the indirect method to determine cash flow from operating activities*

eXcel

Top Brands, Inc. (TBI), presents its statement of cash flows using the indirect method. The following accounts and corresponding balances were drawn from TBI's 2009 and 2008 year-end balance sheets.

Account Title	2009	2008
Accounts receivable	$24,000	$26,000
Merchandise inventory	56,000	52,000
Prepaid insurance	19,000	24,000
Accounts payable	23,000	20,000
Salaries payable	4,600	4,200
Unearned revenue	8,000	9,700

Additional information drawn from the 2009 income statement:

1. Net income amounted to $21,000.
2. Depreciation expense was $6,000.
3. There was a gain on the sale of equipment in the amount of $3,000.

Required

Prepare the operating activities section of the statement of cash flows.

Problem 12-16A   *Determining cash flow from investing activities*

L.O. 4

The following information was drawn from the year-end balance sheets of Desoto Company:

CHECK FIGURES
b. $5,000
c. $35,000

Account Title	2009	2008
Marketable securities	$ 33,500	$ 30,000
Equipment	235,000	220,000
Buildings	845,000	962,000
Land	80,000	69,000

Additional information regarding transactions occurring during 2009:

1. Marketable securities that had cost $5,600 were sold. The 2009 income statement contained a loss on the sale of marketable securities of $600.
2. Equipment with a cost of $50,000 was purchased.
3. The income statement showed a gain on the sale of equipment of $6,000. On the date of sale, accumulated depreciation on the equipment sold amounted to $8,000.
4. A building that had originally cost $158,000 was demolished.
5. Land that had cost $25,000 was sold for $22,000.

Required

a. Determine the amount of cash flow for the purchase of marketable securities during 2009.
b. Determine the amount of cash flow from the sale of marketable securities during 2009.
c. Determine the cost of the equipment that was sold during 2009.
d. Determine the amount of cash flow from the sale of equipment during 2009.
e. Determine the amount of cash flow for the purchase of buildings during 2009.
f. Determine the amount of cash flow for the purchase of land during 2009.
g. Prepare the investing activities section of the 2009 statement of cash flows.

Problem 12-17A   *Determining cash flow from financing activities*

L.O. 5

The following information was drawn from the year-end balance sheets of Pet Doors, Inc.:

CHECK FIGURES
c. $15,000
e. Net Cash Flow from
   Operating Activities:
   ($74,000) outflow

Account Title	2009	2008
Bonds payable	$800,000	$900,000
Common stock	197,000	140,000
Treasury stock	25,000	10,000
Retained earnings	80,000	69,000

Additional information regarding transactions occurring during 2009:

1. Pet Doors, Inc., issued $50,000 of bonds during 2009. The bonds were issued at face value. All bonds retired were retired at face value.
2. Common stock did not have a par value.
3. Pet Doors, Inc., uses the cost method to account for treasury stock
4. The amount of net income shown on the 2009 income statement was $27,000.

Required

a. Determine the amount of cash flow for the retirement of bonds that should appear on the 2009 statement of cash flows.
b. Determine the amount of cash flow from the issue of common stock that should appear on the 2009 statement of cash flows.

c. Determine the amount of cash flow for the purchase of treasury stock that should appear on the 2009 statement of cash flows.

d. Determine the amount of cash flow for the payment of dividends that should appear on the 2009 statement of cash flows.

e. Prepare the financing activities section of the 2009 statement of cash flows.

L.O. 3, 4, 5

CHECK FIGURES
Net Cash Flow from
Operating Activities:
$18,750
Net Increase in Cash:
$21,400

Problem 12-18A *Using financial statements to prepare a statement of cash flows—Indirect method*

The following financial statements were drawn from the records of Pacific Company.

Balance Sheets As of December 31		
	2007	**2006**
Assets		
Cash	$24,200	$ 2,800
Accounts receivable	2,000	1,200
Inventory	6,400	6,000
Equipment	19,000	42,000
Accumulated depreciation—equipment	(9,000)	(17,400)
Land	18,400	10,400
Total assets	$61,000	$45,000
Liabilities and equity		
Accounts payable (inventory)	$ 2,600	$ 4,200
Long-term debt	2,800	6,400
Common stock	22,000	10,000
Retained earnings	33,600	24,400
Total liabilities and equity	$61,000	$45,000

Income Statement For the Year Ended December 31, 2007	
Sales revenue	$35,700
Cost of goods sold	(14,150)
Gross margin	21,550
Depreciation expense	(3,600)
Operating income	17,950
Gain on sale of equipment	500
Loss on disposal of land	(50)
Net income	$18,400

Additional Data

1. During 2007, the company sold equipment for $18,500; it had originally cost $30,000. Accumulated depreciation on this equipment was $12,000 at the time of the sale. Also, the company purchased equipment for $7,000 cash.

2. The company sold land that had cost $4,000. This land was sold for $3,950, resulting in the recognition of a $50 loss. Also, common stock was issued in exchange for title to land that was valued at $12,000 at the time of exchange.

3. Paid dividends of $9,200.

Required

Prepare a statement of cash flows using the indirect method.

Problem 12-19A   *Using financial statements to prepare a statement of cash flows—Indirect method*   **L.O. 3, 4, 5**

The comparative balance sheets for Redwood Corporation for 2006 and 2007 follow:

Balance Sheets As of December 31		
	2007	**2006**
Assets		
Cash	$ 68,800	$ 40,600
Accounts receivable	30,000	22,000
Merchandise inventory	160,000	176,000
Prepaid rent	2,400	4,800
Equipment	256,000	288,000
Accumulated depreciation	(146,800)	(236,000)
Land	192,000	80,000
Total assets	$562,400	$375,400
Liabilities		
Accounts payable (inventory)	$ 67,000	$ 76,000
Salaries payable	28,000	24,000
Stockholders' equity		
Common stock, $25 par value	250,000	200,000
Retained earnings	217,400	75,400
Total liabilities and equity	$562,400	$375,400

Income Statement For the Year Ended December 31, 2007	
Sales	$1,500,000
Cost of goods sold	(797,200)
Gross profit	702,800
Operating expenses	
Depreciation expense	(22,800)
Rent expense	(24,000)
Salaries expense	(256,000)
Other operating expenses	(258,000)
Net income	$ 142,000

eXcel

Other Information

1. Purchased land for $112,000.
2. Purchased new equipment for $100,000.
3. Sold old equipment that cost $132,000 with accumulated depreciation of $112,000 for $20,000 cash.
4. Issued common stock for $50,000.

Required

Prepare the statement of cash flows for 2007 using the indirect method.

Problem 12-20A   *Using transaction data to prepare a statement of cash flows (Appendix)*   **L.O. 3, 4, 5**

Store Company engaged in the following transactions during the 2007 accounting period. The beginning cash balance was $28,600 and ending cash balance was $6,025.

1. Sales on account were $250,000. The beginning receivables balance was $87,000 and the ending balance was $83,000.
2. Salaries expense for the period was $56,000. The beginning salaries payable balance was $3,500 and the ending balance was $2,000.

3. Other operating expenses for the period were $125,000. The beginning operating expense payable balance was $4,500 and the ending balance was $8,500.

4. Recorded $19,500 of depreciation expense. The beginning and ending balances in the Accumulated Depreciation account were $14,000 and $33,500, respectively.

5. The Equipment account had beginning and ending balances of $210,000 and $240,000, respectively. The increase was caused by the cash purchase of equipment.

6. The beginning and ending balances in the Notes Payable account were $50,000 and $150,000, respectively. The increase was caused by additional cash borrowing.

7. There was $6,000 of interest expense reported on the income statement. The beginning and ending balances in the Interest Payable account were $1,500 and $1,000, respectively.

8. The beginning and ending Merchandise Inventory account balances were $90,000 and $108,000, respectively. The company sold merchandise with a cost of $156,000 (cost of goods sold for the period was $156,000). The beginning and ending balances of Accounts Payable were $9,500 and $11,500, respectively.

9. The beginning and ending balances of Notes Receivable were $5,000 and $10,000, respectively. The increase resulted from a cash loan to one of the company's employees.

10. The beginning and ending balances of the Common Stock account were $100,000 and $120,000, respectively. The increase was caused by the issue of common stock for cash.

11. Land had beginning and ending balances of $50,000 and $41,000, respectively. Land that cost $9,000 was sold for $12,200, resulting in a gain of $3,200.

12. The tax expense for the period was $7,700. The Taxes Payable account had a $950 beginning balance and an $875 ending balance.

13. The Investments account had beginning and ending balances of $25,000 and $29,000, respectively. The company purchased investments for $18,000 cash during the period, and investments that cost $14,000 were sold for $9,000, resulting in a $5,000 loss.

Required

Convert the preceding information to cash-equivalent data and prepare a statement of cash flows using the direct method.

L.O. 3, 4, 5

Problem 12-21A *Using financial statements to prepare a statement of cash flows—Direct method (Appendix)*

CHECK FIGURES

Net Cash Flow from Operating Activities: $86,800

Net Increase in Cash: $95,400

The following financial statements were drawn from the records of Raceway Sports:

Balance Sheets As of December 31		
	2007	**2006**
Assets		
Cash	$123,600	$ 28,200
Accounts receivable	57,000	66,000
Inventory	126,000	114,000
Notes receivable	0	30,000
Equipment	147,000	255,000
Accumulated depreciation—equipment	(74,740)	(141,000)
Land	82,500	52,500
Total assets	$461,360	$404,700
Liabilities and equity		
Accounts payable (inventory)	$ 42,000	$ 48,600
Salaries payable	30,000	24,000
Utilities payable	600	1,200
Interest payable	0	1,800
Note payable	0	60,000
Common stock	300,000	240,000
Retained earnings	88,760	29,100
Total liabilities and equity	$461,360	$404,700

Income Statement For the Year Ended December 31, 2007	
Sales revenue	$580,000
Cost of goods sold	(288,000)
Gross margin	292,000
Operating expenses	
Salary expense	(184,000)
Depreciation expense	(17,740)
Utilities expense	(12,200)
Operating income	78,060
Nonoperating items	
Interest expense	(3,000)
Gain or (Loss)	(1,800)
Net income	$ 73,260

Additional Information

1. Sold equipment costing $108,000 with accumulated depreciation of $84,000 for $22,200 cash.
2. Paid a $13,600 cash dividend to owners.

Required

Analyze the data and prepare a statement of cash flows using the direct method.

EXERCISES—SERIES B

Exercise 12-1B *Direct versus indirect method of determining cash flow from operating activities*   L.O. 2

Security Services, Inc. (SSI), recognized $2,400 of sales revenue on account and collected $1,900 of cash from accounts receivable. Further, SSI recognized $900 of operating expenses on account and paid $400 cash as partial settlement of accounts payable.

Required

Based on this information alone:

a. Prepare the operating activities section of the statement of cash flows under the direct method.
b. Prepare the operating activities section of the statement of cash flows under the indirect method.

Exercise 12-2B *Use the indirect method to determine cash flow from operating activities*   L.O. 3

An accountant for Farve Enterprise Companies (FEC) computed the following information by making comparisons between FEC's 2009 and 2008 balance sheets. Further information was determined by examining the company's 2009 income statement.

1. The amount of cash dividends paid to the stockholders.
2. The amount of an increase in the balance of an Unearned Revenue account.
3. The amount of a decrease in the balance of an Inventory account.
4. The amount of a decrease in the balance of a Land account.
5. The amount of an increase in the balance of a Prepaid Rent account.
6. The amount of an increase in the balance of a Treasury Stock account.
7. The amount of a decrease in the balance of the Accounts Receivable account.
8. The amount of a gain arising from the sale of land.
9. The amount of an increase in the balance of the Salaries Payable account.
10. The amount of an increase in the balance of the Bonds Payable account.
11. The amount of depreciation expense shown on the income statement.

Required

For each item described above, indicate whether the amount should be added to or subtracted from the amount of net income when determining the amount of cash flow from operating activities. If an item does not affect cash flow from operating activities, identify it as being not affected.

L.O. 3

Exercise 12-3B   *Use the indirect method to determine cash flow from operating activities*

Haughton Incorporated presents its statement of cash flows using the indirect method. The following accounts and corresponding balances were drawn from the company's 2009 and 2008 year-end balance sheets:

Account Title	2009	2008
Accounts receivable	$26,200	$21,400
Accounts payable	9,700	9,300

The 2009 income statement showed net income of $36,300.

Required

a. Prepare the operating activities section of the statement of cash flows.
b. Explain why the change in the balance in accounts receivable was added to or subtracted from the amount of net income when you completed Requirement *a*.
c. Explain why the change in the balance in accounts payable was added to or subtracted from the amount of net income when you completed Requirement *a*.

L.O. 3

Exercise 12-4B   *Use the indirect method to determine cash flow from operating activities*

Hong Company presents its statement of cash flows using the indirect method. The following accounts and corresponding balances were drawn from Hong's 2009 and 2008 year-end balance sheets:

Account Title	2009	2008
Accounts receivable	$46,000	$38,000
Prepaid rent	2,400	2,800
Interest receivable	900	1,000
Accounts payable	10,500	9,000
Salaries payable	4,200	4,800
Unearned revenue	5,000	4,500

The income statement contained a $500 loss on the sale of equipment, a $700 gain on the sale of land, and $3,200 of depreciation expense. Net income for the period was $47,000.

Required

Prepare the operating activities section of the statement of cash flows.

L.O. 4

Exercise 12-5B   *Determining cash flow from investing activities*

On January 1, 2008, Oswalt Company had a balance of $156,000 in its Land account. During 2008, Oswalt sold land that had cost $66,000 for $98,000 cash. The balance in the Land account on December 31, 2008, was $220,000.

Required

a. Determine the cash outflow for the purchase of land during 2008.
b. Prepare the investing activities section of the 2008 statement of cash flows.

Exercise 12-6B   *Determining cash flow from investing activities*

On January 1, 2008, Artex Company had a balance of $65,600 in its Office Equipment account. During 2008, Artex purchased office equipment that cost $21,600. The balance in the Office Equipment account on December 31, 2008, was $65,000. The 2008 income statement contained a gain from the sale of equipment for $5,000. On the date of sale, accumulated depreciation on the equipment sold amounted to $8,300.

Required

a. Determine the cost of the equipment that was sold during 2008.
b. Determine the amount of cash flow from the sale of office equipment that should be shown in the investing activities section of the 2008 statement of cash flows.

Exercise 12-7B   *Determining cash flow from investing activities*

The following accounts and corresponding balances were drawn from Callon Company's 2009 and 2008 year-end balance sheets:

Account Title	2009	2008
Marketable securities	$ 98,000	$106,000
Machinery	565,000	520,000
Land	90,000	140,000

Other information drawn from the accounting records:

1. Callon incurred a $4,000 loss on the sale of marketable securities during 2009.
2. Old machinery with a book value of $7,000 (cost of $32,000 minus accumulated depreciation of $25,000) was sold. The income statement showed a gain on the sale of machinery of $5,500.
3. Callon incurred a loss of $2,500 on the sale of land in 2009.

Required

a. Compute the amount of cash flow associated with the sale of marketable securities.
b. Compute the amount of cash flow associated with the purchase of machinery.
c. Compute the amount of cash flow associated with the sale of machinery.
d. Compute the amount of cash flow associated with the sale of land.
e. Prepare the investing activities section of the statement of cash flows.

Exercise 12-8B   *Determining cash flow from financing activities*

On January 1, 2008, MMC Company had a balance of $700,000 in its Bonds Payable account. During 2008, MMC issued bonds with a $200,000 face value. There was no premium or discount associated with the bond issue. The balance in the Bonds Payable account on December 31, 2008, was $400,000.

Required

a. Determine the cash outflow for the repayment of bond liabilities assuming that the bonds were retired at face value.
b. Prepare the financing activities section of the 2008 statement of cash flows.

Exercise 12-9B   *Determining cash flow from financing activities*

On January 1, 2008, Graves Company had a balance of $200,000 in its Common Stock account. During 2008, Graves paid $15,000 to purchase treasury stock. Treasury stock is accounted for using the cost method. The balance in the Common Stock account on December 31, 2008, was $240,000. Assume that the common stock is no par stock.

Required

a. Determine the cash inflow from the issue of common stock.

b. Prepare the financing activities section of the 2008 statement of cash flows.

L.O. 5   **Exercise 12-10B**   *Determining cash flow from financing activities*

The following accounts and corresponding balances were drawn from Poole Company's 2009 and 2008 year-end balance sheets:

Account Title	2009	2008
Bonds payable	$300,000	$210,000
Common stock	550,000	450,000

Other information drawn from the accounting records:

1. Dividends paid during the period amounted to $40,000.
2. There were no bond liabilities repaid during the period.

Required

a. Compute the amount of cash flow associated with the issue of bond liabilities.

b. Compute the amount of cash flow associated with the issue of common stock.

c. Prepare the financing activities section of the statement of cash flows.

L.O. 7   **Exercise 12-11B**   *Use the direct method to determine cash flow from operating activities (Appendix)*

The following accounts and corresponding balances were drawn from Pizzazz Company's 2009 and 2008 year-end balance sheets:

Account Title	2009	2008
Unearned revenue	$5,000	$6,500
Prepaid rent	2,400	1,800

During the year, $72,000 of unearned revenue was recognized as having been earned. Rent expense for 2009 was $20,000.

Required

Based on this information alone, prepare the operating activities section of the statement of cash flows assuming the direct approach is used.

L.O. 7   **Exercise 12-12B**   *Use the direct method to determine cash flow from operating activities (Appendix)*

The following accounts and corresponding balances were drawn from Hughes Company's 2009 and 2008 year-end balance sheets:

Account Title	2009	2008
Accounts receivable	$56,000	$41,000
Interest receivable	6,000	5,000
Operating expenses payable	22,000	28,000
Salaries payable	15,000	13,000

The 2009 income statement is shown below:

Income Statement	
Sales	$725,000
Salary expense	(180,000)
Other operating expenses	(310,000)
Operating income	235,000
Nonoperating items: Interest revenue	18,000
Net income	$253,000

Required

a. Use the direct method to compute the amount of cash inflow from operating activities.

b. Use the direct method to compute the amount of cash outflow from operating activities.

Exercise 12-13B *The direct versus the indirect method of determining cash flow from operating activities (Appendix)*   L.O. 2, 7

The following accounts and corresponding balances were drawn from Littlejohn Company's 2009 and 2008 year-end balance sheets:

Account Title	2009	2008
Accounts receivable	$89,000	$92,000
Prepaid rent	1,100	1,500
Utilities payable	2,100	2,600
Other operating expenses payable	42,000	49,000

The 2009 income statement is shown below:

Income Statement	
Sales	$312,000
Rent expense	(36,000)
Utilities expense	(41,900)
Other operating expenses	(189,000)
Net income	$ 45,100

Required

a. Prepare the operating activities section of the statement of cash flows using the direct method.

b. Prepare the operating activities section of the statement of cash flows using the indirect method.

PROBLEMS—SERIES B

Problem 12-14B *Preparing a statement of cash flows*   L.O. 1

The following information can be obtained by examining a company's balance sheet and income statement information.

a. Gains recognized on the sale of noncurrent assets.

b. Cash outflows to pay dividends.

c. Cash inflows from the issue of contributed capital (common stock).

d. Cash inflows from the sale of noncurrent assets.

e. Increases in current liability account balances.

f. Cash inflows from the issue of noncurrent debt.

g. Losses incurred from the sale of noncurrent assets.

h. Decreases in noncash current asset account balances.

i. Cash outflows to repay noncurrent debt.

j. Increases in noncash current asset account balances.

k. Cash outflows made to purchase noncurrent assets.

l. Decreases in current liability account balances.

m. Noncash expenses (e.g., depreciation).

n. Cash outflows to purchase treasury stock.

Required

Construct a table like the one shown below. For each item, indicate whether it would be used in the computation of net cash flows from operating, investing, or financing activities. Also, indicate whether the item would be added or subtracted when determining the net cash flow from operating, investing, or financing activities. Assume the indirect method is used to prepare the operating activities section of the statement of cash flows. The first item has been completed as an example.

Item	Type of Activity	Add or Subtract
a.	Operating	Subtract
b.		
c.		
d.		
e.		
f.		
g.		
h.		
i.		
j.		
k.		
l.		
m.		
n.		

L.O. 3

Problem 12-15B   *Use the indirect method to determine cash flow from operating activities*

Bryan Sports, Inc. (BSI), presents its statement of cash flows using the indirect method. The following accounts and corresponding balances were drawn from BSI's 2009 and 2008 year-end balance sheets:

Account Title	2009	2008
Accounts receivable	$36,000	$45,000
Merchandise inventory	65,000	62,000
Prepaid insurance	24,000	20,000
Accounts payable	20,000	25,000
Salaries payable	4,500	3,900
Unearned revenue	9,500	8,600

Additional information drawn from the 2009 income statement:

1. Net income amounted to $46,000.

2. Depreciation expense was $8,000.

3. There was a gain on the sale of equipment in the amount of $2,500.

Required

Prepare the operating activities section of the statement of cash flows.

Problem 12-16B *Determining cash flow from investing activities*

The following information was drawn from the year-end balance sheets of Madison Company:

Account Title	2009	2008
Marketable securities	$ 46,500	$ 50,000
Equipment	275,000	260,000
Buildings	950,000	920,000
Land	70,000	90,000

Additional information regarding transactions occurring during 2009:

1. Marketable securities that had cost $7,800 were sold. The 2009 income statement contained a loss on the sale of marketable securities of $1,200.
2. Equipment with a cost of $75,000 was purchased.
3. The income statement showed a gain on the sale of equipment of $10,000. On the date of sale, accumulated depreciation on the equipment sold amounted to $52,000.
4. A building that had originally cost $70,000 was demolished.
5. Land that had cost $15,000 was sold for $20,000.

Required

a. Determine the amount of cash flow for the purchase of marketable securities during 2009.
b. Determine the amount of cash flow from the sale of marketable securities during 2009.
c. Determine the cost of the equipment that was sold during 2009.
d. Determine the amount of cash flow from the sale of equipment during 2009.
e. Determine the amount of cash flow for the purchase of buildings during 2009.
f. Determine the amount of cash flow for the purchase of land during 2009.
g. Prepare the investing activities section of the 2009 statement of cash flows.

Problem 12-17B *Determining cash flow from financing activities*

The following information was drawn from the year-end balance sheets of Sports Supply, Inc.:

Account Title	2009	2008
Bonds payable	$700,000	$800,000
Common stock	180,000	140,000
Treasury stock	40,000	25,000
Retained earnings	96,000	80,000

Additional information regarding transactions occurring during 2009:

1. Sports Supply, Inc., issued $70,000 of bonds during 2009. The bonds were issued at face value. All bonds retired were retired at face value.
2. Common stock did not have a par value.
3. Sports Supply, Inc., uses the cost method to account for treasury stock. Sports Supply, Inc., did not resell any treasury stock in 2009.
4. The amount of net income shown on the 2009 income statement was $36,000.

Required

a. Determine the amount of cash flow for the retirement of bonds that should appear on the 2009 statement of cash flows.
b. Determine the amount of cash flow from the issue of common stock that should appear on the 2009 statement of cash flows.
c. Determine the amount of cash flow for the purchase of treasury stock that should appear on the 2009 statement of cash flows.

d. Determine the amount of cash flow for the payment of dividends that should appear on the 2009 statement of cash flows.

e. Prepare the financing activities section of the 2009 statement of cash flows.

L.O. 3, 4, 5   **Problem 12-18B**   *Using financial statements to prepare a statement of cash flows—Indirect method*

The following financial statements were drawn from the records of Healthy Products Co.

Balance Sheets As of December 31		
	2003	**2002**
Assets		
Cash	$16,120	$ 1,940
Accounts receivable	2,400	2,000
Inventory	2,000	2,600
Equipment	13,700	17,100
Accumulated depreciation—equipment	(11,300)	(12,950)
Land	13,000	8,000
Total assets	$35,920	$18,690
Liabilities and equity		
Accounts payable (inventory)	$ 3,600	$ 2,400
Long-term debt	3,200	4,000
Common stock	17,000	10,000
Retained earnings	12,120	2,290
Total liabilities and stockholders' equity	$35,920	$18,690

Income Statement For the Year Ended December 31, 2003	
Sales revenue	$17,480
Cost of goods sold	(6,200)
Gross margin	11,280
Depreciation expense	(1,750)
Operating income	9,530
Gain on sale of equipment	1,800
Loss on disposal of land	(600)
Net income	$10,730

Additional Data

1. During 2003, the company sold equipment for $6,800; it had originally cost $8,400. Accumulated depreciation on this equipment was $3,400 at the time of the sale. Also, the company purchased equipment for $5,000 cash.

2. The company sold land that had cost $2,000. This land was sold for $1,400, resulting in the recognition of a $600 loss. Also, common stock was issued in exchange for title to land that was valued at $7,000 at the time of exchange.

3. Paid dividends of $900.

Required

Prepare a statement of cash flows using the indirect method.

Problem 12-19B *Using financial statements to prepare a statement of cash flows—Indirect method*   L.O. 3, 4, 5

The comparative balance sheets for Lind Beauty Products, Inc., for 2006 and 2007 follow:

Balance Sheets As of December 31		
	2007	**2006**
Assets		
Cash	$ 6,300	$ 48,400
Accounts receivable	10,200	7,260
Merchandise inventory	45,200	56,000
Prepaid rent	700	2,140
Equipment	140,000	144,000
Accumulated depreciation	(73,400)	(118,000)
Land	116,000	50,000
Total assets	$245,000	$189,800
Liabilities and equity		
Accounts payable (inventory)	$ 37,200	$ 40,000
Salaries payable	12,200	10,600
Stockholders' equity		
Common stock, $50 par value	150,000	120,000
Retained earnings	45,600	19,200
Total liabilities and equity	$245,000	$189,800

Income Statement For the Year Ended December 31, 2007	
Sales	$480,000
Cost of goods sold	(264,000)
Gross profit	216,000
Operating expenses	
Depreciation expense	(11,400)
Rent expense	(7,000)
Salaries expense	(95,200)
Other operating expenses	(76,000)
Net income	$ 26,400

Other Information

1. Purchased land for $66,000.
2. Purchased new equipment for $62,000.
3. Sold old equipment that cost $66,000 with accumulated depreciation of $56,000 for $10,000 cash.
4. Issued common stock for $30,000.

Required

Prepare the statement of cash flows for 2007 using the indirect method.

Problem 12-20B *Using transaction data to prepare a statement of cash flows (Appendix)*   L.O. 7

Greenstein Company engaged in the following transactions during 2009. The beginning cash balance was $86,000 and ending cash balance was $37,100.

1. Sales on account were $548,000. The beginning receivables balance was $128,000 and the ending balance was $90,000.
2. Salaries expense was $232,000. The beginning salaries payable balance was $16,000 and the ending balance was $8,000.

3. Other operating expenses were $236,000. The beginning Operating Expense Payable balance was $16,000 and the ending balance was $10,000.

4. Recorded $30,000 of depreciation expense. The beginning and ending balances in the Accumulated Depreciation account were $12,000 and $42,000, respectively.

5. The Equipment account had beginning and ending balances of $44,000 and $56,000, respectively. The increase was caused by the cash purchase of equipment.

6. The beginning and ending balances in the Notes Payable account were $44,000 and $36,000, respectively. The decrease was caused by the cash repayment of debt.

7. There was $4,600 of interest expense reported on the income statement. The beginning and ending balances in the Interest Payable account were $8,400 and $7,500, respectively.

8. The beginning and ending Merchandise Inventory account balances were $22,000 and $29,400, respectively. The company sold merchandise with a cost of $83,600. The beginning and ending balances of Accounts Payable were $8,000 and $6,400, respectively.

9. The beginning and ending balances of Notes Receivable were $100,000 and $60,000, respectively. The decline resulted from the cash collection of a portion of the receivable.

10. The beginning and ending balances of the Common Stock account were $120,000 and $160,000, respectively. The increase was caused by the issue of common stock for cash.

11. Land had beginning and ending balances of $24,000 and $14,000, respectively. Land that cost $10,000 was sold for $6,000, resulting in a loss of $4,000.

12. The tax expense for 2003 was $6,600. The Tax Payable account had a $2,400 beginning balance and a $2,200 ending balance.

13. The Investments account had beginning and ending balances of $20,000 and $60,000, respectively. The company purchased investments for $50,000 cash during 2003, and investments that cost $10,000 were sold for $22,000, resulting in a $12,000 gain.

Required

Convert the preceding information to cash-equivalent data and prepare a statement of cash flows using the direct method.

L.O. 7

Problem 12-21B *Using financial statements to prepare a statement of cash flows—Direct method (Appendix)*

The following financial statements were drawn from the records of Norton Materials, Inc.

Balance Sheets As of December 31		
	2008	2009
Assets		
Cash	$ 94,300	$ 14,100
Accounts receivable	36,000	40,000
Inventory	72,000	64,000
Notes receivable	0	16,000
Equipment	98,000	170,000
Accumulated depreciation—equipment	(47,800)	(94,000)
Land	46,000	30,000
Total assets	$298,500	$240,100
Liabilities and equity		
Accounts payable	$ 24,000	$ 26,400
Salaries payable	15,000	10,000
Utilities payable	800	1,400
Interest payable	0	1,000
Note payable	0	24,000
Common stock	150,000	110,000
Retained earnings	108,700	67,300
Total liabilities and equity	$298,500	$240,100

Income Statement For the Year Ended December 31, 2009	
Sales revenue	$300,000
Cost of goods sold	(144,000)
Gross margin	156,000
Operating expenses	
Salary expense	(88,000)
Depreciation expense	(9,800)
Utilities expense	(6,400)
Operating income	51,800
Nonoperating items	
Interest expense	(2,400)
Loss	(800)
Net income	$ 48,600

Additional Information

1. Sold equipment costing $72,000 with accumulated depreciation of $56,000 for $15,200 cash.
2. Paid a $7,200 cash dividend to owners.

Required

Analyze the data and prepare a statement of cash flows using the direct method.

ANALYZE, THINK, COMMUNICATE

ATC 12-1   Business Applications Case   *Understanding real-world annual reports*

Required—Part 1

Use the Topps Company's annual report in Appendix B to answer the following questions.

The Topps Company, Inc.

a. For the 2006 and 2005 fiscal years, which was larger, Topps' *net income* or its *cash flow from operating activities?* By what amounts did they differ?

b. What two items are most responsible for the difference between Topps' *net income* and its *cash flow from operating activities* in 2006 and 2005?

c. In 2004, Topps generated approximately $22.9 million of cash from operating activities, and its cash balance decreased by about $20.5 million. How did the company use this $43 million of cash?

Required—Part 2

Use the Harley-Davidson's annual report that came with this book to answer the following questions.

Harley-Davidson, Inc.

a. For the 2005 fiscal year, which was larger, Harley-Davidson's *net income* or its *cash flow from operating activities?* By what amount did they differ?

b. In 2005, what are the two items that affect Harley-Davidson's *net income* most differently than its *cash flow from operating activities?* Explain if each of these items cause cash flow from operating activities to be larger or smaller than net income.

c. In 2005, Harley-Davidson generated approximately $961 million of cash from operating activities. What did the company do with this cash?

ATC 12-2   Real-World Case   *Following the cash*

The Curious Accountant story in Chapter 11 noted that by the end of 2005 XM Satellite Holdings, Inc., had accumulated net losses of $2.2 billion. XM's statement of cash flows for 2003, 2004, and 2005 follow.

XM SATELLITE RADIO HOLDINGS, INC., AND SUBSIDIARIES
Consolidated Statements of Cash Flows
(amounts in thousands)

	Years Ended December 31		
	2005	**2004**	**2003**
Cash Flows from Operating Activities			
Net loss	$(666,715)	$(642,368)	$(584,535)
Adjustments to reconcile net loss to net cash used in operating activities:			
Provision for doubtful accounts	8,328	3,218	2,077
Depreciation and amortization	145,870	147,165	158,317
Interest accretion expense	45,579	53,422	45,227
Net noncash loss on redemption of notes	24,154	66,274	24,777
Noncash loss on equity investments	1,411	–	–
Amortization of deferred financing fees and debt discount	30,178	18,524	17,409
Noncash stock-based compensation	5,966	2,020	3,003
Provision for deferred income taxes	2,330	27,317	–
Other	(878)	(15)	(663)
Changes in operating assets and liabilities:			
Increase in accounts receivable	(35,441)	(8,407)	(11,480)
Increase in due from related parties	(3,262)	(191)	(3,698)
Increase in prepaid programming content	(54,348)	(11,390)	–
(Increase) decrease in prepaid and other assets	(45,290)	11,491	(9,611)
Increase in accounts payable and accrued expenses	125,791	57,371	59,435
Increase (decrease) in accrued interest	(8,543)	8,719	(11,224)
Increase in amounts due to related parties	48,130	82,835	24,256
Increase in subscriber deferred revenue	208,291	98,463	41,587
Net cash used in operating activities	(168,449)	(85,552)	(245,123)
Cash Flows from Investment Activities			
Purchase of property and equipment	(61,210)	(25,934)	(15,685)
Additions to system under construction	(118,583)	(143,978)	(4,108)
Purchase of equity investments	(27,000)	–	–
Net maturity (purchase) of restricted investments	(996)	(341)	22,750
Insurance proceeds from satellite recoveries	–	133,924	–
Other investing activities	–	–	11,664
Net cash (used in) provided by investing activities	(207,789)	(36,329)	14,621
Cash Flows from Financing Activities			
Proceeds from sale of common stock, net and exercise of stock options	319,637	236,835	253,102
Proceeds from issuance of 10% senior secured convertible notes	–	–	210,000
Proceeds from issuance of 12% senior secured notes	–	–	185,000
Proceeds from issuance of 1.75% convertible senior notes	100,000	300,000	–
Proceeds from issuance of floating rate notes	–	200,000	–
Proceeds from refinancing of mortgage on corporate facility	–	33,300	–
Repayment of 12% senior secured notes	(15,000)	(70,000)	–
Repayment of 7.75% convertible subordinated notes	–	–	(6,723)
Repayment of 14% senior secured notes	(22,824)	(13,028)	–
Repayment of related party long-term debt	–	(81,194)	–
Payments on mortgages on corporate facilities	(381)	(28,247)	(420)
Payments on related party credit facility	–	(103,034)	–
Repurchase of Series B preferred stock	–	–	(10,162)
Payments on other borrowings	(9,651)	(40,174)	(2,722)
Deferred financing costs	(2,419)	(13,017)	(12,084)
Net cash provided by financing activities	369,362	421,441	615,991
Net increase (decrease) in cash and cash equivalents	(6,876)	299,560	385,489
Cash and cash equivalents at beginning of period	717,867	418,307	32,818
Cash and cash equivalents at end of period	$ 710,991	$ 717,867	$ 418,307

Required

a. This chapter explained that many companies that report a net loss on their earnings statements report positive cash flows from operating activities. How do XM's net earnings compare to its cash flows from operating activities?

b. As is true with many new and growing companies, XM spent considerable sums of cash building and buying property, plant, and equipment. What was the source(s) of the cash used for these purchases?

c. Notice that in 2005 XM repaid $37.8 million of notes payable. Where did the company get the cash used to repay this debt?

d. Do you think the way XM repaid its debt is a positive or negative situation? Explain.

ATC 12-3   Group Assignment   *Preparing a statement of cash flows*

The following financial statements and information are available for Blythe Industries, Inc.

Balance Sheets As of December 31		
	2004	**2005**
Assets		
Cash	$120,600	$ 160,200
Accounts receivable	85,000	103,200
Inventory	171,800	186,400
Marketable securities (available for sale)	220,000	284,000
Equipment	490,000	650,000
Accumulated depreciation	(240,000)	(310,000)
Land	120,000	80,000
Total assets	$967,400	$1,153,800
Liabilities and equity		
Liabilities		
Accounts payable (inventory)	$ 66,200	$ 36,400
Notes payable—long-term	250,000	230,000
Bonds payable	100,000	200,000
Total liabilities	416,200	466,400
Stockholders' equity		
Common stock, no par	200,000	240,000
Preferred stock, $50 par	100,000	110,000
Paid-in capital in excess of par—preferred stock	26,800	34,400
Total paid-in capital	326,800	384,400
Retained earnings	264,400	333,000
Less: Treasury stock	(40,000)	(30,000)
Total stockholders' equity	551,200	687,400
Total liabilities and stockholders' equity	$967,400	$1,153,800

Income Statement For the Year Ended December 31, 2005		
Sales revenue		$1,050,000
Cost of goods sold		(766,500)
Gross profit		283,500
Operating expenses		
Supplies expense	$20,400	
Salaries expense	92,000	
Depreciation expense	90,000	
Total operating expenses		(202,400)

continued

Operating income	$ 81,100
Nonoperating items	
Interest expense	(16,000)
Gain from the sale of marketable securities	30,000
Gain from the sale of land and equipment	12,000
Net income	$ 107,100

Additional Information

1. Sold land that cost $40,000 for $44,000.
2. Sold equipment that cost $30,000 and had accumulated depreciation of $20,000 for $18,000.
3. Purchased new equipment for $190,000.
4. Sold marketable securities, classified as available-for-sale, that cost $40,000 for $70,000.
5. Purchased new marketable securities, classified as available-for-sale, for $104,000.
6. Paid $20,000 on the principal of the long-term note.
7. Paid off a $100,000 bond issue and issued new bonds for $200,000.
8. Sold 100 shares of treasury stock at its cost.
9. Issued some new common stock.
10. Issued some new $50 par preferred stock.
11. Paid dividends. (*Note:* The only transactions to affect retained earnings were net income and dividends.)

Required

Organize the class into three sections, and divide each section into groups of three to five students. Assign each section of groups an activity section of the statement of cash flows (operating activities, investing activities, or financing activities). (Use direct method.)

Group Task

Prepare your assigned portion of the statement of cash flows. Have a representative of your section put your activity section of the statement of cash flows on the board. As each adds its information on the board, the full statement of cash flows will be presented.

Class Discussion

Have the class finish the statement of cash flows by computing the net change in cash. Also have the class answer the following questions:

a. What is the cost per share of the treasury stock?
b. What was the issue price per share of the preferred stock?
c. What was the book value of the equipment sold?

ATC 12-4   Business Applications Case   *Identifying different presentation formats*

In *Statement of Financial Accounting Standards No. 95,* the Financial Accounting Standards Board (FASB) recommended but did not require that companies use the direct method. In Appendix B, Paragraphs 106–121, the FASB discussed its reasons for this recommendation.

Required

Obtain a copy of *Standard No. 95* and read Appendix B Paragraphs 106–121. Write a brief response summarizing the issues that the FASB considered and its specific reaction to those issues. Your response should draw heavily on paragraphs 119–121.

ATC 12-5   Writing Assignment   *Explaining discrepancies between cash flow and operating income*

The following selected information was drawn from the records of Fleming Company:

Assets	2005	2006
Accounts receivable	$ 400,000	$ 840,200
Merchandise inventory	720,000	1,480,000
Equipment	1,484,000	1,861,200
Accumulated depreciation	(312,000)	(402,400)

Fleming is experiencing cash flow problems. Despite the fact that it reported significant increases in operating income, operating activities produced a net cash outflow. Recent financial forecasts predict that Fleming will have insufficient cash to pay its current liabilities within three months.

Required

Write a response explaining Fleming's cash shortage. Include a recommendation to remedy the problem.

ATC 12-6 **Ethical Dilemma** *Would I lie to you, baby?*

Andy and Jean Crocket are involved in divorce proceedings. When discussing a property settlement, Andy told Jean that he should take over their investment in an apartment complex because she would be unable to absorb the loss that the apartments are generating. Jean was somewhat distrustful and asked Andy to support his contention. He produced the following income statement, which was supported by a CPA's unqualified opinion that the statement was prepared in accordance with generally accepted accounting principles.

CROCKET APARTMENTS		
Income Statement		
For the Year Ended December 31, 2009		
Rent revenue		$580,000
Less: Expenses		
Depreciation expense	$280,000	
Interest expense	184,000	
Operating expense	88,000	
Management fees	56,000	
Total expenses		(608,000)
Net loss		$ (28,000)

All revenue is earned on account. Interest and operating expenses are incurred on account. Management fees are paid in cash. The following accounts and balances were drawn from the 2002 and 2003 year-end balance sheets.

Account Title	2008	2009
Rent receivable	$40,000	$44,000
Interest payable	12,000	18,000
Accounts payable (oper. exp.)	6,000	4,000

Jean is reluctant to give up the apartments but feels that she must because her present salary is only $40,000 per year. She says that if she takes the apartments, the $28,000 loss would absorb a significant portion of her salary, leaving her only $12,000 with which to support herself. She tells you that while the figures seem to support her husband's arguments, she believes that she is failing to see something. She knows that she and her husband collected a $20,000 distribution from the business on December 1, 2009. Also, $150,000 cash was paid in 2009 to reduce the principal balance on a mortgage that was taken out to finance the purchase of the apartments two years ago. Finally, $24,000 cash was paid during 2009 to purchase a computer system used in the business. She wonders, "If the apartments are losing money, where is my husband getting all the cash to make these payments?"

Required

a. Prepare a statement of cash flows for the 2009 accounting period.

b. Compare the cash flow statement prepared in Requirement *a* with the income statement and provide Jean Crocket with recommendations.

c. Comment on the value of an unqualified audit opinion when using financial statements for decision-making purposes.

ATC 12-7 Research Assignment *Analyzing cash flow information*

In 2004 and 2005, Google Corporation raised cash by selling its stock to the public for the first time. Using Google's 2005 annual report or Form 10-K, complete the requirements below. The annual report and Form 10-K can be found on the company's website. You can also obtain the Form 10-K using the EDGAR system by following the instructions in Appendix A.

Required

a. How much cash did Google receive in 2004 from issuing stock? How much cash did Google receive from issuing stock in 2005?

b. What did Google do with the cash it raised from the stock it sold in 2004? You will have to use some judgment to answer this, but try to be as specific as possible.

c. What did Google do with the cash it raised from the stock it sold in 2005?

d. Google did not sell any stock to the public in 2003, yet it spent $314 million on investing activities. Where did it get this cash?

Accessing the EDGAR Database Through the Internet

Successful business managers need many different skills, including communication, interpersonal, computer, and analytical. Most business students become very aware of the data analysis skills used in accounting, but they may not be as aware of the importance of "data-finding" skills. There are many sources of accounting and financial data. The more sources you are able to use, the better.

One very important source of accounting information is the EDGAR database. Others are probably available at your school through the library or business school network. Your accounting instructor will be able to identify these for you and make suggestions regarding their use. By making the effort to learn to use electronic databases, you will enhance your abilities as a future manager and your marketability as a business graduate.

These instructions assume that you know how to access and use an Internet browser. Follow the instructions to retrieve data from the Securities and Exchange Commission's EDGAR database. Be aware that the SEC may have changed its interface since this appendix was written. Accordingly, be prepared for slight differences between the following instructions and what appears on your computer screen. Take comfort in the fact that changes are normally designed to simplify user access. If you encounter a conflict between the following instructions and the instructions provided in the SEC interface, remember that the SEC interface is more current and should take precedence over the following instructions.

1. To connect to EDGAR, type in the following address: **http://www.sec.gov/.**

2. After the SEC home page appears, under the heading **Filings & Forms (EDGAR),** click on **Search for Company Filings.**

3. From the screen that appears, click on **Companies & Other Filers.**

4. On the screen that appears, enter the name of the company whose file you wish to retrieve and click on the **Find Companies** button.

5. The following screen will present a list of companies that have the same, or similar, names to the one you entered. Identify the company you want and click on the CIK number beside it.

6. Enter the SEC form number that you want to retrieve in the window titled **Form Type** that appears in the upper right portion of the screen that appears. For example, if you want Form 10-K, which will usually be the case, enter **10-K,** and click on the **Retrieve Filings** button.

7. A list of the forms you requested will be presented, along with the date they were filed with the SEC. You may be given a choice of **[text]** or **[html]** file format. The **[text]** format will present one large file for the form you requested. The **[html]** format will probably present several separate files from which you must choose. These will be named Document 1 . . ., Document 2 . . ., etc. Usually, you should choose the file whose name ends in **10k.txt.** Form 10-K/A is an amended Form 10-K and it sometimes contains more timely information, but usually, the most recent Form 10-K will contain the information you need.

8. Once the 10-K has been retrieved, you can search it online or save it on your hard drive. If you want to save it, do so by using the **Save As** command from the pulldown menu at the top of the screen named **File.**

9. The financial statements are seldom located near the beginning of a company's 10-K, so it is necessary to scroll down the file until you find them. Typically, they are located about one-half to three-fourths of the way through the report.

Annual Report for The Topps Company, Inc.

This appendix contains a portion of the Form 10-K for the Topps Company that was filed with the Securities and Exchange Commission on May 10, 2006. The document included in this appendix is Topps' annual report, which was included *as a part* of its complete Form 10-K for the company's 2006 fiscal year.

This document is included for illustrative purposes, and it is intended to be used for educational purposes only. It should not be used for making investment decisions. Topps Company's complete Form 10-K may be obtained from the SEC's EDGAR website, using the procedures explained in Appendix A. The Form 10-K may also be found on the company's web site at www.topps.com.

UNITED STATES SECURITIES AND EXCHANGE COMMISSION
Washington, D.C. 20549

FORM 10-K

(Mark One)

☑ ANNUAL REPORT PURSUANT TO SECTION 13 OR 15(d) OF THE SECURITIES EXCHANGE ACT OF 1934

For the fiscal year ended February 25, 2006

OR

☐ TRANSITION REPORT PURSUANT TO SECTION 13 OR 15(d) OF THE SECURITIES EXCHANGE ACT OF 1934

For the transition period from   to

Commission file number 0-15817

THE TOPPS COMPANY, INC.
(Exact name of registrant as specified in its charter)

Delaware	11-2849283
(State or other jurisdiction of incorporation or organization)	(I.R.S. Employer Identification No.)
One Whitehall Street, New York, NY	10004
(Address of principal executive offices)	(Zip Code)

(212) 376-0300
(Registrant's telephone number, including area code)

Securities registered pursuant to Section 12(b) of the Act:
Not Applicable

Securities registered pursuant to Section 12(g) of the Act:
Common Stock par value $.01
(Title of class)

Indicate by check mark if the registrant is a well-known seasoned issuer, as defined in Rule 405 of the Securities Act   Yes ☐ No ☑ .

Indicate by check mark if the registrant is not required to file reports pursuant to Section 13 or Section 15(d) of the Act. Yes ☐ No ☑ .

Indicate by check mark whether the registrant (1) has filed all reports required to be filed by Section 13 or 15(d) of the Securities Exchange Act of 1934 during the preceding 12 months (or for such shorter period that the registrant was required to file such reports), and (2) has been subject to such filing requirements for the past 90 days. Yes ☑ No ☐ .

Indicate by check mark if disclosure of delinquent filers pursuant to Item 405 of Regulation S-K is not contained herein, and will not be contained, to the best of registrant's knowledge, in definitive proxy or information statements incorporated by reference in Part III of this form 10-K or any amendment of this Form 10-K. ☐

Indicate by check mark whether the registrant is a large accelerated filer, an accelerated filer or a non-accelerated filer. See definition of "accelerated filer" and "large accelerated filer" in Rule 12b-2 of the Exchange Act.

Large accelerated filer ☐   Accelerated filer ☑   Non-accelerated filer ☐

Indicate by check mark whether the registrant is a shell company (as defined in Rule 12b-2 of the Act). Yes ☐ No ☑ .

The aggregate market value of Common Stock held by non-affiliates as of the last business day of the most recently completed fiscal second quarter was approximately $384,077,750.

The number of outstanding shares of Common Stock as of May 4, 2006 was 39,380,471.

Exhibit 13

Dear Stockholders,

Fiscal 2006 was a busy year for Topps as we made measurable progress on a number of key initiatives aimed at streamlining the business, strengthening our management team and fostering a culture of accountability to drive stockholder value. Although our financial results for the year were below expectations, we enter fiscal 2007 a stronger company, with a clear plan and confidence in our prospects for a more profitable year.

In February 2005, the board authorized the company to pursue, with the assistance of Lehman Brothers, a sale of the candy business believing such a step might provide value for the stockholders, in light of recent industry transactions at attractive multiples.

While the sale process evolved during the first half of fiscal '06, we held off restructuring the organization and implementing certain strategic initiatives, anticipating a successful transaction. That failed to occur, however, and the sale process was ultimately terminated in September 2005.

Since then, the nature and pace of activities, in line with recommendations stemming from a strategic study conducted by independent consultants, has been substantial. Here is a sampling of effected changes:

FISCAL 2006

Restructured The Business To Drive Operating Profitability: We restructured the business to focus on operating profit net of direct overhead rather than contributed margin at our two business units, Confectionery and Entertainment. Beginning in the first quarter of fiscal 2007, financial reporting will reflect this change and lead to more transparency, improved cost management and greater accountability. Now, 80% of our employees report to someone with direct P&L responsibility for a business unit as opposed to 20% before the change.

Created New Culture of Accountability: We redesigned the Company's incentive bonus plan to focus heavily on business unit results and track personal performance against specific, measurable goals identified at the outset of the fiscal year. Our new structure increases the visibility of performance by business unit down to its operating profit net of direct overhead, thus enhancing each individual's accountability.

Reduced Direct and Indirect Costs: With a tight focus on managing costs, we implemented an 8% reduction in U.S. headquarters headcount for annualized savings, net of strategic hires, of $2.5 million. We also reduced indirect costs during the year by freezing the pension plan, modifying our retiree medical plan and reducing certain non-medical insurance, litigation and consulting expenses which will generate an additional $2 million in savings for fiscal 2007.

Strengthened Leadership to Support New Initiatives: We made a number of key hires in a few important areas to support our current strategic initiatives. These include:

- Bazooka brand re-launch
- Improved sales through the hobby channel
- Sports marketing to kids
- New product development for candy
- Confectionery marketing and sales in Europe

1

Improved Efficiency: We progressed major systems upgrades and expect phase one of an enterprise resource planning (ERP) system to be operational this summer. The ERP system will link key areas of the business electronically and provide improved control of our purchasing, order entry, customer service, credit and shipping functions. In addition, we are now operational on a new comprehensive trade spending system to help manage this important business cost.

Achieved Structural Marketing Changes to Benefit Each of our Business Units:
In Entertainment, we successfully negotiated important changes in our agreements with sports card licensors that are already paying dividends. In Confectionery, we relocated Bazooka manufacturing to reduce costs and have re-launched the brand, complete with reformulated product, new packaging, line extensions and marketing programs.

FISCAL 2007

ENTERTAINMENT

We believe that progress made in fiscal '06 sets the stage for growth in fiscal '07 and beyond. We will focus on key priorities to create long term value for our stockholders, employees and distribution partners in fiscal 2007.

On the sports card side, having engineered an important change in the licensing structure of the category, our priorities include capturing additional market share and revenue, engaging more kids to collect our sports products and reducing costs.

With respect to market share, as one of the two licensees marketing Major League baseball cards (last year there were four), Topps will now offer 50% of all baseball card products. We intend to increase our category leadership position by garnering more than our "fair share" of dollars spent. For your information, the football card market witnessed a reduction in licensees from four to three last year and we increased both volume and share.

To generate further success, we have set up a specialized group within our sports department dedicated to developing new products at the medium and high price points for serious collectors. The first two products developed by this team, Topps "Triple Threads" and "Co-Signers Baseball" are both enjoying positive initial trade reception. Moreover, early sales of popularly priced Topps Baseball Series 1 already show considerable improvement over fiscal year 2006.

Among efforts to reconnect with kids, we have entered into agreements with video game publisher, 2KSports and the magazine, Sports Illustrated for Kids, both of which should help promote our products in these kids-focused sports venues. For instance, this year Topps Series 1 Baseball contains cards with special codes by which gamers can apply enhanced powers playing the 2K6 video game. In addition, SI for Kids and Topps have developed a Kids Card Club which is now featured monthly in the magazine and on SIKids.com.

We have also implemented marketing programs at virtually every Major League Baseball ballpark this summer, a first for Topps. Whether through our sponsorship of starting lineups where Topps cards will be featured all season long on in-stadium "Jumbotrons" or special card give-aways, Topps will be on the field, so to speak, not just in the stores. Moreover, we will be part of a $2 million plus industry TV campaign beginning in May, dedicated to showing kids how much fun card collecting truly can be.

Internationally, we intend to devote special efforts to the World Cup this year. We have created a number of World Cup-related collectible products that we will launch in targeted markets. Also, we have extended and expanded our English Premier League Football (Soccer) rights, which we believe will yield good results.

2

Turning to gaming, the market has been soft according to industry sources and we forecast a difficult year for WizKids. Under today's conditions, we believe there is a flight to quality and that the more critical mass one can sustain the better. Accordingly, for the time being we will focus more on our core properties and continue to be extra selective regarding new product introductions such as Horror Clix, planned for launch in the second half of fiscal '07.

Our Entertainment publishing unit will continue to focus on growing franchises and exploiting third party licenses as opportunities are perceived. The Company's own intellectual properties, Wacky Packages and Garbage Pail Kids, enjoy ongoing acceptance in the U.S. marketplace. Series 3 Wacky Packs are heading for a TV advertising test and sampling in select metro markets during the Spring. Later, the product will be packaged with bubble gum qualifying Wackys to appear on candy counters.

On the cost side, we are taking steps to manage operating expenses and grow margins in both the Entertainment and Confectionery businesses. These measures, combined with a planned reduction of obsolescence and returns as a percentage of sales, are expected to result in a further savings of over $2 million in fiscal 2007.

In sports cards, for instance, our initial focus is on pre-press costs which we anticipate reducing by at least 10% beginning in August. In Confectionery, we will apply the new Synectics trade funds management system and use a consultant to help identify means of reducing both operational complexity and costs at facilities manufacturing our confectionery products in Asia. We will also conduct internal reviews to reduce product component costs on a variety of SKU's.

CONFECTIONERY

The Confectionery business unit in fiscal 2007 is executing a number of strategic initiatives including:

- The re-launch of "new" Bazooka in the US
- Refreshing existing brands, and
- Introducing new products at home and abroad, an activity vital to long term growth.

Having relocated our manufacturing operation, Bazooka products will be more competitively priced and offered in a variety of formats and sku's.

Many activities are associated with product refreshment. Among them, our Baby Bottle Pop brand continues to show growth, most recently driven by a line extension called 2 ·D ·Max. Promotional programs with Nickelodeon and new advertising will be used in support of these initiatives. We will also introduce an addition to the Push Pop family this fall. Overseas, we are in our sixth year successfully marketing container candies featuring Pokemon characters.

On the new products front, we have added resources to this important activity and adopted the theme "Fewer, Bigger, Better." Through this process, we are developing a rather revolutionary new candy product for release in January 2007. Called "Vertigo," the product is aimed at tweens and teens, a different consumer segment than our traditional target, and we are excited about it.

CONCLUSION

In totality, the number of concrete activities underway to build stockholder value is unprecedented in our Company's history. Together with fellow employees throughout the Company, our senior leadership team is confident that we have the people, products and vision to see them through.

On behalf of the organization, we thank our stockholders, consumers, fans, collectors, licensors and suppliers for their loyal support.

Officers of the Topps Company, Inc.
(Signatures)

With profound sorrow, we record the passing of our esteemed board member and friend Stanley Tulchin. His vision, warmth and dedication will be well remembered by us all.

Table of Contents

	Page
Stockholders Letter	1
Financial Highlights	6
Management's Discussion and Analysis of Financial Condition and Results of Operations	7
Consolidated Financial Statements	15
Notes to Consolidated Financial Statements	20
Management's Report on Internal Control over Financial Reporting	47
Reports of Independent Registered Public Accounting Firm	48
Market and Dividend Information	50
Selected Consolidated Financial Data	51
Directors, Officers, Subsidiaries and Corporate Information	52

Financial Highlights

	Fiscal Year Ended		
	February 25, 2006	February 26, 2005 (a)	February 28, 2004 (a)
	(in thousands of dollars, except share data)		
Net sales	$ 293,838	$ 294,231	$ 294,917
Net income from continuing operations	3,946	11,268	13,628
Loss from discontinued operations — net of tax	(2,707)	(353)	(744)
Net income	1,239	10,915	12,884
Cash (used in) provided by operations	(6,543)	22,930	11,954
Working capital	127,713	139,910	134,099
Stockholders' equity	204,636	219,168	211,340
Per share items:			
Diluted net income — from continuing operations	$ 0.10	$ 0.27	$ 0.33
Diluted net income — after discontinued operations	$ 0.03	$ 0.26	$ 0.31
Cash dividend paid	$ 0.16	$ 0.16	$ 0.12
Weighted average diluted shares outstanding	41,163,000	41,327,000	41,515,000

(a)   As restated, see Note 2 to Notes to Consolidated Financial Statements

MANAGEMENT'S DISCUSSION AND ANALYSIS OF FINANCIAL CONDITION AND RESULTS OF OPERATIONS

This section provides an analysis of the Company's operating results, cash flow, critical accounting policies, and other matters. It includes or incorporates "forward-looking statements" as that term is defined by the U.S. federal securities laws. In particular, statements using words such as "may", "should", "intend", "estimate", "anticipate", "believe", "predict", "potential", or words of similar import generally involve forward-looking statements. We based these forward-looking statements on our current expectations and projections about future events, and, therefore, these statements are subject to numerous risks and uncertainties. Accordingly, actual results may differ materially from those expressed or implied by the forward-looking statements. We caution readers not to place undue reliance on these forward-looking statements, which speak only as of the date of this report.

The following Management's Discussion and Analysis ("MD&A") gives effect to the restatement discussed in Note 2 to the Consolidated Financial Statements.

CONSOLIDATED NET SALES

The Company has two reportable business segments, Confectionery and Entertainment. The following table sets forth, for the periods indicated, net sales by business segment:

| | Fiscal Year Ended | | |
	February 25, 2006	February 26, 2005	February 28, 2004
	(in thousands of dollars)		
Confectionery	$144,261	$143,762	$147,188
Entertainment	149,577	150,469	147,729
Total	$293,838	$294,231	$294,917

Fiscal 2006 versus 2005*

In fiscal 2006, the Company's consolidated net sales decreased 0.1% to $293.8 million from $294.2 million in fiscal 2005. Weaker foreign currencies versus the prior year reduced fiscal 2006 sales by approximately $600,000. Excluding the impact of stronger foreign currencies, net sales increased by 0.1%.

Worldwide net sales of the Confectionery segment, which includes Ring Pop, Push Pop, Baby Bottle Pop, Juicy Drop Pop and Bazooka brand bubble gum, increased 0.3% to $144.3 million in 2006 from $143.8 million in 2005. Foreign exchange had virtually no impact on full year confectionery sales comparisons. Confectionery products accounted for 49% of the Company's net sales in each of 2006 and 2005.

In the U.S., fiscal 2006 confectionery sales reflected distribution gains and strong retail sales of Juicy Drop Pop, now in its third year. In addition, sales of Baby Bottle Pop increased, driven by a successful new media campaign and initial shipments of 2DMax, a new line extension, which will be officially launched in fiscal 2007.

Confectionery sales in overseas markets were influenced by the introduction of Mega Mouth Candy Spray and continued growth of Pokemon candy products, offset by lower year-on-year performance of core brands in select markets, principally the U.K. and Italy. International sales represented 28% of total confectionery sales in fiscal 2006 versus 31% in 2005.

---

*   *Unless otherwise indicated, all date references to 2006, 2005 and 2004 refer to the fiscal years ended February 25, 2006, February 26, 2005 and February 28, 2004, respectively.*

Going forward, the Company intends to execute a number of strategic initiatives both in the U.S. and abroad aimed at improving the sales and operating profit of the Confectionery segment. Major initiatives include further establishing Topps as a leader in youth-oriented candy products, building the top line through the relaunch of Bazooka, a focus on innovation and the implementation of a disciplined new product process to fuel future growth, enhanced retail distribution and a renewed emphasis on system-wide cost reduction.

Net sales of the Entertainment segment, which includes cards, sticker album collections, Internet activities and strategy games, decreased 0.6% in fiscal 2006 to $149.6 million. Weaker foreign currencies versus the prior year served to reduce fiscal 2006 sales by $0.7 million. Entertainment products represented 51% of the Company's net sales in each of 2006 and 2005.

During the year, the Company reached an agreement on new terms with Major League Baseball and the Players' Association which addressed the industry's product proliferation issues. The deal reduces the number of industry participants from four to two, places a cap on the number of products in the marketplace and requires increased marketing commitments from industry participants targeted at bringing youth back into the market. The combined impact of a positive football season, and to a lesser extent, the new baseball agreement which took effect in January, drove year-over-year increases in sales of sports card products.

Net sales of non-sports products also increased during 2006, a function of successfully marketing products featuring WWE, Star Wars, Pokemon and Wacky Packages. These legacy licenses are a testament to the Company's ability to generate strong publishing sales even in periods of relative licensing inactivity.

Sales of European sports products were below fiscal 2005 levels which was in part a reflection of the absence of products associated with the European Football Championship, which occurs once every four years. In addition, sales of both the Premier League collection in the U.K. and Calcio in Italy were lower than in fiscal 2005. In fiscal 2007, the Company will be marketing products featuring the World Cup, another soccer tournament held every four years.

Finally, sales from WizKids, a developer and marketer of strategy games acquired in July 2003, increased on the strength of a new internally-created category, constructible strategy games, and specifically Pirates products. However, weakness in the gaming industry is expected to put pressure on 2007 sales, at least through the first half, causing the Company to place greater focus on core properties and be more selective in new offerings.

Fiscal 2005 versus 2004

In fiscal 2005, the Company's consolidated net sales decreased 0.2% to $294.2 million from $294.9 million in fiscal 2004. Stronger foreign currencies versus the prior year added $6.6 million to fiscal 2005 sales. Excluding the impact of stronger foreign currencies, net sales decreased 2.5%.

Worldwide net sales of the Confectionery segment decreased 2.3% to $143.8 million in 2005 from $147.2 million in 2004. Stronger foreign currencies provided a $2.7 million benefit to fiscal 2005 sales. Confectionery products accounted for 49% of the Company's net sales in 2005 and 50% in 2004.

Fiscal 2005 U.S. confectionery sales were impacted in part by industry trends such as consumer nutritional concerns and retail consolidation, particularly in the first nine months of the year. Incremental sales of chewy candy products and strong gains on Juicy Drop Pop contributed favorably to results. For the full year, declines in U.S. confectionery sales of 2.8% were in line with trends in the non-chocolate industry.

Net sales of international confectionery products were also down comparatively in fiscal 2005 due to strong 2004 performance of both Push Pop Flip N'Dip in Japan and Yu-Gi-Oh! candy products in Europe. International sales represented 31% of total confectionery sales in each of fiscal 2005 and fiscal 2004.

Net sales of the Entertainment segment increased 1.9% in fiscal 2005 to $150.5 million. Stronger foreign currencies provided a $3.9 million benefit to fiscal 2005 sales. Entertainment products represented 51% of the Company's net sales in 2005 and 50% in fiscal 2004.

Within the Entertainment segment, sales from WizKids increased $6 million to $22 million, reflecting a full year of ownership in fiscal 2005 versus a partial year in fiscal 2004. In late fiscal 2005, WizKids created a new product category, constructible strategy games, and launched two new products, Pirates and Football Flix. In addition, sales of European sports products increased in fiscal 2005, reflecting the inclusion of products featuring the European Football Championship held once every four years.

Net sales of U.S. sports products were below the prior year, a function of the absence of a NHL hockey season and continued industry softness in general. The Company believes that this downtrend is due largely to the proliferation of card and memorabilia products and significantly higher price points.

As anticipated, sales of Internet products were below year ago levels in fiscal 2005 as the Company reduced advertising support and explored new directions for this venture. As a result, Internet operations were virtually breakeven in fiscal 2005 versus a loss of almost $3 million in fiscal 2004.

Finally, fiscal 2005 sales of non-sports publishing products were impacted by the absence of strong licenses, particularly in the fourth quarter. However, during the year, WWE, Barbie, Pokemon and Yu-Gi-Oh! were solid contributors in Europe and Garbage Pail Kids performed well in the U.S.

RESULTS OF OPERATIONS

	Fiscal Year Ended					
	February 25, 2006		February 26, 2005		February 28, 2004	
Net sales	$293,838	100.0%	$294,231	100.0%	$294,917	100.0%
Cost of sales	198,054	67.4%	189,200	64.3%	191,213	64.8%
Gross profit	95,784	32.6%	105,031	35.7%	103,704	35.2%
Sales, general and administrative expenses	98,096	33.4%	92,350	31.4%	87,527	29.7%
(Loss) income from operations	(2,312)	(0.8%)	12,681	4.3%	16,177	5.5%

Fiscal 2006 versus 2005

Fiscal 2006 consolidated gross profit as a percentage of net sales was 32.6% versus 35.7% in 2005. Margins this year were negatively impacted by increases in returns provisions, reported as a net against gross sales. Higher returns resulted from a softer Italian entertainment market and WizKid's expansion into new products and markets. Increased royalty costs driven by the higher mix of royalty-bearing U.S. sports sales and an increase in the effective royalty rate on Premier League products due to lower sales, also put pressure on gross profit margins.

Selling, general & administrative expenses ("SG&A") increased as a percentage of net sales to 33.4% in 2006 from 31.4% in 2005. SG&A dollar spending increased to $98.1 million in 2006 from $92.4 million. The primary cause of higher 2006 SG&A is one-time costs associated with the implementation of strategic initiatives totaling $4.2 million. These include severance and pension costs of $3.7 million related to a corporate restructuring, $0.3 million in costs to move Bazooka production to a less expensive manufacturer and a one-time expense of $0.2 million related to the freeze of our pension plan. Additionally, higher 2006 overhead costs reflect the impact of inflation on salaries and health care costs as well as consulting fees incurred in relation to systems implementation, Sarbanes-Oxley and strategic planning initiatives. Fiscal 2006 overhead cost comparisons benefited from a $1.8 million WizKids' legal settlement net of legal fees and the absence of a $1.9 million fine paid to the European Commission in 2005.

Also within SG&A, full year advertising and marketing expenses of $26.8 million were $3.5 million above 2005 due to the reinstatement of historical levels of spending for the U.S. confectionery business, advertising support for WizKids' new product format and media for Wacky Packages in the U.S.

Net interest income increased slightly to $2.9 million in fiscal 2006 from $2.7 million in fiscal 2005, reflecting rising interest rates.

In fiscal 2006, the Company had a tax benefit versus an effective tax rate of 26.8% in fiscal 2005. The tax benefit was a function of a low earnings base combined with the reversal of tax reserves as a result of a successful IRS tax audit and the Company's tax planning initiatives.

The Company sold thePit.com Internet operations to a third party in January 2006. Accordingly, financial results for this operation have been reclassified and are reported as Loss from discontinued operations – net of tax. In fiscal 2006, this loss, including the asset write-off, totaled $2.7 million.

Net income in fiscal 2006 was $1.2 million, or $0.03 per diluted share, versus $10.9 million, or $0.26 per diluted share in 2005.

Fiscal 2005 versus 2004

Financial results for thePit.com Internet operations have been reclassified to the Discontinued Operations line. See Note 7 – Discontinued Operations – thePit.com.

Fiscal 2005 consolidated gross profit as a percentage of net sales was 35.7%, up from 35.2% in 2004. Fiscal 2005 margins were favorably impacted by lower obsolescence costs following abnormally high write-offs at WizKids and the domestic confectionery and European publishing businesses in fiscal 2004. Improved gross profit margins also reflected lower tooling and mold costs on WizKids and European confectionery products. Partially offsetting these improvements were higher autograph and relic costs on U.S. sports cards and an increase in effective royalties associated with England Premier League products.

Selling, general & administrative expenses increased as a percentage of net sales to 31.4% in 2005 from 29.7% in the prior year. SG&A dollar spending increased to $92.4 million in 2005 from $87.5 million. A $1.9 million fine paid to the European Commission and the full year of WizKids ownership versus a partial year in 2004, were the primary reasons for the dollar increase. Additionally, higher professional fees, in particular legal, Sarbanes-Oxley and consulting-related expenses, impacted fiscal 2005 SG&A. The Company estimates fees paid to third parties related to Sarbanes-Oxley Section 404 compliance were approximately $1.1 million in 2005.

Within SG&A, full year advertising and marketing expenses of $23.3 million were $0.5 million below 2004 due to reduced spending on U.S. confectionery and Internet products, partially offset by increased marketing activity overseas. U.S. confectionery advertising exceeded historical levels in the fourth quarter.

Net interest income increased slightly to $2.7 million in fiscal 2005 from $2.4 million in fiscal 2004, reflecting rising interest rates and higher average investment balances.

The fiscal 2005 effective tax rate was 26.8% versus 26.7% in fiscal 2004.

Net income in fiscal 2005 was $10.9 million, or $0.26 per diluted share, versus $12.9 million, or $0.31 per diluted share in 2004. Excluding the impact of the non-tax deductible European Commission fine, fiscal 2005 net income was $12.8 million, or $0.31 per diluted share.

Quarterly Comparisons

Management believes that quarter-to-quarter comparisons of sales and operating results are affected by a number of factors. The Company's sales of Confectionery products are generally stronger in the first two fiscal quarters of the year. However, sales can be significantly impacted by the introduction of new products and line extensions as well as by advertising and consumer and trade support programs.

In the Entertainment segment, sales of U.S. sports card products are sold throughout the year, spanning the three major sports seasons in which the Company currently participates, i.e. baseball, football, and basketball. The new baseball agreement condensed the period during which baseball products are sold causing certain products previously sold in the third quarter to be pushed to the fourth quarter of fiscal 2006. Topps Europe's sales generally of sports sticker album products are driven largely by shipments of Premier League Soccer products, with much of the sales activity occurring in the fourth fiscal quarter. Sales of non-sports cards, sticker albums and games tend to be impacted by the timing of product introductions and the property on which they are based, often peaking with the release of a movie or the rise in popularity of a particular licensed property.

The net result of the above factors is that quarterly results vary. See Note 22 of Notes to Consolidated Financial Statements.

Inflation

In the opinion of management, inflation has not had a material effect on the operations or financial results of the Company.

Liquidity and Capital Resources

Management believes that the Company has adequate means to meet its liquidity and capital resource needs over the foreseeable future as a result of the combination of cash on hand, anticipated cash from operations and credit line availability.

The Company entered into a credit agreement with Chase Manhattan Bank on September 14, 2004. The agreement provides for a $30.0 million unsecured facility to cover revolver and letter of credit needs and expires on September 13, 2007. With the exception of $0.6 million reserved for letters of credit, the $30.0 million credit line was available as of February 25, 2006. (See Note 11 – Long-Term Debt.)

The Company has presented its portfolio of auction rate securities as short-term investments. Year-over-year changes in the amounts of these securities are being shown under investing activities on the Consolidated Statement of Cash Flows.

As of February 25, 2006, the Company had $28.2 million in cash and cash equivalents and an additional $53.3 million in short-term investments, for a total of $81.4 million.

During fiscal 2006, the Company's net decrease in cash and cash equivalents was $8.3 million versus a decrease of $20.5 million in 2005. The net decrease in cash and cash equivalents and short-term investments combined was $25.0 million in fiscal 2006, versus an increase of $12.6 million in fiscal 2005.

Net cash used by operating activities in 2006 was $6.5 million versus cash generated by operating activities of $22.9 million in 2005. The fiscal 2006 cash use was primarily a function of the low level of net earnings as well as an increase in working capital resulting from a reduction in income taxes payable, higher inventories reflecting the acquisition of sports autographs and a build up of stock prior to a shift in Bazooka production and an increase in receivables driven by the strong sales and timing of U.S. sports card shipments.

Cash generated by investing activities in 2006 of $13.8 million largely reflects the net sale of $16.7 million of short-term investments. The Company also spent $2.9 million in capital expenditures, primarily for computer hardware and software related to the implementation of a the first phase of an ERP system, as well as for other IT-related investments in the U.S. and Europe. Fiscal 2007 capital spending is projected to be approximately $4 million, driven by investments in Ring Pop production equipment and computer software and hardware. Capital spending will be funded out of cash flow from operating activities.

Cash used in financing activities in 2006 of $12.5 million reflects $6.0 million of treasury stock purchases net of options exercised plus $6.5 million in dividend payments, versus $2.3 million in treasury stock purchases net of options exercised and $6.5 million in dividend payments in 2005. The increase in treasury stock purchases in 2006 is a result of the Company's 10b5-1 program, initiated mid-year, which provides for a minimum purchase of 500,000 shares a quarter, assuming the share price remains below a certain threshold.

Finally, the $3.1 million unfavorable effect of exchange rate changes on cash and cash equivalents, which is due to the impact of weaker currencies on foreign subsidiaries' cash balances when translated into U.S. dollars, was $4.1 million worse than in 2005. This change reflects a weakening of European currencies against the U.S. dollar in fiscal 2006, versus a strengthening in fiscal 2005.

In October 2001, the Company's Board of Directors authorized the repurchase of up to 5 million shares of Company common stock. During fiscal 2005, the Company purchased 444,400 shares at an average price of $9.25 per share. During the first half of fiscal 2006, the Company did not purchase any shares due to a strategic business review being performed by investment banking and consulting firms. In September 2005, the Company entered into a written trading plan that complies with Rule 10b5-1 under the Securities Exchange Act of 1934, as amended, which provides for the purchase of 500,000 shares for each of the next four quarters starting in the third quarter of fiscal 2006 at the prevailing market price, per share, subject to certain conditions. In addition, the Board of Directors increased the outstanding share authorization by 3,390,700 shares to 5 million shares. As of February 25, 2006, the Company had purchased 1,027,899 shares under this amended authorization, leaving 3,972,101 shares available for future purchases. See Note 15 - Capital Stock. The Company anticipates purchasing additional shares in the future to complete the authorization.

Contractual Obligations

Future minimum payments under existing key contractual obligations are as follows: (in thousands)

	Total	2007	2008	2009	2010	2011	Thereafter
Future payments under non-cancelable leases	$ 10,600	$ 2,579	$ 2,247	$ 2,128	$ 1,826	$1,284	$ 536
Purchase obligations	16,797	11,011	2,151	952	700	700	1,283
Future payments under royalty contracts	81,642	23,362	20,167	19,793	18,320	—	—
Total	$109,039	$36,952	$24,565	$22,873	$20,846	$1,984	$ 1,819

The Company anticipates making a payment of approximately $1.5 – 2.5 million in fiscal 2007 for the funding of its qualified pension plans.

Critical Accounting Policies

The preparation of financial statements in conformity with accounting principles generally accepted in the United States of America requires Topps management to make estimates and judgments that affect the reported amounts of revenue, expenses, assets, liabilities and the disclosure of contingent assets and liabilities. Actual results may differ from these estimates under different assumptions or conditions.

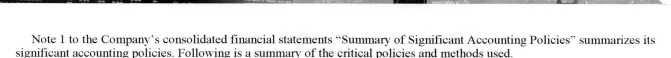

Note 1 to the Company's consolidated financial statements "Summary of Significant Accounting Policies" summarizes its significant accounting policies. Following is a summary of the critical policies and methods used.

Revenue Recognition: Revenue related to sales of the Company's products is generally recognized when products are shipped, the title and risk of loss has passed to the customer, the sales price is fixed or determinable and collectibility is reasonably assured. Sales made on a returnable basis are recorded net of a provision for estimated returns. These estimates are revised, as necessary, to reflect actual experience and market conditions.

Returns Provisions: In determining the provision for returns, the Company performs an in-depth review of wholesale and retail inventory levels, trends in product sell-through by sales channel, and other factors. The provision for returns was $29.8 million in 2006, $22.0 million in 2005 and $17.4 million in 2004, which equates to 10.2%, 7.5% and 5.9% of net sales, respectively. The recent increase in returns provisions is largely the result of a softer Italian entertainment market in fiscal 2006, unusually high returns of products associated with the European Football championship in fiscal 2005 and WizKids' expansion into new products and markets. An increase or decrease in the provision for returns by 1% of sales would decrease or increase operating income by approximately $3.0 million.

Goodwill and Intangible Assets: Management evaluates the recoverability of finite-lived intangible assets under the provisions of Statement of Financial Accounting Standards No. 144 *Accounting for the Impairment or Disposal of Long-lived Assets* ("SFAS 144") based on projected undiscounted cash flows. The recoverability of goodwill is evaluated in accordance with SFAS No. 142 *Goodwill and Other Intangible Assets* ("SFAS 142") and is based on a comparison of the fair value of a reporting unit with its carrying amount. Both the market approach (use of multiples from comparable companies) and the income approach (present value of future income streams) are used in determining the fair value of a reporting unit. The Company performs its annual test of impairment of goodwill as of the first day of its fourth quarter.

Intangible Assets: Intangible assets include trademarks and the value of sports, entertainment and proprietary product rights. Amortization is by the straight-line method over estimated lives of up to fifteen years. Management evaluates the recoverability of finite-lived intangible assets under the provisions of Statement of Financial Accounting Standards No. 144 *Accounting for the Impairment or Disposal of Long-lived Assets* ("SFAS 144") based on the projected undiscounted cash flows attributable to the individual assets, among other methods.

Accruals for Obsolete Inventory: The Company's accrual for obsolete inventory reflects the cost of items in inventory not anticipated to be sold or anticipated to be sold at less than cost. This accrual may be deemed necessary as a result of discontinued items and packaging or a reduction in forecasted sales. The provision for obsolete inventory was $5.4 million in fiscal 2006, $4.9 million in fiscal 2005 and $7.5 million in fiscal 2004, which equates to 1.8%, 1.7% and 2.5% of net sales, respectively. An increase or decrease in the provision for obsolescence by 1% of sales would decrease or increase operating income by approximately $3.0 million.

Income Taxes: Deferred tax assets and liabilities represent the tax effects of temporary book-tax differences which will become payable or refundable in future periods. The Company has accrued tax reserves for probable exposures and, as a result, any assessments resulting from current tax audits should not have a material adverse effect on the Company's consolidated net income.

Disclosures About Market Risk

There is no material risk to financial results due to market risk. The Company's exposure to market risk is largely related to the impact of mark-to-market changes in foreign currency rates on forward contracts. As of February 25, 2006, the Company had $21.0 million in forward contracts which were entered into for the purpose of reducing the impact of changes in foreign currency rates associated with firm and forecasted receipts and disbursements.

13

The Company's primary exchange rate exposure is with the Euro against the British pound, the Japanese yen and the U.S. dollar. At maturity, the proceeds or outlays from the foreign exchange contracts offset a corresponding additional or reduced outlay in the underlying currency. The recognition of mark-to-market gains and losses on these contracts accelerates the gains and losses that would otherwise be recognized when the contracts mature and generally does not result in an incremental impact on earnings or cash flows. The Company has no long-term debt and does not engage in any commodity-related derivative transactions.

New Accounting Pronouncements

In 2004, the Financial Accounting Standards Board ("FASB") issued FASB Statement No. 151, *Inventory Costs,* to clarify the accounting for abnormal amounts of idle facility expense, freight, handling costs, and wasted material (spoilage). This statement is effective for annual periods beginning after June 15, 2005 and requires that those items be recognized as current period charges regardless of whether they meet the criterion of "so abnormal" as defined by Accounting Research Bulletin No. 43. The provisions of this Statement are effective for inventory costs incurred during fiscal years beginning after June 15, 2005. The Company will adopt this Statement on February 26, 2006 and expects that the adoption will not have a material effect on the Company's consolidated financial statements.

In 2004, the FASB issued Statement No. 123 (revised 2004), *Share-Based Payments* ("SFAS 123R"). This Statement requires that the cost resulting from all share-based payment transactions be recognized in the financial statements and establishes fair value as the measurement objective in accounting for all share-based payment arrangements. The Company will adopt SFAS 123R using the modified prospective basis on February 26, 2006. The adoption of this Statement is expected to result in compensation expense of approximately $200,000 in fiscal 2007 (unaudited) related to unvested options outstanding at February 25, 2006. The estimate of future stock-based compensation expense is affected by the Company's stock price, the number of stock-based awards that may be granted in fiscal 2007, fluctuation in the Company's valuation assumptions and the related tax effect.

In 2004, the FASB issued FSP No. 109-2, *Accounting and Disclosure Guidance for the Foreign Earnings Repatriation Provision with the American Job Creation Act of 2004.* FSP No. 109-2 provides guidance for reporting and disclosing certain foreign earnings that are repatriated, as defined by the Act, which was signed into law on October 22, 2004. The Act would have allowed the Company to deduct 85% of certain qualifying foreign earnings available for repatriation to the United States during the fiscal years ended 2005 and 2006. The Company evaluated the potential impact of repatriating earnings and decided not to do so under the provisions of the Act.

In 2004, the FASB issued SFAS No. 153, *Exchanges of Non-monetary Assets,* which eliminates the exception for non-monetary exchanges of similar productive assets and replaces it with a general exception for exchanges of non-monetary assets that do not have commercial substance. SFAS No. 153 will be effective for non-monetary asset exchanges occurring in fiscal periods beginning after June 15, 2005. The Company is currently evaluating the impact of adopting this standard in its future financial statements.

In 2005, FASB Interpretation No. 47, *Accounting for Conditional Asset Retirement Obligations,* an interpretation of FASB Statement No. 143, *Accounting for Asset Retirement Obligations* required that an entity recognize the fair value of a liability for a conditional asset retirement obligation in the period in which it is incurred if a reasonable estimate of fair value can be made. An asset retirement obligation would be reasonably estimable if (a) it is evident that the fair value of the obligation is embodied in the acquisition price of the asset, (b) an active market exists for the transfer of the obligation, or (c) sufficient information exists to apply to an expected present value technique. FASB Interpretation No. 47 became effective for companies with fiscal years ending after December 15, 2005. The adoption of this statement did not have an impact on the Company's consolidated financial statements.

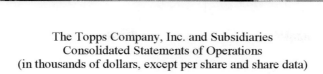

The Topps Company, Inc. and Subsidiaries
Consolidated Statements of Operations
(in thousands of dollars, except per share and share data)

		Fiscal Year Ended	
	February 25, 2006	February 26, 2005 (As restated, see Note 2)	February 28, 2004 (As restated, see Note 2)
Net sales	$ 293,838	$ 294,231	$ 294,917
Cost of sales	198,054	189,200	191,213
Gross profit on sales	95,784	105,031	103,704
Selling, general and administrative expenses	98,096	92,350	87,527
(Loss) income from operations	(2,312)	12,681	16,177
Interest income, net	2,912	2,706	2,426
Income before benefit (provision) for income taxes	600	15,387	18,603
Benefit (provision) for income taxes	3,346	(4,119)	(4,975)
Net income from continuing operations	3,946	11,268	13,628
Loss from discontinued operations — net of tax	2,707	353	744
Net income	$ 1,239	$ 10,915	$ 12,884
Basic net income per share:			
- From continuing operations	$ 0.10	$ 0.28	$ 0.34
- From discontinued operations	$ (0.07)	$ (0.01)	$ (0.02)
Basic net income per share	$ 0.03	$ 0.27	$ 0.32
Diluted net income per share:			
- From continuing operations	$ 0.10	$ 0.27	$ 0.33
- From discontinued operations	(0.07)	$ (0.01)	$ (0.02)
Diluted net income per share	$ 0.03	$ 0.26	$ 0.31
Weighted average shares outstanding			
- basic	40,349,000	40,471,000	40,604,000
- diluted	41,163,000	41,327,000	41,515,000

See Notes to Consolidated Financial Statements

15

The Topps Company, Inc. and Subsidiaries
Consolidated Balance Sheets
(in thousands of dollars, except per share and share data)

	February 25, 2006	February 26, 2005 (As restated, see Note 2)
ASSETS		
Current assets:		
Cash and cash equivalents	$ 28,174	$ 36,442
Short-term investments	53,269	69,955
Accounts receivable, net	31,180	27,851
Inventories	36,781	32,936
Income tax receivable	1,407	338
Deferred tax assets	5,687	5,380
Prepaid expenses and other current assets	11,134	14,541
Total current assets	167,632	187,443
Property, plant and equipment, net	11,028	11,968
Goodwill	63,405	67,566
Intangible assets, net	6,424	8,544
Deferred tax assets	6,334	3,022
Other assets	13,815	11,847
Total assets	$268,638	$ 290,390
LIABILITIES AND STOCKHOLDERS' EQUITY		
Current liabilities:		
Accounts payable	$ 11,263	$ 12,658
Accrued expenses and other liabilities	25,345	27,485
Income taxes payable	3,311	7,390
Total current liabilities	39,919	47,533
Accrued pension obligation	24,083	23,689
Total liabilities	64,002	71,222
Stockholders' equity:		
Preferred stock, par value $.01 per share authorized 10,000,000 shares, none issued	—	—
Common stock, par value $.01 per share, authorized 100,000,000 shares; issued 49,244,000 shares as of February 25, 2006 and February 26, 2005	492	492
Additional paid-in capital	28,644	28,293
Treasury stock, 9,539,000 shares and 8,790,000 shares as of February 25, 2006 and February 26, 2005, respectively	(91,376)	(85,060)
Retained earnings	269,954	275,205
Minimum pension liability adjustment	(5,551)	(5,824)
Cumulative foreign currency adjustment	2,473	6,062
Total stockholders' equity	204,636	219,168
Total liabilities and stockholders' equity	$268,638	$ 290,390

See Notes to Consolidated Financial Statements

16

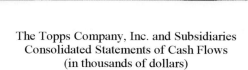

The Topps Company, Inc. and Subsidiaries
Consolidated Statements of Cash Flows
(in thousands of dollars)

	Fiscal Year Ended		
	February 25, 2006	February 26, 2005 (As restated, see Note 2)	February 28, 2004 (As restated, see Note 2)
Cash flows (used in) provided by operating activities:			
Net income from continuing operations	$ 3,946	$ 11,268	$ 13,628
Adjustments to reconcile net income to cash flows:			
Depreciation and amortization	5,829	5,833	5,768
Deferred taxes	(3,749)	2,261	1,523
Net effect of changes in:			
Accounts receivable	(3,335)	2,258	(2,538)
Inventories	(4,086)	84	501
Income tax receivable/payable	(5,153)	585	(2,256)
Prepaid expense and other current assets	3,376	(2,847)	(1,048)
Payables and other current liabilities	(3,068)	2,329	(7,083)
All other	445	781	3,737
Cash (used in) provided by operating activities – continuing operations	(5,795)	22,552	12,232
Cash (used in) provided by operating activities – discontinued operations	(748)	378	(278)
Cash (used in) provided by operating activities – total	(6,543)	22,930	11,954
Cash flows from investing activities:			
Purchase of business	—	—	(28,650)
Purchase of short-term investments	(291,567)	(155,487)	(49,953)
Sale of short-term investments	308,253	122,410	41,650
Purchases of property, plant and equipment	(2,885)	(2,625)	(2,720)
Cash provided by (used in) investing activities – continuing operations	13,801	(35,702)	(39,673)
Cash provided by (used in) investing activities – discontinued operations	—	(9)	(122)
Cash provided by (used in) investing activities – total	13,801	(35,711)	(39,795)
Cash flows from financing activities:			
Dividends paid	(6,490)	(6,477)	(4,868)
Exercise of stock options	1,831	1,814	1,770
Purchase of treasury stock	(7,796)	(4,123)	(2,781)
Cash used in financing activities – continuing operations	(12,455)	(8,786)	(5,879)
Effect of exchange rate changes on cash and cash equivalents	(3,071)	1,050	4,995
Net decrease in cash and cash equivalents	(8,268)	(20,517)	(28,725)
Cash and cash equivalents at beginning of year	36,442	56,959	85,684
Cash and cash equivalents at end of year	$ 28,174	$ 36,442	$ 56,959

17

	Fiscal Year Ended		
	February 25, 2006	February 26, 2005 (As restated, see Note 2)	February 28, 2004 (As restated, see Note 2)
Supplemental disclosures of cash flow information:			
Interest paid	$ 107	$ 258	$ 322
Income taxes paid	$ 2,082	$ 3,883	$ 6,398

See Notes to Consolidated Financial Statements

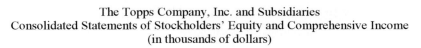

The Topps Company, Inc. and Subsidiaries
Consolidated Statements of Stockholders' Equity and Comprehensive Income
(in thousands of dollars)

	Total	Common Stock	Additional Paid-in Capital	Treasury Stock	Retained Earnings	Accumulated Other Comprehensive (Loss) Income
Balance at March 1, 2003 as originally reported	$196,768	$ 492	$ 27,344	$(80,791)	$262,877	$ (13,154)
Effect of restatement (see Note 2)	(126)				(126)	
Stockholders' equity as of March 1, 2003 (As restated, see Note 2)	196,642	492	27,344	(80,791)	262,751	(13,154)
Net income (As restated, see Note 2)	12,884	—	—	—	12,884	—
Translation adjustment	6,823	—	—	—	—	6,823
Minimum pension liability, net of tax	870	—	—	—	—	870
Total comprehensive income (As restated, see Note 2)	20,577	—	—	—	12,884	7,693
Cash dividends	(4,868)	—	—	—	(4,868)	—
Purchase of treasury stock	(2,781)	—	—	(2,781)	—	—
Exercise of employee stock options	1,770	—	485	1,285	—	—
Stockholders' equity as of February 28, 2004 (As restated, see Note 2)	211,340	492	27,829	(82,287)	270,767	(5,461)
Net income (As restated, see Note 2)	10,915	—	—	—	10,915	—
Translation adjustment	1,864	—	—	—	—	1,864
Minimum pension liability, net of tax	3,835	—	—	—	—	3,835
Total comprehensive income (As restated, see Note 2)	16,614	—	—	—	10,915	5,699
Cash dividends	(6,477)	—	—	—	(6,477)	—
Purchase of treasury stock	(4,123)	—	—	(4,123)	—	—
Exercise of employee stock options	1,814	—	464	1,350	—	—
Stockholders' equity as of February 26, 2005 (As restated, see Note 2)	219,168	492	28,293	(85,060)	275,205	238
Net income	1,239	—	—	—	1,239	—
Translation adjustment	(3,589)	—	—	—	—	(3,589)
Minimum pension liability, net of tax	273	—	—	—	—	273
Total comprehensive income	(2,077)	—	—	—	1,239	(3,316)
Cash dividends	(6,490)	—	—	—	(6,490)	—
Purchase of treasury stock	(7,796)	—	—	(7,796)	—	—
Exercise of employee stock options	1,831	—	351	1,480	—	—
Stockholders' equity as of February 25, 2006	$204,636	$ 492	$ 28,644	$(91,376)	$269,954	$ (3,078)

See Notes to Consolidated Financial Statements

NOTE 1 – SUMMARY OF SIGNIFICANT ACCOUNTING POLICIES

Principles of Consolidation: The consolidated financial statements include the accounts of The Topps Company, Inc. and its subsidiaries (the "Company"). All intercompany items and transactions have been eliminated in consolidation.

The Company and its subsidiaries operate and report financial results on a fiscal year of 52 or 53 weeks which ends on the Saturday closest to the end of February. Fiscal 2004, fiscal 2005 and fiscal 2006 were all comprised of 52 weeks.

Foreign Currency Translation: The financial statements of subsidiaries outside the United States, except those subsidiaries located in highly inflationary economies or where costs are primarily U.S. dollar-based, are generally measured using the local currency as the functional currency. Assets and liabilities of these subsidiaries are translated at the rates of exchange as of the balance sheet date, with the resultant translation adjustments included in accumulated other comprehensive income. Income and expense items are translated at the average exchange rate for the month. Gains and losses from foreign currency transactions of these subsidiaries are included in net income. The Company has no foreign subsidiaries operating in highly inflationary economies or where inventory costs are U.S. dollar-based for which the financial statements are measured using the U.S. dollar as the functional currency.

Derivative Financial Instruments: From time to time, the Company enters into contracts that are intended and effective as hedges of foreign currency risks associated with the anticipated purchase of confectionery inventories from foreign suppliers. It also enters into contracts in order to hedge risks associated with the collection of receivables from certain foreign countries. The Company does not hold or issue derivative financial instruments for trading purposes.

Cash Equivalents: The Company considers investments in highly liquid debt instruments with a maturity of three months or less to be cash equivalents.

Short-term investments: Investments in auction rate instruments as well as bank certificates of deposit and other debt investments with maturities in excess of three months and subject to an early withdrawal penalty are reported as short-term investments.

Inventories: Inventories are stated at lower of cost or market. Cost is determined on the first-in, first-out basis.

Property, Plant and Equipment ("PP&E"): PP&E is stated at cost. Depreciation is computed using the straight-line method based on estimated useful lives of twenty-five years for buildings, three to twelve years for machinery, equipment and software, and the remaining lease period for leasehold improvements. Expenditures for new property, plant or equipment that substantially extend the useful life of an asset are capitalized. Ordinary repair and maintenance costs are expensed as incurred. In accordance with Statement of Financial Accounting Standards ("SFAS") No. 144, *Accounting for the Impairment or Disposal of Long-Lived Assets* ("SFAS 144"), the Company periodically evaluates the carrying value of its PP&E for circumstances which may indicate impairment.

Goodwill and Intangible Assets: Management evaluates the recoverability of finite-lived intangible assets under the provisions of SFAS 144 based on projected undiscounted cash flows. The recoverability of goodwill is evaluated in accordance with SFAS No. 142 *Goodwill and Other Intangible Assets* ("SFAS 142") and is based on a comparison of the fair value of a reporting unit with its carrying amount. Both the market approach (use of multiples from comparable companies) and the income approach (present value of future income streams) are used in determining the fair value of a reporting unit. The Company performs its annual test of impairment of goodwill as of the first day of its fourth quarter.

Revenue Recognition: The Company recognizes revenue when the following criteria are met: the products are shipped, the title and risk of loss has passed to the customer, the sales price is fixed or determinable and collectibility is reasonably assured. Sales made on a returnable basis are recorded net of a provision for estimated returns. These estimates are revised, as necessary, to reflect actual experience and market conditions. In fiscal 2006, approximately 68% of the

Company's sales were made on a returnable basis, and the returns expense for the years ended February 25, 2006, February 26, 2005 and February 28, 2004 were $29.8 million, $22.0 million and $17.4 million, respectively.

Estimates: The preparation of financial statements in conformity with generally accepted accounting principles requires management to make estimates which affect the reporting of assets and liabilities as of the dates of the financial statements and revenues and expenses during the reporting period. These estimates primarily relate to the provision for sales returns, allowance for doubtful accounts and inventory obsolescence. In each case, prior to booking an accounting entry, the Company does an in-depth review of available information including wholesale and retail inventory levels and product sell-through in the case of returns, receivables aging and account credit-worthiness for the allowance for doubtful accounts and component and finished goods inventory levels and product sell-through for obsolescence. Actual results could differ from these estimates.

Income Taxes: The Company provides for deferred income taxes resulting from temporary differences between the valuation of assets and liabilities in the financial statements and the carrying amounts for tax purposes. Such differences are measured using the tax rates and laws in effect for the years in which the differences are expected to reverse.

Employee Stock Options: The Company accounts for stock-based employee compensation based on the intrinsic value of stock options granted in accordance with the provisions of APB 25, *Accounting for Stock Issued to Employees*. The pro forma effect, had the Company accounted for stock-based employee compensation based on the fair value of stock options granted in accordance with SFAS 123, *Accounting for Stock-Based Compensation,* is shown below:

	As Reported	Stock-based Employee Compensation	Pro forma
	(In thousands of dollars, except share data)		
2006			
Net income	$ 1,239	$ (312)	$ 927
Earnings per share			
Basic	$ 0.03		$ 0.02
Diluted	$ 0.03		$ 0.02
2005			
Net income	$10,915	$ (1,054)	$ 9,861
Earnings per share			
Basic	$ 0.27		$ 0.24
Diluted	$ 0.26		$ 0.24
2004			
Net income	$12,884	$ (1,247)	$11,637
Earnings per share			
Basic	$ 0.32		$ 0.29
Diluted	$ 0.31		$ 0.28

Options typically vest within a three-year period. In determining the preceding pro forma amounts under SFAS 123, the fair value of each option grant is estimated as of the date of grant using the Black-Scholes option pricing model. Following are the key assumptions: $0.16 per share dividend on fiscal 2006, 2005 and 2004 options; risk free interest rate, estimated volatility and expected life as follows: fiscal 2006 options — 4.4%, 29% and 5.8 years, respectively; 2005 options — 4.4%, 32% and 5.8 years, respectively; fiscal 2004 options — 4.4%, 38% and 6.5 years, respectively. Changes in assumptions used could have a material effect upon the pro-forma results.

Advertising and Marketing Expenses: Advertising and marketing expenses (which encompass media spending, customer promotions and research) included in selling, general and administrative expenses amounted to $26,772,000 in fiscal 2006, $23,253,000 in fiscal 2005 and $23,820,000 in fiscal 2004. Advertising and marketing expenses are recognized as incurred. Costs relating to future periods are classified as prepaid.

Reclassifications: Certain items in the prior years' financial statements have been reclassified to conform with current year's presentation.

Research and Development Expenses: Research and development costs are included in selling, general and administrative expenses and are recognized as incurred.

New Accounting Pronouncements

In 2004, the Financial Accounting Standards Board ("FASB") issued FASB Statement No. 151, *Inventory Costs,* to clarify the accounting for abnormal amounts of idle facility expense, freight, handling costs, and wasted material (spoilage). This statement is effective for annual periods beginning after June 15, 2005 and requires that those items be recognized as current period charges regardless of whether they meet the criterion of "so abnormal" as defined by Accounting Research Bulletin No. 43. The provisions of this Statement are effective for inventory costs incurred during fiscal years beginning after June 15, 2005. The Company will adopt this Statement on February 26, 2006 and expects that the adoption will not have a material effect on the Company's consolidated financial statements.

In 2004, the FASB issued Statement No. 123 (revised 2004), *Share-Based Payments* ("SFAS 123R"). This Statement requires that the cost resulting from all share-based payment transactions be recognized in the financial statements and establishes fair value as the measurement objective in accounting for all share-based payment arrangements. The Company will adopt SFAS 123R using the modified prospective basis on February 26, 2006. The adoption of this Statement is expected to result in compensation expense of approximately $200,000 in fiscal 2007 (unaudited) related to unvested options outstanding at February 25, 2006. The estimate of future stock-based compensation expense is affected by the Company's stock price, the number of stock-based awards that may be granted in fiscal 2007, fluctuation in the Company's valuation assumptions and the related tax effect.

In 2004, the FASB issued FSP No. 109-2, *Accounting and Disclosure Guidance for the Foreign Earnings Repatriation Provision with the American Job Creation Act of 2004.* FSP No. 109-2 provides guidance for reporting and disclosing certain foreign earnings that are repatriated, as defined by the Act, which was signed into law on October 22, 2004. The Act would have allowed the Company to deduct 85% of certain qualifying foreign earnings available for repatriation to the United States during the fiscal years ended 2005 and 2006. The Company evaluated the potential impact of repatriating earnings and decided not to do so under the provisions of the Act.

In 2004, the FASB issued SFAS No. 153, *Exchanges of Non-monetary Assets,* which eliminates the exception for non-monetary exchanges of similar productive assets and replaces it with a general exception for exchanges of non-monetary assets that do not have commercial substance. SFAS No. 153 will be effective for non-monetary asset exchanges occurring in fiscal periods beginning after June 15, 2005. The Company is currently evaluating the impact of adopting this standard in its future financial statements.

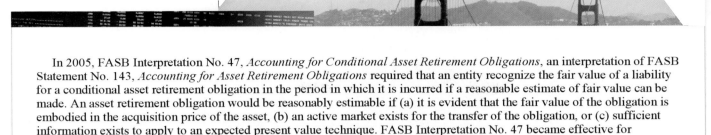

In 2005, FASB Interpretation No. 47, *Accounting for Conditional Asset Retirement Obligations*, an interpretation of FASB Statement No. 143, *Accounting for Asset Retirement Obligations* required that an entity recognize the fair value of a liability for a conditional asset retirement obligation in the period in which it is incurred if a reasonable estimate of fair value can be made. An asset retirement obligation would be reasonably estimable if (a) it is evident that the fair value of the obligation is embodied in the acquisition price of the asset, (b) an active market exists for the transfer of the obligation, or (c) sufficient information exists to apply to an expected present value technique. FASB Interpretation No. 47 became effective for companies with fiscal years ending after December 15, 2005. The adoption of this statement did not have an impact on the Company's consolidated financial statements.

NOTE 2 – RESTATEMENT OF CONSOLIDATED FINANCIAL STATEMENTS

Subsequent to the issuance of the consolidated financial statements for the year ended February 26, 2005, the Company determined (i) that upon performing a full property, plant and equipment analysis and implementation of a new fixed asset tracking system various assets that had been abandoned, sold or impaired, were still being depreciated at their original cost values, as well as that errors had been made in the calculation related to the depreciation of certain assets, and (ii) that there were errors in the prior years' state tax provision raised by the Company while preparing its 2006 tax provision primarily related to a deferred state tax over-accrual in 2004 that was not properly reversed in 2005. As a result, the Company has restated the accompanying fiscal 2005 and 2004 consolidated financial statements.

The impact of the restatement on the Company's beginning retained earnings as of March 1, 2003 was a reduction of $126,000.

The significant impacts of the restatement on the consolidated financial statements are as follows (in thousands, except per share amounts):

	As of February 26, 2005	
	As Previously Reported	As Restated
	(In thousands)	
Consolidated Balance Sheet:		
Deferred tax assets	$ 3,616	$ 5,380
Total current assets	185,679	187,443
Property, plant and equipment, net	12,553	11,968
Deferred tax assets	4,222	3,022
Total assets	290,411	290,390
Retained earnings	275,226	275,205
Total stockholders' equity	$ 219,189	$219,168

	Fiscal Year Ended February 26, 2005			
		Effect of		
	As Previously Reported	Discontinued Operations (1)	Restatement	As Restated
		(In thousands, except per share amounts)		
Consolidated Statement of Operations:				
Selling, general and administrative expenses	$ 93,237	(735)	(152)	$ 92,350
Income from operations	11,967	562	152	12,681
Income before provision for income taxes	14,673	562	152	15,387
Provision for income taxes	3,674	209	236	4,119
Net income	10,999	—	(84)	10,915
Net income per share — basic	0.27	—	—	0.27
Net income per share — diluted	$ 0.27	—	(0.01)	$ 0.26

	Fiscal Year Ended February 28, 2004			
		Effect of		
	As Previously Reported	Discontinued Operations (1)	Restatement	As Restated
		(In thousands, except per share amounts)		
Selling, general and administrative expenses	$ 89,302	(1,454)	(321)	$ 87,527
Income from operations	14,595	1,261	321	16,177
Income before provision for income taxes	17,021	1,261	321	18,603
Provision for income taxes	4,326	517	132	4,975
Net income	12,695	—	189	12,884
Net income per share — basic	0.31	—	0.01	0.32
Net income per share — diluted	$ 0.31	—	—	$ 0.31

(1) See Note 7 for a complete discussion of the discontinued operation.

The restatement did not impact the total amounts presented in the consolidated statements of cash flows for net cash (used in) provided by operating activities, net cash provided by (used in) investing activities or net cash provided by financing activities, although it did impact certain components of cash flows from operating activities.

NOTE 3 – EARNINGS PER SHARE

Earnings per share ("EPS") is computed in accordance with SFAS No. 128 "*Earnings Per Share*". Basic EPS is computed using weighted average shares outstanding. Diluted EPS is computed using weighted average shares outstanding plus additional shares issued as if in-the-money options were exercised (utilizing the treasury stock method).

The following table represents the computation of weighted average diluted shares outstanding:

	Fiscal Year Ended		
	February 25, 2006	February 26, 2005	February 28, 2004
Weighted average shares outstanding:			
Basic	40,349,000	40,471,000	40,604,000
Dilutive stock options	814,000	856,000	911,000
Diluted	41,163,000	41,327,000	41,515,000

In the above calculation, the impact of out-of-the-money options, (i.e. where the exercise price exceeds current market price) was not included as their inclusion would have had an antidilutive effect. These incremental shares totaled approximately 1,198,000 in 2006, 824,000 in 2005 and 1,070,000 in 2004.

NOTE 4 – ACCOUNTS RECEIVABLE

	February 25, 2006	February 26, 2005
	(in thousands of dollars)	
Gross receivables	$ 55,244	$ 51,265
Reserve for estimated returns	(21,181)	(20,824)
Other reserves	(2,883)	(2,590)
Net receivables	$ 31,180	$ 27,851

Other reserves consist of allowances for discounts, doubtful accounts and customer deductions for marketing promotion programs.

NOTE 5 — INVENTORIES

	February 25, 2006	February 26, 2005
	(in thousands of dollars)	
Raw materials	$10,123	$ 7,468
Work in process	4,623	3,703
Finished product	22,035	21,765
Total inventory	$36,781	$32,936

NOTE 6 — PROPERTY, PLANT AND EQUIPMENT, NET

	February 25, 2006	February 26, 2005
	(in thousands of dollars)	
Land	$ 42	$ 42
Buildings and improvements	2,606	2,722
Machinery, equipment and software	27,782	28,384
Total PP&E	30,430	31,148
Accumulated depreciation	(19,402)	(19,180)
Net PP&E	$ 11,028	$ 11,968

NOTE 7 – DISCONTINUED OPERATIONS — thePit.com

In August 2001, the Company acquired all the outstanding common stock of thePit.com, Inc., which operated a sports card exchange, for a net cash purchase price of $5.7 million. The acquisition was accounted for using the purchase method of accounting and resulted in recognizing $0.8 million in intangible assets and $4.1 million in goodwill. The Company included this subsidiary in the Entertainment segment of its business. The Company was unable to operate the subsidiary profitably and in January 2006 sold the subsidiary for $360,000, with scheduled payments to be made over four years.

Per Statement of Accounting Standards No. 144 *Accounting for the Impairment of Long-Lived Assets*, the net book value of the assets of thePit.com, Inc., which consisted primarily of the $4.1 million goodwill from the acquisition as well as smaller amounts of inventory and unamortized intangibles, was written down $2,432,000 net of tax to $360,000, which is the fair value of the assets based on the expected proceeds from the sale of the subsidiary.

The $2,432,000 write-down of the assets to fair value and, additionally, the $275,000 loss from operations net of tax of thePit.com, Inc. for fiscal 2006, which total $2,707,000, are being reported as Loss from discontinued operations – net of tax on a separate line on the Consolidated Statements of Operations.

Revenue for thePit.com for fiscal 2006, 2005, and 2004 was $987,000, $1,634,000 and $2,421,000, respectively, and pre-tax loss for thePit.com for fiscal 2006, 2005 and 2004 was $295,000, $468,000 and $1,167,000, respectively. The purchaser has paid the Company $30,000 of the $360,000 sales price as of February 25, 2006. The remaining $330,000 is reported in Prepaid expenses and other current assets and Other assets on the Consolidated Balance Sheet as of February 25, 2006. The Company has restated its Consolidated Statements of Cash Flows for the years ended February 26, 2005 and February 28, 2004 to reflect this discontinued operation.

NOTE 8 – GOODWILL AND INTANGIBLE ASSETS

Goodwill and Intangible Assets represent amounts paid for the purchase of businesses in excess of the fair value of the acquired assets. Intangible assets consist principally of licenses and contracts, intellectual property, and software; amortization is by the straight-line method over estimated lives of up to fifteen years. Goodwill represents the purchase price less the fair value of acquired assets and less the appraised value of the intangible assets. Goodwill is not amortized.

Licenses and contracts consist primarily of licensing rights to produce sticker albums featuring Premier League soccer players obtained as a part of the Merlin Publishing Group acquisition in July 1995. Intellectual property refers to rights including trademarks and copyrights related to branded products obtained as part of the July 2003 acquisition of Wizkids, LLC. Software and other consists of proprietary software developed by thePit.com for fiscal 2005. In connection with the disposal of thePit.com during fiscal 2006 (see Note 7), $0.1 million of intangible assets and $4.2 million of goodwill were written off in the third quarter of fiscal 2006.

Intangible assets consisted of the following as of February 25, 2006 and February 26, 2005:

| | February 25, 2006 | | |
	Gross Carrying Value	Accumulated Amortization	Net
	(in thousands of dollars)		
Licenses and contracts	$ 21,569	$ (18,611)	$2,958
Intellectual property	18,784	(15,318)	3,466
Software and other	2,482	(2,482)	—
Total intangibles	$ 42,835	$ (36,411)	$6,424

| | February 26, 2005 | | |
	Gross Carrying Value	Accumulated Amortization	Net
	(in thousands of dollars)		
Licenses and contracts	$ 21,569	$ (17,942)	$3,627
Intellectual property	18,784	(14,284)	4,500
Software and other	2,953	(2,811)	142
FAS 132 pension	275	—	275
Total intangibles	$ 43,581	$ (35,037)	$8,544

Useful lives of the Company's intangible assets have been established based on the intended use of such assets and their estimated period of future benefit, which are reviewed periodically. Useful lives are as follows:

Category	Useful Life	Weighted Average Remaining Useful Life
Licenses and contracts	15 years	4.4 years
Intellectual property	6 years	3.4 years

The weighted average remaining useful life for the Company's intangible assets in aggregate is 3.8 years. Over the next five years the Company expects the annual amortization of intangible assets to be as follows:

Fiscal Year	Amount
	(in thousands)
2007	$ 1,703
2008	$ 1,703
2009	$ 1,703
2010	$ 1,036
2011	$ 279

Following the write-down of the goodwill associated with thePit.com, Inc., reported goodwill was reduced from $67,566,000 as of February 26, 2005 to $63,405,000 as of February 25, 2006. Goodwill is broken out by business segment as follows:

	February 25, 2006	February 26, 2005
	(amounts in thousands)	
Confectionery	$ 7,699	$ 7,699
Entertainment	55,706	59,867
Total goodwill	$63,405	$67,566

Intangible assets and goodwill for the reporting units are tested for impairment on an annual basis and between annual tests in certain circumstances. The impairment test is conducted at the reporting unit level by comparing the reporting unit's carrying amount, including intangible assets and goodwill, to the fair value of the reporting unit. If the carrying amount of the reporting unit exceeds its fair value, a second step is performed to measure the amount of impairment, if any. Further, in the event that the carrying amount of the Company as a whole is greater than its market capitalization, there is a potential that some or all of its intangible assets and goodwill would be considered impaired. There can be no assurances given that future impairment tests of goodwill will not result in an impairment.

NOTE 9 — DEPRECIATION AND AMORTIZATION

	Fiscal Year Ended		
	February 25, 2006	February 26, 2005	February 28, 2004
	(in thousands of dollars)		
Depreciation expense	$ 3,542	$ 3,375	$ 3,312
Amortization of:			
Intangible assets	1,703	1,797	1,881
Compensation & other	500	570	452
Deferred financing fees	84	91	123
Total depreciation and amortization	$ 5,829	$ 5,833	$ 5,768

NOTE 10 — ACCRUED EXPENSES AND OTHER LIABILITIES

	Fiscal Year Ended	
	February 25, 2006	February 26, 2005
	(in thousands of dollars)	
Royalties	$ 6,864	$ 5,400
Advertising and marketing expenses	3,659	5,079
Employee compensation	2,938	4,031
Deferred revenue	828	1,555
Inventory in transit	1,647	1,363
Deferred rent expense	1,031	1,123
Other	8,378	8,934
Total accrued expenses and other liabilities	$25,345	$27,485

NOTE 11 — LONG-TERM DEBT

On September 14, 2004, the Company entered into a new credit agreement with JPMorgan Chase Bank. The agreement provides for a $30.0 million unsecured facility to cover revolver and letter of credit needs and expires on September 13, 2007. Interest rates are variable and a function of market rates and the Company's EBITDA. The credit agreement contains restrictions and prohibitions of a nature generally found in loan agreements of this type and requires the Company, among other things, to comply with certain financial covenants, limits the Company's ability to sell or acquire assets or borrow additional money and places certain restrictions on the purchase of Company shares and the payment of dividends. The Company cannot pay dividends and purchase the Company's shares where the total cash outlay exceeds $30 million in three consecutive quarters or $50 million over the term of the credit agreement.

The credit agreement may be terminated by the Company at any point over the three-year term (provided the Company repays all outstanding amounts thereunder) without penalty. With the exception of $0.6 million currently reserved for letters of credit, the $30.0 million credit line was available as of February 25, 2006.

NOTE 12 — INCOME TAXES

The Company provides for deferred income taxes resulting from temporary differences between the valuation of assets and liabilities in the financial statements and the carrying amounts for tax purposes. Such differences are measured using the enacted tax rates and laws that will be in effect when the differences are expected to reverse.

Total Benefit (provision) for income taxes for each year is as follows:

| | Fiscal Year Ended | | |
	February 25, 2006	February 26, 2005	February 28, 2004
	(in thousands of dollars)		
Continuing operations	$ 3,346	$(4,119)	$(4,975)
Discontinued operations	1,865	209	517
Total	$ 5,211	$(3,910)	$(4,458)

U.S. and foreign continuing operations contributed to income (loss) before provision for income taxes as follows :

| | Fiscal Year Ended | | |
	February 25, 2006	February 26, 2005	February 28, 2004
	(in thousands of dollars)		
United States	$ (106)	$12,364	$ 9,163
Europe	1,325	4,049	10,941
Canada	(1,011)	(1,282)	(996)
Latin America	392	256	(505)
Total	$ 600	$15,387	$18,603

Benefit (provision) for income taxes consists of:

	Fiscal Year Ended		
	February 25, 2006	February 26, 2005	February 28, 2004
	(in thousands of dollars)		
Current income tax benefit (provision):			
Federal	$1,074	$ 124	$ 19
Foreign	501	(1,031)	(2,771)
State and local	(532)	(1,081)	(186)
Total current	$1,043	$(1,988)	$(2,938)
Deferred income tax benefit (provision):			
Federal	$1,737	$(1,880)	$(1,454)
Foreign	(101)	(41)	(373)
State and local	667	(210)	(210)
Total deferred	$2,303	$(2,131)	$(2,037)
Total benefit (provision) for income taxes	$3,346	$(4,119)	$(4,975)

The total benefit (provision) for income taxes from continuing operations is less than the amount computed by applying the statutory federal income tax rate to income before benefit (provision) for income taxes. This difference is largely due to the fiscal 2006 reversal of certain tax reserves related to tax audits resolved in the current year and the impact of lower tax rates in foreign countries as shown below:

	Fiscal Year Ended		
	February 25, 2006	February 26, 2005	February 28, 2004
	(in thousands of dollars)		
Computed expected tax provision	$ (210)	$ (5,385)	$ (6,511)
Decrease (increase) in taxes resulting from:			
Effect of foreign operations	292	2,282	967
State and local taxes, net of federal tax effect	87	(917)	(308)
European Commission fine	—	(578)	—
Tax-exempt interest income	489	285	208
Reversal of reserve for tax exposure items	2,536	—	—
R & D tax credits	—	210	310
Meals and entertainment disallowance	(41)	(43)	(24)
Merchandise contributions	111	111	174
Medicare Part D prescription subsidy	84	—	—
Other items, net	(2)	(84)	209
Benefit (provision) for income taxes	$ 3,346	$ (4,119)	$ (4,975)

U.S. income taxes have not been provided on undistributed earnings of foreign subsidiaries as the Company considers such earnings to be permanently reinvested in the businesses. As of February 25, 2006, the cumulative amount of unremitted earnings from foreign subsidiaries that is expected to be permanently reinvested was approximately $21 million. These undistributed foreign earnings could become subject to U.S. income tax if remitted, or deemed remitted, as a dividend. Management has determined that the U.S. income tax liability on these unremitted earnings should not be material, although it is dependent on circumstances existing at the time of the remittance.

The Company is currently under audit by New York State, Pennsylvania, and Ontario, Canada. Taxing authorities periodically challenge positions taken by the Company on its tax returns. On the basis of present information, it is the opinion of the Company's management that the Company has appropriately accrued tax reserves for probable exposures and, as a result, any assessments resulting from current tax audits should not have a materially adverse effect on the Company's consolidated financial statements. To the extent the Company were to prevail in matters for which accrued tax reserves have been established or be required to pay amounts in excess of such reserves, the Company's consolidated financial statements in a given period could be materially impacted. During fiscal 2006, the Company completed certain taxing authority audits which resulted in the reversal of $2.5 million of tax reserves.

The components of current deferred income tax assets and liabilities are as follows:

	February 25, 2006	February 26, 2005
	(in thousands of dollars)	
Deferred income tax assets:		
Pension	$ 1,137	$ 4,047
Inventory	3,192	3,034
Postretirement benefits	3,395	1,969
Foreign tax credits	2,533	1,399
Estimated losses on sales returns	2,578	2,442
Rent	423	463
Other	277	581
Capital loss	1,632	—
Total deferred income tax assets	$15,167	$13,935
Deferred income tax liabilities:		
Depreciation	(2,853)	(3,042)
Package design	—	(1,204)
Prepaid expenses	(293)	(1,287)
Total deferred income tax liabilities	(3,146)	(5,533)
Net deferred	$12,021	$ 8,402

Prior to fiscal 2005, the Company had not recorded a deferred income tax asset relating to its minimum pension obligation (which is included within accumulated other comprehensive income). As of February 25, 2006, the deferred income tax asset relating to the minimum pension obligation is $3.8 million. At the end of fiscal 2005, the deferred income tax asset relating to the minimum pension obligation was $4.0 million. Amounts relating to prior periods were not considered material.

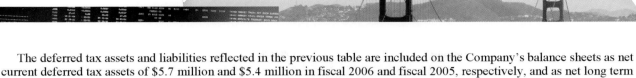

The deferred tax assets and liabilities reflected in the previous table are included on the Company's balance sheets as net current deferred tax assets of $5.7 million and $5.4 million in fiscal 2006 and fiscal 2005, respectively, and as net long term deferred tax assets of $6.3 million and $3.0 million in fiscal 2006 and fiscal 2005, respectively.

As of February 25, 2006, the Company had foreign tax credits of approximately $2.5 million available for use that will expire beginning in fiscal 2009 through fiscal 2016. The Company also had a capital loss of approximately $4.0 million that will expire in fiscal 2011.

NOTE 13 — EMPLOYEE BENEFIT PLANS

The Company maintains qualified and non-qualified defined benefit pensions in the U.S. and Ireland as well as a postretirement healthcare plan in the U.S. for all eligible non-union personnel (the "Plans"). The Company also contributes to a multi-employer defined pension plan for its union employees. The Company's policy is to fund the domestic plans in accordance with the limits defined by the Employee Retirement Income Security Act of 1971 and U.S. income tax regulations. The Ireland plan is funded in accordance with local regulations.

In addition, the Company sponsors a defined contribution plan, which qualifies under Sections 401(a) and 401(k) of the Internal Revenue Code (the "401(k) Plan"). While all non-union employees are eligible to participate in the 401(k) Plan, participation is optional.

Effective April 1, 2006, the Company froze all future benefit accruals under its U.S. qualified defined pension plan and initiated an employer match on 401(k) contributions. In addition, beginning in fiscal 2007, the Company will make non-elective transitional 401(k) contributions with respect to certain employees. As a result of these changes, the Company anticipates a reduction in the amount and volatility of its pension expense and cash contributions. Neither the employee contributions nor matching contributions are invested in the Company's securities.

The Company's investment strategy with respect to its defined benefit plans is to achieve positive return, after adjusting for inflation, and to maximize the long-term total return within prudent levels of risk through a combination of income and capital appreciation. Risk to capital is minimized through the diversification of investments across and within various asset categories. The Company intends to fund its defined benefit plan obligations with the need for future contributions based on changes in the value of plan assets and movements in interest rates. The Company contributed a total of $3.7 million in funding to its pension plans in fiscal 2006 and estimates fiscal 2007 contributions at approximately $1.5 – $2.5 million.

The asset allocation for the Company's U.S. qualified pension plan at the end of 2006 and 2005 and the projection for 2007 are as follows:

| | Percentage of Plan Assets | | |
	2007	2006	2005
Asset Category			
Equity Securities	62%	65%	54%
Debt Securities	38%	35%	40%
Cash	—%	—%	6%

The fair value of plan assets for these plans is $30,260,000 and $29,751,000 as of February 25, 2006 and February 26, 2005, respectively. The expected long-term rate of return on these plan assets was 8.0% in both fiscal 2006 and fiscal 2005. The expected long-term rate of return is estimated using a variety of factors including long-term historical returns, the targeted allocation of plan assets and expectations regarding future market returns for both equity and debt securities. The measurement date for all Topps plans is February 25, 2006.

The following tables summarize benefit costs, benefit obligations, plan assets and the funded status of the Company's U.S. and Ireland pension plans and U.S. postretirement healthcare benefit plan:

	Pension		Postretirement Healthcare	
	February 25, 2006	February 26, 2005	February 25, 2006	February 26, 2005
	(in thousands of dollars)			
Change In Benefit Obligation				
Benefit obligation at beginning of year	$ 45,191	$ 39,709	$ 10,569	$ 10,755
Service cost	1,703	1,419	394	305
Interest cost	2,516	2,414	615	568
Benefits paid	(1,779)	(1,462)	(674)	(619)
Actuarial (gains) / losses	1,627	2,786	1,143	(440)
Participants' contributions	28	19	—	—
Foreign currency impact	(574)	306	—	—
Plan amendments	386	—	(1,729)	—
Curtailments	(4,639)	—	—	—
Settlements	(3,520)	—	—	—
Special termination benefits	573	—	309	—
Benefit obligation at end of year	$ 41,512	$ 45,191	$ 10,627	$ 10,569
Change in Plan Assets				
Fair value of plan assets at beginning of year	$ 29,751	$ 25,551	$ —	$ —
Actual return on plan assets	2,571	1,722	—	—
Employer contributions	3,718	3,666	674	619
Benefits paid	(5,299)	(1,462)	(674)	(619)
Participants' contributions	28	19	—	—
Foreign currency impact	(509)	255	—	—
Fair value of plan assets at end of year	$ 30,260	$ 29,751	$ —	$ —

Below are the assumptions for the pension and postretirement healthcare plans as of the end of the fiscal year:

	Pension Plan		Postretirement Healthcare Plan	
	2006	2005	2006	2005
Discount rate	5.7%	5.6%	5.7%	5.6%
Rate of compensation increase	N/A	4.0%	N/A	N/A
Healthcare cost trend on covered charges	N/A	N/A	10.0%, grading to to 5.0% in 2011	10.0%, grading to to 5.0% in 2010

The discount rate and rate of compensation increase for the Ireland Pension Plan are 4.5% and 3.25%, respectively at year end 2006 and at year end 2005.

	Pension		Postretirement Healthcare	
	February 25, 2006	February 26, 2005	February 25, 2006	February 26, 2005
	(in thousands of dollars)			
Funded status				
Funded status at year end	$(11,253)	$(15,440)	$(10,628)	$(10,568)
Unrecognized actuarial losses	9,058	14,599	2,824	1,789
Unamortized prior service cost	360	276	(1,728)	—
Unrecognized initial transition obligation / (asset)	(611)	(744)	1,701	1,900
Accrued benefit cost	$ (2,446)	$ (1,309)	$ (7,831)	$ (6,879)

The total accumulated benefit obligation for all pension plans was $40,747,000 at the end of fiscal 2006 and $40,592,000 at the end of fiscal 2005.

Amounts recognized in the consolidated balance sheets are as follows:

	Pension		Postretirement Healthcare	
	February 25, 2006	February 26, 2005	February 25, 2006	February 26, 2005
	(in thousands of dollars)			
Prepaid benefit cost	$ 4,602	$ 5,353	$ —	$ —
Accrued benefit liability	(16,252)	(16,808)	(7,831)	(6,879)
Intangible asset	—	275	—	—
Accumulated other comprehensive income	9,204	9,871	—	—
Net amount recognized in the consolidated balance sheets	$ (2,446)	$ (1,309)	$(7,831)	$(6,879)

At the end of fiscal 2006 and 2005, the projected benefit obligation, the accumulated benefit obligation and the fair value of pension assets for pension plans with a projected benefit obligation in excess of plan assets and for pension plans with an accumulated benefit obligation in excess of plan assets were as follows:

	Projected Benefit Obligation Exceeds the Fair Value of Plan Assets		Accumulated Benefit Obligation Exceeds the Fair Value of Plan Assets	
	February 25, 2006	February 26, 2005	February 25, 2006	February 26, 2005
	(in thousands of dollars)			
Projected benefit obligation	$36,761	$45,191	$36,761	$40,081
Accumulated benefit obligation	36,761	40,591	36,761	36,429
Fair value of plan assets	$24,943	$29,751	$24,943	$24,851

The postretirement medical plan has no assets, and the premiums are paid on an on-going basis. The accumulated postretirement benefit obligation at the end of fiscal 2006 and 2005 was $10,627,000 and $10,568,000, respectively.

The weighted-average assumptions used to calculate net periodic benefit costs are as follows:

	U.S. Pension Plan			Postretirement Healthcare Plan		
	2006	2005	2004	2006	2005	2004
Discount rate	5.6%	6.0%	6.3%	5.6%	6.0%	6.3%
Expected return on plan assets	8.0%	8.0%	8.0%	N/A	N/A	N/A
Rate of compensation increase	4.0%	4.0%	4.5%	N/A	N/A	N/A
Healthcare cost trend on covered charges	N/A	N/A	N/A	10.0%, decreasing to 5.0% in 2010	10.0%, decreasing to 5.0% in 2009	10.0%, decreasing to 5.0% in 2008

The discount rate and rate of compensation increase for the Ireland Pension Plan are 4.5% and 3.3% respectively for 2006, 5.3% and 3.3%, respectively, for 2005 and 5.5% and 3.8%, respectively, for 2004. The expected return on assets for the Ireland Pension Plan was 6.75% for 2006, 7.25% for 2005, and 7.25% for 2004.

The components of net periodic benefit costs are as follows:

	Pension Fiscal Years Ended			Postretirement Healthcare Fiscal Years Ended		
	February 25,2006	February 26,2005	February 28,2004	February 25,2006	February 26,2005	February 28,2004
			(in thousands of dollars)			
Service cost	$ 1,703	$ 1,419	$ 1,384	$ 394	$ 304	$ 283
Interest cost	2,516	2,414	2,390	615	568	602
Expected return on plan assets	(2,239)	(2,096)	(1,451)	—	—	—
Amortization of:						
Initial transition obligation (asset)	(62)	(59)	(51)	199	199	199
Prior service cost	81	132	131	—	—	—
Actuarial losses	1,011	808	1,117	109	—	47
Curtailments, settlements, and special termination benefits	1,842	—	—	309	—	336
Net periodic benefit cost	$ 4,852	$ 2,618	$ 3,520	$1,626	$1,071	$1,467

Prior service cost changes are amortized on a straight-line basis over the average remaining service period for employees active on the date of an amendment. Gains and losses are amortized on a straight-line basis over the average remaining service period of employees active on the valuation date.

Expected employer contributions are between $1,500,000 and $2,500,000 for both the qualified plan and the Ireland plan during the fiscal year ending March 3, 2007.

Expected benefit payments are as follows:

Fiscal year ending	Pension	Postretirement	Federal Subsidy
2007	$ 2,491,000	$ 688,000	$ 83,000
2008	$ 2,960,000	$ 749,000	$ 89,000
2009	$ 3,366,000	$ 820,000	$ 96,000
2010	$ 3,192,000	$ 885,000	$102,000
2011	$ 2,917,000	$ 931,000	$108,000
2012-2016	$14,179,000	$4,499,000	$524,000

The above table includes benefits expected to be paid from Company assets.

Assumed health care cost trend rates have a significant effect on the amounts reported for health care plans. A one percentage point change in assumed health care cost trend rates would have the following effect:

	One Percentage Point	
	Increase	Decrease
	(in thousands of dollars)	
On total service and interest cost component	$ 163	$ (133)
On postretirement benefit obligation	$1,251	$(1,059)

NOTE 14 — STOCK OPTION PLAN

The Company has Stock Option Plans that provide for the granting of non-qualified stock options, incentive stock options and stock appreciation rights (SARs) to employees, non-employee directors and consultants within the meaning of Section 422A of the Internal Revenue Code. Options are granted with an exercise price equal to the closing market price of the stock on the grant date, generally vest within three years and expire ten years after the grant date.

The following table summarizes information about the Stock Option Plans.

Stock Options	February 25, 2006 Shares	Wtd. Avg. Exercise Price	February 26, 2005 Shares	Wtd. Avg. Exercise Price	February 28, 2004 Shares	Wtd. Avg. Exercise Price
Outstanding at beginning of year	3,762,919	$7.22	3,800,407	$6.90	3,756,977	$6.73
Granted	60,000	$7.74	262,000	$9.34	890,000	$8.52
Exercised	(261,886)	$5.06	(270,550)	$4.55	(234,680)	$4.85
Forfeited	(146,823)	$9.34	(28,938)	$9.50	(611,890)	$9.01
Outstanding at end of year	3,414,210	$7.30	3,762,919	$7.22	3,800,407	$6.90
Options exercisable at end of year	2,956,624	$7.08	2,973,416	$6.80	2,973,323	$6.44
Weighted average fair value of options granted during the year	$ 2.25		$ 2.99		$ 2.70	

In 2006, of the 146,823 stock options forfeited, 130,498 were unvested options which were lost when employees were terminated from the Company. The remaining 16,325 "forfeited" options were the result of the expiration of options in the normal course. In 2005, the shares forfeited represent those cancelled due to termination of employment; none expired during the year. In 2004, of the 611,890 stock options forfeited, 90,390 were unvested options which were lost when employees were terminated from the Company. The remaining 521,500 "forfeited" options were the result of the expiration of options in the normal course.

Summarized information about stock options outstanding and exercisable at February 25, 2006 is as follows:

	Options Outstanding			Options Exercisable	
Exercise — Price Range	Outstanding as of February 25, 2006	Weighted Average Remaining Contractual Life	Weighted Average Exercise Price	Exercisable as of February 25, 2006	Weighted Average Exercise Price
$1.76-$3.53	673,150	1.9	$ 2.64	673,150	$ 2.64
$3.54-$5.29	416,250	3.0	$ 4.45	416,250	$ 4.45
$5.30-$7.05	96,500	3.3	$ 6.96	96,500	$ 6.96
$7.06-$8.81	1,029,583	6.9	$ 8.27	746,665	$ 8.24
$8.82-$10.57	973,977	6.1	$ 9.84	799,309	$ 9.94
$10.58-$12.34	224,750	4.9	$11.23	224,750	$11.23
	3,414,210	5.0	$ 7.30	2,956,624	$ 7.08

NOTE 15 — CAPITAL STOCK

In October 1999, the Company's Board of Directors authorized the repurchase of up to 5 million shares of the Company's common stock. In October 2001, the Company completed purchases against this authorization and the Company's Board of Directors authorized the repurchase of up to another 5 million shares of the Company's common stock. During fiscal 2004, the Company repurchased 318,800 shares at an average price of $8.69 per share. During fiscal 2005, the Company purchased 444,400 shares at an average price of $9.25 per share.

During the first six months of fiscal 2006, the Company did not purchase any shares due to a strategic business review being performed by investment banking and consulting firms. In September 2005, the Company entered into a written trading plan that complies with Rule 10b5-1 under the Securities and Exchange Act of 1934, as amended, which provides for the purchase of up to 500,000 shares for each of the next four quarters starting in the third quarter of fiscal 2006 at the prevailing market price, per share, subject to certain conditions. In addition, the Board of Directors increased the outstanding share authorization by 3,390,700 shares to 5 million shares. As of February 25, 2006, the Company had purchased 1,027,899 shares under this amended authorization, leaving 3,972,101 shares available for future purchases.

NOTE 16 — DIVIDENDS

On June 26, 2003, the Board of Directors of the Company initiated a regular quarterly cash dividend of $0.04 per share. Four quarterly payments totaling $0.16 per share or $6.5 million were made in fiscal 2006 and 2005, and in 2004, three quarterly payments totaling $0.12 per share, or $4.9 million, were made.

NOTE 17 – LEGAL PROCEEDINGS

In November 2000, the Commission of the European Communities (the "Commission") began an investigation into whether Topps Europe's past distribution arrangements for the sale of Pokemon products complied with European law (the "EU investigation"). On June 17, 2003, the Commission filed a Statement of Objections against The Topps Company, Inc. and its European subsidiaries, therein coming to a preliminary conclusion that these entities infringed Article 81 of the EC

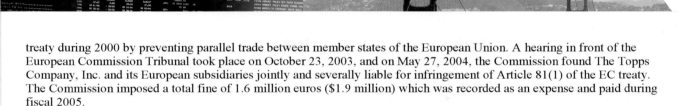

treaty during 2000 by preventing parallel trade between member states of the European Union. A hearing in front of the European Commission Tribunal took place on October 23, 2003, and on May 27, 2004, the Commission found The Topps Company, Inc. and its European subsidiaries jointly and severally liable for infringement of Article 81(1) of the EC treaty. The Commission imposed a total fine of 1.6 million euros ($1.9 million) which was recorded as an expense and paid during fiscal 2005.

In another matter, on November 19, 2001 Media Technologies, Inc. sued the Company and nine other manufacturers of trading cards (the "Defendants") in the Federal District Court for the Central District of California for their sales of all types of "relic" cards that contain an authentic piece of equipment, i.e., a piece of sporting equipment or jersey. Plaintiffs alleged infringement of U.S. Patent Nos. 5,803,501 and 6,142,532. On May 23, 2005 the Company entered into a settlement agreement in which it paid Media Technologies, Inc. a sum of $2,000,000 which is being amortized over the term of the contract. Media Technologies Inc. agreed to dismiss all claims against the Company and to issue a license to the Company to distribute relic cards for seven years. The Company further agreed that under certain conditions which may arise in the future, it would make additional payments to Media Technologies, Inc. as part of the ongoing license.

In another matter, in September of 1999, the Company filed a lawsuit against Cadbury Stani S.A.I.C. ("Stani"), a corporation organized and existing under the laws of Argentina, in federal court in the Southern District of New York. The case centers on the licensing relationship the parties had since 1957 in which the Company had granted Stani the exclusive right to manufacture and distribute gum using the Bazooka brand and related formulas and technologies in Argentina, Bolivia, Chile, Paraguay and Uruguay. In particular, at issue is a 1980 Licensing Agreement (the "Agreement") between the parties and a 1985 Amendment to that Agreement. In its September 17, 2003 Fourth Amended complaint, the Company alleges that Stani continued to use the Company's proprietary and specialized knowledge and experience, and its trade secrets, regarding the production of gum after the Agreement's expiration in April 1996, that it unlawfully disclosed this information to Cadbury Schweppes PLC ("Schweppes") which purchased Stani in 1993 and that it deliberately concealed its use and disclosure from the Company. The Company has filed claims for breach of contract, misappropriation of trade secrets and fraudulent inducement to enter into the 1985 Amendment. The Company is seeking to recover disgorgement of Stani's profits, certain lost royalties and punitive damages, interest and costs. It is also seeking a permanent injunction against Stani's future use and dissemination of the Company's proprietary information and trade secrets. In the Fourth Amended Complaint, the Company demanded damages in excess of $250 million. The Fourth Amended Complaint also initially contained claims against Schweppes, which the parties agreed to dismiss on February 4, 2003.

On December 17, 2003, Stani moved for partial summary judgment and to limit the Company's possible damages. In its August 2, 2005 decision, the Court denied Stani's summary judgment motion, in part, and ruled that (i) the Company's claims were not barred by the statute of limitations; and (ii) disgorgement of profits and punitive damages are available remedies on the Company's misappropriation of trade secrets claims. The Court granted Stani's summary judgment motion, in part, and ruled that (i) disgorgement of profits and punitive damages are not available remedies on the Company's breach of contract and fraudulent inducement claims; and (ii) Stani was not estopped from claiming the 1985 Amendment altered the 1980 Agreement.

On February 9, 2006, the Court adjourned the trial which had been scheduled for March 13, 2006 and ruled it would consider a new motion by Stani for partial summary judgment which argues that the Agreement permitted Stani to use the Company's information and trade secrets after the Agreement's expiration in 1996. Oral argument was held on March 15, 2006 and the parties await a decision. If the Company ultimately prevails in this litigation, it could have a material impact on the Company's consolidated financial statements.

In another matter, on December 12, 2003, WizKids, Inc. ("Wizkids") and Jordan Weisman filed a complaint in Washington state court for professional malpractice, breach of fiduciary duty and disgorgement of fees against the law firm Michael, Best & Friedrich, LLP ("MB&F"), and Timothy Kelley, one of its partners, based on their submission of a PCT patent application for WizKids' combat dial that alleged to have prejudiced WizKids' United States patent rights by failing to designate the United States as one of the member states for subsequent conversion to a national application. In a

settlement reached on October 31, 2005, defendants agreed to pay Wizkids $2,950,000. The Company received the $2,950,000 ($1,833,000 net of legal fees) in the third quarter of fiscal 2006 and has recorded it as a reduction to SG&A.

The Company is a party in several other civil actions which are routine and incidental to its business. In management's opinion, after consultation with legal counsel, these other actions will not have a material adverse effect on the Company's financial condition or results of operations.

NOTE 18 — SEGMENT AND GEOGRAPHIC INFORMATION

Following is the breakdown of industry segments as required by SFAS 131, *Disclosures About Segments of an Enterprise and Related Information.* The Company has two reportable business segments: Confectionery and Entertainment.

The Confectionery segment consists of a variety of candy products including Ring Pop, Push Pop, Baby Bottle Pop, Juicy Drop Pop, the Bazooka bubble gum line and, from time to time, confectionery products based on licensed characters, such as Pokémon and Yu-Gi-Oh!

The Entertainment segment primarily consists of cards and sticker album products featuring sports and non-sports subjects. Trading cards feature players from Major League Baseball, the National Basketball Association, the National Football League as well as characters from popular films, television shows and other entertainment properties. Sticker album products feature players from the English Premier League and characters from entertainment properties such as Pokémon and Yu-Gi-Oh! This segment also includes products from WizKids, a designer and marketer of strategy games acquired in July 2003.

The Company's chief decision-maker regularly evaluates the performance of each segment based upon its contributed margin, which is profit after cost of goods, product development, advertising and promotional costs and obsolescence, but before general and administrative expenses and manufacturing overhead, depreciation and amortization, other income (expense), net interest and income taxes. Beginning in fiscal 2007, segment performance will be evaluated based on contributed margin after direct overhead.

The majority of the Company's assets are shared across both segments, and the Company's chief decision-maker does not evaluate the performance of each segment utilizing asset-based measures. Therefore, the Company does not include a breakdown of assets or depreciation and amortization by segment.

BUSINESS SEGMENTS

	Fiscal Year Ended		
	February 25, 2006	February 26, 2005	February 28, 2004
	(in thousands of dollars)		
NET SALES:			
Candy	$ 134,117	$ 133,214	$ 134,637
Gum	10,144	10,548	12,551
Total Confectionery	144,261	143,762	147,188
Sports	95,376	105,384	107,308
Non-sports	54,201	45,085	40,421
Total Entertainment	149,577	150,469	147,729
Total Net Sales	$ 293,838	$ 294,231	$ 294,917
CONTRIBUTED MARGIN:			
Confectionery	$ 43,842	$ 46,781	$ 45,734
Entertainment	34,983	44,950	42,355
Total Contributed margin	$ 78,825	$ 91,731	$ 88,089
Reconciliation of contributed margin to income before (provision) for income taxes:			
Total contributed margin	$ 78,825	$ 91,731	$ 88,089
Unallocated general and administrative expenses and manufacturing overhead	(76,383)	(73,217)	(66,237)
Depreciation and amortization	(4,754)	(5,833)	(5,675)
(Loss) income from operations	(2,312)	12,681	16,177
Interest income, net	2,912	2,706	2,426
Income before benefit (provision) for income taxes	$ 600	$ 15,387	$ 18,603

Net sales to unaffiliated customers and (Loss) income from operations are based on the location of the ultimate customer (Loss) income from operations is defined as contributed margin less unallocated general and administrative expenses and manufacturing overhead and depreciation and amortization. Certain foreign markets are in part supported from the U.S. and Europe; however, the full cost of this support has not been allocated to them. Identifiable assets are those assets located in each geographic area.

McLane Distribution Services, Inc. ("McLane") accounted for approximately 13% and 12% of consolidated net sales in fiscal 2006 and fiscal 2005, respectively. McLane purchases primarily confectionery products from the Company and distributes them to Wal-Mart, Sam's Club, Southland Corp., and convenience stores in the U.S. The loss of this customer could have a material adverse effect on the Company's results of operations and future plans. The sales to McLane are recorded in the Company's Confectionary segment.

41

GEOGRAPHIC AREAS

	February 25, 2006	Fiscal Year Ended February 26, 2005 (in thousands of dollars)	February 28, 2004
Net Sales:			
United States	$207,834	$ 197,998	$201,181
Europe	61,350	70,252	65,135
Canada, Latin America and Asia	24,654	25,981	28,601
Total Net Sales	$293,838	$ 294,231	$294,917
Income from Operations:			
United States	$ (5,336)	$ 7,029	$ 2,992
Europe	(843)	795	9,535
Canada, Latin America and Asia	3,867	4,857	3,650
Total (Loss) Income from Operations	$ (2,312)	$ 12,681	$ 16,177

	As of February 25, 2006	As of February 26, 2005
Identifiable Assets:		
United States	$ 217,495	$ 236,974
Europe	44,781	47,623
Canada, Latin America and Asia	6,362	5,793
Total Identifiable Assets	$ 268,638	$ 290,390

NOTE 19 – ACQUISITION OF WIZKIDS, LLC

On July 9, 2003, the Company acquired Wizkids, LLC ("WizKids"), a designer and marketer of collectible strategy games, for a cash purchase price of approximately $28.4 million. The intent of the acquisition was to enhance and accelerate the expansion of the Company's entertainment business. The acquisition was accounted for using the purchase method of accounting. The financial statements of WizKids have been consolidated into the financial statements of the Company subsequent to the date of acquisition. The allocation of the purchase price is reflected in the financial statements contained herein.

The total consideration paid by the Company to WizKids' shareholders was comprised of $29,500,000 in cash, net of a working capital adjustment of $1,123,500. The purchase price also reflected a $1,326,130 payment to a third party for associated licenses and legal, accounting, and investment banking fees of $679,075. The purchase price was determined based on discounted cash flow projections, which reflected expected synergies with the Company. The purchase price includes a $6.2 million allocation for intellectual property rights associated with the WizKids product line, which is being amortized over an estimated useful life of 6 years. There were no contingent payments with the purchase price.

Contemporaneous with the acquisition, the Company entered into an employment agreement with Jordan Weisman, the majority shareholder and founder of WizKids, for a forty-eight month period following the closing. As part of this employment agreement, $2 million of the consideration paid to Mr. Weisman as a shareholder is being accounted for as deferred compensation and is being amortized over four years. If Mr. Weisman does not remain a WizKids employee for the full four years of the agreement, he will be required to pay the Company the unamortized balance of his deferred compensation. As an additional part of his employment agreement, Mr. Weisman is entitled to contingent payments during the forty-eight months subsequent to the closing equal to 2% of WizKids' annual net revenue in excess of $35 million, assuming that certain operating margin targets are met. In addition, Mr. Weisman was granted 165,000 options to acquire

the Company's common stock, which were granted at fair market value on the date of grant and vest over a four-year period.

The following table sets forth the components of the purchase price:

Total consideration	$29,500,000
Less: Working capital adjustment	(1,123,500)
Deferred compensation agreement	(2,000,000)
Plus: Purchase of license	1,326,130
Transaction costs	679,075
Total purchase price	$28,381,705

The following table provides the fair value of the acquired assets and liabilities assumed based upon WizKids' July 9, 2003 balance sheet:

Current assets	$ 8,201,851
Property and equipment	564,743
Other assets	115,000
Liabilities assumed, current	(5,426,072)
Fair value of net assets acquired	3,455,522
Intangible assets	6,200,000
Goodwill	18,726,183
Total estimated fair value of net assets acquired and goodwill	$28,381,705

The final purchase price differs slightly from the amount shown for Purchase of business in the Consolidated Statement of Cash Flows as of February 28, 2004 which reflects estimated transaction costs.

The goodwill of $18.7 million is included in the Entertainment business segment and is deductible for tax purposes over a fifteen-year period.

The impact of including WizKids in the consolidated statements of operations on a pro forma basis as if the acquisition had occurred on March 3, 2002, is as follows:

	Fiscal Year Ended February 28, 2004 (restated)
	(amounts in thousands, except share data)
Net sales	$310,726
Income from operations	14,374
Net income	$ 11,773
Net income per share — basic	$ 0.29
— diluted	$ 0.28

NOTE 20 — FAIR VALUE OF FINANCIAL INSTRUMENTS

The carrying value of cash, accounts receivable, accounts payable and accrued liabilities approximates fair value due to their short-term nature.

The Company enters into foreign currency forward contracts to hedge its foreign currency exposure. As of February 25, 2006, the Company had outstanding foreign currency forward contracts, which will mature at various dates during fiscal 2007, in the amount of $20,973,000, as compared to $26,563,000 as of February 26, 2005. Over 62% of the contracts will mature within six months.

The fair value of these forward contracts is the amount the Company would receive or pay to terminate them. The approximate pre-tax benefit or cost to the Company to terminate these agreements as of February 25, 2006 and February 26, 2005 would have been $363,000 and $49,000 respectively. The Company may be exposed to credit losses in the event of non-performance by counterparties to these instruments. Management believes, however, the risk of incurring such losses is remote as the contracts are entered into with major financial institutions.

NOTE 21 – OFF-BALANCE SHEET ARRANGEMENTS

The Company does not have any off-balance sheet arrangements that have, or are reasonably likely to have, a current or future effect on our financial condition, changes in financial condition, revenue or expenses, results of operations, liquidity, capital expenditures or capital resources that is expected to be material.

NOTE 22- QUARTERLY RESULTS OF OPERATIONS (Unaudited)

(in thousands of dollars, except share data)

	Quarter Ended						
	May 28, 2005		Agust 27, 2005		November 26,2005		February 25, 2006
	As Previously Reported (a)	As Restated (b)	As Previously Reported (a)	As Restated (b)	As Previously Reported (a)	As Restated (b)	As reported
Net sales	$78,866	$78,584	$75,277	$74,936	$72,808	$72,808	$67,510
Gross profit on sales	27,674	27,644	28,420	28,376	21,306	21,306	18,458
Income (loss) from continuing operations	397	507	3,285	3,378	(1,300)	(1,300)	(4,897)
(Loss) gain from discontinued operations — net of tax	—	(65)	—	(53)	(3,691)	(3,691)	1,102
Net income (loss)	897	897	4,837	4,837	(3,662)	(3,662)	(833)
Basic net income (loss) per share - From continuing operations	$ 0.02	$ 0.02	$ 0.12	$ 0.12	$ —	$ —	$ (0.05)
- After discontinued operations	$ —	$ 0.02	$ —	$ 0.12	$ (0.09)	$ (0.09)	$ (0.02)
Diluted net income (loss) per share - From continuing operations	$ 0.02	$ 0.02	$ 0.12	$ 0.12	$ —	$ —	$ (0.05)
- After discontinued operations	$ —	$ 0.02	$ —	$ 0.12	$ (0.09)	$ (0.09)	$ (0.02)

| | May 29, 2004 | | August 28, 2004 | | November 27,2004 | | February 26, 2005 | |
	As Previously Reported (a)	As Restated (b)	As Previously Reported (a)	As Restated (b)	As Previously Reported (a)	As Restated (b)	As Previously Reported (a)	As Restated (b)
Net sales	$ 88,089	$ 87,592	$ 68,781	$ 68,405	$ 70,278	$ 70,278	$ 68,345	$ 67,956
Gross profit on sales	33,799	33,738	26,280	26,192	23,621	23,621	21,459	21,480
Income (loss) from continuing operations	5,639	5,804	4,812	4,964	3,367	3,405	(1,712)	(1,492)
(Loss) gain from discontinued operations— net of tax	—	(76)	—	(66)	(82)	(82)	—	(129)
Net income (loss)	4,102	4,125	3,655	3,677	2,791	2,814	451	299
Basic net income (loss) per share								
- From continuing operations	$ 0.10	$ 0.10	$ 0.09	$ 0.09	$ 0.07	$ 0.07	$ 0.01	$ 0.01
- After discontinued operations	$ —	$ 0.10	$ —	$ 0.09	$ 0.07	$ 0.07	$ 0.01	$ 0.01
Diluted net income (loss) per share								
- From continuing operations	$ 0.10	$ 0.10	$ 0.09	$ 0.09	$ 0.07	$ 0.07	$ 0.01	$ 0.01
- After discontinued operations	$ —	$ 0.10	$ —	$ 0.09	$ 0.07	$ 0.07	$ 0.01	$ 0.01

(a) As previously reported amounts have been reclassified to give effect to the discontinued operations as discussed in Note 7.

(b) See Note 2.

NOTE 23- COMMITMENTS

Future minimum payments under non-cancelable leases are as follows: (in thousands)

Fiscal Year	Amount
2007	$ 2,579
2008	2,247
2009	2,128
2010	1,826
2011	1,284
Thereafter	536
	$10,600

The Company anticipates making payments of approximately $1.5 – $2.5 million in fiscal 2007 for the funding of its qualified pension plans.

Historically, lease expense under the Company's contracts was $3,075,000 (2006), $3,141,000 (2005) and $2,752,000 (2004).

Historically, the total royalty expense under the Company's sports and entertainment licensing contracts was $25,117,000 (2006), $24,916,000 (2005), and $23,912,000 (2004).

NOTE 24- RESTRUCTURING CHARGE

On September 29, 2005, a restructuring program was announced which separates the Confectionery and Entertainment businesses to the extent practical and streamlines the organizational structure through headcount reductions. In connection with the headcount reductions, the Company incurred charges of approximately $3.7 million; $1.3 million for termination costs in each of the third and fourth quarters of fiscal 2006 and $1.1 million for pension settlement costs. These charges are reflected in selling, general and administrative expenses in the Consolidated Statements of Operations for the year ended February 25, 2006. The table below reconciles the activity to the liability related to the restructuring from November 26, 2005 through February 25, 2006 (in thousands):

	November 26, 2005	Payments	Additions	February 25, 2006
Termination costs	$ 1,100	$(1,420)	$ 1,300	$ 980
Pension settlement	—	—	1,050	1,050
	$ 1,100	$(1,420)	$ 2,350	$ 2,030

Management's Report on Internal Control Over Financial Reporting

Management of The Topps Company, Inc. (the "Company") is responsible for establishing and maintaining adequate internal control over financial reporting. The Company's internal control over financial reporting is designed to provide reasonable assurance to the Company's management and to the Board of Directors regarding the preparation and presentation of financial statements in accordance with accounting principles generally accepted in the United States of America.

Internal control over financial reporting, no matter how well designed, has inherent limitations. Therefore, even those internal controls determined to be effective can provide only reasonable assurance with respect to financial statement preparation and presentation.

Management assessed the effectiveness of the internal control over financial reporting as of February 25, 2006. In making this assessment, it used the criteria set forth by the Committee of Sponsoring Organizations of the Treadway Commission (COSO) in *Internal Control — Integrated Framework*. Based on this assessment and those criteria, we believe that, as of February 25, 2006, the Company's internal control over financial reporting was effective.

Deloitte & Touche LLP, the Company's independent registered public accounting firm, has issued an attestation report on management's assessment of the Company's internal control over financial reporting, and its report is included herein.

The Topps Company, Inc.
New York, NY
May 9, 2006

REPORT OF INDEPENDENT REGISTERED PUBLIC ACCOUNTING FIRM

To the Board of Directors and Stockholders of
The Topps Company, Inc.

We have audited the accompanying consolidated balance sheets of The Topps Company, Inc. and its subsidiaries (the "Company") as of February 25, 2006 and February 26, 2005, and the related consolidated statements of operations, stockholders' equity and comprehensive income and cash flows for each of the three fiscal years in the period ended February 25, 2006. These consolidated financial statements are the responsibility of the Company's management. Our responsibility is to express an opinion on these financial statements based on our audits.

We conducted our audits in accordance with the standards of the Public Company Accounting Oversight Board (United States). Those standards require that we plan and perform the audit to obtain reasonable assurance about whether the financial statements are free of material misstatement. An audit includes examining, on a test basis, evidence supporting the amounts and disclosures in the financial statements. An audit also includes assessing the accounting principles used and significant estimates made by management, as well as evaluating the overall financial statement presentation. We believe that our audits provide a reasonable basis for our opinion.

In our opinion, such consolidated financial statements present fairly, in all material respects, the financial position of the Company and its subsidiaries as of February 25, 2006 and February 26, 2005, and the results of their operations and their cash flows for each of the three fiscal years in the period ended February 25, 2006, in conformity with accounting principles generally accepted in the United States of America.

As discussed in Note 2 to the Consolidated Financial Statements, the accompanying consolidated financial statements for fiscal 2005 and 2004 have been restated.

We have also audited, in accordance with the standards of the Public Company Accounting Oversight Board (United States), the effectiveness of the Company's internal control over financial reporting as of February 25, 2006, based on the criteria established in *Internal Control—Integrated Framework* issued by the Committee of Sponsoring Organizations of the Treadway Commission and our report dated May 9, 2006 expressed an unqualified opinion on management's assessment of the effectiveness of the Company's internal control over financial reporting and an unqualified opinion on the effectiveness of the Company's internal control over financial reporting.

New York, New York
May 9, 2006

49

REPORT OF INDEPENDENT REGISTERED PUBLIC ACCOUNTING FIRM

To the Board of Directors and Stockholders of The Topps Company, Inc.:

We have audited management's assessment, included in the accompanying Management's Report on Internal Control Over Financial Reporting, that The Topps Company, Inc. and its subsidiaries (the "Company") maintained effective internal control over financial reporting as of February 25, 2006, based on criteria established in *Internal Control—Integrated Framework* issued by the Committee of Sponsoring Organizations of the Treadway Commission. The Company's management is responsible for maintaining effective internal control over financial reporting and for its assessment of the effectiveness of internal control over financial reporting. Our responsibility is to express an opinion on management's assessment and an opinion on the effectiveness of the Company's internal control over financial reporting based on our audit.

We conducted our audit in accordance with the standards of the Public Company Accounting Oversight Board (United States) ("PCAOB"). Those standards require that we plan and perform the audit to obtain reasonable assurance about whether effective internal control over financial reporting was maintained in all material respects. Our audit included obtaining an understanding of internal control over financial reporting, evaluating management's assessment, testing and evaluating the design and operating effectiveness of internal control, and performing such other procedures as we considered necessary in the circumstances. We believe that our audit provides a reasonable basis for our opinions.

A company's internal control over financial reporting is a process designed by, or under the supervision of, the company's principal executive and principal financial officers, or persons performing similar functions, and effected by the company's board of directors, management, and other personnel to provide reasonable assurance regarding the reliability of financial reporting and the preparation of financial statements for external purposes in accordance with generally accepted accounting principles. A company's internal control over financial reporting includes those policies and procedures that (1) pertain to the maintenance of records that, in reasonable detail, accurately and fairly reflect the transactions and dispositions of the assets of the company; (2) provide reasonable assurance that transactions are recorded as necessary to permit preparation of financial statements in accordance with generally accepted accounting principles, and that receipts and expenditures of the company are being made only in accordance with authorizations of management and directors of the company; and (3) provide reasonable assurance regarding prevention or timely detection of unauthorized acquisition, use, or disposition of the company's assets that could have a material effect on the financial statements.

Because of the inherent limitations of internal control over financial reporting, including the possibility of collusion or improper management override of controls, material misstatements due to error or fraud may not be prevented or detected on a timely basis. Also, projections of any evaluation of the effectiveness of the internal control over financial reporting to future periods are subject to the risk that the controls may become inadequate because of changes in conditions, or that the degree of compliance with the policies or procedures may deteriorate.

In our opinion, management's assessment that the Company and its subsidiaries maintained effective internal control over financial reporting as of February 25, 2006, is fairly stated, in all material respects, based on the criteria established in *Internal Control—Integrated Framework* issued by the Committee of Sponsoring Organizations of Treadway Commission. Also in our opinion, the Company and its subsidiaries maintained, in all material respects, effective internal control over financial reporting as of February 25, 2006, based on the criteria established in *Internal Control—Integrated Framework* issued by the Committee of Sponsoring Organizations of Treadway Commission.

We have also audited, in accordance with the standards of the PCAOB, the Company's consolidated financial statements as of and for the year ended February 25, 2006 and our report dated May 9, 2006 expressed an unqualified opinion on those consolidated financial statements.

As discussed in Note 2 to the Consolidated Financial Statements, the accompanying Consolidated Financial Statements for fiscal 2005 and 2004 have been restated.

New York, New York
May 9, 2006

50

Market and Dividend Information

The Company's common stock is traded on the Nasdaq National Market under the symbol *TOPP*. The following table sets forth, for the periods indicated, the high and low stock price for the common stock as reported on the Nasdaq National Market as well as cash dividends per share paid by the Company. As of February 25, 2006, there were approximately 4,200 shareholders of record.

| | Fiscal year ended February 25, 2006 | | | Fiscal year ended February 26, 2005 | | |
| | Stock Price | | Dividends | Stock Price | | Dividends |
	High	Low	Paid	High	Low	Paid
First quarter	$ 9.55	$ 8.47	$ 0.04	$ 9.76	$ 8.40	$ 0.04
Second quarter	$ 10.94	$ 8.97	$ 0.04	$ 10.09	$ 8.82	$ 0.04
Third quarter	$ 10.26	$ 7.11	$ 0.04	$ 10.55	$ 9.23	$ 0.04
Fourth quarter	$ 8.22	$ 6.99	$ 0.04	$ 10.00	$ 9.38	$ 0.04

Selected Consolidated Financial Data

	2006	2005 (1)	2004 (1)	2003 (1)	2002 (1)
			(in thousands of dollars, except share data, unaudited)		
OPERATING DATA:					
Net sales	$ 293,838	$ 294,231	$ 294,917	$ 284,649	$ 296,053
Gross profit on sales	95,784	105,031	103,704	101,684	113,717
Selling, general and administrative expenses	98,096	92,350	87,527	78,801	79,240
(Loss) income from operations	(2,312)	12,681	16,177	22,883	38,403
Interest income, net	2,912	2,706	2,426	2,515	4,892
Loss from discontinued operations — net of tax	(2,707)	(353)	(744)	(1,736)	(1,614)
Net income	$ 1,239	$ 10,915	$ 12,884	$ 16,936	$ 28,462
Basic net income per share					
From continuing operations	$ 0.10	$ 0.28	$ 0.34	$ 0.45	$ 0.70
From discontiinued operations	(0.07)	(0.01)	(0.02)	(0.04)	(0.04)
Basic net income per share	$ 0.03	$ 0.27	$ 0.32	$ 0.41	$ 0.66
Diluted net income per share					
From continuing operations	$ 0.10	$ 0.27	$ 0.33	$ 0.44	$ 0.68
From discontiinued operations	(0.07)	(0.01)	(0.02)	(0.04)	(0.04)
Diluted net income per share	$ 0.03	$ 0.26	$ 0.31	$ 0.40	$ 0.64
Dividends per share	$ 0.16	$ 0.16	$ 0.12	$ —	$ —
Wtd. avg. shares outstanding — basic	40,349,000	40,471,000	40,604,000	41,353,000	43,073,000
Wtd. avg. shares outstanding — diluted	41,163,000	41,327,000	41,515,000	42,065,000	44,276,000
BALANCE SHEET DATA:					
Cash and equivalents	$ 28,174	$ 36,442	$ 56,959	$ 85,684	$ 98,007
Short-term investments	53,269	69,955	36,878	28,575	23,050
Working capital	127,713	139,910	134,099	142,416	137,504
Net property, plant and equipment	11,028	11,968	13,049	13,548	13,102
Total assets	268,638	290,390	275,526	262,875	257,561
Long-term debt	—	—	—	—	—
Stockholders' equity	$ 204,636	$ 219,168	$ 211,340	$ 196,642	$ 193,665

---

(1) See description of restatement at Note 2 to the Consolidated Financial Statements.

BOARD OF DIRECTORS

Arthur T. Shorin*
Chairman and Chief Executive Officer

Allan A. Feder
Independent Business Consultant

Stephen D. Greenberg
Managing Director
Allen & Company, LLC

Ann Kirschner
President
Comma International

David Mauer
Chief Executive Officer
E&B Giftware, LLC

Edward D. Miller*
Former President and CEO
AXA Financial, Inc.

Jack H. Nusbaum
Partner and Chairman
Willkie Farr & Gallagher, LLP

Richard Tarlow
Chairman
Roberts & Tarlow

---

*Nominated to stand for re-election to the Company's Board of Directors at the 2006 Annual Meeting of Stockholders.

OFFICERS

Arthur T. Shorin
Chairman and Chief Executive Officer

Scott Silverstein
President and Chief Operating Officer

John Budd
Vice President – Confectionary Marketing

John Buscaglia
Vice President – Entertainment Sales

Michael P. Clancy
Vice President — International and
Managing Director, Topps International Limited

Ira Friedman
Vice President – Publishing and
New Product Development

Warren Friss
Vice President — General
Manager Entertainment

Catherine K. Jessup
Vice President — Chief
Financial Officer and Treasurer

Michael K. Murray
Vice President — Confectionery Sales

William G. O'Connor
Vice President — Administration

Christopher Rodman
Vice President – Topps Europe

SUBSIDIARIES

Topps Argentina SRL
Managing Director -
Juan P. Georgalos

Topps Europe Limited
Managing Director -
Christopher Rodman

Topps Canada, Inc.
General Manager -
Paul Cherrie

Topps Italia SRL
Managing Director -
Furio Cicogna

Topps International Limited
Managing Director -
Michael P. Clancy

WizKids, Inc.
President -
Jordan Weisman

Topps UK Limited
Managing Director -
Martin Tilney

Topps Finance, Inc.

Topps Enterprises, Inc.

CORPORATE INFORMATION

Annual Meeting
Thursday, July 28, 2006
10:30 A.M.
JPMorgan Chase & Co.
270 Park Avenue
New York, NY 10022

Investor Relations
Brod & Schaffer, LLC
230 Park Avenue, Suite 1831
New York, NY 10169
212-750-5800

Corporate Counsel
Willkie Farr & Gallagher,
LLP
787 Seventh Avenue
New York, NY 10019

Independent Auditors
Deloitte & Touche LLP
Two World Financial Center
New York, NY 10281

Registrar and Transfer Agent
American Stock Transfer & Trust Company
59 Maiden Lane
New York, NY 10038
877-777-0800 ext 6820

54

Summary of Financial Ratios

CHAPTER 1

Price-earnings Ratio

The price-earnings ratio (P/E ratio) gives an indication of how optimistic the financial markets are about a company's future earnings. The higher a company's P/E ratio is, the more investors are willing to pay for each dollar of earnings that the company generates. Typically investors are willing to pay this higher price because they think the company will grow in the future. Lower P/E ratios indicate investors are less optimistic about the company's future growth. The price-earnings ratio is defined as:

$$\frac{\text{Market price of one share of stock}}{\text{Earnings per share}}$$

Earnings per Share Ratio

The earnings per share ratio (EPS) provides an indication of the amount of a company's earnings that are attributable to each share of common stock outstanding. Obviously, the higher this ratio is the better. In companies that have complex equity structures, such as convertible preferred stock and stock option plans, the computation of EPS can be very complex, but in its simplest form, EPS is defined as:

$$\frac{\text{Net earnings}}{\text{Outstanding shares of common stock}}$$

CHAPTER 3

Debt to Assets Ratio

The debt to assets ratio reveals the percentage of a company's assets that is financed with borrowed money. The higher the debt to assets ratio is, the greater its financial risk, other things being equal. The debt to assets ratio is defined as:

$$\frac{\text{Total debt}}{\text{Total assets}}$$

Return on Assets Ratio

The return on assets ratio (ROA) helps measure how well a company is using the assets available to it. The greater the amount of earnings that can be obtained for a given amount of assets, the better a company is doing at utilizing its assets. So, in general, the higher a company's ROA, the better. The ROA ratio is defined as:

$$\frac{\text{Net income}}{\text{Total assets}}$$

Return on Equity Ratio

The return on equity ratio (ROE) helps to measure how much the owners of a company are earning on the money they have invested in the business. The higher a company's ROE, the better. The ROE is defined as:

$$\frac{\text{Net income}}{\text{Equity}}$$

CHAPTER 5

Gross Margin Percentage

The gross margin percentage helps explain a company's pricing strategy. It compares the amount a company pays for the goods it sells to the price the company is able to charge for those goods. The more a company marks up its goods, the higher the gross margin percentage will be. Specialty shops tend to have higher gross margin percentages while discount stores tend to have lower percentages. This ratio is sometimes called the gross profit percentage. The gross margin percentage is defined as:

$$\frac{\text{Gross margin}}{\text{Sales}}$$

Return on Sales Ratio

The return on sales ratio, expressed as a percentage, indicates how much of each dollar of sales remains as profit after all expenses have been deducted. Discount stores do not necessarily have lower return on sales percentages than specialty shops. The higher the return on sales ratio percentage, the better. The return on sales ratio is defined as:

$$\frac{\text{Net income}}{\text{Sales}}$$

CHAPTER 6

Current Ratio

Liquidity refers to how quickly noncash assets can be converted into cash. The more quickly assets can be converted into cash, the more liquid they are, and the more useful they are for paying liabilities that must be paid in the near future. The current ratio provides a measure of how much liquidity a company has. Specifically, it compares a company's more liquid assets (current assets) to its current liabilities. Other things being equal, the higher a company's current ratio, the easier it can pay its currently maturing debts. The current ratio is defined as:

$$\frac{\text{Current assets}}{\text{Current liabilities}}$$

CHAPTER 7

Accounts Receivable Turnover Ratio and Average Days to Collect Receivables

The accounts receivable turnover ratio and the average days to collect receivables ratio indicate how long a company takes to collect its accounts receivable. The first ratio, accounts receivable turnover, explains how many times per year a company's receivables are collected, or "turned over"; generally, the *higher* this ratio is, the better. Because the accounts receivable turnover ratios are not easily understood by everyone, the second ratio, average days to collect receivables, is often used. However, the average days to collect receivables ratio cannot be computed without first computing the accounts receivable turnover ratio. Generally, the *lower* the average days to collect receivables ratio is, the better. The accounts receivable turnover ratio is defined as:

$$\frac{\text{Sales}}{\text{Accounts receivable}}$$

The average days to collect receivables ratio is defined as:

$$\frac{365 \text{ days}}{\text{Accounts receivable turnover}}$$

CHAPTER 8

Inventory Turnover Ratio and Average Days to Sell Inventory

The inventory turnover ratio and the average days to sell inventory ratio indicate how long a company takes to sell the goods it has in merchandise inventory. The first ratio, inventory turnover, explains how many times per year a company's inventory is sold, or "turned over"; generally, the *higher* this ratio is the better. Because the inventory turnover ratio is not easily understood by everyone, the second ratio, average days to sell inventory, is often used. However, the average days to sell inventory ratio cannot be computed without first computing the inventory turnover ratio. Generally, the *lower* the average days to sell inventory ratio is, the better. The inventory turnover ratio is defined as:

$$\frac{\text{Cost of goods sold}}{\text{Inventory}}$$

The average days to sell inventory ratio is defined as:

$$\frac{365 \text{ days}}{\text{Inventory turnover}}$$

A company's operating cycle is the time it takes it to convert cash into inventory, sell the inventory, and collect the cash from accounts receivable that resulted from the sale of the inventory. The time it takes a business to do this can be computed by adding the *average days to sell inventory* and the *average days to collect accounts receivable.*

CHAPTER 10

Times Interest Earned Ratio

The times interest earned ratio helps assess a company's ability to make interest payments on its debt. Failure to make interest (or principal) payments can cause a company to be forced into bankruptcy. Other things being equal, a company with a higher times interest earned ratio is considered to have lower financial risk than a company with a lower ratio.

EBIT is an acronym for "earnings before interest and taxes." In other words, it is what net earnings would have been if the company had had no interest expense or income tax expense. Because net earnings are calculated after interest has been subtracted, a company might have $0 of earnings and still have been able to make its interest payments. Thus, the times interest earned ratio is based on EBIT, and is defined as follows:

$$\frac{\text{EBIT}}{\text{Interest expense}}$$

Return on Assets Ratio (refined)

As discussed in detail in Chapter 3, the return on assets ratio (ROA) helps measure how well a company is using the assets available to it. The greater the amount of earnings that can be obtained for a given amount of assets, the better a company is doing at utilizing its assets, so the higher this ratio is, the better. Throughout most of this textbook, ROA has been based on net earnings. However, the use of net earnings creates an ROA that is biased against companies with relatively more debt versus equity financing. Since the ROA ratio is intended to help assess how efficiently a company is using its assets, not how it is financed, the ROA that is used in the business world is often defined as follows:

$$\frac{\text{EBIT}}{\text{Total assets}}$$

Annual Report and Financial Statement Analysis Projects

ANNUAL REPORT PROJECT FOR THE TOPPS COMPANY, INC. (SEE APPENDIX B FOR THE TOPPS ANNUAL REPORT)

Management's Discussion and Analysis

The annual report for The Topps Company, Inc., opens with a letter to the stockholders that describes the company's mission, products and services, customers, past performance, and future prospects. The letter is followed by a section called "Management's Discussion and Analysis" in which management talks about financial results and trends, liquidity, risk factors, and other matters deemed necessary to provide adequate disclosure to users of the report. Read The Topps Company Stockholders' Letter and Management's Discussion and Analysis on pages 1 through 14 of Appendix B to answer questions 1–6.

1. What are the company's two reportable business segments?
2. What were company's goals for each segment in 2006? What specific achievements resulted from these goals?
3. What percentage of the company's total sales came from the Entertainment segment?
4. What effect has inflation had on the company's operations?
5. What is management's view of the company's liquidity status for the foreseeable future? How does the company plan to meet its cash needs?
6. What caused the changes between the company's fiscal year 2006 and 2005 net sales, gross margin, and selling, general and administrative expenses?

Income Statement—Vertical Analysis

7. Using Excel, compute common-size income statements for all three fiscal years. In common-size income statements, net sales is 100 percent and every other number is a percentage of sales. Attach the spreadsheet to the end of this project.
8. Using the common-size income statements, identify the significant trends.
9. What was the gross margin (gross profit) and the gross margin percentage for fiscal year-end 2006, 2005, and 2004?
10. If the gross margin changed over the three-year period, what caused the change? (The change in the two components of gross margin will reveal what caused any change in the gross margin.)
11. What was the percentage return on sales for fiscal year-end 2006, 2005, and 2004? What do these ratios indicate about Topps?

Income Statement—Horizontal Analysis

12. What were the absolute dollar and the percentage changes in revenues between fiscal 2006 and 2005 and between 2005 and 2004?
13. Describe the trend in revenues. Be specific (e.g., slight/steady/drastic increase or decrease each year, or fluctuating with an initial modest/significant increase or decrease followed by a modest/significant increase or decrease, etc.) to precisely describe the company's situation.

14. What were the absolute dollar and the percentage changes in cost of sales (cost of goods sold) between fiscal 2006 and 2005 and between 2005 and 2004?

15. Describe the trend in cost of sales (cost of goods sold). Be specific (e.g., slight/steady/ drastic increase or decrease each year, or fluctuating with an initial modest/significant increase or decrease followed by a modest/significant increase or decrease, etc.) to precisely describe the company's situation.

16. What were the absolute dollar and the percentage changes in selling, general and administrative expenses (operating expenses) between fiscal 2006 and 2005 and between 2005 to 2004?

17. Describe the trend in selling, general and administrative expenses. Be specific (e.g., slight/steady/drastic increase or decrease each year, or fluctuating with an initial modest/ significant increase or decrease followed by a modest/significant increase or decrease, etc.) to precisely describe the company's situation.

18. What were the absolute dollar and the percentage changes in net income between fiscal 2006 to 2005 and 2005 to 2004?

19. How would you describe the trend for net income? Be specific (e.g., slight/ steady/drastic increase or decrease each year, or fluctuating with an initial modest/ significant increase or decrease followed by a modest/significant increase or decrease, etc.) to precisely describe the company's situation. Do you expect the trend to continue?

20. Which items had the largest percentage change between fiscal 2006 and 2004, revenues or expenses (selling, general and administrative expenses and cost of sales)?

21. Summarize what is causing the changes in net income from fiscal 2004 to 2005 and 2005 to 2006 based on the percentages computed in questions 12 through 20. Do you expect the trend to continue?

Balance Sheet—Vertical Analysis

22. Using Excel, compute common-size balance sheets at the end of fiscal 2005 and 2006. In common-size balance sheets, total assets is 100% and every other number is a percentage of total assets. Attach the spreadsheet to the end of this project.

23. What percentage were current assets of total assets at the end of fiscal 2006 and 2005?

24. What percentage were long-term assets of total assets at the end of fiscal 2006 and 2005?

25. What percentage was inventory of current assets at the end of fiscal 2006 and 2005?

26. Which current asset had the largest balance at the end of fiscal 2006 and 2005?

27. What percentages were current liabilities of total liabilities and long-term liabilities of total liabilities at the end of fiscal 2006 and 2005?

Balance Sheet—Horizontal Analysis

28. What was the absolute dollar and the percentage change between the year-end 2006 and year-end 2005 net accounts receivable balance? Was the change an increase or decrease?

29. What was the absolute dollar and the percentage change between year-end 2006 and year-end 2005 inventory? Was the change an increase or decrease?

30. Compared to year-end 2005, did the amounts reported for the following long-term assets increase or decrease? By how much? Include dollar amounts for each item.

	Dollar Amount	Increase or Decrease
Property, plant and equipment, net		
Goodwill, intangibles, and other		
Total long-term assets		

31. What was the amount of the change in the balance in retained earnings between year-end 2006 and 2005? What caused this change?

Balance Sheet—Ratio Analysis

32. Compute the current ratio at the end of fiscal 2006 and 2005. What does this ratio indicate about Topps?

33. Calculate the accounts receivable turnover and the average number of days to collect accounts receivable for fiscal 2006 and 2005. In which year was the turnover and days to collect more favorable?

34. What was the absolute dollar and the percentage change between year-end 2006 and year-end 2005 inventory? Was the change an increase or decrease?

35. Calculate the inventory turnover ratios and the average number of days to sell inventory for fiscal 2006 and 2005. In which year was the turnover and days to sell inventory more favorable?

36. Calculate the ratio of debt to total assets for fiscal year-end 2006 and 2005.

37. Calculate the ratio of stockholders' equity to total assets for fiscal year-end 2006 and 2005. (Recall: 100 percent Assets = 100 percent (Liabilities + Stockholders' Equity). Percentages for questions 35 and 36 should total 100 percent each year.)

Balance Sheet—Stockholders' Equity Section

38. Does the company's common stock have a par value? _____ If so, how much was the par value per share? _____

39. How many shares of common stock were issued at the end of fiscal 2006 and 2005?

40. How many shares of treasury stock did the company have at the end of fiscal 2005 and 2006? How were the treasury stock purchases reflected on the statement of cash flows? Include the type of cash flow activity.

41. What percentage of stockholders' equity do the following items represent at year-end?

	2006	2005
Total paid-in capital		
Retained earnings		
Other items		
	100%	100%

Statement of Cash Flows

42. Does the company report cash flows from operating activities using the direct or the indirect method? Describe how you can tell.

43. Did the company pay cash to purchase treasury stock in 2006? If so, what was the amount of the cash outflow?

44. What was the dollar amount of the increase or decrease in cash and cash equivalents for the fiscal years ended 2006, 2005, and 2004?

45. Does the ending balance of cash and cash equivalents agree with the amount reported on the balance sheet?

	2006	2005
Balance sheet	$	$
Statement of cash flows	$	$

46. For each of the following revenue and expense items on the income statement, identify the related current asset or current liability item (working capital item) on the balance sheet.

Revenue or Expense Item	Related Current Asset or Current Liability
Sales	
Cost of sales	
Selling, general and administrative expenses	
Provision for income taxes	

47. Calculate the net increase or decrease in each following working capital items. Do your calculations agree with the amounts reported on the statement of cash flows?

Working Capital Item	Increase or Decrease
Accounts receivable, net	
Inventories	
Income tax receivable/payable	
Prepaid expenses and other current assets	
Accounts payable, accrued expenses and other liabilities	

48. On what statement(s) would you expect to find information regarding the declaration and payment of dividends? Did the company declare or pay dividends in 2006?

Notes to the Financial Statements

49. In your own words, briefly summarize two significant accounting policies.

50. How much is the estimated allowance for discounts and doubtful accounts for fiscal 2006?

51. What is the net realizable value of receivables at the end of fiscal 2006?

52. How much is accumulated depreciation and amortization at the end of fiscal 2006? For fiscal 2006, what percent of selling, general and administrative expenses is depreciation and amortization expense?

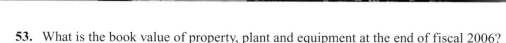

53. What is the book value of property, plant and equipment at the end of fiscal 2006?

54. Did the balance in the goodwill account increase or decrease? Speculate as to what caused this change.

55. Identify three different accrued expenses in addition to "other" liabilities.

56. Comment on Topps' long-term debt agreement. Name the financial institution extending the credit. What kinds of credit restrictions apply to the long-term debt agreement? Identify at least two restrictions. What is the amount of available credit as of March 1, 2006?

57. Identify two kinds of commitments and contingencies.

58. What are the estimated useful lives of the company's depreciable assets?

59. In addition to goodwill, what kinds of intangible assets does the company have? What are their estimated lives?

60. Complete the following schedule contrasting the effect the three inventory cost flow assumptions have on the balance sheet and income statement dollar amounts. Specify for each financial statement the account that is affected by the sale of inventory. Insert the most appropriate term (High, Middle, or Low) to indicate how the specified account would be affected by each of the given cost flow assumptions. Assume an inflationary environment.

	Cost Flow Assumptions		
Account Affected	FIFO	AVG	LIFO
1. Balance Sheet:			
2. Income Statement:			

61. What inventory cost flow method does Topps use?

62. Complete the following schedule contrasting the effect the two types of depreciation methods have on the balance sheet and income statement dollar amounts. Specify for each financial statement the account affected by recording depreciation expense. Designate with an X the method (accelerated or straight-line) that would result in the higher balance in the specified account in the early years of the asset's life.

	Depreciation Methods	
Account Affected	Accelerated	Straight-line
1. Balance Sheet:		
2. Income Statement:		
	(Higher balance early in asset's life)	

63. What method of depreciation does Topps use?

Other Information

64. Topps' financial statements are consolidated. Explain the meaning of the term *consolidated*. Identify two of the company's subsidiaries. (*Hint:* You can find the definition of consolidated statements in your textbook.)

65. On what exchange is the company's stock traded?

Report of Independent Public Accountants (Auditors)

66. What is the name of the company's independent auditors?

67. Who is responsible for the financial statements?

68. What is the outside auditors' responsibility?

69. What type of opinion did the independent auditors issue on the financial statements (unqualified, qualified, adverse, or disclaimer)? What does this opinion mean?

70. The auditors' report indicates the audit was concerned with material misstatements rather than absolute accuracy in the financial statements. What does "material" mean?

Performance Measures

71. Compute the return on assets ratio (use net income rather than EBIT in the numerator) for fiscal years 2006 and 2005.

72. Compute the return on equity ratio for fiscal years 2006 and 2005.

73. For fiscal 2006, was the return on equity ratio greater than the return on assets ratio? Explain why.

74. What was Topps' basic earnings per share (EPS) for fiscal 2006 and 2005?

75. Given an average market price per share of $9.28 for fiscal 2006 and $10.48 for fiscal 2005, calculate the price-earnings (P/E) ratio. What does the P/E ratio mean?

76. Suggest why the company's stock price fell between fiscal 2006 and 2005 while its P/E ratio increased during the same period.

ANNUAL REPORT PROJECT FOR HARLEY-DAVIDSON, INC.

Management's Discussion and Analysis

In addition to financial statements and related footnotes, most corporate annual reports describe the company's mission, products and services, customers, past performance, and future prospects. In Harley-Davidson's annual report[1] this type of information is presented on pages 3 through 35. Annual reports also typically include a section called "Management's Discussion and Analysis (MD&A)" in which management discusses financial results and trends, liquidity, risk factors, and other matters deemed necessary to provide adequate disclosure to users of the reports. Harley-Davidson's MD&A information is included in pages 36 through 46.

1. Read pages 3–28 of the report. What is management's mission for Harley-Davidson?

2. Read the Chairman's letter to shareholders on pages 3 through 6. Assume you own Harley-Davidson stock. Write a brief statement identifying specific details about the company's performance as described by the chairman that impress you favorably or unfavorably. Explain why the items you identify give you a positive or a negative impression.

3. What is the nature of Harley-Davidson's business? What products or services does it produce and sell? *(Hint: Footnote 12 on page 69 also provides information pertinent to this question.)*

---

[1]A Harley-Davidson annual report is packaged with new textbooks. If the annual report is misplaced, you can access it online at www.harley-davidson.com. Because companies change website interfaces from time to time, we cannot provide exact instructions for finding the annual report on the Harley-Davidson website. Explore the website and follow links such as "Investor Relations" to locate the annual report. This project uses the 2005 report.

Income Statement

4. Locate Harley-Davidson's income statements. Are they presented in the single-step or the multi-step format?

5. Use the income statement figures to calculate the percentage growth in net income from 2004 to 2005 and from 2003 to 2004.

6. Is it likely that Harley-Davidson can maintain the rate of net income growth you computed in question 5? *(Hint: The MD&A on pages 36 through 46 provides information pertinent to this question.)*

7. Calculate Harley-Davidson's gross margin (profit) percentage for 2004 and 2005.

8. Did Harley-Davidson's gross margin percentage increase or decrease between 2004 and 2005? What caused the change? *(Hint: Information on page 37 of the report is pertinent to these questions).*

9. Calculate the percentage change in Harley-Davidson's gross margin (profit) between 2004 and 2005. What caused this change?

10. Use the information in footnote 12 on page 69 of the annual report to answer the following questions.
    a. What percent of income from operations is provided by Motorcycles versus Financial Services for the years 2005, 2004, and 2003 (ignore general corporate expenses)? Identify any trend present in the data.
    b. With respect to income from operations, which segment (Motorcycles or Financial Services) grew more rapidly for the two years between 2003 and 2005?
    c. Do you expect the trends you identified in parts a and b to continue?

11. Based on the information in footnote 12 on page 69, the Financial Services segment had more identifiable assets ($2,363,235) than the Motorcycles segment ($1,845,802). Yet the Financial Services segment has significantly less depreciation ($6,872) than the Motorcycles segment ($198,833). Explain this apparent contradiction.

12. Use the income statement figures on page 47 to calculate the percentage change in Financial Services income and Financial Services expense for the two years between 2003 and 2005.

Balance Sheet

13. The current asset section of the balance sheets includes the caption "Cash and cash equivalents." What does Harley-Davidson mean by the term "cash equivalents"? *(Hint: cash equivalents are defined in footnote 1 on page 52.)*

14. What is the amount of the "At beginning of year" balance of "Cash and cash equivalents" reported on the 2005 statement of cash flows? Where is this amount reported on the consolidated balance sheets?

15. The largest current asset reported on the balance sheets is labeled "Current portion of finance receivables, net." *(Hint: Footnote 4 on page 57 and footnote 1 on page 52 provide information pertinent to parts a through d of this question.)*
    a. What is the difference between finance receivables and accounts receivable?
    b. What do the words "current portion" in the asset description mean?
    c. What does the term "net" in the asset description mean?
    d. At what point does Harley-Davidson consider finance receivables (retail loans) to be uncollectible?

16. Calculate the percentage change in the current asset "Current portion of finance receivables, net" between year-end 2004 and year-end 2005. Explain the likely reason for the increase or decrease.

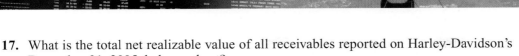

17. What is the total net realizable value of all receivables reported on Harley-Davidson's December 31, 2005, balance sheet?

18. Do the balance sheets report any intangible assets? If so, identify them.

19. Read the section of footnote 1 on page 52 that describes product warranty. The footnote reports an ending warranty balance of $34,319. What caption on the balance sheet most likely includes this amount? Do you expect warranty expense to increase or decrease in 2006?

Statement of Cash Flows

20. How does net income compare to cash flows from operating activities for 2005?

21. Does Harley-Davidson report cash flows from operating activities using the direct or the indirect method?

22. In the presentation of cash flows from operating activities, did Harley-Davidson add depreciation expense to net income or subtract it?

23. Does Harley-Davidson have a pattern of paying cash dividends?

24. What percentage of net income did Harley-Davidson pay out in cash dividends during 2003?

25. The amount of dividends paid in 2005 was almost three times higher than the amount paid in 2003. Provide an explanation for why Harley-Davidson would increase dividends by such a large amount.

26. In 2005 Harley-Davidson generated nearly $960 million in cash from operating activities. What did the company do with all that cash?

27. What are the two largest items reported in the "Cash flows from investing activities" section of the 2005 statement of cash flows? Do you expect these cash flows to recur regularly?

28. What is the total amount of finance debt reported on the balance sheet at December 31, 2005? What individual components are included in the finance debt category? Identify the interest rates and terms to maturity for each debt component. *(Hint: Footnote 4, page 59, provides information pertinent to this question.)*

More on Equity

(Hint: Footnote 8 on page 65 provides information pertinent to questions 29–37.)

29. How many shares of common stock was Harley-Davidson authorized to issue as of December 31, 2005?

30. How many shares of common stock had Harley-Davidson issued as of December 31, 2005?

31. How many shares of common stock did Harley-Davidson have outstanding as of December 31, 2005?

32. What is the par value of the common stock as of December 31, 2005?

33. How many shares of preferred stock was Harley-Davidson authorized to issue as of December 31, 2005?

34. How many shares of preferred stock had Harley-Davidson issued as of December 31, 2005?

35. How many shares of preferred stock were outstanding as of December 31, 2005?

36. What is the par value of the preferred stock as of December 31, 2005?

37. What amount of cash did Harley-Davidson spend to purchase treasury stock during 2005?

Report of Independent Auditors

Hint: The reports of management and accounting firms are presented on pages 71 and 72. These reports provide information pertinent to questions 38 through 43.

38. Who is responsible for preparing the financial statements?

39. What is the independent auditors' responsibility?

40. What type of opinion did the independent auditors issue on the financial statements (unqualified, qualified, adverse, or disclaimer)? Assume you own shares of Harley-Davidson stock. Does the auditors' opinion indicate the company is a good investment?

41. Who establishes GAAP? Do you trust the organization that establishes accounting standards (GAAP)? Why? Answers to these questions do not appear in the Harley-Davidson annual report. Look for answers in your textbook or do a Web search to answer the questions. If you search online, we suggest you begin with the following website: www.fasb.org.

42. The auditors' report indicates the audit was concerned with material misstatements rather than absolute accuracy in the financial statements. What does "material" mean?

43. Identify the name of the company's independent auditors. Perform a Web search to assess the reputation of the audit firm. Assume you own shares of Harley-Davidson stock. Do you feel positive or negative about the audit firm's reputation? Why?

Ratio Analysis

Average ratios computed for the 30 companies that make up the Dow Jones Industrial Average are presented below. The underlying data were drawn from the Compact Disclosure Data Base. Calculate each ratio based on Harley-Davidson's 2005 fiscal year and comment on how Harley-Davidson's ratio compares to the Dow average. Indicate specifically whether Harley-Davidson's ratios are more or less favorable than the Dow average.

Ratio	Dow 30
44. Current ratio	1.34 to 1
45. Average days to collect accounts receivable	241 days for all firms, 61 days for all firms except financial institutions
46. Average days to sell inventory	30 days
47. Debt to assets	.64 to 1
48. Return on equity	19%
49. Price-earnings ratio*	20

*Base your computations for Harley-Davidson on a market price per share of $44.27 and use the basic earnings per common share reported on Harley-Davidson's income statement.

FINANCIAL STATEMENTS PROJECT (SELECTION OF COMPANY TO BE DECIDED BY INSTRUCTOR)

Date Due: _____

Required

Based on the annual report of the company you are reviewing, answer the following questions. If you cannot answer a particular question, briefly explain why. If the question is not applicable to your company's financial statements answer "N/A."

Show all necessary computations in good form. Label all numbers in your computations. If relevant, reference your answers to page(s) in the annual report.

"Current year" means the most recent fiscal year in the company's annual report. "Prior year" means the fiscal year immediately preceding the current year.

1. What products or services does the company sell? Be specific.

2. What do you think the outlook is for these products or services? Why do you think so?

3. By what percentage have sales increased or decreased in each of the last two fiscal years?

4. If the company reported sales by segments, which segment had the largest percentage of total sales? Which segment had the smallest percentage of total sales? **Show computations of the relevant percentages.**

   Largest segment _____   Percentage of total sales _____
   Smallest segment _____   Percentage of total sales _____

5. What is net income for the current year? _____

6. Did the current year's net income increase or decrease since the prior year? By how much? What caused the change?

7. If the company reported earnings by segments, which segment had the largest percentage of total earnings? Which segment had the smallest percentage of total earnings? **Show computations of the relevant percentages.**

   Largest segment _____   Percentage of total earnings _____
   Smallest segment _____   Percentage of total earnings _____

8. Did the company report any special, unusual, or otherwise nonroutine items in either current or prior year net income? If so, explain the item(s).

9. For the current year, how does net income compare to net cash provided (used) by operating activities?

10. For the current year, what one or two items were most responsible for the difference between net income and net cash provided (used) by operating activities?

11. Did the company pay cash dividends during the current year? If so, how much were they?

12. If the company paid cash dividends, what percentage of net income were the cash dividends? If the company did not pay cash dividends, why do you think it did not?

13. Which of the following is the company's largest asset category: accounts receivable, inventory, or land? What is the amount of that asset category?

14. If the company reported assets by segments, which segment had the largest percentage of total assets? Which segment had the smallest percentage of total assets? **Show computations of the relevant percentages.**

   Largest segment _____   Percentage of total assets _____
   Smallest segment _____   Percentage of total assets _____

15. How much **cash** did the company invest in property, plant, and equipment during the current year?

16. Which inventory method(s) did the company use?

17. Which depreciation method(s) did the company use?

18. If the company has any intangible assets, what kind are they?

19. Did the company report any contingent liabilities ("contingencies")? If so, briefly explain.

20. Does the company have any preferred stock authorized? If so, how many shares were authorized?

21. Does the company's common stock have a par value? If so, what was it?

22. In what price range was the company's common stock trading during the last quarter of the current year?

23. What was the market price of the company's common stock on DD/MM/Year?

24. Where (on what stock exchange) is the company's stock traded?

25. Who was the company's independent auditor?

26. Develop one question about the company's financial report that you do not know how to answer.

27. Compute the following ratios for the current year and the prior year. Show the appropriate formulas in the first column. Show all supporting computations in the second and third columns.

Ratio	Current Year	Prior Year
Gross Profit Formula:		
Inventory Turnover Formula:		
Current Ratio Formula:		
Debt to Equity Formula:		
Return on Assets Formula:		
Return on Equity Formula:		

Accounting for Investment Securities

TYPES OF INVESTMENT SECURITIES

A financial investment occurs when one entity provides assets or services to another entity in exchange for a certificate known as a *security.* The entity that provides the assets and receives the security certificate is called the **investor.** The entity that receives the assets or services and gives the security certificate is called the **investee.** This appendix discusses accounting practices that apply to securities held by investors.

There are two primary types of investment securities: debt securities and equity securities. An investor receives a **debt security** when assets *are loaned* to the investee. In general, a debt security describes the investee's obligation to return the assets and to pay interest for the use of the assets. Common types of debt securities include bonds, notes, certificates of deposit, and commercial paper.

An **equity security** is obtained when an investor acquires an *ownership interest* in the investee. An equity security usually describes the rights of ownership, including the right to influence the operations of the investee and to share in profits or losses that accrue from those operations. The most common types of equity securities are common stock and preferred stock. In summary, **investment securities** are certificates that describe the rights and privileges that investors receive when they loan or give assets or services to investees.

Transactions between the investor and the investee constitute the **primary securities market.** There is a **secondary securities market** in which investors exchange (buy and sell) investment securities with other investors. Securities that regularly trade in established secondary markets are called **marketable securities.** Investee companies are affected by secondary-market transactions only to the extent that their obligations are transferred to a different party. For example, assume that Tom Williams (investor) loans assets to American Can Company (investee). Williams receives a bond (investment security) from American Can that describes American Can's obligation to return assets and pay interest to Williams. This exchange represents a primary securities market transaction. Now assume that in a secondary-market transaction Williams sells his investment security (bond) to Tina Tucker. American Can Company is affected by this transaction only to the extent that the company's obligation transfers from Williams to Tucker. In other words, American Can's obligation to repay principal and interest does not change. The only thing that changes is the party to whom American Can makes payments. *An investee's financial statements are not affected when the securities it has issued to an investor are traded in the secondary market.*

The **fair value,** also called **market value,** of an investor's securities is established by the prices at which they sell in the secondary markets. For financial reporting purposes, fair value is established as the closing (last) price paid for an identical security on the investor's fiscal closing date. Whether securities are reported at fair value or historical cost depends on whether the investor intends to sell or hold the securities. Generally accepted accounting principles require companies to classify their investment securities into one of three categories: (1) held-to-maturity securities, (2) trading securities, and (3) available-for-sale securities.

Held-to-Maturity Securities

Since equity securities representing ownership interests have no maturity date, the held-to-maturity classification applies only to debt securities. Debt securities should be classified as held-to-maturity securities if the investor has a *positive intent* and the *ability* to hold the securities until the maturity date. **Held-to-maturity securities** are reported on the balance sheet at *amortized historical cost.*[1]

Trading Securities

Both debt and equity securities can be classified as *trading securities.* **Trading securities** are bought and sold for the purpose of generating profits on the short-term appreciation of stock or bond prices. They are usually traded within three months of when they are acquired. Trading securities are reported on the investor's balance sheet at their fair value on the investor's fiscal closing date.

Available-for-Sale Securities

All marketable securities that are not classified as held-to-maturity or trading securities must be classified as **available-for-sale securities.** These securities are also reported on the investor's balance sheet at fair value as of the investor's fiscal closing date.

Two of the three classifications, therefore, must be reported at fair value, which is a clear exception to the historical cost concept. Other exceptions to the use of historical cost measures for asset valuation are discussed in later sections of this appendix.

REPORTING EVENTS THAT AFFECT INVESTMENT SECURITIES

The effects on the investor's financial statements of four distinct accounting events involving marketable investment securities are illustrated in the following section. The illustration assumes that the investor, Arapaho Company, started the accounting period with cash of $10,000 and common stock of $10,000.

Event 1 Investment Purchase
Arapaho paid $9,000 cash to purchase marketable investment securities.

This event is an asset exchange. One asset (cash) decreases, and another asset (investment securities) increases. The income statement is not affected. The $9,000 cash outflow is reported as either an operating activity or an investing activity, depending on how the securities are classified. Since *trading securities* are short-term assets that are regularly traded for the purpose of producing income, cash flows from the purchase or sale of trading securities are reported in the operating activities section of the statement of cash flows. In contrast, cash flows involving the purchase or sale of securities classified as *held to maturity* or *available for sale* are reported in the investing activities section of the statement of cash flows. The only difference among the three alternatives lies in the classification of the cash outflow reported on the statement of cash flows, as shown in the following statements model:

---

[1]Debt securities are frequently purchased for amounts that are more or less than their face value (the amount of principal due at the maturity date). If the purchase price is above the face value, the difference between the face value and the purchase price is called a *premium.* If the purchase price is below the face value, the difference is called a *discount.* Premiums and discounts increase or decrease the amount of interest revenue earned and affect the carrying value of the bond investment reported on the balance sheet. The presentation in this section of the text makes the simplifying assumption that the bonds are purchased at a price equal to their face value. Accounting for discounts and premiums is discussed in Chapter 10.

Event No.	Type	Assets			=	Liab.	+	Equity	Rev.	−	Exp.	=	Net Inc.	Cash Flow	
		Cash	+	Inv. Sec.											
1	Held	(9,000)	+	9,000	=	NA	+	NA	NA	−	NA	=	NA	(9,000)	IA
1	Trading	(9,000)	+	9,000	=	NA	+	NA	NA	−	NA	=	NA	(9,000)	OA
1	Available	(9,000)	+	9,000	=	NA	+	NA	NA	−	NA	=	NA	(9,000)	IA

Event 2 Recognition of Investment Revenue
Arapaho earned $1,600 of cash investment revenue.

Investment revenue is reported the same way regardless of whether the investment securities are classified as held to maturity, trading, or available for sale. Investment revenue comes in two forms. Earnings from equity investments are called **dividends.** Revenue from debt securities is called **interest.** Both forms have the same impact on the financial statements. Recognizing the investment revenue increases both assets and stockholders' equity. Revenue and net income increase. The cash inflow from investment revenue is reported in the operating activities section of the statement of cash flows regardless of how the investment securities are classified.

Event No.	Assets	=	Liab.	+	Equity	Rev.	−	Exp.	=	Net Inc.	Cash Flow	
	Cash	=			Ret. Earn.							
2	1,600	=	NA	+	1,600	1,600	−	NA	=	1,600	1,600	OA

Event 3 Sale of Investment Securities
Arapaho sold securities that cost $2,000 for $2,600 cash.

This event results in recognizing a $600 realized (actual) gain that increases both total assets and stockholders' equity. The asset cash increases by $2,600 and the asset investment securities decreases by $2,000, resulting in a $600 increase in total assets. The $600 realized gain is reported on the income statement, increasing net income and retained earnings. The $600 gain does not appear on the statement of cash flows. Instead, the entire $2,600 cash inflow is reported in one section of the statement of cash flows. Cash inflows from the sale of held-to-maturity and available-for-sale securities are reported as investing activities. Cash flows involving trading securities are reported as operating activities. These effects are shown below.

Event No.	Type	Assets			=	Liab.	+	Equity	Rev. or Gain	−	Exp. or Loss	=	Net Inc.	Cash Flow	
		Cash	+	Inv. Sec.											
3	Held	2,600	+	(2,000)	=	NA	+	600	600	−	NA	=	600	2,600	IA
3	Trading	2,600	+	(2,000)	=	NA	+	600	600	−	NA	=	600	2,600	OA
3	Available	2,600	+	(2,000)	=	NA	+	600	600	−	NA	=	600	2,600	IA

Event 4 Market Value Adjustment
Arapaho recognized a $700 unrealized gain.

After Event 3, the historical cost of Arapaho's portfolio of remaining investment securities is $7,000 ($9,000 purchased less $2,000 sold). Assume that at Arapaho's fiscal closing date, these securities have a fair value of $7,700, giving Arapaho a $700 unrealized gain on its investment. This type of gain (sometimes called a *paper profit*) is classified as *unrealized* because the securities have not been sold. The treatment of **unrealized gains or losses** in the financial statements depends on whether the securities are classified as held to maturity, trading, or available for sale. Unrealized gains or losses on securities classified as *held to maturity* are not recognized in the financial statements; they have no effect on the balance sheet, income statement, and statement of cash flows. Even so, many companies choose to disclose the market value of the securities as part of the narrative description or in the footnotes that accompany the statements. Whether or not the market value is disclosed, held-to-maturity securities are reported on the balance sheet at amortized cost.

Investments classified as trading securities are reported in the financial statements at fair value. Unrealized gains or losses on *trading securities* are recognized in net income even though the securities have not been sold. In Arapaho's case, the $700 gain increases the carrying value of the investment securities. The gain increases net income, which in turn increases retained earnings. Unrealized gains and losses have no effect on cash flows.

Investments classified as available-for-sale securities are also reported in the financial statements at fair value. However, an important distinction exists with respect to how the unrealized gains and losses affect the financial statements. Even though unrealized gains or losses on available-for-sale securities are included in the assets on the balance sheet, they *are not* recognized in determining net income.[2] On Arapaho's balance sheet, the $700 gain increases the carrying value of the investment securities. A corresponding increase is reported in a separate equity account called Unrealized Gain or Loss on Available-for-Sale Securities. The statement of cash flows is not affected by recognizing unrealized gains and losses on available-for-sale securities.

The effects of these alternative treatments of unrealized gains and losses on Arapaho's financial statements are shown here:

Event No.	Type	Assets	=	Liab.	+	Equity			Rev. or Gain	−	Exp. or Loss	=	Net Inc.	Cash Flow
		Inv. Sec.	=			Ret. Earn.	+	Unreal. Gain						
4	Held	NA	=	NA	+	NA	+	NA	NA	−	NA	=	NA	NA
4	Trading	700	=	NA	+	700	+	NA	700	−	NA	=	700	NA
4	Available	700	=	NA	+	NA	+	700	NA	−	NA	=	NA	NA

FINANCIAL STATEMENTS

As the preceding discussion implies, the financial statements of Arapaho Company are affected by not only the business events relating to its security transactions but also the accounting treatment used to report those events. In other words, the same economic events

---

[2]*Statement of Financial Accounting Standards No. 130* permits companies to report unrealized gains and losses on available-for-sale securities as additions to or subtractions from net income with the result being titled *comprehensive income*. Alternatively, the unrealized gains and losses can be reported on a separate statement or as part of the statement of changes in stockholders' equity.

ARAPAHO COMPANY
Comparative Financial Statements

Income Statements

Investment Securities Classified as	Held	Trading	Available
Investment revenue	$ 1,600	$ 1,600	$ 1,600
Realized gain	600	600	600
Unrealized gain		700	
Net income	$ 2,200	$ 2,900	$ 2,200

Balance Sheets

	Held	Trading	Available
Assets			
Cash	$ 5,200	$ 5,200	$ 5,200
Investment securities, at cost (market value $7,700)	7,000		
Investment securities, at market (cost $7,000)		7,700	7,700
Total assets	$12,200	$12,900	$12,900
Stockholders' equity			
Common stock	$10,000	$10,000	$10,000
Retained earnings	2,200	2,900	2,200
Unrealized gain on investment securities			700
Total stockholders' equity	$12,200	$12,900	$12,900

Statements of Cash Flows

	Held	Trading	Available
Operating Activities			
Cash inflow from investment revenue	$ 1,600	$ 1,600	$ 1,600
Outflow to purchase securities		(9,000)	
Inflow from sale of securities		2,600	
Investing Activities			
Outflow to purchase securities	(9,000)		(9,000)
Inflow from sale of securities	2,600		2,600
Financing Activities*	0	0	0
Net decrease in cash	(4,800)	(4,800)	(4,800)
Beginning cash balance	10,000	10,000	10,000
Ending cash balance	$ 5,200	$ 5,200	$ 5,200

*The $10,000 capital acquisition is assumed to have occurred prior to the start of the accounting period.

are reflected differently in the financial statements depending on whether the securities are classified as held to maturity, trading, or available for sale. Exhibit E.1 displays the financial statements for Arapaho under each investment classification alternative.

The net income reported under the trading securities alternative is $700 higher than that reported under the held-to-maturity and available-for-sale alternatives because unrealized gains and losses on trading securities are recognized on the income statement. Similarly, total

Investment Category	Types of Securities	Types of Revenue Recognized	Reported on Balance Sheet at	Recognition of Unrealized Gains and Losses on the Income Statement	Cash Flow from Purchase or Sale of Securities Classified As
Held to maturity	Debt	Interest	Amortized cost	No	Investing activity
Trading	Debt and equity	Interest and dividends	Market value	Yes	Operating activity
Available for sale	Debt and equity	Interest and dividends	Market value	No	Investing activity

assets and total stockholders' equity are $700 higher under the trading and available-for-sale alternatives than they are under the held-to-maturity category because the $700 unrealized gain is recognized on the balance sheet for those two classifications. The gain is not reported on the income statement for available-for-sale securities; it is reported on the balance sheet in a special equity account called Unrealized Gain on Investment Securities. The statements of cash flows report purchases and sales of trading securities as operating activities while purchases and sales of available-for-sale and held-to-maturity securities are investing activities. Exhibit E.2 summarizes the reporting differences among the three classifications of investment securities.

Alternative Reporting Practices for Equity Securities

If an investor owns 20 percent or more of an investee's equity securities, the investor is presumed able, unless there is evidence to the contrary, to exercise *significant influence* over the investee company. Investors owning more than 50 percent of the stock of an investee company are assumed to have control over the investee. The previous discussion of accounting rules for equity securities assumed the investor did not significantly influence or control the investee. Alternative accounting rules apply to securities owned by investors who exercise significant influence or control over an investee company. Accounting for equity investment securities differs depending on the level of the investor's ability to influence or control the operating, investing, and financing activities of the investee.

As previously demonstrated, investors who do not have significant influence (they own less than 20 percent of the stock of the investee) account for their investments in equity securities at fair value. Investors exercising significant influence (they own 20 to 50 percent of the investee's stock) must account for their investments using the **equity method.** A detailed discussion of the equity method is beyond the scope of this text. However, *be aware that investments reported using the equity method represent a measure of the book value of the investee rather than the cost or fair value of the equity securities owned.*

Investors who have a controlling interest (they own more than 50 percent of the investee's stock) in an investee company are required to issue **consolidated financial statements.** The company that holds the controlling interest is referred to as the **parent company,** and the company that is controlled is called the **subsidiary company.** Usually, the parent and subsidiary companies maintain separate accounting records. However, a parent company is also required to report to the public its accounting data along with that of its subsidiaries in a single set of combined financial statements. These consolidated statements represent a separate accounting entity composed of the parent and its subsidiaries. A parent company that owns one subsidiary will produce three sets of financial statements: statements for the parent company, statements for the subsidiary company, and statements for the consolidated entity.

EXERCISES

Exercise E1   *Identifying asset values for financial statements*

Required

Indicate whether each of the following assets should be valued at fair market value (FMV), lower of cost or market (LCM), or historical cost (HC) on the balance sheet. For certain assets, historical cost may be called amortized cost (AC.)

Asset	FMV	LCM	HC/AC
Supplies			
Land			
Trading securities			
Cash			
Held-to-maturity securities			
Buildings			
Available-for-sale securities			
Office equipment			
Inventory			

Exercise E2   *Accounting for investment securities*

Norris Bros. purchased $36,000 of marketable securities on March 1, 2009. On the company's fiscal year closing date, December 31, 2009, the securities had a market value of $27,000. During 2009, Norris recognized $10,000 of revenue and $2,000 of expenses.

Required

a. Record a +, −, or NA in a horizontal statements model to show how the purchase of the securities affects the financial statements, assuming that the securities are classified as (1) held to maturity, (2) trading, or (3) available for sale. In the Cash Flow column, indicate whether the event is an operating activity (OA), investing activity (IA), or financing activity (FA). Record only the effects of the purchase event.

Event No.	Type	Cash	+	Inv. Sec.	=	Liab.	+	Equity	Rev.	−	Exp.	=	Net Inc.	Cash Flow
1	Held													
2	Trading													
3	Available													

b. Determine the amount of net income that would be reported on the 2009 income statement, assuming that the marketable securities are classified as (1) held to maturity, (2) trading, or (3) available for sale.

Exercise E3   *Effect of investment securities transactions on financial statements*

The following information pertains to Butler Supply Co. for 2011.

1. Purchased $100,000 of marketable investment securities.
2. Earned $10,000 of cash investment revenue.

3. Sold for $30,000 securities that cost $25,000.
4. The fair value of the remaining securities at December 31, 2011, was $89,000.

Required

a. Record the four events in a statements model like the following one. Use a separate model for each classification: (1) held to maturity, (2) trading, and (3) available for sale. The first event for the first classification is shown as an example.

Held to Maturity

Event No.	Cash	+	Inv. Sec.	=	Liab.	+	Ret. Earn.	+	Unreal. Gain.		Rev. or Gains	−	Exp. or Loss	=	Net Inc.		Cash Flow
1	(100,000)	+	100,000	=	NA	+	NA	+	NA		NA	−	NA	=	NA		(100,000) IA

b. What is the amount of net income under each of the three classifications?
c. What is the change in cash from operating activities under each of the three classifications?
d. Are the answers to Requirements *b* and *c* different for each of the classifications? Why or why not?

Exercise E4   *Preparing financial statements for investment securities*

Wright, Inc., began 2012 with $100,000 in both cash and common stock. The company engaged in the following investment transactions during 2012:

1. Purchased $20,000 of marketable investment securities.
2. Earned $600 cash from investment revenue.
3. Sold investment securities for $14,000 that cost $10,000.
4. Purchased $7,000 of additional marketable investment securities.
5. Determined that the investment securities had a fair value of $22,000 at the end of 2012.

Required

Use a vertical statements model to prepare income statements, balance sheets, and statements of cash flow for Wright, Inc., assuming the securities were (*a*) held to maturity, (*b*) trading, and (*c*) available for sale.

Exercise E5   *Differences among marketable investment securities classifications*

Complete the following table for the three categories of marketable investment securities:

Investment Category	Types of Securities	Types of Revenue Recognized	Value Reported on Balance Sheet	Recognition of Unrealized Gains and Losses on the Income Statement	Cash Flow from Purchase or Sale of Securities Is Classified as
Held to maturity	Debt	Interest	Amortized cost	No	Investing activity
Trading					
Available for sale					

Exercise E6   *Effect of marketable investment securities transactions on financial statements*

The following transactions pertain to Harrison Imports for 2007:

1. Started business by acquiring $30,000 cash from the issue of common stock.
2. Provided $90,000 of services for cash.

3. Invested $35,000 in marketable investment securities.
4. Paid $18,000 of operating expense.
5. Received $500 of investment income from the securities.
6. Invested an additional $16,000 in marketable investment securities.
7. Paid a $2,000 cash dividend to the stockholders.
8. Sold investment securities that cost $8,000 for $14,000.
9. Received another $1,000 in investment income.
10. Determined the market value of the investment securities at the end of the year was $42,000.

Required

Use a vertical model to prepare a 2009 income statement, balance sheet, and statement of cash flows, as-suming that the marketable investment securities were classified as (a) held to maturity, (b) trading, and (c) available for sale. (*Hint:* Record the events in T-accounts prior to preparing the financial statements.)

Exercise E7 *Comprehensive horizontal statements model*

Woody's Catering experienced the following independent events.

1. Acquired cash from issuing common stock.
2. Purchased inventory on account.
3. Paid cash to purchase marketable securities classified as trading securities.
4. Recorded unrealized loss on marketable securities that were classified as trading securities.
5. Recorded unrealized loss on marketable securities that were classified as available-for-sale securities.
6. Recorded unrealized loss on marketable securities that were classified as held-to-maturity securities.
7. Wrote down inventory to comply with lower-of-cost-or-market rule. (Assume that the company uses the perpetual inventory system.)
8. Recognized cost of goods sold under FIFO.
9. Recognized cost of goods sold under the weighted-average method.

Required

a. Show the effect of each event on the elements of the financial statements using a horizontal state-ments model like the following one. Use + for increase, − for decrease, and NA for not affected. In the Cash Flow column, indicate whether the item is an operating activity (OA), investing activ-ity (IA), or financing activity (FA). The first transaction is entered as an example.

Event No.	Assets	=	Liab.	+	Equity	Rev. or Gain	−	Exp. or Loss	=	Net Inc.	Cash Flow
1	+		NA		+	NA		NA		NA	+ FA

b. Explain why there is or is not a difference in the way Events 8 and 9 affect the financial statements model.

Time Value of Money

Future Value

Suppose you recently won $10,000 cash in a local lottery. You save the money to have funds available to obtain a masters of business administration (MBA) degree. You plan to enter the program three years from today. Assuming you invest the money in an account that earns 8 percent annual interest, how much money will you have available in three years? The answer depends on whether your investment will earn *simple* or *compound* interest.

To determine the amount of funds available assuming you earn 8 percent **simple interest,** multiply the principal balance by the interest rate to determine the amount of interest earned per year ($10,000 × 0.08 = $800). Next, multiply the amount of annual interest by the number of years the funds will be invested ($800 × 3 = $2,400). Finally, add the interest earned to the principal balance to determine the total amount of funds available at the end of the three-year term ($10,000 principal + $2,400 interest = $12,400 cash available at the end of three years).

Investors can increase their returns by reinvesting the income earned from their investments. For example, at the beginning of the second year, you will have available for investment not only the original $10,000 principal balance but also $800 of interest earned during the first year. In other words, you will be able to earn interest on the interest that you previously earned. Earning interest on interest is called **compounding.** Assuming you earn 8 percent compound interest, the amount of funds available to you at the end of three years can be computed as shown in Exhibit F.1.

EXHIBIT F.1

Year	Amount Invested	×	Interest Rate	=	Interest Earned	+	Amount Invested	=	New Balance
1	$10,000.00	×	0.08	=	$ 800.00	+	$10,000.00	=	$10,800.00
2	10,800.00	×	0.08	=	864.00	+	10,800.00	=	11,664.00
3	11,664.00	×	0.08	=	933.12	+	11,664.00	=	12,597.12
Total interest earned				=	$2,597.12				

Obviously, you earn more with compound interest ($2,597.12 compound versus $2,400 simple). The computations required for **compound interest** can become cumbersome when the investment term is long. Fortunately, there are mathematical formulas, interest tables, and computer programs that reduce the computational burden. For example, a compound interest factor can be developed from the formula

$$(1 + i)^n$$

where i = interest

n = number of periods

The value of the investment is determined by multiplying the compound interest factor by the principal balance. The compound interest factor for a three-year term and an 8 percent interest rate is 1.259712 (1.08 × 1.08 × 1.08 = 1.259712). Assuming a $10,000 original investment, the value of the investment at the end of three years is $12,597.12 ($10,000 × 1.259712). This is, of course, the same amount that was computed in the previous illustration (see final figure in the New Balance column of Exhibit F.1).

The mathematical formulas have been used to develop tables of interest factors that can be used to determine the **future value** of an investment for a variety of interest rates and time periods. For example, Table I on page 739 contains the interest factor for an investment with a three-year term earning 8 percent compound interest. To confirm this point, move down the column marked n to the third period. Next move across to the column marked 8 percent, where you will find the value 1.259712. This is identical to the amount computed using the mathematical formula in the preceding paragraph. Here also, the value of the investment at the end of three years can be determined by multiplying the principal balance by the compound interest factor ($10,000 × 1.259712 = $12,597.12). These same factors and amounts can be determined using computer programs in calculators and spreadsheet software.

Clearly, a variety of ways can be used to determine the future value of an investment, given a principal balance, interest rate, and term to maturity. In our case, we showed that your original investment of $10,000 would be worth $12,597 in three years, assuming an 8 percent compound interest rate. Suppose you determine this amount is insufficient to get you through the MBA program you want to complete. Assume you believe you will need $18,000 three years from today to sustain yourself while you finish the degree. Suppose your parents agree to cover the shortfall. They ask how much money you need today in order to have $18,000 three years from now.

Present Value

The mathematical formula required to convert the future value of a dollar to its **present value** equivalent is

$$\frac{1}{(1 + i)^n}$$

where i = interest

         n = number of periods

For easy conversion, the formula has been used to develop Table II, Present Value of $1. At an 8 percent annual compound interest rate, the present value equivalent of $18,000 to be received three years from today is computed as follows: Move down the far left column to where $n = 3$. Next, move right to the column marked 8%. At this point, you should see the interest factor 0.793832. Multiplying this factor by the desired future value of $18,000 yields the present value of $14,288.98 ($18,000 × 0.793832). This means if you invest $14,288.98 (present value) today at an annual compound interest rate of 8 percent, you will have the $18,000 (future value) you need to enter the MBA program three years from now.

If you currently have $10,000, you will need an additional $4,288.98 from your parents to make the required $14,288.98 investment that will yield the future value of $18,000 you need. Having $14,288.98 today is the same as having $18,000 three years from today, assuming you can earn 8 percent compound interest. To validate this conclusion, use Table I to determine the future value of $14,288.98, given a three-year term and 8 percent annual compound interest. As previously indicated, the future-value conversion factor under these conditions is 1.259712. Multiplying this factor by the $14,288.98 present value produces the expected future value of $18,000 ($14,288.98 × 1.259712 = $18,000). The factors in Table I can be used to convert present values to future values, and the corresponding factors in Table II are used to convert future values to present values.

Future Value Annuities

The previous examples described present and future values of a single lump-sum payment. Many financial transactions involve a series of payments. To illustrate, we return to the example in which you want to have $18,000 available three years from today. We continue the assumption that you can earn 8 percent compound interest. However, now we assume that you do not have $14,288.98 to invest today. Instead, you decide to save part of the money during each of the next three years. How much money must you save each year to have $18,000 at the end of three years? *The series of equal payments made over a number of periods in order to acquire a future value is called an* **annuity.** The factors in Table III, Future Value of an Annuity of $1, can be used to determine the amount of the annuity needed to produce the desired $18,000 future value. The table is constructed so that future values can be determined by multiplying the conversion factor by the amount of the annuity. These relationships can be expressed algebraically as follows:

Amount of annuity payment × Table conversion factor = Future value

To determine the amount of the required annuity payment in our example, first locate the future value conversion factor. In Table III, move down the first column on the left-hand side until you locate period 3. Next move to the right until you locate the 8 percent column. At this location you will see a conversion factor of 3.2464. This factor can be used to determine the amount of the annuity payment as indicated here:

Amount of annuity payment × Table conversion factor = Future value

Amount of annuity payment = Future value ÷ Table conversion factor

Amount of annuity payment = $18,000.00 ÷ 3.2464

Amount of annuity payment = $5,544.60

If you deposit $5,544.60 in an investment account at the end of each of the next three years,[1] the investment account balance will be $18,000, assuming your investment earns 8 percent interest compounded annually. This conclusion is confirmed by the following schedule.

End of Year	Beg. Acct. Bal.	+	Interest Computation	+	Payment	=	End. Acct. Bal.
1	NA	+	NA	+	$5,544.60	=	$ 5,544.60
2	$ 5,544.60	+	$ 5,544.60 × 0.08 = $443.57	+	5,544.60	=	11,532.77
3	11,532.77	+	11,532.77 × 0.08 = 922.62	+	5,544.60	=	18,000.00*

*Total does not add exactly due to rounding.

PRESENT VALUE ANNUITIES

We previously demonstrated that a future value of $18,000 is equivalent to a present value of $14,288.98, given annual compound interest of 8 percent for a three-year period. If the future value of a $5,544.60 annuity for three years is equivalent to $18,000, that same annuity should have a present value of $14,288.98. We can test this conclusion by using the

---

[1] A payment made at the end of a period is known as an *ordinary annuity.* A payment made at the beginning of a period is called an *annuity due.* Tables are generally set up to assume ordinary annuities. Minor adjustments must be made when dealing with an annuity due. For the purposes of this text, we consider all annuities to be ordinary.

conversion factors in Table IV, Present Value of an Annuity of $1. The present value annuity table is constructed so that present values can be determined by multiplying the conversion factor by the amount of the annuity. These relationships can be expressed algebraically as follows:

Amount of annuity payment × Table conversion factor = Present value

To determine the present value of the annuity payment in our example, first locate the present value conversion factor. In Table IV, move down the first column on the left-hand side until you locate period 3. Next move to the right until you locate the column for the 8 percent interest rate. At this location you will see a conversion factor of 2.577097. This factor can be used to determine the amount of the present value of the annuity payment, as indicated:

Amount of annuity payment × Table conversion factor = Present value

$5,544.60 × 2.577097 = $14,288.97*

*The 1 cent difference between this value and the expected value of $14,288.98 is due to rounding.

In summary, Tables III and IV can be used to convert annuities to future or present values for a variety of different assumptions regarding interest rates and time periods.

BUSINESS APPLICATIONS

Long-Term Notes Payable

In the early part of this chapter, we considered a case in which Blair Company borrowed $100,000 from National Bank. We indicated that Blair agreed to repay the bank through a series of annual payments (an *annuity*) of $25,709 each. How was this amount determined? Recall that Blair agreed to pay the bank 9 percent interest over a five-year term. Under these circumstances, we are trying to find the annuity equivalent to the $100,000 present value that the bank is loaning Blair. The first step in determining the annuity (annual payment) is to locate the appropriate present value conversion factor from Table IV. At the fifth row under the 9% column, you will find the value 3.889651. This factor can be used to determine the amount of the annuity payment as indicated here:

Amount of annuity payment × Table conversion factor = Present value

Amount of annuity payment = Present value ÷ Table conversion factor

Amount of annuity payment = $100,000 ÷ 3.889651

Amount of annuity payment = $25,709

There are many applications in which debt repayment occurs through annuities. Common examples with which you are probably familiar include auto loans and home mortgages. Payment schedules for such loans may be determined from the interest tables, as demonstrated here. However, most real-world businesses have further refined the computational process through the use of sophisticated computer programs. The software program prompts the user to provide the relevant information regarding the present value of the amount borrowed, number of payments, and interest rate. Given this information and a few keystrokes, the computer program produces the amount of the amortization payment along with an amortization schedule showing the amounts of principal and interest payments over the life of the loan. Similar results can be obtained with spreadsheet software applications such as Excel and Lotus. Even many handheld calculators have present and future value functions that enable users to quickly compute annuity payments for an infinite number of interest rate and time period assumptions.

Bond Liabilities: Determine Price

We discussed the use of discounts and premiums as means of producing an effective rate of interest that is higher or lower than the stated rate of interest (see Chapter 10). For example, if the stated rate of interest is lower than the market rate of interest at the time the bonds are issued, the issuer can increase the effective interest rate by selling the bonds for a price lower than their face value. At maturity, the issuer will settle the obligation by paying the face value of the bond. The difference between the discounted bond price and the face value of the bond is additional interest. To illustrate, assume that Tower Company issues $100,000 face value bonds with a 20-year term and a 9 percent stated rate of annual interest. At the time the bonds are issued, the market rate of interest for bonds of comparable risk is 10 percent annual interest. For what amount would Tower Company be required to sell the bonds in order to move its 9 percent stated rate of interest to an effective rate of 10 percent?

Information from present value Tables II and IV is required to determine the amount of the discount required to produce a 10 percent effective rate of interest. First, we identify the future cash flows that will be generated by the bonds. Based on the stated interest rate, the bonds will pay $9,000 ($100,000 face value $\times$ 0.09 interest) interest per year. This constitutes a 20-year annuity that should be discounted back to its present value equivalent. Also, at the end of 20 years, the bonds will require a single $100,000 lump-sum payment to settle the principal obligation. This amount must also be discounted back to its present value in order to determine the bond price. The computations required to determine the discounted bond price are shown here:

Present value of principal	$100,000 $\times$ 0.148644	=	$14,864.40
	(Table II, $n = 20$, $i = 10\%$)		
Present value of interest	$9,000 $\times$ 8.513564	=	76,622.08
	(Table IV, $n = 20$, $i = 10\%$)		
Bond price (proceeds received)			$91,486.48

Tower Company bonds sell at an $8,513.52 discount ($100,000 − $91,486.48) to produce a 10 percent effective interest rate. Note that in these computations, the stated rate of interest was used to determine the amount of cash flow, and the effective rate of interest was used to determine the table conversion factors.

TABLE I

Future Value of $1

n	4%	5%	6%	7%	8%	9%	10%	12%	14%	16%	20%
1	1.040000	1.050000	1.060000	1.070000	1.080000	1.090000	1.100000	1.120000	1.140000	1.160000	1.200000
2	1.081600	1.102500	1.123600	1.144900	1.166400	1.188100	1.210000	1.254400	1.299600	1.345600	1.440000
3	1.124864	1.157625	1.191016	1.225043	1.259712	1.295029	1.331000	1.404928	1.481544	1.560896	1.728000
4	1.169859	1.215506	1.262477	1.310796	1.360489	1.411582	1.464100	1.573519	1.688960	1.810639	2.073600
5	1.216653	1.276282	1.338226	1.402552	1.469328	1.538624	1.610510	1.762342	1.925415	2.100342	2.488320
6	1.265319	1.340096	1.418519	1.500730	1.586874	1.677100	1.771561	1.973823	2.194973	2.436396	2.985984
7	1.315932	1.407100	1.503630	1.605781	1.713824	1.828039	1.948717	2.210681	2.502269	2.826220	3.583181
8	1.368569	1.477455	1.593848	1.718186	1.850930	1.992563	2.143589	2.475963	2.852586	3.278415	4.299817
9	1.423312	1.551328	1.689479	1.838459	1.999005	2.171893	2.357948	2.773079	3.251949	3.802961	5.159780
10	1.480244	1.628895	1.790848	1.967151	2.158925	2.367364	2.593742	3.105848	3.707221	4.411435	6.191736
11	1.539454	1.710339	1.898299	2.104852	2.331639	2.580426	2.853117	3.478550	4.226232	5.117265	7.430084
12	1.601032	1.795856	2.012196	2.252192	2.518170	2.812665	3.138428	3.895976	4.817905	5.936027	8.916100
13	1.665074	1.885649	2.132928	2.409845	2.719624	3.065805	3.452271	4.363493	5.492411	6.885791	10.699321
14	1.731676	1.979932	2.260904	2.578534	2.937194	3.341727	3.797498	4.887112	6.261349	7.987518	12.839185
15	1.800944	2.078928	2.396558	2.759032	3.172169	3.642482	4.177248	5.473566	7.137938	9.265521	15.407022
16	1.872981	2.182875	2.540352	2.952164	3.425943	3.970306	4.594973	6.130394	8.137249	10.748004	18.488426
17	1.947900	2.292018	2.692773	3.158815	3.700018	4.327633	5.054470	6.866041	9.276464	12.467685	22.186111
18	2.025817	2.406619	2.854339	3.379932	3.996019	4.717120	5.559917	7.689966	10.575169	14.462514	26.623333
19	2.106849	2.526950	3.025600	3.616528	4.315701	5.141661	6.115909	8.612762	12.055693	16.776517	31.948000
20	2.191123	2.653298	3.207135	3.869684	4.660957	5.604411	6.727500	9.646293	13.743490	19.460759	38.337600

TABLE II

Present Value of $1

n	4%	5%	6%	7%	8%	9%	10%	12%	14%	16%	20%
1	0.961538	0.952381	0.943396	0.934579	0.925926	0.917431	0.909091	0.892857	0.877193	0.862069	0.833333
2	0.924556	0.907029	0.889996	0.873439	0.857339	0.841680	0.826446	0.797194	0.769468	0.743163	0.694444
3	0.888996	0.863838	0.839619	0.816298	0.793832	0.772183	0.751315	0.711780	0.674972	0.640658	0.578704
4	0.854804	0.822702	0.792094	0.762895	0.735030	0.708425	0.683013	0.635518	0.592080	0.552291	0.482253
5	0.821927	0.783526	0.747258	0.712986	0.680583	0.649931	0.620921	0.567427	0.519369	0.476113	0.401878
6	0.790315	0.746215	0.704961	0.666342	0.630170	0.596267	0.564474	0.506631	0.455587	0.410442	0.334898
7	0.759918	0.710681	0.665057	0.622750	0.583490	0.547034	0.513158	0.452349	0.399637	0.353830	0.279082
8	0.730690	0.676839	0.627412	0.582009	0.540269	0.501866	0.466507	0.403883	0.350559	0.305025	0.232568
9	0.702587	0.644609	0.591898	0.543934	0.500249	0.460428	0.424098	0.360610	0.307508	0.262953	0.193807
10	0.675564	0.613913	0.558395	0.508349	0.463193	0.422411	0.385543	0.321973	0.269744	0.226684	0.161506
11	0.649581	0.584679	0.526788	0.475093	0.428883	0.387533	0.350494	0.287476	0.236617	0.195417	0.134588
12	0.624597	0.556837	0.496969	0.444012	0.397114	0.355535	0.318631	0.256675	0.207559	0.168463	0.112157
13	0.600574	0.530321	0.468839	0.414964	0.367698	0.326179	0.289664	0.229174	0.182069	0.145227	0.093464
14	0.577475	0.505068	0.442301	0.387817	0.340461	0.299246	0.263331	0.204620	0.159710	0.125195	0.077887
15	0.555265	0.481017	0.417265	0.362446	0.315242	0.274538	0.239392	0.182696	0.140096	0.107927	0.064905
16	0.533908	0.458112	0.393646	0.338735	0.291890	0.251870	0.217629	0.163122	0.122892	0.093041	0.054088
17	0.513373	0.436297	0.371364	0.316574	0.270269	0.231073	0.197845	0.145644	0.107800	0.080207	0.045073
18	0.493628	0.415521	0.350344	0.295864	0.250249	0.211994	0.179859	0.130040	0.094561	0.069144	0.037561
19	0.474642	0.395734	0.330513	0.276508	0.231712	0.194490	0.163508	0.116107	0.082948	0.059607	0.031301
20	0.456387	0.376889	0.311805	0.258419	0.214548	0.178431	0.148644	0.103667	0.072762	0.051385	0.026084

TABLE III Future Value of an Annuity of $1

n	4%	5%	6%	7%	8%	9%	10%	12%	14%	16%	20%
1	1.000000	1.000000	1.000000	1.000000	1.000000	1.000000	1.000000	1.000000	1.000000	1.000000	1.000000
2	2.040000	2.050000	2.060000	2.070000	2.080000	2.090000	2.100000	2.120000	2.140000	2.160000	2.200000
3	3.121600	3.152500	3.183600	3.214900	3.246400	3.278100	3.310000	3.374400	3.439600	3.505600	3.640000
4	4.246464	4.310125	4.374616	4.439943	4.506112	4.573129	4.641000	4.779328	4.921144	5.066496	5.368000
5	5.416323	5.525631	5.637093	5.750739	5.866601	5.984711	6.105100	6.352847	6.610104	6.877135	7.441600
6	6.632975	6.801913	6.975319	7.153291	7.335929	7.523335	7.715610	8.115189	8.535519	8.977477	9.929920
7	7.898294	8.142008	8.393838	8.654021	8.922803	9.200435	9.487171	10.089012	10.730491	11.413873	12.915904
8	9.214226	9.549109	9.897468	10.259803	10.636628	11.028474	11.435888	12.299693	13.232760	14.240093	16.499085
9	10.582795	11.026564	11.491316	11.977989	12.487558	13.021036	13.579477	14.775656	16.085347	17.518508	20.798902
10	12.006107	12.577893	13.180795	13.816448	14.486562	15.192930	15.937425	17.548735	19.337295	21.321469	25.958682
11	13.486351	14.206787	14.971643	15.783599	16.645487	17.560293	18.531167	20.654583	23.044516	25.732904	32.150419
12	15.025805	15.917127	16.869941	17.888451	18.977126	20.140720	21.384284	24.133133	27.270749	30.850169	39.580502
13	16.626838	17.712983	18.882138	20.140643	21.495297	22.953385	24.522712	28.029109	32.088654	36.786196	48.496603
14	18.291911	19.598632	21.015066	22.550488	24.214920	26.019189	27.974983	32.392602	37.581065	43.671987	59.195923
15	20.023588	21.578564	23.275970	25.129022	27.152114	29.360916	31.772482	37.279715	43.842414	51.659505	72.035108
16	21.824531	23.657492	25.672528	27.888054	30.324283	33.003399	35.949730	42.753280	50.980352	60.925026	87.442129
17	23.697512	25.840366	28.212880	30.840217	33.750226	36.973705	40.544703	48.883674	59.117601	71.673030	105.930555
18	25.645413	28.132385	30.905653	33.999033	37.450244	41.301338	45.599173	55.749715	68.394066	84.140715	128.116666
19	27.671229	30.539004	33.759992	37.378965	41.446263	46.018458	51.159090	63.439681	78.969235	98.603230	154.740000
20	29.778079	33.065954	36.785954	40.995492	45.761964	51.160120	57.274999	72.052442	91.024928	115.379747	186.688000

TABLE IV Present Value of an Annuity of $1

n	4%	5%	6%	7%	8%	9%	10%	12%	14%	16%	20%
1	0.961538	0.952381	0.943396	0.934579	0.925926	0.917431	0.909091	0.892857	0.877193	0.862069	0.833333
2	1.886095	1.859410	1.833393	1.808018	1.783265	1.759111	1.735537	1.690051	1.646661	1.605232	1.527778
3	2.775091	2.723248	2.673012	2.624316	2.577097	2.531295	2.486852	2.401831	2.321632	2.245890	2.106481
4	3.629895	3.545951	3.465106	3.387211	3.312127	3.239720	3.169865	3.037349	2.913712	2.798181	2.588735
5	4.451822	4.329477	4.212364	4.100197	3.992710	3.889651	3.790787	3.604776	3.433081	3.274294	2.990612
6	5.242137	5.075692	4.917324	4.766540	4.622880	4.485919	4.355261	4.111407	3.888668	3.684736	3.325510
7	6.002055	5.786373	5.582381	5.389289	5.206370	5.032953	4.868419	4.563757	4.288305	4.038565	3.604592
8	6.732745	6.463213	6.209794	5.971299	5.746639	5.534819	5.334926	4.967640	4.638864	4.343591	3.837160
9	7.435332	7.107822	6.801692	6.515232	6.246888	5.995247	5.759024	5.328250	4.946372	4.606544	4.030967
10	8.110896	7.721735	7.360087	7.023582	6.710081	6.417658	6.144567	5.650223	5.216116	4.833227	4.192472
11	8.760477	8.306414	7.886875	7.498674	7.138964	6.805191	6.495061	5.937699	5.452733	5.028644	4.327060
12	9.385074	8.863252	8.383844	7.942686	7.536078	7.160725	6.813692	6.194374	5.660292	5.197107	4.439217
13	9.985648	9.393573	8.852683	8.357651	7.903776	7.486904	7.103356	6.423548	5.842362	5.342334	4.532681
14	10.563123	9.898641	9.294984	8.745468	8.244237	7.786150	7.366687	6.628168	6.002072	5.467529	4.610567
15	11.118387	10.379658	9.712249	9.107914	8.559479	8.060688	7.606080	6.810864	6.142168	5.575456	4.675473
16	11.652296	10.837770	10.105895	9.446649	8.851369	8.312558	7.823709	6.973986	6.265060	5.668497	4.729561
17	12.165669	11.274066	10.477260	9.763223	9.121638	8.543631	8.021553	7.119630	6.372859	5.748704	4.774634
18	12.659297	11.689587	10.827603	10.059087	9.371887	8.755625	8.201412	7.249670	6.467420	5.817848	4.812195
19	13.133939	12.085321	11.158116	10.335595	9.603599	8.905115	8.364920	7.365777	6.550369	5.877455	4.843496
20	13.590326	12.462210	11.469921	10.594014	9.818147	9.128546	8.513564	7.469444	6.623131	5.928841	4.869580

EXERCISES

Exercise F1   *Future value and present value*

Required

Using Tables I, II, III, or IV in the appendix, calculate the following:

a. The future value of $30,000 invested at 8 percent for 10 years.
b. The future value of eight annual payments of $2,000 at 9 percent interest.
c. The amount that must be deposited today (present value) at 8 percent to accumulate $60,000 in five years.
d. The annual payment on a 10-year, 6 percent, $50,000 note payable.

Exercise F2   *Computing the payment amount*

Karen Webb is a business major at State U. She will be graduating this year and is planning to start a consulting business. She will need to purchase computer equipment that costs $25,000. She can borrow the money from the local bank but will have to make annual payments of principal and interest.

Required

a. Compute the annual payment Karen will be required to make on a $25,000, four-year, 8 percent loan.
b. If Karen can afford to make annual payments of $8,000, how much can she borrow?

Exercise F3   *Saving for a future value*

Billy Dan and Betty Lou were recently married and want to start saving for their dream home. They expect the house they want will cost approximately $325,000. They hope to be able to purchase the house for cash in 10 years.

Required

a. How much will Billy Dan and Betty Lou have to invest each year to purchase their dream home at the end of 10 years? Assume an interest rate of 9 percent.
b. Billy Dan's parents want to give the couple a substantial wedding gift for the purchase of their future home. How much must Billy Dan's parents give them now if they are to have the desired amount of $325,000 in 12 years? Assume an interest rate of 9 percent.

Exercise F4   *Sale of bonds at a discount using present value*

Carr Corporation issued $50,000 of 6 percent, 10-year bonds on January 1, 2008, for a price that reflected a 7 percent market rate of interest. Interest is payable annually on December 31.

Required

a. What was the selling price of the bonds?
b. Prepare the journal entry to record issuing the bonds.
c. Prepare the journal entry for the first interest payment on December 31, 2008, using the effective interest rate method.

accelerated depreciation method Depreciation method that recognizes more depreciation expense in the early stages of an asset's life than the straight-line method and less later in the asset's life. *p. 450*

account Record of classified and summarized transaction data; component of financial statement elements. *p. 10*

account balance Difference between total debit and total credit amounts in an account. *p. 172*

accounting Service-based profession developed to provide reliable and relevant financial information useful in making decisions. *p. 3*

accounting controls Procedures companies implement to safeguard assets and to ensure accurate and reliable accounting records and reports. *p. 344*

accounting cycle For a given time period, the cycle of recording accounting data, adjusting the accounts, preparing the financial statements, and closing the temporary accounts; when one accounting cycle ends, a new one begins. *p. 67*

accounting equation Algebraic relationship between a company's assets and the claims on those assets, represented as Assets = Liabilities + Equity. *p. 11*

accounting event Economic occurrence that changes a company's assets, liabilities, or equity. *p. 12*

accounting period Time span covered by the financial statements; normally one year, but may be a quarter, a month or some other time interval. *p. 17*

accounts receivable Expected future cash receipts arising from permitting customers to *buy now and pay later;* typically relatively small balances due within a short time period. *pp. 62, 391*

accounts receivable turnover Financial ratio that measures how fast accounts receivable are collected in cash; computed by dividing sales by accounts receivable. *p. 405*

accrual Accounting recognition of revenue or expense in a period before cash is exchanged. *p. 61*

accrual accounting Accounting system which recognizes revenues when earned and expenses when incurred regardless of when the related cash is exchanged. *p. 61*

Accumulated Depreciation Contra asset account that shows the sum of all depreciation expense recognized for an asset since the date of acquisition. *pp. 124, 449*

adjusting entry Entry that updates account balances prior to preparing financial statements; a bookkeeping tool. Adjusting entries never affect the Cash account. *p. 71*

administrative controls Procedures companies implement to evaluate performance and monitor compliance with company policies and public laws. *p. 344*

adverse opinion Opinion issued by a certified public accountant that means one or more departures from GAAP in a company's financial statements are so very material the auditors believe the financial statements do not fairly represent the company's status; contrast with *unqualified opinion. p. 84*

allocation Recognizing expense by systematically assigning the cost of an asset to periods of use. *p. 121*

Allowance for Doubtful Accounts Contra asset account used to record the amount of accounts receivable estimated to be uncollectible. *p. 393*

allowance method of accounting for bad debts Method of accounting for receivables in which the amount of future uncollectible accounts is estimated and recognized as expense in the same period in which the corresponding sales are recognized. Receivables are reported in the financial statements at net realizable value (the amount expected to be collected in cash). *p. 392*

allowances Reductions in the selling price of goods extended to buyers because the goods are defective or of lower quality than the buyer ordered to encourage a buyer to keep merchandise that would otherwise be returned.

American Institute of Certified Public Accountants (AICPA). National association that serves the educational and professional interests of members of the public accounting profession; membership is voluntary. See also *Code of Professional Conduct. p. 78*

amortization (1) Systematic and periodic allocation of the costs of intangible assets to expense over their useful lives; (2) periodically transferring the discount on a note or a bond to interest expense. *pp. 410, 444*

amortization (of loan) Systematic repayment of principal and interest over the life of a loan. *p. 501*

annual report Document companies publish to provide information, including financial statements, to stockholders. *p. 23*

annuity Series of equal cash flows received or paid over equal time intervals at a constant rate of return. *p. 736*

appropriated retained earnings Retained earnings restricted by the board of directors for a specific purpose (e.g., to repay debt or for future expansion); part of total retained earnings, but not available for distribution as dividends. *p. 574*

articles of incorporation Information about a proposed corporation, such as its name, purpose, location, expected life, proposed capital stock, and a list of the members of its board of directors, filed with a state agency when applying for the legal formation of the corporation. *p. 560*

articulation Characteristic of financial statements that means they are interrelated. For example, the amount of net income reported on the income statement is added to beginning retained earnings as a component in calculating the ending retained earnings balance reported on the statement of changes in stockholders' equity. *p. 17*

asset Economic resource used to produce revenue which is expected to provide future benefit to the business. *p. 4*

asset exchange transaction A transaction, such as the purchase of land with cash, that decreases one asset and increases another asset; total assets remain unchanged. *pp. 13, 62*

asset source transaction A transaction that increases both an asset and a claim on assets; the three types of asset source transactions are acquisitions from owners (equity), borrowings from creditors (liabilities), or earnings from operations (revenues). *pp. 12, 62*

asset use transaction A transaction that decreases both an asset and a claim on assets; the three types of asset use transactions are distributions (transfers to owners), liability payments (to creditors), or expenses (costs incurred to operate the business). *pp. 14, 63*

audit Detailed examination of some aspect of a company's accounting records or operating procedures in order to report the results to interested parties. See *financial audit. p. 83*

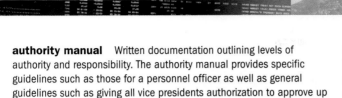

authority manual   Written documentation outlining levels of authority and responsibility. The authority manual provides specific guidelines such as those for a personnel officer as well as general guidelines such as giving all vice presidents authorization to approve up to a designated spending limit. *p. 345*

authorized stock   Number of shares of stock a corporation has state approval to issue. *p. 566*

available-for-sale securities   Classification for marketable securities that are not considered held-to-maturity or trading securities. *p. 726*

average number of days to collect accounts receivable (average collection period)   Measure of how quickly, on average, a business collects its accounts receivable; calculated as 365 divided by the accounts receivable turnover. *p. 405*

average number of days to sell inventory (average days in inventory)   Financial ratio that measures the average number of days that inventory stays in stock before it is sold. *p. 313*

bad debts expense   Expense resulting from failure to collect accounts receivable; the amount recognized may be estimated using the allowance method, or, if not material, actual losses may be recorded using the direct write-off method. *p. 393*

balance sheet   Financial statement that reports a company's assets and the corresponding claims (liabilities and equity) on those assets as of a specific date (usually as of the end of the accounting period). *p. 19*

bank reconciliation   Schedule that identifies and explains differences between the cash balance reported by the bank and the cash balance in the company's accounting records. *p. 350*

bank statement   Record issued by a bank (usually monthly) of all activity in the bank account for that period. *p. 349*

bank statement credit memo   Bank statement enclosure that describes an increase in the account balance. *p. 349*

bank statement debit memo   Bank statement enclosure that describes a decrease in the account balance. *p. 349*

basket purchase   Acquiring several assets at once for a single purchase price; no specific cost is attributed to the individual assets. *p. 445*

board of directors   Group of individuals elected by the stockholders of a corporation to oversee its operations. *p. 563*

bond certificate   Debt security used to obtain long-term financing in which a company borrows funds from a number of lenders, called *bondholders;* usually issued in denominations of $1,000. *p. 505*

bond discount   Difference between the selling price and the face amount of a bond sold for less than the face amount. *p. 512*

bondholder   The party buying a bond (the lender or creditor). *p. 505*

bond premium   Difference between the selling price and the face amount of a bond that is sold for more than the face amount. *p. 517*

book of original entry   A journal in which a transaction is first recorded. *p. 186*

book value   Historical (original) cost of an asset minus accumulated depreciation to date. *pp. 124, 450*

book value per share   An accounting measure of a share of common stock, computed by dividing total stockholders' equity less preferred rights by the number of common shares outstanding. *p. 566*

call premium   Difference between the call price (the price that must be paid for a called bond) and the face amount of the bond. *p. 508*

call price   Specified price an issuer must pay to call bonds; usually higher than the face amount of the bonds. *p. 508*

callable bonds   Bonds which the issuer, at its option, may pay off prior to maturity. *p. 508*

capital expenditures (for an existing asset)   Substantial amounts spent to improve an asset's quality or to extend its life. *p. 457*

capitalized   Initially recorded an expenditure in an asset account for subsequent transfer to expense as the asset is used to produce revenue. *p. 140*

carrying value   Face amount of a bond liability less any unamortized bond discount or plus any unamortized bond premium. *p. 513*

cash   Coins, currency, checks, balances in checking and certain savings accounts, money orders, bank drafts, certificates of deposit, and other items that are payable on demand. *p. 346*

cash discount   Price reduction on merchandise sold offered by sellers to encourage prompt payment; when taken, represents a sales discount to the seller and a purchase discount to the buyer of the merchandise. *p. 247*

cash inflows   Sources of cash. *p. 605*

cash outflows   Uses of cash. *p. 605*

Cash Short and Over   Account used to record the amount of cash shortages or overages; shortages represent expenses and overages represent revenues. *p. 354*

certified check   Check guaranteed by a bank to be drawn on an account with sufficient funds to pay the check. *p. 351*

certified public accountant (CPA)   Accountant who, by meeting certain educational and experiential requirements, is licensed by the state government to provide audit services to the public. *p. 83*

chart of accounts   List of all ledger accounts and their corresponding account numbers. *p. 184*

checks   Prenumbered forms, sometimes multicopy, preprinted on the face with the name of the business issuing them, authorizing the bank to disburse funds from the issuer's account. The issuer enters the transaction date, the desired payee, and the amount in the appropriate places on the check form. *p. 348*

claims   Owners' and creditors' interests in a business's assets. *p. 11*

claims exchange transaction   A transaction that decreases one claim and increases another claim; total claims remain unchanged. For example, accruing interest expense is a claims exchange transaction; liabilities increase, and the expense recognition decreases retained earnings. *p. 63*

classified balance sheet   Balance sheet that distinguishes between current and noncurrent items. *p. 358*

closely held corporation   Corporation whose stock is exchanged among a limited number of individuals. *p. 560*

closing entries   Entries that transfer the balances in the temporary accounts (Revenue, Expense, and Dividends accounts) to the Retained Earnings account at the end of the accounting period. *pp. 21, 188*

closing the books or closing   Bookkeeping technique of transferring balances from the temporary accounts (Revenue, Expense, and Dividends) to the permanent account (Retained Earnings). *p. 67*

Code of Professional Conduct   Guidelines established by the American Institute of Certified Public Accountants (AICPA) to

promote ethical conduct among certified public accountants; AICPA members agree to adhere to this code, which goes beyond legal requirements. *p. 78*

collateral   Assets pledged as security for a loan. *p. 519*

common size financial statements   Financial statements in which dollar amounts are converted to percentages to aid in comparing financial data among periods and among companies. *p. 259*

common stock   Basic class of corporate stock that has no preferential claim on assets or dividends; certificates that evidence ownership in a company. *pp. 11, 566*

compound interest   Interest earned on interest by reinvesting interest so that it is added to the initial principal. Contrast with *simple interest*. *p. 734*

compounding   Earning interest on interest. *p. 734*

consistency   The generally accepted accounting principle that a company should, in most circumstances, continually use the same accounting method(s) so that its financial statements are comparable across time. *p. 305*

consolidated financial statements   Financial statements that represent the combined operations of a parent company and its subsidiaries. *p. 730*

continuity   Presumption that a corporation's existence may extend well beyond the time at which any particular shareholder retires or sells his or her stock. *p. 562*

contra account   Account with a normal balance opposite that of other accounts in the same category (e.g., Accumulated Depreciation is classified as an asset, but it normally has a credit balance). *p. 182*

contra asset account   Account used to reduce the reported value of the asset to which it relates; e.g., subtracting the contra asset Allowance for Bad Debts from Accounts Receivable reduces receivables to their net realizable value. *pp. 124, 449*

contra liability account   Account used to reduce the reported value of the liability to which it relates; e.g., subtracting the contra liability Discount on Note Payable from Notes Payable reduces the amount of liabilities on the balance sheet. *p. 409*

contributed capital   The claim on assets resulting from asset contributions to a business by its owners.

convertible bonds   Bonds which bondholders can convert (exchange) to ownership interests (stock) in the corporation. *p. 508*

copyright   Legal protection of writings, musical compositions, and other intellectual property for the exclusive use of the creator or persons assigned the right by the creator. *p. 460*

corporation   Legal entity separate from its owners, created by the state pursuant to an application submitted according to state laws by a group of individuals with a common purpose. *p. 560*

cost method of accounting for treasury stock   Method of accounting for treasury stock in which treasury stock purchases are recorded in the Treasury Stock account at their cost to the company without regard to the original issue price or par value. *p. 571*

cost of goods available for sale   Total costs paid to obtain goods and ready them for sale, including the cost of beginning inventory plus purchases and transportation-in costs, less purchase returns and allowances and purchase discounts. *pp. 241, 242*

cost of goods sold   Total cost incurred for the goods sold during a specific accounting period. *pp. 241, 242*

credit   Entry on the right side of an account; increases liability and equity accounts or decreases asset accounts. *p. 172*

creditor   Individual or organization that has loaned goods or services to a business. *p. 4*

cumulative dividends   Preferred dividends that accumulate from year to year until paid. *p. 567*

current (short-term) asset   Asset that will be converted to cash or consumed within one year or an operating cycle, whichever is longer. *pp. 357, 443*

current (short-term) liability   Obligation due within one year or an operating cycle, whichever is longer. *p. 357*

current ratio (working capital ratio)   Measure of liquidity; calculated by dividing current assets by current liabilities. *p. 359*

date of record   Date that establishes who will receive the dividend payment: shareholders who actually own the stock on the record date will receive the dividend even if they sell the stock before the dividend is paid. *p. 572*

debenture   Unsecured bond backed by the general credit of the issuing company. *p. 507*

debit   Entry on the left side of an account; increases asset accounts or decreases liability and equity accounts. *p. 172*

debt security   Type of financial instrument that represents a liability to the investee company. *p. 725*

debt to assets ratio   Financial measure of a company's level of risk, calculated as total debt divided by total assets. *p. 137*

declaration date   Date on which the board of directors declares a dividend. *p. 572*

deferral   Accounting recognition of revenue or expense in a period after cash is exchanged. *p. 121*

deferred tax liability   Income tax payment postponed until future years because of the difference in accounting methods selected for financial reporting and methods required for tax purposes (e.g., a company may use straight-line depreciation in financial statements but use MACRS for tax reporting). *p. 456*

depletion   The removal of natural resources from the land; the depletion costs of the natural resources are systematically transferred to expense as the resources are removed. *p. 444*

deposit ticket   Bank form submitted along with funds that identifies the account number, account name, and a record of the checks and cash being put in the account. *p. 348*

deposits in transit   Deposits added to a depositor's books but not received and recorded by the bank prior to the date of the bank statement. *p. 350*

depreciable cost   Original cost minus salvage value (of a long-term depreciable asset). *p. 451*

depreciation   Decline in value of long-term tangible assets such as buildings, furniture, or equipment. It is systematically recognized by accountants as depreciation expense over the useful lives of the affected assets. *p. 444*

depreciation expense   Portion of the original cost of a long-term tangible asset allocated to an expense account in a given period. *p. 124*

direct method   Method of reporting cash flows from operating activities on the statement of cash flows that shows individual categories of cash receipts from and cash payments for major activities (collections from customers, payments to suppliers, etc.). *p. 609*

direct write-off method   Accounting practice of recognizing uncollectible accounts expense when accounts are determined to be uncollectible, regardless of the period in which the related sale occurred. *p. 400*

disclaimer of audit opinion   Report on financial statements issued when the auditor is unable to obtain enough information to determine if the statements conform to GAAP; is neither positive nor negative. *p. 85*

discount   Amount of interest included in the face of a discount note; the discount (interest) is subtracted from the face amount of the note to determine the amount of cash borrowed (principal). *p. 409*

discount notes   Notes with interest included in their face value, which is also the maturity value. *p. 409*

Discount on Bonds Payable   Contra liability account used to record the amount of discount on a bond issue. *p. 513*

Discount on Notes Payable   Contra liability account subtracted from the Notes Payable account to determine the carrying value of the liability. *p. 409*

dividend   Transfer of wealth from a business to its owners. *pp. 15, 727*

dividends in arrears   Cumulative dividends on preferred stock that were not paid in prior periods; must be paid before paying any dividends to holders of common stock. *p. 567*

double taxation   Recognition that corporate profits distributed to owners are taxed twice, once when the income is reported on the corporation's income tax return and again when the dividends are reported on the individual's return. *p. 561*

double-declining-balance depreciation   Depreciation computations that produce larger amounts of depreciation in the early years of an asset's life and progressively smaller amounts as the asset ages. *p. 446*

double-entry accounting (double-entry bookkeeping)   Recordkeeping system that provides checks and balances by recording two sides for every transaction. *pp. 12, 172*

earnings (net income)   The difference between revenues and expenses. Sometimes called *profit. p. 4*

effective interest rate   Yield rate of bonds, equal to the market rate of interest on the day the bonds are sold. *p. 513*

effective interest rate method   Method of amortizing bond discounts and premiums that bases interest computations on the carrying value of liability. As the liability increases or decreases, the amount of interest expense also increases or decreases. *p. 523*

elements   The primary financial statement categories: assets, liabilities, equity, contributed capital, revenue, expenses, gains, losses, distributions, and net income. *p. 10*

entity   Economic unit (individual, business, or other organization) for which accounting records are separately maintained; it is distinct from its owners, creditors, managers, and employees.

entrenched management   Management that may be difficult to remove, even if it has become ineffective, because of the organization's political dynamics. *p. 563*

equity   Owners' interest in company assets; secondary to creditors' claims (i.e., Assets − Liabilities = Equity); also called *residual interest* or *net assets. p. 11*

equity method   Method of accounting for investments in marketable equity securities required when the investor company owns 20 percent or more of the investee company. Under the equity method, the amount of the investment asset represents a measure of the book value of the investee rather than the cost or market value of the investment security. *p. 730*

equity security   Type of financial instrument that evidences an ownership interest in a company, such as a common stock certificate. *p. 725*

estimated useful life   Time period for which a business expects to use an asset. *p. 447*

ex-dividend   Stock traded after the date of record but before the payment date; does not receive the benefit of the upcoming dividend. *p. 572*

expense   An economic sacrifice (decrease in assets or increase in liabilities) that is incurred in the process of generating revenue. *pp. 14, 65*

expense transactions   Business events that decrease assets or increase liabilities in order to produce revenue in the course of operating a business.

face value (of bond)   Amount to be paid to the bondholder at bond maturity; base for computing periodic cash interest payments. *p. 505*

fair value   The price at which securities or other assets sell in free markets. Also called market value. *p. 725*

fidelity bond   Insurance policy that a company buys to insure itself against loss due to employee dishonesty. *p. 344*

financial accounting   Branch of accounting focused on the business information needs of external users (creditors, investors, governmental agencies, financial analysts, etc.); its objective is to classify and record business events and transactions to produce external financial reports (income statement, balance sheet, statement of cash flows, and statement of changes in equity). *p. 6*

Financial Accounting Standards Board (FASB)   Private, independent standard-setting body established by the accounting profession that has been delegated the authority by the SEC to establish most of the accounting rules and regulations for public financial reporting. *p. 8*

financial audit   Detailed examination of a company's accounting records and the documents that support the information reported in the financial statements; includes testing the reliability of the underlying accounting system used to produce the financial reports. *p. 84*

financial leverage   Principle of increasing earnings through debt financing by investing money at a higher rate than the rate paid on the borrowed money. *pp. 138, 520*

financial resources   Money or credit supplied to a business by investors (owners) and creditors. *p. 4*

financial statements   Reports used to communicate a company's financial information to interested external parties. The four general-purpose financial statements are the income statement, statement of changes in equity, balance sheet, and statement of cash flows. *p. 10*

financing activities   Cash inflows and outflows from transactions with investors and creditors (except interest), including cash receipts from issuing stock, borrowing activities, and cash disbursements to pay dividends; one of the three categories of cash inflows and outflows reported on the statement of cash flows. This category shows the amount of cash supplied by these resource providers and the amount of cash that is returned to them. *pp. 20, 606*

first-in, first-out (FIFO) cost flow method   Inventory cost flow method in which cost of goods sold is computed as if the earliest items purchased are the first items sold. *p. 300*

fiscal year   The annual time period for which a company provides financial statements. *p. 171*

fixed interest rate   Interest rate (charge for borrowing money) that remains constant over the life of the loan. *p. 501*

FOB (free on board) destination   Shipping term that means the seller bears the freight (transportation-in) costs. *p. 248*

FOB (free on board) shipping point   Shipping term that means the buyer bears the freight (transportation-in) costs. *p. 248*

footnotes to the financial statements   Written explanations accompanying the financial statements that provide information about such items as estimates used and accounting methods chosen when GAAP permits alternatives. *p. 191*

franchise   Exclusive right to sell products or perform services in certain geographic areas. *p. 460*

full disclosure   The accounting principle that financial statements should include all information relevant to an entity's operations and financial condition. Full disclosure frequently requires adding footnotes to the financial statements. *p. 305*

future value   Amount an investment will be worth at some point in the future, assuming a specified interest rate and the reinvestment of interest each period that it is earned. *p. 735*

gains   Increases in assets or decreases in liabilities that result from peripheral or incidental transactions. *p. 251*

general authority   Company guidelines that apply to various levels of a company's management, such as requiring everyone at that level to fly coach class. *p. 345*

general journal   Book of original entry in which any accounting transaction could be recorded, though commonly limited to adjusting and closing entries and unusual transactions. *p. 186*

general ledger   The set of all accounts used in given accounting system, typically organized in financial statement order. *p. 16*

generally accepted accounting principles (GAAP)   Rules and practices that accountants agree to follow in financial reports prepared for public distribution. *p. 8*

going concern assumption   Accounting presumption that a company will continue to operate indefinitely, benefiting from its assets and paying its obligations in full; justifies reporting assets and liabilities in the financial statements. *p. 392*

goodwill   Intangible added value of a successful business attributable to such factors as reputation, location, and superior products that enables the business to earn above-average profits; measured by an entity acquiring the business as the excess paid over the appraised value of the net assets. *p. 461*

gross margin (gross profit)   Difference between sales revenue and cost of goods sold; the amount a company makes from selling goods before subtracting operating expenses. *pp. 241, 242*

gross margin method   Technique for estimating the ending inventory amount without a physical count; useful when the percentage of gross margin to sales remains relatively stable from one accounting period to the next. *p. 310*

gross margin percentage   Expressing gross margin as a percentage of sales by dividing gross margin by net sales; the amount of each dollar of sales that is profit before deducting any operating expenses. *p. 260*

half-year convention   Tax rule that requires recognizing six months of depreciation expense on an asset both in the year of purchase and in the year of disposal regardless of the actual purchase date. *p. 455*

held-to-maturity securities   Classification for marketable debt securities the purchasing company intends to hold (rather than sell) until the securities mature. *p. 726*

historical cost concept   Accounting practice of reporting assets at the actual price paid for them when purchased regardless of estimated changes in market value. *pp. 15, 445*

horizontal statements model   Concurrent representation of several financial statements horizontally across a page. *p. 21*

imprest basis   Maintaining an account at a specified fixed amount, such as periodically replenishing a petty cash fund to its imprest amount. *p. 355*

income   Increase in value created by providing goods and services through resource transformation. *p. 4*

income statement   Financial report of profitability; measures the difference between revenues and expenses for the accounting period (whether or not cash has been exchanged). *p. 17*

independent auditor   Licensed certified public accountant engaged to audit a company's financial statements; not an employee of the audited company. *p. 84*

indirect method   Method of reporting cash flows from operating activities on the statement of cash flows that starts with the net income from the income statement, followed by adjustments necessary to convert accrual-based net income to a cash-basis equivalent. *p. 609*

installment notes   Obligations that require regular payments of principal and interest over the life of the loan. *p. 502*

intangible assets   Long-term assets having no physical substance that benefit their owners through providing rights and privileges, such as a trademark. *p. 444*

interest   Fee paid for the use of funds; represents expense to the borrower and revenue to the lender. *pp. 5, 727*

interest-bearing notes   Notes that require face value plus accrued interest be paid at maturity. *p. 409*

internal controls   Policies and procedures companies establish to provide reasonable assurance of reducing fraud, providing reliable accounting records, and accomplishing organization objectives. *p. 80*

inventory   Goods under production or finished and ready for sale; also stockpiles of supplies used in the business (office supplies, cleaning supplies).

inventory cost flow methods   Alternative ways to allocate the cost of goods available for sale between cost of goods sold and ending inventory. *p. 302*

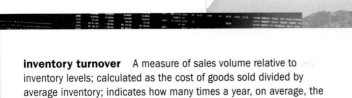

inventory turnover A measure of sales volume relative to inventory levels; calculated as the cost of goods sold divided by average inventory; indicates how many times a year, on average, the inventory is sold (turned over). *p. 312*

investee Company that receives assets or services in exchange for a debt or equity security. *p. 725*

investing activities Cash inflows and outflows associated with buying or selling long-term assets and cash inflows and outflows associated with lending activities and investments in the debt and equity of other companies; one of the three categories of cash inflows and outflows reported on the statement of cash flows. *pp. 20, 606*

investment Commitment of assets (usually cash) by a business to acquire other assets that will be used to produce revenue. *p. 70*

investment securities Certificates that describe the rights and privileges that investors receive when they loan or give assets or services to investees. *p. 725*

investor Company or individual who gives assets or services in exchange for security certificates representing ownership interests. *pp. 4, 725*

issued stock Stock a company has sold to the public. *p. 566*

issuer (of a bond) Party that issues the bond (the borrower). *pp. 75, 505*

issuer of the note Individual or business borrowing funds (the party receiving the cash when a note is issued). *pp. 75, 409*

journal Book (or electronic record) of original entry in which accounting data are entered chronologically before posting to the ledger accounts.

labor resources Both intellectual and physical efforts of individuals used in the process of providing goods and services to customers. *p. 5*

last-in, first-out (LIFO) cost flow method Inventory cost flow method in which cost of goods sold is computed as if the most recently purchased items are the first items sold. *p. 300*

ledger Collection of all accounts used by a business; primary source of financial statement information. *p. 184*

legal capital Amount of assets that should be maintained as protection for creditors; the number of shares multiplied by the par value. *p. 565*

liabilities Obligations of a business to relinquish assets, provide services, or accept other obligations. *p. 11*

limited liability Concept that investors in a corporation may not be held personally liable for the actions or debts of the corporation; stockholders' liability is limited to the amount they paid for their stock. *p. 562*

limited liability company (LLC) Organizational form that offers many of the favorable characteristics and legal benefits of a corporation (e.g., limited liability and centralized management) but is permitted by federal law to be taxed as a partnership, thereby avoiding double taxation of profits. *p. 562*

line of credit Preapproved financing arrangement with a lending institution in which a business can borrow money up to the approved limit by simply writing a check. *p. 505*

liquidation Process of dividing up an organization's assets and returning them to the resource providers. In business liquidations,

creditors normally have first priority; after creditor claims have been satisfied, any remaining assets are distributed to the company's owners (investors). *p. 4*

liquidity Ability to convert assets to cash quickly and meet short-term obligations. *pp. 19, 359*

long-term liabilities Liabilities with maturity dates beyond one year or the company's operating cycle, whichever is longer; non-current liabilities. *p. 501*

long-term operational assets Assets used by a business, normally over multiple accounting periods, to generate revenue; contrast with assets that are sold (inventory) or held (investments) to generate revenue; also called *productive assets. p. 443*

losses Decreases in assets or increases in liabilities that result from peripheral or incidental transactions. *p. 251*

lower-of-cost-or-market rule Accounting principle of reporting inventory at its replacement cost (market) if replacement cost has declined below the inventory's original cost, regardless of the cause. *p. 308*

management's discussion and analysis (MD&A) Section of a company's annual report in which management explains many different aspects of the company's past performance and future plans. *p. 192*

managerial accounting Branch of accounting focused on the information needs of managers and others working within the business; its objective is to gather and report information that adds value to the business. Managerial accounting information is not regulated or reported to the public. *p. 6*

manufacturing businesses Companies that make the goods they sell customers. *p. 22*

market Group of people or entities organized to buy and sell resources. *p. 4*

market interest rate Interest rate currently available on a wide range of alternative investments with similar levels of risk. *p. 518*

market value The price at which securities sell in the secondary market; also called *fair value. pp. 566, 725*

marketable securities Securities that are readily traded in the secondary securities market. *p. 725*

matching concept Accounting principle of recognizing expenses in the same accounting period as the revenues they produce, using one of three methods: match expenses directly with revenues (e.g. cost of goods sold); match expenses to the period in which they are incurred (e.g. rent expense), and match expenses systematically with revenues (e.g. depreciation expense). *pp. 71, 126*

material error Error or other reporting problem that, if known, would influence the decision of an average prudent investor. *p. 84*

materiality The point at which knowledge of information would influence a user's decision; can be measured in absolute, percentage, quantitative, or qualitative terms. The concept allows nonmaterial matters to be handled in any convenient way, such as charging a pencil sharpener to expense rather than recording periodic depreciation over its useful life. *p. 127*

merchandise inventory Finished goods held for resale to customers. *p. 243*

merchandising businesses Companies that buy and resell merchandise inventory. *p. 22*

modified accelerated cost recovery system (MACRS)
Prescribed method of depreciation for tax purposes that provides the maximum depreciation expense deduction permitted under tax law. *p. 455*

mortgage bond   Type of secured debt that conditionally transfers title of designated property to the bondholder until the bond is paid. *p. 507*

multistep income statement   Income statement format that matches various revenues with related expenses in order to present subtotals (steps) such as gross margin and operating income; distinguishes between routine operating items and nonoperating items such as gains, losses, and interest. Contrast with *single-step income statement. p. 254*

natural resources   Wasting assets originally attached to land such as mineral deposits, oil and gas reserves, and reserves of timber, mines, and quarries; the land value declines as the resources are removed. *p. 444*

net assets   See *equity. p. 11*

net income   Increase in equity resulting from operating the business. *p. 17*

net income percentage   See *return on sales. p. 260*

net loss   Decrease in equity resulting from operating the business. *p. 17*

net realizable value   The amount of accounts receivable a company expects to actually collect in cash; the face amount of receivables less an allowance for estimated uncollectible accounts. *p. 392*

net sales   Sales less returns from customers and allowances or cash discounts granted to customers. *p. 259*

noncash investing and financing activities   Certain business transactions, usually long-term, that do not involve cash, such as exchanging stock for land or purchasing property by using debt; reported separately on the statement of cash flows. *p. 606*

non-sufficient-funds (NSF) check   Customer's check deposited but returned by the bank on which it was drawn because the customer did not have enough money in its account to pay the check. *p. 351*

note payable   Liability represented by a legal document called a *note* that describes pertinent details such as principal amount, interest charges, maturity date, and collateral. *p. 74*

notes receivable   Notes that evidence rights to receive cash in the future; usually specify the maturity date, rate of interest, and other credit terms. *p. 391*

not-for-profit entities   Organizations (also called *nonprofit* or *nonbusiness entities*) established primarily for motives other than making a profit, such as providing goods and services for the social good. Examples include state-supported universities and colleges, hospitals, public libraries, and public charities. *p. 6*

operating activities   Cash inflows from and outflows for routine, everyday business operations, normally resulting from revenue and expense transactions including interest; one of the three categories of cash inflows and outflows reported on the statement of cash flows. *pp. 20, 606*

operating cycle   Process of converting cash into inventory, inventory into receivables, and receivables back to cash; its length can be measured in days using financial statement data. *pp. 357, 407*

operating income   Income after subtracting operating expenses from operating revenues. Gains and losses and other peripheral activities are added to or subtracted from operating income to determine net income or loss. *p. 253*

opportunity   An element of the fraud triangle that recognizes weaknesses in internal controls that enable the occurrence of fraudulent or unethical behavior. *p. 80*

outstanding checks   Checks the depositor company has written and deducted from its cash account balance that have not yet been presented to its bank for payment. *p. 350*

outstanding stock   Shares of stock a corporation has issued that are still owned by outside parties, i.e. all stock that has been issued less any treasury stock the corporation has repurchased. *p. 566*

paid-in capital in excess of par (or stated) value   Any amount received above the par or stated value of stock when stock is issued. *p. 568*

par value   Arbitrary value assigned to stock by the board of directors; like *stated value*, designates *legal capital. p. 565*

parent company   Company that holds a controlling interest (more than 50 percent ownership) in another company. *p. 730*

partnership   Business entity owned by at least two people who share talents, capital, and the risks of the business. *p. 560*

partnership agreement   Legal document that defines the rights and responsibilities of each partner and describes how income and losses are to be divided. *p. 560*

patent   Legal right granted by the U.S. Patent Office ensuring a company or an individual the exclusive right to a product or process. *pp. 444, 460*

payables   Obligations to make future economic sacrifices, usually cash payments. *p. 391*

payment date   Date on which a dividend is actually paid. *p. 572*

period costs   Expenses recognized in the period in which they are incurred regardless of when cash payments for them are made; costs that cannot be directly traced to products. *pp. 67, 241*

periodic inventory system   Method of accounting for inventory which requires a physical count of goods on hand at the end of the accounting period in order to determine the amount of cost of goods sold and to update the Inventory account. *p. 264*

permanent accounts   Balance sheet accounts; contain information carried forward from one accounting period to the next (ending account balance one period becomes beginning account balance next period). *p. 21*

perpetual inventory system   Method of accounting for inventory in which the amount of cost of goods sold is recorded for each sale of inventory; the Inventory account is increased and decreased with each purchase and sale of merchandise. *p. 241*

petty cash fund   Small amount of currency kept on company premises to pay for minor items when writing checks is not practical. *p. 355*

petty cash voucher   Document that verifies a petty cash disbursement, signed by the person who received the money. Supporting documents, such as an invoice, restaurant bill, or parking fee receipt, should be attached to the petty cash voucher. *p. 355*

physical flow of goods   Physical movement of goods through a business, normally on a FIFO basis so that the first goods purchased are the first goods delivered to customers, reducing the likelihood of inventory obsolescence. *p. 300*

physical resources   Natural resources businesses transform create more valuable resources. *p. 5*

posting   Copying transaction data from journals to ledger accounts. *p. 186*

preferred stock Class of stock, usually nonvoting, that has preferential claims (usually to dividends) over common stock. *p. 567*

premium on bonds payable *p. 517*

present value A measure of the value today of an amount of money expected to be exchanged on a specified future date. *p. 735*

pressure An element of the fraud triangle that recognizes conditions that motivate fraudulent or unethical behavior. *p. 81*

price-earnings (P/E) ratio Measure that reflects the values of different stocks in terms of earnings; calculated as market price per share divided by earnings (net income) per share; a higher P/E ratio generally indicates that investors are optimistic about a company's future. *p. 25*

primary securities market Market in which investee companies issue debt and equity securities to investors in exchange for assets; contrast with *secondary securities market. p. 725*

principal Amount of cash actually borrowed, to be repaid in the future with interest. *p. 409*

procedures manual Written documentation of a company's accounting policies and procedures. *p. 345*

product costs All costs directly traceable to acquiring inventory and getting it ready for sale, including transportation-in. Contrast with *selling and administrative costs. p. 241*

productive assets See *long-term operational assets. p. 20*

profit Value added by transforming resources into products or services desired by customers. *p. 4*

property, plant, and equipment Assets such as machinery and equipment, buildings, and land, used to produce products or to carry on the administrative and selling functions of a business; sometimes called *plant assets. p. 444*

purchase discount Reduction in the gross price of merchandise offered to a buyer if the buyer pays cash for the merchandise within a stated time (usually within 10 days of the date of the sale). *p. 247*

purchase returns and allowances A reduction in the cost of purchases resulting from dissatisfaction with merchandise purchased. *p. 246, 247*

qualified opinion Opinion issued by a certified public accountant that means the company's financial statements are, for the most part, in compliance with GAAP, but there is some circumstance (explained in the auditor's report) about which the auditor has reservations; contrast with *unqualified opinion. p. 84*

rationalization An element of the fraud triangle that recognizes a human tendency to justify fraudulent or unethical behavior. *p. 81*

realization Accounting term that usually refers to actual cash collection (e.g., collecting accounts receivable). *p. 61*

recognition Reporting an accounting event in the financial statements. *p. 61*

reinstate Recording an account receivable previously written off back into the accounting records, generally when cash is collected long after the original due date.

relative fair market value method Method of allocating the purchase price among individual assets acquired in a basket purchase; each asset is assigned a percentage of the total price paid for all assets. The percentage assigned equals the market value of a particular asset divided by the total of the market values of all assets acquired in the basket purchase. *p. 445*

reliability concept The accounting principle that supports reporting most assets at historical cost, because historical cost , unlike the market value of many assets, can be independently verified. Reliable information is not subjective. *p. 15*

reporting entities Businesses or other organizations for which financial statements are prepared. *p. 9*

residual interest See *equity. p. 11*

restrictive covenants Provisions specified in a loan agreement that are designed to reduce creditor risk, such as limiting additional borrowing or dividend payments. *p. 519*

retail companies Businesses that sell merchandise directly to consumers. *p. 239*

retained earnings Portion of stockholders' equity that includes all earnings retained in the business since inception (revenues minus expenses and distributions for all accounting periods). *p. 11*

return on assets Profitability measure based on earnings a company generates relative to its asset base; calculated as net income divided by average total assets. *p. 136*

return on equity Profitability measure based on earnings a company generates relative to its stockholders' equity; calculated as net income divided by average stockholders' equity. *p. 138*

return on sales Profitability measure that reflects the percent of net income each sales dollar generates; computed by dividing net income by net sales. Also called *net income percentage. p. 260*

revenue The economic benefit (increase in assets or decrease in liabilities) gained by providing goods or services to customers. *pp. 14, 82*

salaries payable Amounts owed but not yet paid to employees for services they have already performed. *p. 63*

sales discount Cash discount offered by the seller of merchandise to encourage a customer to pay promptly. When the customer takes the discount and pays less than the original selling price, the difference between the selling price and the cash collected is the sales discount. *p. 256*

sales returns and allowances A reduction in sales revenue resulting from dissatisfaction with merchandise sold. *p. 259*

salvage value Expected selling price of an asset at the end of its useful life. *p. 447*

Sarbanes-Oxley Act of 2002 Federal legislation enacted to promote ethical corporate governance and fair financial reporting. The act requires a company's chief executive officer (CEO) and chief financial officer (CFO) to certify in writing that the financial reports being issued present fairly the company's financial status. An executive who falsely certifies the company's financial reports is subject to significant fines and imprisonment. The act also establishes the Public Company Accounting Oversight Board (PCAOB) which has the primary responsibility for developing and enforcing auditing standards for CPAs who audit SEC companies. The Sarbanes-Oxley Act also prohibits auditors from providing most types of nonaudit services to companies they audit. *p. 561*

schedule of cost of goods sold Internal report used with the periodic inventory system that reflects the computation of cost of goods sold. *p. 265*

secondary securities market Market in which investors exchange securities with each other; contrast with *primary securities market*. *p. 725*

secured bonds Bonds secured by specific identifiable assets. *p. 507*

Securities Act of 1933 and Securities Exchange Act of 1934 Federal legislation passed after the stock market crash of 1929 to regulate the issuance and subsequent trading of public company stocks and bonds; created the Securities and Exchange Commission (SEC). *p. 561*

Securities and Exchange Commission (SEC) Federal agency authorized by Congress to establish financial reporting practices of public companies; requires companies that issue securities to the public to file audited financial statements with the government annually. *p. 192*

selling and administrative costs Costs such as advertising expense and rent expense that cannot be directly traced to inventory; recognized as expenses in the period in which they are incurred. Contrast with *product costs*. *p. 241*

separation of duties Internal control feature of assigning the functions of authorization, recording, and custody to different individuals. *p. 344*

serial bonds Bonds that mature at specified intervals throughout the life of the total issue. *p. 507*

service businesses Organizations such as accounting and legal firms, dry cleaners, and insurance companies that provide services to consumers. *p. 22*

service charges Fees charged by a bank for such things as services performed or penalties for overdrawn accounts or failure to maintain a specified minimum cash balance. *p. 351*

shrinkage Decreases in inventory for reasons other than sales to customers. *p. 255*

signature card Bank form that documents the bank account number and signatures of persons authorized to write checks on an account. *p. 348*

simple interest Interest computed by multiplying the principal by the interest rate by the number of periods. Previously earned interest is not added to the principal, so no interest is earned on the interest of past periods. Contrast with *compound interest*. *p. 734*

single-step income statement Income statement format which presents net income in one step, the difference between total revenues and total expenses. Contrast with *multistep income statement*. *p. 254*

sinking fund Fund to which the bond issuer contributes cash annually to ensure sufficient funds will be available to pay the face amount on the maturity date. *p. 508*

sole proprietorship Business (usually small) owned by one person. *p. 560*

solvency Ability of a business to pay liabilities in the long run. *p. 359*

source document Record such as a cash register tape, invoice, time card, or check stub that provides accounting information to be recorded in the accounting journals and ledgers. *p. 186*

special journals Journals designed to improve recording efficiency for specific routine, high-volume transactions such as credit sales. *p. 186*

specific authorizations Policies and procedures that apply to designated levels of management, such as the policy that only the plant manager can authorize overtime pay. *p. 345*

specific identification Inventory costing method in which cost of goods sold and ending inventory are computed using the actual costs of the specific goods sold or those on hand at the end of the period. *p. 300*

spread Difference between the rate a bank pays to obtain money (e.g., interest paid on savings accounts) and the rate the bank earns on money it lends to borrowers. *p. 520*

stakeholders Parties interested in the operations of a business, including owners, lenders, employees, suppliers, customers, and government agencies. *p. 6*

stated interest rate Rate of interest specified in the bond contract that is the percentage of face value used to calculate the amount of interest paid in cash at specified intervals over the life of the bond. *p. 506*

stated value Arbitrary value assigned to stock by the board of directors; like *par value*, designates *legal capital*. *p. 565*

statement of cash flows The financial statement that reports a company's cash inflows and outflows for an accounting period, classifying them as operating, investing, or financing activities. *p. 20*

statement of changes in stockholders' equity Statement that summarizes the transactions that affected the owners' equity during the accounting period. *p. 19*

stock certificate Document showing ownership interest issued to an investor in exchange for contributing assets to a corporation; describes ownership rights and privileges. *p. 560*

stock dividend Proportionate distribution of additional shares of the declaring corporation's stock. *p. 573*

stockholders Owners of a corporation. *pp. 11, 563*

stockholders' equity The interest in a corporation's assets that is owned by the stockholders. *p. 11*

stock split Corporate action that proportionately reduces the par value and increases the number of outstanding shares; designed to reduce the market value of the split stock. *p. 573*

straight-line amortization Method of amortization in which equal amounts of the account being reduced (e.g., Bond Discount, Bond Premium, Patent) are transferred to the appropriate expense account over the relevant time period. *p. 514*

straight-line depreciation Depreciation computations that produce equal amounts of depreciation to allocate to expense each period over an asset's life; computed by subtracting the salvage value from the asset's cost and then dividing by the number of years of useful life. *pp. 124, 446*

straight-line method Allocation method that produces equal amounts in each accounting period.

subordinated debentures Unsecured bonds with a lower claim on assets than general creditors; in the case of liquidation, holders are paid off after the general creditors are paid. *p. 507*

subsidiary company Company controlled (more than 50 percent owned) by another company. *p. 730*

systematic allocation of cost Process of allocating the cost of an asset to expense over several accounting periods in an orderly manner. *p. 127*

T-account   Simple account representation, using two bars arranged in the form of the letter "T"; the account title is written across the top on the horizontal bar, debit entries are recorded on the left side of the vertical bar, and credit entries on the right side. *p. 172*

tangible assets   Assets that have physical form, such as equipment, machinery, natural resources, and land. *p. 444*

temporary accounts   Accounts used to collect retained earnings data applicable to only the current accounting period (revenues, expenses and distributions); sometimes called *nominal accounts*. *p. 21*

term bonds   Bonds in an issue that mature on a specified date in the future. *p. 507*

time value of money   The concept that the present value of one dollar to be exchanged in the future is less than one dollar because of interest, risk, and inflation factors. For example, a person may be willing to pay $0.90 today for the right to receive $1.00 one year from today.

times interest earned   Ratio that measures a company's ability to make its interest payments; calculated by dividing the amount of earnings available for interest payments (net income before interest and income taxes) by the amount of the interest payments. *p. 521*

trademark   Name or symbol that identifies a company or an individual product. *p. 460*

trading securities   Classification for marketable securities companies plan to buy and sell quickly to generate profits from short-term appreciation in stock and bond prices. *p. 726*

transaction   Business event that involves transferring something of value between two entities. *p. 12*

transferability   Characteristic of corporations referring to the ease of exchanging ownership interests since ownership is divided into small, readily traded ownership units (shares of stock). *p. 563*

transportation-in (freight-in)   Cost of freight on goods purchased under FOB shipping point terms; a product cost usually added to the cost of inventory. *p. 248*

transportation-out (freight-out)   Freight cost for goods delivered to customers under FOB destination terms; a period cost expensed when incurred. *p. 248*

treasury stock   Stock previously issued to the public that the issuing corporation has bought back. Contrast with *outstanding stock*. *p. 566*

trial balance   Schedule listing the balances of all ledger accounts; verifies mathematical accuracy of the accounting records and provides a convenient reference of current account balances. *p. 190*

true cash balance   Actual amount of cash owned by a company at the close of business on the date of the bank statement. *p. 350*

2/10, n/30   Common payment terms indicating the seller is offering the purchaser a 2 percent discount off the gross invoice price if the purchaser pays the reduced amount in cash within 10 days from the merchandise purchase date. *p. 247*

unadjusted bank balance   Depositor's cash balance reported by the bank as of the date of the bank statement. *p. 350*

unadjusted book balance   Cash account balance in the depositor's accounting records as of the date of the bank reconciliation before making any adjustments. *p. 350*

unearned revenue   Liability arising when customers pay cash in advance for services a business will perform in the future. *p. 122*

units-of-production depreciation   Depreciation computations that produce varying amounts of depreciation based on the level of an asset's usage each period rather than a measure of time; for example, automobile depreciation may be based on total estimated miles to be driven rather than total estimated years to be used. *pp. 446*

unqualified opinion   Opinion issued by a certified public accountant that means the company's financial statements are, in all material respects, in compliance with GAAP; the auditor has no reservations. Contrast with *qualified opinion. p. 84*

unrealized gains or losses   Paper gains or losses on investment securities the company still owns; not realized until the securities are sold or otherwise disposed of. *p. 728*

unsecured bonds (debentures)   Bonds backed by the general credit of the organization. *p. 507*

unsubordinated debentures   Unsecured bonds with claims on assets equal to those of general creditors. *p. 507*

users   Individuals or organizations that use financial information for decision making. *p. 6*

variable interest rate   Interest rate that fluctuates (changes) from period to period over the life of the loan. *p. 501*

voluntarily disclosing   Professional responsibility to clients that prohibits CPAs, in most circumstances, from revealing information obtained as a result of their client–accountant relationships. *p. 85*

warranty   Promise to correct a deficiency in or dissatisfaction with quality, quantity, or performance of a product or service sold. *p. 402*

weighted-average cost flow method   Inventory cost flow method in which the cost allocated between inventory and cost of goods sold is based on the weighted average cost per unit, which is determined by dividing total costs of goods available for sale during the accounting period by total units available for sale during the period. If the weighted average is recomputed with each successive purchase, the result is moving average. *p. 300*

wholesale companies   Companies that sell goods to other businesses. *p. 239*

withdrawals   Distributions of assets to the owners of proprietorships and partnerships. *p. 564*

Chapter 1

p. 3: © The McGraw-Hill Companies, Inc./John Flournoy, photographer, P. 4: © David Buffington/Getty Images, P. 8: © Brand X Pictures/Punch-Stock; p. 9: © Royalty-Free/CORBIS; p. 11: © Amy Etra/Photo Edit; p. 23 (left): © Royalty-Free/CORBIS; p. 23 (middle): © PhotoLink/Getty Images; p. 23 (right): © Kim Steele/Getty Images; p. 24: © David Tietz/Editorial Image, LLC

Chapter 2

p. 61: © Donovan Reese/Getty Images; p. 71: © Digital Vision/Getty Images; p. 76: © Digital Vision/Getty Images; p. 85: © Reuters/CORBIS

Chapter 3

p. 121: © David Tietz/Editorial Image, LLC; p. 122: © Michael Newman/PhotoEdit; p. 127: © Royalty-Free/CORBIS; p. 138: © Janis Christie/Getty Images; p. 139: Royalty-Free/CORBIS

Chapter 4

p. 171: © The McGraw-Hill Companies, Inc./Andrew Resek, photographer; p. 186: © Joel Gordon; p. 191: © Chad Rachman/AP Photo; p. 193 (top): © Archivo Icongrafico, S.A./Corbis; p. 193 (bottom): AP Photo/Paul Sancya

Chapter 5

p. 239: © Steve Cole/Getty Images; p. 241: © BananaStock/Punch-Stock; p. 246: © Steve Allen/Getty Image; p. 256: © John S. Reid; p. 259: © The McGraw-Hill Companies, Inc./Lars A. Niki, photographer; p. 262: © Stockdisc/PunchStock

Chapter 6

p. 299: © Royalty-Free/CORBIS; p. 300: © Ron Chapple/Thinkstock; p. 304, 307, 308: © Royalty-Free/CORBIS; p. 313: © Photolink/Getty Images

Chapter 7

p. 343: © Adam Rountree/Getty Images; p. 345 (both): Courtesy of Nordstrom; p. 348: © Royalty-Free/CORBIS; p. 351: © Keith Brofsky/Getty Images; p. 360: © Royalty-Free/CORBIS

Chapter 8

p. 391: © Royalty-Free/CORBIS; p. 401: © Janis Christie/Getty Images; p. 406: © Rick Friedman/Corbis; p. 408: © Lawrence Lawry/Getty Images

Chapter 9

p. 443: © Comstock Images/Alamy; p. 444: © The McGraw-Hill Companies, Inc./John Flournoy, photographer; p. 461: © Brand X Pictures/PunchStock; p. 462: © Photodisc Collection/Getty Images; p. 466: © Comstock Images/Alamy

Chapter 10

p. 501: © Lucas Jackson/AP Photo; p. 508: © AP Photo/Pat Sullivan; p. 519: © Keith Brofsky/Getty Images

Chapter 11

p. 559: © BananaStock/PunchStock ; p. 561: © Royalty-Free/CORBIS; p. 563: © Chad Baker/Ryan McVay/Getty Images p. 566: © Simon Fell/Getty Images; p. 576: © BD Lanphere/Stock Boston

Chapter 12

p. 605: © Nick Coudis/Getty Images; p. 617: © The McGraw-Hill Companies, Inc/Lars A. Niki, Photographer; p. 622: © Steve Allen/Getty Image

Page numbers followed by n indicate material found in notes.

A

Abercrombie & Fitch, 171, 191, 192
Account(s), 10. *See also* T-accounts;
     specific account names
   chart of, 184
   liability, contra, 409
   permanent, 21
   temporary (nominal), 21, 74
Account balance, 172
Accounting
   careers in, 7–8
   defined, 3
   private, 8
   public, 7–8
   role in society, 4–8
Accounting cycles, 67
   closing process and, 67, 68
Accounting equation, 11, 12–15
   asset exchange transactions and, 13
   asset source transactions and, 12–13, 14
   asset use transactions and, 14–15
   deferral accounting and, 130–132, 134–136
Accounting events, 12
Accounting information, 5–6
   types of, 6
Accounting period, 17
Accounts receivable, 391
   average number of days to collect, 405–406, 712
   collection of, 351
Accounts receivable turnover ratio, 405, 712
Accrual(s), 25
Accrual accounting, 60–78
   adjusting accounts and, 71
   closing process and, 67, 68, 74
   converting to cash-basis accounting from, 607–611
   defined, 60
   financial statements and, 65–67, 72–74
   in first accounting cycle, 62–69
   ledger accounts and, 64, 65
   matching concept and, 67–69
   notes payable and, 74–78
   in second accounting cycle, 70–74
   steps in accounting cycle and, 74
Accrued interest, 71
Adjusting entries, 71
   year-end, allowance method of accounting for bad
        debts and, 398
Adjustments
   to bank balance, 350, 351–352
   to book balance, 350–351, 352
   for lost, damaged, or stolen inventory, 255–256
Administrative controls, 344
Advance Auto Parts, Inc., 550
Advanced Micro Devices (AMD), 76
Adverse opinion, 84
Alaska Airlines, 622
Albertson's, 299, 312
Alcoa, Inc., 294, 576
Aldila, Inc., 137

Allocation
   of cost, systematic, 127
   defined, 121
Allowance for Doubtful Accounts account, 393
Allowance method of accounting for bad debts,
        392–400
   estimating bad debts expense and, 396
   financial statements and, 395, 399, 400
   T-accounts and, 394, 395, 398, 399
   year-end adjusting entries and, 398
American Electric Power, 350
American Greetings Corporation, 494
American Institute of Certified Public Accountants
        (AICPA), Code of Professional Conduct of, 78
American Red Cross (ARC), 3, 10
American Stock Exchange, 561
Amortization, 444
   of costs of intangible assets with identifiable useful
        lives, 462–463
   defined, 501
   of discounts, 410
   straight-line, 514
Anheuser Bush Companies, Inc., 493
Annual reports, 23, 191–194
   footnotes to financial statements in, 191
   independent auditor's role and, 192
   management's discussion and analysis in, 192
   SEC and, 192–194
Annuities
   future value, 736
   ordinary, 736n
   present value, 736–737
Annuities due, 736n
Applebee's International, 493
Appropriated Retained Earnings account, 574
Arthur Andersen, 85
Articles of incorporation, 560
Asset(s), 4, 11
   assessing effective use of, 136–138
   claims on, 11
   current (short-term), 357, 443
   intangible. *See* Intangible assets
   long-term, 444. *See also* Depreciation;
        Long-term operational assets
   productive, 20–21
   ratio of debt to, 137–138, 350, 711
   return on, 136–137, 521, 711, 713
   tangible, intangible assets versus, 444–445
Asset exchange transactions, 13
   in double-entry accounting system, 176–177
Asset source transactions, 12–13, 14
   in double-entry accounting system, 172–175
Asset use transactions, 14–15
   in double-entry accounting system, 177–179
AT&T, 563
Audit(s)
   external, 83–86
   financial, 84
Audit opinions, 84–85
   disclaimer of, 85

Auditors, independent, 192
Auditor's report, 23
Audit services, 7
Authority manuals, 345
Authorized stock, 566
Automated accounting systems, 186
AutoZone, Inc., 538
Available-for-sale securities, 726
Average collection period, 405–406, 712
Average days in inventory, 313
Average number of days to collect accounts
        receivable, 405–406, 712
Average number of days to sell inventory, 313, 713
A&W All American Foods, 118

B

Bad debts expense, 392n, 393
   allowance method of accounting for, 392–400
   direct write-off method for recognizing, 400–401
   estimating, 386
Balance, trial, 190–191
Balance sheet, 18
   accrual accounting and, 65, 66, 73, 74
   classified, 358
   cost flow and, 301
   defined, 19
   long-term operational assets and, 464
   preparing, 19
   vertical statements model and, 77
Bank balance
   adjustments to, 350, 351–352
   true, 350
   unadjusted, 350
Bank checks, 348–349
Bank loans, 135
Bank reconciliation, 350–354
Bank statement(s), 349–350
   bank reconciliation and, 350–354
Bank statement credit memos, 349
Bank statement debit memos, 349
Basket purchases, 445–446
Biogen Idec, Inc., 166
Black & Decker, 521
Blue Nile, 239, 240, 241, 254, 261
Boards of directors, 563
Boeing, 538, 622
Bond(s), 505–519
   advantages of issuing, 506–507
   callable, 508, 518
   convertible, 508
   face value of, 505–506, 509
   financial leverage and, 520
   financial statements and, 510–512
   holder of, 505
   issued at a discount. *See* Bond discounts
   issued at a premium, 517–518, 526
   issued at face value, 509
   issuer of, 505

Bond(s)—*Cont.*
journal entries for, 509
maturity of, 507–508
mortgage, 507
prices of. *See* Bond prices
ratings of, 508
redemptions of, 518–519
secured, 507
semiannual interest payments and, 517
serial, 507
tax advantage of debt financing and, 520
term, 507
unsecured, 507
Bond certificates, 505
Bond discounts, 512–517
amortizing under effective interest rate method, 523–526
bond prices and, 513
effective interest rate and, 512–513
financial statements and, 515–516
Bonded employees, 344
Bondholders, 505
Bond premiums, 517–518
amortizing under effective interest rate method, 526
Bond prices
bond discount and, 513
call price, 508
determining, time value of money and, 738
Bond ratings, 508
Book(s), closing. *See* Closing
Book balance, adjustments to, 350–351
Book of original entry, 186–188
Book value per share, 566
BorgWarner, Inc., 538
Burger King, 6
Businesses, 4
financing of, international differences in, 566
forms of, 560–563. *See also specific business forms*
liquidation of, 4
real-world financial reports of, 22–24
BusinessWeek, 7

C

Callable bonds, 508, 518
Callaway Gold, 137
Call premium, 508
Call price, 508
Campbell Soup Company, 337
Capital
legal, 565, 568
raising of, by corporations, 563
Capital expenditures, 457–458
Capital structure
and financial statements, 563–565
in financial statements, 563–565
Capitalized costs, 457–458
Careers in accounting, 7–8
Cash, petty cash funds and, 355–357
Cash balance, determining, 350
Cash-basis accounting, converting from accrual basis accounting to, 607–611

Cash controls, 346–354
bank reconciliation and, 350–354
for cash payments, 347–348
for cash receipts, 347
Cash discounts, 247, 248
inventory purchases and, 245
Cash dividends, 572–573
Cash flow statement. *See* Statement of cash flows
Cash inflows, 605
Cash outflows, 605
Cash Short and Over account, 354
checking account documents and, 348–350
cost of, 348
Caterpillar, Inc., 292
CBS Corporation, 501, 503
Certified checks, 351
Certified Internal Auditor (CIA) designation, 8
Certified Management Accounting (CMA) designation, 8
Certified public accountants (CPAs), 7, 8
external audits conducted by, 83
Chain of command, 345
Chart of accounts, 184
Check(s), 348–349
certified, 351
NSF, 351
outstanding, 350
Checking accounts
bank reconciliation and, 350–354
documents related to, 348–350
Chevron, 139, 391, 393
Circuit City, 406
Citicorp, 54
Claims, on assets, 11
Claims exchange transactions, in double-entry accounting system, 179–180
Classified balance sheets, 358
Closely held corporations, 560, 577
Closing, 21
accrual accounting and, 67, 68
of temporary accounts, 74
Closing entries, 188–190
Closing the books. *See* Closing
Coca-Cola, 460
Code of Professional Conduct (AICPA), 78
Coke, 460
Colgate Palmolive, 538
Collateral, 519
Collection, of accounts receivable, 351
Common size financial statements, 259, 260
Common stock, 11, 566–567
Compounding, 735
Compound interest, 735
Concha y Toro, 313, 406–407
Confidentiality, external audits and, 85–86
Conoco Phillips, 117, 139
Conservatism, 68–69
Consistency, inventory cost flow and, 305
Consolidated financial statements, 730
Consulting services, 7
Consumers, 4
Continuity, of corporations, 562

Contra liability accounts, 409
Controls. *See* Cash controls; Internal controls
Conversion agents. *See* Businesses; *specific types of businesses*
Convertible bonds, 508
Cooper, Cynthia, 347
Cooper Tire Rubber Company, 494
Copyrights, 460
Corporate governance, 78–82
common features of criminal and ethical misconduct and, 80–82
importance of ethics and, 78–79
Sarbanes-Oxley Act of 2002 and, 79–80
Corporations, 560
closely held, 560, 577
continuity of, 562
equity in, on financial statements, 565
limited liability of, 562
management structure of, 563
raising of capital by, 563
regulation of, 560–561
stock and. *See* Stock *entries*
taxes of, 561–562
transferability of ownership of, 563
widely held, 577
Cost(s)
capitalized, 457–458
of credit sales, 405–406
expensed, 457
of financing inventory, 248
of goods available for sale, 241, 302–303
of goods sold, 23
historical, 15, 445
of long-term assets, 445–446
period, 68, 241
product, 241
of protecting cash, 348
selling and administrative, 241
systematic allocation of, 127
transportation, 245, 248–250
Costco, 259, 313
Cost flow methods for inventory, 300
Cost method of accounting for treasury stock, 571
Cost of goods sold, 444
Cost of Goods Sold account, 241
Cox Communications, 466
Credit(s)
debit/credit relationships and, 183–184
defined, 172
lines of, 505, 506
Credit card sales, 401–402
Credit memos, bank statement, 349
Creditors, 4
Credit sales, costs of, 405–406
Criminal misconduct, common features of ethical misconduct and, 80–82
CSX Corporation, 494
Cumulative dividends, 567
Current assets, 357, 443
Current liabilities, 357–358
Current ratio, 350, 712
CVS, 262

D

DaimlerChrysler, 551
Dana Corporation, 551
Date of record for cash dividends, 572
Debentures, 507
Debit(s), defined, 172
Debit/credit relationships, 183–184
Debit memos, bank statement, 349
Debt, long-term. *See* Long-term debt
Debt risk, assessing, 137–138
Debt securities, 725
Debt to assets ratio, 137–138, 350, 711
Declaration date for cash dividends, 572
Deere & Company, 493
Deferral(s), defined, 121
Deferral accounting, 120–136
    financial statements and, 125, 130–132,
        134–136
    in first accounting period, 122–127
    ledger accounts and, 124–125
    matching concept and, 125–127
    in second accounting period, 127, 129–132
    in third accounting period, 132–136
Deferred tax liability, 456
Deflation, inventory cost flow and, 305
Del Monte Foods Company, Inc., 562
Depletion, 444–445
Deposits in transit, 350
Deposit tickets, 348
Depreciation, 124, 444, 446–453
    double-declining-balance method for, 446,
        450–452, 453, 454
    income taxes and, 455–456
    judgment and estimation and, 464–465
    modified accelerated cost recovery system and, 455
    straight-line, 124
    straight-line method for, 446, 447–450,
        453, 454
    units-of-production method for, 446, 452–453, 454
Digg.com, 24
Dillard's, Inc., 617
Direct method for statement of cash flows, 609,
    624–625
Direct write-off method for recognizing bad debts
    expense, 400–401
Disclaimer of audit opinion, 85
Disclosure, voluntary, 85–86
Discount(s), 726n
    amortization of, 410
    on bonds. *See* Bond discounts
    cash, 245, 247, 248
    on notes payable, 409
    purchase, inventory purchases and, 247
    sales, 256, 258–259
Discount notes, 409–413
    financial statements and, 410–411, 413
    T-accounts and, 410–411, 413
Discount on Notes Payable account, 409
Dividends, 15, 567–568
    in arrears, 567
    cash, 572–573

Dividends—*Cont.*
    cumulative, 567
    receiving, 575
    stock, 573
Documents, prenumbered, 345
Dominion Resources, 350
Double-declining-balance method for depreciation,
    446, 450–452, 453, 454
Double-entry accounting system, 170–191, 172
    adjustments and, 180–183
    asset exchange transactions and, 176–177
    asset source transactions and, 172–175
    asset use transactions and, 177–179
    claims exchange transactions and, 179–180
    closing entries and, 188–190
    debit/credit relationships and, 183, 184
    debit/credit terminology and, 172
    financial statements and, 188, 189
    general journal and, 186–188
    inventory events in, 243–245, 251–255
    ledger and, 184, 185
    T-accounts and, 184
    trial balance and, 190–191
Double-entry bookkeeping, 13
Double taxation, of corporations, 561–562

E

Earnings, 4
Earnings before interest and taxes (EBIT), 521
Earnings per share (EPS), 25, 711
Eastman Kodak Company, 385
Ebbers, Bernie, 347
EDGAR (Electronic Data Gathering, Analysis, and
    Retrieval) system, 193–194, 655
Effective interest rate, bond discount and, 512–513
Effective interest rate method, 523–526
    amortizing bond discounts under, 523–526
    amortizing bond premiums under, 526
Elements of financial statements, 10
Employees
    authority of, 345
    bonded, 344
    performance evaluations for, 346
    procedural manuals for, 345
    quality of, 344
    required absences for, 344
    responsibility of, 345
Ending inventory, estimating, 310–313
Enron Corporation, 79, 80, 85, 508
Entrenched management, 563
Equity
    return on, 138, 711
    stockholders', 11, 570–574. *See also* Statement of
        changes in stockholders' equity
Equity method, 730
Equity securities, 725
    reporting practices for, 730
Errors
    correcting in bank reconciliation, 351
    material, financial audits and, 84

Estimates
    of bad debts expense, 386
    depreciation expense and, 464–465
    of ending inventory, 310–313
    revision of, 456
Ethics
    importance of, 78–79
    as international issue, 79
Expenditures, capital, 457–458
Expense(s), 14
Expensed costs, 457
External audits, 83–86
    confidentiality and, 85–86
    financial, 84
    materiality and, 84
    types of opinions and, 84–85
ExxonMobil, 84, 563, 576

F

Face value, bonds issued at, 505–506, 509
Fair value, 566, 725
Fastow, Andrew, 85
Federal Express, 54
Federated Department Stores, 262
FedEx Corporation, 54
Fidelity bonds, 344
Financial accounting, accounting information and, 7
Financial Accounting Standards Board (FASB),
    8, 9, 561
    on direct method for statement of cash flows, 610
    on noncash investing and financing activities, 606
    Statement of Financial Accounting Standard 95
        issued, 254
Financial audits, 84
    materiality and, 84
Financial leverage, 138, 520
Financial resources, 4–5
Financial statements. *See also* Annual reports;
    specific statements
    accrual accounting and, 65–67, 72–74
    allowance method of accounting for bad debts
        and, 395, 399, 400
    bond discount and, 515–516
    bonds and, 510–512
    capital structure and, 563–565
    common size, 259, 260
    consistency and, 305
    cost flow and, 300–301, 303–304
    deferral accounting and, 130–132, 134–136
    defined, 10
    discount notes and, 410–411, 413
    double-declining-balance method and, 451–452
    double-entry accounting system and, 188, 189
    elements of, 10
    footnotes to, 191
    full disclosure and, 305
    horizontal financial statements model and, 21–22
    international differences among, 360
    investment securities and, 728–730
    of merchandising businesses, 22, 244–245,
        246, 259, 260

Financial statements—*Cont.*
preparing, 17–21
real-world, 22–24
stock and, 574–575
stock issuance and, 570
vertical statements model and, 76–78
warranties and, 403–404
Financing, international differences in, 566
Financing activities, 20–21
statement of cash flows and, 606, 617–619, 620
First-in, first-out (FIFO) cost flow method, 300
under perpetual system, 302–303
when sales and purchases occur intermittently, 306–307
First-in, first-out (FIFO) method, for physical flow of goods, 308
Fiscal year, 171
Fixed interest rate, 501
FOB destination, 248
FOB shipping point, 248
Footnotes to the financial statements, 191
Ford, 538, 551
Franchises, 460
Fraud
avoiding in merchandising businesses, 309–310
internal controls to prevent, 344–346
Full disclosure, inventory cost flow and, 305
Future value, 734–735
annuities and, 736
tables of, 739, 740

G

Gains, 251
unrealized, 728
Gap, Inc., 339
GEICO Insurance, 13
Gekko, Gordon, 79
Genentech, Inc., 166
General authority, 345
General journal, 186–188
General ledger, 16–17
Generally accepted accounting principles (GAAP), 8
external audits and, 83
international accounting and, 461
as international issue, 9
tax accounting and, 307
General Motors Corporation, 135, 193, 343, 521, 551, 576
Going concern assumption, 392
Goods, physical flow of, 300, 308
Goodwill, 461–462
Goodyear Tire & Rubber Company, 494
Google, Inc., 54, 599, 654
Gross margin (profit), 241
Gross margin method, for estimating ending inventory, 310–312
Gross margin percentage, 260, 261, 712
Growth, percentage analysis for measuring, 26

H

Half-year convention, 455
Harley-Davidson, 53, 116, 164, 165, 231, 291, 336, 383, 437, 492, 550, 597, 649, 719–724
Hartford, 138, 139
Haverty's, 538
HCA, 462
Healthy Choice, 460
Held-to-maturity securities, 725–726
Hershey Foods Corporation, 538
Hilton Hotels, 521
Historical cost, 15, 445
Home Depot, 350
Horizontal financial statements model, 21–22

I

Imprest basis, 355
Income, 4
net, 17, 253
operating, 253
Income statement, 18
accrual accounting and, 65, 66, 72–74
cost flow and, 300–301, 305
defined, 17
matching concept and, 17
multistep, 253–255
single-step, 254
vertical statements model and, 77
Income taxes
of corporations, 561–562
debt financing and, 520
deferred tax liability and, 456
depreciation and, 455–456
earnings before interest and taxes and, 521
GAAP and, 307
inventory cost flow methods and, 304–305
Independent auditors, 192
Indirect method, for statement of cash flows, 609, 610–615
Industry characteristics, financial performance measures and, 466
Inflation, inventory cost flow and, 305
Initial public offerings (IPOs), 562
Installment notes payable, 502–504
Insurance, prepaid, 132, 135
Intangible assets, 460–463
expense recognition for, 462–463
tangible assets versus, 444–445
Intel Corporation, 83, 495
Interest, 5
accrued, 71
on bank account, 351
on bonds, semiannual payments of, 517
compound, 735
simple, 735
Interest-bearing notes, 409
Interest rates
effective, bond discount and, 512–513
effective interest rate method and, 523–526

Interest rates—*Cont.*
fixed, 501
markets, 518
variable, 501
Internal controls, 80–81, 343–346
accounting, 344
administrative, 344
limitations of, 346
International Accounting Standards Board (IASB), 138
International Business Machine Corporation (IBM), 135, 599, 622
International issues
ethics as, 79
financial statements, 360
financing of businesses, 566
GAAP, 9, 461
IASB and, 138
tax accounting and GAAP, 307
terminology, 408
Inventory
average number of days to sell (average days in inventory), 313, 713
counting, 256
in double-entry system, 243–245, 251–255
ending, estimating, 310–313
inventory cost allocation between asset and expense accounts and, 241
periodic inventory system and, 264–265
perpetual inventory system and, 241–243
Inventory cost flow methods, 300–307
financial statements and, 300–301, 303–305
income taxes and, 304–305
under perpetual system, 302–305
ratio analysis and, 314
when sales and purchases occur intermittently, 306–307
Inventory purchases, 245–250
cost of financing inventory and, 248
financial statements and, 246
purchase discounts and, 247
purchase returns and allowances and, 246–247
transportation costs and, 248–250
Inventory turnover ratio, 312–314, 713
Investees, 725
Investing activities, 20–21
statement of cash flows and, 606, 615–616
Investment(s), 70
Investment securities, 725–731
available-for-sale, 726
debt, 725
equity, 725, 730
financial statements and, 728–730
held-to-maturity, 725–726
investment, 725
marketable, 725
reporting events that affect, 726–728
trading, 726
Investors, 4–5, 725
Issued stock, 566
Issuers
of bonds, 505
of notes, 75

J

JC Penney's, 384
Jobs and Growth Tax Relief Reconciliation Act
   (JGTRRA) of 2003, 562n
Jos. A. Bank Clothiers, Inc., 552
Journal(s), 188
   general, 186–188
   special, 186–188
Journal entries
   adjustments and. See Adjusting entries
   for bank reconciliation, 354
   for bonds, 509
   closing, 188–190

K

Karma Capitalism, 79
Kellogg's, 521
Kelly Services, 466
KFC, 118
K&G Fashion Superstores, 552
Kinko's, Inc., 54
Kleenex, 460
Kmart, 259
Kroger, 76, 350

L

Labor resources, 5
Last-in, first-out (LIFO) cost flow method, 300
   under perpetual system, 303
   when sales and purchases occur
      intermittently, 307
Last-in, first-out (LIFO) method, for physical flow
   of goods, 308
Lay, Kenneth, 85
Ledger, 184
   general, 16–17
Ledger accounts
   accrual accounting and, 64, 65
   deferral accounting and, 124–125
Legal capital, 565, 568
Liabilities, 11
   current (short-term), 357–358
   long-term, 501. See also Long-term debt
Life
   of corporations, 562
   expected, revision of, 456
   extending, 458
Life cycle, of operational assets, 446
Limited liability companies (LLCs), 562
Limited liability of corporations, 562
Lines of credit, 505, 506
Liquidation, 4
Liquidity, 19, 359–360
Loans
   collateral for, 519
   restrictive covenants and, 519
Long John Silver's, 118
Long-term debt, 500–522
   bonds. See Bond(s)

Long-term debt—Cont.
   financial leveraging and, 520
   installment notes payable, 502–504
   lines of credit, 505, 506
   security for loan agreements and, 519
   taxes and debt financing and, 520–521
   times interest earned ratio and,
      521–522, 713
Long-term liabilities, 501. See also Bond(s);
   Long-term debt
Long-term operational assets, 442–467
   balance sheet presentation of, 464
   basket purchase allocation and, 445–446
   continuing expenditures for plant assets and,
      457–459
   cost of, 445–446
   depreciation expense and. See Depreciation
   industry characteristics and, 466
   intangible, 460–463
   judgment and estimation and, 464–465
   life cycle of, 446
   natural resources, 459–460
   revising estimates related to, 456
   tangible, 444
   tangible versus intangible, 444–445
Losses, 251
   net, 17
   unrealized, 728
Lower-of-cost-or-market (LCM) rule, 308–309
Lowe's, 350

M

Machine Import Company (MIC), 54–55
Macy's, 262
Management
   business type and, 563
   entrenched, 563
Management's discussion and analysis (MD&A),
   23, 192
Management structure, business types
   and, 563
Managerial accounting, 7, 8
Manufacturing businesses, financial
   reports of, 22
Marathon Oil, 139
Margin, gross, 241
Market(s), setting resource priorities and, 4
Marketable securities, 725
Market-based resource allocation, 4–5
Market interest rate, 518
Market value, 566, 725
Marriott, 521
Matching concept, 71
   accrual accounting and, 67–69
   deferral accounting and, 125–127
Material errors, financial audits and, 84
Materiality concept, 127
McAfee, 622
McDonald's Corporation, 3, 10, 57, 313,
   406, 445
MCI, 347

Measurement rules, 8
The Men's Wearhouse, Inc., 552
Merchandise inventory
   defined, 239
   in double-entry system, 251–255
   gains and losses and, 251
   lost, damaged, or stolen, 255–256
   purchases of. See Inventory purchases
Merchandising businesses, 238–263
   avoiding fraud in, 309–310
   common size financial statements and, 259, 260
   financial reports of, 22
   financial statements of, 244–245, 246
   inventory and. See Inventory; Merchandise
      inventory
   product costs versus selling and administrative
      costs of, 241
   ratio analysis and, 260–262
   sales and, 256–259
Merck & Company, 262, 598
Meredith Corporation, 121, 127
MetLife, 138–139
Microsoft Corporation, 495
Modified accelerated cost recovery
   system (MACRS), 455
Moody's, 508, 550
Moores Clothing for Men, 552
Mortgage bonds, 507
Multistep income statement, 253–255

N

Nationwide, 139
Natural resources, 444, 459–460
Neiman Marcus, 259, 313
Net income, 17, 253
Net income percentage, 260
Net losses, 17
Net realizable value, 392
Net sales, 259
Newmont Mining Corporation, 117
New York Stock Exchange, 561
Nike Company, 235, 460
Nominal accounts, 21, 74
Nonbusiness organizations.
   See Not-for-profit entities
Noncash investing and financing activities,
   statement of cash flows and, 606, 621
Nonprofit accounting, accounting information
   and, 7
Nonprofit organizations. See Not-for-profit entities
Non-sufficient-funds (NSF) checks, 351
Notes payable, 74–78
   discount, 409–413
   installment, 502–504
   interest-bearing, 409
   long-term, time value of money and, 737
   principal of, 409
Notes receivable, 391
Not-for-profit entities, 6
   financial reports of, 22
Nusbaum, Edward, 561

O

Office Depot, 262, 313
OfficeMax, 313, 407
Operating activities, 20–21
    statement of cash flows and, 606, 610–615
Operating cycle, 357
Operating income, 253
Operational assets, long-term. *See* Long-term
    operational assets
Opportunity, ethical misconduct and, 80
Oracle Corporation, 292
Ordinary annuities, 736n
Outstanding checks, 350
Outstanding stock, 566
Ownership, transferability of, of corporations, 563

P

Paid-in Capital in Excess of Par (Stated) Value
    account, 568
Parent companies, 730
Partnership(s), 560
    equity in, on financial statements, 564–565
    liability and, 562
    management structure of, 563
Partnership agreements, 560
Par value, 565
Patents, 444, 460
Payables, 391
Payless Shoe Source, Inc., 54
Payment(s)
    cash, 347–348
    of interest on bonds, semiannual, 517
Payment date for cash dividends, 572–573
Peace Corps, 6
Pep Boys Manny, Moe & Jack, 386
PepsiCo, 118, 600
Percentage analysis, 26
Performance evaluations, 346
Period costs, 68, 241
Periodic inventory system, 264–265
    perpetual inventory system versus, 265
Permanent accounts, 21
Perpetual inventory system, 241–243
    inventory cost flow under, 302–305
    periodic inventory system versus, 265
Petty cash custodian, 355
Petty cash funds, 355–357
Petty cash vouchers, 35, 354
Physical control, 345–346
Physical flow of goods, 300, 308
Physical resources, 5
Pier 1 Imports, 383
Pizza Hut, 118, 406
Polo Ralph Lauren, 171, 191, 192
Posting, 186–188
Preferred stock, 567–568
Premium(s), 726n
    bonds issued at, 517–518, 526
    call, 508
Premium on Bonds Payable account, 517–518

Prenumbered documents, 345
Prepaid insurance, 132, 135
Present value, 735
    annuities and, 736–737
    tables of, 739, 740
Pressure, ethical misconduct and, 81
Price(s). *See* Bond prices; Stock prices
Price/earnings (P/E) ratio, 25, 576, 711
Primary securities market, 725
Principal of notes payable, 409
Private accounting, 8
Procedural manuals, 345
Product costs, 241
Productive assets, 20–21
Profit, 4
    gross, 241
Property, plant, and equipment, 444
    continuing expenditures for, 457–459
Proprietorships, equity in, on financial
    statements, 563–564
Public accounting, 7–8
Public Company Accounting Oversight Board (PCAOB),
    80, 194, 561
Pulte Homes, 165, 622, 623
Purchase(s), intermittent, inventory cost
    flow with, 306–307
Purchase discounts, inventory purchases and, 247
Purchase returns, inventory purchases and,
    245, 246–247

Q

Qualified opinion, 84
Quality, improving, 457–458
QuickBooks, 186

R

Ratio analysis
    accounts receivable turnover and, 405, 712
    average days to collect receivables and,
        405–406, 712
    average number of days to sell inventory and,
        313, 713
    for comparisons between companies, 261
    for comparisons within a company, 260–261
    current ratio and, 350, 712
    debt to assets ratio and, 137–138, 350, 711
    earnings per share and, 25, 711
    gross margin percentage and, 260, 261, 712
    inventory cost flow methods and, 314
    inventory turnover and, 312–314, 713
    for manufacturing businesses, 260–262
    for measuring effective use of assets, 136–138
    price/earnings ratio and, 25, 576, 711
    return on assets and, 136–137, 521, 711, 713
    return on sales and, 260, 261, 712
    times interest earned and, 521–522, 713
Rationalization, ethical misconduct and, 81
Reader's Digest Association, Inc., 167
Realization, 61
Receipts, cash, 347

Receivables, bad debts and, 392n
Recognition, 61
Redemption of bonds, 518–519
Red Hat, Inc., 54
Regulation of corporations, 560–561
Relative fair market value method, 445
Reliability concept, 15
Rent-A-Center, 405
Reporting entities, 9
Resource(s)
    financial, 4
    labor, 5
    natural, 459–460
    nonbusiness usage of, 7
    physical, 5
Resource allocation, market-based, 4–5
Resource owners, 4
Restrictive covenants, 519
Retail companies, 239.
    See also Merchandising businesses
Retained earnings, 11–12
    appropriation of, 574
Return on assets (ROA) ratio, 136–137, 521,
    711, 713
Return on equity ratio (ROE), 138, 711
Return on sales, 260, 261, 712
Revenue, 14
    unearned, 127, 128, 136
Rose, Kevin, 24
Ruby Tuesday's, Inc., 338
Ryland Group, 165

S

Safeway, Inc., 338
Saks Fifth Avenue, 259
Sales, 256–259
    credit card, 401–402
    intermittent, inventory cost flow with, 306–307
    net, 259
    return on, 260, 261, 712
Sales discounts, 256, 258–259
Sales returns and allowances, 257–258, 259
Salvage value, expected, revision of, 456
Sarbanes-Oxley Act of 2002 (SOX), 79–80, 561
Save-A-Lot, 293
Schedule of cost of goods sold, 265
Sears, Roebuck and Company, 13, 54, 135
Secondary securities market, 725
Secured bonds, 507
Securities Act of 1933, 561
Securities Act of 1934, 561
Securities and Exchange Commission (SEC), 561
    annual reports and, 192–194
    reports required by, 23, 192–193
Selling and administrative costs, 241
Separation of duties, 344
Serial bonds, 507
Service businesses, financial reports of, 22
Service charges on bank account, 351
Sharper Image Corp., 232, 233
Short-term assets, 357

Short-term liabilities, 357–358
Shrinkage of inventory, 255–256
Signature cards, 348
Simple interest, 735
Single-entry system, 186
Single-step income statements, 254
Sinking fund, 508
Six Flags, Inc., 232
Skilling, Jeffrey, 85
Sole proprietorships, 560
    liability and, 562
    management structure of, 563
Solvency, 359–360
Sonic Corporation, 551
Source documents, 188
Southwest Airlines, 383, 622
Special journals, 186–188
Specific authorizations, 345
Specific identification cost flow method, 300
Spread, 520
Sprint Nextel, 622
Stakeholders of accounting information, 6
Standard & Poor's (S&P), 550
Stanley Works, 521
Staples, 262, 313
Starbucks, 292, 313
Stated value, 565, 569
Statement of activities, 10
Statement of cash flows, 10, 18, 604–623
    accrual accounting and, 65, 66, 67, 73, 74
    converting from accrual to cash-basis accounting
        and, 607–611
    defined, 20
    direct method for preparing, 609, 624–625
    financing activities and, 606, 617–619, 620
    indirect method for preparing, 609–615
    investing activities and, 606, 615–616
    noncash investing and financing activities and,
        606, 621
    operating activities and, 606, 610–615
    preparing, 20–21
    reporting format for, 606–607
    vertical statements model and, 77
Statement of changes in stockholders' equity, 18
    accrual accounting and, 65, 66, 73, 74
    defined, 19
    preparing, 19
    vertical statements model and, 77
Statement of Financial Accounting
        Standard 95, 254
Statement of financial position, 10
Stock
    authorized, 566
    characteristics of, 565
    common, 566–567
    control through ownership of, 577
    dividends on. See Dividends
    earnings per share of, 25, 711
    financial statements and, 574–575
    issuance of. See Stock issuance
    issued, 566
    outstanding, 566

Stock—Cont.
    par value, 565, 568
    preferred, 567–568
    stated value, 565, 569
    treasury, 566, 570–571
Stock certificates, 560
Stock dividends, 573
Stock exchanges, 561
Stockholders, 11, 563
Stockholders' equity, 11, 570–574. See also
        Statement of changes in stockholders' equity
Stock issuance, 135
    financial statements and, 570
    with no par value, 569
    of par value stock, 568
    at stated value, 569
    stock classification and, 568–569
Stock prices
    increasing, 576
    price/earnings ratio and, 25, 576, 711
Stock splits, 573–574
Straight-line amortization, 514
Straight-line depreciation method, 124
Straight-line method for depreciation, 446, 447–450,
        453, 454
Subordinated debentures, 507
Subsidiary companies, 730
Sullivan, Scott, 347
Sun Trust Bank, 165
Sun Tzu, 79
Supervalu, Inc., 293
Supplies, 130, 135
Systematic allocation of cost, 127

T

T-accounts, 172, 184, 185
    allowance method of accounting for bad debts,
        394, 395, 398, 399
    discount notes and, 410–411, 413
    warranties and, 403–404
Taco Bell, 118
Tangible assets
    intangible assets versus, 444–445
    long-term, 444
Target, 261
Taxes. See Income taxes
Tax services, 7
TaylorMade Golf, 137
Temporary accounts, 21, 74
10-K report, 23
Term bonds, 507
Terminology, international differences
        in, 408
Texas Instruments, Inc., 385
Thornton, Grant, 561
Tiffany & Company, 292
Times interest earned ratio, 521–522, 713
Time value of money, 734–740
    bond price determination and, 738
    future value and, 734–735, 739, 740

Time value of money—Cont.
    future value annuities and, 736
    long-term notes payable and, 737
    present value and, 735, 739, 740
    present value annuities and, 736–737
Time Warner (TW), 136, 137
Toll Brothers, Inc., 232
Tommy Hilfiger, 192
Topps Company, Inc., 23, 53, 116, 164, 165,
        231, 291, 336, 383, 437, 492, 550,
        596, 649, 656–710, 714–719
Toro Company, 440
Trademarks, 460
Trading securities, 726
Transactions
    defined, 12
    in general ledger, 16–17
    recording under accounting
        equation, 12–15
Transportation cost, 245, 248–250
Transportation-in, 248
Transportation-out, 248
Treasury stock, 566, 570–571
    cost method of accounting for, 571
Trial balance, 190–191
True bank balance, 350
Tupperware Company, 384
2/10, n/30, 247

U

Unadjusted bank balance, 350
Unearned revenue, 127, 128, 136
Union Pacific (UNP) Corporation, 61, 69, 554
United Airlines, 466
United Parcel Service, Inc. (UPS), 551
Units-of-production method for depreciation,
        446, 452–453, 454
Unqualified opinion, 84
Unsecured bonds, 507
Unsubordinated debentures, 507
Useful life
    identifiable, intangible assets with,
        462–463
    indefinite, 444–445, 463
Users, of accounting information, 6

V

Vail Resorts, Inc., 232
Value
    book, per share, 566
    future, 734–735, 739, 740
    market (fair), 566, 725
    par, 565
    present, 735, 739, 740
    stated, 565, 569
Value Line Investment Survey, 622
Variable interest rate, 501
Vaseline, 460
Verizon Communications, Inc., 117

Vertical statements model, 76–78
Voluntary disclosure, 85–86
Vonage, 605, 608–609
Vulcan Materials Co., 308

W

Wachovia Corporation, 117
Walgreen's, 262
Wal-Mart, 259, 261, 262, 343, 563
The Walt Disney Company, 55
Warranties, 402–404
    financial statements and, 403–404
    T-accounts and, 403–404
Waste Management, 343

Weighted-average cost flow method, 300
    under perpetual system, 303
    when sales and purchases occur
        intermittently, 307
Weight Watchers International, Inc., 493
Wells Fargo & Co., 165
Wendy's, 6, 383
Weyerhaeuser Company, 443
Whole Foods Market, 293, 350
Wholesale companies, 239.
    See also Merchandising businesses
Widely held corporations, 577
Willamette Valley Vineyards, 313, 406
Withdrawals, 564
WorldCom, 79, 80, 343, 347

X

Xerox, 460
XM Satellite Holdings, Inc., 562, 649–650

Y

Yahoo, Inc., 166
Yum! Brands, 313, 406

Z

Zales Corporation, 239, 240, 241,
    254, 261, 338